ORACLE

IN A NUTSHELL

ORACLE

IN A NUTSHELL

Rick Greenwald and David C. Kreines

O'REILLY®

Beijing • Cambridge • Farnham • Köln • Paris • Sebastopol • Taipei • Tokyo

Oracle in a Nutshell
by Rick Greenwald and David C. Kreines

Published by O'Reilly & Associates, Inc., 1005 Gravenstein Highway North,
Sebastopol, CA 95472.

O'Reilly & Associates books may be purchased for educational, business, or sales
promotional use. Online editions are also available for most titles (*safari.oreilly.com*). For
more information contact our corporate/institutional sales department: (800) 998-9938 or
corporate@oreilly.com.

Editor:	Deborah Russell
Production Editor:	Philip Dangler
Cover Designer:	Ellie Volckhausen
Interior Designer:	David Futato

Printing History:

December 2002:   First Edition.

ISBN: 0-596-00336-6
[M]   [2/03]

For my father, Robert Greenwald.
—Rick Greenwald

For Suzanne, who keeps it all together.
—David C. Kreines

Table of Contents

Part II. Languages

Part III. Tools and Utilities

Part IV. Appendixes

Preface

Introduced a quarter-century ago, the Oracle database remains the leading enterprise-strength relational database management system (RDBMS) in the world. Oracle is a complex system, offering a myriad of products, languages, and tools. Frequent updates, releases, and editions complicate the ability of Oracle users to keep up with the huge amount of frequently changing information about Oracle. A large number of books, articles, and web sites endeavor to clarify a confusing and demanding situation. Is there really a need for yet another book?

The goal of *Oracle in a Nutshell* is to provide just what you need to know about Oracle in a volume whose content and format combine to put necessary information at your fingertips. This book is a quick reference for the commands and parameters used with Oracle's core languages and tools. In this book, we've tried to pull together, in the most concise fashion possible, the information that database administrators and developers need as they manage Oracle databases and write code for these databases.

As with other books in O'Reilly's "In a Nutshell" series, this book is geared toward users who know what they want to do, but just can't remember the right command or default, the right parameter or range of values, or the right package header format and datatypes. We generally assume that you are already at least somewhat familiar with the languages and tools described here. For tutorials, detailed discussions of usage, and subtle details, you may need to consult the Oracle documentation and other, more focused books (see Appendix E for many suggestions for books and other resources that you can go to for additional information in the various topic areas). But for most tasks, we think you will find the answers you need in this volume. We hope that this book will become an invaluable desktop reference for Oracle users of all kinds.

A word about what this book is—and what it is not. It is a succinct reference to the information that most Oracle users need to know. There is something here for all types of Oracle users: DBAs; PL/SQL and Java developers; and system, network, and security administrators. Most chapters consist mainly of quick-reference material (e.g., initialization parameter summaries; syntax for SQL and PL/SQL statements, function calls, and built-in package procedure and function headers; commands and options for SQL*Plus, SQL*Loader, Import/Export, and RMAN; data dictionary views; Oracle/Java interfaces and classes; and optimization hints). But in the interest of keeping the length of this book from being unwieldy (we do acknowledge that the phrase "In a Nutshell" is close to being an oxymoron), we chose not to go down some other interesting technical highways and byways.

One of the greatest challenges that faced us was the most basic—how to create a Nutshell book for Oracle and still have a volume that you could actually lift without mechanical assistance. We arrived at a few decisions as to how to achieve this end:

1. We sought to follow the 90/10 rule. Similar to the 80/20 rule, this corollary implies that we could deliver 90% of the most important information about Oracle in 10% of the pages. Because this book boils down in excess of 13,000 pages of Oracle documentation (in Oracle9i), we hope that we have achieved this target.

2. We wanted to make sure that the level of detail offered, while reduced, still was helpful and made sense. So we made decisions like the one evident in Chapter 10: we provided the header and a brief description of each call to the many PL/SQL built-in packages, but nothing else. If you choose to learn more about any particular package in depth, you can go look for the detail available in the Oracle documentation, but Chapter 10 provides the information you need to use the functionality.

3. We reluctantly kept the number of examples to a minimum, because providing examples for each statement, command, and parameter would increase the page count to an impossibly large number. The omission of examples is most striking in the (already very long) chapter on SQL. As we've said, though, we hope to provide the necessary information and structure to allow you to go elsewhere in those few cases where you need more detail.

4. Whenever possible, we tried to make the actual structure and format of the book offer information. A prime example of this is the fact that we grouped the initialization parameters in Chapter 2, instead of arranging them in strict alphabetical order. It has been our experience that constellations of related parameters are typically used together, so we arranged the chapter in that way. We also hoped that this organization would allow you to find out about related parameters that you might not otherwise be aware of.

5. Finally, we decided to cover only topics that are used by the mainstream of Oracle users. So we reluctantly left out Advanced Queuing, Streams, Advanced Security, and a number of other niche options. It would have been impossible to reach our first goal if we had had to offer even a cursory quick-reference to these and other areas.

All in all, we hope that we have made the right decisions. We look forward to hearing from you if you disagree—but please, be gentle!

Which Platform and Version?

Oracle runs on an enormous number of hardware and operating system platforms. Most of the information in this book applies to all platforms. When a command or parameter works differently on Windows, Linux, or some other system, we've noted that fact.

At the time we went to press, the latest version of Oracle was Oracle9i Release 2. Because Oracle9i is still relatively new, we've noted when features were introduced (or removed). So in many sections you will find comments like this: "new with Oracle9i" and "not support after in Oracle8i." In this way, we hope to accommodate readers who may be running on older versions of Oracle. We have not tried to address systems earlier than Oracle8.

Structure of This Book

This book is divided into four parts:

Part I, *Foundations*

This part of the book contains fundamental information about the Oracle database, which applies no matter what language or tools you are using.

- Chapter 1, *Architecture and Packaging*, provides an overview of the architecture and underlying components of the Oracle database and briefly describes the various Oracle editions.

- Chapter 2, *Configuration*, describes the initialization parameters (*INIT.ORA* and/or *SPFILE* parameters) that allow you to configure your Oracle database.

- Chapter 3, *Concurrency*, describes Oracle's multiversion read consistency (MVRC) scheme and provides a brief discussion of transactions, locks, and other concurrency concepts.

- Chapter 4, *Security*, briefly describes authentication, profiles, privileges, roles, and auditing and specifies the syntax for controlling security in an Oracle database.

- Chapter 5, *Networking*, briefly describes Oracle networking concepts and summarizes the syntax of the configuration files you must define in order to use a network with Oracle; these files include *TNSNAMES.ORA, SQLNET. ORA, LISTENER.ORA, LDAP.ORA, NAMES.ORA,* and *CMAN.ORA.*

- Chapter 6, *Data Dictionary*, summarizes the Oracle data dictionary views that maintain information about the objects and users in an Oracle database; it covers both the static views and the dynamic performance views.

Part II, *Languages*

This part of the book focuses on the syntax used to construct SQL statements and functions, PL/SQL programs, and Java interfaces to Oracle.

- Chapter 7, *SQL*, summarizes the syntax of Oracle's version of SQL (Structured Query Language).

- Chapter 8, *Functions*, summarizes the syntax of the functions that may be called from SQL and PL/SQL.

- Chapter 9, *PL/SQL,* briefly describes the capabilities of Oracle's procedural language and summarizes the syntax of all statements.
- Chapter 10, *PL/SQL Packages,* lists the header specifications for all of the procedures and functions included in Oracle's built-in packages, along with parameter descriptions.
- Chapter 11, *Java and Oracle,* provides a summary of the Java interfaces to the Oracle database, including Java drivers available for Oracle, the mapping between Java datatypes and Oracle datatypes, and the syntax for the SQLJ and JDBC interfaces to Oracle

Part III, *Tools and Utilities*

This part of the book summarizes the commands and file specifications for a variety of tools and utilities used to manage and interact with the Oracle database.

- Chapter 12, *SQL*Plus,* summarizes the commands and formatting elements available with SQL*Plus, the command-line interface to the Oracle database that you use to enter SQL statements and PL/SQL code and execute script files.
- Chapter 13, *Export and Import,* summarizes the commands available with the Export utility (which copies data from the database into a binary file) and the Import utility (which bring data into the Oracle database from a binary file). You can use these utilities to capture both the structures and the data in an Oracle database.
- Chapter 14, *SQL*Loader,* summarizes the commands available with SQL*Loader, a utility that allows you to load data in standard operating system file formats into an Oracle database and to perform a variety of data manipulation and transformation operations during the load.
- Chapter 15, *Backup and Recovery,* briefly describes Oracle backup and recovery concepts, outlines the procedures you can follow to perform user-managed backup and recovery, and summarizes the commands available with the Recovery Manager (RMAN), the Oracle backup and recovery utility.
- Chapter 16, *Enterprise Manager,* summarizes the features of Enterprise Manager, a graphical user interface console that allows you to manage Oracle databases.
- Chapter 17, *Performance,* summarizes the main Oracle tools that help you examine and improve Oracle performance. It describes the SQL optimizers and hints and provides syntax for using the Explain Plan, *TKPROF,* AUTOTRACE, UTLBSTAT, UTLESTAT, and Statspack optimization tools.

Part IV, *Appendixes*

This part of the book contains summary and reference information.

- Appendix A, *Datatypes,* summarizes the Oracle datatypes and conversion rules.
- Appendix B, *Expressions, Operators, and Conditions,* lists the valid expressions, operators, and conditions that can be included in SQL, PL/SQL, and SQL*Plus statements.

- Appendix C, *Numeric Formats*, lists numeric format elements that can be included in SQL, PL/SQL, and SQL*Plus statements.
- Appendix D, *Date Formats*, lists date format elements that can be included in SQL, PL/SQL, and SQL*Plus statements.
- Appendix E, *Additional Resources*, provides a list of books and online resources containing additional information on the topics included in this book.

Conventions Used in This Book

The following typographical conventions are used in this book:

Italic
> Used for filenames, directory names, URLs, the first use of technical terms, and occasional emphasis.

`Constant width`
> Used for syntax models and code examples.

`Constant width italic`
> In syntax models, indicates an element (e.g., a filename) you supply.

`Constant width bold`
> Used in examples that show interaction between an Oracle utility (e.g., SQL*Plus, RMAN) and a user; commands typed by the user are shown in bold, while output from the program is shown in normal text. Bold is also used to show defaults.

UPPERCASE
> In syntax models, generally indicates keywords.

Lowercase
> In syntax models, generally indicates user-defined terms, such as variables and parameters.

[ ]
> In syntax models, square brackets enclose optional items

{ }
> In syntax models, curly braces enclose a set of items from which you must choose only one.

|
> In syntax models, a vertical bar, or pipe, separates the items enclosed in curly brackets, such as {VARCHAR2 | DATE | NUMBER}.

Indicates a tip, suggestion, or general note. For example, we'll tell you if a certain feature is version-specific.

Indicates a warning or caution. For example, we'll tell you if a certain operation has some kind of negative impact on the system.

Comments and Questions

We have tested and verified the information in this book and in the source code to the best of our ability, but given the number of tools described in this book and the rapid pace of technological change, you may find that features have changed or that we have made mistakes. If so, please notify us by writing to:

O'Reilly & Associates
1005 Gravenstein Highway
Sebastopol, CA 95472
800-998-9938 (in the U.S. or Canada)
707-829-0515 (international or local)
707-829-0104 (fax)

You can also send messages electronically. To be put on the mailing list or request a catalog, send email to:

· *info@oreilly.com*

To ask technical questions or comment on the book, send email to:

bookquestions@oreilly.com

We have a web site for this book where you can find errata and other information about this book. You can access this page at:

http://www.oreilly.com/catalog/oraclenut

For more information about this book and others, see the O'Reilly web site:

http://www.oreilly.com

Acknowledgments

As you might expect, a tremendous number of people have helped us put this book together. We are very grateful to them all.

First, a huge thank-you to those whose original books provided source material on which we built the chapters in this book: Jonathan Gennick, Steven Feuerstein, Bill Pribyl, Chip Dawes, Brian Laskey, Don Bales, Darl Kuhn, and Scott Schulze. In particular, we would like to send a special thanks to Steven Feuerstein, our friend and hero; Chip Dawes, who provided a wealth of accurate and timely information; and Don Bales, whose patience and gentle insistence helped to produce the sections of this book on Java.

We are also very grateful to the reviewers of this book: Jonathan Gennick, Sanjay Mishra, Darl Kuhn, and Alan Beaulieu. All of them were not only thorough but also willing to work under unreasonable deadlines. We take back all of the curses muttered under our breath during the last days of preparation as we tried to correct all the errors they found and make all the changes they suggested.

In addition, a special thanks to Debby Russell, our editor, who, as usual, acted as a cross between a guide and a relentless enforcer, but without whom this book would never have been published. And thanks as well to the entire O'Reilly production team for turning this mass of pages, syntax diagrams, and tables into a cohesive and beautifully formatted whole.

We do acknowledge, however, that despite all of this help, any and all errors or missteps are exclusively the responsibility of the authors.

From Rick

Creating a book is a laborious process. To make it through the long haul, you need the support of many of those people mentioned earlier. Even more importantly, you need the help of those closest to you. For me, that would be the rest of my immediate family—LuAnn, Elinor, and Josephine Greenwald. LuAnn has given me a life full of happiness. Ellie and Josie can't even spell Oracle (and wonder why their daddy can't play with them more), but they are the reason for virtually everything I do.

Throughout this long process, I have been able to keep plugging along. This project has made me understand and value the work ethic that is deeply a part of me. For this, I can only thank my father, who passed away during the writing of the book. Thank you, Dad.

From Dave

When I first thought about writing Oracle in a Nutshell, I discussed it with a few people and excitedly sent an outline to Debby Russell, my editor for previous book projects at O'Reilly. Unfortunately, it turned out that Rick Greenwald had already submitted an outline for the same book. My disappointment was short-lived, however, when Rick invited me to work on the book as his coauthor. After all the grief and anxiety I have caused Rick with deadlines, content, format, and all the other details that are the responsibility of the primary author, he may by now regret his decision! But, I would like to take this opportunity to thank Rick for including me in this project. It was a lot of work, and I learned a lot from it. Thanks, Rick! I'll try to make up for some of those sleepless nights!

There are many friends and acquaintances who have encouraged my work with Oracle, including John Beresniewicz, Buff Emslie, Steven Feuerstein, Jonathan Gennick, Steve Hazeldine, Ken Jacobs, Brian Laskey, Rich Niemiec, Matt Reagan, and Marlene Theriault. Special thanks also to my colleagues at Rhodia, including Claude Cohen, Deb Irwin, Dave Flood, Raphael Hevia, Joaquin Lucero, Paul Mars, Brian McMahon, Bin Pan, and Christian Tiberghien. I know I've missed a few others, but you know who you are.

Finally, I would like to thank my family for once again putting up with the "lost night" of researching, writing, checking, and editing.

I

Foundations

This part of the book contains fundamental information about the Oracle database, which applies no matter what language or tools you are using. It consists of the following chapters:

Chapter 1, *Architecture and Packaging*, provides an overview of the architecture and underlying components of the Oracle database and briefly describes the various Oracle editions.

Chapter 2, *Configuration*, describes the initialization parameters (*INIT.ORA* and/or *SPFILE* parameters) that allow you to configure your Oracle database.

Chapter 3, *Concurrency*, describes Oracle's multiversion read consistency (MVRC) scheme and provides a brief discussion of transactions, locks, and other concurrency concepts.

Chapter 4, *Security*, briefly describes authentication, profiles, privileges, roles, and auditing and specifies the syntax for controlling security in an Oracle database.

Chapter 5, *Networking*, briefly describes Oracle networking concepts and summarizes the syntax of the configuration files you must define in order to use a network with Oracle; these files include *TNSNAMES.ORA, SQLNET.ORA, LISTENER.ORA, LDAP.ORA, NAMES.ORA,* and *CMAN.ORA*.

Chapter 6, *Data Dictionary*, summarizes the Oracle data dictionary views that maintain information about the objects and users in an Oracle database; it covers both the static views and the dynamic performance views.

1

Architecture and Packaging

The architecture of the Oracle relational database management system is a unique one. Features such as rollback buffers and Real Application Clusters are part of the innate Oracle architecture and make it possible for the Oracle database to provide a wide range of features not found in any other database.

This chapter provides a brief overview of the architecture and underlying components of the Oracle database, as well as a description of the different "flavors" of the database currently offered by Oracle Corporation: its various editions, versions, and major features. By understanding how Oracle accomplishes its tasks, you'll be better equipped to understand the rest of the information in this book—the Oracle initialization parameters and data dictionary views, its various language statements, the details of the various Oracle tools and utilities, and the major aspects of tuning and optimization.

Oracle Instances and Databases

Two entities are sometimes referred to as an Oracle database—the instance and the database—and people often confuse them.

In the Oracle world, the term *database* refers to the physical storage of information, while *instance* refers to the software executing on the server that provides access to the information in the database. The instance runs on the computer or server; the database is stored on the disks attached to the server, as shown in Figure 1-1.

The database is physical: it consists of files stored on disks. The instance is logical: it consists of in-memory structures and processes on the server. An instance can connect to one and only one database. Instances are temporal, but databases, with proper maintenance, last forever.

Users do not directly access the information in an Oracle database. Instead, they pass requests for information to an Oracle instance.

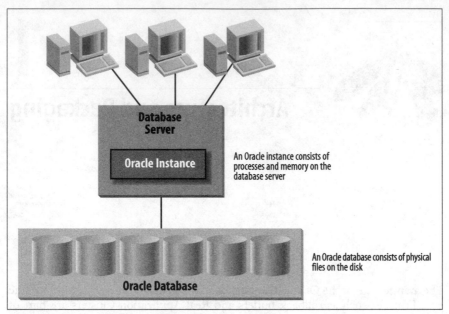

Figure 1-1. An instance and a database

The Components of a Database

A database consists of a collection of physical files and logical structures, described in the following sections.

A database has a specific name, assigned when you create it. You cannot change the name of a database once you have created it, although you can change the name of the instance that accesses the database.

Tablespaces

A *tablespace* is a logical structure, which exists only within the context of an Oracle database. Each tablespace is composed of physical structures called *datafiles*; each tablespace must consist of one or more datafiles, and each datafile can belong to only one tablespace. When you create a table, you can specify the tablespace in which you want to create it. Oracle will then find space for it in one of the datafiles that make up the tablespace.

Figure 1-2 shows the relationship of tablespaces to datafiles for a database. This figure shows two tablespaces within an Oracle database. When you create a new table in this Oracle database, you may place it in the DATA1 tablespace or the DATA2 tablespace. It will physically reside in one of the datafiles that make up the specified tablespace.

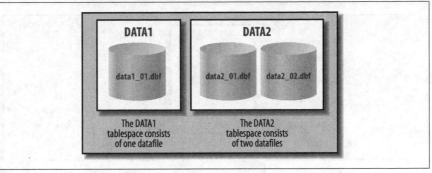

Figure 1-2. Tablespaces and datafiles

Physical Files in an Oracle Database

A tablespace is a logical view of the physical storage of information in an Oracle database. Three fundamental types of physical files make up an Oracle database:

- Control files
- Datafiles
- Redo log files

Other files, such as password files and instance initialization files, are used within a database environment, but the three fundamental types listed represent the physical database itself. Figure 1-3 illustrates the three types of files and their interrelationships.

Oracle9*i* introduces the concept of Oracle managed files (OMFs). You indicate that you want to use OMFs by specifying values for the initialization parameters DB_CREATE_FILE_DEST and DB_CREATE_ONLINE_LOG_DEST_*n* (these and all of the Oracle initialization parameters are described in detail in Chapter 2). If you request OMFs, Oracle9*i* will automatically create, name, and delete (when appropriate) all the files for your Oracle database. OMFs are designed to reduce the maintenance overhead of naming and tracking the names for your Oracle database, as well as to avoid the problems that can occur when fallible human beings do not correctly identify a file in an Oracle database.

The following sections describe the role of these three types of files and their interactions.

Control Files

The control file contains a list of all the other files that make up the database, such as the datafiles and redo log files. It also contains key information about the contents and state of the database, such as:

- The name of the database
- When the database was created
- The current state of the datafiles: whether they need recovery, are in a read-only state, and so on

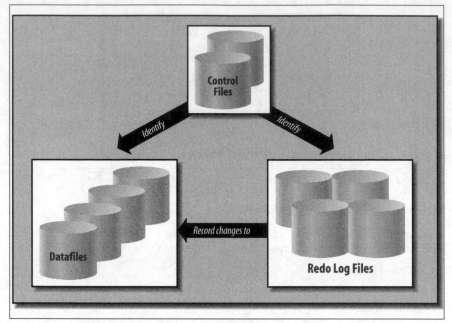

Figure 1-3. The files that make up a database

- Whether the database closed cleanly the last time it was shut down
- The time period covered by each archived redo log
- What backups have been performed for the database

Prior to Oracle8, control files were typically under a megabyte in size. With Oracle8, there is more information in the control file, such as the details of database backups. The control files in Oracle8 and beyond can easily grow to the 10 MB range or beyond. The size of a control file is influenced by a number of initialization parameters, including MAXLOGFILES, MAXLOGMEMBERS, MAXLOGHISTORY, MAXDATAFILES, and MAXINSTANCES.

You can have your Oracle instance maintain multiple copies of control files. Although you can potentially rebuild a control file if it is damaged or deleted, this process takes time and in some scenarios you cannot rebuild the control file to its correct state. You cannot run an Oracle database without a control file, so having multiple copies of your control file can be an important safety option. You use the initialization parameter CONTROL_FILES to list the locations of multiple copies of the control file.

Datafiles

Datafiles contain the actual data stored in the database. This data includes the tables and indexes created by users of the database; the data dictionary, which keeps information about these data structures; and the rollback segments, which are used to implement Oracle's consistency scheme.

A datafile is composed of Oracle database blocks that are, in turn, composed of operating system blocks on a disk. Oracle block sizes range from 2K to 32K. If you're using Oracle with very large memory (VLM) support, you may use big Oracle blocks (BOBs), which can be as large as 64K in size.

Prior to Oracle9*i*, you could have only a single block size for an entire database. With Oracle9*i*, you still set a default block size for the database, but you can also have five different nonstandard block sizes in the database. Each datafile can support only one block size, but you can have mixed block sizes within the database.

Figure 1-4 illustrates the relationship of Oracle blocks to operating system blocks.

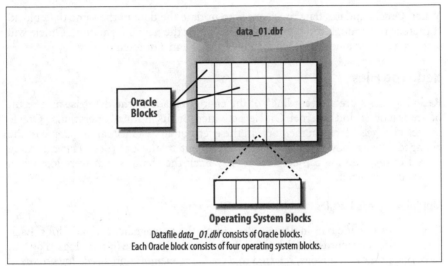

Figure 1-4. Oracle blocks and operating system blocks

Datafiles belong to only one database and to only one tablespace within that database. Data is read in units of Oracle blocks from the datafiles into memory as needed, based on the work users are doing. Blocks of data are written from memory to the datafiles stored on disk, as needed, to ensure that the database reliably records changes made by users.

Datafiles are the lowest level of granularity between an Oracle database and the operating system. When you lay a database out on the I/O subsystem, the smallest physical piece you place in any particular location is a datafile. Tuning the I/O subsystem to improve Oracle performance typically involves moving datafiles from one set of disks to another.

Datafile structure

The first block of each datafile is called the *datafile header*. It contains critical information used to maintain the overall integrity of the database. One of the most crucial pieces of information in this header is the *checkpoint structure*, a logical timestamp that indicates the last point at which changes were written to the datafile. This timestamp is critical for recovery situations. The Oracle recovery process uses the timestamp in the header of a datafile to determine which redo logs to apply to bring the datafile up to the current point in time.

Extents and segments

From a physical point of view, a datafile is stored as operating system blocks. From a logical point of view, datafiles have three intermediate organizational levels: data blocks, extents, and segments. An *extent* is a set of data blocks that are contiguous within an Oracle datafile. A *segment* is an object that takes up space in an Oracle database, such as a table or an index, that is comprised of one or more extents.

When Oracle updates data, it attempts to update the data in the same data block. If there is not enough room in the data block for the new information, Oracle will write the data to a new data block, which may be in a different extent.

Redo Log Files

Redo log files store a "recording" of the changes made to the database as a result of transactions and internal Oracle activities. In its normal operations, Oracle caches changed blocks in memory; in the event of an instance failure, some of the changed blocks may not have been written out to the datafiles. The recording stored in the redo log can be used to play back the changes that were lost when the failure occurred.

Multiplexing redo log files

Oracle uses specific terminology in describing the management of redo logs. Each Oracle instance records the changes it makes to the database in redo logs. You can have one or more redo logs, referred to as *redo log members*, in a *redo log group*.

Logically, you can think of a redo log group as a single redo log file. However, Oracle allows you to specify multiple copies of a redo log to protect the log against media failure. Multiple copies of the same log are grouped together in a redo log group. All redo log groups for an instance are referred to as a *redo thread*.

There are ways you can rebuild the static part of the control file if you lose it, but there is no way to reproduce a lost redo log file; be sure that you have multiple copies of the redo file.

How Oracle uses the redo logs

Once Oracle fills one redo log file, it automatically begins to use the next log file. Once the server cycles through all the available redo log files, it returns to the first one and reuses it. Oracle keeps track of the different redo logs by using a sequence number. As the server fills each redo log file and moves on to the next one, it increments an internal counter called the *redo log sequence number*. This sequence number is recorded inside the redo log files as they are used. Oracle uses this internal number to properly sequence the logs, even though a reused log file may have the name initially created for an earlier redo log.

Archived redo logs

While reading the previous explanation, you might have wondered how to avoid losing the critical information in the redo log when Oracle cycles over a previously used redo log.

There are actually two ways to address this issue. The first is quite simple: you don't avoid losing the information, and you suffer the consequences in the event of a failure. You will lose the history stored in the redo file when it's overwritten. If a failure occurs that damages the datafiles, you must restore the entire database to the point in time when the last backup occurred. No redo log history exists to reproduce the changes made since the time the last backup occurred, so you will be out of luck. Very few Oracle shops make this choice, because the inability to recover to the point of failure is unacceptable—it results in lost data.

The second and more practical way to address the issue caused by recycling redo logs is to archive the redo logs as they fill. To understand archiving redo logs, you must first understand that there are actually two types of redo logs for Oracle:

Online redo logs
> The operating system files that Oracle cycles through to log the changes made to the database

Archived redo logs
> Copies of the filled online redo logs made to avoid losing redo data as the online redo logs are overwritten

An Oracle database can run in one of two modes with respect to archiving redo logs:

NOARCHIVELOG
> As the name implies, no redo logs are archived. As Oracle cycles around the logs, the filled logs are reinitialized and overwritten, which erases the history of the changes made to the database. This mode essentially is the first choice mentioned before, when a failure could lead to a loss of data.
>
> Choosing not to archive redo logs significantly reduces your choices and options for database backups.

ARCHIVELOG
> When Oracle rolls over to a new redo log, it archives the previous redo log. To prevent gaps in the history, a given redo log cannot be reused until it's successfully archived. The archived redo logs, plus the online redo logs, provide a complete history of all changes made to the database. Together, they allow Oracle to recover all committed transactions up to the exact time a failure occurred.

To enable ARCHIVELOG mode, you must turn on archive logging with the ALTER DATABASE ARCHIVELOG command in SQL*Plus and set the LOG_ARCHIVE_START initialization parameter to TRUE. This will start archiving logs to the location specified by the LOG_ARCHIVE_DEST parameters with names specified by the LOG_ARCHIVE_FORMAT parameter.

The Components of an Instance

An Oracle instance can be defined as an area of shared memory and a collection of background processes.

The area of shared memory for an instance is called the System Global Area, or SGA. The SGA is not really one large undifferentiated section of memory—it's made up of various components described in the next section, "Memory Structures for an Instance." All the processes of an instance—system processes and user processes—share the SGA.

Prior to Oracle9*i*, the size of the SGA was set when the Oracle instance started. The only way you could change the size of the SGA or any of its components was to change the appropriate initialization parameters and stop and restart the instance. With Oracle9*i*, you can now change the size of the SGA or its components while the Oracle instance is still running.

The background processes interact with the operating system and each other to manage the memory structures for the instance. These processes also manage the actual database on disk and perform general housekeeping for the instance.

Other physical files can be considered as part of the instance as well:

Instance initialization file
> The initialization file contains a variety of parameters that configure how the instance will operate: how much memory it will use, how many users it will allow to connect, what database the instance actually provides access to, and so on. You can alter many of these parameters dynamically at either the systemwide or session-specific level. Up until Oracle9*i*, the initialization file was called *INIT.ORA*.* Oracle9*i* introduced the *SPFILE*, which performs the same function as the *INIT.ORA* file but can also persistently store changes to initialization parameters that are made while Oracle9*i* is running. Refer to your operating system–specific documentation for the default location of the *INIT.ORA* file on your system.

Instance configuration file
> The configuration file, called *CONFIG.ORA*, is an optional parameter file, included if you want to segregate a set of initialization parameters (for example, those used for Oracle Parallel Server or Real Application Clusters).

Password file
> Oracle can use an optional password file, stored as an operating system file, to provide additional flexibility for managing Oracle databases. This file is encrypted and contains user IDs and passwords that can be used to perform administrative tasks, such as starting and stopping the instance. Use of a password file is a standard method for implementing remote access security in addition to access security by operating system. The latter is typically used locally (i.e., on the database server). For example, on a Unix system, any user in the DBA group can start up or shut down Oracle—the operating system

---

* The specific name of your *INIT.ORA* file will depend upon your instance name. See Chapter 2 for details.

group gives that user the authority. Validating a password against the value stored in the database for a user is not possible when the database is not open. The password file forces a user to authenticate himself with a password in order to start up the database.

Additional background processes may exist when you use certain other features of the database: for example, the Shared Server/Multi-Threaded Server (MTS), job queues, or replication.

Memory Structures for an Instance

The SGA is actually composed of four main areas: the database buffer cache, the shared pool, the redo log buffer, and the large pool, as shown in Figure 1-5.

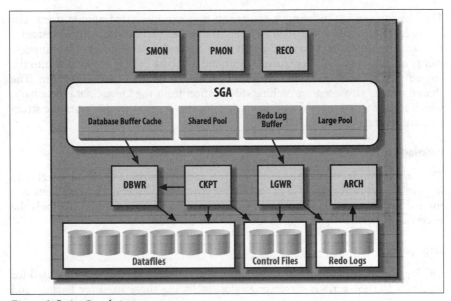

Figure 1-5. An Oracle instance

Database buffer cache

The database buffer cache caches blocks of data retrieved from the database. This buffer between the users' requests and the actual datafiles improves the performance of the Oracle database. If a piece of data can be found in the buffer cache, you can retrieve it from memory without the overhead of having to go to disk. Oracle manages the cache using a least recently used (LRU) algorithm. This means that if a user requests data that has been recently used, the data is more likely to be in the database buffer cache and can be delivered immediately without having to execute a disk read operation.

Oracle7 had one pool of buffers for database blocks. Oracle8 introduced multiple buffer pools. Three pools are available in Oracle8 and beyond:

DEFAULT
> The standard Oracle database buffer cache. All objects use this cache unless otherwise indicated.

KEEP

For frequently used objects you wish to cache.

RECYCLE

For objects that you're less likely to access again.

Both the KEEP and the RECYCLE buffer pools remove their objects from consideration by the LRU algorithm.

You can mark a table or index for caching in a specific buffer pool. This helps to keep more desirable objects in the cache and avoids the "churn" of all objects fighting for space in one central cache.

Shared pool

The shared pool caches various constructs that can be shared among users. For example, SQL statements issued by users are cached so that they can be reused if the same statement is submitted again. Another example is stored procedures—pieces of code stored and executed within the database. These are loaded into the shared pool for execution and then cached, again using an LRU algorithm. The shared pool is also used for caching information from the Oracle *data dictionary*, which is the metadata (or data describing data structures) that describes the structure and content of the database itself.

Redo log buffer

The redo log buffer caches redo information until it is written to the physical redo log files stored on a disk. Use of this buffer improves performance. Oracle caches the redo until it can be written to disk at a more optimal time, which avoids the overhead of constantly writing to the disk with the redo logs.

Large pool

The large pool, introduced with Oracle8, is an optional area of the SGA used for buffering I/O for various server processes, including those used for backup and recovery. The area is also used to store session memory for the Multi-Threaded Server and when using the XA protocol for distributed transactions.

Background Processes for an Instance

The background processes shown in Figure 1-5 are:

Database Writer (DBWR)

This process writes database blocks from the database buffer cache in the SGA to the datafiles on disk. An Oracle instance can have up to 10 DBWR processes, named DBW0 through DBW9, if needed, to handle the I/O load to multiple datafiles. Most instances run one DBWR. DBWR writes blocks out of the cache for two main reasons:

- To perform a checkpoint. A *checkpoint* is the technical term for updating the blocks of the datafiles so that they "catch up" to the redo logs. Oracle writes the redo for a transaction when it is committed and later writes the actual blocks. Periodically, Oracle performs a checkpoint to bring the datafile contents in line with the redo that was written out for the committed transactions.

- To free space in the cache. If Oracle needs to read blocks requested by users into the cache and there is no free space in the buffer cache, DBWR is called to write out some blocks to free space. The blocks written out are the least recently used blocks. Writing blocks in this order minimizes the performance impact of losing them from the buffer cache.

Log Writer (LGWR)

This process writes the redo information from the log buffer in the SGA to all copies of the current redo log file on disk. As transactions proceed, the associated redo information is stored in the redo log buffer in the SGA. When a transaction is committed, Oracle makes the redo information permanent by invoking the Log Writer to write it to disk.

System Monitor (SMON)

This process maintains overall health and safety for an Oracle instance. SMON performs crash recovery when the instance is started after a failure. SMON coordinates and performs recovery for a failed instance when you have more than one instance accessing the same database, as with Oracle Parallel Server/Real Application Clusters. SMON also cleans up adjacent pieces of free space in the datafiles by merging them into one piece, and it gets rid of space used for sorting rows when that space is no longer needed.

Process Monitor (PMON)

This process watches over the user processes that access the database. If a user process terminates abnormally, PMON is responsible for cleaning up any of the resources left behind (such as memory) and for releasing any locks held by the failed process.

Archiver (ARCH)

This process reads the redo log files once Oracle has filled them and writes a copy of the used redo log files to the specified archive log destination(s). Oracle8i and beyond support up to 10 ARCH processes, named ARC0 through ARC9. LGWR will start additional archivers as needed, based on the load, up to the limit specified by the initialization parameter LOG_ARCHIVE_MAX_PROCESSES.

Checkpoint (CKPT)

This process works with DBWR to perform checkpoints. CKPT updates the control file and database file headers to update the checkpoint data when the checkpoint is complete.

Recover (RECO)

This process automatically cleans up failed or suspended distributed transactions.

Oracle Versions

Oracle version numbers, like the product packaging we discuss in the next section, have more to do with the marketplace than the technology. The Oracle database, like all software products, has a periodic release cycle, but the exact timing and contents of those releases is shaped, to some degree, by sales requirements as well as the development cycle. Because of nontechnical factors, the naming conventions for versions can change at any time.

As of this writing, Oracle seems to have settled on a consistent version naming scheme. Up until Oracle8, each major version was named with an increasing version number (e.g., Oracle6, Oracle7, Oracle8). However, the release after Oracle8 was named Oracle8i, connecting it with the Internet (and causing formatting problems for authors ever since!). The next version was named Oracle9i, and the upcoming version is slated to be called Oracle10i—although that may change by the time the version is released.

Typically, the OracleNi versions have had an intermediate release, also typically identified as Release 2. Release 2s generally are the first major maintenance release; they follow the main release and frequently contain enhancements that were planned for the main release but that could not make the deadline.

This book assumes that Oracle8 was the beginning of time. Any features that were not present in that version are not discussed. Any features that were added or dropped since then are duly noted.

Oracle Packaging

Even more so than versions, the actual packaging of Oracle releases is controlled primarily by sales forces, rather than by technical forces. The decision to include a feature in one or more versions of the database, as well as the decision to segregate functionality in an extra-cost option, is, for the most part, arbitrary.

Editions

There are four basic editions of the Oracle database:

Standard Edition
    The lowest cost server edition of Oracle, which does not include all the capabilities of the Oracle database. The extra options described in the next section cannot be used with Standard Edition.

Enterprise Edition
    The complete Oracle database, which is required for the use of the extra options described in the next section.

Personal Edition
    A single-user version of the Oracle database, available only for Windows. This edition includes all the functionality of all the options for Enterprise Edition, where appropriate.

Lite
    A trimmed-down version of the Oracle database designed for mobile use.

Although Oracle sometimes decides to fold formerly extra-cost options into one or more editions of the standard product, the company has never yet decided to take functionality out of a lesser edition in order to force upgrades.

Most of the functionality described in this book is included in all versions of the database. The following functionality is available in Enterprise Edition, but not Standard Edition, as of the time of this writing:

Data Guard
> Provides a set of routines and a management tool that make it easier to implement standby databases.

Fast-start recovery
> Implements a method of recovery that allows the database to be opened as soon as the rollback is applied from the log files.

Online index build and coalesce
> Allows index build and coalesce operations to be performed without requiring the index to be taken offline.

Online table reorganization and redefinition
> Allows table reorganization and redefinition operations to be performed without requiring the index to be taken offline.

Block-level media recovery
> Enables the recovery of specific blocks on the media, reducing the need to recover an entire file.

Incremental backup and recovery
> Allows the backup and recovery of data that has been changed since the time of the last full or incremental backup; this approach can significantly reduce the time for these operations.

Parallel backup and recovery
> Allows backup and recovery operations that use parallel execution, which can significantly reduce the time for these operations.

Tablespace point-in-time recovery
> Gives you the ability to recover a tablespace to a particular point in time; this feature can be used to recover data from a damaged log file or to recover to a point in time just before a data error occurred.

Trial recovery
> Lets you test the validity of a backup without having to run the entire process.

Virtual Private Database (VPD)
> Gives you the ability to define security on a row based on the outcome of a security procedure. This capability allows you to grant access to a row based on the value of the data in the row, among other implementation strategies.

Fine-grained auditing
> Allows auditing to be performed based on the content of a row.

Database Resource Manager (DRM)
> Allows you to limit the amount of database resources allocated to a single user or group of users.

Bitmapped index and bitmapped join index
> Supports additional types of indexes that can speed the performance of data warehouse-type queries.

Automated parallel query degree
Allows Oracle to choose the best degree of parallelism for a particular query.

Parallel operations
Allow parallel operations (e.g., query, load, analyze, bitmap star query optimization, DML, index build, and index scan) to run faster, because they can take advantage of multiple processes.

Export of transportable tablespaces
Supports transportable tablespaces, which allow you to move a tablespace as easily as copying a file. This approach can be more efficient than an import/export process.

Advanced replication
Allows the replication of changed data from one database instance to another. This feature allows you to build custom conflict resolution methods.

Options

Oracle provides a number of options that can be purchased with Oracle Enterprise Edition. As with the packaging in general, the content, price, and availability of these options are subject to change.

At the time of this writing (with Oracle9*i* Release 2), the following options are available:

Real Application Clusters
Allows the use of a clustered database spread over multiple servers

Partitioning
Allows data to be spread over multiple disks to improve performance

OLAP
Includes a set of analytical functions that can be used for Online Analytical Processing

Data Mining
Includes a set of data mining functionality for creating business intelligence applications

Spatial
Enables the use of features and the manipulation of data for spatial information, such as that used in geographic information systems (GIS)

Advanced Security
Provides the ability to use strong authentication and encryption

Label Security
Provides the ability to define fine-grained security for data

In addition to these options, Oracle supports a series of expansion, or add-on, packs that can be used to extend the functionality of Enterprise Manager. These packs are described in Chapter 16.

2

Configuration

Oracle is designed to be a very flexible and configurable system. These qualities are absolute necessities for a database that can be run on dozens of different hardware platforms in a multitude of configurations, supporting an almost infinite variety of applications and users. In order to achieve the needed flexibility, Oracle must provide the DBA with a simple method of specifying certain operational characteristics of the database in a clear and consistent manner. DBAs specify most of these characteristics by setting and resetting values for the database *initialization parameters*, commonly referred to as *INIT.ORA parameters*. The fundamental goal is to set or reset these parameters in a way that gets the database running at its peak performance level.

Each initialization parameter controls a specific aspect of the Oracle server. Together, all of the parameters combine to shape the generic Oracle database technology to fit your particular needs.

The following is a typical initialization file for a general-purpose installation of Oracle9*i*:

```
DB_NAME = "ORA9"
DB_DOMAIN = homeserver
INSTANCE_NAME = ORA9
SERVICE_NAMES = ORA9.homeserver

DB_FILES = 1024
DB_BLOCK_SIZE = 8192

COMPATIBLE = 9.0.0
SORT_AREA_SIZE = 65536
SORT_AREA_RETAINED_SIZE = 65536

CONTROL_FILES = ("C:\Oracle\oradata\ORA9\control01.ctl",
"D:\Oracle\oradata\ORA9\control02.ctl",
"E:\Oracle\oradata\ORA9\control03.ctl")
```

```
OPEN_CURSORS = 100
CURSOR_SHARING = similar

MAX_ENABLED_ROLES = 30
DB_FILE_MULTIBLOCK_READ_COUNT = 8
DB_BLOCK_BUFFERS = 2048

SHARED_POOL_SIZE = 19728640
LARGE_POOL_SIZE = 614400
JAVA_POOL_SIZE = 25971520

LOG_CHECKPOINT_INTERVAL = 10000
LOG_CHECKPOINT_TIMEOUT = 1800

PROCESSES = 200
PARALLEL_MAX_SERVERS = 5
LOG_BUFFER = 32768
MAX_DUMP_FILE_SIZE = 10240   # limit trace file size to 5M each
GLOBAL_NAMES = true

ORACLE_TRACE_COLLECTION_NAME = ""
BACKGROUND_DUMP_DEST = D:\Oracle\admin\ORA9\bdump
RESOURCE_MANAGER_PLAN = system_plan
USER_DUMP_DEST = D:\Oracle\admin\ORA9\udump
TRACEFILE_IDENTIFIER = ORA9

REMOTE_LOGIN_PASSWORDFILE = exclusive
OS_AUTHENT_PREFIX = ""

PLSQL_COMPILER_FLAGS = debug
UNDO_MANAGEMENT = auto
```

This example shows only some of the basic parameters in the initialization file. In an operational system, you would probably include additional parameters; you would typically also include comments describing the specific effects of the parameters in your environment and the revision history of changes to the parameters. Such comments must be preceded by the # character, as with the MAX_DUMP_FILE_SIZE parameter in the example.

The bulk of this chapter consists of a comprehensive list of initialization parameters, although we start with a brief discussion of the parameters and the files used to store them.

Parameter Files and Types

The name and location of the database initialization parameter file on your system depends upon the Oracle version and the operating system you are running, as described in the following sections.

INIT.ORA: The Initialization File

In Oracle releases prior to Oracle9*i*, initialization parameters are specified in the *INIT.ORA* file. This file is usually named in the form *INITsid.ORA*, where *sid* is the SID, or system identifier, for your particular Oracle instance. The SID is a unique name used to identify a particular instance across your entire environment.

Refer to the Oracle documentation for the default location of this file for your particular operating system.

SPFILE: The Server Parameter File

Beginning with Oracle9*i*, Oracle introduced the concept of the server parameter file. This file, known as *SPFILE*, differs from the standard *INIT.ORA* file in a number of ways:

- It is a binary file, rather than a text-based file.
- It is stored on the server, rather than on a client machine.
- It can maintain changes to parameter values over the shutdown and startup of an instance.

This last point is the important part of *SPFILE*. If your database is running under Oracle9*i*, any changes you make to configuration parameters via the ALTER SYSTEM statement will be saved as part of the permanent configuration file. That means that if you change any of your database parameter values for tuning purposes, you won't also have to change one or more *INIT.ORA* files so that the new values will persist. You also have the option of making dynamic changes to parameters without making them a part of the *SPFILE*; you do this by including the SCOPE clause in the ALTER SYSTEM statement, using the following syntax:

```
ALTER SYSTEM SET parameter_name = parameter_value
    SCOPE = {MEMORY | SPFILE | BOTH};
```

For a complete description of the ALTER SYSTEM syntax, see Chapter 7.

With Oracle9*i*, you can still use a local *INIT.ORA* file by specifying the location of that file with a PFILE=*name* clause in the STARTUP statement. Oracle9*i* also provides a simple way to migrate the parameters in an existing *INIT.ORA* file to the binary *SPFILE* for an instance. You can copy the *INIT.ORA* file to the server machine and issue the following command, substituting the complete actual pathname for *pathname*:

```
CREATE SPFILE FROM PFILE='pathname/initsid.ora';
```

The SPFILE parameter, which you can specify in your *INIT.ORA* file, allows you to point to a nondefault location for the *SPFILE*; simply include a line such as the following in your *INIT.ORA* file:

```
SPFILE=$ORACLE_HOME/dbs/spfile.ora;
```

Dynamically Modifiable Parameters

While most initialization parameters are static, taking their values from the initial-ization file as it exists at the time of database startup, some may be dynamically modified while the instance is up and the database is open.

Dynamic modification is different from dynamic storage of a changed value in the *SPFILE*. In all versions of Oracle, you can dynamically modify a setting using the ALTER SYSTEM or ALTER SESSION command. Starting with Oracle9i, these changes may also be dynamically stored in the *SPFILE*, depending on the value of the SCOPE clause of the ALTER command.

In the individual parameter descriptions in the following sections, we indicate which parameters may be dynamically modifiable (the Dynamic entry in the parameter description) and how they can be modified (via ALTER SYSTEM, ALTER SESSION, or both).

Initialization Parameters

The remainder of this chapter describes the Oracle initialization parameters. We show the parameter names here in uppercase for readability, but you can specify parameters in upper, lower, or mixed case in the parameter file.

In addition to the initialization parameters listed in this chapter, which apply to most Oracle systems, some additional parameters are specific to a particular hardware platform or operating system. These parameters are documented in the *Installation Guide*, *User Guide*, and/or *Release Notes* for your release of Oracle.

We've grouped the parameters presented in the following sections in a number of functional categories; within each category, they are listed alphabetically. We've arranged the parameters this way because you will frequently use a group of parameters to control a particular area of operation, such as auditing or job management. If you need to find a particular parameter, however, check the index; you'll find an alphabetical listing of all parameters under "initialization parameters."

These functional categories are:

Auditing	National Language Support (NLS)
Backup and recovery	Optimization and performance
Clustered databases	Oracle Trace
Cursors	Parallel execution
Database links	Parameters
Distributed operations and	PL/SQL
Heterogeneous Services	Remote sites
I/O and space management	Rollback (undo/redo) management
Java	Security
Jobs	Shared Server/Multi-Threaded
Licenses	Server (MTS)

Locking and transactions	Sorts
Logging and archiving	Standby databases
Memory management	System operations
Names	Miscellaneous parameters

For each parameter, we include the following information, where appropriate:

- Valid values for the parameter; note that you can specify the following abbreviations in many parameter values: K (kilobytes), M (megabytes), G (gigabytes)
- The default value
- Whether the parameter may be dynamically modified and the command that can be used to modify it (ALTER SESSION, ALTER SYSTEM)
- The syntax for specifying the parameter (included only for complicated parameter assignments)
- Keywords you may specify in setting the parameter's value
- A brief description, including information about which Oracle versions and/or editions support the parameter, if relevant

A few parameters are not supported in all versions covered in this book (Oracle8, Oracle8i, and Oracle9i.) This limited support is also noted in the parameter descriptions.

Auditing

The following parameters shape how auditing is performed in the Oracle database.

AUDIT_FILE_DEST

Value: valid directory pathname   **Default:** *$ORACLE_HOME/RDBMS/AUDIT*

Specifies the directory where auditing files are stored.

AUDIT_TRAIL

Value: NONE | FALSE | DB | TRUE | OS   **Default:** NONE

Enables or disables the writing of rows to the audit trail. The SQL AUDIT statements can set auditing options regardless of the setting of this parameter.

Keywords

NONE	Audited records are not written
FALSE	Supported for backward compatibility. Same as NONE
DB	Enables systemwide auditing and causes audited records to be written to the database audit trail (the SYS.AUD$ table)
TRUE	Supported for backward compatibility. Same as DB
OS	Enables systemwide auditing and causes audited records to be written to the operating system's audit trail

TRANSACTION_AUDITING

Value: TRUE | FALSE   **Default:** TRUE   **Dynamic:** ALTER SYSTEM DEFERRED

Specifies whether the transaction layer generates a special redo record that contains session and user information.

Backup and Recovery

The following parameters shape and control the options and operations of backup and recovery. See the descriptions of related parameters in the "Logging and Archiving" and "Rollback (Undo/Redo) Management" sections.

BACKUP_DISK_IO_SLAVES

Value: 0–15   **Default:** 0

Specifies the number of I/O slaves used by the Recovery Manager to back up, copy, or restore data to disk. Obsolete with Oracle9i.

BACKUP_TAPE_IO_SLAVES

Value: TRUE | FALSE   **Default:** FALSE   **Dynamic:** ALTER SYSTEM DEFERRED

Specifies whether I/O slaves are used by the Recovery Manager to back up, copy, or restore data to tape.

FAST_START_IO_TARGET

Value: 0 | 1000–all buffers in the cache   **Default:** all buffers in the cache   **Dynamic:** ALTER SYSTEM

Specifies the number of buffer I/O operations expected to be used during crash or instance recovery. Lower values cause the DB writer process to write dirty buffers to disk more often in order to keep buffer I/O at recovery within the target set, at the expense of overall performance. 0 disables fast-start checkpointing. New with Oracle8i and available only with Enterprise Edition.

With Oracle9i, Oracle recommends that you use FAST_START_MTTR_TARGET instead of this parameter.

FAST_START_MTTR_TARGET

Value: 0–3600   **Default:** 0   **Dynamic:** ALTER SYSTEM

Specifies the number of seconds expected to be used during crash or instance recovery. Works like FAST_START_IO_TARET, but ignored if that parameter or LOG_CHECKPOINT_INTERVAL is specified. New with Oracle9i.

FAST_START_PARALLEL_ROLLBACK

Value: HIGH | LOW | FALSE   **Default:** LOW   **Dynamic:** ALTER SYSTEM

Specifies the maximum number of processes that will perform parallel rollback. FALSE disables parallel rollback, LOW sets the number to 2 * CPU_COUNT, HIGH sets the number to 4 * CPU_COUNT. New with Oracle9i.

FREEZE_DB_FOR_FAST_INSTANCE_RECOVERY

Value: TRUE | FALSE   **Default:** see description   **Dynamic:** ALTER SYSTEM

Parallel Server parameter that controls whether Oracle freezes the entire database during instance recovery. If TRUE, Oracle freezes the entire database during instance recovery, which stops all other disk activities except those for instance recovery, allowing instance recovery to complete faster. If FALSE, Oracle does not freeze the entire database, unless Oracle is responsible for resilvering some of the mirrored datafiles. If all online datafiles use hash locks, the default is FALSE. If any datafiles use fine-grained locks, the default is TRUE. Multiple instances must have identical values. Obsolete with Oracle8i.

RECOVERY_PARALLELISM

Value: 0–PARALLEL_MAX_SERVERS   **Default:** operating system dependent

Specifies the number of processes to participate in instance or media recovery. New with Oracle9i.

Clustered Databases

The following parameters apply to either Oracle Parallel Server (prior to Oracle9i) or Real Application Clusters (new with Oracle9i).

CLUSTER_DATABASE

Value: TRUE | FALSE   **Default:** FALSE

Specifies whether Real Application Clusters is enabled. Must be set to TRUE for all instances in a Real Application Cluster. New with Oracle9i.

CLUSTER_DATABASE_INSTANCES

Value: positive integer   **Default:** 1

Specifies the number of instances participating in a Real Application Cluster. Should be set to the same value in each instance. New with Oracle9i.

CLUSTER_INTERCONNECTS

Value: one or more valid IP addresses, separated by colons (:)

Specifies additional interconnect IP addresses in a Real Application Cluster, in order to improve performance in large clusters. New with Oracle9*i*.

DELAYED_LOGGING_BLOCK_CLEANOUTS

Value: TRUE | FALSE   **Default:** TRUE

Turns the delayed block cleanout feature on or off. This reduces pinging in an Oracle Parallel Server. Keeping this feature set to TRUE sets a fast path and results in no logging block cleanout at commit time. Obsolete with Oracle8*i*.

DRS_START

Value: TRUE | FALSE   **Default:** FALSE   **Dynamic:** ALTER SYSTEM

Specifies whether the disaster recovery process (DRMON) is started. Should be specified only if the instance will be part of a disaster recovery configuration.

GC_DEFER_TIME

Value: any positive integer   **Default:** 10   **Dynamic:** ALTER SYSTEM

Specifies the time in hundredths of a second that the server waits before responding to forced-write requests for hot blocks from other instances. The default value means that the feature is disabled. Obsolete with Oracle9*i*.

GC_FILES_TO_LOCKS

Value: see description

Parallel Server parameter that controls the mapping of Parallel Cache Management (PCM) locks to datafiles. The parameter can be used to limit the number of locks used per datafile and also to specify that each lock should cover a set of contiguous blocks. If this parameter is specified, Oracle will disable the Cache Fusion processing feature of Oracle9*i* Real Application Clusters. Multiple instances must have identical values.

Syntax

```
GC_FILES_TO_LOCKS = '{file_list=lock_count[!blocks][EACH]}[:]...'
```

Keywords

file_list   One or more datafiles listed by their file numbers, or ranges of file numbers, with comma separators

lock_count   The number of PCM locks assigned to *file_list*. If *lock_count* is set to 0, then fine-grained locking is used for these files.

!blocks   Optionally indicates the number of contiguous blocks covered by one lock.

EACH   Optionally specifies that each datafile in *file_list* is assigned a separate set of *lock_count* PCM locks; the default is noncontiguous blocks.

GC_LCK_PROCS

Value: 1–10, or 0 for a single instance running in exclusive mode   **Default:** 1

Sets the number of background lock processes (LCK0 through LCK9) for an instance in a Parallel Server. The default of 1 is normally sufficient, but the value can be increased if the distributed lock request rate saturates the lock process. Multiple instances must have identical values.

GC_RELEASABLE_LOCKS

Value: 50–unlimited   **Default:** value of DB_BLOCK_BUFFERS

Specifies a value used to allocate space for fine-grained locking. There is no maximum value, except as imposed by memory restrictions. Specific to Oracle Parallel Server in shared mode. Obsolete with Oracle9i.

GC_ROLLBACK_LOCKS

Value: 1 – unlimited   **Default:** 20

Specifies, for each rollback segment, the number of distributed locks available for simultaneously modified rollback segment blocks for Parallel Server. The default is adequate for most applications. Each instance must have identical values. Obsolete with Oracle9i.

Syntax

```
GC_ROLLBACK_LOCKS = 'rs_list = lock_count[!blocks][R][EACH][:...]'
```

Keywords

rs_list	One or more rollback segments listed by their segment numbers, or ranges of segment numbers, with comma separators.
lock_count	Number of PCM locks assigned to *rs_list*.
!blocks	Number of contiguous blocks covered by one lock. The default is noncontiguous blocks.
R	Indicates that these locks are releasable and are drawn as needed from the pool of releasable locks.
EACH	Indicates that each rollback segment in *rs_list* is assigned a separate set of *lock_count* PCM locks.

INSTANCE_GROUPS

Value: comma-separated string of group names   **Default:** none

Assigns the current instance to the specified groups. This is a Real Application Clusters/Parallel Server parameter. See PARALLEL_INSTANCE_GROUP under "Parallel Execution."

INSTANCE_NAME

Value: string containing instance name   **Default:** current instance SID

Specifies the name of the instance. Primarily useful in Real Application Clusters or Parallel Server, where it may be desirable to specify a particular instance by which to connect to the database. New with Oracle8i.

INSTANCE_NUMBER

Value: 1–maximum number of instances specified in CREATE DATABASE statement
Default: lowest available number

Specifies a unique number that maps the instance to one group of free space lists for each table created with the storage option FREELIST GROUPS. The INSTANCE option of the ALTER TABLE ALLOCATE EXTENT statement assigns an extent to a particular group of free lists. If INSTANCE_NUMBER is set to the value specified for the INSTANCE option, the instance uses that extent for inserts and updates that expand rows. INSTANCE_NUMBER is a Parallel Server parameter. Multiple instances must have different values.

LM_LOCKS

Value: 512–available shared memory   **Default:** 12000

Specifies the number of locks that will be configured for the Lock Manager when running Parallel Server. The number of locks is represented by the following equation:

$$L = R + (R*(N - 1))/N$$

where:

R is the number of resources
N is the total number of nodes
L is the total number of locks

Multiple instances must have the same value. Obsolete with Oracle9i.

LM_PROCS

Value: 36–PROCESSES + maximum number of instances + safety factor
Default: 64 + maximum instances supported

Parallel Server parameter that specifies the value of the PROCESSES parameter plus the maximum number of instances. Must be the same for all instances. Obsolete with Oracle8i.

LM_RESS

Value: 256–available shared memory   **Default:** 6000

Parallel Server parameter that controls the number of resources that can be locked by each Lock Manager instance. The value specified for LM_RESS should be much less than 2 * DML_LOCKS plus an overhead of about 20 locks. Multiple instances must have the same value. Obsolete with Oracle9i.

LOG_FILE_NAME_CONVERT

Value: character string (see description)   **Default:** none

Converts the filename of a new log file on the primary database to the filename of a log file on the standby database. The file must exist and be writable on the standby database or the recovery process will halt with an error.

Syntax
    LOG_FILE_NAME_CONVERT = [(]'string1','string2'[,'string1,string2...][)]

Keywords
string1   The pattern found in the log file names on the primary database.

string2   The pattern found in the log file names on the standby database.

MAX_COMMIT_PROPAGATION_DELAY

Value: 0–90000   **Default:** 90000

Specifies the maximum amount of time in hundredths of seconds allowed before the System Change Number (SCN) held in the SGA of an instance is refreshed by LGWR. It determines if the local SCN should be refreshed from the lock value when getting the snapshot SCN for a query.

This parameter should not be changed except under a limited set of circumstances specific to Oracle Parallel Server. It must be identical for all nodes in the cluster.

OPS_ADMIN_GROUP

Value: valid group name   **Default:** all active instances

Allows instances to be partitioned in a Parallel Server environment for monitoring or administration purposes. The database must be mounted in Parallel Server mode. The value of OPS_ADMIN_GROUP determines which instances return information in a GV$ view query. Obsolete with Oracle8*i*.

PARALLEL_SERVER

Value: TRUE | FALSE   **Default:** FALSE

Specifies that the Parallel Server option is to be enabled for this instance. Multiple instances must have same value. Obsolete with Oracle9*i*.

PARALLEL_SERVER_IDLE_TIME

Value: 0–operating system dependent   **Default:** operating system dependent

Specifies the amount of idle time after which Oracle terminates a query server process, expressed in minutes. Obsolete with Oracle8*i*.

PARALLEL_SERVER_INSTANCES

Value: 0–operating system dependent   **Default:** operating system dependent

Specifies the number of instances to use for sizing SGA structures in a Parallel Server environment. Available only in Oracle8i.

Cursors

The following parameters shape the use of cursors.

CLOSE_CACHED_OPEN_CURSORS

Value: TRUE | FALSE   **Default:** FALSE

Specifies whether cursors opened and cached in memory by PL/SQL are automatically closed at each COMMIT. If PL/SQL cursors are reused frequently, FALSE can cause subsequent executions to be faster. TRUE causes open cursors to be closed at each COMMIT or ROLLBACK, and the cursor can then be reopened as needed. Obsolete with Oracle8i.

CURSOR_SHARING

Value: SIMILAR | EXACT | FORCE   **Dynamic:** ALTER SYSTEM, ALTER SESSION

Specifies the way that SQL statements can share cursors in memory. New with Oracle9i.

Keywords

SIMILAR   Specifies that SQL that is the same except for literals will share the same cursor in memory unless the literals affect the meaning of the SQL statement.

EXACT   Specifies that SQL must be identical to share the same cursor in memory.

FORCE   Specifies that SQL that is the same except for literals will share the same cursor.

CURSOR_SPACE_FOR_TIME

Value: TRUE | FALSE   **Default:** FALSE

Controls the use of memory used to store cursors. If this parameter is set to TRUE, the database uses more space for cursors to save time. Because the shared SQL areas never leave memory while they are in use, however, this parameter should be set to TRUE only when the shared pool is large enough to hold all open cursors simultaneously. Setting this parameter to TRUE also retains the private SQL area allocated for each cursor between executes instead of discarding it after cursor execution, which saves cursor allocation and initialization time.

OPEN_CURSORS

Value: 1–4294967297   **Default:** 50

Specifies the maximum number of open cursors a session can have at once, preventing a session from opening an excessive number of cursors. No added overhead is incurred by setting this value too high. Also constrains the size of the PL/SQL cursor cache used to avoid having to reparse statements.

ROW_CACHE_CURSORS

Value: 10–3300   **Default:** 10

Specifies the maximum number of cached recursive cursors used by the Dictionary Cache Manager for selecting rows from the data dictionary. Obsolete with Oracle8*i*.

SERIAL_REUSE

Value: DISABLE | SELECT | DML | PLSQL | ALL | NULL
Default: DISABLE

Specifies which types of SQL cursors should make use of the serially reusable memory feature. Moves well-structured private cursor memory into the SGA shared pool so that it can be reused by sessions executing the same cursor.

Keywords

DISABLE   Disables the option for all SQL statement types. This value overrides any other values included in the list.

SELECT   Enables the option for SELECT statements.

DML   Enables the option for DML statements.

PLSQL   Currently has no effect.

ALL   Enables the option for both DML and SELECT statements.

NULL   Equivalent to DISABLE.

SESSION_CACHED_CURSORS

Value: 0–operating system dependent   **Default:** 0   **Dynamic:** ALTER SYSTEM

Specifies the maximum number of session cursors to keep in the session cursor cache. Repeated parse calls of the same SQL statement cause the session cursor for that statement to be moved into the session cursor cache. Subsequent parse calls need not reopen the cursor.

Database Links

The following parameters concern the use of database links (DB links) to remote databases.

DBLINK_ENCRYPT_LOGIN

Value: TRUE | FALSE   **Default:** FALSE

Specifies whether attempts to connect to other Oracle servers through database links should use encrypted passwords. If TRUE, and the connection fails, Oracle does not re-attempt a failed connection. If FALSE, Oracle re-attempts the connection using an unencrypted version of the password.

OPEN_LINKS

Value: 0–255   **Default:** 4

Specifies the maximum number of concurrent open connections to remote databases in one session. The value should equal or exceed the number of databases referred to in a single SQL statement that references multiple databases so that all the databases can be open to execute the statement. Can also avoid the overhead of re-opening database links in sequential access.

OPEN_LINKS_PER_INSTANCE

Value: 0–4294967297   **Default:** 4

Specifies the maximum number of migratable open connections. XA transactions use migratable open connections so that the connections are cached after a transaction is committed. OPEN_LINKS_PER_INSTANCE differs from the OPEN_LINKS parameter in that OPEN_LINKS indicates the number of connections from a session and is not applicable to XA applications.

Distributed Operations and Heterogeneous Services

The following parameters control distributed operations and Heterogeneous Services (HS) used with Oracle.

COMMIT_POINT_STRENGTH

Value: 0–255   **Default:** operating system dependent

Specifies a value that determines the commit point site in a distributed transaction. The node in the transaction with the highest value for COMMIT_POINT_STRENGTH will be the commit point site. A database's commit point strength should be set relative to the amount of critical shared data in the database.

DISTRIBUTED_LOCK_TIMEOUT

Value: 1–unlimited   **Default:** 60

Specifies the amount of time in seconds for distributed transactions to wait for locked resources. Obsolete with Oracle8*i*.

DISTRIBUTED_RECOVERY_CONNECTION_HOLD_TIME

Value: 0–1800   **Default:** 200

Specifies the length of time in seconds to hold a remote connection open after a distributed transaction fails. (The purpose of holding the connection open is the hope that communication will be restored without having to reestablish the connection.) Values larger than 1800 seconds can be specified, but because the reconnection and recovery background process run every 30 minutes (1800 seconds) whether or not a failure occurs, a value of 1800 means that the connection never closes. Obsolete with Oracle8*i*.

DISTRIBUTED_TRANSACTIONS

Value: 0–TRANSACTIONS   **Default:** TRANSACTIONS * 25

Specifies the maximum number of distributed transactions in which this database can concurrently participate. The value of this parameter cannot exceed the value of the TRANSACTIONS parameter. If DISTRIBUTED_TRANSACTIONS is set to 0, no distributed transactions are allowed, and the recovery process does not start when the instance starts up.

HS_AUTOREGISTER

Value: TRUE | FALSE   **Default:** TRUE   **Dynamic:** ALTER SYSTEM

Specifies whether automatic self-registration of Heterogeneous Services agents is enabled. Oracle recommends setting this parameter to TRUE, because overhead will thus be reduced when establishing subsequent connections through the same agent. New with Oracle8*i*.

MAX_TRANSACTION_BRANCHES

Value: 1–32   **Default:** 8

Controls the number of branches in a distributed transaction, allowing up to 32 servers or server groups per instance to work on one distributed transaction.

I/O and Space Management

The following parameters shape and control I/O operations and space management.

DB_BLOCK_CHECKING

Value: TRUE | FALSE   **Default:** FALSE
Dynamic: ALTER SYSTEM, ALTER SESSION

Specifies whether data blocks are checked for corruption before being written. Setting this parameter to TRUE will result in a performance penalty of up to 10%, so use it with caution. New with Oracle8*i*.

DB_BLOCK_SIZE

Value: 2048–32768 at most, but may be less depending on operating system
Default: operating system dependent

Specifies the size in bytes of Oracle database blocks. The value for DB_BLOCK_SIZE when the database is created determines the size of the blocks, and at all other times the value must be set to the original *valuemum* value of the FREELISTS storage parameter for tables and indexes.

This value can be set only at database creation time and must not be changed afterward.

DB_FILE_DIRECT_IO_COUNT

Value: operating system dependent   **Default:** 64

Specifies the number of blocks to be used for I/O operations performed by backup, restore, or direct path read and write functions. The I/O buffer size is a product of DB_FILE_DIRECT_IO_COUNT and DB_BLOCK_SIZE and cannot exceed the maximum I/O size for the platform. Obsolete with Oracle9*i*.

DB_FILE_MULTIBLOCK_READ_COUNT

Value: 1–operating system dependent   **Default:** 8
Dynamic: ALTER SYSTEM, ALTER SESSION

Specifies the maximum number of blocks read in one I/O operation during a sequential scan. Batch environments typically have values for this parameter in the range of 4 to 16. DSS (decision support/data warehouse) database environments tend to benefit from maximizing the value for this parameter. The actual maximum varies by operating system; it is always less than or equal to the operating system's maximum I/O size expressed as Oracle blocks (maximum I/O size / DB_BLOCK_SIZE).

DB_FILE_SIMULTANEOUS_WRITES

Value: 1 to 4 * number of disks in a striped file, or 4 if no striping
Default: 4

Specifies the maximum number of simultaneous writes that can be made to a given database file. Oracle also uses the value of this parameter in computing various internal parameters that affect read and write operations to database files. Also used to determine the number of reads-per-file in the redo read-ahead when reading redo during recovery. Obsolete with Oracle8*i*.

DB_FILES

Value: specified in the MAXDATAFILES clause the last time CREATE DATABASE or CREATE CONTROLFILE was executed, or the current actual number of datafiles in the data
Default: operating system dependent

Specifies the maximum number of database files that can be opened for this database. This parameter should be set for the maximum number of files, subject to operating system constraints, that will ever be specified for the database, including files to be added via the ADD DATAFILE statement. If the value of DB_FILES is increased, all instances accessing the database must be shut down and restarted before the new value can take effect.

DISK_ASYNCH_IO

Value: TRUE | FALSE   **Default:** TRUE

Controls whether I/O to datafiles, control files, and log files is asynchronous. If a platform does not support asynchronous I/O to disk, this parameter has no effect. If DISK_ASYNCH_IO is set to FALSE, then the DBWR_IO_SLAVES parameter should be set to a nonzero value in order to simulate asynchronous I/O.

HASH_MULTIBLOCK_IO_COUNT

Value: operating system dependent   **Default:** 1   **Dynamic:** ALTER SESSION

Specifies how many sequential blocks a hash join reads and writes in one I/O. When operating in multi-threaded server mode, this parameter is ignored and a value of 1 is used. The maximum value is always less than the operating system's maximum I/O size expressed as Oracle blocks. This parameter strongly affects performance because it controls the number of partitions into which the input is divided. Obsolete with Oracle9*i*.

LGWR_IO_SLAVES

Value: 0–operating system dependent   **Default:** 0

Specifies the number of I/O slaves used by the LGWR process. Obsolete with Oracle8*i*.

Java

The following parameters apply to the use of Java in the database.

JAVA_MAX_SESSIONSPACE_SIZE

Value: 0–4 GB   **Default:** 0

Specifies the maximum amount of session space in bytes that will be made available to a Java program executing on the server. New with Oracle8*i*.

If the user session attempts to allocate more memory than specified here, the Java Virtual Manager (JVM) will generate an out-of-memory condition and the session will be killed.

JAVA_POOL_SIZE

Value: 1000000–1000000000   Default: 20000

Specifies the size of the Java pool in the SGA in bytes. New with Oracle8i.

JAVA_SOFT_SESSIONSPACE_LIMIT

Value: 0–4 GB   Default: 0

Specifies the amount in bytes of Java memory that can be used in a session before a warning is generated in a trace file. New with Oracle8i.

Jobs

The following parameters apply to jobs and the job queue.

JOB_QUEUE_INTERVAL

Value: 1–3600   Default: 60

Specifies the interval in seconds between wake-ups for the SNPn background processes of the instance. Oracle8 and Oracle8i only.

JOB_QUEUE_KEEP_CONNECTIONS

Value: TRUE | FALSE   Default: FALSE

Specifies whether job queue processes keep network connections open between jobs. Obsolete with Oracle8i.

JOB_QUEUE_PROCESSES

Value: 0–1000   Default: 0   Dynamic: ALTER SYSTEM

Specifies the maximum number of background processes per instance that can be created for the execution of jobs.

Licenses

The following parameters apply to licensing.

LICENSE_MAX_SESSIONS

Value: 0–number of session licenses   Default: 0

Specifies the maximum number of concurrent user sessions allowed simultaneously. When this limit is reached, only users with the RESTRICTED SESSION privilege can connect to the server, and users who are not able to connect receive a warning message indicating that the system has reached maximum capacity.

Usage licensing and user licensing should not be enabled concurrently; you must always set either LICENSE_MAX_SESSIONS or LICENSE_MAX_USERS to zero. If this parameter is set to a nonzero number, LICENSE_SESSIONS_WARNING should also be set.

LICENSE_MAX_USERS

Value: 0–number of user licenses   **Default:** 0

Specifies the maximum number of users that can be created in the database. When this limit is reached, additional users cannot be created. Multiple instances should have the same value.

LICENSE_SESSIONS_WARNING

Value: 0–LICENSE_MAX_SESSIONS   **Default:** 0

Specifies a warning limit on the number of concurrent user sessions. When this limit is reached, additional users can connect, but Oracle writes a message in the alert file for each new connection. Users with RESTRICTED SESSION privilege who connect after the limit is reached receive a warning message stating that the system is nearing its maximum capacity.

Locking and Transactions

The following parameters change the ways that Oracle handles locking behavior and transactions.

DISCRETE_TRANSACTIONS_ENABLED

Value: TRUE | FALSE   **Default:** FALSE

Implements a simpler, faster rollback mechanism that improves performance for certain kinds of transactions. There are limits on the kinds of transactions that can occur in discrete mode; for details, see the Oracle documentation. Obsolete with Oracle8*i*.

DML_LOCKS

Value: 0 | 20–unlimited   **Default:** 4 * TRANSACTIONS

Specifies the maximum number of DML locks; include one for each table modified in a transaction. The value should equal the grand total of locks on tables currently referenced by all users. If the value is set to 0, enqueues are disabled and performance is slightly increased. However, you will not be able to use DROP TABLE, CREATE INDEX, or explicit lock statements such as LOCK TABLE IN EXCLUSIVE MODE. Multiple instances must all have positive values or must all be 0.

ENQUEUE_RESOURCES

Value: 10–unlimited   **Default:** Derived from SESSIONS

Sets the number of resources that can be concurrently locked by the Lock Manager. For fewer than 4 sessions, the default value is 20; for 4 to 10 sessions, the default value is ((SESSIONS - 3) * 5) + 20; and for more than 10 sessions, it is ((SESSIONS - 10) * 2) + 55. If ENQUEUE_RESOURCES is explicitly set to a value higher than DML_LOCKS + 20, then the value provided is used. If there are many tables, the value may be increased. Allow one per resource, regardless of the number of sessions or cursors using that resource. Increase the value if Oracle returns an error specifying that enqueues are exhausted.

ROW_LOCKING

Value: ALWAYS | DEFAULT | INTENT   **Default:** ALWAYS

Specifies whether row locks are acquired when a table is updated. ALWAYS or DEFAULT means that only row locks are acquired when a table is updated. INTENT means that only row locks are used on a SELECT FOR UPDATE, but at update time, table locks are acquired.

SPIN_COUNT

Value: 1–1000000   **Default:** 1

Specifies the number of times a process will request a latch until it obtains one. If the number of requests reaches SPIN_COUNT, the process fails to acquire the latch, sleeps, and then tries to acquire the latch again. Because a latch is a low-level lock, a process does not hold it long, and it is less expensive to use CPU time by spinning a process than it is to make a process sleep. Obsolete with Oracle8i.

TRANSACTIONS

Value: 4–232   **Default:** 11 * SESSIONS

Specifies the maximum number of concurrent transactions.

TRANSACTIONS_PER_ROLLBACK_SEGMENT

Value: 1–operating system dependent   **Default:** 21

Specifies the number of concurrent transactions allowed per rollback segment. The minimum number of rollback segments acquired at startup is TRANSACTIONS divided by the value for this parameter.

Logging and Archiving

The following parameters shape and control logging and archiving. See also the related parameters under "Rollback (Undo/Redo) Management."

ARCH_IO_SLAVES

Value: 0–15 **Default: 0**

Specifies the number of I/O slaves used by the ARCH process to archive redo log files. The ARCH process and its slaves always write to disk. This parameter is normally adjusted when an I/O bottleneck has been detected in the ARCH process. Obsolete with Oracle8i.

ARCHIVE_LAG_TARGET

Value: 0 or 60–7200 **Default: 0** **Dynamic: ALTER SYSTEM**

Specifies the time, in seconds, that will elapse before a log switch is forced. A value of 0 indicates that the time-based thread advance feature is disabled. New with Oracle9i.

CPU_COUNT

Value: 0–unlimited **Default: 0 or actual number of CPUs**

Specifies the number of CPUs available to Oracle. Oracle uses this setting to set the default value of the LOG_SIMULTANEOUS_COPIES parameter. On single-CPU computers, the value of CPU_COUNT is 0.

On most platforms Oracle automatically sets the value of CPU_COUNT to the number of CPUs available to the Oracle instance. If there is heavy contention for latches, change the value of LOG_SIMULTANEOUS_COPIES to twice the number of CPUs available, but do not change the value of CPU_COUNT.

DB_CREATE_ONLINE_LOG_DEST_*n*

Value: string containing directory name
Dynamic: ALTER SYSTEM, ALTER SESSION

Specifies the default location where online log files and control files will be created. To provide fault tolerance, you should specify this parameter at least twice. The directory specified must already exist and must have sufficient permissions to allow Oracle to create files in it. New with Oracle9i.

Syntax

```
DB_CREATE_ONLINE_LOG_DEST_n = directory
```

Keywords

n Integer between 1 and 5 specifying the multiplexed file instance

directory Specifies the name of a directory that will contain one member of each online redo log group and one control file

FAL_CLIENT

Value: valid client name **Default: none** **Dynamic: ALTER SYSTEM**

Specifies the name of the fetch archive log (FAL) client used by the FAL service. New with Oracle9i.

FAL_SERVER

Value: valid server name   **Default:** none   **Dynamic:** ALTER SYSTEM

Specifies the fetch archive log (FAL) server for a standby database and must point to the FAL server. New with Oracle9*i*.

LOG_ARCHIVE_BUFFER_SIZE

Value: 1–operating system dependent   **Default:** operating system dependent

Specifies the size of each archival buffer, in redo log blocks. The default should be adequate for most applications. With LOG_ARCHIVE_BUFFERS, this parameter can be used to tune archiving. Obsolete with Oracle8*i*.

LOG_ARCHIVE_BUFFERS

Value: operating system dependent   **Default:** operating system dependent

Specifies the number of buffers to allocate for archiving. With LOG_ARCHIVE_BUFFER_SIZE, can tune archiving to run as fast as necessary, but not so fast that it reduces system performance. Obsolete with Oracle8*i*.

LOG_ARCHIVE_DEST

Value: valid path or device name   **Default:** operating system dependent
Dynamic: ALTER SYSTEM

Specifies the default location of the disk file directory or tape device when archiving redo log files. Note that archiving to tape is not supported on all operating systems.

Oracle recommends that if the Enterprise Edition of Oracle8*i* or Oracle9*i* is used, then you should set LOG_ARCHIVE_DEST_*n* instead of LOG_ARCHIVE_DEST.

LOG_ARCHIVE_DEST_*n*

Value: see description   **Default:** none
Dynamic: ALTER SYSTEM, ALTER SESSION

Specifies up to 10 archived log destinations. This parameter is valid for only the Oracle8*i* or Oracle9*i* Enterprise Edition. If you use this parameter, you must not also use LOG_ARCHIVE_DEST.

Syntax

```
LOG_ARCHIVE_DEST_n = ((SERVICE = service | LOCATION = location)
    [AFFIRM | NOAFFIRM]
    [ALTERNATE = destination | NOALTERNATE]
    [ARCH | LGWR]
    [DELAY[= minutes] | NODELAY]
    [DEPENDENCY = destination | NODEPENDENCY]
    [MANDATORY | OPTIONAL]
    [MAX_FAILURE = count | NOMAX_FAILURE]
    [QUOTA_SIZE = blocks | NOQUOTA_SIZE]
```

```
[QUOTA_USED = blocks | NOQUOTA_USED]
[REGISTER | NOREGISTER]
[REOPEN=seconds | NOREOPEN]
[SYNC | ASYNC=blocks])
```

Keywords

n
> Number from 1 to 10 that identifies the destination.

SERVICE=service
> Specifies the name of a network service used to transmit the archived log file to a standby instance.

LOCATION=location
> Specifies a local filesystem destination. At least one location must be specified.

MANDATORY
> Specifies that archiving to the destination must succeed before the redo log file can be reused.

OPTIONAL
> Specifies that successful archiving to the destination is not required before the redo log file can be reused. This is the default.

REOPEN=seconds
> Specifies the number of seconds that must pass before the destination can be used for archiving after an error. The default is 300 seconds.

LOG_ARCHIVE_DEST_STATE_*n*

Value: ENABLE | DEFER   **Default:** ENABLE
Dynamic: ALTER SYSTEM, ALTER SESSION

Specifies whether the corresponding LOG_ARCHIVE_DEST_*n* is available. You can use this parameter only in conjunction with the LOG_ARCHIVE_DEST_*n* parameter. Oracle recommends that if the Enterprise Edition of Oracle8*i* or Oracle9*i* is used, then you should set LOG_ARCHIVE_DEST_*n* instead of LOG_ARCHIVE_DEST.

LOG_ARCHIVE_DUPLEX_DEST

Value: valid path or device name or NULL **Default:** NULL
Dynamic: ALTER SYSTEM

Specifies a second archive destination: the duplex archive destination. This duplex archive destination can be either a must-succeed or a best-effort archive destination, depending on how many archive destinations must succeed (see the LOG_ARCHIVE_MIN_SUCCEED_DEST description later in this section).

Oracle recommends that you set LOG_ARCHIVE_DEST_*n* instead of this parameter if the Enterprise Edition is used. Do not also specify LOG_ARCHIVE_DEST_*n* if this parameter is used.

LOG_ARCHIVE_FORMAT

Value: valid filename format   **Default:** operating system dependent

Specifies the default filename format when archiving redo log files when running in ARCHIVELOG mode. The string generated from this format is appended to the string specified in the LOG_ARCHIVE_DEST parameter.

The following variables can be used in the format:

%s   Log sequence number

%t   Thread number

The default is operating system dependent, but is usually *%t_%s.dbf*. Using uppercase letters (for example, %S) for the variables causes the value to be a fixed length padded to the left with zeros.

LOG_ARCHIVE_MAX_PROCESSES

Value: 1–10   **Default:** 1   **Dynamic:** ALTER SYSTEM

Specifies the maximum number of archiver processes, named ARC0 through ARC9, that Oracle will initially create. New with Oracle8*i*.

LOG_ARCHIVE_MIN_SUCCEED_DEST

Value: 1–10   **Default:** 1   **Dynamic:** ALTER SYSTEM, ALTER SESSION

Specifies the minimum number of archive log destinations that must succeed. When automatic archiving is enabled and LOG_ARCHIVE_DEST is used, the allowable values are 1 and 2. If this parameter is 1, LOG_ARCHIVE_DEST is a must-succeed destination, and LOG_ARCHIVE_DUPLEX_DEST is a best-effort destination. If this parameter is 2, both LOG_ARCHIVE_DEST and LOG_ARCHIVE_DUPLEX_DEST are must-succeed destinations.

If LOG_ARCHIVE_DEST or LOG_ARCHIVE_DUPLEX_DEST is used, then you may not dynamically modify this parameter.

LOG_ARCHIVE_START

Value: TRUE | FALSE   **Default:** FALSE

Specifies whether archiving should be automatic or manual when the instance starts up in ARCHIVELOG mode. The Server Manager or SQL*Plus commands ARCHIVE LOG START or ARCHIVE LOG STOP override this parameter.

To use ARCHIVELOG mode while creating a database, set this parameter to TRUE. Normally, a database is created in NOARCHIVELOG mode and then altered to ARCHIVELOG mode after creation.

LOG_ARCHIVE_TRACE

Value: 0–255   **Default:** 0
Dynamic: ALTER SYSTEM (changes with next archiving operation)

Specifies the level of output generated by background archiver processes into the alert file. The values for the parameter are:

0   Disable ARCHIVELOG tracing; log only errors.

1   Track archival of redo log file.

2   Track archival status of each ARCHIVELOG destination.

4   Track archival operational phase.

8   Track ARCHIVELOG destination activity.

16 Track detailed ARCHIVELOG destination activity.

32 Track ARCHIVELOG destination parameter modifications.

64 Track ARC*n* process state activity.

128 Track FAL (fetch archive log) server–related activities.

These tracing levels may be combined by adding together the values corresponding to the desired levels. For example, if you wanted to trace the archiving of the redo log file (1) and the archive status of each ARCHIVELOG destination (2), you would specify a value of 3. New with Oracle9*i*.

LOG_FILES

Value: 2–255   **Default:** 255

Multiple instances must have the same value.

Specifies the maximum log group number and sets the upper limit on the group numbers that can be specified when issuing log-related commands. Obsolete with Oracle8*i*.

REMOTE_ARCHIVE_ENABLE

Value: TRUE | FALSE   **Default:** TRUE

Specifies whether archiving of redo logs to remote destinations is allowed. New with Oracle9*i*.

TAPE_ASYNCH_IO

Value: TRUE | FALSE   **Default:** TRUE

Controls whether I/O to sequential devices (for example, backup or restore of Oracle data to or from tape) is asynchronous. If a platform does not support asynchronous I/O to sequential devices, this parameter has no effect. Obsolete with Oracle8*i*.

Memory Management

The following parameters shape and control the way memory is allocated and used.

BITMAP_MERGE_AREA_SIZE

Value: operating system dependent   **Default:** 1000000

Specifies the amount of memory used to merge bitmaps retrieved from a range scan of the index. A larger value should improve performance because the bitmap segments must be sorted before being merged into a single bitmap.

BUFFER_POOL_KEEP

Value: integer | BUFFERS:integer | LRU_LATCHES:integer

Specifies the number of buffers (of size DB_BLOCK_BUFFER) to be set aside as a KEEP buffer pool and optionally specifies the number of LRU latches to be allocated to the KEEP buffer pool.

Beginning with Oracle9i, Oracle recommends that you use the DB_KEEP_CACHE_ SIZE parameter instead of BUFFER_POOL_KEEP.

If this parameter is specified, then DB_KEEP_CACHE_SIZE may not be specified, or an error will result.

BUFFER_POOL_RECYCLE

Value: integer | BUFFERS:integer | LRU_LATCHES:integer

Specifies the number of buffers (of size DB_BLOCK_BUFFER) to be set aside as a RECYCLE buffer pool and optionally specifies the number of LRU latches to be allocated to the RECYCLE buffer pool.

Beginning with Oracle9i, Oracle recommends that you use the DB_RECYCLE_ CACHE_SIZE parameter instead of BUFFER_POOL_RECYCLE.

If this parameter is specified, then DB_RECYCLE_CACHE_SIZE may not be specified, or an error will result.

CACHE_SIZE_THRESHOLD

Value: 0–DB_BLOCK_BUFFERS   **Default:** 01 * DB_BLOCK_BUFFERS

Specifies the maximum size of a cached partition of a table split among the caches of multiple instances. If the partition is larger than the value of this parameter, the table is not split among the instances' caches. Multiple instances should have the same value. This parameter can also specify the maximum cached partition size for a single instance. Obsolete with Oracle8i.

CREATE_BITMAP_AREA_SIZE

Value: operating system dependent   **Default:** 8 MB

Specifies the amount of memory allocated for bitmap creation. The default value is 8 MB, and a larger value might lead to faster index creation. If the cardinality (the number of unique values) of the index is very small, you can set a small value for this parameter.

DB_CACHE_ADVICE

Value: ON | OFF | READY   **Default:** OFF   **Dynamic:** ALTER SYSTEM

Specifies how statistics gathering used for predicting database performance with different cache sizes will be performed. If this parameter is set to OFF and then changed to ON using the ALTER SYSTEM statement, an error is likely to occur, because memory will not be allocated. Use the READY setting to allow this parameter to be changed to ON at a later time. New with Oracle9i.

Keywords

ON   Cache advisory is turned on and statistics are gathered.

OFF   Cache advisory is turned off, and no memory is allocated for gathering of statistics.

READY   Cache advisory is turned off, but memory is allocated for statistics.

DB_nK_CACHE_SIZE

Value: 2 | 4 | 8 | 16 | 32   **Default:** not configured   **Dynamic:** ALTER SYSTEM

Specifies the size of cache for nK buffers, when DB_BLOCK_SIZE is set to a value different from nK. May not be less than the minimum block size and may not exceed the maximum block size on the platform. New with Oracle9i.

DB_BLOCK_BUFFERS

Value for Oracle8/8i: 4–operating system dependent   **Default:** 50
Value for Oracle9i: 50–operating system dependent   **Default:** 48M / DB_BLOCK_SIZE

Specifies the number of database buffers available in the buffer cache. This is one of the primary parameters that contribute to the total memory requirements of the SGA on the Oracle instance. The DB_BLOCK_BUFFERS parameter, together with the DB_BLOCK_SIZE parameter, determines the total size of the buffer cache.

With Oracle9i, Oracle recommends that you use DB_CACHE_SIZE instead of DB_BLOCK_BUFFERS.

DB_CACHE_SIZE

Value: integer [K | M | G]   **Default:** 48M   **Dynamic:** ALTER SYSTEM

Specifies the size of the DEFAULT buffer pool in the SGA buffers with the primary block size (which is specified by DB_BLOCK_SIZE). New with Oracle9i.

DB_KEEP_CACHE_SIZE

Value: integer [K | M | G]   **Default:** 0   **Dynamic:** ALTER SYSTEM

Specifies the number of buffers (of size DB_BLOCK_SIZE) in the KEEP buffer pool. New with Oracle9i.

DB_RECYCLE_CACHE_SIZE

Value: integer [K | M | G]   **Default:** 0   **Dynamic:** ALTER SYSTEM

Specifies the number of buffers (of size DB_BLOCK_SIZE) in the RECYCLE buffer pool. New with Oracle9i.

HASH_AREA_SIZE

Value: 0–operating system dependent   **Default:** 2 * SORT_AREA_SIZE   **Dynamic:** ALTER SESSION

Specifies the maximum amount of memory in bytes to be used for hash joins.

HI_SHARED_MEMORY_ADDRESS

Value: integer address   **Default:** 0

Specifies the starting address of the SGA. A value of 0 causes the SGA address to default to a system-specific address. On 64-bit platforms, this parameter is used to specify the high-order 32 bits of the address, and SHARED_MEMORY_ADDRESS is used to specify the low-order 32 bits.

LARGE_POOL_MIN_ALLOC

Value: 16K–64M   **Default:** 16K

Specifies the minimum allocation size from the large pool in bytes, megabytes (M), or kilobytes (K). Obsolete with Oracle8i.

LARGE_POOL_SIZE

Value: 300K–2 GB or higher (maximum is operating system specific)
Default: 0

Specifies the size in bytes of the large pool allocation heap. If specified, the minimum size is 600K (300K in Oracle8) or LARGE_POOL_MIN_ALLOC, whichever is larger. The value of the parameter can be specified in bytes, megabytes (M), or kilobytes (K). The default of 0 means that no large pool is allocated.

LOCK_SGA

Value: TRUE | FALSE   **Default:** FALSE

Specifies whether the entire SGA is locked into real (physical) memory. Should be TRUE if there is a potential for the SGA being swapped to disk, because this could significantly degrade performance.

OBJECT_CACHE_MAX_SIZE_PERCENT

Value: 0–operating system dependent   **Default:** 10
Dynamic: ALTER SYSTEM DEFERRED, ALTER SESSION

Specifies the percentage of the optimal cache size that the session object cache can grow past the optimal size. The maximum size is equal to the optimal size plus the product of this percentage and the optimal size. When the cache size exceeds this maximum size, the system will attempt to shrink the cache to it.

OBJECT_CACHE_OPTIMAL_SIZE

Value: 102400–operating system dependent   Default: 102400   Dynamic: ALTER SYSTEM, ALTER SESSION

Specifies the size to which the session object cache is reduced when the size of the cache exceeds the maximum size.

PGA_AGGREGATE_TARGET

Value: 10 MB–4000 GB   Default: 0

Specifies the target aggregate PGA memory available to all server processes attached to the instance. Must be set to enable automatic sizing of SQL working areas used by memory-intensive SQL operators. New with Oracle9i.

PRE_PAGE_SGA

Value: TRUE | FALSE   Default: FALSE

If TRUE, Oracle touches all of the SGA pages during instance startup, causing them to be brought into memory. As a result, setting this parameter increases instance startup time and user login time, but it can reduce the number of page faults that occur shortly thereafter. The reduction in page faults allows the instance to reach its maximum performance capability more quickly. This parameter is most useful on systems that have sufficient memory to hold all the SGA pages without degrading performance in other areas. You should ensure that the SGA be sized properly in relation to existing physical memory in order to avoid swapping.

SEQUENCE_CACHE_ENTRIES

Value: 10–32000   Default: 10

Specifies the number of sequences that can be cached in the SGA for immediate access. The highest concurrency is achieved when this value is set to the highest possible number of sequences that will be used on an instance at one time. Sequences created with the NOCACHE option do not reside in this cache and are written through to the data dictionary on every use. Obsolete with Oracle8i.

SGA_MAX_SIZE

Value: 1–operating system dependent   Default: initial size of SGA at startup

Specifies the maximum size, in bytes, for the SGA during the life of the instance. New with Oracle9i.

SHARED_MEMORY_ADDRESS

Value: integer address   Default: 0

Specifies the starting address of the SGA. 0 causes the SGA address to default to a system-specific address. On 32-bit systems, this parameter is used to provide the entire address. On 64-bit platforms, this parameter is used to specify the low-order 32 bits of the address, and HI_SHARED_MEMORY_ADDRESS is used to specify the high-order 32 bits.

SHARED_POOL_RESERVED_MIN_ALLOC

Value: 5000–SHARED_POOL_RESERVED_SIZE
Default: 5000

Controls allocation of reserved memory. Memory allocations larger than this value can allocate space from the reserved list if a chunk of memory of sufficient size is not found on the shared pool free lists. If this parameter is increased, the Oracle Server will allow fewer allocations from the reserved list and will request more memory from the shared pool list. Can be specified as a numeric value or a number followed by K (1000) or M (1,000,000). Obsolete with Oracle8i.

SHARED_POOL_RESERVED_SIZE

Value: SHARED_POOL_RESERVED_MIN_ALLOC – SHARED_POOL_SIZE / 2
Default: SHARED_POOL_SIZE * 05

Specifies the shared pool space that is reserved for large contiguous requests for shared pool memory. With the SHARED_POOL_RESERVED_MIN_ALLOC parameter, this parameter can be used to avoid performance degradation in the shared pool from situations in which pool fragmentation forces Oracle to search for and free chunks of unused pool to satisfy the current request. If SHARED_POOL_RESERVED_SIZE exceeds 1/2 SHARED_POOL_SIZE, Oracle signals an error. In general, you should set SHARED_POOL_RESERVED_SIZE to 10% of SHARED_POOL_SIZE. Can be specified as a numeric value or a number followed by K (1000) or M (1,000,000).

SHARED_POOL_SIZE

Value: 300K–operating system dependent

Default: 64M for 64-bit systems, otherwise 16M. **Dynamic:** ALTER SYSTEM.

Specifies the size of the shared pool in bytes. Can be specified as a numeric value or a number followed by K (kilobytes) or M (megabytes).

SORT_AREA_RETAINED_SIZE

Value: 2 * DB_BLOCK_SIZE – SORT_AREA_SIZE
Default: SORT_AREA_SIZE   **Dynamic:** ALTER SYSTEM DEFERRED, ALTER SESSION

Specifies the maximum amount, in bytes, of user memory retained after a sort run completes. The retained size controls the size of the read buffer used to maintain a portion of the sort in memory. You may allocate multiple sort spaces of this size.

SORT_AREA_SIZE

Value: 6 * DB_BLOCK_SIZE – operating system dependent
Default: operating system dependent   **Dynamic:** ALTER SYSTEM DEFERRED, ALTER SESSION

Specifies the maximum amount, in bytes, of Program Global Area (PGA) memory to use for a sort. If Shared Server/MTS is enabled, the sort area is allocated from the SGA. After the sort is complete, and all that remains to do is to fetch the rows, the memory is released down to the size specified by SORT_AREA_RETAINED_SIZE. After the last row is fetched, all memory is freed. The memory is released back to the PGA, not to the operating system.

With Oracle9i, Oracle recommends that you use this parameter only for an instance configured with the Shared Server option. Otherwise, Oracle recommends that you use PGA_AGGREGATE_TARGET instead.

USE_INDIRECT_DATA_BUFFERS

Value: TRUE | FALSE   **Default:** FALSE

Specifies how the SGA uses memory. If TRUE, enables the use of the extended buffer cache mechanism for 32-bit platforms that can support more than 4 GB of physical memory. If FALSE, this capability is disabled. New with Oracle8i.

WORKAREA_SIZE_POLICY

Value: AUTO | MANUAL   **Default:** derived   **Dynamic:** ALTER SYSTEM, ALTER SESSION

Specifies the policy for sizing work areas. If AUTO, work areas used by memory-intensive operations are sized automatically, based on the PGA memory used by the system. This value can be specified only if PGA_AGGREGATE_TARGET is defined and is the default if PGA_AGGREGATE_TARGET is defined. If MANUAL, the sizing of work areas is manual and is based on the value of the corresponding *_AREA_SIZE parameter that applies (e.g., a sort uses SORT_AREA_SIZE) to the operation being performed. MANUAL is the default if PGA_AGGREGATE_TARGET is not defined. Obsolete with Oracle9i.

Names

The following parameters control and assign names to different files and objects.

DB_CREATE_FILE_DEST

Value: string with directory name   **Default:** not defined   **Dynamic:** ALTER SYSTEM, ALTER SESSION

Specifies the default location where datafiles, control files, and online log files will be created. The directory specified must already exist and must have sufficient permissions to allow Oracle to create files in it. New with Oracle9i.

DB_DOMAIN

Value: any legal string of name components, separated by periods and up to 128 characters long
Default: WORLD

Specifies the extension components of a global database name, consisting of valid identifiers separated by periods. The database domain name may be composed of alphabetic characters, numbers, underscore (_), and pound (#).

DB_FILE_NAME_CONVERT

Value: valid datafile name pattern

Converts the filename of a new datafile on the primary database to a filename on the standby database. The file must exist and be writable on the standby database, or the recovery process will halt with an error. The value of this parameter is two strings: the first string is the pattern found in the datafile names on the primary database; the second string is the pattern found in the datafile names on the standby database.

DB_NAME

Value: any valid database name up to eight characters
Default: NULL

This parameter is optional. If specified, it must correspond to the name specified in the CREATE DATABASE statement. If it is not specified, a database name must appear on either the STARTUP or the ALTER DATABASE MOUNT command line for each instance of the Parallel Server. Multiple instances must have the same value, or else the same value must be specified in STARTUP OPEN *db_name* or ALTER DATABASE *db_name* MOUNT.

ENT_DOMAIN_NAME

Value: valid domain name   **Default:** none

Specifies the enterprise domain name. Applies only to Oracle8*i*.

GLOBAL_NAMES

Value: TRUE | FALSE   **Default:** FALSE   **Dynamic:** ALTER SESSION, ALTER SYSTEM

Specifies whether a database link is required to have the same name as the database to which it connects. If FALSE, no check is performed. If TRUE, forces the use of consistent naming conventions for databases and links. If distributed processing is used, set GLOBAL_NAMES to TRUE to ensure a unique identifying name for each database in a networked environment.

SERVICE_NAMES

Value: valid service names   **Default:** value of DB_NAMEDB_DOMAIN
Dynamic: ALTER SYSTEM

Specifies one or more names for the database service to which this instance connects. If the service name is not qualified with a domain, the value of DB_DOMAIN is used if set; otherwise, the domain of the local database as defined in the data dictionary is used. This parameter must be set for every multiple instance. New with Oracle8*i*.

National Language Support (NLS)

The following parameters control the use of NLS character sets.

NLS_CALENDAR

Value: valid calendar format name   **Default:** none   **Dynamic:** ALTER SESSION

Specifies the calendar system to be used in this database; you can specify one of the following values:

ARABIC HIJRAH	PERSIAN
ENGLISH HIJRAH	ROC OFFICIAL
GREGORIAN	THAI BUDDHA
JAPANESE IMPERIAL	

NLS_COMP

Value: BINARY | ANSI   **Default:** BINARY   **Dynamic:** ALTER SESSION

Specifies how comparisons in the WHERE clause of queries are performed. If ANSI, comparisons will use the linguistic sort specified in the NLS_SORT parameter instead of the normal binary comparison. You must have an index on the column on which you want to do a linguistic sort. New with Oracle8*i*.

NLS_CURRENCY

Value: any valid character string, up to 10 bytes
Default: derived   **Dynamic:** ALTER SESSION

Specifies the string to use as the local currency symbol for the L number format element. The default value is determined by NLS_TERRITORY.

NLS_DATE_FORMAT

Value: any valid date format mask   **Default:** derived   **Dynamic:** ALTER SESSION

Specifies the default date format to use with the TO_CHAR and TO_DATE functions. The default value is determined by NLS_TERRITORY. The value can be any valid date format mask enclosed in double quotation marks.

NLS_DATE_LANGUAGE

Value: any valid NLS_LANGUAGE value   **Default:** value for NLS_LANGUAGE
Dynamic: ALTER SESSION

Specifies the language to use for the spelling of day and month names and date abbreviations (AD, BC, AM, PM).

NLS_DUAL_CURRENCY

Value: any valid format name   **Default:** derived   **Dynamic:** ALTER SESSION

Specifies the dual currency symbol (e.g., the Euro) for the territory. The default value is the dual currency symbol defined in the territory of your current language environment. New with Oracle8*i*.

NLS_ISO_CURRENCY

Value: any valid NLS_TERRITORY value   **Default:** derived   **Dynamic:** ALTER SESSION

Specifies the string to use as the international currency symbol for the C number format element. Default value is determined by NLS_TERRITORY.

NLS_LANGUAGE

Value: any valid language name   **Default:** derived   **Dynamic:** ALTER SESSION

Specifies the default language of the database. Used for messages; the day and month names; the symbols for AD, BC, AM, and PM; and the default sorting mechanism. This parameter determines the default values of the parameters NLS_DATE_LANGUAGE and NLS_SORT. For a complete list of languages, see the *Oracle9i Globalization Support Guide, Oracle Server Reference Manual,* and appropriate server *Release Notes.*

NLS_LENGTH_SEMANTICS

Value: BYTE | CHAR   **Default:** BYTE   **Dynamic:** ALTER SYSTEM, ALTER SESSION

Specifies whether CHAR and VARCHAR2 columns are created with byte or character length semantics. Tables created by SYS and SYSTEM always use byte semantics. NCHAR, NVARCHAR, CLOB, and NCLOB columns are always character based. New with Oracle9*i*.

NLS_NUMERIC_CHARACTERS

Value: see description   **Default:** derived   **Dynamic:** ALTER SESSION

Specifies the characters to use as the group separator and decimal. This parameter setting overrides those defined implicitly by NLS_TERRITORY.

The two characters specified must be single-byte, and the characters must be different from each other. The characters cannot be any numeric character or any of the following characters: plus (+), hyphen (-), less-than sign (<), greater-than sign (>). The characters are specified in the following format:

```
NLS_NUMERIC_CHARACTERS = "<decimal_character><group_separator>"
```

NLS_SORT

Value: BINARY or valid language name   **Default:** derived   **Dynamic:** ALTER SESSION

Specifies the collating sequence for ORDER BY queries. If the value is BINARY, the collating sequence for ORDER BY queries is based on the numeric value of characters (a binary sort that requires less system overhead).

If the value is a named language, sorting is based on the order of the defined linguistic sort. The default value of this parameter depends on the value of the NLS_LANGUAGE parameter. The NLS_SORT operator must be used with comparison operations if the linguistic sort behavior is desired.

Setting NLS_SORT to anything other than BINARY causes a sort to use a full table scan, regardless of the path chosen by the optimizer.

NLS_TERRITORY

Value: any valid territory name   **Default:** operating system dependent
Dynamic: ALTER SESSION

Specifies the name of the territory whose conventions are to be followed for day and week numbering, the default date format, the default decimal character and group separator, and the default ISO and local currency symbols. For a complete list of territories, see the *Oracle9i Globalization Support Guide* or *Oracle Server Reference Manual*.

NLS_TIMESTAMP_FORMAT

Value: any valid datetime format mask   **Default:** derived   **Dynamic:** ALTER SESSION

Specifies the default timestamp format to use with the TO_CHAR and TO_TIMESTAMP_TZ functions. You must enclose this value in single quotes. Default value is determined by NLS_TERRITORY. New with Oracle9i.

NLS_TIMESTAMP_TZ_FORMAT

Value: any valid date/time format mask   **Default:** derived   **Dynamic:** ALTER SESSION

Specifies the default timestamp with time zone format to use with the T_CHAR and TO_TIMESTAMP functions. You must enclose this value in single quotes. Default value is determined by NLS_TERRITORY. New with Oracle9i.

Optimization and Performance

The following parameters apply to the optimizer and to various Oracle performance features.

B_TREE_BITMAP_PLANS

Value: TRUE | FALSE   **Default:** FALSE

Specifies that the optimizer consider a bitmap access path even when a table has only regular B-tree indexes. Do not change this parameter unless you are instructed by Oracle Support. Obsolete with Oracle8i.

BLANK_TRIMMING

Value: TRUE | FALSE   **Default:** FALSE

A value of TRUE allows the data assignment of a source character string/variable to a destination character column/variable even though the source length is longer than the destination length, as long as the additional length over the destination length is all blanks. A value of FALSE disallows this type of data assignment.

FAST_FULL_SCAN_ENABLED

Value: TRUE | FALSE   **Default:** FALSE

Specifies whether the fast full scan query access path will be enabled. Obsolete with Oracle8i.

HASH_JOIN_ENABLED

Value: TRUE | FALSE   **Default:** TRUE   **Dynamic:** ALTER SESSION

Specifies whether the optimizer will consider using a hash join.

OPTIMIZER_FEATURES_ENABLE

Value: 8.0.0 | 8.0.3 | 8.0.4 | 8.0.5 | 8.0.6 | 8.1.0 | 8.1.3 | 8.1.4 | 8.1.5 | 8.1.6 | 8.1.7 | 9.0.0 |9.0.1 | 9.2.0
Default: current release

Specifies the behavior of the Oracle optimizer based on features available in specific release numbers.

OPTIMIZER_INDEX_CACHING

Value: 0–100   **Default:** 0

Specifies an estimated percentage of index blocks that will be cached. Higher values favor the use of index-based execution plans.

OPTIMIZER_INDEX_COST_ADJ

Value: 4–232　　　　　**Default:** 100　　　　　**Dynamic:** ALTER SESSION

Specifies a "discount" to the cost of index-based execution plans.

OPTIMIZER_MAX_PERMUTATIONS

Value: 0–100　　　　　**Default:** 100　　　　　**Dynamic:** ALTER SYSTEM, ALTER SESSION

Specifies the maximum number of permutations of the tables that the optimizer will consider in queries with joins. If this parameter is too low, parse times for queries will be reduced at the added risk of overlooking a better execution plan. A value of 80,000 means no limit.

OPTIMIZER_MODE

Value: RULE | CHOOSE | FIRST_ROWS_{1 | 10 | 100 | 1000} | FIRST_ROWS | ALL_ROWS
Default: CHOOSE　　　　　**Dynamic:** ALTER SESSION

Specifies the behavior of the optimizer. See Chapter 7 for an explanation of these values. Cost-based optimization will always be used for any query that references an object with a nonzero degree of parallelism.

OPTIMIZER_PERCENT_PARALLEL

Value: 0–100　　　　　**Default:** 0　　　　　**Dynamic:** ALTER SESSION

Specifies the amount of parallelism that the optimizer uses in its cost functions. Default means that the optimizer chooses the best serial plan. A value of 100 means that the optimizer uses each object's degree of parallelism in computing the cost of a full table scan operation. Obsolete with Oracle9i.

OPTIMIZER_SEARCH_LIMIT

Value: 0–10　　　　　**Default:** 5　　　　　**Dynamic:** ALTER SESSION

Specifies the number of tables for which Cartesian products will be considered during join operations. Obsolete with Oracle9i.

PARTITION_VIEW_ENABLED

Value: TRUE | FALSE　　　　　**Default:** FALSE

Specifies optimizer behavior for partitioned views. If TRUE, the optimizer prunes or skips unnecessary table accesses in a partition view. Also changes the way the cost-based optimizer computes statistics on a partition view from statistics on underlying tables.

QUERY_REWRITE_ENABLED

Value: TRUE | FALSE   **Default:** FALSE
Dynamic: ALTER SYSTEM, ALTER SESSION

Specifies whether query rewrites of materialized views will be enabled globally for the database. To take advantage of query rewrites, you must enable this option for each materialized view, and you must enable cost-based optimization. New with Oracle9i.

QUERY_REWRITE_INTEGRITY

Value: STALE_TOLERATED | TRUSTED | ENFORCED
Default: ENFORCED   **Dynamic:** ALTER SYSTEM, ALTER SESSION

Specifies the degree to which Oracle will enforce query rewriting.

Keywords

STALE_TOLERATED
> Allows rewrites using unenforced relationships. Materialized views may be rewritten even if they are known to be inconsistent with underlying detail data.

TRUSTED   Allows rewriting using relationships that have been declared but not enforced by Oracle.

ENFORCED   Oracle enforces and guarantees consistency and integrity.

READ_ONLY_OPEN_DELAYED

Value: TRUE | FALSE   **Default:** FALSE

Specifies when tables in read-only tablespaces are accessed. If TRUE, datafiles are opened only when an attempt is made to read from them. If FALSE, files are opened at database open time.

SEQUENCE_CACHE_HASH_BUCKET

Value: 10–SEQUENCE_CACHE_ENTRIES   **Default:** 7

Specifies the number of buckets used to speed lookup for newly requested sequences in the cache, which is arranged as a hash table. You should specify a prime number as the value for this parameter; if it is not prime, Oracle will raise the value to the next prime number. Obsolete with Oracle8i.

STAR_TRANSFORMATION_ENABLED

Value: TRUE | FALSE   **Default:** FALSE   **Dynamic:** ALTER SESSION

Determines whether a cost-based query transformation will be applied to star queries.

TIMED_OS_STATISTICS

Value: 0–unlimited   **Default:** 0   **Dynamic:** ALTER SYSTEM, ALTER SESSION

Specifies the interval in seconds at which Oracle collects operating system statistics. 0 means no statistics will be collected. Obsolete with Oracle8i.

TIMED_STATISTICS

Value: TRUE | FALSE   **Default:** FALSE   **Dynamic:** ALTER SYSTEM, ALTER SESSION

Specifies whether statistics related to time are collected. If FALSE, the statistics are always zero and the server can avoid the overhead of requesting the time from the operating system.

Parallel Execution

The following parameters configure parallel execution.

PARALLEL_ADAPTIVE_MULTI_USER

Value: TRUE | FALSE   **Default:** derived   **Dynamic:** ALTER SYSTEM

Specifies whether Oracle will dynamically adjust the requested degree of parallelism based on system load at the time the query begins execution. The default is taken from the value of PARALLEL_AUTOMATIC_TUNING. The algorithm used assumes that the system is tuned for optimal performance in a single-user environment.

PARALLEL_AUTOMATIC_TUNING

Value: TRUE | FALSE   **Default:** FALSE

Specifies whether Oracle will choose the default values for most parallel tuning parameters.You must also specify the PARALLEL clause for the target tables in the system. New with Oracle8i.

PARALLEL_BROADCAST_ENABLED

Value: TRUE | FALSE   **Default:** FALSE   **Dynamic:** ALTER SESSION

Specifies whether Oracle can choose to copy all the source rows of the small result set and broadcast a copy to each cluster database that is processing rows from the larger set, when applicable.

PARALLEL_DEFAULT_MAX_INSTANCES

Value: 0–number of instances   **Default:** operating system dependent

Specifies the default number of instances to split a table across for parallel query processing. Used if INSTANCES DEFAULT is specified in the PARALLEL clause of a table's definition. New with Oracle8i.

PARALLEL_EXECUTION_MESSAGE_SIZE

Value: 2148–65535   **Default:** operating system dependent

Specifies the size in bytes of messages for parallel execution. On most systems, the default is 2148 if PARALLEL_AUTOMATIC_TUNING is FALSE and 4096 if it is TRUE. Multiple instances must have same value. Larger values result in better performance at the cost of higher memory use.

PARALLEL_INSTANCE_GROUP

Value: valid group name   **Default:** group of all instances currently active

Identifies the parallel instance group to be used for spawning parallel query slaves. Parallel operations will spawn parallel query slaves only on instances that specify a matching group in their INSTANCE_GROUPS parameter.

PARALLEL_MAX_SERVERS

Value: 0–3599   **Default:** derived

Specifies the maximum number of parallel query servers or parallel recovery processes for an instance. Oracle will increase the number of query servers to this value, as demand requires, from the number created at instance startup. If the value is too low, some queries may not have a query server available during query processing. If it is too high, memory resource shortages may occur during peak periods. Multiple instances must have the same value.

PARALLEL_MIN_MESSAGE_POOL

Value: 0–SHARED_POOLSIZE * 90
Default: CPUs * PARALLEL_MAX_SERVERS * 15 * (OS message buffer size) or CPUs * 5 * 15 * (OS message size)

Specifies the minimum permanent amount of memory that will be allocated from the shared pool for messages in parallel execution. Allocated at startup time if PARALLEL_MIN_SERVERS is set to a nonzero value or when the server is first allocated. This parameter cannot be set to a number higher than 90% of the shared pool. Obsolete with Oracle8*i*.

PARALLEL_MIN_PERCENT

Value: 0–100   **Default:** 0   **Dynamic:** ALTER SESSION

Specifies the minimum percent of threads required for parallel execution. Ensures that a parallel operation will not be executed sequentially if adequate resources are not available. If too few query slaves are available, an error message is displayed and the query is not executed.

PARALLEL_MIN_SERVERS

Value: 0–PARALLEL_MAX_SERVERS   **Default:** 0

Specifies the minimum number of parallel execution server processes for an instance.

PARALLEL_THREADS_PER_CPU

Value: 0–unlimited   **Default:** usually 2   **Dynamic:** ALTER SYSTEM

Specifies the default degree of parallelism for the instance and represents the number of parallel execution processes that a CPU can handle during parallel execution or in a multiple instance environment. In general, you should reduce the value if the machine appears to be overloaded when a typical parallel operation is executed, and you should increase it if the system is I/O-bound.

PARALLEL_TRANSACTION_RESOURCE_TIMEOUT

Value: 0–operating system dependent   **Default:** 300   **Dynamic:** ALTER SYSTEM

Specifies the maximum amount of time that can pass before a session executing a parallel operation times out while waiting for a resource held by another session in an incompatible lock mode. Obsolete with Oracle8*i*.

Parameters

The following parameters point to other parameter files.

IFILE

Value: valid filename   **Default:** none

Embeds another parameter file within the current parameter file. Up to three levels of nesting can be used. You can include multiple parameters in one parameter file by listing IFILE several times with different values.

SPFILE

Value: any valid server parameter file (*SPFILE*) name
Default: *$ORACLE_HOME/dbs/spfile.ora*

Specifies the name of the current server parameter file in use. If you have multiple instances, they should all have the same value.

PL/SQL

The following parameters apply to the PL/SQL language

PLSQL_COMPILER_FLAGS

Value: DEBUG | NON_DEBUG [INTERPRETED | NATIVE]
Default: NON_DEBUG INTERPRETED
Dynamic: ALTER SYSTEM, ALTER SESSION

Specifies compiler flags associated with PL/SQL modules. This parameter has no effect on compiled PL/SQL modules. New with Oracle9*i*.

PLSQL_LOAD_WITHOUT_COMPILE

Value: TRUE | FALSE   **Default:** FALSE   **Dynamic:** ALTER SESSION

Specifies whether PL/SQL can be loaded without the compilation flag.

PLSQL_NATIVE_C_COMPILER

Value: any valid pathname   **Default:** in shipped make file   **Dynamic:** ALTER SYSTEM

Specifies the full pathname of the C compiler used to compile generated C code into an object file. New with Oracle9*i*.

PLSQL_NATIVE_LIBRARY_DIR

Value: any valid directory pathname   **Default:** none   **Dynamic:** ALTER SYSTEM

Specifies the full pathname of the directory where the shared objects produced by the native compiler are stored. New with Oracle9*i*.

PLSQL_NATIVE_LIBRARY_SUBDIR_COUNT

Value: $0 - 2^{32} - 1$ **Default:** 0   **Dynamic:** ALTER SYSTEM

Specifies the number of subdirectories created by the DBA in the directory specified by PLSQL_NATIVE_LIBRARY_DIR. Allows multiple subdirectories to be created in order to avoid creating a large number of files in a single directory, which can adversely affect performance. New with Oracle9*i*.

PLSQL_NATIVE_LINKER

Value: any valid pathname   **Default:** in shipped make file   **Dynamic:** ALTER SYSTEM

Specifies the full pathname of the linker used to link an object file into a shared object file or DLL. New with Oracle9*i*.

PLSQL_NATIVE_MAKE_UTILITY

Value: any valid pathname   **Default:** none   **Dynamic:** ALTER SYSTEM

Specifies the full pathname of the make utility used to generate a shared object file or DLL from generated C code. New with Oracle9*i*.

PLSQL_V2_COMPATIBILITY

Value: TRUE | FALSE   **Default:** FALSE   **Dynamic:** ALTER SYSTEM, ALTER SESSION

Sets the compatibility level for PL/SQL. If FALSE, PL/SQL Version 8 behavior is enforced and Version 2 behavior is not allowed. If TRUE, then the following PL/SQL Version 2 behaviors are accepted when running PL/SQL Version 8:

- Allows elements of an index table passed in as an IN parameter to be modified or deleted.

- Allows OUT parameters to be used in expression contexts in some cases. This behavior is restricted to a few cases: fields of OUT parameters that are records and OUT parameters referenced in the from list of a SELECT statement.

- Allows OUT parameters in the FROM clause of a select list, where their values are read.

- Allows the passing of an IN parameter into another procedure as an OUT parameter restricted to fields of IN parameters that are records.

- Allows a type to be referenced earlier than its definition in the source.

UTL_FILE_DIR

Value: valid directory name   **Default:** NULL

Specifies a directory that is permitted for PL/SQL file I/O. You can specify multiple directories, but each directory must be specified with a separate UTL_FILE_DIR parameter.

Remote Sites

The following parameters control how you interact with remote sites.

REMOTE_DEPENDENCIES_MODE

Value: TIMESTAMP | SIGNATURE   **Default:** TIMESTAMP

Specifies how dependencies upon remote stored procedures are to be handled by the database. If set to TIMESTAMP, the client running the procedure compares the timestamp recorded on the server-side procedure with the current timestamp of the local procedure and executes the procedure only if the timestamps match. If set to SIGNATURE, the procedure is allowed to execute as long as the signatures are considered safe, which allows client PL/SQL applications to be run without recompilation.

REMOTE_LISTENER

Value: valid network name   **Default:** none

Specifies a network name that resolves to an address or address list of Oracle network remote listeners, as specified in the *tnsnames.ora* file. New with Oracle9*i*.

REMOTE_OS_AUTHENT

Value: TRUE | FALSE   **Default:** FALSE

Allows authentication of remote clients using the value specified for the OS_AUTHENT_PREFIX initialization parameter (see the later section, "Security") when TRUE.

REMOTE_OS_ROLES

Value: TRUE | FALSE   **Default:** FALSE

Allows operating system roles for remote clients when set to TRUE.

Rollback (Undo/Redo) Management

The following parameters apply to management and use of rollback buffers, undo tablespaces, and redo logs.

CLEANUP_ROLLBACK_ENTRIES

Value: integer   **Default:** 20

Specifies the number of undo records processed at one time when rolling back a transaction, preventing long transactions from freezing out shorter transactions that also need to be rolled back. Obsolete with Oracle8*i*.

LOG_BLOCK_CHECKSUM

Value: TRUE | FALSE   **Default:** FALSE

Specifies whether redo log blocks will include a checksum. Obsolete with Oracle9*i*.

LOG_BUFFER

Value: 2048–512K   **Default:** operating system dependent

Specifies the amount of memory, in bytes, that is used when buffering redo entries to a redo log file. In general, larger values for LOG_BUFFER reduce redo log file I/O, particularly if transactions are long or numerous. If the system contains multiple CPUs, this value may be as high as 128K * CPU_COUNT.

LOG_CHECKPOINT_INTERVAL

Value: 0–unlimited   **Default:** operating system dependent
Dynamic: ALTER SYSTEM.

Specifies the frequency of checkpoints in terms of the number of redo log file operating system blocks that are written between consecutive checkpoints. If the value exceeds the actual redo log file size, checkpoints occur only when switching logs. If the intervals are so close together that the checkpoint requests are arriving faster than the rate at which the server can satisfy them, Oracle may ignore some of these requests to avoid excessive checkpointing activity.

LOG_CHECKPOINT_TIMEOUT

Value: 0–unlimited   **Default:** 0   **Dynamic:** ALTER SYSTEM

Specifies the maximum amount of time (in seconds) before another checkpoint occurs. The time begins at the start of the previous checkpoint.

LOG_CHECKPOINTS_TO_ALERT

Value: TRUE | FALSE   **Default:** FALSE   **Dynamic:** ALTER SYSTEM

Specifies that checkpoints be logged to the alert file. This parameter is useful in determining if checkpoints are occurring at the desired frequency.

LOG_SIMULTANEOUS_COPIES

Value: 0–unlimited   **Default:** CPU_COUNT

Specifies the maximum number of redo buffer copy latches available to write log entries simultaneously. For good performance, specify up to twice as many redo copy latches as CPUs. Obsolete with Oracle8*i*.

LOG_SMALL_ENTRY_MAX_SIZE

Value: operating system dependent   **Default:** operating system dependent
Dynamic: ALTER SYSTEM

Specifies the size, in bytes, of the largest copy to the log buffers that can occur under the redo allocation latch without obtaining the redo buffer copy latch. Obsolete with Oracle8*i*.

MAX_ROLLBACK_SEGMENTS

Value: 2–65535
Default: MAX (30, TRANSACTION / TRANSACTIONS_PER_ROLLBACK_SEGMENT)

Specifies the maximum size of the rollback segment cache in the SGA, which also signifies the maximum number of rollback segments that can be kept online simultaneously by one instance.

ROLLBACK_SEGMENTS

Value: comma-separated list of rollback segment names (except SYSTEM)
Default: NULL

Specifies one or more rollback segments to allocate by name to this instance. If this parameter is set, an instance acquires all of the rollback segments named in this parameter, even if the number of rollback segments exceeds the minimum number required by the instance (calculated from the ratio TRANSACTIONS / TRANSACTIONS_PER_ROLLBACK_SEGMENT). You can also specify public rollback segments if they are not already in use. If this parameter is not set, the instance uses all public rollback segments by default. Multiple instances must have their own rollback segments.

UNDO_MANAGEMENT

Value: MANUAL | AUTO   **Default:** MANUAL

Specifies which undo space management mode is used. If MANUAL, undo space is allocated as rollback segments. If AUTO, automatic undo management is used. New with Oracle9*i*.

UNDO_RETENTION

Value: $0-2^{32}-1$ **Default:** 900   **Dynamic:** ALTER SYSTEM

Specifies in seconds how long committed undo information is to be retained in the database. Multiple instances must have the same value. New with Oracle9*i*.

UNDO_SUPPRESS_ERRORS

Value: TRUE | FALSE   **Default:** FALSE   **Dynamic:** ALTER SYSTEM, ALTER SESSION

Specifies whether errors are suppressed while executing manual undo management operations in automatic undo management mode. Used with pre-Oracle9*i* scripts with undo management commands used with Oracle9*i*.

UNDO_TABLESPACE

Value: name of an existing undo tablespace
Default: first available undo tablespace   **Dynamic:** ALTER SYSTEM

Specifies the undo tablespace to be used when the instance starts. If no undo tablespaces are specified or available, Oracle uses the SYSTEM rollback segment, which is not recommended. The instance will not start if a value is provided for this parameter and the database is in manual management mode. New with Oracle9*i*.

Security

The following parameters affect how security is enforced.

MAX_ENABLED_ROLES

Value: 0–148   **Default:** 20

Specifies the maximum number of database roles that a user can enable in addition to the user's own role and PUBLIC.

07_DICTIONARY_ACCESSIBILITY

Value: TRUE | FALSE   **Default:** FALSE

Controls restrictions on SYSTEM privileges. If the value is TRUE, access to objects in the SYS schema is allowed (Oracle7 behavior). If the value is FALSE, SYSTEM privileges that allow access to objects in other schemas do not allow access to objects in the dictionary schema. Prior to Oracle9*i*, the default for this parameter was TRUE.

OS_AUTHENT_PREFIX

Value: any valid string   **Default:** OPS$

Specifies the prefix that is concatenated to the beginning of every user's operating system username to allow Oracle to authenticate users with the user's operating system account name and password. The value of this prefixed username is compared with the Oracle usernames in the database when a connection request is attempted. This mechanism has no effect for Oracle accounts that are not created using the IDENTIFIED EXTERNALLY keywords.

OS_ROLES

Value: TRUE | FALSE   **Default:** FALSE

Specifies whether Oracle allows the operating system to identify the username's roles. If the value is TRUE, when a user attempts to create a session, the username's security domain is initialized using the roles identified by the operating system. In addition, if TRUE, the operating system completely manages the role grants for all database usernames. Any revokes of roles granted by the operating system are ignored, and any previously granted roles are ignored. If the value is FALSE, roles are identified and managed by the database.

RDBMS_SERVER_DN

Value: any X500 distinguished name   **Default:** none

Specifies the distinguished name (DN) of the server in order to retrieve roles for an enterprise directory service. Do not set this parameter if you want SSL authentication alone. New with Oracle9*i*.

REMOTE_LOGIN_PASSWORDFILE

Value: NONE | EXCLUSIVE | SHARED   **Default:** NONE

Specifies whether Oracle checks for a password file and how many databases can use the password file. NONE indicates that Oracle should ignore any password file, which means that privileged users must be authenticated by the operating system. EXCLUSIVE signifies that the password file can be used by only one database and that the password file can contain names other than SYS and INTERNAL. SHARED allows more than one database to use a password file, but the only users recognized by the password file are SYS and INTERNAL. Multiple instances must have the same value.

SQL92_SECURITY

Value: TRUE | FALSE   **Default:** FALSE

Specifies whether table-level SELECT privileges are required to execute an update or delete that references table column values.

Shared Server/Multi-Threaded Server

The following parameters control and shape the operation of Shared Server (with Oracle9*i*) and Multi-Threaded Server (MTS) (prior to Oracle9*i*).

CIRCUITS

Value: integer   **Default:** see description

Specifies the total number of virtual circuits available for network connections in a Shared Server environment. The default is the value of SESSIONS if MTS is in use; otherwise, the default is 0. New with Oracle9i.

DISPATCHERS

Value: see description   **Default:** none   **Dynamic:** ALTER SYSTEM

Configures dispatcher processes in a Shared Server environment. New with Oracle9i.

Syntax

```
DISPATCHERS =
'{ (PROTOCOL = protocol)
 | (ADDRESS = address)
 | (DESCRIPTION = description}
}
[({DISPATCHERS = integer
  | SESSIONS = integer
  | CONNECTIONS = integer
  | TICKS = seconds
  | POOL = {1 | ON | YES | TRUE | BOTH |({IN | OUT} = integer) |
           0 | OFF | NO | FALSE | integer}
| MULTIPLEX = {1 | ON | YES | TRUE |
              0 | OFF | NO | FALSE | BOTH | IN | OUT}
| LISTENER = tnsname
| SERVICE = service
| INDEX = integer
})]'
```

Keywords

protocol   Network protocol for the dispatcher.

address   Network protocol address for the dispatcher.

description   Network description for the dispatcher.

DISPATCHERS
        Initial number of dispatchers.

SESSIONS   Maximum number of network sessions per dispatcher.

CONNECTIONS
        Maximum number of network connections per dispatcher.

TICKS   Length of a network tick in seconds.

POOL   Controls connection pooling. ON, YES, TRUE, and BOTH specify connection pooling for IN and OUT network connections. NO, OFF, and FALSE specify no connection pooling for IN and OUT network connections. IN and OUT specify connection pooling for their respective network connections. An integer by itself indicates the timeout for both types of connections. You can include an integer with IN or OUT, such as (IN = 20)(OUT = 10), to specify the ticks for each direction. The default timout is 10.

MULTIPLEX Enables network session multiplexing for both IN and OUT connections with 1, ON, YES, TRUE, or BOTH. Disables with 0, NO, OFF, or FALSE. IN and OUT enable multiplexing in their respective directions.

LISTENER The network name of an address or address list of the Oracle Net listener that will register the dispatcher.

SERVICE Service names the dispatchers register with the listeners.

INDEX Used to identify a particular dispatcher when used with the ALTER SYSTEM SET DISPATCHERS statement. Note that 0 is the index base.

MAX_DISPATCHERS

Value: 1–number of dispatchers   **Default:** 5

Specifies the maximum number of dispatcher processes allowed to be running simultaneously and applies only if dispatchers have been configured. You should set this parameter to at least the maximum number of concurrent sessions divided by the number of connections for each dispatcher (250 sessions per dispatcher provides good performance). New with Oracle9*i*.

MAX_SHARED_SERVERS

Value: 0–65535   **Default:** 2 * SHARED_SERVERS

Specifies the maximum number of Shared Server processes that can be running simultaneously.

MTS_CIRCUITS

Value: integer   **Default:** see description

Specifies the total number of virtual circuits available for network connections in a Shared Server environment. The default is the value of SESSIONS if MTS is in use; otherwise, it is 0. New with Oracle8*i*. Starting with Oracle9*i*, Oracle recommends that you use the CIRCUITS parameter instead.

MTS_DISPATCHERS

Value: string   **Default:** none   **Dynamic:** ALTER SYSTEM

Configures dispatcher processes in an MTS or Shared Server environment. With Oracle9*i*, Oracle recommends that you use the DISPATCHERS parameter instead.

Syntax

```
DISPATCHERS =
'{ (PROTOCOL = protocol)
 | (ADDRESS = address)
 | (DESCRIPTION = description}
}
[({DISPATCHERS = integer
 | SESSIONS = integer
```

```
 | CONNECTIONS = integer
 | TICKS = seconds
 | POOL = {1 | ON | YES | TRUE | BOTH |({IN | OUT} = integer) |
           0 | OFF | NO | FALSE | integer}
 | MULTIPLEX = {1 | ON | YES | TRUE |
               0 | OFF | NO | FALSE | BOTH | IN | OUT}
 | LISTENER = tnsname
 | SERVICE = service
 | INDEX = integer
 })]'
```

Keywords

See the descriptions of the keywords under the DISPATCHERS parameter earlier in this section.

MTS_LISTENER_ADDRESS

Value: valid MTS_LISTENER_ADDRESS specification
Default: NULL

Specifies the configuration of the listener process, which requires an address to listen for connection requests for each network protocol that is used on the system. Each address must have its own parameter. Replaced with LOCAL_LISTENER and LISTENER with Oracle8. Obsolete with Oracle9i.

MTS_MAX_DISPATCHERS

Value: greater of 5 or number of dispatchers**Default:** 5

Specifies the maximum number of dispatcher processes allowed to be running simultaneously. Starting with Oracle9i, you should use the MAX_DISPATCHERS parameter instead.

MTS_MAX_SERVERS

Value: 0 – 65535   **Default:** 2 * SHARED_SERVERS

Specifies the maximum number of Shared Server processes that can be running simultaneously. Starting with Oracle9i, you should use the MAX_SHARED_SERVERS parameter instead.

MTS_MULTIPLE_LISTENERS

Value: TRUE | FALSE   **Default:** FALSE

Controls the syntax of the MTS_LISTENER_ADDRESS parameter. Obsolete with Oracle9i.

MTS_RATE_LOG_SIZE

Value: see description   **Default:** 10 for each name listed

Specifies the sample size used to calculate dispatcher rate statistics. The sample size determines how much memory will be used and the frequency with which maximum rates will be determined. Obsolete with Oracle8i.

MTS_RATE_LOG_SIZE accepts a string consisting of one or more (*name* = *value*) sections, and the values are shared among all dispatchers. Valid names are:

DEFAULTS	Overrides default number of events to log for unspecified statistics
EVENT_LOOPS	Number of event loops to log
MESSAGES	Number of messages to log
SERVER_BUFFERS	Number of buffers going to the server to log
CLIENT_BUFFERS	Number of buffers going to the client to log
TOTAL_BUFFERS	Number of buffers going in either direction to log
IN_CONNECTS	Number of inbound connections to log
OUT_CONNECTS	Number of outbound connections to log
RECONNECTS	Number of connection pool reconnections to log

MTS_RATE_SCALE

Value: see description   **Default:** see description

Specifies the scale at which dispatcher rate statistics are reported, in hundredths of a second. Obsolete with Oracle8i. Valid default values are:

DEFAULTS	None
EVENT_LOOPS	6000
MESSAGES	100
SERVER_BUFFERS	10
CLIENT_BUFFERS	10
TOTAL_BUFFERS	10
IN_CONNECTS	6000
OUT_CONNECTS	6000
RECONNECTS	6000

MTS_SERVERS

Value: operating system dependent   **Default:** 1 if using MTS, otherwise 0

Specifies the number of server processes that are to be created when an instance is started. Starting with Oracle9i, you should use SHARED_SERVERS instead.

MTS_SERVICE

Value: service name   **Default:** NULL

Specifies the name of the service to be associated with the dispatcher. Using this name in the CONNECT string allows users to connect to an instance through a dispatcher.

Make sure to specify a unique name, and do not enclose it in quotation marks. If this parameter is not specified, MTS_SERVICE defaults to the value specified by DB_NAME. If DB_NAME also is not specified, the Oracle Server returns an error at startup indicating that the value for this parameter is missing. Obsolete with Oracle9i.

SHARED_SERVER_SESSIONS

Value: 0–SESSIONS - 5   **Default:** lesser of CIRCUITS or SESSIONS - 5

Specifies the total number of Shared Server user sessions. New with Oracle9i.

Sorts

The following parameters shape the way that sorts are performed.

SORT_DIRECT_WRITES

Value: AUTO | TRUE | FALSE   **Default:** AUTO   **Dynamic:** ALTER SYSTEM, ALTER SESSION

Controls whether sort data will bypass the buffer cache to write intermediate sort results to disk. If AUTO, and the value of the sort area size is greater than 10 times the block size, memory is allocated from the sort area to do this. If TRUE, additional buffers are allocated from memory during each sort, and additional temporary segment space can be required. If FALSE, the sorts that write to disk write through the buffer cache. Obsolete with Oracle8i.

SORT_READ_FAC

Value: operating system dependent   **Default:** operating system dependent
Dynamic: ALTER SYSTEM, ALTER SESSION

Specifies a ratio that describes the amount of time to read a single database block divided by the block transfer rate. Obsolete with Oracle8i.

SORT_SPACEMAP_SIZE

Value: operating system dependent   **Default:** operating system dependent

Specifies the size, in bytes, of the sort space map. This parameter should be adjusted only if very large indexes exist. A sort automatically increases its space map if necessary, but it does not necessarily do so when it will make best use of disk storage. The sort makes optimal use of disk storage if SORT_SPACEMAP_SIZE is set to total_sort_bytes = (number_of_records) * [sum_of_average_column_sizes + (2 * number_of_columns)]. Obsolete with Oracle8i.

SORT_WRITE_BUFFER_SIZE

Value: 32768–65536   **Default:** 32768   **Dynamic:** ALTER SYSTEM, ALTER SESSION

Sets the size of the sort I/O buffer when the SORT_DIRECT_WRITES parameter is set to TRUE. Recommended for use with symmetric replication. Obsolete with Oracle8i.

SORT_WRITE_BUFFERS

Value: 1 – 8   **Default:** 1   **Dynamic:** ALTER SYSTEM, ALTER SESSION

Specifies the number of sort buffers when the SORT_DIRECT_WRITES parameter is TRUE. Recommended for use with symmetric replication. Obsolete with Oracle8*i*.

Standby Databases

The following parameters apply to the use of standby databases.

ACTIVE_INSTANCE_COUNT

Value: positive integer

In a cluster of exactly two instances, a value of 1 indicates that the first instance started is the primary instance, while the second instance acts as a standby. Any other value is ignored. New with Oracle9*i*.

LOCK_NAME_SPACE

Value: 8 characters maximum, no special characters allowed
Default: none

Specifies the namespace that the Distributed Lock Manager (DLM) uses to generate lock names.

STANDBY_ARCHIVE_DEST

Value: any valid path or device name   **Default:** operating system specific
Dynamic: ALTER SYSTEM

Specifies the location of archived log files arriving for a standby database in managed recovery mode. New with Oracle9*i*.

STANDBY_FILE_MANAGEMENT

Value: MANUAL | AUTO   **Default:** MANUAL   **Dynamic:** ALTER SYSTEM

Specifies whether automatic standby file management is enabled. If AUTO, file management operations like adding and deleting files are performed automatically on the standby database. New with Oracle9*i*.

STANDBY_PRESERVES_NAMES

Value: TRUE | FALSE   **Default:** FALSE   **Dynamic:** ALTER SYSTEM

Specifies whether filenames on the standby database are the same (preserved) as those on the primary database. New with Oracle9*i*.

System Operations

The following parameters apply to various system processes, the overall operation of Oracle, dump files, and control files.

BACKGROUND_CORE_DUMP

Value: FULL | PARTIAL   **Default:** FULL

If FULL, the SGA is dumped as part of the generated core file. If PARTIAL, the SGA is not dumped as part of the generated core file.

BACKGROUND_DUMP_DEST

Value: string containing valid directory name
Default: operating system dependent   **Dynamic:** ALTER SYSTEM

Specifies the pathname for a directory where debugging trace files for the background processes (LGWR, DBWR, and so on) are written during Oracle operations.

CONTROL_FILE_RECORD_KEEP_TIME

Value: 0–365   **Default:** 7   **Dynamic:** ALTER SYSTEM

Specifies the minimum age, in days, that a record in the circularly reusable section of the control file must be before it can be reused. If a new record needs to be added to a reusable section and the oldest record has not aged enough, the record section expands. If this parameter is set to 0, then reusable sections never expand and records are reused as needed. The names of the reusable sections of the control file are:

ARCHIVED LOG	COPY CORRUPTION
BACKUP CORRUPTION	DATAFILE COPY
BACKUP DATAFILE	DELETED OBJECT
BACKUP PIECE	LOGHISTORY
BACKUP REDO LOG	OFFLINE RANGE
BACKUP SET	

CONTROL_FILES

Value: 1–8 filenames   **Default:** operating system dependent

Specifies one or more names of control files, separated by commas.

CORE_DUMP_DEST

Value: valid directory pathname   **Default:** $ORACLE_HOME/dbs.   **Dynamic:** ALTER SYSTEM

Specifies the directory where core dump files are written.

DB_BLOCK_CHECKPOINT_BATCH

Value: 0–derived   **Default:** 8   **Dynamic:** ALTER SYSTEM

Specifies the number of buffers that will be added to each batch of buffers that DBWR writes in order to advance checkpoint processing. Reducing DB_BLOCK_CHECK-POINT_BATCH prevents the I/O system from being flooded with checkpoint writes and allows other modified blocks to be written to disk. Setting it to a higher value allows checkpoints to complete more quickly. Setting DB_BLOCK_CHECKPOINT_BATCH to zero causes the default value to be used. If the specified value is too large, Oracle limits it to the number of blocks that can be written in a database writer write batch. Obsolete with Oracle8i.

DB_BLOCK_CHECKSUM

Value: TRUE | FALSE   **Default:** FALSE   **Dynamic:** ALTER SYSTEM

Specifies whether DBWR and the direct loader will calculate a checksum and store it in the cache header of every data block when writing it to disk. Setting DB_BLOCK_CHECKSUM to TRUE can incur additional performance overhead. Set this parameter to TRUE only if advised to do so by Oracle Support.

DB_BLOCK_LRU_EXTENDED_STATISTICS

Value: 0–dependent on system memory   **Default:** 0

Disables or enables compilation of statistics in the X$KCBRBH table, which measures the effects of increasing the number of buffers in the buffer cache in the SGA. Effective with Oracle8, these statistics are also available in V$RECENT_BUCKET. Set this parameter to 0 when you are not actively tuning. Obsolete with Oracle8i.

DB_BLOCK_LRU_LATCHES

Value: 1–number of CPUs   **Default:** CPU_COUNT / 2

Specifies the upper bound of the number of LRU latch sets. If the parameter is not set, Oracle calculates a value that is usually adequate. Increase this value only if misses are higher than 3% in V$LATCH. Obsolete with Oracle9i.

DB_BLOCK_LRU_STATISTICS

Value: TRUE | FALSE   **Default:** FALSE

Disables or enables compilation of statistics in the X$KCBCBH table, which measures the effect of decreasing the number of buffers in the SGA buffer cache. These statistics are also available in V$CURRENT_BUCKET. This parameter is a tuning tool; you should set it to FALSE during normal operation. Obsolete with Oracle8i.

DB_BLOCK_MAX_DIRTY_TARGET

Value: 100–all buffers in the cache   **Default:** all buffers in the cache

Specifies the number of buffers that can be dirty (modified and different from what is on disk). If the number of dirty buffers in a buffer cache exceeds this value, DBWR will write out buffers in order to try to keep the number of dirty buffers below the specified value. This parameter can be used to influence the amount of time it takes to perform instance recovery because recovery is related to the number of buffers that were dirty at the time of the crash. The smaller the value of this parameter, the faster the instance recovery. Setting this value to 0 disables the writing of buffers for incremental checkpointing purposes; all other write activity continues as is. Obsolete with Oracle9*i*.

DB_WRITER_PROCESSES

Value: 1-20   **Default:** 1

Specifies the number of DB writer processes created for an instance.

DBWR_IO_SLAVES

Value: 0–operating system dependent   **Default:** 0

Specifies the number of I/O slaves used by the DBW0 process to perform writes to disk and to simulate asynchronous I/O on platforms that do not support asynchronous I/O or that implement it inefficiently. This parameter is valid only when DB_WRITER_PROCESSES is set to 1. If specified, it will force DB_WRITER_PROCESSES to be set to 1.

MAX_DUMP_FILE_SIZE

Value: 0–UNLIMITED   **Default:** UNLIMITED   **Dynamic:** ALTER SYSTEM, ALTER SESSION

Specifies the maximum size of trace files to be written. Can accept a numeric value (operating system blocks) or a number followed by the suffix K or M.

PROCESSES

Value: 6–operating system dependent   **Default:** derived

Specifies the maximum number of operating system user processes that can simultaneously connect to an Oracle Server. In calculating this number, make sure to allow for all background processes, including LCK processes, job queue processes, and parallel query processes. The default value is derived from PARALLEL_MAX_SERVERS. The default values of SESSIONS is derived from this parameter, so if it is altered, you may also need to adjust the value of SESSIONS.

RESOURCE_LIMIT

Value: TRUE | FALSE   **Default:** FALSE   **Dynamic:** ALTER SYSTEM

Specifies the enforcement status of resource limits set in database profiles.

RESOURCE_MANAGER_PLAN

Value: any valid character string   **Default:** none   **Dynamic:** ALTER SYSTEM

Specifies the top-level resource plan for use with the instance. If this parameter is not specified, the Resource Manager is off by default.

SESSION_MAX_OPEN_FILES

Value: 1–the smaller of 50 or MAX_OPEN_FILES
Default: 10

Specifies the maximum number of BFILEs that can be opened in any given session. Once this number is reached, subsequent attempts to open more files in the session will fail. This parameter is also dependent on the equivalent parameter defined for the underlying operating system.

SESSIONS

Value: 1–231   **Default:** 11 * PROCESSES + 5

Specifies the total number of user and system sessions. The default values of ENQUEUE_RESOURCES and TRANSACTIONS are derived from SESSIONS. If you alter the value of SESSIONS, you may also need to adjust the values for these other parameters. With the Shared Server or Multi-Threaded Server, you should set the value of SESSIONS to approximately 1.1 * (total number of connections).

SHADOW_CORE_DUMP

Value: FULL | PARTIAL   **Default:** PARTIAL

Determines whether the SGA will be included in core dumps. If FULL, the SGA is included in the core dump. If PARTIAL, the SGA is not dumped.

TEMPORARY_TABLE_LOCKS

Value: 0–operating system dependent   **Default:** SESSIONS

Specifies the number of temporary tables that can be created in the temporary segment space. A temporary table lock is needed any time a sort occurs that is too large to hold in memory. This may occur as the result of a SELECT on a large table with ORDER BY or as the result of sorting a large index. Obsolete with Oracle8*i*.

THREAD

Value: 0–maximum number of enabled threads
Default: 0

Specifies the number of the redo thread that is to be used by the instance. THREAD is applicable only to instances that intend to run with Real Application Clusters or Parallel Server. Any available redo thread number can be used, but an instance cannot use the same thread number as another instance and cannot start when its redo thread is disabled. A value of 0 causes an available, enabled public thread to be chosen. Redo threads are specified with the THREAD option of the ALTER DATABASE ADD LOGFILE statement and enabled with the ALTER DATABASE ENABLE [PUBLIC] THREAD statement. The PUBLIC keyword signifies that the redo thread may be used by any instance. Thread 1 is the default thread in exclusive mode, but an instance running in exclusive mode can specify THREAD to use the redo log files in a thread other than thread 1.

USE_ISM

Value: TRUE, FALSE **Default:** TRUE

Specifies whether the shared page table is enabled. Obsolete with Oracle8i.

Oracle Trace

The following parameters affect the operation of Oracle Trace.

ORACLE_TRACE_COLLECTION_NAME

Value: valid name up to 16 characters **Default:** none

Specifies the Oracle Trace collection name. This parameter is also used in the output filenames of the collection definition file *.cdf* and the datafile *.dat*, along with the ORACLE_TRACE_COLLECTION_PATH parameter described next.

ORACLE_TRACE_COLLECTION_PATH

Value: valid directory pathname **Default:** operating system dependent

Specifies the directory where Oracle Trace collection definition and datafiles are located.

ORACLE_TRACE_COLLECTION_SIZE

Value: 0–4294967295 **Default:** 5242880

Specifies the maximum size, in bytes, of the Oracle Trace collection file. Once the collection file reaches this maximum, the collection is disabled.

ORACLE_TRACE_ENABLE

Value: TRUE | FALSE **Default:** FALSE **Dynamic:** ALTER SYSTEM, ALTER SESSION

Specifies whether the Oracle Trace collections for the server should be enabled. If TRUE, does not start an Oracle Trace collection but allows Oracle Trace to be used for that server. Oracle Trace can then be started by using the Oracle Trace Manager application with the Oracle Enterprise Manager Diagnostic Pack, by using the Oracle Trace command-line interface, or by specifying a name in the ORACLE_TRACE_COLLECTION_NAME parameter.

ORACLE_TRACE_FACILITY_NAME

Value: ORACLED | ORACLEE | ORACLESM | ORACLEC
Default: ORACLED

Specifies the Oracle Trace product definition file (*.fdf*). The file must be located in the directory pointed to by the ORACLE_TRACE_FACILITY_PATH parameter. The product definition file contains definition information for all the events and data items that can be collected for a product that uses the Oracle Trace Data Collection API. The available product definition files are:

ORACLE	The ALL event set
ORACLED	The DEFAULT event set
ORACLEE	The EXPERT event set
ORACLESM	The SUMMARY event set
ORACLEC	The CACHEIO event set

ORACLE_TRACE_FACILITY_PATH

Value: valid pathname   **Default:** operating system dependent

Specifies the directory pathname where Oracle Trace facility definition files are located.

SQL_TRACE

Value: TRUE | FALSE   **Default:** FALSE

Disables or enables the SQL Trace facility. Can also be changed using the DBMS_SYSTEM package.

TRACE_ENABLED

Value: TRUE | FALSE   **Default:** TRUE   **Dynamic:** ALTER SYSTEM, ALTER SESSION

Specifies whether tracing of the execution history or code path is performed. Multiple instances must have the same value. New with Oracle9*i*.

TRACEFILE_IDENTIFIER

Value: any valid filename   **Default:** none   **Dynamic:** ALTER SESSION

Specifies a custom identifier that becomes a part of the Oracle Trace filename for foreground processes. New with Oracle9*i*.

USER_DUMP_DEST

Value: valid directory pathname   **Default:** operating system dependent
Dynamic: ALTER SYSTEM.

Specifies the directory where the server will write debugging trace files on behalf of a user process.

Miscellaneous Parameters

The following parameters do not fit into any of the previous categories.

ALWAYS_ANTI_JOIN

Value: NESTED_LOOPS | MERGE | HASH   **Default:** NESTED_LOOPS

Sets the type of antijoin that the Oracle Server uses. Obsolete with Oracle9i.

Keywords

NESTED_LOOPS
> Server uses a nested loop antijoin algorithm.

MERGE   Server uses the sort merge antijoin algorithm.

HASH   Server uses the hash antijoin algorithm to evaluate the subquery.

AQ_TM_PROCESSES

Value: 0 | 1   **Default:** 0   **Dynamic:** ALTER SYSTEM

If this parameter is set to 1, a one-time manager process is created to monitor the messages. If the parameter is not specified or is set to 0, the manager is not created.

COMPATIBLE

Value: 7.3.0–current Oracle release   **Default:** current Oracle release (eg, 9.2.0)

Allows the use of a new release, while at the same time guaranteeing backward compatibility with an earlier release. Some features of the current release may be restricted.

When you are using the standby database feature, this parameter must have the same value on both databases, and the value must be 7.3.0.0.0 or higher.

COMPATIBLE_NO_RECOVERY

Value: default Oracle version – current Oracle version
Default: release dependent

Functions like the COMPATIBLE parameter, except that the earlier version may not be usable on the current database if recovery is needed. The default value is the earliest version with which compatibility can be guaranteed. Obsolete with Oracle8i.

COMPLEX_VIEW_MERGING

Value: TRUE | FALSE   **Default:** FALSE

Specifies whether complex view merging should be enabled. Obsolete with Oracle9i.

EVENT

Value: provided by Oracle Support   **Default:** none

Used to debug the system. Set this parameter only at the direction of Oracle Support.

FIXED_DATE

Value: valid date as shown   **Default:** none

Specifies a constant date that SYSDATE will always return instead of the current date. The format of the date is:

```
YYYY-MM-DD-HH24:MI:SS
```

Also accepts the default Oracle date format, without a time. Specify the value with double quotes (not single quotes) or without quotes; for example, FIXED_DATE = "30-nov-02" or FIXED_DATE = 30-nov-02.

LOCAL_LISTENER

Value: valid listener specification   **Default:** see description

Identifies "local" listeners so that they can complete client connections to dedicated servers. Specifies the network name of either a single address or an address list, which must be on the same machine as the instance. When present, LOCAL_LISTENER overrides MTS_LISTENER_ADDRESS and MTS_MULTIPLE_LISTENERS. The default value is:

```
(ADDRESS_LIST = (ADDRESS = (PROTOCOL = TCP) (HOST=localhost) (Port=1521))
                (ADDRESS =(PROTOCOL = IPC)
                (KEY= dbname)))
```

LOGMNR_MAX_PERSISTENT_SESSIONS

Value: 1–unlimited   **Default:** 1

Specifies the maximum number of persistent LogMiner sessions that are concurrently active. In a clustered environment, you should set the value for the number of nodes in the cluster. New with Oracle9i.

REPLICATION_DEPENDENCY_TRACKING

Value: TRUE | FALSE   **Default:** TRUE

Specifies dependency tracking for read/write operations to the database. Dependency tracking is essential for the Replication Server to propagate changes in parallel. TRUE turns on dependency tracking. FALSE allows read/write operations to the database to run faster but does not produce dependency information for the Replication Server to perform parallel propagations. Do not specify this parameter unless applications will perform absolutely no read/write operations to replicated tables.

3

Concurrency

One of the most important features of a database is the way that it supports multiple users. The Oracle database has a concurrency scheme to support concurrent access by multiple users called *multiversion read consistency* (MVRC) that is unique among major databases. This feature is a great benefit to application developers, because it removes the need for them to worry about handling most locking issues in their own code. The ability to support MVRC is built deeply into the architecture of the Oracle database.

This chapter summarizes the concepts involved in implementing a concurrency scheme and describes briefly how Oracle's MVRC features work.

Concurrency Concepts

Several important concepts are necessary to understanding concurrency and how it works in the Oracle system.

Transactions

The *transaction* is the bedrock of data integrity in multiuser databases and the foundation of all concurrency schemes. A transaction is defined as a single indivisible piece of work that affects some data. All of the modifications made to data within a transaction are either uniformly applied to a relational database with a COMMIT statement, or the data affected by the changes is uniformly returned to its initial state with a ROLLBACK statement. Once a transaction is committed, the changes made by that transaction become permanent and are made visible to other transactions and other users.

Transactions always occur over time, although most transactions occur over a very short period of time. Because the changes made by a transaction are not official until the transaction is committed, this means that each individual transaction must be isolated from the effects of other transactions. The mechanism used to enforce *transaction isolation* is the lock.

Locks

A database uses a system of *locks* to prevent transactions from interfering with each other. One transaction could interfere with another by attempting to change a piece of data that another transaction is in the process of also changing. Figure 3-1 illustrates this potential problem. Transaction A reads a piece of data. Transaction B reads the same piece of data and commits a change to the data. When Transaction A goes to commit the data, its change unwittingly overwrites the changes made by Transaction B, resulting in a loss of data integrity.

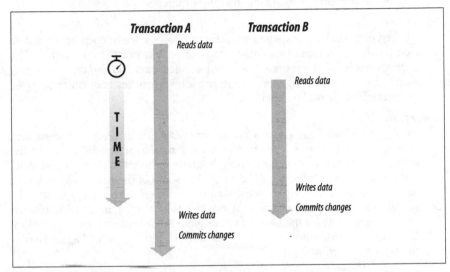

Figure 3-1. Transactions over time

Normally, two types of locks are used to avoid this problem. The first type of lock is called a *write lock*, or an *exclusive lock*. An exclusive lock is applied and held while changes are made to data in the course of a transaction and is released when the transaction is ended by either a COMMIT or a ROLLBACK. A write lock can be held by only one user at a time, so only one user at a time can change that data.

Some databases also use *read locks*, or *shared locks*. A read lock can be held by any number of users who are merely reading the data, because there are no potential conflicts with read-only access. However, a read lock prevents a write lock from being placed on the data, as the write lock is an exclusive lock. In Figure 3-1, if a read lock were placed on the data when Transaction A began, Transaction B would not be prevented from reading the same data, but it would be prevented from acquiring a write lock on the data until Transaction A ended.

Normally, Oracle uses read locks only when a SQL operation specifically requests them with the FOR UPDATE clause in a SELECT statement.

Concurrency and Contention

The locks used to enforce isolation between concurrent users of data can lead to their own problems. As the example described in the previous section illustrates, a single transaction could cause significant performance problems as the locks it places on the database prevent other transactions from completing. The interference caused by conflicting locks is called *contention*. Contention can degrade the performance of the database.

Integrity Problems

Although locks can introduce contention and performance degradation, locks are still required to prevent the following integrity problems:

Dirty reads
> This type of read occurs when a database allows a transaction to read data that has been changed by another transaction but not yet committed. The changes made by the transaction may be rolled back, so the data read may turn out to be incorrect. Many databases allow dirty reads in order to avoid the contention caused by read locks.

Nonrepeatable reads
> This type of read occurs as a result of changes made by another transaction. A transaction performs a query based on a particular condition. After the data has been sent to this transaction, but before this transaction is complete, another transaction changes the data so that some of the previously retrieved data would no longer satisfy the selection condition. If the query were to be repeated in the same transaction, it would return a different set of results, so any changes made on the basis of the original results may no longer be valid. Data that was read once may return different results if it is read again later in the same transaction.

Phantom reads
> This type of read also occurs as a result of changes made by another transaction. One transaction performs a query based on a particular condition. After the data has been sent to this transaction, but before this transaction is complete, another transaction inserts new rows into the database that would have been selected by the first transaction. If the transaction is making changes based on the assumption that the only rows that satisfied the condition were returned, a phantom read could result in improper data. Although all the data that was read by the first query is returned for the second query, additional data could have also been returned, so any changes made on the basis of the original results may no longer be valid.

Serialization

The goal of a complete concurrency solution is to provide the highest level of isolation between the actions of different users accessing the same data. As defined by the SQL92 standard, this highest level is called *serializable*. As the name implies, serializable transactions appear as though they have been executed in a series of distinct, ordered transactions. When one transaction begins, it is isolated from any changes that occur to its data from subsequent transactions.

To the user, a serializable transaction looks as though it has the exclusive use of the database for the duration of the transaction. Serializable transaction are predictable and reproducible, the two cardinal virtues of data integrity.

Of course, it is nontrivial to have a database server support thousands of users and have each user think that she is the only one. But MVRC in Oracle enables this feat.

Oracle and Concurrent User Access

Oracle's concurrency scheme, multiversion read consistency (MVRC), guarantees that a user sees a consistent view of the data he requests. If another user changes the underlying data during the query execution, Oracle maintains a version of the data as it existed at the time the query began. If transactions were underway but uncommitted at the time the query began, Oracle will ensure that the query does not see the changes made by those transactions. The data returned to the query will reflect all committed transactions at the time the query started.

This feature has several effects on the way that queries impact the database and its performance:

- Oracle does not place any locks on data for read operations. This means that a read operation will never block a write operation. Even if a database places a single lock on a single row as part of a read operation, it can still cause contention in the database, especially because most database tables tend to concentrate update operations around a few hot spots of active data.

- A write operation will never block a read operation, because MVRC will simply provide a version of the data that existed before the write operation began.

- A user gets a complete snapshot view of the data, accurate at the point in time that the query began. A row that is retrieved at the end of a result set may have been changed since the time the result set retrieval began. But because Oracle keeps a version of the row as it existed at the start of the query, you always get a consistent view of the data at a single point in time.

- A write operation will block another write operation only if it attempts to write the same row.

MVRC Implementation Features

Three data structures are used by Oracle to implement multiversion read consistency:

Rollback segments
Rollback segments are structures in the Oracle database used to store undo information for transactions in case of rollback. This undo information is used to restore database rows to the state they were in before the transaction in question started. When a transaction starts changing some data in a block, it first writes the old image of the data to a rollback segment. The information stored in a rollback segment is used for two main purposes: to provide

the information necessary to roll back a transaction and to support multiversion read consistency.

A rollback segment is different from a redo log. The redo log is used to log all transactions to the database and to recover the database in the event of a system failure, while the rollback segment is used to provide rollback for transactions and read consistency.

Blocks of rollback segments are cached in the System Global Area (SGA) just like blocks of tables and indexes. If rollback segment blocks are unused for a period of time, they may be aged out of the cache and written to disk

System Change Number (SCN)

In order to preserve the integrity of the data in the database, it is critical to keep track of the order in which transactions were performed. The mechanism Oracle uses to preserve the ordering of transactions with respect to time is the System Change Number, or SCN.

The SCN is a logical timestamp that is used to track the order in which transactions occurred. Oracle uses the SCN information in the redo log to reproduce transactions in the original and correct order when applying redo. Oracle also uses the SCN to determine when to clean up information in rollback segments that is no longer needed, as you will see in the following sections.

Locks in data blocks

A database must have a way of determining if a particular row is locked. Most databases keep a list of locks in memory that are managed by a Lock Manager process. Oracle keeps locks with an indicator in the actual block in which the row is stored. A data block is the smallest amount of data that can be read from disk for an Oracle database, so whenever the row is requested, the block is read, and the lock is available within the block. Although the lock indicators are kept within a block, each lock affects only an individual row within the block.

In addition to the preceding data structures, which directly pertain to multiversion read consistency, another implementation feature in Oracle provides a greater level of concurrency in large user populations:

Nonescalating row locks

In order to reduce the overhead of the lock management process, non-Oracle database management systems sometimes *escalate* locks to a higher level of granularity within the database. For example, if a certain percentage of rows in a table are locked, the database escalates the lock to a table lock, which locks all of the rows in a table, including rows that are not specifically used by the SQL statement in question. Although lock escalation reduces the number of locks the Lock Manager process has to handle, it causes unaffected rows to be locked. However, because Oracle maintains each row's lock within its data block, there is no need for Oracle to escalate a lock—and it never does.

MVRC Syntax

MVRC basically works behind the scenes, so there is very little syntax associated with it. However, you do need to be aware of what isolation levels are and how to set them.

An *isolation level* is the degree to which the operations of one user are isolated from the operations of another user. There are two basic isolation levels that can be used with Oracle. These levels have different implications for users and developers:

READ COMMITED
> This level enforces serialization at the statement level. This means that every statement will get a consistent view of the data as it existed at the start of the statement. However, because a transaction can contain more than one statement, nonrepeatable reads and phantoms can occur within the context of the complete transaction. The READ COMMITTED isolation level is the default isolation level for Oracle.

SERIALIZABLE
> This level enforces serialization at the transaction level. This means that every statement within a transaction will get the same consistent view of data as it existed at the start of the transaction.

Because of their differing spans of control, these two isolation levels also react differently when they encounter a transaction that blocks their operation with a lock on a requested row. Both isolation levels wait for the lock to be released. Once the lock has been released by the blocking transaction, an operation executing with the READ COMMITTED isolation level simply retries the operation. Because this operation is concerned only with the state of data when the statement begins, this is a perfectly logical approach.

On the other hand, if the blocking transaction commits changes to the data, an operation executing with a SERIALIZABLE isolation level returns an error indicating that it cannot serialize operations. This error makes sense, because the blocking transaction will have changed the state of the data from the beginning of the SERIALIZABLE transaction, making it impossible to perform any more write operations on the changed rows. In this situation, an application programmer will have to add logic to his program to return to the start of the SERIALIZABLE transaction and begin it again.

One other isolation level is supported by Oracle:

READ ONLY
> You can declare a session or a transaction to have an isolation level of READ ONLY. As the name implies, this level explicitly does not allow any write operations. As with the other isolation levels, the READ ONLY level provides an accurate view of all the data at the time the transaction began.

Isolation levels can be set with the following SQL statements. Here we include only the syntax needed to handle concurrency. For complete explanations of the full syntax of these statements, see Chapter 7 (refer to the index for the specific location of the statements in that chapter).

ALTER SESSION

```
ALTER SESSION SET ISOLATION_LEVEL = SERIALIZABLE | READ COMMITTED
```

Sets the isolation level for the session.

Keywords

SERIALIZABLE
> Enforces serialization at the transaction level.

READ COMMITTED
> Enforces serialization at the statement level. This value is the default for Oracle.

SET TRANSACTION

```
SET TRANSACTION ISOLATION LEVEL SERIALIZABLE | READ COMMITTED
```

Sets the isolation level for the transaction.

Keywords

SERIALIZABLE
> Enforces serialization at the transaction level for this transaction.

READ COMMITTED
> Enforces serialization at the statement level for this transaction. This value is the default for Oracle.

4

Security

Oracle provides a variety of features that can help secure your database from unauthorized access and can help protect your data from being seen or manipulated by unauthorized users. This chapter focuses on the major security-related concepts for Oracle—authentication, profiles, privileges, roles, and auditing—and specifies the syntax for controlling security in an Oracle database.

In addition, we include brief discussions of some of the more advanced security options for Oracle. Detailed information on these more specialized and/or extra-cost options is outside the scope of this book. If your site has purchased the Advanced Security or Label Security options, consult Oracle documentation for information.

Authentication

Authentication is the process of recognizing authorized users. Basically, authentication is the system's way of confirming that you are who you say you are. Oracle security is primarily based on the concept of individual authorized users.

System Users

The Oracle database creates two users when you install Oracle:

SYS
> The schema for SYS contains the base tables and views used for the data dictionary. You should never change any of these tables. The SYS user has the DBA role. (Roles are described in the "Roles" section later in this chapter.) The default password for SYS is CHANGE_ON_INSTALL.

SYSTEM
> The SYSTEM username is used to create additional tables and views for administrative information. The SYSTEM user has the DBA role. The default password for SYSTEM is MANAGER.

When you create an Oracle database using the CREATE DATABASE statement, you can use the USER SYS IDENTIFIED BY *password* and USER SYSTEM IDENTIFIED BY *password* clauses to protect access by these powerful precreated users.

Creating Users

You can create your own users with the CREATE USER statement. You can modify user characteristics with the ALTER USER statement.

CREATE USER

```
CREATE USER username
    IDENTIFIED {BY password | EXTERNALLY | GLOBALLY AS 'external_name'}
    [DEFAULT TABLESPACE tablespace_name]
    [TEMPORARY TABLESPACE tablespace_name]
    [QUOTA {integer (K | M) | UNLIMITED} ON tablespace_name]
        [QUOTA {integer (K | M) | UNLIMITED} ON tablespace_name ...]
    [PROFILE profilename]
    [PASSWORD EXPIRE]
    [ACCOUNT LOCK | UNLOCK]
```

Creates a user and specifies basic characteristics of the user.

Keywords

IDENTIFIED BY

Specifies the way the user will be authenticated. There are three options for authentication:

PASSWORD

Identified with a locally stored password. The password can contain only single-byte characters from the database character set.

EXTERNALLY

Identified by an external service, such as the operating system. If you want the user to have access only through the operating system account, add the OS_AUTHENT_PREFIX parameter value before the username.

GLOBALLY AS 'external_name'

Identified by an enterprise directory service. The *external_string* can be either the Distinguished Name from the directory or NULL, which indicates that the directory will map users to the appropriate database schema.

DEFAULT TABLESPACE

Specifies the default tablespace for objects created by the user. The default is the SYSTEM tablespace.

TEMPORARY TABLESPACE

Specifies the tablespace used for the user's temporary storage. The default is the SYSTEM tablespace.

QUOTA

Specifies the amount of space the user can use in the specified tablespace. You can have multiple QUOTA clauses for multiple tablespaces. You can specify kilobytes (K) or megabytes (M). UNLIMITED means the user will have no restrictions on space usage.

PROFILE

Specifies the profile assigned to the user. For more information, see the later "Profiles" section.

PASSWORD EXPIRE

Specifies that the user or the DBA will have to change the user's password before the user can log into the database.

ACCOUNT LOCK | UNLOCK

Disables or enables access through the user account.

ALTER USER

```
ALTER USER username
    [IDENTIFIED {BY password [REPLACE old_password]
        EXTERNALLY | GLOBALLY AS 'external_name'}]
    [DEFAULT TABLESPACE tablespace_name]
    [TEMPORARY TABLESPACE tablespace_name]
    [QUOTA {integer [K | M] | UNLIMITED} ON tablespace_name]
        [QUOTA {integer [K | M] | UNLIMITED} ON tablespace_name]
    [PROFILE profile_name]
    [DEFAULT ROLE {[role_name[,role_name . . .] |
        ALL {EXCEPT [role_name[, role_name . . .]} | NONE
    [PASSWORD EXPIRE]
    [ACCOUNT LOCK | UNLOCK]
    [username [,username . . .] proxy_clause]
```

Changes the characteristics of an existing user.

Keywords

Most keywords for the ALTER USER statement have the same meaning as those in the CREATE USER statement. The following keywords apply to only the ALTER USER statement:

REPLACE old_password

If the password complexity verification function is turned on, you must specify your old password when you change it with the ALTER USER command.

DEFAULT ROLE

A role is a way to manage groups of user privileges for groups of users. You can specify multiple roles for a user, ALL or ALL EXCEPT roles for a user, or no role for a user. For more information on roles, see the later "Roles" section.

proxy_clause

The proxy clause can be used with more than one user's name. This was new in Oracle8*i*. In Oracle8*i*, a user could be identified by a proxy, but the proxy would pass the password to the database for re-authentication. With Oracle9*i*, the user identity, in the form of a Distinguished Name or a full X.509 certificate, can be passed to the database for identification without re-authentication.

The proxy clause has the following syntax:

```
{GRANT | REVOKE} CONNECT THROUGH proxy
    [WITH {ROLE [role_name[, role_name . . .]] |
        ALL [EXCEPT] [role_name[, role_name . . .]] |
        NO ROLES}]
    AUTHENTICATED USING {PASSWORD | DISTINGUISHED NAME |
        CERTIFICATE [TYPE 'type_name'][VERSION 'version_name']}
```

GRANT | REVOKE
> Allows or prohibits the proxy connection.

CONNECT THROUGH proxy
> Identifies the proxy connecting to Oracle. For more information on proxies, see the section "Other Security Features" near the end of this chapter.

WITH ROLE
> Assigns a role to the proxy user. The syntax is the same as the DEFAULT ROLE keyword.

AUTHENTICATED USING
> Specifies if the proxy will be authenticated by a source other than the proxy. The DISTINGUISHED NAME and CERTIFICATE indicate that the proxy is acting on behalf of a global database user.

Profiles

A *profile* can be associated with a user to limit the resources available to that user or to specify a condition on how passwords are administered. By limiting the computing resources that any one individual can use, you can prevent any one user from exhausting too many resources and affecting other users. (This is known as *denial of service*.) By placing limits on how passwords are administered, you can help to safeguard the authentication process for your Oracle database.

Profiles can be used if you enable dynamic resource limits with either the RESOURCE_LIMIT initialization parameter or the ALTER SYSTEM SET statement. Once a profile has been defined with the CREATE PROFILE command, you can assign a user to a profile with either the CREATE USER or ALTER USER statement.

CREATE PROFILE

CREATE PROFILE *profile_name* LIMIT {*resource_parameter* | *password_parameter*}

Allows you to create a profile and assign different types of resource limits to the profile. You can specify multiple parameters for a role.

Keywords—all parameters

The following values can be used for both resource and password parameters, unless specified otherwise in the parameter descriptions:

UNLIMITED
> Specifies no limit for the particular parameter.

DEFAULT
> Specifies that the parameter assumes the value specified for the DEFAULT profile. Initially, all values for the DEFAULT profile are specified as UNLIMITED. You can change the values for the DEFAULT profile with the ALTER PROFILE statement.

resource_parameter | password_parameter
> For resource parameters, the value is an integer. For password parameters, the value is an expression.

Keywords—resource parameters

Except as noted, if a user attempts to perform an operation that exceeds any of the resource limits, Oracle aborts the operation, rolls back the current statement, returns an error, and leaves the transaction intact.

SESSIONS_PER_USER
> Limits the number of concurrent sessions for the user.

CPU_PER_SESSION
> Limits the CPU time for a user session, in hundredths of seconds.

CPU_PER_CALL
> Limits the CPU time for an individual call by the user, in hundredths of seconds.

CONNECT_TIME
> Limits the total elapsed time for a session for the user, in minutes. If a user exceeds this parameter, Oracle rolls back the current transaction and ends the session. The next call made by the user will return an error.

IDLE_TIME
> Limits the amount of continuous idle time for the user, in minutes. Idle time does not apply to long-running queries or other operations. If a user exceeds this parameter, Oracle rolls back the current transaction and ends the session. The next call made by the user will return an error.

LOGICAL_READS_PER_SESSION
> Limits the number of logical data blocks read in a user's session, from either memory or disk.

LOGICAL_READS_PER_CALL
> Limits the number of logical data blocks read in for each call by the user, from either memory or disk.

COMPOSITE_LIMIT
> Limits the total resource cost of a session, as a number of service units. Oracle calculates service units as a weighted sum of the following initialization parameters: CPU_PER_SESSION, CONNECT_TIME, LOGICAL_READS_PER_SESSION, and PRIVATE_SGA. You can modify the weight given to each of these resources with the ALTER RESOURCE COST statement.

PRIVATE_SGA (integer (K | M)| UNLIMITED | DEFAULT)
> Limits the amount of private space a user's session can allocate from the shared pool of the SGA, in kilobytes (K) or megabytes (M).

Keywords—password parameters

FAILED_LOGIN_ATTEMPTS
> Limits the number of failed login attempts by a user before the user account is locked.

PASSWORD_LIFE_TIME
> Sets a limit on the maximum time a single password can be used by the user, in days. At the end of this time, the password expires.

PASSWORD_REUSE_TIME
> Specifies how many days must pass before a password can be reused. If you use an integer value for this parameter, you must set the PASSWORD_REUSE_MAX parameter to UNLIMITED.

PASSWORD_REUSE_MAX

Specifies the number of password changes before a previous password can be reused. If you use an integer value for this parameter, you must set the PASSWORD_REUSE_TIME parameter to UNLIMITED.

PASSWORD_LOCK_TIME

Specifies the number of days a user's account will be locked if the number of login attempts is exceeded.

PASSWORD_GRACE_TIME

Specifies the number of days a warning is issued, prior to a password expiring.

PASSWORD_VERIFY_FUNCTION function | NULL | DEFAULT

Allows the use of a PL/SQL function to verify password complexity.

ALTER PROFILE

`ALTER PROFILE profile_name LIMIT {resource_parameter | password_parameter}`

Changes the resource or parameter limits for an existing profile.

Keywords

The ALTER PROFILE statement uses the same keywords and values as the CREATE PROFILE statement.

DROP PROFILE

`DROP PROFILE profile_name (CASCADE)`

Deletes an existing profile.

Keywords

CASCADE

Specifies that the profile will be desassigned from any active users and replaced with the DEFAULT profile. You must use this clause to drop a profile for a currently active user.

Privileges

Privileges are rights that are assigned to individual users or roles. There are two basic types of privileges:

System privileges

Give the user or role the ability to perform certain system operations

Schema object privileges

Give the user or role access privileges on individual schema objects

System privileges relate to the Oracle instance as a whole—for example, a privilege on all of a type of object (such as all tables), while schema privileges relate to a specific schema object within an Oracle database (for example, a particular accounting table).

System Privileges

This section provides summary information for all of the Oracle system privileges. Several varieties of system privileges apply to more than one type of privilege:

ANY
> Gives the privilege to perform the action on objects in any schema. Without this keyword, a privilege is granted only on objects within the user's schema. By default, the ANY keyword gives the user privilege on all objects in all schemas, including the SYS schema. To prevent access to the SYS schema with the ANY privilege, you can set the O7_DICTIONARY_ACCESSIBILITY initialization parameter to FALSE.

ALTER
> Gives the privilege to alter the type of object.

CREATE
> Gives the privilege to create the type of object.

DROP
> Gives the privilege to drop the type of object.

EXECUTE
> Gives the privilege to execute or reference the type of object.

SELECT ANY
> Gives the privilege to access objects. Because users always have the ability to access objects in their own schema, this variety is used only with the ANY keyword.

Each of these varieties of system privilege can be used with many of the system privilege types described in the following entries.

In each of the privilege entries, we've noted two categories of privileges: the common (those listed in the previous section, which apply to many different types of privileges) and the unique (those unique to that particular privilege type).

AUDIT

Allows auditing functions.

Unique privileges   *AUDIT SYSTEM*
> Gives the privilege to issue AUDIT statements in SQL.

Common privileges ANY.

CLUSTER

Provides the ability to work with clusters.

Unique privileges   None.

Common privileges CREATE [ANY], ALTER ANY, DROP ANY.

CONTEXT

Provides the ability to work with contexts. New with Oracle8*i*.

Unique privileges   None.

Common privileges CREATE ANY, DROP ANY.

DATABASE

Provides the ability to use the ALTER DATABASE statement.

Unique privileges   None.

Common privileges ALTER.

DATABASE LINKS

Provides the ability to work with database links.

Unique privileges   *CREATE PUBLIC*
Gives the privilege to create public database links.
DROP PUBLIC
Gives the privilege to drop public database links.

Common privileges CREATE.

DEBUG

Provides the ability to work with the debugger. New with Oracle9*i*.

Unique privileges   *DEBUG CONNECT SESSION*
Gives the privilege to connect the current session to a debugger that uses the Java Debug Wire Protocol.
DEBUG ANY PROCEDURE
Gives the privilege to debug any PL/SQL and Java code in any database object, as well as display all SQL statements executed by the application.

Common privileges None.

DIMENSION

Provides the ability to work with dimensions. New with Oracle8*i*.

Unique privileges   None.

Common privileges CREATE [ANY], ALTER ANY, DROP ANY.

DIRECTORY

Provides the ability to work with directories.

Unique privileges   None.

Common privileges CREATE ANY, DROP ANY.

INDEX

Provides the ability to work with indexes.

Unique privileges   See the entry for [GLOBAL] QUERY REWRITE under "Miscellaneous Privileges."

Common privileges CREATE ANY, ALTER ANY, DROP ANY.

INDEXTYPE

Provides the ability to work with user-created index types. New with Oracle8i.

Unique privileges   None.

Common privileges CREATE [ANY], ALTER ANY (new in Oracle9i), DROP ANY, EXECUTE ANY.

LIBRARY

Provides the ability to work with libraries.

Unique privileges   None.

Common privileges CREATE [ANY], DROP ANY.

MATERIALIZED VIEW

Provides the ability to work with materialized views. The MATERIALIZED VIEW privileges were known as the SNAPSHOT privileges prior to Oracle8i.

Unique privileges   *ON COMMIT REFRESH*
Gives the privilege to create a materialized view that is refreshed on COMMITs. New with Oracle8i.

See the entries for [GLOBAL] QUERY REWRITE and FLASHBACK ANY TABLE under "Miscellaneous Privileges."

Common privileges CREATE [ANY], ALTER ANY, DROP ANY.

OPERATOR

Provides the ability to work with user-defined operators. New with Oracle8*i*.

Unique privileges None.

Common privileges CREATE [ANY], DROP, EXECUTE.

OUTLINE

Provides the ability to work with stored outlines. New with Oracle8*i*.

Unique privileges *SELECT ANY*
Although this uses a common keyword for objects, these keywords give the privilege to create a private outline from a public outline. New with Oracle9*i*.

Common privileges CREATE ANY, ALTER ANY, DROP ANY.

PROCEDURE

Provides the ability to work with procedures.

Unique privileges None.

Common privileges CREATE [ANY], ALTER ANY, DROP ANY, EXECUTE ANY.

PROFILE

Provides the ability to work with profiles.

Unique privileges None.

Common privileges CREATE, ALTER, DROP.

RESOURCE COST

Provides the ability to assign costs to resources.

Unique privileges None.

Common privileges ALTER.

ROLE

Provides the ability to work with roles.

Unique privileges *GRANT ANY*
Gives the privilege to grant any role in the database.

Common privileges CREATE, ALTER ANY, DROP ANY.

ROLLBACK SEGMENT

Provides the ability to work with rollback segments.

Unique privileges None.

Common privileges CREATE, ALTER, DROP.

SEQUENCE

Provides the ability to work with sequences.

Unique privileges None.

Common privileges CREATE [ANY], ALTER ANY, DROP ANY, SELECT ANY.

SESSION

Provides the ability to work with sessions.

Unique privileges *ALTER RESOURCE COST*
  Gives the privilege to set the costs for session resources.
  RESTRICTED SESSION
  Gives the privilege to log on after the Oracle instance is started with the STARTUP RESTRICT statement.

Common privileges CREATE, ALTER.

SNAPSHOT

The SNAPSHOT object keyword has been replaced by the MATERIALIZED VIEW keywords in Oracle9i. In Oracle8i, the SNAPSHOT object keyword and the MATERIALIZED VIEW object keyword were interchangeable.

SYNONYM

Provides the ability to work with synonyms.

Unique privileges None.

Common privileges CREATE [ANY] [PUBLIC], DROP ANY, DROP PUBLIC.

SYSTEM

Provides the ability to alter system parameters.

Unique privileges None.

Common privileges ALTER.

TABLE

Provides the ability to work with tables.

Unique privileges   *BACKUP ANY*

Gives the privilege to use the Export utility on objects in other users' schemas.

COMMENT ANY

Gives the privilege to comment on any table, view, or column in any schema.

INSERT ANY

Gives the privilege to insert rows into tables in other users' schemas.

LOCK ANY

Gives the privilege to lock tables and views in other users' schemas.

FLASHBACK ANY

Gives the ability to issue a SQL flashback query on any table, view, or materialized view in other users' schemas. You can still use the DBMS_FLASHBACK built-in package's procedures without this privilege. New with Oracle9i.

UPDATE ANY

Gives the privilege to update rows in tables and views in other users' schemas.

See the entry on FLASHBACK ANY TABLE under "Miscellaneous Privileges."

Common privileges CREATE [ANY] (CREATE supported only in Oracle8 and before), ALTER ANY, DELETE ANY, DROP ANY, SELECT ANY.

TABLESPACES

Provides the ability to work with tablespaces.

Unique privileges   *MANAGE*

Gives the privilege to take tablespaces offline and online and to begin and end tablespace backups.

UNLIMITED TABLESPACE

Gives the privilege to override any specific tablespace quotas assigned. If this privilege is revoked, a user cannot allocate an additional tablespace unless allowed by existing tablespace quotas. This privilege cannot be granted to a role.

Common privileges CREATE, ALTER, DROP.

TRIGGER

Provides the ability to work with triggers.

Unique privileges   *ADMINISTER DATABASE*
> Gives the privilege to create a trigger on the database. To obtain this privilege, the user or role must also have the CREATE [ANY] TRIGGER privilege. New with Oracle8i.

Common privileges CREATE [ANY], ALTER ANY, DROP.

TYPES

Provides the ability to work with user-defined types.

Unique privileges   *UNDER ANY*
> Gives the privilege to create subtypes under any types not defined as final. New with Oracle9i.

Common privileges CREATE [ANY], ALTER ANY, DROP ANY, EXECUTE ANY.

USER

Provides the ability to work with database users.

Unique privileges   *BECOME*
> Gives the privilege to become another user, which is required to perform a full database import.

Common privileges CREATE, ALTER, DROP.

VIEWS

Provides the ability to work with views.

Unique privileges   *UNDER ANY*
> Gives the privilege to create subviews under any object view. New with Oracle9i.
>
> See the entry for FLASHBACK ANY TABLE under "Miscellaneous Privileges."

Common privileges CREATE [ANY], DROP.

Miscellaneous Privileges

The following system privileges do not fall into any of the earlier categories:

ANALYZE ANY
> Gives the privilege to analyze any table, cluster, or index in any schema.

EXEMPT ANY
> Gives the privilege to bypass application-driven security policies. New with Oracle9*i*.

FLASHBACK ANY TABLE
> Gives the privilege to issue a SQL flashback query on any table, view, or materialized view in any schema. You can still use the DBMS_FLASHBACK built-in package's procedures without this privilege. New with Oracle9*i*.

FORCE TRANSACTION
> Gives the privilege to force the commit or rollback of any of the user's distributed transaction in the local database.

FORCE ANY TRANSACTION
> Gives the privilege to force the commit or rollback of any distributed transaction in the local database or induce the failure of a distributed transaction.

GRANT ANY PRIVILEGE
> Gives the privilege to grant any system privilege.

GRANT ANY OBJECT PRIVILEGE
> Gives the privilege to grant any object privilege. New with Oracle9*i*.

[GLOBAL] QUERY REWRITE
> Gives the privilege to enable query rewrite on a materialized view or to create a function-based index. The GLOBAL keyword acts like the ANY keyword. New with Oracle8*i*.

RESUMABLE
> Gives the privilege to enable resumable space allocation. New with Oracle9*i*.

SELECT ANY DICTIONARY
> Gives the privilege to query any data dictionary object in the SYS schema, which lets the user selectively override the setting of the O7_DICTIONARY_ACCESSIBILITY initialization parameter. New with Oracle9*i*.

Special System Privileges

The following system privileges are used to give the user permission to perform an entire set of operations. These system privileges are special because a single privilege grants multiple underlying permissions.

SYSDBA
> Gives a user all the permissions needed to start up and shut down an Oracle database. It includes the RESTRICTED SESSION privilege and the following permissions:
>
> > ALTER DATABASE
> > CREATE DATABASE
> > ARCHIVELOG and RECOVERY
> > CREATE SPFILE (new with Oracle9*i*)

SYSOPER
> Gives a user a slightly more limited set of permissions, designed for a system operator. It includes the RESTRICTED SESSION privilege and these permissions:
>
> > ALTER DATABASE OPEN | MOUNT | BACKUP
> > ARCHIVELOG and RECOVERY
> > CREATE SPFILE (new with Oracle9*i*)

Schema Object Privileges

There are several different varieties of schema object privileges. These can be applied to a number of different types of schema objects, as described in the following sections.

Varieties of schema object privileges

ALTER
> Changes the definition of the object.

DEBUG
> Accesses PL/SQL code or information about SQL statements that access the object directly through a debugger. New with Oracle9*i*.

DELETE
> Removes rows from the object.

EXECUTE
> Compiles or executes a procedure or function in the object or accesses a program object declared in the object.

FLASHBACK
> Executes a flashback query on the object. New with Oracle9*i*.

INSERT
> Adds new rows to the object.

REFERENCES
> Creates a constraint that references the object.

SELECT
> Queries the object.

UNDER
> Creates a subobject under the level of an object. New with Oracle9*i*.

UPDATE
> Changes existing data in the object.

Schema objects and their privileges

Each type of schema object is listed in the following sections, with the common and particular varieties of the privilege.

Directories

Provides privileges to perform operations on directories.

Unique privileges *READ*
> Reads files in a directory.

WRITE
> Writes to files in a directory, with the exception of BFILEs. Applies to external tables in the directory. New with Oracle9*i*.

Common privileges None.

External Tables

Provides privileges to perform operations on external tables.

Unique privileges None.

Common privileges ALTER, SELECT.

Indextypes

Provides privileges to perform operations on indextype objects, which are user-defined indexes introduced in Oracle8*i*.

Unique privileges None.

Common privileges EXECUTE.

Libraries

Provides privileges to perform operations on libraries.

Unique privileges None.

Common privileges EXECUTE.

Materialized Views

Provides privileges to perform operations on materialized views. Materialized views are preaggregated summaries used for business intelligence operations. Materialized views were new in Oracle8*i*. In Oracle8*i*, both materialized views and snapshots could have these privileges. For Oracle8 and previous versions, only snapshots could have these privileges.

Unique privileges None.

Common privileges DELETE, FLASHBACK, INSERT, SELECT, UPDATE. The DELETE, INSERT, and UPDATE privileges can be granted only on updatable materialized views.

Operators

Provides privileges to perform operations on operators—that is, user-defined operators for specific types of comparisons. Operators were new with Oracle8*i*.

Unique privileges None.

Common privileges EXECUTE.

Procedures, Functions, and Packages

Provides privileges to perform operations on three types of program units: procedures, functions, and packages.

Unique privileges   None.

Common privileges DEBUG, EXECUTE.

Sequences

Provides privileges to perform operations on sequences.

Unique privileges   None.

Common privileges ALTER, SELECT.

Tables

Provides privileges to perform operations on tables.

Unique privileges   *INDEX*
>   Creates an index on the table.
>   *ON COMMIT REFRESH*
>   Creates a materialized view that is refreshed on a COMMIT operation. New with Oracle9i.
>   *QUERY REWRITE*
>   Creates a materialized view for query rewrite on a specific table.

Common privileges ALTER, DELETE, DEBUG, FLASHBACK, INSERT, REFERENCES, SELECT, UPDATE.

User-defined Types

Provides privileges to perform operations on user-defined types. User-defined types are unique datatypes created by a user. User-defined types were new with Oracle8i.

Unique privileges   None.

Common privileges DEBUG, EXECUTE, UNDER.

Views

Provides privileges to perform operations on views. To grant a privilege on a view, you must have that privilege with the GRANT OPTION on all of the view's base tables.

Unique privileges   None.

Common privileges DEBUG, DELETE, FLASHBACK, INSERT, REFERENCES, SELECT, UNDER.

Privileges and Users

To assign privileges to a user or a role, you use the GRANT command. To remove a privilege from a user or a role, you use the REVOKE command.

Common Keywords and Clauses

The following keywords and clauses are valid for both the GRANT and REVOKE commands:

system_privilege
   A system privilege, as described in the earlier "System Privileges" section.

role
   An existing role.

ALL PRIVILEGES
   Grants or revokes all system privileges except SELECT ANY DICTIONARY. For objects, grants all privileges that you have for the object, and the keyword PRIVILEGES is optional.

grantee
   Can be one or more users, roles, or the keyword PUBLIC, which grants or revokes the privilege to all database users. If multiple grantees are specified, they should be separated by commas.

object_privilege
   An object privilege, as described earlier in this chapter.

column_name
   One or more columns on which to grant or revoke the INSERT, REFERENCES, or UPDATE object privileges. If you do not specify a column, the grantee has privilege on all columns in the table or view.

schema.object
   Specifies the object on which to grant or revoke the privilege. If you do not specify a schema, Oracle assumes that the object is in your own schema.

DIRECTORY directory_name
   Specifies the directory on which to grant or revoke a privilege.

GRANT

To grant system privileges or roles:
```
GRANT {system_privilege | role | ALL PRIVILEGES} TO grantee
    [IDENTIFIED BY password] [WITH ADMIN OPTION]
```

To grant object privileges:
```
GRANT {object_privilege | ALL [PRIVILEGES]}
        [column_name [,column_name . . .]]
    ON {schema.object | DIRECTORY directory_name |
        JAVA (SOURCE | RESOURCE) [schema.]object}
    TO grantee [WITH GRANT OPTION] [WITH HIERARCHY OPTION]
```

Grants privileges or roles to a user or role. In order to grant a privilege, you must have previously been granted the privilege or role with the WITH ADMIN OPTION, described in the following "Keywords" section. You can also grant privileges if you have GRANT ANY PRIVILEGE (for system privileges), GRANT ANY ROLE (for roles), GRANT OPTION (for schema objects), or own the object.

System privileges and schema object privileges cannot be granted in the same GRANT statement.

Keywords

IDENTIFIED BY password
> Can be used to identify an existing user by password or to create a new user with the specified password. New with Oracle9i.

ALL PRIVILEGES
> Grants all privileges to the user or role, except the SELECT ANY DICTIONARY privilege. New with Oracle9i.

WITH ADMIN OPTION
> Allows the user to grant or revoke the system privilege or role or to alter or drop the role.

WITH GRANT OPTION
> Like the WITH ADMIN OPTION, allows the user or role to grant or revoke object privilege to other users or roles.

JAVA SOURCE | RESOURCE
> Grants access to Java source code or a Java resource. New with Oracle8i.

WITH HIERARCHY OPTION
> Allows grantee to have privilege on all subobjects of the specified schema object. New with Oracle9i.

Security

REVOKE

To revoke system privileges or roles:
```
REVOKE {system_privilege | role | ALL PRIVILEGES} FROM grantee
```
To revoke object privileges:
```
REVOKE {object_privilege | ALL [PRIVILEGES]}
       [column_name [,column_name . . .]]
   ON {schema.object | DIRECTORY directory_name |
       JAVA [SOURCE | RESOURCE] [schema.]object}
   FROM grantee [CASCADE CONSTRAINTS] [FORCE]
```

Revokes privileges previously granted to a user or role. This command can only revoke privileges that were previously granted with the GRANT command. If you revoke a role from a user currently using the role, the role will remain but will not be available for the user again after he has left the role.

If multiple grantors have given a privilege to a user (or PUBLIC), all grantors must revoke the privilege before it becomes unavailable to the user.

Keywords

ALL PRIVILEGES
> Revokes all existing system privileges for the user or role. New with Oracle9i.

JAVA SOURCE | RESOURCE
> Revokes access to Java source code or a Java resource. New with Oracle8i.

CASCADE CONSTRAINTS

Used only when you revoke the REFERENCES privilege or ALL object privileges. Drops any constraints the revoked user has defined on the object.

FORCE

Used when you revoke the EXECUTE object privilege on user-defined type objects with table or type dependencies. Causes all dependent objects to be marked INVALID, disallows access to data in dependent tables, and marks all dependent function-based indexes as UNUSABLE.

Roles

Granting individual privileges to individual users can incur a substantial amount of overhead, especially for enterprise systems with large numbers of users. Roles are designed to simplify the management of privileges.

Privileges can be granted to roles and then users assigned to roles. Privilege maintenance is performed on roles and affects users with those roles. In addition, roles can be selectively enabled and disabled for users, depending on context. In this way, you can use roles to combine together sets of privileges that will be granted as a whole. For instance, you could have an ADMIN role that would give the appropriate permissions to an administrator.

A role can be granted to another role. If you give a user the parent role, by default that user will also be granted all of the roles granted to that parent role.

A user can be granted multiple roles. The number of roles that can be enabled at one time is limited by the initialization parameter MAX_ENABLED_ROLES. Multiple roles allow a single user to assume different sets of privileges at different times. If a role has other roles granted to it, using the parent role will have the effect of using all the child roles.

You can set one or more default roles using the ALTER USER statement. Default roles take effect when a user logs in to the Oracle database.

System Roles

Oracle comes with a number of predefined system roles:

CONNECT

Includes system privileges ALTER SESSION, CREATE CLUSTER, CREATE DATABASE LINK, CREATE SEQUENCE, CREATE SESSION, CREATE SYNONYM, CREATE TABLE, and CREATE VIEW. According to Oracle Corporation, this role is provided to provide compatability with earlier versions of Oracle and may not be supported in releases past Oracle9*i*.

RESOURCE

Includes system privileges CREATE CLUSTER, CREATE INDEXTYPE, CREATE OPERATOR, CREATE PROCEDURE, CREATE SEQUENCE, CREATE TABLE, CREATE TABLE, and CREATE TYPE. According to Oracle Corporation, this role is provided to provide compatability with earlier versions of Oracle and may not be supported in releases past Oracle9*i*.

DBA

Includes all system privileges with WITH ADMIN OPTION. According to Oracle Corporation, this role is provided to provide compatability with earlier versions of Oracle and may not be supported in releases past Oracle9i.

CREATE TYPE

Includes the CREATE TYPE, EXECUTE, EXECUTE ANY TYPE, ADMIN OPTION, and GRANT OPTION privileges. This role was dropped after Oracle8.

EXP_FULL_DATABASE

Designed to provide all the privileges necessary to perform full and incremental database exports. Includes privileges SELECT ANY TABLE, BACKUP ANY TABLE, EXECUTE ANY PROCEDURE, EXECUTE ANY TYPE, ADMINISTER RESOURCE MANAGER, and the INSERT, DELETE, and UPDATE privileges on the SYS.INCVID, SYS.INCFIL, and SYS.INCEXP tables. Also includes EXECUTE_CATALOG_ROLE and SELECT_CATALOG_ROLE roles.

IMP_FULL_DATABASE

Designed to provide all the privileges necessary to perform full database imports. Includes many system privileges and the EXECUTE_CATALOG_ROLE and SELECT_CATALOG_ROLE roles.

DELETE_CATALOG_ROLE

Includes DELETE privilege on the system audit table (AUD$).

EXECUTE_CATALOG_ROLE

Includes EXECUTE privilege on the system audit table (AUD$) and the HS_ADMIN_ROLE role.

SELECT_CATALOG_ROLE

Includes SELECT privilege on the system audit table (AUD$) and the HS_ADMIN_ROLE role.

RECOVERY_CATALOG_OWNER

Designed to provide all the privileges required for the owner of the recovery catalog. Includes system privileges CREATE SESSION, ALTER SESSION, CREATE CLUSTER, CREATE DATABASE LINK, CREATE PROCEDURE, CREATE SEQUENCE, CREATE SYNONYM, CREATE TABLE, CREATE TRIGGER, and CREATE VIEW.

HS_ADMIN_ROLE

Designed to protect Heterogeneous Services (HS) data dictionary views and packages.

AQ_USER_ROLE

Provides EXECUTE privilege on the DBMS_AQ and DBMS_AQIN Advanced Queuing built-in packages. Obsolete in Oracle9i.

AQ_ADMINISTRATOR_ROLE
 Designed to provide privileges needed to administer Advanced Queing. Includes ENQUEUE ANY QUEUE, DEQUEUE ANY QUEUE, MANAGE ANY QUEUE, SELECT privileges on Advanced Queing tables, and EXECUTE privileges on Advanced Queing packages.

SNMPAGENT
 Used by the Enterprise Manager Intelligent Agent and includes ANALYZE ANY and SELECT privileges on various views.

Defining Roles

The commands described in the following sections allow you to create, alter, and drop roles.

You can set one or more default roles using the ALTER USER statement. Default roles take effect when a user logs in to the Oracle database.

CREATE ROLE

```
CREATE ROLE rolename {NOT IDENTIFIED | IDENTIFIED
    {EXTERNALLY | GLOBALLY |
    BY PASSWORD |
    USING [schema.]package}}
```

Creates a role. When you create a role, it is automatically granted to you as a default role.

Keywords

NOT IDENTIFIED
 Specifies that no password is required for the role.

IDENTIFIED
 Indicates the way the user will be authenticated before being allowed to enable the role or assume the role as a default role. Options are:

 BY password
  Local user must provide password to enable role.

 USING (schema.)package
  A package will verify the user. Used for application roles. If a schema name is not provided, the package is assumed to be in your schema. New with Oracle9i.

 EXTERNALLY
  External user is authorized by a third-party service, like the operating system.

 GLOBALLY
  User is authorized by an enterprise directory service.

ALTER ROLE

```
CREATE ROLE rolename {NOT IDENTIFIED | IDENTIFIED
    {EXTERNALLY | GLOBALLY |
    BY PASSWORD |
    USING [schema.]package}}
```

Alters the way that the user of a role is authenticated.

Keywords
The keywords are identical to the keywords listed for the CREATE ROLE command.

DROP ROLE

```
DROP ROLE role_name
```

Drops a role from the database. If a user currently has the role enabled, that user will not be immediately affected but will not be able to enable the role again.

SET ROLE

```
SET ROLE {role [IDENTIFIED BY password] [,role [IDENTIFIED BY PASSWORD...]] |
    ALL [EXCEPT role[, role...]]
    NONE}
```

Enables one or more roles for a user or disables all roles for a user.

Keywords
ALL
> Enables all roles granted to a user.

EXCEPT
> Used to exclude some roles from being enabled with the ALL keyword.

NONE
> Used to disable all roles for the user.

Auditing

Just as monitoring resource usage is an important way to understand performance issues, auditing is a way to track usage in the database and to become aware of potential security issues.

For some time, Oracle has allowed three different types of auditing:

Statement auditing
> Audits the statements issued on the database, for specific users or for all users.

Privilege auditing
> Audits the use of system privileges for specific users or for all users.

Schema object auditing
> Audits a specific set of SQL statements on a particular schema object.

Oracle9*i* also allows a fourth type of auditing, called *fine-grained auditing*, which is explained in the final section of this chapter.

For all types of auditing, Oracle writes audit records to a database audit trail or the SYS.FGA_LOG$ table or in binary format to an operating system file. The audit trail records contain different information, depending on the type of auditing and the options set for the auditing.

Auditing of System Actions

Whether auditing is enabled for your Oracle database or not, the following actions always generate records for the operating system audit trail:

- Instance startup
- Instance shutdown
- Access by users with administrator privileges

Using Auditing

You enable and disable auditing with the AUDIT and NOAUDIT commands.

AUDIT

```
AUDIT sql_statement_clause | schema_object_clause
    [BY SESSION | ACCESS]
    [WHENEVER [NOT] SUCCESSFUL]
```

Enables auditing on your Oracle database.

Clauses

sql_statement_clause

This clause is used to specify statement and system privilege auditing and has the following syntax:

```
{[statement_option | ALL][, ...]} |
    {[system_privilege | ALL PRIVILEGES] [, ...]}
    BY {proxy(, proxy ...,] ON BEHALF OF [{user [, user ...]} | ANY |
    {user[, user ...]}
```

schema_object_clause

This clause is used to specify schema object auditing and has the following syntax:

```
{object_option[, object_option ...] | ALL }
    ON {[schema.]object | DIRECTORY directory_name | DEFAULT }
```

Keywords

BY SESSION | ACCESS

Specifies whether you want an audit record written once for each session or for each time a particular type of access is attempted. All statement auditing and all privilege auditing on DDL statements can only be set BY ACCESS.

WHENEVER [NOT] SUCCESSFUL

Specifies whether to modify only successful or failed SQL statements. The only failed SQL statements that are audited with the NOT keyword are those that fail or result in errors based on insufficient privileges or that a referenced object does not exist. The default is to audit all statements, regardless of whether they succeed or fail for the reasons mentioned.

BY user

Specifies auditing on the basis of one or more usernames.

BY proxy ON BEHALF OF
> Specifies auditing of actions taken by a proxy on behalf of a user. New with Oracle8*i*.

statement_option
> The values for this keyword, and the statements each value will audit for that type of object, are listed. The first section of this list includes all statements that are audited if you specify the ALL keyword.

CLUSTER
> CREATE, AUDIT, DROP, TRUNCATE.

CONTEXT
> CREATE, DROP. New with Oracle8*i*.

[PUBLIC] DATABASE LINK
> CREATE, DROP.

DIMENSION
> CREATE, ALTER, DROP. New with Oracle8*i*.

DIRECTORY
> CREATE, DROP.

INDEX
> CREATE, ALTER, DROP.

NOT EXISTS
> All statements that fail because an object does not exist.

PROCEDURE
> CREATE FUNCTION, CREATE LIBRARY, CREATE PACKAGE, CREATE PACKAGE BODY, CREATE PROCEDURE, DROP FUNCTION, DROP LIBRARY, DROP PACKAGE, DROP PROCEDURE.

PROFILE
> CREATE, ALTER, DROP.

ROLE
> CREATE, ALTER, DROP, SET.

ROLLBACK SEGMENT
> CREATE, ALTER, DROP.

SEQUENCE
> CREATE, DROP.

SESSION
> Logons for the session.

[PUBLIC] SYNONYM
> CREATE, DROP.

SYSTEM AUDIT
> AUDIT system privileges and roles; NOAUDIT system privileges and roles.

SYSTEM GRANT
> GRANT system privileges and roles; REVOKE system privileges and roles.

TABLE
> CREATE, DROP, TRUNCATE.

TABLESPACE
> CREATE, ALTER, DROP.

TRIGGER
> CREATE, ALTER with ENABLE or DISABLE clauses, DROP, ALTER TABLE with ENABLE or DISABLE clauses.

TYPE
> CREATE, CREATE TYPE BODY, ALTER, DROP, DROP TYPE BODY.

USER
> CREATE, ALTER, DROP.

VIEW
> CREATE, DROP.

The following keywords can be used to specify statement auditing, but these are not audited if you specify the ALL keyword. Unless noted, the keywords only cause auditing on the statement they specify.

ALTER SEQUENCE

ALTER TABLE

COMMENT TABLE
> Audits COMMENT statement on table, view, materialized view, or columns in each of these objects.

DELETE TABLE

EXECUTE PROCEDURE
> Audits CALL.

GRANT DIRECTORY
> GRANT and REVOKE on directory.

GRANT PROCEDURE
> GRANT and REVOKE on procedure.

GRANT SEQUENCE
> GRANT and REVOKE on sequence.

GRANT TABLE
> GRANT and REVOKE on table, view, or materialized view.

GRANT TYPE
> GRANT and REVOKE on type.

INSERT TABLE
> INSERT INTO table or view.

LOCK TABLE
> LOCK table or view.

SELECT SEQUENCE
> Any statement containing CURRVAL or NEXTVAL for the sequence.

SELECT TABLE
> SELECT FROM table, view, or materialized view.

UPDATE TABLE
> UPDATE table or updatable view.

ALL (statement_option)
> See the definition of *statement_option*, earlier, for a list of the statements ALL will audit.

system_privilege
> Specifies the system privileges to audit. You can specify the CONNECT, RESOURCE, or DBA role to audit all the system privileges included in that role.

ALL PRIVILEGES
> Audits all system privileges.

proxy
> Specifies whether to audit all actions by a proxy or only those taken by the proxy on behalf of a particular user.

user
> The user(s) to be audited.

object_option
> Each object has one or more types of access that can be audited. Objects and their auditing options are:

Context
> GRANT. This type of auditing was new with Oracle8*i*.

Directory
> AUDIT, GRANT, READ.

Library
> GRANT, READ.

Materialized view
> ALTER, AUDIT, COMMENT, DELETE, INDEX, INSERT, LOCK, RENAME, SELECT, UPDATE. For Oracle8 and previous versions, these object options existed under the name of the snapshot object. For Oracle8*i*, these object options could be used with either materialized views or snapshots.

Object type
> ALTER, AUDIT, GRANT. This type of auditing was new with Oracle8*i*.

Procedure, function, package
> AUDIT, EXECUTE, GRANT, RENAME. This type of auditing is available in PL/SQL or Java in Oracle8*i* and beyond.

Sequence
> ALTER, AUDIT, GRANT, SELECT.

Table
> ALTER, AUDIT, COMMENT, DELETE, GRANT, INDEX, INSERT, LOCK, RENAME, SELECT, UPDATE.

View
> AUDIT, COMMENT, DELETE, GRANT, INSERT, LOCK, RENAME, SELECT, UPDATE.

[schema.]object
> Object to be audited. If the schema is not present, Oracle assumes that the object is in your schema.

directory_name
> Name of the directory to be audited.

DEFAULT
> Sets the default auditing options for all objects created after this statement is issued.

NOAUDIT

```
NOAUDIT sql_statement_clause | schema_object_clause
    [BY SESSION | ACCESS]
```

Turns off any previously started audits.

Keywords

The keywords and clauses for NOAUDIT have the same meaning as for the AUDIT statement.

Other Security Features

The security features described in the following sections are most relevant to Oracle system administrators or security administrators. We provide only a brief overview of these features; see the Oracle documentation for complete details.

Views and Stored Procedures

In addition to the security features described in previous sections are other ways to provide security for data in your Oracle database. Until Oracle8*i*, the most common approaches to limiting access to data based on the value of the data were through the use of views or stored procedures:

Views
> With views, you define a subset of data in a table and then grant access to the view only to a user. Starting with Oracle8*i*, you can achieve the same security by selection with the use of fine-grained access control, described in the next section.

Stored procedures
> You can impose a similar limitation by accessing a table only through a stored procedure or package and then granting access to the stored procedure or package to users. The stored procedure could have its own validation rules within its code.

We'll look at some additional access controls in the following sections.

Fine-grained Access Control and Security Policy

Fine-grained access control provides the type of context-sensitive security that used to be implemented in application code or views. But because fine-grained access control is enforced by the database, it is consistently applied across all applications.

Fine-grained access control, introduced in Oracle8*i*, is implemented by having a security policy associated with a table implement security on that table. The *security policy* is a program unit that can grant access based on any kind of logical condition. The security policy creates a predicate (a condition added to the WHERE clause to limit data accessed) for any SQL statements issued against the database, which automatically can be used to implement security based on the content of data in the table.

Virtual Private Databases

Content-sensitive security can be used to implement a Virtual Private Database, or VPD. With a VPD, many different users can essentially see their own views of one or more tables in the database. This is the type of security that used to be performed by the creation and maintenance of views, as mentioned earlier, but without the overhead of creating views and having different users, or groups of users, access different database views.

Label Security and Policy Manager

Label security was introduced in Oracle9i. Label security is an extension of the VPD, except that the program units to support the VPD are already written and act on the value in a single column, which contains the label. Because of this, label security requires no programming to implement. Label security is an add-on product for Oracle9i Enterprise Edition.

Policy Manager, a GUI management tool that is a part of Enterprise Manager, was also introduced with Oracle9i. With Policy Manager, you can implement label security.

Application Context

Application context, introduced in Oracle8i, is a way to allow certain attributes to be set for a user that last for the duration of the user's session. By using these attributes to grant access, you can create an application-dependent role that persists in the database across different portions of the application. Application context can be used to implement fine-grained access control.

Fine-grained Auditing

Fine-grained auditing was introduced with Oracle9i. Like fine-grained access control, fine-grained auditing is implemented by defining a predicate to limit the SQL statements that will be audited. By using these audit policies, you can focus auditing activity on a small set of vital data. Reducing the overall number of audit records makes it much easier to spot potential security violations.

LogMiner

LogMiner is a tool that lets you use SQL statements to analyze events in the database log. With LogMiner, you can track transactions as they are processed or locate specific functions that result in data modifications. LogMiner was introduced with Oracle8i.

LogMiner can be used, along with audit trails, to determine what has happened in your Oracle database. A LogMiner viewer is included as part of Enterprise Manager with Oracle9i.

A complete discussion of LogMiner is outside the scope of this book. For more information, see the Oracle documentation.

Oracle Advanced Security

Oracle Advanced Security, formerly known as Secure Network Services and then Advanced Network Services, is an add-on package that provides encryption services. Oracle Advanced Security provides additional security functionality in three main areas:

Network security
> Includes encrypting messages going over Oracle Net Services, implementing Secure Sockets Layer (SSL) encryption and support for RADIUS, Kerberos, smart cards, token cards, and biometric authentication.

Enterprise user security
> Includes the use of a wide variety of third-party directory support, such as LDAP directories, which can be used to implement single signon capability. Oracle Internet Directory (OID), described in the next section, is included with Oracle Advanced Security.

Public key infrastructure security
> Includes support for standard X.509 Version 3 certificates. Oracle works with major PKI service vendors, such as Baltimore Technologies and VeriSign, to ensure coordination with their trusted roots.

Oracle Advanced Security embeds these services in the Oracle Net Services layer, which implements communications between a client and a server, as discussed in Chapter 5. Oracle Advanced Security can also be used with a thin JDBC driver that does not include Oracle Net Services.

Oracle Advanced Security includes Oracle Enterprise Security Manager, a GUI interface for managing enterprise users and domains.

You also can encrypt data on your server with Oracle9*i*, through the use of the DBMS_OBFUSCATION_TOOLKIT package (without requiring Oracle Advanced Security). For more information on this package, see Chapter 10.

Oracle Internet Directory

Several times in this chapter, we've mentioned external directories. An *external directory* is a way to store information about a database, such as usernames and permissions. An external directory can relate to many different instances of Oracle across an enterprise. Oracle has its own external directory offering, the Oracle Internet Directory (OID). OID is a fully compliant LDAP (Lightweight Directory Access Protocol) directory. LDAP is a directory access protocol that was developed at the University of Michigan (Go Blue!).

With OID or other LDAP directories, you can create an authentication method that can span multiple databases, as well as be used for other purposes in your overall IT architecture. OID supports three types of authentication—anonymous, password based, and certificate based.

OID includes its own Replication Manager, for support of multiple directories, and a GUI interface tool.

Invoker Rights

Prior to Oracle8i, a stored procedure had its own set of privileges. Anyone using that stored procedure to access data used the privileges granted to the procedure, regardless of her own set of privileges.

Starting with Oracle8i, you can now create a function, procedure, package, object type, or Java code with an invoker rights clause. This clause causes the object to execute with the rights of the user invoking it, rather than the rights of the object itself.

5

Networking

The Oracle database is more than just a server. Clients have to be able to connect to an Oracle instance, and Oracle instances have to be able to communicate with other instances, as well as with application servers, foreign databases, and external procedures.

This chapter provides a quick introduction to Oracle networking and then summarizes the syntax of the configuration files you must define in order to use a network as part of your Oracle environment. These files include *TNSNAMES.ORA, SQLNET.ORA, LISTENER.ORA, LDAP.ORA, NAMES.ORA,* and *CMAN.ORA.*

Oracle Networking Fundamentals

Oracle networking software has been known by a few different names over the years. Prior to Oracle8, the name was SQL*Net; with Oracle8, the name of the software was changed to Net8; and with Oracle9*i*, the name was changed to the more generic Oracle Net Services. For the remainder of this chapter, we use the term Oracle Net Services to refer to all versions of Oracle networking software, with version-specific differences noted.

Regardless of name, the purpose of the networking software has remained the same. If a client of an Oracle instance needs to connect to an Oracle database—whether that client is a traditional client, an application server, or some other type of server—that client must connect to one end of a network connection as implemented by the Oracle network software. The network software transparently implements the communication to the Oracle instance.

Oracle Net Services supports many different client and server platforms and many different network protocols. The underlying architecture and complexity of the network infrastructure is all handled by Oracle Net Services. However, you have to manage Oracle Net Services. This chapter focuses on the configuration files used to accomplish this management task.

Oracle Net Services provides the implementation of the network transport of data and communications, but more as well. Certain features, such as Shared Server (known as Multi-Threaded Server prior to Oracle9i), which can help to improve performance by reducing network resource requirements, failover, or client load balancing, are also implemented with Oracle Net Services.

Making the Connection

Oracle Net Services provides the transport of information to and from a server. Figure 5-1 illustrates this connection, with the components of Oracle Net Services and their associated configuration files.

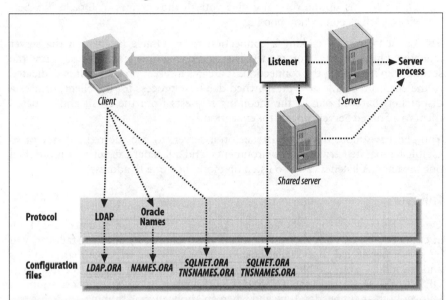

Figure 5-1. Network communication and configuration

When a client creates a connection to a server, there are two basic steps in the process. In the first step, the client locates the appropriate server. The location can be accomplished through several means, including:

- Looking in the local *TNSNAMES.ORA* file.
- Getting the information from an external LDAP (Lightweight Directory Access Protocol) directory (new in Oracle8i) or an external naming service.
- Using a centralized naming service, such as Oracle Names (scheduled to be desupported after Oracle9i).

Oracle Names was designed to act as a centralized directory for network services. Unfortunately, it is a proprietary technology, whereas the new LDAP directories fulfill the same purpose and are open technologies. For this reason, Oracle has announced that Oracle Names will not be enhanced any more and has provided Oracle Names users with both a migration path to LDAP directories and a way to have Oracle Names servers act as proxy servers for LDAP directories.

- Directly connecting to the host using a TCP/IP or DNS identifier (new with Oracle8); this option does not give you all the services of Oracle Net Services, such as connection pooling.

The client is actually making a connection to an Oracle listener on the server machine. Once a connection request is received, the Oracle listener performs the second step in making the connection. It creates a server process that is dedicated to the client process, uses a prespawned database process for the client, or uses a dispatcher that will handle the incoming requests from the client and dispatch them to a Shared Server process for execution.

You can have more than one listener on a server, to provide redundancy or to establish separate networking environments, and a listener can support more than one instance. A listener can also listen on more than one IP address.

Failover

Oracle Net Services supports failover, which occurs when an instance fails, both at connection time and when an application is running. By allowing failover, you let a user connected to the failed instance fail over to an instance that is still up and running. You enable failover by simply listing multiple listeners in a DESCRIPTION entry in the *TNSNAMES.ORA* file. Oracle Net Services supports failover both at connection time and when an application is running.

Connect-time failover allows you to direct connection requests to a backup instance in the event that the primary instance is down and is perhaps most useful when used in connection with Real Application Clusters (where you have multiple instances running against a single database). You enable connect-time failover by simply listing multiple listeners in a DESCRIPTION entry in the *TNSNAMES. ORA* file. (Failover might also be used in standby database environments to redirect a connect request to a standby database in case the primary database is down.)

Transparent Application Failover (TAF) provides failover when an application is running. If a connection fails, and TAF is enabled, the user automatically fails over to another listener. You can even specify that the connection to the other listener be established when the user makes the initial connection to the first listener, to reduce the failover time. In addition, most queries currently running with TAF enabled will maintain their location, so that the next row retrieved after failover will be the same as the next row would have been without the failure. Keep in mind, though, that the new connection will have to read through all the previous rows to get to this next row, which could cause a performance glitch, depending on the size of the result set and the position within the result set.

In order to use TAF, an application has to be written using the Oracle Call Interface (OCI) directly or with the use of failover-aware calls. There are other limitations associated with the use of TAF. See the Oracle documentation for more details on these limitations in your version of Oracle.

Load Balancing

Load balancing can be performed on both the client side and the server side:

- On the client side, you request load balancing by specifying multiple listeners in the *TNSNAMES.ORA* file (similar to the way that you specify multiple listeners for failover). Load balancing causes a client connection to randomly choose one of the listener addresses in the *TNSNAMES.ORA* file.
- On the server side, Shared Servers, described in the next section, provide load balancing through the listener. With this type of load balancing, new connections are distributed to the dispatcher that is the least busy.

Shared Servers

Normally, Oracle Net Services creates a single dedicated server process for each user connection. Each server process requires some memory overhead to maintain, even if the process is not doing any active work.

To avoid the excessive use of these connection resources, Oracle Net Services provides a feature called *Shared Server*, called Multi-Threaded Server (or MTS) prior to Oracle9i. A Shared Server is a server process that can be used for more than one user connection. Instead of creating a dedicated server process, the Shared Server feature uses the listener to route a connection request through a dispatcher. The dispatcher assumes the responsibility of coordinating communication between the database and the client, and routes subsequent requests to one of a number of Shared Servers.

You can have more than one dispatcher process and can configure the number of Shared Servers for an instance. You can have both dedicated and Shared Servers on the same instance. For example, you could create different service names for the same instance, one for dedicated server processes and one for Shared Servers.

Shared Servers are initialized by specifying the appropriate parameters in the instance initialization file, not in any of the Oracle Net Services configuration files described in this chapter. For more details on these initialization parameters, see Chapter 2. You can specify the use of a dedicated server, even when Shared Servers are running as part of the instance, with the MTS_SERVERS or SHARED_SERVERS parameter in either the *TNSNAMES.ORA* file or the *SQLNET.ORA* file.

Shared Servers work best in an environment in which many users are accessing the database, and each user is idle a significant part of the time. The opposite of this environment would be a batch job, which you should always assign to a dedicated server.

Shared Servers reduce memory requirements but typically do not perform faster than dedicated servers, because there is some latency, or delay, that can occur when no servers are available.

Networking

Dedicated servers use memory from the dedicated process's Program Global Area (PGA). Shared Servers, on the other hand, use memory from the large pool or the shared pool, because information about the connection has to potentially be accessed by multiple Shared Server processes.

Connection Manager

Just as dedicated server processes take up overhead, so do network connections. Each network connection uses up some of the bandwidth of the network. Oracle Connection Manager, which first became available with Oracle8 Enterprise Edition, can use a single network connection to provide three key benefits:

Multiple network sessions
Connection Manager works in conjunction with Shared Servers to provide the ability to handle multiple network sessions. This multiplexing reduces overhead.

Translation between two different network protocols
Connection Manager can also be used as a way to translate between different network protocols in a heterogeneous network. A client can be running one protocol to Connection Manager and another one from Connection Manager to the Oracle Server.

Translation of network addresses
You can also use Connection Manager to handle network address translation (NAT). When a client connects to an Oracle listener, its connection is redirected to either a dedicated server process or a dispatcher. This server entity sends its address back to the client. If the server is inside a firewall, the internal address returned may not be accessible to the client. This problem can be overcome by having Connection Manager act as an intermediary.*

Connection Manager can also be used to filter TCP/IP communications based on the IP addresses of the source or the destination or on the database service name.

You can have multiple machines with Connection Manager running on them, with each separate link between machines using connection multiplexing, protocol conversion, or IP filtering.

For more information on Connection Manager, see the Oracle documentation.

Configuration Files

The operation of Oracle Net Services is shaped by the information stored in its configuration files. These files are:

---

* See a very helpful article by Jonathan Gennick entitled "Lock the Door on Connection Manager" at *http://gennick.com/lock_the_door.html*.

TNSNAMES.ORA

This client file contains text definitions for Oracle service names. It provides all the information needed to translate local service names into network addresses that can be used by Oracle Net Services, as well as information needed for some of the special features supported by Oracle Net Services. You don't need to use this file if you are using an external naming service or host naming or if you are using Oracle Names or LDAP (directory naming).

SQLNET.ORA

This file contains configuration information for Oracle Net Services. It includes information such as:

- The list of naming methods to use and the order in which to try them
- The default domain
- The directory and filename to use for network trace files
- The directory and filename to use for network log files

LISTENER.ORA

This server file contails configuration information about the Oracle listener(s) on the server.

LDAP.ORA

This parameter file contains information about the LDAP server that will be used. It is new with Oracle8*i*.

NAMES.ORA

This parameter file is used only if you are running Oracle Net Services with Oracle Names. It contains configuration details used to control the operation of the Oracle Names server. Oracle is phasing out Oracle Names, and only a small subset of Oracle users currently implement this product, so this book does not include detailed information on *NAMES.ORA*. For detailed information on this file, see the Oracle documentation.

CMAN.ORA

This parameter file is used only if you are running Oracle Net Services with Connection Manager. It contains configuration details used to control the operation of Connection Manager. Because only a small subset of Oracle users currently implement Connection Manager, this book does not include detailed information on *CMAN.ORA*. For detailed information on this file, see the Oracle documentation.

The following sections describe the syntax and keywords used in the *TNSNAMES.ORA*, *SQLNET.ORA*, *LISTENER.ORA*, and *LDAP.ORA* files. In syntax entries, bold face indicates default options.

SQLNET.ORA

SQLNET.ORA is a configuration file used to control the operation of Oracle Net Services. You must have a *SQLNET.ORA* file on both the client and server.

The default location for the *SQLNET.ORA* file is in the *network\admin* directory in the *ORACLE_HOME* location (for Oracle8, the file was in *net80\admin*). Use the TNS_ADMIN environment variable to point to the directory for this file.

Keywords and syntax

BEQUEATH_DETACH=YES | NO

Controls whether or not Unix signal handling is used to terminate server processes spawned by Bequeath connections. YES turns over responsibility for terminating the server process to the Unix *init* process. Signal handling is not used in this case. NO leaves the parent process, the one that used Bequeath to spawn the server process, with the responsibility of terminating that server process once it is no longer needed. Signal handling is used in this case. The default is NO.

DAEMON.TRACE_DIRECTORY = directory_path

Specifies the directory to use for trace files generated by the Oracle Enterprise Manager (EM) daemon. This parameter is relevant only for 1.x releases of Enterprise Manager. The default is *$ORACLE_HOME/network/trace*. This parameter is no longer supported with Oracle9i.

DAEMON.TRACE_LEVEL = OFF | USER | ADMIN | SUPPORT

Specifies the trace level for the Oracle Enterprise Manager daemon. It is relevant only for 1.x releases of Oracle Enterprise Manager. The default value is OFF. This parameter is no longer supported with Oracle9i.

OFF

No trace output is generated.

USER

Generates user-level trace output.

ADMIN

Generates administrative-level trace output. This gets you more details than the USER setting.

SUPPORT

Generates extremely detailed trace information. This is the highest setting possible and results in a great deal more trace output than either USER or ADMIN.

DAEMON.TRACE_MASK = (mask)

Limits the entries written to the trace file to those that match the specified mask. This parameter is relevant only for 1.x releases of Oracle Enterprise Manager. This parameter is no longer supported with Oracle9i.

DISABLE_OOB = OFF | ON

Specifies whether out-of-band (OOB) breaks are enabled. These represent Oracle Net Service's mechanism for urgent messages between client and server and are what enable you to interrupt long-running queries by pressing CTRL-C. The default value is OFF, which allows out-of-band breaks to occur. A setting of ON disables out-of-band breaks.

LOG_DIRECTORY_CLIENT = directory_path

Specifies the directory to which Oracle Net Services client log files are written. Client log files are generated whenever you use Oracle Net Services in a client mode. Prior to Oracle9i, the default log directory for the log was *$ORACLE_HOME/network/log*; with Oracle9i, the default is the directory from which the executable is started.

LOG_DIRECTORY_SERVER = directory_path

Specifies the directory to which Oracle Net Services server log files are written. Prior to Oracle9i, the default log directory for the log was *$ORACLE_HOME/network/log*; with Oracle9i, the default is the directory from which the executable is started.

LOG_FILE_CLIENT = *filename*

Specifies the filename to use for Oracle Net Services client log files. The default filename is *sqlnet.log*.

LOG_FILE_SERVER = *filename*

Specifies the filename to use for Oracle Net Services server log files. The default filename is *sqlnet.log*.

NAMES.CONNECT_TIMEOUT = *seconds*

The amount of time a client will wait for a connection to an Oracle Names server. This parameter was new with Oracle9*i*.

NAMES.DCE.PREFIX = *prefix*

Used in a Distributed Computing Environment (DCE) to specify a cell name, or prefix, to use when performing a name lookup. This applies only when DCE's Cell Directory Services (CDS) has been chosen as the naming method.

NAMES.DEFAULT.DOMAIN = *ONS_domain*

Specifies a default domain that is appended to net service names that do not already include a domain component. Any net service name that does not already include a dot (.), will have this domain appended to it. The default value is an empty string, or NULL. Prior to the release of Oracle8, the default value was WORLD.

NAMES.DIRECTORY_PATH = *(naming_method[, naming_method...])*

Specifies the naming method, or methods, that Oracle Net Services will use when trying to resolve a net service name. The values for *naming_method* are:

> TNSNAMES
> LDAP (new with Oracle9*i*)
> ONAMES
> HOSTNAME
> DCE (prior to Oracle9*i*) or CDS (with Oracle9*i*)
> NIS
> NOVELL (desupported in Oracle9*i*)

NAMES.INITIAL_RETRY_TIMEOUT = *seconds*

Specifies the number of seconds to wait for a response from one Oracle Names server before attempting to contact the next Names server on the list. The default value is operating system dependent but is often 15 seconds. The valid range is from 1 to 600 seconds.

NAMES.MAX_OPEN_CONNECTIONS = *max_connections*

Specifies the maximum number of Oracle Net Services connections that an Oracle Names client may have at any given time. The default value is 10. The valid range is from 3 to 64.

NAMES.MESSAGE_POOL_START_SIZE = *num_of_messages*

Specifies the initial allocation of messages in the client's message pool. The default value is 10. The valid range is from 3 to 256.

NAMES.NIS.META_MAP = *map_name*

Valid only when Sun's Network Information Service (NIS) naming is used and specifies the map file that defines the manner in which NIS attributes are used to define a net service name. The default map filename is *sqlnet.maps*.

NAMES.PREFERRED_SERVERS=*(ADDRESS_LIST = (address) [(address)...])*

Specifies the list of Names servers to be used when using Oracle Names to resolve a net service name. Although there is no default value, if you used Names Control or the administrative assistant to discover available Names servers on the network, the $ORACLE_HOME/network/names/sdns.ora* file will also contain a list of Names servers to use. The NAMES.PREFERRED_SERVERS setting, if it's used, overrides the list in *sdns.ora*.

NAMES.REQUEST_RETRIES = retry_count

Specifies the number of attempts that a client should make to contact a given Names server before giving it up as unreachable. When Oracle Names is used as the naming method, you will often have a list of Names servers to use when resolving net service names (see NAMES. PREFERRED_SERVERS earlier in this list). When resolving a specific net service name, an attempt is made to contact the first Names server in that list. If contact is not made, Oracle Net Services will retry the number of times specified by NAMES.REQUEST_RETRIES. If contact still has not been made, Oracle Net Services moves on to the next Names server in the list. The default value is 1. The valid range is from 1 to 5.

NAMESCTL.ECHO=TRUE | FALSE

Specifies whether the Oracle Names Control utility echoes commands with prompts in the output log. New with Oracle9*i*.

NAMESCTL.INTERNAL_ENCRYPT_PASSWORD = TRUE | FALSE

Controls whether or not the Names Control utility encrypts passwords when sending them to a Names server. The default is TRUE, which means that passwords are encrypted. A value of FALSE causes passwords to be transmitted in the clear.

NAMESCTL.INTERNAL_USE = TRUE | FALSE

Allows you to enable a set of undocumented Names Control utility commands. These are used for troubleshooting, and they all begin with an underscore (_). A value of TRUE enables these commands. The default value is FALSE, which disables the undocumented commands. You can see documentation for the undocumented commands by enabling them and then issuing the HELP command from within the Names Control utility.

NAMESCTL.NO_INITIAL_SERVER = TRUE | FALSE

Controls whether or not the Names Control utility attempts to connect to a default Names server when you first start the utility. The default value is FALSE. The result is a slight delay when you first start Names Control while the utility attempts to contact a Names server on your network. Setting this parameter to TRUE prevents Names Control from contacting a Names server until you issue a SET SERVER command. The result is that Names Control will start more quickly than it would otherwise.

NAMESCTL.NOCONFIRM = ON | OFF

Controls whether or not Names Control prompts you to confirm the execution of certain critical commands; these critical commands are STOP, SHUTDOWN, RELOAD, and RESTART. The default value is OFF, which means that you won't be prompted. Set this parameter to ON in order to be prompted for confirmation when issuing one of these commands.

NAMESCTL.SERVER_PASSWORD = password

Allows you to specify the Names server password in the *SQLNET.ORA* file rather than using the SET PASSWORD command to supply it each time that you run the Names Control utility. The password must match the one set by the NAMES. PASSWORD parameter in the server's *NAMES.ORA* file.

NAMESCTL.TRACE_DIRECTORY = directory_path
Specifies the directory in which Names Control trace files should be created. The default is *$ORACLE_HOME/network/trace*.

NAMESCTL.TRACE_FILE = filename
Specifies the name of the file to which Names Control trace information should be written. This file is created and written to only when *NAMESCTL.TRACE_LEVEL* is at a setting other than OFF. The default filename is *namesctl_pid.trc*, where *pid* represents your process ID number.

*NAMESCTL.TRACE_LEVEL = **OFF** | USER | ADMIN | SUPPORT*
Controls the amount of trace information generated when running the Names Control utility. See DAEMON.TRACE_LEVEL earlier in this list for an explanation of the keywords.

*NAMESCTL.TRACE_UNIQUE = **ON** | OFF*
Controls whether or not a process identifier is appended to trace filenames. See NAMESCTL.TRACE_FILE earlier in this list. The default value is ON, which means that trace filenames are qualified by process identifiers. This parameter has no effect under Windows NT.

OSS.SOURCE.LOCATION = (SOURCE = (METHOD = ORACLE)
(METHOD_DATA = (SQLNET_ADDRESS = net_service_name)))
Tells Oracle Net Services how, and from where, to retrieve encrypted private keys. This parameter is no longer supported with Oracle9*i*.

OSS.SOURCE.MY_WALLET = (SOURCE = (METHOD = FILE)
(METHOD_DATA = (DIRECTORY = directory_path)))
Specifies the directory in which SSL wallets are stored. The only method currently supported is FILE. This parameter is no longer supported with Oracle9*i*.

SQLNET.AUTHENTICATION_GSSAPI_SERVICE = principal
Used with Oracle Advanced Security to define the CyberSafe service principal.

SQLNET.AUTHENTICATION_KERBEROS5 = kerberos_service_name
If Kerberos authentication is used, this parameter specifies the name of the Kerberos5 service. There is no default value.

SQLNET.AUTHENTICATION_SERVICES = (method [,method...])
The SQLNET.AUTHENTICATION_SERVICES parameter enables Net8 support for various services used to authenticate users when they log in to a database. Note that this parameter simply enables the various methods; it does not select the method to be used for a given connection. The default value for this parameter is NONE. The *method* keywords supported are:

NONE
No special authentication is performed. Users log in using their usernames and passwords.

ALL
Enables all the authentication methods.

BEQ
Enables the BEQ (Bequeath) authentication method. This parameter is no longer supported with Oracle9*i*.

CYBERSAFE
Allows users to be authenticated using CyberSafe. This parameter is valid only with Oracle Advanced Security.

DCEGSSAPI

Allows users to be authenticated using DCE GSSAPI. This parameter is valid only with Oracle Advanced Security.

IDENTIX

Allows users to be authenticated using Identix. This parameter is no longer supported with Oracle9*i*.

KERBEROS5

Allows users to be authenticated using Kerberos. This parameter is valid only with Oracle Advanced Security.

NDS

Allows users to be authenticated using Netware Directory Services. This parameter is no longer supported with Oracle9*i*.

NTS

Allows users to be authenticated using Windows NT Native Security.

RADIUS

Allows users to be authenticated using RADIUS.

SECURID

Allows users to be authenticated using SecureID. This parameter is no longer supported with Oracle9*i*.

TCPS

Allows users to be authenticated using SSL. This parameter is no longer supported with Oracle9*i*.

SQLNET.CLIENT_REGISTRATION = client_id

Allows you to set a unique Oracle Net Services identifier for a client computer. This identifier is passed to the Oracle Net Services listener whenever the client connects and is included in the Oracle Net Services audit trail on the server. The *client_id* value may be any alphanumeric string up to 128 characters in length. There is no default value.

SQLNET.CRYPTO_CHECKSUM_CLIENT = checksum_method

Specifies the manner in which an Oracle Net Services client negotiates the use of checksums with a server when a new connection is made. If a client and server cannot agree on the use of checksums, then the connection attempt fails. See SQLNET.CRYPTO_CHECKSUM_SERVER, next in this list. The default setting is REJECTED in Oracle9*i* and ACCEPTED in previous versions. The *checksum_method* keywords are:

ACCEPTED

The client does not request the use of checksums but goes along if the server requests them. Compatible server parameters are REJECTED, REQUESTED, and REQUIRED.

REJECTED

The client does not support the use of checksums at all. Compatible server parameters are REJECTED, ACCEPTED, and REQUESTED.

REQUESTED

The client prefers to use checksums, but does not force the issue if the server rejects their use. Compatible server parameters are ACCEPTED, REQUESTED, and REQUIRED.

REQUIRED
> The client demands the use of checksums and does not connect otherwise. Compatible server parameters are ACCEPTED, REQUESTED, and REQUIRED.

SQLNET.CRYPTO_CHECKSUM_SERVER = checksum_method
> Specifies the manner in which an Oracle Net Services server negotiates the use of checksums with a client when a new connection is made. If a client and server cannot agree on the use of checksums, then the connection attempt fails. See the previous entry for SQLNET.CRYPTO_CHECKSUM_CLIENT. The default setting is REJECTED in Oracle9*i* and ACCEPTED before. The *checksum_method* keywords are the same as for the SQLNET.CRYPTO_CHECKSUM_CLIENT parameter.

SQLNET.CRYPTO_CHECKSUM_TYPES_CLIENT = (MD5 | SHAL)
> Specifies the list of checksum algorithms that a client is allowed to use. This parameter affects all Oracle Net Services client connections from a given machine. When a connection is made, one of the checksum types supported by the server (see SQLNET.CRYPTO_CHECKSUM_TYPES_ SERVER, next) must match one of the checksum types supported by the client. The default and only allowed value until Oracle9*i* was MD5 (for RSA Data Security's MD5 algorithm); in Oracle9*i*, SHAL (for secure hash algorithm) is also an accepted value. MD5 refers to RSA Data Security's MD5 algorithm.

SQLNET.CRYPTO_CHECKSUM_TYPES_SERVER = (MD5 | SHAL)
> Specifies the list of checksum algorithms that a server is allowed to use. When a connection is made, client and server must be able to agree on a common checksum algorithm. The default and only allowed value until Oracle9*i* was MD5 (for RSA Data Security's MD5 algorithm); in Oracle9*i*, SHAL (for secure hash algorithm) is also an accepted value. MD5 refers to RSA Data Security's MD5 algorithm.

SQLNET.CRYPTO_SEED = "seed_string"
> Specifies the character string used when generating cryptographic keys. The string may be any sequence of characters and must be between 10 and 70 characters in length.

SQLNET.ENCRYPTION_CLIENT = encryption
> Specifies the manner in which an Oracle Net Services client negotiates the use of encryption with a server when a new connection is made. If a client and server cannot agree on the use of encryption, then the connection attempt fails. See SQLNET.ENCRYPTION_SERVER, next. The default setting is REJECTED in Oracle9*i* and ACCEPTED in previous versions. The *encryption* keywords are the same as for the SQLNET.CRYPTO_CHECKSUM_CLIENT parameter.

SQLNET.ENCRYPTION_SERVER = encryption
> Specifies the manner in which an Oracle Net Services server negotiates the use of encryption with a client when a new connection is made. If a client and server cannot agree on the use of encryption, then the connection attempt fails. See SQLNET.ENCRYPTION_CLIENT. The default setting is REJECTED in Oracle9*i* and ACCEPTED in previous versions. The *encryption* keywords are the same as for the SQLNET.CRYPTO_CHECKSUM_CLIENT parameter.

SQLNET.ENCRYPTION_TYPES_CLIENT = (method [,method...])
> This parameter specifies the encryption methods that a client may choose from when initiating an encrypted Oracle Net Services session. The default is to choose

from among all possible algorithms. Key sizes greater than 40 bits are allowed only by the "domestic" (United States and Canada) version of Oracle Net Services. One of the types listed here must match a type listed in the SQLNET. ENCRYPTION_TYPES_SERVER for an encrypted connection to be made. The *method* keywords are:

RC4_40
> Use 40-bit RSA RC4 encryption.

RC4_56
> Use 56-bit RSA RC4 encryption.

RC4_128
> Use 128-bit RSA RC4 encryption.

RC4_256
> Use 256-bit RSA RC4 encryption (only with Oracle9i).

DES
> Use standard 56-bit DES encryption.

DES40
> Use 40-bit DES encryption.

3DES_112
> Use triple DES with a two-key (112-bit) limit (only with Oracle9i).

3DES_168
> Use triple DES with a three-key (168-bit) limit (only with Oracle9i).

SQLNET.ENCRYPTION_TYPES_SERVER = (method [,method...])
> This parameter specifies the encryption methods that a server may choose from when accepting an encrypted Oracle Net Services session from a client. The default is to choose from among all possible algorithms. Key sizes greater than 40 bits are allowed only by the "domestic" (United States and Canada) version of Net8. The *method* keywords are the same as for the SQLNET.ENCRYPTION_ TYPES_CLIENT parameter.

SQLNET.EXPIRE_TIME = time_interval
> Sets an expiration time for Oracle Net Services sessions. The expiration time represents an interval that is specified in terms of seconds for Oracle9i, minutes for earlier versions. The clock begins ticking when a connection is made. At the specified interval, Oracle Net Services verifies that the connection still exists. If the probe fails, the Oracle Net Services session is terminated.

SQLNET.IDENTIX_FINGERPRINT_DATABASE = net_service_name
> If Identix fingerprint authentication is used, this parameter specifies the net service name for the database containing the fingerprints. This parameter is no longer supported with Oracle9i.

SQLNET.IDENTIX_FINGERPRINT_DATABASE_METHOD = ORACLE
> Specifies the type of database used to store fingerprint definitions. Currently, the only supported method is ORACLE. This parameter is not supported as of Oracle9i.

SQLNET.IDENTIX_FINGERPRINT_DATABASE_PASSWORD = password
> Specifies the password to use when connecting to the fingerprint database to verify a print. This parameter is no longer supported with Oracle9i.

SQLNET.IDENTIX_FINGERPRINT_DATABASE_USER = *username*

Specifies the username to use when connecting to the fingerprint database to verify a print. This parameter is no longer supported with Oracle9*i*.

SQLNET.KERBEROS5_CC_NAME = *path_filename*

Specifies the full path and name of a Kerberos credentials cache file. This applies only when Kerberos authentication is used. See SQLNET.AUTHENTICATION_ SERVICES earlier. The default value under Unix is */usr/tmp/krbcache*. Under Windows, the default is *C:\temp\ krbcache*.

SQLNET.KERBEROS5_CLOCKSKEW = *seconds*

Specifies the number of seconds for which a Kerberos credential is considered valid. Credentials expire after the specified time elapses. The default is 300 seconds (which works out to 5 minutes).

SQLNET.KERBEROS5_CONF = *path_filename*

Specifies the full path and name of a Kerberos configuration file. The default value under Unix is */krb5/krb.conf*. Under Windows, the default is *C:\krb5\krb. conf*.

SQLNET.KERBEROS5_KEYTAB = *path_filename*

Specifies the full path and name of a Kerberos secret key mapping file. The default value under Unix is */etc/v5srvtab*. Under Windows, it is *C:\krb5\v5srvtab*.

SQLNET.KERBEROS5_REALMS = *path_filename*

Specifies the full path and name of a Kerberos realm translation file. The default value under Unix is */krb5/krb.realms*. Under Windows, the default is *C:\krb\krb. realms*.

SQLNET.RADIUS_ALTERNATE = *host_name*

Specifies the hostname, or numeric TCP/IP address if you prefer to use that, of an alternate RADIUS server to use in case the primary RADIUS server is not available. There is no default value. RADIUS support was new in Oracle8*i*.

SQLNET.RADIUS_ALTERNATE_PORT = *port_number*

Specifies the TCP/IP port number to use when contacting the alternate RADIUS server. The default port number is 1645. RADIUS support was new in Oracle8*i*.

SQLNET.RADIUS_ALTERNATE_RETRIES = *retry_count*

Specifies the number of times to retry a connection to the alternate RADIUS server. The default is to retry three times. RADIUS support was new in Oracle8*i*.

SQLNET.RADIUS_AUTHENTICATION = *host_name*

Specifies the hostname, or numeric TCP/IP address if you prefer to use that, of the primary RADIUS server. The default is to contact the local host. RADIUS support was new in Oracle8*i*.

SQLNET.RADIUS_AUTHENTICATION_INTERFACE = *interface_class*

Specifies the Java class that defines the user interface used to interact with the user when RADIUS is in a challenge-response mode. The default class is *Default-RadiusInterface*. See SQLNET.RADIUS_CLASSPATH. RADIUS support was new in Oracle8*i*.

SQLNET.RADIUS_AUTHENTICATION_PORT = *port_number*

Specifies the TCP/IP port number to use when contacting the primary RADIUS server. The default port number is 1645. RADIUS support was new in Oracle8*i*.

SQLNET.RADIUS_AUTHENTICATION_RETRIES = *retry_count*

Specifies the number of times to retry a connection to the primary RADIUS server. The default is to retry three times. RADIUS support was new in Oracle8*i*.

SQLNET.RADIUS_AUTHENTICATION_TIMEOUT = seconds

Specifies the number of seconds to wait for a response when attempting to contact a RADIUS server. The default is to wait 5 seconds. RADIUS support was new in Oracle8*i*.

SQLNET.RADIUS_CHALLENGE_KEYWORD = keyword

Sets the keyword used to request a challenge from the RADIUS server. The default keyword is "challenge". RADIUS support was new in Oracle8*i*. This parameter is no longer supported with Oracle9*i*.

SQLNET.RADIUS_CHALLENGE_RESPONSE = ON | OFF

Enables or disables the RADIUS challenge/response feature. The default is OFF. RADIUS support was new in Oracle8*i*.

SQLNET.RADIUS_CLASSPATH = classpath

Defines the path to the Java classes that implement the challenge/response interface. See SQLNET.RADIUS_AUTHENTICATION_INTERFACE. There is no default value. RADIUS support was new in Oracle8*i*. This parameter is no longer supported with Oracle9*i*.

SQLNET.RADIUS_SECRET = path_filename

Specifies the full path and name of the RADIUS shared secret file. The default location is *$ORACLE_HOME/network/security/radius.key*. RADIUS support was new in Oracle8*i*.

SQLNET.RADIUS_SEND_ACCOUNTING = ON | OFF

Enables or disables RADIUS accounting. If accounting is enabled, then packets are sent to the RADIUS server using a port number that is 1 higher than the port number set by SQLNET.RADIUS_AUTHENTICATION_PORT. In other words, if SQLNET.RADIUS_ AUTHENTICATION_PORT is set to 1645, then port 1646 is used when accounting is enabled. The default for this parameter is OFF, which disables RADIUS accounting. New in Oracle8*i*.

SSL_CIPHER_SUITES = (suite_name [,suite_name...])

Specifies the list of SSL cipher suites that you want to support. See the Oracle documentation for the appropriate list of suite name variables.

SSL_CLIENT_AUTHENTICATION = TRUE | FALSE

Specifies whether or not a client should be authenticated using SSL. The default value is TRUE but applies only when SSL authentication is used. See SQLNET. AUTHENTICATION_SERVICES.

SSL_SERVER_DN_MATCH = {YES | ON | TRUE} | {NO | OFF | FALSE}

Requires that the database server's Distinguished Name match its service name. The default is NO. New with Oracle9*i*.

SSL_VERSION = UNDETERMINED | 2.0 | 3.0

Specifies the version of SSL to use for an SSL-encrypted Oracle Net Services connection. The default value is UNDETERMINED, which allows the version to be determined by the client and the server at connect time.

TCP.EXCLUDED_NODES = (hostname | ip_address[, hostname | ip_address] . .)

Specifies which clients are denied access to the database. This parameter is new with Oracle9*i* and is meant to replace the functionality in the no longer supported *protocol.ora* file.

TCP.INVITED_NODES = (hostname | ip_address[, hostname | ip_address] . .)

Specifies which clients are allowed access to the database. If both this list and the TCP.EXCLUDED_NODES are present, this parameter takes precedence. This parameter is new with Oracle9*i* and is meant to replace the functionality in the no longer supported *protocol.ora* file.

TCP. NODELAY = YES | NO

Specifies whether to preempt delays in buffer flushing within the TCP/IP protocol stack. The default is NO. This parameter is new with Oracle9*i* and is meant to replace the functionality in the no longer supported *protocol.ora* file.

TCP.VALIDNODE_CHECKING=YES | NO

Specifies whether to use the TCP.EXCLUDED_NODES and the TCP.INVITED_ NODES for checking client access. The default is NO. This parameter is new with Oracle9*i* and is meant to replace the functionality in the now longer supported *protocol.ora* file.

TNSPING.TRACE_DIRECTORY = directory_path

Specifies the directory to use for *TNSPING* trace files. The default value is *$ORACLE_HOME/ network/trace*.

TNSPING.TRACE_LEVEL = OFF | USER | ADMIN | SUPPORT

Specifies the level of trace detail that the *tnsping* utility should generate. The default value is OFF. Please see DAEMON.TRACE_LEVEL earlier in this for an explanation of the keywords.

TRACE_DIRECTORY_CLIENT = directory_path

Specifies the directory into which Oracle Net Services trace files should be written when Oracle Net Services is acting as a client. The default is *$ORACLE_HOME/ network/trace*.

TRACE_DIRECTORY_SERVER = directory_path

Specifies the directory into which Oracle Net Services trace files should be written when Oracle Net Services is acting as a server. The default is *$ORACLE_HOME/ network/trace*.

TRACE_FILE_CLIENT = filename

Specifies the filename to use for client trace files. The default trace filename is *sqlnet.trc*, or sometimes *cli.trc*. Client trace filenames may optionally include a process ID number. See TRACE_UNIQUE_CLIENT.

TRACE_FILE_SERVER = filename

Specifies the filename to use for server trace files. The default trace filename is *svr_pid.trc*, where *pid* represents the process ID number.

TRACE_FILELEN_CLIENT = kilobytes

Specifies the size of the client trace file. New with Oracle9*i*.

TRACE_FILELEN_SERVER = kilobytes

Specifies the size of the server trace file. New with Oracle9*i*.

TRACE_FILENO_CLIENT = number

Specifies the number of client trace files. When used in conjunction with TRACE_FILELEN_CLIENT, the trace files are used in a circular fashion. New with Oracle9*i*.

TRACE_FILENO_server = number

Specifies the number of server trace files. When used in conjunction with TRACE_FILELEN_SERVER, the trace files are used in a circular fashion. New with Oracle9*i*.

Networking

TRACE_LEVEL_CLIENT = OFF | USER | ADMIN | SUPPORT
> Enables Oracle Net Services client-side tracing and specifies the amount of detail to be written to the trace file. See DAEMON.TRACE_LEVEL, earlier, for an explanation of the keywords.

TRACE_LEVEL_SERVER = OFF | USER | ADMIN | SUPPORT
> Enables Oracle Net Services server-side tracing and specifies the amount of detail to be written to the trace file. See DAEMON.TRACE_LEVEL, earlier, for an explanation of the keywords.

TRACE_TIMESTAMP_CLIENT = ON | OFF
> Specifies adding a timestamp to every client trace event. The default is ON. New with Oracle9*i*.

TRACE_TIMESTAMP_SERVER = ON | OFF
> Specifies adding a timestamp to every server trace event. The default is ON. New with Oracle9*i*.

TRACE_UNIQUE_CLIENT = ON | OFF
> Controls whether or not client trace files should have unique names. Uniqueness is accomplished by appending a process ID number, or a thread ID number, to the names of client trace files. A value of ON results in that happening. The default value is OFF, which leaves process and thread IDs out of the name. See TRACE_FILE_CLIENT, earlier.

USE_CMAN = TRUE | FALSE
> Allows you to force all Oracle Net Services sessions to go through Oracle Connection Manager. The default setting is FALSE. When set to TRUE, Oracle Net Services connections will automatically be routed through Connection Manager in order to get to the server.

USE_DEDICATED_SERVER = OFF | ON
> Allows you to force the use of dedicated server processes for all connections from a given client. The default value is OFF. When set to ON, any connection to a remote Oracle Net Services service results in a new dedicated server process being spawned.

WALLET_LOCATION
> Used with Oracle Advanced Security to specify the location of wallets on the system. New with Oracle9*i*. See the Oracle documentation for more information on this parameter and the use of wallets.

TNSNAMES.ORA

TNSNAMES.ORA is a configuration file that associates a net service name with the addresses and network protocols used to connect to that service. This file is used for *local naming*, in which a local file identifies and configures communications to the listener.

For ease of reference, the following description of the syntax for the *TNSNAMES.ORA* file is divided into sections for each clause in the file. See an example of the file after the syntax sections.

Syntax

The basic syntax for the file is:

```
service_name =
    (description_information
        (connect_information)
    )
```

where *service_name* is the name of the net service, *description_information* is the clause that provides the characteristics of the service, and *connect_information* is the clause that provides the connection details for that service.

Specify *service_name* by providing the name you want Oracle Net Services to use for the connection, followed by a period (.) and the name of the Oracle Net Services domain for the service name.

The *TNSNAMES.ORA* file can have multiple entries, each taking this form. Note that the parentheses are required for this file. The formatting shown is optional, but most Oracle users find it the most readable format, because there can be many sets of parentheses in any one entry.

---

description_information

```
DESCRIPTION_LIST=
    [(DESCRIPTION=
        [(ADDRESS LIST=]
            (ADDRESS=address_info)
            [(ADDRESS=address_info). . .]
        (address_parameters)
        ()]
    [(description_list_parameter
    ) (description_list_parameter])]
    [(description_parameter
    ) (description_parameter])]
    ()]
```

Used to specify information about the connection. There can be more than one *description_information* clause for a service. If the client attempts to connect to a service, Oracle Net Services will try to connect using the first description clause. If this fails, Oracle Net Services will move on to the second clause, and so on.

Keywords and clauses

DESCRIPTION LIST

> An optional keyword, used if you want to specify one or more description parameters. If this keyword is omitted, you also should not use the trailing parenthesis. If you use this parameter, client load balancing is turned on by default.

description_parameter

> If you use the DESCRIPTION LIST parameter, you can specify description parameters. These parameters are:

FAILOVER=({ON | YES | TRUE} | {OFF | NO | FALSE})

> Enables or disables connect-time failover for descriptions in the list. By default, failover is ON. When failover is ON, a failure to connect using one description causes Oracle Net Services to try another description in the list. Oracle Net Services works through addresses in order unless client load balancing is used. New with Oracle8*i*.

LOAD_BALANCE=({ON | YES | TRUE} | {OFF | NO | FALSE})

Enables or disables client load balancing. When a description list is used, client load balancing is ON by default. When making a new connection, Oracle Net Services randomly chooses a description from the description list. If failover is also ON, then Oracle Net Services randomly progresses from one description to another until either all descriptions have been tried or a connection is made. New with Oracle8*i*.

SOURCE_ROUTE=({ON | YES} | {OFF | NO})

Used to route connections through Connection Manager. The default setting is OFF. When enabled, the description list must include two or more descriptions. The first description must point to a Connection Manager instance. Oracle Net Services then connects by hopping from one description to the next until a database listener is reached. New with Oracle8*i*.

Each description parameter must be enclosed by parentheses and is typically placed on its own line.

description_list_parameters

Uses the same parameters as the *description_list*, except for FAILOVER and LOAD_BALANCE.

ADDRESS LIST

An optional keyword starting with Oracle8*i*. If this keyword is omitted, you also should not use the trailing parenthesis. An entry can have more than one address list. If it does, Oracle Net Services will randomly choose one address from the first list. If this fails, Oracle Net Services will randomly choose an address from the second list, and so on.

address_info

Specifes the type of protocol used to connect to the listener and configuration information for the protocol. The protocols supported, and the information needed for each, are:

BEQUEATH—not supported in Oracle9i

```
(PROTOCOL=BEQ)(PROGRAM=program_name)
(ARGV0=program_instance_name)(
    ARGS='(DESCRIPTION=(LOCAL=YES)(ADDRESS=(PROTOCOL=beq)))')
```

TCP/IP

```
(PROTOCOL = TCP)(HOST={hostname | IP_address})
(PORT = port_number)
```

TPC/IP with SSL—new with Oracle8i

```
(PROTOCOL = TCPS) (HOST = {hostname | IP_address})
(PORT = port_number)
```

IPC

```
(PROTOCOL = IPC)(KEY = key_name)
```

Named Pipes

```
(PROTOCOL = NMP)(SERVER = server_name)(PIPE = pipe_name)
```

SPX—desupported in Oracle9i

```
(PROTOCOL = SPX)(SERVICE = spx_service_name)
```

LU6.2—desupported in Oracle9i

```
(PROTOCOL=LU6.2)(LU_NAME = qualified_server_name)
    (LLU_NAME | LOCAL_LLU_NAME = qualified_local_LU_alias)
    (MODE | MDN = log_mode_entry)
    (PLU_LA | PARTNER_LU_LOCAL_ALIAS = partner_LU_alias)
    (TP_NAME | TPN = host_transaction_program)
```

address_parameters

Uses most of the same parameters as the *description_list* (except that FAILOVER and LOAD_BALANCE have no effect here), as well as the following parameters:

SDU = number

Specifies the transfer rate of data packets sent across the network, the session data unit (SDU). For greatest efficiency, the SDU should be a multiple of the underlying network transport's frame size, which you can set using the TDU parameter. This parameter cannot be set for a database that dynamically registers with the listener and a dedicated server connection. The default value for *number* is 2048 bytes. The maximum value for *number* is 32,768 (32K) bytes.

TYPE_OF_SERVICE

Specifies whether the description connects you to an Oracle database (ORACLE8_DATABASE), the default, or an Oracle Rdb database (RDB_DATABASE). You need only specify this parameter when connecting to an Oracle Rdb database.

connect_information

```
(CONNECT_DATA=
    [(connect_parameter)]
    [(connect_parameter)] . . .
)
```

Provides connection information. For each service, there is one section containing the appropriate connect information.

Keywords and clauses

The following parameters can be used for connect parameters, each enclosed by parentheses:

FAILOVER_MODE = failover_clause

Used for Transparent Application Failover (TAF). The *failover_clause* can be one or more of the following parameters, each surrounded by parentheses:

BACKUP = backup_net_service_name

Specifies the net service name for the backup connection.

TYPE = SESSION | SELECT | NONE

Specifies what Oracle Net Services does if a failure on the primary instance occurs. SESSION establishes a session with the backup instance. SELECT establishes a session with the backup instance, reopens cursors for any outstanding SELECT statements, and repositions those cursors so that fetching continues from the point the client was at when the primary connection failed. NONE doesn't failover at all, which allows you to explicitly specify the default behavior.

METHOD = BASIC | PRECONNECT

BASIC establishes the backup connection only when the connection to the primary instance fails. PRECONNECT establishes the connection to the backup when the primary connection is made.

RETRIES = retry_attempts

Specifies the number of attempts to retry a connection to the backup instance when a failover occurs. The default is normally 0, but if a value is specified for DELAY, the default number of retry attempts becomes 5. New with Oracle8*i*.

DELAY = retry_delay

Specifies the delay in seconds between retries. The default delay is 1 second. New in Oracle8*i*.

GLOBAL_NAME = global_database_name

Identifies an Oracle Rdb database. Specify this parameter only when connecting to an Oracle Rdb database.

HS = OK

Tells Oracle Net Services that you are connecting to a service that is not an Oracle or Oracle Rdb database. The HS is an abbreviation for Heterogeneous Services.

INSTANCE_NAME = instance_name

Identifies a specific Oracle instance to which you want to connect. This is useful when a service has more than one instance, and you want to connect specifically to one of those instances. An instance name should always be specified in conjunction with a service name. New with Oracle8*i*.

RDB_DATABASE = rdb_filename

Identifies an Oracle Rdb database by its filename. You may include the path and extension as part of the filename.

SDU=number

Identical to the SDU parameter from the address section.

SERVER = DEDICATED | SHARED

Specifies whether the connection is to a dedicated server process or to a Shared Server process. Use the SHARED keyword only if the server is configured for Shared Servers. You can use the DEDICATED keyword to indicate that you want to make a dedicated server connection to a database that is otherwise set up for Shared Servers.

SERVICE_NAME = database_service

Identifies an Oracle database service. This must match a service name specified by an instance's SERVICE_NAMES parameter, or it must match the database's global name.

SID = system_identifier

Allows you to identify an instance by its system identifier. SID may be used in place of SERVICE_NAME. SID may also be used alongside SERVICE_NAME when you need to support both clients using Oracle8*i* or a later release and those using prior versions of the Oracle Networking software with one *TNSNAMES.ORA* file.

Example

The following *TNSNAMES.ORA* file makes the following assumptions:

- The net service name is Bailey in the *greenie.org* domain.
- The protocol used is TCP.
- The hosts in this domain are TREATS, BAGELS, and FRIES.
- There is load balancing between these addresses.
- There is failover to the net service CHUCK in the same domain.
- The failover connection is established when the primary connection is made.

```
BAILEY.GREENIE.ORG =
(DESCRIPTION =
    (ADDRESS_LIST =
    (ADDRESS=(PROTOCOL=TCP)(HOST=TREATS.GREENIE.ORG)(PORT=1521))
        (ADDRESS=(PROTOCOL=TCP)(HOST=BAGELS.GREENIE.ORG)(PORT=1521))
        (ADDRESS=(PROTOCOL=TCP)(HOST=FRIES.GREENIE.ORG)(PORT=1521))
        (LOAD_BALANCE=ON)
        (FAILOVER=ON)
    )
    (CONNECT_DATA =
        (SERVICE_NAME=CHUCK.GREENIE.ORG)
        (FAILOVER_MODE=
            (TYPE=SESSION)
            (METHOD=PRECONNECT))
    )
)
```

LDAP.ORA

LDAP.ORA is a configuration file on a client machine that is used to point to the LDAP server used for net service names. *LDAP.ORA* is used when you are storing network service configuration in an LDAP directory instead of using the local method with *TNSNAMES.ORA*.

Because most of the network information is stored in the LDAP directory, the *LDAP. ORA* file is fairly concise. The *LDAP.ORA* file is normally created by the Oracle Net Configuration Assistant utility, and Oracle suggests not modifying it.

Keywords and clauses

DIRECTORY_SERVERS = host:port[:sslport][, host:port[:sslport] . . .]
> Lists the hostnames, ports, and SSL ports for primary and alternate LDAP servers.

DIRECTORY_SERVER_TYPE = type_id
> Identifies the type of LDAP server. As of Oracle9i, the only supported values for *type_id* are '*oid*' for Oracle Internet Directory and '*ad*' for Microsoft Active Directory, which was not supported before Oracle9i.

DEFAULT_ADMIN_CONTEXT = distinguished_name
> Specifies the directory entry that contains an Oracle Context, from which connect identifiers can be created, modified, or looked up.

LISTENER.ORA

LISTENER.ORA is a configuration file used to control the operation of an Oracle listener on the server. You can have more than one listener configured in one *LISTENER.ORA* file if each has a unique name.

The syntax for the *LISTENER.ORA* file is similar to the *TNSNAMES.ORA* file syntax.

Syntax
```
LISTENER=
    (DESCRIPTION_LIST
        (DESCRIPTION=
         (ADDRESS LIST=
             (ADDRESS=address_info)
             [(ADDRESS=address_info). . .]
             [(PROTOCOL_STACK=
             (PRESENTATION=GIOP)
             (SESSION=RAW))]
    )
SID_LIST_LISTENER=
    (SID_LIST=
        (SID_DESC=
            (sid_parameters)
            [(sid_parameters) . . .]
        )
        [(SID_DESC=
            (sid_parameters)
            [(sid_parameters) . . .]
        ) . . .]
(control_parameters)
[(control_parameters). . .]
```

Keywords and clauses
address_info
> Uses the same syntax as the *address_info* for *TNSNAMES.ORA* described earlier. In addition to the keywords listed for each protocol, *LISTENER.ORA address_ info* for TCP/IP also accepts:
>
> *QUEUESIZE = number*
> > Specifies the number of concurrent connection requests a listener can accept on a TCP/IP listening endpoint. This keyword must be the last one in the *address_info*. The default for *number* is 5 on Sun SPARC Solaris and Windows NT 4.0 Workstation and 60 on Windows NT 4.0 Server.

(PROTOCOL_STACK =
(PRESENTATION = GIOP)
(SESSION = RAW))
> Used for IIOP (Internet Intra-Orb Protocol) communication to the Java option in the database. This parameter was new in Oracle8*i*.

SID_LIST_LISTENER
> For Oracle8*i* and Oracle9*i*, instances automatically register themselves with their listeners at startup. For Oracle8 and previous versions, as well as for external procedure calls or Heterogeneous Services, you will need to use this clause to statically configure services for the listener.

sid_parameters

The following parameters are allowed for a statically configured SID (Oracle system identifier), each enclosed in parentheses.

ENVS = "variable = value[,variable = value . . .]"

Allows you to set environment variables for the listener; these are set prior to executing a dedicated server program or a program specified with the PROGRAM parameter. This parameter will not work with Windows NT, as any process spawned by the listener will inherit the listener's environment and variables.

GLOBAL_DBNAME = database_name.database_domain

Specifies the global database name, which is made from the database name and the database domain. This name should match one of the values specified in the SERVICE_NAMES parameter of the *INIT.ORA* file.

ORACLE_HOME = home_path

Specifies the Oracle home directory for the service.

PROGRAM = program_name

Identifies the service's executable program name.

SID_NAME = sid_name

Specifies the SID name of the Oracle instance. Must match the value from the INSTANCE_NAME parameter of the *INIT.ORA* file.

control_parameters

Controls the operation of the listener. The control parameters, each of which has the name of the listener appended to the end of it, are listed here:

ADMIN_RESTRICTIONS_listener_name = ON | OFF

Disables or reenables runtime modification of *LISTENER.ORA* parameters. This parameter is not necessary if you use a password to secure the listener. For more details, refer to the later "Listener Control Utility" section.

LOG_DIRECTORY_listener_name = listener_log_path

Specifies the directory for the listener log file.

LOG_FILE_listener_name = logfile_name

Specifies the name of the listener log file.

LOGGING_listener_name = ON | OFF

Turns logging on and off for the specified listener.

PASSWORDS_listener_name = (encrypted_password)

Allows you to specify an encrypted password for the listener. Has the same effect as the CHANGE_PASSWORD command of the Listener Control utility.

SAVE_CONFIG_ON_STOP_listener_name = TRUE|FALSE

Specifies whether to save changes made to the listener configuration file using SET commands from the Listener Control utility.

SSL_CLIENT_AUTHENTICATION = TRUE | FALSE

Specifies whether a client is authenticated with SSL. If this parameter is set to TRUE, the listener attempts to authenticate the user.

STARTUP_WAIT_TIME_listener_name = number

Specifies the number of seconds a listener waits before responding to a START command from the Listener Control utility.

TRACE_DIRECTORY_listener_name = tracefile_directory

Specifies the directory for the listener trace file.

TRACE_FILE_listener_name = tracefile_name
Specifies the file name for the listener trace file. The default is *listener.trc*.

TRACE_FILELEN_listener_name = number
Specifies the size of the listener trace files (in kilobytes). Once this limit is reached, the trace starts writing to the next file. The default is unlimited.

TRACE_FILENO_listener_name = number
Specifies the number of listener trace files. If this parameter is specified, an integer is added to the end of the trace filename.

*TRACE_LEVEL_listener_name = **OFF** | USER | ADMIN | SUPPORT*
Specifies the level of information in the listener trace file.

*TRACE_TIMESTAMP_listener_name = ON | **OFF***
Specifies whether to add a timestamp to entries in the trace file.

WALLET_LOCATION
Used in conjunction with wallets with Oracle Advanced Security. For more information about this parameter, see the Oracle documentation.

Networking Management Utilities

This section describes a variety of utilities used to manage Oracle Net Services. The general goal of these utilities is to make it easier to implement and manage network communication. We provide descriptions for the network management utilities most commonly used for Oracle9*i*. For command-line utilities, the executable names are shown in the list:

Listener Control utility (lsnrctl)
A command-line utility for managing the Oracle listener. You can also start the listener automatically as a service on some operating system platforms, like Windows, and you can embed your *lsnrctl* commands in a startup script on Unix and Linux systems.

Oracle Names Control utility (namesctl)
A command-line utility for managing Oracle Names. For more information on the commands used by the Oracle Names Control utility, see the Oracle documentation.

Oracle Connection Manager Control utility (cmctl)
A command-line utility for managing the Oracle Connection Manager. For more information on the commands used by the Oracle Connection Manager utility, see the Oracle documentation.

TNSPing utility (tnsping)
A command-line utility used to check the connection between an Oracle Net Services client and server.

Oracle Net Manager
A GUI management tool that allows you to create, discover, and test configurations for the listener, connection, and Oracle Names.

Configuration Assistant

A GUI management tool used during the installation process to configure listener names, protocol addresses, naming methods, net service names, and directory usage.

Listener Control Utility

The Listener Control utility allows you to manage the Oracle listener. This utility generally has the executable name *lsnrctl*. Note, however, that the name may vary by platform and release. The Listener Control commands and their parameters are listed in the following sections.

Calling the utility

The Listener Control utility is generally called with its program name (normally *lsnrctl*) from the command prompt of your operating system. You start the Listener Control with any one of these commands:

```
lsnrctl [command] [listener]
```

or

```
lsnrctl @filename
```

The optional parameters are:

command

Any valid Listener Control utility command.

listener

The name of a listener. If you do not specify a specific listener name in a command, the Listener Control utility looks for a listener named LISTENER.

@filename

Executes the statements in the filename. You can include comments in the file by preceding them with either REM or the number sign (#).

If you call the Listener Control utility without a command or a file, the Listener Control utility will open up its own session with the lsnrctl> prompt.

Listener Control utility commands

You can specify the following commands for the Listener Control utility

CHANGE_ PASSWORD	CHANGE_PASSWORD [listener] Changes the password on the Listener Control utility to an encrypted password. After issuing this command, the Listener Control utility prompts you for your old password (if one exists) and your new password without echoing either entry. Typically, you issue a SAVE_CONFIG command after changing the password.
EXIT	EXIT Exits the Listener Control utility.

HELP	HELP [*listener*]
	Displays a list of Listener Control utility commands.

QUIT	QUIT
	Exits the Listener Control utility. This command is identical to the EXIT command.

RELOAD	RELOAD [*listener*]
	Reloads the *LISTENER.ORA* file, so that the specifications in this configuration file are applied. In many cases, issuing RELOAD allows you to implement changes without having to stop and restart the listener.

SAVE_CONFIG	SAVE_CONFIG [*listener*]
	Saves all changes made to the listener configuration to the *LISTENER.ORA* file.

SERVICES	SERVICES [*listener*]
	Returns detailed information about database services, instances, dedicated servers, and dispatchers with which the listener interacts.

SET	SET *command*
	Allows you to set the parameter values for the listener. If you issue the command without a parameter, it will return a list of parameters that can be set.

Keywords

command

One of the parameters from the following list:

CURRENT_LISTENER
Specifies the default listener for all subsequent Listener Control utility commands.

*DISPLAYMODE = COMPAT | **NORMAL** | VERBOSE | RAW*
Specifies the amount of information displayed for the SERVICE and STATUS commands:

COMPAT displays output that is compatible with older versions of the listener.

VERBOSE displays all information about the listener

RAW displays information without formatting and should be used only if requested by Oracle Support.

LOG_DIRECTORY directory
Specifies the directory for Listener Control utility log files.

LOG_FILE logfile_name
> Specifies the log filename for the Listener Control utility log file. The default is *listener.log*.

LOG_STATUS ON | OFF
> Turns logging for the Listener Control utility on and off.

PASSWORD
> Specifies the password for the user. After this command, the Listener Control utility will prompt you for the password. You have to issue this command before using password-protected commands like START, STOP, or SAVE_CONFIG.

SAVE_CONFIG_ON_STOP ON | OFF
> Specifies that any changes to the configuration file should be saved (or not) to the *LISTENER.ORA* file when you exit the Listener Control utility.

STARTUP_WAITTIME seconds
> Specifies the amount of time, in seconds, the listener should wait after you issue a START command for the listener. This command is deprecated in Oracle9*i* and will be desupported in a future release.

TRC_DIRECTORY directory
> Specifies the directory for Listener Control utility trace files.

TRC_FILE filename
> Specifies the filename for Listener Control utility trace files.

TRC_LEVEL OFF | USER | ADMIN | SUPPORT
> Specifies the level of detail for information in the trace file.

SHOW [parameter]
> Specifies the value for a parameter, or, if no parameter is specified, for all parameters.

SPAWN [listener] [alias] [arguments = 'arg1, arg2, . . .]
> Runs a program specified in the PROGRAM parameter of the *LISTENER.ORA* file. The *alias* is the name specified in the PROGRAM parameter.

START [listener]
> Starts the specified listener.

STATUS [listener]
> Displays concise information about the listener, including configuration settings, protocol addresses, and a summary of services registered with the listener.

STOP [listener]
> Stops the listener.

TRACE {OFF | USER | ADMIN | SUPPORT} [listener]
> Starts a trace file for the listener. The effect is the same as using the SET TRC_LEVEL command.

VERSION
> Displays the current version of the listener.

Networking

TNSPing	tnsping *net_service_name* [*count*]

TNSPing is a command-line utility used to check the connection between an Oracle Net Services client and server. The operation performed by TNSPing is similar to that performed by the *ping* command for TCP.

This utility is called from the command line with the program name *tnsping*.

The *net_service_name* is the name of a net service as defined in the *TNSNAMES.ORA* file or a name service. *count* defines how many times the TNSPing program will attempt to connect to the server.

TNSPing returns a message containing the connection information it found to access the net service, a success ·message (if appropriate) of "OK" for each connection attempt specified, and the time it took to complete the connection.

Oracle Net Manager

Oracle Net Manager is a GUI management tool that you can use to create, discover, and test configurations for the listener, connection, and Oracle Names. You can use Oracle Net Manager as a standalone utility or as a part of Oracle Enterprise Manager. Oracle Net Manager also includes some wizards that walk you through different configuration tasks, including:

Net Service Name wizard
    Used for creating a *TNSNAME.ORA* file

Directory Server Migration wizard
    Used for migrating information from a *TNSNAMES.ORA* file to a directory-based system

Names wizard
    Used for creating and configuring an Oracle Names server

In Oracle8*i*, the tasks of Oracle Net Manager were accomplished with the Net8 Configuration Assistant. In Oracle8, these tasks were accomplished with the Oracle Net8 Assistant and the Net8 Easy Configuration Tool.

Oracle Net Configuration Assistant

The Configuration Assistant, which was known as the Net8 Configuration Assistant in Oracle8*i* and the Net8 Easy Configuration Tool in Oracle8, is used during the installation process to configure listener names and protocol addresses, naming methods, net service names, and directory usage.

For Oracle8*i*, the Database Configuration Assistant also adds some information about the database to the *LISTENER.ORA* file, which is used by Oracle Enterprise Manager.

6

Data Dictionary

The Oracle data dictionary is a collection of tables and related views that enable you to see the inner workings and structure of the Oracle database. By querying these views, you can obtain information about every object and every user of the database. All of the Oracle monitoring tools look at the information available in the data dictionary and present it in an easy-to-use format.

Traditionally, the data dictionary has consisted of a series of views owned by the SYS user. These views, known as *static data dictionary views*, present information contained in tables that are updated when Oracle processes a DDL statement. The SYS tables and views, as well as a set of public synonyms for the views, are all created by the *catalog.sql* script. In addition, the installation of some Oracle features creates tables and views in the SYSTEM schema. In general, tables and views owned by SYSTEM exist to support functionality provided by PL/SQL stored procedures (described in Chapter 9) rather than fundamental Oracle functionality.

A second set of views is known as the *dynamic performance data dictionary views*, commonly referred to as the *V$ views*. These V$ views are based on a set of internal memory structures maintained by Oracle as virtual tables, which all begin with an "X$" prefix. Just as the static data dictionary views provide information about the database, the V$ views and underlying X$ tables provide information about the active instance.

Static Data Dictionary Views

The static data dictionary views have existed in their current format since Oracle Version 6. These are views owned by SYS that are built upon tables owned by SYS and give you the ability to find information about database objects.

Families of Views

Most of the data dictionary is constructed in a matrix fashion. The first way to categorize data dictionary views is by the breadth of information they cover. Views can be divided into four groups:

USER_ views
: Views that allow you to see objects you own. Most of these views begin with USER_.

ALL_ views
: Views that allow you to see objects that you own or that were granted to you. Most of these views begin with ALL_.

DBA_ views
: Views that allow you to see all objects in the database. These are primarily for use by the DBA. Most of these views begin with DBA_.

Other views
: A handful of other views that provide information of general interest about the database.

The second way to categorize data dictionary views is by content. Many of the USER_, ALL_, and DBA_ views are grouped in families, according to how their view names end (e.g., TABLES, COLUMNS, and so on). Groups of views provide information about various topics, including:

Tables
Storage
Columns
Views
Objects
Networking objects

The ALL_ views have the same structure as the DBA_ views. The USER_ views have the same structure as the DBA_ views with the exception that they do not include the OWNER column. In this chapter we'll list the "family" views and the other views of interest. We'll reference those views that exist in multiple forms (i.e., ALL_, DBA_, USER_) in the form *_viewname. So, for example, there are three *_INDEXES views:

ALL_INDEXES
DBA_INDEXES
USER_INDEXES

If any of the following views do not support all three varieties, we'll note the exception. Some views have only one form or do not follow this naming pattern, and we show those without the wildcard character (*).

Commonly Used Static Data Dictionary Views

This section summarizes the Oracle static data dictionary views that are commonly used. Views are divided into functional categories and are arranged alphabetically within category.

Advanced Queuing

The following views provide information about the message queues:

*_ATTRIBUTE_TRANSFORMATIONS
> Lists all the transformation functions for these transformations. There is no ALL_ATTRIBUTE_TRANSFORMATIONS view. New with Oracle9*i*.

DBA_TRANSFORMATIONS
> Provides information about Advanced Queuing message transformations. New with Oracle9*i*.

*_QUEUE_SCHEDULES
> Shows when particular queued messages are to be delivered.

*_QUEUE_TABLES
> Lists the tables used to hold the queues defined as part of the Advanced Queuing facility.

*_QUEUES
> Lists the queues defined as part of the Advanced Queuing facility.

Audit trail

The following views provide information about the status of auditing and audit trails:

ALL_DEF_AUDIT_OPTS
> Lists the default auditing options in effect for new objects.

AUDIT_ACTIONS
> Lists the audit codes and descriptions.

*_AUDIT_EXISTS
> Contains audit trail information generated by AUDIT EXISTS and AUDIT NOEXISTS.

*_AUDIT_OBJECT
> Contains audit trail information for object auditing.

*_AUDIT_SESSION
> Contains audit trail information for all connects and disconnects.

*_AUDIT_STATEMENT
> Contains audit trail information for all audited statements.

*_AUDIT_TRAIL
> Contains all audit trail information. The other _AUDIT_ views are subsets of this view.

*_OBJ_AUDIT_OPTS
> Lists all object auditing options in effect.

*_PRIV_AUDIT_OPTS
> Lists all system privilege auditing options in effect.

STMT_AUDIT_OPTION_MAP
> Lists the valid SQL statements that can be specified for statement auditing.

_STMT_AUDIT_OPTS
Lists all statement auditing options in effect.

SYSTEM_PRIVILEGE_MAP
Lists the valid system privileges that can be specified for system privilege auditing.

TABLE_PRIVILEGE_MAP
Lists the valid object audit options that can be specified for schema object auditing.

Change Data Capture

Oracle9*i* introduces a feature known as Change Data Capture, used primarily in data warehouses, which allows a user to create a set of change tables that can be used to publish changes to a set of underlying tables:

_SOURCE_TAB_COLUMNS
Lists the columns in the source tables that are contained in change tables.

_SOURCE_TABLES
Lists the links between change tables and their source tables.

_SUBSCRIBED_COLUMNS
Lists the columns of published tables that have been subscribed to.

_SUBSCRIBED_TABLES
Lists all published tables that have been subscribed to.

_SUBSCRIPTIONS
Lists all subscriptions.

Constraints

The following views provide information about constraints and columns included in the constraints:

_CONS_COLUMNS
Shows which columns are affected by each constraint.

_CONSTRAINTS
Lists all constraints defined in the database.

Data dictionary

The following views provide information about the objects in the data dictionary:

_CATALOG
Lists all tables, views, sequences, and synonyms in the database.

_DEPENDENCIES
Lists dependencies between database objects. Used to determine which objects become invalid after other objects are altered or dropped.

_OBJECTS
Lists all objects in the database. This name predates the Oracle Objects Option and is not restricted to objects created using the Objects Option.

DICT_COLUMNS
> Lists all columns defined in the data dictionary views.

DICTIONARY
> Lists all data dictionary views.

External tables

With Oracle9*i*, you can access data in files that reside outside of the Oracle database; these are referred to as *external tables*. The following views provide metadata about external tables:

*_EXTERNAL_LOCATIONS
> Lists the sources for external tables.

*_EXTERNAL_TABLES
> Describes the attributes of external tables.

Indexes

These views provide information about indexes and indexed columns:

*_IND_COLUMNS
> Lists all indexed columns.

*_INDEXES
> Lists all indexes.

INDEX_HISTOGRAM
> Contains information about the distribution of index keys within the table. Populated for one index at a time by the ANALYZE INDEX ... VALIDATE STRUCTURE command.

INDEX_STATS
> Contains information about the structure of an index. Populated for one index at a time by the ANALYZE INDEX ... VALIDATE STRUCTURE command.

Jobs

The following views provide information about the job queues managed by the Oracle built-in DBMS_JOBS package. These job queues are used by the replication facilities and by Oracle Enterprise Manager but are available for use by any application:

*_JOBS
> Lists all jobs defined.

*_JOBS_RUNNING
> Lists all currently running jobs.

Large objects (LOBs)

The following views provide information about large objects (LOBs):

*_DIRECTORIES
> Lists all defined external directories where BFILEs are stored.

*_LOBS
> Lists all large objects defined in the database.

Locks

The following views provide information about the current status of locks in the database:

*_BLOCKERS
> Lists all sessions holding locks for whose release others are waiting.

DBMS_LOCK_ALLOCATED
> Shows which locks the current user has allocated.

*_DDL_LOCKS
> Lists all existing DDL locks.

*_DML_LOCKS
> Lists all existing DML locks.

*_KGLLOCK
> Lists all KGL (Kernel Generic Library cache) locks in the database.

*_LOCK_INTERNAL
> Contains internal information for each lock defined in *_LOCKS.

*_LOCKS
> Lists all locks held or requested in the database.

*_WAITERS
> Lists all sessions that are waiting on a lock held by another session.

Log groups

A log group is used to multiplex log files across different locations and contains multiple members, which are identical log files. Log groups are used to reduce the impact of a disk failure disaster on the recovery process:

*_LOG_COLUMNS
> Lists the columns assigned to log groups. New with Oracle9i.

*_LOG_GROUPS
> Lists the tables that are associated with log groups and indicates whether the log group is always used for the table or only when certain columns in the table are modified. New with Oracle9i.

Materialized views

A materialized view is a view that is used to speed up data warehouse queries with precalculated aggregates. The following views provide more information about materialized views in Oracle9i:

*_BASE_TABLE_MVIEWS
> Lists information about existing materialized views.

*_MVIEW_LOGS
> Lists information about materialized view logs, which track changes to the master tables that can be used to refresh the materialized views.

Networking and distributed transactions

The following views provide information about the status of Oracle networking, remote databases, and distributed transactions to these remote databases:

*_2PC_NEIGHBORS
> Contains information about the commit point for distributed transactions listed in *_2PC_PENDING.

*_2PC_PENDING
> Lists information about distributed transactions requiring recovery.

*_DB_LINKS
> Lists all database links.

GLOBAL_NAME
> Shows the value of the global name. Can be used to determine which database the application is connected to.

*_PENDING_TRANSACTIONS
> Contains further information used by XA for distributed transactions listed in *_ 2PC_PENDING.

TRUSTED_SERVERS
> Specifies which servers have been identified as trusted.

Objects Option

The following views provide information relating to objects created using Oracle's Objects Option:

*_COLL_TYPES
> Lists collection types created.

*_METHOD_PARAMS
> Lists all parameters for methods defined in *_TYPE_METHODS.

*_METHOD_RESULTS
> Lists all method results for methods defined in *_TYPE_METHODS.

*_NESTED_TABLES
> Lists all nested tables created using features from the Objects Option.

Data
Dictionary

_OBJECT_TABLES

    Lists all tables created using features from the Objects Option.

_REFS

    Lists the REF columns and attributes for objects.

_TYPE_ATTRS

    Lists attributes of all types.

_TYPE_METHODS

    Lists methods created to support each type defined in *_TYPES.

_TYPES

    Lists all types created.

Partitioning

The following views provide information about partitioned tables and indexes:

_IND_PARTITIONS

    Lists all index partitions. One row exists for each index partition.

_PART_COL_STATISTICS

    Contains distribution information about partitioned columns that have been analyzed—for example, *_TAB_COL_STATISTICS for partitioned tables.

_PART_HISTOGRAMS

    Contains information about histograms created on individual partitions.

_PART_INDEXES

    Lists all partitioned indexes. One row exists for each index partition.

_PART_KEY_COLUMNS

    Lists the partition key columns for all partitions.

_PART_TABLES

    Lists all partitioned tables. One row exists for each partitioned table.

_TAB_PARTITIONS

    Lists all table partitions. One row exists for each table partition.

PL/SQL

The following views provide information about PL/SQL stored programs, including functions, procedures, packages, and triggers:

ALL_ARGUMENTS

    Lists all valid arguments for stored procedures and functions.

_ERRORS

    Shows all errors from compiling objects.

_LIBRARIES

    Lists the external libraries that can be called from PL/SQL packages, procedures, and functions.

_OBJECT_SIZE
>   Shows the size of the compiled code for each PL/SQL package, procedure, function, and trigger.

PUBLIC_DEPENDENCY
>   Lists dependencies using only object numbers.

_SOURCE
>   Shows PL/SQL source for packages, procedures, and functions.

_TRIGGER_COLS
>   Lists columns that are referenced in triggers.

_TRIGGERS
>   Shows PL/SQL code for database triggers.

Replication

The following views provide information used by Oracle's advanced replication facilities. Oracle currently recommends using the Replication Manager to obtain the information in these views:

_ANALYZE_OBJECTS
>   Lists analyze objects. Obsolete with Oracle9i.

_REGISTERED_SNAPSHOT_GROUPS, _REGISTERED_MVIEW_GROUPS
>   Lists registered snapshot groups.

_REPAUDIT_ATTRIBUTE
>   Lists replication audit attributes.

_REPAUDIT_COLUMN
>   Lists replication audit columns.

_REPCAT
>   Lists the interim status of any asynchronous administrative requests and any error messages generated.

_REPCATLOG
>   Lists the interim status of any asynchronous administrative requests and any error messages generated.

_REPCOLUMN
>   Lists replicated columns for a group.

_REPCOLUMN_GROUP
>   Lists column groups defined for a table. There is no USER_REPCOLUMN_GROUP view.

_REPCONFLICT
>   Lists tables with replication conflict resolution methods and the methods for the tables. There is no USER_ALL_REPCONFLICT view.

_REPDDL
>   Lists DDL for replication objects.

*_REPGENOBJECTS

Lists objects generated to support replication.

*_REPGROUP

Lists users who are registered for object group privileges.

*_REPGROUPED_COLUMN

Lists columns in column groups for each table.

*_REPKEY_COLUMNS

Lists information about primary key columns for replicated tables.

*_REPOBJECT

Lists objects in each replicated object group.

*_REPPARAMETER_COLUMN

Lists information about columns used to resolve conflicts.

*_REPPRIORITY

Lists value and priority level of each priority group.

*_REPPRIORITY_GROUP

Lists priority and site priority groups for a replicated object group.

*_REPPROP

Lists technique used to propagate an object.

*_REPRESOL_STATS_CONTROL

Lists information for statistics collection for conflict resolution.

*_REPRESOLUTION

Lists routines used to resolve conflicts for a given schema.

*_REPRESOLUTION_METHOD

Lists conflict resolution routines.

*_REPRESOLUTION_STATISTICS

Lists information about resolved replication conflicts.

*_REPSITES

Lists members of replicated object's group.

DBA_REPEXTENSIONS

Lists current operations that are adding new master sites to a master group without quiescing the master group. New with Oracle9i.

DBA_REPSITES_NEW

Lists the new replication sites that you plan to add to your replication environment. New with Oracle9i.

DEFCALLDEST

Lists destinations for each deferred remote procedure call. New with Oracle9i.

Security

The following views provide information about users, grants, and security policies that implement fine-grained access control (FGAC):

_APPLICATION_ROLES
Describes all application roles that have authentication policy roles defined for them. There is no ALL_ view. New with Oracle9*i*.

_COL_PRIVS
Lists all column grants made in the database.

_GLOBAL_CONTEXT
Lists all the global contexts; these are sets of application-defined attributes that can be used for determining access rights available to the instance. There is no USER_GLOBAL_CONTEXT view. New with Oracle9*i*.

_POLICY_CONTEXTS
Lists policies and their associated contexts. New with Oracle9*i*.

_POLICY_GROUPS
Lists the various groups for the different security policies. This view is new with Oracle9*i*.

_PROFILES
Lists all defined profiles.

RESOURCE_COST
Shows the assigned cost of each resource for composite limits.

RESOURCE_MAP
Maps profile resource numbers to resource names.

_ROLES
Lists all roles.

_ROLE_PRIVS
Lists all roles granted to users and to other roles.

ROLE_ROLE_PRIVS
Lists roles granted to other roles. A subset of *_ROLE_PRIVS.

ROLE_SYS_PRIVS
Lists system privileges granted to roles. A subset of *_SYS_PRIVS.

ROLE_TAB_PRIVS
Lists table grants granted to roles. A subset of *_TAB_PRIVS.

SESSION_PRIVS
Shows which system privileges are active for the current session.

SESSION_ROLES
Shows which roles are active for the current session

_SYS_PRIVS
Shows which system privileges have been assigned to which users.

*_TAB_PRIVS

　　Shows all object privileges. Includes not only tables but also views, sequences, packages, procedures, and functions.

USER_PASSWORD_LIMITS

　　Shows the password limits in effect for the current session.

*_USERS

　　Lists all users.

Sequences

This view provides information about sequences:

*_SEQUENCES

　　Lists all sequences in the database.

Server management

The following views provide information about the current status of the database:

NLS_DATABASE_PARAMETERS

　　Shows the National Language Support (NLS) parameters in effect at the database level.

NLS_INSTANCE_PARAMETERS

　　Shows the NLS parameters in effect at the instance level.

NLS_SESSION_PARAMETERS

　　Shows the NLS parameters in effect at the session level.

PRODUCT_COMPONENT_VERSION

　　Shows the current release level of all installed Oracle options.

SM$VERSION

　　Shows the Oracle version level packaged for Server Manager to use.

SQLJ

SQLJ (described in Chapter 11) is a way of embedding static SQL statements into a Java program. SQLJ statements access SQLJ objects, which are composite data structures related to the SQLJ statements. SQLJ objects are stored in the Oracle database and are described through the following views:

*_SQLJ_TYPES

　　Describes the SQLJ object types. New with Oracle9i.

*SQLJ_TYPE_ATTRS

　　Lists the attributes associated with each SQLJ object type. New with Oracle9i.

*_SQLJ_TYPE_METHODS

　　Describes the methods associated with each SQLJ object type. New with Oracle9i.

Storage

The following views provide information about internal storage in the database, including datafiles, tablespaces, free extents, used extents, and segments:

*_DATA_FILES
> Lists all datafiles in use by the database.

*_EXTENTS
> Lists every allocated extent for every segment.

*_FREE_SPACE
> Lists every free extent. This view, combined with *_EXTENTS, should account for all storage in *_ DATA_FILES.

*_FREE_SPACE_COALESCED
> Lists every extent that is at the start of a block of free extents.

*_ROLLBACK_SEGS
> Lists all rollback segments.

*_SEGMENTS
> Lists all segments.

*_TABLESPACES
> Lists all tablespaces.

*_TS_QUOTAS
> Shows the granted quota and used storage in tablespaces by user.

Synonyms

This view provides information about synonyms:

*_SYNONYMS
> Lists all synonyms in the database.

Tables, clusters, and views

These views provide information about tables, clusters, and views:

*_ALL_TABLES
> Lists all object and relational tables.

*_CLU_COLUMNS
> Lists all cluster keys.

*_CLUSTER_HASH_EXPRESSIONS
> Lists the hash values used for the optional cluster hash indexes.

*_CLUSTERS
> Lists all clusters in the database.

*_COL_COMMENTS
> Shows comments on all table and view columns.

*_TAB_COL_STATISTICS
> Contains column information about analyzed columns.

_TAB_COLUMNS
: Shows all table and view columns.

_TAB_COMMENTS
: Shows all comments on tables and views.

_TAB_HISTOGRAMS
: Shows all table histograms.

_TABLES
: Shows all relational tables.

_UPDATABLE_COLUMNS
: Lists columns in views with joins that can be updated.

_VIEWS
: Shows all views.

Others

These other views and tables are used by individual users:

DBA_UNDO_EXTENTS
: Lists the commit time of each extent in the UNDO tablespace. New with Oracle9i.

CHAINED_ROWS
: Populated by the ANALYZE TABLE command to show all chained rows in a table. Created using the *utlchain.sql* script.

EXCEPTIONS
: Contains a list of all rows that have a constraint violation. Populated when attempting to create or enable a constraint. Created using the *utlexcpt.sql* script.

_JOIN_IND_COLUMNS
: Describes the columns used in the join that the bitmapped index is associated with. New with Oracle9i.

PLAN_TABLE
: Used by the EXPLAIN_PLAN process to show the execution plan for a SQL statement. Created using the *utlxplan.sql* script.

_PROCEDURES
: Lists information about procedures defined within the database, such as whether they are aggregate functions, pipelined table functions, or parallel-enabled functions. New with Oracle9i.

_PROXIES
: Lists information about all proxy connections in the system. There is no ALL_ PROXIES view. New with Oracle9i.

*_RESUMABLE

Lists all RESUMABLE statements. When the database runs out of space, these statements allow the DBA to suspend an operation, add more space, and then resume the operation. There is no ALL_RESUMABLE view. New with Oracle9*i*.

*_STORED_SETTINGS

Provides information about persistent parameter settings for stored PL/SQL units. New with Oracle9*i*.

Other Static Data Dictionary Views

The following views show important information about the structure of the database but are normally not referenced directly. They are listed here for completeness.

Export

The following views provide information to the Export and Import utilities:

*_EXP_FILES
*_EXP_OBJECTS
*_EXP_VERSION

Gateways

The following views provide information needed to support foreign data sources (FDSs) or data gateways:

HS_ALL_CAPS
HS_ALL_DD
HS_ALL_INITS
HS_BASE_CAPS
HS_BASE_DD
HS_CLASS_CAPS
HS_CLASS_DD
HS_CLASS_INIT
HS_EXTERNAL_OBJECT_PRIVILEGES
HS_EXTERNAL_OBJECTS
HS_EXTERNAL_USER_PRIVILEGES
HS_FDS_CLASS
HS_FDS_INST
HS_INST_CAPS
HS_INST_DD
HS_INST_INIT

Oracle Parallel Server/Real Application Clusters

The following views provide information about the status of the Oracle Parallel Server/Real Application Clusters environment. Note, however, that standard use of Real Application Clusters does not involve these type of locks and pings:

FILE_LOCK
FILE_PING

Remote procedure calls

The following views provide information about the status of remote procedure calls (RPCs):

```
DEFCALL
DEFDEFAULTDEST
DEFERRCOUNT
DEFERROR
DEFLOB
DEFPROPAGATOR
DEFSCHEDULE
DEFTRAN
DEFTRANDEST
ORA_KGLR7_DB_LINKS
ORA_KGLR7_DEPENDENCIES
ORA_KGLR7_IDL_CHAR
ORA_KGLR7_IDL_SB4
ORA_KGLR7_IDL_UB1
ORA_KGLR7_IDL_UB2
```

Snapshots

The following views provide information about snapshots or their replacement, materialized views (MVIEWS):

```
DBA_REGISTERED_SNAPSHOT_GROUPS
DBA_SNAPSHOT_LOG_FILTER_COLS
*_RCHILD
*_REFRESH
*_REFRESH_CHILDREN
*_REGISTERED_SNAPSHOTS/_REGISTERED_MVIEWS
*_RGROUP
*_SNAPSHOT_LOGS/MVIEW_LOGS
*_SNAPSHOT_REFRESH_TIMES/MVIEW_REFRESH_TIMES
*_SNAPSHOTS/MVIEWS
```

SQL*Loader

The following views provide information used by the SQL*Loader direct path option:

```
LOADER_CONSTRAINT_INFO
LOADER_FILE_TS
LOADER_PARAM_INFO
LOADER_PART_INFO
LOADER_TAB_INFO
LOADER_TRIGGER_INFO
```

The following views provide information required for tablespace point-in-time recovery (PITR):

> STRADDLING_RS_OBJECTS
> TS_PITR_CHECK
> TS_PITR_OBJECTS_TO_BE_DROPPED

Dynamic Data Dictionary Views

The dynamic performance data dictionary views (the V$ views) primarily cover information about the Oracle instance, as well as information that the instance maintains about the database. These views are considered dynamic because their contents change based upon how the instance is performing. The contents respond to the total workload, rather than to any one specific SQL statement or command.

Availability of Dynamic Data Dictionary Views

Specific dynamic performance data dictionary views are available based on the status of the instance, as follows:

- Dynamic performance data dictionary views that provide information specifically about the instance (e.g., V$PARAMETER). These are available immediately upon the instance being started.

- Dynamic performance data dictionary views that provide information stored in the control files. These are available once the database has been mounted (as noted in the view description).

- Dynamic performance data dictionary views that provide information about how the kernel is processing SQL statements. These are available once the database has been opened (as noted in the view description).

How Dynamic Data Dictionary Views Are Built

Unlike the static data dictionary views, which are views on existing tables, the dynamic performance data dictionary views are views on a set of tables that do not physically exist in the database; instead, they are actually views on X$ tables, which are representations of internal memory structures in the Oracle instance. For example:

- V$DATABASE is a public synonym for the view SYS.V_$DATABASE.
- SYS.V_$DATABASE is a view on SYS.V$DATABASE.
- V$DATABASE is a view on the memory structure X$KCCDI.

The exact specification of how the V$ views are built is maintained within the Oracle kernel. The view V$FIXED_VIEW_DEFINITION defines all V$ views as views based upon the X$ tables.

How these views are built is important to understanding how they work. Initially defined within the Oracle kernel, these hardcoded V$ tables are accessible once the instance has been started or once the database has been mounted. Once the database is opened, the normal SQL processing takes over, and the public synonyms referencing the views are used. With public synonyms, the same name is available whether you are CONNECTed INTERNAL before the database is opened, or are connected as a user with DBA privileges after the database is opened.

The relatively few V$ views that are available only once the database is open turn out to be true views, based upon X$ or other V$ tables.

Global Dynamic Performance Views (GV$ Views)

Beginning with Oracle8, the dynamic performance data dictionary views (V$ views) were augmented with a complementary set of global dynamic performance data dictionary views (GV$ views). The V$ views provide information about the instance to which you are connected and its management of the database. The GV$ views provide the same information for all other instances that have the same database mounted and are primarily of interest in a Real Applications Cluster or Oracle Parallel Server environment.

The global dynamic performance data dictionary views add the column INST_ID to their names, which allows you to identify the instance for which information is being provided.

Dynamic Views

This section summarizes the dynamic performance data dictionary views. For convenience, the dynamic performance data dictionary views are divided into families based upon general areas of functionality, which are listed alphabetically. Most of the views described in the following sections are listed as *$viewname*; the wildcard character (*) indicates that the view can be referenced either as V$*viewname* or GV$*viewname*.

Advanced Queuing

This view provides throughput statistics for the Advanced Queuing facility:

*$AQ
> Provides message statistics for each of the Advanced Queuing message queues. Available after database is opened.

Configuration

The following views provide information about the current configuration of the Oracle environment:

*$COMPATIBILITY
> Lists features in use by the current instance that would preclude reverting to a previous release of the Oracle software. Because these are instance based, some of the features may disappear if the database is shut down normally.

*$COMPATSEG
> Lists permanent features in the database that would preclude reverting to a previous release of the Oracle software.

*$EVENT_NAME
Contains descriptive information about all possible wait events.

*$LICENSE
Contains a single row specifying the maximum numbers of concurrent and named users allowed, as well as the highwater marks.

*$MLS_PARAMETERS
Lists the initialization parameters and their current values for Trusted Oracle. The format is the same as *$PARAMETER. Available after database is opened.

*$NLS_PARAMETERS
Contains the current values for each of the National Language Support (NLS) parameters.

*$NLS_VALID_VALUES
Lists the valid values that each of the NLS parameters can take.

*$OPTION
Lists the Oracle options that have been installed with the Oracle software.

*$PARAMETER
Lists all initialization parameters and their current settings. Also indicates whether the current value is specified in the initialization file or is the default value, as well as whether the parameter is modifiable with an ALTER SYSTEM or ALTER SESSION command.

*$RMAN_CONFIGURATION
Lists the persistent configuration parameters for RMAN, the standard Oracle backup and recovery utility (described in Chapter 15). New with Oracle9i.

*$SPPARAMETER
Lists the contents of the SPFILE. New with Oracle9i.

*$STATNAME
Lists the name for each statistic stored in *$SYSSTAT and *$SESSTAT.

*$SYSTEM_PARAMETER
Lists all initialization parameters and their current settings and indicates whether the current value is specified in the initialization file or is the default value, as well as whether the parameter is modifiable with an ALTER SYSTEM or ALTER SESSION command.

*$TIMEZONE_NAMES
Lists the names and accepted abbreviations for valid time zones for the Oracle database. New with Oracle9i.

*$VERSION
Lists current version numbers of the library components of the Oracle kernel.

Data dictionary cache

The following views provide information about how the Oracle kernel is managing the data dictionary and library caches:

$DB_OBJECT_CACHE
Lists tables, indexes, clusters, synonyms, PL/SQL procedures, packages, and triggers that are in the library cache.

$LIBRARYCACHE
Contains statistics about library cache performance.

$ROWCACHE
Contains statistics about data dictionary cache performance.

$SUBCACHE
Lists each subordinate cache in the library cache.

Database

The following views provide information about the physical database:

$CONTROLFILE
Provides the names of all control files.

$CONTROLFILE_RECORD_SECTION
Provides information about the amount of information stored in each section of the control file. Available after database is mounted.

$DATABASE
Provides information about the database that is stored in the control file. Available after database is mounted.

$DATAFILE
Contains information about each datafile, based upon information from the control file. Available after database is mounted.

$DATAFILE_HEADER
Contains information about each datafile, based upon information in the datafile header. Available after database is mounted.

$DBFILE
Contains the name for each datafile. Maintained for upward compatibility. Oracle recommends that you now use *$DATAFILE instead. Available after database is mounted.

$OFFLINE_RANGE
Provides information about the offline status of datafiles. The information is provided from the control file. Available after database is mounted.

$TABLESPACE
Provides information about tablespaces, based upon information in the control file. Available after database is mounted.

$TYPE_SIZE
Specifies the size in bytes for the various components of an Oracle data or index block.

*$UNDOSTAT
> Lists a variety of information about the use of undo space by the database. This information can be used to estimate the amount of undo space needed by the database and is used by the database to tune the use of undo space. New with Oracle9*i*.

V$FILESTAT
> Provides information about the I/O activity for each file used in the database. New with Oracle9*i*. Available after database is mounted.

Instance

The following views provide information related to the status of the instance:

*$BGPROCESS
> Provides information about each of the background processes.

*$INSTANCE
> Provides status information about the current instance.

Locks and latches

The following views provide information about the status of locks and latches within the instance:

*$ACCESS
> Lists all locked objects in the database and the sessions accessing these objects.

*$BUFFER_POOL
> Provides information about the available buffer pools. The number of buffer pools is related to the initialization parameter DB_BLOCK_LRU_LATCHES.

*$ENQUEUE_LOCK
> Lists all locks owned by enqueue state objects.

*$LATCH
> Provides statistics for all latches. If the latch is a parent latch, provides a summation of the statistics for each of its children latches. Available after database is opened.

*$LATCH_CHILDREN
> Provides statistics for all children latches.

*$LATCH_MISSES
> Provides statistics about all failures to acquire a latch.

*$LATCH_PARENT
> Provides statistics for all parent latches.

*$LATCHHOLDER
> Provides information about current latch holders.

*$LATCHNAME
> Provides a decoded latch name for every latch listed in *$LATCH. Available after database is mounted.

*$LOCK
Lists all locks held and all outstanding requests for locks or latches.

*$LOCKED_OBJECT
Lists all objects currently locked by transactions within the system.

*$RESOURCE
Contains the names, types, and addresses of all resources in the system.

Multi-Threaded Server/Shared Server

The following views provide information on how the Multi-Threaded Server (MTS) or Shared Server (with Oracle9i) systems are configured and performing:

*$CIRCUIT
Contains information about the virtual circuits used to connect users to the instance.

*$DISPATCHER
Provides information about the various configured dispatcher processes.

*$DISPATCHER_RATE
Provides statistics about the dispatcher processes' throughput.

*$MTS
Provides information about the overall activity of the MTS/Shared Server.

*$QUEUE
Provides statistics about the MTS message queue.

*$REQDIST
Provides a 12-bucket histogram of the distribution of request service times. This width-balanced histogram shows the number of hits in each of the 12 consistent times. The sizes of the buckets are allowed to change over time.

*$SHARED_SERVER
Shows the status of the each of the Shared Servers.

Oracle Parallel Server/Real Application Clusters

The following views are specific to an Oracle Parallel Server/Real Application Clusters environment:

*$ACTIVE_INSTANCES
Lists all current instances that have the database mounted.

*$BH
Provides the status and pings of every data buffer in the System Global Area (SGA). Available after database is opened.

*$CACHE
Provides information about the block header of every object the current instance has in its SGA. Available after database is opened.

*$CACHE_LOCK
Provides the lock status of every data block the current instance has in its SGA. Available after database is opened.

*$CLASS_PING

Shows statistics on the number of pings per data block class.

*$FALSE_PING

Lists buffers that are getting excessive pings because they are covered under a different lock. Buffers that are identified can be remapped using the initialization parameter GC_FILES_TO_LOCKS. Available after database is opened.

*$ENQUEUE_STAT

Lists statistics about each of the different types of enqueue request for a particular database instance. An enqueue is used to prevent multiple users or processes from writing to the same data block at the same time. New with Oracle9i.

*$FILES_CACHE_TRANSFER

Shows the number of block pings per datafile. Prior to Oracle9i this view was called *$FILE_PING. Available after database is mounted.

*$GCSHVMASTER

Tracks the mastering of Global Cache Service resources, except those that are in files that are mapped to a specific instance. New with Oracle9i.

*$GCSPFMASTER

Tracks the mastering of Global Cache Service resources that are in files that are mapped to a specific instance. New with Oracle9i.

*$GES_CONVERT_LOCAL

Shows elapsed times for local DLM lock conversions. Prior to Oracle9i this view was called *$DLM_CONVERT_LOCAL.

*$GES_CONVERT_REMOTE

Shows elapsed times for remote DLM lock conversions. Prior to Oracle9i this view was called *$DLM_CONVERT_REMOTE.

*$GES_LATCH

Shows the total count and number of immediate gets of DLM latches acquired by latch type. Prior to Oracle9i this view was called *$DLM_LATCH. Available after database is opened.

*$GES_LOCKS

Shows all DLM locks and lock requests that are blocked or are blocking other lock requests. Prior to Oracle9i this view was called *$DLM_LOCKS.

*$GES_MISC

Provides statistics on various DLM parameters. Prior to Oracle9i this view was called *$DLM_MISC.

*$HVMASTER

Tracks the mastering of Global Enqueue Service resources. New with Oracle9i.

*$LOCK_ACTIVITY

Provides an overall view of DLM locks within the current instance.

*$LOCK_ELEMENT

Provides information about each PCM lock in the data buffers.

*$LOCKS_WITH_COLLISIONS
Shows locks with high numbers of false pings.

*$PING
A subset of *$CACHE; shows only those buffers that have been pinged at least once. Available after database is opened.

Parallel Query

The following views provide information in support of Parallel Query operations:

*$EXECUTION
Provides information about each Parallel Query execution.

*$PQ_SESSTAT
Provides statistics on Parallel Query activity for the current session.

*$PQ_SLAVE
Provides statistics on each of the Parallel Query servers in the system.

*$PQ_SYSSTAT
Provides a summary of Parallel Query statistics for the entire system.

*$PQ_TQSTAT
Provides statistics for each Parallel Query session while it is active.

Recovery

The following views provide information about the current status of the online and offline redo logs, as well as backup processes controlled by the Recovery Manager (RMAN):

*$ARCHIVE
Lists redo logs that must be archived. Available after database is mounted.

*$ARCHIVE_DEST
Shows the status of all archive log destinations specified for the instance. See the discussion of the initialization parameters LOG_ARCHIVE_DEST, LOG_ARCHIVE_DUPLEX_DEST, and LOG_ARCHIVE_MIN_SUCCEED_DEST in Chapter 2.

*$ARCHIVE_DEST_STATUS
Provides runtime information about archived log redo destinations. Can be used to see the progress of archiving multiple redo logs to multiple locations. New with Oracle9i.

*$ARCHIVE_GAP
Provides information about any gaps in archived redo logs, which can block database recovery operations. New with Oracle9i.

*$ARCHIVED_LOG
Provides information from the control file for all archive logs, using a time-based view of the log files. Available after database is mounted.

$BACKUP

Shows the backup status of all online datafiles managed by RMAN. Available after database is mounted.

$BACKUP_CORRUPTION

Details any datafile corruption detected as part of a backup managed by RMAN. Available after database is mounted.

$BACKUP_DATAFILE

Shows the location of the backup datafile used by RMAN. Available after database is mounted.

$BACKUP_DEVICE

Provides a list of available backup devices supported by RMAN.

$BACKUP_PIECE

Provides information about each backup piece (a subset of an RMAN backup set). Available after database is mounted.

$BACKUP_REDOLOG

Provides information about archived redo logs that have been backed up by RMAN. Available after database is mounted.

$BACKUP_SET

Provides information about all RMAN backup sets. Available after database is mounted.

$COPY_CORRUPTION

Details any datafile corruption detected as part of a datafile copy managed by RMAN. Available after database is mounted.

$DATAFILE_COPY

Provides information about datafile copies from the control file. This information is maintained by RMAN. Available after database is mounted.

$DELETED_OBJECT

Provides information about archived redo logs, datafile pieces, and datafile copies that have been deleted from the control file. Available after database is mounted.

$LOG

Contains information about redo logs from the control file. Available after database is mounted.

$LOG_HISTORY

Contains information about archived redo logs from the control file. Provides an SCN view of the archived log files. Available after database is mounted.

$LOGFILE

Provides the current status of all redo logs. Available after database is mounted.

$LOGHIST

Contains redo log history from the control file. Oracle Corporation recommends that you now use *$LOG_HISTORY instead. Available after database is mounted.

$MANAGED_STANDBY

Views that contain information about various Data Guard processes. Can also be used to monitor the process of recovery with Data Guard. New with Oracle9*i*.

$RECOVER_FILE

Lists datafiles used in media recovery. Available after database is mounted.

$RECOVERY_FILE_STATUS

Contains information relevant to the current file recovery process. Available only to the Recovery Manager process, not to users. Available after database is mounted.

$RECOVERY_LOG

Contains derived information from *$LOG_HISTORY that is useful to the Recovery Manager process. Returns no rows when queried directly by users. Available after database is mounted.

$RECOVERY_PROGRESS

Contains a subset of *$SESSION_LONGOPS that provides the current status of recovery operations.

$RECOVERY_STATUS

Maintains current statistics for the recovery process. The information is available only to the Recovery Manager process and will return no rows when queried directly by users.

$STANDBY_LOG

Lists information on the redo logs for a standby database. New with Oracle9*i*.

$THREAD

Contains information about all current redo log threads from the control file. Available after database is mounted.

Replication

The following views help to monitor and understand the use of replication in the database:

$MVREFRESH

Provides information about any materialized views that are currently being refreshed. New with Oracle9*i*.

$REPLPROP

Provides information about how parallel propagation is operating as part of the replication process. New with Oracle9*i*.

$REPLQUEUE

Provides information about any deferred replication transactions. New with Oracle9*i*.

Resource allocation

The Database Resource Manager (DRM) can be used to set up rules on how to allocate resources between different groups of users. With Oracle9i, two dynamic views allow you to see the available resource allocation methods:

ACTIVE_SESSION_POOL_MTH
Lists all of the currently available active session pool resource allocation methods. New with Oracle9i.

QUEUEING_MTH
Lists all of the currently available queuing resource allocation methods. New with Oracle9i.

Security

The following views provide information about privileges:

$ENABLEDPRIVS
Lists all system privileges that are enabled for the current session. Includes those explicitly granted and those available through a role.

$PWFILE_USERS
Lists all users who have been identified in the password file as having SYSDBA or SYSOPER privileges.

Session

The following views provide information about the current Oracle session:

$MYSTAT
Provides information about current session statistics. One row exists for every entry in *$STATNAME.

$PROCESS
Lists each process in the instance. You can join this view to *$SESSION to gain more information.

$SESS_IO
Provides up-to-date I/O information for each session in the database. Available after database is opened.

$SESSION
Lists each session in the instance.

$SESSION_CONNECT_INFO
Provides information about the network connection of the current session.

$SESSION_CURSOR_CACHE
Provides information about the current session's cursor usage.

$SESSION_EVENT
Provides information about how much time each session spends waiting on each event specified in *$EVENT_NAME.

$SESSION_LONGOPS

Provides information about the status of long-running operations for sessions. Details the number of work units already accomplished and the expected amount of work required to complete the operation.

$SESSION_OBJECT_CACHE

Provides object cache statistics for the current session in the current instance.

$SESSION_WAIT

Lists the resources upon which each active session is waiting and how long each session has been waiting for each resource.

$SESSTAT

Provides information about each session's session statistics. There is one row for each session for each statistic specified in *$STATNAME.

SGA

The following views provide information about the System Global Area (SGA):

$CURRENT_BUCKET

Lists the number of increased buffer misses if the value of the DB_BLOCK_BUFFERS initialization parameter were to be reduced. Obsolete after Oracle 8.1. Available after database is opened.

$PGASTAT

Provides memory usage statistics that are used by the Oracle Memory Manager to allocate the maximum amount of memory a particular work area can have at any one time. New with Oracle9i.

$RECENT_BUCKET

Lists the number of increased buffer hits if the value of DB_BLOCK_BUFFERS were to be increased. See the initialization parameter DB_BLOCK_LRU_EXTENDED_STATISTICS in Chapter 2. Available after database is opened.

$SGA

Contains information about the size, in bytes, of each of the various SGA components.

$SGASTAT

Provides more detailed information about SGA utilization than *$SGA. Shows the breakdown of the SHARED_POOL and LARGE_POOL areas.

$SHARED_POOL_RESERVED

Contains statistics about the SHARED_POOL area of the SGA. Some of the columns are meaningful only if the initialization parameter SHARED_POOL_RESERVED_SIZE has been set.

$VPD_POLICY

Lists all the security policies and predicates that are associated with the cursors that are currently in the library cache. (VPD stands for Virtual Private Database, which we describe in Chapter 4. VPDs can be used to implement completely separate logical databases in the same Oracle database using fine-grained security policies.)

SQL

The following views provide information about the processing of all SQL statements in the instance:

$OBJECT_DEPENDENCY
Lists all objects that a package, procedure, or cursor in the SGA is depending upon. This view can be joined to the *$SQL and *$SESSION views to obtain a list of all objects being referenced by a user.

$OPEN_CURSOR
Lists all open cursors in the system.

$SORT_SEGMENT
Provides information about all sort segments in tablespaces specified as TEMPORARY.

$SORT_USAGE
Provides information about sort segments in all tablespaces.

$SQL
Provides information about all SQL statements in the shared SQL area.

$SQL_BIND_DATA
Provides information about bind variables in each SQL statement.

$SQL_BIND_METADATA
Provides metadata about all bind variables used in SQL statements.

$SQL_CURSOR
Provides debugging information about every cursor in the shared SQL area.

$SQL_PLAN
Shows the plan used to execute recent SQL statements. Similar to the information you would get from using the EXPLAIN PLAN command, except that this information is a log of the plan actually used, rather than a description of the plan that will probably be used. New with Oracle9i.

$SQL_REDIRECTION
Lists the SQL statements that have been redirected, along with the reason for the redirection, such as a query rewrite, with materialized views, or an invalid object that was referenced. New with Oracle9i.

$SQL_SHARED_MEMORY
Provides information about how memory is allocated for every cursor in the shared SQL area.

$SQL_WORKAREA
Provides information on resource usage for the work areas used by SQL cursors. New with Oracle9i.

$SQL_WORKAREA_ACTIVE
Provides instantaneous information on the currently active work areas. The information provided in this view is slightly different from that provided in the previous view. New with Oracle9i.

*$SQLAREA
Provides information on all SQL statements in the shared SQL area. Available after database is opened.

*$SQLTEXT
Provides the text of all SQL statements in the shared SQL area. All newline and tab information is replaced by spaces.

*$SQLTEXT_WITH_NEWLINES
Provides the text of all SQL statements in the shared SQL area, but includes the original newline and tab characters.

SQL*Loader direct path

The following views provide information relevant to the current SQL*Loader direct path operation:

*$LOADCSTAT
View in which Oracle stores statistics about the number of rows processed during the current load. However, because you cannot query the view when the load is in progress, all queries of the view return "no rows found."

*$LOADPSTAT
View used by SQL*Loader to track statistics for the current direct load. Because this information applies only to the current session, it will always return zero rows when queried by a user.

*$LOADTSTAT
View in which Oracle stores additional statistics about the number of rows discarded during the current load. However, because you cannot query the view when the load is in progress, all queries of the view return "no rows found."

System environment

The following views provide miscellaneous information about the current environment:

*$DB_PIPES
Provides information about database pipes currently defined in the database.

*$DBLINK
Provides information about all currently open database links.

*$FILESTAT
Provides information about the current read/write status of all datafiles.

*$FIXED_TABLE
Lists all *$ and X$ tables defined in the kernel.

*$FIXED_VIEW_DEFINITION
Provides a view definition for each dynamic performance view based upon the X$ tables.

$GLOBAL_TRANSACTION

Provides information on all current global transactions.

$INDEXED_FIXED_COLUMN

Lists each index column in the tables listed in *$FIXED_TABLE.

$RESOURCE_LIMIT

Shows the current utilization of system resources that can be specified in the initialization file. Shoes the initial allocation, the current usage, and the maximum allowed value for each resource.

$ROLLNAME

Lists the names of all rollback segments. Available after database is opened.

$ROLLSTAT

Provides statistics about each rollback segment.

$SYSSTAT

Provides the current values for each of the system statistics defined in *$STATNAME.

$SYSTEM_CURSOR_CACHE

Provides information about cursor usage across all sessions.

$SYSTEM_EVENT

Provides information about time spent waiting for each system event defined in *$EVENT_NAME.

$TIMER

Provides access to a timer that increments every one-hundredth of a second.

$TRANSACTION

Lists all active transactions in the system.

$TRANSACTION_ENQUEUE

Lists all enqueues held by active transactions in the system.

$WAITSTAT

Provides information about the number of waits and how long the system had to wait for each class of data block.

Data
Dictionary

Languages

This part of the book focuses on the syntax used to construct SQL statements and functions, PL/SQL programs, and Java interfaces to Oracle. It consists of the following chapters:

Chapter 7, *SQL*, summarizes the syntax of Oracle's SQL (Structured Query Language).

Chapter 8, *Functions*, summarizes the syntax of the functions that may be called from SQL and PL/SQL.

Chapter 9, *PL/SQL*, briefly describes the capabilities of Oracle's procedural language and summarizes the syntax of all statements.

Chapter 10, *PL/SQL Packages*, lists the header specifications for all of the procedures and functions included in Oracle's built-in packages, along with parameter descriptions.

Chapter 11, *Java and Oracle*, provides a summary of the Java interfaces to the Oracle database, including Java drivers available for Oracle, the mapping between Java datatypes and Oracle datatypes, and the syntax for the SQLJ and JDBC interfaces to Oracle.

7

SQL

Structured Query Language (SQL) has evolved over the years into the standard language for operations on relational databases. While each database vendor has implemented its own version of SQL, Oracle has remained fairly compliant with the ANSI SQL standard, although the company has certainly added its share of extensions and enhancements with each new release of the database.

SQL statements fall into two categories: Data Definition Language (DDL) and Data Manipulation Language (DML). You invoke DDL statements when you need to manipulate the structure of your Oracle database. You can use DDL statements to define, modify, and remove every type of object that can exist in an Oracle database. Many of the DDL statements require special database privileges and are normally executed by the DBA.

Data Manipulation Language (DML) statements, on the other hand, access and manipulate data stored in the Oracle database. You can use DML statements to insert, update, delete, and read data, as well as to control how Oracle operates when accessing data in the database.

This chapter provides a quick reference to the two types of SQL statements and their syntax. The common keywords and identifiers, summarized in the first section, apply to both types of statements.

Common Keywords and Identifiers

Many keywords are used in multiple SQL statements. To conserve pages, these common keywords are listed here, rather than repeated in each SQL statement in which they are used.

See also the discussion of datatypes in Appendix A, of expressions, operators, and conditions in Appendix B, of numeric format elements in Appendix C, and of date format elements in Appendix D.

alias
Alternate name by which an object, such as a table, can be referenced.

column
Name of a column in a table or view.

COMPRESS integer
Specifies that key compression be enabled during creation of an index. *integer* specifies the number of prefix columns to compress.

date
Specifies a date in Oracle date format. This date format must match the default date format for the database (see Appendix A).

dblink
Name of a database link, which provides access to schema objects that reside in a remote database.

expr
Any valid Oracle expression, usually involving one or more columns from the table, view, or snapshot. See Appendix B for details.

filename
Name of a file in operating system–specific format.

indexname
Name of an index. The name may be prefixed by the owner name (schema).

integer
Any number without a decimal point or decimal component.

LOGGING
Specifies that redo log records will be written during creation of the object. This is the default.

NOCOMPRESS
Specifies that key compression be disabled during index creation. This is the default.

NOLOGGING
Specifies that redo log records will not be written during creation of the object. This option generally speeds creation, but in the case of a database failure, the creation operation cannot be recovered by applying log files. Instead, the object must be re-created.

NOPARALLEL
Specifies that the operation be performed serially. This is the default.

OR REPLACE
Specifies that if the object being created already exists, then that object should be dropped and re-created without causing an error as a result of its prior existence.

PARALLEL [integer]
Specifies that Oracle will select a degree of parallelism equal to the number of CPUs available on all participating instances, multiplied by the value of the

PARALLEL_THREADS_PER_CPU initialization parameter. If *integer* is specified, it indicates the degree of parallelism.

partition_name
  Name of a partition.

schema
  Specifies the name of a schema, which is the Oracle user account that owns an object. If *schema* is not provided when referencing the name of an object, then the Oracle user currently logged into the session will be used as the schema by default.

subpartition_name
  Name of a subpartition.

table_name
  Name of a table. The name may be prefixed by the owner name (schema).

tablespace_name
  Name of a tablespace.

Common SQL Clauses

A clause is a set of keywords that are related and used as a unit in a variety of SQL statements. The commonly used SQL clauses are listed in this section. In the statement summaries later in this chapter, we simply reference their names and syntactical positions in the individual SQL syntax descriptions.

Autoextend_Clause

```
AUTOEXTEND
{OFF
| ON [NEXT integer [K | M]] [MAXSIZE {integer [K | M] | UNLIMITED}]
}
```

Specifies whether or not files will be permitted to grow in size. When files are allowed to grow in size, this clause also specifies the growth parameters.

Keywords

OFF
  Specifies that the autoextend feature should not be enabled and that the file will not be permitted to grow in size.

ON
  Specifies that when the file becomes full and additional space is requested, the file will be extended in size by the amount specified by the NEXT parameter, up to the limit specified by the MAXSIZE parameter.

NEXT
  Specifies the amount of space in bytes, kilobytes (K), or megabytes (M) that will be added to the file when growth occurs.

MAXSIZE
  Specifies the maximum size in bytes, kilobytes (K), or megabytes (M) for the file. The autoextend feature does not extend the file beyond this size.

UNLIMITED
  Specifies that the file is permitted to grow up to the capacity of the physical disk or the maximum size permitted by the operating system, whichever is less.

Column_Constraint_Clause

```
[CONSTRAINT constraint_name]
{ {NULL | NOT NULL}
| {UNIQUE | PRIMARY KEY (column[,column ...])}
| REFERENCES [schema.]table_name [(column[,column ...])
  [ON DELETE {CASCADE | SET NULL}]
| CHECK (condition)
}
[Constraint_State_Clause]
```

Defines column constraints.

Keywords

CONSTRAINT

Specifies the name for the constraint. If omitted, Oracle will assign a name in the form SYS_C*nnn*, where *nnn* is an integer number.

NULL

Specifies that the column may contain a value of NULL.

NOT NULL

Specifies that the column may not contain a value of NULL.

UNIQUE

Specifies that the value in this column must not duplicate a value for the same column in any other row of the table; that is, the value of this column must be unique for all rows of the table. Note, however, that more than one row may contain NULL in this column.

PRIMARY KEY

Specifies that the column or combination of columns serves as the primary key for the table in which it is defined. A primary key column may not contain NULL, and no value of the primary key may appear in the same column of any other row in the table (i.e., the key value must be unique).

REFERENCES

Specifies the table and column(s) that are referenced by a foreign key. The combination of referenced columns must represent either a PRIMARY KEY constraint or a UNIQUE constraint on the target table.

ON DELETE CASCADE

Specifies that when a row containing a primary or unique key is deleted, rows containing dependent foreign keys will also be automatically deleted.

ON DELETE SET NULL

Specifies that when a row containing a primary or unique key is deleted, dependent foreign keys will be automatically changed to NULL.

CHECK

Specifies a condition that must evaluate to TRUE or NULL for the constraint to be satisfied.

Constraint_State_Clause

Specifies how the constraint will be applied to data in the column. See the next section.

Constraint_State_Clause

```
{DEFERRABLE [INITIALLY {IMMEDIATE | DEFERRED}
| NOT DEFERRABLE [INITIALLY IMMEDIATE ]
}
{ INITIALLY IMMEDIATE  [[NOT] DEFERRABLE]
| INITIALLY  DEFERRED
}
[RELY | NORELY]
[USING INDEX
  [INITRANS integer]
  [MAXTRANS integer]
  [PCTFREE  integer]
  [TABLESPACE tablespace_name]
  [NOSORT]
  [LOGGING | NOLOGGING]
  [Storage_Clause]
  [ENABLE | DISABLE]
  [VALIDATE | NOVALIDATE]
  [EXCEPTIONS INTO [schema.]table_name]
]
```

Allows a constraint to be selectively enabled or disabled.

Keywords

DEFERRABLE

Specifies that the constraint may be deferred. A deferred constraint will not be checked until the transaction is committed.

INITIALLY IMMEDIATE

Specifies that the constraint should initially be evaluated immediately after the execution of each DML statement. The SET CONSTRAINTS statement may be used within a transaction to alter this behavior.

INITIALLY DEFERRED

Specifies that the constraint should initially be checked only when a transaction is committed. The SET CONSTRAINTS statement may be used within a transaction to alter this behavior.

NOT DEFERRABLE

Specifies that constraint checking may not be deferred for this constraint.

RELY

Specifies that a materialized view (or snapshot) will be eligible for query rewrite even if an associated constraint is not validated. This keyword is valid only for materialized views.

NORELY

Specifies that a materialized view (or snapshot) will be not be eligible for query rewrite if an associated constraint is not validated. This keyword is valid only for materialized views.

USING INDEX

Specifies that an index will be used to validate a unique or primary key constraint.

INITRANS

Specifies the initial number of transaction entries allocated in each data block of an index. One transaction entry is required for each concurrent transaction that updates the block.

MAXTRANS

Specifies the largest number of transaction entries that may be allocated in each data block for this index. This keyword limits the number of concurrent transactions that can update the block. The default is based on the block size.

PCTFREE

Specifies the percentage of space in each index block reserved for updates of index values.

TABLESPACE

Specifies the name of the tablespace in which the index for a constraint will be stored.

NOSORT

Specifies that the data rows are stored in the database in ascending order, so no sort is required when creating the index.

Storage_Clause

Specifies the storage characteristics for the index used to enforce the constraint. See the "Storage_Clause" entry later in this section.

ENABLE

Specifies that the constraint be applied immediately to all new data in the table or view.

DISABLE

Specifies that the constraint be disabled and not applied to data in the table or view.

VALIDATE

Specifies that any existing data in the table or view must comply with the constraint.

NOVALIDATE

Specifies that any existing data in the table or view should not be checked for compliance with the constraint.

EXCEPTIONS INTO

Specifies a table into which Oracle will place the row IDs of rows violating this constraint. The table must already exist and can be created with the script *ultexcpt1.sql*. Note that if you are going to specify EXCEPTIONS INTO, you must also specify VALIDATE.

Index_Attributes_Clause

```
[Physical_Attributes_Clause]
[Storage_Clause]
[{LOGGING | NOLOGGING}]
[ONLINE]
[COMPUTE STATISTICS]
[TABLESPACE {Tablespace_name | DEFAULT}]
[{COMPRESS integer | NOCOMPRESS}]
[{NOSORT | REVERSE}]
[{PARALLEL | NOPARALLEL}]
```

Specifies a set of physical and logical characteristics of an index..

Keywords

Physical_Attributes_Clause
> Specifies the physical attributes for the index; see the "Physical_Attributes_Clause" entry later in this section.

Storage_Clause
> Specifies the storage characteristics for the index. See the "Storage_Clause" entry later in this section.

ONLINE
> Specifies that DML operations on the indexed table will be permitted during index creation.

COMPUTE STATISTICS
> Specifies that statistics will be collected during the creation of an index.

TABLESPACE
> Specifies the name of the tablespace where this index will be stored. If you omit TABLESPACE, the default tablespace for the schema owner will be used. The keyword DEFAULT may also be specified.

NOSORT
> Specifies that the rows being indexed were loaded in ascending order and do not have to be sorted during index creation.

REVERSE
> Specifies that (except for ROWID) bytes of the index block will be stored in reverse order. This keyword cannot be used with NOSORT.

LOB_Parameter_Clause

```
[TABLESPACE tablespace_name]
[{ENABLE | DISABLE} STORAGE IN ROW]
[Storage_Clause]
[CHUNK integer]
[RETENTION]
[FREEPOOLS integer]
[PCTVERSION integer ]
[CACHE READS | NOCACHE [LOGGING | NOLOGGING]]
```

Specifies storage parameters to be applied to large object (LOB) data segments.

TABLESPACE
> Specifies the name of the tablespace in which the LOB will be stored.

ENABLE STORAGE IN ROW
> Specifies that the LOB data may be stored in the data row if its size is less than approximately 4000 bytes. This option is the default behavior.

DISABLE STORAGE IN ROW
> Specifies that the LOB data is always stored outside the data row.

STORAGE
> Specifies the storage parameters for the LOB segment. See the "Storage_Clause" entry later in this section for details.

CHUNK

Specifies that integer bytes should be allocated for LOB manipulation. Note that *integer* will be rounded up to a multiple of the Oracle block size.

PCTVERSION

Specifies the maximum percentage of LOB storage space to be used for creating new versions of the LOB. The default is 10%.

CACHE READS

Specifies that LOB data will be retained in memory for faster access.

NOCACHE

Specifies that LOB data will not be retained in memory. This option is the default behavior.

LOB_Storage_Clause

```
LOB
{(lob_item[,lob_item...]) STORE AS
 (LOB_Parameter_Clause)
|(lob_item) STORE AS [(lob_segname)]
 (LOB_Parameter_Clause)
}
```

Specifies how LOB data segments are to be stored in a table, partition, or subpartition.

Keywords

LOB   Specifies that LOB storage parameters are provided for the listed LOB items. Any unlisted LOB item will use the same storage parameters as the table, partition, or subpartition. Note that Oracle automatically creates a system-managed index for each LOB item listed with this keyword.

STORE AS   Indicates that the storage parameters to be applied immediately follow this keyword.

STORE AS lob_segname

Specifies the name of a LOB segment, which can be used only when listing a single LOB item.

Partition_Clause

```
{PARTITION BY RANGE (column[,column...])
 (PARTITION [partition_name]
   VALUES LESS THAN ({value | MAXVALUE}[,({value | MAXVALUE}...])
   [LOB_Storage_Clause]
   [Physical_Attributes_Clause]
   [TABLESPACE tablespace_name]
   [LOGGING | NOLOGGING]
   [{ SUBPARTITIONS integer [STORE IN (tablespace_name[,tablespace_name...]])
    | (SUBPARTITION [subpartition_name] [TABLESPACE tablespace_name]
        [LOB_Storage_Clause]
        [, SUBPARTITION [subpartition_name] [TABLESPACE tablespace_name]
          [LOB_Storage_Clause] ...])
     }
   [,(PARTITION [partition_name]
```

```
      VALUES LESS THAN ({value | MAXVALUE}[,({value | MAXVALUE}...)
      [LOB_Storage_Clause]
      [Physical_Attributes_Clause]
      [TABLESPACE tablespace_name]
      [LOGGING | NOLOGGING]
      [{ SUBPARTITIONS integer [STORE IN (tablespace_name[,tablespace_name ...])
       | (SUBPARTITION [subpartition_name] [TABLESPACE tablespace_name]
            [LOB_Storage_Clause]
            [, SUBPARTITION [subpartition_name] [TABLESPACE tablespace_name]
              [LOB_Storage_Clause] ...])
         }
| PARTITION BY LIST (column)
  (PARTITIONS partition_name VALUES ({value | NULL}
    [,{value | NULL}...]
  [Partition_Description_Clause]
  [,PARTITIONS partition_name VALUES ({value | NULL}
    [,{value | NULL}...]
  [Partition_Description_Clause]...])

| PARTITION BY HASH (column[,column ...])
  [{PARTITIONS integer [STORE IN (tablespace_name[,tablespace_name ...])
   | (PARTITION [partition_name] [TABLESPACE tablespace_name]
      [LOB_Storage_Clause]
      [, PARTITION [partition_name] [TABLESPACE tablespace_name]
      [LOB_Storage_Clause]
      ...]
    }
}
```

Specifies partitioning parameters and is also used to define range partitioning, composite partitioning, list partitioning, or hash partitioning.

Keywords

PARTITION BY RANGE
> Specifies that the table is to be partitioned by ranges of values in the listed columns.

PARTITION ... VALUES LESS THAN
> Specifies a name for the partition and one or more values (corresponding one-to-one with the column list of the PARTITION BY RANGE keyword) serving as maximum values for inclusion in the partition. The value list may contain the keyword MAXVALUE, which represents the highest possible value for a given column.

LOB_Storage_Clause
> Specifies the LOB storage parameters for this partition. See the previous entry, "LOB_Storage_Clause".

Physical_Attributes_Clause
> Specifies the physical attributes for this partition; see the "Physical_Attributes_ Clause" later in this section.

TABLESPACE
> Specifies the name of the tablespace in which this partition or subpartition will be stored.

SUBPARTITIONS

Specifies that *integer* subpartitions are to be created for this partition.

STORE IN

Specifies the name(s) of one or more tablespaces in which subpartitions are to be created. New with Oracle8i.

SUBPARTITION

Specifies subpartitions by name.

PARTITION BY LIST

Specifies that partitions are to be created using an explicit list of values. New with Oracle9i.

PARTITION BY HASH

Specifies that hash subpartitions are to be created based on the column list supplied. New with Oracle8i.

PARTITIONS

Specifies that *integer* partitions are to be created.

PARTITION

Specifies the name for a partition. If *partition_name* is omitted, Oracle assigns a name using the format SYS_P*nnn*, where *nnn* is a sequential number maintained by Oracle.

 Partitioning is an extra-cost option and is available only in the Oracle Enterprise Edition.

Partition_Description_Clause

```
[Physical_Attributes_Clause]
[TABLESPACE tablespace_name]
[LOGGING | NOLOGGING]
[COMPRESS integer | NOCOMPRESS]
[OVERFLOW [Physical_Attributes_Clause]
  [TABLESPACE tablespace_name]
  [LOGGING | NOLOGGING]]
[{LOB_Storage_Clause| Varray_Storage_Clause}
  [,{LOB_Storage_Clause| Varray_Storage_Clause}...]]
[{SUBPARTITIONS integer [STORE IN (tablespace_name[,tablespace_name ...])]}
  | SUBPARTITION [subpartition_name] [TABLESPACE tablespace_name]
  [OVERFLOW [TABLESPACE tablespace_name]]
  [{LOB_Storage_Clause| Varray_Storage_Clause}
    [,{LOB_Storage_Clause| Varray_Storage_Clause}...]]
  [,SUBPARTITION [subpartition_name] [TABLESPACE tablespace_name]
  [OVERFLOW [TABLESPACE tablespace_name]]
  [{LOB_Storage_Clause| Varray_Storage_Clause}
    [,{LOB_Storage_Clause| Varray_Storage_Clause}...]
  ...)]
}]
```

Specifies various physical storage parameters for partitions.

Keywords

Physical_Attributes_Clause
> Specifies the physical attributes for this partition; see the next entry, "Physical_Attributes_Clause".

LOB_Storage_Clause
> Specifies the LOB storage parameters for this partition. See the "LOB_Storage_Clause" entry earlier in this section.

OVERFLOW
> Specifies that table rows of an index-organized table that exceed the PCTTHRESHOLD value be placed in a segment described in this clause.

Physical_Attributes_Clause

```
[INITRANS integer]
[MAXTRANS integer]
[PCTFREE integer]
[PCTUSED integer]
```

Specifies schema object characteristics affecting space utilization in an Oracle block.

Keywords

INITTRANS
> Specifies the number of transaction entries allocated to each block of the object. The allowed range of values is 1 to 255 and should not normally be changed from the default of 1 (although a value as high as 4 to 8 may be beneficial for an OLTP system with a high transaction rate).

MAXTRANS
> Specifies the maximum number of concurrent transactions that can update a block of the object. Values are 1 to 255 and should not normally be changed from the default. The default is a function of the Oracle block size.

PCTFREE
> Specifies the percentage of space in each data block kept free for future updates to the object. The permissible range of values is 0 to 99. The default value is 10.

PCTUSED
> Specifies the percentage of space in each data block that Oracle attempts to keep filled. The permissible range of values is 0 to 99, and the default is 40. Note that this keyword does not apply to indexes.

Storage_Clause

```
STORAGE (
  [INITIAL integer [K | M]]
  [NEXT integer [K | M]]
  [MINEXTENTS integer]
  [MAXEXTENTS [integer | UNLIMITED] ]
  [PCTINCREASE integer ]
  [FREELISTS integer ]
  [FREELIST GROUPS integer ]
  [OPTIMAL [integer [K | M]]]
  [BUFFER_POOL {KEEP | RECYCLE | DEFAULT}]
)
```

Specifies how storage within an Oracle tablespace is allocated to an individual object.

Keywords

STORAGE

Specifies the database object's physical storage characteristics.

INITIAL

Specifies the size of the first extent for the database object in bytes, kilobytes (K), or megabytes (M). If this size is not a multiple of the database block size, it will be rounded up to a multiple of the database block size.

NEXT

Specifies the size of the next extent for the database object in bytes, kilobytes (K), or megabytes (M). If this size is not a multiple of the database block size, it will be rounded up to a multiple of the database block size.

MINEXTENTS

Specifies the number of extents to be allocated when the database object is created. The minimum and default value is 1, except for rollback segments, which have a minimum and default of 2.

MAXEXTENTS

Specifies the maximum number of extents that may be allocated for the database object. The default varies according to the database block size. If the keyword UNLIMITED is specified, there is no upper limit to the number of extents allowed.

PCTINCREASE

Specifies the percentage by which each extent grows over the previous extent. The default is 50, which means that each extent will be one and one-half times larger than the previous extent.

> Because extent growth will be difficult to manage if PCTIN-CREASE is set, it is probably best to set PCTINCREASE to 0 and define appropriately sized INITIAL and NEXT values.

FREELISTS

Specifies the number of freelists contained in each freelist group for this database object. The default is 1, and the maximum depends on the database block size. Systems with high insert rates will benefit from FREELISTS set between 2 and 4.

FREELIST GROUPS

Specifies the number of groups of free lists for this database object. The default is 1. This parameter should be used only in an Oracle Parallel Server or Real Application Clusters environment.

OPTIMAL

For rollback segments only. The integer specifies the optimal size Oracle attempts to maintain by deallocating unused rollback segment extents. If no size is specified, the rollback segment will never be reduced in size. The default behavior, which you get when you omit the OPTIMAL clause, is to never shrink rollback segments at all.

BUFFER_POOL
Specifies how schema objects are to be assigned to buffer pools:

KEEP
Object will be assigned to the KEEP buffer pool and retained in memory permanently, if possible.

RECYCLE
Object will be assigned to the RECYCLE buffer pool and removed from memory as soon as it is not needed.

DEFAULT
Object will be assigned to the DEFAULT buffer pool, which will utilize the standard least recently used (LRU) algorithm for buffer reuse.

Note that the KEEP and RECYCLE pools must be configured by the DBA prior to use.

Table_Constraint_Clause

```
[CONSTRAINT constraint_name]
{{UNIQUE | PRIMARY KEY} (column[,column ...])
| CHECK (condition)
| FOREIGN KEY (column[,column ...])
   REFERENCES [schema.] table_name [(column[,column ...])]
   [ON DELETE {CASCADE | SET NULL}]
}
[Constraint_State_Clause]
```

Defines constraints on a table.

Keywords

CONSTRAINT
Specifies a name for the constraint. If omitted, Oracle assigns a name in the form SYS_C*nnn*, where *nnn* is an integer number.

UNIQUE
Specifies that the value in the columns identified by *column* must not duplicate a value for the same column(s) in any other row of the table. The value of the column(s) in the constraint must be unique for each row in the table. Note, however, that more than one column may contain the value NULL.

PRIMARY KEY
Specifies that the column(s) identified by *column* will serve as the primary key for the table in which it is defined. A primary key column must not contain NULL, and no value of the primary key may appear in the same column(s) of any other row in the table.

CHECK
Specifies a condition that must evaluate to TRUE or NULL for the constraint to be satisfied.

FOREIGN KEY
Specifies that one or more columns in this table participate in a foreign key referential integrity relationship.

SQL

REFERENCES

Specifies the table and column(s) that are referenced by this foreign key constraint.

ON DELETE CASCADE

Specifies that when a row containing a primary or unique key is deleted, dependent foreign keys will be deleted automatically.

ON DELETE SET NULL

Specifies that when a row containing a primary or unique key is deleted, dependent foreign keys will be changed to NULL automatically.

Constraint_State_Clause

Specifies how the constraint will be applied to data in the table. See the "Constraint_State_Clause" entry earlier in this section.

Varray_Storage Clause

```
VARRAY varray_item
{ {[ELEMENT] IS OF [TYPE] (ONLY type)
  | [NOT] SUBSTITUTABLE AT ALL LEVELS
  }
| STORE AS LOB
  { LOB_segname
    [([TABLESPACE tablespace_name]
    [{ENABLE | DISABLE} STORAGE IN ROW]
    [Storage_Clause]
    [CHUNK integer]
    [PCTVERSION integer ]
    [CACHE | NOCACHE [LOGGING | NOLOGGING]]
    )]
  | ([TABLESPACE tablespace_name]
    [{ENABLE | DISABLE} STORAGE IN ROW]
    [Storage_Clause]
    [CHUNK integer]
    [PCTVERSION integer ]
    [CACHE | NOCACHE [LOGGING | NOLOGGING]]
    )
  }
}
```

Defines the storage characteristics of a VARRAY (variable array, a type of Oracle collection). New with Oracle8i.

varray_item   Specifies the name of the VARRAY item.

ELEMENT   Specifies that the element type of a collection column or attribute is to be constrained to a subtype of its declared *type*.

IS OF TYPE   Specifies that the type of the object column is to be constrained to a subtype of its declared *type*.

NOT SUBSTITUTABLE AT ALL LEVELS

Specifies that the object column cannot hold instances corresponding to any of its subtypes and that substitution is disabled for any embedded object attributes and elements of embedded nested tables and VARRAYs. The default is SUBSTITUTABLE AT ALL LEVELS.

STORE AS LOB
> Specifies that the VARRAY is to be stored as a LOB and that the storage parameters to be applied follow this keyword.

TABLESPACE
> Specifies the name of the tablespace in which the LOB will be stored.

ENABLE STORAGE IN ROW
> Specifies that the LOB data may be stored in the data row if its size is less than approximately 4000 bytes. This option is the default behavior.

DISABLE STORAGE IN ROW
> Specifies that the LOB data is always stored outside the data row.

STORAGE　Specifies the storage parameters for the LOB segment. See the "Storage_ Clause" entry earlier in this section.

CHUNK　Specifies that integer bytes should be allocated for LOB manipulation. Note that *integer* will be rounded up to a multiple of the Oracle block size.

PCTVERSION
> Specifies the maximum percentage of LOB storage space to be used for creating new versions of the LOB. The default is 10 percent.

CACHE　Specifies that LOB data will be retained in memory for faster access.

NOCACHE　Specifies that LOB data will not be retained in memory. This option is the default behavior.

Data Definition Statements

Data Definition Language (DDL) statements are used to create and maintain Oracle database objects. Because DDL statements can perform so many different functions, there are a large number of them, and many have a wide range of options and syntax choices. This section provides a reference to the syntax of these DDL SQL statements. (Data Manipulation Language, or DML, statements are described separately later in this chapter.)

In many cases, multiple DDL statements may operate on the same object type. For example, CREATE TABLE, ALTER TABLE, and DROP TABLE are all related DDL statements that operate on Oracle tables. For convenience, we have grouped these related DDL statements together in a single list. When you see a heading like CREATE/ALTER/DROP TABLE, this means that we provide the syntax for all three statements under that heading.

Many DDL statements are normally used only for administration of a database and are typically issued by a DBA. For this reason, many statements require specific privileges. Some statements also apply only when specific Oracle options, such as the Partition Option or Real Application Clusters, are installed.

ALTER RESOURCE COST

```
ALTER RESOURCE COST
[CPU_PER_SESSION weight]
[CONNECT_TIME weight]
[LOGICAL_READS_PER_SESSION weight]
[PRIVATE_SGA weight]
```

Modifies the formula used to calculate the session's total resource cost. This cost may then be limited by the COMPOSITE_LIMIT parameter in a user's profile.

 The total resource cost is calculated by multiplying the amount of each resource used in the session by the weight assigned to that resource and adding the products for all four resources. The result is expressed in service units. You must activate the ALTER RESOURCE COST privilege to issue this statement.

Keywords

CPU_PER_SESSION
  Specifies the amount of CPU time used in a session (in hundredths of a second).

CONNECT_TIME
  Specifies the total elapsed time for a session (in minutes).

LOGICAL_READS_PER_SESSION
  Specifies the number of database blocks read in a session, including those read from memory and disk.

PRIVATE_SGA
  Specifies the amount of memory a session can allocate in the shared pool of the System Global Area (SGA) (in bytes). Applies only when using the Multi-Threaded Server/Shared Server and allocating private space in the SGA for the session.

weight
  Integer weight of each resource.

ALTER SYSTEM

```
ALTER SYSTEM
{SET
 {[RESOURCE_LIMIT = TRUE | FALSE] |
  [GLOBAL_NAMES = TRUE | FALSE] |
  [MTS_SERVERS = integer] |
  [MTS_DISPATCHERS = 'protocol, integer'] |
  [LICENSE_MAX_SESSIONS = integer] |
  [LICENSE_SESSIONS_WARNING = integer] |
  [LICENSE_MAX_USERS = integer] |
 }
  [COMMENT 'text']
  [DEFERRED]
  [SCOPE = {MEMORY | SPFILE | BOTH}]
  [SID = {'sid' | .}]
| [RESET
```

```
{[RESOURCE_LIMIT = TRUE | FALSE] |
 [GLOBAL_NAMES = TRUE | FALSE] |
 [MTS_SERVERS = integer] |
 [MTS_DISPATCHERS = 'protocol, integer'] |
 [LICENSE_MAX_SESSIONS = integer] |
 [LICENSE_SESSIONS_WARNING = integer] |
 [LICENSE_MAX_USERS = integer]
}]
 [SCOPE = {MEMORY | SPFILE | BOTH}]
 [SID = {'sid' | *}]
| [{ENABLE | DISABLE} RESTRICTED SESSION]
| [FLUSH SHARED POOL]
| [CHECKPOINT [{GLOBAL | LOCAL}]]
| [CHECK DATAFILES {GLOBAL | LOCAL}]
| [SWITCH LOGFILE]
| [{ENABLE | DISABLE} DISTRIBUTED RECOVERY]
| [QUIESCE RESTRICTED | UNQUIESCE]
| [SHUTDOWN [IMMEDIATE] dispatcher_name]
| [REGISTER]
| [{SET | RESET} parameter_name
     [SCOPE={MEMORY | SPFILE | BOTH}] [SID = 'sid'[,sid...]]]
| [SUSPEND | RESUME]
| [KILL SESSION 'sid_integer, session_integer' [IMMEDIATE]]
| [DISCONNECT SESSION 'sid_integer, session_integer '
    [POST_TRANSACTION | IMMEDIATE]
| [ARCHIVE_LOG [THREAD integer]
  {[START [TO 'destination']]
  | [STOP]
  | [SEQUENCE integer [TO 'destination']]
  | [CHANGE integer [TO 'destination']]
  | [CURRENT [TO 'destination']]
  | [GROUP integer [TO 'destination']]
  | [LOGFILE 'filename' [TO 'destination']]
  | [NEXT [TO 'destination']]
  | [ALL [TO 'destination']]
  }
}
```

Makes dynamic changes to a database instance.

 Except as noted in the following keyword descriptions, the database must be mounted and open to use the ALTER SYSTEM statement.

Keywords

RESOURCE_LIMIT
> Specifies whether resource limits will be enforced (TRUE) or not enforced (FALSE).

GLOBAL_NAMES
> Specifies whether global naming will be enforced (TRUE) or not enforced (FALSE).

MTS_SERVERS

Changes the minimum number of shared Multi-Threaded Server/Shared Server processes.

MTS_DISPATCHERS

Changes the number of dispatcher processes for the named protocol. The database must be open to issue this statement.

LICENSE_MAX_SESSIONS

Specifies the maximum number of sessions permitted on this instance. A value of 0 indicates no limit.

LICENSE_SESSIONS_WARNING

Specifies the maximum number of sessions permitted on this instance before a warning message is written to the alert log file. A value of 0 indicates no limit.

LICENSE_MAX_USERS

Specifies the maximum number of users in this database. A value of 0 indicates no limit.

COMMENT

Specifies a comment string that will be associated with this change in the value of the parameter. If you also specify SPFILE, this comment will appear in the initialization parameter file to indicate the most recent change made to this parameter. New with Oracle9i.

DEFERRED

Specifies that the parameter change is to be effective for future sessions but that current sessions retain the old value. New with Oracle9i.

SCOPE

Specifies when the change takes effect, depending on whether you are started up the database using a parameter file (INITsid_ORA) or a server parameter file (SPFILE). If a server parameter file was used to start up the database, BOTH is the default. New with Oracle9i.

MEMORY

Specifies that the change is made in memory, takes effect immediately, and persists until the database is shut down. If you started up the database using a parameter file, this is the only scope you can specify.

SPFILE

Specifies that the change is made in the server parameter file and that the new setting takes effect when the database is next shut down and started up again. You must specify SPFILE when changing the value of a static parameter.

BOTH

Specifies that the change is made in memory and in the server parameter file. The new setting takes effect immediately and persists after the database is shut down and started up again.

SID

Specifies the SID of the instance where the value will take effect. Specify SID = 'sid' if you want Oracle to change the value of the parameter only for the instance sid, or specify SID = * if you want Oracle to change the value of the parameter for all instances. This clause is used only in a Real Application Cluster and is new with Oracle9i.

ENABLE RESTRICTED SESSION

Allows only users with the RESTRICTED SESSION privilege to log on to the instance. The database may be dismounted, mounted, open, or closed when issuing this statement.

DISABLE RESTRICTED SESSION

Allows any user with the CREATE SESSION privilege to log on to the instance. The database may be dismounted, mounted, open, or closed when issuing this statement.

FLUSH SHARED POOL

Clears all data from the instance's shared pool. The database may be dismounted, mounted, open, or closed when issuing this statement.

CHECKPOINT

Causes Oracle to perform a global or local checkpoint. GLOBAL performs a checkpoint for all instances that have opened the database; LOCAL performs a checkpoint for only the instance to which you are connected. The database may be open or closed when issuing this statement.

CHECK DATAFILES

Verifies access to online datafiles. GLOBAL verifies that all instances that have opened the database can access the datafiles, while LOCAL verifies that the instance to which you are connected can access the datafiles. The database may be open or closed when issuing this statement.

SWITCH LOGFILE

Causes Oracle to switch redo log file groups.

ENABLE DISTRIBUTED RECOVERY

Specifies that distributed recovery is to be enabled and, in a single-process environment, is used to initiate distributed recovery.

DISABLE DISTRIBUTED RECOVERY

Specifies that distributed recovery is to be disabled.

QUIESCE RESTRICTED

Specifies that the database is to be placed in a quiesced state, which enables DBAs to perform administrative operations that cannot be safely performed in the presence of concurrent transactions, queries, or PL/SQL operations. New with Oracle9i.

UNQUIESCE

Specifies that the database is to be taken out of a quiesced state. New with Oracle9i.

DISCONNECT SESSION

Disconnects the specified session from the database by killing the dedicated server process or the MTS virtual circuit.

POST_TRANSACTION

Specifies that ongoing transactions be completed before the session is disconnected.

IMMEDIATE

Specifies that the session be disconnected immediately, without waiting for transactions to complete. If POST_TRANSACTION is specified, this keyword will be ignored.

KILL SESSION

Terminates a session using SID and SERIAL# from the V$SESSION view. If the session is waiting for an activity, such as an operation on a remote database, to complete, Oracle will wait until this activity is complete unless IMMEDIATE is specified.

SUSPEND

Specifies that all I/O activity for all instances should be suspended until an ALTER SYSTEM RESUME statement is issued. All tablespaces should be in hot backup mode before you issue this statement. New with Oracle8*i*.

RESUME

Specifies that normal I/O operations should be resumed following an ALTER SYSTEM SUSPEND statement.

ARCHIVE_LOG

Manually archives redo log file groups or enables/disables automatic archiving.

SET *parameter_name*

Specifies that a dynamically modifiable initialization parameter is to be set. (For more information on initialization parameters, see Chapter 2.) New with Oracle9*i*.

SCOPE

Specifies how changes to dynamic initialization parameters are to be handled:

MEMORY

Sets the parameter for the running instance, but does not change the *SPFILE*.

SPFILE

Changes the value of this parameter in the *SPFILE*, but does not apply it to the running instance.

BOTH

Sets the parameter for the running instance and also saves it in the *SPFILE*.

SID

Specifies the SID of the instance where the value will take effect in a Parallel Server or Real Application Clusters environment. Specify SID = * if you want Oracle to change the value of the parameter for all instances

THREAD

Specifies the thread containing the redo log file group to be archived. This parameter is required only when running the Parallel Server or Real Application Clusters option in parallel mode.

START

Enables automatic archiving of redo log groups.

STOP

Disables automatic archiving of redo log groups.

SEQUENCE

Specifies the log sequence number of the redo log file group to be manually archived. The database must be mounted but may be open or closed to specify SEQUENCE.

CHANGE

Manually archives the online redo log file group containing the redo log entry with the System Change Number (SCN) specified by the integer. If the SCN is the current log group, a log switch is performed. The database must be open to specify CHANGE.

CURRENT
> Manually forces a log switch and archives the current redo log file group. The database must be open to specify CURRENT.

GROUP
> Manually archives the online redo log file group with the specified GROUP value, which can be found in the DBA_LOG_FILES parameter in the initialization file. The database must be mounted but may be open or closed to specify GROUP.

LOGFILE
> Manually archives the online redo log file group containing the log file member identified by *filename*. The database must be mounted but may be open or closed to specify LOGFILE.

NEXT
> Manually archives the next online redo log file group that is full but has not yet been archived. The database must be mounted but may be open or closed to specify NEXT.

ALL
> Manually archives all online redo log file groups that are full but that have not yet been archived. The database must be mounted but may be open or closed to specify ALL.

Common keywords and clauses: *filename*, *integer*.

ASSOCIATE STATISTICS

```
ASSOCIATE STATISTICS WITH
{COLUMNS [schema.] table_name.column[, [schema.] table_name.column...]
| FUNCTIONS [schema.]function[,[schema.]function...]
| PACKAGES [schema.]package[,[schema.]package...]
| INDEXES [schema.]index[,[schema.]index...]
}
{USING [schema.]statistics_type
| DEFAULT COST (cpu_cost,io_cost,network_cost)
| DEFAULT SELECTIVITY default_selectivity
| TYPES [schema.]type[,[schema.]type...]
}
```

Defines how statistics are to be computed for the specified database objects. To remove or disassociate statistics from an object, use the DISASSOCIATE STATISTICS statement. New with Oracle8*i*.

Keywords

COLUMNS   Specifies that a list of columns will be provided.

FUNCTIONS Specifies that one or more functions will be associated.

PACKAGES   Specifies that one or more packages will be associated.

INDEXES   Specifies that one or more indexes will be associated.

USING statistics_type
> Specifies the statistics type being associated.

DEFAULT COST
> Specifies that default costs will be provided for CPU, I/O, and the network. This keyword is not valid if the COLUMNS keyword is used.

cpu_cost	Integer representing the CPU cost of a single execution or access.
io_cost	Integer representing the I/O cost of a single execution or access.
network_cost	Integer representing the network cost of a single execution or access.

DEFAULT SELECTIVITY default_selectivity
> Specifies an integer between 1 and 100, representing the default selectivity as a percentage. This keyword is not valid if the COLUMNS keyword is used.

TYPES   Specifies that one or more types will be associated.

Common keywords and clauses: *schema, table_name.*

AUDIT (Schema Objects)

```
AUDIT {object_option[,object_option ...] | ALL}
ON {[schema.]object_name | DIRECTORY directory_name | DEFAULT}
[BY SESSION [WHENEVER [NOT] SUCCESSFUL]
[BY ACCESS [WHENEVER [NOT] SUCCESSFUL]
```

Sets up auditing for a specific schema object.

Keywords

object_option Indicates that a particular operation will be audited. The following operations are valid: ALTER, AUDIT, COMMENT, DELETE, EXECUTE, GRANT, INDEX, INSERT, LOCK, RENAME, SELECT, and UPDATE. The keyword ALL specifies all of these operations.

object_name Name of the schema object to be audited.

DIRECTORY directory_name
> Specifies the name of a directory to audit.

DEFAULT   Establishes the specified object option as the default for objects that have not yet been created.

BY SESSION Causes Oracle to write a single record for all SQL statements of the same type issued in the same session.

BY ACCESS Causes Oracle to write a single record for each audited statement.

WHENEVER SUCCESSFUL
> Chooses auditing only for SQL statements that complete successfully.

WHENEVER NOT SUCCESSFUL
> Chooses auditing only for SQL statements that fail or result in errors.

Common keywords and clauses: *schema.*

AUDIT (SQL Statements)

```
AUDIT {system_option | sql_option}[,{system_option | sql_option ...}]
{[BY username[,username ...]]
| [BY proxy [ON BEHALF OF {ANY | username[,username]] }
}
{[BY SESSION] [WHENEVER [NOT] SUCCESSFUL]
| [BY ACCESS] [WHENEVER [NOT] SUCCESSFUL]
}
```

Sets up auditing for specific SQL statements in subsequent user sessions. Audit records are written to the audit trail, which is a database table containing audit records that can be accessed through data dictionary views. Auditing must be enabled using the AUDIT_TRAIL parameter in the initialization file. (See Chapter 2 for information on auditing parameters.)

Keywords

system_option
Specifies that SQL statements authorized by the named system privilege be audited. See Chapter 4 for details.

sql_option
Specifies a set of SQL statements to be audited. See Chapter 4 for details.

BY username Specifies that SQL statements issued by the named user be audited.

BY proxy Specifies that SQL statements issued by the specified proxy be audited.

ON BEHALF OF ANY
Specifies that SQL statements issued on behalf of any user be audited.

ON BEHALF OF username
Specifies the user on whose behalf the proxy executes the specified statement.

BY SESSION Causes Oracle to write a single record for all SQL statements of the same type issued in the same session.

BY ACCESS Causes Oracle to write a single record for each audited statement.

WHENEVER SUCCESSFUL
Chooses auditing only for SQL statements that complete successfully.

WHENEVER NOT SUCCESSFUL
Chooses auditing only for SQL statements that fail or result in errors.

CALL

CALL [*schema.*][*package.*]{*function* | *procedure*}[*@dblink*]
   (*expr*[,*expr* ...]) [INTO :*host_variable* [[INDICATOR] :*indicator_variable*]]

Executes a stored PL/SQL function or procedure.

Keywords

package Name of the package that contains the function or procedure.

function Name of a function to be executed.

procedure Name of a procedure to be executed.

expr Argument to the function or procedure.

INTO Specifies (for a function) the name of the host variable that will hold the return value.

INDICATOR Specifies the name of a variable that will indicate the condition of the host variable.

Common keywords and clauses: *dblink, expr, schema.*

COMMENT

```
COMMENT ON
{TABLE [schema.]{ table_name | view | snapshot}
| COLUMN [schema.]{ table_name | view | snapshot}.column
}
IS 'text'
```

Adds a comment about a table, view, snapshot, or column into the data dictionary.

Keywords

TABLE Specifies that the comment be associated with a table, view, or snapshot.

view Name of a view with which the comment will be associated.

snapshot Name of a snapshot with which the comment will be associated.

COLUMN Specifies that the comment be associated with a column.

text Actual text of the comment. This text will be recorded in the data dictionary.

Common keywords and clauses: *schema, table_name*.

CREATE/ALTER/DROP CLUSTER

CREATE Syntax:
```
CREATE CLUSTER [schema.]cluster_name
(column  datatype[, column  datatype ...])
[Physical_Attributes_Clause]
[SIZE integer [K | M]]
[TABLESPACE tablespace_name]
[Storage_Clause]
[INDEX]
[[SINGLE TABLE] HASHKEYS integer HASH IS expr]
[{PARALLEL [integer] | NOPARALLEL}]
[CACHE | NOCACHE]
```

ALTER Syntax:
```
ALTER CLUSTER [schema.]clustername
[SIZE integer [K | M]]
[Physical_Attributes_Clause]
[Storage_Clause]
[PARALLEL [integer] | NOPARALLEL]
[ALLOCATE EXTENT
  (EXTSIZE integer [K | M] [DATAFILE 'filename'] [INSTANCE integer])]
```

DROP Syntax:
```
DROP CLUSTER [schema.]clustername
[INCLUDING TABLES]
[CASCADE CONSTRAINTS]
```

Creates, modifies, or drops a cluster, which is a schema object containing one or more tables with one or more columns in common. Clustering can improve database performance and efficiency. With clustering, common columns are stored only once, and the data from all tables is normally stored contiguously.

Keywords

cluster_name Name of the cluster.

datatype Datatype of the column.

TABLESPACE
> Specifies the name of the tablespace where this cluster will be stored. If omitted, the default tablespace for the schema owner will be used.

INDEX Specifies that an indexed cluster be created. This keyword is not valid for a hash cluster.

SINGLE TABLE
> Specifies that this cluster is a special type containing only one table. New with Oracle8*i*.

HASHKEYS *integer*
> Specifies that a hash cluster be created with *integer* hash keys.

HASH IS *expr*
> Specifies an expression to be used as the hash function for the hash cluster.

CACHE Specifies that the blocks retrieved for this table be placed at the most recently used end of the buffer cache when a full table scan is performed.

NOCACHE Specifies that the blocks retrieved for this table be placed at the least recently used end of the buffer cache when a full table scan is performed. This is the default.

EXTSIZE *integer*
> Specifies the size of the new extent in bytes, kilobytes (K), or megabytes (M).

DATAFILE Specifies the name of the operating system datafile in the tablespace containing this cluster that is to hold the new extent. If omitted, Oracle will select a datafile.

INSTANCE Makes the new extent available to the specified instance, which is identified by the initialization parameter INSTANCE_NUMBER. This parameter can be used only when running in parallel mode.

INCLUDING TABLES
> Specifies that all tables belonging to the cluster be dropped.

CASCADE CONSTRAINTS
> Specifies that all referential integrity constraints from tables outside the cluster referring to primary and unique keys in the cluster's tables be dropped.

Common keywords and clauses: *column, integer, Physical_Attributes_Clause, Storage_Clause.*

CREATE/DROP CONTEXT

CREATE Syntax:
```
CREATE [OR REPLACE] CONTEXT namespace USING [schema .] package
[INITIALIZED {EXTERNALLY | GLOBALLY } | ACCESSED GLOBALLY ]
```

DROP Syntax:
```
  DROP CONTEXT namespace
```

Creates or drops a namespace for a context. New with Oracle8i.

Keywords

OR REPLACE
> Specifies that an existing context namespace is to be replaced

namespace
> Name of the context namespace to be created.

package
> Name of the PL/SQL package that sets the context attributes.

INITIALIZED
> Specifies that an entity other than Oracle can initialize the context namespace.

> *EXTERNALLY*
>> Specifies that the namespace can be initialized using an OCI interface when establishing a session.

> *GLOBALLY*
>> Specifies that the namespace can be initialized by the LDAP directory when a global user connects to the database.

ACCESSED GLOBALLY
> Specifies that any application context set in the namespace is accessible throughout the entire instance. This setting lets multiple sessions share application attributes.

Common keywords and clauses: *schema*.

CREATE CONTROLFILE

```
CREATE CONTROLFILE [REUSE] [SET] DATABASE dbname
LOGFILE [GROUP integer] filename[,[GROUP integer] filename ...]
{RESETLOGS | NORESETLOGS}
[MAXLOGFILES integer]
[MAXLOGMEMBERS integer]
[MAXLOGHISTORY integer]
[MAXDATAFILES integer]
[MAXINSTANCES integer]
[ARCHIVELOG | NOARCHIVELOG]
DATAFILE (filename[,filename ...])
CHARACTER SET character_set
```

Re-creates a control file, allowing changes to some parameters.

Keywords

REUSE
> Specifies that one or more existing control files specified in the initialization file can be reused and overwritten. If this keyword is omitted and if any of the control files named in *INIT.ORA* or *SPFILE* exists, an error results.

SET
> Specifies that the supplied *dbname* will be a new name for the database. Valid names are one to eight characters long.

DATABASE
> Specifies the name of the database. Unless you use the SET statement, this must be the current name of the database.

LOGFILE
> Specifies members of all redo log file groups, all of which must exist.

RESETLOGS
> Specifies that the contents of the log files listed in the LOGFILE clause be ignored. Each file listed in the LOGFILE clause must have a SIZE specified.

NORESETLOGS
> Specifies that all files listed in the LOGFILE clause (which must be current redo log files and not restored from backups) be reused with their original sizes.

MAXLOGFILES
> Specifies the maximum number of redo log file groups that can ever be created for the database. The default and maximum values are operating system dependent. This value must be at least 2 and should be at least 3.

MAXLOGMEMBERS
> Specifies the maximum number of redo log group copies that may exist in the database. The minimum is 1, and the default and maximum are operating system dependent.

MAXLOGHISTORY
> Specifies the maximum number of archived redo log file groups for automatic media recovery of Parallel Server or Real Application Clusters. The minimum value is 1, and the default and maximum are operating system dependent.

MAXDATAFILES
> Specifies the maximum number of datafiles that can ever be created for the database. The minimum is 1, but it should never be set lower than the largest number of datafiles ever created in the database.

MAXINSTANCES
> Specifies the maximum number of instances that can have the database mounted and open. This parameter applies only to the Parallel Server/Real Application Clusters environment.

ARCHIVELOG
> Specifies that the database will be run in ARCHIVELOG mode.

NOARCHIVELOG
> Specifies that the database will not be run in ARCHIVELOG mode and that online redo log files will be reused. This option is the default.

DATAFILE
> Specifies the names of all datafiles in the database, all of which must exist.

character_set
> Specifies the name of the character set used to create the database, if different from the default.

Common keywords and clauses: *filename, integer.*

CREATE/ALTER DATABASE

CREATE Syntax:
```
CREATE DATABASE [dbname]
CONTROLFILE [REUSE]
LOGFILE [GROUP integer] (filename[,[GROUP integer] filename ...])
[MAXLOGFILES integer]
[MAXLOGMEMBERS integer]
[MAXLOGHISTORY integer]
[MAXDATAFILES integer]
[MAXINSTANCES integer]
[ARCHIVELOG | NOARCHIVELOG]
[CHARACTER SET charset]
[NATIONAL CHARACTER SET charset]
[SET TIME_ZONE = '{{+ | -} hh:mi | time_zone_region}']
[USER SYS IDENTIFIED BY password]
[USER SYSTEM IDENTIFIED BY password]
[DEFAULT TEMPORARY TABLESPACE tablespace_name [TEMPFILE filename]
   [EXTENT MANAGEMENT LOCAL] [UNIFORM [SIZE integer [ K | M ]]]]
[UNDO TABLESPACE tablespace_name [DATAFILE filename [autoextend_clause]
DATAFILE (filename[,filename ...])[Autoextend_Clause]]]
[EXTENT MANAGEMENT LOCAL]
```

ALTER Syntax:
```
ALTER DATABASE [dbname]
{ ARCHIVELOG | NOARCHIVELOG
| MOUNT [[STANDBY | CLONE] DATABASE]
| CONVERT
| OPEN
  [{READ WRITE [{RESETLOGS | NORESETLOGS}] [MIGRATE]
  | READ ONLY
  }]
| ACTIVATE [PHYSICAL | LOGICAL] STANDBY DATABASE
  [SKIP [STANDBY LOGFILE]]
| SET STANDBY DATABASE TO MAXIMIZE
  {PROTECTION | AVAILABILITY | PERFORMANCE}
| REGISTER [OR REPLACE] {PHYSICAL | LOGICAL }
  LOGFILE logfile_descriptor[,logfile_descriptor ...]
| START LOGICAL STANDBY APPLY [NEW PRIMARY dblink | INITIAL scn_value]
| {STOP | ABORT} LOGICAL STANDBY APPLY
| COMMIT TO SWITCHOVER TO {PHYSICAL | LOGICAL} {PRIMARY | STANDBY}
  [{WITH | WITHOUT} SESSION SHUTDOWN] [WAIT | NOWAIT]
}
{ RESET COMPATIBILITY
| CONVERT
| ENABLE [PUBLIC] THREAD integer
| DISABLE THREAD integer
| GUARD {ALL | STANDBY | NONE}
| RENAME GLOBAL_NAME TO database[.domain[.domain ...]]
| CHARACTER SET character_set
| NATIONAL CHARACTER SET character_set
| DEFAULT TEMPORARY TABLESPACE tablespace_name
| SET TIME_ZONE = '{{+ | -} hh:mi | time_zone_region}'
}
```

```
{ CREATE DATAFILE 'filename'[,'filename' ...] [AS filename]
| DATAFILE 'filename'[,'filename' ...]
  {ONLINE | OFFLINE [DROP}
  | RESIZE integer [K | M]
  | END BACKUP
  | Autoextend_Clause
  }
| TEMPFILE 'filename'[,'filename' ...]
  {ONLINE | OFFLINE [DROP]
  | RESIZE integer [K | M]
  | Autoextend_Clause
  }
| RENAME FILE 'filename' [,'filename' ...] TO 'filename' [,'filename' ...]
{ ADD [STANDBY] LOGFILE [THREAD integer]
  [GROUP integer] filename[,[GROUP integer] filename ...]
| ADD [STANDBY] LOGFILE MEMBER 'filename' [RESUSE] [,'filename' [RESUSE] ...]
  TO logfile_descriptor[,logfile_descriptor ...]
| ADD SUPPLEMENTAL LOG DATA ({PRIMARY KEY | UNIQUE INDEX}
  [,{PRIMARY KEY | UNIQUE INDEX...}]) COLUMNS
| DROP {GROUP integer | 'filename'|('filename','filename'[,'filename' ...])
  }
| DROP [STANDBY] LOGFILE MEMBER 'filename'[,'filename' ...]
| CLEAR [UNARCHIVED] LOGFILE logfile_descriptor[,logfile_descriptor ...]
  UNRECOVERABLE DATAFILE
}
{ CREATE STANDBY CONTROLFILE AS 'filename' [REUSE]
| BACKUP CONTROLFILE TO {'filename' [REUSE] | TRACE}
  [{RESETLOGS | NORESETLOGS}]
}
{ RECOVER [AUTOMATIC] [FROM 'location']
  {[STANDBY] DATABASE
    [{ UNTIL {CANCEL | TIME date | CHANGE integer }
     | USING BACKUP CONTROLFILE}
    | TABLESPACE tablespace_name [, tablespace_name]...
    | DATAFILE 'filename' [, 'filename']...
    | STANDBY
      {TABLESPACE tablespace_name [, tablespace_name]...
      | DATAFILE filename' [, 'filename']...
      }
      UNTIL [CONSISTENT  WITH] CONTROLFILE
    | LOGFILE 'filename'
    }
      TEST
      ALLOW integer CORRUPTION
      NOPARALLEL | PARALLEL [integer]} |
      CONTINUE [DEFAULT] | CANCEL}
    | CONTINUE [DEFAULT]
    | CANCEL
    }
| RECOVER MANAGED STANDBY DATABASE
  { {[DISCONNECT [FROM SESSION]] [FINISH [NOWAIT]]
    | [TIMEOUT integer | NOTIMEOUT]
  }
| {NODELAY | DELAY integer | DEFAULT DELAY}
```

```
 | [NEXT integer] |
 | [EXPIRE integer | NO EXPIRE]
 | [PARALLEL integer | NOPARALLEL]
 | [THROUGH [THREAD integer] SEQUENCE integer]
   | [ALL ARCHIVELOG]
   | [{ALL | LAST | NEXT} SWITCHOVER]]
   }
   | CANCEL [IMMEDIATE] [NOWAIT] |
   | [DISCONNECT [FROM SESSION]]
       [PARALLEL integer | NOPARALLEL]
       [FINISH [SKIP [STANDBY LOG FILE]][{WAIT | NOWAIT}]]
 }
 | END BACKUP
 }
```

Creates or alters a database and specifies parameters associated with it.

Keywords

dbname

> Name of the database. May be one to eight characters long and must not be a reserved word.

CONTROLFILE REUSE

> Specifies that one or more existing control files specified in the initialization file can be reused and overwritten. If this keyword is omitted and any of the control files named in *INIT.ORA* or *SPFILE* exists, an error will result. If the parameters specified require that the control file be larger than the current size, the statement will fail. Note that this option is not normally used for a new database creation.

LOGFILE

> Specifies the names of one or more redo log files to be created.

MAXLOGFILES

> Specifies the maximum number of redo log file groups that can ever be created for the database. The default and maximum value are operating system dependent. This value must be at least 2 and should be at least 3.

MAXLOGMEMBERS

> Specifies the maximum number of copies of a redo log group that may exist in the database. The minimum is 1, and the default and maximum are operating system dependent.

MAXLOGHISTORY

> Specifies the maximum number of archived redo log file groups for automatic media recovery of Parallel Server or Real Application Clusters. The minimum value is 1, and the default and maximum are operating system dependent.

MAXDATAFILES

> Specifies the maximum number of datafiles that can ever be created for the database. The minimum is 1, but it should never be set lower than the largest number of datafiles ever created in the database.

MAXINSTANCES

> Specifies the maximum number of instances that can have the database mounted and open. This parameter applies only to the Parallel Server/Real Application Clusters environment.

ARCHIVELOG

Specifies that the database will be run in ARCHIVELOG mode, which means that a redo log group must be archived before the redo log group can be reused. If the group has not been archived, the database will halt until archiving occurs successfully. This mode is required to perform media recovery.

NOARCHIVELOG

Specifies that redo log groups will not be archived and may be reused immediately by Oracle. This option is the default.

CHARACTER SET

Specifies the character set that the database will use to store data (e.g., US7ASCII or JA16SJIS). This character set cannot be changed after database creation. The choices and default are operating system dependent.

NATIONAL CHARACTER SET

Specifies the national character set that will be used for specifically designated columns. If omitted, the default database character set is used.

SET TIME_ZONE

Specifies the time zone of the database. *hh:mm* specifies an offset (positive or negative) from Coordinated Universal Time (UTC, which is basically equivalent to GMT), or you may specify a region name. This keyword is new with Oracle9i.

> To see a list of valid region names, query the TZNAME column of the V$TIMEZONE_NAMES dynamic view.

DEFAULT TEMPORARY TABLESPACE

Specifies that a temporary tablespace will be created and will be used as the default tablespace for users. If this clause is not specified, then SYSTEM will be used as the default temporary tablespace. This clause is new with Oracle9i.

TEMPFILE *filename*

Specifies the name of the datafile for the temporary tablespace. This clause is new with Oracle9i Release 2.

EXTENT MANAGEMENT

Specifies how Oracle will handle space management for the temporary tablespace. New with Oracle9i.

LOCAL

Specifies that some part of the tablespace be set aside for a bitmap. All temporary tablespaces have locally managed extents, so this clause is optional.

UNIFORM

Specifies the size of the extents of the temporary tablespace in bytes and that all extents of temporary tablespaces are the same size. The default is uniform extents of 1M.

UNDO TABLESPACE

Specifies that Oracle will create an undo tablespace named *tablespace_name*. Oracle will handle management of undo data using this undo tablespace. New with Oracle9i Release 2.

DATAFILE

Specifies the names of all datafiles in the database. If omitted, a single datafile will be created by default for the SYSTEM tablespace. In Oracle9*i* Release 2, EXTENT MANAGEMENT LOCAL can be specified to create a locally managed SYSTEM tablespace.

Additional ALTER Keywords

MOUNT STANDBY DATABASE

Specifies that the standby database be mounted. New with Oracle9*i*.

MOUNT CLONE DATABASE

Specifies that the clone database be mounted. New with Oracle9*i*.

CONVERT

Specifies that the database data dictionary be converted from Oracle7 to Oracle8 or Oracle8*i*.

OPEN READ WRITE

Specifies that the database be opened in read/write mode. This option is the default.

RESETLOGS

Resets the log sequence number to 1 and invalidates all redo entries in the existing online and archived log files. Use this option only after performing incomplete media recovery or when opening the database after performing media recovery with a backup control file; otherwise, use NORESETLOGS. If the database is opened with the RESETLOGS keyword, you should immediately perform a complete backup of the database.

NORESETLOGS

Makes no change to the status of the current log sequence number and redo log entries.

MIGRATE

Specifies that the database is to be upgraded from Release 7.3.4 to the current release. If upgrading from a release other than 7.3.4, you can use the SQL*Plus command STARTUP MIGRATE. New with Oracle9*i*.

READ ONLY

Specifies that the database be opened in read-only mode, which makes queries possible but disables write operations. New with Oracle8*i*.

ACTIVATE STANDBY DATABASE

Specifies that the state of the database be changed from standby to active. New with Oracle9*i*.

PHYSICAL

Specifies that a physical standby database is to be activated.

LOGICAL

Specifies that a logical standby database is to be activated.

SKIP

Specifies that Oracle is to force the operation to proceed even if standby redo log files contain data that could be recovered using the RECOVER MANAGED STANDBY DATABASE statement.

SET STANDBY DATABASE TO MAXIMIZE

Specifies the level of protection for the database. New with Oracle9*i*.

PROTECTION
> Establishes "maximum protection mode."

AVAILABILITY
> Establishes "maximum availability mode."

PERFORMANCE
> Establishes "maximum performance mode."

REGISTER LOGFILE
> Specifies that the log files from the failed primary database be manually regis-
> tered. For a logical standby database, you can use this statement to seed the initial
> starting point for a new logical standby database. Then when you issue an ALTER
> DATABASE START LOGICAL STANDBY APPLY INITIAL statement, use the
> lowest registered log file as its starting point. New with Oracle9*i*.

START LOGICAL STANDBY
> Specifies that Oracle begin applying redo logs to a logical standby database.

> *NEW PRIMARY*
>> Specifies a new primary database after the ALTER DATABASE COMMIT
>> TO SWITCHOVER TO LOGICAL STANDBY statement or when a standby
>> database has completed processing logs from one primary, and now a new
>> database becomes the primary

> *INITIAL*
>> Specifies that this is the first time logs are being applied to the standby
>> database.

COMMIT TO SWITCHOVER
> Specifies that Oracle perform a "graceful switchover," in which the current
> primary database takes on standby status, and one standby database becomes the
> primary database. In a Real Application Clusters environment, all instances other
> than the instance from which you issue this statement must be shut down
> normally.

> *PHYSICAL*
>> Prepares the database to run in the role of a physical standby database.

> *LOGICAL*
>> Prepares the database to run in the role of a logical standby database. If you
>> specify LOGICAL, you must then issue an ALTER DATABASE START
>> LOGICAL STANDBY APPLY statement.

> *WITH SESSION SHUTDOWN*
>> Specifies that Oracle is to shut down any open application sessions and roll
>> back uncommitted transactions as part of the execution of this statement.

> *WITHOUT SESSION SHUTDOWN*
>> Specifies that the statement will fail if there are any open application
>> sessions. This is the default.

RESET COMPATIBILITY
> Specifies that the compatibility of the database be reset to the version specified.
> This change is effective the next time the database is started.

ENABLE THREAD
> Specifies that the thread of redo log files be enabled in a Parallel Server/Real
> Application Clusters environment. If the keyword PUBLIC is specified, the
> enabled thread is available to any instance. Otherwise, the thread is available only
> to an instance that specifically requests it.

SQL

DISABLE THREAD

Specifies that the thread of redo log files be disabled and made unavailable to all instances of a Parallel Server/Real Application Clusters environment.

GUARD

Specifies that data in the database be protected from change. ALL prevents users other than SYS from making changes to any data in the database. STANDBY prevents users other than SYS from making changes to any database object being maintained by logical standby; this setting is useful if you want report operations to be able to modify data as long as it is not being replicated by logical standby.

RENAME FILE 'filename1' TO 'filename2'

Specifies that the name of a datafile, temporary file, or log file be changed in the control file. Note that this keyword does not affect the name of the operating system file.

RENAME GLOBAL NAME TO

Specifies that the global name of the database be changed to the supplied value, which may be up to eight characters.

CREATE DATAFILE

Specifies that a new empty datafile be created in place of an old one (which may have been lost without backup). Media recovery must be performed before the datafile is usable.

ONLINE

Specifies that the datafile is to be brought online.

OFFLINE

Specifies that the datafile is to be brought offline.

RESIZE

Specifies that the size of the datafile is to be increased or decreased to the indicated size.

END BACKUP

Specifies that media recovery will not be performed when the database starts after a hot backup was interrupted. New with Oracle9*i*.

TEMPFILE

Specifies that changes be made to a temporary datafile.

ONLINE

Datafile should be brought online.

OFFLINE

Datafile should be taken offline.

DROP

For a database in NOARCHIVELOG mode, a datafile is to be taken offline. If the database is in ARCHIVELOG mode, this keyword is ignored.

The DROP clause does not remove the datafile from the database. To do that, you must drop the tablespace in which the datafile resides. Until you do so, the datafile remains in the data dictionary.

ADD LOGFILE

Specifies that one or more redo log file groups be added. THREAD may be indicated in a Parallel Server/Real Application Clusters environment.

ADD LOGFILE MEMBER

Specifies that a new member filename be added to an existing redo log file group. Include REUSE to indicate that the *filename* already exists.

logfile_descriptor

Specifies an existing redo log file group either as GROUP *integer* or as a list of filenames.

DROP GROUP

Specifies that the entire redo log file group is to be dropped after an ALTER SYSTEM SWITCH LOGFILE statement has been issued. The dropped group may be specified either as GROUP *integer* or as a list of filenames.

DROP LOGFILE MEMBER 'filename'

Specifies that one or more individual redo log file members be dropped.

CLEAR LOGFILE

Specifies that an online redo log be reinitialized, optionally without archiving the redo log. CLEAR LOGFILE is similar to adding and dropping a redo log, except that the statement may be issued even if there are only two logs for the thread and also may be issued for the current redo log of a closed thread. You must specify UNARCHIVED if you want to reuse a redo log that was not archived

UNRECOVERABLE DATAFILE

Must be specified if the datafile has been taken offline with the database in ARCHIVELOG mode (that is, you specified ALTER DATABASE ... DATA-FILE OFFLINE without the DROP keyword) and if the unarchived log to be cleared is needed to recover the datafile before bringing it back online. In this case, you must drop the datafile and the entire tablespace once the CLEAR LOGFILE statement completes

CREATE STANDBY CONTROL FILE

Specifies that a control file be created to maintain a standby database.

BACKUP CONTROL FILE TO

Specifies that the current control file be backed up to the indicated filename. If the keywords TO TRACE are specified, a set of SQL statements will be written to the trace file instead of creating a backup of the control file. If RESETLOGS is specified, the SQL statements written will include ALTER DATABASE OPEN RESETLOGS. If NORESETLOGS is specified, the SQL statement ALTER DATA-BASE OPEN NORESETLOGS will be written.

RECOVER FROM

Specifies the location from which archived redo log files required for recovery will be read. If the keyword AUTOMATIC is specified, the name of the next archived redo log file required for recovery will be generated, using the LOG_ARCHIVE_DEST and LOG_ARCHIVE_FORMAT initialization parameters.

DATABASE

Specifies that the entire database be recovered. If the STANDBY keyword is supplied, the standby database will be recovered using the control file and archived redo log files from the primary database. The keywords UNTIL CANCELLED may be supplied, specifying that the database be recovered until the operation is canceled using the RECOVER CANCEL clause. The TIME keyword specifies that time-based recovery be performed up to the supplied time. The CHANGE keyword indicates that recovery will be performed to just before the specified System Change Number.

USING BACKUP CONTROLFILE
Specifies that a backup control file (instead of the current control file) be used.

STANDBY TABLESPACE UNTIL CONSISTENT WITH CONTROLFILE
Specifies that *tablespace* on an old standby database be recovered using the control file from the current standby database. New with Oracle8*i*.

STANDBY DATAFILE UNTIL CONSISTENT WITH CONTROLFILE
Specifies that *datafile* on an old standby database be recovered using the control file from the current standby database. New with Oracle8*i*.

TABLESPACE
Specifies one or more tablespaces (which must be offline) to be recovered.

DATAFILE
Specifies one or more datafiles (which must be offline) to be recovered.

LOGFILE
Specifies that media recovery should continue using the log file(s) supplied.

TEST
Specifies that a trial recovery be performed.

ALLOW CORRUPTION
Specifies the number of corrupted blocks that can be tolerated in a log file before recovery will stop.

CONTINUE DEFAULT
Specifies that recovery will continue using the redo log file that would be automatically generated. This keyword is equivalent to RECOVER AUTOMATIC, except that no prompt for filenames exists.

CONTINUE
Specifies that recovery of multiple instances should continue after it was interrupted to disable a thread.

CANCEL
Specifies that cancel-based recovery be ended.

RECOVER MANAGED STANDBY DATABASE
Specifies that recovery should occur using sustained standby recovery mode, which assumes the standby database as an active component. New with Oracle8*i*.

DELAY
Specifies that Oracle should wait the specified number of minutes before applying the archived redo logs. NODELAY specifies that the logs should be applied immediately.

DEFAULT DELAY
Specifies that Oracle should wait the number of minutes specified in the LOG_ARCHIVE_DEST_*n* initialization parameter on the primary database before applying archived redo logs.

TIMEOUT
Specifies the number of minutes to wait for a requested archived redo log file to become available for writing to the standby database.

CANCEL
Specifies that sustained recovery be ended after the current archived redo file has been applied, unless the IMMEDIATE keyword, which terminates after applying the next redo log file read, is specified.

DISCONNECT

Specifies that the managed redo process (MRP) should apply archived redo files as a detached background process, thereby leaving the current session available for other tasks. (The FROM SESSION keywords are optional and are provided for clarity.) New with Oracle9*i*.

NEXT

Specifies that Oracle should apply the specified number of archived redo logs as soon as possible after they have been archived. This parameter temporarily overrides any delay setting in the LOG_ARCHIVE_DEST_*n* initialization parameter on the primary database and overrides any DELAY values specified in an earlier ALTER DATABASE ... MANAGED STANDBY RECOVERY statement. Once the *integer* archived redo logs are processed, any such delay again takes effect.

EXPIRE

Specifies the number of minutes from the current time after which the managed recovery operation terminates automatically. The process may actually expire after the interval specified, because Oracle will finish processing any archived redo log that is being processed at the time of expiration.

NOEXPIRE

Disables a previously issued EXPIRE statement.

THROUGH

Specifies when to terminate managed recovery. New with Oracle9*i*.

ALL ARCHIVELOG

Specifies that Oracle is to manage the recovery process until all archived redo log files have been applied.

SWITCHOVER

The managed standby recovery process normally stops when it encounters a switchover operation, because these operations produce an end-of-redo archival indicator. The SWITCHOVER clause is useful if you have more than one standby database, all but one of which will remain in the standby role after the switchover. This clause keeps the managed standby recovery process operational. It lets these "secondary" standby databases wait to receive the redo stream from the new primary database, rather than stopping the recovery process and then starting it again after the new primary database is activated.

ALL keeps managed standby recovery operational through all switchover operations. LAST cancels managed standby recovery operations after the final end-of-redo archival indicator. NEXT cancels managed standby recovery after recovering the next end-of-redo archival indicator encountered; this is the default

Common keywords and clauses: *Autoextend_Clause, filename, integer, tablespace_name*.

CREATE/DROP DATABASE LINK

CREATE Syntax:
```
CREATE [SHARED] [PUBLIC] DATABASE LINK dblink
[CONNECT TO
  {CURRENT USER
  | username IDENTIFIED BY password
    [AUTHENTICATED BY username IDENTIFIED BY password]
  }]
[USING 'connectstring']
```

DROP Syntax:
```
DROP [PUBLIC] DATABASE LINK dblink
```

Creates or removes a database link, which allows access to objects on a remote database.

Keywords

dblink   Specifies the name of the database link being created. Must be a valid Oracle object name.

SHARED   Specifies that a single network connection be shared across users when the Multi-Threaded Server/Shared Server is configured.

PUBLIC   Specifies that the database link be available to all users. If omitted, the database link is private and available only to you.

CONNECT TO CURRENT USER

Specifies that a current user database link be created, which requires a global user with a valid account on the remote database.

CONNECT TO username IDENTIFIED BY password

Specifies the username and password used to connect to the remote database.

AUTHENTICATED BY

Specifies a username and password on the remote database to be used for authentication when the SHARED keyword is used.

USING   Specifies the Oracle Net Services database specification (*connectstring*) for the remote database.

 If the CONNECT TO clause is omitted, the account username and password currently logged in, not the username and password of the creator, will be used when the database link is invoked.

CREATE/DROP DIMENSION

CREATE Syntax:
```
CREATE [FORCE | NOFORCE] DIMENSION [schema.]dimension
LEVEL level IS
  { level_ table.level_column
  |(level_ table.level_column, table_name _ table_name.level_column ...)
  }
HIERARCHY hierarchy (child_level CHILD OF parent_level)
[JOIN KEY {child_key_column | (child_key_column,child_key_column ...)}
  REFERENCES parent_level] |
```

```
ATTRIBUTE level DETERMINES
  { dependent_column
  |(dependent_column, dependent_column ...)
  }
```

DROP Syntax:
```
DROP DIMENSION [schema.]dimension
```

Creates or removes a dimension, which defines a parent-child relationship between pairs of column sets. New with Oracle9i.

Keywords

FORCE — Specifies that the dimension be created, even if the referenced tables do not exist.

NOFORCE — Specifies that the dimension be created only if the referenced objects exist. This is the default.

dimension — Name of the dimension.

LEVEL — Defines a level with a name that defines dimension hierarchies and attributes.

level_table.level_column — Specifies the columns (up to 32) for the level.

HIERARCHY — Specifies the name of a hierarchy.

child_level — Name of a level that has an *n*-to-1 relationship with a parent level.

CHILD OF — Specifies the name of a parent level.

JOIN KEY — Specifies the name of a column in the JOIN condition with a parent table.

REFERENCES — Specifies the name of the parent level.

ATTRIBUTE — Specifies the name of a level or hierarchy.

DETERMINES dependent_column — Specifies the name of a column that is dependent on an attribute level.

Common keywords and clauses: *column, schema, table_name*.

CREATE/DROP DIRECTORY

CREATE Syntax:
```
CREATE [OR REPLACE] DIRECTORY directory_name AS 'path_name'
```

DROP Syntax:
```
DROP DIRECTORY directory_name
```

Creates or removes a directory object that specifies an operating system directory for storing BFILE objects.

 Oracle does not check to see if the directory actually exists on the host operating system, so be sure to check the path you provide carefully.

Keywords

OR REPLACE

Specifies that this directory object should replace any existing directory object with the same name.

directory_name

Name of the directory object.

path_name

Operating system directory's full case-sensitive pathname.

CREATE/ALTER/DROP FUNCTION

Creates, modifies, or removes a PL/SQL function in the database. See Chapter 9 for information on syntax and use.

CREATE/ALTER/DROP INDEX

CREATE Syntax:

```
CREATE [OR REPLACE] [UNIQUE | BITMAP] INDEX [schema.]indexname ON
{ CLUSTER [schema.]cluster
    Index_Attributes_Clause
| [schema.] table_name [alias] ({column | col_expr} [ASC | DESC]
  [,{column|col_expr} [ASC | DESC] ...])
  [{ { {GLOBAL PARTITION BY RANGE (column_list)
         (PARTITION partition_name VALUES LESS THAN (value[, value...])
         [Physical_Attributes_Clause]
         [TABLESPACE tablespace_name]
         [LOGGING | NOLOGGING]
      | LOCAL (PARTITION partition_name
        [Physical_Attributes_Clause]
        [TABLESPACE tablespace_name]
        [LOGGING | NOLOGGING]
        [,PARTITION partition_name
        [Physical_Attributes_Clause]
        [TABLESPACE tablespace_name]
        [LOGGING | NOLOGGING] ...])
      | LOCAL
        {STORE IN ({tablespace_name[,tablespace_name...]|DEFAULT})
        | (PARTITION [partition_name] [TABLESPACE tablespace_name]
        [,PARTITION [partition_name] [TABLESPACE tablespace_name] ...])
        }
      | LOCAL STORE IN ({tablespace_name[,tablespace_name ...] | DEFAULT})
        (PARTITION [partition_name]
        [Index_Attributes_Clause]
        { STORE IN { tablespace_name[,tablespace_name ...] | DEFAULT}
        | (SUBPARTITION subpartition_name [TABLESPACE tablespace_name]
          [,SUBPARTITION subpartition_name [TABLESPACE tablespace_name] ...])
        }
      }
    | Index_Attributes_Clause
    }
  | INDEXTYPE IS indextype
```

```
    [PARALLEL | NOPARALLEL]
    [PARAMETERS('parmstring')]
  }
| [schema.] table_name ([schema.]table_name column [{ASC | DESC}]
  [,[schema.]table_name column [{ASC | DESC}]...])
  FROM [schema.] table_name [,[schema.] table_name...]
  WHERE condition
  { LOCAL (PARTITION partition_name
    [Physical_Attributes_Clause]
    [TABLESPACE tablespace_name]
    [LOGGING | NOLOGGING]
    [,PARTITION partition_name
    [Physical_Attributes_Clause]
    [TABLESPACE tablespace_name]
    [LOGGING | NOLOGGING] ...])
  | LOCAL
    {STORE IN ({tablespace_name[,tablespace_name...]|DEFAULT})
    | (PARTITION [partition_name] [TABLESPACE tablespace_name]
      [,PARTITION [partition_name] [TABLESPACE tablespace_name] ...])
    }
  | LOCAL STORE IN ({tablespace_name[,tablespace_name ...] | DEFAULT})
    (PARTITION [partition_name]
    [Index_Attributes_Clause]
    { STORE IN { tablespace_name[,tablespace_name ...] | DEFAULT}
    | (SUBPARTITION subpartition_name [TABLESPACE tablespace_name]
      [,SUBPARTITION subpartition_name [TABLESPACE tablespace_name] ...])
    }
  }
}
```

ALTER Syntax:

```
ALTER INDEX [schema.]indexname
[DEALLOCATE UNUSED [KEEP integer [K | M]]]
[ALLOCATE EXTENT (
  [SIZE integer [K | M]]
  [DATAFILE 'filename']
  [INSTANCE integer])]
[PARALLEL integer | NOPARALLEL]
[Physical_Attributes_Clause]
[Storage_Clause]
[LOGGING | NOLOGGING]
[REBUILD
  [{ {PARTITION partition_name | SUBPARTITION subpartition_name}
    | REVERSE | NOREVERSE}
  }]
  [PARALLEL integer | NOPARALLEL]
  [TABLESPACE tablespace_name]
  [ONLINE]
  [Physical_Attributes_Clause]
  [Storage_Clause]
  [{COMPRESS integer | NOCOMPRESS}]
  [{LOGGING | NOLOGGING}]
  [COMPUTE STATISTICS]
  [PARAMETERS ('rebuild_parameters')]
```

```
[PARAMETERS ('alter_parameters')]
[{ENABLE | DISABLE}]
[UNUSABLE]
[RENAME [PARTITION partition_name] TO new _name]
[COALESCE]
[{MONITORING | NOMONITORING} USAGE]
[Partition_Clause]
```

DROP Syntax:

```
DROP INDEX [schema.]indexname
```

Creates, modifies, or removes an index on one or more columns of a table or a cluster.

If the *Storage_Clause* is omitted from the CREATE INDEX or ALTER INDEX statement, Oracle allocates storage for the index as follows:

- If the indexed table has no rows, Oracle uses the default storage values for the tablespace.

- If the indexed table has rows and the resulting index can be contained in no more than 25 data blocks, Oracle allocates a single extent for this index.

- If the indexed table has rows and the resulting index is more than 25 data blocks, Oracle allocates five equal-sized extents for this index.

Keywords

UNIQUE
: Specifies that the value of the column(s) upon which the index is based must be unique.

BITMAP
: Specifies that the index be created as a bitmap rather than using the normal B-tree structure.

ON CLUSTER
: Specifies that the index be built on a cluster (which cannot be a hash cluster) and specifies the cluster name.

ON table_name
: Specifies that the index be built on a table and specifies the table name.

INDEXTYPE IS indextype
: Specifies that a domain index be created. *indextype* is the name of the indextype object, which must already exist. New with Oracle8i.

PARAMETERS
: Specifies the parameter string that is passed to the *indextype* routine.

alias
: Alias name for the table on which the index is being built. This option is required if the index references any object type attributes or object type methods.

ASC
: Specifies that the index should be created in ascending order, based on the database character set's character values.

DESC
: Specifies that the index should be created in descending order, based on the database character set's character values.

ONLINE
: Specifies that DML operations may be performed on the table being indexed during the index creation. New with Oracle 8i.

COMPUTE STATISTICS
: Specifies that statistics be computed and inserted into the data dictionary during index creation. New with Oracle8i.

GLOBAL PARTITION BY RANGE
> Specifies that the global index be partitioned on the range of values from the specified columns.

column_list Name(s) of the column(s) on which the index is partitioned. Beginning with Oracle8*i*, this list can include functions or columns.

LOCAL Specifies that the index be partitioned on the same columns, the same number of partitions, and the same partition bounds as the table on which the index is built.

PARTITION Specifies the name of individual partitions, which must be equal to the number of table partitions and provided in the same order.

LOCAL STORE IN
> Specifies how index hash partitions or index subpartitions will be distributed across tablespaces.

DEFAULT Specifies that for a local index on a hash or composite-partitioned table, the tablespace specified at the index level will be overridden, and the same partition or subpartition that the table resides in will be used.

SUBPARTITION
> Specifies the name of a subpartition.

Additional ALTER Keywords

DEALLOCATE UNUSED
> Specifies that unused space at the end of the index be freed and made available for other uses in the database.

KEEP Specifies a number of bytes above the highwater mark that should remain as part of the index after deallocation.

ALLOCATE EXTENT
> Specifies that a new extent be allocated for this index.

SIZE Specifies the size of the extent to be allocated.

DATAFILE Specifies the name of the datafile to contain the new extent. If omitted, Oracle chooses a datafile from those available for this index.

INSTANCE Specifies that the new extent be made available to this instance only. If omitted, the extent will be made available to all instances.

REBUILD PARTITION
> Specifies a partition of the index to be rebuilt.

REBUILD SUBPARTITION
> Specifies a subpartition of the index to be rebuilt.

REVERSE Specifies that the bytes of the index block be stored in reverse order (without ROWID) when the index is rebuilt.

NOREVERSE
> Specifies that the bytes of the index block be stored without reversing when the index is rebuilt.

rebuild_ parameters
> Parameter string to be passed to the *indextype* routine for rebuilding a global index.

alter_ parameters
    Parameter string to be passed to the *indextype* routine when altering a global index.

ENABLE   Specifies that a disabled function-based index be enabled.

DISABLE   Specifies that a function-based index be disabled.

UNUSABLE   Specifies that the index be marked unusable.

RENAME TO Specifies that the index be renamed.

COALESCE   Specifies that the contents of index blocks be merged to free blocks for reuse. New with Oracle8*i*.

MONITOR   Specifies that monitoring is to begin on the index. New with Oracle9*i*.

NOMONITOR
    Specifies that monitoring of the index be terminated. New with Oracle9*i*.

Common keywords and clauses: *column*, *filename*, *Index_Attributes_Clause*, *index-name*, *integer*, LOGGING, NOLOGGING, NOPARALLEL, OR REPLACE, PARALLEL, *Partition_Clause*, *partition_name*, *Physical_Attributes_Clause*, *schema*, *Storage_Clause*, *subpartition_name*, *table_name*, *tablespace_name*.

CREATE/DROP INDEXTYPE

CREATE Syntax:
```
CREATE INDEXTYPE [schema.]indextype
FOR [schema.]operator (parm_type[,parm_type...])[,[schema.]operator...]
USING [schema.]implementation_type
```

DROP Syntax:
```
DROP INDEXTYPE [schema.]indextype
```

Creates or removes an indextype object for use in managing a domain index. New with Oracle8*i*.

Keywords

indextype   Name of the indextype object.

FOR   Specifies a list of operators supported by this indextype.

operator   Name of an operator.

parm_type   Specifies a type of parameter to the operator.

USING   Specifies the type that provides the implementation for the indextype.

implementation_type
    Name of a type that implements an Oracle Data Cartridge interface (ODCI).

Common keywords and clauses: *schema*.

CREATE/ALTER/DROP JAVA

CREATE Syntax:
```
CREATE [OR REPLACE]    [AND {RESOLVE | COMPILE}] [NOFORCE]
JAVA
{ {SOURCE | RESOURCE} NAMED [schema.]object_name
| CLASS [SCHEMA schema]
```

```
}
[AUTHID {CURRENT_USER | DEFINER}]
RESOLVER ((match_string[,]{schema_name | -})[(match_string...)])]
{ USING
  {BFILE (directory_object_name,server_file_name)
  | { BLOB subquery
    | CLOB
    | BFILE
    }
  | 'key_for_BLOB'
  }
|
  AS source_text
}
```

ALTER Syntax:
```
ALTER JAVA
{SOURCE | CLASS} [schema.]object_name
[RESOLVER ((match_string[,]{schema_name | -})[(match_string...)])]
{COMPILE | RESOLVE}
[AUTHID {CURRENT_USER | DEFINER}]
```

DROP Syntax:
```
DROP JAVA {SOURCE | CLASS | RESOURCE} [schema.]object_name
```

Creates an object containing a Java source, class, or resource; or forces the resolution of a Java class schema object or the compilation of a Java source schema object; or removes a Java object from the database. New with Oracle8i.

Keywords

OR REPLACE
> Specifies that the Java object is to be replaced if it already exists.

RESOLVE | COMPILE
> Specifies that Oracle should attempt to resolve the Java schema object that is created. The two keywords have identical meaning and are interchangeable.

NOFORCE   Specifies that the results of this statement are to be rolled back if RESOLVE or COMPILE is specified and the resolution fails.

SOURCE   Specifies that a Java source file is to be loaded.

RESOURCE Specifies that a Java resource file is to be loaded.

object_name Name of the schema object in which source code is held or which should hold the Java resource.

CLASS   Specifies that a Java class file is to be loaded.

SCHEMA   Specifies the schema in which the object containing the Java file resides. If omitted, the user's schema is used.

AUTHID CURRENT_USER
> Specifies that the methods execute with the privileges of the current user.

DEFINER   Specifies that the methods execute with the privileges of the Java schema object's creator.

RESOLVER	Specifies that the Java schema object is to be mapped to a fully qualified Java name.
match_string	A fully qualified Java name or a wildcard that will match one or more Java names.
schema_name	
	Specifies a schema to be searched for the matching Java object.
- (dash)	Specifies that if the match_string matches a valid Java name, the schema can remain unresolved.
USING	Specifies a sequence of data for the Java class or resource.
BFILE	Specifies the directory object and operating system filename containing the Java sequence.
BLOB	Specifies a subquery that returns a single row of type BLOB.
CLOB	Specifies a subquery that returns a single row of type CLOB.
BFILE	Specifies a subquery that returns a single row of type BFILE.
'key_for_BLOB'	
	Specifies the use of an implicit query using the table CREATEJVATABLE in the current schema.
AS source_text	
	Specifies a sequence of characters for Java or SQLJ.

Common keywords and clauses: *schema*.

CREATE/DROP LIBRARY

CREATE Syntax:
```
CREATE [OR REPLACE]LIBRARY [schema.]library_name
{IS | AS} 'filename'
```
DROP Syntax:
```
DROP LIBRARY [schema.]library_name
```
Creates or removes a schema object associated with an operating system shared library.

Keywords
OR REPLACE
Specifies that the library schema object is to be replaced if it already exists in the schema.

library_name
Name of the library schema object.

Common keywords and clauses: *filename, schema*.

CREATE/ALTER/DROP MATERIALIZED VIEW

CREATE Syntax:
```
CREATE MATERIALIZED VIEW [schema.]materialized_view_name
[Physical_Attributes_Clause]
[TABLESPACE tablespace_name]
[Storage_Clause]
[REFRESH [FAST | COMPLETE | FORCE]
  [START WITH date] [NEXTREF date]]
AS materialized_view_query
```

ALTER syntax:
```
ALTER MATERIALIZED VIEW [schema.]materialized_view_name
[Physical_Attributes_Clause]
[Storage_Clause]
[REFRESH [FAST | COMPLETE | FORCE][START WITH date][NEXTREF date]
```

DROP Syntax:
```
DROP MATERIALIZED VIEW [schema.]materialized_view_name
```

Creates, modifies, or removes a materialized view (also called a snapshot), which is the result of a query run against one or more tables or views. The script *dbmssnap.sql* must be run by SYS before you attempt to create a materialized view. New with Oracle*8i*.

Keywords

materialized_view_name
> Name of the materialized view. Because Oracle appends 7-character identifiers to the name when creating materialized view objects in the schema, you should limit the *materialized_view_name* to 27 characters or fewer.

TABLESPACE
> Specifies the name of the tablespace in which this materialized view will be created. The default tablespace for the schema owner is the default.

REFRESH
> Specifies the mode and times for automatic refreshes.

> *FAST*
>> Use the materialized view log associated with the master table.

> *COMPLETE*
>> Refresh by reexecuting the materialized view's query.

> *FORCE*
>> Oracle will decide if a FAST refresh is possible and, if not, will do a COMPLETE refresh. FORCE is the default.

START WITH
> Specifies a date for the next automatic refresh time using a standard Oracle date expression.

NEXTREF
> Specifies a new date expression for calculating the interval between automatic refreshes.

AS materialized_view_query
> Provides the actual SQL query that is used to populate the materialized view and is subject to the same restrictions as a view.

Common keywords and clauses: *date, Physical_Attributes_Clause, schema, Storage_Clause.*

CREATE/ALTER/DROP MATERIALIZED VIEW LOG

CREATE Syntax:
```
CREATE MATERIALIZED VIEW LOG ON [schema.]table_name
[Physical_Attributes_Clause]
[TABLESPACE tablespace_name]
[Storage_Clause]
```

ALTER Syntax:
```
ALTER MATERIALIZED VIEW LOG ON [schema.]table_name
[Physical_Attributes_Clause]
[Storage_Clause]
```

DROP Syntax:
```
DROP MATERIALIZED VIEW LOG ON [schema.]table_name
```

Creates, modifies, or removes a materialized view log, which is a table associated with the master table of a materialized view used to control materialized view refreshes. New with Oracle8i.

Keywords

table_name   Specifies the name of the table for which the materialized view log will be maintained.

Common keywords and clauses: Physical_Attributes_Clause, schema, Storage_Clause, table_name, tablespace_name.

CREATE/ALTER/DROP OPERATOR

CREATE Syntax:
```
CREATE OPERATOR [schema.] operator
BINDING ( parameter_type [, parameter_type]... )
RETURN return_type
  {[ANCILLARY TO
    primary_operator ( parameter_type [, parameter_type]... )
    [, primary_operator ( parameter_type [, parameter_type]... )]...]
  | WITH INDEX CONTEXT, SCAN CONTEXT implementation_type
    [COMPUTE ANCILLARY DATA]
  }
  USING [schema .] [ package . | type . ] function_name]...
```

ALTER Syntax:
```
ALTER OPERATOR [schema.] operator  COMPILE
```

DROP Syntax:
```
DROP OPERATOR operator [FORCE]
```

Creates, alters, or removes a new operator and defines its bindings. New with Oracle8i. Note that the ALTER syntax shown here is new with Oracle9i Release 2.

Keywords

operator   Name to be assigned to this operator.

BINDING   Specifies one or more parameter types for binding the operator to a function.

RETURN   Specifies the return datatype of the binding.

ANCILLARY TO
   Indicates that the operator binding is ancillary to the specified primary operator binding (primary_operator).

COMPUTE ANCILLARY DATA
   Specifies that the operator binding computes ancillary data.

function_name
> Function that provides the implementation for the binding. *function_name* can be a standalone function, a packaged function, a type method, or a synonym for any of these.

ALTER OPERATOR COMPILE
> Specifies that the existing operator should be recompiled. New with Oracle9i Release 2.

FORCE   Specifies that the operator is to be dropped even if it is currently being referenced by one or more schema objects (indextypes, packages, functions, procedures, and so on) and marks those dependent objects INVALID. Without FORCE, you cannot drop an operator if any schema objects reference it.

Common keywords and clauses: *schema*.

CREATE/ALTER/DROP OUTLINE

CREATE Syntax:
```
CREATE [{PUBLIC | PRIVATE}] OUTLINE [outline_name]
[FROM [{PUBLIC | PRIVATE}] source_outline]
[FOR CATEGORY category] [ON statement]
```

ALTER Syntax:
```
ALTER OUTLINE [{PUBLIC | PRIVATE}] outline_name
{ REBUILD
| RENAME TO new_outline_name
| CHANGE CATEGORY TO new_category_name
}
```

DROP Syntax:
```
DROP OUTLINE outline_name
```

Creates, modifies, or removes a set of attributes used by the optimizer to generate an execution plan. New in Oracle8i.

Keywords

PUBLIC   Specifies that the outline is available to all users. This is the default. The use of this keyword in the ALTER OUTLINE statement is new with Oracle9i.

PRIVATE   Specifies that the outline is private to the current session. The use of this keyword in the ALTER OUTLINE statement is new with Oracle9i.

source_outline
> Name of an existing outline from which this outline will be copied.

category   Name of the category for grouped outlines.

ON statement
> Specifies the SQL statement for which Oracle will create an outline when the statement is compiled. This clause is optional only if you are creating a copy of an existing outline using the FROM clause.

REBUILD   Specifies that Oracle is to regenerate the execution plan for *outline_name* using current conditions.

RENAME TO
> Specifies that the outline is to be renamed.

CHANGE CATEGORY TO
> Specifies that this outline will be placed in a new category.

CREATE/ALTER/DROP PACKAGE

Creates,SQL: modif

or removes a stored package of PL/SQL functions, procedures, and other program objects in the database. See Chapter 9 for information on syntax and use.

CREATE/ALTER/DROP PACKAGE BODY

Creates, modifies, or removes the body of a stored package, which defines a collection of PL/SQL functions, procedures, and other program objects in the database. See Chapter 9 for information on syntax and use.

CREATE/ALTER/DROP PROCEDURE

Creates, modifies, or removes a PL/SQL procedure in the database. See Chapter 9 for information on syntax and use.

CREATE PFILE

```
CREATE PFILE [= 'pfile_name'] FROM SPFILE [= 'spfile_name']
```

Creates a text file containing initialization parameters. New with Oracle9*i* Release 2.

Keywords

pfile_name   Specifies the name of the output text file that will be created and that will contain parameter information in text form. If *pfile_name* is not specified, Oracle uses a platform-specific filename, usually *INIT*sid*ORA*.

spfile_name   Specifies the name of the existing binary server parameter file from which parameters will be written. If *spfile_name* is not specified, Oracle uses a platform-specific filename.

CREATE/ALTER/DROP PROFILE

CREATE Syntax:
```
CREATE PROFILE profile_name LIMIT
[SESSIONS_PER_USER  integer | UNLIMITED | DEFAULT]
[CPU_PER_SESSION  integer | UNLIMITED | DEFAULT]
[CPU_PER_CALL  integer | UNLIMITED | DEFAULT]
[CONNECT_TIME  integer | UNLIMITED | DEFAULT]
[IDLE_TIME  integer | UNLIMITED | DEFAULT]
[LOGICAL_READS_PER_SESSION  integer | UNLIMITED | DEFAULT]
[LOGICAL_READS_PER_CALL  integer | UNLIMITED | DEFAULT]
[PRIVATE_SGA  {integer [K | M] | UNLIMITED | DEFAULT}]
```

```
[COMPOSITE_LIMIT  {integer | UNLIMITED | DEFAULT}]
[FAILED_LOGIN_ATTEMPTS expr | UNLIMITED | DEFAULT]
[PASSWORD_LIFE_TIME expr | UNLIMITED | DEFAULT]
[PASSWORD_REUSE_TIME expr| UNLIMITED | DEFAULT]
[PASSWORD_REUSE_MAX expr| UNLIMITED | DEFAULT]
[PASSWORD_LOCK_TIME expr | UNLIMITED | DEFAULT]
[PASSWORD_GRACE_TIME expr | UNLIMITED | DEFAULT]
[PASSWORD_VERIFY_FUNCTION function | NULL | DEFAULT]
```

ALTER Syntax:
```
ALTER PROFILE profile_name LIMIT
[SESSIONS_PER_USER  integer | UNLIMITED | DEFAULT]
[CPU_PER_SESSION  integer | UNLIMITED | DEFAULT]
[CPU_PER_CALL  integer | UNLIMITED | DEFAULT]
[CONNECT_TIME  integer | UNLIMITED | DEFAULT]
[IDLE_TIME  integer | UNLIMITED | DEFAULT]
[LOGICAL_READS_PER_SESSION  integer | UNLIMITED | DEFAULT]
[LOGICAL_READS_PER_CALL  integer | UNLIMITED | DEFAULT]
[PRIVATE_SGA  integer [K | M] | UNLIMITED | DEFAULT]
[COMPOSITE_LIMIT  integer | UNLIMITED | DEFAULT]
[FAILED_LOGIN_ATTEMPTS expr | UNLIMITED | DEFAULT]
[PASSWORD_LIFE_TIME expr | UNLIMITED | DEFAULT]
[PASSWORD_REUSE_TIME expr | UNLIMITED | DEFAULT]
[PASSWORD_REUSE_MAX expr | UNLIMITED | DEFAULT]
[PASSWORD_LOCK_TIME expr | UNLIMITED | DEFAULT]
[PASSWORD_GRACE_TIME expr | UNLIMITED | DEFAULT]
[PASSWORD_VERIFY_FUNCTION function | NULL | DEFAULT]
```

DROP Syntax:
```
DROP PROFILE profile_name [CASCADE]
```

Creates, modifies, or removes a profile that sets limits on database resources.

 To apply the limits associated with the profile to a specific user, you must assign the profile to the user with the CREATE USER or ALTER USER statement. Resource limits must also be enabled either via the RESOURCE_LIMIT initialization parameter or by using the ALTER SYSTEM statement.

Keywords

profile_name
> Name of the profile to be created.

SESSIONS_PER_USER
> Limits the number of concurrent sessions for a user.

CPU_PER_SESSION
> Limits the amount of CPU time that can be used in a session (in hundredths of a second).

CPU_PER_CALL
> Limits the amount of CPU time for a call (a parse, execute, or fetch) (in hundredths of a second).

CONNECT_TIME
> Limits the total elapsed time for a session (in minutes).

IDLE_TIME

Limits the amount of continuous inactive time during a session (in minutes).

LOGICAL_READS_PER_SESSION

Limits the number of database blocks read in a session, including those read from memory and disk.

LOGICAL_READS_PER_CALL

Limits the number of database blocks read for a call (a parse, execute, or fetch).

PRIVATE_SGA

Limits the amount of memory a session can allocate in the SGA's shared pool (in bytes).

COMPOSITE_LIMIT

Limits the total resource cost for a session (in service units). See the ALTER RESOURCE COST entry earlier in this section for additional information.

UNLIMITED

Specifying this value means that no limit will be imposed on this resource.

DEFAULT

Specifying this value means that the limit specified in the DEFAULT profile will be used for this resource.

FAILED_LOGIN_ATTEMPTS

Specifies the number of failed login attempts allowed before the account is locked.

PASSWORD_LIFE_TIME

Specifies the number of days the password may be used before it expires and must be changed.

PASSWORD_REUSE_TIME

Specifies the number of days before which a previously used password may be reused. If set to *integer*, PASSWORD_REUSE_MAX must be set to UNLIMITED.

PASSWORD_REUSE_MAX

Specifies the number of password changes required before the current password can be reused. If set to *integer*, PASSWORD_REUSE_TIME must be set to UNLIMITED.

PASSWORD_LOCK_TIME

Specifies the number of days an account will remain locked after the FAILED_LOGIN_ATTEMPTS limit is exceeded.

PASSWORD_GRACE_TIME

Specifies the number of days after password expiration that a login will be allowed with a warning message.

PASSWORD_VERIFY_FUNCTION

Specifies the name of a PL/SQL function used to verify passwords. Setting this parameter to NULL indicates that no verification will be performed.

Common keywords and clauses: *expr*.

CREATE/ALTER/DROP ROLE

CREATE Syntax:
```
CREATE ROLE rolename
{NOT IDENTIFIED
```

```
| IDENTIFIED
  { EXTERNALLY
  | GLOBALLY
  | BY password
  | USING [schema.]package
  }
}
```

ALTER Syntax:
```
ALTER ROLE rolename
{NOT IDENTIFIED
| IDENTIFIED
  { EXTERNALLY
  | GLOBALLY
  | BY password
  | USING [schema.]package
  }
}
```

DROP Syntax:
```
DROP ROLE rolename
```

Creates, modifies, or removes a role, which is a set of privileges that can be granted to users. When you create a role, you are automatically granted that role WITH ADMIN OPTION, which allows you to grant or revoke the role or to modify it using the ALTER ROLE statement.

Keywords

rolename
> Name of the role to be created.

NOT IDENTIFIED
> Specifies that a user who was granted the role does not need to be verified when enabling it.

IDENTIFIED BY password
> Specifies that the password must be provided when enabling the role.

IDENTIFIED EXTERNALLY
> Specifies that the operating system verifies the user enabling the role.

IDENTIFIED GLOBALLY
> Specifies that a global user is to be created. A global user must be authorized to use the role by the enterprise directory service before the role is enabled with the SET ROLE statement or at login time.

IDENTIFIED USING
> Specifies that this is an application role, which is a role that can be enabled only by applications using packages. New with Oracle9i.

Common keywords and clauses: *schema*.

CREATE/ALTER/DROP ROLLBACK SEGMENT

CREATE Syntax:
```
CREATE [PUBLIC] ROLLBACK SEGMENT segment_name
TABLESPACE tablespace_name
  [Storage_Clause]
```

ALTER Syntax:
```
ALTER ROLLBACK SEGMENT segment_name
[Storage_Clause]
[ONLINE | OFFLINE]
[SHRINK]
```

DROP Syntax:
```
DROP ROLLBACK SEGMENT segment_name
```

Creates, modifies, or removes a rollback segment, which Oracle uses to store data necessary to roll back changes made by transactions.

 When a rollback segment is created, it will be offline. It must be brought online by using the ALTER ROLLBACK SEGMENT statement or by restarting the database with the rollback segment named in the initialization file.

Keywords

PUBLIC
Specifies that this rollback segment is available to any instance. If omitted, it is available only to the instance naming it in the ROLLBACK_SEGMENTS parameter in the initialization file.

segment_name
Name of the rollback segment to be created.

TABLESPACE
Specifies the name of the tablespace in which this rollback segment will be created.

ONLINE
Specifies that the named rollback segment be brought online.

OFFLINE
Specifies that the named rollback segment be taken offline.

SHRINK
Specifies that the named rollback segment should be reduced to the size specified or to the OPTIMAL size if no size is specified.

Common keywords and clauses: *Storage_Clause, tablespace_name*.

CREATE SCHEMA

```
CREATE SCHEMA AUTHORIZATION schema
[CREATE TABLE statement]
[CREATE VIEW statement]
[GRANT statement]
```

Creates multiple tables and/or views and issues grants in a single statement.

 You must have the same privileges required for the CREATE TABLE, CREATE VIEW, and GRANT statements to issue this statement. Individual statements within the CREATE SCHEMA statement must not be terminated with the SQL termination character.

Keywords

schema
    Name of the schema to be created, which must be the same as your username.

CREATE TABLE statement
    This is a CREATE TABLE statement, as shown later in the CREATE TABLE entry.

CREATE VIEW statement
    This is a CREATE VIEW statement, as shown later in the CREATE VIEW entry.

GRANT statement
    This is a GRANT statement, as shown later in the GRANT entry.

CREATE/ALTER/DROP SEQUENCE

CREATE Syntax:
```
CREATE SEQUENCE [schema.]sequence_name
[INCREMENT BY integer]
[START WITH integer]
[MAXVALUE integer | NOMAXVALUE]
[MINVALUE integer | NOMINVALUE]
[CYCLE | NOCYCLE]
[CACHE integer | NOCACHE]
[ORDER | NOORDER]
```

ALTER Syntax:
```
ALTER SEQUENCE [schema.]sequence_name
[INCREMENT BY integer]
[MAXVALUE integer | NOMAXVALUE]
[MINVALUE integer | NOMINVALUE]
[CYCLE | NOCYCLE]
[CACHE integer | NOCACHE]
[ORDER | NOORDER]
```

DROP Syntax:
```
DROP SEQUENCE [schema.]sequence_name
```

Creates, modifies, or removes an Oracle sequence that can be used to automatically generate sequential numbers during database operations. The generation of a sequence number is not affected by the subsequent rollback of the transaction; once generated, that sequence number will not be available again, so gaps can occur. Sequence numbers are accessed by using the pseudocolumns CURRVAL and NEXTVAL.

The DROP SEQUENCE and CREATE SEQUENCE statements can be issued sequentially to restart a sequence at a lower number. However, all GRANTs to the sequence will also have to be re-created.

Keywords

INCREMENT BY
    Specifies the increment between sequence numbers and can be positive or negative (but not 0). The default is 1.

START WITH
    Specifies the first sequence number to be generated. The default is the MINVALUE for ascending sequences and MAXVALUE for descending sequences.

SQL

MAXVALUE   Specifies the largest value the sequence number can reach. The default is NOMAXVALUE, which means the maximum value is 1027.

MINVALUE   Specifies the smallest value the sequence number can reach. The default is NOMINVALUE, which means the minimum value is 1.

CYCLE   Specifies that when sequence numbers reach MAXVALUE they will begin again at MINVALUE. The default is NOCYCLE.

NOCYCLE   Specifies that after reaching the maximum value, no additional sequence numbers will be generated.

CACHE   Specifies how many sequence numbers Oracle will pregenerate and keep in memory. Note that when the database is shut down, unused sequence numbers stored in cache will be lost. The default is 20.

NOCACHE   Specifies that no sequence numbers are pregenerated to memory.

ORDER   Specifies that sequence numbers are guaranteed to be issued in the order of request. The default is NOORDER.

NOORDER   Specifies that sequence numbers are not guaranteed to be generated in the order of request.

Common keywords and clauses: *integer, schema.*

CREATE/ALTER/DROP SNAPSHOT

CREATE Syntax:
```
CREATE SNAPSHOT [schema.]snapshot_name
[Physical_Attributes_Clause]
[TABLESPACE tablespace_name]
[Storage_Clause]
[REFRESH [FAST | COMPLETE | FORCE]
[START WITH date][NEXTREF date]]
AS snapshot_query
```

ALTER Syntax:
```
ALTER SNAPSHOT [schema.]snapshot_name
[Physical_Attributes_Clause] [Storage_Clause]
[REFRESH [FAST | COMPLETE | FORCE]
 [START WITH date][NEXTREF date]]
```

DROP Syntax:
```
DROP SNAPSHOT [schema.]snapshot_name
```

Creates, modifies, or removes a snapshot, which is the result of a query run against one or more tables or views. Note that before you can attempt to create a snapshot, the *dbmssnap.sql* script must be run by SYS to create the built-in DBMS_SNAPSHOT package.

Keywords

snapshot_name
> Name of the snapshot. Because Oracle appends 7-character identifiers to the snapshot name when creating snapshot objects in the schema, you should limit *snapshot_name* to 23 characters or fewer.

TABLESPACE
> Specifies the name of the tablespace where this snapshot will be stored. If omitted, the default tablespace for the schema owner will be used.

REFRESH

Specifies the mode and times for automatic refreshes.

FAST

Uses the snapshot log associated with the master table.

COMPLETE

Refreshes by reexecuting the snapshot's query.

FORCE

Oracle decides if a FAST refresh is possible or if a COMPLETE refresh is necessary; FORCE is the default.

START WITH

Specifies a date for the next automatic refresh time using a standard Oracle date expression.

NEXTREF

Specifies a new date expression for calculating the interval between automatic refreshes.

AS

Provides the actual SQL query used to populate the snapshot and subject to the same restrictions as a view.

Common keywords and clauses: *date, Physical_Attributes_Clause, schema, Storage_Clause, tablespace_name.*

CREATE/ALTER/DROP SNAPSHOT LOG

CREATE Syntax:
```
CREATE SNAPSHOT LOG ON [schema.]table_name
[Physical_Attributes_Clause]
[TABLESPACE tablespace_name]
[Storage_Clause]
```

ALTER Syntax:
```
ALTER SNAPSHOT LOG ON [schema.]table_name
[Physical_Attributes_Clause]
[Storage_Clause]
```

DROP Syntax:
```
DROP SNAPSHOT LOG ON [schema.]table_name
```

Creates, modifies, or removes a snapshot log (a table associated with the master table of a snapshot and used to control refreshes of snapshots).

Keywords

TABLESPACE

Specifies the name of the tablespace where this snapshot will be stored. If omitted, the default tablespace for the schema owner will be used.

Common keywords and clauses: *Physical_Attributes_Clause, Storage_Clause, schema, table_name, tablespace_name.*

CREATE SPFILE

```
CREATE SPFILE [= 'pfile_name'] FROM PFILE [= 'spfile_name']
```

Creates a binary server parameter file by importing the contents of a text initialization parameter file (*INIT.ORA* or *SPFILE*). New with Oracle9*i* Release 2.

Keywords

'spfile_name'
> Name of the binary server parameter file that will be created. If *spfile_name* is not specified, Oracle uses a platform-specific filename, usually *INIT*sid*.ORA*.

'pfile_name'
> Name of the existing text initialization parameter file. If *pfile_name* is not specified, Oracle uses a platform-specific filename.

CREATE/DROP SYNONYM

CREATE Syntax:
```
CREATE [PUBLIC] SYNONYM synonym_name
FOR [schema.]object_name[@dblink]
```

DROP Syntax:
```
DROP [PUBLIC] SYNONYM [schema.]synonym_name
```

Creates or removes a public or private synonym for a database object.

Keywords

PUBLIC
> Specifies that this synonym will be available to all users. If omitted, the synonym will be available only to the schema owner.

synonym_name
> Name of the new synonym.

object_name
> Name of the object to which the synonym will refer. It may include a reference to a remote database by appending the *@dblink* syntax.

> Oracle resolves object names in the current schema first, so a PUBLIC synonym will be used only if the object name is not prefaced with a schema name, is not followed by a *dblink*, and does not exist in the current schema.

Common keywords and clauses: *dblink, schema.*

CREATE/ALTER/DROP TABLE (Relational Syntax)

CREATE Syntax:
```
CREATE [GLOBAL] [TEMPORARY] TABLE [schema.]table_name
(column   datatype [DEFAULT expr] [Column_Constraint_Clause]
  [,column   datatype [DEFAULT expr] [Column_Constraint_Clause]...]
[Table_Constraint_Clause])
[ON COMMIT {DELETE | PRESERVE} ROWS]
[Physical_Attributes_Clause]
[TABLESPACE tablespace_name]
[Storage_Clause]
[{LOGGING | NOLOGGING}]
[{COMPRESS | NOCOMPRESS}]
{ CLUSTER (column[,column ...])
```

```
|  ORGANIZATION HEAP
    [Physical_Attributes_Clause]
    [TABLESPACE tablespace_name]
    [Storage_Clause]
    [{LOGGING | NOLOGGING}]
    [{COMPRESS | NOCOMPRESS}]
|  ORGANIZATION INDEX
    [Physical_Attributes_Clause]
    [TABLESPACE tablespace_name]
    [Storage_Clause]
    [{LOGGING | NOLOGGING}]
    { {MAPPING TABLE | NOMAPPING}
    | PCTTHRESHOLD integer
    | {COMPRESS integer | NOCOMPRESS}
    }
    [[INCLUDING colummn] OVERFLOW
    [Physical_Attributes_Clause]
    [TABLESPACE tablespace_name]
    [Storage_Clause]
    [LOGGING | NOLOGGING]
|  ORGANIZATION EXTERNAL
    ([TYPE access_data_type]
    DEFAULT DIRECTORY directory
    [ACCESS PARAMETERS {(opaque_format_spec) | USING CLOB subquery}]
    LOCATION ([directory:]'location_specifier'
      [,[directory:]'location_specifier'])
    [REJECT LIMIT {integer | UNLIMITED}]
}
[Partition_Clause]
{
  [ { varray_storage_clause
    | [LOB
      { (lob_item[,lob_item ...]) STORE AS
        ([TABLESPACE tablespace_name]
        [{ENABLE | DISABLE} STORAGE IN ROW]
        [Storage_Clause]
        [CHUNK integer]
        [PCTVERSION integer]
        [CACHE | NOCACHE [LOGGING | NOLOGGING]])
      | (lob_item) STORE AS [(lob_segname)]
        [([TABLESPACE tablespace_name]
        [{ENABLE | DISABLE} STORAGE IN ROW]
        [Storage_Clause]
        [CHUNK integer]
        [PCTVERSION integer]
        [CACHE | NOCACHE [LOGGING | NOLOGGING]])
      }
    }]
}
[ENABLE | DISABLE ROW MOVEMENT]
[CACHE | NOCACHE]
[MONITORING | NOMONITORING]
[ROWDEPENDENCIES | NOROWDEPENDENCIES]
[PARALLEL integer | NOPARALLEL]
```

```
[ENABLE | DISABLE [VALIDATE | NOVALIDATE]]
  {UNIQUE (column[, column ...]
  | PRIMARY KEY
  | CONSTRAINT constraint_name
  }
  [USING INDEX
    [TABLESPACE tablespace_name]
    [Physical_Attributes_Clause]
    [Storage_Clause]
    [NOSORT]
    [LOGGING | NOLOGGING]]
  [EXCEPTIONS INTO [schema.]table_name]
  [CASCADE]
  [{KEEP | DROP} INDEX]
[AS subquery]
```

ALTER Syntax:

```
ALTER TABLE [schema.]table_name
{ Physical_Attributes_Clause
  [{LOGGING | NOLOGGING}]
  [{COMPRESS | NOCOMPRESS}]
  [ADD SUPPLEMENTAL LOG GROUP lg_group (column[,column...]) [ALWAYS]
  | DROP SUPPLEMENTAL LOG GROUP lg_group
  }
  [ALLOCATE EXTENT (
  [SIZE integer[K | M]]
  [DATAFILE 'filename']
  [INSTANCE integer]
  )]
  [DEALLOCATE UNUSED [KEEP integer[K | M]]]
  [CACHE | NOCACHE]
  [MONITORING | NOMONITORING]
  [UPGRADE [[NOT] INCLUDING DATA]
    [Column_Properties_Clause]
  [{MINIMIZE | NOMINIMIZE} RECORDS_PER_BLOCK]
  [PARALLEL integer | NOPARALLEL]
  [ENABLE | DISABLE ROW MOVEMENT]
  [RENAME TO new_table_name]
| { ADD (column datatype [DEFAULT expr] [Column_Constraint_Clause]
    [,column datatype [DEFAULT expr] [Column_Constraint_Clause] ...)]
    [Column_Properties_Clause]
  | MODIFY
    { (column datatype [DEFAULT expr] [Column_Constraint_Clause]
      [,column datatype [DEFAULT expr] [Column_Constraint_Clause] ...)]
      [LOB_Storage_Clause]
    | COLUMN column [NOT] SUBSTITUTABLE AT ALL LEVELS [FORCE]
    }
  | DROP
    { {PRIMARY KEY | UNIQUE (column[,column...])}
    | CONSTRAINT constraint_name [CASCADE]
    }
  | RENAME COLUMN column to new_column_name
  | MODIFY VARRAY varray_item ([Storage_Clause] [LOB_Parameters_Clause])
  }
```

```
    | { ADD Constraint_Clause
      | MODIFY CONSTRAINT constraint_name constraint_state
      | RENAME CONSTRAINT constraint_name TO new_constraint_name
      | DROP
        { {PRIMARY KEY | UNIQUE (column[,column...])}
        | CONSTRAINT constraint_name [CASCADE]
        }
    }
| MODIFY DEFAULT ATTRIBUTES [FOR PARTITION partition_name]
    [TABLESPACE tablespace_name]
    [LOGGING | NOLOGGING]
    [Physical_Attriobutes_Clause]
    [PCTTHRESHOLD integer]
    [{COMPRESS integer | NOCOMPRESS}]
    [OVERFLOW [Physical_Attributes_Clause]
    [ALLOCATE EXTENT ([SIZE integer [K | M]]
     [DATAFILE 'filename']
     [INSTANCE integer])]
   [DEALLOCATE UNUSED [KEEP integer[K | M]]
| MODIFY PARTITION partition_name
    Partition_Attributes_Clause
    [REBUILD] UNUSABLE LOCAL INDEXES]
    { ADD PARTITION partition_name
      Partition_Clause
      COALESCE SUBPARTITION {UPDATE | INVALIDATE} GLOBAL INDEXES
    | MAPPING TABLE
      {UPDATE BLOCK REFERENCES
      | ALLOCATE EXTENT ([SIZE integer [K | M]]
        [DATAFILE 'filename']
        [INSTANCE integer])
      | DEALLOCATE UNUSED [KEEP integer[K | M]]
      }
    | {ADD | DROP} VALUES (value[,value...])
    }
| MODIFY SUBPARTITION subpartition_name
    Partition_Attributes_Clause
    [REBUILD] UNUSABLE LOCAL INDEXES]
    { ADD PARTITION partition_name
      Partition_Clause
      COALESCE SUBPARTITION {UPDATE | INVALIDATE} GLOBAL INDEXES
    | MAPPING TABLE
      {UPDATE BLOCK REFERENCES
      | ALLOCATE EXTENT ([SIZE integer [K | M]]
        [DATAFILE 'filename']
        [INSTANCE integer])
      | DEALLOCATE UNUSED [KEEP integer[K | M]]
      }
    | {ADD | DROP} VALUES (value[,value...])
    }
| MOVE PARTITION partition_name [MAPPING TABLE]
    [Partition_Description_Clause]
    [{UPDATE | INVALIDATE} GLOBAL INDEXES]
    [PARALLEL integer | NOPARALLEL]
| MOVE SUBPARTITION subpartition_name
```

SQL

```
        [{UPDATE | INVALIDATE} GLOBAL INDEXES]
          [PARALLEL integer | NOPARALLEL]
   | ADD PARTITION partition_name Partition_Clause
       COALESCE SUBPARTITION {UPDATE | INVALIDATE} GLOBAL INDEXES
          [PARALLEL integer | NOPARALLEL]
   | DROP {PARTITION partition_name | SUBPARTITION subpartition_name}
       [{UPDATE | INVALIDATE} GLOBAL INDEXES]
          [PARALLEL integer | NOPARALLEL]
   | RENAME
       { PARTITION partition_name TO new_partition_name
       | SUBPARTITION subpartition_name TO new_subpartition_name
       }
   | TRUNCATE {PARTITION partition_name | SUBPARTITION subpartition_name}
   | SPLIT PARTITION partition_name {AT | VALUES} (value[,value...])
       [INTO (PARTITION partition_name Partition_Clause)]
       [{UPDATE | INVALIDATE} GLOBAL INDEXES]
       [PARALLEL integer | NOPARALLEL]
   | SPLIT SUBPARTITION subpartition_name
       VALUES ({value | NULL}[,{value | NULL ...})
       [INTO (PARTITION subpartition_name Partition_Clause)]
       [{UPDATE | INVALIDATE} GLOBAL INDEXES]
       [PARALLEL integer | NOPARALLEL]
   | MERGE PARTITIONS partition_name, partition_name
       [INTO (PARTITION partition_name Partition_Clause)]
       [{UPDATE | INVALIDATE} GLOBAL INDEXES]
       [PARALLEL integer | NOPARALLEL]
   | MERGE SUBPARTITIONS subpartition_name, sub partition_name
       [INTO (PARTITION subpartition_name Partition_Clause)]
       [{UPDATE | INVALIDATE} GLOBAL INDEXES]
       [PARALLEL integer | NOPARALLEL]
   | EXCHANGE {PARTITION partition_name | subpartition_name}
       WITH TABLE table_name
       [{INCLUDING | EXCLUDING} INDEXES]
       [{WITH | WITHOUT} VALIDATION]
       [EXCEPTIONS INTO [schema.]table_name]
       [{UPDATE | INVALIDATE} GLOBAL INDEXES]
   }
```

DROP Syntax:
```
DROP TABLE [schema.]table_name
[CASCADE CONSTRAINTS]
```

Creates (either by defining structure or by copying an existing table), modifies, or drops a relational table.

When you drop a table, all rows are deleted. Any indexes remaining on the table are also automatically deleted, regardless of what schema created or currently owns them. If the table to be dropped is a base table for a view or if it is referenced in any stored procedure, the view or procedure will be marked INVALID (but not dropped). If the table is the master table for a snapshot, the snapshot is not dropped. Likewise, if the table has a snapshot log, that snapshot log is not dropped.

Keywords

GLOBAL TEMPORARY

Specifies that the table to be created will be a temporary table with a structure visible to all sessions, but with data visible only to the creating session. A temporary table must be created in a temporary tablespace. New with Oracle9*i*.

datatype

Datatype to be associated with *column.*

DEFAULT

Specifies a default value for the column, which will be used if rows inserted into the table omit values for the column. The expression must match the *datatype* of the column.

ON COMMIT

Specifies whether the data in the temporary table persists for the duration of a transaction or a session. This clause applies only to temporary tables. New with Oracle9*i*.

TABLESPACE

Specifies the name of the tablespace where this table will be stored. If omitted, Oracle uses the default tablespace for the schema owner.

CLUSTER

Specifies that the table is to be part of the cluster. The columns listed in this clause are the table columns that correspond to the cluster's columns.

ORGANIZATION HEAP

Specifies that no order is associated with the storage of rows of data in this table. This option is the default.

ORGANIZATION INDEX

Specifies that the table be created as an index-organized table, meaning that the data rows are actually held in an index that is defined on the primary key of the table.

MAPPING TABLE

Specifies that Oracle is to create a mapping of local to physical ROWIDs and store them in a heap-organized table. This mapping is needed in order to create a bitmap index on the index-organized table. NOMAPPING is the default. New in Oracle9*i*.

PCTTHRESHOLD

Specifies the percentage of space in each index block reserved for data rows. Any part of a data row that cannot fit in this space will be placed in the overflow segment. New in Oracle9*i*.

INCLUDING

Specifies the point at which a table row is to be divided between index and overflow portions. All columns following *column* (except primary key columns) will be stored in the overflow segment.

OVERFLOW

Specifies that index-organized table rows that exceed the PCTTHRESHOLD value be placed in a segment described in this clause.

ORGANIZATION EXTERNAL

Specifies that Oracle is to create an external table, which is a read-only table whose metadata is stored in the database but whose data in stored outside the database. New in Oracle9i.

TYPE

Access driver of the external table. The access driver is the API that interprets the external data for the database. If you do not specify TYPE, then Oracle uses the default access driver, ORACLE_LOADER.

DEFAULT DIRECTORY

Default directory object corresponding to a directory on the filesystem where the external data sources may reside. The default directory can also be used by the access driver to store auxiliary files such as error logs.

ACCESS PARAMETERS

Values for the parameters of the specific access driver for this external table. The *opaque_format_spec* lets you list the parameters and their values. USING CLOB *subquery* lets you derive the parameters and their values through a subquery, which cannot contain any set operators or an ORDER BY clause and must return one row containing a single item of datatype CLOB. Oracle does not interpret anything in this clause; it is up to the access driver to interpret this information in the context of the external data.

LOCATION

One or more external data sources. Usually the *location_specifier* is a file, but it need not be. Oracle does not interpret this clause; it is up to the access driver to interpret this information in the context of the external data.

REJECT LIMIT

Number of conversion errors that can occur during a query of the external data before an Oracle error is returned and the query is aborted. The default value is 0.

LOB

Specifies storage attributes for LOB data.

lob_item

Name of a LOB column.

STORE AS

Specifies the name of the LOB data segment.

ENABLE STORAGE IN ROW

Specifies that the LOB value is stored in the row. If these keywords are specified for an index-organized table, OVERFLOW must also be specified. This option is the default.

DISABLE STORAGE IN ROW

Specifies that the LOB value be stored outside the row.

CHUNK

Specifies the number of bytes (rounded up to the nearest database block size) allocated for LOB manipulation.

PCTVERSION

Specifies the maximum percentage of the LOB storage space used in creating a new version of the LOB.

ENABLE ROW MOVEMENT
Specifies that a row may be moved to a different partition or subpartition if required as the result of an update of the key. New with Oracle8*i*.

DISABLE ROW MOVEMENT
Specifies that rows may not be moved to a different partition or subpartition and returns an error if an update to a key would require such a move. New with Oracle8*i*.

MONITORING
Specifies that modification statistics can be collected for this table. New with Oracle8*i*.

NOMONITORING
Specifies that modification statistics will not be collected for this table. This option is the default. New with Oracle9*i*.

ROWDEPENDENCIES
Specifies that row-level dependency tracking is to be enabled for this table. This feature is used primarily in replicated environments and adds 6 bytes to the length of each row. New with Oracle9*i*.

NOROWDEPENDENCIES
Specifies that row-level dependency tracking is not enabled. This is the default.

ENABLE
Specifies that a constraint be applied to all new data in the table.

DISABLE
Specifies that a constraint be disabled for the table.

VALIDATE
When specified with ENABLE, causes Oracle to verify that all existing data in the table comply with the constraint.

NOVALIDATE
When specified with ENABLE, prevents Oracle from verifying that existing data in the table comply with the constraint but ensures that new data added to the table does comply with the constraint.

UNIQUE
Specifies that the unique constraint defined on the specified column or combination of columns be enabled or disabled.

PRIMARY KEY
Specifies that the table's primary key constraint be enabled or disabled.

CONSTRAINT
Specifies that the integrity constraint named *constraint_name* be enabled or disabled.

USING INDEX
Specifies the characteristics of an index used to enforce a constraint.

EXCEPTIONS INTO
Specifies the name of a table into which Oracle places information about rows violating the constraint. You must explicitly create this table by running the *UTLEXCPT1.SQL* script before using this keyword.

KEEP
Specifies that the index Oracle has been using to enforce a unique or primary key constraint be preserved.

SQL

DROP

Specifies that the index Oracle has been using to enforce a unique or primary key constraint be dropped.

CASCADE

Specifies that any integrity constraints that depend on the specified integrity constraint be disabled. To disable a primary or unique key that is part of a referential integrity constraint, you must specify this clause.

Additional ALTER Keywords

ADD SUPPLEMENTAL LOG GROUP

Specifies that a supplemental log group be added and supplies the filename. New with Oracle9*i*.

DROP SUPPLEMENTAL LOG GROUP

Specifies that the supplemental log group identified be dropped. New with Oracle9*i*.

ALLOCATE EXTENT

Explicitly allocates a new extent for the table using the specified parameters.

SIZE

Specifies the size of the extent to be allocated.

DATAFILE

Specifies the name of a datafile to which the extent is to be added.

INSTANCE

Specifies the instance number to which the extent is to be added.

DEALLOCATE UNUSED

Specifies that unused space at the end of the table, partition, subpartition, overflow data segment, LOB data segment, or LOB index be deallocated and the space made available for other segments in the tablespace.

KEEP

Specifies the number of bytes above the highwater mark that the table overflow data segment, LOB data segment, or LOB index is to have after deallocation.

UPGRADE

Specifies that metadata of the table be converted to conform to the latest version of each referenced type. This keyword applies only to tables that contain object columns. New with Oracle9*i*.

INCLUDING DATA

Specifies that Oracle convert the data in the table to the latest type version format (if it was not converted when the type was altered). You can define the storage for any new column while upgrading the table. This is the default. If NOT INCLUDING DATA is specified, Oracle will leave column data unchanged.

MINIMIZE RECORDS_PER_BLOCK

Specifies that Oracle should calculate the largest number of rows in any block of the table (by examining existing table data) and limiting future inserts so that no more than this number of rows may occur in any block. NOMINIMIZE, which is the default, may be specified to disable this behavior.

RENAME TO
>Specifies that the table be renamed to the new name provided.

ADD
>Specifies the name and characteristics of a new column being added to the table.

MODIFY
>Specifies that the column characteristics be modified.

DROP PRIMARY KEY
>Specifies that the primary key constraint on this table be removed.

DROP UNIQUE
>Specifies that the unique key on the column indicated be dropped.

RENAME COLUMN
>Specifies that the name of a column in this table be changed. New with Oracle9*i*.

MODIFY VARRAY
>Specifies that the storage characteristics of the VARRAY be changed. New with Oracle9*i*.

ADD Constraint_Clause
>Specifies that a constraint be added to the table.

MODIFY CONSTRAINT
>Specifies that the named constraint be modified.

RENAME CONSTRAINT
>Changes the name of an existing constraint on the table. New with Oracle9*i* Release 2.

DROP CONSTRAINT
>Drops an integrity constraint.

RENAME COLUMN
>Changes the name of an existing column in the table. New with Oracle9*i* Release 2.

MODIFY DEFAULT ATTRIBUTES
>Specifies new default values for the attributes of the table. Partitions and LOB partitions created subsequently will inherit these values unless overridden explicitly when creating the partition or LOB partition. Existing partitions and LOB partitions are not affected by this clause.

>*FOR PARTITION*
>>Specifies that the default attributes apply only to the named partition. FOR PARTITION applies only to composite-partitioned tables.

MODIFY PARTITION
>Specifies that the characteristics of the named partition be changed.

>*REBUILD UNUSABLE LOCAL INDEXES*
>>Specifies that local indexes for the partition being modified be rebuilt. If this clause is not specified the index will be marked

>*ADD PARTITION*
>>Specifies that a new partition be created for this table.

>*COALESCE SUBPARTITION*
>>Specifies that Oracle select a hash subpartition, distribute its contents into one or more remaining subpartitions (determined by the hash function), and then drop the selected subpartition. New with Oracle8*i*.

UPDATE GLOBAL INDEXES

Specifies that if a global index is defined on the table, Oracle update the entire index, not only the partition being operated on.

INVALIDATE GLOBAL INDEXES

Specifies that if a global index is defined on the table, Oracle invalidate the entire index, not only the partitions being operated on.

ADD VALUES

Specifies that Oracle extend the partition (or subpartition) value list to include additional values. New with Oracle9i Release 2.

DROP VALUES

Specifies that Oracle reduce the partition (or subpartition) value list by removing the supplied values. New with Oracle9i Release 2.

MODIFY SUBPARTITION

Specifies that the characteristics of the named subpartition be changed.

MOVE PARTITION

Specifies that Oracle move the specified partition to another segment.

MOVE SUBPARTITION

Specifies that Oracle move the specified subpartition to another segment.

DROP PARTITION

Specifies that the named partition be removed.

DROP SUBPARTITION

Specifies that the named subpartition be removed.

RENAME PARTITION

Specifies that the name of a table partition be changed from *partition_name* to *new_partition_name*.

RENAME SUBPARTITION

Specifies that the name of a table subpartition be changed from *subpartition_name* to *new_subpartition_name*.

TRUNCATE PARTITION

Specifies that all data rows in a partition be removed in a manner similar to the TRUNCATE TABLE statement. If the table is index-organized, any corresponding mapping table partitions are also truncated.

TRUNCATE SUBPARTITION

Specifies that all data rows in a subpartition be removed in a manner similar to the TRUNCATE TABLE statement. If the table is index-organized, any corresponding mapping table subpartitions are also truncated.

SPLIT

Specifies that Oracle create two new partitions or subpartitions, each with a new segment and new physical attributes and new initial extents. The segment associated with the original partition or subpartition is discarded.

MERGE

Specifies that Oracle merge the contents of two partitions or subpartitions of the table into one new partition, and then drop the original two partitions.

EXCHANGE

Specifies that Oracle exchange the data and index segments of one of the following: one nonpartitioned table with one hash, list, or range partition (or one hash or list subpartition), or one hash-partitioned table with the hash subpartitions of a range partition of a range-hash composite-partitioned table, or one list-partitioned table with the list subpartitions of a range partition of a range-list composite-partitioned table. In all cases, the structure of the table and the partition or subpartition being exchanged, including their partitioning keys, must be identical. In the case of list partitions and subpartitions, the corresponding value lists must also match.

Additional DROP Keywords

CASCADE CONSTRAINTS
Specifies that all referential integrity constraints referring to primary and unique keys in the table to be dropped will also be dropped.

Common keywords and clauses: *column,* COMPRESS, *expr, integer,* LOGGING, NOCOMPRESS, NOLOGGING, NOPARALLEL, PARALLEL, *partition_name, schema, subpartition_name, table_name, tablespace_name, Column_Constraint_Clause, Constraint_State_Clause, LOB_Parameter_Clause, LOB_Storage_Clause, Partition_ Clause, Partition_Description_Clause, Physical_Attributes_Clause, Storage_Clause, Table_Constraint_Clause, VARRAY_Storage_Clause.*

CREATE/ALTER/DROP TABLE (Object Syntax)

CREATE Syntax:
```
CREATE [GLOBAL TEMPORARY] TABLE [schema.]table_name
  OF [schema.]object_type
( { { column | attribute} [DEFAULT expr]
    { SCOPE IS [schema.]scope_table_name]
    | WITH ROWID
    | [CONSTRAINT constraint_name]  REFERENCES [schema.]object_table
      [ON DELETE CASCADE]
    }
|     { SCOPE FOR ({column | attribute}) IS [schema.]table_name |
        REF ({column | attribute}) WITH ROWID
    | [CONSTRAINT constraint_name] FOREIGN KEY (column)
        REFERENCES [schema.]object_table [ON DELETE CASCADE]
        [Constraint_State_Clause]
    }
)
[OBJECT ID {SYSTEM GENERATED | PRIMARY KEY}]
[ON COMMIT {DELETE | PRESERVE} ROWS]
[OIDINDEX [indexname] ([physical_attributes_clause]
[TABLESPACE tablespace_name])]
[Physical_Attributes_Clause]
[TABLESPACE_NAME tablespace_name]
[Storage_Clause]
[LOGGING | NOLOGGING]
[CLUSTER (column[,column ...]]
[ { ORGANIZATION HEAP
    [Physical_Attributes_Clause]
    [TABLESPACE tablespace_name]
    [Storage_Clause]
    [LOGGING | NOLOGGING]
  | ORGANIZATION INDEX
    [PCTTHRESHOLD integer]
```

```
         [COMPRESS integer | NOCOMPRESS]
         [Physical_Attributes_Clause]
         [TABLESPACE tablespace_name]
         [Storage_Clause]
         [LOGGING | NOLOGGING]
         [[INCLUDING column] OVERFLOW
           [Physical_Attributes_Clause]
           [TABLESPACE tablespace_name]
           [Storage_Clause]
           [LOGGING | NOLOGGING]]
     }
[LOB
  {(lob_item[,lob_item...]) STORE AS
     (LOB_Parameter_Clause)
   | (lob_item) STORE AS [(lob_segname)]
     [(LOB_Parameter_Clause)] ]
     [VARRAY varray_item STORE AS LOB [lob_segname]
       [(LOB_Parameter_Clause)]]
     [NESTED TABLE nested_table STORE AS storage_table
       (table_name [Physical_Attributes_Clause]
       [TABLESPACE tablespace_name] [LOGGING | NOLOGGING]]
       [[LOB {(lob_item[,lob_item...]) STORE AS
         ([LOB_Parameter_Clause)
   |    (lob_item) STORE AS [(lob_segname)]
       [(LOB_Parameter_Clause)]}
} ]
[RETURN AS {LOCATOR | VALUE}]
[Partitioning_Clause]
[ENABLE | DISABLE ROW MOVEMENT]
[CACHE | NOCACHE]
[MONITORING | NOMONITORING]
[PARALLEL integer | NOPARALLEL]
[{ENABLE | DISABLE} [VALIDATE | NOVALIDATE]
  { UNIQUE (column[, column...]
  | PRIMARY KEY
  | CONSTRAINT constraint_name
  }
  [USING INDEX
    [TABLESPACE tablespace_name]
    [Physical_Attributes_Clause]
    [Storage_Clause]
    [NOSORT]
    [LOGGING | NOLOGGING]]
    [EXCEPTIONS INTO [schema.]table_name [CASCADE]]
[AS subquery]
```

ALTER Syntax:

```
ALTER TABLE [schema.]table_name
{ Physical_Attributes_Clause
| { ADD ([column   datatype [DEFAULT expr] [Column_Constraint_Clause]
    [,column datatype [DEFAULT expr] [Column_Constraint_Clause] ...)]
  | MODIFY
    { ([column   datatype [DEFAULT expr] [Column_Constraint_Clause]
      [,column datatype [DEFAULT expr] [Column_Constraint_Clause] ...)]
```

```
        [LOB_Storage_Clause]
    | COLUMN column [NOT] SUBSTITUTABLE AT ALL LEVELS [FORCE]
    }
  }
  { { column | attribute} [DEFAULT expr]
    { SCOPE IS [schema.]scope_table_name]
    | WITH ROWID
    | [CONSTRAINT constraint_name]  REFERENCES [schema.]object_table
        [ON DELETE CASCADE]
    }
  |   { SCOPE FOR ({column | attribute}) IS [schema.]table_name
  | REF ({column | attribute}) WITH ROWID
  | [CONSTRAINT constraint_name] FOREIGN KEY (column)
        REFERENCES [schema.]object_table [ON DELETE CASCADE]
        [Constraint_State_Clause]
}
)
[OBJECT ID {SYSTEM GENERATED | PRIMARY KEY}]
[ON COMMIT {DELETE | PRESERVE} ROWS]
[OIDINDEX [indexname] ([physical_attributes_clause]
[TABLESPACE tablespace_name])]
[Physical_Attributes_Clause]
[TABLESPACE_NAME tablespace_name]
[Storage_Clause]
[LOGGING | NOLOGGING]
[LOB
 {(lob_item[,lob_item...]) STORE AS
    (LOB_Parameter_Clause)
  | (lob_item) STORE AS [(lob_segname)]
    [(LOB_Parameter_Clause)] ]
    [VARRAY varray_item STORE AS LOB [lob_segname]
        [(LOB_Parameter_Clause)]]
    [NESTED TABLE nested_table STORE AS storage_table
        (table_name [Physical_Attributes_Clause]
        [TABLESPACE tablespace_name] [LOGGING | NOLOGGING]]
        [LOB (lob_item[,lob_item...]) STORE AS
        (LOB_Parameter_Clause)]
  | (lob_item) STORE AS [(lob_segname)]
    [(LOB_Parameter_Clause)]
 ) ]
[RETURN AS {LOCATOR | VALUE}]
[Partitioning_Clause]
[ENABLE | DISABLE ROW MOVEMENT]
[CACHE | NOCACHE]
[MONITORING | NOMONITORING]
[PARALLEL integer | NOPARALLEL]
[{ENABLE | DISABLE} [VALIDATE | NOVALIDATE]
  { UNIQUE (column[, column...])
  | PRIMARY KEY
  | CONSTRAINT constraint_name
  }
  [USING INDEX
    [TABLESPACE tablespace_name]
    [Physical_Attributes_Clause]
```

SQL

```
[Storage_Clause]
[NOSORT]
[LOGGING | NOLOGGING]]
[EXCEPTIONS INTO [schema.]table_name
[CASCADE]]]
```

DROP Syntax:
```
DROP TABLE [schema.]table_name
[CASCADE CONSTRAINTS]
```

Creates, modifies, or drops an object table.

Keywords

GLOBAL TEMPORARY
: Specifies that the table to be created will be a temporary table whose structure will be visible to all sessions but whose data is visible only to the creating session. New with Oracle9*i*.

OF
: Specifies the underlying object type for the object table being created. See the CREATE TYPE entry later in this section for more information.

attribute
: Qualified column name of an item in an object.

DEFAULT
: Specifies a default value for the column, which will be used with INSERT statements if a value is omitted. The expression must match the datatype of the column.

SCOPE IS
: Specifies that each REF value in the column be restricted to referencing the *scope_table_name* table.

WITH ROWID
: Specifies that the ROWID is to be stored along with the REF value for this column.

CONSTRAINT
: Specifies the name of a constraint.

REFERENCES
: Specifies the name of a table to be used in the referential integrity constraint on the REF value of this column.

ON DELETE CASCADE
: Specifies that when a row is deleted from this table, rows containing the dependent foreign key will also be deleted.

SCOPE FOR
: Specifies that a REF value for the *column* or *attribute* is restricted to referencing the table *table_name*.

REF WITH ROWID
: Specifies that the ROWID is to be stored along with the REF value for this column.

FOREIGN KEY
: Specifies the name of a column to be used in the foreign key constraint on the REF value of this column.

OBJECT ID
: Specifies whether the object identifier should be SYSTEM GENERATED (this is the default) or based on the primary key of the table. Note that if PRIMARY KEY is specified, the primary key constraint must be defined.

ON COMMIT

Specifies whether rows of a temporary table are to be deleted or preserved when a COMMIT is issued. New with Oracle9*i*.

OIDINDEX Specifies either the name of an index or the physical attributes for an index to hold Object ID values for this table.

TABLESPACE

Specifies the name of the tablespace where this table will be stored. If TABLESPACE is omitted, Oracle uses the default tablespace for the schema owner.

ORGANIZATION HEAP

Specifies that there is no order associated with the storage of rows of data in this table. This is the default.

ORGANIZATION INDEX

Specifies that the table is to be created as an index-organized table, which means that the data rows are actually held in an index defined on the primary key of the table.

PCTTHRESHOLD

Specifies the percentage of space in each index block reserved for data rows. Any part of a data row that cannot be fit in this space will be placed in the overflow segment.

INCLUDING *column*

Specifies the point at which a table row is to be divided between the index and overflow portions. All columns that follow *column* (except primary key columns) will be stored in the overflow segment.

LOB Specifies storage attributes for LOB data identified by *lob_item*.

STORE AS Specifies the name of the LOB data segment.

VARRAY Specifies storage characteristics for a LOB in which a VARRAY type will be stored.

NESTED TABLE

Specifies storage characteristics for *nested_table* that will be stored in *storage_table*.

RETURN AS LOCATOR

Specifies that a collection locator for a copy of this nested table be returned.

RETURN AS VALUE

Specifies that a copy of the nested table be returned.

ENABLE ROW MOVEMENT

Specifies that a row may be moved to a different partition or subpartition if required as the result of an update of the key.

DISABLE ROW MOVEMENT

Specifies that rows may not be moved to a different partition or subpartition and returns an error if an update to a key would require such a move.

USING INDEX

Specifies the characteristics of an index used to enforce a constraint.

SQL

EXCEPTIONS INTO
Specifies the name of a table into which Oracle will place information about rows that violate the constraint. You must explicitly create this table by running the *UTLEXCPT1.SQL* script before using this keyword.

CASCADE   When specifying DISABLE, this keyword disables all integrity constraints that depend on the constraint being disabled.

AS subquery   Specifies a *subquery* to be used to insert rows into the table upon creation. If column definitions are omitted from the CREATE TABLE statement, then the column names, datatypes, and constraints will be copied from the table referenced in the *subquery*.

Common keywords and clauses: *column, Column_Constraint_Clause,* COMPRESS, *Constraint_State_Clause, expr, filename, indexname, integer, LOB_Parameter_Clause,* LOGGING, NOCOMPRESS, NOLOGGING, NOPARALLEL, PARALLEL, *Partition_ Clause, partition_name, Physical_Attributes_Clause, schema, Storage_Clause subpartition_name, table_name, tablespace_name.*

CREATE/ALTER/DROP TABLE (XML Syntax)

CREATE Syntax:
```
CREATE TABLE [schema.]table OF XMLTYPE
[XMLTYPE STORE AS
  {OBJECT RELATIONAL
  | CLOB
    [{LOB_segname [(LOB_Parameter_Clause)]
    | LOB_Parameter_Clause
    }]
  }]
[[XMLSCHEMA XMLSchema_URL] ELEMENT
  {element
  | XMLSchema_URL # element
  }]
```

ALTER Syntax:
```
ALTER TABLE [schema.]table_name
{ ADD (column  datatype [DEFAULT expr] [Column_Constraint_Clause]
  [,column datatype [DEFAULT expr] [Column_Constraint_Clause] ...)]
| MODIFY
  { (column  datatype [DEFAULT expr] [Column_Constraint_Clause]
    [,column datatype [DEFAULT expr] [Column_Constraint_Clause] ...)]
XMLTYPE COLUMN column STORE AS
  {OBJECT RELATIONAL
  | CLOB
    [{ LOB_segname [(LOB_Parameter_Clause)]
    | LOB_Parameter_Clause
    }]
  }]
[[XMLSCHEMA XMLSchema_URL] ELEMENT
  {element
  | XMLSchema_URL # element
  }]
```

DROP Syntax:
```
DROP TABLE [schema.]table_name
[CASCADE CONSTRAINTS]
```

Creates, modifies, or drops an XML table. New with Oracle9*i* Release 2.

Keywords

STORE AS

Specifies how Oracle manages the storage of the underlying columns. New with Oracle9*i*.

OBJECT RELATIONAL

Specifies that Oracle is to store the XMLType data in object-relational columns. If you specify OBJECT RELATIONAL, then you must also specify an XMLSchema in the XMLSCHEMA clause, and you must already have registered the schema (using the built-in DBMS_XMLSCHEMA package). Oracle will create the table conforming to the registered schema.

CLOB

Specifies that Oracle is to store the XML data in a CLOB column. If you specify CLOB, then you may also specify either a LOB segment name or the *LOB_Parameter_Clause* or both.

XMLSCHEMA

Specifies the URL of a registered XMLSchema (in the XMLSCHEMA clause or as part of the ELEMENT clause) and an XML element name. You must specify an element, although the XMLSchema URL is optional. If you do specify an XMLSchema URL, you must already have registered the XMLSchema using the DBMS_XMLSCHEMA package.

XMLTYPE COLUMN

Identifies the XML column to be added or modified. New with Oracle9*i*.

Common keywords and clauses: *column, Column_Constraint_Clause, expr, LOB_Parameter_Clause, schema, table_name, tablespace_name.*

CREATE/ALTER/DROP TABLESPACE

CREATE Syntax:
```
CREATE [UNDO] TABLESPACE tablespace_name
DATAFILE 'filename' [SIZE integer [K | M] [REUSE]] [Autoextend_Clause]
[,'filename' [SIZE integer [K | M] [REUSE]] [Autoextend_Clause]]
DEFAULT Storage_Clause
[ONLINE | OFFLINE]
[PERMANENT | TEMPORARY]
[LOGGING | NOLOGGING]
[MINIMUM EXTENT integer]
[EXTENT MANAGEMENT
 {DICTIONARY
 | LOCAL [AUTOALLOCATE
 | UNIFORM [SIZE integer [ K | M ]]]
 }]
[SEGMENT SPACE MANAGEMENT {MANUAL | AUTO}]
```

ALTER Syntax:
```
ALTER TABLESPACE tablespace_name
{[ADD DATAFILE filename [SIZE integer [K | M]] [REUSE]]
```

```
| [Autoextend_Clause]
| [RENAME DATAFILE 'filename1' TO 'filename2']
| [DEFAULT Storage_Clause
| [{ONLINE]|OFFLINE}]
| [{PERMANENT | TEMPORARY}]
| [{BEGIN BACKUP | END BACKUP}]
| [{LOGGING | NOLOGGING}]
| [MAXIMUM EXTENT integer]
}
```

DROP Syntax:
```
DROP TABLESPACE tablespace_name
[INCLUDING CONTENTS [AND DATAFILES]] [CASCADE CONSTRAINTS]
```

Creates, modifies, or removes a tablespace, optionally specifying default storage characteristics for objects subsequently created in the tablespace.

Keywords

UNDO

Specifies that an UNDO tablespace is to be created. New with Oracle9*i*.

DATAFILE

Specifies the name of the operating system datafile for this tablespace. SIZE is required unless the file already exists. If the file does exist, you must specify the REUSE keyword.

DEFAULT Storage_Clause

Specifies the physical storage characteristics. See the *Storage Clause* entry under the earlier "Common SQL Clauses" section for detailed information.

ONLINE

Brings the tablespace online after creation. This is the default.

OFFLINE

Leaves the tablespace offline after creation.

PERMANENT

Specifies that the tablespace may contain permanent objects.

TEMPORARY

Specifies that the tablespace will create only temporary objects.

MINIMUM EXTENT

Specifies that every used or free extent size in the tablespace is at least as large as, and is a multiple of, *integer*. This parameter controls free space fragmentation.

EXTENT MANAGEMENT

Specifies how extents in the tablespace will be managed. New with Oracle9*i*.

> *DICTIONARY*
>
> Space is to be managed using dictionary tables.
>
> *LOCAL*
>
> Space will be locally managed, using a bitmap in the tablespace.
>
> *AUTOALLOCATE*
>
> Tablespace is system-managed, and users cannot specify an extent size.
>
> *UNIFORM*
>
> Tablespace is managed with uniform extents of SIZE *integer* bytes. Use K or M to specify the extent size in kilobytes or megabytes. The default SIZE is 1 megabyte

---

SEGMENT SPACE MANAGEMENT

Specifies whether Oracle should track the used and free space in the segments in the tablespace using free lists or bitmaps. This clause applies only to locally managed permanent tablespaces. New with Oracle9*i*.

MANUAL

Oracle will manage the free space of segments in the tablespace using freelists.

AUTO

Oracle will manage the free space of segments in the tablespace using a bitmap. If you specify AUTO, Oracle ignores any specification for FREELIST and FREELIST GROUPS in subsequent storage specifications for objects in this tablespace.

BEGIN BACKUP

Signals to Oracle that the tablespace is being backed up, thereby changing log file behavior to accumulate all block changes for this tablespace. Note that this statement does not actually perform a backup; it signals to Oracle that the backup is about to begin.

END BACKUP

Signals to Oracle that the tablespace backup is complete, thereby restoring log file behavior to normal.

INCLUDING CONTENTS

Specifies that any objects contained in this tablespace be dropped automatically. If this keyword is not included and any objects exist in the tablespace, the statement will fail.

AND DATAFILES

Specifies that Oracle should delete the associated operating system files. New with Oracle9*i*.

CASCADE CONSTRAINTS

Specifies that referential integrity constraints from tables outside this tablespace that refer to primary and unique keys in the tables of this tablespace be dropped.

Common keywords and clauses: *Autoextend_Clause, filename, integer,* LOGGING, NOLOGGING, *schema, Storage_Clause, tablespace_name.*

CREATE TEMPORARY TABLESPACE

```
CREATE TEMPORARY TABLESPACE
TEMPFILE 'filename' [SIZE integer [K | M] [REUSE]]
[Autoextend_clause]
[EXTENT MANAGEMENT LOCAL]
[UNIFORM] [SIZE integer [K | M]]
```

Creates a temporary tablespace, which is used to hold temporary objects (which are retained only for the duration of a session). Like any other tablespace, a temporary tablespace can be dropped with the DROP TABLESPACE command. Temporary tablespaces are not affected by media recovery.

Keywords

TEMPFILE   Specifies the name of the operating system datafile for this temporary tablespace.

SIZE
: Specifies the size of the file in bytes, kilobytes (K), or megabytes (M). SIZE is required unless the file already exists. If the file already exists, you must specify the REUSE keyword.

REUSE
: Specifies that the operating system file must already exist and be reused for this temporary tablespace.

INITIAL
: Specifies the size of the first extent for a new object in bytes, kilobytes (K), or megabytes (M). If the specified size is not a multiple of the database block size, *integer* will be rounded up to a multiple of it.

EXTENT MANAGEMENT LOCAL
: Specifies that the temporary tablespace be locally managed, meaning that some portion of this tablespace is set aside for a bitmap. New with Oracle9*i*.

UNIFORM SIZE
: Specifies the size for all extents in this tablespace in bytes, kilobytes (K), or megabytes (M) and indicates that all extents will be equally sized. If *integer* is omitted, the extent size defaults to 1 megabyte.

Common keywords and clauses: *filename, integer*.

CREATE/ALTER/DROP TRIGGER

Creates, modifies, or removes a PL/SQL trigger that is stored in the database and is executed when defined database events occur. See Chapter 9 for information on syntax and use.

CREATE/ALTER/DROP TYPE

CREATE Incomplete Syntax:

```
CREATE [OR REPLACE] TYPE [schema.]type_name
```

CREATE Object Syntax:

```
CREATE [OR REPLACE] TYPE [schema.]type_name
[AUTHID {CURRENT_USER | DEFINER}]
{IS | AS} OBJECT (attribute datatype[, attribute datatype...]),
  {MEMBER | STATIC} {procedure_spec | function_spec}
  [,PRAGMA RESTRICT_REFERENCES ({method_name | DEFAULT},
  {RNDS|WNDS | RNPS | WNPS | TRUST}
   [,{RNDS | WNDS | RNPS | WNPS | TRUST}...] [,PRAGMA...]
  {MEMBER | STATIC} {procedure_spec | function_spec}
  [,PRAGMA RESTRICT_REFERENCES ({method_name | DEFAULT},
  {RNDS | WNDS | RNPS | WNPS | TRUST}
   [,{RNDS | WNDS | RNPS | WNPS | TRUST}...] [,PRAGMA...] ...]
  [, {MAP | ORDER} MEMBER function_spec]
```

Create VARRAY Syntax:

```
CREATE [OR REPLACE] TYPE [schema.]type_name
{IS | AS} {VARRAY | VARYING ARRAY} (limit) OF datatype
```

CREATE Nested Table Syntax:

```
CREATE [OR REPLACE] TYPE [schema.]type_name
{IS | AS} TABLE OF datatype
```

ALTER Syntax:

```
ALTER TYPE [schema.]type_name
```

```
{ COMPILE [DEBUG] [SPECIFICATION | BODY] [REUSE SETTINGS]
| REPLACE [AUTHID {CURRENT_USER | DEFINER}]
  AS OBJECT (attribute datatype[, attribute datatype...]),
 {MEMBER | STATIC} {procedure_spec | function_spec}
  [,PRAGMA RESTRICT_REFERENCES ({method_name | DEFAULT},
  {RNDS | WNDS | RNPS | WNPS | TRUST}]
    [,{RNDS | WNDS | RNPS | WNPS | TRUST}...]),PRAGMA...]
 {MEMBER | STATIC} {procedure_spec | function_spec}
  [,PRAGMA RESTRICT_REFERENCES ({method_name | DEFAULT},
  {RNDS | WNDS | RNPS | WNPS | TRUST}
    [,{RNDS | WNDS | RNPS | WNPS | TRUST}...])[,PRAGMA...] ...]
| [{ADD | DROP}
{ {MAP | ORDER} MEMBER function_spec]
| {MEMBER | STATIC} {procedure_spec | function_spec}}
  [INVALIDATE | CASCADE [[NOT] INCLUDING TABLE DATA] [FORCE]]
| [{ADD | MODIFY} ATTRIBUTE
    {attribute [datatype] | (attribute datatype, attribute datatype...)}]
| DROP ATTRIBUTE {attribute | (attribute, attribute...}
| [NOT] {INSTANTIABLE | FINAL}
```

DROP Syntax:
```
DROP TYPE [schema.]type_name [FORCE]
```

Creates, modifies, or removes an incomplete, object, VARRAY, or nested table type.

Keywords

type_name   Name of the type.

AUTHID CURRENT_USER

Specifies that the member functions and procedures execute with the privileges of the current user (invoker rights).

AUTHID DEFINER

Specifies that the member functions and procedures execute with the privileges of the object's creator (definer rights).

attribute   Name of an attribute of this type.

datatype   Oracle datatype of the attribute. *datatype* cannot be ROWID, LONG, or LONG ROW.

MEMBER   Specifies that a function or procedure is associated with the object type that is referenced in an attribute. This class of method has an implicit first parameter referenced as SELF. Because the member function is specific to each instance of an object, this function can reference the attributes of its particular instance of the class.

STATIC   Specifies that a function or procedure is associated with the object type that is referenced in an attribute, but has no implicit parameters. A static function is specific to the class as a whole, and so it can accept inputs and generate outputs, but cannot reference any nonstatic member functions or variables.

procedure_spec

Specification for a procedure. See Chapter 9 for details.

function_spec

Specification for a function. See Chapter 9 for details.

PRAGMA RESTRICT_REFERENCES

Specifies that read/write access to database tables and/or packaged variables will be denied to a member function.

method_name

Name of the MEMBER function to which the pragma is being applied.

DEFAULT   Specifies that the pragma should be applied to all methods in the type for which a pragma has not been specified.

RNDS   Specifies that database tables are not queried (read no database state).

WNDS   Specifies that database tables are not modified (write no database state).

RNPS   Specifies that package variables are not referenced (read no package state).

WNPS   Specifies that package variables are not modified (write no package state).

TRUST   Specifies that restrictions in this pragma are not to be enforced but are trusted to be true.

MAP MEMBER

Specifies a member function that returns the relative position of a given instance in the ordering of all instances of the object.

ORDER MEMBER

Specifies a member function that takes an instance of an object as an explicit argument, compares that to the implicit SELF argument, and returns -1, 0, or a positive integer to indicate the relationship between the two objects. A value of 1 means that the object passed explicitly is the "greater" of the two objects. A value of -1 indicates that the object passed explicitly is the "lesser" of the two objects. A value of 0 indicates that the two objects should be considered equivalent for purposes of ordering and sorting.

limit   Maximum number of elements returned by the VARRAY type.

COMPILE   Specifies that the object type specification and/or body is to be compiled. If neither SPECIFICATION nor BODY is specified, then by default both will be compiled.

DEBUG   Specifies that code will be generated for use by the PL/SQL debugger.

REPLACE AS OBJECT

Specifies that new member subprogram specifications are to be added. This keyword is valid only for object types.

ADD   Specifies that a new attribute or method definition is to be added to this type. New with Oracle9*i*.

DROP   Specifies that an attribute or method definition is to be removed from this type. New with Oracle9*i*.

INVALIDATE

Specifies that all dependent objects will be invalidated.

CASCADE   Specifies that the type change is to be propagated to dependent types and tables.

INCLUDING TABLE DATA

Specifies that data stored in user-defined columns is to be converted.

FORCE	Specifies that the type will be dropped even if it has dependent database objects.
MODIFY	Specifies that one or more attributes are to be modified in this type. New with Oracle9*i*.

 If you use FORCE to drop a type with dependent objects, the data in the dependent objects may become inaccessible. For this reason, we strongly recommend that you not use this option.

Common keywords and clauses: *schema*.

CREATE/DROP TYPE BODY

CREATE Syntax:
```
CREATE [OR REPLACE] TYPE BODY [schema.]type_name
{IS | AS} {MEMBER | STATIC} {procedure_spec | function_spec}
[{MEMBER | STATIC} {procedure_spec | function_spec} ...]
[, {MAP | ORDER} MEMBER function_spec]
END
```

DROP Syntax:
```
DROP TYPE BODY [schema.]type_name
```

Creates or removes a type body.

Note that there is no ALTER TYPE BODY statement. However, if you DROP a type body, the corresponding object type declaration will still exist, and you can issue a new CREATE TYPE BODY statement to create a new, and possibly different, type body.

Keywords

type_name	Name of the object type to which this type body corresponds.
MEMBER	Specifies that a function or procedure is associated with the object type that is referenced in an attribute. This class of method has an implicit first parameter referenced as SELF.
STATIC	Specifies that a function or procedure is associated with the object type that is referenced in an attribute, but has no implicit parameters.

procedure_spec
> Specification for a procedure. See Chapter 9 for details.

function_spec
> Specification for a function. See Chapter 9 for details.

MAP MEMBER function_spec
> Specifies a member function that returns the relative position of a given instance in the ordering of all instances of the object.

ORDER MEMBER function_spec
> Specifies a member function that takes an instance of an object as an explicit argument and the implicit SELF argument and returns -1, 0, or a positive integer.

Common keywords and clauses: *schema*.

CREATE/ALTER/DROP USER

CREATE Syntax:
```
CREATE USER username
[IDENTIFIED {BY password | EXTERNALLY | GLOBALLY AS 'external_name'}]
[DEFAULT TABLESPACE tablespace_name]
[TEMPORARY TABLESPACE tablespace_name]
[QUOTA [integer [K | M] | UNLIMITED] ON tablespace_name]
 [QUOTA [integer [K | M] | UNLIMITED] ON tablespace_name]...]
[PROFILE profilename]
[PASSWORD EXPIRE] [ACCOUNT {LOCK | UNLOCK}]
```

ALTER Syntax:
```
ALTER USER username
[REPLACE old_password]
[IDENTIFIED {BY password | EXTERNALLY | GLOBALLY AS 'external_name'}]
[DEFAULT TABLESPACE tablespace_name]
[TEMPORARY TABLESPACE tablespace_name]
[QUOTA [integer [K | M] | UNLIMITED] ON tablespace_name]
 [QUOTA [integer [K | M] | UNLIMITED] ON tablespace_name]...]
[PROFILE profilename]
[PASSWORD EXPIRE] [ACCOUNT {LOCK | UNLOCK}]
[DEFAULT ROLE
 {rolename[,rolename ...]
 | ALL [EXCEPT rolename[,rolename ...]]
 |  NONE
 }]
[username [,username ...] proxy_clause]
```

DROP Syntax:
```
DROP USER username [CASCADE]
```

Creates, modifies, or removes a database user together with associated security and storage properties.

Keywords

IDENTIFIED BY
> Specifies how the user will be authenticated. There are three options for authentication:

> *PASSWORD*
>> Identified with a locally stored password. The password can contain only single-byte characters from the database character set.

> *EXTERNALLY*
>> Identified by an external service, such as the operating system. If you want the user to have access only through the operating system account, add the OS_AUTHENT_PREFIX parameter value before the username.

> *GLOBALLY AS 'external_name'*
>> Identified by an enterprise directory service. The *external_string* can be either the Distinguished Name from the directory or NULL, which indicates that the directory will map users to the appropriate database schema.

DEFAULT TABLESPACE
> Specifies the name of the tablespace used by default when this user creates a database object.

TEMPORARY TABLESPACE

Specifies the name of the tablespace used for the creation of temporary segments when operations such as sorts require more memory than is available.

PASSWORD EXPIRE

Specifies that the user or the DBA will have to change the user's password before the user can log into the database.

ACCOUNT LOCK | UNLOCK

Disables or enables access through the user account.

QUOTA

Specifies the amount of space this user is permitted to use for object storage in the specified tablespace. UNLIMITED means that there is no limit to the storage used (subject to the total size of the tablespace).

PROFILE

Sets the user's profile to *profilename*, which subjects the user to the limits specified in that profile.

CASCADE

Specifies that all objects in the user's schema be dropped before removing the user. This keyword must be specified if the user schema contains any objects; otherwise, the command will fail. If you specify the CASCADE option, referential integrity constraints on tables in other schemas that refer to primary and unique keys on tables in this schema will also be dropped. If tables or other database objects in this schema are referred to by views or synonyms, or stored procedures, functions, or packages in another schema, then those referring objects will be marked INVALID, but not dropped.

Common keywords and clauses: *integer*, *tablespace_name*.

CREATE/ALTER/DROP VIEW

CREATE Syntax:

```
CREATE [OR REPLACE] [[NO] FORCE] VIEW [schema.]view_name
[ { ( { alias [Column_Constraint_Clause [Column_Constraint_Clause]...]
        | Table_Constraint_Clause } [,[Table_Constraint_Clause]... ]
      } )
  | OF [schema.] type_name
    { WITH OBJECT IDENTIFIER { DEFAULT | (attribute [,attribute]...)}
    | UNDER [schema.] superview
    }
    ( { Table_Constraint_Clause
      | attribute Table_Constraint_Clause [Table_Constraint_Clause...]
      })
  | OF XMLTYPE
    [[XMLSCHEMA XML_Schema_URL] ELEMENT {element | XML_Schema_URL#element]
    WITH OBJECT IDENTIFIER {(expr[,expr...]) | DEFAULT}

}]
AS viewquery [WITH
{READ ONLY
| CHECK OPTION [CONSTRAINT constraint_name]
}]
```

ALTER Syntax:
```
ALTER VIEW [schema .] view_name
{ADD Table_Constraint_Clause
| MODIFY CONSTRAINT Table_Constraint_Clause {RELY | NORELY}
| DROP {CONSTRAINT constraint_name | PRIMARY KEY | UNIQUE (column[,column]... )}
| COMPILE
}
```

DROP Syntax:
```
DROP VIEW [schema.view_name]
```

Creates, modifies, or removes a view.

The ALTER VIEW statement explicitly recompiles a view. We recommend that you issue it after making changes to any of the view's underlying base tables.

Keywords

Table_Constraint_Clause

> May be included in the CREATE/ALTER VIEW statement beginning in Oracle9*i*. See the discussion under "Common Keywords and Identifiers" for more information.

FORCE   Specifies that the view be created regardless of whether the view's base tables exist or whether the owner of the schema has privileges on them.

NOFORCE   Specifies that the view be created only if the base tables exist and the owner of the schema has privileges on them. This is the default.

view_name   Name of the view to be created.

alias   One or more aliases that correspond to columns or expressions returned by the view's query.

OF type_name

> Specifies that this view is on an object type identified by *type_name*.

WITH OBJECT IDENTIFIER

> Specifies that this view is a top-level (root) object view. This clause lets you specify the attributes of the object type that will be used as a key to identify each row in the object view.

UNDER   Specifies that this view is a subview based on the named object superview.

OF XMLTYPE

> Specifies that this view is an XMLType view, which displays data from an XMLSchema-based table of datatype XMLType. The XMLSchema_ spec indicates the XMLSchema to be used to map the XML data to its object-relational equivalents. The XMLSchema must already have been created before you can create an XMLType view.

WITH OBJECT IDENTIFIER

> Object tables (as well as XMLType tables, object views, and XMLType views) do not have any column names specified for them. Therefore, Oracle defines a system-generated column SYS_NC_ROWINFO$. You can use this column name in queries and to create object views with the WITH OBJECT IDENTIFIER keyword.

viewquery   Any SQL SELECT statement.

WITH CHECK OPTION
> Specifies that inserts and updates performed through the view must result in rows that the view query can select.

READ ONLY
> Specifies that this view cannot be updated.

CONSTRAINT
> Specifies a name for the CHECK OPTION constraint. The default is a system-assigned name in the form SYS_C*n*, for which *n* is an integer resulting in a unique name.

ADD   Specifies that a constraint is to be added to the view. New with Oracle9*i*.

MODIFY   Specifies whether a constraint in NOVALIDATE mode is to be taken into account for query rewrite. Specify RELY to activate an existing constraint in NOVALIDATE mode for query rewrite in an unenforced query rewrite integrity mode. The constraint is in NOVALIDATE mode, so Oracle does not enforce it. The default is NORELY.

COMPILE   Causes the view to be recompiled.

Common keywords and clauses: *alias, Column_Constraint_Clause*, OR REPLACE, *schema, Table_Constraint_Clause*.

DISASSOCIATE STATISTICS

```
DISASSOCIATE STATISTICS FROM
{ COLUMNS [schema.]table_name.column[, [schema.]table_name.column ...]
| FUNCTIONS [schema.]function[,[schema.]function ...]
| PACKAGES [schema.]package[,[schema.]package ...]
| INDEXES [schema.]indexname[,[schema.]indexname ...]
}
```

Disassociates a method of statistics computation from database objects. New with Oracle8*i*.

Keywords

COLUMNS Specifies that a list of one or more columns be provided.

column   Column name for which an association is defined.

FUNCTIONS Specifies that one or more functions will be disassociated.

PACKAGES Specifies that one or more packages will be disassociated.

INDEXES   Specifies that one or more indexes will be disassociated.

Common keywords and clauses: *column, Column_Constraint_Clause, schema, table_ name*.

GRANT (Object Privileges)

```
GRANT {object_priv[,object_priv ...] | ALL [PRIVILEGES]}
   [column [,column...]] ON
{ [schema.]object_name
| DIRECTORY directory_name
| JAVA {SOURCE | RESOURCE} [schema.]java_object
}
```

```
TO {username | role | PUBLIC}
[WITH GRANT OPTION]
```
Grants privileges on a database object to one or more users or roles.

Keywords

object_priv
: Specifies the name of the object privilege to be granted. Valid privileges are ALTER, DELETE, EXECUTE, INDEX, INSERT, REFERENCES, SELECT, and UPDATE.

object_name
: Name of the object on which privileges are to be granted.

DIRECTORY
: Specifies the name of a directory object on which privileges are to be granted.

JAVA SOURCE
: Specifies the name of a Java source object on which privileges are to be granted.

JAVA RESOURCE
: Specifies the name of a Java resource object on which privileges are to be granted.

username
: Name of the user who will be granted the object privilege.

role
: Name of a role that will be granted the object privilege.

PUBLIC
: Specifies that the object privilege be granted to all current and future users.

WITH GRANT OPTION
: Specifies that the grantee of the privilege can grant the privilege to others.

Common keywords and clauses: *column*, *schema*.

GRANT (System Privilege or Role)

```
GRANT {{privilege | role}[,{privilege | role} ...]
   | ALL PRIVILEGES}}
TO {username | rolename | PUBLIC}
 [,{username | rolename | PUBLIC} ...]
[WITH ADMIN OPTION]
```
Grants a system privilege or role to one or more users and/or roles.

Keywords

privilege
: Name of a system privilege to be granted. See Chapter 4 for details.

role
: Name of a role to be granted. See Chapter 4 for details.

username
: Name of a user to be granted a privilege or role.

rolename
: Name of a role to be granted a privilege or role.

PUBLIC
: Specifies that the granted privilege or role be granted to all users, including those not yet created.

WITH ADMIN OPTION
: Specifies that the grantee of the privilege or role can grant the privilege or role to others, and may alter or drop the role.

NOAUDIT (Schema Objects)

```
NOAUDIT object_option[,object_option ...]
ON {[schema.]object_name | DIRECTORY directory_name | DEFAULT}
[WHENEVER [NOT] SUCCESSFUL]
```

Stops auditing defined by a prior AUDIT statement for schema objects.

Keywords

object_option Indicates that auditing on a particular operation will be stopped. The following operations are valid: ALTER, AUDIT, COMMENT, DELETE, EXECUTE, GRANT, INDEX, INSERT, LOCK, RENAME, SELECT, and UPDATE. The keyword ALL is equivalent to specifying all of the operations.

object_name Name of the schema object for which auditing will be stopped.

DIRECTORY Specifies the name of a directory for which auditing will be stopped.

DEFAULT Specifies that no auditing will be performed as the default for objects that have not yet been created for the specified object option.

WHENEVER SUCCESSFUL
Turns off auditing only for SQL statements that complete successfully.

WHENEVER NOT SUCCESSFUL
Turns off auditing only for SQL statements that fail or result in errors.

Common keywords and clauses: *schema*.

NOAUDIT (SQL Statements)

```
NOAUDIT {statement_opt | system_priv}[,{statement_opt | system_priv} ...] [BY
{ username[,username ...]
| proxy [ON BEHALF OF
  {ANY
  | username [,username ...]
  }]
}]
[WHENEVER [NOT] SUCCESSFUL]
```

Stops auditing defined by a prior AUDIT statement for SQL statements.

Keywords

statement_opt
Statement option for which auditing will be stopped. See Chapter 4 for details.

system_priv System privilege for which auditing will be stopped. See Chapter 4 for details.

BY username Stops auditing only for SQL statements issued by a username in this list. The default option is to stop auditing for all users.

BY proxy Stops auditing only for SQL statements issued by proxy on behalf of a user or a list of specific users.

WHENEVER SUCCESSFUL

Stops auditing only for SQL statements that complete successfully. If NOT is specified, auditing stops only for SQL statements that result in an error. If this clause is omitted, auditing stops for all SQL statements, successful or not.

RENAME

```
RENAME oldname TO newname
```

Changes the name of an existing table, view, sequence, or private synonym. Integrity constraints, indexes, and grants on the old object are automatically transferred to the new object.

 Objects that depend on the renamed object (e.g., views, synonyms, stored procedures, or functions) will be marked INVALID.

Keywords

oldname   Name of the existing object for which you want to assign a new name.

newname   New name for the database object.

REVOKE (Object Privileges)

```
REVOKE
{object_priv[,object_priv ...]
| ALL [PRIVILEGES]
}
ON [schema.]object_name
FROM {username | role | PUBLIC}
```

Revokes privileges on a database object from one or more users or roles.

Keywords

object_priv   Name of the object privilege to be granted. Valid privileges are ALTER, DELETE, EXECUTE, INDEX, INSERT, REFERENCES, SELECT, and UPDATE.

object_name   Name of the object on which privileges are granted.

username   Name of the user who will be granted the object privilege.

role   Name of a role that will be granted the object privilege.

PUBLIC   Specifies that the object privilege be granted to all current and future users.

Common keywords and clauses: *schema*.

REVOKE (System Privilege or Role)

```
REVOKE {{privilege | role}[,{privilege | role} ...]
| ALL PRIVILEGES
FROM {username | rolename | PUBLIC}
[,{username | rolename | PUBLIC} ...]
```

Removes a system privilege or role from one or more users and/or roles.

Keywords

privilege   Name of a system privilege to be revoked. See Chapter 4 for details.

role   Name of a role to be revoked. See Chapter 4 for details.

username   Name of a user from whom a privilege or role is to be revoked.

rolename   Name of a role from which a privilege or role is to be revoked.

PUBLIC   Specifies that the granted privilege or role no longer be available to all users by default.

Data Manipulation Statements

Data Manipulation Language (DML) statements access and manipulate data stored in the Oracle database. You can use these statements to insert, update, delete, and read data, as well as to modify how Oracle operates when accessing data in the database. There are fewer DML statements than there are DDL (Data Definition Language) statements, but many do have a wide range of options and syntax choices, shown in the following syntax descriptions.

ALTER SESSION

```
ALTER SESSION
{ { SET
  | [CONSTRAINT[S] = IMMEDIATE | DEFERRED | DEFAULT]
  | [CREATE_STORED_OUTLINES = TRUE | FALSE | category_name]
  | [CURRENT_SCHEMA = schema]
  | [CURSOR_SHARING = FORCE | EXACT]
  | [DB_BLOCK_CHECKING = TRUE | FALSE]
  | [DB_FILE_MULTIBLOCK_READ_COUNT = integer]
  | [FAST_START_IO_TARGET = integer]
  | [FLAGGER = ENTRY | INTERMEDIATE | FULL | OFF]
  | [GLOBAL_NAMES = [TRUE | FALSE]
  | [HASH_AREA_SIZE = integer]
  | [HASH_JOIN_ENABLED = TRUE | FALSE]
  | [HASH_MULTIBLOCK_IO_COUNT = integer]
  | [INSTANCE = integer]
  | [ISOLATION_LEVEL = SERIALIZABLE | READ COMMITTED]
  | [LABEL = 'text' | DBHIGH | DBLOW | OSLABEL]
  | [LOG_ARCHIVE_DEST_integer =
      {''
      | LOCATION = pathname
      | SERVICE = tnsnames_service
      }
      [MANDATORY | OPTIONAL] [REOPEN[ = integer]]]
  | [LOG_ARCHIVE_DEST_STATE_integer = ENABLE | DEFER]
  | [LOG_ARCHIVE_MINIMUM_SUCCEED_DEST = integer]
  | [MAX_DUMP_FILE_SIZE = integer | UNLIMITED]
  | [NLS_CALENDAR = 'text']
  | [NLS_COMP = 'text']
```

```
      | [NLS_CURRENCY = 'text']
      | [NLS_DATE_FORMAT = 'date_format']
      | [NLS_DATE_LANGUAGE = language]
      | [NLS_DUAL_CURRENCY = 'text']
      | [NLS_ISO_CURRENCY = territory]
      | [NLS_LABEL_FORMAT = label_format]
      | [NLS_NUMERIC_CHARACTERS = 'text']
      | [NLS_LANGUAGE = language]
      | [NLS_SORT = sort | BINARY]
      | [NLS_TERRITORY = territory]
      | [OBJECT_CACHE_MAX_SIZE_PERCENT = integer]
      | [{OPTIMIZER_GOAL | OPTIMIZER_MODE} =
          ALL_ROWS | FIRST_ROWS | RULE | CHOOSE]
      | [OBJECT_CACHE_OPTIMAL_SIZE = integer]
      | [OPTIMIZER_INDEX_CACHING = integer]
      | [OPTIMIZER_INDEX_COST_ADJ = integer]
      | [OPTIMIZER_MAX_PERMUTATIONS = integer]
      | [OPTIMIZER_PERCENT_PARALLEL = integer]
      | [PARALLEL_BROADCAST_ENABLED = TRUE | FALSE]
      | [PARALLEL_INSTANCE_GROUP = 'text']
      | [PARTITION_VIEW_ENABLED = TRUE | FALSE]
      | [PLSQL_V2_COMPATIBILITY = TRUE | FALSE]
      | [QUERY_REWRITE_ENABLED = TRUE | FALSE]
      | [QUERY_REWRITE_INTEGRITY = ENFORCED | TRUSTED | STALE_TOLERATED]
      | [REMOTE_DEPENDENCIES_MODE = TIMESTAMP | SIGNATURE]
      | [SESSION_CACHED_CURSORS = integer]
      | [SKIP_UNUSABLE_INDEXES = TRUE | FALSE]
      | [SORT_AREA_RETAINED_SIZE = integer]
      | [SORT_AREA_SIZE = integer]
      | [SORT_MULTIBLOCK_READ_COUNT = integer]
      | [SQL_TRACE = TRUE | FALSE]
      | [STAR_TRANSFORMATION_ENABLED = TRUE | FALSE]
      | [TIMED_STATISTICS = TRUE | FALSE]
      | [USE_STORED_OUTLINES = TRUE | FALSE | 'category_name']
      }
  | [CLOSE DATABASE LINK dblink]
  | [ADVISE COMMIT | ROLLBACK | NOTHING]
  | [{ENABLE | DISABLE} COMMIT IN PROCEDURE]
  | [{ENABLE | DISABLE | FORCE} PARALLEL {DML | DDL} [PARALLEL integer]]
  | {[ENABLE RESUMABLE [TIMEOUT integer][NAME string]
     | DISABLE RESUMABLE]
     }
  }
```

Changes the current database session's functional characteristics, including several National Language Support (NLS) characteristics.

Many of the parameters that may be set using this command are defined on an instance-wide basis by parameters in the initialization file (*INIT.ORA* or *SPFILE)*. Although defaults are indicated here when appropriate, the values of the initialization parameters will override those defaults and be the de facto default values. Be sure that you understand the use of each parameter before attempting to set it for a session.

Keywords

CONSTRAINT[S]

Specifies when conditions defined by a deferrable constraint are enforced.

IMMEDIATE

Conditions are checked immediately after each DML statement.

DEFERRED

Indicates that the conditions are checked when the transaction is committed.

DEFAULT

Restores all constraints to their initial state, as defined when they were created.

CREATE_STORED_OUTLINES

Specifies whether Oracle will store an outline for each query. If you specify category_name, then outlines will be created and stored in the category_ name category.

CURRENT_SCHEMA

Changes the current schema to the specified schema. Although the schema is changed, the user is not, and no additional privileges are available.

CURSOR_SHARING

Specifies the kinds of SQL statements that can share a cursor. If FORCE is specified, statements may share a cursor if they are identical except for some literals and if the differences do not affect the meaning of the statement. EXACT means that only identical SQL statements may share a cursor.

DB_BLOCK_CHECKING

Specifies whether data block checking is performed.

DB_FILE_MULTIBLOCK_READ_COUNT

Specifies the number of blocks read during a single I/O operation when performing a sequential scan. The default is 8.

FAST_START_IO_TARGET

Specifies the target number of reads and writes to and from cache that should be performed during crash or instance recovery.

FLAGGER

Specifies a FIPS flagging level, which causes an error message to be generated whenever a SQL statement does not conform to ANSI SQL-92 standards. Note that there is currently no difference among ENTRY, INTERMEDIATE, and FULL.

GLOBAL_NAMES

Controls whether global name resolution will be enforced for this session.

HASH_AREA_SIZE

Specifies the amount of memory (in bytes) used for hash joins.

HASH_JOIN_ENABLED

Specifies whether hash joins will be performed in queries.

HASH_MULTIBLOCK_IO_COUNT

Specifies the number of data blocks to be read or written during a hash join.

INSTANCE

Specifies that in a Parallel Server/Real Application Clusters environment, database files should be accessed as though the session were connected to the specified instance.

ISOLATION_LEVEL
Specifies how database modifications are to be handled.

SERIALIZABLE
If an attempt is made to update a row that has been updated and not yet committed by another session, the statement will fail; this option is consistent with the serializable transaction isolation mode specified in the SQL-92 standard.

READ COMMITTED
Oracle's default behavior will be in effect, and if a row is locked by another uncommitted transaction, the statement will wait until the row locks are released.

LABEL
Changes the DBMS session label to the label specified by *text*, the label equivalent of DBHIGH or DBLOW, or the operating system label (OSLABEL).

LOG_ARCHIVE_DEST_*integer*
Specifies a location for archived redo log file groups. Up to five locations may be defined (as specified by *integer*) and the archiving process will attempt to archive redo log files to each.

''
Specifies that no destination is defined for this archive log destination. However, at least one archive log destination (1–5) must have a location defined.

LOCATION
Specifies the operating system location for archived redo log files.

SERVICE
Specifies the name of an Oracle Net Services service running a standby database. *tnsnames_service* must be an entry in the *TNSNAMES.ORA* file.

MANDATORY
Specifies that archiving to the destination must succeed before the redo log file is made available for reuse.

OPTIONAL
Specifies that archiving to the destination does not have to succeed before the redo log file is made available for reuse.

REOPEN
Specifies the number of seconds that must pass after an error is encountered during archiving to the destination before future archives to the destination can be attempted.

LOG_ARCHIVE_DEST_STATE_*integer*
Specifies the state to be associated with the corresponding LOG_ARCHIVE_DEST_*integer*. ENABLE means that any valid LOG_ARCHIVE_DEST can be used. DEFER indicates that the LOG_ARCHIVE_DEST_*integer* with the same value of *integer* will not be used.

LOG_ARCHIVE_MINIMUM_SUCCEED_DEST
Specifies the minimum number of destinations that must be written to successfully before a redo log file can be reused.

MAX_DUMP_FILE_SIZE
Specifies the maximum size for a trace dump file in blocks. If UNLIMITED is specified, there is no size limit.

NLS_CALENDAR
> Specifies a new calendar type—for example, GREGORIAN or JAPANESE IMPERIAL.

NLS_COMP
> Specifies the linguistic comparison to be performed using the rules associated with the NLS_SORT parameter supplied as text—for example, FRENCH or AMERICAN.

NLS_CURRENCY
> Specifies the local currency symbol returned by the number format element L. This parameter overrides the defaults set by NLS_TERRITORY.

NLS_DATE_FORMAT
> Specifies the default date format. The *date_format* must be a valid Oracle date format mask. This parameter overrides the defaults set by NLS_TERRITORY.

NLS_DATE_LANGUAGE
> Specifies the language (e.g., FRENCH, JAPANESE) to use for day and month names, as well as for other specified date values. This parameter overrides the defaults set by NLS_LANGUAGE.

NLS_DUAL_CURRENCY
> Specifies the value to be returned by the number format element U (normally used for the Euro).

NLS_ISO_CURRENCY
> Specifies the territory (e.g., AMERICA, FRANCE) whose ISO currency symbol should be used. This parameter may override the defaults set by NLS_TERRITORY.

NLS_LABEL_FORMAT
> For Trusted Oracle only; changes the default label format for the session.

NLS_NUMERIC_CHARACTERS
> Specifies the decimal character and group separator (for example, comma and period). The value of *'text'* must be in the form *'dg'*, where *d* is the decimal character, and *g* is the group character. This parameter may override the defaults set by NLS_TERRITORY.

NLS_LANGUAGE
> Specifies the language (e.g., FRENCH, JAPANESE) for Oracle messages, day and month names, and sort sequences.

NLS_SORT
> Specifies the collating sequence for character sorts. BINARY specifies a binary sort, while *sort* specifies the name of a specific sort sequence, such as FRENCH or GERMAN.

NLS_TERRITORY
> Specifies the territory (e.g., FRANCE, JAPAN) whose date format, numeric decimal, group separator, and local and ISO currency symbols are to be used as defaults. This parameter may override the defaults set by NLS_LANGUAGE.

OBJECT_CACHE_MAX_SIZE_PERCENT
> Specifies the percentage by which the object cache can grow beyond the optimal size. The default is 10.

OBJECT_CACHE_OPTIMAL_SIZE
> Specifies the optimal size (in kilobytes) for the object cache. The default is 100.

OPTIMIZER_GOAL

For Oracle7, specifies the optimization goal for this session. Replaced by OPTIMIZER_MODE beginning with Oracle8.

OPTIMIZER_INDEX_CACHING

Specifies the percentage of index blocks assumed to be in the cache.

OPTIMIZER_INDEX_COST_ADJ

Specifies a percentage indicating the importance that the optimizer attaches to the availability of an index path instead of a full table scan.

OPTIMIZER_MAX_PERMUTATIONS

Specifies the number of table permutations the optimizer will consider for large join operations.

OPTIMIZER_MODE

Beginning with Oracle8, specifies the optimization goal for this session. The following goals are valid:

ALL_ROWS

Optimize for best overall throughput.

FIRST_ROWS

Optimize for best response time.

RULE

Use rule-based optimization.

CHOOSE

Use cost-based optimization if possible; otherwise, use rule-based optimization.

OPTIMIZER_PERCENT_PARALLEL

Specifies the amount of parallelism the optimizer uses when computing costs. The default is 0, which indicates no parallelism.

PARALLEL_BROADCAST_ENABLED

Specifies that parallel processing can be used to enhance performance during hash and merge joins.

PARALLEL_INSTANCE_GROUP

Specifies the parallel instance group used when spawning parallel query slave processes. This option is valid only when running Parallel Server or Real Application Clusters in parallel mode.

PARTITION_VIEW_ENABLED

Specifies that unnecessary table access can be eliminated during operations on partitioned views.

PLSQL_V2_COMPATIBILITY

Specifies whether or not PL/SQL constructs that were legal in Oracle7 (under PL/SQL 2.0), but are illegal starting in Oracle8, are allowed. A value of TRUE allows the old constructs. A value of FALSE disallows them.

QUERY_REWRITE_ENABLED

Specifies whether query rewrite will be in effect for materialized views. Query rewrite is disabled if OPTIMIZER_MODE is set to RULE.

QUERY_REWRITE_INTEGRITY

Specifies consistency levels for query rewrites.

ENFORCED

System-enforced relationships are relied on so that data integrity can be guaranteed.

TRUSTED

Materialized views created with the ON PREBUILD TABLE clause are supported, and unenforced join relationships are accepted.

STALE_TOLERATED

Any stale but usable materialized view may be used.

REMOTE_DEPENDENCIES_MODE

Specifies how dependencies of remote stored procedures are handled.

SESSION_CACHED_CURSORS

Specifies the number of cursors for this session that may be retained in cache.

SKIP_UNUSABLE_INDEXES

Specifies whether operations will be permitted on tables with unusable indexes or index partitions. TRUE means all such operations will be allowed, while FALSE causes such operations to return an error.

SORT_AREA_RETAINED_SIZE

Specifies the maximum amount of memory in bytes that will be retained by each sort operation after the first fetch.

SORT_AREA_SIZE

Specifies the maximum amount of memory in bytes that each sort operation will use.

SORT_MULTIBLOCK_READ_COUNT

Specifies the number of blocks to read each time the sort performs a read from temporary segments. The default is 2.

SQL_TRACE

Controls whether performance statistics are generated. The initial value is set in the initialization file.

STAR_TRANSFORMATION_ENABLED

Specifies whether cost-based optimization will be applied to star queries.

TIMED_STATISTICS

Specifies whether (TRUE) or not (FALSE) Oracle requests time information from the operating system when generating time-based statistics.

USE_STORED_OUTLINES

Specifies whether the optimizer will use stored outlines when generating execution plans. If you specify *category_name,* only outlines stored under that category will be used.

CLOSE DATABASE LINK

Closes a connection to a remote database using the database link *dblink.* This command succeeds only if the database link is not in use and there is no pending commit across the link.

ADVISE

Sends advice for forcing a distributed transaction to a remote database by placing the value 'C' (COMMIT), 'R' (ROLLBACK), or '' (NOTHING) in DBA_ 2PC_ PENDING_ADVICE on the remote database.

SQL

ENABLE COMMIT IN PROCEDURE

Specifies that procedures and stored functions can issue COMMIT and ROLL-BACK statements.

DISABLE COMMIT IN PROCEDURE

Specifies that procedures and stored functions may not issue COMMIT and ROLLBACK statements.

ENABLE PARALLEL

Specifies that the DML or DDL statements following in the session be executed in parallel, if possible. This option is the default for DDL statements.

DISABLE PARALLEL

Specifies that the DML or DDL statements following in the session be executed serially. This option is the default for DML statements.

FORCE PARALLEL

Specifies that subsequent statements in the session be executed in parallel.

DML

Specifies that the ENABLE, DISABLE, or FORCE PARALLEL keyword applies to Data Manipulation Language (DML) statements.

DDL

Specifies that the ENABLE, DISABLE, or FORCE PARALLEL keyword applies to Data Definition Language (DDL) statements.

PARALLEL

Specifies the degree of parallelism. The integer overrides a parallel clause specified in a DDL statement, but not a parallel hint specified in a subsequent DML statement.

ENABLE RESUMABLE

Specifies that resumable space allocation for the session is enabled. New with Oracle9*i*.

TIMEOUT

Specifies the time (in seconds) during which an operation can remain suspended while waiting for the error condition to be fixed. If the error condition is not fixed within the TIMEOUT period, Oracle aborts the suspended operation.

NAME

Specifies a user-defined text string to help users identify the statements issued during the session while the session is in resumable mode. Oracle inserts the specified *string* into the USER_RESUMABLE and DBA_RESUMABLE data dictionary views. If you do not specify NAME, Oracle inserts the default string 'User *username(userid)*, Session *sessionid*, Instance *instanceid*'.

DISABLE RESUMABLE

Specifies that resumable space allocation for the session is disabled. New with Oracle9*i*.

Common keywords and clauses: *integer, schema.*

ANALYZE

```
ANALYZE {TABLE [schema.]table_name
 [PARTITION partition_name | SUBPARTITION subpartition_name]
 | INDEX [schema.]indexname
```

```
[PARTITION partition_name | SUBPARTITION subpartition_name]
| CLUSTER [schema.]clustername}
}
{ COMPUTE [SYSTEM] STATISTICS
| ESTIMATE [SYSTEM] STATISTICS [SAMPLE integer {ROWS | PERCENT}]
  {[FOR {TABLE
  | ALL [INDEXED] COLUMNS [SIZE integer]
  | COLUMNS [SIZE integer] {column_name | attribute} [SIZE integer]
  | ALL [LOCAL] INDEXES]
  }
}
| DELETE [SYSTEM] STATISTICS
| VALIDATE STRUCTURE [CASCADE]
| LIST CHAINED ROWS [INTO [schema.]table_name]
| VALIDATE REF UPDATE [SET DANGLING TO NULL]
}
```

Collects or deletes statistics about an object in the database, validates the structure of an object, or identifies migrated and chained rows in a table or cluster.

Statistics are accessible in the ALL_TABLES, USER_TABLES, and DBA_TABLES views. Some column statistics are accessible in the ALL_TAB_COLUMNS, USER_TAB_COLUMNS, and DBA_TAB_COLUMNS views. Cluster statistics also appear in USER_CLUSTERS and DBA_CLUSTERS.

Keywords

COMPUTE STATISTICS
> Computes the exact statistics for the entire named object and stores them in the data dictionary.

ESTIMATE STATISTICS
> Estimates statistics for the named object and stores them in the data dictionary. The optional SAMPLE clause may be used to specify the sample size to use; this clause contains the following keywords:

ROWS
> Causes *integer* rows of a table or cluster, or *integer* entries from an index, to be sampled.

PERCENT
> Causes *integer* percent of the rows of a table or cluster, or *integer* percent of the entries in an index, to be sampled. The valid range for PERCENT is 1–99. If SAMPLE is not specified, a default value of 1050 rows will be used as the sample size.

COMPUTE STATISTICS results in more accurate statistics but is likely to take longer. ESTIMATE STATISTICS is normally much faster and almost as accurate. The object being analyzed will be locked while statistics are being collected, so the faster ESTIMATE STATISTICS may be preferable in a heavy transaction environment.

FOR
> Specifies whether an entire table or index, or just particular columns, will be analyzed. New with Oracle9i.

TABLE

Specifies that only table statistics (and not column statistics) will be collected.

ALL COLUMNS

Specifies that statistics are to be collected for all columns in the table. If INDEXED is specified, then only those columns participating in an index for this table will be analyzed.

COLUMNS

Specifies that only specific columns (and not the table) will have statistics collected. Columns may be specified by name or attributes.

ALL INDEXES

Specifies that all indexes associated with this table will be analyzed. If the LOCAL keyword is included, then local indexes will be analyzed (this keyword is required if the PARTITION clause is used).

SIZE

Specifies the number of buckets in the histogram. *integer* can range from 1 to 254, and the default is 75.

DELETE STATISTICS

Causes all statistics stored in the data dictionary for the named object to be deleted.

VALIDATE STRUCTURE

Causes the structure of the named object to be validated. The CASCADE keyword will also cause indexes associated with the named object to be validated.

LIST CHAINED ROWS

Generates a list of chained and migrated rows for the named table or cluster (this operation is not permitted on an index). Entries are made in a table named CHAINED_ROWS, which is assumed to exist in the user's schema. Include the INTO clause to specify a different name for the target table.

VALIDATE REF UPDATE

Causes the REFs of the named object to be validated.

SET DANGLING TO NULL

Specifies that any REF pointing to an invalid or nonexistent object be set to NULL.

Common keywords and clauses: *schema, table_name.*

DELETE

```
DELETE [FROM]
{ table_name[@dblink]
| table_name PARTITION (partition_name)
| table_name SUBPARTITION (subpartition_name)
| view[@dblink]
| snapshot[@dblink]
| [(subquery)]
| [TABLE(subquery)]
}
[table_alias] |
ONLY (
{ table_name[@dblink]
```

```
|  table_name PARTITION (partition_name)
|  table_name SUBPARTITION (subpartition_name)
|  view[@dblink]
|  snapshot[@dblink]
|  [(subquery)]
|  [TABLE(subquery)]
}
[table_alias])
[WHERE condition]
    [RETURNING expression[,expression ...] INTO data_item[,data_item ...]]
```

Deletes rows from a table, view, or snapshot.

Keywords

FROM   Optional keyword to aid readability.

PARTITION Specifies that rows are to be deleted from a partition (named *partition*) of the specified table.

SUBPARTITION

        Specifies that rows are to be deleted from a subpartition (named *subpartition*) of the specified table.

subquery   Specifies a subquery, which determines the rows that are candidates for deletion. See the SELECT entry for more information on subqueries.

TABLE subquery

        Specifies a SELECT statement that returns a single column value, which must be a nested table. The TABLE keyword informs Oracle that the value is a collection, not a scalar value.

table_alias Specifies an alias (or alternate name) for the table, view, or subquery. If a *table_alias* is specified, any columns referenced in the DELETE statement with a specific table reference must be qualified using the *table_alias* and not the table name.

ONLY   This clause is relevant only for views, and is used if the view in the FROM clause belongs to a view hierarchy and you do not want to delete rows from any of its subviews.

WHERE   Specifies the *condition* that will be used to identify the rows to be deleted. The specified condition may be any valid WHERE condition.

RETURNING

        Specifies that the value(s) of the specified expression(s) be returned for rows deleted by this command. Valid only from within a PL/SQL program.

INTO   Specifies the PL/SQL variables into which the values returned for rows deleted by this command are to be stored.

Common keywords and clauses: *dblink, table_name*.

EXPLAIN PLAN

```
EXPLAIN PLAN
SET STATEMENT_ID = 'text'
[INTO [schema.]table_name[@dblink]]
FOR SQL_statement
```

Creates an explanation of the execution plan for a SQL statement.

You must have INSERT privilege on the destination table (specified by INTO) before issuing this command. The destination table is usually called PLAN_TABLE, and can be created by running the script *utlxplan.sql*. The value specified in the SET clause appears in the STATEMENT_ID column of the destination table

Keywords

SET STATEMENT_ID

Specifies a text string used to identify the result of this EXPLAIN PLAN statement. The default is NULL.

INTO Specifies the name and location of the plan table. The default is to use a table named PLAN_TABLE in your current schema.

FOR Specifies the SQL statement for which the plan is to be generated.

Common keywords and clauses: *dblink, schema, table_name.*

INSERT

```
INSERT INTO
{ table_name[@dblink]
| table_name PARTITION (partition_name)
| table_name SUBPARTITION (subpartition_name)
| view[@dblink]
}
[table_alias]
[(column[,column...])]
{ VALUES (expr
    | DEFAULT[,expr
    | DEFAULT...]
    )
| subquery
}
[RETURNING expr[,expr...] INTO data_item[,data_item...]]
```

Inserts a row of data into a table or view.

Keywords

PARTITION Specifies that rows be inserted into a partition (named *partition*) of the specified table.

SUBPARTITION

Specifies that rows be inserted into a subpartition (named *subpartition*) of the specified table.

view Name of a view into which rows are to be inserted.

table_alias Alias (or alternate name) for the table or view. If a *table_alias* is specified, any columns referenced in the INSERT statement with a specific table reference must be qualified using the *table_alias* and not the table name.

column Name(s) of one or more columns in the table or view into which values will be stored. If the VALUES keyword is specified, then for each column specified, a corresponding *expr* must be specified in the VALUES clause. If the list of column names is omitted, the list is considered to contain all columns of the table or view.

VALUES	Specifies the value(s) to be stored in each column of the row to be inserted. *expr* can be any valid SQL expression, and there must be exactly as many *exprs* listed as there are columns specified for the table or view. If no column list is supplied, there must be the same number of expressions as columns in the table or view.
DEFAULT	Specifies that Oracle should use the default value for the column. If no default is declared, then NULL is used. New with Oracle9*i*.
subquery	Specifies a subquery, which returns values to be stored in the row to be inserted. If a list of columns is specified for the table or view into which rows are to be inserted, *subquery* must return exactly the same number of columns, in the same sequence. If no column list is specified, *subquery* must return the same number of columns as the table or view. See the SELECT entry later in this chapter for more information on subqueries.

RETURNING

Specifies that the value(s) of the expression *(expr)* for rows inserted by this command be returned. Valid only from within a PL/SQL program.

INTO	Specifies that the value(s) returned for rows inserted by this command are to be stored in the PL/SQL variable(s) *data_item*.

Common keywords and clauses: *dblink, expr, partition_name, subpartition_name, table_name*.

MERGE

```
MERGE INTO table_name [alias]
  USING {table_name | viewname | subquery}
ON (condition)
WHEN MATCHED THEN merge_update_clause
WHEN NOT MATCHED THEN merge_insert_clause
```

Selects rows from a table for update of or insert into another table. This statement is used to avoid multiple INSERT and UPDATE statements. New with Oracle9*i* Release 2.

Keywords

INTO	Specifies the name of the target table, that is, the table that will be updated or have rows inserted.
USING	Specifies the name of the table, view, or subquery from which rows are to be selected.

ON (condition)

Specifies a condition that will evaluate to either TRUE or FALSE. This is a SQL clause, and is typically a test for equality.

merge_update_clause

Specifies a SQL DML statement to be performed if *condition* is TRUE. This is normally an UPDATE statement.

merge_insert_clause

Specifies a SQL DML statement to be performed if *condition* is not TRUE. This is normally an INSERT statement.

Common keywords and clauses: *alias, table_name*.

SAVEPOINT

```
SAVEPOINT savepoint
```

Identifies a point in a transaction to which you can roll back using the ROLLBACK statement.

Keyword

SAVEPOINT savepoint
> Specifies a name for the *savepoint* being created.

SELECT

```
SELECT [{DISTINCT | UNIQUE | ALL}]
{ [schema.]{table_name. | view. | snapshot.}
|  expr [[AS] alias][,expr [[AS] alias] ...]
| *
}
FROM
{table_name[@dblink] [AS OF {SCN | TIMESTAMP} expr]
| table_name PARTITION (partition_name) [AS OF {SCN | TIMESTAMP} expr]
| table_name SUBPARTITION (subpartition_name) [AS OF {SCN | TIMESTAMP} expr]
| table_name SAMPLE [BLOCK] sample_percent [AS OF {SCN | TIMESTAMP} expr]
| view[@dblink] [AS OF {SCN | TIMESTAMP} expr]
| snapshot[@dblink] [AS OF {SCN | TIMESTAMP} expr]
| (subquery)
| table_name
  { [join_type] JOIN table_name
    { ON condition
    | USING (column [, column]... )
  | { CROSS JOIN | NATURAL [join_type] JOIN table_name }
  }
[,[table_alias]
[,table_name[@dblink] [AS OF {SCN | TIMESTAMP} expr]
| table_name PARTITION (partition_name) [AS OF {SCN | TIMESTAMP} expr]
| table_name SUBPARTITION (subpartition_name) [AS OF {SCN | TIMESTAMP} expr]
| table_name SAMPLE [BLOCK] sample_percent [AS OF {SCN | TIMESTAMP} expr]
| view[@dblink] [AS OF {SCN | TIMESTAMP} expr]
| snapshot[@dblink] [AS OF {SCN | TIMESTAMP} expr]
| (subquery)
| table_name
  { [join_type] JOIN table_name
    { ON condition
    | USING (column [, column]... )}
  | { CROSS JOIN | NATURAL [join_type] JOIN table_name }
  }
}
[table_alias]]
[WHERE condition]
{[GROUP BY {expr | {expr[,expr ...}}
| CUBE (expr[,expr ...])
| ROLLUP (expr[,expr ...])
}
```

```
GROUPING SETS (
  {expr | {expr[,expr ...]}
  | CUBE (expr[,expr ...])
  | ROLLUP (expr[,expr ...])
  }
[HAVING condition]
[[START WITH condition] CONNECT BY condition]
[{UNION [ALL] | INTERSECT | MINUS} {subquery)
 [,{UNION [ALL] | INTERSECT | MINUS} {subquery) ...]]
[ORDER BY {expr | position | alias} [ASC | DESC]
 [, {expr | position | alias} [ASC | DESC] ...]
[FOR UPDATE OF {table | view}.column
 [{ table_name | view}.column ...]]
[NOWAIT]
```

Retrieves data from tables, views, or snapshots.

Keywords

DISTINCT
> Specifies that only one copy of a row should be returned, even if there are dupli-cate rows. A duplicate row is one that returns the same values for all columns listed in the select list.

view
> Name of a view.

snapshot
> Name of a snapshot.

* Specifies that all columns are to be returned and is the equivalent of listing each column of the table, view, or snapshot.

AS Specifies an alias (or alternate name) for a column or expression. The keyword AS is optional.

FROM
> Specifies the name(s) of one or more tables, views, or snapshots from which data is to be retrieved.

ALL
> Specifies that all rows should be returned, including duplicates. This option is the default.

AS OF
> Specifies that the query should operate on data as it existed at a particular SCN or timestamp as specified by *expr*. This clause cannot be used with a database link and is new with Oracle9*i* Release 2.

PARTITION
> Specifies that data be retrieved from the partition of *table_name* identified by partition.

SUBPARTITION
> Specifies that data be retrieved from the subpartition of *table_name* identified by subpartition.

SAMPLE [BLOCK]

Specifies that a random sample of the rows in the table be selected. Replace *sample_percent* with the percentage that you want to use. If you specify BLOCK, Oracle performs block sampling instead of row sampling.

subquery

Any valid SELECT statement. Note that a subquery may not contain a FOR UPDATE clause.

table_alias

Specifies an alias (or alternate name) for a table, view, or snapshot. If a *table_alias* is specified, any ambiguously defined columns referenced in the SELECT statement must be qualified using the *table_alias,* and not the table name.

JOIN

Specifies explicitly that a join is being performed. You can use this syntax to replace the comma-delimited table expressions used in Oracle joins. New with Oracle9i.

join_type

Specifies the kind of join being performed. New with Oracle9i.

INNER

Inner join is being performed. This is the default.

RIGHT

Right outer join is being performed.

LEFT

Left outer join is being performed.

FULL

Full or two-sided outer join. In addition to the inner join, rows from both tables that have not been returned in the result of the inner join will be preserved and extended with NULLs.

ON condition

Specifies a join condition separate from any search or filter conditions in the WHERE clause. New with Oracle9i.

USING

Specifies the columns to be used when specifying an equijoin of columns that have the same name in both tables This clause can be used only if the join columns in both tables have the same name.

CROSS JOIN

Specifies that a cross join is being performed. A cross join produces the cross-product of two relations.

NATURAL

Specifies that a natural join is being performed. A natural join is based on all columns in the two tables that have the same name. It selects rows from the two tables that have equal values in the relevant columns. New with Oracle9i.

WHERE

Specifies that only rows meeting *condition* will be retrieved. *condition* will be evaluated, and only rows that evaluate to TRUE will be returned. If you omit this clause, all rows will be returned.

GROUP BY

Specifies that rows are to be grouped according to the provided expression(s) (*expr*) and a single row of summary information be returned for each group. Beginning with Oracle9*i*, multiple groupings are allowed.

CUBE

Specifies that rows are to be grouped based on all possible combinations of values from the provided list of expressions. New with Oracle8*i*.

ROLLUP

Specifies that rows are to be grouped based on values from the provided list of expressions and summary rows returned for each *expr*, along with an additional superaggregate row. New with Oracle8*i*.

GROUPING SETS

Specifies multiple groupings of data to facilitate efficient aggregation. If you specify only the desired groups, Oracle does not need to perform the full set of aggregations generated by CUBE or ROLLUP. New with Oracle9*i*.

START WITH

Specifies the row(s) used as the root of a hierarchical query. If you omit these keywords, all rows of the table are considered root rows.

CONNECT BY

Specifies the relationship between parent and child rows in the hierarchy.

UNION [ALL]

Specifies that the results of the SELECT statement that precedes this keyword be combined with the results of the SELECT statement that follows.

INTERSECT

Specifies that the results of the SELECT statement preceding this keyword be combined with the results of the SELECT statement that follows, and that only the rows appearing in both are to be returned.

MINUS

Specifies that the results of the SELECT statement preceding this keyword be combined with the results of the SELECT statement that follows. Any row appearing in the following SELECT will be removed from the set of rows to be returned by the first.

ORDER BY

Specifies that rows are to be sorted before being returned. The sort may be performed on expression(s), alias(es), or position(s). In the syntax, *position* is an integer referring to the expression's position in the select list. The first item in the select list is considered to be in position 1.

ASC

Values are to be sorted in ascending sequence—from lowest to highest. This is the default.

DESC

Values are to be sorted in descending sequence—from highest to lowest.

FOR UPDATE

Specifies that the selected rows are to be locked. If the keyword OF is specified, only rows in the table specified will be locked.

NOWAIT
> Specifies that if a table is already locked, Oracle should not wait for the lock to be released. If you do not specify NOWAIT, Oracle will wait for the lock to be released.

Common keywords: *column, dblink, expr, partition_name, schema, subpartition_name, table_name*.

SET CONSTRAINT

```
SET {CONSTRAINT | CONSTRAINTS} {ALL | constraint_name[,constraint_name...]}
{IMMEDIATE | DEFERRED}
```

Specifies at the transaction level whether specific constraints are checked after each DML statement or are deferred until the end of a transaction. This statement applies only to deferrable constraints. The success of deferrable constraints can be tested by issuing the statement SET CONSTRAINTS ALL IMMEDIATE before the COMMIT statement is issued.

Keywords

ALL　　　Specifies that all deferrable constraints for the transaction are affected by this statement.

constraint_name
> Name of a deferrable constraint.

IMMEDIATE
> Specifies that the conditions enforced by the constraints be checked after each DML statement is completed.

DEFERRED　Specifies that the conditions enforced by the constraints be checked after the entire transaction is complete and committed.

SET ROLE

```
SET ROLE
{ role [IDENTIFIED BY password][,role [IDENTIFIED BY password ...]]
| ALL [EXCEPT role[,role ...]]
| NONE
}
```

Enables or disables roles for the current session.

Keywords

role　　　Name of the role to be enabled.

IDENTIFIED BY
> Specifies the password for the role. This option is required if the role is password protected.

ALL　　　Specifies that all roles granted to you are to be enabled. If the EXCEPT clause is included, the specified roles will not be enabled, but all other roles granted to you will be.

NONE　　Specifies that all roles granted to you be disabled for this session.

SET TRANSACTION

```
SET TRANSACTION [NAME 'name']
{READ ONLY
| READ WRITE
| ISOLATION LEVEL {SERIALIZABLE | READ COMMITTED}
| USE ROLLBACK SEGMENT seg_name
}
```

Establishes the current transaction as read-only or read/write or specifies the rollback segment to be used by the transaction. If used, this statement must be the first in your transaction. A transaction is ended with a COMMIT or COMMIT WORK statement.

Keywords

NAME
> Specifies a name for this transaction. New with Oracle9*i*.

READ ONLY
> Specifies that the current transaction is read-only.

READ WRITE
> Specifies that the current transaction is read/write.

ISOLATION_LEVEL
> Specifies how database modifications are to be handled.

> *SERIALIZABLE*
>> If an attempt is made to update a row that has been updated and not yet committed by another session, the statement will fail; this situation is consistent with the serializable transaction isolation mode specified in the ANSI SQL-92 standard.

> *READ COMMITTED*
>> Oracle's default behavior will be in effect, and if a row is locked by another uncommitted transaction, the statement will wait until the row locks are released.

USE ROLLBACK SEGMENT
> Assigns this transaction to the rollback segment specified by *seg_name*. This clause implies READ WRITE and cannot be specified with READ ONLY.

TRUNCATE

```
TRUNCATE
{ TABLE table_name [{PRESERVE | PURGE}
| {SNAPSHOT | MATERIALIZED VIEW} LOG]
| CLUSTER cluster
}
[{DROP | REUSE} STORAGE]
```

Removes all rows from a table or cluster.

The TRUNCATE statement does not create rollback records, so it cannot be rolled back. This characteristic makes TRUNCATE extremely fast, and it is preferable to DELETE FROM, unless the rollback capability is required. When a table is truncated and the DROP STORAGE clause is specified, only the initial extent of the table is retained; all other storage is deallocated.

Keywords

cluster
> Specifies the name of the cluster from which rows are to be removed.

PRESERVE ... LOG
> Specifies that existing materialized view or snapshot logs on this table should be preserved when the table is truncated. This option is useful when a table is being reloaded during an Export/TRUNCATE/Import operation, because a fast refresh will not be triggered.

PURGE ... LOG
> Specifies that existing snapshot logs on this table should be purged when the table is truncated.

DROP STORAGE
> Deallocates storage used by the rows and returns the space to the free space pool. This is the default.

REUSE STORAGE
> Retains the space used by the deleted rows. This option is useful if the table or cluster will be reloaded with data.

Common keywords and clauses: *table_name*.

UPDATE

```
UPDATE
{table_name[@dblink]
|table_name PARTITION (partition_name)
|table_name SUBPARTITION (subpartition_name)
|view[@dblink]
|snapshot[@dblink]
}
[table_alias]
SET
{ column={expr | (subquery) | DEFAULT}
   [,column={expr | (subquery) | DEFAULT} ... ]
| (column[,column ...])=subquery
}
[WHERE condition]
[RETURNING expr[,expr ...] INTO data_item[,data_item ...]]
```

Changes the value stored in one or more columns of data in one or more tables, views, or snapshots.

Keywords

view   Name of a view to be updated.

snapshot   Name of a snapshot to be updated.

PARTITION   Specifies that data be updated in the partition of *table_name* identified by *partition*.

SUBPARTITION
> Specifies that data be updated in the subpartition of *table_name* identified by *subpartition*.

subquery	Any valid SELECT statement. Note that a subquery may not contain a FOR UPDATE clause.
DEFAULT	Specifies that Oracle should use the default value for the column. If no default is declared, then NULL is used. New with Oracle9i.
table_alias	Alias (or alternate name) for a table, view, or snapshot.
column	Name of a column in the table, view, or snapshot that will be updated.
WHERE	Specifies that only rows meeting *condition* will be updated. The *condition* will be evaluated, and only rows that evaluate to TRUE will be updated. If you omit this clause, all rows will be updated.
RETURNING	Specifies that the value(s) of *expr* for rows updated by this statement be returned. Valid only from within a PL/SQL program.
INTO	Specifies that value(s) returned for rows updated by this statement are to be stored in the PL/SQL variable(s) *data_item*.

Common keywords and clauses: *column, dblink, expr, table_name.*

8

Functions

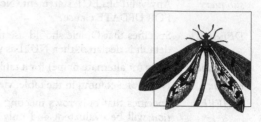

Oracle provides a large number of built-in functions that you can use in SQL or in PL/SQL stored procedures. These functions extend the capabilities of the SQL language in order to provide commonly used capabilities. For example, in the following SQL statement you call the built-in AVG function, which returns the average value of the salary column for each department:

```
SELECT dept, AVG (salary) FROM emp GROUP BY dept
```

You can also create your own functions, which can be used in the same manner as Oracle's built-in functions. Chapter 9 includes information about how you can create and call functions with the PL/SQL language.

This chapter provides brief descriptions of all of the Oracle built-in functions. We've divided the functions into the following categories; within each category, the functions are listed alphabetically:

Aggregate and analytic functions
Numeric functions
Character functions
Date and time functions
Conversion functions
Object functions
XML functions
Miscellaneous functions

Each function description contains a syntax block showing the parameters that may be passed to a function. In most cases, we describe each parameter. When the parameters have already been described in the "Common Keywords and Clauses" section, we simply provide a reference. In some cases, the parameters are obvious (e.g., an expression), so we won't provide the details.

Common Keywords and Clauses

You can specify the following keywords in calling many of the functions described in this chapter:

ASC

Specifies that the ordering sequence should be ascending.

DESC

Specifies that the ordering sequence should be descending.

dfmt

Specifies a date format specification made up of the elements shown in Appendix D.

fmt

Specifies a numeric format specification made up of the elements shown in Appendix C

nlsparams

Specifies a character string made up of one or more of the following elements, allowing you to specify various National Language Support (NLS) characteristics for the result:

NLS_NUMERIC_CHARACTERS = ''*dg*''

Allows you to specify the characters to use for decimal points, *d*, and group separators, *g*. You also must use D and G in your format specification to mark the location of the decimal point and group separators.

NLS_CURRENCY = ''*text*''

Allows you to specify the currency symbol (up to 10 characters long) to use in place of any L characters contained in the format specification.

NLS_ISO_CURRENCY = ''*territory*''

Allows you to specify the NLS territory whose currency symbol you want to use in place of any C characters contained in the format specification.

The *nlsparams* settings are strings embedded within a string. Note that the quotes in this clause are doubled single quotes, not double quotes.

nlsdateparam

Specifies a string in the form NLS_DATE_LANGUAGE = *langname*, where *langname* represents a valid NLS language name. The NLS language name affects the spelling used for day and month names.

NULLS FIRST

Specifies that NULL values should appear first in the ordering sequence.

NULLS LAST

Specifies that NULL values should appear last in the ordering sequence.

Functions

Aggregate and Analytic Functions

Aggregate functions are SQL functions designed to allow data from multiple rows of a table or a view to be summarized. You can invoke the functions in this category only from PL/SQL expressions.

Analytic functions also summarize data from multiple rows, but they differ from aggregate functions because they can return multiple rows from each group, while aggregate functions return only a single row.

Most of the functions in this section may be used as either aggregate or analytic functions. The analytic portion of the syntax can be readily identified by the OVER keyword, which introduces the analytic clause. (See the upcoming "Analytic Clause" section for details.)

GROUP BY

When used with an aggregate function, the GROUP BY clause causes Oracle to report the aggregate value for each distinct value of the column(s) being grouped.

The GROUP BY clause causes the results to be sorted into different buckets—one for each distinct value in the GROUP BY column. The results of aggregate functions are returned for each of these values.

DISTINCT and ALL

Most aggregate functions optionally accept the DISTINCT and ALL keywords in their parameter list. These keywords allow you to control the manner in which duplicate column values are handled. The keywords have the following meanings:

DISTINCT
:   Causes the aggregate function to look only at distinct values, and to ignore duplicates.

ALL
:   Causes the aggregate function to look at all values including any duplicates. This is the default behavior.

Analytic Clause

When a function is used as an analytic function, the analytic clause is always preceded by the keyword OVER. Analytic functions always use the analytic clause, which has the following general syntax:

```
[PARTITION BY expr [,expr...] ]
[ORDER [SIBLINGS] BY
    {expr | position | c_alias} [ASC | DESC] [NULLS FIRST | NULLS LAST]
    [,{expr | position | c_alias} [ASC | DESC] [NULLS FIRST | NULLS LAST]...]
{ROWS | RANGE} BETWEEN
    {UNBOUNDED PRECEDING | CURRENT ROW | value_expr
            {PRECEDING | FOLLOWING}} AND
    {UNBOUNDED PRECEDING | CURRENT ROW | value_expr
            {PRECEDING | FOLLOWING}}}]
```

Parameters

PARTITION

Specifies that the query result set should be partitioned into one or more groups based on one or more expressions (*expr*).

ORDER BY

Specifes how data is to be ordered within a partition.

position

Specifies that the partition should be ordered according to the expression in this relative position in the expression list.

c_alias

Specifies that the partition should be ordered according to the column identified by this alias.

ROWS

Specifies that a window is defined in terms of physical rows.

RANGE

Specifies that a window is defined in terms of a logical offset.

BETWEEN

Specifies that a starting and ending point for a window will be defined.

UNBOUNDED PRECEDING

Specifies that the window ends at the last row of the query.

UNBOUNDED FOLLOWING

Specifies that the window starts at the first row of the query.

CURRENT ROW

Specifies that the window begins at the current row or value, depending on whether ROWS or RANGE was specified.

value_expr

Resolves to a number representing a physical offset if ROWS is specified or to a number representing a logical offset if RANGE is specified.

Common keywords and clauses: ASC, DESC, NULLS FIRST, NULLS LAST.

AVG   AVG ([DISTINCT | ALL] *expr*) [OVER (*analytic_clause*)]

Computes the average value of a column or expression over the set of rows returned by a query or the set of rows specified by a GROUP BY clause.

CORR   CORR (*expr1*,*expr2*) [OVER (*analytic_clause*)]

Computes the correlation coefficient of a set of number pairs provided by *expr1* and *expr2*. Both *expr1* and *expr2* must return numbers.

Functions

COUNT

COUNT ([DISTINCT | ALL] *expr* [,DISTINCT | ALL] *expr*...] | *)
   [OVER (*analytic_clause*)]

Counts the number of rows returned by *expr*. If you use a wildcard
(*) as the subject of this function, the function will cause all rows,
including those with NULL values, to be counted.

COVAR_POP

COVAR_POP (*expr1*,*expr2*) [OVER (*analytic_clause*)]

Computes the population covariance of a set of number pairs
provided by *expr1* and *expr2*. Both *expr1* and *expr2* must return
numbers. After eliminating pairs of *exp1* and *exp2* where either is
NULL, Oracle makes the following calculation.

   (SUM (*expr1* * *expr2*) - SUM (*expr2*) * SUM (*expr1*) / *n*) / *n*

where *n* is the number of rows returned.

COVAR_SAMP

COVAR_SAMP (*expr1*,*expr2*) [OVER (*analytic_clause*)]

Computes the sample covariance of a set of number pairs provided
by *expr1* and *expr2*. Both *expr1* and *expr2* must return numbers.
After eliminating pairs of *exp1* and *exp2* where either is NULL,
Oracle makes the following calculation

   (SUM(*expr1* * *expr2*) - SUM(*expr1*) * SUM(*expr2*) / *n*) / (*n*-1)

where *n* is the number of rows returned.

CUME_DIST

Aggregate syntax:
CUME_DIST (*expr*[,*expr*...]) WITHIN GROUP
   (ORDER BY *expr* [ASC | DESC][NULLS {FIRST | LAST}]
      [, *expr* [ASC | DESC] [NULLS {FIRST | LAST}]...])

Analytic syntax:
CUME_DIST ( ) OVER (*analytic_clause*)

Computes the relative position of a row among all rows of the
aggregation group for a hypothetical row identified by the arguments to the function and the ORDER BY specification. The value
returned is > 0 and < = 1. All arguments to this function must evaluate to a constant expression. Expressions in the main function
must match the positions of those in the ORDER BY clause.

Parameters

Common keywords and clauses: ASC, DESC, NULLS FIRST,
NULLS LAST.

DENSE_RANK

Aggregate syntax:
```
DENSE_RANK (expr[,expr...]) WITHIN GROUP
    (ORDER BY expr [ASC | DESC][NULLS {FIRST | LAST}]
        [, expr [ASC | DESC] [NULLS {FIRST | LAST}]...])
```

Analytic syntax:
```
DENSE_RANK ( ) OVER (analytic_clause)
```

Computes the dense rank position of that row among all rows of the aggregation group for a hypothetical row identified by the arguments to the function and the ORDER BY specification. The value returned is an integer > = 1, and the highest possible value is the number of unique values returned by the query. All arguments to this function must evaluate to a constant expression. Expressions in the main function must match the positions of those in the ORDER BY clause. Parameters are the same as for CUME_DIST

FIRST_VALUE

```
FIRST_VALUE (expr) OVER (analytic_clause)
```

Returns the first value in an ordered set of values. Analytic function only.

GROUP_ID

```
GROUP_ID ( )
```

Assigns a unique integer number, beginning with 0, to duplicate groups resulting from a GROUP BY specification. You must include parentheses in this function call. New with Oracle9i.

GROUPING

```
GROUPING (expr)
```

Designed for use in SELECT statements that make use of the CUBE and ROLLUP operators. CUBE and ROLLUP both cause extra rows, with NULL values, to be inserted into a query to summarize a group of records. Returns a 1 if the NULL value is the result of an additional row returned as a result of using CUBE or ROLLUP; otherwise, returns a 0. New with Oracle8i.

GROUPING_ID

```
GROUPING_ID (expr[,expr...])
```

Assigns an integer number corresponding to the GROUPING bit vector associated with a row, thereby avoiding the need for multiple GROUPING functions. Used in a SELECT statement that contains a GROUP BY extension like ROLLUP or CUBE. New with Oracle9i.

KEEP

```
aggregate_function KEEP (DENSE_RANK {FIRST | LAST}
    ORDER BY expr [ASC | DESC][NULLS {FIRST | LAST}]
        [, expr [ASC | DESC] [NULLS {FIRST | LAST}]...])
    [OVER (analytic_clause)]
```

Used in conjunction with another aggregate function (MIN, MAX, SUM, AVG, COUNT, VARIANCE, or STDDEV) to operate on a set of values from a set of rows that rank as the FIRST or LAST rows, as specified by the ORDER BY specification. Expressions must match the positions of those in the ORDER BY clause.

Parameters

aggregate_function
> MIN, MAX, SUM, AVG, COUNT, VARIANCE, or STDDEV function.

DENSE RANK
> Specifies that aggregation will occur only over those rows with minimum or maximum dense rank.

analytic_clause
> Can use only the PARTITION BY portion of the analytic clause.

Common keywords and clauses: ASC, DESC, NULLS FIRST, NULLS LAST.

LAG

LAG (*expr* [,*offset*][,*default*]) OVER (*analytic_clause*)

Provides access to more than one row of a table at the same time without a self-join. Analytic function only.

Parameters

offset
> Physical offset prior to the current row for an additional row to be retrieved.

default
> Value returned if the offset goes beyond the scope of the window.

LAST_VALUE

LAST_VALUE (*expr*) OVER (*analytic_clause*)

Returns the last value in an ordered set of values. Analytic function only.

LEAD

LEAD (*expr* [,*offset*][,*default*]) OVER (*analytic_clause*)

Provides access to more than one row of a table at the same time without a self-join. Analytic function only.

Parameters

offset
> Physical offset after the current row for an additional row to be retrieved.

default
> Value returned if the offset goes beyond the scope of the window.

MAX

MAX ([DISTINCT | ALL] *expr*)

Computes the maximum value of a column or expression over the set of rows returned by a query or the set of rows specified by a GROUP BY clause. The use of ALL or DISTINCT does not affect the value returned by the MAX function.

MIN

MIN ([DISTINCT | ALL] *expr*)

Computes the minimum value of a column or expression over the set of rows returned by a query or the set of rows specified by a GROUP BY clause. The use of ALL or DISTINCT does not affect the value returned by the MIN function.

NTILE

NTILE (*ntile_expr*) OVER (*analytic_clause*)

Divides an ordered data set into a number of buckets and assigns the appropriate bucket number to each row. Analytic function only.

Parameters

ntile_expr
> Resolves to a number that specifies the number of buckets to be assigned to rows.

PERCENT_RANK

Aggregate syntax:
PERCENT_RANK (*pct_expr*[,*pct_expr*...]) WITHIN GROUP
   (ORDER BY *expr* [ASC | DESC][NULLS {FIRST | LAST}]
     [, *expr* [ASC | DESC] [NULLS {FIRST | LAST}]...])

Analytic syntax:
PERCENT_RANK ( ) OVER (*analytic_clause*)

Computes an interpolated value that would fall into a specified percentile value *pct_expr* with respect to the ORDER BY clause. This function assumes a continuous distribution model. New with Oracle9i.

Parameters

Common keywords and clauses: ASC, DESC, NULLS FIRST, NULLS LAST.

PERCENTILE_ CONT

PERCENTILE_CONT (*pct_expr*) WITHIN GROUP
   (ORDER BY *expr* [ASC | DESC]) [OVER (*analytic_clause*)]

Computes an interpolated value that would fall into a specified percentile value *pct_expr* with respect to the ORDER BY clause. This function assumes a continuous distribution model. New with Oracle9i.

Parameters

pct_expr
> Must evaluate to a number between 0 and 1 that specifies the percentile value.

Common keywords and clauses: ASC, DESC.

**PERCENTILE_
DISC**

```
PERCENTILE_DISC (pct_expr) WITHIN GROUP
   (ORDER BY expr [ASC | DESC]) [OVER (analytic_clause)]
```

Computes an interpolated value that would fall into a specified percentile value *pct_expr* with respect to the ORDER BY clause. This function assumes a discrete distribution model. New with Oracle9*i*.

Parameters

pct_expr
> Must evaluate to a number between 0 and 1 that specifies the percentile value.

Common keywords and clauses: ASC, DESC.

RANK

Aggregate syntax:
```
RANK (expr[,expr...]) WITHIN GROUP
   (ORDER BY expr [ASC | DESC][NULLS {FIRST | LAST}]
      [, expr [ASC | DESC] [NULLS {FIRST | LAST}]...])
```

Analytic syntax:
```
RANK ( ) OVER (analytic_clause)
```

As an aggregate function, computes for the row identified by the arguments to the function and the ORDER BY specification, the rank of that row among all rows of the aggregation group. As an analytic function, computes the rank of each row returned with respect to the other rows returned. The value returned is an integer > = 1, and the highest possible value is the number of unique values returned by the query. All arguments to this function must evaluate to a constant expression. Expressions must match the positions of those in the ORDER BY clause.

Parameters

Common keywords and clauses: ASC, DESC, NULLS FIRST, NULLS LAST.

**RATIO_TO_
REPORT**

```
RATIO_TO_REPORT (rr_expr) OVER (analytic_clause)
```

Computes the ratio of a value to the sum of a set of values. Analytic function only.

Parameters

rr_expr
> Resolves to a number that will be compared to the sum of the set of values returned by the *analytic_clause*.

REGR...   REGR_regr_type (expr1,expr2) [OVER (analytic_clause)]

Computes the least-squares regression line to a set of number pairs
returned by *expr1* and *expr2*.

Parameters

regr_type

May be any one of the following:

SLOPE	Returns the slope of the line.
INTERCEPT	Returns the Y intercept of the line.
COUNT	Returns the number of non-NULL pairs used to calculate the line.
R2	Returns the coefficient of determination (also known as the Chi-Squared or Goodness of Fit) for the line.
AVGX	Returns the average of the independent variable (*expr2*) of the line after eliminating NULL values. The returned value can be NULL.
AVGY	Returns the average of the dependent variable (*expr1*) of the line after eliminating NULL values. The returned value can be NULL.
SXX	Computes the value of REGR_COUNT (*expr1*,*expr2*) * VAR_POP(*expr2*) after elimination of NULL *expr1*,*expr2* pairs.
SYY	Computes the value of REGR_COUNT *expr1*,*expr2*) * VAR_POP(*expr1*, *expr2*) after elimination of NULL *expr1*,*expr2* pairs.
SXY	Computes the value of REGR_COUNT (*expr1*,*expr2*) * VAR_POP(*expr1*,*expr2*) after elimination of NULL *expr1*,*expr2* pairs.

ROW_NUMBER   ROW_NUMBER ( ) OVER (analytic_clause)

Assigns a unique sequential number, beginning with 1, to each row
returned to the query. Analytic function only.

STDDEV   STDDEV ([DISTINCT | ALL] expr) [OVER (analytic_clause)]

Computes the sample standard deviation of the values of a column
or expression over the set of rows returned by a query or the set of
rows specified by a GROUP BY clause. The sample standard deviation uses the number of rows returned by the query in the
denominator. STDDEV is similar to STDDEV_SAMP, but this
function returns 0, rather than NULL, when *expr* returns only one
row.

STDDEV_POP   STDDEV_POP ([DISTINCT | ALL] *expr*) [OVER (*analytic_clause*)]

Computes the population standard deviation of the values of a column or expression over the set of rows returned by a query or the set of rows specified by a GROUP BY clause. The population variance uses the number of rows returned by the query in the denominator.

STDDEV_SAMP   STDDEV_SAMP ([DISTINCT | ALL] *expr*) [OVER (*analytic_clause*)]

Computes the sample standard deviation of the values of a column or expression over the set of rows returned by a query or the set of rows specified by a GROUP BY clause. The sample standard deviation uses the number of rows returned by the query in the denominator.

SUM   SUM ([DISTINCT | ALL] *expr*) [OVER (*analytic_clause*)]

Computes the sum of the values of a column or expression over the set of rows returned by a query or the set of rows specified by a GROUP BY clause.

VAR_POP   VARIANCE ([DISTINCT | ALL] *expr*) [OVER (*analytic_clause*)]

Computes the population variance of the values of a column or expression over the set of rows returned by a query or the set of rows specified by a GROUP BY clause. The population variance uses the number of rows returned by the query in the denominator.

VAR_SAMP   VARIANCE ([DISTINCT | ALL] *expr*) [OVER (*analytic_clause*)]

Computes the sample variance of the values of a column or expression over the set of rows returned by a query or the set of rows specified by a GROUP BY clause. The sample standard deviation uses the number of rows returned by the query in the denominator. VAR_SAMP is almost identical to VARIANCE, but this function returns NULL when *expr* returns only one row, whereas VARIANCE returns 0 in that case.

VARIANCE   VARIANCE ([DISTINCT | ALL] *expr*) [OVER (*analytic_clause*)]

Computes the sample variance of the values of a column or expression over the set of rows returned by a query or the set of rows specified by a GROUP BY clause. The sample standard deviation uses the number of rows returned by the query in the denominator.

Numeric Functions

Numeric functions are those that take numbers as arguments and that return numeric values.

ABS	ABS (*n*)
	Returns the absolute value of a number *n*.

ACOS	ACOS (*n*)
	Returns the arc cosine of a value between -1 and 1, an angle expressed in radians. The value will fall in the range 0 to π inclusive. Reverses the output of the COS function.

ASIN	ASIN (*n*)
	Returns the arc sine of a value between -1 and 1, an angle expressed in radians. The value will fall in the range $-\pi/2$ and $\pi/2$ inclusive. Reverses the output of the SIN function.

ATAN	ATAN (*n*)
	Returns the arc tangent of a value, an angle expressed in radians. The value will fall in the range $-\pi/2$ and $\pi/2$ inclusive. Reverses the output of the TAN function.

ATAN2	ATAN2 (*n*,*m*)
	Returns the arc tangent of the value *n/m*, an angle expressed in radians. The value will fall in the range $-\pi/2$ and $\pi/2$ inclusive. ATAN2(*n*,*m*) is the same as ATAN(*n/m*).

BITAN	BITAN (*n*,*m*)
	Computes an AND operation on the bits of arguments *n* and *m*, which must be non-negative integers. The datatype of the returned value is not determined, so this function should always be wrapped in another function, such as TO_NUMBER.

CEIL	CEIL (*n*)
	Returns the lowest valued integer that is greater than or equal to the input. If *n* is already an integer, *n* will be returned.

COS	COS (*n*)
	Returns the cosine of an angle, where that angle is expressed in radians.

COSH   COSH (*n*)

Returns the hyperbolic cosine of an angle, where that angle is expressed in radians.

EXP   EXP (*n*)

Returns the value of *e* raised to the power *n*.

FLOOR   FLOOR (*n*)

Returns the largest integer value that is less than or equal to the input value.

GREATEST   GREATEST (*expr* [,*expr*...])

Returns the highest value from the list of arguments supplied. Can be used with character strings and dates, as well as with numbers. If you mix datatypes, Oracle uses the datatype of the first argument as a base and converts (if possible) all other arguments to that type before choosing the greatest value.

LEAST   LEAST (*expr* [,*expr*...])

Returns the lowest value from the list of arguments supplied. Can be used with character strings and dates, as well as with numbers. If you mix datatypes, Oracle uses the datatype of the first argument as a base and converts (if possible) all other arguments to that type before choosing the greatest value.

LN   LN (*n*)

Returns the natural logarithm of number *n*.

LOG   LOG (*m*,*n*)

Returns the base *m* logarithm of the number *n*.

MOD   MOD (*m*,*n*)

Returns the remainder left over when *m* is divided by *n*.

POWER   POWER (*m*,*n*)

Returns m^n. m^{-n} is equivalent to $1/m^n$

Parameters

m   Nonzero number.

n   Power. If *m* is positive, *n* may be any positive or negative number. If *m* is negative, *n* must be an integer.

| **ROUND** | ROUND (*n,m*) |
| | Rounds a value *n* to the number of decimal places specified by *m*. |

SIGN	SIGN (*n*)
	Returns a value indicating the sign of *n*. The number returned by the SIGN function will be one of the following:
	-1 The number is negative.
	0 The number is zero.
	1 The number is positive.

| **SIN** | SIN (*n*) |
| | Returns the sine of the angle *n*, which must be expressed in radians. |

| **SINH** | SINH (*n*) |
| | Returns the hyperbolic sine of the angle *n*, which must be expressed in radians. |

| **SQRT** | SQRT(*n*) |
| | Returns the square root of *n*, which must be a positive number. |

| **TAN** | TAN (*n*) |
| | Returns the tangent of the angle *n*, which must be expressed in radians. |

| **TANH** | TANH (*n*) |
| | Returns the hyperbolic tangent of the angle *n*, which must be expressed in radians. |

| **TRUNC** | TRUNC (*n* [,*m*]) |
| | Truncates a number *n* to the number of decimal places specified by *m*. |

Functions

WIDTH_BUCKET   WIDTH_BUCKET (*expr, min, max, n*)

This function is intended for the construction of histograms. Returns a bucket number into which the value of *expr* will fall when it is evaluated. If Oracle encounters values lower than *min* and/or higher than *max*, they will be placed in "overflow" buckets 0 and *n*+1, respectively. New with Oracle9*i*.

Parameters

expr Specifies an expression for which a histogram is being constructed. This expression must evaluate to either a number or a DATE value.

min Specifies the lowest acceptable value for *expr*.

max Specifies the highest acceptable value for *expr*.

n Specifies the number of buckets

Character Functions

Character functions are those that operate on character values. Functions in this category can return either character or numeric values. Note that the GREATEST and LEAST functions, described under "Numeric Functions" can also operate on character values.

ASCII   ASCII (*char*)

Returns the decimal representation of a character, based on the character set in effect for the database. A true ASCII value will be returned only if a 7-bit ASCII character set is in use for the database. If *char* is a string, returns the ASCII value of the first character of the string.

CHR   CHR (*n* [USING NCHAR_CS])

Returns the character from the database character set that is associated with *n*.

Parameters

n   Numeric value that represents the character to be returned.

USING NCHAR_CS
                       Specifies that the national character set of the database is to be used.

CONCAT   CONCAT (*string1, string2*)

Concatenates two input strings and returns the result.

INITCAP   INITCAP (*string*)

Returns the string provided with the first letter of each word in the string changed to uppercase, and all other letters in lowercase.

INSTR...   INSTR (*string1*, *string2*[, *n*[, *m*]])

Searches *string1* to find *string2* and returns the character position in *string1* where *string2* begins. INSTR can take the following forms:

INSTR	Uses standard character set
INSTRB	Uses input character set
INSTRC	Uses Unicode complete characters (new with Oracle9*i*)
INSTR2	Uses UCS2 codepoints (new with Oracle9*i*)
INSTR4	Uses UCS4 codepoints (new with Oracle9*i*)

Parameters

string1	String that you want to search.
string2	String that you want to find.
n	Character position from which the search should begin. The default is to begin searching from the first character, which is position 1. Negative values specify the starting position relative to the right end of *string1* rather than the left.
m	Which occurrence of *string2* you want to find (if it occurs more than once). The default is to find the first occurrence.

LENGTH...   LENGTH (*string*)

Returns the number of characters in a string. LENGTH can take the following forms:

LENGTH	Uses standard character set.
LENGTHB	Uses input character set.
LENGTHC	Uses Unicode complete characters (new with Oracle9*i*)
LENGTH2	Uses UCS2 codepoints (new with Oracle9*i*)
LENGTH4	Uses UCS4 codepoints (new with Oracle9*i*)

LOWER   LOWER (*string*)

Converts all the characters in a string to lowercase.

LPAD   LPAD (*string1*, *n*[, *string2*])

Pads the left side of *string1* with spaces, or with copies of the character string specified by *stringr2*, until the size of the resulting string reaches *n* characters.

Parameters

string1   String that will be padded.

n   Final length of *string1* after padding occurs.

string2   String that will be added to the left side of *string1*. The default is a single space.

LTRIM   LTRIM (*string1* [,*string2*])

Removes the character specified by *string2* from the left side of *string1*.

Parameters

string1   String to be searched.

string2   String that will be removed from the left side of *string1*. The default is a single blank.

NLS_INITCAP   NLS_INITCAP (*string*[, 'NLS_SORT=*sort*'])

Performs like INITCAP but uses the national character set.

Parameters

string   The input character string.

sort   Name of the linguistic sort sequence that specifies the capitalization rules for the language being used.

NLS_LOWER   NLS_LOWER (*string*[, 'NLS_SORT=*sort*'])

Performs like LOWER but uses the national character set.

Parameters

string   Input character string.

sort   Name of the linguistic sort sequence that specifies the capitalization rules for the language being used.

NLS_UPPER   NLS_UPPER (*string*[, 'NLS_SORT=*sort*'])

Performs like UPPER but uses the national character set.

Parameters

string   Input character string.

sort   Name of the linguistic sort sequence that specifies the capitalization rules for the language being used.

NLSSORT   NLSSORT (*string*[, 'NLS_SORT=*sort*'])

Returns the byte string used to represent a value that is being sorted using a linguistic sort sequence.

Parameters

string   Input character string.

sort   Name of a linguistic sort sequence or the keyword BINARY, which returns the exact byte values of the input string.

REPLACE   REPLACE (*string, search_string* [,*replacement_string*])

Searches a string and replaces one substring with another.

Parameters

string   String to search.

search_string   Substring to search for.

replacement_string

                  String that you want to use in place of the *search_string*. Without this optional argument, all occurrences of *search_string* are deleted.

RPAD   RPAD (*string1, n*[, *string2*])

Pads the right side of *string1* with spaces or with copies of the character string specified by *string2*, until the size of the resulting string reaches *n* characters.

Parameters

string1   String that will be padded.

n   Final length of *string1* after padding occurs.

string2   String that will be added to the right side of *string1*. The default is a single space.

RTRIM   RTRIM (*string1* [,*string2*])

Removes the characters specified by *string2* from the right side of *string1*.

Parameters

string1   String to be searched.

string2   String that will be removed from the right side of *string1*. The default is a single blank.

Functions

SOUNDEX

SOUNDEX (*string*)

Returns a string of digits that represents the phonetic pronunciation of *string*. Using SOUNDEX can make it easier to search for a given string, because you don't need to spell it correctly in order to get a match.

Use the following steps to derive the output string:

1. Retain the first letter of the string.

2. Remove all occurrences of the following letters: a, e, h, i, o, u, w, y.

3. Replace any remaining letters with digits, as shown in Table 8-1.

4. Truncate the resulting string to four characters in length.

Table 8-1. SOUNDEX letter-to-digit correspondence

Letters	SOUNDEX digit
b, f, p, v	1
c, g, j, k, q, s, x, z	2
d, t	3
l	4
m, n	5
r	6

SUBSTR . . .

SUBSTR (*string*, *m* [,*n*])

Searches *string* and returns the substring that is *n* characters long, beginning in postion *m* offset from the left end of the string. SUBSTR can take the following forms:

SUBSTR	Uses standard character set.
SUBSTRB	Uses input character set.
SUBSTRC	Uses Unicode complete characters (new with Oracle9*i*).
SUBSTR2	Uses UCS2 codepoints (new with Oracle9*i*).
SUBSTR4	Uses UCS4 codepoints (new with Oracle9*i*).

Parameters

string	String to be searched.
m	Starting position in the string, starting from the left. If *m* is negative, the offset will be calculated from the right end of the string.
n	Number of characters to be returned. If not specified, then all characters beginning at position *m* are returned.

TRANSLATE	TRANSLATE (*string*, *from_string*, *to_string*)

Modifies the input string *string* by replacing any occurrence of *from_string* with *to_string*.

Parameters

string	String to be modified.
from_string	String to be replaced.
to_string	String to be used to replace *from_string*.

TREAT	TREAT (*expr* AS [REF] [*schema.*]*type*)

Changes the declared type of an expression *expr* to the type specified by *type*. *type* must be a supertype or subtype of the type of *expr*. If it is not, the function returns NULL. New with Oracle9*i*.

Parameters

REF	Specifies that the value for *expr* is a REF.
schema	Owner of *type*.
type	Type to be used for *expr*.

TRIM	TRIM ([LEADING | TRAILING | BOTH] [*trim_character* FROM] *string*)

Removes characters from a string.

Parameters

LEADING	Specifies that only leading spaces are to be trimmed.
TRAILING	Specifies that only trailing spaces are to be trimmed.
BOTH	Specifies that both leading and trailing spaces are to be trimmed. This is the default.
trim_character	Specifies some other character to trim instead of a space.
string	Input string.

UPPER	UPPER (*string*)

Converts all the characters in *string* to uppercase.

Date and Time Functions

Date and time functions are those that operate on and/or return date or time values. This section describes the traditional date functions, as well as the new interval and timestamp functions introduced in Oracle9*i*.

Throughout the following sections, *date* always indicates an expression of the standard Oracle DATE datatype.

ADD_MONTHS   ADD_MONTHS (*date,n*)

Adds *n* months to the date *date*. Negative values of *n* subtract months from *d*. The following rules control whether or not the day of the month is affected:

- If the original date represents the last day of its month, then the resulting date will be adjusted so that it is also the last day of the month.
- If keeping the same day of the month results in an invalid date because the new month has fewer days than the original, then the day will be adjusted downward to fit the new month.

Parameter

n   Number of months to be added to *date*.

CURRENT_DATE   CURRENT_DATE

Returns the current date and time in the session time zone as a DATE datatype. Unless you use ALTER SESSION to change the session time zone, CURRENT_DATE will return the datetime for the server you are logged into. New with Oracle9*i*.

CURRENT_
TIMESTAMP   CURRENT_TIMESTAMP [(*precision*)]

Returns the current date and time in the session time zone as a TIMESTAMP WITH TIMEZONE datatype. The default *precision* is 6. CURRENT TIMESTAMP is similar to LOCAL_TIMESTAMP but returns a TIMESTAMP WITH TIME ZONE value, instead of a TIMESTAMP value. New with Oracle9*i*.

DBTIMEZONE   DBTIMEZONE

Returns the time zone of the database. This may be either a time zone offset or a time zone region name, depending on how it was specified in the most recent CREATE DATABASE or ALTER DATABASE statement. New with Oracle9*i*.

EXTRACT   EXTRACT ({
          [YEAR | MONTH | DAY | HOUR | MINUTE | SECOND] |
          [TIMEZONE_HOUR | TIMEZONE_MINUTE] |
          [TIMEZONE_REGION | TIMEZONE_ABBR] }
          FROM {*datetime_expr* | *interval_value_expr*})

Extracts the value of the selected datetime field from the specified datetime expression or interval value expression. The field being extracted must be a valid part of the specified expression. New with Oracle9*i*.

Parameters

datetime_expr Expression that resolves to an Oracle DATE.

interval_value_expr
  Expression that resolves to an Oracle interval value.

FROM_TZ

FROM_TZ (*timestamp_value*,*timezone_value*)

Converts *timestamp_value* at a time zone to a TIMESTAMP WITH TIMEZONE value. New with Oracle9*i*.

Parameters

timestamp_value
  Timestamp value to be converted.

timezone_value Character string in the form TZH:TZM or a character expression that returns a string in TZR with the optional TZD format.

INTERVAL DAY TO SECOND

```
INTERVAL '{int1 | int1 time_exp | time_exp}'
   {[DAY | HOUR | MINUTE] (lead_precision)|
    SECOND (lead_precision[, frac_precision ])}
   [TO {DAY | HOUR | MINUTE | SECOND [(frac_precision)]}]]
```

Translates literal integers representing days, hours, minutes, and seconds into an interval of time. This function may have one or two units of time. If two units are specified, the first unit must be greater than the second, as in INTERVAL ... DAY TO SECOND or INTERVAL ... HOUR TO MINUTE. New with Oracle9*i*.

You can use the INTERVAL functions to perform date arithmetic, as shown in the following "Examples" section. For more information about INTERVAL datatypes and all of the Oracle datatypes, see Appendix A.

Parameters

int1 Integer representing the first unit of time.

time_expression
  Time expression that can take one of the following forms:

  HH:MI:SS[.*n*]
  MI:SS[.*n*]
  SS[.*n*]
  If used with *int1*, the leading field must be DAY.

lead_precision Integer representing the precision of the leading field. Default is 2.

frac_precision Integer representing the precision of the fractional part of the SECOND field. Default is 6.

Examples

The following examples illustrate various forms of the INTERVAL syntax and show the values to which they translate; see the next entry for INTERVAL YEAR TO MONTH syntax:

INTERVAL '10-4' YEAR(3) TO MONTH
    10 years, 4 months

INTERVAL '10-4' YEAR TO MONTH
    Error because first value exceeds default precision of 2

INTERVAL '240' MONTH
    20 years

INTERVAL '5 4' DAY TO MINUTE
    5 days and 4 minutes

INTERVAL '5 4' DAY TO HOUR
    5 days and 4 hours

INTERVAL '3 11:15' DAY TO MINUTE
    3 days, 11 hours, and 15 minutes

INTERVAL '20' DAY - INTERVAL '120' HOUR
    15 days

INTERVAL YEAR TO MONTH

INTERVAL 'int1 [- int2]' YEAR | MONTH [int_precision] [TO MONTH]

Translates literal integers representing years, months, or years and months into an interval of time. This function may have one or two units of time. If two units are specified, the first unit must be greater than the second, as in INTERVAL ... YEAR TO MONTH. New with Oracle9i.

You can use the INTERVAL functions to perform date arithmetic, as shown in the "Examples" section of the preceding INTERVAL DAY TO SECOND entry.

Parameters

int1
    Integer representing the first unit of time: YEAR or MONTH.

int2
    Optional integer that represents the second optional unit of time, MONTH. Has a range of 0–11.

int_precision
    Optional precision of the leading field. Default is 2. If the number of digits exceeds this value, the function returns an error.

LAST_DAY

LAST_DAY(date)

Returns the date corresponding to the last day of the month in which date falls.

LOCAL_ TIMESTAMP	CURRENT_TIMESTAMP [(precision)]

Returns the current date and time in the session time zone as a TIMESTAMP datatype. Default *precision* is 6. New with Oracle9*i*.

MONTHS_ BETWEEN	MONTHS_BETWEEN (date1, date2)

Returns the number of months between the two dates *date1* and *date2*. If both dates represent the same day of the month or if both represent the last day of their respective months, this function returns an integer value. Otherwise, it returns a fractional value, based on a 31-day month.

NEW_TIME	NEW_TIME (date, z1, z2)

Converts a datetime value date from time zone *z1* to a date/time value in time zone *z2*. Time zones must be chosen from the time zone identifiers listed in Table 8-2. Note that There is no relation between these identifiers and the TZD and TZR format elements used for time zones in the timestamp values introduced in Oracle9*i*.

Table 8-2. Time zone identifiers

Time zone identifier	Time zone
AST	Atlantic Standard Time
ADT	Atlantic Daylight Time
BST	Bering Standard Time
BDT	Bering Daylight Time
CST	Central Standard Time
CDT	Central Daylight Time
EST	Eastern Standard Time
EDT	Eastern Daylight Time
GMT	Greenwich Mean Time
HST	Alaska-Hawaii Standard Time
HDT	Alaska-Hawaii Daylight Time
MST	Mountain Standard Time
MDT	Mountain Daylight Time
NST	Newfoundland Standard Time
PST	Pacific Standard Time
PDT	Pacific Daylight Time
YST	Yukon Standard Time
YDT	Yukon Daylight Time

Functions

NEXT_DAY	NEXT_DAY (date, string)

Returns the next occurrence of the day *string* following the datetime specified by *date*. Any time component in the date is preserved and returned in the result. NEXT_DAY always looks forward. If the date you pass in as a parameter happens to fall on the day you are searching for, NEXT_DAY will return the subsequent occurrence of that day.

Parameters

string	Day of the week. *string* must be a full name such as Wednesday or an abbreviation such as Wed. Day names must be valid for your current NLS_DATE_LANGUAGE setting.

NUMTODS-INTERVAL	NUMTODSINTERVAL (n,'expr')

Converts *n* to an INTERVAL DAY TO SECOND literal. New with Oracle9*i*.

Parameters

n	Number to be converted to an INTERVAL DAY TO SECOND literal.
expr	Unit to be returned; must one of the following: 'DAY,' 'HOUR,' 'MINUTE,' or 'SECOND.'

NUMTOYM-INTERVAL	NUMTOYMINTERVAL (n,'expr')

Converts *n* to an INTERVAL YEAR TO MONTH literal. New with Oracle9*i*.

Parameters

n	Number to be converted to an INTERVAL YEAR TO MONTH literal.
expr	Unit to be returned; must be either 'YEAR' or 'MONTH.'

ROUND	ROUND (date [,dfmt])

Rounds *date* to the nearest datetime unit specified by *dfmt*. Rounding a date may result in a new date that is greater than the date you started with. If you don't want to round up, use the TRUNC function instead.

Common keywords and clauses: *dfmt*.

SESSIONTIME-ZONE	SESSIONTIMEZONE

Returns the value of the current session's time zone. This may be either a time zone offset or a time zone region name, depending on how the time zone value was specified in the most recent ALTER SESSION statement. New with Oracle9*i*.

SYS_EXTRACT_UTC	SYS_EXTRACT_UTC (*datetime_expr*)

Returns the UTC (or GMT) time from *datetime_expr*. (UTC stands for Coordinated Universal Time, GMT for Greenwich Mean Time.) New with Oracle9*i*.

Parameter

datetime_expr Expression that resolves to a datetime with time zone displacement.

SYSDATE	SYSDATE

Returns the current date and time, which includes hours, minutes, and seconds.

SYSTIMESTAMP	SYSTIMESTAMP

Returns the system date and time, including the time zone of the database, as a TIMESTAMP WITH TIME ZONE datatype. New with Oracle9*i*.

TO_DSINTERVAL	TO_DSINTERVAL (*string*['NLS_NUMERIC_CHARACTERS="dg"'])

Converts *string* to an INTERVAL DAY SECOND type. See the earlier introduction to the INTERVAL entries. New with Oracle9*i*.

Parameters

string String containing the characters to be converted.

d Character representing the decimal separator.

g Character representing the group separator.

TO_TIMESTAMP	TO_TIMESTAMP (*string*[,*dfmt*['NLS_NUMERIC_CHARACTERS="dg"']])

Converts *string* to a TIMESTAMP type. If *dfmt* is not provided, *string* must match the default format for the TIMESTAMP datatype. New with Oracle9*i*.

Parameters

string String containing the characters to be converted.

d Character representing the decimal separator.

g Character representing the group separator.

Common keywords and clauses: *dfmt*.

TO_TIMESTAMP_TZ	TO_TIMESTAMP_TZ (*string*[,*dfmt*['NLS_NUMERIC_CHARACTERS="dg"']])

Converts *string* to a TIMESTAMP WITH TIME ZONE type. If *dfmt* is not provided, *string* must match the default format for the TIMESTAMP WITH TIME ZONE datatype. New with Oracle9*i*.

Functions

Parameters

string	String containing the characters to be converted.
d	Specifies the character representing the decimal separator.
g	Specifies the character representing the group separator.

Common keywords and clauses: *dfmt*.

TO_
YMINTERVAL

TO_YMINTERVAL (*string*)

Converts *string* to an INTERVAL YEAR TO MONTH type. See the earlier introduction to the INTERVAL entries. New with Oracle9*i*.

TRUNC

TRUNC (*date* [,*dfmt*])

Returns a datetime value truncated to the unit specified. Use TRUNC whenever you want to be sure that you are working with only a date and not a date combined with a time component

Common keywords and clauses: *dfmt*.

TZ_OFFSET

TZ_OFFSET ({'*timezone_name*' | '{+ | -}*hh:mi*' |
    SESSIONTIMEZONE | DBTIMEZONE})

Returns the time zone offset. New with Oracle9*i*.

Parameters

timezone_name	Time zone name.
+	Specifies that the offset will be positive—that is, in the future.
-	Specifies that the offset will be negative—that is, in the past.
hh	Minutes of offset.
mi	Hours of offset.
SESSIONTIMEZONE	Specifies that the offset is to be the time zone setting for the current session.
DBTIMEZONE	Specifies that the offset is to be the time zone setting for the database.

Conversion Functions

Conversion functions are those that allow you to convert a value from one datatype to another.

ASCIISTR

ASCIISTR (*'char_string'*)

Converts *char_string* to an ASCII string in the database character set. New with Oracle9*i*.

BIN_TO_NUM

BIN_TO_NUM (*expr*[,*expr*...])

Converts one or more expressions that resolve into bits into an Oracle NUMBER. New with Oracle9*i*.

CAST

CAST {*expr* | (*subquery*) | MULTISET (*subquery*)} AS *type*)

Converts a built-in datatype or collection-typed value into another of type *type*.

Parameters

subquery	Subquery which must return a single value of collection type or built-in type.
MULTISET	Specifies that Oracle is to take the result set of the subquery and return a collection value.
type	Name of a built-in datatype or collection type.

CHARTOROWID

CHARTOROWID (*string*)

Converts a string value *string* to a ROWID value.

COMPOSE

COMPOSE (*'string'*)

Converts *string* in any datatype to a Unicode string in its fully normalized form with same character set as the input. New with Oracle9*i*.

CONVERT

CONVERT (*string*, *dest_char_set*[, *source_char_set*])

Converts a character string from one character set to another.

Parameters

string	Character string to convert.
dest_char_set	Name of the destination character set.
source_char_set	Name of the source character set. Defaults to the database character set.

DECOMPOSE

DECOMPOSE (*'string'*)

Converts a string in any datatype to a Unicode string after canonical decomposition in the same character set as the input. New with Oracle9*i*.

Functions

HEXTORAW	HEXTORAW (*string*)
	Converts hexadecimal digits in *string* to a RAW value of bytes.

NUMTODS-INTERVAL	NUMTODSINTERVAL (*n*,{'DAY' | 'HOUR' | 'MINUTE' | 'SECOND'}.)
	Converts *n* into an INTERVAL DAY TO SECOND literal. See the earlier introduction to the INTERVAL entries. New with Oracle9*i*.

Parameters

n	Number value to be converted.
DAY	Specifies that *n* is to be treated as *n* days.
HOUR	Specifies that *n* is to be treated as *n* hours.
MINUTE	Specifies that *n* is to be treated as *n* minutes.
SECOND	Specifies that *n* is to be treated as *n* seconds.

NUMTOYM-INTERVAL	NUMTOYMINTERVAL (*n*,{'YEAR' | 'MONTH'})
	Converts *n* into an INTERVAL YEAR TO MONTH literal. See the earlier introduction to INTERVALs. New with Oracle9*i*.

Parameters

n	Number value to be converted
YEAR	Specifies that *n* is to be treated as *n* years.
MONTH	Specifies that *n* is to be treated as *n* months.

RAWTOHEX	RAWTOHEX (*raw*)
	Converts *raw* to a VARCHAR2 string of hexadecimal digits where each two-character hex digit corresponds to one byte of *raw*.

RAWTONHEX	RAWTONHEX (*raw*)
	Converts *raw* to an NVARCHAR2 string of hexadecimal digits where each two-character hex digit corresponds to one byte of *raw*. New with Oracle9*i*.

ROWIDTOCHAR	ROWIDTOCHAR (*rowid*)
	Converts *rowid* to a character string. ROWID values are also implicitly converted to character strings whenever you select them from a table using SQL*Plus. New with Oracle9*i*.

ROWIDTONCHAR	ROWIDTONCHAR (*rowid*)
	Converts *rowid* to an NCHAR string. New with Oracle9*i*.

TO_CHAR (character)

TO_CHAR (*value*)

Converts NCHAR, NVARCHAR2, CLOB, or NCLOB *value* into the database character set. New with Oracle9i.

TO_CHAR (datetime)

TO_CHAR (*date* [, *dfmt* [,'*nlsparams*']])

Converts *date* into a character-based representation with *dfmt*.

Parameter

date   Specifies a datetime value (of type DATE).

Common keywords and clauses: *dfmt*, *nlsparams*.

TO_CHAR (number)

TO_CHAR (*n* [, *fmt* [,'*nlsparams*']])

Converts a numeric value into a character-based representation of that value.

Parameter

n   Numeric value to convert.

Common keywords and clauses: *fmt*, *nlsparams*.

TO_CLOB

TO_CLOB ({*lob_column* | *char_string*})

Converts NCLOB in *lob_column* or a character string *char_string* to a CLOB value. New with Oracle9i

Parameters

lob_column   Name of a LOB column.

char_string   Name of a character string.

TO_DATE

TO_DATE (*string* [, *dfmt* [,'*nlsdateparam*']])

Converts *string* into a value of type DATE.

Parameters

string   Character string representation of the datetime value to be converted.

Common keywords and clauses: *dfmt*, *nlsdateparam*.

TO_DSINTERVAL

TO_DSINTERVAL (*string*['NLS_NUMERIC_CHARACTERS="dg"'])

Converts *string* to an INTERVAL DAY SECOND type. See the earlier introduction to the INTERVAL entries. New with Oracle9i.

Parameters

string   String containing the characters to be converted.

d   Character representing the decimal separator.

g   Character representing the group separator.

Functions

TO_LOB

TO_LOB (*long_column*)

Converts a LONG or LONG RAW value *long_column* into a CLOB, BLOB, or NCLOB. Can be used only in the subquery of an INSERT ... SELECT FROM statement when using that statement to populate a LOB column. LONG values are converted to either CLOB or NCLOB values depending on the datatype of the destination column. LONG RAW values are converted to BLOB values.

TO_MULTI_ BYTE

TO_MULTI_BYTE (*string*)

Converts single-byte characters in *string* to their multibyte equivalents.

TO_NCHAR (character)

TO_NCHAR (*value* [, *dfmt* [,'*nlsparams*']])

Converts *value*, which can be a character string, CLOB, or NCLOB, into a character-based representation of that value in the national character set.

Common keywords and clauses: *dfmt, nlsparams*.

TO_NCHAR (datetime)

TO_NCHAR ({*datetime* | *interval*}[, *dfmt* [,'*nlsparams*']])

Converts *datetime* or *interval* in the database character set to the national character set.

Parameters

datetime   Datetime value.

interval   Interval value.

Common keywords and clauses: *dfmt, nlsparams*.

TO_NCHAR (number)

TO_NCHAR (*value* [, *fmt* [, '*nlsparams*']])

Converts numeric *value* to the national character set. New with Oracle9*i*.

Common keywords and clauses: *fmt, nlsparams*.

TO_NCLOB

TO_NCLOB (*value*)

Converts *value* to NCLOB. *value* can be a LOB column, CHAR, VARCHAR2, NCHAR, NVARCHAR2, CLOB, or NCLOB. New with Oracle9*i*.

TO_NUMBER

TO_NUMBER (*string* [, *fmt*[, '*nlsparams*']])

Converts *string* to a NUMBER value.

Parameters

string   Character string containing the character-based representation that you want to convert.

Common keywords and clauses: *fmt, nlsparams*.

TO_SINGLE_ **BYTE**	TO_SINGLE_BYTE (*string*)
	Converts multibyte characters contained in *string* to their single-byte equivalents.

TO_ **YMINTERVAL**	TO_YMINTERVAL (*char_string*)
	Converts *char_string* of type CHAR, VARCHAR2, NCHAR, or NVARCHAR2 into an INTERVAL YEAR TO MONTH type. See the earlier introduction to the INTERVAL entries. New with Oracle9*i*.

TRANSLATE ... **USING**	TRANSLATE (*text* USING {CHAR_CS | NCHAR_CS})
	Converts text into either the database character set or the national character set.

Parameters

text	String that you want to translate.
CHAR_CS	Causes the string to be converted from the national character set into the database character set. The result is returned as a VARCHAR2 value.
NCHAR_CS	Causes the string to be converted from the database character set into the national character set. The result is returned as an NVARCHAR2 value.

UNISTR	UNISTR ('*string*')
	Converts *string* of any character set to Unicode in the database Unicode character set. UCS2 codepoint characters are represented by the backslash (\) followed by a number. New with Oracle9*i*.

Object Functions

The following functions are used to manipulate reference pointers (REFs) to object types.

DEREF	DEREF (*expr*)
	Returns the object reference of *expr*, which must return a REF to an object. By default, Oracle returns the object ID of an object in a query. New with Oracle8*i*.

MAKE_REF	MAKE_REF (*table* | *view* , *key* [, *key* . . .])
	Creates a REF to a row of an object *view* or an object *table*. The object identifier for the row must be primary key based (*key*). New with Oracle8*i*.

REF	REF (*correlation_variable*)
	Returns a REF for the object instance in the object table, aliased by *correlation_variable*. New with Oracle8*i*.
REFTOHEX	REFTOHEX (*expr*)
	Converts REF *expr* to its hexadecimal equivalent. New with Oracle8*i*.
VALUE	VALUE (*correlation_variable*)
	Returns object instances stored in the object table, aliased by the *correlation_variable*. New with Oracle8*i*.

XML Functions

The following functions are used to manipulate XML documents.7

EXISTSNODE	EXISTSNODE (*XMLtype_instance,XMLpath_string*)
	Determines whether traversing the document *XMLtype_instance* using the path supplied results in any nodes. The function returns 0 if no nodes remain; otherwise, it returns a positive number. New with Oracle9*i*.

Parameters

XMLtype_instance Name of an XMLtype instance containing an XML document.

XMLpath_string VARCHAR2 string containing the XML path.

EXTRACT (XML)	EXTRACT (*XMLTypeInstance, XPath_string*)
	Similar to the EXISTSNODE function. Extracts an XMLType instance of *XPath_string* from *XMLTypeInstance*. New with Oracle9*i*.

Parameters

XMLTypeInstance Name of an XMLType instance.

XMLpath_string VARCHAR2 string containing the XML path.

EXTRACTVALUE	EXTRACTVALUE (*XMLTypeInstance, XPath_string*)
	Extracts the scalar value of *XPath_string* from *XMLTypeInstance*. New with Oracle9*i*.

Parameters

XMLTypeInstance Name of an XMLType instance.

XMLpath_string VARCHAR2 string containing the XML path.

SYS_XMLAGG

SYS_XMLAGG (*expr* [*xmlfmt*])

Returns a single XML document that is an aggregate of all of the XML documents represented by *expr*. The function adds a new enclosing element with a default name ROWSET. If *xmlfmt* (an instance of the SYS.XMLGenFormatType object) is provided, the XML document will be formatted accordingly. New with Oracle9*i*.

SYS_XMLGEN

SYS_XMLGEN (*expr* [*xmlfmt*])

Returns an instance of type SYS.XMLType containing an XML document from *expr*, which evaluates to a particular row and column of the database. *xmlfmt* (an instance of the SYS.XMLGen-FormatType object), may be specified to format the XML document differently. New with Oracle9*i*.

UPDATEXML

UPDATEXML (*XMLType_instance*, *Xpath_string*, *value_expr*)

Returns an XMLType instance of *XMLType_instance* type found on *Xpath_string* having *value_expr*.

Parameters

XMLTypeInstance Name of an XMLType instance.

XMLpath_string   VARCHAR2 string containing the XML path.

XMLAGG

XMLAGG (*XMLTypeInstance* [ORDER BY *sort_list*])

Returns an aggregated XML document from a collection of XML fragments. XMLAGG is similar to SYS_XMLAGG except that XMLAGG returns a collection of nodes. However, it does not accept formatting using the XMLFormat object and does not enclose the output in an element tag as does SYS_XMLAGG. New with Oracle9*i*.

Parameters

XMLTypeInstance Name of an XMLType instance.

sort_list   List of values used to sort.

XMLCOLATTVAL

XMLCOLATTVAL (*value_expr* [AS *c_alias*])

Creates an XML fragment with *value_expr*, a column name, and expands it so that it has the name column with the attribute column. If *c_alias* is present, replaces column name. New with Oracle9*i*.

XMLCONCAT

XMLCONCAT(*XMLTypeInstance*[,*XMLTypeInstance*. . .])

Returns a concatenated series from *XMLType_instance*s. New with Oracle9*i*.

Parameters

XMLTypeInstance Name of an XMLType instance.

XMLELEMENT	XMLELEMENT ([NAME] *identifier* [, XMLATTRIBUTES(*value_expr* [AS *c_alias*] [, *value_expr* [AS *c_alias*]. . .]] [,*value_expr*[, *value_expr* . . .])])

Returns an instance of XMLType named *identifier*, with the attributes listed in *XML_attributes_clauses* and a value of *value_expr*. *c_alias* is an optional alternative name for the XML value. Typically used to format values returned from columns into XML fragments. New with Oracle9*i*.

XMLFOREST	XMLFOREST (*value_expr* [AS *c_alias*])

Converts each *value_expr* to XML and returns an XML fragment with the concatenation of the expressions. *c_alias* is an optional alternative name for the XML value. New with Oracle9*i*.

XMLSEQUENCE	XMLSEQUENCE (*XMLTypeInstance* | *REF_cursor* [, *xmlfmt*])

Returns a VARRAY of XMLTypes. If *xmlfmt* (an instance of the SYS.XMLGenFormatType object) is provided, the XML document will be formatted accordingly. New with Oracle9*i*.

Parameters

XMLTypeInstance With this variable, returns a VARRAY of top-level nodes in the XMLType.

REF_cursor A REF CURSOR instance, with optional *fmt* XMLFormat object. With this variable, returns XMLSequence type and an XML document for each row of the cursor.

XMLTRANSFORM	XMLTRANSFORM (*XMLTypeInstance, XSLTypeInstance*)

Transforms *XMLTypeInstance* with *XSLTypeInstance*. New with Oracle9*i*.

Parameters

XMLTypeInstance With this variable, returns a VARRAY of top-level nodes in the XMLType.

Miscellaneous Functions

The remaining functions don't fall neatly into any of the other categories listed in this chapter.

BFILENAME	BFILENAME (*directory, filename*)

Returns a BFILE locator that points to a file that you specify.

Parameters

directory	A directory (previously created using the CREATE DIRECTORY statement) containing the file.
filename	Name of the file to which you want the locator to point.

COALESCE

COALESCE (*expr[,expr...]*)

Returns the first non-NULL expression in the argument list. If all expressions are NULL, the function returns NULL. New with Oracle9*i*.

DECODE

DECODE (*expr, search, result* [*,search, result...*] [*,default*])

Provides the capabilities of an inline IF statement. DECODE receives an input value and a list of up to 255 value/result pairs. DECODE then looks for the pair where the value matches the input. When that pair is found, DECODE returns the result from that pair as the result of the function. If no matching value is found, DECODE returns the default result.

Datatypes are controlled by the first *search, result* pair. The input expression and all *search* values are converted to the datatype of the first *search* value. The return value is converted to the datatype of the first *result* value.

Parameters

expr	Input value. DECODE compares this value with subsequent *search* values in order to find the matching value/result pair.
search	Value portion of a value/result pair.
result	Rsult portion of a value/result pair.
default	Optional default result that DECODE returns if none of the *search* values matches the input expression.

DEPTH

DEPTH (*correlation_integer*)

Returns the number of levels in the path specified with the UNDER_PATH or EQUALS_PATH conditions. The *correlation_integer* is used to correlate the function with a primary condition if the statement contains multiple primary conditions. New with Oracle9*i*.

DUMP

DUMP (*expr* [*,return_format* [*,start_position* [*,length*]]])

Returns a VARCHAR2 showing the datatype and the internal representation of data stored within a column or of the data returned by an expression.

Parameters

expr   Data to be dumped. Can be a column name or a valid SQL expression.

return_format Format that controls the manner in which the dumped data is formatted. Select from the following values:

8   Use octal notation.

10 Use decimal notation. This is the default.

16 Use hexadecimal notation.

17 Display the result using characters.

If you add 1000 to the format specifier, DUMP also returns the name of the character set.

start_position Specifies the starting byte for the data to be dumped. The default is to start with the first byte of data.

length   Specifies the number of bytes to dump. The default is to dump all the data.

EMPTY_BLOB

EMPTY_BLOB ( )

Returns an empty BLOB locator, which can then be used to initialize a BLOB column. You must include parentheses in this function call.

EMPTY_CLOB

EMPTY_CLOB ( )

Returns an empty CLOB locator, which can then be used to initialize a CLOB column. You must include parentheses in this function call.

NLS_CHARSET_ DECL_LEN

NLS_CHARSET_DECL_LEN (*bytecnt,csid*)

Returns the declaration width of an NCHAR column (in terms of the number of characters), based on the *bytecnt*.

Parameters

bytecnt   Size, in bytes, of the NCHAR column.

csid   Number identifying the NLS character set you are using for the column. You can use the NLS_ CHARSET_ID function to get the character set number corresponding to a character set name.

NLS_CHARSET_ ID

NLS_CHARSET_ID (*text*)

Returns the ID number corresponding to a given NLS character set name of *text*.

NLS_CHARSET_ **NAME**	NLS_CHARSET_NAME (*n*) Returns the name corresponding to the NLS character set ID number *n*.
NULLIF	NULLIF (*expr1,expr2*) Compares *expr1* to *expr2*. If they are equal, the function returns NULL; otherwise, it returns *expr1*. *expr1* cannot be set to the literal NULL. New with Oracle9*i*.
NVL	NVL (*expr1,expr2*) Returns an alternative value to use if the given input value is NULL. NVL returns *expr2* if *expr1* is NULL; otherwise, it simply returns *expr1*.
NVL2	NVL2 (*expr1,expr2,expr3*) Returns either *expr2* or *expr3*. If *expr1* is NULL, the function returns *expr2*; otherwise, it returns *expr3*. *expr2* and *expr3* cannot be LONG.
PATH	PATH (*correlation_integer*) Returns the relative path that leads to the resource defined with the UNDER_PATH or EQUALS_PATH condition. The *correlation_integer* is used to correlate the function with a primary condition if the statement contains multiple primary conditions. New with Oracle9*i*.
SYS_CONNECT_ **BY_PATH**	SYS_CONNECT_BY_PATH (*column,char*) Returns the path of a column value from root to node, with column values separated by *char* for each row returned by CONNECT BY. New with Oracle9*i*.
SYS_CONTEXT	SYS_CONTEXT (*namespace, attribute_name* [,*length*]) Returns the value of an attribute in an application context namespace.

Parameters

namespace	Name of a namespace previously created using the CREATE CONTEXT statement. You can also specify the default namespace USERENV.
attribute_name	Name of an attribute within the namespace, which is then returned by this function. Several predefined attributes are available for use with the default USERENV namespace and are listed in Table 8-3.

Functions

	length	Length that you want to allow for an attribute's return value. This optional parameter is only available beginning with Oracle 8.1.6 and only for the AUTHENTICATION_DATA attribute; in addition, it cannot be more than 4000.0	

Table 8-3. Predefined attributes in the USERENV namespace

Attribute name	Description	Max length	Since version
AUTHENTICATION_ DATA	Data being used to authenticate a user. If authentication is via an X. 503 certificate, the content of the certificate will be returned in hexa-decimal format.	256– 4000	8.1.6
AUTHENTICATION_ TYPE	Indicates how the user was authenticated: DATABASE: A username and password were used. OS: Operating system authentication was used. NETWORK: Authentication was via a network protocol or via the Advanced Networking Option (ANO). PROXY: Authentication was by an Oracle Call Interface (OCI) proxy.	30	8.1.6
BG_JOB_ID	If the current session was created by an Oracle background process, this is the job ID of the session; otherwise, it is NULL.	30	8.1.6
CLIENT_INFO	Returns up to 64 bytes of user session information stored using the DBMS_APPLICATION_INFO package.	64	8.1.6
CURRENT_SCHEMA	Current schema name.	30	8.1.5
CURRENT_SCHEMAID	ID number associated with the current schema.	30	8.1.5
CURRENT_USER	Current username. If a stored procedure has been invoked, this may not be the same as the login username returned by SESSION_USER.	30	8.1.5
CURRENT_USERID	ID number associated with the current user.	30	8.1.5
DB_DOMAIN	Database domain as specified by the DB_DOMAIN initialization parameter.	256	8.1.6
DB_NAME	Database name as specified by the DB_NAME initialization parameter.	30	8.1.6
ENTRYID	Your auditing entry identifier. This attribute is not valid in distributed SQL statements. In addition, the AUDIT_TRAIL initialization parameter must be set to TRUE.	30	8.1.6
EXTERNAL_NAME	External name of the database user. For users authenticated using SSL, this is the distinguished name (DN) from the user's v.503 certificate.	256	8.1.6
FG_JOB_ID	Session's job ID if the session was created by a client's foreground process.	30	8.1.6
HOST	Name of the machine from which the client is connecting.	54	8.1.6
INSTANCE	Number identifying the instance to which you are currently connected.	30	8.1.6
IP_ADDRESS	User's IP address. This applies only to TCP/IP connections.	30	8.1.5
ISDBA	TRUE or FALSE depending on whether the ISDBA role is enabled.	30	8.1.6
LANG	ISO abbreviation for your current language name.	62	8.1.6
LANGUAGE	Your current language setting, territory setting, and database char-acter set name.	52	8.1.6
NETWORK_ PROTOCOL	Name of the network protocol being used for the connection.	256	8.1.6
NLS_CALENDAR	Current NLS calendar name.	62	8.1.5
NLS_CURRENCY	Current NLS currency indicator.	62	8.1.5

Table 8-3. Predefined attributes in the USERENV namespace (continued)

Attribute name	Description	Max length	Since version
NLS_DATE_FORMAT	Current NLS date format.	62	8.1.5
NLS_DATE_LANGUAGE	Current NLS date language.	62	8.1.5
NLS_SORT	Current sort base.	62	8.1.5
NLS_TERRITORY	Current NLS territory name.	62	8.1.5
OS_USER	Operating system username of the client process that initiated the database connection.	30	8.1.6
PROXY_USER	Name of the user who opened the current session on behalf of the current session user.	30	8.1.6
PROXY_USERID	User ID of the user who opened the current session on behalf of the current session user.	30	8.1.6
SESSION_USER	Name that the current user logged in with. Does not change even when a stored procedure owned by another user is invoked.	30	8.1.5
SESSION_USERID	ID number associated with the session user.	30	8.1.5
SESSIONID	Your auditing session identifier. Not valid in distributed SQL statements.	30	8.1.6
TERMINAL	Operating system identifier for the current session's client. In a distributed environment, can be used only for remote SELECT statements and returns the identifier for the local session.	10	8.1.6

SYS_DBURIGEN

    SYS_DBURIGEN ({column | attribute}[rowid]
    [,{column | attribute}[rowid]...][,'text()'])

Returns a URL of datatype DBUriType to a column or row object, which can be used to retrieve an XML document from the database. New with Oracle9*i*.

SYS_EXTRACT_UTC

    SYS_EXTRACT_UTC (datetime_with_timezone)

Returns the UTC/GMT from a datetime with the time zone displacement.

SYS_GUID

    SYS_GUID ( )

Returns a 16-byte RAW value that can be used as a globally unique identifier. On most platforms, the value is a combination of the host ID, a process (or thread) ID, and a sequence number. You must include parentheses in this function call.

SYS_TYPEID

    SYS_TYPEID (object_type_value)

Returns the type ID of the most specific type of *object_type_value*.

UID   UID

Returns an integer value that uniquely identifies the current data-base user. The value comes from the V$SESSION view's USER# column.

USER   USER

Returns the current username. Normally, USER returns the user-name used to log into the database. When invoked from within a stored procedure or function, this function returns the name of the procedure or function's owner. When invoked from within a trigger, it returns the login username.

USERENV   USERENV (*option*)

Returns information about the current user as a VARCHAR2. Beginning with the Oracle 8.1.6 release, SYS_CONTEXT may also be used to retrieve these user environment values. For ENTRYID and SESSIONID, the AUDIT_TRAIL initialization parameter must be TRUE, and these variables cannot be used in a distributed environment.

Parameters

option   Returns one of the values from Table 8-4.

Table 8-4. USERENV option values

Option	Description
ENTRYID	Returns an auditing entry identifier
INSTANCE	Returns the instance identifier
ISDBA	Returns a Boolean indicating whether the ISDBA role is enabled
LANG	Returns the abbreviation for the current ISO language
LANGUAGE	Returns the user's current language and territory settings
SESSIONID	Returns the auditing session identifier
TERMINAL	Returns the current session's operating system terminal identifier

VSIZE   VSIZE (*expr*)

Returns the size, in bytes, of the internal representation of a value specified by *expr*.

9

PL/SQL

PL/SQL, which stands for Procedural Language extensions to the Structured Query Language, is a highly structured, readable, and accessible language that is tightly integrated with the Oracle database. PL/SQL was the first procedural language supported by the Oracle database, and it continues to be the most popular language for creating program units, such as procedures, functions, packages, and triggers, in the database.

This chapter briefly summarizes PL/SQL fundamentals and syntax. To the extent possible, we've organized descriptions of PL/SQL statements in accordance with the block structure of PL/SQL code. (PL/SQL programs are generally organized into four sections: the header section, declaration section, execution section, and exception section.) So, for example, within the discussion under the "Execution Section" heading, you will find descriptions of the syntax and entities you will work with in that section. If a particular type of data, such as a cursor, must be declared before it can be used, you will find declarative information under the "Declaration Section" heading and information on its use under the "Execution Section" heading. Certain topics, such as packages, triggers, and external procedures are described under separate heads toward the end of the chapter.

There is much more to learn about this powerful language. For an excellent discussion of the language syntax and use, see *Oracle PL/SQL Programming* by Steven Feuerstein with Bill Pribyl (O'Reilly & Associates).

PL/SQL Fundamentals

This section provides basic information on PL/SQL's character set, identifiers, literals, delimiters, comments, and block structure.

Character Set

The PL/SQL language is constructed from letters, digits, symbols, and whitespace as follows:

- Letters: A–Z, a–z
- Digits: 0–9
- Symbols: ~ ! @ # $ % & * ( ) _ - + = | [ ] { } : ; " ' < > , . ? / ^
- Whitespace: space, tab, carriage return, newline

These characters are used for PL/SQL identifiers, literals, and delimiters.

Identifiers

Identifiers are names for PL/SQL objects, including constants, scalar variables, composite variables (records or collections), exceptions, procedures, functions, packages, types, cursors, reserved words, and labels. Identifiers have the following characteristics:

- Can be up to 30 characters in length
- Cannot include whitespace (space, tab, carriage return, newline)
- Must start with a letter
- Can include a dollar sign ($), an underscore (_), or a pound sign (#)
- Are not case-sensitive

If you enclose an identifier within double quotes, then all but the first of these rules are ignored.

Literals

Literals are specific values, not represented by identifiers. There are several different types of literals.

Numeric, string, and Boolean literals

Most literals used in PL/SQL are composed of number (e.g. 29 or 6.001), string (e. g., "Rick" or "This is a fine book") or Boolean (e.g., TRUE or FALSE) values. They may also be NULL. Literals are not represented by identifiers. There are no complex datatype literals as they are internal representations. Unlike the rest of PL/SQL, literals are case-sensitive. To embed single quotes within a string literal, place two single quotes next to each other.

Datetime interval literals

Two new datetime interval datatypes, INTERVAL YEAR TO MONTH and INTERVAL DAY TO SECOND, were introduced in Oracle9i. They represent a chronological interval, expressed either as years and months or as days, hours, minutes, seconds, and fractional seconds. Literals of these datatypes have the form INTERVAL YEAR (*year_precision*) TO MONTH or INTERVAL DAY (*day_precision*) to SECOND (*fractional_seond_precision*). See Appendix A for details and examples.

Delimiters

Delimiters are symbols or combinations of symbols with a special meaning to PL/
SQL. PL/SQL delimiters are listed in Table 9-1.

Table 9-1. PL/SQL delimiters

Delimiter	Usage
;	Terminator (for statements and declarations)
+ - * / ** =	Arithmetic operators
<> != ^= ~=	Inequality operators
< > <= >= <>	Comparison operators
||	Concatenation operator
:=	Assignment operator
( )	Expression or list delimiter
,	Comma. Item separator
'	Single quote. Literal delimiter
"	Double quote. Quoted literal delimiter
<< >>	Label delimiters
:	Host variable delimiter
%	Attribute delimiter
.	Period. Component indicator, as with fields in a record (*record.field*) or elements in a package (*package.element*)
@	dblink (database link) indicator
=>	Association indicator for parameters in a call
..	Two periods. Range operator used in a FOR loop
--	Single-line comment indicator
/* */	Multiline comment indicator

Block Structure

Each PL/SQL program is a block consisting of a standard set of elements, identified by keywords The block determines the scope of declared elements and controls how exceptions are handled and propagated.

The block structure has the following syntax:

```
[CREATE OR REPLACE name [(parameter datatype [,parameter datatype . . .])
    {IS | AS}]                      -- Header section
[[DECLARE]
    variable variable_type;
    [variable variable_type; . . .]  -- Declaration section
BEGIN
    execution_code;
    [execution_code; . . ]
END;                                -- Execution section
[EXCEPTION
    exception_code;
    [exception_code; . . ] ]        -- Exception section
```

The sections are:

Header section
> Provides the name of the block. Required for named blocks and not allowed for anonymous blocks.

Declaration section
> Declares variables, constants, cursors, TYPEs, and local programs used in the block. Optional.

Execution section
> Contains execution code. Generally used, but optional in package and TYPE specifications.

Exception section
> Handles error conditions. Optional.

Descriptions of these four sections of code and their main characteristics follow.

Header Section

The header section provides a name for a PL/SQL block or program unit. The header section is optional, depending on the type of PL/SQL block.

Types of Blocks

There are two basic types of blocks:

Anonymous block
> Cannot be called from outside of the block that contains it. Optional declaration section begins with the keyword DECLARE. This type of block has the following form:

```
DECLARE
    today DATE DEFAULT SYSDATE;
BEGIN
    -- Display the date.
    DBMS_OUTPUT.PUT_LINE ('Today is ' || today);
END;
```

Named block
> Requires a header. Can be called outside of the block that contains it. Does not use the keyword DECLARE for the declaration section. This type of block is shown in the following example:

```
CREATE OR REPLACE PROCEDURE show_the_date
IS
    today DATE DEFAULT SYSDATE;
BEGIN
    -- Display the date.
    DBMS_OUTPUT.PUT_LINE ('Today is ' || today);
END show_the_date;
```

You can declare parameters for a block in the header section. Parameters are optional, enclosed by parentheses, and comma-separated. Each parameter name must be followed by a datatype.

Parameters

Procedures, functions, and cursors use parameters to pass information back and forth between a subprogram and the calling program. You specify these parameters in a list that may contain one or more parameters. Each parameter is defined by its name, datatype, mode, and optional default value.

Syntax

```
parameter_name [mode] [NOCOPY] datatype
   [(:= | DEFAULT) value]
```

Keywords

mode
> Specifies whether the parameter can be read from or written to, with the following acceptable values:
>
> *IN*
>> Read-only variable. The value of the actual parameter can be referenced inside the program, but the parameter cannot be changed. This is the default.
>
> *OUT*
>> Read/write variable.
>
> *IN OUT*
>> Read/write variable.
>
> If an exception is raised during execution of a procedure or function, assignments made to OUT or IN OUT parameters get rolled back, unless NOCOPY is specified.

NOCOPY
> Compiler hint for parameters makes the parameter a call-by-reference instead of a call-by-value parameter. Normally, PL/SQL passes IN OUT parameters by value—a copy of the parameter is created for the subprogram. When parameter items get large (as collections and objects do), the copy can eat memory and slow down processing. NOCOPY directs PL/SQL to pass the parameter by reference, using a pointer to the single copy of the parameter. The disadvantage of NOCOPY is that when an exception is raised during execution of a program that has modified an OUT or IN OUT parameter, the changes to the actual parameters are not rolled back because the parameters were passed by reference instead of being copied.

datatype
> Can be any PL/SQL or programmer-defined datatype but cannot be constrained by a size. The actual size of the parameter is determined from the calling program or via a %TYPE constraint, which is explained later in this chapter.

```
CREATE OR REPLACE PROCEDURE empid_to_name
(in_id              emp.emp_id%TYPE  -- Compiles OK.
,out_last_name      VARCHAR2         -- Compiles OK.
,out_first_name     VARCHAR2(10)     -- Won't compile.
) IS
...
```

The lengths of out_last_name and out_first_name are determined by the calling program:

```
DECLARE
    surname      VARCHAR2(10);
    first_name   VARCHAR2(10);
BEGIN
    empid_to_name(10, surname, first_name);
END;
```

DEFAULT

Indicates a default value for an IN parameter. If an IN parameter has a default value, then you do not have to provide an explicit value for that parameter when you call the program unit. It automatically uses the default value.

Parameter-Passing Notation

Formal parameters are the names that are declared in the header of a procedure or function. *Actual parameters* are the values or expressions placed in the parameter list when a procedure or function is called.

PL/SQL lets you use either of two styles of notation for passing arguments in parameter lists:

Positional notation

Associates each value in the list of arguments supplied in the program call with the parameter in the corresponding position. This is the default.

Named notation

Explicitly associates the argument value with its parameter by name, not by position. When you use named notation, you can supply the arguments in any order, and you can skip over IN arguments that have default values.

The call to the empid_to_name procedure is shown here with both types of notation:

```
BEGIN
    -- Implicit positional notation.
    empid_to_name(10, surname, first_name);

    -- Explicit named notation.
    empid_to_name(in_id=>10
        ,out_last_name=>surname
        ,out_first_name=>first_name);
END;
```

You can combine positional and named notation. Just make sure that positional arguments appear to the left of any named notation arguments. When calling PL/SQL stored functions from SQL, named notation is not supported.

Declaration Section

The declaration section contains declarations for any program variables, constants, cursors, object types, or local programs used in the block. The section is optional; if the block does not need any of these entities, you need not include this section. (For information about how to use the entities declared in this section, see the description under the "Execution Section" heading, later in this chapter.)

Datatypes

A variable declaration includes a datatype. PL/SQL uses all the datatypes allowed with Oracle SQL, as well as some of its own datatypes. For a complete listing of datatypes, see Appendix A.

Constrained/unconstrained declarations

The datatype in a declaration can be constrained or unconstrained. Constrained datatypes have a size, scale, or precision limit that is less than the unconstrained datatype. For example:

```
total_sales    NUMBER(15,2);   -- Constrained.
emp_id         VARCHAR2(9);    -- Constrained.
company_number NUMBER;         -- Unconstrained.
book_title     VARCHAR2;       -- Not valid.
```

Constrained declarations require less memory than unconstrained declarations. Not all datatypes can be specified as unconstrained. You cannot, for example, declare a variable to be of type VARCHAR2—you must declare the maximum size of this datatype.

Variables

Before you can use a variable, you must first declare it in the declaration section of your PL/SQL block or in a package as a global. When you declare a variable, PL/SQL allocates memory for the variable's value and names the storage location so that the value can be retrieved and changed. The syntax for a variable declaration is:

```
variable_name datatype [CONSTANT] [NOT NULL]
   [:= | DEFAULT initial_value]
```

Default values

Whenever you declare a variable, it is assigned a default value of NULL. Initializing all variables is distinctive to PL/SQL; in this way, PL/SQL differs from languages such as C and Ada. If you want to initialize a variable to a value other than NULL, you do so in the declaration with either the assignment operator (:=) or the DEFAULT keyword:

```
counter    BINARY_INTEGER := 0;
priority   VARCHAR2(8)    DEFAULT 'LOW';
```

NOT NULL

You can append a NOT NULL constraint to the variable's datatype declaration to indicate that NULL is not a valid value. If you add the NOT NULL constraint, you must explicitly assign an initial value for that variable.

Constants

If you declare a constant by including the CONSTANT keyword in a declaration, you must specify an initial value, which you cannot change. For example:

```
min_order_qty   NUMBER(1) CONSTANT := 5;
```

Cursor Variables

A *cursor* is essentially a pointer into a result set in the database. Cursors are used to access data in a result set on a row-by-row basis. The two types of cursors are:

Explicit cursors
    SELECT statements DECLAREd explicitly in the declaration section of the current block or in a package specification

Implicit cursors
    Automatically created in response to an SQL statement in the execution section of the PL/SQL block

See the discussion of using explicit and implicit cursors under the later "Execution Section" heading.

Declaring explicit cursors

To declare an explicit cursor as a cursor variable in the declaration section of a block or package (discussed later), you can use one of the following forms:

- A cursor without parameters, such as:

  ```
  CURSOR company_cur
      IS
      SELECT company_id FROM company;
  ```

- A cursor that accepts arguments through a parameter list, described under the "Heading Section" header:

  ```
  CURSOR company_cur (id_in IN NUMBER) IS
      SELECT name FROM company
      WHERE   company_id = id_in;
  ```

- A cursor *header* that contains a RETURN clause in place of the SELECT statement:

  ```
  CURSOR company_cur (id_in IN NUMBER)
      RETURN company%ROWTYPE
  ```

The last example shows that the cursor can be declared separately from its implementation—for example, the header in a package specification and the implementation in the package body.

Restrictions on cursor variables

There are a number of restrictions on cursor variables:

- You cannot declare a package-level cursor variable. (You can declare such variables in packaged procedures and functions, however.)
- You cannot assign NULLs to a cursor variable nor use comparison operators to test for equality, inequality, or nullity.
- Neither database columns nor collections can store cursor variables.
- You cannot use remote procedure calls (RPCs) to pass cursor variables from one server to another.

REF CURSOR Variables

A CURSOR points to a specific result set, while a REF CURSOR variable can be used to point to different result sets. A REF CURSOR can also have the SQL it uses assigned in the execution section of a PL/SQL block, which means you can use it to implement dynamic SQL statements.

The cursor and result set are objects in the database. The result set is maintained as long as a database cursor points to it. For this reason, you can use a REF CURSOR to pass result sets of data between different PL/SQL program units. You can also use REF CURSOR variables to hide minor variations in queries.

The syntax for a REF_CURSOR type is:

```
TYPE ref_cursor_name IS REF CURSOR
   [RETURN record_type];
```

where *record_type* is a row that exists in the database.

If you do not include a RETURN clause, then you are declaring a weak REF CURSOR. REF CURSOR variables declared from weak REF CURSORs can be associated with any query at runtime. A REF CURSOR declaration with a RETURN clause defines a strong REF CURSOR. A REF CURSOR variable based on a strong REF CURSOR can be associated with queries whose result sets match the number and datatype of the record structure after the RETURN at runtime.

To use REF CURSOR variables, you must first create a REF_CURSOR type, then declare an instance based on that type. The following example shows the declaration of both weak and strong REF CURSORs:

```
DECLARE
    -- Create a cursor type based on the companies table.
    TYPE company_curtype IS REF CURSOR
        RETURN companies%ROWTYPE;

    -- Create the variable based on the REF CURSOR.
    company_cur company_curtype;

    -- The weak, general approach.
    TYPE any_curtype IS REF CURSOR;
    generic_curvar any_curtype;
```

Anchored Declarations

Use the %TYPE attribute to *anchor* the datatype of a scalar variable (which contains a single value) either to another variable or to a column in a database table or view. Use %ROWTYPE to anchor a declaration to a cursor or table.

The following block shows several variations of anchored declarations:

```
DECLARE
    tot_sales NUMBER(20,2);
    -- Anchor to a PL/SQL variable.
    monthly_sales tot_sales%TYPE;

    -- Anchor to a database column.
    v_ename employee.last_name%TYPE;

    CURSOR mycur IS
        SELECT * FROM employee;

    -- Anchor to a cursor.
    myrec mycur%ROWTYPE;
```

The NOT NULL clause on a variable declaration (but not on a database column definition) can follow the %TYPE anchoring and requires anchored declarations to have a default in their declaration. The default value for an anchored declaration can be different from that for the base declaration.

Programmer-Defined Subtypes

PL/SQL allows you to define unconstrained scalar subtypes. An unconstrained subtype provides an alias to the original underlying datatype; for example:

```
CREATE OR REPLACE PACKAGE std_types
IS
    -- Declare standard types as globals.
    SUBTYPE dollar_amt_t IS NUMBER;
END std_types;

CREATE OR REPLACE PROCEDURE process_money
IS
    -- Use the global type declared above.
    credit std_types.dollar_amt_t;
    ...
```

A constrained subtype limits or constrains the new datatype to a subset of the original datatype.

You can define your own constrained subtypes in your programs (starting with Oracle8*i*), as you would typically do in the package section:

```
PACKAGE std_types
IS
    SUBTYPE currency_t IS NUMBER (15, 2);

END;
```

Records

A *record* is a composite data structure that is similar in concept and structure to a row in a database table. It consists of multiple pieces of information called *fields*. The record as a whole does not have a value of its own; instead, each individual field has a value, and the record gives you a way to store and access these values as a group. To use a record, you must first define it and declare a variable of this type.

Types of records

There are three types of records: table based, cursor based, and programmer defined. You need not explicitly define table-based or cursor-based records, because they are implicitly defined with the same structure as a table or cursor. Variables of these types are declared via the %ROWTYPE attribute. The record's fields correspond to the table's columns or the columns in the select list.

On the other hand, programmer-defined records must be explicitly defined with the TYPE statement in the PL/SQL declaration section or in a package specification. Variables of this type can then be declared or used as part of another type:

```
DECLARE
   TYPE name_rectype IS RECORD(
      prefix        VARCHAR2(15)
      ,first_name   VARCHAR2(30)
      ,middle_name VARCHAR2(30)
      ,sur_name     VARCHAR2(30)
      ,suffix       VARCHAR2(10) );

   -- Declare a variable of this type.
   new_emp_rec name_rectype;
BEGIN
```

Nested records

Nested records are records contained in fields that are records themselves. Nesting records is a powerful way to normalize data structures and hide complexity within PL/SQL programs. For example:

```
DECLARE
   -- Define a record.
   TYPE phone_rectype IS RECORD (
      area_code  VARCHAR2(3),
      exchange   VARCHAR2(3),
      phn_number VARCHAR2(4),
      extension  VARCHAR2(4));

   -- Define a record composed of records.
   TYPE contact_rectype IS RECORD (
      day_phone#  phone_rectype,
      eve_phone#  phone_rectype,
      cell_phone# phone_rectype);

  -- Declare a variable for the nested record.
  auth_rep_info_rec contact_rectype;
BEGIN
```

Collections

A *collection* is a composite data structure that acts like a list or a single-dimensional array (traditional arrays are not supported in PL/SQL).

There are three different types of collections in PL/SQL: *associative arrays* (called *index-by tables* in Oracle8 and Oracle8i and *PL/SQL tables* before that), *nested tables*, and *VARRAYs* (variable arrays). The following sections briefly describe the declarations for these different types, but for information about using and comparing these collection types, see "Using Collections" under "Execution Section" later in this chapter. Table 9-2 compares the three collection types.

Collections are implemented as TYPEs. Like any programmer-defined type, you must first define the type; then you can declare instances of that type. The TYPE definition can be stored in the database or declared in the PL/SQL program. Each instance of the TYPE is a collection.

Table 9-2. Comparison of collection types

Characteristic	Associative array	Nested table	VARRAY
Dimensionality	Single	Single	Single
Usable in SQL?	No	Yes	Yes
Usable as a column datatype in a table?	No	Yes; data stored "out of line" (in a separate table)	Yes; data typically stored "in line" (in the same table)
Uninitialized state	Empty (cannot be NULL); elements are undefined	Atomically null; illegal to reference elements	Atomically null; illegal to reference elements
Initialization	Automatic, when declared	Via constructor, fetch, assignment	Via constructor, fetch, assignment
In PL/SQL, elements referenced by	BINARY_INTEGER (-2,147,483,647... 2,147,483,647) or character string (VARCHAR2)	Positive integer between 1 and 2,147,483,647	Positive integer between 1 and 2,147,483,647
Sparse?	Yes	Initially no; after deletions, yes	No
Bounded?	No	Can be extended	Yes
Can assign a value to any element at any time?	Yes	No; may need to EXTEND first	No; may need to EXTEND first, and cannot EXTEND past the upper bound
Means of extending	Assign value to element with a new subscript	Use built-in EXTEND procedure or TRIM to condense, with no predefined maximum	EXTEND or TRIM, but only up to declared maximum size.
Can be compared for equality	No	No	No
Elements retain ordinal position and subscript when from the database	N/A—can't be stored in database	No	Yes

Associative Array

```
CREATE [OR REPLACE] TYPE type_name IS TABLE OF element_type [NOT NULL]
    INDEX BY BINARY_INTEGER| PLS_INTEGER | VARCHAR2(n);
```

A singly-dimensioned, unbounded, sparse collection of homogeneous elements available only in PL/SQL, not in the database. Associative arrays can be indexed by a BINARY_INTEGER, a PLS_INTEGER, or a VARCHAR2.

Keywords

type_name   Any valid identifier that will be used later to declare the collection.

element_type Type of the collection's elements. All elements are of a single type, which may be most scalar datatypes, an object type, or a REF object type. If the elements are objects, the object type itself cannot have an attribute that is a collection. Explicitly disallowed collection datatypes are BOOLEAN, NCHAR, NCLOB, NVARCHAR2, REF CURSOR, TABLE, and VARRAY.

max_elements
                Maximum number of elements for this associative array.

NOT NULL   Indicates that a collection of this type cannot have any NULL elements. However, the collection can be atomically NULL (uninitialized).

BINARY_INTEGER | PLS_INTEGER | VARCHAR(n)
                An associative array can be indexed by a BINARY_INTEGER, a PLS_INTEGER, or a VARCHAR value.

Nested Table

```
[CREATE [OR REPLACE]] TYPE type_name IS TABLE OF element_type [NOT NULL];
```

A singly dimensioned, unbounded collection of homogeneous elements available in both PL/SQL and the database as a column or a table. Nested tables are initially dense (they have consecutive subscripts) but can become sparse as a result of deletions.

Keywords

type_name   Any valid identifier that will be used later to declare the collection.

element_type Type of the collection's elements. All elements are of a single type, which can be most scalar datatypes, an object type, or a REF object type. If the elements are objects, the object type itself cannot have an attribute that is a collection. Explicitly disallowed collection datatypes are BOOLEAN, NCHAR, NCLOB, NVARCHAR2, REF CURSOR, TABLE, and VARRAY.

NOT NULL   Indicates that a collection of this type cannot have any NULL elements. However, the collection can be atomically NULL (uninitialized).

VARRAY

```
[CREATE [OR REPLACE]] TYPE type_name IS VARRAY |
    VARYING ARRAY (max_elements) OF element_type [NOT NULL];
```

A singly dimensioned, bounded collection of homogeneous elements available in both PL/SQL and the database. VARRAYs (variable arrays) are always bounded and never

PL/SQL

sparse. Unlike nested tables, their element order is preserved when you store and retrieve them from the database.

Keywords

type_name   Any valid identifier that will be used later to declare the collection.

max_elements

      Maximum number of elements for this VARRAY.

element_type   Type of the collection's elements. All elements are of a single type, which can be most scalar datatypes, an object type, or a REF object type. If the elements are objects, the object type itself cannot have an attribute that is a collection. Explicitly disallowed collection datatypes are BOOLEAN, NCHAR, NCLOB, NVARCHAR2, REF CURSOR, TABLE, and VARRAY.

NOT NULL   Indicates that a collection of this type cannot have any NULL elements. However, the collection can be atomically NULL (uninitialized).

Creating Collections

Once you have declared any of these collections, you must create an instance of the collection, as in:

```
TYPE index_table IS TABLE OF NUMBER INDEX BY BINARY_INTEGER;
indtab index_table;
```

where *indtab* is an instance of *index_table*.

You can use the %TYPE attribute of a collection to link another collection's datatype to it—for example:

```
TYPE varray1 IS VARRAY(20) OF NUMBER;
v1 varray1;
v2 v1%type;
```

If the definition of v1 changes, the definition of v2 will change along with it.

Exceptions

An *exception* is returned when an error occurs in your PL/SQL code. When an exception occurs (or is "raised"), control leaves the execution section and passes directly to the exception section of your PL/SQL block.

Some exceptions have been predefined by Oracle in the STANDARD package, or you can declare your own exception with the datatype EXCEPTION, as in:

```
DECLARE
    exception_name EXCEPTION;
```

An exception can be declared only once in a block, but nested blocks can declare an exception with the same name as an outer block. If this multiple declaration occurs, scope takes precedence over name when handling the exception. The inner block's declaration takes precedence over a global declaration.

All declared exceptions have an error code of 1 and the error message "User-defined exception," unless you use the EXCEPTION_INIT pragma. (See the later "Pragmas" section for a discussion of pragmas in PL/SQL.)

You can associate an error number with a declared exception with the PRAGMA EXCEPTION_INIT statement:

```
DECLARE
    exception_name EXCEPTION;
    PRAGMA EXCEPTION_INIT (exception_name, error_number);
```

where *error_number* is a literal value (variable references are not allowed). This number can be an Oracle error, such as -1855, or an error in the user-definable range of -20000 to -20999.

Forward Declarations

Programs must be declared before they can be used. PL/SQL supports *mutual recursion*, in which program A calls program B, whereupon program B calls program A. To implement this mutual recursion, you must use a *forward declaration* of the programs. This technique declares a program in advance of the program definition, thus making it available for other programs to use. The forward declaration is the program header up to the IS/AS keyword:

```
PROCEDURE perform_calc(year_in IN NUMBER)
IS
    /* Forward declaration for total_cost function. */
    FUNCTION total_cost (...) RETURN NUMBER;

    /* The net_profit function can now use total_cost. */
    FUNCTION net_profit(...) RETURN NUMBER
    IS
    BEGIN
        RETURN total_sales(...) - total_cost(...);
    END;

    /* The Total_cost function calls net_profit. */
    FUNCTION total_cost (...) RETURN NUMBER
    IS
    BEGIN
        IF net_profit(...) < 0
        THEN
            RETURN 0;
            ELSE
            RETURN...;
        END IF;
    END;
BEGIN /* procedure perform_calc */
    ...
END perform_calc;
```

Execution Section

This section contains the code used to implement the functionality of the block. The code can consist of any SQL statement, as well as some PL/SQL-specific logical control structures.

Statements

The execution section of a PL/SQL block is composed of one or more logical statements. A statement is terminated by a semicolon delimiter. A physical end-of-line marker in a PL/SQL program is ignored by the compiler, except to terminate a single-line comment (initiated by --).

Conditional Control Statements

PL/SQL includes three variations of IF-THEN-ELSE control statements and a CASE statement and expression. The CASE syntax is new with Oracle9*i*.

IF-THEN-ELSE

IF-THEN combination:
```
IF condition THEN
    executable_statement(s)
END IF;
```

IF-THEN-ELSE combination:
```
IF condition THEN
    sequence_of_executable_statement(s)
ELSE
    sequence_of_executable_statement(s)
END IF;
```

IF-THEN-ELSIF combination:
```
IF condition-1 THEN
    statements-1
ELSIF condition-N THEN
    statements-N
[ELSE
    else_statements]
END IF;
```

Allows you to design conditional logic in your programs. There are three variations of IF-THEN-ELSE structures:

CASE (Statement)

```
CASE expression
    WHEN value_expr THEN action;
    [WHEN value_expr THEN action; . . .]
    [ELSE
        action;]
END CASE;
```

Allows you to select one sequence of statements to execute out of many possible sequences. The CASE statement is similar to an IF-THEN-ELSIF statement. However, the CASE statement has a switch expression immediately after the keyword CASE. The expression is evaluated and compared to the value in each WHEN clause. The first WHEN clause evaluating TRUE is executed, and then control passes to the next statement following the END CASE.

If a switch expression evaluates to NULL, the ELSE case is the only one that can possibly match. WHEN NULL will never match because Oracle performs an equality comparison on the expressions.

Both the CASE statement and the CASE expression (see the next section) should include an ELSE clause that will execute statements if no WHEN clause evaluates to TRUE because PL/SQL's runtime engine will raise an error if it finds no matching case.

CASE (Expression)

```
CASE
    WHEN expression = value_expr THEN
        action;
    [WHEN expression = value_expr THEN
        action; . . .]
        [ELSE
            action;]
END CASE;
```

Unlike the CASE statement, the CASE expression does not have a switch expression; instead, each WHEN clause has a complete Boolean expression. The first matching WHEN clause is executed and control passes to the next statement following the END CASE.

Sequential Control Statements

There are two types of sequential control statements, GOTO and NULL.

GOTO

```
GOTO label_name;
```

Performs unconditional branching to a named label. In general, use of the GO statement is not recommended. At least one executable statement must follow the label (if you wish, the NULL statement can be this necessary executable statement).

Restrictions

The following scope restrictions apply to the GOTO statement:

- Can branch out of an IF statement, LOOP, or sub-block
- Cannot branch into an IF statement, LOOP, or sub-block
- Cannot branch from one section of an IF statement to another (from the IF/THEN section to the ELSE section is illegal)
- Cannot branch into or out of a subprogram

- Cannot branch from the exception section to the executable section of a PL/SQL block
- Cannot branch from the executable section to the exception section of a PL/SQL block, although a RAISE does this

NULL

```
NULL;
```

An executable statement that does nothing. The NULL statement is useful when you need an executable (but "do nothing") statement following a GOTO label or in aiding readability in an IF-THEN-ELSE structure.

Loop Statements

The LOOP construct allows you to repeatedly execute a sequence of statements. There are three kinds of loops: simple, WHILE, and FOR; there are two variants on the FOR loop: the numeric FOR loop and the CURSOR FOR loop.

All loops can have a label or contain an EXIT statement.

Loops can be optionally labeled to improve readability and execution control. The label must appear immediately in front of the statement that initiates the loop.

The EXIT statement is used to break out of the loop and pass control to the statement following the END LOOP. The syntax for the EXIT statement is:

```
EXIT [WHEN Boolean_condition];
```

If you do not include a WHEN clause in the EXIT statement, it will terminate the loop unconditionally. Otherwise, the loop terminates only if *Boolean_condition* evaluates to TRUE. The EXIT statement is optional and can appear anywhere in the loop.

Simple Loop

```
LOOP
    executable_statement(s)
END LOOP;
```

The simplest of the loop constructs. This type of loop consists simply of the LOOP and END LOOP statements, enclosing at least one executable statement. You typically use the simple loop when you want to ensure that the body of the loop executes at least once. The simple loop will terminate only when an EXIT or EXIT WHEN statement is executed (or when an exception is raised and goes unhandled) in its body. If that does not occur, the loop will execute indefinitely.

Numeric FOR Loop

```
FOR loop_index IN [REVERSE] lowest_number..
    highest_number
LOOP
    executable_statement(s)
END LOOP;
```

The traditional "counted" loop in which you specify the number of iterations. The PL/SQL runtime engine automatically declares the loop index a PLS_INTEGER variable; make sure to never declare a variable with that name yourself. The *lowest_number* and *highest_number* ranges can be variables but are evaluated only once—on initial entry into the loop. The REVERSE keyword causes PL/SQL to start with the *highest_number* and decrement down to the *lowest_number*.

Cursor FOR Loop

```
FOR record_index IN [cursor_name | (SELECT statement)]
LOOP
    executable_statement(s)
END LOOP;
```

A loop that is associated with (and defined by) an explicit cursor or a SELECT statement. This type of loop automatically opens the cursor, fetches all rows identified by the cursor, and then closes the cursor. You can embed the SELECT statement directly in the cursor FOR loop.

The PL/SQL runtime engine automatically declares the loop index a record of *cursor_name*%ROWTYPE; make sure that you never declare a variable with that name yourself.

WHILE Loop

```
WHILE condition
LOOP
    executable_statement(s)
END LOOP;
```

A conditional loop that continues to execute as long as the Boolean *condition* defined in the loop boundary evaluates to TRUE. Use the WHILE loop when you don't know in advance the number of times a loop must execute. You might also use the WHILE loop instead of the simple loop when you might not want the loop body to execute even once.

Explicit Cursors

A cursor is a pointer into a result set in the database. An explicit cursor is a cursor that you name and manipulate explicitly in your program. An explicit cursor is static; the SQL statement is determined at compile time. Static cursors are used only for DML statements (SELECT, INSERT, UPDATE, DELETE, MERGE, or SELECT FOR UPDATE).

Use the following syntax when working with explicit cursors.

OPEN

```
OPEN cursor_name [(argument [,argument ...])];
```

Opens an explicit cursor. You must open an explicit cursor before you can fetch rows from that cursor. When the cursor is opened, the processing includes the parse, bind, open, and execute phases of SQL statement execution.

When using a cursor FOR loop, the OPEN is implicit in the FOR statement. If you try to open a cursor that is already open, PL/SQL will raise an "ORA-06511: PL/SQL: cursor already open" exception.

Keywords

cursor_name   Name of the cursor as declared in the declaration section.

argument   Required if the definition of the cursor contains a parameter list.

FETCH

FETCH *cursor_name* INTO *record_or_variable_list*;

Fetches an explicit cursor. Places the contents of the current row into local variables. To retrieve all rows in a result set, each row needs to be fetched.

Keyword

cursor_name   Name of the cursor as declared and opened.

CLOSE

CLOSE *cursor_name*;

Closes an explicit cursor. After all rows have been fetched, a cursor needs to be closed. Closing a cursor enables the PL/SQL memory optimization algorithm to release the associated memory at an appropriate time.

If you declare a cursor in a local anonymous, procedure, or function block, that cursor will automatically close when the block terminates. Cursors that are declared in a package must be closed explicitly, or they stay open for the duration of your session. Closing a cursor that is not open raises an INVALID CURSOR exception.

Keyword

cursor_name   Name of the cursor declared and opened.

Explicit Cursor Attributes

cursor_name%attribute

Four attributes are associated with cursors: ISOPEN, FOUND, NOTFOUND, and ROWCOUNT.

Keywords

cursor_name
    Name of the explicit cursor.

attribute
    One of four keywords:

    %ISOPEN
        Returns TRUE if cursor is open, FALSE if cursor is not open.

%FOUND
> Returns NULL before the first fetch, TRUE if record was fetched success-fully, FALSE if no row was returned. INVALID_CURSOR is raised if cursor has not been OPENed or is CLOSEd.

%NOTFOUND
> Returns NULL before the first fetch, FALSE if record was fetched success-fully, TRUE if no row was returned. INVALID_CURSOR is raised if cursor has not been OPENed or has been CLOSEd.

%ROWCOUNT
> Returns number of records fetched from the cursor. INVALID_CURSOR is raised if cursor has not been OPENed or is CLOSEd.

Implicit Cursors

PL/SQL declares and manages an implicit cursor whenever you execute a SQL DML statement (INSERT, UPDATE, DELETE, or MERGE) or a SELECT INTO that returns a single row from the database directly into a PL/SQL data structure. Whenever you use a SQL statement directly in the execution or exception section of a PL/SQL block, you are working with implicit cursors. Unlike explicit cursors, implicit cursors do not need to be declared, OPENed, FETCHed, or CLOSEd.

Like an explicit cursor, an implicit cursor is associated with a static SQL statement (in contrast to the dynamic statements described in the next section).

Syntax

```
sql_statement
    [RETURNING value[, value . . .]
        INTO variable[, variable . . .] ]
    %attribute
```

Keywords

sql_statement
> INSERT, UPDATE, DELETE, MERGE, or SELECT INTO statement.

RETURNING
> Use the RETURNING clause in INSERT, UPDATE, and DELETE state-ments to obtain data modified by the associated DML statement. This clause allows you to avoid an additional SELECT statement to query the results of the DML statement. For example:

```
BEGIN
    UPDATE activity SET last_accessed := SYSDATE
    WHERE UID = user_id
    RETURNING last_accessed, cost_center
    INTO timestamp, chargeback_acct;
```

attribute
> Keyword directly follows last line in SQL statement, without a space. May be:

SQL%ISOPEN
> Always returns FALSE for implicit cursors because the cursor is opened implicitly and closed immediately after the statement is executed.

SQL%FOUND
> Returns TRUE if one or more rows were inserted, merged, updated, or deleted or if only one row was selected; FALSE if no row was affected.

SQL%NOTFOUND
> Returns NULL before the statement; TRUE if no row was selected, merged, updated, inserted, or deleted; FALSE if one or more rows were affected.

SQL%ROWCOUNT
> Returns the number of rows affected by the cursor.

SQL%BULK_ROWCOUNT
> Pseudo associative array containing number of records modified by FORALL statement (see the "FORALL" entry later in this chapter) for each collection element.

SQL%BULK_EXCEPTIONS
> Pseudo associatve array containing number of rows modified by the FORALL statement (see the "FORALL" entry later in this chapter) for each collection element.

Dynamic Cursors and SQL

With a dynamic cursor, the SQL statement is determined at runtime. Dynamic cursors are used for any type of valid SQL statement, such as CREATE, TRUNCATE, ALTER, GRANT, and REVOKE.

EXECUTE IMMEDIATE

```
EXECUTE IMMEDIATE sql_statement
    [INTO {variable [,variable ...] | record| object_variable}]
    [USING [IN | OUT | IN OUT] bind_argument
        [,[IN | OUT | IN OUT] bind_argument ...] ]
    [{RETURNING | RETURN} INTO bind_argument [,bind_argument]...];
```

Parses and executes a SQL statement in a single step. It can be used for any SQL statement except a multirow query. With Oracle9*i*, the EXECUTE IMMEDIATE statement can be used for bulk fetches and bulk INSERTs or UPDATEs, even if they encounter errors in the bulk processing.

To use dynamic SQL with queries that return multiple rows, use a CURSOR variable, described in the next section.

 The EXECUTE IMMEDIATE statement requires a terminating semicolon, but the *sql_statement* must not have a trailing semicolon.

Keywords
The keywords are the same as for standard SQL and explicit cursors.

Using Cursor Variables

With Oracle8*i*, you can use cursor variables for dynamic SQL.

A cursor variable can be declared in the declaration section of the PL/SQL program as an instance of a REF CURSOR datatype. To use a CURSOR variable, you open it with a SQL statement with the OPEN. . .FOR syntax shown in the following entry. Once you have opened a cursor variable, you can use FETCH and CLOSE with the same syntax as that shown for explicit cursors.

OPEN. . .FOR

```
OPEN cursor_name FOR select_statement;
```
Opens a previously declared cursor variable.

Using Cursor Expressions

New with Oracle9*i*, a *cursor expression* is a cursor that is used as a column expression in the select list of an explicit cursor.

Cursor expressions can reduce the amount of redundant data returned to a calling program; for this reason, you may wish to use it in place of techniques that involve joining the tables together. The cursor expression is automatically opened when the parent row is fetched. Cursor expressions can be nested as well. These nested cursors are closed when one of the following occurs:

- The nested cursor is explicitly closed by the program.
- The parent cursor is closed.
- The parent cursor is re-executed.
- An exception is raised during the fetch of the parent row.

CURSOR

```
CURSOR (subquery)
```
Returns a nested cursor from within a query.

Using Records

Individual fields of records are referenced via dot notation:

```
record_name.field_name
```

Individual fields within a record can be read from or written to. They can appear on either the left or right side of the assignment operator. An entire record can be assigned to another record of the same type, but one record cannot be compared to another record via Boolean operators. For example, the following is a valid assignment:

```
shipto_address_rec := customer_address_rec
```

But the next example is not a valid comparison (you must compare the individual fields of the record instead):

```
IF shipto_address_rec = customer_address_rec
THEN
...
END IF;
```

Values can be assigned to records or to the fields within a record in four different ways:

- You can use the assignment operator to assign a value to a field:

  ```
  new_emp_rec.hire_date := SYSDATE;
  ```

- You can SELECT INTO a whole record or the individual fields:

  ```
  SELECT emp_id,dept,title,hire_date,college_recruit
    INTO new_emp_rec
    FROM emp
   WHERE surname = 'LI'
  ```

- You can FETCH INTO a whole record or the individual fields:

  ```
  FETCH emp_cur INTO new_emp_rec;
  FETCH emp_cur INTO new_emp_rec.emp_id,
     new_emp_rec.name;
  ```

- You can assign all of the fields of one record variable to another record variable of the same type:

  ```
  IF rehire THEN
    new_emp_rec := former_emp_rec;
  ENDIF;
  ```

This aggregate assignment technique works only for records declared with the same TYPE statement.

Using Collections

This section explores how to work with collections. The three different types of collections (associative arrays, nested tables, and VARRAYs) were introduced earlier under the "Declaration Section" heading.

Collection functions and methods

You can manipulate collections with the following functions:

CAST
   Maps a collection of one type to a collection of another type.

   ```
   SELECT column_value
   FROM TABLE(SELECT CAST(colors AS color_tab_t)
              FROM color_models_a
              WHERE model_type ='RGB');
   ```

MULTISET
   Maps a database table to a collection. With MULTISET and CAST, you can retrieve rows from a database table as a collection-typed column. You can use

CAST and MULTISET to extract nested columns for use in trigger logic (described later in the chapter.)

```
SELECT b.genus ,b.species,
       CAST(MULTISET(SELECT bh.country
                        FROM bird_habitats bh
                       WHERE bh.genus = b.genus
                         AND bh.species = b.species)
            AS country_tab_t)
  FROM birds b;
```

TABLE

Maps a collection to a database table; the inverse of MULTISET.

```
SELECT *
  FROM color_models c
 WHERE 'RED' IN (SELECT * FROM TABLE(c.colors));
```

You can use TABLE( ) to unnest a transient collection:

```
DECLARE
   birthdays Birthdate_t :=
      Birthdate_t('24-SEP-1984', '19-JUN-1993');
BEGIN
   FOR the_rec IN
      (SELECT COLUMN_VALUE
         FROM TABLE(CAST(birthdays AS Birthdate_t)))
```

Collections also support a set of methods, described in the "Collection Datatypes" section in Appendix A. These methods are:

COUNT
DELETE
EXISTS
EXTEND
FIRST
LAST
LIMIT
PRIOR
NEXT
TRIM

The syntax for using these methods is:

```
collection_name.method_name[(parameters)]
```

Initializing collections

Simply declaring an associative array also initializes it. Initializing a nested table or VARRAY can also be done as follows:

- Explicitly, with a constructor
- Implicitly with a fetch from the database
- Implicitly, with a direct assignment of another collection variable

The constructor is a built-in function with the same name as the collection. It constructs the collection from the elements passed to it. For example, you can

create a nested table of colors and explicitly initialize it to three elements with a
constructor, as shown here:

```
DECLARE
    TYPE colors_tab_t IS TABLE OF VARCHAR2(30);

    colors_tab_t('RED','GREEN','BLUE');
BEGIN
```

Using the second initialization technique, you can create our nested table of colors
and implicitly initialize it with a fetch from the database:

```
-- Create the nested table to exist in the database.
CREATE TYPE colors_tab_t IS TABLE OF VARCHAR2(32);

-- Initialize a collection of colors from the table.
DECLARE
    basic_colors colors_tab_t;
BEGIN
    SELECT colors INTO basic_colors
      FROM color_models
     WHERE model_type = 'RGB';
...
END;
```

Using the third initialization technique, you can implicitly initialize the table using
an assignment from an existing collection:

```
DECLARE
    basic_colors Color_tab_t :=
        Color_tab_t ('RED','GREEN','BLUE');

    my_colors Color_tab_t;
BEGIN
    my_colors := basic_colors;
    my_colors(2) := 'MUSTARD';
```

Adding and removing elements

You can add elements in an associative array simply by referencing new
subscripts. To add elements to nested tables or VARRAYs, you must first enlarge
the collection with the EXTEND function and then assign a value to a new
element using one of the methods described earlier.

Use the DELETE function to remove an element in a nested table regardless of its
position. You can also use the TRIM function to remove elements, but only from
the end of a collection. To avoid unexpected results, do not use both DELETE
and TRIM on the same collection.

Privileges

As with other TYPEs in the database, you need the EXECUTE privilege on a
TYPE from another schema to create a collection type based on it.

Nested collections

Nested collections are collections contained in members that are collections themselves. Nesting collections is a powerful way to implement object-oriented programming constructs within PL/SQL programs. This discussion is beyond the scope of this chapter but is well described in *Oracle PL/SQL Programming*.

Here is a simple example of specifying a nested collection:

```
CREATE TYPE books IS TABLE OF VARCHAR2(64);
CREATE TYPE our_books IS TABLE OF books;
```

Bulk Binds

You can use collections to improve the performance of SQL operations executed iteratively by using *bulk binds*. Bulk binds reduce the number of context switches between the PL/SQL engine and the database engine. Bulk binds can also be used to implement dynamic SQL with Oracle9*i*.

Two PL/SQL language constructs implement bulk binds: FORALL and BULK COLLECT INTO.

FOR ALL

```
FORALL bulk_index IN lower_bound..upper_bound [SAVE EXCEPTIONS]
   {EXECUTE IMMEDIATE sql_statement | sql_statement };
```

When PL/SQL processes this statement, the whole collection, instead of each individual collection element, is sent to the database server for processing. You can use FOR ALL, as well as BULK COLLECT INTO, with the EXECUTE IMMEDIATE syntax for dynamic SQL.

Keywords

bulk_index
> Integer variable. Can be used only in the *sql_statement* and only as a collection index (subscript).

lower_bound..upper_bound
> Limits of elements in the collection that will be processed by the database engine.

SAVE EXCEPTIONS
> Allows bulk processing to continue even if errors on individual operations fail. The details of these failures are available in SQL%BULK_EXCEPTIONS after the loop has completed processing

BULK COLLECT INTO

```
sql_statement BULK COLLECT INTO collection_name_list;
```

When PL/SQL processes this statement, the whole collection, instead of each individual collection element, is returned from the database server for processing. You can include the BULK COLLECT INTO clause in the SELECT INTO, FETCH INTO, or RETURNING INTO statements. You can use the BULK COLLECT INTO clause with dynamic SQL executed with the EXECUTE IMMEDIATE syntax.

You can use the SQL%BULK_ROWCOUNT cursor attribute for bulk bind operations. That attribute is like an associative array containing the number of rows affected by the executions of the bulk bound statements. The *n*th element of SQL%BULK_ROWCOUNT contains the number of rows affected by the *n*th execution of the SQL statement.

You cannot pass SQL%BULK_ROWCOUNT as a parameter to another program, nor can you use an aggregate assignment to another collection. %ROWCOUNT contains a summation of all %BULK_ROWCOUNT elements. %FOUND and %NOTFOUND reflect only the last execution of the SQL statement

Keywords

sql_statement
> SQL statement such as SELECT INTO, FETCH INTO, RETURNING INTO, or EXECUTE IMMEDIATE.

collection_name_list
> Comma-delimited list of collections, one for each column in the SELECT. Collections of records cannot be a target of a BULK COLLECT INTO clause. However, Oracle does support retrieving a set of typed objects and "bulk collecting" them into a collection of objects.

Transaction Management

The Oracle RDBMS provides a *transaction* model based on a unit of work. The PL/SQL language supports most, but not all, of the database model for transactions.* A transaction begins implicitly with the start of a session or with the first SQL statement issued since the last COMMIT or ROLLBACK (essentially, with the first change to data). A transaction ends with either a COMMIT or ROLLBACK.

Transactions are independent of PL/SQL blocks. Transactions can span multiple PL/SQL blocks, or there can be multiple transactions in a single PL/SQL block (with the help of autonomous transactions, described later). The PL/SQL-supported transaction statements, described next, are COMMIT, ROLLBACK, SAVEPOINT, SET TRANSACTION, and LOCK TABLE.

COMMIT

```
COMMIT [WORK] [COMMENT text];
```

Makes the database changes permanent and visible to other database sessions. Note that PL/SQL does not support the database statement COMMIT FORCE for distributed transactions.

Keywords

WORK
> Optional. Provided only to aid in readability.

COMMENT text
> Optional. Can be up to 50 characters in length.

---

* You cannot, for example, specify ROLLBACK FORCE.

ROLLBACK

```
ROLLBACK [WORK] [TO [SAVEPOINT] savepoint_name];
```

Undoes the outstanding changes made in the current transaction either to the beginning of the transaction or to a specified *savepoint*.

Keyword

savepoint

> Named processing point in a transaction, created with the SAVEPOINT statement.

SAVEPOINT

```
SAVEPOINT savepoint_name;
```

Establishes a savepoint (a named processing point) in the current transaction. Specifying a savepoint then allows you to perform partial rollbacks.

Keyword

savepoint_name

> Undeclared identifier. More than one savepoint can be established within a transaction. If you reuse a savepoint name, that savepoint is moved to the later position and you will not be able to roll back to the initial savepoint position.

SET TRANSACTION

```
SET TRANSACTION trans_type  NAME name
```

Controls the type of transaction.

Keyword

trans_type

> Can be one of these values:
>
> *READ ONLY*
>
>> Marks the beginning of a read-only transaction. Tells the RDBMS to enforce a read-consistent view of the database for the transaction (the default is for the statement). The transaction is ended with either a COMMIT or a ROLLBACK. Only LOCK TABLE, SELECT, SELECT INTO, OPEN, FETCH, CLOSE, COMMIT, and ROLLBACK statements are permitted during a read-only transaction. Issuing other statements, such as INSERT or UPDATE, in a read-only transaction results in an ORA-1456 error.
>
> *READ WRITE*
>
>> Marks the beginning of a READ WRITE transaction; this is the default.
>
> *ISOLATION LEVEL SERIALIZABLE*
>
>> Similar to a READ ONLY transaction in that transaction-level read consistency is enforced instead of the default statement-level read consistency. Serializable transactions do allow changes to data. For more information about isolation levels, see Chapter 3.

   If the transaction requires rows that are locked by other transactions, will wait.

USE ROLLBACK SEGMENT rbseg_name

   Tells the RDBMS to use the specifically named rollback segment *rbseg_name*. Useful when only one rollback segment is large and a program knows that it needs to use the large rollback segment, such as during a month-end close operation.

name

  Name for the transaction, which is available for the duration of the transaction.

LOCK TABLE

```
LOCK TABLE table_list IN lock_mode MODE [NOWAIT];
```

Bypasses the implicit database row-level locks by explicitly locking one or more entire tables in the specified mode.

Keywords

table_list Comma-delimited list of tables.

lock_mode Can be ROW SHARE, ROW EXCLUSIVE, SHARE UPDATE, SHARE, SHARE ROW EXCLUSIVE, or EXCLUSIVE.

NOWAIT Specifies that the RDBMS should not wait for a lock to be released. If there is a lock when NOWAIT is specified, the RDBMS raises the exception:

```
ORA-00054: resource busy and acquire with NOWAIT specified
```

  The default RDBMS locking behavior is to wait indefinitely.

Autonomous Transactions

Autonomous transactions, new in Oracle8i, execute within a block of code as separate transactions from the outer (main) transaction. Changes can be committed or rolled back in an autonomous transaction without committing or rolling back the main transaction. Changes committed in an autonomous transaction are visible to the main transaction, even though they occur after the start of the main transaction. Changes committed in an autonomous transaction are visible to other transactions as well. The RDBMS suspends the main transaction while the autonomous transaction executes.

  Autonomous transactions also allow you to commit and rollback transactions in triggers without interfering with the operation of the trigger.

Changes made in the main transaction are not visible to the autonomous transaction, and if the main transaction holds any locks that the autonomous transaction waits for, a deadlock occurs. Using the NOWAIT option on UPDATE statements in autonomous transactions can help to minimize this kind of deadlock. Functions and procedures, database triggers, top-level anonymous PL/SQL blocks, and object methods can be declared autonomous via the compiler directive PRAGMA AUTONOMOUS_TRANSACTION.

If you are using autonomous transactions, you must do the following:

- Include the PRAGMA AUTONOMOUS_TRANSACTIONS directive
- Specify COMMIT or ROLLBACK at each exit point in the autonomous program. If you do not do this, the following error is raised:

  ```
  ORA-06519: active autonomous transaction detected and rolled back
  ```

The following example illustrates these two requirements:

```
PROCEDURE main IS
BEGIN
   UPDATE ...-- Main transaction begins here.
   DELETE ...
   at_proc;  -- Call the autonomous transaction.
   SELECT ...
   INSERT ...
   COMMIT;    -- Main transaction ends here.
END;

PROCEDURE at_proc IS
   PRAGMA AUTONOMOUS_TRANSACTION;
BEGIN           -- Main transaction suspends here.
   SELECT ...
   INSERT ...-- Autonomous transaction begins here.
   UPDATE ...
   DELETE ...
   COMMIT;    -- Autonomous transaction ends here.
END;           -- Main transaction resumes here.
```

Exception Section

PL/SQL allows developers to raise and handle errors (exceptions) in a very flexible and powerful way. Each PL/SQL block can have its own exception section in which exceptions can be trapped and handled. When an exception is raised in a PL/SQL block, its execution section immediately terminates. Control is passed to the exception section. Every exception in PL/SQL has an error number and error message; some exceptions also have names.

When an exception occurs (or is raised), the control leaves the execution section and passes directly to the exception section of your PL/SQL block. If the exception is not handled by the exception section, control leaves the block.

Raising Exceptions

An exception can be raised in three ways:

- By the PL/SQL runtime engine
- By an explicit RAISE statement in your code
- By a call to the built-in function RAISE_APPLICATION_ERROR

RAISE

RAISE *exception_name*;

Raises an exception explicitly. If you use the RAISE statement inside an exception handler, you can leave off an exception name to reraise the current exception. This syntax is not valid outside the exception section.

Keyword

exception_name

Name of an exception that you have declared or one that is declared in the STANDARD package.

RAISE_APPLICATION_ERROR

```
RAISE_APPLICATION_ERROR (
   num BINARY_INTEGER,
   msg VARCHAR2,
   keeperrorstack BOOLEAN DEFAULT FALSE);
```

You can also raise an exception by issuing a call to this built-in function.

Keywords

num   Error number, an integer between -20999 and -20000.

msg   Associated error message.

keeperrorstack

Controls the contents of the error stack.

Exception Scope

An exception handler will handle or attempt to handle only exceptions raised in the executable section of the PL/SQL block. Exceptions raised in the declaration or exception sections are automatically passed to the outer block. You can limit the exception scope by placing any line or set of PL/SQL code inside its own block and given its own exception section.

Exception Propagation

Exceptions raised in a PL/SQL block propagate to an outer block if they are unhandled or reraised in the exception section.

When an exception occurs, PL/SQL looks for an exception handler that checks for the exception (or is the WHEN OTHERS clause documented later in this section) in the current block. If a match is not found, then PL/SQL propagates the exception to the enclosing block or calling program. This propagation continues until the exception is handled or propagated out of the outermost block, back to the calling program. In this case, the exception is "unhandled" and it stops the calling program.

When an exception is raised in a PL/SQL block, it does *not* roll back your current transaction, even if the block itself issued an INSERT, UPDATE, or DELETE. You must issue your own ROLLBACK statement if you want to clean up your transaction as a result of the exception.

If your exception goes unhandled (propagates out of the outermost block), however, most host environments will then force an automatic, unqualified rollback of any outstanding changes in your session.

Once an exception is handled, it will not propagate upward. If you want to trap an exception, display a meaningful error message, and have the exception propagate upward as an error, you must reraise the exception. The RAISE statement, described earlier, can reraise the current exception or raise a new exception.

WHEN OTHERS Clause

```
EXCEPTION
   WHEN OTHERS
      THEN...
```

Clause in the exception handler. You can use WHEN OTHERS as a catch-all to trap any exceptions that are not handled by specific WHEN clauses in the exception section. If present, this clause must be the last exception handler in the exception section.

SQLCODE

Built-in function that returns the SQL error code for the current exception. You can include this function inside the exception section's WHEN OTHERS clause in order to handle specific errors by number. The EXCEPTION_INIT pragma allows you to handle errors by name. See the SQLERRM entry, next, for an example of using this function.

SQLERRM

Built-in function that returns the SQL error message for the current exception. You can include this function inside the exception section's WHEN OTHERS clause in order to handle specific errors by number. The EXCEPTION_INIT pragma allows you to handle errors by name.

The following examples illustrate the use of SQLERRM and SQLCODE:

```
CREATE TABLE err_test
   (widget_name   VARCHAR2(100)
   ,widget_count  NUMBER
   ,CONSTRAINT no_small_numbers CHECK
      (widget_count > 1000));
BEGIN
   INSERT INTO err_test (widget_name, widget_count)
   VALUES ('Athena',2);
EXCEPTION
   WHEN OTHERS THEN
   IF SQLCODE = -2290
```

```
              AND SQLERRM LIKE '%NO_SMALL_NUMBERS%'
        THEN
            DBMS_OUTPUT.PUT_LINE('widget_count is too small');
        ELSE
            DBMS_OUTPUT.PUT_LINE('Exception not handled,'
                ||'SQLcode='||SQLCODE);
            DBMS_OUTPUT.PUT_LINE(SQLERRM);
        END IF;
    END;
```

When PL/SQL executes this code, it produces the following output:

```
widget_count is too small
```

Pragmas

The PRAGMA keyword allows you to give instructions to the compiler. There are four types of pragmas in PL/SQL:

EXCEPTION_INIT
> Tells the compiler to associate the specified error number with an identifier that has been declared an EXCEPTION in your current program or in an accessible package.

RESTRICT_REFERENCES
> Tells the compiler the purity level of a packaged program. The purity level is the degree to which a program does not read or write database tables and/or package variables. No longer necessary with Oracle8*i*.

SERIALLY_REUSABLE
> Tells the runtime engine that package data should not persist between references. This is used to reduce per-user memory requirements when the package data is needed only for the duration of the call and not for the duration of the session.

AUTONOMOUS_TRANSACTION
> Tells the compiler that the function, procedure, top-level anonymous PL/SQL block, object method, or database trigger executes in its own transaction space. New with Oracle8*i*.

Program Units

The PL/SQL programming language allows you to create a variety of named program units (containers for code). They include:

Procedure
> Program that executes one or more statements.

Function
> Program that executes one or more statements and that directly returns a value.

Package
> Container for procedures, functions, and data structures.

Triggers
Program that executes in response to database changes.

Object type
Oracle's version of a class in an object-oriented language; object types can contain member procedures and functions. An object type can contain PL/SQL code in its methods.

Common Attributes

The following keywords can be used in defining either a procedure or a function:

OR REPLACE
Used to rebuild an existing program unit, preserving its privileges.

AUTHID
Defines whether the program will execute with the privileges of, and resolve names like, the object owner (DEFINER) or as the user executing the function (CURRENT_USER). Prior to Oracle8i, only the built-in packages DBMS_SQL and DBMS_UTILITY executed as CURRENT_USER. The default AUTHID is DEFINER. New with Oracle8i.

Stored SQL supports two models for addressing privileges at runtime. The default, definer rights, tells Oracle to use the privileges of the owner or definer of the program. With the definer rights model, the owner of the program must have the required prvileges granted directly to him—he cannot inherit the privileges from a role.

With invoker rights, the user who executes the program does so using his own privileges. Anonymous PL/SQL blocks always execute with invoker rights. To create a program that uses the invoker rights model, specify AUTHID CURRENT_USER in your program's declaration.

AGGREGATE USING
Required for aggregate functions. Tells Oracle that the function evaluates a group of rows and returns a single result. The built-in AVG is an aggregate function. New with Oracle9i.

DETERMINISTIC
Required for function-based indexes. A function is DETERMINISTIC if it always returns the same value when called with the same parameters. Deterministic functions do not meaningfully reference package variables or the database. The built-in INITCAP is deterministic, but SYSDATE is not. New with Oracle8i.

PARALLEL_ENABLED [(PARTITION in_parm BY {ANY | HASH | RANGE})]
Tells the optimizer that a function is safe for parallel execution. The PARTITION BY clause is available only to functions that have a REF CURSOR IN parameter. This clause is used with table functions and tells the optimizer how the input can be partitioned. New with Oracle8i.

PIPELINED
> Used with table functions. Tells Oracle that the function can start to return data as it is generated instead of all at once after processing is complete. New with Oracle9*i*.

Procedures

```
CREATE [OR REPLACE] PROCEDURE name
   [ (parameter [,parameter]) ]
   [AUTHID {CURRENT_USER | DEFINER} ]
   [DETERMINISTIC]
{IS | AS}
   declaration_section
BEGIN
   executable_section
[EXCEPTION
   exception_section]
END [name];
```

Program unit, or module, that execute one or more statements and that can receive or return zero or more values through its parameter list. You can call a procedure as a standalone executable PL/SQL statement as shown in this example:

```
apply_discount(new_company_id, 0.15) --15% discount
```

Common keywords: AGGREGATE USING, AUTHID, DETERMINISTIC, PARALLEL_ENABLE, and PIPELINED.

Functions

```
CREATE [OR REPLACE] FUNCTION name
   [ (parameter [,parameter]) ]
   RETURN return_datatype
   [AUTHID {CURRENT_USER | DEFINER} ]
   [DETERMINISTIC]
   [PARALLEL_ENABLED]
   [PIPELINED]
   [AGGREGATE USING]
{IS | AS}
   [declaration_section]
BEGIN
   executable_section
[EXCEPTION
   exception_section]
END [name];
```

Program unit, or module, that executes zero or more statements and that returns a value through the RETURN clause. Like procedures, functions can also receive or return zero or more values through their parameter lists. A function must have at least one RETURN statement in the execution section. The RETURN clause in the function header specifies the datatype of the returned value.

A function can be called anywhere an expression of the same type can be used. You can call a function as follows:

- In an assignment statement:
    ```
    sales95 := tot_sales(1995,'C');
    ```

- To set a default value:
  ```
  DECLARE
    sales95 NUMBER DEFAULT tot_sales(1995,'C');
  BEGIN
  ```
- In a Boolean expression:
  ```
  IF tot_sales(1995,'C') > 10000
  THEN
     ...
  ```
- In a SQL statement:
  ```
  SELECT first_name ,surname
      FROM sellers
  WHERE tot_sales(1995,'C') > 1000;
  ```
- As an argument in another program unit's parameter list.

Common keywords: AUTHID, DETERMINISTIC, PARALLEL_ENABLE AGGRE-
GATE USING, and PIPELINED.

Table Functions

Functions that take a collection or REF CURSOR (set of rows) as input and return a
collection of records (set of rows) as output. Table functions were introduced in
Oracle8i. Starting with Oracle9i, you can use the PIPE ROW statement to identify the
input and output streams. Streamlining in this way allow you to pipeline table funtions
together, eliminating the need to stage tables between transformations. Table funtions
typically appear in the FROM clause of a query.

Local Programs

Procedure or function that is defined in the declaration section of a PL/SQL block. The
declaration of a local program must appear at the end of the declaration section, after
the declarations of any types, records, cursors, variables, and exceptions. A program
defined in a declaration section may be referenced only within that block's executable
and exception sections. It is not defined outside that block.

The following program defines a local procedure and a local function:

```
PROCEDURE track_revenue
IS
    PROCEDURE calc_total (year_in IN INTEGER) IS
    BEGIN
       calculations here ...
    END;

    FUNCTION below_minimum (comp_id IN INTEGER)
        RETURN BOOLEAN
    IS
    BEGIN
       ...
    END;
```

Local programs may be overloaded with the same restrictions as overloaded packaged programs.

Program Overloading

PL/SQL allows you to define two or more programs with the same name within any declaration section (including a package specification or body, described in the next section). This technique is called *overloading*. If two or more programs have the same name, they must be different in some other way so that the compiler can determine which program should be used.

Here is an example of overloaded programs in one of Oracle's own built-in package specifications:

```
PACKAGE DBMS_OUTPUT
IS
    PROCEDURE PUT_LINE (a VARCHAR2);
    PROCEDURE PUT_LINE (a NUMBER);
    PROCEDURE PUT_LINE (a DATE);
END;
```

Each PUT_LINE procedure is identical, except for the datatype of the parameter. That is enough difference for the compiler.

To overload programs successfully, one or more of the following conditions must be true:

- Parameters must differ by datatype family (number, character, datetime, or Boolean).
- The program type must be different (you can overload a function and a procedure of the same name with identical parameter lists).
- The numbers of parameters must be different.

You *cannot* overload programs if:

- Only the datatypes of the functions' RETURN clauses are different.
- Parameter datatypes are within the same family (CHAR and VARCHAR2, NUMBER and INTEGER, etc.).
- Only the modes of the parameters are different.

Packages

A package is a group of PL/SQL code elements. Elements that can be placed in a package include procedures, functions, constants, variables, cursors, exception names, and TYPE statements (for associative arrays, records, REF CURSORs, etc.).

Package Structure

A package can have two parts, a package specification and a package body, described in the following sections.

Package Specification

```
CREATE [OR REPLACE] PACKAGE package_name
[ AUTHID {CURRENT_USER | DEFINER} ]
{IS | AS}
```

```
[definitions of public TYPEs
,declarations of public variables, types and objects
,declarations of exceptions
,pragmas
,declarations of cursors, procedures and functions
,headers of procedures and functions]
```

```
END [package_name];
```

Lists all the objects that are publicly available for use in applications. A package specification also provides all the information a developer needs in order to use objects in the package; essentially, it is the package's Application Programming Interface (API.). The package specification is required. A package does not need a body if the specification or that package does not contain any procedures or functions and if no private code is needed.

Package Body

```
CREATE [OR REPLACE] PACKAGE BODY package_name
{IS | AS}

   [definitions of private TYPEs
   ,declarations of private variables, types and objects
   ,full definitions of cursors
   ,full definitions of procedures and functions]

[BEGIN
   executable_statements

[EXCEPTION
   exception_handlers ] ]

END [package_name];
```

Contains all of the code needed to implement procedures, functions, and cursors listed in the specification, as well as any private objects accessible only to other elements defined in that package, and an optional initialization section.

The declarations in the specifications cannot be repeated in the body. Both the executable section and the exception section are optional in a package body. The package body itself can have an execution section, which follows the declaration of procedures and functions within the package body. If the executable section is present, it is called the *initialization section* and executes only once—the first time any package element is referenced during a session.

You must compile the package specification before the body specification. When you grant EXECUTE authority on a package to another schema or to PUBLIC, you are giving access only to the specification; the body remains hidden.

Here's an example of a package:

```
CREATE OR REPLACE PACKAGE time_pkg IS
   FUNCTION GetTimestamp  RETURN DATE;
   PRAGMA RESTRICT_REFERENCES (GetTimestamp, WNDS);
```

PL/SQL

```
    PROCEDURE ResetTimestamp;
END time_pkg;

CREATE OR REPLACE PACKAGE BODY time_pkg IS
    StartTimeStamp    DATE := SYSDATE;
    -- StartTimeStamp is package data.

    FUNCTION GetTimestamp RETURN DATE IS
    BEGIN
        RETURN StartTimeStamp;
    END GetTimestamp;

    PROCEDURE ResetTimestamp IS
    BEGIN
        StartTimeStamp := SYSDATE;
    END ResetTimestamp;

END time_pkg;
```

Referencing Package Elements

The elements declared in the specification are referenced from the calling application via dot notation:

```
package_name.package_element
```

For example, the built-in package DBMS_OUTPUT has a procedure named PUT_LINE, so a call to this package would look like this:

```
DBMS_OUTPUT.PUT_LINE('This is parameter data');
```

Package Data

Data structures declared within a package specification or body, but outside any procedure or function in the package, are known as *package data*. The scope of package data is your entire session; it spans transaction boundaries, so package data essentially constitutes the globals for your programs.

Keep the following guidelines in mind as you work with package data:

- The state of your package variables is not affected by COMMITs and ROLL-BACKs.

- A cursor declared in a package has global scope. It remains open until you close it explicitly or your session ends.

- A good practice is to hide your data structures in the package body and provide "get and set" programs to read and write that data.

SERIALLY_REUSABLE Pragma

If you need package data to exist only during a call to the packaged functions or procedures and not between calls of the current session, you can potentially save runtime memory by using the pragma SERIALLY_REUSABLE. You must include this pragma in both the specification and the body. After each call, PL/SQL closes the cursors and releases the memory used in the package.

This technique is applicable only to large user communities executing the same routine. Normally, the database server's memory requirements grow in linear fashion, with the number of users. If you use SERIALLY_REUSABLE, this growth can be less than linear, because work areas for package states are kept in a pool in the SGA (System Global Area) and are shared among all users.

Package Initialization

The first time a user references a package element, the entire package is loaded into the SGA of the database instance to which the user is connected. That code is then shared by all sessions that have EXECUTE authority on the package.

Any package data are then instantiated into the session's UGA (User Global Area), a private area in either the SGA or PGA (Program Global Area). If the package body contains an initialization section, that code will be executed. The initialization section is optional and appears at the end of the package body, beginning with a BEGIN statement and ending with the EXCEPTION section if present or the END of the package.

Triggers

A *trigger* is a program that executes in response to a change in table data or to certain events that occur in the database. There is a predefined set of events that can be "hooked" with a trigger, enabling you to integrate your own processing with that of the database. A triggering event fires, or executes, the trigger.

Triggers are enabled on creation (via a CREATE TRIGGER statement) and can be disabled (so they do not fire) via an ALTER TRIGGER or ALTER TABLE statement:

```
ALTER TRIGGER trigger_name {ENABLE | DISABLE};

ALTER TABLE table_name {ENABLE | DISABLE} ALL
    TRIGGERS;
```

Triggers cannot be created on SYS-owned objects.

CREATE TRIGGER

```
CREATE [OR REPLACE] TRIGGER trigger_name
    {BEFORE | AFTER | INSTEAD OF} trigger_event
ON
    [ NESTED TABLE nested_table_column OF view ]
      | table_or_view_reference | DATABASE [referencing_clause]
[FOR EACH ROW [WHEN trigger_condition]]
trigger_body;
```

Creates a trigger. The trigger body included in the CREATE TRIGGER statement is a standard PL/SQL block.

Keywords

BEFORE | AFTER

Triggers can fire BEFORE or AFTER the triggering event. AFTER data triggers are slightly more efficient than BEFORE triggers.

INSTEAD OF

Typically used with views, to allow updating of underlying tables for views through an INSERT, UPDATE, or DELETE statement.

trigger_event

One of the following events:

INSERT

Fires whenever a row is added to the *table_or_view_reference*.

UPDATE

Fires whenever an UPDATE changes the *table_or_view_reference*. UPDATE triggers can additionally specify an OF clause to restrict firing to updates OF certain columns.

DELETE

Fires whenever a row is deleted from the *table_or_view_reference*. Does not fire on a TRUNCATE of the table.

CREATE

Fires whenever a CREATE statement adds a new object to the database. In this context, objects are things like tables or packages (found in ALL_OBJECTS). Can apply to a single schema or the entire database.

ALTER

Fires whenever an ALTER statement changes a database object. In this context, objects are things like tables or packages (found in ALL_OBJECTS). Can apply to single schema or the entire database.

DROP

Fires whenever a DROP statement removes an object from the database. In this context, objects are things like tables or packages (found in ALL_OBJECTS). Can apply to a single schema or the entire database.

SERVERERROR

Fires whenever a server error message is logged. Only AFTER triggers are allowed in this context.

LOGON

Fires whenever a session is created (a user connects to the database). Only AFTER triggers are allowed in this context.

LOGOFF

Fires whenever a session is terminated (a user disconnects from the database). Only BEFORE triggers are allowed in this context.

STARTUP

Fires when the database is opened. Only AFTER triggers are allowed in this context.

Fires when the database is closed. Only BEFORE triggers are allowed in this context.

referencing_clause
Allowed only for the data events INSERT, UPDATE, and DELETE. Lets you give a nondefault name to the old and new pseudo-records. These pseudo-records give the program visibility to the pre- and post-change values in row-level triggers. Such records are defined like %ROWTYPE records, except that columns of type LONG or LONG RAW cannot be referenced. They are prefixed with a colon in the trigger body and are referenced with dot notation. Unlike other records, these fields can only be assigned individually—aggregate assignment is not allowed. All old fields are NULL within INSERT triggers, and all new fields are NULL within DELETE triggers.

FOR EACH ROW
Defines the trigger to be a row-level trigger. Row-level triggers fire once for each row affected. The default is a statement-level trigger, which fires only once for each triggering statement.

WHEN trigger_condition
Specifies the conditions that must be met for the trigger to fire. Stored functions and object methods are not allowed in the trigger condition.

trigger_body
A standard PL/SQL block.

Event Sequences

As you can see from the preceding description, many different types of triggers can be defined on a single table. You need to understand the order in which these triggers fire.

The most basic sequencing syntax is the FOR EACH ROW syntax. The FOR EACH ROW keywords specify whether a trigger fires for a row or for a table. Other factors also affect the order in which triggers are executed, as described in the following sections.

DML events

The DML events include INSERT, UPDATE, or DELETE statements on a table or view. Triggers on these events can be statement-level (table only) or row-level triggers and can fire before or after the triggering event. BEFORE triggers can modify the data in affected rows and are generally used to determine whether the triggering statement should complete. AFTER triggers do not perform this additional logical read and therefore perform slightly better; however, AFTER triggers are not able to change the *:new* values.

The order in which DML triggers fire, if present, is as follows:

1. BEFORE statement-level trigger
2. For each row affected by the statement
3. BEFORE row-level trigger

4. The triggering statement
5. AFTER row-level trigger
6. AFTER statement-level trigger

DDL events

The DDL events include CREATE, ALTER, and DROP. These triggers fire whenever the respective DDL statement is executed. DDL triggers can apply to either a single schema or the entire database. New with Oracle8*i*.

Database events

The database events include SERVERERROR, LOGON, LOGOFF, STARTUP, and SHUTDOWN. Only BEFORE triggers are allowed for LOGOFF and SHUTDOWN events. Only AFTER triggers are allowed for LOGON, STARTUP, and SERVERERROR events. A SHUTDOWN trigger will fire on a SHUTDOWN NORMAL and a SHUTDOWN IMMEDIATE, but not on a SHUTDOWN ABORT. New with Oracle8*i*.

Trigger Predicates

When using a single trigger for multiple events, use the trigger predicates INSERTING, UPDATING, and DELETING in the trigger condition to identify the triggering event. The following example illustrates the use of trigger predicates:

```
CREATE OR REPLACE TRIGGER emp_log_t
    AFTER INSERT OR UPDATE OR DELETE ON emp
    FOR EACH ROW
DECLARE
    dmltype  CHAR(1);
BEGIN
    IF INSERTING THEN
        dmltype := 'I';
        INSERT INTO emp_log (emp_no, who, operation)
            VALUES (:new.empno, USER, dmltype);
    ELSIF UPDATING  THEN
        dmltype := 'U';
        INSERT INTO emp_log (emp_no, who, operation)
            VALUES (:new.empno, USER, dmltype);
    END IF;
END;
```

Calling PL/SQL Functions in SQL

Stored functions can be called from SQL statements in a manner similar to built-in functions like DECODE, NVL, or RTRIM. There are a number of caveats and restrictions, which we'll summarize in the following sections.

Specifying the Function

Use the following syntax to call your own custom-built functions from within SQL. This feature essentially allows you to customize the SQL language to meet your application requirements.

Syntax

```
[schema_name.][pkg_name.]func_name[@db_link]
   [parm_list]
```

Keywords

schema_name
: User/owner of the function or package. Optional.

pkg_name
: Package containing the called function. Optional.

func_name
: Function name.

db_link
: Database link name to the remote database containing the function. Optional.

parm_list
: List of parameters for the function. Optional.

Requirements and restrictions

There are a number of requirements for calling stored functions in SQL:

- All parameters must be IN; no IN OUT or OUT parameters are allowed.
- The datatypes of the function's parameters and RETURN must be compatible with RDBMS datatypes. You cannot have arguments or RETURN types like BOOLEAN, programmer-defined record, associative arrays, and so on.
- The parameters passed to the function must use positional notation; named notation is not supported.
- The function must be stored in the database, not in a local program.

RESTRICT_REFERENCES Pragma

Prior to Oracle8*i*, it was necessary to assert the purity level of a packaged procedure or function when using it directly or indirectly in a SQL statement. Beginning with Oracle8*i*, the PL/SQL runtime engine determines a program's purity level automatically if no assertion exists. The RESTRICT REFERENCES pragma is still supported for backwards compatibility but it has been deprecated in Oracle9*i*.

The RESTRICT_REFERENCES pragma asserts a purity level. The syntax for the RESTRICT_REFERENCES pragma is:

```
PRAGMA RESTRICT_REFERENCES (program_name | DEFAULT, purity_level);
```

PL/SQL

The keyword DEFAULT applies to all methods of an object type or all programs in a package.

You can specify from one to five purity levels, in any order, in a comma-delimited list. The purity level describes to what extent the program or method is free of *side effects*. Side effects are listed in the Table 9-3 with the purity levels they address.

Table 9-3. Purity levels and side effects

Purity level	Description	Restriction
WNDS	Write No Database State	Executes no INSERT, UPDATE, or DELETE statements
RNDS	Read No Database State	Executes no SELECT statements
WNPS	Write No Package State	Does not modify any package variables
RNPS	Read No Package State	Does not read any package variables
TRUST		Does not enforce the restrictions declared but allows the compiler to trust they are true

Caveats on Calling PL/SQL Functions From SQL

The most notable caveat is that stored functions executed from SQL are not by default guaranteed to follow the statement-level read consistency model of the database. Unless the SQL statement and any stored functions in that statement are in the same read-consistent transaction, each execution of the stored function may look at a different time-consistent set of data. To avoid this potential problem, you need to ensure read consistency programmatically by issuing the SET TRANSACTION READ ONLY or SET TRANSACTION ISOLATION LEVEL SERIALIZABLE statement before executing your SQL statement containing the stored function. A COMMIT or ROLLBACK then needs to follow the SQL statement to end this read-consistent transaction.

If your function has the same name as a table column in your SELECT statement and if the function has no parameter, then the column takes precedence over the function. To force the RDBMS to resolve the name to your function, you must prepend the schema name to it.

Native Compilation of PL/SQL

Beginning with Oracle9*i*, you can speed up many of your PL/SQL programs by compiling the stored programs natively. Oracle will translate your PL/SQL program into C code and compile it into a shared library (a DLL on Windows). You must have a supported C compiler on your database server machine to support native compilation.

We've summarized the steps needed to compile your PL/SQL program natively, but refer to the Oracle documentation for details:

1. Edit the makefile *spnc_makefile.mk*, which should be in the *$ORACLE HOME/plsql* subdirectory.

2. Set the initialization parameter PLSQL_COMPILER_FLAGS = 'NATIVE'. You may also need to set these additional parameters (see Chapter 2 for information):

> PLSQL_NATIVE_C_COMPILER
> PLSQL_NATIVE_LINKER
> PLSQL_NATIVE LIBRARY_DIR
> PLSQL_NATIVE_MAKE_UTILITY
> PLSQL_NATIVE_MAKE_FILE_NAME

You can set these in the *SPFILE/INIT.ORA* file or with an ALTER SYSTEM statement.

3. Create or replace your stored programs.

4. Verify the native compilation by querying the data dictionary view USER_STORED_SETTINGS and also by locating the shared library or DLL in the database server's filesystem.

External Procedures

External procedures provide a mechanism for calling a nondatabase program (such as a DLL under Windows or a shared library under Unix) from a PL/SQL program. Every session calling an external procedure will have its own *extproc* process started by the listener. This *extproc* process is started with the first call to the external procedure and terminates when the session exits. The shared library needs to have a corresponding library created for it in the database.

The following is a brief summary of the steps you need to follow in order to create an external procedure. For details and examples of external procedures, see Chapter 23 in *Oracle PL/SQL Programming*, 3ed edition.

1. Set up the listener.

External procedures require a listener. If you are running an Oracle Net Services listener, that listener can be used as the *extproc* listener as well, although you may increase security by separating it from the external procedure listener and launching it from an account that has more limited privileges. See the *Oracle9i Administrators' Guide* or the *Oracle9i Net Services Administrators' Guide* for the details on configuring your listener.

2. Identify or create the shared library or DLL.

This step has nothing to do with PL/SQL and may or may not have anything to do with the database. You must write your own C routines and link them into a shared library/DLL or use an existing library's functions or procedures. The simple example shown later will use the existing random number-generating calls available from the operating system.

3. Create the library in the database.

Create a library in the database for the shared library or DLL using the CREATE LIBRARY statement (described in Chapter 7).

To remove libraries from the database, use the DROP LIBRARY statement.

To call out to the C runtime library's *rand* function, you don't have to code any C routines at all, because the call is already linked into a shared library, and because its arguments are directly type-mappable to PL/SQL. If the *rand* function is in the standard */lib/libc.so* shared library, as on Solaris, you would issue the following CREATE LIBRARY statement:

```
CREATE OR REPLACE LIBRARY libc_1 AS
    '/lib/libc.so';  -- References C runtime library.
```

This is the typical corresponding statement for Windows:

```
CREATE OR REPLACE LIBRARY libc_1 AS
    'C:\WINDOWS\SYSTEM32\CRTDLL.DLL';
```

4. Create the PL/SQL wrapper for the external procedure.

The next step requires a specific use of the CREATE PROCEDURE statement, described in the following section

---

CREATE PROCEDURE

```
CREATE [OR REPLACE] PROCEDURE proc_name
    [parm_list]
{IS | AS} LANGUAGE C
    [NAME external_name]
    LIBRARY library_name
    [AGENT IN (agent_name)]
    [WITH CONTEXT]
    [PARAMETERS (external_parameter_list)];
```

Creates a procedure—in this case, a wrapper procedure for the external procedure.

Keywords

proc_name
Name of the wrapper procedure.

LANGUAGE C
Language in which the external routine was written (default is C).

library_name
Name of the library created with the CREATE LIBRARY statement.

external_name
Name of the external routine as it appears in the library. This name defaults to the wrapper package name. PL/SQL package names are usually saved in uppercase, so the *external_name* may need to be enclosed in double quotes to preserve case.

AGENT IN (agent_name)
Specifies the value of the agent as a formal PL/SQL parameter to the call spec.

WITH CONTEXT
Used to pass a context pointer to the external routine, so it can make Oracle Call Interface (OCI) calls back to the database.

PARAMETERS
Identify the *external_parameter_list*, which is a comma-delimited list containing the position and datatype of parameters that get passed to the external routine.

The purpose of this clause is to resolve inconsistencies between the way PL/SQL and C handle variables. The syntax for each parameter in the list is:

```
{CONTEXT | RETURN | parameter_name [property]}
    [BY REFERENCE] [external_datatype]
```

where:

CONTEXT

Indicates the position in the parameter list at which the context pointer will be passed. It is required if the WITH CONTEXT clause is being used to pass a context pointer to the called program. By convention, CONTEXT appears as the first parameter in the external parameter list. If CONTEXT is used, the *property,* BY REFERENCE, and *external_datatype* optional sections are invalid.

RETURN

Indicates that the descriptions are for the return value from the external routine. By default, RETURN is passed by value. You can use the keywords BY REFERENCE to pass by reference (use pointers).

parameter_name

PL/SQL formal parameter name. By default, IN formal parameters are passed by value. You can use the keywords BY REFERENCE to pass by reference (as a pointer). IN OUT and OUT formal parameters are always passed by reference.

property

Breaks out further to the general syntax:

```
INDICATOR [STRUCT | TDO ] | LENGTH | MAXLEN | CHARSETID |
CHARSETFORM | SELF
```

INDICATOR indicates whether the corresponding parameter is NULL. In the C program, if the indicator equals the constant OCI_IND_NULL, the parameter is NULL. If the indicator equals the constant OCI_IND_NOTNULL, the indicator is not NULL. For IN parameters, INDICATOR is passed by value (by default). For IN OUT, OUT, and RETURN parameters, INDICATOR is passed by reference.

You can pass a user-defined type to an external procedure. To do so, you typically pass three parameters: the actual object value, a TDO (Type Descriptor Object) parameter as defined in C by the Oracle Type Translator; and an INDICATOR STRUCT parameter, to designate whether the object is NULL.

Use LENGTH and MAXLEN to pass the current and maximum length of strings or RAWs. For IN parameters, LENGTH is passed by value (by default). For IN OUT, OUT, and RETURN parameters, LENGTH is passed by reference. MAXLEN is not valid for IN parameters. For IN OUT, OUT, and RETURN parameters, MAXLEN is passed by reference and is read-only.

CHARSETID and CHARSETFORM are used to support NLS character sets. They are the same as the OCI attributes OCI_ATTR_CHARSET_ID and OCI_ATTR_CHARSET_FORM. For IN parameters, CHARSETID and CHARSETFORM are passed by value (by default) and are read-only. For IN OUT, OUT, and RETURN parameters, CHARSETID and CHARSETFORM are passed by reference and are read-only.

Use SELF if an object member function is implemented as a callout instead of a PL/SQL routine.

The wrapper PL/SQL function or procedure is usually in a package.

Using the preceding random number generator example, you could create the wrapper package as follows:

```
CREATE OR REPLACE PACKAGE random_utl
AS
    FUNCTION rand RETURN PLS_INTEGER;
    PRAGMA RESTRICT_REFERENCES(rand,WNDS,RNDS,WNPS,RNPS);

    PROCEDURE srand (seed IN PLS_INTEGER);
    PRAGMA RESTRICT_REFERENCES(srand,WNDS,RNDS,WNPS,RNPS);
END random_utl;

CREATE PACKAGE BODY random_utl
AS
    FUNCTION rand RETURN PLS_INTEGER
    IS
        LANGUAGE C    -- Language of routine.
        NAME "rand"    -- Function name in the library.
        LIBRARY libc_1 -- The library created above.

    PROCEDURE srand (seed IN PLS_INTEGER)
    IS
        LANGUAGE C
        NAME "srand"                -- Name is lowercase in this library.
        LIBRARY libc_1
        PARAMETERS (seed ub4); -- Map to unsigned INT.
END random_utl;
```

To use this external random number function, simply call the package procedure *srand* to seed the generator, then the package function *rand* to get random numbers:

```
DECLARE
    random_nbr  PLS_INTEGER;
    seed        PLS_INTEGER;
BEGIN
    SELECT TO_CHAR(SYSDATE,'SSSSS') INTO seed
        FROM dual;

    random_utl.srand(seed);              -- Seed the generator.

    random_nbr := random_utl.rand;      -- Get the number.
    DBMS_OUTPUT.PUT_LINE('number='||random_nbr);

    random_nbr := random_utl.rand;      -- Get the number.
    DBMS_OUTPUT.PUT_LINE('number='||random_nbr);
END;
```

You could, of course, accomplish the same purpose with the DBMS_RANDOM built-in package, which is described in Chapter 10.

Java and PL/SQL

For information on using Java with PL/SQL, see Chapter 11.

10

PL/SQL Packages

A *package* is a collection of PL/SQL or Java objects that are packaged or grouped together. Packages may contain procedures, functions, variables, constants, and a variety of other objects.

Oracle uses the package construct to extend the capabilities of the core database through built-in packages (written in PL/SQL) for developers to call from their PL/SQL programs. Many new Oracle features are implemented in the form of packages. For example, the Advanced Queuing facility uses the DBMS_AQ and DBMS_AQADM packages. Some packages, like DBMS_STATISTICS, encapsulate commonly used functionality in an enhanced form.

You can also write your own packages, as described in Chapter 9.

This chapter consists of brief descriptions of the procedures and functions included in the PL/SQL packages that are a part of the Oracle database. The packages are listed alphabetically. For each package, we include a listing of the interfaces for the procedures and functions, along with brief summaries of the parameters passed to each program unit. In general, optional parameters are enclosed in square brackets ([ ]) throughout this book. In this chapter, we've used a special convention to indicate parameters used only in Oracle9*i*: these are enclosed in square brackets with the sharp character (#) appended to distinguish such parameters from ordinary optional parameters.

For detailed information on these packages and their use, see the Oracle documentation. For packages available through Oracle8, see also the excellent descriptions in *Oracle Built-in Packages* by Steven Feuerstein, Charles Dye, and John Beresniewicz (O'Reilly & Associates).

DBMS_ALERT

Provides mechanisms for synchronous, transaction-based notification to multiple sessions that specific database events have occurred.

Calls

PROCEDURE DBMS_ALERT.REGISTER
  (*name* IN VARCHAR2);
    Registers the calling session to receive notification of alert *name*.

PROCEDURE DBMS_ALERT.REMOVE
  (*name* IN VARCHAR2);
    Unregisters the calling session from receiving notification of alert *name*.

PROCEDURE DBMS_ALERT.REMOVEALL;
    Unregisters the calling session from notification of all alerts. New with Oracle8*i*.

PROCEDURE DBMS_ALERT.SET_DEFAULTS
  (*sensitivity* IN NUMBER);
    Defines configurable settings for the calling session in seconds.

PROCEDURE DBMS_ALERT.SIGNAL
  (*name* IN VARCHAR2,
  message IN VARCHAR2);
    Signals the occurrence of alert *name* and attaches *message*. Sessions registered for alert *name* are notified only when the signaling transaction commits.

PROCEDURE DBMS_ALERT.WAITANY
  (*name* OUT VARCHAR2,
  message OUT VARCHAR2,
  status OUT INTEGER,
  timeout IN NUMBER DEFAULT MAXWAIT);
    Waits for up to *timeout* seconds to be notified of any alerts for which the session is registered. If *status* = 0, then *name* and *message* contain alert information. If *status* = 1, then *timeout* seconds have elapsed without notification of any alert.

PROCEDURE DBMS_ALERT.WAITONE
  (*name* IN VARCHAR2,
  message OUT VARCHAR2,
  status OUT INTEGER,
  timeout IN NUMBER DEFAULT MAXWAIT);
    Waits for up to *timeout* seconds for notification of alert *name*.

DBMS_APPLICATION_INFO

Allows applications to register their current execution status into several of the Oracle V$ virtual tables in the data dictionary.

Calls

PROCEDURE DBMS_APPLICATION_INFO.READ_CLIENT_INFO
  (*client_info* OUT VARCHAR2);
    Returns the currently registered *client_info* for the session.

PROCEDURE DBMS_APPLICATION_INFO.READ_MODULE
  (*module_name* OUT VARCHAR2,
  action_name OUT VARCHAR2);
    Returns the currently registered *module_name* and *action_name* for the session.

PROCEDURE DBMS_APPLICATION_INFO.SET_ACTION
  (*action_name* IN VARCHAR2);
    Registers *action_name* into V$SESSION and V$SQLAREA as the current action for the session.

PROCEDURE DBMS_APPLICATION_INFO.SET_CLIENT_INFO
    (*client_info* IN VARCHAR2);
      Registers *client_info* into V$SESSION as the current client information for the session.

PROCEDURE DBMS_APPLICATION_INFO.SET_MODULE
    (*module_name* IN VARCHAR2,
    action_name IN VARCHAR2);
      Registers *module_name* and *action_name* into V$SESSION and V$SQLAREA as the current module and action for the session.

PROCEDURE DBMS_APPLICATION_INFO.SET_SESSION_LONGOPS
    (*rindex* IN OUT BINARY_INTEGER,
    slno IN OUT BINARY_INTEGER,
    op_name   IN VARCHAR2 DEFAULT NULL,
    target IN BINARY_INTEGER DEFAULT 0,
    context IN BINARY_INTEGER DEFAULT 0,
    sofar IN NUMBER DEFAULT 0,
    totalwork IN NUMBER DEFAULT 0,
    target_desc IN VARCHAR2 DEFAULT 'unknown target',
    units IN VARCHAR2 DEFAULT NULL);
      Inserts or updates runtime data for long-running operations in the V$SESSION_LONGOPS virtual table. Rows are identified by the value of *rindex*. A new row is acquired when *rindex* is set to the package constant SET_SESSION_LONGOPS_NOHINT. Unique combinations of other parameters may also force a new row. *op_name* specifies the name of the long-running target; *target* is the name of the object; *context*, *sofar*, and *totalwork* are client-defined values in *units*. New with Oracle8*i*.

DBMS_APPLY_ADM

Provides procedures that allow you to start, stop, and modify apply processes. Apply processes are used with Oracle Streams, which are new with Oracle9*i*.

Calls

PROCEDURE DBMS_APPLY_ADM.ALTER_APPLY
    (*apply_name* IN VARCHAR2,
    rule_set_name IN VARCHAR2 DEFAULT NULL,
    remove_rule_set IN BOOLEAN DEFAULT FALSE,
    message_handler IN VARCHAR2 DEFAULT NULL,
    remove_message handler IN BOOLEAN DEFAULT FALSE,
    ddl_handler IN VARCHAR2 DEFAULT NULL,
    remove_ddl_handler IN BOOLEAN DEFAULT FALSE,
    apply_user IN VARCHAR2 DEFAULT NULL,
    apply_tag IN RAW DEFAULT NULL,
    remove_apply_tag IN BOOLEAN DEFAULT FALSE);
      Alters the characteristics of an apply process by changing or canceling the rule set, message handler, DDL handler, or tag or changes the user who applies all DML and DDL changes and runs apply handlers. The apply process is stopped and restarted when you change any of the characteristics except the user.

PROCEDURE DBMS_APPLY_ADM.CREATE_APPLY
    (*queue_name* IN VARCHAR2,
    apply_name IN VARCHAR2,
    rule_set_name IN VARCHAR2 DEFAULT NULL,

```
    message_handler IN VARCHAR2 DEFAULT NULL,
    ddl_handle IN VARCHAR2 DEFAULT NULL,
    apply_user IN VARCHAR2 DEFAULT NULL,
    apply_database_link IN VARCHAR2 DEFAULT NULL,
    apply_tag IN RAW DEFAULT '00',
    apply_captured IN BOOLEAN DEFAULT FALSE);
```
Creates an apply process.

PROCEDURE DBMS_APPLY_ADM.DELETE_ALL_ERRORS
```
    (apply_name IN VARCHAR2 DEFAULT NULL);
```
Deletes all error transactions for the specified apply process.

PROCEDURE DBMS_APPLY_ADM.DELETE_ERROR
```
    (local_transaction_id IN VARCHAR2);
```
Deletes a specific error transaction.

PROCEDURE DBMS_APPLY_ADM.DROP_APPLY
```
    (apply_name IN VARCHAR2);
```
Drops the specified apply process.

PROCEDURE DBMS_APPLY_ADM.EXECUTE_ALL_ERRORS
```
    (apply_name IN VARCHAR2 DEFAULT NULL,
    execute_as_user IN BOOLEAN DEFAULT FALSE);
```
Used to reexecute error transactions, in the security context of either the current user or the original user.

PROCEDURE DBMS_APPLY_ADM.EXECUTE_ERROR
```
    (local_transaction_name IN VARCHAR2,
    execute_as_user IN BOOLEAN DEFAULT FALSE);
```
Used to reexecute a specific error transaction.

PROCEDURE DBMS_APPLY_ADM.GET_ERROR_MESSAGE
```
    (message_number IN NUMBER,
    local_transaction_id IN VARCHAR2)
    RETURN Sys.Anydata;
```
Returns message for specified message number and transaction queue.

PROCEDURE DBMS_APPLY_ADM.SET_DML_HANDLER
```
    (object_name IN VARCHAR2,
    object_type IN VARCHAR2,
    operation_name IN VARCHAR2,
    error_handler IN BOOLEAN DEFAULT FALSE,
    user_procedure IN VARCHAR2,
    apply_database_link IN VARCHAR2 DEFAULT NULL);
```
Sets up a DML (Data Manipulation Language) handler on a specific object.

PROCEDURE DBMS_APPLY_ADM.SET_GLOBAL_INSTANTIATION_SCN
```
    (source_database_name IN VARCHAR2,
    instantiation_scn IN NUMBER,
    apply_database_link IN VARCHAR2 DEFAULT NULL);
```
Sets the instantiation System Change Number (SCN) for the specified source database.

PROCEDURE DBMS_APPLY_ADM.SET_KEY_COLUMNS
```
    (object_name IN VARCHAR2,
    {column_list IN VARCHAR2 | column_table IN DBMS_UTILITY.NAME_ARRAY},
    apply_database_link IN VARCHAR2 DEFAULT NULL);
```
Sets up columns to be used as the substitute primary key columns for the object.

PROCEDURE DBMS_APPLY_ADM.SET_PARAMETER
　　(*apply_name* IN VARCHAR2,
　　parameter IN VARCHAR2,
　　value IN VARCHAR2);
　　　Sets the value for an apply parameter.

PROCEDURE DBMS_APPLY_ADM.SET_SCHEMA_INSTANTIATION_SCN
　　(*source_schema_name* IN VARCHAR2,
　　source_database_name IN VARCHAR2,
　　instantiation_scn IN NUMBER,
　　apply_database_link IN VARCHAR2 DEFAULT NULL);
　　　Sets the instantiation SCN in a specific schema.

PROCEDURE DBMS_APPLY_ADM.SET_TABLE_INSTANTIATION_SCN
　　(*source_object_name* IN VARCHAR2,
　　source_database_name IN VARCHAR2,
　　instantiation_scn IN NUMBER,
　　apply_database_link IN VARCHAR2 DEFAULT NULL);
　　　Sets the instantiation SCN for a specific table.

PROCEDURE DBMS_APPLY_ADM.SET_UPDATE_CONFLICT_HANDLER
　　(*object_name* IN VARCHAR2,
　　method_name IN VARCHAR2,
　　resolution_column IN VARCHAR2,
　　column_list IN DBMS_UTILITY.NAME_ARRAY,
　　apply_database_link IN VARCHAR2 DEFAULT NULL);
　　　Manages an update conflict handler.

PROCEDURE DBMS_APPLY_ADM.START_APPLY
　　(*apply_name* IN VARCHAR2);
　　　Starts an apply process.

PROCEDURE DBMS_APPLY_ADM.STOP_APPLY
　　(*apply_name* IN VARCHAR2,
　　force IN BOOLEAN DEFAULT FALSE);
　　　Stops an apply process. The *force* parameter controls whether to immediately
　　　stop the apply process or to wait for applied transactions to complete.

DBMS_AQ

Provides calls to enqueue to and dequeue messages from queues created in the
Advanced Queuing facility. Advanced Queuing is Oracle's messaging infrastructure,
used for job queuing and communication.

Calls

PROCEDURE DBMS_AQ.ENQUEUE
　　(*queue_name* IN VARCHAR2,
　　enqueue_options IN DBMS_AQ.ENQUEUE_OPTIONS_T,
　　message_properties IN DBMS_AQ.MESSAGE_PROPERTIES_T,
　　payload IN <*payload_type*>,
　　msgid OUT RAW);
　　　Adds the message *payload* to the queue *queue_name*, using the options specified
　　　by the *enqueue_options* record. The *payload_type* is either *RAW* or the name of an
　　　object TYPE. Returns the pointer to the message in *msgid*.

```
PROCEDURE DBMS_AQ.DEQUEUE
    (queue_name IN VARCHAR2,
    dequeue_options IN DBMS_AQ.DEQUEUE_OPTIONS_T,
    message_properties OUT DBMS_AQ.MESSAGE_PROPERTIES_T,
    payload OUT <payload_type>,
    msgid OUT RAW);
```
This procedure has the same parameter meanings as DBMS_AQ.ENQUEUE.

```
DBMS_AQ.LISTEN
    (agent_list IN AQ$_AGENT_LIST_T,
    wait IN BINARY_INTEGER DEFAULT DBMS_AQ.FOREVER,
    agent OUT SYS.AQ$_AGENT);
```
Listens on one or more queues on behalf of a list of agents. New with Oracle8*i*.

```
DBMS_AQ.REGISTER
    (reg_list IN SYS.AQ$_REG_INFO_LIST,
    count IN NUMBER);
```
Registers an email address, PL/SQL procedure, or URL for message notification. New with Oracle9*i*.

```
DBMS_AQ.UNREGISTER
    (reg_list IN SYS.AQ$_REG_INFO_LIST,
    count IN NUMBER);
```
Unregisters a message notification destination. New with Oracle9*i*.

```
DBMS_AQ.POST
    (post_list IN SYS.AQ$_POST_INFO_LIST,
    count IN NUMBER);
```
Posts to a list of anonymous subscriptions for all clients who are registered for subscriptions. New with Oracle9*i*.

```
DBMS_AQ.BIND_AGENT
    (agent IN SYS.AQ$_AGENT,
    certificate IN VARCHAR2 DEFAULT NULL);
```
Creates an entry for the AQ agent in the LDAP directory. New with Oracle9*i*.

```
DBMS_AQ.UNBIND_AGENT
    (agent IN SYS.AQ$_AGENT);
```
Removes the entry for the AQ agent in the LDAP directory. New with Oracle9*i*.

DBMS_AQADM

Provides a set of programs you can use to create, manage, and drop queues and queue tables in the Oracle Advanced Queuing facility.

Calls

```
PROCEDURE DBMS_AQADM.CREATE_QUEUE_TABLE
    (queue_table IN VARCHAR2,
    queue_payload_type IN VARCHAR2,
    storage_clause IN VARCHAR2 DEFAULT NULL,
    sort_list IN VARCHAR2 DEFAULT NULL,
    multiple_consumers IN BOOLEAN DEFAULT FALSE,
    message_grouping IN BINARY_INTEGER DEFAULT NONE,
    comment IN VARCHAR2 DEFAULT NULL,
    auto_commit IN BOOLEAN DEFAULT TRUE,
    primary_instance IN BINARY_INTEGER DEFAULT 0,
```

```
    secondary_instance IN BINARY_INTEGER DEFAULT 0,
    compatible IN VARCHAR2 DEFAULT NULL]);
```
Creates a queue table named *queue_table* of *queue_payload_type* (RAW or the name of an object TYPE). The *primary_instance*, *secondary_instance*, and *compatible* parameters were new with Oracle8*i*.

PROCEDURE DBMS_AQADM.ALTER_QUEUE_TABLE
```
    (queue_table IN VARCHAR2,
    comment IN VARCHAR2 DEFAULT NULL,
    primary_instance IN BINARY_INTEGER DEFAULT NULL,
    secondary_instance IN BINARY_INTEGER DEFAULT NULL);
```
Alters the properties of an existing queue. New with Oracle8*i*.

PROCEDURE DBMS_AQADM.DROP_QUEUE_TABLE
```
    (queue_table IN VARCHAR2,
    force IN BOOLEAN DEFAULT FALSE,
    auto_commit IN BOOLEAN DEFAULT TRUE);
```
Drops the queue table *queue_table*.

PROCEDURE DBMS_AQADM.CREATE_QUEUE
```
    (queue_name IN VARCHAR2,
    queue_table IN VARCHAR2,
    queue_type IN BINARY_INTEGER DEFAULT NORMAL_QUEUE,
    max_retries IN NUMBER DEFAULT NULL,
    retry_delay IN NUMBER DEFAULT 0,
    retention_time IN NUMBER DEFAULT 0,
    dependency_tracking IN BOOLEAN DEFAULT FALSE,
    comment IN VARCHAR2 DEFAULT NULL,
    auto_commit IN BOOLEAN DEFAULT TRUE);
```
Creates a queue named *queue_name* in the queue table *queue_table*.

PROCEDURE DBMS_AQADM.CREATE_NP_QUEUE
```
    (queue_name IN VARCHAR2,
    multiple_consumers IN BOOLEAN DEFAULT FALSE,
    comment IN VARCHAR2 DEFAULT NULL);
```
Creates a nonpersistent queue. New with Oracle8*i*.

PROCEDURE DBMS_AQADM.ALTER_QUEUE
```
    (queue_name IN VARCHAR2,
    max_retries IN NUMBER DEFAULT NULL,
    retry_delay IN NUMBER DEFAULT NULL,
    retention_time IN NUMBER DEFAULT NULL,
    auto_commit IN BOOLEAN DEFAULT TRUE,
    comment IN VARCHAR2 DEFAULT NULL);
```
Alters the specified characteristics of the *queue_name* queue. New with Oracle8*i*.

PROCEDURE DBMS_AQADM.DROP_QUEUE
```
    (queue_name IN VARCHAR2,
    auto_commit IN BOOLEAN DEFAULT TRUE);
```
Drops the *queue_name* queue.

PROCEDURE DBMS_AQADM.START_QUEUE
```
    (queue_name IN VARCHAR2,
    enqueue IN BOOLEAN DEFAULT TRUE,
    dequeue IN BOOLEAN DEFAULT TRUE);
```
Starts the *queue_name* queue with *enqueue* and/or *dequeue* capabilities.

```
PROCEDURE DBMS_AQADM.STOP_QUEUE
   (queue_name IN VARCHAR2,
   enqueue IN BOOLEAN DEFAULT TRUE,
   dequeue IN BOOLEAN DEFAULT TRUE,
   wait IN BOOLEAN DEFAULT TRUE);
```
Stops the *queue_name* queue for *enqueue* and/or *dequeue* capabilities with or without waiting for completion of outstanding transactions.

```
PROCEDURE DBMS_AQADM.GRANT_SYSTEM_PRIVILEGE
   (privilege IN VARCHAR2,
   grantee IN VARCHAR2,
   admin_option IN BOOLEAN := FALSE);
```
Grants AQ system privileges to users and roles. Initially, only SYS and SYSTEM can use this procedure. New with Oracle8*i*.

```
PROCEDURE DBMS_AQADM.REVOKE_SYSTEM_PRIVILEGE
   (privilege IN VARCHAR2,
   grantee IN VARCHAR2);
```
Revokes AQ system privileges from users and roles. New with Oracle8*i*.

```
PROCEDURE DBMS_AQADM.GRANT_QUEUE_PRIVILEGE
   (privilege IN VARCHAR2,
   queue_name IN VARCHAR2,
   grantee IN VARCHAR2,
   admin_option IN BOOLEAN := FALSE);
```
Grants privileges on a queue to users and roles. New with Oracle8*i*.

```
PROCEDURE DBMS_AQADM.REVOKE_QUEUE_PRIVILEGE
   (privilege IN VARCHAR2,
   queue_name IN VARCHAR2,
   grantee IN VARCHAR2);
```
Revokes privileges on a queue from users and roles. New with Oracle8*i*.

```
PROCEDURE DBMS_AQADM.ADD_SUBSCRIBER
   (queue_name IN VARCHAR2,
   subscriber IN SYS.AQ$_AGENT,
   ,rule IN VARCHAR2 DEFAULT NULL
   [,transformation IN VARCHAR2 DEFAULT NULL]#);
```
Adds the *subscriber* agent to the *queue_name* queue. The *rule* parameter was new with Oracle8*i*. The *transformation* parameter was new with Oracle9*i*.

```
PROCEDURE DBMS_AQADM.ALTER_SUBSCRIBER
   (queue_name IN VARCHAR2,
   subscriber IN SYS.AQ$_AGENT,
   rule IN VARCHAR2
   [,transformation IN VARCHAR2]#);
```
Alters the properties of an existing subscriber. This procedure was new with Oracle8*i*. The *transformation* parameter was new with Oracle9*i*.

```
PROCEDURE DBMS_AQADM.REMOVE_SUBSCRIBER
   (queue_name IN VARCHAR2,
   subscriber IN SYS.AQ$_AGENT);
```
Removes the *subscriber* agent from the *queue_name* queue.

```
PROCEDURE DBMS_AQADM.SCHEDULE_PROPAGATION
   (queue_name IN VARCHAR2,
   destination IN VARCHAR2 DEFAULT NULL,
   start_time IN DATE DEFAULT SYSDATE,
```

    duration IN NUMBER DEFAULT NULL,
    next_time IN VARCHAR2 DEFAULT NULL,
    latency IN NUMBER DEFAULT 60);
      Schedules propagation of messages from a *queue_name* to a *destination* with properties specified by the other parameters.

PROCEDURE DBMS_AQADM.UNSCHEDULE_PROPAGATION
    (*queue_name* IN VARCHAR2,
    destination IN VARCHAR2 DEFAULT NULL);
      Unschedules a previously scheduled message propagation for *queue_name*.

PROCEDURE DBMS_AQADM.VERIFY_QUEUE_TYPES
    (*src_queue_name* IN VARCHAR2,
    dest_queue_name IN VARCHAR2,
    destination IN VARCHAR2 DEFAULT NULL,
    rc OUT BINARY_INTEGER);
      Verifies that source and destination queues have identical types.

PROCEDURE DBMS_AQADM.ALTER_PROPAGATION_SCHEDULE
    (*queue_name* IN VARCHAR2,
    destination IN VARCHAR2 DEFAULT NULL,
    duration IN NUMBER DEFAULT NULL,
    next_time IN VARCHAR2 DEFAULT NULL,
    latency IN NUMBER DEFAULT 60);
      Alters properties of an existing propagation schedule for *queue_name*. New with Oracle8*i*.

PROCEDURE DBMS_AQADM.ENABLE_PROPAGATION_SCHEDULE
    (*queue_name* IN VARCHAR2,
    destination IN VARCHAR2 DEFAULT NULL);
      Enables previously disabled propagation schedule. New with Oracle8*i*.

PROCEDURE DBMS_AQADM.DISABLE_PROPAGATION_SCHEDULE
    (*queue_name* IN VARCHAR2,
    destination IN VARCHAR2 DEFAULT NULL);
      Disables propagation schedule. New with Oracle8*i*.

PROCEDURE DBMS_AQADM.MIGRATE_QUEUE_TABLE
    (*queue_table* IN VARCHAR2,
    compatible IN VARCHAR2);
      Migrates an Oracle8 queue to an Oracle8*i* queue (*compatible* = '8.1'), or vice versa (*compatible* = '8.0'). New with Oracle8*i*.

PROCEDURE DBMS_AQADM.CREATE_AQ_AGENT
    (*agent_name* IN VARCHAR2,
    certificate_location IN VARCHAR2 DEFAULT NULL,
    enable_http IN BOOLEAN DEFAULT FALSE,
    enable_smtp IN BOOLEAN DEFAULT FALSE,
    enable_anyp IN BOOLEAN DEFAULT FALSE);
      Registers an *agent_name* for a queue using HTTP, SMTP, or any protocol. New with Oracle9*i*.

PROCEDURE DBMS_AQADM.ALTER_AQ_AGENT
    (*agent_name* IN VARCHAR2,
    certificate_location IN VARCHAR2 DEFAULT NULL,
    enable_http IN BOOLEAN DEFAULT FALSE,
    enable_smtp IN BOOLEAN DEFAULT FALSE,
    enable_anyp IN BOOLEAN DEFAULT FALSE);
      Changes characteristics of an existing AQ agent. New with Oracle9*i*.

PROCEDURE DBMS_AQADM.DROP_AQ_AGENT
    (*agent_name* IN VARCHAR2);
        Drops existing AQ agent. New with Oracle9*i*.

PROCEDURE DBMS_AQADM.ENABLE_DB_ACCESS
    (*agent_name* IN VARCHAR2,
    db_username IN VARCHAR2);
        Gives an AQ agent the privileges of a specific database user. New with Oracle9*i*.

PROCEDURE DBMS_AQADM.DISABLE_DB_ACCESS
    (*agent_name* IN VARCHAR2,
    db_username IN VARCHAR2);
        Revokes privileges of a specific database user from an AQ agent. New with Oracle9*i*.

PROCEDURE DBMS_AQADM.ADD_ALIAS_TO_LDAP
    (*alias* IN VARCHAR2,
    obj_location IN VARCHAR2);
        Creates an alias in an LDAP directory for a queue, agent, or JMSConnectionFactory. New with Oracle9*i*.

PROCEDURE DBMS_AQADM.DEL_ALIAS_TO_LDAP
    (*alias* IN VARCHAR2);
        Drops existing alias from an LDAP directory. New with Oracle9*i*.

PROCEDURE DBMS_AQADM.GRANT_TYPE_ACCESS
    (*user_name* IN VARCHAR2);
        Grants to *user_name* the ability to create queues that work with multiple consumers. This procedure is not supported from Oracle8*i*.

FUNCTION DBMS_AQADM.QUEUE_SUBSCRIBERS
    (*queue_name* IN VARCHAR2)
    RETURN AQ$_SUBSCRIBER_LIST_T;
        Returns the list of subscribers for the *queue_name* queue. This procedure is not supported from Oracle8*i*.

PROCEDURE DBMS_AQADM.START_TIME_MANAGER;
        Starts the Queue Monitor process. This procedure is not supported from Oracle8.

PROCEDURE DBMS_AQADM.STOP_TIME_MANAGER;
        Stops the Queue Monitor process. This procedure is not supported from Oracle8.

DBMS_AQELM

Provides procedures to manage Advanced Queuing asynchronous notification. New with Oracle9*i*.

Calls

PROCEDURE DBMS_AQELM.SET_MAILHOST
    (*mailhost* IN VARCHAR2);
        Sets the hostname for the SMTP server.

PROCEDURE DBMS_AQELM.GET_MAILHOST
    (*mailhost* OUT VARCHAR2);
        Gets the hostname for the SMTP server.

PROCEDURE DBMS_AQELM.SET_MAILPORT
   (*mailport* IN NUMBER);
     Sets the port for the SMTP server.

PROCEDURE DBMS_AQELM.GET_MAILPORT
   (*mailport* OUT NUMBER);
     Gets the port for the SMTP server.

PROCEDURE DBMS_AQELM.SET_SENDFROM
   (*sendfrom* IN VARCHAR2);
     Sets the address from which to send.

PROCEDURE DBMS_AQELM.GET_SENDFROM
   (*sendfrom* OUT VARCHAR2);
     Gets the address to which to send.

PROCEDURE DBMS_AQELM.SET_PROXY
   (*proxy* IN VARCHAR2,
   no_proxy_domains IN VARCHAR2 DEFAULT NULL);
     Sets the proxy server name for HTTP requests, except requests from hosts in the
     no_proxy_domains parameter.

PROCEDURE DBMS_AQELM.GET_PROXY
   (*proxy* OUT VARCHAR2,
   no_proxy_domains OUT VARCHAR2 DEFAULT NULL);
     Gets the proxy server name for HTTP requests and the hosts excluded in the *no_proxy_domains* parameter.

DBMS_CAPTURE_ADM

Includes procedures for managing capture processes, a part of Oracle Streams. New with Oracle9*i*.

Calls

PROCEDURE DBMS_CAPTURE_ADM.ABORT_GLOBAL_INSTANTIATION;
     Removes data dictionary information about the database instantiation. This procedure is the opposite of the PREPARE_GLOBAL_INSTANTIATION procedure.

PROCEDURE DBMS_CAPTURE_ADM.ABORT_SCHEMA_INSTANTIATION
   (*schema_name* IN VARCHAR2);
     Removes data dictionary information about the schema instantiation. This procedure is the opposite of the PREPARE_SCHEMA_INSTANTIATION procedure.

PROCEDURE DBMS_CAPTURE_ADM.ABORT_TABLE_INSTANTIATION
   (*table_name* IN VARCHAR2);
     Removes data dictionary information about the table instantiation. This procedure is the opposite of the PREPARE_TABLE_INSTANTIATION procedure.

PROCEDURE DBMS_CAPTURE_ADM.ALTER_CAPTURE
   (*capture_name* IN VARCHAR2,
   rule_set_name IN VARCHAR2 DEFAULT NULL,
   remove_rule_set IN BOOLEAN DEFAULT FALSE,
   start_scn IN NUMBER DEFAULT NULL);
     Alters an existing capture process.

```
PROCEDURE DBMS_CAPTURE_ADM.CREATE_CAPTURE
   (queue_name IN VARCHAR2,
   capture_name IN VARCHAR2,
   rule_set_name IN VARCHAR2 DEFAULT NULL,
   start_scn IN NUMBER DEFAULT NULL);
```
   Creates a capture process.

```
PROCEDURE DBMS_CAPTURE_ADM.DROP_CAPTURE
   (capture_name IN VARCHAR2);
```
   Drops an existing capture process.

```
PROCEDURE DBMS_CAPTURE_ADM.PREPARE_GLOBAL_INSTANTIATION;
```
   Performs the synchronization necessary to instantiate all the tables in a database at another database.

```
PROCEDURE DBMS_CAPTURE_ADM.PREPARE_SCHEMA_INSTANTIATION
   (schema_name IN VARCHAR2);
```
   Performs the synchronization necessary to instantiate all the tables in a schema at another database.

```
PROCEDURE DBMS_CAPTURE_ADM.PREPARE_TABLE_INSTANTIATION
   (table_name IN VARCHAR2);
```
   Performs the synchronization necessary to instantiate a table in another database.

```
PROCEDURE DBMS_CAPTURE_ADM.SET_PARAMETER
   (capture_name IN VARCHAR2,
   parameter IN VARCHAR2,
   value IN VARCHAR2);
```
   Sets a parameter for a capture process.

```
PROCEDURE DBMS_CAPTURE_ADM.START_CAPTURE
   (capture_name IN VARCHAR2);
```
   Starts a capture process.

```
PROCEDURE DBMS_CAPTURE_ADM.STOP_CAPTURE
   (capture_name IN VARCHAR2,
   force IN BOOLEAN DEFAULT FALSE);
```
   Stops a capture process. If *force*, the capture process is stopped immediately; otherwise, the capture process stops after it captures its current transaction.

DBMS_DDL

Contains procedures to recompile stored code, analyze and compute statistics for database objects, and modify the referenceability of object identifiers in Oracle.

Calls

```
PROCEDURE DBMS_DDL.ALTER_COMPILE
   (type IN VARCHAR2,
   schema IN VARCHAR2,
   name IN VARCHAR2);
```
   Recompiles the stored PL/SQL object *name* (case-sensitive) owned by *schema* of type *type*. A NULL *schema* uses the current schema. Valid values for *type* are PROCEDURE, FUNCTION, PACKAGE, PACKAGE BODY, and PACKAGE SPECIFICATION.

PROCEDURE DBMS_DDL.ALTER_TABLE_NOT_REFERENCEABLE
   (*table_name* IN VARCHAR2,
   table_schema IN VARCHAR2 DEFAULT NULL,
   affected_schema IN VARCHAR2 DEFAULT NULL);
     Reverts references to object *table_name* by schema *affected_schema* from *table_name* owned by *table_schema* to the default. New with Oracle9*i*.

PROCEDURE DBMS_DDL.ALTER_TABLE_REFERENCEABLE
   (*table_name* IN VARCHAR2,
   table_schema IN VARCHAR2 DEFAULT NULL,
   affected_schema IN VARCHAR2 DEFAULT NULL);
     Makes the object table owned by *table_schema* the table referenced from schema *affected_schema* for object name *table_name*. New with Oracle9*i*.

PROCEDURE DBMS_DDL.ANALYZE_OBJECT
   (*type* IN VARCHAR2,
   schema IN VARCHAR2,
   name IN VARCHAR2,
   method IN VARCHAR2,
   estimate_rows IN NUMBER DEFAULT NULL,
   estimate_percent IN NUMBER DEFAULT NULL,
   method_opt IN VARCHAR2 DEFAULT NULL,
   partname VARCHAR2 DEFAULT NULL);
     Analyzes database object *name* owned by *schema* of type *type* (TABLE, INDEX, or CLUSTER) using option *method* (ESTIMATE, NULL, or DELETE). When *method* is ESTIMATE, you must specify either *estimate_rows* or *estimate_percent* to identify sample size. Additional analyze options specifiable by *method_opt* are *FOR TABLE, FOR ALL COLUMNS [SIZE N], FOR ALL INDEXED COLUMNS [SIZE N]*, and *FOR ALL INDEXES*. The *partname* parameter refers to a partition name.

PROCEDURE DBMS_DDL.SET_TRIGGER_FIRING_PROPERTY
   (*trig_owner* IN VARCHAR2,
   trig_name IN VARCHAR2,
   fire_once IN BOOLEAN);
     Sets the firing property of *trig_name* with the *fire_once* value. New with Oracle9*i*.

PROCEDURE DBMS_DDL.IS_TRIGGER_FIRE_ONCE
   (*trig_owner* IN VARCHAR2,
   trig_name IN VARCHAR2);
     Returns TRUE if *trig_name* is set to fire once, FALSE if not. New with Oracle9*i*.

DBMS_DEBUG

Provides an API into the PL/SQL debugger layer. To use this API, you must have two sessions active—one session for the PL/SQL code and one for the debugger. You must also enable debugging for the session with the command:

    ALTER SESSION SET PLSQL_DEBUG = TRUE

and recompile the target of debugging with the commands:

    ALTER unit_type unit_name COMPILE DEBUG;
    ALTER PACKAGE | TYPE unit_name COMPILE DEBUG BODY;

You can call the PROBE_VERSION, SELF_CHECK, and SET_TIMEOUT procedures from either session. You must call the INITIALIZE, DEBUG_ON, and DEBUG_OFF procedures from the target session. You can make all other calls from the debugging session.

This package was new with Oracle8*i*.

Calls

PROCEDURE DBMS_DEBUG.PROBE_VERSION
  (*major* OUT BINARY_INTEGER,
  minor OUT BINARY_INTEGER))
> Specifies major and minor version number of the package.

PROCEDURE DBMS_DEBUG.SELF_CHECK
  (*timeout* IN BINARY_INTEGER DEFAULT 60);
> If this call does not return successfully in *timeout* seconds, an incorrect version of DBMS_DEBUG exists on the server.

FUNCTION DBMS_DEBUG.SET_TIMEOUT
  (*timeout* IN BINARY_INTEGER)
  RETURN BINARY_INTEGER;
> Sets and returns the *timeout* in seconds.

FUNCTION DBMS_DEBUG.INITIALIZE
  (*debug_session_id* IN VARCHAR2 := NULL,
  diagnostics IN BINARY_INTEGER := 0)
  RETURN VARCHAR2;
> Initializes *debug_session_id*. If no value is supplied, an ID is automatically generated. *diagnostics* can be either 0, for no diagnostics in the trace file, or 1, to include diagnostics. The procedure returns the session ID.

PROCEDURE DBMS_DEBUG.DEBUG_ON
  (*no_client_side_plsql_engine* BOOLEAN := TRUE,
  immediate BOOLEAN := FALSE);
> Turns on debugging on the server, unless the first parameter is set to FALSE. If *immediate* is not TRUE, the session turns on debugging at the completion of the call; otherwise, debugging starts immediately.

PROCEDURE DBMS_DEBUG.DEBUG_OFF;
> Turns debugging off.

PROCEDURE DBMS_DEBUG.ATTACH_SESSION
  (*debug_session_id* IN VARCHAR2,
  diagnostics IN BINARY_INTEGER := 0);
> Notifies the debugging session about the target program. If *diagnostics* is not the default of 0, will generate diagnostic output.

FUNCTION DBMS_DEBUG.SYNCHRONIZE
  (*run_info* OUT runtime_info,
  info_requested IN BINARY_INTEGER := NULL)
  RETURN BINARY_INTEGER;
> When the target program signals an event, if *info_requested* is not NULL, it calls DBMS_DEBUG.GET_RUNTIME_INFO. The function returns a code indicating success, timeout, or another error.

PROCEDURE DBMS_DEBUG.SHOW_SOURCE
  (*first_line* IN BINARY_INTEGER,
  last_line IN BINARY_INTEGER,
  source OUT vc2_table);

```
PROCEDURE DBMS_DEBUG.SHOW_SOURCE
    (first_line IN BINARY_INTEGER,
    last_line IN BINARY_INTEGER,
    window IN BINARY_INTEGER,
    print_arrow IN BINARY_INTEGER,
    buffer IN OUT VARCHAR2,
    buflen IN BINARY_INTEGER,
    pieces OUT BINARY_INTEGER);
```

Returns the source of nonpersistent programs. The first version returns all the source in a table; the second returns formatted source but may not include all the source code.

```
PROCEDURE DBMS_DEBUG.PRINT_BACKTRACE
    (listing IN OUT VARCHAR2 | backtrace_table);
```

Prints a backtrace listing from the current execution stack.

```
FUNCTION DBMS_DEBUG.CONTINUE
    (run_info IN OUT runtime_info,
    breakflags IN BINARY_INTEGER,
    info_requested IN BINARY_INTEGER := NULL)
    RETURN BINARY_INTEGER;
```

Returns the status of program in *run_info*. *breakflags* provides a mask for events desired. *info_requested* designates what information should be returned when the program stops. The procedure returns a success code like the DBMS_DEBUG. SYNCHRONIZE procedure.

```
FUNCTION DBMS_DEBUG.SET_BREAKPOINT
    (program IN program_info,
    line# IN BINARY_INTEGER,
    breakpoint# OUT BINARY_INTEGER,
    fuzzy IN BINARY_INTEGER := 0,
    iterations IN BINARY_INTEGER := 0)
    RETURN BINARY_INTEGER;
```

Sets a breakpoint in the target session code. The *fuzzy* parameter applies if there is no executable code at the indicated line; 1 indicates a search forward for a line, while -1 indicates a search backward. As of Oracle9i Release 2, *fuzzy* and *iterations* were not yet implemented, but they should be available in a later release. The procedure returns a success code like the DBMS_DEBUG.SYNCHRONIZE procedure.

```
FUNCTION DBMS_DEBUG.DELETE_BREAKPOINT
    (breakpoint IN BINARY_INTEGER)
    RETURN BINARY_INTEGER;
```

Deletes an existing breakpoint. The procedure returns a success code similar to the codes offered by the DBMS_DEBUG.SYNCHRONIZE procedure.

```
FUNCTION DBMS_DEBUG.DISABLE_BREAKPOINT
    (breakpoint IN BINARY_INTEGER)
    RETURN BINARY_INTEGER;
```

Disables a breakpoint. The procedure returns a success code similar to the codes offered by the DBMS_DEBUG.SYNCHRONIZE procedure.

FUNCTION DBMS_DEBUG.ENABLE_BREAKPOINT
    (*breakpoint* IN BINARY_INTEGER)
    RETURN BINARY_INTEGER;
> Enables a breakpoint. The procedure returns a success code similar to the codes offered by the DBMS_DEBUG.SYNCHRONIZE procedure.

PROCEDURE DBMS_DEBUG.SHOW_BREAKPOINTS
    (*listing* {IN OUT VARCHAR2|OUT breakpoint_table});
> Returns a listing of existing breakpoints.

FUNCTION DBMS_DEBUG.GET_VALUE
    (*variable_name* IN VARCHAR2,
    {*frame#* IN BINARY_INTEGER | *handle* IN program_info},
    scalar_value OUT VARCHAR2,
    format IN VARCHAR2 := NULL)
    RETURN BINARY_INTEGER;
> Returns the value of package variables. The procedure returns a success code similar to the codes offered by the DBMS_DEBUG.SYNCHRONIZE procedure.

FUNCTION DBMS_DEBUG.SET_VALUE
    ({*frame#* IN BINARY_INTEGER | *handle* IN program_info},
    assignment_statement IN VARCHAR2)
    RETURN BINARY_INTEGER;
> Sets the value for a package variable. The procedure returns a success code similar to the codes offered by the DBMS_DEBUG.SYNCHRONIZE procedure.

PROCEDURE DBMS_DEBUG.DETACH_SESSION;
> Stops debugging the target session.

FUNCTION DBMS_DEBUG.GET_RUNTIME_INFO
    (*info_requested* IN BINARY_INTEGER,
    run_info OUT runtime_info)
    RETURN BINARY_INTEGER;
> Returns information about current program. Beginning with Oracle8*i*, used only with client-side PL/SQL.

FUNCTION DBMS_DEBUG.GET_INDEXES
    (*varname* IN VARCHAR2,
    frame# IN BINARY_INTEGER,
    handle IN program_info,
    entries OUT index_table)
    RETURN BINARY_INTEGER;
> Returns the set of *varname*'s indexes. Returns an error if *varname* is not an indexed table.

PROCEDURE DBMS_DEBUG.EXECUTE
    (*what* IN VARCHAR2,
    frame# IN BINARY_INTEGER,
    bind_results IN BINARY_INTEGER,
    results IN OUT NOCOPY dbms_debug_vc2coll,
    errm IN OUT NOCOPY VARCHAR2);
> Executes code in *what* in the target session. *bind_results* indicates whether to bind the source to results in order to return values (value 1) or not (value 0).

PROCEDURE DBMS_DEBUG.PRINT_INSTANTIATIONS
   (*pkgs* IN OUT NOCOPY backtrace_table,
   flags IN BINARY_NUMBER);

>Returns list of packages that have been instantiated in the target session. The *flags* parameter indicates the scope of the report. New with Oracle9*i*.

FUNCTION DBMS_DEBUG.TARGET_PROGRAM_RUNNING RETURN BOOLEAN;

>Returns TRUE if target session is currently executing a procedure. New with Oracle9*i*.

PROCEDURE DBMS_DEBUG.PING;

>Pings target session to prevent it from timing out. Timeout options are set on session with DBMS_DEBUG.SET_TIMEOUT_BEHAVIOR. New with Oracle9*i*.

PROCEDURE DBMS_DEBUG.SET_TIMEOUT_BEHAVIOR
   (*behavior* IN PLS_INTEGER);

>Sets action for a timeout in the target session. New with Oracle9*i*.

FUNCTION DBMS_DEBUG.GET_TIMEOUT_BEHAVIOR
   RETURN BINARY_INTEGER;

>Returns timeout behavior. New with Oracle9*i*.

FUNCTION DBMS_DEBUG.SET_OER_BREAKPOINT
   (*oer* IN PLS_INTEGER)
   RETURN PLS_INTEGER;

>Sets an OER breakpoint. (An OER is an Oracle error returned from the Oracle kernel.) For more information about OER breakpoints, see the Oracle documentation. New with Oracle9*i*.

FUNCTION DBMS_DEBUG.DELETE_OER_BREAKPOINT
   (*oer* IN PLS_INTEGER)
   RETURN PLS_INTEGER;

>Deletes an OER breakpoint. New with Oracle9*i*.

PROCEDURE DBMS_DEBUG.SHOW_BREAKPOINTS
   (*code_breakpoints* OUT breakpoint_table,
   oer_breakpoints OUT oer_table);

>Returns existing breakpoints.

DBMS_DEFER

Provides procedures that allow you to interact with a replicated transactional deferred remote procedure call used in replication. New with Oracle8*i*.

Calls

PROCEDURE DBMS_DEFER.CALL
   (*schema_name* IN VARCHAR2,
   package_name IN VARCHAR2,
   proc_name IN VARCHAR2,
   arc_count IN NATURAL,
   {*node* IN node_list_t | *group_name* IN VARCHAR DEFAULT ''});

>Builds a deferred call to a remote procedure. The last parameter was new with Oracle8*i*.

```
PROCEDURE DBMS_DEFER.COMMIT_WORK
   (commit_work_comment IN VARCHAR2);
```
   Performs a transaction commit after checking for well-formed deferred remote procedure calls.

```
PROCEDURE DBMS_DEFER.datatype_ARG
   (arg IN datatype);
```
   Specifies datatype for parameters. Used after the DBMS_DEFER.CALL procedure.

```
PROCEDURE DBMS_DEFER.TRANSACTION
   (nodes IN node_list_t);
```
   where *nodes* is a list of fully qualified database names to which you want to propagate the deferred transactions.

DBMS_DEFER_QUERY

Allows you to query the deferred transactions queue data that is not exposed through normal data dictionary views.

```
FUNCTION DBMS_DEFER_QUERY.GET_ARG_FORM
   (callno IN NUMBER,
   arg_no IN NUMBER,
   deferred_tran_id IN VARCHAR2)
   RETURN NUMBER;
```
   Returns the character set form of the deferred call parameter.

```
FUNCTION DBMS_DEFER_QUERY.GET_ARG_TYPE
   (callno IN NUMBER,
   arg_no IN NUMBER,
   deferred_tran_id IN VARCHAR2)
   RETURN NUMBER;
```
   Determines the type of an argument in a deferred call.

```
PROCEDURE DBMS_DEFER_QUERY.GET_CALL_ARGS
   (callno IN NUMBER,
   startarg IN NUMBER := 1,
   argcnt IN NUMBER,
   argsize IN NUMBER,
   tran_id IN VARCHAR2,
   date_fmt IN VARCHAR2,
   types OUT TYPE_ANY,
   forms OUT TYPE_ANY,
   vals OUT VAL_ANY);
```
   Returns the text version of the arguments of *callno*.

```
FUNCTION DBMS_DEFER_QUERY.GET_datatype_ARG
   (callno IN NUMBER,
   arg_no IN NUMBER,
   deferred_tran_id IN VARCHAR2)
   RETURN datatype;
```
   Determines the value of an argument in *callno*.

FUNCTION DBMS_DEFER_QUERY.GET_OBJECT_NULL_VECTOR_ARG
    (*callno* IN NUMBER,
    arg_no IN NUMBER,
    deferred_tran_id IN VARCHAR2)
    RETURN SYSTEM.REPCAT$_OBJECT_NULL_VECTOR;
    Returns type information for a column object. New with Oracle9*i*.

DBMS_DEFER_SYS

Provides procedures that allow you to manage default replication nodes used in replication.

Calls

PROCEDURE DBMS_DEFER_SYS.ADD_DEFAULT_DEST
    (*dblink* IN VARCHAR2);
    Adds the fully qualified database name (*dblink*) to the DEFDEFAULTDEST data dictionary view.

PROCEDURE DBMS_DEFER_SYS.CLEAR_PROP_STATISTICS
    (*dblink* IN VARCHAR2);
    Clears propagation statistics for *dblink* from the DEFSCHEDULE data dictionary view. New with Oracle9*i*.

PROCEDURE DBMS_DEFER_SYS.DELETE_DEFAULT_DEST
    (*dblink* IN VARCHAR2);
    Removes the *dblink* database from the DEFDEFAULTDEST data dictionary view.

PROCEDURE DBMS_DEFER_SYS.DELETE_DEF_DESTINATION
    (*destination* IN VARCHAR2,
    force IN BOOLEAN := FALSE);
    Removes the *destination* database from the DEFSCHEDULE view. If *force* is TRUE, Oracle ignores all safety checks and deletes the destination.

PROCEDURE DBMS_DEFER_SYS.DELETE_ERROR
    (*deferred_tran_id* IN VARCHAR2,
    destination IN VARCHAR2);
    Deletes *deferred_tran_id* in *destination* from the DEFERROR data dictionary view.

PROCEDURE DBMS_DEFER_SYS.DELETE_TRAN
    (*deferred_tran_id* IN VARCHAR2,
    destination IN VARCHAR2);
    Deletes *deferred_tran_id* in *destination* from the DEFTRANDEST data dictionary view.

FUNCTION DBMS_DEFER_SYS.DISABLED
    (*destination* IN VARCHAR2)
    RETURN BOOLEAN;
    Returns if propagation from current site to *destination* is enabled.

FUNCTION DBMS_DEFER_SYS.EXCLUDE_PUSH
    (*timeout* IN INTEGER)
    RETURN INTEGER;
    Prevents deferred transaction PUSHes for the duration of the transaction. If lock to prevent PUSHes cannot be acquired in *timeout* seconds, returns 1.

PROCEDURE DBMS_DEFER_SYS.EXECUTE_ERROR
   (*deferred_tran_id* IN VARCHAR2,
   destination IN VARCHAR2);
     Reexecutes *deferred_tran_id* in *destination* if it failed because of an error in the
     original security context.

PROCEDURE DBMS_DEFER_SYS.EXECUTE_ERROR_AS_USER
   (*deferred_tran_id* IN VARCHAR2,
   destination IN VARCHAR2);
     Reexecutes *deferred_tran_id* in *destination* if it failed because of an error in the
     context of the connected user.

FUNCTION DBMS_DEFER_SYS.PURGE
   (*purge_method* IN BINARY_INTEGER := purge_method,
   rollback_segment IN VARCHAR2 := NULL,
   startup_seconds IN BINARY_INTEGER := 0,
   execution_seconds IN BINARY_INTEGER := NULL | SECONDS_INFINITY,
   delay_seconds IN BINARY_INTEGER := 0,
   transaction_count IN BINARY_INTEGER := NULL | TRANSACTIONS_INFINITY,
   write_trace IN BOOLEAN := NULL)
   RETURN BINARY_INTEGER;
     Purges pushed transactions from the deferred transaction view on the current
     master site. Default values SECONDS_INFINITY and TRANSACTIONS_
     INFINITY were changed in Oracle9*i*.

FUNCTION DBMS_DEFER_SYS.PUSH
   (*destination* IN VARCHAR2,
   parallelism IN BINARY_INTEGER := 0,
   heap_size IN BINARY_INTEGER := 0,
   stop_on_error IN BOOLEAN := FALSE,
   write_trace IN BOOLEAN := FALSE,
   startup_seconds IN BINARY_INTEGER := 0,
   execution_seconds IN BINARY_INTEGER := SECONDS_INFINITY,
   delay_seconds IN BINARY_INTEGER := 0,
   transaction_count IN BINARY_INTEGER := TRANSACTIONS_INFINITY,
   deliver_order_limit IN BOOLEAN := NULL)
   RETURN BINARY_INTEGER;
     Forces a deferred RPC queue to be pushed (propagated) to *destination*.

PROCEDURE DBMS_DEFER_SYS.REGISTER_PROPAGATOR
   (*username* IN VARCHAR2);
     Registers *username* as the propagator for the local database and grants necessary
     privileges.

PROCEDURE DBMS_DEFER_SYS.SCHEDULE_PURGE
   (*interval* IN VARCHAR2,
   next_date IN DATE,
   reset IN BOOLEAN DEFAULT NULL,
   purge_method IN BINARY_INTEGER DEFAULT NULL,
   rollback_segment IN VARCHAR2 DEFAULT NULL,
   startup_seconds IN BINARY_INTEGER DEFAULT 0,
   execution_seconds IN BINARY_INTEGER := NULL | SECONDS_INFINITY,
   delay_seconds IN BINARY_INTEGER := 0,
   transaction_count IN BINARY_INTEGER := NULL | TRANSACTIONS_INFINITY,
   write_trace IN BOOLEAN := NULL);
     Schedules a purge job for deferred transactions. Default values SECONDS_
     INFINITY and TRANSACTIONS_INFINITY were changed in Oracle9*i*.

```
PROCEDURE DBMS_DEFER_SYS.SCHEDULE_PUSH
   (destination IN VARCHAR2,
   interval IN VARCHAR2,
   next_date IN DATE,
   reset IN BOOLEAN := FALSE,
   parallelism IN BINARY_INTEGER := NULL,
   heap_size IN BINARY_INTEGER := NULL,
   stop_on_error IN BOOLEAN := NULL,
   write_trace IN BOOLEAN := NULL,
   startup_seconds IN BINARY_INTEGER := 0,
   execution_seconds IN BINARY_INTEGER := NULL | SECONDS_INFINITY,
   delay_seconds IN BINARY_INTEGER := 0,
   transaction_count IN BINARY_INTEGER := NULL | TRANSACTIONS_INFINITY
   [,write_trace IN BOOLEAN := NULL]#);
```

Schedules a job to push the deferred transaction queue to *destination*. Default values SECONDS_INFINITY and TRANSACTIONS_INFINITY were changed in Oracle9*i*. The *write_trace* parameter was new with Oracle9*i*.

```
PROCEDURE DBMS_DEFER_SYS.SET_DISABLED
   (destination IN VARCHAR2,
   disabled IN BOOLEAN := TRUE
   [,catchup IN RAW := '00']#
   [,override IN BOOLEAN := FALSE]#);
```

Disables or enables propagation of deferred transaction queue to *destination*. Parameters *catchup*, which is the extension identifier for adding new master sites to a master group without quiescing the master group, and *override*, which can force Oracle to ignore the disable state set internally for synchronization, were new with Oracle9*i*.

```
PROCEDURE DBMS_DEFER_SYS.UNREGISTER_PROPAGATOR
   (username IN VARCHAR2,
   timeout IN INTEGER DEFAULT DBMS_LOCK.MAXWAIT);
```

Removes *username* from local database and removes privileges from that user.

```
PROCEDURE DBMS_DEFER_SYS.UNSCHEDULE_PURGE( );
```

Stops automatic purges of pushed transactions.

```
PROCEDURE DBMS_DEFER_SYS.UNSCHEDULE_PUSH
   (destination IN VARCHAR2);
```

Stops automatic pushes from *destination*.

DBMS_DESCRIBE

Contains a single procedure used to describe the arguments of a stored PL/SQL procedure or function.

Call

```
PROCEDURE DBMS_DESCRIBE.DESCRIBE_PROCEDURE
   (object_name IN VARCHAR2,
   reserved1 IN VARCHAR2,
   reserved2 IN VARCHAR2,
   overload OUT DBMS_DESCRIBE.NUMBER_TABLE,
   position OUT DBMS_DESCRIBE.NUMBER_TABLE,
   level OUT DBMS_DESCRIBE.NUMBER_TABLE,
```

```
argument_name OUT DBMS_DESCRIBE.VARCHAR2_TABLE,
datatype OUT DBMS_DESCRIBE.NUMBER_TABLE,
default_value OUT DBMS_DESCRIBE.NUMBER_TABLE,
in_out OUT DBMS_DESCRIBE.NUMBER_TABLE,
length OUT DBMS_DESCRIBE.NUMBER_TABLE,
precision OUT DBMS_DESCRIBE.NUMBER_TABLE,
scale OUT DBMS_DESCRIBE.NUMBER_TABLE,
radix OUT DBMS_DESCRIBE.NUMBER_TABLE,
spare OUT DBMS_DESCRIBE.NUMBER_TABLE);
```
Returns information about the parameters and RETURN type (if a function) of the specified object (procedure or function) in a set of PL/SQL tables, whose types are described in the same package.

DBMS_DISTRIBUTED_TRUST_ADMIN

Procedures used to maintain Trusted Servers. The program units in this package maintain the Trusted Server list. If a database is not trusted, Oracle will refuse database links from it.

Calls

```
DBMS_DISTRIBUTED_TRUST_ADMIN.ALLOW_ALL;
```
Empties the Trusted Server list and indicates that all servers are members of a trusted domain.

```
DBMS_DISTRIBUTED_TRUST_ADMIN.ALLOW_SERVER
   (server IN VARCHAR2);
```
Ensures that server is trusted, even if you have previously issued the DENY_ALL procedure in this package.

```
DBMS_DISTRIBUTED_TRUST_ADMIN.DENY_ALL;
```
Empties the Trusted Server list and denies access to all servers.

```
DBMS_DISTRIBUTED_TRUST_ADMIN.DENY_SERVER
   (server IN VARCHAR2);
```
Ensures that server is not trusted, even if you have previously issued the ALLOW_ALL procedure in this package.

DBMS_FGA

Provides procedures that allow you to administer policies used for fine-grained auditing. New with Oracle9i.

Calls

```
PROCEDURE DBMS_FGA.ADD_POLICY
   (object_schema IN VARCHAR2,
   object_name IN VARCHAR2,
   policy_name IN VARCHAR2,
   audit_condition IN VARCHAR2,
   audit_column IN VARCHAR2,
   handler_schema IN VARCHAR2,
   handler_module IN VARCHAR2,
   enable BOOLEAN);
```
Assigns audit policy_name and handler_module to object_name in object_schema.

```
PROCEDURE DBMS_FGA.DROP_POLICY
    (object_schema IN VARCHAR2,
    object_name IN VARCHAR2,
    policy_name IN VARCHAR2);
```
   Drops audit *policy_name* for *object_name* in *object_schema*.

```
PROCEDURE DBMS_FGA.ENABLE_POLICY
    (object_schema IN VARCHAR2 DEFAULT NULL,
    object_name IN VARCHAR2,
    policy_name IN VARCHAR2,
    enable BOOLEAN DEFAULT TRUE);
```
   Enables audit *policy_name*.

```
PROCEDURE DBMS_FGA.DISABLE_POLICY
    (object_schema IN VARCHAR2 DEFAULT NULL,
    object_name IN VARCHAR2,
    policy_name IN VARCHAR2);
```
   Disables audit *policy_name*.

DBMS_FLASHBACK

Provides procedures that allow you to manage flashback query. New with Oracle9*i*.

Calls

```
PROCEDURE DBMS_FLASHBACK.ENABLE_AT_TIME
    (query_time IN TIMESTAMP);
```
   Enables flashback mode for the entire session for snapshot at *query_time*.

```
PROCEDURE DBMS_FLASHBACK.ENABLE_AT_SYSTEM_CHANGE_NUMBER
    (query_scn IN NUMBER);
```
   Enables flashback mode for the entire session for snapshot at *query_scn*.

```
FUNCTION DBMS_FLASHBACK.GET_SYSTEM_CHANGE_NUMBER( )
    RETURN NUMBER;
```
   Returns current SCN for later use.

```
PROCEDURE DBMS_FLASHBACK.DISABLE;
```
   Disables flashback mode for entire session.

DBMS_HS

Provides procedures that allow you to work with Heterogeneous Services (HS). Not supported in Oracle9*i*.

Calls

```
PROCEDURE DBMS_HS.ALTER_BASE_CAPS
    (CAP_number IN NUMBER,
    new_CAP_number IN NUMBER := -1e-130,
    new_CAP_description IN VARCHAR2 := '-');
```
   Alters the row identified by *CAP_number* in the HS$_BASE_CAPS table. New with Oracle8*i*.

```
PROCEDURE DBMS_HS.ALTER_BASE_DD
   (DD_table_name IN VARCHAR2,
   new_DD_table_name IN VARCHAR := '-',
   new_DD_table_name_descr IN VARCHAR2 := '-');
```
Alters the row identified by *DD_table_name* in the HS$_BASE_DD table. New with Oracle8*i*.

```
PROCEDURE DBMS_HS.ALTER_CLASS_CAPS
   (FDS_class_name IN VARCHAR2,
   CAP_number IN NUMBER,
   new_FDS_class_name IN VARCHAR2 := '-',
   new_CAP_number IN NUMBER := -1e-130,
   new_context IN NUMBER := -1e-130,
   new_translation IN VARCHAR2 := '-',
   new_additional_info NUMBER := -1e-130);
```
Alters the row identified by *CAP_number* in the HS$_CLASS_CAPS table. New with Oracle8*i*.

```
PROCEDURE DBMS_HS.ALTER_CLASS_DD
   (FDS_class_name IN VARCHAR2,
   DD_table_name IN VARCHAR2,
   new_FDS_class_name IN VARCHAR2 := '-',
   new_DD_table_name IN NUMBER := -1e-130,
   new_translation_type IN CHAR := '-',
   new_translation_text IN VARCHAR2 := '-');
```
Alters the contents of the HS$_CLASS_DD table. New with Oracle8*i*.

```
PROCEDURE DBMS_HS.ALTER_CLASS_INIT
   (FDS_class_name IN VARCHAR2,
   init_value_name IN VARCHAR2,
   new_FDS_class_name IN VARCHAR2 := '-',
   new_init_value_name IN VARCHAR2 := '-',
   new_init_value IN VARCHAR2 := '-',
   new_init_value_type IN VARCHAR2 := '-');
```
Alters the contents of the HS$_CLASS_INIT table. New with Oracle8*i*.

```
PROCEDURE DBMS_HS.ALTER_FDS_CLASS
   (FDS_class_name IN VARCHAR2,
   new_FDS_class_name IN VARCHAR2 := '-',
   new_FDS_class_comments IN VARCHAR2 := '-');
```
Alters the contents of the HS$_FDS_CLASS table for *FDS_class_name*. New with Oracle8*i*.

```
PROCEDURE DBMS_HS.ALTER_FDS_INST
   (FDS_inst_name IN VARCHAR2,
   FDS_class_name IN VARCHAR2,
   new_FDS_inst_name IN VARCHAR2 := '-',
   new_FDS_class_name IN VARCHAR2 := '-',
   new_FDS_class_comments IN VARCHAR2 := '-');
```
Alters the contents of the HS$_FDS_INST table for *FDS_inst_name* of *FDS_class_name*. New with Oracle8*i*.

```
PROCEDURE DBMS_HS.ALTER_INST_CAPS
   (FDS_inst_name IN VARCHAR2,
   FDS_class_name IN VARCHAR2,
   CAP_number IN NUMBER,
   new_FDS_inst_name IN VARCHAR2 := '-',
```

```
new_FDS_class_name IN VARCHAR2 := '-',
new_CAP_number IN NUMBER := -1e-130,
new_context IN NUMBER := -1e-130,
new_translation IN VARCHAR2 := '-',
new_additional_info IN NUMBER := -1e-130);
```
Alters the contents of the HS$_INST_CAPS table for *FDS_inst_name* of *FDS_class_name*. New with Oracle8*i*.

PROCEDURE DBMS_HS.ALTER_INST_DD
```
(FDS_inst_name IN VARCHAR2,
FDS_class_name IN VARCHAR2,
DD_table_name IN VARCHAR2,
new_FDS_inst_name IN VARCHAR2 := '-',
new_FDS_class_name IN VARCHAR2 := '-',
new_DD_table_name IN VARCHAR2 := '-',
new_translation_type IN CHAR := '-',
new_transation_text VARCHAR2 := '-');
```
Alters the contents of the HS$_INST_DD table for *FDS_inst_name* of *FDS_class_name* and *DD_table_name*. New with Oracle8*i*.

PROCEDURE DBMS_HS.ALTER_INST_INIT
```
(FDS_inst_name IN VARCHAR2,
FDS_class_name IN VARCHAR2,
init_value_name IN VARCHAR2,
new_FDS_inst_name IN VARCHAR2 := '-',
new_FDS_class_name IN VARCHAR2 := '-',
new_init_value_name IN VARCHAR2 := '-',
new_init_valee IN VARCHAR2 := '-',
new_init_value_type IN VARCHAR2 := '-');
```
Alters the contents of the HS$_INST_INIT table for *FDS_inst_name* of *FDS_class_name*. New with Oracle8*i*.

PROCEDURE DBMS_HS.COPY_CLASS
```
(old_FDS_class_name IN VARCHAR2);
```
Copies everything from the *old_FDS_class_name* to another class. New with Oracle8*i*.

PROCEDURE DBMS_HS.COPY_INST
```
(FDS_inst_name IN VARCHAR2,
FDS_class_name IN VARCHAR2,
new_FDS_inst_name IN VARCHAR2 := '-',
new_FDS_class_comments IN VARCHAR2 := '-');
```
Creates a new instance *new_FDS_inst_name* in the HS$_FDS_INST table for *FDS_inst_name* of *FDS_class_name*. New with Oracle8*i*.

PROCEDURE DBMS_HS.CREATE_BASE_CAPS
```
(CAP_number IN NUMBER,
CAP_description IN VARCHAR2 := NULL);
```
Creates a row in the HS$_BASE_CAPS table. New with Oracle8*i*.

PROCEDURE DBMS_HS.CREATE_BASE_DD
```
(DD_table_name IN VARCHAR2,
DD_table_descr IN VARCHAR2 := NULL);
```
Creates a row in the HS$_BASE_DD table. New with Oracle8*i*.

PROCEDURE DBMS_HS.CREATE_CLASS_CAPS
```
(FDS_class_name IN VARCHAR2,
CAP_number IN NUMBER,
```

```
  context IN NUMBER := NULL,
  translation IN VARCHAR2 := NULL,
  additional_info NUMBER := NULL);
```
    Creates a row in the HS$_CLASS_CAPS table. New with Oracle8*i*.

```
PROCEDURE DBMS_HS.CREATE_CLASS_DD
  (FDS_class_name IN VARCHAR2,
  DD_table_name IN VARCHAR2,
  translation_type IN CHAR,
  translation_text IN VARCHAR2);
```
    Creates a row for the HS$_CLASS_DD table. New with Oracle8*i*.

```
PROCEDURE DBMS_HS.CREATE_CLASS_INIT
  (FDS_class_name IN VARCHAR2,
  init_value_name IN VARCHAR2,
  init_value IN VARCHAR2,
  init_value_type IN VARCHAR2);
```
    Creates a row in the HS$_CLASS_INIT table. New with Oracle8*i*.

```
PROCEDURE DBMS_HS.CREATE_FDS_CLASS
  (FDS_class_name IN VARCHAR2,
  FDS_class_comments IN VARCHAR2);
```
    Creates a row in the HS$_FDS_CLASS table. New with Oracle8*i*.

```
PROCEDURE DBMS_HS.CREATE_FDS_INST
  (FDS_inst_name IN VARCHAR2,
  FDS_class_name IN VARCHAR2,
  FDS_inst_comments IN VARCHAR2 := NULL);
```
    Creates a row in the HS$_FDS_INST table.

```
PROCEDURE DBMS_HS.CREATE_INST_CAPS
  (FDS_inst_name IN VARCHAR2,
  FDS_class_name IN VARCHAR2,
  CAP_number IN NUMBER,
  context IN NUMBER := NULL,
  translation IN VARCHAR2 := NULL,
  new_additional_info IN NUMBER);
```
    Creates a row in the HS$_INST_CAPS table. New with Oracle8*i*.

```
PROCEDURE DBMS_HS.CREATE_INST_DD
  (FDS_inst_name IN VARCHAR2,
  FDS_class_name IN VARCHAR2,
  DD_table_name IN VARCHAR2,
  translation_type IN CHAR,
  transation_text VARCHAR2 := NULL);
```
    Creates a row in the HS$_INST_DD table. New with Oracle8*i*.

```
PROCEDURE DBMS_HS.CREATE_INST_INIT
  (FDS_inst_name IN VARCHAR2,
  FDS_class_name IN VARCHAR2,
  init_value_name IN VARCHAR2,
  init_value IN VARCHAR2,
  init_value_type IN VARCHAR2);
```
    Creates a row in the HS$_INST_INIT table. New with Oracle8*i*.

```
PROCEDURE DBMS_HS.DROP_BASE_CAPS
  (CAP_number IN NUMBER);
```
    Drops a row from the HS$_BASE_CAPS table. New with Oracle8*i*.

```
PROCEDURE DBMS_HS.CREATE_BASE_DD
    (DD_table_name IN VARCHAR2,);
```
Drops a row from the HS$_BASE_DD table. New with Oracle8*i*.

```
PROCEDURE DBMS_HS.DROP_CLASS_CAPS
    (FDS_class_name IN VARCHAR2,
    CAP_number IN NUMBER);
```
Drops a row from the HS$_CLASS_CAPS table. New with Oracle8*i*.

```
PROCEDURE DBMS_HS.DROP_CLASS_DD
    (FDS_class_name IN VARCHAR2,
    DD_table_name IN VARCHAR2);
```
Drops a row from the HS$_CLASS_DD table. New with Oracle8*i*.

```
PROCEDURE DBMS_HS.DROP_CLASS_INIT
    (FDS_class_name IN VARCHAR2,
    init_value_name IN VARCHAR2);
```
Drops a row from the HS$_CLASS_INIT table. New with Oracle8*i*.

```
PROCEDURE DBMS_HS.DROP_FDS_CLASS
    (FDS_class_name IN VARCHAR2);
```
Drops a row from the HS$_FDS_CLASS table. New with Oracle8*i*.

```
PROCEDURE DBMS_HS.DROP_FDS_INST
    (FDS_inst_name IN VARCHAR2,
    FDS_class_name IN VARCHAR2);
```
Drops a row from the HS$_FDS_INST table. New with Oracle8*i*.

```
PROCEDURE DBMS_HS.DROP_INST_CAPS
    (FDS_inst_name IN VARCHAR2,
    FDS_class_name IN VARCHAR2,
    CAP_number IN NUMBER);
```
Drops a row from the HS$_INST_CAPS table. New with Oracle8*i*.

```
PROCEDURE DBMS_HS.DROP_INST_DD
    (FDS_inst_name IN VARCHAR2,
    FDS_class_name IN VARCHAR2,
    DD_table_name IN VARCHAR2);
```
Drops a row from the HS$_INST_DD table. New with Oracle8*i*.

```
PROCEDURE DBMS_HS.CREATE_INST_INIT
    (FDS_inst_name IN VARCHAR2,
    FDS_class_name IN VARCHAR2,
    init_value_name IN VARCHAR2);
```
Drops a row from the HS$_INST_INIT table.

```
PROCEDURE DBMS_HS.REPLACE_BASE_CAPS
    (CAP_number IN NUMBER,
    new_CAP_number IN NUMBER := NULL,
    new_CAP_description IN VARCHAR2 := NULL);
```
Performs a create or replace on the HS$_BASE_CAPS table. New with Oracle8*i*.

```
PROCEDURE DBMS_HS.REPLACE_BASE_DD
    (DD_table_name IN VARCHAR2,
    new_ DD_table_name IN VARCHAR := NULL,
    new_ DD_table_name_descr IN VARCHAR2 := NULL);
```
Performs a create or replace on the HS$_BASE_DD table. New with Oracle8*i*.

```
PROCEDURE DBMS_HS.REPLACE_CLASS_CAPS
   (FDS_class_name IN VARCHAR2,
    CAP_number IN NUMBER,
    new_FDS_class_name IN VARCHAR2 := NULL,
    new_CAP_number IN NUMBER := NULL,
    new_context IN NUMBER := NULL,
    new_translation IN VARCHAR2 := NULL,
    new_additional_info NUMBER := NULL);
```
Performs a create or replace on the HS$_CLASS_CAPS table. New with Oracle8*i*.

```
PROCEDURE DBMS_HS.REPLACE_CLASS_DD
   (FDS_class_name IN VARCHAR2,
    DD_table_name IN VARCHAR2,
    new_FDS_class_name IN VARCHAR2 := NULL,
    new_DD_table_name IN NUMBER := NULL,
    new_translation_type IN CHAR := NULL,
    new_translation_text IN VARCHAR2 := NULL);
```
Performs a create or replace on the HS$_CLASS_DD table. New with Oracle8*i*.

```
PROCEDURE DBMS_HS.REPLACE_CLASS_INIT
   (FDS_class_name IN VARCHAR2,
    init_value_name IN VARCHAR2,
    new_FDS_class_name IN VARCHAR2 := NULL,
    new_init_value_name IN VARCHAR2 := NULL,
    new_init_value IN VARCHAR2 := NULL,
    new_init_value_type IN VARCHAR2 := NULL);
```
Performs a create or replace on the HS$_CLASS_INIT table. New with Oracle8*i*.

```
PROCEDURE DBMS_HS.REPLACE_FDS_CLASS
   (FDS_class_name IN VARCHAR2,
    new_FDS_class_name IN VARCHAR2 := NULL,
    new_FDS_class_comments IN VARCHAR2 := NULL);
```
Performs a create or replace on the HS$_FDS_CLASS table. New with Oracle8*i*.

```
PROCEDURE DBMS_HS.REPLACE_FDS_INST
   (FDS_inst_name IN VARCHAR2,
    FDS_class_name IN VARCHAR2,
    new_FDS_inst_name IN VARCHAR2 := NULL,
    new_FDS_class_name IN VARCHAR2 := NULL,
    new_FDS_class_comments IN VARCHAR2 := NULL);
```
Performs a create or replace on the HS$_FDS_INST table. New with Oracle8*i*.

```
PROCEDURE DBMS_HS.REPLACE_INST_CAPS
   (FDS_inst_name IN VARCHAR2,
    FDS_class_name IN VARCHAR2,
    CAP_number IN NUMBER,
    new_FDS_inst_name IN VARCHAR2 := NULL,
    new_FDS_class_name IN VARCHAR2 := NULL,
    new_CAP_number IN NUMBER := NULL,
    new_context IN NUMBER := NULL,
    new_translation IN VARCHAR := NULL,
    new_additional_info IN NUMBER := NULL);
```
Performs a create or replace on the HS$_INST_CAPS table. New with Oracle8*i*.

```
PROCEDURE DBMS_HS.REPLACE_INST_DD
   (FDS_inst_name IN VARCHAR2,
    FDS_class_name IN VARCHAR2,
    DD_table_name IN VARCHAR2,
```

```
new_FDS_inst_name IN VARCHAR2 := NULL,
new_FDS_class_name IN VARCHAR2 := NULL,
new_DD_table_name IN VARCHAR2 := NULL,
new_translation_type IN CHAR := NULL,
new_translation_text VARCHAR2 := NULL);
```
   Performs a create or replace on the HS$_INST_DD table. New with Oracle8*i*.

PROCEDURE DBMS_HS.REPLACE_INST_INIT
```
   (FDS_inst_name IN VARCHAR2,
   FDS_class_name IN VARCHAR2,
   init_value_name IN VARCHAR2,
   new_FDS_inst_name IN VARCHAR2 := NULL,
   new_FDS_class_name IN VARCHAR2 := NULL,
   new_init_value_name IN VARCHAR2 := NULL,
   new_init_valee IN VARCHAR2 := NULL,
   new_init_value_type IN VARCHAR2 := NULL);
```
   Performs a create or replace on the HS$_INST_INIT table. New with Oracle8*i*.

DBMS_HS_PASSTHROUGH

Manages sending statements directly to a non-Oracle server without interpretation (Heterogeneous Services). All of these program units run as if they were located on the remote server.

Calls

PROCEDURE DBMS_HS_PASSTHROUGH.BIND_VARIABLE
```
   (c IN BINARY_INTEGER NOT NULL,
   pos IN BINARY_INTEGER NOT NULL,
   val IN {DATE | NUMBER | VARCHAR2},
   name IN VARCHAR2);
```
   Binds *val* to cursor *c* in postion *pos* on remote system.

PROCEDURE DBMS_HS_PASSTHROUGH.BIND_VARIABLE_RAW
```
   (c IN BINARY_INTEGER NOT NULL,
   pos IN BINARY_INTEGER NOT NULL,
   val IN RAW,
   name IN VARCHAR2);
```
   Binds raw *val* to cursor *c* in postion *pos* on remote system.

PROCEDURE DBMS_HS_PASSTHROUGH.BIND_OUT_VARIABLE
```
   (c IN BINARY_INTEGER NOT NULL,
   pos IN BINARY_INTEGER NOT NULL,
   val OUT {DATE | NUMBER | VARCHAR2},
   name IN VARCHAR2);
```
   Binds OUT *val* to cursor *c* in postion *pos* in a PL/SQL program variable.

PROCEDURE DBMS_HS_PASSTHROUGH.BIND_OUT_VARIABLE_RAW
```
   (c IN BINARY_INTEGER NOT NULL,
   pos IN BINARY_INTEGER NOT NULL,
   val OUT RAW,
   name IN VARCHAR2);
```
   Binds OUT RAW *val* to cursor *c* in postion *pos* in a PL/SQL program variable.

PROCEDURE DBMS_HS_PASSTHROUGH.BIND_INOUT_VARIABLE
   (*c* IN BINARY_INTEGER NOT NULL,
   pos IN BINARY_INTEGER NOT NULL,
   val IN OUT {DATE | NUMBER | VARCHAR2},
   name IN VARCHAR2);
     Binds IN OUT *val* to cursor *c* in postion *pos* in a PL/SQL program variable.

PROCEDURE DBMS_HS_PASSTHROUGH.BIND_INOUT_VARIABLE_RAW
   (*c* IN BINARY_INTEGER NOT NULL,
   pos IN BINARY_INTEGER NOT NULL,
   val IN OUT RAW,
   name IN VARCHAR2);
     Binds IN OUT RAW *val* to cursor *c* in postion *pos* in a PL/SQL program variable.

PROCEDURE DBMS_HS_PASSTHROUGH.CLOSE_CURSOR
   (*c* IN BINARY_INTEGER NOT NULL);
     Closes cursor *c* and releases memory after statement run on a non-Oracle system.

FUNCTION DBMS_HS_PASSTHROUGH.EXECUTE_IMMEDIATE
   (*s* IN VARCHAR2 NOT NULL)
   RETURN BINARY_INTEGER;
     Executes SQL statement *s* immediately. Note that SELECT statements cannot be run immediately.

FUNCTION DBMS_HS_PASSTHROUGH.EXECUTE_NON_QUERY
   (*c* IN BINARY_INTEGER NOT NULL)
   RETURN BINARY_INTEGER;
     Executes parsed SQL statement of cursor *c*. The specified statement must not be a SELECT.

FUNCTION DBMS_HS_PASSTHROUGH.FETCH_ROW
   (*c* IN BINARY_INTEGER NOT NULL,
   first IN BOOLEAN)
   RETURN BINARY_INTEGER;
     Fetches rows from the result set on cursor *c*. If *first* is TRUE, the SELECT statement is re-executed; otherwise, the next row (or the first row for a query that has not been run) is retrieved.

PROCEDURE DBMS_HS_PASSTHROUGH.GET_VALUE
   (*c* IN BINARY_INTEGER NOT NULL,
   pos IN BINARY_INTEGER NOT NULL,
   val OUT {DATE | NUMBER | VARCHAR2});
     Retrieves either the list of items in a SELECT statement or the list of OUT bind values after the SQL statement has been run.

PROCEDURE DBMS_HS_PASSTHROUGH.GET_VALUE_RAW
   (*c* IN BINARY_INTEGER NOT NULL,
   pos IN BINARY_INTEGER NOT NULL,
   val OUT RAW);
     Gets RAW values. This procedure is similar to the GET_VALUE procedure.

FUNCTION DBMS_HS_PASSTHROUGH.OPEN_CURSOR
   RETURN BINARY_INTEGER;
     Opens a cursor on a non-Oracle system.

PROCEDURE DBMS_HS_PASSTHROUGH.PARSE
    (*c* IN BINARY_INTEGER NOT NULL,
    stmt IN VARCHAR2 NOT NULL);
        Parses the statement *stmt* on cursor *c* on a non-Oracle system.

DBMS_IOT

Provides procedures that allow you to create tables to manage references to chained rows or rows that violate a constraint in index-organized tables. New with Oracle8*i*.

Calls

PROCEDURE DBMS_IOT.BUILD_CHAIN_ROWS_TABLE
    (*owner* IN VARCHAR2,
    iot_name IN VARCHAR2.
    chainrow_table_name IN VARCHAR2 DEFAULT 'IOT_CHAINED_ROWS');
        Builds table *chainrow_table_name* to hold references to chained rows in *iot_name* owned by *owner*.

PROCEDURE DBMS_IOT.BUILD_EXCEPTIONS_TABLE
    (*owner* IN VARCHAR2,
    iot_name IN VARCHAR2.
    exceptions_table_name IN VARCHAR2 DEFAULT 'IOT_EXCEPTIONS_ROWS');
        Builds table *exceptions_table_name* to hold rows of *iot_name* table owned by *owner* which violate constraints.

DBMS_JOB

Provides an interface into the Oracle job queue subsystem that allows automated, unattended scheduling and execution of PL/SQL programs.

Calls

PROCEDURE DBMS_JOB.BROKEN
    (*job* IN BINARY_INTEGER,
    broken IN BOOLEAN,
    next_date IN DATE DEFAULT SYSDATE);
        Sets or unsets the Boolean *broken* flag for the *job*, and optionally sets the next execution date specified by *next_date*. Jobs flagged with *broken* = TRUE are not automatically executed.

PROCEDURE DBMS_JOB.CHANGE
    (*job* IN BINARY_INTEGER,
    what IN VARCHAR2,
    next_date IN DATE,
    interval IN VARCHAR2,
    instance IN BINARY_INTEGER DEFAULT NULL,
    force IN BOOLEAN DEFAULT FALSE);
        Changes one or more of the parameters *what, next_date, interval,* or *instance* (new with Oracle8*i*) for *job*. If *force* (new with Oracle8*i*) is TRUE, any positive integer is acceptable for the *instance*; if *force* is FALSE, *instance* must be running.

```
PROCEDURE DBMS_JOB.INTERVAL
    (job IN BINARY_INTEGER,
    interval IN VARCHAR2);
```
Changes the date expression used to determine the next execution date for *job* to *interval*.

```
PROCEDURE DBMS_JOB.SUBMIT
    (job IN BINARY_INTEGER,
    what IN VARCHAR2,
    next_date IN VARCHAR2,
    interval IN VARCHAR2 DEFAULT 'null',
    no_parse IN BOOLEAN DEFAULT FALSE,
    instance IN BINARY_INTEGER DEFAULT any_instance,
    force IN BOOLEAN DEFAULT FALSE);
```
Submits a job with the specified *job* number and PL/SQL definition *what*, scheduled to execute at *next_date* and every *interval* thereafter, on instance *instance* (new with Oracle8*i*). If *no_parse* is TRUE, parsing of the PL/SQL in *what* is deferred until execution. If *force* (new with Oracle8*i*) is TRUE, any positive integer is acceptable for the *instance*; if *force* is FALSE, *instance* must be running.

```
PROCEDURE DBMS_JOB.NEXT_DATE
    (job IN BINARY_INTEGER,
    next_date IN DATE);
```
Changes the next scheduled date of execution for *job* to *next_date*.

```
PROCEDURE DBMS_JOB.REMOVE
    (job IN BINARY_INTEGER);
```
Removes *job* from the queue. If *job* is currently executing, it will run to normal completion but will not be rescheduled.

```
PROCEDURE DBMS_JOB.RUN
    (job IN BINARY_INTEGER
    force IN BOOLEAN DEFAULT TRUE);
```
Immediately executes *job* in the current session. If *force* (new with Oracle8*i*) is FALSE, the job can be run only in the foreground in the specified instance.

```
PROCEDURE DBMS_JOB.USER_EXPORT
    (job IN BINARY_INTEGER,
    mycall IN OUT VARCHAR2
    [myinst IN OUT VARCHAR2]);
```
Returns a character string in *mycall* that can be used to resubmit *job* to the job queue. If *myinst* (new with Oracle8*i*) is used, the procedure modifies the instance affinity. New with Oracle8*i*.

```
PROCEDURE DBMS_JOB.WHAT
    (job IN BINARY_INTEGER,
    what IN VARCHAR2);
```
Changes the PL/SQL definition for *job* to *what*.

```
PROCEDURE DBMS_JOB.INSTANCE
    (job IN BINARY_INTEGER,
    instance IN BINARY_INTEGER,
    force IN BOOLEAN DEFAULT FALSE);
```
Changes the job affinity to the instance. If *force* is TRUE, any positive integer is acceptable for the *instance*; if *force* is FALSE, *instance* must be running. New with Oracle8*i*.

DBMS_LDAP

Provides functions and procedure that you can use to access data from LDAP servers. The data must be loaded into the database with the *catldap.sql* script. New with Oracle9*i*.

Calls

FUNCTION DBMS_LDAP.INIT
   (*hostname* IN VARCHAR2,
   portnum IN PLS_INTEGER)
   RETURN SESSION;
     Establishes a session with the LDAP server on *hostname* port *portnum*.

FUNCTION DBMS_LDAP.SIMPLE_BIND_S
   (*ld* IN SESSION,
   dn IN VARCHAR2,
   passwd IN VARCHAR2)
   RETURN PLS_INTEGER;
     Performs simple username (*dn*)/password (*passwd*) authentication. Returns a success flag.

FUNCTION DBMS_LDAP.BIND_S
   (*ld* IN SESSION,
   dn IN VARCHAR2,
   cred IN VARCHAR2,
   meth IN PLS_INTEGER)
   RETURN PLS_INTEGER;
     Performs complex authentication using *meth*. Returns a success flag.

FUNCTION DBMS_LDAP.UNBIND_S
   (*ld* IN SESSION)
   RETURN PLS_INTEGER;
     Unbinds the session for *ld*. Returns a success flag.

FUNCTION DBMS_LDAP.COMPARE_S
   (*ld* IN SESSION,
   dn IN VARCHAR2,
   attr IN VARCHAR2,
   value IN VARCHAR2)
   RETURN PLS_INTEGER;
     Compares *attr* in *dn* with *value*. Returns a success flag.

FUNCTION DBMS_LDAP.SEARCH_S
   (*ld* IN SESSION,
   base IN VARCHAR2,
   scope IN PLS_INTEGER,
   filter IN VARCHAR2,
   attrs IN STRING_COLLECTION,
   attronly IN PLS_INTEGER,
   res OUT MESSAGE)
   RETURN PLS_INTEGER;
     Performs a synchronous search of the *ld* server for *attrs*. Returns a success flag.

```
FUNCTION DBMS_LDAP.SEARCH_ST
    (ld IN SESSION,
    base IN VARCHAR2,
    scope IN PLS_INTEGER,
    filter IN VARCHAR2,
    attrs IN STRING_COLLECTION,
    attronly IN PLS_INTEGER,
    tv IN TIMEVAL,
    res OUT MESSAGE)
    RETURN PLS_INTEGER;
```

Performs a synchronous search of the *ld* server for *attrs* with a client-side timeout *tv*. Returns a success flag.

```
FUNCTION DBMS_LDAP.FIRST_ENTRY
    (ld IN SESSION,
    msg IN MESSAGE)
    RETURN MESSAGE;
```

Retrieves the first entry in the result set (*msg*) returned by the SEARCH_S or SEARCH_ST functions.

```
FUNCTION DBMS_LDAP.NEXT_ENTRY
    (ld IN SESSION,
    msg IN MESSAGE)
    RETURN MESSAGE;
```

Retrieves the next entry in the result set (*msg*) returned by the SEARCH_S or SEARCH_ST functions.

```
FUNCTION DBMS_LDAP.COUNT_ENTRIES
    (ld IN SESSION,
    msg IN MESSAGE)
    RETURN PLS_INTEGER;
```

Returns the count of entries in the result set (*msg*) returned by the SEARCH_S or SEARCH_ST functions.

```
FUNCTION DBMS_LDAP.FIRST_ATTRIBUTE
    (ld IN SESSION,
    msg IN MESSAGE,
    ber_elem OUT BER_ELEMENT)
    RETURN VARCHAR2;
```

Returns the first attribute of a given entry.

```
FUNCTION DBMS_LDAP.NEXT_ATTRIBUTE
    (ld IN SESSION,
    msg IN MESSAGE,
    ber_elem IN BER_ELEMENT)
    RETURN VARCHAR2;
```

Returns the next attribute of a given entry.

```
FUNCTION DBMS_LDAP.GET_DN
    (ld IN SESSION,
    msg IN MESSAGE)
    RETURN VARCHAR2;
```

Returns the distinguised name for session.

```
FUNCTION DBMS_LDAP.GET_VALUES
    (ld IN SESSION,
    ldapentry IN MESSAGE,
```

    attr IN VARCHAR2)
    RETURN STRING_COLLECTION;
      Returns all values for *attr* in *ldapentry*.

FUNCTION DBMS_LDAP.GET_VALUES_LENGTH
    (*ld* IN SESSION,
    ldapentry IN MESSAGE,
    attr IN VARCHAR2)
    RETURN BINVAL_COLLECTION;
      Returns the lengths for all values for *attr* in *ldapentry*.

FUNCTION DBMS_LDAP.DELETE_S
    (*ld* IN SESSION,
    entrydn IN VARCHAR2)
    RETURN PLS_INTEGER;
      Removes a leaf entry *entrydn* in the *ld* directory. Returns a success flag.

FUNCTION DBMS_LDAP.MODRDN2_S
    (*ld* IN SESSION,
    entrydn IN VARCHAR2,
    newrdn IN VARCHAR2,
    deleteoldrdn IN PLS_INTEGER)
    RETURN PLS_INTEGER;
      Renames the relative distinguished name for *entrydn* to *newrdn*. If *deleteoldrdn* is nonzero, the old relative distinguished name should be removed. Returns a success flag.

FUNCTION DBMS_LDAP.ERR2STRING
    (*ldap_err* IN PLS_INTEGER)
    RETURN VARCHAR2;
      Translates an error number to error message.

FUNCTION DBMS_LDAP.CREATE_MOD_ARRAY
    (*num* IN PLS_INTEGER)
    RETURN MOD_ARRAY;
      Allocates memory for *num* of array modification entries that are applied with the MODIFY_S or ADD_S functions.

PROCEDURE DBMS_LDAP.POPULATE_MOD_ARRAY
    (*modptr* IN DBMS_LDAP.MOD_ARRAY,
    mod_op IN PLS_INTEGER,
    mod_type IN VARCHAR2,
    modval IN {DBMS_LDAP.STRING_COLLECTION | DBMS_LDAP.BERVAL_COLLECTION});
      Passes a pointer (*modptr*) for modification of type *mod_op* on attribute type of *mod_type* with value *modval*. The same procedure call works for strings or binary values with differing datatypes for *modval*.

FUNCTION DBMS_LDAP.MODIFY_S
    (*ld* IN SESSION,
    entrydh IN VARCHAR2,
    modptr IN DBMS_LDAP.MOD_ARRAY)
    RETURN PLS_INTEGER;
      Performs a synchronous update to the LDAP directory structure identified by *modptr*. Returns a success code.

FUNCTION DBMS_LDAP.MODIFY_S
    (*ld* IN SESSION,
    entrydh IN VARCHAR2,

```
       modptr IN DBMS_LDAP.MOD_ARRAY)
    RETURN PLS_INTEGER;
```
Adds a value to the LDAP directory structure identified by *modptr*. You must call CREATE_MOD_ARRAY and POPULATE_MOD_ARRAY before calling this function. Returns a success code.

```
PROCEDURE DBMS_LDAP.FREE_MOD_ARRAY
    (modptr IN DBMS_LDAP.MOD_ARRAY);
```
Frees memory allocated for *modptr*.

```
FUNCTION DBMS_LDAP.COUNT_VALUES
    (values IN DBMS_LDAP.STRING_COLLECTION_
    RETURN PLS_INTEGER;
```
Returns the number of values returned by a GET_VALUES call.

```
FUNCTION DBMS_LDAP.COUNT_VALUES_LEN
    (values IN DBMS_LDAP.STRING_COLLECTION_
    RETURN PLS_INTEGER;
```
Returns the number of values returned by a GET_VALUES_LEN call.

```
FUNCTION DBMS_LDAP.RENAME_S
    (ld IN SESSION,
    entrydn IN VARCHAR2,
    newrdn IN VARCHAR2,
    deleteoldrdn IN PLS_INTEGER,
    serverctrls IN LDAPCONTROL,
    clientcntrls IN LDAPCONTROL)
    RETURN PLS_INTEGER;
```
Renames an LDAP entry synchronously. If *deleteoldrdn* is nonzero, the old relative distinguished name should be removed. *serverctrls* and *clientcntrls* are not supported in Oracle9*i*. Returns a success flag.

```
FUNCTION DBMS_LDAP.EXPLODE_DN
    (dn IN VARCHAR2,
    notypes IN PLS_INTEGER)
    RETURN STRING_COLLECTION;
```
Returns the distinguished name (*dn*) broken up into parts. If *notypes* is 0, attribute tags are included.

```
FUNCTION DBMS_LDAP.OPEN_SSL
    (ld IN SESSION,
    sslwr1 IN VARCHAR2,
    sslwalletpasswd IN VARCHAR2,
    sslauth IN PLS_INTEGER)
    RETURN PLS_INTEGER;
```
Establishes a Secure Systems Layer (SSL) connection over an existing LDAP collection. Returns success flag.

DBMS_LIBCACHE

Prepares the library cache on an Oracle instance by retrieving SQL and PL/SQL from a remote instance and recompiling it locally. New with Oracle9*i*.

Call

PROCEDURE DBMS_LIBCACHE.COMPILE_CURSORS_FROM_REMOTE
  (*dblink* IN VARCHAR2,
  username IN VARCHAR2,
  execution_threshold IN NUMBER,
  shared_mem_threshold IN NUMBER);

Retrieves SQL in batch from *dblink* and parses it with *username* user. Only SQL-parsed *execution_threshold* times and above *shared_mem_threshold* will be retrieved.

DBMS_LOB

Provides a mechanism for accessing and manipulating large objects (LOBs). LOBs include BLOBs (binary large objects), CLOBs (character large objects), NCLOBs (National Language Support character large objects), and BFILEs (binary files). The CHARACTER SET ANY_CS clauses in the CLOB declarations allow either CLOB or NCLOB locators.

Calls

PROCEDURE DBMS_LOB.APPEND
  ({*dest_lob* IN OUT BLOB | *dest_lob* IN OUT CLOB CHARACTER SET ANY_CS},
  {*src_lob* IN BLOB | *src_lob* IN CLOB CHARACTER SET *dest_lob*%CHARSET});

Appends the contents of the source LOB *src_lob* to the destination LOB *dest_lob*. Both *src_lob* and *dest_lob* must be of the same LOB type: BLOB, CLOB, or NCLOB.

PROCEDURE DBMS_LOB.CLOSE
  ({*lob_loc* IN OUT NOCOPY BLOB |
  lob_loc IN OUT NOCOPY CLOB CHARACTER SET ANY_CS |
  file_loc IN OUT NOCOPY BFILE});

Closes a previously opened BLOB, CLOB, or external file. New with Oracle9*i*.

FUNCTION DBMS_LOB.COMPARE
  (*lob_1* IN {BLOB | CLOB CHARACTER SET ANY_CS},
  lob_2 IN {BLOB | CLOB CHARACTER SET lob_1%CHARSET},
  amount IN INTEGER DEFAULT 4294967295,
  offset_1 IN INTEGER DEFAULT 1,
  offset_2 IN INTEGER DEFAULT 1)
RETURN INTEGER;

FUNCTION DBMS_LOB.COMPARE
  (*file_1* IN BFILE,
  file_2 IN BFILE,
  amount IN INTEGER,
  offset_1 IN INTEGER DEFAULT 1,
  offset_2 IN INTEGER DEFAULT 1)
RETURN INTEGER;

Compares input LOBs *lob_1* and *lob_2* or *file_1* and *file_2* across *amount* bytes, optionally starting the comparison *offset_1* and *offset_2* bytes into the input files. Both inputs must be of the same LOB type: BLOB, CLOB, NCLOB, or BFILE.

Returns 0 if the inputs exactly match, nonzero if they don't match, or NULL if *amount*, *offset_1*, or *offset_2* is either less than 1 or greater than LOBMAXSIZE, a constant in this package with a value of 4,294,967,295.

PROCEDURE DBMS_LOB.COPY
   (*dest_lob* IN OUT {BLOB | CLOB CHARACTER SET ANY_CS},
   src_lob IN {BLOB | CLOB CHARACTER SET *dest_lob*%CHARSET},
   amount IN INTEGER,
   dest_offset IN INTEGER DEFAULT 1,
   src_offset IN INTEGER DEFAULT 1);

   Copies *amount* bytes (BLOB) or characters (CLOB) from source LOB *lob_loc*, starting *src_offset* bytes or characters into the source LOB to the destination (target) LOB, *dest_lob*, starting *dest_offset* into the destination LOB. Both *src_lob* and *dest_lob* must be the same LOB type: BLOB, CLOB, or NCLOB.

PROCEDURE DBMS_LOB.CREATETEMPORARY
   (*lob_loc* IN OUT NOCOPY {BLOB | CLOB CHARACTER SET ANY_CS},
   cache IN BOOLEAN,
   dur IN PLS_INTEGER DEFAULT 10);

   Creates a temporary copy of *lob_loc*, reads it into the buffer cache depending on *cache*, and specifies whether *dur*ation is SESSION (the default) or CALL. New with Oracle8*i*.

PROCEDURE DBMS_LOB.ERASE
   (*lob_loc* IN OUT {BLOB | CLOB CHARACTER SET ANY_CS},
   amount IN OUT INTEGER,
   offset IN INTEGER DEFAULT 1);

   Erases (zero byte fill) *amount* bytes (BLOB) or characters (CLOB) in the LOB *lob_loc*, beginning *offset* bytes or characters into the LOB *lob_loc*.

PROCEDURE DBMS_LOB.FILECLOSE
   (*file_loc* IN OUT BFILE);

   Closes the BFILE *file_loc*, whether it is open or not.

PROCEDURE DBMS_LOB.FILECLOSEALL;

   Closes all open BFILEs in the current session.

FUNCTION DBMS_LOB.FILEEXISTS
   (*file_loc* IN BFILE)
   RETURN INTEGER;

   Returns 1 if BFILE *file_loc* exists; returns 0 otherwise.

PROCEDURE DBMS_LOB.FILEGETNAME
   (*file_loc* IN BFILE,
   dir_alias OUT VARCHAR2,
   filename OUT VARCHAR2);

   Gets a directory alias (as previously defined via the CREATE DIRECTORY command) and filename for the given file locator *file_loc*.

FUNCTION DBMS_LOB.FILEISOPEN
   (*file_loc* IN BFILE)
   RETURN INTEGER;

   Returns 1 if the BFILE *file_loc* is open; returns 0 otherwise.

PROCEDURE DBMS_LOB.FILEOPEN
   (*file_loc* IN OUT BFILE,
   open_mode IN BINARY_INTEGER DEFAULT FILE_READONLY);

   Opens BFILE *file_loc* for read-only access.

PROCECURE DBMS_LOB.FREETEMPORARY
    (*lob_loc* IN OUT NOCOPY {BLOB | CLOB CHARACTER SET ANY_CS});
       Frees temporary BLOB or CLOB in *lob_loc*, which is then marked as invalid. New with Oracle9*i*.

FUNCTION DBMS_LOB.GETCHUNKSIZE
    (*lob_loc* IN OUT NOCOPY {BLOB | CLOB CHARACTER SET ANY_CS})
    RETURN INTEGER;
       Returns the chunk size for *lob_loc*. New with Oracle8*i*.

FUNCTION DBMS_LOB.GETLENGTH
    (*lob_loc* IN {BLOB | CHARACTER SET ANY_CS | BFILE})
    RETURN INTEGER;
       Returns the size in bytes or characters of the LOB *lob_loc*.

FUNCTION DBMS_LOB.INSTR
    (*lob_loc* IN {BLOB | CHARACTER SET ANY_CS | BFILE},
    pattern IN {RAW | VARCHAR2 CHARACTER SET *lob_loc*%CHARSET | RAW},
    offset IN INTEGER DEFAULT 1,
    nth IN INTEGER DEFAULT 1)
    RETURN INTEGER;
       Similar to the built-in function INSTR. Returns the byte (BLOB) or character (CLOB) offset in LOB *lob_loc* where the *nth* occurrence of *pattern* is found. The search begins *offset* bytes or characters into *lob_loc*.

FUNCTION DBMS_LOB.ISOPEN
    ({*lob_loc* | *file_loc*} IN {BLOB | CHARACTER SET ANY_CS | BFILE})
    RETURN INTEGER;
       Returns TRUE if LOB or file is already open. New with Oracle8*i*.

FUNCTION DBMS_LOB.ISTEMPORARY
    (*lob_loc* IN {BLOB | CHARACTER SET ANY_CS})
    RETURN INTEGER;
       Returns TRUE if *lob_loc* is pointing to a temporary LOB. New with Oracle8*i*.

PROCEDURE DBMS_LOB.LOADFROMFILE
    (*dest_lob* IN OUT NOCOPY {BLOB | CLOB CHARACTER SET ANY_CS},
    src_lob IN BFILE,
    amount IN INTEGER,
    dest_offset IN INTEGER := 1,
    src_offset IN INTEGER := 1);
       Copies *amount* bytes of data from the source BFILE *src_lob* to the destination (target) LOB *dest_lob*, starting *src_offset* bytes into the source BFILE and *dest_offset* bytes into the destination (target) LOB. Prior to Oracle9*i*, this call could use the CLOB datatype; with Oracle9*i*, it can accept only a BLOB datatype.

PROCEDURE DBMS_LOB.LOADBLOBFROMFILE
    (*dest_lob* IN OUT NOCOPY BLOB,
    src_lob IN BFILE,
    amount IN INTEGER,
    dest_offset IN OUT INTEGER := 1,
    src_offset IN OUT INTEGER := 1);
       Loads data from BFILE *src_lob* to internal BLOB *dest_lob*. Equivalent to LOADFROMFILE and new with Oracle9*i*.

PROCEDURE DBMS_LOB.LOADCLOBFROMFILE
    (*dest_lob* IN OUT NOCOPY BLOB,
    src_lob IN BFILE,
    amount IN INTEGER,
    dest_offset IN OUT INTEGER := 1,
    src_offset IN OUT INTEGER := 1,
    lang_context IN OUT INTEGER,
    warning OUT INTEGER);

    Loads a BFILE *src_lob* into internal CLOB/NCLOB *dest_lob* with necessary character set conversion. The *lang_context* IN parameter is for the current load, and the OUT parameter is for the language context when the current load stops. The *warning* parameter is returned if an anomaly occurred during the load. New with Oracle9*i*.

PROCEDURE DBMS_LOB.OPEN
    (*lob_loc* IN OUT NOCOPY {BLOB | CLOB CHARACTER SET ANY_CS | BFILE},
    open_mode IN BINARY_INTEGER);

    Opens a LOB in *open_mode* mode. For a BFILE, only file_readonly mode is supported. New with Oracle8*i*.

PROCEDURE DBMS_LOB.READ
    (*lob_loc* IN {BLOB | CLOB CHARACTER SET ANY_CS | BFILE},
    amount IN OUT [NOCOPY] BINARY_INTEGER,
    offset IN INTEGER,
    buffer OUT {RAW | CHARACTER SET *lob_loc*%CHARSET});

    Copies *amount* bytes (BLOB) or characters (CLOB) from source LOB *lob_loc*, starting *offset* bytes or characters into the LOB to the destination (target) variable, *buffer*. Returns the actual number of bytes or characters copied in *amount*.

FUNCTION DBMS_LOB.SUBSTR
    (*lob_loc* IN {BLOB | CLOB CHARACTER SET ANY_CS | BFILE},
    amount IN INTEGER := 32767,
    offset IN INTEGER := 1)
    RETURN {RAW | VARCHAR2 CHARACTER SET *lob_loc*%CHARSET};

    Similar to the built-in function SUBSTR. Returns *amount* bytes (BLOB) or characters (CLOB) of the LOB *lob_loc* starting *offset* bytes or characters into the LOB.

PROCEDURE DBMS_LOB.TRIM
    (*lob_loc* IN OUT {BLOB | CLOB CHARACTER SET ANY_CS},
    newlen IN INTEGER);

    Truncates the LOB *lob_loc* to *newlen* bytes (BLOB) or characters (CLOB).

PROCEDURE DBMS_LOB.WRITE
    (*lob_loc* IN OUT {BLOB | CLOB CHARACTER SET ANY_CS},
    amount IN BINARY_INTEGER,
    offset IN INTEGER,
    buffer IN {RAW | VARCHAR2 CHARACTER SET *lob_loc*%CHARSET);

    Copies *amount* bytes from source variable *buffer* to the destination LOB *lob_loc*, starting *offset* bytes (BLOB) or characters (CLOB) into the LOB, overwriting any existing data in *lob_loc*.

PROCEDURE DBMS_LOB.WRITEAPPEND
    (*lob_loc* IN OUT NOCOPY {BLOB | CLOB CHARACTER SET ANY_CS},
    amount IN BINARY_INTEGER,
    buffer IN {RAW | VARCHAR2 CHARACTER SET lob_lob%CHARSET});

    Writes *amount* of data from the *buffer* to the end of *lob_loc*. New with Oracle8*i*.

DBMS_LOCK

Makes Oracle lock management services available for implementation of specialized, non-data locking and serialization requirements within applications.

Calls

PROCEDURE DBMS_LOCK.ALLOCATE_UNIQUE
  (*lockname* IN VARCHAR2,
  lockhandle OUT VARCHAR2,
  expiration_secs IN INTEGER DEFAULT 864000);
    Allocates a unique *lockhandle* for the lock identified by *lockname* to last for *expiration_secs* seconds. Also performs a COMMIT.

FUNCTION DBMS_LOCK.CONVERT
  ({*id* IN INTEGER | *lockhandle* IN VARCHAR2},
  lockmode IN INTEGER,
  timeout IN NUMBER DEFAULT MAXWAIT)
  RETURN INTEGER;
    Converts the lock identified by either *id* or *lockhandle* to the mode specified by *lockmode*, waiting for up to *timeout* seconds for successful completion. *lockmode* must be a valid constant as defined in the DBMS_LOCK package. Return values are 0 = success; 1 = timed out; 2 = deadlock; 3 = parameter error; 4 = do not own lock, cannot convert; or 5 = illegal lockhandle.

FUNCTION DBMS_LOCK.RELEASE
  ({*id* IN INTEGER | *lockhandle* IN VARCHAR2})
  RETURN INTEGER;
    Releases the lock identified by either *id* or *lockhandle*. Return values are the same as for the CONVERT function.

FUNCTION DBMS_LOCK.REQUEST
  ({*id* IN INTEGER | *lockhandle* IN VARCHAR2},
  lockmode IN INTEGER DEFAULT X_MODE,
  timeout IN INTEGER DEFAULT MAXWAIT,
  release_on_commit IN BOOLEAN DEFAULT FALSE)
  RETURN INTEGER;
    Acquires the lock identified by either *id* or *lockhandle* in the mode specified by *lockmode*, waiting for up to *timeout* seconds for successful completion. When *release_on_commit* is TRUE, the lock is automatically released as the result of the transaction COMMIT or ROLLBACK. *lockmode* must be a valid constant as defined in the DBMS_LOCK package. Return values are the same as for the CONVERT function.

PROCEDURE DBMS_LOCK.SLEEP
  (*seconds* IN NUMBER);
    Suspends the session for *seconds* seconds.

DBMS_LOGMNR

Provides procedures used to initialize LogMiner. New with Oracle8*i*.

Calls

```
PROCEDURE DBMS_LOGMINER.ADD_LOGFILE
  (logfilename IN VARCHAR2,
  options IN BINARY_INTEGER DEFAULT ADDFILE);
```
  Adds a file to the existing list of archive files to process.

```
PROCEDURE DBMS_LOGMINER.START_LOGMNR
  (startSCN IN NUMBER DEFAULT 0,
  endSCN IN NUMBER DEFAULT 0,
  starttime IN DATE DEFAULT '01-JAN-1988',
  endtime IN DATE DEFAULT '01-JAN-2988',
  dict_file_name IN VARCHAR2 DEFAULT '',
  options IN BINARY_INTEGER DEFAULT 0);
```
  Starts a LogMiner session with either a starting and ending SCN or time. (If the SCNs are present, times are ignored.) *dict_file_name* is a flat file that contains a snapshot of the database catalog. For information on *options*, see the Oracle documentation.

```
PROCEDURE DBMS_LOGMINER.END_LOGMNR;
```
  Ends a LogMiner session.

```
FUNCTION DBMS_LOGMINER.MINE_VALUE
  (sql_redo_undo IN RAW,
  column_name IN VARCHAR2 DEFAULT '')
  RETURN VARCHAR2;
```
  Extracts data about *column_name* from *sql_redo_undo* column in V$LOGMNR_ CONTENTS and returns either NULL or non_NULL. New with Oracle9*i*.

```
FUNCTION DBMS_LOGMINER.COLUMN_PRESENT
  (sql_redo_undo IN RAW,
  column_name IN VARCHAR2 DEFAULT '')
  RETURN NUMBER;
```
  Extracts data about *column_name* from *sql_redo_undo* column in V$LOGMNR_ CONTENTS and returns either 0, which indicates the column is not present, or 1, that it is. New with Oracle9*i*.

DBMS_LOGMNR_CDC_PUBLISH

Used to set up Oracle Change Data Capture to set up a CDC system and publish information from it. New with Oracle9*i*.

Calls

```
PROCEDURE DBMS_LOGMNR_CDC_PUBLISH.
  (owner IN VARCHAR2,
  change_table_name IN VARCHAR2,
  change_set_name IN VARCHAR2,
  source_schema IN VARCHAR2,
  source_table IN VARCHAR2,
  column_type_list IN VARCHAR2,
```

```
capture_values IN VARCHAR2,
rs_id IN CHAR,
row_id IN CHAR,
user_id IN CHAR,
timestamp IN CHAR,
object_id IN CHAR,
source_colmap IN CHAR,
target_colmap IN CHAR,
options_string IN VARCHAR2);
```
Creates a *change_table_name* in *owner* schema to monitor *source_table* in *source_schema*.

PROCEDURE DBMS_LOGMNR_CDC_PUBLISH.ALTER_CHANGE_TABLE
```
(owner IN VARCHAR2,
change_table_name IN VARCHAR2,
operation IN VARCHAR2,
column_list IN VARCHAR2,
capture_values IN VARCHAR2,
rs_id IN CHAR,
row_id IN CHAR,
user_id IN CHAR,
timestamp IN CHAR,
object_id IN CHAR,
source_colmap IN CHAR,
target_colmap IN CHAR);
```
Adds columns to (*operation* ADD) or drops columns from (*operation* DROP) *change_table_name*.

PROCEDURE DBMS_LOGMNR_CDC_PUBLISH.DROP_SUBSCRIBER_VIEW
```
(subscription_handle IN NUMBER,
source_schema IN VARCHAR2,
source_table IN VARCHAR2);
```
Drop a *subscriber_handle* view in *source_schema*.

PROCEDURE DBMS_LOGMNR_CDC_PUBLISH.DROP_SUBSCRIPTION
```
(subscription_handle IN NUMBER);
```
Drops *subscription_handle* obtained with the DBMS_LOGMNR_CDC_SUBSCRIBE.GET_SUBSCRIPTION_HANDLE call.

PROCEDURE DBMS_LOGMNR_CDC_PUBLISH.DROP_CHANGE_TABLE
```
(owner IN VARCHAR2,
change_table_name IN VARCHAR2,
force IN CHAR);
```
Drops *change_table_name* in *owner*. If *force* is Y, the table is dropped even if there are subscribers making references to the table; if *force* is N, the procedure will not drop the table if there are subscriptions making reference to it.

PROCEDURE DBMS_LOGMNR_CDC_PUBLISH.PURGE;
Removes unneeded rows from change tables.

DBMS_LOGMNR_CDC_SUBSCRIBE

Provides procedures that allow publisher to view and query change data that was captured with DBMS_LOGMNR_CDC_PUBLISH. New with Oracle9*i*.

Calls

PROCEDURE DBMS_LOGMNR_CDC_SUBSCRIBE.GET_SUBSCRIPTION_HANDLE
   (*change_set* IN VARCHAR2,
   description IN VARCHAR2 := NULL,
   subscription_handle OUT NUMBER);
     Gets a *subscription_handle* associated with *change_set*.

PROCEDURE DBMS_LOGMNR_CDC_SUBSCRIBE.SUBSCRIBE
   (*subscription_handle* IN NUMBER,
   source_schema IN VARCHAR2,
   source_table IN VARCHAR2,
   column_list IN VARCHAR2);

PROCEDURE DBMS_LOGMNR_CDC_SUBSCRIBE.SUBSCRIBE
   (*subscription_handle* IN NUMBER,
   publication_id IN NUMBER,
   column_list IN VARCHAR2);
     Specifies the source tables and columns for the subscriber, by their identities or by the *publication_id* of a specific publication.

PROCEDURE DBMS_LOGMNR_CDC_SUBSCRIBE.ACTIVATE_SUBSCRIBER
   (*subscription_handle* IN NUMBER);
     Makes *subscription_handle* ready to start accessing change data.

PROCEDURE DBMS_LOGMNR_CDC_SUBSCRIBE.EXTEND_WINDOW
   (*subscription_handle* IN NUMBER);
     Sets window boundaries for *subscription_handle* so that new change data can be seen.

PROCEDURE DBMS_LOGMNR_CDC_SUBSCRIBE.PREPARE_SUBSCRIBER_VIEW
   (*subscription_handle* IN NUMBER,
   source_schema IN VARCHAR2,
   source_table IN VARCHAR2,
   view_name OUT VARCHAR2);
     Creates *view_name* in subscriber's schema to receive change data from *source_table*.

PROCEDURE DBMS_LOGMNR_CDC_SUBSCRIBE.DROP_SUBSCRIBER_VIEW
   (*subscription_handle* IN NUMBER,
   source_schema IN VARCHAR2,
   source_table IN VARCHAR2);
     Drops subscriber view for *subscription_handle* in subscriber's schema.

PROCEDURE DBMS_LOGMNR_CDC_SUBSCRIBE.PURGE_WIND)W
   (*subscription_handle* IN NUMBER);
     Resets the low-water mark for *subscription_handle*, which effectively makes the window empty.

PROCEDURE DBMS_LOGMNR_CDC_SUBSCRIBE.DROP_SUBSCRIPTION
   (*subscription_handle* IN NUMBER);
     Drops *subscription_handle*.

DBMS_LOGMNR_D

Contains procedures that allow you to work with alternative tablespaces and the data dictionary. New with Oracle8*i*.

Calls

```
PROCEDURE DBMS_LOGMNR_D.BUILD
  (dictionary_filename IN VARCHAR2,
  dictionary_location IN VARCHAR2
  [,options IN NUMBER]#);
```
Writes data dictionary information to *dictionary_filename* in *dictionary_location*, either as a flat file (*options* = STORE_IN_FLAT_FILE) or as redo logs (*options* = STORE_IN_REDO_LOGS). *options* are new with Oracle9*i*.

```
PROCEDURE DBMS_LOGMNR_D.SET_TABLESPACE
  (tablespace IN VARCHAR2);
```
Re-creates LogMiner tables in a *tablespace* other than the default of SYS. New with Oracle9*i*.

DBMS_LOGSTNDBY

Logical standby is a new feature of Oracle9*i* Release 2 that allows the use of a standby database that is not an exact physical copy of the active database. This package provides procedures that permit you to manage a logical standby environment.

Calls

```
PROCEDURE DBMS_LOGSTNDBY.APPLY_SET
  (parameter IN VARCHAR2,
  value IN VARCHAR2);
```
Lets you set *parameter* to *value*. For more information on the parameters that can be set, see the Oracle documentation.

```
PROCEDURE DBMS_LOGSTDBY.APPLY_UNSET
  (parameter IN VARCHAR);
```
Reverses the values applied with the APPLY_SET procedure.

```
PROCEDURE DBMS_LOGSTDBY.BUILD;
```
Used to preserve LogMiner dictionary information in the redo logs.

```
PROCEDURE DBMS_LOGSTDBY.GUARD_BYPASS_OFF;
```
Reenables the database guard feature that was previously bypassed with the GUARD_BYPASS_ON procedure.

```
PROCEDURE DBMS_LOGSTDBY.GUARD_BYPASS_ON;
```
Turns off the database guard that protects the logical standby from modifications. Typically used for maintenance or problem correction on the standby, but not for transactions, because triggers and constraints are not used.

```
PROCEDURE DBMS_LOGSTDBY.INSTANTIATE_TABLE
  (table_name IN VARCHAR2,
  schema IN VARCHAR2,
  dblink IN VARCHAR2);
```
Creates *table_name* in *schema* of *dblink*.

```
PROCEDURE DBMS_LOGSTDBY.SKIP
    (statement_option IN VARCHAR2,
    schema_name IN VARCHAR2,
    object_name IN VARCHAR2,
    proc_name IN VARCHAR2);
```
Defines filter, defined by keywords in *statement_option*, to prevent certain SQL statements on *object_name* in *schema_name* from being applied to the logical standby database, based on rules defined in *proc_name*.

```
PROCEDURE DBMS_LOGSTDBY.SKIP_ERROR
    (statement_option IN VARCHAR2,
    schema_name IN VARCHAR2,
    object_name IN VARCHAR2,
    proc_name IN VARCHAR2);
```
Called when log apply services encounter an error.

```
PROCEDURE DBMS_LOGSTDBY.SKIP_TRANSACTION
    (XIDUSN NUMBER STRING,
    XIDSLT NUMBER STRING,
    XIDSQN NUMBER STRING);
```
Called to skip a particular transaction, identified by the undo segment number, slot number, and sequence number of the transaction.

```
PROCEDURE DBMS_LOGSTDBY.UNSKIP
    (statement_option IN VARCHAR2,
    schema_name IN VARCHAR2,
    object_name IN VARCHAR2,
```
Undoes the action of the SKIP procedure.

```
PROCEDURE DBMS_LOGSTDBY.UNDO_ERROR
    (statement_option IN VARCHAR2,
    schema_name IN VARCHAR2,
    object_name IN VARCHAR2);
```
Undoes the action of the SKIP_ERROR procedure.

```
PROCEDURE DBMS_LOGSTDBY.UNSKIP_TRANSACTION
    (XIDUSN NUMBER STRING,
    XIDSLT NUMBER STRING,
    XIDSQN NUMBER STRING);
```
Undoes the action of the SKIP_TRANSACTION procedure.

DBMS_METADATA

Allows you to retrieve complete database object definitions from the data dictionary. New with Oracle9*i*.

Calls

```
PROCEDURE DBMS_METADATA.OPEN
    (object_type IN VARCHAR2,
    version IN VARCHAR2 DEFAULT 'COMPATIBLE',
    model IN VARCHAR2 DEFAULT 'ORACLE')
    RETURN NUMBER;
```
Specifies *object_type*, *version,* and object *model* and returns a context handle used in subsequent calls.

```
PROCEDURE DBMS_METADATA.SET_FILTER
    (handle IN NUMBER,
     name IN VARCHAR2,
     value IN {VARCHAR2 | BOOLEAN DEFAULT TRUE});
```
Specifies restrictions on objects to be retrieved. The *name* parameter refers to the name of a filter, as explained in the Oracle documentation.

```
PROCEDURE DBMS_METADATA.SET_COUNT
    (handle IN NUMBER,
     value IN NUMBER);
```
Specifies the maximum number of objects (*value*) to be retrieved with a FETCH_* procedure.

```
PROCEDURE DBMS_METADATA.GET_QUERY
    (handle IN NUMBER)
    RETURN VARCHAR2;
```
Returns the text of queries used by the FETCH_* procedure.

```
PROCEDURE DBMS_METADATA.SET_PARSE_ITEM
    (handle IN NUMBER,
     name IN VARCHAR2);
```
Specifies an output attribute (*name*) to be parsed and returned with the FETCH_ DDL procedure.

```
PROCEDURE DBMS_METADATA.ADD_TRANSFORMATION
    (handle IN NUMBER,
     name IN VARCHAR2,
     encoding IN VARCHAR2 DEFAULT NULL)
    RETURN NUMBER;
```
Requests that a transformation be applied to the XML representation of objects retrieved. Returns a handle to the transformed representation.

```
PROCEDURE DBMS_METADATA.SET_TRANSFORM_PARAM
    (transform_handle IN NUMBER,
     name IN VARCHAR2,
     value IN {VARCHAR2 | BOOLEAN DEFAULT TRUE});
```
Specifies parameters to the XSLT stylesheet identified by *transform_handle* used to modify output of the transformation.

```
PROCEDURE DBMS_METADATA.FETCH_XML
    (handle IN NUMBER)
    RETURN SYS.XMLTYPE;
```
Returns metadata as XML.

```
PROCEDURE DBMS_METADATA.FETCH_DDL
    (handle IN NUMBER)
    RETURN SYS.KU$_DDLS;
```
Returns metadata as DDL.

```
PROCEDURE DBMS_METADATA.FETCH_CLOB
    (handle IN NUMBER)
    RETURN CLOB;
```

```
PROCEDURE DBMS_METADATA.FETCH_CLOB
    (handle IN NUMBER,
     doc IN OUT NOCOPY CLOB);
```
Returns the object itself as a CLOB.

```
PROCEDURE DBMS_METADATA.CLOSE
    (handle IN NUMBER);
      Closes the handle and cleans up its state.

FUNCTION DBMS_METADATA.GET_XML
    (object_type IN VARCHAR2,
    name IN VARCHAR2,
    schema IN VARCHAR2 DEFAULT NULL,
    version IN VARCHAR2 DEFAULT 'COMPATIBLE',
    model IN VARCHAR2 DEFAULT 'ORACLE',
    transform IN VARCHAR2 DEFAULT NULL)
    RETURN CLOB;
      Returns metadata for object name in schema as XML.

FUNCTION DBMS_METADATA.GET_DDL
    (object_type IN VARCHAR2,
    name IN VARCHAR2,
    schema IN VARCHAR2 DEFAULT NULL,
    version IN VARCHAR2 DEFAULT 'COMPATIBLE',
    model IN VARCHAR2 DEFAULT 'ORACLE',
    transform IN VARCHAR2 DEFAULT 'DDL')
    RETURN CLOB;
      Returns metadata for object name in schema as DDL.

FUNCTION DBMS_METADATA.GET_DEPENDENT_XML
    (object_type IN VARCHAR2,
    base_object_name IN VARCHAR2,
    base_object_schema IN VARCHAR2 DEFAULT NULL,
    version IN VARCHAR2 DEFAULT 'COMPATIBLE',
    model IN VARCHAR2 DEFAULT 'ORACLE',
    transform IN VARCHAR2 DEFAULT NULL,
    object_count) IN NUMBER DEFAULT 10000)
    RETURN CLOB;
      Returns metadata for dependent objects as XML.

FUNCTION DBMS_METADATA.GET_DEPENDENT_DDL
    (object_type IN VARCHAR2,
    base_object_name IN VARCHAR2,
    base_object_schema IN VARCHAR2 DEFAULT NULL,
    version IN VARCHAR2 DEFAULT 'COMPATIBLE',
    model IN VARCHAR2 DEFAULT 'ORACLE',
    transform IN VARCHAR2 DEFAULT 'DDL',
    object_count IN NUMBER DEFAULT 10000)
    RETURN CLOB;
      Returns metadata for dependent objects as DDL.

PROCEDURE DBMS_METADATA.GET_GRANTED_XML
    (object_type IN VARCHAR2,
    grantee IN VARCHAR2 DEFAULT NULL,
    version IN VARCHAR2 DEFAULT 'COMPATIBLE',
    model IN VARCHAR2 DEFAULT 'ORACLE',
    transform IN VARCHAR2 DEFAULT NULL,
    object_count IN NUMBER DEFAULT 10000)
    RETURN CLOB;
      Returns metadata for granted objects as XML.
```

```
PROCEDURE DBMS_METADATA.GET_GRANTED_XML
    (object_type IN VARCHAR2,
    grantee IN VARCHAR2 DEFAULT NULL,
    version IN VARCHAR2 DEFAULT 'COMPATIBLE',
    model IN VARCHAR2 DEFAULT 'ORACLE',
    transform IN VARCHAR2 DEFAULT 'DDL',
    object_count IN NUMBER DEFAULT 10000)
    RETURN CLOB;
```
Returns metadata for granted objects as DDL.

DBMS_MGWADM

Provides procedures that serve as the administrative interface for the Messaging Gateway, a part of Oracle Advanced Queuing. In order to use this package, you must run the *catmgw.sql* script. New in Oracle9*i*.

Calls

```
PROCEDURE DBMS_MGWADM.ALTER_AGENT
    (max_connections IN BINARY_INTEGER DEFAULT NULL,
    max_memory IN BINARY_INTEGER DEFAULT NULL);
```
Sets resource limits on connections and memory used by the Messaging Gateway agent.

```
PROCEDURE DBMS_MGWADM.DB_CONNECT_INFO
    (username IN VARCHAR2,
    password IN VARCHAR2,
    database IN VARCHAR2 DEFAULT NULL);
```
Specifies Oracle connection information used by the Messaging Gateway agent.

```
PROCEDURE DBMS_MGWADM.STARTUP
    (instance IN BINARY_INTEGER DEFAULT 0,
    force IN BINARY_INTEGER DEFAULT DBMS_MGWADM.NO_FORCE);
```
Starts the Messaging Gateway agent on *instance*. If *instance* is 0, the agent can use any instance. If *force* has the default value, it must use the specified instance.

```
PROCEDURE DBMS_MGWADM.SHUTDOWN
    (sdmode IN BINARY_INTEGER DEFAULT DBMS_MGWADM.SHUTDOWN_NORMAL);
```
If *sdmode* has the default value, the Messaging Gateway agent attempts to complete its current propagation work. If *sdmode* is SHUTDOWN_IMME-DIATE, the gateway terminates immediately.

```
PROCEDURE DBMS_MGWADM.CLEANUP_GATEWAY
    (action IN BINARY_INTEGER);
```
Performs cleanup or recovery operations left in the wake of an abnormal shutdown. The only acceptable value is DBMS_MGWADM.CLEAN_STARTUP_STATE.

```
PROCEDURE DBMS_MGWADM.SET_LOG_LEVEL
    (log_level IN BINARY_INTEGER);
```
Sets the log level to either DBMS_MGWADM.BASIC_LOGGING or DBMS_MGWADM.TRACE_DEBUG_LOGGING.

```
PROCEDURE DBMS_MGWADM.CREATE_MSGSYSTEM_LINK
    (linkname IN VARCHAR2,
    properties IN SYS.MGW_MQSERIES_PROPERTIES,
```

```
    options IN SYS.MGW_PROPERTIES DEFAULT NULL,
    comment IN VARCHAR2 DEFAULT NULL);
```
Creates a *linkname* link to an MQSeries messaging system with specified *properties*.

```
PROCEDURE DBMS_MGWADM.ALTER_MSGSYSTEM_LINK
    (linkname IN VARCHAR2,
    properties IN SYS.MGW_MQSERIES_PROPERTIES,
    options IN SYS.MGW_PROPERTIES DEFAULT NULL,
    comment IN VARCHAR2 DEFAULT DBMS_MGWADM.NO_CHANGE);
```
Alters the *properties* of the *linkname* link to an MQSeries messaging system.

```
PROCEDURE DBMS_MGWADM.REMOVE_MSGSYSTEM_LINK
    (linkname IN VARCHAR2);
```
Removes the *linkname* link.

```
PROCEDURE DBMS_MGWADM.REGISTER_FOREIGN_QUEUE
    (name IN VARCHAR2,
    linkname IN VARCHAR2,
    provider_queue IN VARCHAR2 DEFAULT NULL,
    domain IN INTEGER DEFAULT NULL,
    options IN SYS.MGW_PROPERTIES DEFAULT NULL,
    comment IN VARCHAR2 DEFAULT NULL);
```
Registers *name* on foreign system with *linkname* to *provider_queue* in the domain.

```
PROCEDURE DBMS_MGWADM.UNREGISTER_FOREIGN_QUEUE
    (name IN VARCHAR2,
    linkname IN VARCHAR2);
```
Drops queue *name*, which uses *linkname*.

```
PROCEDURE DBMS_MGWADM.ADD_SUBSCRIBER
    (subscriber_id IN VARCHAR2,
    propagation_type IN BINARY_INTEGER,
    queue_name IN VARCHAR2,
    destination IN VARCHAR2,
    rule IN VARCHAR2 DEFAULT NULL,
    transformation IN VARCHAR2 DEFAULT NULL,
    exception_queue IN VARCHAR2 DEFAULT NULL);
```
Adds *subscriber_id* to consume messages from *queue_name*.

```
PROCEDURE DBMS_MGWADM.ALTER_SUBSCRIBER
    (subscriber_id IN VARCHAR2,
    rule IN VARCHAR2 DEFAULT NULL,
    transformation IN VARCHAR2 DEFAULT NULL,
    exception_queue IN VARCHAR2 DEFAULT NULL);
```
Alters *subscriber_id*.

```
PROCEDURE DBMS_MGWADM.REMOVE_SUBSCRIBER
    (subscriber_id IN VARCHAR2,
    force IN BINARY_INTEGER DEFAULT DBMS_MGWADM.NO_FORCE);
```
Drops *subscriber_id*. If *force* has the default value, the action will fail without valid cleanup; if *force* is FORCE, the action will succeed even if cleanup cannot be done.

```
PROCEDURE DBMS_MGWADM.RESET_SUBSCRIBER
    (subscriber_id IN VARCHAR);
```
Resets the propagation error state for *subscriber_id*.

PROCEDURE DBMS_MGWADM.SCHEDULE_PROPAGATION
    (*schedule_id* IN VARCHAR2,
    propagation_type IN BINARY_INTEGER,
    source IN VARCHAR2,
    destination IN VARCHAR2,
    start_time IN DATE DEFAULT SYSDATE,
    duration IN NUMBER DEFAULT NULL,
    next_time IN VARCHAR2 DEFAULT NULL,
    latency IN NUMBER DEFAULT 60);
    Schedules *schedule_id* message propagation from *source* to *destination*.

PROCEDURE DBMS_MGWADM.UNSCHEDULE_PROPAGATION
    (*schedule_id* IN VARCHAR2);
    Removes *schedule_id* from propagation schedule.

PROCEDURE DBMS_MGWADM.SCHEDULE_PROPAGATION
    (*schedule_id* IN VARCHAR2,
    duration IN NUMBER DEFAULT NULL,
    next_time IN VARCHAR2 DEFAULT NULL,
    latency IN NUMBER DEFAULT 60);
    Alters *schedule_id* message propagation.

PROCEDURE DBMS_MGWADM.ENABLE_PROPAGATION_SCHEDULE
    (*schedule_id* IN VARCHAR2);
    Enables *schedule_id* propagation.

PROCEDURE DBMS_MGWADM.DISABLE_PROPAGATION_SCHEDULE
    (*schedule_id* IN VARCHAR2);
    Disables *schedule_id* propagation.

DBMA_MGWMSG

Provides procedures for working with Messaging Gateway message types, as well as the object types used. In order to use this package, you must run the *catmgw.sql* script. New with Oracle9*i*.

Calls

PROCEDURE DBMS_MGWMSG.NVARRAY_ADD
    (*p_array* IN OUT SYS.MGW_NAME_ARRAY_T,
    p_value IN SYS.MGS_NAME_VALUE_T);
    Appends *p_value* to *p_array*.

FUNCTION DBMS_MGWMSG.NVARRAY_GET
    (*p_array* IN SYS.MGW_NAME_ARRAY_T,
    p_name IN VARCHAR2,
    p_compare IN BINARY_INTEGER DEFAULT CASE_SENSITIVE)
    RETURN SYS.MGW_NAME_VALUE_T;
    Returns a value for *p_name* in *p_array*. *p_compare* is either CASE_SENSITIVE or CASE_INSENSITIVE and controls how *p_name* is compared to the names in *p_array*.

FUNCTION DBMS_MGWMSG.NVARRAY_GET_BOOLEAN
    (*p_array* IN SYS.MGW_NAME_ARRAY_T,
    p_name IN VARCHAR2,

```
p_compare IN BINARY_INTEGER DEFAULT CASE_SENSITIVE)
RETURN INTEGER;
```
Returns a value for BOOLEAN *p_name* in *p_array*. *p_compare* is either CASE_ SENSITIVE or CASE_INSENSITIVE and controls how *p_name* is compared to the names in *p_array*.

```
FUNCTION DBMS_MGWMSG.NVARRAY_GET_BYTE
    (p_array IN SYS.MGW_NAME_ARRAY_T,
    p_name IN VARCHAR2,
    p_compare IN BINARY_INTEGER DEFAULT CASE_SENSITIVE)
    RETURN INTEGER;
```
Returns a value for BYTE *p_name* in *p_array*. *p_compare* is either CASE_SENSI-TIVE or CASE_INSENSITIVE and controls how *p_name* is compared to the names in *p_array*.

```
FUNCTION DBMS_MGWMSG.NVARRAY_GET_SHORT
    (p_array IN SYS.MGW_NAME_ARRAY_T,
    p_name IN VARCHAR2,
    p_compare IN BINARY_INTEGER DEFAULT CASE_SENSITIVE)
    RETURN INTEGER;
```
Returns a value for SHORT *p_name* in *p_array*. *p_compare* is either CASE_ SENSITIVE or CASE_INSENSITIVE and controls how *p_name* is compared to the names in *p_array*.

```
FUNCTION DBMS_MGWMSG.NVARRAY_GET_INTEGER
    (p_array IN SYS.MGW_NAME_ARRAY_T,
    p_name IN VARCHAR2,
    p_compare IN BINARY_INTEGER DEFAULT CASE_SENSITIVE)
    RETURN INTEGER;
```
Returns a value for INTEGER *p_name* in *p_array*. *p_compare* is either CASE_ SENSITIVE or CASE_INSENSITIVE and controls how *p_name* is compared to the names in *p_array*.

```
FUNCTION DBMS_MGWMSG.NVARRAY_GET_LONG
    (p_array IN SYS.MGW_NAME_ARRAY_T,
    p_name IN VARCHAR2,
    p_compare IN BINARY_INTEGER DEFAULT CASE_SENSITIVE)
    RETURN INTEGER;
```
Returns a value for LONG *p_name* in *p_array*. *p_compare* is either CASE_SENSI-TIVE or CASE_INSENSITIVE and controls how *p_name* is compared to the names in *p_array*.

```
FUNCTION DBMS_MGWMSG.NVARRAY_GET_FLOAT
    (p_array IN SYS.MGW_NAME_ARRAY_T,
    p_name IN VARCHAR2,
    p_compare IN BINARY_INTEGER DEFAULT CASE_SENSITIVE)
    RETURN INTEGER;
```
Returns a value for FLOAT *p_name* in *p_array*. *p_compare* is either CASE_SENSI-TIVE or CASE_INSENSITIVE and controls how *p_name* is compared to the names in *p_array*.

```
FUNCTION DBMS_MGWMSG.NVARRAY_GET_DOUBLE
    (p_array IN SYS.MGW_NAME_ARRAY_T,
    p_name IN VARCHAR2,
```

```
    p_compare IN BINARY_INTEGER DEFAULT CASE_SENSITIVE)
    RETURN INTEGER;
```
Returns a value for DOUBLE *p_name* in *p_array*. *p_compare* is either CASE_
SENSITIVE or CASE_INSENSITIVE and controls how *p_name* is compared to
the names in *p_array*.

```
FUNCTION DBMS_MGWMSG.NVARRAY_GET_TEXT
    (p_array IN SYS.MGW_NAME_ARRAY_T,
    p_name IN VARCHAR2,
    p_compare IN BINARY_INTEGER DEFAULT CASE_SENSITIVE)
    RETURN VARCHAR2;
```
Returns a value for text *p_name* in *p_array*. *p_compare* is either CASE_SENSI-
TIVE or CASE_INSENSITIVE and controls how *p_name* is compared to the
names in *p_array*.

```
FUNCTION DBMS_MGWMSG.NVARRAY_GET_RAW
    (p_array IN SYS.MGW_NAME_ARRAY_T,
    p_name IN VARCHAR2,
    p_compare IN BINARY_INTEGER DEFAULT CASE_SENSITIVE)
    RETURN RAW;
```
Returns a value for RAW *p_name* in *p_array*. *p_compare* is either CASE_SENSI-
TIVE or CASE_INSENSITIVE and controls how *p_name* is compared to the
names in *p_array*.

```
FUNCTION DBMS_MGWMSG.NVARRAY_GET_DATE
    (p_array IN SYS.MGW_NAME_ARRAY_T,
    p_name IN VARCHAR2,
    p_compare IN BINARY_INTEGER DEFAULT CASE_SENSITIVE)
    RETURN DATE;
```
Returns a value for date *p_name* in *p_array*. *p_compare* is either CASE_SENSI-
TIVE or CASE_INSENSITIVE and controls how *p_name* is compared to the
names in *p_array*.

```
FUNCTION DBMS_MGWMSG.NVARRAY_FIND_NAME
    (p_array IN SYS.MGW_NAME_ARRAY_T,
    p_name IN VARCHAR2,
    p_compare IN BINARY_INTEGER DEFAULT CASE_SENSITIVE)
    RETURN BINARY_INTEGER;
```
Returns the position of *p_name* in *p_array*. *p_compare* is either CASE_SENSI-
TIVE or CASE_INSENSITIVE and controls how *p_name* is compared to the
names in *p_array*.

```
FUNCTION DBMS_MGWMSG.NVARRAY_FIND_NAME_TYPE
    (p_array IN SYS.MGW_NAME_ARRAY_T,
    p_name IN VARCHAR2,
    p_type IN BINARY_INTEGER,
    p_compare IN BINARY_INTEGER DEFAULT CASE_SENSITIVE)
    RETURN BINARY_INTEGER;
```
Returns the position of *p_name* of *p_type* in *p_array*. *p_compare* is either CASE_
SENSITIVE or CASE_INSENSITIVE and controls how *p_name* is compared to
the names in *p_array*.

DBMS_MVIEW

Provides procedures and functions used to manage materialized views. This package was renamed from DBMS_SNAPSHOT with Oracle9i.

Calls

PROCEDURE DBMS_MVIEW.BEGIN_TABLE_REORGANIZATION
  (*tabowner* IN VARCHAR2,
  tabname IN VARCHAR2);
  Preserves materialized view data of *tabname* in *tabowner* schema.

PROCEDURE DBMS_MVIEW.END_TABLE_REORGANIZATION
  (*tabowner* IN VARCHAR2,
  tabname IN VARCHAR2);
  Called after *tabname* in *tabowner* schema is reorganized to ensure that materialized view data is valid and that *tabname* is in proper state.

PROCEDURE DBMS_MVIEW.EXPLAIN_MVIEW
  (*mv* IN VARCHAR2,
  {*statement_id* IN VARCHAR2 := NULL |
  msg_array OUT SYS.EXPLAINMVARRAYTYPE});
  Returns an explanation of the capabilities of *mv*. If you use the *statement_id* parameter, the output goes to the MV_CAPABILITIES_TABLE, which must exist. You must run the *utlxmv.sql* script before using. New with Oracle8i.

PROCEDURE DBMS_MVIEW.EXPLAIN_MVIEW
  (*query* IN VARCHAR2,
  mv IN VARCHAR2,
  {*statement_id* IN VARCHAR2 := NULL |
  msg_array OUT SYS.EXPLAINMVARRAYTYPE});
  Returns an explanation of the rewrite of *query* using *mv*. If you use the *statement_id* parameter, the output goes to the REWRITE_TABLE, which is created when you run the *utlxrw.sql* script. New with Oracle9i.

FUNCTION DBMS_MVIEW.I_AM_A_REFRESH( )
  RETURN BOOLEAN;
  Returns TRUE if all local replication triggers for materialized views are disabled and FALSE if not. We like a function that identifies itself!

FUNCTION DBMS_MVIEW.PMARKER
  (*rid* IN ROWID)
  RETURN NUMBER;
  Returns a partition marker from *rid* (the ROWID), which is used for Partition Change Tracking. New with Oracle9i.

PROCEDURE DBMS_MVIEW.PURGE_DIRECT_LOAD_LOG;
  Removes entries from the direct loader log. New with Oracle8i.

PROCEDURE DBMS_MVIEW.PURGE_LOG
  (*master* IN VARCHAR2,
  num IN BINARY_INTEGER := 1,
  flag IN VARCHAR2 := 'NOP');
  Removes rows from the materialized view log of *master*. *num* is the amount of the least most recently refreshed materialized views. If *flag* is 'DELETE', this guarantees that rows are deleted for at least one materialized view.

PROCEDURE DBMS_MVIEW.PURGE_{SNAPSHOT | MVIEW}_FROM_LOG
  ({*snapshot_id* | *mview* IN BINARY_INTEGER |
  {*snapowner* | *mviewowner*} IN VARCHAR2},
  {*snapname* | *mviewname*} IN VARCHAR2,
  {*snapsite* | *mviewsite*} IN VARCHAR2);

> Deletes rows from materialized view refresh-related data dictionary views. The materialized view is either identified with *mview_id* or the owner, name, and site of the view. New with Oracle8*i*.

PROCEDURE DBMS_MVIEW.REFRESH
  ({*list* IN VARCHAR2 | *tab* IN OUT DBMS_UTILITY.UNCL_ARRAY},
  method IN VARCHAR2 := NULL,
  rollback_seg IN VARCHAR2 := NULL,
  push_deferred_rpc IN BOOLEAN := TRUE,
  refresh_after_errors IN BOOLEAN := FALSE,
  purge_option IN BINARY_INTEGER := 1,
  parallelism IN BINARY_INTEGER := 0,
  heap_size IN BINARY_INTEGER := 0,
  atomic_refresh IN BOOLEAN := TRUE);

> Refreshes a list of materialized views specified in *list* or *tab*. *atomic_refresh* is new with Oracle8*i*.

PROCEDURE DBMS_MVIEW.REFRESH_ALL_MVIEWS
  (*number_of_failures* OUT BINARY_INTEGER,
  method IN VARCHAR2 := NULL,
  rollback_seg IN VARCHAR2 := NULL,
  refresh_after_errors IN BOOLEAN := FALSE,
  atomic_refresh IN BOOLEAN := TRUE);

> Refreshes all materialized views that have not been refreshed since the most recent change to the master table. The materialized view and all master tables and materialized views must be local and in the view DBA_MVIEWS. New with Oracle8*i*.

PROCEDURE DBMS_MVIEW.REFRESH_DEPENDENT
  ([*number_of_failures* OUT BINARY_INTEGER,]
  {*list* IN VARCHAR2 | *tab* IN OUT DBMS_UTILITY.UNCL_ARRAY},
  method IN VARCHAR2 := NULL,
  rollback_seg IN VARCHAR2 := NULL,
  refresh_after_errors IN BOOLEAN := FALSE,
  atomic_refresh IN BOOLEAN := TRUE);

> Refreshes all materialized views that are dependent on the master tables or materialized views in *list* or *tab* and that have not been refreshed since the most recent change to the master table. The materialized view and all master tables and materialized views must be local and in the view DBA_MVIEWS. The *number_of_failures* parameter is not supported in Oracle9*i*. The procedure was new with Oracle8*i*.

PROCEDURE DBMS_MVIEW.REGISTER_{SNAPSHOT | MVIEW}
  (*snapowner* | *mviewowner*} IN VARCHAR2,
  {*snapname* | *mviewname*} IN VARCHAR2,
  {*snapsite* | *mviewsite*} IN VARCHAR2,
  {*snapid* | *mview_id*} IN {DATE | BINARY_INTEGER},
  {*flag* IN BINARY_INTEGER,
  qry_txt IN VARCHAR2,
  rep_type IN BINARY_INTEGER := DBMS_{SNAPSHOT | MVIEW.REG_UNKNOWN}};

> Used to register individual materialized views.

```
PROCEDURE DBMS_SNAPSHOT.SET_I_AM_A_REFRESH
    (value IN BOOLEAN);
```
Sets the I_AM_A_REFRESH package to *value*. Not supported after Oracle8.
```
PROCEDURE DBMS_MVIEW.UNREGISTER_{SNAPSHOT | MVIEW}
    ({snapowner | mviewowner} IN VARCHAR2,
    {snapname | mviewname} IN VARCHAR2,
    {snapsite | mviewsite} IN VARCHAR2);
```
Unregisters individual materialized views.

DBMS_OBFUSCATION_TOOLKIT

Provides procedures that allow an application to encrypt data with the Data Encryption Standard (DES) or the Triple DES standard. New with Oracle9*i*.

Calls

```
PROCEDURE DBMS_OBFUSCATION_TOOLKIT.DESENCRYPT
    (input IN {RAW | VARCHAR2},
    key IN {RAW | VARCHAR2},
    encrypted_data OUT {RAW | VARCHAR2});
```
Returns a form of *input*, encrypted with *key*, in *encrypted_data*.

```
PROCEDURE DBMS_OBFUSCATION_TOOLKIT.DESDECRYPT
    (input IN {RAW | VARCHAR2},
    key IN {RAW | VARCHAR2},
    decrypted_data OUT {RAW | VARCHAR2});
```
Returns a form of *input*, decrypted with *key*, in *decrypted_data*.

```
PROCEDURE DBMS_OBFUSCATION_TOOLKIT.DES3ENCRYPT
    (input IN {RAW | VARCHAR2},
    key IN {RAW | VARCHAR2},
    encrypted_data OUT {RAW | VARCHAR2},
    which IN PLS_INTEGER);
```
Returns a form of *input*, triple or double encrypted with *key*, in *encrypted_data*, which is either 0 (uses TwoKeyMode) or 1 (uses ThreeKeyMode).

```
PROCEDURE DBMS_OBFUSCATION_TOOLKIT.DESDECRYPT
    (input IN {RAW | VARCHAR2},
    key IN {RAW | VARCHAR2},
    decrypted_data OUT {RAW | VARCHAR2});
```
Returns a form of *input*, triple or double decrypted with *key*, in *decrypted_data*, which is either 0 (uses TwoKeyMode) or 1 (uses ThreeKeyMode).

DBMS_ODCI

Returns the CPU cost of a user function, based on the elapsed time of the function, which is used by extensible optimizer routines. New with Oracle9*i*.

Call

```
FUNCTION DBMS_ODCI.ESTIMATE_CPU_UNITS
    (elapsed_time NUMBER)
    RETURN NUMBER;
```
Returns the cost of the function, based on the *elapsed_time* in seconds and the processor speed of the machine.

DBMS_OFFLINE_OG

Provides procedures used to manage offline instantiations of master groups, which are used in a multimaster environment.

Calls

```
PROCEDURE DBMS_OFFLINE_OG.BEGIN_INSTANTIATION
    (gname IN VARCHAR2,
    new_site IN VARCHAR2,
    fname IN VARCHAR2);
```
Starts offline instantiation of *new_site* for *gname* replication group. The *fname* parameter is for internal use only.

```
PROCEDURE DBMS_OFFLINE_OG.BEGIN_LOAD
    (gname IN VARCHAR2,
    new_site IN VARCHAR2);
```
Disables triggers while data is being imported into the *new_site* master site. Must be called from the master site.

```
PROCEDURE DBMS_OFFLINE_OG.END_INSTANTIATION
    (gname IN VARCHAR2,
    new_site IN VARCHAR2);
```
Ends instantiation of *new_site*. Must be called from the master definition site.

```
PROCEDURE DBMS_OFFLINE_OG.END_LOAD
    (gname IN VARCHAR2,
    new_site IN VARCHAR2,
    fname IN VARCHAR2);
```
Reenables triggers in *new_site* at the end of the offline instantiation and load. The *fname* parameter is for internal use only.

```
PROCEDURE DBMS_OFFLINE_OG.RESUME_SUBSET_OF_MASTERS
    (gname IN VARCHAR2,
    new_site IN VARCHAR2,
    override IN BOOLEAN := FALSE);
```
Resumes replication at existing sites during replication activity to *new_site*. If *override* (new with Oracle8*i*) is FALSE, replication is restored at each master as quickly as possible; if *override* is TRUE, replication begins only when there are no pending replication requests for *gname* at each master.

DBMS_OFFLINE_SNAPSHOT

Provides procedures for management of offline instantiation of materialized views.

Calls

```
PROCEDURE DBMS_OFFLINE_SNAPSHOT.BEGIN_LOAD
    (gname IN VARCHAR2,
    sname IN VARCHAR2,
    master_site IN VARCHAR2,
    snapshot_oname IN VARCHAR2,
    storage_c IN VARCHAR2 := '',
```

```
comment IN VARCHAR2 := '',
min_communication IN BOOLEAN := TRUE);
```
Prepares a materialized view in *sname* for import of a new materialized view, *snapshot_oname*. If *min_communications* is TRUE, the update sends a new value of a column only if the value is modified with an UPDATE statement.

PROCEDURE DBMS_OFFLINE_SNAPSHOT.END_LOAD
```
(gname IN VARCHAR2,
sname IN VARCHAR2,
snapshot_oname IN VARCHAR2);
```
Completes offline instantiation of *snapshot_oname*.

DBMS_OLAP

Provides a collection of materialized view analysis and Summary Advisor procedures and functions. New with Oracle8*i*.

Calls

PROCEDURE DBMS_OLAP.ADD_FILTER_ITEM
```
(filter_id IN NUMBER,
filter_name IN VARCHAR2,
string_list IN VARCHAR2,
number_min IN NUMBER,
number_max IN NUMBER,
date_min IN VARCHAR2,
date_max IN VARCHAR2);
```
Adds another filter to an existing filter, *filter_id*. The *filter_name* parameter describes the type of filter, while the remainder of the parameters are used by different types of filters. New with Oracle9*i*.

PROCEDURE DBMS_OLAP.CREATE_ID
```
(id OUT NUMBER);
```
Creates a unique *id* used to identify a filter, workload, or results of a Summary Advisor or validation run. New with Oracle9*i*.

PROCEDURE DBMS_OLAP.ESTIMATE_{SUMMARY_SIZE | MVIEW_SIZE}
```
(stmt_id IN VARCHAR2,
select_clause IN VARCHAR2,
num_rows OUT NUMBER,
num_bytes OUT NUMBER);
```
Returns *num_rows* and *num_bytes* that would be in a materialized view created by the *select_clause*. ESTIMATE_SUMMARY_SIZE was used with Oracle8*i* and ESTIMATE_MVIEW_SIZE with Oracle9*i*.

PROCEDURE DBMS_OLAP.EVALUATE_UTILIZATION;
Measures utilization of materialized views. The output is in MVIEW$_EVALUATIONS. Only in Oracle8*i*.

PROCEDURE DBMS_OLAP.EVALUATE_UTILIZATION_W;
Measures utilization of materialized views based on a workload in the default schema. Only in Oracle8*i*.

PROCEDURE DBMS_OLAP.EVALUATE_MVIEW_STRATEGY
```
(run_id IN NUMBER,
```

workload_id IN NUMBER,
filter_id IN NUMBER);

Estimates utilization of a materialized view, based on a *workload_id* and *filter_id* and returns *run_id* as an ID to identify the results of the run. New with Oracle9*i*.

PROCEDURE DBMS_OLAP.GENERATE_MVIEW_REPORT
(*filename* IN VARCHAR2,
id IN NUMBER
flags IN NUMBER);

Generates a *filename* report on a Summary Advisor run (*id*). The *flags* parameter controls the information in the report. New with Oracle9*i*.

PROCEDURE DBMS_OLAP.GENERATE_MVIEW_SCRIPT
(*filename* IN VARCHAR2,
id IN NUMBER
tspace IN VARCHAR2);

Generates SQL commands into *filename* that implement Summary Advisor recommendations. *tspace* is a tablespace name to use when creating materialized views. New with Oracle9*i*.

PROCEDURE DBMS_OLAP.LOAD_WORKLOAD_CACHE
(*workload_id* IN NUMBER,
flags IN NUMBER,
filter_id IN NUMBER,
application IN VARCHAR2,
priority IN NUMBER);

Loads a SQL cache workload *workload_id*. *flags* are WORKLOAD_OVER-WRITE, WORKLOAD_APPEND, or WORKLOAD_NEW; *filter_id* is a previously defined filter; *application* is the default business application, and *priority* assigns a business priority to the queries in the target workload. New with Oracle9*i*.

PROCEDURE DBMS_OLAP.LOAD_WORKLOAD_TRACE
(*collection_id* IN NUMBER,
flags IN NUMBER,
filter_id IN NUMBER,
application IN VARCHAR2,
priority IN NUMBER,
owner_name IN VARCHAR2);

Loads a SQL Trace workload *collection_id*. *flags* are WORKLOAD_OVER-WRITE, WORKLOAD_APPEND, or WORKLOAD_NEW; *filter_id* is a previously defined filter; *application* is the default business application; *priority* assigns a business priority to the queries in the target workload; and *owner_name* is the schema that contains the SQL Trace data. New with Oracle9*i*.

PROCEDURE DBMS_OLAP.LOAD_WORKLOAD_USER
(*workload_id* IN NUMBER,
flags IN NUMBER,
filter_id IN NUMBER,
owner_name IN VARCHAR2,
table_name IN VARCHAR2);

Loads a user-defined workload *workload_id*. *flags* are WORKLOAD_OVER-WRITE, WORKLOAD_APPEND, or WORKLOAD_NEW. *filter_id* is a previously defined filter. *owner_name* is the schema that contains *table_name*, which holds valid workload data. New with Oracle9*i*.

PROCEDURE DBMS_OLAP.PURGE_FILTER
   (*filter_id* IN NUMBER);
   Removes *filter_id*. New with Oracle9*i*.

PROCEDURE DBMS_OLAP.PURGE_RESULTS
   (*run_id* IN NUMBER);
   Removes results from recommendation, evaluation, or validation run identified by *run_id*. New with Oracle9*i*.

PROCEDURE DBMS_OLAP.PURGE_WORKLOAD
   (*workload_id* IN NUMBER);
   Removes *workload_id*. New with Oracle9*i*.

PROCEDURE DBMS_OLAP.RECOMMEND_MV[_W]
   (*fact_table_filter* IN VARCHAR2,
   storage_in_bytes IN NUMBER,
   retention_list IN VARCHAR2,
   retention_pct IN NUMBER := 50);
   Recommends which materialized views should be created, retained, or dropped. *fact_table_filter* is a comma-separated list of fact table names, *storage_in_bytes* is the maximum storage that can be used for storing materialized views, *retention_list* is a comma-separated list of materialized view table names that are excluded from a drop list, and *retention_pct* is the percentage of existing materialized view storage that must be maintained. RECOMMEND_MV_W is based on the workload gathered by Oracle Trace. Only in Oracle8*i*.

PROCEDURE DBMS_OLAP.RECOMMEND_MVIEW_STRATEGY
   (*run_id* IN NUMBER,
   workload_id IN NUMBER,
   filter_id IN NUMBER,
   storage_in_bytes IN NUMBER,
   retention_pct IN NUMBER,
   retention_list IN VARCHAR2,
   fact_table_filter IN VARCHAR2);
   Generates recommendations about existing and proposed materialized views. You must run DBMS_STATS.GATHER_TABLE_STATS prior to running this procedure. New with Oracle9*i*.

PROCEDURE DBMS_OLAP.SET_CANCELLED
   (*run_id* IN NUMBER);
   Stops a Summary Advisor *run_id*. New with Oracle9*i*.

PROCEDURE DBMS_OLAP.VALIDATE_DIMENSION
   (*dimension_name* IN VARCHAR2,
   dimension_owner IN VARCHAR2,
   incremental IN BOOLEAN,
   check_nulls IN BOOLEAN,
   run_id IN NUMBER);
   Verifies that *dimension_name*, owned by *dimension_owner*, has valid hierarchical, attribute and join relationships. *incremental* and *check_nulls* are validation checks, and *run_id* is an ID generated by DBMS_OLAP.CREATE_ID.

PROCEDURE DBMS_OLAP.VALIDATE_WORKLOAD_CACHE
   (*valid* OUT NUMBER,
   error OUT VARCHAR2);
   Validates SQL cache workload before a load and returns a success flag in *valid* and an error set in *error*, if appropriate. New with Oracle9*i*.

```
PROCEDURE DBMS_OLAP.VALIDATE_WORKLOAD_TRACE
    (owner_name IN VARCHAR2,
    valid OUT NUMBER,
    error OUT VARCHAR2);
```
Validates SQL Trace workload before a load and returns success flag in *valid* and an error set in *error*, if appropriate. *owner_name* is the owner of the trace workload table. New with Oracle9*i*.

```
PROCEDURE DBMS_OLAP.VALIDATE_WORKLOAD_USER
    (owner_name IN VARCHAR2,
    table_name IN VARCHAR2,
    valid OUT NUMBER,
    error OUT VARCHAR2);
```
Validates user-supplied workload for *table_name* before a load and returns a success flag in *valid* and an error set in *error*, if appropriate. *owner_name* is the owner of the user workload table. New with Oracle9*i*.

DBMS_ORACLE_TRACE_AGENT

Provides a procedure that lets you collect trace data for another session. Normally, the package is accessible only to user SYS. New in Oracle8*i*.

Call

```
PROCEDURE DBMS_ORACLE_TRACE_AGENT.SET_ORACLE_TRACE_IN_SESSION
    (sid NUMBER DEFAULT 0,
    serial# NUMBER DEFAULT 0,
    on_off IN BOOLEAN DEFAULT FALSE,
    collection_name IN VARCHAR2 DEFAULT '',
    facility_name IN VARCHAR2 DEFAULT '');
```
Collects SQL Trace data for a *sid* with *serial#*. *on_off* turns the trace on or off, and *collection_name* and *facility_name* identify the SQL Trace entities.

DBMS_ORACLE_TRACE_USER

Provides public access to SQL Trace instrumentation for the calling user. New with Oracle8*i*.

Call

```
PROCEDURE DBMS_ORACLE_TRACE_USER.SET_ORACLE_TRACE
    (on_off IN BOOLEAN DEFAULT FALSE,
    collection_name IN VARCHAR2 DEFAULT '',
    facility_name IN VARCHAR2 DEFAULT '');
```
on_off turns the trace on or off, and *collection_name* and *facility_name* identify the SQL Trace entities.

DBMS_OUTLN

Provides the ability to manage stored outlines. In Oracle8*i*, the DROP_UNUSED, DROP_BY_CAT, and UPDATE_BY_CAT procedures were a part of the OUTLN_PKG package.

Calls

PROCEDURE DBMS_OUTLN.DROP_BY_CAT
  (*cat* VARCHAR2);
> Drops outlines of category *cat*.

PROCEDURE DBMS_OUTLN.DROP_COLLISION;
> Drops an outline with an OL$.HINTCOUNT that does not match the number of hints for the outline in OL$HINTS.

PROCEDURE DBMS_OUTLN.DROP_EXTRA;
> Drops extra hint rows not accounted for by OL$.HINTCOUNT.

PROCEDURE DBMS_OUTLN.DROP_UNREFD_HINTS;
> Drops hint rows that have no corresponding outline in the OL$ table.

PROCEDURE DBMS_OUTLN.DROP_UNUSED;
> Drop outlines generated by an application for one-time use only.

PROCEDURE DBMS_OUTLN.UPDATE_BY_CAT
  (*oldcat* VARCHAR2 DEFAULT 'DEFAULT',
  newcat VARCHAR2 DEFAULT 'DEFAULT');
> Changes the category of all outlines in *oldcat* to *newcat*.

PROCEDURE DBMS_OUTLN.GENERATE_SIGNATURE
  (*sqltxt* IN VARCHAR2,
  signature OUT RAW);
> Generates a *signature* for *sqltext*.

DBMS_OUTLN_EDIT

Used to edit stored outlines. New with Oracle9*i*.

Calls

PROCEDURE DBMS_OUTLN_EDIT.CHANGE_JOIN_POS
  (*name* VARCHAR,
  hintno NUMBER,
  newpos NUMBER);
> Changes the join position in *hintno* of *outline* name to *newpos*.

PROCEDURE DBMS_OUTLN_EDIT.CREATE_EDIT_TABLES;
> Creates the outline editing tables in the user's schema.

PROCEDURE DBMS_OUTLN_EDIT.DROP_EDIT_TABLES;
> Drops the outline edit tables in the user's schema.

PROCEDURE DBMS_OUTLN_EDIT.REFRESH_PRIVATE_OUTLINE
  (*name* IN VARCHAR2);
> Refreshes the in-memory copy of the outline *name* to synchronize it with edits made to outline hints.

DBMS_OUTPUT

Provides a mechanism for displaying information on your session's output device from within a PL/SQL program. Can be used as a crude debugger or trace facility.

Calls

PROCEDURE DBMS_OUTPUT.DISABLE;
>   Disables output from the package and purges the DBMS_OUTPUT buffer.

PROCEDURE DBMS_OUTPUT.ENABLE
>   (*buffer_size* IN INTEGER DEFAULT 20000);
>   Enables output from the package and sets to *buffer_size* the maximum number of bytes that can be stored in the buffer.

PROCEDURE DBMS_OUTPUT.GET_LINE
>   (*line* OUT VARCHAR2,
>   *status* OUT INTEGER);
>   Gets the next line from the buffer and places it in *line*. A *status* of 0 means successful retrieval; 1 means failure.

PROCEDURE DBMS_OUTPUT.GET_LINES
>   (*lines* OUT DBMS_OUTPUT.CHARARR,
>   *numlines* IN OUT INTEGER);
>   Gets *numlines* number of lines from the buffer and places them in the *lines* PL/SQL table.

PROCEDURE DBMS_OUTPUT.NEW_LINE;
>   Writes a newline character to the DBMS_OUTPUT buffer. New with Oracle8*i*.

PROCEDURE DBMS_OUTPUT.PUT
>   (*a* IN DATE|NUMBER|VARCHAR2);
>   Puts the data contained in *a* in the DBMS_OUTPUT buffer and does not append a newline character.

PROCEDURE DBMS_OUTPUT.PUT_LINE
>   (*a* IN DATE|NUMBER|VARCHAR2);
>   Puts the data contained in *a* in the DBMS_OUTPUT buffer and then appends a newline character.

DBMS_PCLXUTIL

Provides intrapartition parallelism used in creating partition-wise local indexes. New with Oracle8*i*.

Call

PROCEDURE DBMS_PCLXUTIL.BUILD_PART_INDEX
>   ([*jobs_per_batch* IN NUMBER DEFAULT 1,]
>   *procs_per_job* IN NUMBER DEFAULT 1,
>   *tab_name* IN VARCHAR2 DEFAULT NULL,
>   *idx_name* IN VARCHAR2 DEFAULT NULL,
>   *force_opt* IN BOOLEAN DEFAULT FALSE);
>   Builds the local index *idx_name* on partitioned table *tab_name* with *procs_per_job* query processes. If *force_opt* is TRUE, forces a rebuild of all partitioned indexes; otherwise, rebuilds only partitions marked UNUSABLE. *jobs_per_batch* is supported only until Oracle8*i*.

DBMS_PIPE

Enables communication of messages between database sessions using memory-based structures. Communication is asynchronous, is nontransactional, and persists beyond session lifetime.

Calls

FUNCTION DBMS_PIPE.CREATE_PIPE
  (*pipename* IN VARCHAR2,
  maxpipesize IN INTEGER DEFAULT 8192,
  private IN BOOLEAN DEFAULT TRUE)
  RETURN INTEGER;
   Creates a pipe identified by *pipename* with maximum size *maxpipesize* and returns 0. When *private* is FALSE, the pipe is publicly accessible.

FUNCTION DBMS_PIPE.NEXT_ITEM_TYPE
  RETURN INTEGER;
   Returns an integer identifying the datatype of the next item in the session message buffer.

PROCEDURE DBMS_PIPE.PACK_MESSAGE
  (*item* IN {VARCHAR2 | NUMBER | DATE});
   Packs *item* into the session message buffer.

PROCEDURE DBMS_PIPE.PACK_MESSAGE_RAW
  (*item* IN RAW);
   Packs the raw data in *item* into the session message buffer.

PROCEDURE DBMS_PIPE.PACK_MESSAGE_ROWID
  (*item* IN ROWID);
   Packs the ROWID data in *item* into the session message buffer.

PROCEDURE DBMS_PIPE.PURGE
  (*pipename* IN VARCHAR2);
   Purges all messages from *pipename*.

FUNCTION DBMS_PIPE.RECEIVE_MESSAGE
  (*pipename* IN VARCHAR2,
  timeout IN INTEGER DEFAULT MAXWAIT)
  RETURN INTEGER;
   Receives a message from *pipename* into the session message buffer, waiting for up to *timeout* seconds for successful completion. Returns 0 for success and 1 for timeout.

FUNCTION DBMS_PIPE.REMOVE_PIPE
  (*pipename* IN VARCHAR2)
  RETURN INTEGER;
   Removes *pipename* and frees its memory back to the shared pool, returning 0.

PROCEDURE DBMS_PIPE.RESET_BUFFER;
   Resets the session message buffer's pack and unpack indicators, effectively discarding all contents.

FUNCTION DBMS_PIPE.SEND_MESSAGE
  (*pipename* IN VARCHAR2,
  timeout IN INTEGER DEFAULT MAXWAIT,

```
maxpipesize IN INTEGER DEFAULT 8192)
RETURN INTEGER;
```
Sends the contents of the session message buffer onto *pipename*, waiting for up to *timeout* seconds for successful completion and optionally increasing the maximum size of *pipename* to *maxpipesize*. Returns 0 for success and 1 for timeout.

```
FUNCTION DBMS_PIPE.UNIQUE_SESSION_NAME
RETURN VARCHAR2;
```
Returns a string identifier unique to the session up to 30 bytes in length.

```
PROCEDURE DBMS_PIPE.UNPACK_MESSAGE
(item OUT {VARCHAR2 | NUMBER | DATE});
```
Unpacks the next data item in the message buffer into *item*.

```
PROCEDURE DBMS_PIPE.UNPACK_MESSAGE_RAW
(item OUT RAW);
```
Unpacks the next data item in the message buffer into *item* when it is of datatype RAW.

```
PROCEDURE DBMS_PIPE.UNPACK_MESSAGE_ROWID
(item OUT ROWID);
```
Unpacks the next data item in the message buffer into *item* when it is of datatype ROWID.

DBMS_PROFILER

Provides procedures and functions to profile PL/SQL applications in order to identify performance bottlenecks. Each function returns a success code; 0 indicates success and other positive integers are error codes. New with Oracle8*i*.

Calls

```
FUNCTION DBMS_PROFILER.START_PROFILER
(run_comment IN VARCHAR2 := SYSDATE
[,run_comment1 IN VARCHAR := '']#
[,run_number OUT BINARY_INTEGER]#)
RETURN BINARY_INTEGER;
```
Starts the profiler with comments. *run_number* is an optional OUT parameter that stores the run number to access the information later. The last two parameters are new with Oracle9*i*.

```
FUNCTION DBMS_PROFILER.STOP_PROFILER
RETURN BINARY_INTEGER;
```
Stops the profiler run.

```
FUNCTION DBMS_PROFILER.FLUSH_DATA
RETURN BINARY_INTEGER;
```
Flushes the data to pre-existing database tables.

```
FUNCTION DBMS_PROFILER.PAUSE_PROFILER
RETURN BINARY_INTEGER;
```
Pauses profiler data collection. New with Oracle9*i*.

```
FUNCTION DBMS_PROFILER.RESUME_PROFILER
RETURN BINARY_INTEGER;
```
Resumes profiler data collection. New with Oracle9*i*.

```
PROCEDURE DBMS_PROFILER.GET_VERSION
   (major OUT BINARY_INTEGER,
   minor OUT BINARY_INTEGER);
```
   Returns the version of the package.

```
FUNCTION DBMS_PROFILER.INTERNAL_VERSION_CHECK
   RETURN BINARY_INTEGER;
```
   Checks to make sure this version of the package can work with the version of the database.

DBMS_PROPAGATION_ADM

Provides procedures to administer propagation from a source queue to a destination queue. Used with Oracle Streams. New with Oracle9i.

Calls
```
PROCEDURE DBMS_PROPAGATION_ADM.ALTER_PROPAGATION
   (propagation_name IN VARCHAR2,
   rule_set_name IN VARCHAR2);
```
   Alters, adds, or removes *rule_set_name* from *propagation_name*.

```
PROCEDURE DBMS_PROPAGATION_ADM.CREATE_PROPAGATION
   (propagation_name IN VARCHAR2,
   source_queue IN VARCHAR2,
   destination_queue IN VARCHAR2,
   destination_dblink IN VARCHAR2 DEFAULT NULL,
   rule_set_name IN VARCHAR2 DEFAULT NULL);
```
   Creates *propagation_name* from *source_queue* to *destination_queue* at *destination_dblink* with *rule_set_name*.

```
PROCEDURE DBMS_PROPAGATION_ADM.DROP_PROPAGATION
   (propagation_name IN VARCHAR2);
```
   Drops *propagation_name* and all its messages.

DBMS_RANDOM

Provides a random number–generating utility. New in Oracle8.

Calls
```
PROCEDURE DBMS_RANDOM.INITIALIZE
   (seed IN BINARY_INTEGER);
```
   Initializes the random number generator with the value of *seed*, which should be at least five digits in length.

```
FUNCTION DBMS_RANDOM.RANDOM
   RETURN BINARY_INTEGER;
```
   Returns a random integer value from the random number generator.

```
PROCEDURE DBMS_RANDOM.SEED
   (seed IN BINARY_INTEGER);
```
   Changes the random number generator's seed value to *seed*, which should be at least five digits in length.

```
PROCEDURE DBMS_RANDOM.TERMINATE;
```
   Releases resources used by the random number generator when no longer needed.

DBMS_RECTIFIER_DIFF

Provides procedures to detect and resolve inconsistencies between data in two replicated sites.

Calls

```
PROCEDURE DBMS_RECTIFIER_DIFF.DIFFERENCES
  (sname1 IN VARCHAR2,
  oname1 IN VARCHAR2,
  reference_site IN VARCHAR2 := '',
  sname2 IN VARCHAR2,
  oname2 IN VARCHAR2,
  comparison_site IN VARCHAR2 := '',
  where_clause IN VARCHAR2 := '',
  {column_list IN VARCHAR2 := '' |
    array_columns IN DBMS_UTILITY.NAME_ARRAY},
  missing_rows_sname IN VARCHAR2,
  missing_rows_oname1 IN VARCHAR2,
  missing_rows_oname2 IN VARCHAR2,
  missing_rows_site IN VARCHAR2:= '',
  max_missing IN INTEGER,
  commit_rows IN INTEGER := 500);
```
Compares the *column_list* or *array_columns* of *sname1.oname1* at *reference_site* to *sname2.oname2* at *comparison_site*. Inserts up to *max_missing* rows into *missing_ rows_sname.missing_rows_oname1* and information about the missing rows in *missing_rows_oname2*, with a commit every *commit_rows*.

```
PROCEDURE DBMS_RECTIFIER_DIFF.RECTIFY
  (sname1 IN VARCHAR2,
  oname1 IN VARCHAR2,
  reference_site IN VARCHAR2 := '',
  sname2 IN VARCHAR2,
  oname2 IN VARCHAR2,
  comparison_site IN VARCHAR2 := '',
  where_clause IN VARCHAR2 := '',
  {column_list IN VARCHAR2 := '' |
    array_columns IN DBMS_UTILITY.NAME_ARRAY},
  missing_rows_sname IN VARCHAR2,
  missing_rows_oname1 IN VARCHAR2,
  missing_rows_oname2 IN VARCHAR2,
  missing_rows_site IN VARCHAR2:= '',
  max_missing IN INTEGER,
  commit_rows IN INTEGER := 500);
```
Resolves the differences between the two tables found with the DIFFERENCES procedure. The *max_missing* parameter is new with Oracle8*i*.

DBMS_REDEFINITION

Provides procedures to perform an online redefinition of a table. New with Oracle9*i*.

Calls

```
PROCEDURE DBMS_REDEFINITION.CAN_REDEF_TABLE
   (uname IN VARCHAR2,
   tname IN VARCHAR2,
   options_flag IN BINARY_INTEGER := 1);
```
   If the *uname.tname* table cannot be redefined with *options_flag* of either DBMS_ REDEFINITION.CONS_USE_PK (redefinition done using primary key, the default) or DBMS_REDEFINITION.CONS_USE_ROWID (redefinition done using ROWID), an error is returned.

```
PROCEDURE DBMS_REDEFINITION.START_REDEF_TABLE
   (uname IN VARCHAR2,
   orig_table IN VARCHAR2,
   int_table IN VARCHAR2,
   col_mapping IN VARCHAR2:= NULL,
   options_flag IN BINARY_INTEGER := 1);
```
   Starts redefinition of *uname.orig_table* into interim table *int_table* with *col_ mapping* list. If *col_mapping* is NULL, all columns of *orig_table* are used. *options_ flag* has the same value as for CAN_REDEF_TABLE.

```
PROCEDURE DBMS_REDEFINITION.FINISH_REDEF_TABLE
   (uname IN VARCHAR,
   orig_table IN VARCHAR2,
   int_table IN VARCHAR2);
```
   Completes redefinition of *uname.orig_table*. You can create new indexes, triggers, grants, and constraints on the *int_table* before this call.

```
PROCEDURE DBMS_REDEFINITION.SYNCH_REDEF_TABLE
   (uname IN VARCHAR,
   orig_table IN VARCHAR2,
   int_table IN VARCHAR2);
```
   Synchronizes *int_table* with *uname.orig_table*. If there is a long-running process, this procedure can reduce the final work performed by FINISH_REDEF_TABLE.

```
PROCEDURE DBMS_REDEFINITION.ABORT_REDEF_TABLE
   (uname IN VARCHAR,
   orig_table IN VARCHAR2,
   int_table IN VARCHAR2);
```
   Cleans up errors that occur during the redefinition process.

DBMS_REFRESH

Lets you create groups of materialized views that can be refreshed together at a point in time that is transactionally consistent.

Calls

```
PROCEDURE DBMS_REFRESH.ADD
   (name IN VARCHAR2,
   {list IN VARCHAR2 | tab IN DBMS_UTILITY.UNCL_ARRAY},
   lax IN BOOLEAN := FALSE);
```
   Adds members in *list* or *tab* to group *name*. If you are moving a materialized view from one group to another, *lax* must be TRUE.

```
PROCEDURE DBMS_REFRESH.CHANGE
    (name IN VARCHAR2,
    next_date IN DATE := NULL,
    interval IN VARCHAR2 := NULL,
    implicit_destroy IN BOOLEAN := NULL,
    rollback_seg IN VARCHAR2 := NULL,
    push_deferred_rpc IN BOOLEAN := NULL,
    refresh_after_errors IN BOOLEAN := NULL,
    purge_option IN BINARY_INTEGER := NULL
    parallelism IN BINARY_INTEGER := NULL,
    heap_size IN BINARY_INTEGER := NULL);
```
Changes the *interval* for refresh group *name*, starting with *next_date*. The remaining parameters alter other characteristics of the refresh group, as described in the MAKE procedure.

```
PROCEDURE DBMS_REFRESH.DESTROY
    (name IN VARCHAR);
```
Removes materialized views from *name* and deletes the group.

```
PROCEDURE DBMS_REFRESH.MAKE
    (name IN VARCHAR2,
    {list IN VARCHAR2 | tab IN DBMS_UTILITY.UNCL_ARRAY},
    next_date IN DATE := NULL,
    interval IN VARCHAR2 := NULL,
    implicit_destroy IN BOOLEAN := FALSE,
    lax IN BOOLEAN := NULL,
    job IN  BINARY_INTEGER := 0,
    rollback_seg IN VARCHAR2 := NULL,
    push_deferred_rpc IN BOOLEAN := TRUE,
    refresh_after_errors IN BOOLEAN := FALSE,
    purge_option IN BINARY_INTEGER := NULL
    parallelism IN BINARY_INTEGER := NULL,
    heap_size IN BINARY_INTEGER := NULL);
```
Creates refresh group *name* from *list* or *tab*. The *interval* for refresh group *name* is the time between refreshes, starting with *next_date*. *implicit_destroy* deletes *name* if there are no members. *lax* is used if any of the materialized views being moved into *name* are already part of another group. *job* is needed by the Import utility and should be left at 0. *rollback_seg* is the name of the segment to use when refreshing materialized views. *push_deferred_rpc* pushes changes from an updatable materialized view to the master table or view. *refresh_after_errors* allows this update to process even if there are conflicts. *purge_option* controls how queues are purged if parallel propagation is used. *parallelism* indicates the number of parallel processes used for propagation, and *heap_size* specifies the maximum number of transactions examined for parallel propagation scheduling. This last parameter should not be set unless Oracle Support requests it.

```
PROCEDURE DBMS_REFRESH.REFRESH
    (name IN VARCHAR2);
```
Refreshes *name* manually.

```
PROCEDURE DBMS_REFRESH.SUBTRACT
    (name IN VARCHAR2,
```

```
{list IN VARCHAR2 | tab IN DBMS_UTILITY.UNCL_ARRAY},
lax IN BOOLEAN := FALSE);
```
Adds the members in *list* or *tab* to group *name*. If *lax* is FALSE, an error is returned if a materialized view is not a member of *name*.

DBMS_REPAIR

Allows you to detect and repair corrupt blocks in tables and indexes. The objects being repaired can still be used while they are being repaired. New with Oracle8*i*.

Calls

```
PROCEDURE DBMS_REPAIR.ADMIN_TABLES
  (table_name IN VARCHAR2,
  table_type IN BINARY_INTEGER,
  action IN BINARY_INTEGER,
  tablespace IN VARCHAR2 DEFAULT NULL);
```
Repairs administrative tables (ORPHAN_TABLE or REPAIR_TABLE in *table_type*) for *table_name*. *action* is either CREATE_ACTION to create the table, PURGE_ACTION to delete rows from the table for nonexistent objects, or DROP_ACTION to drop the table. *tablespace* is the tablespace used when creating a table.

```
PROCEDURE DBMS_REPAIR.CHECK_OBJECT
  (schema_name IN VARCHAR2,
  object_name IN VARCHAR2,
  partition_name IN VARCHAR2 DEFAULT NULL
  object_type IN BINARY_INTEGER DEFAULT TABLE_OBJECT,
  repair_table_name IN VARCHAR2 DEFAULT 'REPAIR_TABLE',
  flags IN BINARY_OBJECT DEFAULT NULL,
  relative_fno IN BINARY_INTEGER DEFAULT NULL,
  block_start IN BINARY_INTEGER DEFAULT NULL,
  block_end IN BINARY_INTEGER DEFAULT NULL,
  corrupt_count OUT BINARY_INTEGER);
```
Checks *schema_name.object_name*, in *partition_name* (if relevant) of *object_type* (TABLE_TYPE or INDEX_TYPE). Adds rows to *repair_table*, which must exist in the *SYS* schema. *relative_fno* is the relative file number and *block_start* and *block_end* specify the block range. *repair_table_name* is the name of the repair table that will be populated. *flags* is reserved for future use. Returns *corrupt_count* of number of corruptions reported.

```
PROCEDURE DBMS_REPAIR.DUMP_ORPHAN_KEYS
  (schema_name IN VARCHAR2,
  object_name IN VARCHAR2,
  partition_name IN VARCHAR2 DEFAULT NULL
  object_type IN BINARY_INTEGER DEFAULT INDEX_OBJECT,
  repair_table_name IN VARCHAR2 DEFAULT 'REPAIR_TABLE',
  orphan_table_name IN VARCHAR2 DEFAULT 'ORPHAN_KEYS_TABLE',
  flags IN BINARY_OBJECT DEFAULT NULL,
  key_count OUT BINARY_INTEGER);
```
Reports index entries in *schema_name.object_name*, in *partition_name* (if relevant) of *object_type* (TABLE_TYPE or INDEX_TYPE) that point to corrupt data blocks and inserts a row into *orphan_table_name*. *repair_table_name* has information about corrupt blocks in the base table. *flags* is reserved for future use. Returns *key_count* of number of index entries processed.

```
PROCEDURE DBMS_REPAIR.FIX_CORRUPT_BLOCKS
    (schema_name IN VARCHAR2,
    object_name IN VARCHAR2,
    partition_name IN VARCHAR2 DEFAULT NULL
    object_type IN BINARY_INTEGER DEFAULT TABLE_OBJECT,
    repair_table_name IN VARCHAR2 DEFAULT 'REPAIR_TABLE',
    flags IN BINARY_OBJECT DEFAULT NULL,
    fix_count OUT BINARY_INTEGER);
```
Fixes objects in *schema_name.object_name*, in *partition_name* (if relevant) of *object_type* (TABLE_TYPE or INDEX_TYPE) previously reported with the CHECK_OBJECT procedure. *repair_table_name* has information repair directives. *flags* is reserved for future use. Returns *fix_count* of number of index entries processed.

```
PROCEDURE DBMS_REPAIR.REBUILD_FREELISTS
    (schema_name IN VARCHAR2,
    partition_name IN VARCHAR2 DEFAULT NULL
    object_type IN BINARY_INTEGER DEFAULT TABLE_OBJECT);
```
Rebuilds freelists for *schema_name* in *partition_name* (if relevant).

```
PROCEDURE DBMS_REPAIR.SKIP_CORRUPT_BLOCKS
    (schema_name IN VARCHAR2,
    object_name IN VARCHAR2,
    object_type IN BINARY_INTEGER DEFAULT TABLE_OBJECT,
    flags IN BINARY_INTEGER DEFAULT SKIP_FLAG);
```
Enables skipping of corrupt blocks on index or table scans of *schema_name*. *object_name* when *flags* is SKIP_FLAG, rather than NOSKIP_FLAG.

```
PROCEDURE DBMS_REPAIR.SEGMENT_FIX_STATUS
    (segment_owner IN VARCHAR2,
    segment_name IN VARCHAR2,
    segment_type IN BINARY_INTEGER DEFAULT TABLE_OBJECT,
    file_number IN BINARY_INTGER DEFAULT NULL,
    block_number IN BINARY_INTGER DEFAULT NULL,
    status_value IN BINARY_INTGER DEFAULT NULL,
    partition_name IN VARCHAR2 DEFAULT NULL);
```
Fixes corrupted bitmap entry for *segment_owner.segment_name* in *partition_name* (if relevant). You can specify *file_number* and *block_number* to specify the data block location more exactly and *status_value* to override setting the block status to the current state of the block. New with Oracle9*i*.

DBMS_REPCAT

Provides procedures and functions to manage the replication catalog and its environment.

Calls

```
PROCEDURE DBMS_REPCAT.ADD_GROUPED_COLUMNS
    (sname IN VARCHAR2,
    oname IN VARCHAR2,
    column_group IN VARCHAR2,
    list_of_column_names IN {VARCHAR2 | DBMS_REPCAT.VARCHAR2s});
```
Adds *list_of_column_names* to existing *column_group* for *sname.oname*.

```
PROCEDURE DBMS_REPCAT.ADD_MASTER_DATABASE
    (gname IN VARCHAR2,
    master IN VARCHAR2,
    use_existing_objects IN BOOLEAN := TRUE,
    copy_rows IN BOOLEAN := TRUE,
    comment IN VARCHAR2 := '',
    propagation_mode IN VARCHAR2 := 'ASYNCHRONOUS',
    fname IN VARCHAR2 := NULL);
```
Adds *master* to *gname* replication group. *use_existing_objects* lets you indicate if you want to reuse objects of the same type at the existing master site, *copy_rows* indicates that you want to copy the contents of a table to the new master site, *comment* is added to the MASTER_COMMENT column of the DBA_REPSITES view, *propagation_mode* can be either ASYNCHRONOUS or SYNCHRONOUS, and *fname* is for internal Oracle use only.

```
PROCEDURE DBMS_REPCAT.ADD_NEW_MASTERS
    (export_required IN BOOLEAN,
    {available_master_list IN VARCHAR2 |
     available_master_table DBMS_UTILITY.DBLINK_ARRAY},
    masterdef_flashback_scn OUT NUMBER,
    extension_id OUT RAW,
    break_trans_to_masterdef IN BOOLEAN := FALSE,
    break_trans_to_new_masters IN BOOLEAN := FALSE,
    percentage_for_catchup_mdef IN BINARY_INTEGER := 100,
    cycle_seconds_mdef IN BINARY_INTEGER := 60,
    percentage_for_catchup_new IN BINARY_INTEGER := 100,
    cycle_seconds_new IN BINARY_INTEGER := 60);
```
Adds new master sites to the master groups from the SPECIFY_NEW_MASTERS procedure. For more information, see the Oracle documentation. New with Oracle9*i*.

```
PROCEDURE DBMS_REPCAT.ADD_PRIORITY_datatype
    (gname IN VARCHAR2,
    pgroup IN VARCHAR2,
    value IN datatype,
    priority IN NUMBER);
```
Adds *gname* to *pgroup* with priority group *value* of *priority*. *datatype* can be replaced with NUMBER, VARCHAR2, CHAR, DATE, RAW, NCHAR, or NCHAR2.

```
PROCEDURE DBMS_REPCAT.ADD_SITE_PRIORITY
    (gname IN VARCHAR2,
    group IN VARCHAR2,
    site IN VARCHAR2,
    priority IN NUMBER);
```
Adds *site* to *name* site priority group of *gname* with priority level *priority*.

```
PROCEDURE DBMS_REPCAT.ADD_UPDATE_RESOLUTION
    (sname IN VARCHAR2,
    oname IN VARCHAR2,
    column_group IN VARCHAR2,
    sequence_no IN NUMBER,
    method IN VARCHAR2,
    parameter_column_name IN {VARCHAR2 | DBMS_REPCAT.VARCHAR2s |
      DBMS_UTILITY.LNAME_ARRAY},
```

```
    priority_group IN VARCHAR2 := NULL,
    function_name IN VARCHAR2 := NULL,
    comment IN VARCHAR2 := NULL);
```

Designates a method for resolving update conflicts for *column_group* in *sname*. *oname*. *sequence_no* designates the sequence in which the conflict resolution method should be applied. *method* is the type of method used, either one of the standard *function_name*s or 'USER_FUNCTION'. *parameter_column_name* provides a list of columns used to resolve the conflict, if applicable. *priority_group* is an existing priority group. *comment* is a user comment.

PROCEDURE DBMS_REPCAT.ADD_DELETE_RESOLUTION
```
    (sname IN VARCHAR2,
    oname IN VARCHAR2,
    sequence_no IN NUMBER,
    parameter_column_name IN {VARCHAR2 | DBMS_REPCAT.VARCHAR2s},
    function_name IN VARCHAR2,
    comment IN VARCHAR2 := NULL,
    method IN VARCHAR2 := 'USER FUNCTION');
```

Designates a method for resolving delete conflicts for *sname.oname*. *sequence_no* designates the sequence in which the conflict resolution method should be applied. *parameter_column_name* provides a list of columns used to resolve the conflict, if applicable. *method* (new with Oracle8*i*) is the type of method used, either one of the standard *function_name*s or 'USER_FUNCTION'. *priority_group* is an existing priority group. *comment* is a user comment.

PROCEDURE DBMS_REPCAT.ADD_UNIQUE_RESOLUTION
```
    (sname IN VARCHAR2,
    oname IN VARCHAR2,
    constraint IN VARCHAR2,
    sequence_no IN NUMBER,
    parameter_column_name IN {VARCHAR2 | DBMS_REPCAT.VARCHAR2s |
        DBMS_UTLITY.LNAME_ARRAY},
    function_name IN VARCHAR2,
    comment IN VARCHAR2 := NULL);
```

Designates the method for resolving uniqueness conflicts for *sname.oname* coming from *constraint*. *sequence_no* designates the sequence in which the conflict resolution method should be applied. *parameter_column_name* provides a list of columns used to resolve the conflict, if applicable. *method* is the type of method used, either one of the standard *function_name*s or 'USER_FUNCTION'. *priority_group* is an existing priority group. *comment* is a user comment.

PROCEDURE DBMS_REPCAT.ALTER_CATCHUP_PARAMETERS
```
    (extension_id IN RAW,
    percentage_for_catchup_mdef IN BINARY_INTEGER := NULL,
    cycle_seconds_mdef IN BINARY_INTEGER := NULL,
    percentage_for_catchup_new IN BINARY_INTEGER := NULL,
    cyc_seconds_new IN BINARY_INTEGER := NULL);
```

Changes catchup parameters as identified. The *extension_id* is for the current pending request to add to the master database without quiesce. New with Oracle9*i*.

PROCEDURE DBMS_REPCAT.ALTER_MASTER_PROPAGATION
```
    (gname IN VARCHAR2,
    master IN VARCHAR2,
    {dblink_list IN VARCHAR2 | dblink_table IN DBMS_UTILITY.DBLINK_ARRAY},
```

```
[copy_rows IN BOOLEAN := TRUE,]#
propagation_mode IN VARCHAR2 := 'ASYNCHRONOUS',
comment IN VARCHAR2 := '');
```
Alters the propagation method. If the master site appears in *dblink_list* or *dblink_table*, that database link is ignored. Other parameters are described in ADD_MASTER_DATABASE. *copy_rows* is new with Oracle9i.

PROCEDURE DBMS_REPCAT.ALTER_MASTER_REPOBJECT
```
(sname IN VARCHAR2,
oname IN VARCHAR2,
type IN VARCHAR2,
ddl_text IN VARCHAR2,
comment IN VARCHAR2 := '',
retry IN BOOLEAN := FALSE
[,safe_table_change IN BOOLEAN := FALSE]#);
```
Alters *sname.oname* of *type* with *ddl_text*. If *retry* is TRUE, the object is altered only at masters whose object status is not VALID. A *safe_table_change* can be made without quiescing the master group that contains the table and is new with Oracle9i.

PROCEDURE DBMS_REPCAT.ALTER_MVIEW_PROPAGATION
```
(gname IN VARCHAR2,
propagation_mode IN VARCHAR2,
comment IN VARCHAR2 := '',
gowner IN VARCHAR2 := 'PUBLIC');
```
Alters the propagation method for *gname* replication group owned by *gowner*. New with Oracle9i.

PROCEDURE DBMS_REPCAT.ALTER_PRIORITY
```
(gname IN VARCHAR2,
pgroup IN VARCHAR2,
old_priority IN NUMBER,
new_priority IN NUMBER);
```
Changes *old_priority* to *new_priority* of *pgroup* in master *gname*.

PROCEDURE DBMS_REPCAT.ALTER_PRIORITY_datatype
```
(gname IN VARCHAR2,
pgroup IN VARCHAR2,
old_value IN datatype,
new_value IN datatype);
```
Changes *old_value* to *new_value* of *pgroup* in master *gname*. The datatype of the priority column determines which value for *datatype* is used: NUMBER, VARCHAR2, CHAR, DATE, RAW, NCHAR, or NCHAR2.

PROCEDURE DBMS_REPCAT.ALTER_SITE_PRIORITY
```
(gname IN VARCHAR2,
name IN VARCHAR2,
old_priority IN NUMBER,
new_priority IN NUMBER);
```
Changes *old_priority* to *new_priority* of site *name* in master *gname*.

PROCEDURE DBMS_REPCAT.ALTER_SITE_PRIORITY_SITE
```
(gname IN VARCHAR2,
name IN VARCHAR2,
```

```
old_site IN VARCHAR2,
new_site IN VARCHAR2);
```
Changes *old_site* name to *new_site* name of *name* site priority group in master *gname*.

PROCEDURE DBMS_REPCAT.ALTER_SNAPSHOT_PROPAGATION
```
(gname IN VARCHAR2,
propagation_mode IN VARCHAR2,
comment IN VARCHAR2 := '');
```
Changes *propagation_mode* for group *gname* with *comment*. Only in Oracle8*i*.

PROCEDURE DBMS_REPCAT.CANCEL_STATISTICS
```
(sname IN VARCHAR2,
oname IN VARCHAR2);
```
Stops the collection of statistics about conflicts for *sname.oname* table.

PROCEDURE DBMS_REPCAT.COMMENT_ON_COLUMN_GROUP
```
(sname IN VARCHAR2,
oname IN VARCHAR2,
column_group IN VARCHAR2,
comment IN VARCHAR2);
```
Adds *comment* for *column_group* in *sname.oname*.

PROCEDURE DBMS_REPCAT.COMMENT_ON_MVIEW_REPSITES
```
(gowner IN VARCHAR2,
name IN VARCHAR2,
comment IN VARCHAR2);
```
Updates *comment* for *name* site priority group owned by *gowner*. New with Oracle9*i*.

PROCEDURE DBMS_REPCAT.COMMENT_ON_PRIORITY_GROUP
```
(gname IN VARCHAR2,
pgroup IN VARCHAR2,
comment IN VARCHAR2);
```
Updates *comment* for *pgroup* priority group in *gname* master group.

PROCEDURE DBMS_REPCAT.COMMENT_ON_REPGROUP
```
(gname IN VARCHAR2,
comment IN VARCHAR2);
```
Updates *comment* for *gname* replication group.

PROCEDURE DBMS_REPCAT.COMMENT_ON_REPOBJECT
```
(sname IN VARCHAR2,
oname IN VARCHAR2,
type IN VARCHAR2,
comment IN VARCHAR2);
```
Updates *comment* for *type* of object of *sname.oname* object.

PROCEDURE DBMS_REPCAT.COMMENT_ON_REPSITES
```
(gname IN VARCHAR2,
[master IN VARCHAR2,]
comment IN VARCHAR2);
```
Updates *comment* for *gname_group* of *sname.oname* replication group. If *master* is present, updates MASTER_COMMENT column of DBA_REPSITES; otherwise, updates SCHEMA_COMMENT for materialized view site. New with Oracle8*i*.

PROCEDURE DBMS_REPCAT.COMMENT_ON_SITE_PRIORITY
    (*gname* IN VARCHAR2,
    name IN VARCHAR2,
    comment IN VARCHAR2);
    Updates *comment* for *name* site priority group in *gname* master group.

PROCEDURE DBMS_REPCAT.COMMENT_ON_UPDATE_RESOLUTION
    (*sname* IN VARCHAR2,
    oname IN VARCHAR2,
    column_group IN VARCHAR2,
    sequence_no IN NUMBER,
    comment IN VARCHAR2);
    Adds *comment* for *sname.oname* for *column_group* of update conflict resolution.
    sequence_no is the number of the sequence in the conflict resolution process.

PROCEDURE DBMS_REPCAT.COMMENT_ON_UNIQUE_RESOLUTION
    (*sname* IN VARCHAR2,
    oname IN VARCHAR2,
    constraint_name IN VARCHAR2,
    sequence_no IN NUMBER,
    comment IN VARCHAR2);
    Adds *comment* for *sname.oname* for the *constraint_name* that causes a conflict.
    sequence_no is the number of the sequence in the conflict resolution process.

PROCEDURE DBMS_REPCAT.COMMENT_ON_DELETE_RESOLUTION
    (*sname* IN VARCHAR2,
    oname IN VARCHAR2,
    sequence_no IN NUMBER,
    comment IN VARCHAR2);
    Adds *comment* for *sname.oname* for delete conflict resolution. *sequence_no* is the
    number of the sequence in the conflict resolution process.

PROCEDURE DBMS_REPCAT.COMPARE_OLD_VALUES
    (*sname* IN VARCHAR2,
    oname IN VARCHAR2,
    {*column_list* IN VARCHAR2 |
      column_table IN {DBMS_UTILITY.VARCHAR2s | DBMS_UTILITY.LNAME_ARRAY}},
    operation IN VARCHAR2 := 'UPDATE',
    compare IN BOOLEAN := TRUE);
    Compares *column_list/column_table* columns in *sname.oname* table if *compare* is
    TRUE for *operation* UPDATE, DELETE, or *, meaning both. New with Oracle8*i*.

PROCEDURE DBMS_REPCAT.CREATE_MASTER_REPGROUP
    (*gname* IN VARCHAR2,
    group_comment IN VARCHAR2 := '',
    master_comment IN VARCHAR2 := '',
    qualifier IN VARCHAR2 := '');
    Creates a new master group *gname* with connection *qualifier* and comments.

PROCEDURE DBMS_REPCAT.CREATE_MASTER_REPOBJECT
    (*sname* IN VARCHAR2,
    oname IN VARCHAR2,
    type IN VARCHAR2,
    use_existing_object IN BOOLEAN := TRUE,
    ddl_text IN VARCHAR2,
    comment IN VARCHAR2 := '',
    retry IN BOOLEAN := FALSE,

```
copy_rows IN BOOLEAN := FALSE,
gname IN VARCHAR2 := '');
```

Creates a replica of *sname.oname* of *type* with *ddl_text* into replication group *gname*. *use_existing_object* is TRUE if you want to reuse any objects of the same type and shape. If *retry* is TRUE, Oracle will reattempt to create an object it was previously unable to create. If *copy_rows* is TRUE, the rows of the object will be initially copied to the replica.

PROCEDURE DBMS_REPCAT.CREATE_{SNAPSHOT`| MVIEW}_REPOBJECT
```
(sname IN VARCHAR2,
oname IN VARCHAR2,
type IN VARCHAR2,
ddl_text IN VARCHAR2,
comment IN VARCHAR2 := '',
gname IN VARCHAR2 := '',
gen_object_owner IN VARCHAR2 := '',
min_communication IN BOOLEAN := TRUE,
generate_80_compatible  IN BOOLEAN := TRUE
[,gowner IN VARCHAR2 := 'PUBLIC']#);
```

Creates a replica of *sname.oname* of *type* with *ddl_text* (for objects of *type* SNAPSHOT) into replication group *gname*. *gname* and *gowner* (only with Oracle9*i*) are the name and owner of the replication materialized view group to which you are adding the object. *min_communication* is FALSE if you are running Oracle 7.3. *generate_80_compatible* is TRUE if you are running a version of Oracle prior to Oracle8*i*. This procedure is called CREATE_SNAPSHOT_REPOBJECT prior to Oracle9*i*.

PROCEDURE DBMS_REPCAT.CREATE_SNAPSHOT_REPGROUP
```
(gname IN VARCHAR2,
master IN VARCHAR2,
comment IN VARCHAR2 := '',
propagation_mode := 'ASYNCHRONOUS',
fname IN VARCHAR2 := NULL);
```

Creates a propagation method for *gname* replication group of *master* database. *propagation_mode* is either 'ASYNCHRONOUS' or 'SYNCHRONOUS'. *fname* is for internal use only. Not supported in Oracle9*i*.

PROCEDURE DBMS_REPCAT.DEFINE_COLUMN_GROUP
```
(sname IN VARCHAR2,
oname IN VARCHAR2,
column_group IN VARCHAR2,
comment IN VARCHAR2 := NULL);
```

Defines an empty *column_group* for *sname.oname*, with *comment* if desired.

PROCEDURE DBMS_REPCAT.DEFINE_PRIORITY_GROUP
```
(gname IN VARCHAR2,
pgroup IN VARCHAR2,
datatype IN VARCHAR2,
fixed_length IN INTEGER := NULL,
comment IN VARCHAR2 := NULL);
```

Creates priority group *pgroup* for *gname* master group, with *datatype* type of priority group members (CHAR, VARCHAR2, NUMBER, DATE, RAW, NCHAR, NCHAR2) of *fixed_length* length for CHAR datatype, with optional *comment*.

PROCEDURE DBMS_REPCAT.DEFINE_SITE_PRIORITY
  (*gname* IN VARCHAR2,
  name IN VARCHAR2,
  comment IN VARCHAR2 := NULL);
  Creates site priority group *name* for master group *gname* with optional *comment*.

PROCEDURE DBMS_REPCAT.DO_DEFERRED_REPCAT_ADMIN
  (*gname* IN VARCHAR2,
  all_sites IN BOOLEAN := FALSE);
  Executes local outstanding deferred administrative procedures for *gname* master group. If *all_sites*, uses a job to execute local administrative procedures at each master site.

PROCEDURE DBMS_REPCAT.DROP_COLUMN_GROUP
  (*sname* IN VARCHAR2,
  oname IN VARCHAR2,
  column_group IN VARCHAR2);
  Drops *column_group* of *sname.oname*.

PROCEDURE DBMS_REPCAT.DROP_GROUPED_COLUMN
  (*sname* IN VARCHAR2,
  oname IN VARCHAR2,
  column_group IN VARCHAR2,
  list_of_column_names IN {VARCHAR2 | DBMS_REPCAT.VARCHAR2s});
  Drops *list_of_column_names* from *column_group* of *sname.oname*.

PROCEDURE DBMS_REPCAT.DROP_MASTER_REPGROUP
  (*gname* IN VARCHAR2,
  drop_contents IN BOOLEAN := FALSE,
  all_sites IN BOOLEAN := FALSE);
  Drops *gname* master group. If *drop_contents*, the replicated objects are dropped from the schema. If *all_sites*, the call is multicast to all the masters.

PROCEDURE DBMS_REPCAT.DROP_MASTER_REPOBJECT
  (*sname* IN VARCHAR2,
  oname IN VARCHAR2,
  type IN VARCHAR2,
  drop_objects IN BOOLEAN := FALSE);
  Drops *sname.oname* of *type* from master group. If *drop_objects*, the object is dropped from each master site.

PROCEDURE DBMS_REPCAT.DROP_MVIEW_REPGROUP
  (*gname* IN VARCHAR2,
  drop_contents IN BOOLEAN := FALSE,
  gowner IN VARCHAR2 := 'PUBLIC');
  Drops materialized view *gname*, owned by *gowner*. If *drop_contents*, the object is dropped from its schemas. New with Oracle9*i*.

PROCEDURE DBMS_REPCAT.DROP_MVIEW_REPOBJECT
  (*sname* IN VARCHAR2,
  oname IN VARCHAR2,
  type IN VARCHAR2,
  drop_objects IN BOOLEAN := FALSE);
  Drops *sname.oname* of *type* from materialized view. If *drop_objects*, the object is dropped from each master site. New with Oracle9*i*.

PROCEDURE DBMS_REPCAT.DROP_PRIORITY
   (*gname* IN VARCHAR2,
   pgroup IN VARCHAR2,
   priority_num IN NUMBER);
     Drops *pgroup* from *gname* with *priority_num*.

PROCEDURE DBMS_REPCAT.DROP_PRIORITY_GROUP
   (*gname* IN VARCHAR2,
   pgroup IN VARCHAR2);
     Drops *pgroup* from *gname*.

PROCEDURE DBMS_REPCAT.DROP_PRIORITY_*datatype*
   (*gname* IN VARCHAR2,
   pgroup IN VARCHAR2,
   value IN *datatype*);
     Drops *pgroup* from *gname* with *value*. The datatype can be NUMBER, VARCHAR2, CHAR, DATE, RAW, NCHAR, or NCHAR2.

PROCEDURE DBMS_REPCAT.DROP_SITE_PRIORITY
   (*gname* IN VARCHAR2,
   name IN VARCHAR2);
     Drops *name* site priority group from *gname* master group.

PROCEDURE DBMS_REPCAT.DROP_SITE_PRIORITY_SITE
   (*gname* IN VARCHR2,
   name IN VARCHAR2,
   site IN VARCHAR2);
     Drops *site* from *name* site priority group from *gname* master group.

PROCEDURE DBMS_REPCAT.DROP_SNAPSHOT_REPGROUP
   (*gname* IN VARCHR2,
   drop_contents IN BOOLEAN := FALSE);
     Drops *gname* from the current snapshot site. If *drop_contents*, replicated objects are also dropped. Not supported in Oracle9*i*.

PROCEDURE DBMS_REPCAT.DROP_SNAPSHOT_REPOBJECTS
   (*sname* IN VARCHR2,
   oname IN VARCHAR2,
   type IN VARCHAR2,
   drop_objects IN BOOLEAN := FALSE);
     Drops *sname.oname* of *type* from the current snapshot site. If *drop_objects*, replicated objects are also dropped. Only in Oracle8*i*.

PROCEDURE DBMS_REPCAT.DROP_UPDATE_RESOLUTION
   (*sname* IN VARCHAR2,
   oname IN VARCHAR2,
   column_group IN VARCHAR2,
   sequence_no IN NUMBER);
     Drops update conflict resolution routine for *column_group* in *sname.oname*. *sequence_no* is the ID of the conflict resolution method.

PROCEDURE DBMS_REPCAT.DROP_DELETE_RESOLUTION
   (*sname* IN VARCHAR2,
   oname IN VARCHAR2,
   sequence_no IN NUMBER);
     Drops delete conflict resolution routine for *sname.oname*. *sequence_no* is the ID of the conflict resolution method.

PROCEDURE DBMS_REPCAT.DROP_UNIQUE_RESOLUTION
   (*sname* IN VARCHAR2,
   oname IN VARCHAR2,
   constraint_name IN VARCHAR2,
   sequence_no IN NUMBER);

    Drops uniqueness conflict resolution routine for *sname.oname*, which uses *constraint_name*. *sequence_no* is the ID of the conflict resolution method.

PROCEDURE DBMS_REPCAT.EXECUTE_DDL
   (*gname* IN VARCHAR2,
   {*master_list* IN VARCHAR2 := NULL |
   master_table IN DBMS_UTILITY.DBLINK.ARRAY},
   ddl_text IN VARCHAR2);

    Executes *ddl_text* for master group *gname*. *master_list*/*master_table* provides a list of master sites to execute the DDL.

PROCEDURE DBMS_REPCAT.GENERATE_MVIEW_SUPPORT
   (*sname* IN VARCHAR2,
   oname IN VARCHAR2,
   type IN VARCHAR2,
   gen_object_owner IN VARCHAR2 := '',
   min_communication IN BOOLEAN := TRUE
   [,*generate_80_compatible* IN BOOLEAN := TRUE]);

    Generates triggers and packages in *gen_object_owner* (or *sname* if NULL) needed to support a materialized view on *sname.oname* of *type*. *min_communication* is FALSE if you are running Oracle 7.3, *generate_80_compatible* is TRUE if you are running a version of Oracle prior to Oracle8*i*. New with Oracle9*i*.

PROCEDURE DBMS_REPCAT.GENERATE_REPLICATION_PACKAGE
   (*sname* IN VARCHAR2,
   oname IN VARCHAR2);

    Generates a replication package for *sname.oname*. Not available in versions later than Oracle8.

PROCEDURE DBMS_REPCAT.GENERATE_REPLICATION_SUPPORT
   (*sname* IN VARCHAR2,
   oname IN VARCHAR2,
   type IN VARCHAR2,
   package_prefix IN VARCHAR2 := NULL,
   procedure_prefix IN VARCHAR2 := NULL,
   distributed IN BOOLEAN := TRUE,
   gen_object_owner IN VARCHAR2 := '',
   min_communication IN BOOLEAN := TRUE
   [, *generate_80_compatible* IN BOOLEAN := TRUE]);

    Generates triggers and packages needed to support an object *sname.oname* of *type*. *package_prefix* and *procedure_prefix* control the generated code, and *distributed* must be left at TRUE. *min_communication* is FALSE if you are running Oracle 7.3. *generate_80_compatible* (new in Oracle8*i*) is TRUE if you are running a version of Oracle prior to Oracle8*i*.

PROCEDURE DBMS_REPCAT.GENERATE_REPLICATION_TRIGGER
   ({*sname* IN VARCHAR2,
   oname IN VARCHAR2 |
   gname IN VARCHAR2},

```
    gen_objs_owner IN VARCHAR2 := NULL,
    min_communication IN BOOLEAN := TRUE);
```
Generates replication package for either *sname.oname* or group *gname*. *gen_objs_ owner* must be true for compatibility releases of Oracle prior to Oracle 7.3. *min_ communication* should be FALSE if any master site is running Version 7.3. Not present after Oracle8.

PROCEDURE DBMS_REPCAT.GENERATE_SNAPSHOT_SUPPORT
```
    (sname IN VARCHAR2,
    oname IN VARCHAR2,
    type IN VARCHAR2,
    gen_object_owner IN VARCHAR2 := '',
    min_communication IN BOOLEAN := TRUE
    [, generate_80_compatible  IN BOOLEAN := TRUE]);
```
Generates triggers and packages needed to support a snapshot *sname.oname* of *type*. *min_communication* is FALSE if you are running Oracle 7.3. *generate_80_ compatible* (new in Oracle8i) is TRUE if you are running a version of Oracle prior to Oracle8i.

PROCEDURE DBMS_REPCAT.MAKE_COLUMN_GROUP
```
    (sname IN VARCHAR2,
    oname IN VARCHAR2,
    column_group IN VARCHAR2,
    list_of_column_names IN {VARCHAR2 | DBMS_REPCAT.VARCHAR2s});
```
Creates *column_group* with *list_of_column_names* for *sname.oname*.

PROCEDURE DBMS_REPCAT.PREPARE_INSTANTIATED_MASTER
```
    (extension_id IN RAW);
```
Enables the propagation of pending request *extension_id* to add master databases to a master group without quiesce. New with Oracle9i.

PROCEDURE DBMS_REPCAT.PURGE_MASTER_LOG
```
    (id IN BINARY_INTEGER,
    source IN VARCHAR2,
    gname IN VARCHAR2);
```
Removes *id* request from *source* site in *gname* group.

PROCEDURE DBMS_REPCAT.PURGE_STATISTICS
```
    (sname IN VARCHAR2,
    oname IN VARCHAR2,
    start_date IN DATE,
    end_date IN DATE);
```
Removes statistics for *sname.oname* from *start_date* to *end_date*. Only in Oracle8i.

PROCEDURE DBMS_REPCAT.REFRESH_{SNAPSHOT | MVIEW}_REPGROUP
```
    (gname IN VARCHAR2,
    drop_missing_contents IN BOOLEAN := FALSE,
    refresh_mviews IN BOOLEAN := FALSE,
    refresh_other_objects  IN BOOLEAN := FALSE
    [,gowner IN VARCHAR2 := 'PUBLIC']#);
```
Refreshes materialized view group *gname* owned by *gowner* (new in Oracle9i). *drop_missing_contents* drops objects previously dropped from replication group from the materialized view schema. *refresh_mviews* refreshes contents of materialized views, *refresh_other_objects* refreshes other objects not in materialized view in *gname*. Called REFRESH_SNAPSHOT_REPGROUP prior to Oracle8i.

```
PROCEDURE DBMS_REPCAT.REGISTER_{SNAPSHOT | MVIEW}_REPGROUP
    (gname IN VARCHAR2,
    mviewsite IN VARCHAR2,
    [comment IN VARCHAR2 := NULL,]
    rep_type IN NUMBER := REG_UNKNOWN,
    fname IN VARCHAR2 := NULL
    [,gowner IN VARCHAR2 := 'PUBLIC']);
```
Registers *gname* materialized view group with global name *mviewsite* owned by *gowner* (only in Oracle9*i*). *comment* is optional, *rep_type* is the version of the materialized view group, and *fname* is for internal Oracle use only in Oracle8*i* and later. This procedure is called REGISTER_SNAPSHOT_REPGROUP prior to Oracle8*i*.

```
PROCEDURE DBMS_REPCAT.REGISTER_STATISTICS
    (sname IN VARCHAR2,
    oname IN VARCHAR2);
```
Registers statistics on conflict resolution for *sname.oname*.

```
PROCEDURE DBMS_REPCAT.RELOCATE_MASTERDEF
    (gname IN VARCHAR2,
    old_masterdef IN VARCHAR2,
    new_masterdef IN VARCHAR2,
    notify_masters IN BOOLEAN := TRUE,
    include_old_masterdef  IN BOOLEAN := TRUE,
    require_flavor_change IN BOOLEAN := FALSE);
```
Moves *gname* replication group from *old_masterdef* to *new_masterdef* site. If *notify_masters*, broadcasts change to all masters. If also *include_old_masterdef*, the old master definition site also hears of its loss. *require_flavor_change* is an internal Oracle parameter in Oracle8*i* and later.

```
PROCEDURE DBMS_REPCAT.REMOVE_MASTER_DATABASES
    (gname IN VARCHAR2,
    {master_list IN VARCHAR2 | master_table IN DBMS_UTILITY.DBLINK_ARRAY});
```
Removes master databases in the second parameter from the replication environment associated with *gname* replication group.

```
PROCEDURE DBMS_REPCAT.RENAME_SHADOW_COLUMN_GROUP
    (sname IN VARCHAR2,
    oname IN VARCHAR2,
    new_col_group_name IN VARCHAR2);
```
Places columns in a shadow group of *sname.oname* in *new_col_group_name*. New with Oracle9*i*.

```
PROCEDURE DBMS_REPCAT.IMPORT_CHECK
    (gname IN VARCHAR2,
    master IN BOOLEAN
    [,gowner IN VARCHR2 := 'PUBLIC']#);
```
Checks to see if objects in the master group have appropriate identifers and status values after an import/export of a replicated object. If there is no value for *gname* master group and *gowner* (new with Oracle9*i*), all master groups are checked at the current site. *master* means to check a master site.

PROCEDURE DBMS_REPCAT.RESUME_MASTER_ACTIVITY
   (*gname* IN VARCHAR2,
   override IN BOOLEAN := FALSE);
     Restores replication for *gname*. If *override*, ignores pending administrative requests and resumes activity as quickly as possible.

PROCEDURE DBMS_REPCAT.RESUME_PROPAGATION_TO_MDEF
   (*extension_*id IN RAW);
     Adds new master sites to master group without quiesce. The pending request is identified by pending request *extension_id*. New with Oracle9*i*.

PROCEDURE DBMS_REPCAT.SEND_[AND_COMPARE_]OLD_VALUES
   (*sname* IN VARCHAR2,
   oname IN VARCHAR2,
   {*column_list* IN VARCHAR2 |
   column_table IN {DBMS_UTILITY.VARCHAR2s | DBMS_UTILITY.LNAME_ARRAY}},
   operation IN VARCHAR2 := 'UPDATE',
   send IN BOOLEAN := 'TRUE');
     Sends old column values durring propagation of deferred transactions for columns that are not key columns in *column_list/column_table* for *sname.oname* for *operation* (UPDATE, DELETE, or *, indicating both), if *send*. This procedure was called SEND_AND_COMPARE_OLD_VALUES in Oracle8.

PROCEDURE DBMS_REPCAT.SET_COLUMNS
   (*sname* IN VARCHAR2,
   oname IN VARCHAR2,
   {*column_list* IN VARCHAR2 |
   column_table IN {DBMS_UTILITY.VARCHAR2s | DBMS_UTILITY.LNAME_ARRAY}});
     Uses *column_list/column_table* for comparison on replication of *sname.oname*.

PROCEDURE DBMS_REPCAT.SPECIFY_NEW_MASTERS
   (*gname* IN VARCHAR2,
   {*master_list* IN VARCHAR2, *master_table* IN DBMS_UTILITY.DBLINK_ARRAY});
     Adds new masters listed in the second parameter to *gname* master group. New with Oracle9*i*.

PROCEDURE DBMS_REPCAT.SUSPEND_MASTER_ACTIVITY
   (*gname* IN VARCHAR2);
     Suspends activity for *gname* master group.

PROCEDURE DBMS_REPCAT.SWITCH_{SNAPSHOT | MVIEW}_MASTER
   (*gname* N VARCHAR2,
   master IN VARCHAR2
   [,*gowner* IN VARCHAR2 := 'PUBLIC']#);
     Switches *gname* materialized view group owned by *gowner* (new with Oracle9*i*) to the *master* site. This procedure was called SWITCH_SNAPSHOT_MASTER prior to Oracle9*i*.

PROCEDURE DBMS_REPCAT.UNDO_ADD_NEW_MASTERS_REQUEST
   (*extension_id* IN RAW,
   drop_contents IN BOOLEAN := TRUE);
     Undoes all changes made by SPECIFY_NEW_MASTERS and ADD_NEW_MASTERS for the *extension_id* request. If *drop_contents*, the contents of objects in new replication groups are dropped. New with Oracle9*i*.

PROCEDURE DBMS_REPCAT.UNREGISTER_{SNAPSHOT | MVIEW}_REPGROUP
    (*gname* IN VARCHAR2,
    mviewsite IN VARCHAR2
    [,*gowner* IN VARCHAR := 'PUBLIC']#);

    Removes registration for *gname* owned by *gowner* (with Oracle9*i*) from *mviewsite*. This procedure was called UNREGISTER_SNAPSHOT_REPGROUP prior to Oracle9*i*.

FUNCTION DBMS_REPCAT.VALIDATE
    (*gname* IN VARCHAR2,
    check_genflags IN BOOLEAN := FALSE,
    check_valid_objs IN BOOLEAN := FALSE,
    check_links_sched IN BOOLEAN := FALSE,
    check_links IN BOOLEAN := FALSE,
    {*error_table* OUT DBMS_REPCAT.VALIDATE_ERR_TABLE |
    error_msg_table OUT DBMS_UTILITY.UNCL_ARRAY,
    error_num_table OUT DBMS_UTILITY.NUMBER_ARRAY})
    RETURN BINARY_INTEGER;

    Validates conditions specified by the various *check_** parameters for *gname*, and returns errors in the last parameter(s) and the number of errors as a return from the function.

PROCEDURE DBMS_REPCAT.WAIT_MASTER_LOG
    (*gname* IN VARCHAR,
    record_count IN NATURAL,
    timeout IN NATURAL,
    true_count OUT NATURAL);

    Determines the number of incomplete activities *true_count* for the *gname* master group over *timeout* seconds. *record_count* determines the number of incomplete activities that will force the return of the procedure.

DBMS_REPCAT_ADMIN

Creates users with privileges needed for symmetric replication facility. New with Oracle8*i*.

Calls

PROCEDURE DBMS_REPCAT_ADMIN.GRANT_ADMIN_ANY_SCHEMA
    (*username* IN VARCHAR2),

    Grants *username* privileges to administer any replication groups at the current site.

PROCEDURE DBMS_REPCAT_ADMIN.GRANT_ADMIN_SCHEMA
    (*username* IN VARCHAR2),

    Grants *username* privileges to administer replication groups with the same schema at the current site.

PROCEDURE DBMS_REPCAT_ADMIN.REGISTER_USER_REPGROUP
    (*username* IN VARCHAR2,
    privilege_type IN VARCHAR2,

```
      {list_of_gnames IN VARCHAR2 |
      table_of_gnames IN DBMS_UTILITY.NAME_ARRAY});
```
    Assigns *privilege_type* (RECEIVER for receiver privileges or PROXY_ SNAPADMIN for proxy materialized view administrative privileges) to *username* for a list of the groups in the last parameter. New with Oracle8*i*.

PROCEDURE DBMS_REPCAT_ADMIN.REVOKE_ADMIN_ANY_SCHEMA
```
      (username IN VARCHAR2);
```
    Revokes all privileges assigned to *username* by GRANT_ADMIN_ANY_ SCHEMA.

PROCEDURE DBMS_REPCAT_ADMIN.REVOKE_ADMIN_SCHEMA
```
      (username IN VARCHAR2);
```
    Revokes all privileges assigned to *username* by GRANT_ADMIN_SCHEMA.

PROCEDURE DBMS_REPCAT_ADMIN.UNREGISTER_USER_REPGROUP
```
      (username IN VARCHAR2,
      privilege_type IN VARCHAR2,
      {list_of_gnames IN VARCHAR2 |
      table_of_gnames IN DBMS_UTILITY.NAME_ARRAY});
```
    Removes *privilege_type* (RECEIVER for receiver privileges or PROXY_ SNAPADMIN for proxy materialized view administrative privileges) to *username* for a list of the groups in the last parameter. New with Oracle8*i*.

DBMS_REPCAT_AUTH

Grants and revokes surrogate privileges for replication. Not present in Oracle8*i* and beyond.

Calls

PROCEDURE DBMS_REPACT_AUTH.GRANT_SURROGATE_REPCAT
```
      (userid IN VARCHAR2);
```
    Grants privileges needed for the advanced replication facility to *userid*.

PROCEDURE DBMS_REPACT_AUTH.REVOKE_SURROGATE_REPCAT
```
      (userid IN VARCHAR2);
```
    Revokes privileges needed for the advanced replication facility from *userid*.

DBMS_REPCAT_INSTANTIATE

Instantiates deployment templates. New with Oracle8*i*.

Calls

PROCEDURE DBMS_REPCAT_INSTANTIATE.DROP_SITE_INSTANTIATION
```
      (refresh_template_name IN VARCHAR2,
      site_name IN VARCHAR2,
      repapi_site_id IN NUMBER := -1e-130);
```
    Drops the *refresh_template_name* template from *site_name*. The *repapi_site_id* parameter is new with Oracle8*i*.

FUNCTION DBMS_REPCAT_INSTANTIATE.OFFLINE
```
      (refresh_template_name IN VARCHAR2,
      site_name IN VARCHAR2,
      runtime_parm_id IN NUMBER := -1e-130,
```

```
next_date IN DATE := SYSDATE,
interval IN VARCHAR := 'SYSDATE+1'
[,user_default_gowner IN BOOLEAN := TRUE]#);
RETURN NUMBER;
```

> Generates a file used to create the materialized view environment from *refresh_template_name* at *site_name* while offline. *runtime_parm_id* is an ID returned from the INSERT_RUNTIME_PARMS procedure. *next_date* is the next date to be used to create the refresh group, and *interval* is the interval to be used. If *user_default_gowner* (new with Oracle9*i*) is TRUE, any materialized view groups are owned by PUBLIC; otherwise, they are owned by the user performing the instantiation. Returns an ID to retrieve the generated script.

```
FUNCTION DBMS_REPCAT_INSTANTIATE.INSTANTIATE_ONLINE
    (refresh_template_name IN VARCHAR2,
    site_name IN VARCHAR2,
    runtime_parm_id IN NUMBER := -1e-130,
    next_date IN DATE := SYSDATE,
    interval IN VARCHAR := 'SYSDATE+1'
[, user_default_gowner IN BOOLEAN := TRUE]#);
RETURN NUMBER;
```

> Generates a file used to create the materialized view environment from *refresh_template_name* at *site_name* while online. *runtime_parm_id* is an ID returned from the INSERT_RUNTIME_PARMS procedure. *next_date* is the next date to be used to create the refresh group, and *interval* is the interval to be used. If *user_default_gowner* (new with Oracle9*i*) is TRUE, any materialized view groups are owned by PUBLIC; otherwise, they are owned by the user performing the instantiation. Returns an ID to retrieve the generated script.

DBMS_REPCAT_RGT

Creates and maintains replication refresh templates. New with Oracle8*i*.

Calls

```
PROCEDURE DBMS_REPCAT_RGT.ALTER_REFRESH_TEMPLATE
    (refresh_template_name IN VARCHAR2,
    new_owner IN VARCHAR2 := '-',
    new_refresh_group_name IN VARCHAR2 := '-',
    new_refresh_template_name IN VARCHAR2 := '-',
    new_template_comment IN VARCHAR2 := '-',
    new_public_template IN VARCHAR2 := '-',
    new_last_modified IN DATE := to_date('1', 'J'),
    new_modified_by IN NUMBER := -1e-130);
```

> Alters *refresh_template_name*. To keep the same template owner, do not enter a value for *new_owner*.

```
PROCEDURE DBMS_REPCAT_RGT.ALTER_TEMPLATE_OBJECT
    (refresh_template_name IN VARCHAR2,
    object_name IN VARCHAR2,
    object_type IN VARCHAR2,
    new_refresh_template_name IN VARCHAR2 := '-',
    new_object_name IN VARCHAR2 := '-',
    new_object_type IN VARCHAR2 := '-',
    new_ddl_text IN CLOB := '-',
```

```
    new_master_rollback_seg IN VARCHAR2 := '-',
    [new_last_modified IN DATE := to_date('1', 'J'),]#
    new_flavor_id IN NUMBER := -1e-130);
```

Alters *object_name* of *object_type* in *refresh_template_name*. To keep the same refresh template, do not enter a value for *refresh_template_name*. The *new_last_ modified* parameter is new with Oracle9i.

PROCEDURE DBMS_REPCAT_RGT.ALTER_TEMPLATE_PARM

```
    (refresh_template_name IN VARCHAR2,
    parameter_name IN VARCHAR2,
    new_refresh_template_name IN VARCHAR2 := '-',
    new_parameter_name IN VARCHAR2 := '-',
    new_default_parm_value IN CLOB := NULL,
    new_prompt_string IN VARCHAR2 := '-',
    new_user_override IN VARCHAR2 := '-');
```

Alters *parameter_name* for *refresh_template_name*. To keep the same refresh template, do not enter a value for *refresh_template_name*.

PROCEDURE DBMS_REPCAT_RGT.ALTER_USER_AUTHORIZATION

```
    (user_name IN VARCHAR2,
    refresh_template_name IN VARCHAR2,
    new_user_name IN VARCHAR2:= '-',
    new_refresh_template_name IN VARCHAR2 := '-');
```

Alters *user_name* to *new_user_name* for *refresh_template_name*. To keep the same refresh template, do not enter a value for *refresh_template_name*.

PROCEDURE DBMS_REPCAT_RGT.ALTER_USER_PARM_VALUE

```
    (refresh_template_name IN VARCHAR2,
    parameter_name IN VARCHAR2,
    user_name IN VARCHAR2,
    new_refresh_template_name IN VARCHAR2 := '-',
    new_parameter_name IN VARCHAR2 := '-',
    new_user_name IN VARCHAR2 := '-',
    new_parm_value IN CLOB := NULL);
```

Alters *parameter_name* for *user_name* of *refresh_template_name*. To keep the same parameter value, do not enter a value for the *new_* parameter.

FUNCTION DBMS_REPCAT_RGT.COMPARE_TEMPLATES

```
    (source_template_name IN VARCHAR2,
    compare_template_name IN VARCHAR2)
    RETURN NUMBER;
```

Compares *source_template_name* to *source_template_name*. Returns a handle to view differences in the USER_REPCAT_TEMP_OUTPUT view.

FUNCTION DBMS_REPCAT_RGT.COPY_TEMPLATE

```
    (old_refresh_template_name IN VARCHAR2,
    new_refresh_template_name IN VARCHAR2,
    copy_user_authorizations IN VARCHAR2,
    dblink IN VARCHAR2 := NULL)
    RETURN NUMBER;
```

Copies *old_refresh_template* (optionally from *dblink*) to *new_refresh_template*. *copy_user_authorizations* specifies whether template authorizations should be copied from the original template (Y) or not (N). Returns a number used internally by Oracle.

FUNCTION DBMS_REPCAT_RGT.CREATE_OBJECT_FROM_EXISTING
   (*refresh_template_name* IN VARCHAR2,
   object_name IN VARCHAR2,
   sname IN VARCHAR2,
   oname IN VARCHAR2,
   otype IN VARCHAR2)
   RETURN NUMBER;

    Creates an *object_name* of *otype* from *sname.oname* and adds it to *refresh_template_name*. Returns a number used internally by Oracle.

FUNCTION DBMS_REPCAT_RGT.CREATE_REFRESH_TEMPLATE
   (*owner* IN VARCHAR2,
   refresh_group_name IN VARCHAR2,
   refresh_template_name IN VARCHAR2,
   template_comment IN VARCHAR2 := NULL,
   public_template IN VARCHAR2 := NULL,
   last_modified IN DATE := SYSDATE,
   modified_by IN VARCHAR2 := USER,
   creation_date IN DATE := SYSDATE,
   created_by IN VARCHAR2 := USER)
   RETURN NUMBER;

    Creates *refresh_template_name* in *refresh_template_group*, owned by *owner*. *public_template* is either Y or N. Returns a number used internally by Oracle.

FUNCTION DBMS_REPCAT_RGT.CREATE_TEMPLATE_OBJECT
   (*refresh_template_name* IN VARCHAR2,
   object_name IN VARCHAR2,
   object_type IN VARCHAR2,
   ddl_text IN CLOB,
   master_rollback_seg IN VARCHAR2 := NULL,
   flavor_id IN NUMBER := -1e-130)
   RETURN NUMBER;

    Creates *object_name* of *object_type* with *ddl_text* in *refresh_template_name*, which uses *master_rollback_seg*. *flavor_id* and the returned number are used internally by Oracle.

FUNCTION DBMS_REPCAT_RGT.CREATE_TEMPLATE_PARM
   (*refresh_template_name* IN VARCHAR2,
   parameter_name IN VARCHAR2,
   default_parm_value IN CLOB := NULL,
   new_prompt_string IN VARCHAR2 := NULL,
   user_override IN VARCHAR2 := NULL)
   RETURN NUMBER;

    Creates *parameter_name* for *refresh_template_name*. If *user_override* is Y, the user can override *default_parm_value* at instantiation. Returns a number used internally by Oracle.

FUNCTION DBMS_REPCAT_RGT.CREATE_USER_AUTHORIZATION
   (*user_name* IN VARCHAR2,
   refresh_template_name IN VARCHAR2)
   RETURN NUMBER;

    Creates *user_name* for *refresh_template_name*. Returns a number used internally by Oracle.

FUNCTION DBMS_REPCAT_RGT.CREATE_USER_PARM_VALUE
   (*refresh_template_name* IN VARCHAR2,
   parameter_name IN VARCHAR2,
   user_name IN VARCHAR2,
   parm_value IN CLOB := NULL)
   RETURN NUMBER;
   Alters *parameter_name* for *user_name* of *refresh_template_name*. Returns a number used internally by Oracle.

PROCEDURE DBMS_REPCAT_RGT.DELETE_RUNTIME_PARMS
   (*runtime_parm_id* IN NUMBER,
   parameter_name IN VARCHAR2);
   Deletes *parameter_name* from *runtime_parm_id* created with the INSERT_RUNTIME_PARMS procedure before instantiating the deployment template.

PROCEDURE DBMS_REPCAT_RGT.DROP_ALL_OBJECTS
   (*refresh_template_name* IN VARCHAR2,
   object_type IN VARCHAR2 := NULL)
   Drops all objects of *object_type* from *refresh_template_name*. If *object_type* is NULL, drops all objects.

PROCEDURE DBMS_REPCAT_RGT.DROP_ALL_TEMPLATE_PARMS
   (*refresh_template_name* IN VARCHAR2,
   drop_objects IN VARCHAR2 := N);
   Drops all objects in *refresh_template_name* not referenced by a template object. If *drop_objects* is Y, objects that reference any template parameter and the template parameters are dropped from the template.

PROCEDURE DBMS_REPCAT_RGT.DROP_ALL_TEMPLATE_SITES
   (*refresh_template_name* IN VARCHAR2);
   Drops all sites in *refresh_template_name*.

PROCEDURE DBMS_REPCAT_RGT.DROP_ALL_TEMPLATES;
   Drops all templates at the site where the procedure is called.

PROCEDURE DBMS_REPCAT_RGT.DROP_ALL_USER_AUTHORIZATIONS
   (*refresh_template_name* IN VARCHAR2);
   Drops all user authorizations for *refresh_template_name*.

PROCEDURE DBMS_REPCAT_RGT.DROP_ALL_USER_PARMS
   (*refresh_template_name* IN VARCHAR2,
   user_name IN VARCHAR2,
   parameter_name IN VARCHAR2):
   Can use any combination of the second two parameters to specify dropping all parameters for a user, all parameters for a template, an individual parameter for a user, or all parameters for all users for the template.

PROCEDURE DBMS_REPCAT_RGT.DROP_REFRESH_TEMPLATE
   (*refresh_template_name* IN VARCHAR2);
   Drops the *refresh_template_name* template.

PROCEDURE DBMS_REPCAT_RGT.DROP_SITE_INSTANTIATION
   (*refresh_template_name* IN VARCHAR2,
   user_name IN VARCHAR2,
   site_name IN VARCHAR2,
   repapi_site_id IN NUMBER :=-1e-130);
   Drops *refresh_template_name* at *site_name* originally instantiated by *user_name*. The *repapi_site_id* parameter is used only with Oracle8*i*.

PROCEDURE DBMS_REPCAT_RGT.DROP_TEMPLATE_OBJECT
    (*refresh_template_name* IN VARCHAR2,
    object_name IN VARCHAR2,
    object_type IN VARCHAR2);
    Drops *object_name* of *object_type* from *refresh_template_name*.

PROCEDURE DBMS_REPCAT_RGT.DROP_TEMPLATE_PARM
    (*refresh_template_name* IN VARCHAR2,
    parameter_name IN VARCHAR2);
    Drops *parameter_name* from *refresh_template_name*.

PROCEDURE DBMS_REPCAT_RGT.DROP_USER_AUTHORIZATION
    (*refresh_template_name* IN VARCHAR2
    user_name IN VARCHAR2);
    Drops *user_name* from *refresh_template_name*.

PROCEDURE DBMS_REPCAT_RGT.DROP_USER_PARM_VALUE
    (*refresh_template_name* IN VARCHAR2,
    parameter_name IN VARCHAR2,
    user_name IN VARCHAR2);
    Drops *parameter_name* from *user_name* of *refresh_template_name*.

FUNCTION DBMS_REPCAT_RGT.GET_RUNTIME_PARM_ID
    RETURN NUMBER;
    Returns ID to be used when defining a runtime parameter value.

PROCEDURE DBMS_REPCAT_RGT.INSERT_RUNTIME_PARMS
    (*runtime_parm_id* IN NUMBER,
    parameter_name IN VARCHAR2,
    parameter_value IN CLOB);
    Gives *parameter_name* the value of *parameter_value* for the template identified by *runtime_parm_id*.

FUNCTION DBMS_REPCAT_RGT.INSTANTIATE_OFFLINE
    (*refresh_template_name* IN VARCHAR2,
    site_name IN VARCHAR2 := NULL,
    user_name IN VARCHAR := NULL,
    runtime_parm_id IN NUMBER := -1e-130,
    next_date IN DATE := SYSDATE,
    interval IN VARCHAR2 := 'SYSDATE+1'
    [,*use_default_gowner* IN BOOLEAN := TRUE]#)
    RETURN NUMBER;
    Generates a script at the master site that is used to create a remote materialized view site based on *refresh_template_name* at *site_name* by *user_name* while the remote site is not connected to the master. *runtime_parm_id* is the ID used with INSERT_RUNTIME_PARMS. *next_date* and *interval* control the refresh group. If *use_default_gowner* (new with Oracle9i) is TRUE, materialized view groups are owned by PUBLIC. Returns an ID for retrieving the generated instantiation script.

FUNCTION DBMS_REPCAT_RGT.INSTANTIATE_ONLINE
    (*refresh_template_name* IN VARCHAR2,
    site_name IN VARCHAR2 := NULL,
    user_name IN VARCHAR := NULL,
    runtime_parm_id IN NUMBER := -1e-130,
    next_date IN DATE := SYSDATE,
    interval IN VARCHAR2 := 'SYSDATE+1'

[, *use_default_gowner* IN BOOLEAN := TRUE]#)
RETURN NUMBER;
>   Generates a script at the master site that is used to create a remote materialized
>   view site based on *refresh_template_name* at *site_name* by *user_name* while the
>   remote site is connected to the master. *runtime_parm_id* is the ID used with
>   INSERT_RUNTIME_PARMS. *next_date* and *interval* control the refresh group. If
>   *use_default_gowner* (new with Oracle9*i*) is TRUE, materialized view groups are
>   owned by PUBLIC. Returns an ID for retrieving the generated instantiation script.

PROCEDURE DBMS_REPCAT_RGT.LOCK_TEMPLATE_EXCLUSIVE;
>   Locks a template while it is being updated or modified.

PROCEDURE DBMS_REPCAT_RGT.LOCK_TEMPLATE_SHARED;
>   Locks a template to make it read-only.

DBMS_REPUTIL

Provides procedures and functions to generate shadow tables, triggers, and packages
for table replication.

Calls

PROCEDURE DBMS_REPUTIL.REPLICATION_OFF;
>   Allows you to modify tables without replicating the modification to other sites.

PROCEDURE DBMS_REPUTIL.REPLICATION_ON;
>   Turns replication back on.

FUNCTION DBMS_REPUTIL.REPLICATION_IS_ON
RETURN BOOLEAN;
>   Used to determine if replication is on. New with Oracle8*i*.

PROCEDURE DBMS_REPUTIL.FROM_REMOTE
RETURN BOOLEAN;
>   Returns TRUE at the beginning of internal replication procedures and FALSE at
>   the end. New with Oracle8*i*.

PROCEDURE DBMS_REPUTIL.GLOBAL_NAME
RETURN VARCHAR2;
>   Returns the global database name of a local database. New with Oracle8*i*.

PROCEDURE DBMS_REPUTIL.MAKE_INTERNAL_PKG
(*canon_sname* IN VARCHAR2,
canon_oname IN VARCHAR2);
>   Synchronizes internal packages with the *canon_sname.canon_oname* table or
>   materialized view in replication catalog. Use this procedure only when suggested
>   by Oracle Support. New with Oracle8*i*.

PROCEDURE DBMS_REPUTIL.SYNC_UP_REP
(*canon_sname* IN VARCHAR2,
canon_oname IN VARCHAR2);
>   Synchronizes internal packages with the *canon_sname.canon_oname* table or
>   materialized view in the replication catalog. Use this procedure only when
>   suggested by Oracle Support. New with Oracle8*i*.

DBMS_RESOURCE_MANAGER

Provides procedures to manage plans, consumer groups, and plan directives used by the Database Resource Manager (DRM). New with Oracle8i.

Calls

```
PROCEDURE DBMS_RESOURCE_MANAGER.CREATE_PLAN
   (plan IN VARCHAR2,
   comment IN VARCHAR2,
   cpu_mth IN VARCHAR DEFAULT 'EMPHASIS',
   active_sess_pool_mth | max_active_sess_target
     IN VARCHAR2 DEFAULT 'ACTIVE_SESSION_POOL_ABSOLUTE',
   parallel_degree_limit_mth IN VARCHAR2 DEFAULT
     'PARALLEL_DEGREE_LIMIT_ABSOLUTE',
   queueing_mth IN VARCHAR2 DEFAULT 'FIFO_TIMEOUT');
```

> Creates a resource plan *plan* with methods indicated in the parameters. In Oracle 8.2, *max_active_sess_target* was renamed to *active_sess_pool_mth* and *queueing_mth* was added.

```
PROCEDURE DBMS_RESOURCE_MANAGER.CREATE_SIMPLE_PLAN
   (simple_plan IN VARCHAR2,
   consumer_group1 in VARCHAR2,
   group1_cpu IN VARCHAR2,
   consumer_group2 in VARCHAR2,
   group2_cpu IN VARCHAR2,
   consumer_group3 in VARCHAR2,
   group3_cpu IN VARCHAR2,
   consumer_group4 in VARCHAR2,
   group4_cpu IN VARCHAR2,
   consumer_group5 in VARCHAR2,
   group5_cpu IN VARCHAR2,
   consumer_group6 in VARCHAR2,
   group6_cpu IN VARCHAR2,
   consumer_group7 in VARCHAR2,
   group7_cpu IN VARCHAR2,
   consumer_group8 in VARCHAR2,
   group8_cpu IN VARCHAR2);
```

> Creates *simple_plan* resource plan with up to eight consumer groups in one call. New with Oracle9i.

```
PROCEDURE DBMS_RESOURCE_MANAGER.UPDATE_PLAN
   (plan IN VARCHAR2,
   new_comment IN VARCHAR2,
   new_cpu_mth IN VARCHAR DEFAULT NULL,
   new_active_sess_pool_mth | new_max_active_sess_target
     IN VARCHAR2 DEFAULT NULL,
   new_parallel_degree_limit_mth IN VARCHAR2 DEFAULT NULL,
   new_queueing_mth IN VARCHAR2 DEFAULT NULL
[,new_group_switch_mth IN VARCHAR2 DEFAULT NULL)]#;
```

> Updates a resource plan *plan* with methods indicated in the parameters. In Oracle 8.2, *max_active_sess_target* was renamed to *new_active_sess_pool_mth* and *new_queueing_mth* was added. The *new_group_switch_mth* parameter was added in Oracle9i.

PROCEDURE DBMS_RESOURCE_MANAGER.DELETE_PLAN
    (*plan* IN VARCHAR2);
       Deletes *plan* and plan directives to which it refers.

PROCEDURE DBMS_RESOURCE_MANAGER.DELETE_PLAN_CASCADE
    (*plan* IN VARCHAR2);
       Deletes *plan* and plan directives to which it refers and all its descendants.

PROCEDURE DBMS_RESOURCE_MANAGER.CREATE_CONSUMER_GROUP
    (*consumer_group* IN VARCHAR2,
    comment IN VARCHAR2,
    cpu_mth IN VARCHAR2 DEFAULT 'ROUND-ROBIN');
       Creates *consumer_group* with *comment*, which uses *cpu_mth*.

PROCEDURE DBMS_RESOURCE_MANAGER.CREATE_CONSUMER_GROUP
    (*consumer_group* IN VARCHAR2,
    new_comment IN VARCHAR2 DEFAULT NULL,
    new_cpu_mth IN VARCHAR2 DEFAULT NULL);
       Updates *consumer_group* with *new_comment*, which uses *new_cpu_mth*.

PROCEDURE DBMS_RESOURCE_MANAGER.DELETE_CONSUMER_GROUP
    (*consumer_group* IN VARCHAR2);
       Deletes *consumer_group*.

PROCEDURE DBMS_RESOURCE_MANAGER.CREATE_PLAN_DIRECTIVE
    (*plan* IN VARCHAR2,
    group_or_subplan IN VARCHAR2,
    comment IN VARCHAR2,
    cpu_p1 IN NUMBER DEFAULT NULL,
    cpu_p2 IN NUMBER DEFAULT NULL,
    cpu_p3 IN NUMBER DEFAULT NULL,
    *cpu_p14*IN NUMBER DEFAULT NULL,
    cpu_p5 IN NUMBER DEFAULT NULL,
    cpu_p6 IN NUMBER DEFAULT NULL,
    cpu_p7 IN NUMBER DEFAULT NULL,
    cpu_p8 IN NUMBER DEFAULT NULL,
    {*active_sess_pool_pl* | *max_active_sess_target_pl*}
      IN NUMBER DEFAULT UNLIMITED,
    [,*queueing_pl* IN NUMBER DEFAULT UNLIMITED]#
    [,*switch_group* IN VARCHAR2 DEFAULT NULL]#
    [,*switch_time* IN NUMBER DEFAULT UNLIMITED]#
    [,*switch_estimate* IN BOOLEAN DEFAULT FALSE]#
    [,*max_est_exec_time* IN NUMBER DEFAULT UNLIMITED]#
    [,*undo_pool* IN NUMBER DEFAULT UNLIMITED,]#
    parallel_degree_limit_pl IN NUMBER DEFAULT UNLIMITED);
       Creates *plan*, as part of consumer *group_or_subplan*, with parameters for eight CPU allocations *cpu_p**. *switch_group* uses *switch_time*, which is estimated if *switch_estimate*. In Oracle 8.2, *max_active_sess_target* was renamed to *active_sess_pool_pl*. The other parameters control their associated values. The parameters from *queueing_pl* through *undo_pool* were new with Oracle9i.

PROCEDURE DBMS_RESOURCE_MANAGER.UPDATE_PLAN_DIRECTIVE
    (*plan* IN VARCHAR2,
    group_or_subplan IN VARCHAR2,
    comment IN VARCHAR2,
    new_cpu_p1 IN NUMBER DEFAULT NULL,
    new_cpu_p2 IN NUMBER DEFAULT NULL,

```
new_cpu_p3 IN NUMBER DEFAULT NULL,
new_cpu_p4IN NUMBER DEFAULT NULL,
new_cpu_p5 IN NUMBER DEFAULT NULL,
new_cpu_p6 IN NUMBER DEFAULT NULL,
new_cpu_p7 IN NUMBER DEFAULT NULL,
new_cpu_p8 IN NUMBER DEFAULT NULL,
{new_active_sess_pool_p1 | new_max_active_sess_target}
   IN NUMBER DEFAULT NULL
[,new_queueing_p1 IN NUMBER DEFAULT NULL]#
[,new_parallel_degree_limit_p1 IN NUMBER DEFAULT NULL]#
[,new_switch_group IN VARCHAR2 DEFAULT NULL]#
[,new_switch_time IN NUMBER DEFAULT NULL]#
[,new_switch_estimate IN BOOLEAN DEFAULT FALSE]#
[,new_max_est_exec_time IN NUMBER DEFAULT NULL]#
[,new_undo_pool IN NUMBER DEFAULT NULL]#);
```
Updates *plan*, as part of consumer *group_or_subplan*, with parameters for eight CPU allocations *cpu_p**. *new_switch_group* uses *new_switch_time*, which is estimated if *new_switch_estimate*. The other parameters control their associated values. In Oracle 8.2, *new_max_active_sess_target* was renamed to *new_active_sess_pool_pl*. The other parameters control their associated values. The parameters from *new_queueing_pl* through *new_undo_pool* were new with Oracle9i.

PROCEDURE DBMS_RESOURCE_MANAGER.DELETE_PLAN_DIRECTIVE
```
(plan IN VARCHAR2,
group_or_subplan IN VARCHAR2);
```
Deletes *plan*, part of consumer *group_or_subplan*.

PROCEDURE DBMS_RESOURCE_MANAGER.CREATE_PENDING_AREA;
Creates a pending area where changes to the plan schema of Resource Manager objects can be made.

PROCEDURE DBMS_RESOURCE_MANAGER.VALIDATE_PENDING_AREA;
Validates changes in the pending area.

PROCEDURE DBMS_RESOURCE_MANAGER.CLEAR_PENDING_AREA;
Clears changes in the pending area for the Resource Manager.

PROCEDURE DBMS_RESOURCE_MANAGER.SUBMIT_PENDING_AREA;
Submits changes for the Resource Manager in the pending area. Clears the pending area after validating and commiting the changes.

PROCEDURE DBMS_RESOURCE_MANAGER.SET_INITIAL_CONSUMER_GROUP
```
(user IN VARCHAR2,
consumer_group IN VARCHAR2);
```
Sets the initial *consumer_group* for *user*.

PROCEDURE DBMS_RESOURCE_MANAGER.SWITCH_CONSUMER_GROUP_FOR_SESSION
```
(session_id IN NUMBER,
session_serial IN NUMBER,
consumer_group IN VARCHAR2);
```
Switches the session identified by *session_id* (SID) and *session_serial* (SERIAL# column from V$SESSION) to *consumer_group* and any slave session.

PROCEDURE DBMS_RESOURCE_MANAGER.SWITCH_CONSUMER_GROUP_FOR_USER
```
(user IN VARCHAR2,
consumer_group IN VARCHAR2);
```
Switches all sessions for *user* to *consumer_group* and any slave session.

DBMS_RESOURCE_MANAGER_PRIVS

Used to maintain privileges associated with Database Resource Manager. New with Oracle8*i*.

Calls

```
PROCEDURE DBMS_RESOURCE_MANAGER_PRIVS.GRANT_SYSTEM_PRIVILEGE
    (grantee_name IN VARCHAR2,
    privilege_name IN VARCHAR2 DEFAULT 'ADMINISTER_RESOURCE_MANAGER',
    admin_option IN BOOLEAN);
```
> Grants *privilege_name* to *grantee_name*. If *admin_option*, *grantee_name* can regrant privilege.

```
PROCEDURE DBMS_RESOURCE_MANAGER_PRIVS.REVOKE_SYSTEM_PRIVILEGE
    (grantee_name IN VARCHAR2,
    privilege_name IN VARCHAR2 DEFAULT 'ADMINISTER_RESOURCE_MANAGER');
```
> Revokes *privilege_name* from *grantee_name*.

```
PROCEDURE DBMS_RESOURCE_MANAGER_PRIVS.GRANT_SWITCH_CONSUMER_GROUP
    (grantee_name IN VARCHAR2,
    consumer_group IN VARCHAR2,
    grant_option IN BOOLEAN);
```
> Grants *grantee_name* the ability to switch to *consumer_group*. If *grant_option*, *grantee_name* can regrant access.

```
PROCEDURE DBMS_RESOURCE_MANAGER_PRIVS.REVOKE_SWITCH_CONSUMER_GROUP
    (grantee_name IN VARCHAR2,
    consumer_group IN VARCHAR2);
```
> Revokes *grantee_name* the ability to switch to *consumer_group*.

DBMS_RESUMABLE

Provides procedures and functions to handle resumable operations that run out of space or reach space limits. New with Oracle9*i*.

Calls

```
PROCEDURE DBMS_RESUMABLE.ABORT
    (session_id IN NUMBER);
```
> Aborts the suspended *session_id*.

```
FUNCTION DBMS_RESUMABLE.GET_SESSION_TIMEOUT
    (session_id IN NUMBER);
```
> Returns the timeout value of resumable space allocations for *session_id*.

```
FUNCTION DBMS_RESUMABLE.GET_SESSION_TIMEOUT
    (session_id IN NUMBER,
    timeout IN NUMBER);
```
> Sets *timeout* for resumable space allocations for *session_id*.

```
FUNCTION DBMS_RESUMABLE.GET_TIMEOUT;
```
> Returns the timeout value of the current session.

```
PROCEDURE DBMS_RESUMABLE.SET_TIMEOUT
    (timeout IN NUMBER);
```
> Sets *timeout* of the current session.

```
FUNCTION DBMS_RESUMABLE.SPACE_ERROR_INFO
   (error_type OUT VARCHAR2,
   object_type OUT VARCHAR2,
   object_owner OUT VARCHAR2,
   table_space_name OUT VARCHAR2,
   object_name OUT VARCHAR2,
   sub_object_name OUT VARCHAR2)
   RETURN BOOLEAN;
```
   If there is a space-related error, returns information in parameters and TRUE for
   the function; otherwise, returns FALSE.

DBMS_RLS

Provides access to Oracle's fine-grained access control administrative interface. This
package is new with Oracle8*i* and available only with Enterprise Edition.

Calls

```
PROCEDURE DBMS_RLS.ADD_POLICY
   (object_schema IN VARCHAR2 DEFAULT NULL,
   object_name IN VARCHAR2,
   policy_name IN VARCHAR2,
   function_schema IN VARCHAR2 DEFAULT NULL,
   policy_function IN DEFAULT VARCHAR2,
   statement_types IN VARCHAR2 DEFAULT NULL,
   update_check IN BOOLEAN DEFAULT FALSE,
   enable IN BOOLEAN DEFAULT TRUE
   [,static_policy IN BOOLEAN DEFAULT FALSE]#);
```
   Adds *policy_name* to *object_schema.object_name*. The policy uses *function_
   schema.policy_schema* and applies to *statement_types*, which can include any
   combination of SELECT, INSERT, UPDATE, and DELETE. If *update_check*, the
   server checks the policy against the value after an INSERT or UPDATE. If *static_
   policy* (new with Oracle9*i*), the server assumes that the policy produces the same
   predicate for all users except SYS or any user with EXEMPT ACCESS POLICY
   privilege.

```
PROCEDURE DBMS_RLS.DROP_POLICY
   (object_schema IN VARCHAR2 DEFAULT NULL,
   object_name IN VARCHAR2,
   policy_name IN VARCHAR2);
```
   Drops *policy_name* for *object_schema.object_name*.

```
PROCEDURE DBMS_RLS.REFRESH_POLICY
   (object_schema IN VARCHAR2 DEFAULT NULL,
   object_name IN VARCHAR2,
   policy_name IN VARCHAR2);
```
   Forces all cached statements associated with *object_schema.object_name* to be
   reparsed.

```
PROCEDURE DBMS_RLS.ENABLE_POLICY
   (object_schema IN VARCHAR2 := NULL,
   object_name IN VARCHAR2,
```

```
    policy_name IN VARCHAR2,
    enable IN BOOLEAN);
```
Enables (if *enable* is TRUE) or disables (if *enable* is FALSE) *policy_name* for *object_schema.object_name*.

```
PROCEDURE DBMS_RLS.CREATE_POLICY_GROUP
    (object_schema IN VARCHAR2 DEFAULT NULL,
    object_name IN VARCHAR2,
    policy_group IN VARCHAR2);
```
Creates *policy_group* for *object_schema.object_name*. New with Oracle9*i*.

```
PROCEDURE DBMS_RLS.ADD_GROUPED_POLICY
    (object_schema IN VARCHAR2,
    object_name IN VARCHAR2,
    policy_group IN VARCHAR2,
    policy_name IN VARCHAR2,
    function_schema IN VARCHAR2,
    policy_function IN DEFAULT VARCHAR2,
    statement_types IN VARCHAR2,
    update_check IN BOOLEAN,
    enable IN BOOLEAN,
    static_policy IN BOOLEAN DEFAULT FALSE);
```
Adds *policy_name* to *policy_group* for *object_schema.object_name*. The parameters are the same as those for ADD_POLICY. New with Oracle9*i*.

```
PROCEDURE DBMS_RLS.ADD_POLICY_CONTEXT
    (object_schema IN VARCHAR2,
    object_name IN VARCHAR2,
    namespace IN VARCHAR2,
    attribute IN VARCHAR2);
```
Adds *attribute* and *namespace* context for *object_schema.object_name*. New with Oracle9*i*.

```
PROCEDURE DBMS_RLS.DELETE_POLICY_GROUP
    (object_schema IN VARCHAR2 DEFAULT NULL,
    object_name IN VARCHAR2,
    policy_group IN VARCHAR2);
```
Deletes *policy_group* for *object_schema.object_name*. New with Oracle9*i*.

```
PROCEDURE DBMS_RLS.ADD_GROUPED_POLICY
    (object_schema IN VARCHAR2,
    object_name IN VARCHAR2,
    policy_group IN VARCHAR2,
    policy_name IN VARCHAR2);
```
Drops *policy_name* of *policy_group* for *object_schema.object_name*. New with Oracle9*i*.

```
PROCEDURE DBMS_RLS.DROP_POLICY_CONTEXT
    (object_schema IN VARCHAR2,
    object_name IN VARCHAR2,
    namespace IN VARCHAR2,
    attribute IN VARCHAR2);
```
Drops *attribute* and *namespace* context of *object_schema.object_name*. New with Oracle9*i*.

```
PROCEDURE DBMS_RLS.ENABLE_GROUPED_POLICY
    (object_schema IN VARCHAR2,
    object_name IN VARCHAR2,
```

```
group_name IN VARCHAR2,
policy_name IN VARCHAR2,
enable IN BOOLEAN);
```
   If *enable* is TRUE, enables *policy_name* of *group_name* for *object_schema.object_
   name*; otherwise, disables it. New with Oracle9*i*.

PROCEDURE DBMS_RLS.REFRESH_GROUPED_POLICY
```
(object_schema IN VARCHAR2,
object_name IN VARCHAR2,
group_name IN VARCHAR2,
policy_name IN VARCHAR2);
```
   Forces all cached SQL statements associated with *policy_name* of *group_name* for
   object_schema.object_name to be re-parsed. New with Oracle9*i*.

DBMS_ROWID

Provides routines for working with ROWIDs. ROWIDs changed structure in Oracle8;
for Oracle8 and later versions, this package works with both the old and the new
ROWID types.

An Oracle7 (restricted) ROWID has three parts in base 16 (hex):

   BBBBBBBB.RRRR.FFFF

An Oracle8 (extended) ROWID has four parts in base 64:

   OOOOOOFFFBBBBBBRRR

where:

   OOOOOO is the object number.
   FFFF (FFF) is the absolute (Oracle7) or relative (Oracle8) file number.
   BBBBBBBB (BBBBBB) is the block number within the file.
   RRRR (RRR) is the row number within the block.

Calls

FUNCTION DBMS_ROWID.ROWID_BLOCK_NUMBER
```
(row_id IN ROWID)
RETURN NUMBER;
```
   Returns the block number component of *row_id*.

FUNCTION DBMS_ROWID.ROWID_CREATE
```
(rowid_type IN NUMBER,
object_number IN NUMBER,
relative_fno IN NUMBER,
block_number IN NUMBER,
row_number IN NUMBER)
RETURN ROWID;
```
   Creates a *rowid_type* ROWID composed of *object_number*, *relative_fno*, *block_
   number*, and *row_number*. *rowid_type* can be ROWID_TYPE_EXTENDED or
   ROWID_TYPE_ RESTRICTED. *object_number* can be ROWID_OBJECT_
   UNDEFINED or the object number (OID).

PROCEDURE DBMS_ROWID.ROWID_INFO
```
(rowid_in IN ROWID,
rowid_type OUT NUMBER,
object_number OUT NUMBER,
relative_fno OUT NUMBER,
```

```
block_number OUT NUMBER,
row_number OUT NUMBER);
```
Parses *rowid_in* into its individual components. *rowid_type* can be ROWID_
TYPE_EXTENDED or ROWID_TYPE_RESTRICTED. *object_number* can be
ROWID_OBJECT_UNDEFINED or the object number (OID).

```
FUNCTION DBMS_ROWID.ROWID_OBJECT
   (row_id IN ROWID)
   RETURN NUMBER;
```
Returns the object number component of *row_id*.

```
FUNCTION DBMS_ROWID.ROWID_RELATIVE_FNO
   (row_id IN ROWID)
   RETURN NUMBER;
```
Returns the relative file number component of *row_id*.

```
FUNCTION DBMS_ROWID.ROWID_ROW_NUMBER
   (row_id IN ROWID)
   RETURN NUMBER;
```
Returns the row number component of *row_id*.

```
FUNCTION DBMS_ROWID.ROWID_TO_ABSOLUTE_FNO
   (row_id IN ROWID,
   schema_name IN VARCHAR2,
   object_name IN VARCHAR2)
   RETURN NUMBER;
```
Returns the absolute file number for *row_id*, *schema_name*, and *object_name*.

```
FUNCTION DBMS_ROWID.ROWID_TO_EXTENDED
   (old_rowid IN ROWID,
   schema_name IN VARCHAR2,
   object_name IN VARCHAR2,
   conversion_type IN INTEGER)
   RETURN ROWID;
```
Returns the extended ROWID for the restricted *old_rowid*, *schema_ name*, and
object_name using *conversion_type*. The *conversion_type* (new with Oracle8*i*) can
be either ROWID_CONVERT_INTERNAL (indicating that ROWID was stored
in a column of type ROWID) or ROWID_CONVERT_EXTERNAL (indicating
that ROWID was stored in a column of type CHAR/VARCHAR/VARCHAR2).

```
FUNCTION DBMS_ROWID.ROWID_TO_RESTRICTED
   (old_rowid IN ROWID,
   conversion_type IN INTEGER)
   RETURN ROWID;
```
Returns a restricted ROWID for the extended *old_rowid* using *conversion_type*.
The *conversion_type* can be either ROWID_CONVERT_INTERNAL (indicating
that ROWID will be stored in a column of type ROWID) or ROWID_
CONVERT_EXTERNAL (indicating that ROWID will be stored in a column of
type CHAR/VARCHAR/ VARCHAR2).

```
FUNCTION DBMS_ROWID.ROWID_TYPE
   (row_id IN ROWID)
   RETURN NUMBER;
```
Returns ROWID_TYPE_EXTENDED or ROWID_TYPE_RESTRICTED for *row_
id*.

```
FUNCTION DBMS_ROWID.ROWID_VERIFY
   (rowid_in IN ROWID,
```

```
schema_name IN VARCHAR2,
object_name IN VARCHAR2,
conversion_type IN INTEGER)
RETURN NUMBER;
```
Returns ROWID_VALID or ROWID_INVALID for *rowid_in*, *schema_name*, and *object_name*, using *conversion_type*. The *conversion_type*, new in Oracle8i, can be either ROWID_CONVERT_INTERNAL (*rowid_in* is stored in a column of type ROWID) or ROWID_CONVERT_ EXTERNAL (*rowid_in* is stored in a column of type CHAR/ VARCHAR/VARCHAR2).

DBMS_RULE

Evaluates rules in a rule set for a specific evaluation context. New with Oracle9i.

Call

```
PROCEDURE DBMS_RULE.EVALUATE
  (rule_set_name IN VARCHAR2,
  evaluation_context IN VARCHAR2,
  event_context IN SYS.RE$NVLIST DEFAULT NULL,
  table_values IN SYS.RE$TABLE_VALUE_LIST DEFAULT NULL,
  [column_values IN SYS.RE$COLUMN_VALUE_LIST,]
  variable_values IN SYS.RE$VARIABLE_VALUE_LIST DEFAULT NULL,
  [attribute_values IN SYS.RE$ATTRIBUTE_VALUE_LIST,]
  stop_on_first_hit IN BOOLEAN DEFAULT FALSE,
  simple_rules_only IN BOOLEAN DEFAULT FALSE,
  true_rules OUT SYS.RE$RULE_HIT_LIST,
  maybe_rules OUT SYS.RE$RULE_HIT_LIST);
```
Evaluates *rule_set_name* using *evaluation_context* and *event_context* (a list of name/value pairs that identify events that cause evaluation). The different values come from the specified tables. *stop_on_first_hit* causes the engine to stop when it hits the first rule that evaluates as TRUE or, in the absence of a TRUE rule, on one that may evaluate as TRUE if more data were present. If *simple_rules_only*, the procedure evaluates rules simple enough to be evaluated without issuing SQL statements. *true_rules* returns the rules that evaluate to TRUE based on the specified data. *maybe_rules* returns rules that could not be evaluated due to lack of data or the complexity of the rule, with *simple_rules_only*. *column_values* and *attribute_values* are either both present or both absent from this call.

DBMS_RULE_ADMIN

Provides procedures for administering rules, rule sets, and rule evaluation contexts. New with Oracle9i.

Calls

```
PROCEDURE DBMS_RULE_ADMIN.ADD_RULE
  (rule_name IN VARCHAR2,
  rule_set_name IN VARCHAR2,
  evaluation_context IN VARCHAR2 DEFAULT NULL,
  rule_comment IN VARCHAR2 DEFAULT NULL);
```
Adds *rule_name* to *rule_set_name*, with optional *evaluation_context* and *rule_ comment*.

PROCEDURE DBMS_RULE_ADMIN.ALTER_RULE
    (*rule_name* IN VARCHAR2,
    condition IN VARCHAR2 DEFAULT NULL,
    evaluation_context IN VARCHAR2 DEFAULT NULL,
    remove_evaluation_context IN BOOLEAN DEFAULT FALSE,
    action_context IN SYS.RE$NV_LIST DEFAULT NULL,
    remove_action_context IN BOOLEAN DEFAULT FALSE,
    rule_comment IN VARCHAR2 DEFAULT NULL,
    remove_rule_comment IN BOOLEAN DEFAULT FALSE);

> Alters *rule_name* by changing *condition* and either changing or removing the evaluation context, action context, or rule.

PROCEDURE DBMS_RULE_ADMIN.CREATE_EVALUATION_CONTEXT
    (*evaluation_context_name* IN VARCHAR2,
    table_aliases IN SYS.RE$TABLE_ALIAS_LIST DEFAULT NULL,
    variable_types IN SYS.RE$VARIABLE_TYPE_LIST DEFAULT NULL,
    evaluation_function IN VARCHAR2 DEFAULT NULL,
    evaluation_context_comment IN VARCHAR2 DEFAULT NULL);

> Creates *evaluation_context_name* with table aliases and variables specified in tables. *evaluation_function* is an optional function that will be used to evaluate rules using this context and which has the same form as the DBMS_RULE.EVALUATE procedure.

PROCEDURE DBMS_RULE_ADMIN.CREATE_RULE
    (*rule_name* IN VARCHAR2,
    condition IN VARCHAR2 DEFAULT NULL,
    evaluation_context IN VARCHAR2 DEFAULT NULL,
    action_context IN SYS.RE$NV_LIST DEFAULT NULL,
    rule_comment IN VARCHAR2 DEFAULT NULL);

> Creates *rule_name* with *condition* that can be evaluated as a Boolean with optional *evaluation_context* and *rule_set_comment*.

PROCEDURE DBMS_RULE_ADMIN.CREATE_RULE_SET
    (*rule_set_name* IN VARCHAR2,
    evaluation_context IN VARCHAR2 DEFAULT NULL,
    rule_set_comment IN VARCHAR2 DEFAULT NULL);

> Creates *rule_set_name* with optional evaluation context and comment.

PROCEDURE DBMS_RULE_ADMIN.DROP_EVALUATION_CONTEXT
    (*evaluation_context* IN VARCHAR2,
    force IN BOOLEAN DEFAULT FALSE);

> Drops *rule_name*. If *force*, removes the *evaluation_context* and all rules and rule sets that use it; otherwise, drops the evaluation context if no rules or rule sets use it or returns an exception.

PROCEDURE DBMS_RULE_ADMIN.DROP_RULE
    (*rule_name* IN VARCHAR2,
    force IN BOOLEAN DEFAULT FALSE);

> Drops *rule_name*. If *force*, removes the rule and all rule sets that use it; otherwise, drops the rule if no rule sets use it or returns an exception.

PROCEDURE DBMS_RULE_ADMIN.DROP_RULE_SET
    (*rule_set_name* IN VARCHAR2,
    delete_rules IN BOOLEAN DEFAULT FALSE);

> Drops *rule_set_name*. If *delete_rules*, drops any rules in the rule set; otherwise, does not drop the rules.

```
PROCEDURE DBMS_RULE_ADMIN.GRANT_OBJECT_PRIVILEGE
    (privilege IN BINARY_INTEGER,
    object_name IN VARCHAR2,
    grantee IN VARCHAR2,
    grant_option IN BOOLEAN DEFAULT FALSE);
```
   Grants rule *privilege* on *object_name* to *grantee*. If *grant_option*, *grantee* can regrant privilege.

```
PROCEDURE DBMS_RULE_ADMIN.GRANT_SYSTEM_PRIVILEGE
    (privilege IN BINARY_INTEGER,
    grantee IN VARCHAR2,
    grant_option IN BOOLEAN DEFAULT FALSE);
```
   Grants rule system *privilege* to *grantee*. If *grant_option*, *grantee* can regrant privilege.

```
PROCEDURE DBMS_RULE_ADMIN.REMOVE_RULE
    (rule_name IN VARCHAR2,
    rule_set_name IN VARCHAR2,
    evaluation_context IN VARCHAR2 DEFAULT NULL,
    all_evaluation_contexts IN BOOLEAN DEFAULT FALSE);
```
   Removes *rule_name* from *rule_set_name*. If an *evaluation_context* was specified with the ADD_RULE procedure, must also be specified in this procedure. If *all_evaluation_contexts*, the rule is removed from all evaluation contexts; otherwise, it is removed only from rule sets with the specified evaluation context.

```
PROCEDURE DBMS_RULE_ADMIN.REVOKE_OBJECT_PRIVILEGE
    (privilege IN BINARY_INTEGER,
    object_name IN VARCHAR2,
    revokee IN VARCHAR2);
```
   Revokes rule *privilege* on *object_name* from *revokee*.

```
PROCEDURE DBMS_RULE_ADMIN.REVOKE_SYSTEM_PRIVILEGE
    (privilege IN BINARY_INTEGER,
    revokee IN VARCHAR2);
```
   Revokes rule system *privilege* from *revokee*.

DBMS_SESSION

Provides facilities to set and modify session settings, enable or disable roles, and manage session resources.

Calls

```
PROCEDURE DBMS_SESSION.CLEAR_IDENTIFIER;
```
   Removes the value of the session's client ID. New with Oracle9*i*.

```
PROCEDURE DBMS_SESSION.CLOSE_DATABASE_LINK
    (dblink IN VARCHAR2);
```
   Closes the database link *dblink* or raises an exception if *dblink* is not open or is in use.

```
PROCEDURE DBMS_SESSION.FREE_UNUSED_USER_MEMORY;
```
   Releases freeable session memory back to the operating system (for a dedicated connection) or the Oracle shared pool (for a Shared Server connection).

FUNCTION DBMS_SESSION.IS_ROLE_ENABLED
    (*rolename* IN VARCHAR2)
  RETURN BOOLEAN;
    Returns TRUE if the *rolename* is currently enabled in the session.

FUNCTION DBMS_SESSION.IS_SESSION_ALIVE
  (*uniqueid* IN VARCHAR2)
  RETURN BOOLEAN;
    Returns TRUE if the session identified by *uniqueid* is still alive. New with
    Oracle8*i*.

PROCEDURE DBMS_SESSION.LIST_CONTEXT
  (*list* OUR AppCtxTabTyp,
  size OUT NUMBER);
    Returns information about the current context in a table of AppCtxTabType. *size*
    is the number of entries returned in the buffer. New with Oracle8*i*.

PROCEDURE DBMS_SESSION.MODIFY_PACKAGE_STATE
  (*action_flags* IN PLS_INTEGER);
    Modifies the package state either with FREE_ALL_RESOURCES, which frees all
    memory associated with the previously run PL/SQL programs, clears the value of
    package globals, and closes cached cursors, or with REINITIALIZE, which reini-
    tializes packages and reuses package memory. New with Oracle9*i*.

PROCEDURE DBMS_SESSION.LIST_CONTEXT
  (*list* OUT AppCtxTabTyp,
  size OUT NUMBER);
    Returns a *list* of namespaces, attributes, and values in the current session. *size* is
    the number of entries returned. New with Oracle9*i*.

PROCEDURE DBMS_SESSION.RESET_PACKAGE;
    Resets all package states in the session, destroying the values of all persistent
    package variables.

PROCEDURE DBMS_SESSION.SET_CLOSE_CACHED_OPEN_CURSORS
  (*close_cursors* IN BOOLEAN);
    Overrides the CLOSE_CACHED_OPEN_CURSORS database parameter at the
    session level with the value in *close_cursors*.

PROCEDURE DBMS_SESSION.SET_CONTEXT
  (*namespace* IN VARCHAR2,
  attribute IN VARCHAR2,
  [,*value* IN VARCHAR2]#
  [,*user_name* IN VARCHAR2]#
  client_id IN VARCHAR2);
    Sets *attribute* of application context to *value* for *namespace*. *user_name* and *client_*
    id can both be supplied. New with Oracle8*i*. The *user_name* and *value* parame-
    ters are new with Oracle9*i*.

PROCEDURE DBMS_SESSION.SET_IDENTIFIER
  (*client_id* IN VARCHAR);
    Sets *client_id* in session. New with Oracle9*i*.

PROCEDURE DBMS_SESSION.SET_LABEL
  (*lbl* IN VARCHAR2);
    Sets the session's Trusted Oracle session label to *lbl*. Beginning with Oracle8*i*, no
    longer supported.

PROCEDURE DBMS_SESSION.SET_MLS_LABEL_FORMAT
  (*fmt* IN VARCHAR2);
  Sets the session's default Trusted Oracle label format to *fmt*. Beginning with
  Oracle8*i*, no longer supported.

PROCEDURE DBMS_SESSION.SET_NLS
  (*param* IN VARCHAR2,
  value IN VARCHAR2);
  Sets the National Language Support parameter *param* to *value*. When *value* is a
  format mask, use a triple-quoted string.

PROCEDURE DBMS_SESSION.SET_ROLE
  (*role_cmd* IN VARCHAR2);
  Enables role(s) by appending *role_cmd* to the SET_ROLE command and
  executing. You can disable all roles by setting *role_cmd* to NONE.

PROCEDURE DBMS_SESSION.SET_SQL_TRACE
  (*sql_trace* IN BOOLEAN);
  Turns SQL tracing on or off in the session according to *sql_trace* (TRUE = on,
  FALSE = off). The functionality of this procedure used to be found in the DBMS_
  SYSTEM.SET_SQL_TRACE_IN_SESSION procedure.

PROCEDURE DBMS_SESSION.SWITCH_CURRENT_CONSUMER_GROUP
  (*new_consumer_group* IN VARCHAR2,
  old_consumer_group OUT VARCHAR2,
  initial_group_on_error IN BOOLEAN);
  Switches the current consumer group to the *new_consumer_group* and returns the
  name of the *old_consumer_group*. If *initial_group_on_error*, sets the current
  consumer group to the initial consumer group in the event of an error.

FUNCTION DBMS_SESSION.UNIQUE_SESSION_ID
  RETURN VARCHAR2;
  Returns a string identifier unique to the session up to 24 bytes in length.

DBMS_SHARED_POOL

Contains programs to help manage the System Global Area (SGA) shared pool.

Calls

PROCEDURE DBMS_SHARED_POOL.ABORTED_REQUEST_THRESHOLD
  (*threshold_size* IN NUMBER);
  Sets the maximum object size for which the shared pool will flush other objects to
  make room. If you attempt to load objects larger than *threshold_size* bytes,
  returns an ORA-04031 error if sufficient space is not available. New in Oracle8*i*.

PROCEDURE DBMS_SHARED_POOL.KEEP
  (*name* IN VARCHAR2,
  flag IN CHAR DEFAULT 'P');
  Pins the object identified by *name* in the shared pool. The object's type is identified by *flag*: 'P' or 'p' for package, procedure, or function; 'C' or 'c' for cursor (in
  Oracle8); 'Q' or 'q' for sequences; and 'R' or 'r' for triggers. Specifies any other
  character *flag* to pin a cursor identified by address and hash value (from
  V$SQLAREA) in *name*.

```
PROCEDURE DBMS_SHARED_POOL.SIZES
    (minsize IN NUMBER);
```
Displays objects and cursors in the shared pool that exceed *minsize* kilobytes in size.

```
PROCEDURE DBMS_SHARED_POOL.UNKEEP
    (name IN VARCHAR2,
    flag IN CHAR DEFAULT 'P');
```
Unpins the object of type *flag* and identified by *name* from the shared pool. Valid *flag* values are the same values as for DBMS_ SHARED_POOL.KEEP.

DBMS_SNAPSHOT

This package was replaced by DBMS_MVIEW in Oracle9*i*.

DBMS_SPACE

Provides procedures that provide internal space utilization and freelist information about table, index, and cluster segments.

Calls

```
PROCEDURE DBMS_SPACE.FREE_BLOCKS
    (segment_owner IN VARCHAR2,
    segment_name IN VARCHAR2,
    segment_type IN VARCHAR2,
    freelist_group_id IN NUMBER,
    free_blks OUT NUMBER
    [,scan_limit IN NUMBER DEFAULT NULL]
    [,partition_name IN VARCHAR2 DEFAULT NULL]);
```
Returns into *free_blks* the number of blocks on the freelist on instance *freelist_group_id* for segment *segment_name* of type *segment_type* (TABLE, INDEX, or CLUSTER) owned by *segment_owner* in partition *partition_name* (optional, new with Oracle8). *scan_limit* (optional) limits the number of free blocks scanned.

```
PROCEDURE DBMS_SPACE.SPACE_USAGE
    (segment_owner IN VARCHAR2,
    segment_name IN VARCHAR2,
    segment_type IN VARCHAR2,
    unformatted_blocks OUT NUMBER,
    unformatted_bytes OUT NUMBER,
    fs1_blocks OUT NUMBER,
    fs1_bytes OUT NUMBER,
    fs2_blocks OUT NUMBER,
    fs2_bytes OUT NUMBER,
    fs3_blocks OUT NUMBER,
    fs3_bytes OUT NUMBER,
    fs4_blocks OUT NUMBER,
    fs4_bytes OUT NUMBER,
    full_blocks OUT NUMBER,
```

```
full_bytes OUT NUMBER,
partition_name IN VARCHAR2 DEFAULT NULL);
```

Returns unused space in *segment_name* owned by *segment_owner* in *partition_name* of *segment_type* (TABLE, INDEX, or CLUSTER). Parameters display the number of blocks and bytes that are *unformatted*, with less than 25% free space (*fs1*), 25–50% free space (*fs2*), 50–75% free space (*fs3*), and at least 75% free space (*fs4*), as well as the number of blocks and bytes that are *full*. New with Oracle9*i*.

```
PROCEDURE DBMS_SPACE.UNUSED_SPACE
    (segment_owner IN VARCHAR2,
    segment_name IN VARCHAR2,
    segment_type IN VARCHAR2,
    total_blocks OUT NUMBER,
    total_bytes OUT NUMBER,
    unused_blocks OUT NUMBER,
    unused_bytes OUT NUMBER,
    last_used_extent_file_id OUT NUMBER,
    last_used_extent_block_id OUT NUMBER,
    last_used_block OUT NUMBER
    [,partition_name IN VARCHAR2 DEFAULT NULL]);
```

Returns the high-water mark (*last_used_extent_file_id*, *last_used_ extent_block_id*, and *last_used_block*), space used (*total_blocks*, *total_bytes*), and space unused (*unused_blocks*, *unused_bytes*) in segment *segment_name* of type *segment_type* (TABLE, INDEX, or CLUSTER) owned by *segment_owner* in partition *partition_name*. The *partition_name* parameter, which is optional, is new with Oracle8.

DBMS_SPACE_ADMIN

Provides procedures to manage locally managed tablespaces. A locally managed tablespace must be managed by the user, so these procedures perform a lot of the maintenance normally done automatically by the Oracle server. New with Oracle8*i*.

Calls

```
PROCEDURE DBMS_SPACE_ADMIN.SEGMENT_VERIFY
    (tablespace_name IN VARCHAR2,
    header_relative_file IN POSITIVE,
    header_block IN POSITIVE
    verify_option IN POSITIVE DEFAULT SEGMENT_VERIFY_EXTENTS);
```

For *tablespace_name*, with relative file number of *header_relative_file* and block number of header of *header_block*, uses *verify_option* of either SEGMENT_VERIFY_EXTENTS or SEGMENT_VERIFY_EXTENTS_GLOBAL to verify the segments.

```
PROCEDURE DBMS_SPACE_ADMIN.SEGMENT_CORRUPT
    (tablespace_name IN VARCHAR2,
    header_relative_file IN POSITIVE,
    header_block IN POSITIVE
    corrupt_option IN POSITIVE DEFAULT SEGMENT_MARK_CORRUPT);
```

For *tablespace_name*, with relative file number of *header_relative_file* and block number of header of *header_block*, uses *corrupt_option* of either SEGMENT_MARK_CORRUPT or SEGMENT_MARK_VALID to check the segments.

PROCEDURE DBMS_SPACE_ADMIN.SEGMENT_DROP_CORRUPT
  (*tablespace_name* IN VARCHAR2,
  header_relative_file IN POSITIVE,
  header_block IN POSITIVE);
> Drops a segment marked as corrupt in *tablespace_name*, with the relative file number of *header_relative_file* and the block number of header of *header_block*.

PROCEDURE DBMS_SPACE_ADMIN.SEGMENT_DUMP
  (*tablespace_name* IN VARCHAR2,
  header_relative_file IN POSITIVE,
  header_block IN POSITIVE
  dump_option IN POSITIVE DEFAULT SEGMENT_DUMP_EXTENT_MAP);
> The segment residing in *tablespace_name*, with relative file number of *header_relative_file* and block number of header of *header_block*, dumps the segment header and extent block maps. There is only one valid value for *dump_option*: SEGMENT_DUMP_EXTENT_MAP.

PROCEDURE DBMS_SPACE_ADMIN.TABLESPACE_VERIFY
  (*tablespace_name* IN VARCHAR2,
  verify_option IN POSITIVE := TABLESPACE_VERIFY_BITMAP);
> Verifies that bitmap and extent maps are in sync for segments in *tablespace_name*. The options for *verify_option* are TABLESPACE_EXTENT_MAKE_FREE or TABLESPACE_EXTENT_MAKE_USED.

PROCEDURE DBMS_SPACE_ADMIN.TABLESPACE_FIX_BITMAPS
  (*tablespace_name* IN VARCHAR2,
  dbarange_relative_file IN POSITIVE,
  dbarange_begin_block IN POSITIVE,
  dbarange_end_block IN POSITIVE,
  fix_option IN POSITIVE);
> Marks the extent (DBA range) *dbarange_relative_file* beginning with *dbarange_begin_block* and ending with *dbarange_end_block* in *tablespace_name* as free or used in bitmap, depending on *fix_option* of TABLESPACE_EXTENT_MAKE_FREE or TABLESPACE_EXTENT_MAKE_USED.

PROCEDURE DBMS_SPACE_ADMIN.TABLESPACE_REBUILD_BITMAPS
  (*tablespace_name* IN VARCHAR2,
  bitmap_relative_file IN POSITIVE DEFAULT NULL,
  bitmap_block IN POSITIVE DEFAULT NULL);
> Rebuilds *bitmap_block* of *bitmap_relative_file* in *tablespace_name*.

PROCEDURE DBMS_SPACE_ADMIN.REBUILD_QUOTAS
  (*tablespace_name* IN VARCHAR2);
> Rebuilds quotas for *tablespace_name*.

PROCEDURE DBMS_SPACE_ADMIN.MIGRATE_FROM_LOCAL
  (*tablespace_name* IN VARCHAR2);
> Migrates a locally managed *tablespace_name* to a dictionary-managed tablespace.

PROCEDURE DBMS_SPACE_ADMIN.MIGRATE_TO_LOCAL
  (*tablespace_name* IN VARCHAR,
  allocation_unit IN INTEGER,
  relative_fno IN INTEGER);
> Migrates dictionary-managed *tablespace_name* to a locally managed tablespace, with an *allocation_unit* and an optional relative file number (*relative_fno*) where the bitmaps should be placed. New with Oracle9*i*.

PROCEDURE DBMS_SPACE_ADMIN.RELOCATE_BITMAPS
  (*tablespace_name* IN VARCHAR,
  relative_fno IN INTEGER,
  block_number IN NUMBER);
> Migrates bitmaps of *tablespace_name* to relative file number (*relative_fno*) and *block_number*. New with Oracle9*i*.

PROCEDURE DBMS_SPACE_ADMIN.TABLESPACE_FIX_SEGMENT_STATES
  (*tablespace_name* IN VARCHAR);
> Fixes states of segments for a *tablespace_name* where migration was aborted. New with Oracle9*i*.

DBMS_SQL

Provides procedures and functions for using dynamic SQL within PL/SQL. For Oracle8 and later, these procedures provide support for array operations in PL/SQL. With Oracle8*i*, Oracle introduced native dynamic SQL, which can be used instead of these procedures.

Calls

PROCEDURE DBMS_SQL.BIND_ARRAY
  (*c* IN INTEGER,
  name IN VARCHAR2,
  <*table_variable* IN *datatype*>
  [,*index1* IN INTEGER
  ,*index2* IN INTEGER]);
> Binds the *table_variable* array to the placeholder name in the parsed (but not executed) SQL statement in the cursor *c* (returned by the OPEN_CURSOR call). For Oracle8 and later, used to perform array processing. The <*table_variable* IN *datatype*> can be any of the following:
>
>> *n_tab* IN DBMS_SQL.NUMBER_TABLE
>> *c_tab* IN DBMS_SQL.VARCHAR2_TABLE
>> *d_tab* IN DBMS_SQL.DATE_TABLE
>> *bl_tab* IN DBMS_SQL.BLOB_TABLE
>> *cl_tab* IN DBMS_SQL.CLOB_TABLE
>> *bf_tab* IN DBMS_SQL.BFILE_TABLE
>
> The optional argument *index1* defines the lower bound (first row) within the table, and *index2* defines the upper bound (last row). Available in Oracle8 and later.

PROCEDURE DBMS_SQL.BIND_VARIABLE
  (*c* IN INTEGER,
  name IN VARCHAR2,
  value IN {NUMBER | VARCHAR2 | DATE | BLOB | CLOB
    CHARACTER SET ANY_CS | BFILE}
  [,*out_value_size* IN INTEGER]);
> Binds the scalar value to the placeholder name in the parsed SQL statement in the cursor *c*, optionally with the maximum expected size of value being *out_value_size*. You can also use the following syntax for variables of CHAR, RAW, or ROWID datatypes:

```
PROCEDURE DBMS_SQL.BIND_VARIABLE_CHAR
    (c IN INTEGER,
    name IN VARCHAR2,
    value IN CHAR CHARACTER SET ANY_CS
    [,out_value_size IN INTEGER]);

PROCEDURE DBMS_SQL.BIND_VARIABLE_RAW
    (c IN INTEGER,
    name IN VARCHAR2,
    value IN RAW
    [,out_value_size IN INTEGER]);

PROCEDURE DBMS_SQL.BIND_VARIABLE_ROWID
    (c IN INTEGER,
    name IN VARCHAR2,
    value IN ROWID);
```

See the earlier explanation for BIND_VARIABLE.

```
PROCEDURE DBMS_SQL.CLOSE_CURSOR
    (c IN OUT INTEGER);
```

Closes cursor c.

```
PROCEDURE DBMS_SQL.COLUMN_VALUE
    (c IN INTEGER,
    position IN INTEGER,
    value OUT {NUMBER | VARCHAR | DATE | BLOB | CLOB
        CHARACTER SET ANY_CS | BFILE | MLSLABEL }
    [,column_error OUT NUMBER
    [,actual_length OUT INTEGER]]);
```

Transfers the contents of column number *position* in the select list of the fetched cursor *c* into the variable *value*, optionally setting *actual_length* to the pretruncated length in bytes and *column_error* to the error code for the specified value. Truncation may occur if there is a difference in size between the retrieved value in the cursor and the variable length. MLSLABEL is for Trusted Oracle, which is no longer supported in Oracle9*i*. The COLUMN_VALUE procedure can also have the following syntax:

```
PROCEDURE DBMS_SQL.COLUMN_VALUE
    (c IN INTEGER,
    position IN INTEGER,
    <table_parameter> IN <table_type>);
```

The *table_parameter* and *table_type* can be any of the following:

```
    n_tab IN DBMS_SQL.NUMBER_TABLE
    c_tab IN DBMS_SQL.VARCHAR2_TABLE
    d_tab IN DBMS_SQL.DATE_TABLE
    bl_tab IN DBMS_SQL.BLOB_TABLE
    cl_tab IN DBMS_SQL.CLOB_TABLE
    bf_tab IN DBMS_SQL.BFILE_TABLE
```

The procedure can also have the following syntax for CHAR, LONG, RAW, and ROWID datatypes:

```
PROCEDURE DBMS_SQL.COLUMN_VALUE_CHAR
    (c IN INTEGER,
    position IN INTEGER,
    value OUT CHAR CHARACTER SET ANY_CS
```

```
          [,column_error OUT NUMBER
          [,actual_length OUT INTEGER]]);.
      PROCEDURE DBMS_SQL.COLUMN_VALUE_LONG
          (c IN INTEGER,
          position IN INTEGER,
          length IN INTEGER,
          offset IN INTEGER,
          value OUT VARCHAR2,
          value_length OUT INTEGER);
      PROCEDURE DBMS_SQL.COLUMN_VALUE_RAW
          (c IN INTEGER,
          position IN INTEGER,
          value OUT RAW
          [,column_error OUT NUMBER
          [,actual_length OUT INTEGER]]);
      PROCEDURE DBMS_SQL.COLUMN_VALUE_ROWID
          (c IN INTEGER,
          position IN INTEGER,
          value OUT ROWID);
          [,column_error OUT NUMBER
          [,actual_length OUT INTEGER]]);
```

For information on these procedures, see COLUMN_VALUE.

```
PROCEDURE DBMS_SQL.DEFINE_ARRAY
    (c IN INTEGER,
    position IN INTEGER,
    <table_parameter IN table_type>,
    cnt IN INTEGER,
    lower_bound IN INTEGER);
```
Defines the datatype and size of the elements in the fetch array for column number *position* in the SELECT list of the cursor *c* as the same datatype and size as the nested table *table_parameter*, beginning with row *lower_bound*, and having a maximum array size of *cnt* rows. For Oracle8 and beyond, *table_parameter* and *table_type* can be any of these:

```
        n_tab IN DBMS_SQL.NUMBER_TABLE
        c_tab IN DBMS_SQL.VARCHAR2_TABLE
        d_tab IN DBMS_SQL.DATE_TABLE
        bl_tab IN DBMS_SQL.BLOB_TABLE
        cl_tab IN DBMS_SQL.CLOB_TABLE
        bf_tab IN DBMS_SQL.BFILE_TABLE
```

```
PROCEDURE DBMS_SQL.DEFINE_COLUMN
    (c IN INTEGER,
    position IN INTEGER,
    column IN NUMBER | DATE | BLOB | CLOB CHARACTER SET
        ANY_CS | BFILE | MLSLABEL);
```
The variable or expression *column* defines the datatype for column number *position* in the select list of the cursor *c*. MLSLABEL is for Trusted Oracle only, which is no longer supported in Oracle9i. The following syntax is also supported for DEFINE_COLUMN:

PROCEDURE DBMS_SQL.DEFINE_COLUMN
   (*c* IN INTEGER,
   position IN INTEGER,
   column IN VARCHAR2 CHARACTER SET ANY_CS,
   column_size IN INTEGER);

The following syntax is also supported for specific datatypes CHAR, LONG, RAW, and ROWID:

PROCEDURE DBMS_SQL.DEFINE_COLUMN_CHAR
   (*c* IN INTEGER,
   position IN INTEGER,
   column IN CHAR CHARACTER SET ANY_CS,
   column_size IN INTEGER);

PROCEDURE DBMS_SQL.DEFINE_COLUMN_LONG
   (*c* IN INTEGER,
   position IN INTEGER);

PROCEDURE DBMS_SQL.DEFINE_COLUMN_RAW
   (*c* IN INTEGER,
   position IN INTEGER,
   column IN RAW,
   column_size IN INTEGER);

PROCEDURE DBMS_SQL.DEFINE_COLUMN_ROWID
   (*c* IN INTEGER,
   position IN INTEGER,
   column IN ROWID);

   For an explanation of these procedures, see the DEFINE_COLUMN procedure.

PROCEDURE DBMS_SQL.DESCRIBE_COLUMNS
   (*c* IN INTEGER,
   col_cnt OUT INTEGER,
   desc_t OUT DESC_TAB);
   Populates PL/SQL table *desc_t* of type DBMS_SQL.DESC_REC with the description of columns of cursor *c*. *col_cnt* is the number of columns in *c* and the number of rows in *desc_t*.

FUNCTION DBMS_SQL.EXECUTE
   (*c* IN INTEGER)
   RETURN INTEGER;
   For INSERT, UPDATE, or DELETE statements, returns the number of rows processed by executing the cursor *c*. For all other SQL statements, executes the cursor *c* and returns an undefined value.

FUNCTION DBMS_SQL.EXECUTE_AND_FETCH
   (*c* IN INTEGER,
   exact IN BOOLEAN DEFAULT FALSE)
   RETURN INTEGER;
   Returns the number of rows fetched by executing and fetching cursor *c*. Raises an exception if more than one row is fetched when *exact* is set to TRUE. Multiple rows require Oracle8 or later and array processing.

```
FUNCTION DBMS_SQL.FETCH_ROWS
  (c IN INTEGER)
  RETURN INTEGER;
```
Fetches and returns the number of rows fetched from cursor *c* or 0 when there are no more rows to fetch.

```
FUNCTION DBMS_SQL.IS_OPEN
  (c IN INTEGER)
  RETURN BOOLEAN;
```
Returns TRUE if cursor *c* is open, FALSE otherwise.

```
FUNCTION DBMS_SQL.LAST_ERROR_POSITION
  RETURN INTEGER;
```
Returns the byte offset in the SQL statement where the last error occurred. Must be called immediately after an EXECUTE or EXECUTE_AND_FETCH.

```
FUNCTION DBMS_SQL.LAST_ROW_COUNT
  RETURN INTEGER;
```
Returns the total number of rows fetched so far; this is similar to the %ROWCOUNT attribute of static cursors.

```
FUNCTION DBMS_SQL.LAST_ROW_ID
  RETURN ROWID;
```
Returns the ROWID of the most recently fetched row. Must be called immediately after a FETCH_ROWS or EXECUTE_AND_FETCH.

```
FUNCTION DBMS_SQL.LAST_SQL_FUNCTION_CODE
  RETURN INTEGER;
```
Returns the SQL function code for the SQL statement. A complete list of these function codes can be found in Oracle Corporation's *Server Reference Manual* in the section describing the table column V$SESSION.COMMAND.

```
FUNCTION DBMS_SQL.OPEN_CURSOR
  RETURN INTEGER;
```
Returns an INTEGER pointer to memory allocated for a dynamic cursor.

```
PROCEDURE DBMS_SQL.PARSE
  (c IN INTEGER,
  statement IN VARCHAR2,
  language_flag IN INTEGER);
```
Parses a SQL statement less than 32K bytes in length and associates it with cursor *c*, following database behavior specified by *language_flag* (which may be DBMS_SQL.NATIVE, DBMS_SQL.V7, or DBMS_SQL.V6). Do not terminate your SQL string with a semicolon unless it is a PL/SQL block. For DDL statements (e.g., TRUNCATE TABLE), this also executes the statement. You can also use the following form for large SQL statements:

```
PROCEDURE DBMS_SQL.PARSE
  (c IN INTEGER,
  statement IN VARCHAR2S,
  lb IN INTEGER,
  ub IN INTEGER,
  lfflg IN BOOLEAN,
  language_flag IN INTEGER);
```
Parses a SQL statement contained in rows *lb* through *ub* in the PL/SQL table and associates it with cursor *c*, following the database behavior specified by *language_flag* (which may be DBMS_SQL.NATIVE, DBMS_SQL.V7, or DBMS_SQL.V6) and appending a line feed after each row from statement if *lfflg* is set to TRUE.

```
PROCEDURE DBMS_SQL.VARIABLE_VALUE
   (c IN INTEGER,
   name IN VARCHAR2,
   value OUT {NUMBER | VARCHAR2 | DATE | BLOB | CLOB
      CHARACTER SET ANY_CS| BFILE | MLSLABEL});
```

Retrieves the value of the host variable *name* in cursor *c* into the PL/SQL NUMBER variable value. MLSLABEL is for Trusted Oracle only, which is no longer supported in Oracle9*i*. The following syntax can also be used for VARIABLE_VALUE:

```
PROCEDURE DBMS_SQL.VARIABLE_VALUE
   (c IN INTEGER,
   name IN VARCHAR2,
   value IN <table_type>);
```

Retrieves the values of the host variable *name* in cursor *c* into the PL/SQL table *value*. For Oracle8 and later, the *table_type* can be one of the following:

```
   DBMS_SQL.NUMBER_TABLE
   DBMS_SQL.VARCHAR2_TABLE
   DBMS_SQL.DATE_TABLE
   DBMS_SQL.BLOB_TABLE
   DBMS_SQL.CLOB_TABLE
   DBMS_SQL.BFILE_TABLE
```

The following syntax is also supported for the specific datatypes CHAR, RAW, and ROWID:

```
PROCEDURE DBMS_SQL.VARIABLE_VALUE_CHAR
   (c IN INTEGER,
   name IN VARCHAR2,
   value OUT CHAR CHARACTER SET ANY_CS);

PROCEDURE DBMS_SQL.VARIABLE_VALUE_RAW
   (c IN INTEGER,
   name IN VARCHAR2,
   value OUT RAW);

PROCEDURE DBMS_SQL.VARIABLE_VALUE_ROWID
   (c IN INTEGER,name IN VARCHAR2,
   value OUT ROWID);
```

For information on these procedures, see VARIABLE_VALUE.

DBMS_STATS

Provides procedures used to gather statistics for the cost-based optimizer. New with Oracle8*i*.

Calls

```
PROCEDURE DBMS_STATS.PREPARE_COLUMN_VALUES[_NVARCHAR | _ROWID]
   (srec IN OUT STATREC,
   values IN values_type
   [,rwmin IN ROWID,
   rwmax IN ROWID]);
```

```
[,rwmin IN ROWID,
rwmax IN ROWID]);
```
STATREC is a record type with the following structure:
```
(epc NUMBER,
minval RAW(2000),
maxval RAW(2000),
bkvals NUMARRAY,
novals NUMARRAY)
```

srec holds the number of *values* in values in the *epc* column of the record and the number of occurences of each of the *values* in *bkvals*. *values* can support *values_types* of CHARARRAY, DATEARRAY, NUMARRAY, or RAWARRAY for the corresponding value types. For PREPARE_COLUMNS_NVARCHAR, use the first set of *rw* parameters. For PREPARE_COLUMNS_ROWID, use the second set of *rw* parameters.

```
PROCEDURE DBMS_STATS.SET_COLUMN_STATS
  (ownname IN VARCHAR2,
  tabname IN VARCHAR2,
  colname IN VARCHAR2,
  partname IN VARCHAR2 DEFAULT NULL,
  stattab IN VARCHAR2 DEFAULT NULL,
  statid IN VARCHAR2 DEFAULT NULL,
  distcnt IN NUMBER DEFAULT NULL,
  density IN NUMBER DEFAULT NULL,
  nullcnt IN NUMBER DEFAULT NULL,
  srec IN STATREC DEFAULT NULL,
  avgclen IN NUMBER DEFAULT NULL,
  [flags IN NUMBER DEFAULT NULL,]
  statown IN VARCHAR2 DEFAULT NULL
  [, no_invalidate IN BOOLEAN DEFAULT FALSE]#);
```
This version is used for standard statistics. Sets statistics for *ownname.tabname. colname* in partition *partname* in *statown.stattab* with optional identifier *statid*. (If *stattab* is NULL, statistics are stored in the dictionary.) Sets the *density*, number of nulls (*nullcnt*), and average length for column (*avgclen*). If *no_invalidate*, dependent cursors are not invalidated. *srec* is the STATREC filled with PREPARE_COLUMN_VALUES or GET_COLUMN_STATS. *flags* is an internal parameter that is no longer supported in Oracle9i. The *no_invalidate* parameter was new with Oracle9i.

For user-defined statistics, which are new with Oracle9i, the call takes the following form:

```
PROCEDURE DBMS_STATS.SET_COLUMN_STATS
  (ownname IN VARCHAR2,
  tabname IN VARCHAR2,
  colname IN VARCHAR2,
  partname IN VARCHAR2 DEFAULT NULL,
  stattab IN VARCHAR2 DEFAULT NULL,
  statid IN VARCHAR2 DEFAULT NULL,
  ext_stats IN RAW,
  stattypown IN VARCHAR2 DEFAULT NULL,
  stattypname IN VARCHAR2 DEFAULT NULL,
```

```
      statown IN VARCHAR2 DEFAULT NULL,
      no_invalidate IN BOOLEAN DEFAULT FALSE);
```

with *ext_stats* as the user-defined statistics for *stattypname* statistic from the *stattypown* schema.

```
PROCEDURE DBMS_STATS.SET_INDEX_STATS
   (ownname IN VARCHAR2,
   indname IN VARCHAR2,
   partname IN VARCHAR2 DEFAULT NULL,
   stattab IN VARCHAR2 DEFAULT NULL,
   statid IN VARCHAR2 DEFAULT NULL,
   numrows IN NUMBER DEFAULT NULL,
   numlblks IN NUMBER DEFAULT NULL,
   numdist IN NUMBER DEFAULT NULL,
   avglblk IN NUMBER DEFAULT NULL,
   avgdblk IN NUMBER DEFAULT NULL,
   clstfct IN NUMBER DEFAULT NULL,
   indlevel IN NUMBER DEFAULT NULL,
   flags IN NUMBER DEFAULT NULL,
   statown IN VARCHAR2 DEFAULT NULL
   [,no_invalidate IN BOOLEAN DEFAULT FALSE#);
```

This version is used for standard statistics for indexes. Sets statistics for *ownname*. *indname* in partition *partname* in *statown.stattab* with optional identifier *statid*. (If *stattab* is NULL, statistics are stored in the dictionary.) Sets the number of rows in the index (*numrows*), number of leaf blocks in the index (*numlblks*), number of distinct keys in the index (*numdist*), average number of leaf blocks in which each distinct key appears (*avglblk*), average number of data blocks in the table pointed to by a distinct key in the index (*avgdblk*), clustering factor (*clstfct*), and height of the index (*indlevel*). If *no_invalidate* (new with Oracle9*i*), dependent cursors are not invalidated.

For user-defined statistics, which are new with Oracle9*i*, the call takes the following form.

```
PROCEDURE DBMS_STATS.SET_INDEX_STATS
   (ownname IN VARCHAR2,
   indname IN VARCHAR2,
   partname IN VARCHAR2 DEFAULT NULL,
   stattab IN VARCHAR2 DEFAULT NULL,
   statid IN VARCHAR2 DEFAULT NULL,
   ext_stats IN RAW,
   stattypown VARCHAR2 DEFAULT NULL,
   stattypname VARCHAR2 DEFAULT NULL,
   statown IN VARCHAR2 DEFAULT NULL,
   no_invalidate IN BOOLEAN DEFAULT FALSE);
```

with *ext_stats* the user-defined statistics for *stattypname* from the *stattypown* schema.

```
PROCEDURE DBMS_STATS.SET_SYSTEM_STATS
   (pname IN VARCHAR2,
   pvalue IN NUMBER,
   stattab IN VARCHAR2 DEFAULT NULL,
```

```
statid IN VARCHAR2 DEFAULT NULL,
statown IN VARCHAR2 DEFAULT NULL);
```

Sets system stat *pname* to *pvalue* in *statown.stattab* with optional identifier *statid*. (If *stattab* is NULL, statistics are stored in the dictionary.) Parameter values for *pname* are average time in milliseconds to read a single block (*sreadtim*), average time in milliseconds to read an *mbrc* block at once (*mreadtim*), average CPU speed in millions of cycles per second (*cpuspeed*), average multiblock read count in blocks (*mbrc*), maximum I/O system throughput in bytes per second (*maxthr*), and average slave I/O throughput in bytes per second (*slavethr*). New with Oracle9*i*.

PROCEDURE DBMS_STATS.SET_TABLE_STATS
```
(ownname IN VARCHAR2,
indname IN VARCHAR2,
partname IN VARCHAR2 DEFAULT NULL,
stattab IN VARCHAR2 DEFAULT NULL,
statid IN VARCHAR2 DEFAULT NULL,
numrows IN NUMBER DEFAULT NULL,
numlblks IN NUMBER DEFAULT NULL,
avgrlen IN NUMBER DEFAULT NULL,
flags IN NUMBER DEFAULT NULL,
statown IN VARCHAR2 DEFAULT NULL
[,no_invalidate IN BOOLEAN DEFAULT FALSE]#);
```

Sets statistics for *ownname.indname* in partition *partname* in *statown.stattab* with optional identifier *statid*. (If *stattab* is NULL, statistics are stored in the dictionary.) Sets number of rows in the table (*numrows*), number of blocks in the table (*numlblks*), and average row length for the table (*avgrlen*). *flags* is for internal Oracle use. If *no_invalidate* (new with Oracle9*i*), dependent cursors are not invalidated.

PROCEDURE DBMS_STATS.CONVERT_RAW_VALUE[_NVARCHAR | _ROWID]
```
(rawval IN RAW,
resval OUT {VARCHAR2 | DATE | NUMBER | NVARCHAR2 | ROWID});
```

Converts column minimum or maximum *rawval* into datatype of *resval*. For NVARCHAR2 and ROWID, the datatype name is added to the end of the procedure name.

PROCEDURE DBMS_STATS.GET_COLUMN_STATS
```
(ownname IN VARCHAR2,
tabname IN VARCHAR2,
colname IN VARCHAR2,
partname IN VARCHAR2 DEFAULT NULL,
stattab IN VARCHAR2 DEFAULT NULL,
statid IN VARCHAR2 DEFAULT NULL,
distcnt OUT NUMBER DEFAULT NULL,
density OUT NUMBER DEFAULT NULL,
nullcnt OUT NUMBER DEFAULT NULL,
srec OUT STATREC DEFAULT NULL,
avgclen OUT NUMBER DEFAULT NULL,
statown IN VARCHAR2 DEFAULT NULL);
```

This version is used for standard statistics. Gets statistics for *ownname.tabname. colname* in partition *partname* in *statown.stattab* with optional identifier *statid*. (If *stattab* is NULL, statistics are stored in the dictionary.) Sets *density*, number of NULLs (*nullcnt*), and average length for column (*avgclen*).

For user-defined statistics, which are new with Oracle9*i*, the call takes the following form:

```
PROCEDURE DBMS_STATS.GET_COLUMN_STATS
    (ownname IN VARCHAR2,
    tabname IN VARCHAR2,
    colname IN VARCHAR2,
    partname IN VARCHAR2 DEFAULT NULL,
    stattab IN VARCHAR2 DEFAULT NULL,
    statid IN VARCHAR2 DEFAULT NULL,
    ext_stats OUT RAW,
    stattypown OUT VARCHAR2 DEFAULT NULL,
    stattypname OUT VARCHAR2 DEFAULT NULL,
    statown IN VARCHAR2 DEFAULT NULL);
```

with *ext_stats* the user-defined statistics for *stattypname* from the *stattypown* schema.

```
PROCEDURE DBMS_STATS.GET_INDEX_STATS
    (ownname IN VARCHAR2,
    indname IN VARCHAR2,
    partname IN VARCHAR2 DEFAULT NULL,
    stattab IN VARCHAR2 DEFAULT NULL,
    statid IN VARCHAR2 DEFAULT NULL,
    numrows OUT NUMBER,
    numlblks OUT NUMBER,
    numdist OUT NUMBER,
    avglblk OUT NUMBER,
    avgdblk OUT NUMBER,
    clstfct OUT NUMBER,
    indlevel OUT NUMBER,
    [flags IN NUMBER DEFAULT NULL,]
    statown IN VARCHAR2 DEFAULT NULL
    [guessq OUT NUMBER]#);
```

This version is used for standard statistics for indexes. Gets statistics for *ownname. indname* in partition *partname* in *statown.stattab* with optional identifier *statid*. If *stattab* is NULL, statistics are stored in the dictionary. Sets number of rows in the index (*numrows*), number of leaf blocks in the index (*numlblks*), number of distinct keys in the index (*numdist*), average number of leaf blocks in which each distinct key appears (*avglblk*), average number of data blocks in the table pointed to by a distinct key in the index (*avgdblk*), clustering factor (*clstfct*), height of the index (*indlevel*), and guess quality for the index (*guessq*), new with Oracle9*i*.

For user-defined statistics, which are new with Oracle9*i*, the call takes the following form:

```
PROCEDURE DBMS_STATS.GET_INDEX_STATS
    (ownname IN VARCHAR2,
    indname IN VARCHAR2,
    partname IN VARCHAR2 DEFAULT NULL,
    stattab IN VARCHAR2 DEFAULT NULL,
    statid IN VARCHAR2 DEFAULT NULL,
    ext_stats OUT RAW,
    stattypown OUT VARCHAR2 DEFAULT NULL,
```

```
    stattypname OUT VARCHAR2 DEFAULT NULL,
    statown IN VARCHAR2 DEFAULT NULL);
```

with *ext_stats* as the user-defined statistics for *stattypname* statistics from the *stattypown* schema.

PROCEDURE DBMS_STATS.GET_SYSTEM_STATS
```
(status OUT VARCHAR2,
dstart OUT DATE,
dstop OUT DATE,
pname IN VARCHAR2,
pvalue OUT NUMBER,
stattab IN VARCHAR2 DEFAULT NULL,
statid IN VARCHAR2 DEFAULT NULL,
statown IN VARCHAR2 DEFAULT NULL);
```
Gets system stat *pname* in *pvalue* from *statown.stattab* with optional identifier *statid*. If *stattab* is NULL, statistics come from the dictionary. *status* is COMPLETED, AUTOGATHERING, BADSTATS, or MANUALGATHERING. If MANUALGATHERING, *dstart* and *dstop* are the start and stop dates for the manual gathering of statistics. Parameter values for *pname* are the average time in milliseconds to read a single block *(sreadtim)*, average time in milliseconds to read an *mbrc* block at once *(mreadtim)*, average CPU speed in millions of cycles per second *(cpuspeed)*, average multiblock read count in blocks *(mbrc)*, maximum I/O system throughput in bytes per second *(maxthr)*, and average slave I/O throughput in bytes per second *(slavethr)*. New with Oracle9i.

PROCEDURE DBMS_STATS.SET_TABLE_STATS
```
(ownname IN VARCHAR2,
indname IN VARCHAR2,
partname IN VARCHAR2 DEFAULT NULL,
stattab IN VARCHAR2 DEFAULT NULL,
statid IN VARCHAR2 DEFAULT NULL,
numrows OUT NUMBER DEFAULT NULL,
numlblks OUT NUMBER DEFAULT NULL,
avgrlen OUT NUMBER DEFAULT NULL,
statown VARCHAR2 DEFAULT NULL);
```
Gets statistics for *ownname.indname* in partition *partname* in *statown.stattab* with optional identifier *statid*. If *stattab* is NULL, statistics are stored in the dictionary. Sets number of rows in the table *(numrows)*, number of blocks in the table *(numlblks)*, and average row length for the table *(avgrlen)*.

PROCEDURE DBMS_STATS.DELETE_COLUMN_STATS
```
(ownname IN VARCHAR2,
tabname IN VARCHAR2,
colname IN VARCHAR2,
partname IN VARCHAR2 DEFAULT NULL,
stattab IN VARCHAR2 DEFAULT NULL,
statid IN VARCHAR2 DEFAULT NULL,
cascade_parts IN NUMBER DEFAULT NULL,
statown IN VARCHAR2 DEFAULT NULL
[,no_invalidate IN BOOLEAN DEFAULT FALSE]#);
```
Deletes statistics for *ownname.tabname.colname* in partition *partname* in *statown. stattab* with optional identifier *statid*. If *stattab* is NULL, statistics are stored in the dictionary. If the table is partitioned and *partname* is NULL, *cascade_parts* causes deletion of underlying partitions as well. If *no_invalidate* (new with Oracle9i), dependent cursors are not invalidated.

PROCEDURE DBMS_STATS.DELETE_INDEX_STATS
    (*ownname* IN VARCHAR2,
    indname IN VARCHAR2,
    partname IN VARCHAR2 DEFAULT NULL,
    stattab IN VARCHAR2 DEFAULT NULL,
    statid IN VARCHAR2 DEFAULT NULL,
    cascade_parts IN NUMBER DEFAULT NULL,
    statown IN VARCHAR2 DEFAULT NULL
    [,*no_invalidate* IN BOOLEAN DEFAULT FALSE]#);

> Deletes statistics for *ownname.indname* in partition *partname* from *statown. stattab* with optional identifier *statid*. If *stattab* is NULL, statistics are stored in the dictionary. If table is partitioned and *partname* is NULL, *cascade_parts* causes deletion of underlying partitions as well. If *no_invalidate* (new with Oracle9i), dependent cursors are not invalidated.

PROCEDURE DBMS_STATS.DELETE_SYSTEM_STATS
    (*stattab* IN VARCHAR2 DEFAULT NULL,
    statid IN VARCHAR2 DEFAULT NULL,
    statown IN VARCHAR2 DEFAULT NULL);

> Deletes system statistics from *statown.stattab* with optional identifier *statid*. If *stattab* is NULL, statistics are stored in the dictionary. New with Oracle9i.

PROCEDURE DBMS_STATS.DELETE_TABLE_STATS
    (*ownname* IN VARCHAR2,
    tabname IN VARCHAR2,
    partname IN VARCHAR2 DEFAULT NULL,
    stattab IN VARCHAR2 DEFAULT NULL,
    statid IN VARCHAR2 DEFAULT NULL,
    cascade_parts IN BOOLEAN DEFAULT TRUE,
    cascade_columns IN BOOLEAN DEFAULT TRUE,
    cascade_indexes IN BOOLEAN DEFAULT TRUE,
    statown VARCHAR2 DEFAULT NULL
    [,*no_invalidate* IN BOOLEAN DEFAULT FALSE]#);

> Deletes statistics for *ownname.tabname* in partition *partname* from *statown. stattab* with optional identifier *statid*. If *stattab* is NULL, statistics are stored in the dictionary. If *tabname* is partitioned and *partname* is NULL, *cascade_parts* deletes statistics for underlying partitions. If *cascade_columns* or *cascade_indexes*, calls DELETE_COLUMN_STATS or DELETE_INDEX_STATS with *cascade_ parts* parameter. If *no_invalidate* (new with Oracle9i), dependent cursors are not invalidated.

PROCEDURE DBMS_STATS.DELETE_SCHEMA_STATS
    (*ownname* IN VARCHAR2,
    stattab IN VARCHAR2 DEFAULT NULL,
    statid IN VARCHAR2 DEFAULT NULL,
    statown VARCHAR2 DEFAULT NULL
    [,*no_invalidate* IN BOOLEAN DEFAULT FALSE]#);

> Deletes statistics for schema *ownname* from *statown.stattab* with optional identifier *statid*. If *stattab* is NULL, statistics are stored in the dictionary. If *no_ invalidate* (new with Oracle9i), dependent cursors are not invalidated.

PROCEDURE DBMS_STATS.DELETE_DATABASE_STATS
    (*stattab* IN VARCHAR2 DEFAULT NULL,
    statid IN VARCHAR2 DEFAULT NULL,

```
statown VARCHAR2 DEFAULT NULL
[,noinvalidate IN BOOLEAN DEFAULT FALSE]#);
```
Deletes statistics for database from *statown.stattab* with optional identifier *statid*. If *stattab* is NULL, statistics are stored in the dictionary. If *no_invalidate* (new with Oracle9*i*), dependent cursors are not invalidated.

PROCEDURE DBMS_STATS.CREATE_STAT_TABLE
```
(ownname IN VARCHAR2,
stattab IN VARCHAR2,
tblspace IN VARCHAR2 DEFAULT NULL);
```
Creates *stattab* in *ownname* for statistics. If *tblspace* is not specified, *ownname* schema is used.

PROCEDURE DBMS_STATS.DROP_STAT_TABLE
```
(ownname IN VARCHAR2,
stattab IN VARCHAR2);
```
Drops *stattab* from *ownname*.

PROCEDURE DBMS_STATS.EXPORT_COLUMN_STATS
```
(ownname IN VARCHAR2,
tabname IN VARCHAR2,
colname IN VARCHAR2,
partname IN VARCHAR2 DEFAULT NULL,
stattab IN VARCHAR2 DEFAULT NULL,
statid IN VARCHAR2 DEFAULT NULL,
statown IN VARCHAR2 DEFAULT NULL);
```
Exports statistics for *ownname.tabname.colname* in partition *partname* in *statown*. *stattab* with optional identifier *statid*. If *stattab* is NULL, statistics are stored in the dictionary.

PROCEDURE DBMS_STATS.EXPORT_INDEX_STATS
```
(ownname IN VARCHAR2,
indname IN VARCHAR2,
partname IN VARCHAR2 DEFAULT NULL,
stattab IN VARCHAR2 DEFAULT NULL,
statid IN VARCHAR2 DEFAULT NULL,
statown IN VARCHAR2 DEFAULT NULL);
```
Exports statistics for *ownname.indname* in partition *partname* from *statown*. *stattab* with optional identifier *statid*. If *stattab* is NULL, statistics are stored in the user's schema.

PROCEDURE DBMS_STATS.EXPORTS_SYSTEM_STATS
```
(stattab IN VARCHAR2 DEFAULT NULL,
statid IN VARCHAR2 DEFAULT NULL,
statown IN VARCHAR2 DEFAULT NULL);
```
Exports system statistics and stores them in *statown.stattab* with optional identifier *statid*. If *stattab* is NULL, statistics are stored in the user's schema. This procedure was called EXPORT_DATABASE_STATS in Oracle8*i*.

PROCEDURE DBMS_STATS.EXPORT_TABLE_STATS
```
(ownname IN VARCHAR2,
tabname IN VARCHAR2,
partname IN VARCHAR2 DEFAULT NULL,
stattab IN VARCHAR2 DEFAULT NULL,
statid IN VARCHAR2 DEFAULT NULL,
```

```
cascade IN BOOLEAN DEFAULT TRUE,
statown VARCHAR2 DEFAULT NULL);
```

Exports statistics for *ownname.tabname* in partition *partname* to *statown.stattab* with optional identifier *statid*. If *cascade*, also exports column and index statistics.

PROCEDURE DBMS_STATS.EXPORT_SCHEMA_STATS

```
(ownname IN VARCHAR2,
stattab IN VARCHAR2 DEFAULT NULL,
statid IN VARCHAR2 DEFAULT NULL,
statown VARCHAR2 DEFAULT NULL);
```

Exports statistics for schema *ownname* to *statown.stattab* with optional identifier *statid*. If *stattab* is NULL, statistics are stored in *ownname*.

PROCEDURE DBMS_STATS.EXPORT_DATABASE_STATS

```
(stattab IN VARCHAR2 DEFAULT NULL,
statid IN VARCHAR2 DEFAULT NULL,
statown VARCHAR2 DEFAULT NULL);
```

Deletes statistics for database from *statown.stattab* with optional identifier *statid*. If *stattab* is NULL, statistics are stored in the dictionary.

PROCEDURE DBMS_STATS.IMPORT_COLUMN_STATS

```
(ownname IN VARCHAR2,
tabname IN VARCHAR2,
colname IN VARCHAR2,
partname IN VARCHAR2 DEFAULT NULL,
stattab IN VARCHAR2 DEFAULT NULL,
statid IN VARCHAR2 DEFAULT NULL,
statown IN VARCHAR2 DEFAULT NULL
[,no_invalidate IN BOOLEAN DEFAULT FALSE]#);
```

Imports statistics for *ownname.tabname.colname* in partition *partname* from *statown.stattab* with optional identifier *statid*. If *stattab* is NULL, statistics are imported from *ownname*. If *no_invalidate* (new with Oracle9i), dependent cursors are not invalidated.

PROCEDURE DBMS_STATS.IMPORT_INDEX_STATS

```
(ownname IN VARCHAR2,
indname IN VARCHAR2,
partname IN VARCHAR2 DEFAULT NULL,
stattab IN VARCHAR2 DEFAULT NULL,
statid IN VARCHAR2 DEFAULT NULL,
statown IN VARCHAR2 DEFAULT NULL
[,no_invalidate IN BOOLEAN DEFAULT FALSE]#);
```

Imports statistics for *ownname.indname* in partition *partname* from *statown.stattab* with optional identifier *statid*. If *stattab* is NULL, statistics are stored in *ownname*. If *no_invalidate* (new with Oracle9i), dependent cursors are not invalidated.

PROCEDURE DBMS_STATS.IMPORT_SYSTEM_STATS

```
(stattab IN VARCHAR2 DEFAULT NULL,
statid IN VARCHAR2 DEFAULT NULL,
statown IN VARCHAR2 DEFAULT NULL);
```

Imports system statistics from *statown.stattab* with optional identifier *statid*.

PROCEDURE DBMS_STATS.IMPORT_TABLE_STATS

```
(ownname IN VARCHAR2,
tabname IN VARCHAR2,
partname IN VARCHAR2 DEFAULT NULL,
```

```
stattab IN VARCHAR2 DEFAULT NULL,
statid IN VARCHAR2 DEFAULT NULL,
cascade IN BOOLEAN DEFAULT TRUE,
statown VARCHAR2 DEFAULT NULL
[,no_invalidate IN BOOLEAN DEFAULT FALSE]#);
```

Imports statistics for *ownname.tabname* in partition *partname* from *statown*. *stattab* with optional identifier *statid*. If *stattab* is NULL, statistics are stored in *ownname*. If *cascade*, also imports column and index stats for the table. If *no_ invalidate* (new in Oracle9*i*), dependent cursors are not invalidated.

PROCEDURE DBMS_STATS.IMPORT_SCHEMA_STATS
```
(ownname IN VARCHAR2,
stattab IN VARCHAR2 DEFAULT NULL,
statid IN VARCHAR2 DEFAULT NULL,
statown VARCHAR2 DEFAULT NULL
[,no_invalidate IN BOOLEAN DEFAULT FALSE]#);
```

Imports statistics for schema *ownname* from *statown.stattab* with optional identifier *statid*. If *stattab* is NULL, statistics are stored in *ownname*. If *no_invalidate* (new with Oracle 9*i*), dependent cursors are not invalidated.

PROCEDURE DBMS_STATS.IMPORT_DATABASE_STATS
```
(stattab IN VARCHAR2 DEFAULT NULL,
statid IN VARCHAR2 DEFAULT NULL,
statown VARCHAR2 DEFAULT NULL,
[,no_invalidate IN BOOLEAN DEFAULT FALSE]#);
```

Imports statistics for database from *statown.stattab* with optional identifier *statid*. If *stattab* is NULL, statistics are stored in *ownname*. If *no_invalidate* (new with Oracle9*i*), dependent cursors are not invalidated.

PROCEDURE DBMS_STATS.GATHER_INDEX_STATS
```
(ownname IN VARCHAR2,
indname IN VARCHAR2,
partname IN VARCHAR2 DEFAULT NULL,
estimate_percent IN NUMBER DEFAULT NULL,
stattab IN VARCHAR2 DEFAULT NULL,
statid IN VARCHAR2 DEFAULT NULL,
statown IN VARCHAR2 DEFAULT NULL
[,degree IN NUMBER DEFAULT NULL]#
[,granularity IN VARCHAR2 DEFAULT 'DEFAULT']#
[,no_invalidate IN BOOLEAN DEFAULT FALSE]#);
```

Gathers statistics for *ownname.indname* in partition *partname* from *statown*. *stattab* with optional identifier *statid*. If *stattab* is NULL, statistics are stored in *ownname*. *estimate_percent* is the percentage of rows to sample. If *estimate_ percent* is NULL, statistics are computed. *degree* (new with Oracle9*i*) is the degree of parallelism to use. Oracle can recommend the best *estimate_percent* with DBMS_STATS.AUTO_SAMPLE_SIZE and the best *degree* with DBMS_STATS. DEFAULT_DEGREE. *granularity* (new with Oracle9*i*) can be DEFAULT, SUBPARTITION, PARTITION, GLOBAL, or ALL. If *no_invalidate* (new with Oracle9*i*), dependent cursors are not invalidated.

PROCEDURE DBMS_STATS.GATHER_TABLE_STATS
```
(ownname IN VARCHAR2,
tabname IN VARCHAR2,
partname IN VARCHAR2 DEFAULT NULL,
estimate_percent IN NUMBER BOOLEAN,
```

```
block_sample IN BOOLEAN DEFAULT FALSE,
method_opt IN VARCHAR2 DEFAULT 'FOR ALL COLUMNS SIZE 1',
degree IN NUMBER DEFAULT NULL,
granularity IN VARCHAR2 DEFAULT 'DEFAULT',
cascade IN BOOLEAN DEFAULT FALSE,
stattab IN VARCHAR2 DEFAULT NULL,
statid IN VARCHAR2 DEFAULT NULL,
statown VARCHAR2 DEFAULT NULL
[,noinvalidate IN BOOLEAN DEFAULT FALSE]#);
```

Gathers statistics for *ownname.tabname* in partition *partname* from *statown*. *stattab* with optional identifier *statid*. If *stattab* is NULL, statistics are stored in *ownname*. *estimate_percent* is the percentage of rows to sample. If *estimate_ percent* is NULL, statistics are computed. *degree* is the degree of parallelism to use. Oracle can recommend the best *estimate_percent* with DBMS_STATS. AUTO_SAMPLE_SIZE and the best *degree* with DBMS_STATS.DEFAULT_ DEGREE. If *block_sample*, the procedure uses random block sampling instead of random row sampling. *method_opt* is the optimization method; for more information on this parameter, see the Oracle documentation. *granularity* can be DEFAULT, SUBPARTITION, PARTITION, GLOBAL, or ALL. If *cascade*, the procedure also gathers index stats for the table. If *no_invalidate* (new with Oracle9i), dependent cursors are not invalidated.

```
PROCEDURE DBMS_STATS.GATHER_SCHEMA_STATS
    (ownname IN VARCHAR2,
    estimate_percent IN NUMBER BOOLEAN,
    block_sample IN BOOLEAN DEFAULT FALSE,
    method_opt IN VARCHAR2 DEFAULT 'FOR ALL COLUMNS SIZE 1',
    degree IN NUMBER DEFAULT NULL,
    granularity IN VARCHAR2 DEFAULT 'DEFAULT',
    cascade IN BOOLEAN DEFAULT FALSE,
    stattab IN VARCHAR2 DEFAULT NULL,
    statid IN VARCHAR2 DEFAULT NULL,
    options IN VARCHAR2 DEFAULT 'GATHER',
    [objList OUT OBJECTTAB,]#
    statown VARCHAR2 DEFAULT NULL
    [,noinvalidate IN BOOLEAN DEFAULT FALSE]
    [,gather_temp IN BOOLEAN DEFAULT FALSE]#);
```

Gathers statistics for schema *ownname* from *statown.stattab* with optional identifier *statid*. If *stattab* is NULL, statistics are stored in *ownname*. *estimate_percent* is the percentage of rows to sample. If *estimate_percent* is NULL, statistics are computed. *degree* is the degree of parallelism to use. Oracle can recommend the best *estimate_percent* with DBMS_STATS.AUTO_SAMPLE_SIZE and the best *degree* with DBMS_STATS.DEFAULT_DEGREE. If *block_sample*, the procedure uses random block sampling instead of random row sampling. *method_opt* is the optimization method; for more information on this parameter, see the Oracle documentation. *granularity* can be DEFAULT, SUBPARTITION, PARTITION, GLOBAL, or ALL. If *cascade*, the procedure also gathers index stats for the table. *options* specifies which objects to gather statistics for and can be GATHER, GATHER | LIST AUTO, GATHER | LIST STALE, GATHER | LIST EMPTY. *objList* (new with Oracle 9i) is the list of objects that were found to be stale or empty. If *no_invalidate* (new with Oracle9i), dependent cursors are not invalidated. If *gather_temp* (new with Oracle9i), the procedure gathers statistics on global temporary tables.

```
PROCEDURE DBMS_STATS.GATHER_DATABASE_STATS
   (ownname IN VARCHAR2,
   estimate_percent IN NUMBER BOOLEAN,
   block_sample IN BOOLEAN DEFAULT FALSE,
   method_opt IN VARCHAR2 DEFAULT 'FOR ALL COLUMNS SIZE 1',
   degree IN NUMBER DEFAULT NULL,
   granularity IN VARCHAR2 DEFAULT 'DEFAULT',
   cascade IN BOOLEAN DEFAULT FALSE,
   stattab IN VARCHAR2 DEFAULT NULL,
   statid IN VARCHAR2 DEFAULT NULL,
   options IN VARCHAR2 DEFAULT 'GATHER',
   [objList OUT OBJECTTAB,]#
   statown VARCHAR2 DEFAULT NULL
   [,no_invalidate IN BOOLEAN DEFAULT FALSE]#
   [,gather_temp IN BOOLEAN DEFAULT FALSE]#);
```

Gathers statistics for database to *statown.stattab* with optional identifier *statid*. If *stattab* is NULL, statistics are stored in *ownname*. *estimate_percent* is the percentage of rows to sample. If *estimate_percent* is NULL, statistics are computed. *degree* is the degree of parallelism to use. Oracle can recommend the best *estimate_percent* with DBMS_STATS.AUTO_SAMPLE_SIZE and the best *degree* with DBMS_STATS.DEFAULT_DEGREE. If *block_sample*, the procedure uses random block sampling instead of random row sampling. *method_opt* is the optimization method; for more information on this parameter, please refer to the Oracle documentation. *granularity* can be DEFAULT, SUBPARTITION, PARTITION, GLOBAL, or ALL. If *cascade*, the procedure also gathers index statistics for the table. *options* specifies which objects to gather statistics for and can be GATHER, GATHER | LIST AUTO, GATHER | LIST STALE, GATHER | LIST EMPTY. *objList* (new with Oracle9*i*) is the list of objects that were found to be stale or empty. If *no_invalidate* (new with Oracle9*i*), dependent cursors are not invalidated. If *gather_temp* (new with Oracle9*i*), the procedure gathers statistics on global temporary tables.

```
PROCEDURE DBMS_STATS.GATHER_SYSTEM_STATS
   (gathering_mode IN VARCHAR2 DEFAULT 'NOWORKLOAD',
   interval IN INTEGER DEFAULT NULL,
   stattab IN VARCHAR2 DEFAULT NULL,
   statid IN VARCHAR2 DEFAULT NULL,
   statown VARCHAR2 DEFAULT NULL);
```

Gathers statistics for the system. *gathering_mode* can be NOWORKLOAD, INTERVAL, START, or STOP. *interval* is the length of time to gather statistics and is used only when *gathering_mode* is INTERVAL. Statistics are stored in *statown.stattab* with optional identifier *statid*. If *stattab* is NULL, statistics are stored in user's schema. New with Oracle9*i*.

```
PROCEDURE DBMS_STATS.GENERATE_STATS
   (ownname IN VARCHAR2,
   objname IN VARCHAR2,
   organized IN NUMBER DEFAULT 7);
```

Gathers statistics for *ownname.objname* from previously collected statistics on related objects. *organized* is the amount of ordering between an index and its associated table (from 0 to 10). The smaller the number, the more organized, such as having consecutive keys referring to consecutive rows on disk.

PROCEDURE DBMS_STATS.FLUSH_SCHEMA_MONITORING_INFO
  (*ownname* VARCHAR2 DEFAULT NULL);
> Flushes in-memory monitoring for tables in *ownname* or the current user's schema if *ownname* is NULL. New with Oracle9*i*.

PROCEDURE DBMS_STATS.FLUSH_DATABASE_MONITORING_INFO;
> Flushes in-memory monitoring for all tables in the dictionary. New with Oracle9*i*.

PROCEDURE DBMS_STATS.ALTER_SCHEMA_TABLE_MONITORING
  (*ownname* IN VARCHAR2 DEFAULT NULL,
  monitoring IN BOOLEAN DEFAULT TRUE);
> Enables or disables the DML monitoring feature for all tables in the *ownname* schema, depending on the value of *monitoring*. New with Oracle9*i*.

PROCEDURE DBMS_STATS.ALTER_DATABASE_TABLE_MONITORING
  (*monitoring* IN BOOLEAN DEFAULT TRUE,
  sysobjs IN BOOLEAN DEFAULT FALSE);
> Enables or disables the DML monitoring feature for all tables in the database, depending on the value of *monitoring*. If *sysobjs*, changes monitoring on the dictionary objects. New with Oracle9*i*.

DBMS_STORAGE_MAP

Used to communicate with FMON (a background process responsible for handling file mapping) to invoke mapping operations and populate mapping views. New with Oracle9*i*.

Calls

PROCEDURE DBMS_STORAGE_MAP.MAP_ELEMENT
  (*elemname* IN VARCHAR2,
  cascade IN BOOLEAN,
  dictionary_update IN BOOLEAN DEFAULT TRUE);
> Builds mapping information for *elemname*. If *cascade*, all elements with the *elemname* I/O stack directed acyclic graph (DAG) are mapped. If *dictionary_update*, mapping information in the data dictionary is also updated.

PROCEDURE DBMS_STORAGE_MAP.MAP_FILE
  (*filename* IN VARCHAR2,
  filetype IN VARCHAR2,
  cascade IN BOOLEAN,
  max_num_fileextent IN NUMBER DEFAULT 100,
  dictionary_update IN BOOLEAN DEFAULT TRUE);
> Builds mapping information for *filename* of *filetype*, which is DATAFILE, SPFILE, TEMPFILE, CONTROLFILE, LOGFILE, or ARCHIVEFILE. If *cascade*, all elements within the *filename* I/O stack DAG are mapped. *max_num_fileextent* is the maximum number of file extents to be mapped. If *dictionary_update*, mapping information in the data dictionary is also updated.

PROCEDURE DBMS_STORAGE_MAP.MAP_OBJECTS
  (*objname* IN VARCHAR2,
  owner IN VARCHAR2,
  objtype IN VARCHAR2);
> Builds mapping information for *owner.objname* of *objtype*.

```
PROCEDURE DBMS_STORAGE_MAP.MAP_ALL
    (max_num_fileext IN NUMBER DEFAULT 100,
    dictionary_update IN BOOLEAN DEFAULT TRUE);
```
Builds mapping information for all type of Oracle files except archive logs. *max_num_fileext* is the maximum number of file extents to be mapped. If *dictionary_update*, mapping information in the data dictionary is also updated.

```
PROCEDURE DBMS_STORAGE_MAP.DROP_ELEMENT
    (elemname IN VARCHAR2,
    cascade IN BOOLEAN,
    dictionary_update IN BOOLEAN DEFAULT TRUE);
```
Drops mapping information for *elemname*. If *cascade*, all elements with the *elemname* I/O stack DAG are dropped. If *dictionary_update*, mapping information in the data dictionary is also updated.

```
PROCEDURE DBMS_STORAGE_MAP.DROP_FILE
    (filename IN VARCHAR2,
    cascade IN BOOLEAN,
    dictionary_update IN BOOLEAN DEFAULT TRUE);
```
Drops mapping information for *filename*. If *cascade*, all elements within the *filename* I/O stack DAG are dropped. If *dictionary_update*, mapping information in the data dictionary is also updated.

```
PROCEDURE DBMS_STORGE_MAP.DROP_ALL
    (dictionary_update IN BOOLEAN DEFAULT TRUE);
```
Drops all mapping information for the instance. If *dictionary_update*, mapping information in the data dictionary is also updated.

```
PROCEDURE DBMS_STORAGE_MAP.SAVE;
```
Saves information needed to regenerate mapping information into the data dictionary.

```
PROCEDURE DBMS_STORAGE_MAP.RESTORE;
```
Restores mapping information from the data dictionary previously saved.

```
PROCEDURE DBMS_STORAGE_MAP.LOCK_MAP;
```
Locks mapping information into the shared memory of the instance.

```
PROCEDURE DBMS_STORAGE_MAP.UNLOCK_MAP;
```
Unlocks mapping information into the shared memory of the instance.

DBMS_STREAM_ADM

Provides an administrative interface for adding and removing simple rules for capture, propagation, and apply for tables, schemas, and the database for use with Oracle Streams. New with Oracle9*i*.

Calls

```
PROCEDURE DBMS_STREAM_ADM.ADD_GLOBAL_PROPAGATION_RULES
    (streams_name IN VARCHAR2,
    source_queue_name IN VARCHAR2,
    destination_queue_name IN VARCHAR2,
    include_dml IN BOOLEAN DEFAULT TRUE,
    include_ddl IN BOOLEAN DEFAULT FALSE,
    include_lcr IN BOOLEAN DEFAULT FALSE,
    source_database IN VARCHAR2 DEFAULT NULL,
```

```
dml_rule_name OUT VARCHAR2,
ddl_rule_name OUT VARCHAR2);
```

Adds a rule to a propagation job *streams_name* that propagates all the logical change records (LCRs) in a *source_queue_name* from *source_database* to *destination_queue_name*. If *include_dml*, returns *dml_rule_name*. If *include_ddl*, returns *ddl_rule_name*. If *include_lcr*, a logical change record is always considered for propagation.

PROCEDURE DBMS_STREAM_ADM.ADD_GLOBAL_RULES
```
(streams_name IN VARCHAR2,
streams_type IN VARCHAR2 DEFAULT NULL,
queue_name IN VARCHAR2 DEFAULT 'STREAMS_QUEUE',
include_dml IN BOOLEAN DEFAULT TRUE,
include_ddl IN BOOLEAN DEFAULT FALSE,
include_lcr IN BOOLEAN DEFAULT FALSE,
source_database IN VARCHAR2 DEFAULT NULL,
dml_rule_name OUT VARCHAR2,
ddl_rule_name OUT VARCHAR2);
```

Adds a rule to *streams_name* of *streams_type* (CAPTURE or APPLY) for all the LCRs in *queue_name* from *source_database*. (For capture rules, *queue_name* enqueues the changes; for apply rules, the changes are dequeued from *queue_name*.) If *include_dml*, returns *dml_rule_name*. If *include_ddl*, returns *ddl_rule_name*. If *include_lcr*, an LCR is always considered for propagation.

PROCEDURE DBMS_STREAM_ADM.ADD_SCHEMA_PROPAGATION_RULES
```
(schema_name IN VARCHAR2,
streams_name IN VARCHAR2,
source_queue_name IN VARCHAR2,
destination_queue_name IN VARCHAR2,
include_dml IN BOOLEAN DEFAULT TRUE,
include_ddl IN BOOLEAN DEFAULT FALSE,
include_lcr IN BOOLEAN DEFAULT FALSE,
source_database IN VARCHAR2 DEFAULT NULL,
dml_rule_name OUT VARCHAR2,
ddl_rule_name OUT VARCHAR2);
```

Adds propagation rules to *streams_name* for all the LCRs from *schema_name* in *source_database* to *destination_queue_name*. If *include_dml*, returns *dml_rule_name*. If *include_ddl*, returns *ddl_rule_name*. If *include_lcr*, an LCR is always considered for propagation.

PROCEDURE DBMS_STREAM_ADM.ADD_SCHEMA_RULES
```
(schema_name IN VARCHAR2,
streams_name IN VARCHAR2,
streams_type IN VARCHAR2 DEFAULT NULL,
queue_name IN VARCHAR2 DEFAULT 'STREAMS_QUEUE',
include_dml IN BOOLEAN DEFAULT TRUE,
include_ddl IN BOOLEAN DEFAULT FALSE,
include_lcr IN BOOLEAN DEFAULT FALSE,
source_database IN VARCHAR2 DEFAULT NULL,
dml_rule_name OUT VARCHAR2,
ddl_rule_name OUT VARCHAR2);
```

Adds a capture or apply (*streams_type*) rule to *streams_name* for all the LCRs in *queue_name* from *schema_name* in *source_database*. (For capture rules, *queue_name* enqueues the changes; for apply rules, the changes are dequeued from *queue_name*.) If *include_dml*, returns *dml_rule_name*. If *include_ddl*, returns *ddl_rule_name*. If *include_lcr*, an LCR is always considered for propagation.

```
PROCEDURE DBMS_STREAM_ADM.ADD_SUBSET_RULES
    (table_name IN VARCHAR2,
    dml_condition IN VARCHAR2,
    streams_type IN VARCHAR2 DEFAULT 'APPLY',
    streams_name IN VARCHAR2,
    queue_name IN VARCHAR2 DEFAULT 'STREAMS_QUEUE',
    include_lcr IN BOOLEAN DEFAULT FALSE,
    source_database IN VARCHAR2 DEFAULT NULL,
    insert_rule_name OUT VARCHAR2,
    update_rule_name OUT VARCHAR2,
    delete_rule_name OUT VARCHAR2);
```
Adds apply rules for a subset of rows in *table_name*, as limited by *dml_condition*, for *streams_name* of *streams_type* (CAPTURE or APPLY) in *queue_name* in *source_database*. If *include_lcr*, an LCR is always considered for propagation. Returns rules for INSERTs, UPDATEs, and DELETEs.

```
PROCEDURE DBMS_STREAM_ADM.ADD_TABLE_PROPAGATION_RULES
    (table_name IN VARCHAR2,
    streams_name IN VARCHAR2,
    source_queue_name IN VARCHAR2,
    destination_queue_name IN VARCHAR2,
    include_dml IN BOOLEAN DEFAULT TRUE,
    include_ddl IN BOOLEAN DEFAULT FALSE,
    include_lcr IN BOOLEAN DEFAULT FALSE,
    source_database IN VARCHAR2 DEFAULT NULL,
    dml_rule_name OUT VARCHAR2,
    ddl_rule_name OUT VARCHAR2);
```
Adds propagation rules for rows in *table_name* for *streams_name* from *source_queue_name* in *destination_queue_name* in *source_database*. If *include_dml*, returns *dml_rule_name*. If *include_ddl*, returns *ddl_rule_name*. If *include_lcr*, an LCR is always considered for propagation.

```
PROCEDURE DBMS_STREAM_ADM.ADD_TABLE_RULES
    table_name IN VARCHAR2,
    streams_type IN VARCHAR2,
    streams_name IN VARCHAR2 DEFAULT NULL,
    queue_name IN VARCHAR2 DEFAULT 'streams_queue',
    include_dml IN BOOLEAN DEFAULT TRUE,
    include_ddl IN BOOLEAN DEFAULT FALSE,
    include_lcr IN BOOLEAN DEFAULT FALSE,
    source_database IN VARCHAR2 DEFAULT NULL,
    dml_rule_name OUT VARCHAR2,
    ddl_rule_name OUT VARCHAR2);
```
Adds apply or capture (*streams_type*) rules for rows in *table_name* for *streams_name* in *queue_name* in *source_database*. If *include_dml*, returns *dml_rule_name*. If *include_ddl*, returns *ddl_rule_name*. If *include_lcr*, an LCR is always considered for propagation.

```
PROCEDURE DBMS_STREAM_ADM.PURGE_SOURCE_CATALOG
    (source_database IN VARCHAR2,
    source_object_name IN VARCHAR2,
    source_object_type IN VARCHAR2);
```
Removes all information regarding streams from the *source_database* for *source_object_name* of *source_object_type*.

PROCEDURE DBMS_STREAM_ADM.REMOVE_RULE
   (*rule_name* IN VARCHAR2,
   streams_type IN VARCHAR2,
   streams_name IN VARCHAR2,
   drop_unused_rule IN BOOLEAN DEFAULT TRUE);

Drops *rule_name* from *streams_name* of *streams_type* (which may be CAPTURE, APPLY, or PROPAGATE). If *drop_unused_rule* and the rule is no longer in a rule set, the rule is dropped from the database.

PROCEDURE DBMS_STREAM_ADM.SET_UP_QUEUE
   (*queue_table* IN VARCHAR2 DEFAULT 'streams_queue_table',
   storage_clause IN VARCHAR2 DEFAULT NULL,
   queue_name IN VARCHAR2 DEFAULT 'streams_queue',
   queue_user IN VARCHAR2 DEFAULT NULL,
   comment IN VARCHAR2 DEFAULT NULL);

Sets up *queue_name* in *queue_table* with any valid *storage_clause*, which is included as part of the CREATE TABLE statement generated. *queue_user* receives ENQUEUE and DEQUEUE privileges for the queue.

DBMS_STREAMS

Provides procedures and functions that allow you to work with data from Oracle Streams. New with Oracle9*i*.

Calls

FUNCTION DBMS_STREAMS.CONVERT_ANYDATA_TO_LCR
   (*source* IN SYS.ANYDATA);
   RETURN SYS.LCR$_DDL_RECORD;

Converts *source* of datatype SYS.ANYDATA to a SYS.LCR$_DDL_RECORD, a logical change record (LCR).

FUNCTION DBMS_STREAMS.CONVERT_ANYDATA_TO_LCR_ROW
   (*source* IN SYS.ANYDATA);
   RETURN SYS.LCR$_ROW_RECORD;

Converts *source* of datatype SYS.ANYDATA to a SYS.LCR$_ROW_RECORD, a logical change record.

FUNCTION DBMS_STREAMS.GET_INFORMATION
   (*name* IN VARCHAR2);
   RETURN SYS.ANYDATA;

Gets information about *name*, which can be SENDER or CONSTRAINT_NAME.

FUNCTION DBMS_STREAMS.GET_TAG( )
   RETURN RAW;

Returns a binary tag for all redo entries generated by the current session.

PROCEDURE DBMS_STREAMS.SET_TAG
   (*tag* IN RAW DEFAULT NULL);

Sets a binary tag for all redo entries subsequently generated by the current session.

DBMS_SYSTEM

Contains procedures for setting special internal trace events, including SQL tracing, at the session level. This package is no longer supported with Oracle8i.

Calls

```
PROCEDURE DBMS_SYSTEM.READ_EV
  (iev BINARY_INTEGER,
  oev OUT BINARY_INTEGER);
```
Returns the current session's event level setting for trace event number *iev* into variable *oev*. This functionality is now included in the DBMS_TRACE package.

```
PROCEDURE DBMS_SYSTEM.SET_EV
  (si BINARY_INTEGER,
  se BINARY_INTEGER,
  ev BINARY_INTEGER,
  le BINARY_INTEGER,
  nm IN VARCHAR2);
```
Sets the level for event number *ev* in the session identified by sid *si* and serial number *se* to the value specified by *le*. Variable *nm* is used to specify the event name. This functionality is now included in DBMS_TRACE package.

```
PROCEDURE DBMS_SYSTEM.SET_SQL_TRACE_IN_SESSION
  (sid IN NUMBER,
  serial# IN NUMBER,
  sql_trace IN BOOLEAN);
```
Turns SQL tracing on or off in the session identified by sid *(sid)* and serial number *(serial#)* according to the value of *sql_trace* (TRUE = on; FALSE = off).

DBMS_TRACE

Provides procedures to manage tracing on execution of PL/SQL programs. New with Oracle8i.

Calls

```
PROCEDURE DBMS_TRACE.SET_PLSQL_TRACE
  (trace_level IN INTEGER);
```
Sets *trace_level* to either 1, which traces all lines (TRACE_ALL_LINES), or 2, which only traces lines in enabled program units (TRACE_ENABLE_LINES).

```
PROCEDURE DBMS_TRACE.CLEAR_PLSQL_TRACE;
```
Disables the existing PL/SQL trace.

```
PROCEDURE DBMS_TRACE.PLSQL_TRACE_VERSION
  (major OUT BINARY_INTEGER,
  minor OUT BINARY_INTEGER);
```
Returns the version of the current PL/SQL trace utility.

DBMS_TRANSACTION

Provides procedures and functions for local and distributed transaction management.

Calls

PROCEDURE DBMS_TRANSACTION.ADVISE_COMMIT;
> Advises remote databases that in-doubt distributed transactions should be committed if possible.

PROCEDURE DBMS_TRANSACTION.ADVISE_NOTHING;
> Removes advice from remote databases regarding in-doubt distributed transactions.

PROCEDURE DBMS_TRANSACTION.ADVISE_ROLLBACK;
> Advises remote databases that in-doubt distributed transactions should be rolled back.

PROCEDURE DBMS_TRANSACTION.BEGIN_DISCRETE_TRANSACTION;
> Sets the current transaction to use discrete transaction processing.

PROCEDURE DBMS_TRANSACTION.COMMIT;
> Commits the current transaction.

PROCEDURE DBMS_TRANSACTION.COMMIT_COMMENT
  (cmnt IN VARCHAR2);
> Commits the current transaction and sends cmnt as the in-doubt transaction comment to remote databases during distributed transactions.

PROCEDURE DBMS_TRANSACTION.COMMIT_FORCE
  (xid IN VARCHAR2
  [,scn IN VARCHAR2 DEFAULT NULL]);
> Forces the local portion of the in-doubt distributed transaction identified by transaction id xid and (optionally) system change number scn to commit.

FUNCTION DBMS_TRANSACTION.LOCAL_TRANSACTION_ID
  (create_transaction IN BOOLEAN := FALSE)
  RETURN VARCHAR2;
> Returns Oracle's unique identifier for the current transaction, optionally beginning a new transaction when create_transaction is TRUE.

PROCEDURE DBMS_TRANSACTION.PURGE_LOST_DB_ENTRY
  (xid IN VARCHAR2);
> Forces Oracle to purge all local entries for the distributed transaction identified by xid when a participating node has been permanently lost. New with Oracle8i.

PROCEDURE DBMS_TRANSACTION.PURGE_MIXED
  (xid IN VARCHAR2);
> Forces Oracle to purge local entries for the mixed-outcome distributed transaction identified locally by xid.

PROCEDURE DBMS_TRANSACTION.READ_ONLY;
> Establishes transaction-level read consistency, where all queries return read-consistent images of data as of the transaction's start time.

PROCEDURE DBMS_TRANSACTION.READ_WRITE;
> Establishes statement-level read consistency, which is also the default behavior.

PROCEDURE DBMS_TRANSACTION.ROLLBACK;
> Rolls back the current transaction.

PROCEDURE DBMS_TRANSACTION.ROLLBACK_FORCE
   (*xid* IN VARCHAR2);
     Rolls back the local portion of the in-doubt distributed transaction identified by *xid*.

PROCEDURE DBMS_TRANSACTION.ROLLBACK_SAVEPOINT
   (*savept* IN VARCHAR2);
     Rolls back the current transaction to the savepoint *savept*.

PROCEDURE DBMS_TRANSACTION.SAVEPOINT
   (*savept* IN VARCHAR2);
     Sets a savepoint named *savept* in the current transaction.

FUNCTION DBMS_TRANSACTION.STEP_ID
   RETURN NUMBER;
     Returns a unique positive integer that orders the DML operations of the current transaction.

PROCEDURE DBMS_TRANSACTION.USE_ROLLBACK_SEGMENT
   (*rb_name* IN VARCHAR2);
     Assigns the current transaction to rollback segment *rb_name*.

DBMS_TRANSFORM

Provides an interface to the transformation features of Oracle Advanced Queueing. New with Oracle9*i*.

Calls

PROCEDURE DBMS_TRANSFORM.CREATE_TRANSFORMATION
   (*schema* IN VARCHAR2(30),
   name IN VARCHAR2(30),
   from_schema IN VARCHAR2(30),
   from_type IN VARCHAR2(30),
   to_schema IN VARCHAR2(30),
   to_type IN VARCHAR2(30),
   transformation IN VARCHAR(4000));
     Transforms from *from_schema* of *from_type* to *to_schema* of *to_type* using *name* of *schema* with *transformation* expression.

PROCEDURE DBMS_TRANSFORM.CREATE_TRANSFORMATION
   (*schema* IN VARCHAR2(30),
   name IN VARCHAR2(30),
   attribute_number IN INTEGER,
   transformation IN VARCHAR(4000));
     Modifies the mapping for *attribute_number* of target type of *name* of *schema* with *transformation* expression.

PROCEDURE DBMS_TRANSFORM.CREATE_TRANSFORMATION
   (*schema* IN VARCHAR2(30),
   name IN VARCHAR2(30));
     Drops transformation *name* in *schema*.

DBMS_TTS

Checks to determine if a transportable table set is self-contained. New with Oracle8i.

Calls

PROCEDURE DBMS_TTS.TRANSPORT_SET_CHECK
(ts_list IN VARCHAR2,
incl_constraints IN BOOLEAN DEFAULT
[,full_closure IN BOOLEAN DEFAULT FALSE]#);
> Checks a list of comma-separated tablespaces in *ts_list*. If *incl_constraints*, includes referential integrity constraints on check of self-containment. If *full_closure* (new with Oracle9i), considers all IN and OUT pointers (dependencies) and treats them as violations if they are not self-contained.

PROCEDURE DBMS_TTS.DOWNGRADE;
> Downgrades transportable tablespace-related data.

DBMS_TYPES

Contains constants that represent built-in and user-defined datatypes used with *inter*Media. New with Oracle9i.

DBMS_UTILITY

Provides procedures and functions used to perform a number of useful tasks, including parsing and tokenizing name references, obtaining database configuration information, analyzing objects, obtaining error and call stack information, and timing code execution.

Calls

FUNCTION DBMS_UTILITY.CURRENT_INSTANCE
RETURN NUMBER;
> Returns the currently connected instance or NULL if the instance is down. New with Oracle8i.

PROCEDURE DBMS_UTILITY.CURRENT_INSTANCES
(instance_table OUT INSTANCE_TABLE,
instance_count OUT NUMBER);
> Returns a list of active instances and their names in *instance_table* and the number of active instances in *instance_count*. New with Oracle8i. This procedure was called ACTIVE_INSTANCES with Oracle8i.

PROCEDURE DBMS_UTILITY.ANALYZE_DATABASE
(method IN VARCHAR2,
estimate_rows IN NUMBER DEFAULT NULL,
estimate_percent IN NUMBER DEFAULT NULL,
method_opt IN VARCHAR2 DEFAULT NULL);
> Analyzes all tables, clusters, and indexes in the database using option *method* (ESTIMATE, COMPUTE, or DELETE). When *method* is ESTIMATE, either *estimate_rows* or *estimate_percent* must be specified to identify the sample size. Additional analyze options specifiable by *method_opt* are FOR TABLE, FOR ALL COLUMNS [SIZE N], FOR ALL INDEXED COLUMNS [SIZE N], and FOR ALL INDEXES. New with Oracle8i.

PROCEDURE DBMS_UTILITY.ANALYZE_PART_OBJECT
    (*schema* IN VARCHAR2 DEFAULT NULL,
    object_name IN VARCHAR2 DEFAULT NULL,
    object_type IN CHAR DEFAULT 'T',
    command_type IN CHAR DEFAULT 'E',
    command_opt IN VARCHAR2 DEFAULT NULL,
    sample_clause IN VARCHAR2 DEFAULT 'SAMPLE 5 PERCENT');

> Analyzes the partitioned table or index *object_name* owned by *schema* of type *object_type* ('T' for table, 'I' for index) in parallel using Oracle job queue processes. *command_type* indicates the type of analysis to perform, and *command_opt* specifies additional options. *sample_clause* specifies the sample size when *command_type* is 'E' (estimate) using 'SAMPLE N ROWS' or 'SAMPLE N PERCENT'.

> Valid *command_type* values are 'C' for compute statistics, 'E' for estimate statistics, 'D' for delete statistics, or 'V' for validate structure.

> Valid *command_opt* values for *command_type* 'C' or 'T' are FOR TABLE, FOR ALL LOCAL INDEXES, FOR ALL COLUMNS, or any combination of FOR options of the ANALYZE command.

> Valid *command_opt* values for *command_type* 'V' are CASCADE when *object_type* is 'T' (table).

PROCEDURE DBMS_UTILITY.ANALYZE_SCHEMA
    (*schema* IN VARCHAR2,
    method IN VARCHAR2,
    estimate_rows IN NUMBER DEFAULT NULL,
    estimate_percent IN NUMBER DEFAULT NULL,
    method_opt IN VARCHAR2 DEFAULT NULL);

> Analyzes all tables, clusters, and indexes in *schema* using *method* (ESTIMATE, COMPUTE, or DELETE). When *method* is ESTIMATE, either *estimate_rows* or *estimate_percent* must be specified to identify the sample size. Additional analyze options specifiable by *method_opt* (new with Oracle8*i*) are FOR TABLE, FOR ALL COLUMNS [SIZE *N*], FOR ALL INDEXED COLUMNS [SIZE *N*], or FOR ALL INDEXES.

PROCEDURE DBMS_UTILITY.COMMA_TO_TABLE
    (*list* IN VARCHAR2,
    tablen OUT BINARY_INTEGER,
    tab OUT UNCL_ARRAY);

> Parses the comma-delimited *list* and returns the tokens in the PL/SQL table *tab* of type DBMS_UTILITY.UNCL_ARRAY. The number of rows in *tab* is returned in *tablen*. New with Oracle8*i*.

PROCEDURE DBMS_UTILITY.COMPILE_SCHEMA
    (*schema* IN VARCHAR2);

> Compiles all stored PL/SQL programs (procedures, functions, and packages) owned by *schema*.

FUNCTION DBMS_UTILITY.DATA_BLOCK_ADDRESS_BLOCK
    (*dba* IN NUMBER)
    RETURN NUMBER;

> Returns the block offset number of the data block address specified in *dba*. New with Oracle8*i*.

```
FUNCTION DBMS_UTILITY.DATA_BLOCK_ADDRESS_FILE
   (dba IN NUMBER)
   RETURN NUMBER;
```
Returns the file number component of the data block address specified in *dba*. New with Oracle8*i*.

```
PROCEDURE DBMS_UTILITY.DB_VERSION
   (version OUT VARCHAR2,
   compatibility OUT VARCHAR2);
```
Returns the Oracle version of the database in *version* and the setting of the *INIT. ORA* or *SPFILE* COMPATIBLE parameter in *compatibility* (or NULL). New with Oracle8*i*.

```
PROCEDURE DBMS_UTILITY.EXEC_DDL_STATEMENT
   (parse_string IN VARCHAR2);
```
Executes the DDL statement specified by *parse_string*. New with Oracle8*i*.

```
FUNCTION DBMS_UTILITY.FORMAT_CALL_STACK
   RETURN VARCHAR2;
```
Returns the current PL/SQL call stack as a formatted string.

```
FUNCTION DBMS_UTILITY.FORMAT_ERROR_STACK
   RETURN VARCHAR2;
```
Returns the current PL/SQL error stack as a formatted string.

```
FUNCTION DBMS_UTILITY.GET_HASH_VALUE
   (name IN VARCHAR2,
   base IN NUMBER,
   hash_size IN NUMBER)
   RETURN NUMBER;
```
Returns a hash function value for *name* with a minimum possible value of *base* using a hash table of size *hash_size*. New with Oracle8*i*.

```
FUNCTION DBMS_UTILITY.GET_PARAMETER_VALUE
   (parnam IN VARCHAR2,
   intval IN OUT BINARY_INTEGER,
   strval IN OUT VARCHAR2)
   RETURN BINARY_INTEGER;
```
Returns information about the current setting of the database initialization (*INIT. ORA* or *SPFILE*) parameter *parnam*. New with Oracle8*i*. *intval* returns the following values:

- The value of a numeric *parnam*
- The length of a string *parnam*
- 0 for FALSE or 1 for TRUE when *parnam* is Boolean

strval returns NULL or the value of a string parameter: 0 if the parameter is Boolean or numeric, 1 if the parameter is a string.

```
FUNCTION DBMS_UTILITY.GET_TIME
   RETURN NUMBER;
```
Returns a number indicating the number of 1/100ths of a second elapsed since an (unknown) arbitrary time in the past. New with Oracle8*i*.

FUNCTION DBMS_UTILITY.IS_[PARALLEL_SERVER | CLUSTER_SERVER]
    RETURN BOOLEAN;
    Returns TRUE if the instance is running in Parallel Server mode (prior to Oracle9*i*) or with Real Application Clusters with Oracle9*i*; returns FALSE otherwise. New with Oracle8*i*.

FUNCTION DBMS_UTILITY.MAKE_DATA_BLOCK_ADDRESS
    (*file* IN NUMBER,
    block IN NUMBER)
    RETURN NUMBER;
    Returns a valid data block address for *file* at block offset *block*. New with Oracle8*i*.

PROCEDURE DBMS_UTILITY.NAME_RESOLVE
    (*name* IN VARCHAR2,
    context IN NUMBER,
    schema OUT VARCHAR2,
    part1 OUT VARCHAR2,
    part2 OUT VARCHAR2,
    dblink OUT VARCHAR2,
    part1_type OUT NUMBER,
    object_number OUT NUMBER);
    Resolves the reference *name* and returns specific identification information about the object referenced as follows: *schema* is the object's owner; *part1* is the object name or package name for a package; *part2* is the program name when the object is a package; *dblink* is the database link if *name* resolves to a remote object; *part1_type* identifies the type of object; *object_number* is the local object number or NULL if *name* could not be fully resolved locally.

    part1_type is 5 if the object is a synonym, 7 if the object is a procedure, 8 if the object is a function, or 9 if the object is a package.

    The *context* parameter must be set to 1.

PROCEDURE DBMS_UTILITY.NAME_TOKENIZE
    (*name* IN VARCHAR2,
    a OUT VARCHAR2,
    b OUT VARCHAR2,
    c OUT VARCHAR2,
    dblink OUT VARCHAR2,
    nextpos OUT BINARY_INTEGER);
    Uses the PL/SQL parser to tokenize the reference *name* into its constituent components according to the following format:
        a [. *b* [. *c*]] [*@dblink*]
    nextpos is the starting position of the next token. New with Oracle8*i*.

FUNCTION DBMS_UTILITY.PORT_STRING
    RETURN VARCHAR2;
    Returns a string with operating system–specific identifying information about the version of Oracle that is running. New with Oracle8*i*.

```
PROCEDURE DBMS_UTILITY.TABLE_TO_COMMA
  (tab IN UNCL_ARRAY,
  tablen OUT BINARY_INTEGER,
  list OUT VARCHAR2);
```
Converts the PL/SQL table *tab* of type DBMS_UTILITY.UNCL_ARRAY into a comma-delimited string returned in *list*, with the number of rows converted returned in *tablen*. New with Oracle8*i*.

DBMS_WM

Provides an interface to Oracle Database Workspace Manager. New with Oracle9*i*.

Calls

```
PROCEDURE DBMS_WM.AlterSavepoint
  (workspace IN VARCHAR2,
  sp_name IN VARCHAR2,
  sp_description IN VARCHAR2);
```
Changes *sp_description* in *sp_name* in *workspace*.

```
PROCEDURE DBMS_WM.AlterWorkspace
  (workspace IN VARCHAR2,
  workspace_description IN VARCHAR2);
```
Changes *workspace_description* for *workspace*.

```
PROCEDURE DBMS_WM.BeginDDL
  (table_name IN VARCHAR2);
```
Starts DDL session for *table_name* and creates a table with the name *table_name_* LTS.

```
PROCEDURE DBMS_WM.BeginResolve
  (workspace IN VARCHAR2);
```
Starts a conflict resolution session for *workspace*.

```
PROCEDURE DBMS_WM.CommitDDL
  (table_name IN VARCHAR2
  [, ignore_last_error IN BOOLEAN DEFAULT FALSE]);
```
Commits DDL changes made during the DDL session for *table_name*. If *ignore_last_error*, ignores the last error that may have occurred during the last call to this procedure.

```
PROCEDURE DBMS_WM.CommitResolve
  (workspace IN VARCHAR2);
```
Ends conflict resolution session and commits any changes made since the DBMS_WM.BeginResolve procedure was called.

```
PROCEDURE DBMS_WM.CompressWorkspace
  (workspace IN VARCHAR2,
  [, compress_view_wo_overwrite IN BOOLEAN]
  [, firstSP IN VARCHAR2 DEFAULT NULL]
  [, secondSP IN VARCHAR2 DEFAULT NULL]
  [, auto_commit IN BOOLEAN DEFAULT TRUE]);
```
Deletes removable savepoints and minimizes Workspace Manager metadata structures for *workspace*. If only *firstSP* is specified, works on all removable savepoints from creation to *firstSP*. If both *firstSP* and *secondSP* are specified, all

removable savepoints between them are deleted. If *secondSP* is LATEST, all save-points from *firstSP* to the end of *workspace* are deleted. If *compress_view_wo_overwrite*, deletes history information between *firstSP* and *secondSP*. If *auto_commit*, the operation is automatically committed after execution.

PROCEDURE DBMS_WM.CompressWorkspaceTree
(*workspace* IN VARCHAR2,
[, *compress_view_wo_overwrite* IN BOOLEAN]
[, *auto_commit* IN BOOLEAN DEFAULT TRUE]);
Deletes removable savepoints and minimizes Workspace Manager metadata structures for *workspace*. If *compress_view_wo_overwrite*, deletes history information. If *auto_commit*, the operation is automatically committed after execution.

PROCEDURE DBMS_WM.CopyForUpdate
(*table_name* IN VARCHAR2
[, *where_clause* IN VARCHAR DEFAULT '']);
Allows LOB columns in *table_name* to be modified. Modification is limited to those rows that pass the *where_clause*, if present.

PROCEDURE DBMS_WM.CreateSavepoint
(*workspace* IN VARCHAR2,
savepoint_name IN VARCHAR2
[, *description* IN VARCHAR DEFAULT NULL]
[, *auto_commit* IN BOOLEAN DEFAULT TRUE]);
Creates *savepoint_name* for *workspace*, with *description*. If *auto_commit*, the operation is automatically committed after execution.

PROCEDURE DBMS_WM.CreateWorkspace
(*workspace* IN VARCHAR2
[, *isref_refreshed* IN BOOLEAN]
[, *description* IN VARCHAR DEFAULT NULL]
[, *auto_commit* IN BOOLEAN DEFAULT TRUE]);
Creates *workspace* with *description*. If *isref_refreshed*, the workspace is continually refreshed. If *auto_commit*, the operation is automatically committed after execution.

PROCEDURE DBMS_WM.DeleteSavepoint
(*workspace* IN VARCHAR2,
savepoint_name IN VARCHAR2
[, *compress_view_wo_overwrite* IN BOOLEAN DEFAULT FALSE]
[, *auto_commit* IN BOOLEAN DEFAULT TRUE]);
Deletes *savepoint_name* from *workspace*. If *compress_view_wo_overwrite*, deletes history information. If *auto_commit*, the operation is automatically committed after execution.

PROCEDURE DBMS_WM.DisableVersioning
(*table_name* IN VARCHAR2
[, *force* IN BOOLEAN DEFAULT FALSE]
[, *ignore_last_error* IN BOOLEAN DEFAULT FALSE]);
Disables versioning for *table_name* and deletes structures created to support this. If *force*, forces all data in workspaces other than LIVE to be discarded. If *ignore_last_error*, ignores the last error that may have occurred during the last call to this procedure.

PROCEDURE DBMS_WM.DropReplicationSupport;
Deletes replication support objects created by the GenerateReplicationSupport procedure.

PROCEDURE DBMS_WM.EnableVersioning
   (*table_list* IN VARCHAR2
   [, *hist* IN VARCHAR DEFAULT 'NONE']);
    Enables versioning on comma-separated *table_list*. *hist* can have the values NONE, VIEW_W_OVERWRITE (which will show only the most recent modifications), or VIEW_WO_OVERWRITE (which will track the history of changes).

PROCEDURE DBMS_WM.FreezeWorkspace
   (*workspace* IN VARCHAR
   [, *session_duration* IN BOOLEAN]
   [, *freezemode* IN VARCHAR2 DEFAULT 'NO ACCESS']
   [, *freezewriter* IN VARCHAR2 DEFAULT NULL]
   [, *force* IN BOOLEAN DEFAULT FALSE]);
    Restricts access to *workspace*. If *session_duration*, *workspace* will be automatically unfrozen when calling session disconnects. *freezemode* can be NO_ACCESS, READ_ONLY, lWRITER (which allows only *freezewriter* to perform writes) or WM_ONLY (which allows only Workspace Manager operations). If not *force*, the workspace will not be frozen if it is already frozen.

PROCEDURE DBMS_WM.GenerateReplicationSupport
   (*mastersites* IN VARCHAR2,
   groupname IN VARCHAR2
   [, *groupdescription* IN VARCHAR2 DEFAULT 'Replication Group for OWM']);
    Creates structures necessary to replicate from the comma-delimited *mastersites* list as part of the *groupname.groupdescription* optional comment.

FUNCTION DBMS_WM.GetConflictWorkspace
   RETURN VARCHAR2;
    Returns the name of the conflict workspace set with SetConflictWorkspace.

FUNCTION DBMS_WM.GetDiffVersions
   RETURN VARCHAR2;
    Returns the names of workspace and savepoint pairs used with SetDiffVersions.

FUNCTION DBMS_WM.GetLockMode
   RETURN VARCHAR2;
    Returns the locking mode for the current session.

FUNCTION DBMS_WM.GetMultiWorkspaces
   RETURN VARCHAR2;
    Returns the workspaces visible in multiworkspace views for version-enabled tables.

FUNCTION DBMS_WM.GetOpContext
   RETURN VARCHAR2;
    Returns the context of the current operation.

FUNCTION DBMS_WM.GetPrivs
   (*workspace* IN VARCHAR2)
   RETURN VARCHAR2;
    Returns a comma-separated list of all privileges that the current user has for *workspace*.

PROCEDURE DBMS_WM.GetSessionInfo
   (*workspace* OUT VARCHAR2,
   context OUT VARCHAR2,
   context_type OUT VARCHAR2);
    Returns *context* for the current session of *workspace* with a *context_type* of LATEST, SAVEPOINT, or INSTANT.

```
FUNCTION DBMS_WM.GetWorkspace
   RETURN VARCHAR2;
```
Returns the current workspace for the session.

```
PROCEDURE DBMS_WM.GotoDate
   (in_date IN DATE);
```
Goes to a point in or near the *in_date*.

```
PROCEDURE DBMS_WM.GotoSavepoint
   ([savepoint_name IN VARCHAR2 DEFAULT 'LATEST']);
```
Goes to *savepoint_name*. If *savepoint_name* is not specified, goes to LATEST.

```
PROCEDURE DBMS_WM.GotoWorkspace
   (workspace IN VARCHAR2);
```
Goes to *workspace*.

```
PROCEDURE DBMS_WM.GrantSystemPriv
   (priv_types IN VARCHAR2,
   grantee IN VARCHAR2
   [, grant_option IN VARCHAR2 DEFAULT 'NO']
   [, auto_commit IN BOOLEAN DEFAULT TRUE]);
```
Grants *priv_types* to *grantee*. If *grant_option* is YES, the grantee can regrant privileges. If *auto_commit*, the operation is automatically committed after execution.

```
PROCEDURE DBMS_WM.GrantWorkspacePriv
   (priv_types IN VARCHAR2,
   workspace IN VARCHAR2,
   grantee IN VARCHAR2
   [, grant_option IN VARCHAR2 DEFAULT 'NO']
   [, auto_commit IN BOOLEAN DEFAULT TRUE]);
```
Grants *priv_types* to *grantee* for *workspace*. If *grant_option* is YES, the grantee can regrant privileges. If *auto_commit*, the operation is automatically committed after execution.

```
FUNCTION DBMS_WM.IsWorkspaceOccupied
   (workspace IN VARCHAR2)
   RETURN VARCHAR2;
```
Returns YES if *workspace* has any active sessions.

```
PROCEDURE DBMS_WM.LockRows
   (workspace IN VARCHAR2,
   table_name IN VARCHAR2
   [, where_clause IN VARCHAR2 DEFAULT '']
   [, lock_mode IN VARCHAR2 DEFAULT 'E']);
```
Locks the latest versions of rows of *table_name* in *workspace*. The *where_clause* specifies a subset of rows to be locked and can reference only primary key columns. *lock_mode* can be 'E'(xclusive) or 'S'(hared).

```
PROCEDURE DBMS_WM.MergeTable
   (workspace IN VARCHAR2,
   table_id IN VARCHAR2
   [, where_clause IN VARCHAR2 DEFAULT '']
   [, create_savepoint IN BOOLEAN DEFAULT FALSE]
   [, remove_data IN BOOLEAN DEFAULT FALSE]
   [, auto_commit IN BOOLEAN DEFAULT TRUE]);
```
Applies changes to *table_id* in *workspace*. The *where_clause* specifies a subset of rows to be locked and can reference only primary key columns. If *create_savepoint*, an implicit savepoint is created. If *remove_data*, data is removed in the

child workspace, if *workspace* is the leaf workspace. If *auto_commit*, the operation is automatically committed after execution.

PROCEDURE DBMS_WM.MergeWorkspace
  (*workspace* IN VARCHAR2
  [, *create_savepoint* IN BOOLEAN DEFAULT FALSE]
  [, *remove_workspace* IN BOOLEAN DEFAULT FALSE]
  [, *auto_commit* IN BOOLEAN DEFAULT TRUE]);

  Applies changes in child *workspace* to its parent. If *create_savepoint*, an implicit savepoint is created. If *remove_workspace*, *workspace* is after the operation. If *auto_commit*, the operation is automatically committed after execution.

PROCEDURE DBMS_WM.RecoverAllMigratingTables
  ([*ignore_last_error* IN BOOLEAN DEFAULT FALSE]);

  Attempts to complete the migration of all tables that were left in an inconsistent state after Workspace Manager failed. If *ignore_last_error*, the procedure ignores the last error that occurred during the migration process.

PROCEDURE DBMS_WM.RecoverMigratingTable
  (*table_id* IN VARCHAR2
  [, *ignore_last_error* IN BOOLEAN DEFAULT FALSE]);

  Attempts to complete the migration of *table_id* that were left in an inconsistent state after Workspace Manager failed. If *ignore_last_error*, the procedure ignores the last error that occurred during the migration process.

PROCEDURE DBMS_WM.RefreshTable
  (*workspace* IN VARCHAR2,
  table_id IN VARCHAR2
  [, *where_clause* IN VARCHAR2 DEFAULT '']
  [, *create_savepoint* IN BOOLEAN DEFAULT FALSE]
  [, *auto_commit* IN BOOLEAN DEFAULT TRUE]);

  Applies changes to *table_id* in *workspace* from its parent workspace. The *where_clause* specifies a subset of rows to be refreshed and can reference only primary key columns. If *create_savepoint*, an implicit savepoint is created. If *auto_commit*, the operation is automatically committed after execution.

PROCEDURE DBMS_WM.RefreshWorkspace
  (*workspace* IN VARCHAR2
  [, *auto_commit* IN BOOLEAN DEFAULT TRUE]);

  Applies all changes made in a parent workspace to *workspace*. If *auto_commit*, the operation is automatically committed after execution.

PROCEDURE DBMS_WM.RelocateWriterSite
  (*newwritersite* IN VARCHAR2,
  oldwritersiteavailable IN BOOLEAN);

  Makes a nonwriter workspace *newwritersite* the new writer site. If *oldwritersiteavailable*, the old writer site is updated to show that the writer site has not been changed. Otherwise, you must use the SynchronizeSite procedure when the old writer site becomes available.

PROCEDURE DBMS_WM.RemoveWorkspace
  (*workspace* IN VARCHAR2
  [, *auto_commit* IN BOOLEAN DEFAULT TRUE]);

  Discards all row versions associated with *workspace* and deletes *workspace*. If *auto_commit*, the operation is automatically committed after execution.

PROCEDURE DBMS_WM.RemoveWorkspaceTree
    (*workspace* IN VARCHAR2
    [, *auto_commit* IN BOOLEAN DEFAULT TRUE]);
    Discards all row versions associated with *workspace* and its descendant work-
    spaces and deletes all of the workspaces. If *auto_commit*, the operation is
    automatically committed after execution.

PROCEDURE DBMS_WM.ResolveConflicts
    (*workspace* IN VARCHAR2,
    table_name IN VARCHAR2,
    where_clause IN VARCHAR2,
    keep IN VARCHAR2);
    Checks *table_name* in *workspace* for conflicts with other workspaces. The *where_
    clause* identifies rows to be refreshed from the parent workspace and can refer-
    ence only primary key columns. *keep* specifies how to resolve conflicts; its values
    are PARENT (which causes the parent workspace rows to be copied to the child),
    CHILD (which resolves the conflict and waits for a merge operation to copy the
    child rows to the parent), or BASE (which causes base rows to be copied to the
    child workspace but not the parent).

PROCEDURE DBMS_WM.RevokeSystemPriv
    (*priv_types* IN VARCHAR2,
    grantee IN VARCHAR2
    [, *auto_commit* IN BOOLEAN DEFAULT TRUE]);
    Revokes *priv_types* from *grantee*. If *auto_commit*, the operation is automatically
    committed after execution.

PROCEDURE DBMS_WM.GrantWorkspacePriv
    (*priv_types* IN VARCHAR2,
    workspace IN VARCHAR2,
    grantee IN VARCHAR2
    [, *auto_commit* IN BOOLEAN DEFAULT TRUE]);
    Revokes workspace *priv_types* from *grantee* for *workspace*. If *auto_commit*, the
    operation is automatically committed after execution.

PROCEDURE DBMS_WM.RollbackDDL
    (table_name IN VARCHAR2);
    Rolls back DDL changes for *table_name* and ends the session.

PROCEDURE DBMS_WM.RollbackResolve
    (*workspace* IN VARCHAR2);
    Quits the conflict resolution session and discards all changes to *workspace* since
    the BeginResolve procedure was called.

PROCEDURE DBMS_WM.RollbackTable
    (*workspace* IN VARCHAR2,
    table_id IN VARCHAR2
    [, *sp_name* IN VARCHAR2 DEFAULT ''']
    [, *where_clause* IN VARCHAR2 DEFAULT ''']
    [, *remove_locks* IN BOOLEAN DEFAULT TRUE]
    [, *auto_commit* IN BOOLEAN DEFAULT TRUE]);
    Discards changes to *table_id* in *workspace*. *sp_name* is the name of the savepoint
    to roll back to. The *where_clause* specifies a subset of rows to be locked and can
    reference only primary key columns.. If *remove_locks*, the procedure releases
    locks on rows in the parent workspace that satisfy the *where_clause*, but this has
    no effect if *sp_name* is present. If *auto_commit*, the operation is automatically
    committed after execution.

PROCEDURE DBMS_WM.RollbackToSP
   (*workspace* IN VARCHAR2,
   savepoint_name IN VARCHAR2
   [, *auto_commit* IN BOOLEAN DEFAULT TRUE]);
> Discards changes to *workspace* to *savepoint_name*. If *auto_commit*, the operation is automatically committed after execution.

PROCEDURE DBMS_WM.RollbackWorkspace
   (workspace IN VARCHAR2
   [, *auto_commit* IN BOOLEAN DEFAULT TRUE]);
> Discards changes to *workspace* for version-enabled tables. If *auto_commit*, the operation is automatically committed after execution.

PROCEDURE DBMS_WM.SetConflictWorkspace
   (*workspace* IN VARCHAR2);
> Determines whether conflicts exist between *workspace* and its parent.

PROCEDURE DBMS_WM.SetDiffVersions
   (*workspace1* IN VARCHAR2,
   [*savepoint1* IN VARCHAR2,]
   workspace2 IN VARCHAR2
   [, *savepoint2* IN VARCHAR2]);
> Compares differences between *workspace1* and *workspace2* and modifies the contents of different views to reflect the differences. If the *savepoint* variables are not present, uses LATEST savepoint.

PROCEDURE DBMS_WM.SetLockingOff;
> Disables Workspace Manager locking for the current session.

PROCEDURE DBMS_WM.SetLockingOn
   (*lockmode* IN VARCHAR2);
> Turns on locking with *lockmode* of 'E'(xclusive), 'S'(hared), or 'C'(arry-forward), which locks the rows in the current workspace with the same mode as their corresponding rows in the previous version.

PROCEDURE DBMS_WM.SetMultiWorkspaces
   (*workspaces* IN VARCHAR2);
> Makes comma-separated *workspaces* visible.

PROCEDURE DBMS_WM.SetWOOverwriteOff;
> Disables VIEW_WO_OVERWRITE history by changing the option to VIEW_W_OVERWRITE.

PROCEDURE DBMS_WM.SetWOOverwriteOn;
> Enables VIEW_WO_OVERWRITE history by changing the option to VIEW_WO_OVERWRITE.

PROCEDURE DBMS_WM.SetWorkspaceLockModeOff
   (*workspace* IN VARCHAR2);
> Disables Workspace Manager locking for *workspace*.

PROCEDURE DBMS_WM.SetWorkspaceLockModeOn
   (*workspace* IN VARCHAR2,
   lockmode IN VARCHAR2
   [, *override* IN BOOLEAN DEFAULT FALSE]);
> Sets the lock mode for *workspace* to *lockmode* of 'E'(xclusive), 'S'(hared), or 'C'(arry-forward), which locks the rows in the current workspace with the same mode as their corresponding rows in the previous version. If *override*, a change to lock mode is allowed.

PROCEDURE DBMS_WM.SynchronizeSite
  (*newwritersite* IN VARCHAR2);
    Updates the *newwritersite* after it was moved using RelocateWriterSite.

PROCEDURE DBMS_WM.UnfreezeWorkspace
  (*workspace* IN VARCHAR2);
    Removes the freeze on *workspace*.

PROCEDURE DBMS_WM.UnlockRows
  (*workspace* IN VARCHAR2,
  table_name IN VARCHAR2
  [, *where_clause* IN VARCHAR2 DEFAULT '']
  [, *all_or_user* IN VARCHAR2 DEFAULT 'USER']
  [, *lock_mode* IN VARCHAR2 DEFAULT 'ES']);
    Unlocks versioned rows in *table_name* of *workspace* and its parent workspace.
    The *where_clause* identifies rows to be unlocked and can reference only primary
    key columns. *all_or_user* can have two choices for the scope of the procedure: all
    locks or only the user's locks. *lock_mode* can be 'E'(xclusive), 'S'(hared), or both
    ('ES'), specifying which locks are considered.

DBMS_XDB

Provides procedures and functions to interface with XML data stored in the Oracle
database. New with Oracle9*i*.

Calls

FUNCTION DMBS_XDB.getAclDocument
  (*abspath* IN VARCHAR);
  RETURN SYS.XMLTYPE;
    Retrieves the ACL document from the XML document with a pathname of
    abspath.

FUNCTION DMBS_XDB.getPrivileges
  (*res_path* IN VARCHAR2)
  RETURN SYS.XMLTYPE;
    Returns privileges granted to the current user on the XML document with the
    absolute path of *res_path*.

FUNCTION DMBS_XDB.changePrivileges
  (*res_path* IN VARCHAR2,
  ace IN XMLTYPE)
  RETURN PLS_INTEGER;
    Adds the *ace* privilege to XML document with the absolute path of *res_path*.
    Returns a positive integer if the ACL was successfully modified.

FUNCTION DMBS_XDB.checkPrivileges
  (*res_path* IN VARCHAR2,
  privs IN XMLTYPE)
  RETURN PLS_INTEGER;
    Checks to see if the XML document with the absolute path of *res_path* has privi-
    lege *privs*. Returns a positive integer if it does.

PROCEDURE DMBS_XDB.setacl
    (*res_path* IN VARCHAR2,
    acl_path IN VARCHAR2);
      Sets the ACL (specified by *acl*) on the XML document with the absolute path of
      res_path to *acl_path*.

FUNCTION DMBS_XDB.AclCheckPrivileges
    (*acl_path* IN VARCHAR2,
    owner IN VARCHAR2,
    privs IN XMLTYPE)
    RETURN PLS_INTEGER;
      Checks *privs* in the document owned by *owner* against *acl_path*. Returns a posi-
      tive integer if all privileges were granted.

FUNCTION DMBS_XDB.LockResource
    (*path* IN VARCHAR2,
    depthzero IN BOOLEAN,
    shared IN BOOLEAN)
    RETURN BOOLEAN;
      Creates a lock on XML resource *path*. If *shared*, the function will create a shared
      lock. *depthzero* is currently unsupported. Returns TRUE if the lock was obtained.

PROCEDURE DMBS_XDB.GetLockToken
    (*path* IN VARCHAR2,
    locktoken OUT VARCHAR2);
      Gets a lock token for XML resource *path*.

FUNCTION DMBS_XDB.UnlockResource
    (*path* IN VARCHAR2,
    deltoken IN VARCHAR2)
    RETURN BOOLEAN;
      Unlocks the XML resource *path* by removing *deltoken*. Returns TRUE if
      successful.

FUNCTION DMBS_XDB.CreateResource
    (*path* IN VARCHAR2,
    input IN *datatype*)
    RETURN BOOLEAN;
      Creates the XML resource *path*. The *datatypes* can be VARCHAR2, SYS.
      XMLTYPE, REF SYS.XMLTYPE, CLOB, or BFILE. Returns TRUE if successful.

FUNCTION DMBS_XDB.CreateFolder
    (*path* IN VARCHAR2)
    RETURN BOOLEAN;
      Creates a folder in the XML hierarchy with *path*. Returns TRUE if successful.

PROCEDURE DMBS_XDB.DeleteResource
    (*path* IN VARCHAR2);
      Deletes the XML resource *path*.

PROCEDURE DMBS_XDB.Link
    (*srcpath* IN VARCHAR2,
    linkfolder IN VARCHAR2,
    linkname IN VARCHAR2);
      Creates the *linkname* in *linkfolder* to *srcpath*.

PROCEDURE DMBS_XDB.CFGRefresh;
      Refreshes the session's configuration information.

```
FUNCTION DMBS_XDB.CFG_Get
   RETURN SYS.XMLTYPE;
```
   Returns the session's configuration information.

```
PROCEDURE DMBS_XDB.CFG_Update
   (xdbconfig IN SYS.XMLTYPE);
```
   Updates the configuration information to *xdbconfig*.

DBMS_XDBT

Provides an interface to create an Oracle ConText index on the XML DB hierarchy. New with Oracle9*i*.

Calls

```
PROCEDURE DBMS_XDBT.dropPreferences;
```
   Drops preferences for a ConText index on the XML hierarchy.

```
PROCEDURE DBMS_XDBT.createPreferences;
```
   Creates default preferences for a ConText index on the XML hierarchy.

```
PROCEDURE DBMS_XDBT.createDatastorePreferences
```
   Creates a USER datastore preference for a ConText index on the XML hierarchy.

```
PROCEDURE DBMS_XDBT.createFilterPref;
```
   Creates a NULL filter preference for a ConText index on the XML hierarchy.

```
PROCEDURE DBMS_XDBT.createLexerPref;
```
   Creates a BASIC lexer filter preference for a ConText index on the XML hierarchy.

```
PROCEDURE DBMS_XDBT.createWordlistPref;
```
   Creates a wordlist preference for a ConText index on the XML hierarchy.

```
PROCEDURE DBMS_XDBT.createStoplistPref;
```
   Creates a stoplist preference for a ConText index on the XML hierarchy.

```
PROCEDURE DBMS_XDBT.createStoragePref;
```
   Creates a BASIC_STORAGE preference for a ConText index on the XML hierarchy.

```
PROCEDURE DBMS_XDBT.createSectiongroupPref;
```
   Creates a section group preference for a ConText index on the XML hierarchy.

```
PROCEDURE DBMS_XDBT.createIndex;
```
   Creates a ConText index on the XML hierarchy.

```
PROCEDURE DBMS_XDBT.configureAutoSync
```
   Sets up jobs for automatic synchronization of a ConText index on the XML hierarchy.

DBMS_XDB_VERSION

Provides procedures and functions used to create and manage versions in XDB. New with Oracle9*i*.

Calls

FUNCTION DBMS_XDB_VERSION.MakeVersioned
    (*pathname* IN VARCHAR2)
    RETURN DBMS_XDD.RESID_TYPE;
       Creates a version-controlled resource for *pathname*.

PROCEDURE DBMS_XDB_VERSION.Checkout
    (*pathname* IN VARCHAR2);
       Checks out *pathname* before updating or deleting it. Returns the resource ID of the first version.

FUNCTION DBMS_XDB_VERSION.Checkin
    (*pathname* IN VARCHAR2)
    RETURN DBMS_XDD.RESID_TYPE;
       Checks in *pathname* and returns the resource ID of the new version.

FUNCTION DBMS_XDB_VERSION.Uncheckout
    (*pathname* IN VARCHAR2)
    RETURN DBMS_XDD.RESID_TYPE;
       Checks in *pathname* and returns the resource ID of the old version.

PROCEDURE DBMS_XDB_VERSION.GetPredecessors
    (*pathname* IN VARCHAR2)
    RETURN DBMS_XDD.RESID_TYPE;
       Returns a list of predecessors of *pathname*.

FUNCTION DBMS_XDB_VERSION.GetPredsByResID
    (*resid* IN RESID_TYPE)
    RETURN RESID_LIST_TYPE;
       Returns a list of predecessors of *resid*.

FUNCTION DBMS_XDB_VERSION.GetResourceByResID
    (*resid* IN RESID_TYPE)
    RETURN XMLTYPE;
       Returns the resource identified by *resid*.

FUNCTION DBMS_XDB_VERSION.GetSuccessors
    (*pathname* IN VARCHAR2)
    RETURN RESID_LIST_TYPE;
       Returns a list of successors to *pathname*.

FUNCTION DBMS_XDB_VERSION.GetSuccsByResId
    (*resid* IN RESID_TYPE)
    RETURN RESID_LIST_TYPE;
       Returns a list of successors to *resid*.

DBMS_XMLDOM

Allows you to access XMLType objects through the Document Object Model (DOM). This extensive package is used to implement different parts of the World Wide Web Consortium (W3C) interfaces to different parts of the DOM and are grouped accordingly.

You must have specified read-from and write-to directories as part of the *INIT.ORA/ SPFILE* file (e.g., in parameters such as UTL_FILE_DIR). New in Oracle9*i*.

Calls

This section specifies the DBMS_XMLDOM calls in several different categories: general calls, DOM node methods, DOM node named methods, DOM list node map methods, DOM node list methods, DOM attribute methods, DOM character data methods, DOM Implementation methods, DOM Document Type methods, DOM Element methods, DOM Entity methods, DOM Notation methods, DOM Processing Instruction methods, DOM Text methods, and DOM Document methods.

General calls

The following calls can be used for most parts of the DOM. The possible values for *DOMdatatype* are DOMNode, DOMNamedNodeMap, DOMNodeList, DOMAttr, DOMCDateSection, DOMCharacterData, DOMComment, DOMImplementation, DOMDocumentFragment, DOMDocumentType, DOMElement, DOMEntity, DOMEntityRef, DOMNotation, DOMText, and DOMDocument.

```
FUNCTION DBMS_XMLDOM.isNull
  (n IN DOMdatatype)
  RETURN BOOLEAN;
```
Returns whether *n* is NULL.

```
FUNCTION DBMS_XMLDOM.makeNode
  (n IN DOMdatatype)
  RETURN DOMNode;
```
Creates a node from *n* and returns a DOMNode. This function can be used for any part of the DOM except for DOMNode, DOMNamedNodeMap, DOMNodeList, and DOMImplementation.

DOM node methods

```
FUNCTION isNull
  ( n DOMNode)
  RETURN BOOLEAN;
```
Returns whether *n* is null.

```
FUNCTION DBMS_XMLDOM.makeAttr
  (n IN DOMNode)
  RETURN DOMAttr;
```
Returns *n* as a DOMAttr.

```
FUNCTION DBMS_XMLDOM.makeCDataSection
  (n IN DOMNode)
  RETURN DOMDataSection;
```
Returns *n* as a DOMDataSection.

```
FUNCTION DBMS_XMLDOM.makeCharacterData
    (n IN DOMNode)
    RETURN DOMCharacterData;
```
Returns *n* as a DOMCharacterData.

```
FUNCTION DBMS_XMLDOM.makeComment
    (n IN DOMNode)
    RETURN DOMComment;
```
Returns *n* as a DOMComment.

```
FUNCTION DBMS_XMLDOM.makeDocumentFragment
    (n IN DOMNode)
    RETURN DOMDocumentFragment;
```
Returns *n* as a DOMDocumentFragment.

```
FUNCTION DBMS_XMLDOM.makeDocumentType
    (n IN DOMNode)
    RETURN DOMDocumentType;
```
Returns *n* as a DOMDocumentType.

```
FUNCTION DBMS_XMLDOM.makeElement
    (n IN DOMNode)
    RETURN DOMElement;
```
Returns *n* as a DOMElement.

```
FUNCTION DBMS_XMLDOM.makeEntity
    (n IN DOMNode)
    RETURN DOMEntity;
```
Returns *n* as a DOMEntity.

```
FUNCTION DBMS_XMLDOM.makeEntityReference
    (n IN DOMNode)
    RETURN DOMEntityReference;
```
Returns *n* as a DOMEntityReference.

```
FUNCTION DBMS_XMLDOM.makeNotation
    (n IN DOMNode)
    RETURN DOMNotation;
```
Returns *n* as a DOMNotation.

```
FUNCTION DBMS_XMLDOM.makeProcessingInstruction
    (n IN DOMNode)
    RETURN DOMProcessingInstruction;
```
Returns *n* as a DOMProcessingInstruction.

```
FUNCTION DBMS_XMLDOM.makeText
    (n IN DOMNode)
    RETURN DOMText;
```
Returns *n* as a DOMText.

```
FUNCTION DBMS_XMLDOM.makeDocument
    (n IN DOMNode)
    RETURN DOMDocument;
```
Returns *n* as a DOMDocument.

```
PROCEDURE DBMS_XMLDOM.WriteToFile
    (n IN DOMNode,
    filename IN VARCHAR2
    [, charset IN VARCHAR2);
```
Writes *n* to *filename*, using *charset* if present, or the database character set if not.

PROCEDURE DBMS_XMLDOM.WriteToBuffer
    (n IN DOMNode,
    buffer IN OUT VARCHAR2
    [, charset IN VARCHAR2);
    Writes *n* to *buffer*, using *charset* if present, or the database character set if not.

PROCEDURE DBMS_XMLDOM.WriteToBuffer
    (n IN DOMNode,
    cl IN OUT CLOB
    [, charset IN VARCHAR2);
    Writes *n* to *cl*, using *charset* if present, or the database character set if not.

FUNCTION DBMS_XMLDOM.getNodeName
    (n IN DOMNode)
    RETURN VARCHAR2;
    Returns the name of *n*.

FUNCTION DBMS_XMLDOM.getNodeValue
    (n IN DOMNode)
    RETURN VARCHAR2;
    Returns the value of *n*.

PROCEDURE DBMS_XMLDOM.setNodeValue
    (n IN DOMNode,
    modeValue IN VARCHAR2);
    Sets the value of *n* to *modeValue*.

FUNCTION DBMS_XMLDOM.getNodeType
    (n IN DOMNode)
    RETURN NUMBER;
    Returns the type of *n*.

FUNCTION DBMS_XMLDOM.getParentNode
    (n IN DOMNode)
    RETURN DOMNode;
    Returns the parent node of *n*.

FUNCTION DBMS_XMLDOM.getChildNodes
    (n IN DOMNode)
    RETURN DOMNodeList;
    Returns the child nodes of *n*.

FUNCTION DBMS_XMLDOM.getFirstChild
    (n IN DOMNode)
    RETURN DOMNode;
    Returns the first child of *n*.

FUNCTION DBMS_XMLDOM.getLastChild
    (n IN DOMNode)
    RETURN DOMNode;
    Returns the last child of *n*.

FUNCTION DBMS_XMLDOM.getPreviousSibling
    (n IN DOMNode)
    RETURN DOMNode;
    Returns the sibling immediately preceding *n*.

FUNCTION DBMS_XMLDOM.getNextSibling
    (*n* IN DOMNode)
    RETURN DOMNode;
      Returns the sibling immediately following *n*.

FUNCTION DBMS_XMLDOM.getAtributes
    (*n* IN DOMNode)
    RETURN DOMNamedNodeMap;
      Returns the attributes of *n*.

FUNCTION DBMS_XMLDOM.getOwnerDocument
    (*n* IN DOMNode)
    RETURN DOMDocument;
      Returns the document object associated with *n*.

FUNCTION DBMS_XMLDOM.insertBefore
    (*n* IN DOMNode,
    newChild IN DOMNode,
    refChild IN DOMNode)
    RETURN DOMNode;
      Inserts *newChild* before *refChild* in *n*.

FUNCTION DBMS_XMLDOM.replaceChild
    (*n* IN DOMNode,
    newChild IN DOMNode,
    oldChild IN DOMNode)
    RETURN DOMNode;
      Replaces *oldChild* with *newChild* in *n*.

FUNCTION DBMS_XMLDOM.removeChild
    (*n* IN DOMNode,
    oldChild IN DOMNode)
    RETURN DOMNode;
      Removes and returns *oldChild* in *n*.

FUNCTION DBMS_XMLDOM.appendChild
    (*n* IN DOMNode,
    newChild IN DOMNode)
    RETURN DOMNode;
      Appends *newChild* to list of children of *n*.

FUNCTION DBMS_XMLDOM.hasChildNodes
    (*n* IN DOMNode)
    RETURN BOOLEAN;
      Returns whether *n* has child nodes.

PROCEDURE DBMS_XMLDOM.cloneNode
    (*n* IN DOMNode,
    deep IN BOOLEAN)
    RETURN DOMNode;
      Creates and returns a clone of *n*. If *deep*, children of *n* are also cloned.

DOM named node map methods

FUNCTION DBMS_XMLDOM.getNamedItem
    (*nnm* DOMNamedNodeMap,
    name IN VARCHAR2)
    RETURN DOMNode;
      Retrieves a node DOMNode from *nnm* by *name*.

```
FUNCTION DBMS_XMLDOM.setNamedItem
   (nnm DOMNamedNodeMap,
   arg IN VARCHAR2)
   RETURN DOMNode;
```
Adds a node to *nnm* by using its NodeName *arg*.

```
FUNCTION DBMS_XMLDOM.removeNamedItem
   (nnm DOMNamedNodeMap,
   name IN VARCHAR2)
   RETURN DOMNode;
```
Remove a node *name* from *nnm*.

```
FUNCTION DBMS_XMLDOM.item
   (nnm DOMNamedNodeMap,
   index IN NUMBER)
   RETURN DOMNode;
```
Returns the item in *nnm* indicated by the *index*. If *index* is greater than or equal to the number of nodes in the map, returns NULL.

```
FUNCTION DBMS_XMLDOM.getLength
   (nnm DOMNamedNodeMap,
   RETURN NUMBER;
```
Returns the number of items in *nnm*.

DOM node list methods

```
FUNCTION DBMS_XMLDOM.item
   (nl IN DOMNodeList,
   index IN NUMBER)
   RETURN DOMNode;
```
Returns the item in *nl* indicated by the *index*. If *index* is greater than or equal to the number of nodes in the map, returns NULL.

```
FUNCTION DBMS_XMLDOM.getLength
   (nl DOMNodeList,
   RETURN NUMBER;
```
Returns the number of items in *nl*.

DOM attribute methods

```
FUNCTION DBMS_XMLDOM.getQualifiedName
   (a IN DOMAttr)
   RETURN VARCHAR2;
```
Returns the qualified name of *a*.

```
FUNCTION DBMS_XMLDOM.getNamespace
   (a IN DOMAttr)
   RETURN VARCHAR2;
```
Returns the namespace of *a*.

```
FUNCTION DBMS_XMLDOM.getLocalName
   (a IN DOMAttr)
   RETURN VARCHAR2;
```
Returns the local name of *a*.

```
FUNCTION DBMS_XMLDOM.getExpandedName
   (a IN DOMAttr)
   RETURN VARCHAR2;
```
Returns the expanded name of *a*.

FUNCTION DBMS_XMLDOM.getName
   (*a* IN DOMAttr)
   RETURN VARCHAR2;
     Returns the name of *a*.

FUNCTION DBMS_XMLDOM.getSpecified
   (*a* IN DOMAttr)
   RETURN BOOLEAN;
     Returns TRUE if *a* was explicitly given a value in the original document.

FUNCTION DBMS_XMLDOM.getValue
   (*a* IN DOMAttr)
   RETURN VARCHAR2;
     Returns the value of *a*.

FUNCTION DBMS_XMLDOM.setValue
   (*a* IN DOMAttr,
   value IN VARCHAR2);
     Sets *value* of *a*.

DOM character data methods

FUNCTION DBMS_XMLDOM.getData
   (*cd* IN DOMCharacterData)
   RETURN VARCHAR2;
     Returns character data for *cd*.

FUNCTION DBMS_XMLDOM.setData
   (*cd* IN DOMCharacterData,
   data IN VARCHAR2);
     Sets character data for *cd* to *data*.

FUNCTION DBMS_XMLDOM.getLength
   (*cd* IN DOMCharacterData)
   RETURN NUMBER;
     Returns the number of 16-bit units available through data and substringData()
     method for *cd*.

FUNCTION DBMS_XMLDOM.substringData
   (*cd* IN DOMCharacterData,
   offset IN NUMBER,
   cnt IN NUMBER)
   RETURN VARCHAR2;
     Returns data from *cd* from *offset* for *cnt* characters.

PROCEDURE DBMS_XMLDOM.appendData
   (*cd* IN DOMCharacterData,
   arg IN VARCHAR2);
     Appends *arg* to *cd*.

PROCEDURE DBMS_XMLDOM.insertData
   (*cd* IN DOMCharacterData,
   offset IN NUMBER,
   arg IN VARCHAR2);
     Inserts *arg* to *cd* at position *offset*.

```
PROCEDURE DBMS_XMLDOM.deleteData
   (cd IN DOMCharacterData,
   offset IN NUMBER,
   cnt IN NUMBER);
```
   Deletes *cnt* characters from *cd* at position *offset*.

```
PROCEDURE DBMS_XMLDOM.replaceData
   (cd IN DOMCharacterData,
   offset IN NUMBER,
   cnt IN NUMBER,
   arg IN VARCHAR2);
```
   Replaces *cnt* characters with *arg* to *cd* at position *offset*.

DOM Implementation methods

```
FUNCTION DBMS_XMLDOM.hasFeature
   (di IN DOMImplementation,
   feature IN VARCHAR2,
   version IN VARCHAR2);
```
   Returns whether *di* has *feature* of *version*.

DOM Document Type methods

```
FUNCTION DBMS_XMLDOM.findEntity
   (dt IN DOMDocumentType,
   name IN VARCHAR2,
   par IN BOOLEAN)
   RETURN DOMEntity;
```
   Finds entity *name* in *dt* and returns it. If *par*, it is a parameter entity; if not, it is a normal entity.

```
FUNCTION DBMS_XMLDOM.findNotation
   (dt IN DOMDocumentType,
   name IN VARCHAR2)
   RETURN DOMEntity;
```
   Finds entity *name* in *dt* and returns it.

```
FUNCTION DBMS_XMLDOM.getPublicId
   (dt IN DOMDocumentType)
   RETURN VARCHAR2;
```
   Returns the public ID of *dt*.

```
FUNCTION DBMS_XMLDOM.getSystemId
   (dt IN DOMDocumentType)
   RETURN VARCHAR2;
```
   Returns the system ID of *dt*.

```
PROCEDURE DBMS_XMLDOM.writeExternalDTDToFile
   (dt IN DOMDocumentType,
   filename IN VARCHAR2
   [, charset IN VARCHAR2]);
```
   Writes *dt* to *filename*, using *charset* if present, or the database character set if not.

```
PROCEDURE DBMS_XMLDOM.writeExternalDTDToBuffer
   (dt IN DOMDocumentType,
   buffer IN OUT VARCHAR2
   [, charset IN VARCHAR2]);
```
   Writes *dt* to *buffer*, using *charset* if present, or the database character set if not.

PROCEDURE DBMS_XMLDOM.writeExternalDTDToClob
  (*dt* IN DOMDocumentType,
  cl IN CLOB
  [, *charset* IN VARCHAR2]);
    Writes *dt* to *cl*, using *charset* if present or the database character set if not.

FUNCTION DBMS_XMLDOM.getName
  (*dt* IN DOMDocumentType)
  RETURN VARCHAR2;
    Returns the name of *dt*.

FUNCTION DBMS_XMLDOM.getEntities
  (*dt* IN DOMDocumentType)
  RETURN DOMNamedNodeMap;
    Returns NamedNodeMap containing general internal and external entities of *dt*.

FUNCTION DBMS_XMLDOM.getNotations
  (*dt* IN DOMDocumentType)
  RETURN DOMNamedNodeMap;
    Returns NamedNodeMap containing notations of *dt*.

DOM Element methods

FUNCTION DBMS_XMLDOM.getQualifiedName
  (*elem* IN DOMElement)
  RETURN VARCHAR2;
    Returns the qualified name of *elem*.

FUNCTION DBMS_XMLDOM.getNamespace
  (*elem* IN DOMElement)
  RETURN VARCHAR2;
    Returns the namespace of *elem*.

FUNCTION DBMS_XMLDOM.getLocalName
  (*elem* IN DOMElement)
  RETURN VARCHAR2;
    Returns the local name of *elem*.

FUNCTION DBMS_XMLDOM.getExpandedName
  (*elem* IN DOMElement)
  RETURN VARCHAR2;
    Returns the expanded name of *elem*.

FUNCTION DBMS_XMLDOM.getChildrenByTagName
  (*elem* IN DOMElement,
  name IN VARCHAR2
  [, *ns* IN VARCHAR2])
  RETURN DOMNodeList;
    Returns a list of children of *elem*, based on *name* alone or *name* and *ns*.

FUNCTION DBMS_XMLDOM.getElementsByTagName
  (*elem* IN DOMElement,
  name IN VARCHAR2
  [, *ns* IN VARCHAR2])
  RETURN DOMNodeList;
    Returns a list of element children of *elem*, based on *name* alone or *name* and *ns*.

```
FUNCTION DBMS_XMLDOM.resolveNamespacePrefix
  (elem IN DOMElement,
  prefix IN VARCHAR2
  RETURN VARCHAR2;
```
Returns the namespace of *elem*, based on *prefix*.

```
FUNCTION DBMS_XMLDOM.getTagName
  (elem IN DOMElement)
  RETURN VARCHAR2;
```
Returns the attribute tag name of *elem*.

```
FUNCTION DBMS_XMLDOM.getTagName
  (elem IN DOMElement,
  name IN VARCHAR2)
  RETURN VARCHAR2;
```
Returns the value of attribute *name* of *elem*.

```
PROCEDURE DBMS_XMLDOM.setTagName
  (elem IN DOMElement,
  name IN VARCHAR2,
  value IN VARCHAR);
```
Sets *value* of attribute *name* of *elem*.

```
PROCEDURE DBMS_XMLDOM.getTagName
  (elem IN DOMElement,
  name IN VARCHAR2);
```
Removes the attribute *name* of *elem*.

```
FUNCTION DBMS_XMLDOM.getAttributeNode
  (elem IN DOMElement,
  name IN VARCHAR2)
  RETURN DOMAttr;
```
Returns attribute node of attribute *name* of *elem*.

```
FUNCTION DBMS_XMLDOM.setAttributeNode
  (elem IN DOMElement,
  newAttr IN DOMAttr)
  RETURN DOMAttr;
```
Adds *newAttr* to *elem*.

```
FUNCTION DBMS_XMLDOM.removeAttributeNode
  (elem IN DOMElement,
  oldAttr IN DOMAttr)
  RETURN DOMAttr;
```
Removes *oldAttr* to *elem*.

```
PROCEDURE DBMS_XMLDOM.normalize
  (elem IN DOMElement);
```
Normalizes the text children of *elem*.

DOM Entity methods

```
FUNCTION DBMS_XMLDOM.getPublicID
  (ent IN DOMEntity)
  RETURN VARCHAR2;
```
Returns the public ID of *ent*.

```
FUNCTION DBMS_XMLDOM.getSystemID
   (ent IN DOMEntity)
   RETURN VARCHAR2;
```
   Returns the system ID of *ent*.

```
FUNCTION DBMS_XMLDOM.getNotationName
   (ent IN DOMEntity)
   RETURN VARCHAR2;
```
   Returns the notational name of *ent*.

DOM Notation methods

```
FUNCTION DBMS_XMLDOM.getPublicID
   (n IN DOMNotation)
   RETURN VARCHAR2;
```
   Returns the public ID of *n*.

```
FUNCTION DBMS_XMLDOM.getSystemID
   (n IN DOMNotation)
   RETURN VARCHAR2;
```
   Returns the system ID of *n*.

DOM Processing Instruction methods

```
FUNCTION DBMS_XMLDOM.getData
   (pi IN DOMProcessingInstruction)
   RETURN VARCHAR2;
```
   Returns the content data of *pi*.

```
FUNCTION DBMS_XMLDOM.getTarget
   (pi IN DOMProcessingInstruction)
   RETURN VARCHAR2;
```
   Returns the target of *pi*.

```
PROCEDURE DBMS_XMLDOM.setData
   (pi IN DOMProcessingInstruction,
   data IN VARCHAR2);
```
   Sets the content data of *pi* to *data*.

DOM Text methods

```
FUNCTION DBMS_XMLDOM.splitText
   (t IN DOMText,
   offset IN NUMBER)
   RETURN DOMText;
```
   Breaks *t* into two DOMText nodes at *offset*.

DOM Document methods

```
FUNCTION DBMS_XMLDOM.newDOMDocument
   RETURN DOMDocument;
```
   Returns a new DOMDocument instance.

```
PROCEDURE DBMS_XMLDOM.freeDocument
   (doc IN DOMDocument);
```
   Frees *doc*.

```
FUNCTION DBMS_XMLDOM.getVersion
  (doc IN DOMDocument)
  RETURN VARCHAR2;
```
Returns the version information for *doc*.

```
PROCEDURE DBMS_XMLDOM.setVersion
  (doc IN DOMDocument
  version IN VARCHAR2);
```
Sets *version* for *doc*.

```
FUNCTION DBMS_XMLDOM.getCharset
  (doc IN DOMDocument)
  RETURN VARCHAR2;
```
Returns character set of *doc*.

```
PROCEDURE DBMS_XMLDOM.setCharset
  (doc IN DOMDocument
  charset IN VARCHAR2);
```
Sets *charset* for *doc*.

```
FUNCTION DBMS_XMLDOM.getStandalone
  (doc IN DOMDocument)
  RETURN VARCHAR2;
```
Returns standalone information for *doc*.

```
PROCEDURE DBMS_XMLDOM.setStandalone
  (doc IN DOMDocument
  value IN VARCHAR2);
```
Sets standalone information *value* for *doc*.

```
PROCEDURE DBMS_XMLDOM.writeToFile
  (doc IN DOMDocument,
  filename IN VARCHAR2
  [, charset IN VARCHAR2]);
```
Writes *doc* to *filename*, using *charset* if present, or the database character set if not.

```
PROCEDURE DBMS_XMLDOM.writeToBuffer
  (doc IN DOMDocument,
  buffer IN OUT VARCHAR2
  [, charset IN VARCHAR2]);
```
Writes *doc* to *buffer*, using *charset* if present, or the database character set if not.

```
PROCEDURE DBMS_XMLDOM.writeToClob
  (doc IN DOMDocument,
  cl IN CLOB
  [, charset IN VARCHAR2]);
```
Writes *doc* to *cl*, using *charset* if present, or the database character set if not.

```
PROCEDURE DBMS_XMLDOM.writeExternalDTDToFile
  (doc IN DOMDocument,
  filename IN VARCHAR2
  [, charset IN VARCHAR2]);
```
Writes the external DTD (Document Type Definition) *doc* to *filename*, using *charset* if present, or the database character set if not.

PROCEDURE DBMS_XMLDOM.writeExternalDTDToBuffer
  (*doc* IN DOMDocument,
  buffer IN OUT VARCHAR2
  [, *charset* IN VARCHAR2]);
    Writes the external DTD *doc* to *buffer*, using *charset* if present, or the database character set if not.

PROCEDURE DBMS_XMLDOM.writeExternalDTDToClob
  (*doc* IN DOMDocument,
  cl IN CLOB
  [, *charset* IN VARCHAR2]);
    Writes the external DTD *doc* to *cl*, using *charset* if present, or the database character set if not.

FUNCTION DBMS_XMLDOM.getDoctype
  (*doc* IN DOMDocument)
  RETURN DOMDocumentType;
    Returns the DTD associated with *doc*.

FUNCTION DBMS_XMLDOM.getImplementation
  (*doc* IN DOMDocument)
  RETURN DOMImplementation;
    Returns the DOMImplementation object that handles *doc*.

FUNCTION DBMS_XMLDOM.getDocumentElement
  (*doc* IN DOMDocument)
  RETURN DOMDocumentElement;
    Returns the child node (the document element) of *doc*.

FUNCTION DBMS_XMLDOM.createElement
  (*doc* IN DOMDocument,
  tagName in VARCHAR2)
  RETURN DOMElement;
    Creates and returns the element for *doc* with name *tagName*.

FUNCTION DBMS_XMLDOM.createDocumentFragment
  (*doc* IN DOMDocument)
  RETURN DOMDocumentFragment;
    Creates and returns the document fragment for *doc*.

FUNCTION DBMS_XMLDOM.createTextNode
  (*doc* IN DOMDocument,
  data in VARCHAR2)
  RETURN DOMText;
    Creates and returns the text node for *doc* with *data* as content.

FUNCTION DBMS_XMLDOM.createComment
  (*doc* IN DOMDocument,
  data in VARCHAR2)
  RETURN DOMComment;
    Creates and returns the comment node for *doc* with *data* as content.

FUNCTION DBMS_XMLDOM.createCDataSection
  (*doc* IN DOMDocument,
  data in VARCHAR2)
  RETURN DOMCDATASection;
    Creates and returns the CDataSection node for *doc* with *data* as content.

```
FUNCTION DBMS_XMLDOM.createProcessingInstruction
  (doc IN DOMDocument,
  target IN VARCHAR2,
  data in VARCHAR2)
  RETURN DOMProcessingInstruction;
```
Creates and returns the processing instruction node for *doc* with *target* and *data* as content.

```
FUNCTION DBMS_XMLDOM.createAttribute
  (doc IN DOMDocument,
  data in VARCHAR2)
  RETURN DOMAttr;
```
Creates and returns the attribute node for *doc* with *data* as content.

```
FUNCTION DBMS_XMLDOM.createEntityReference
  (doc IN DOMDocument,
  name in VARCHAR2)
  RETURN DOMEntityReference;
```
Creates and returns the entity reference node for *doc* with *name* as name.

```
FUNCTION DBMS_XMLDOM.getElementsByTagName
  (doc IN DOMDocument,
  tagname IN VARCHAR)
  RETURN DOMNodeList;
```
Returns a list of elements in *doc* with tag name *tagname*.

DBMS_XMLGEN

Converts the results of a SQL query to XML and returns it as a CLOB. New with Oracle9*i*.

Calls

```
PROCEDURE DBMS_XMLGEN.newContext
  (query IN VARCHAR2 | SYS_REFCURSOR)
  RETURN ctxHandle;
```
Generates a context handle ctxHandle from either a query sting or a PL/SQL reference cursor.

```
PROCEDURE DBMS_XMLGEN.setRowTag
  (ctx IN ctxHandle,
  rowTag IN VARCHAR2);
```
Sets the name of the element separating the rows to *rowTag* in *ctx*.

```
PROCEDURE DBMS_XMLGEN.setRowSetTag
  (ctx IN ctxHandle,
  rowSetTag IN VARCHAR2);
```
Sets the name of the root element for the document *ctx* to *rowSetTag*.

```
FUNCTION DBMS_XMLGEN.getXML[Type]
  ({ctx IN ctxHandle | sqlQuery IN VARCHAR2},
  [clobval IN OUT NCOPY clob,]
  dtdOrSchema IN NUMBER := NONE)
  RETURN {BOOLEAN | CLOB | SYS.XMLType};
```
This function has five forms:

- Using *ctx* for the query and *clobval*, which appends rows to *clobval*
- Using *ctx* and returning the XML document as a CLOB

- Using *sqlQuery* to send the query string and returning a CLOB
- Using *ctx* and returning the XML document as SYS.XMLType, which uses the call getXMLType
- Using *sqlQuery* and returning the XML document as SYS.XMLType, which uses the call getXMLType

All forms use *dtdOrSchema*, which supports only the default.

FUNCTION DBMS_XMLGEN.getNumRowsProcessed
    (*ctx* IN ctxHandle)
    RETURN NUMBER;

Returns the number of rows in XML document *ctx*.

PROCEDURE DBMS_XMLGEN.setMaxRows
    (*ctx* IN ctxHandle,
    maxRows IN NUMBER);

Sets the maximum number of rows *maxRows* to fetch for each invocation getXML call for XML document *ctx*.

PROCEDURE DBMS_XMLGEN.setSkipRows
    (*ctx* IN ctxHandle,
    skipRows IN NUMBER);

Sets the number of rows to skip (*skipRows*) for each invocation getXML call for XML document *ctx*.

PROCEDURE DBMS_XMLGEN.setConvertSpecialCharacters
    (*ctx* IN ctxHandle,
    conv IN BOOLEAN);

Sets whether to convert special characters returned for a query for XML document *ctx*.

FUNCTION DBMS_XMLGEN.convert
    (*xmlData* IN {VARCHAR2 | CLOB},
    flag IN NUMBER := ENTITY_ENCODE)
    RETURN {VARCHAR2 | CLOB};

Converts XML data *xmlData* into its escaped or unescaped equivalent and returns as either a CLOB or a VARCHAR. The datatype of *xmlData* must match the returned datatype. *flag* can be either the default or ENTITY_DECODE.

PROCEDURE DBMS_XMLGEN.useItemTagsForColl
    (*ctx* IN ctxHandle);

Forces the use of tags in the format *itemname*_ITEM for the columns of XML document *ctx*.

PROCEDURE DBMS_XMLGEN.restartQUERY
    (*ctx* IN ctxHandle);

Restarts the query for XML document *ctx*.

PROCEDURE DBMS_XMLGEN.restartQUERY
    (*ctx* IN ctxHandle);

Closes context and releases resources for XML document *ctx*.

DBMS_XMLPARSER

Provides procedures and functions to access the contents and structure of XML documents. New with Oracle9i.

Calls

```
FUNCTION DBMS_XMLPARSER.parse
  (url IN VARCHAR2)
  RETURN DOMDocument;

PROCEDURE DBMS_XMLPARSER.parse
  (p IN PARSER,
  url IN VARCHAR2);
```
  The function uses the default parser behavior on *url* and returns the XML document. The procedure uses parser *p* on *url*.

```
FUNCTION DBMS_XMLPARSER.newParser
  RETURN Parser;
```
  Returns a new parser instance. Must be called before the behavior of the parser is changed or other parser methods need to be used.

```
PROCEDURE DBMS_XMLPARSER.parseBuffer
  (p IN Parser,
  doc IN VARCHAR2);
```
  Parses *doc* with *p*.

```
PROCEDURE DBMS_XMLPARSER.parseClob
  (p IN Parser,
  doc IN CLOB);
```
  Parses *doc* with *p*.

```
PROCEDURE DBMS_XMLPARSER.parseDTD
  (p IN Parser,
  url IN VARCHAR2,
  root IN VARCHAR2);
```
  Parses *url* with root element *root p*.

```
PROCEDURE DBMS_XMLPARSER.parseDTDBuffer
  (p IN Parser,
  dtd IN VARCHAR2,
  root IN VARCHAR2);
```
  Parses *dtd* with root element *root p*.

```
PROCEDURE DBMS_XMLPARSER.parseDTDClob
  (p IN Parser,
  dtd IN CLB,
  root IN VARCHAR2);
```
  Parses *dtd* with root element *root p*.

```
PROCEDURE DBMS_XMLPARSER.setBaseDir
  (p IN Parser,
  dir IN VARCHAR2);
```
  Sets root directory *dir* for *p*.

PROCEDURE DBMS_XMLPARSER.showWarnings
  (*p* IN Parser,
  yes IN BOOLEAN);
    Sets whether warnings are shown for *p*.

PROCEDURE DBMS_XMLPARSER.setErrorLog
  (*p* IN Parser,
  fileName IN BOOLEAN);
    Sets error log to *fileName* for *p*.

PROCEDURE DBMS_XMLPARSER.setPreserveWhitespace
  (*p* IN Parser,
  yes IN BOOLEAN);
    Sets whether whitespace is preserved for *p*.

PROCEDURE DBMS_XMLPARSER.setValidationMode
  (*p* IN Parser,
  yes IN BOOLEAN);
    Sets validation mode for *p*.

FUNCTION DBMS_XMLPARSER.getValidationMode
  (*p* IN Parser)
  RETURN BOOLEAN;
    Gets validation mode for *p*.

PROCEDURE DBMS_XMLPARSER.setDoctype
  (*p* IN Parser,
  dtd IN DOMDocument);
    Sets *dtd* to be used for *p*.

FUNCTION DBMS_XMLPARSER.getDoctype
  (*p* IN Parser)
  RETURN DOMDocument;
    Gets DTD used for *p*. Called after DTD is parsed.

FUNCTION DBMS_XMLPARSER.getDocument
  (*p* IN Parser)
  RETURN DOMDocument;
    Gets root of DOM tree document used for *p*. Called after DTD is parsed.

PROCEDURE DBMS_XMLPARSER.freeParser
  (*p* IN Parser);
    Frees *p*.

FUNCTION DBMS_XMLPARSER.getReleaseVersion
  RETURN VARCHAR2;
    Returns version of Oracle XML parser.

DBMS_XMLQUERY

Provides database-to-XMLType functionality. Oracle recommends using DBMS_XMLGEN instead of this package whenever possible. New with Oracle9*i*.

Calls

FUNCTION DBMS_XMLQUERY.newContext
  (*sqlQuery* IN VARCHAR2 | CLOB)
  RETURN ctxType;
    Creates a query context from *sqlQuery* and returns handle.

PROCEDURE DBMS_XMLQUERY.closeContext
   (*ctxHandle* IN ctxType);
     Closes *ctxHandle*.

PROCEDURE DBMS_XMLQUERY.setRowsetTag
   (*ctxHandle* IN ctxType,
   tag IN VARCHAR2);
     Sets *tag* used to enclose data set for *ctxHandle*.

PROCEDURE DBMS_XMLQUERY.setRowTag
   (*ctxHandle* IN ctxType,
   tag IN VARCHAR2);
     Sets *tag* used to enclose database record for *ctxHandle*.

PROCEDURE DBMS_XMLQUERY.setErrorTag
   (*ctxHandle* IN ctxType,
   tag IN VARCHAR2);
     Sets *tag* used to enclose error documents for *ctxHandle*.

PROCEDURE DBMS_XMLQUERY.setRowIdAttrName
   (*ctxHandle* IN ctxType,
   attrName IN VARCHAR2);
     Sets *attrName* for the id attribute of the row-enclosing tag for *ctxHandle*.

PROCEDURE DBMS_XMLQUERY.setRowAttrValue
   (*ctxHandle* IN ctxType,
   colName IN VARCHAR2);
     Sets *colName* for the column whose value will be used for the id attribute of the
     row-enclosing tag for *ctxHandle*.

PROCEDURE DBMS_XMLQUERY.setCollIdAttrName
   (*ctxHandle* IN ctxType,
   attrName IN VARCHAR2);
     Sets *attrName* for the id attribute of the element-separating tag for *ctxHandle*.

PROCEDURE DBMS_XMLQUERY.useNullAttributeIndicator
   (*ctxHandle* IN ctxType,
   tag IN BOOLEAN);
     Sets whether or not to use XML attribute for NULLs.

PROCEDURE DBMS_XMLQUERY.useTypeForCollElemTag
   (*ctxHandle* IN ctxType,
   tag IN BOOLEAN :=);
     Sets whether to use the collection element's type name as the collection element
     tag name for *ctxHandle*.

PROCEDURE DBMS_XMLQUERY.setTagCase
   (*ctxHandle* IN ctxType,
   tCase IN NUMBER);
     Sets the case for generated XML tags to 0 (as is), 1 (lower), or 2 (upper) for
     ctxHandle.

PROCEDURE DBMS_XMLQUERY.setDateFormat
   (*ctxHandle* IN ctxType,
   mask IN VARCHAR2);
     Sets the date format to *mask* for *ctxHandle*.

```
PROCEDURE DBMS_XMLQUERY.setMaxRows
    (ctxHandle IN ctxType,
    rows IN NUMBER);
```
Sets the maximum number of *rows* for *ctxHandle*.

```
PROCEDURE DBMS_XMLQUERY.setSkipRows
    (ctxHandle IN ctxType,
    rows IN NUMBER);
```
Sets the number of *rows* to skip for *ctxHandle*.

```
PROCEDURE DBMS_XMLQUERY.setStylesheetHeader
    (ctxHandle IN ctxType,
    uri IN VARCHAR2,
    type IN VARCHAR2 DEFAULT := 'text/xsl');
```
Sets the stylesheet header to *uri* of *type* for *ctxHandle*.

```
PROCEDURE DBMS_XMLQUERY.setXSLT
    (ctxHandle IN ctxType,
    uri IN VARCHAR2 | CLOB,
    ref IN VARCHAR2 DEFAULT := NULL);
```
Registers the stylesheet at *uri* or included as a CLOB with *ref* (URL to include, export, and external entities) for *ctxHandle*.

```
PROCEDURE DBMS_XMLQUERY.setXSLTParam
    (ctxHandle IN ctxType,
    name IN VARCHAR2,
    value IN VARCHAR2);
```
Sets *value* of parameter *name* for top-level stylesheet for *ctxHandle*.

```
PROCEDURE DBMS_XMLQUERY.removeXSLTParam
    (ctxHandle IN ctxType,
    name IN VARCHAR2);
```
Removes parameter *name* from top-level stylesheet for *ctxHandle*.

```
PROCEDURE DBMS_XMLQUERY.setBindValue
    (ctxHandle IN ctxType,
    bindName IN VARCHAR2,
    bindValue IN VARCHAR2);
```
Sets *bindValue* of *bindName* for *ctxHandle*.

```
PROCEDURE DBMS_XMLQUERY.setMetaHeader
    (ctxHandle IN ctxType,
    header IN CLOB := NULL);
```
Sets XML metaheader *header* for *ctxHandle*.

```
PROCEDURE DBMS_XMLQUERY.setDataHeader
    (ctxHandle IN ctxType,
    header IN CLOB := NULL,
    tag IN VARCHAR2 := NULL);
```
Sets XML data header *header*, enclosed by *tag*, for *ctxHandle*.

```
PROCEDURE DBMS_XMLQUERY.setEncodingTag
    (ctxHandle IN ctxType,
    enc IN VARCHAR2 := DB_ENCODING);
```
Sets encoding processing instruction *enc* for *ctxHandle*.

PROCEDURE DBMS_XMLQUERY.setRaiseException
  (*ctxHandle* IN ctxType,
  flag IN BOOLEAN);
    Sets whether to throw raised exceptions for *ctxHandle*.

PROCEDURE DBMS_XMLQUERY.setRaiseNoRowsException
  (*ctxHandle* IN ctxType,
  flag IN BOOLEAN);
    Sets whether to throw the OracleXMLNoRowsException for *ctxHandle*.

PROCEDURE DBMS_XMLQUERY.setRaiseException
  (*ctxHandle* IN ctxType,
  flag IN BOOLEAN);
    Sets whether to throw raised exceptions for *ctxHandle*.

PROCEDURE DBMS_XMLQUERY.setSQLToXMLNamesEscaping
  (*ctxHandle* IN ctxType,
  flag IN BOOLEAN := TRUE);
    Sets whether to turn escaping of XML tags on or off if the SQL object name is not
    a valid XML identifier for *ctxHandle*.

PROCEDURE DBMS_XMLQUERY.propagateOriginalException
  (*ctxHandle* IN ctxType,
  flag IN BOOLEAN);
    Sets whether to throw exceptions rather than wrapping them with
    OracleXMLSQLException for *ctxHandle*.

PROCEDURE DBMS_XMLQUERY.getExceptionContent
  (*ctxHandle* IN ctxType,
  errNo OUT NUMBER,
  errMsg OUT VARCHAR2);
    Returns *errNo* and *errMsg* for exceptions for *ctxHandle*. Used to work around the
    fact that the Java Virtual Machine (JVM) throws its own exception on top of the
    original exception.

FUNCTION DBMS_XMLQUERY.getDTD
  (*ctxHandle* IN ctxType,
  withVer IN BOOLEAN := FALSE)
  RETURN CLOB;

PROCEDURE DBMS_XMLQUERY.getDTD
  (*ctxHandle* IN ctxType,
  xDoc IN CLOB,
  withVer IN BOOLEAN := FALSE);
    Generates DTD for *ctxHandle* and returns it either in a CLOB from the function
    or in *xDoc* from the procedure.

FUNCTION DBMS_XMLQUERY.getNumRowProcessed
  RETURN NUMBER;
    Returns the number of rows processed for the query.

PROCEDURE DBMS_XMLQUERY.getVersion;
    Prints the version number of the XSU (XML SQL Utility).

FUNCTION DBMS_XMLQUERY.getXML
  ({*sqlQuery* IN VARCHAR2 | *sqlQuery* IN CLOB | *ctxHandle* IN ctxType},
  metaType IN NUMBER := NONE)
  RETURN CLOB;

```
PROCEDURE DBMS_XMLQUERY.getXML
   (ctxHandle IN ctxType,
   xDoc IN CLOB,
   metaType IN NUMBER := NONE);
```
   The function can take the *sqlQuery* as a VARCHAR2, a CLOB, or *ctxHandle* and returns a CLOB. The procedure receives the XML in *xDoc*. *metaType* can be NONE, DTD, or SCHEMA.

DBMS_XMLSAVE

Implements XML-to database-type functionality. New with Oracle9*i*.

Calls

```
FUNCTION DBMS_XMLSAVE.newContext
   (targetTable IN VARCHAR2)
   RETURN ctxType;
```
   Returns the context handle for *targetTable*.

```
PROCEDURE DBMS_XMLSAVE.closeContext
   (ctxHandle IN ctxType);
```
   Closes and deallocates *ctxHandle*.

```
PROCEDURE DBMS_XMLSAVE.setRowTag
   (ctxHandle IN ctxType,
   tag IN VARCHAR2);
```
   Gives row *tag* for *ctxHandle*.

```
PROCEDURE DBMS_XMLSAVE.setIgnoreCase
   (ctxHandle IN ctxType,
   flag IN NUMBER);
```
   Specifies whether to ignore case on mapping of XML elements to database columns and attributes for *ctxHandle*.

```
PROCEDURE DBMS_XMLSAVE.setDateFormat
   (ctxHandle IN ctxType,
   mask IN VARCHAR2);
```
   Sets the date format to *mask* for *ctxHandle*.

```
PROCEDURE DBMS_XMLSAVE.setBatchSize
   (ctxHandle IN ctxType,
   batchsize IN NUMBER);
```
   Sets the batch size to *batchsize* for *ctxHandle*.

```
PROCEDURE DBMS_XMLSAVE.setCommitBatch
   (ctxHandle IN ctxType,
   batchsize IN NUMBER);
```
   Sets the commit batch size to *batchsize* for *ctxHandle*.

```
PROCEDURE DBMS_XMLSAVE.setSQLToXMLNameEscaping
   (ctxHandle IN ctxType,
   flag IN BOOLEAN := TRUE);
```
   Turns on and off escaping XML tags in case the SQL object name is not a valid XML identifier for *ctxHandle*.

PROCEDURE DBMS_XMLSAVE.setUpdateColumn
   (*ctxHandle* IN ctxType,
   colname IN VARCHAR2);
     Adds *colname* to update column list for *ctxHandle*.

PROCEDURE DBMS_XMLSAVE.clearUpdateColumnList
   (*ctxHandle* IN ctxType);
     Clears update column list for *ctxHandle*.

PROCEDURE DBMS_XMLSAVE.setPreserveWhitespace
   (*ctxHandle* IN ctxType,
   flag IN BOOLEAN := TRUE);
     Turns on and off whitespace preservation for *ctxHandle*.

PROCEDURE DBMS_XMLSAVE.setKeyColumn
   (*ctxHandle* IN ctxType,
   colname IN VARCHAR2);
     Adds *colname* to key column list for *ctxHandle*.

PROCEDURE DBMS_XMLSAVE.clearKeyColumnList
   (*ctxHandle* IN ctxType);
     Clears key column list for *ctxHandle*.

PROCEDURE DBMS_XMLQUERY.setXSLT
   (*ctxHandle* IN ctxType,
   uri IN {VARCHAR2 | CLOB},
   ref IN VARCHAR2 DEFAULT := NULL);
     Registers XSL transform at *uri* or included as a CLOB with *ref* (URL to include,
     export, and external entities) for *ctxHandle*.

PROCEDURE DBMS_XMLSAVE.setXSLTParam
   (*ctxHandle* IN ctxType,
   name IN VARCHAR2,
   value IN VARCHAR2);
     Sets *value* of parameter *name* in top-level stylesheet for *ctxHandle*.

PROCEDURE DBMS_XMLSAVE.setXSLTParam
   (*ctxHandle* IN ctxType,
   name IN VARCHAR2);
     Removes value for parameter *name* in top-level stylesheet for *ctxHandle*.

FUNCTION DBMS_XMLSAVE.insertXML
   (*ctxHandle* IN ctxType,
   xDoc IN VARCHAR2 | CLOB)
   RETURN NUMBER;
     Inserts *xDoc* into *ctxHandle* and returns number of rows inserted.

FUNCTION DBMS_XMLSAVE.updateXML
   (*ctxHandle* IN ctxType,
   xDoc IN VARCHAR2 | CLOB)
   RETURN NUMBER;
     Updates the table specified for *ctxHandle* with *xDoc* and returns the number of
     rows updated.

FUNCTION DBMS_XMLSAVE.deleteXML
   (*ctxHandle* IN ctxType,
   xDoc IN VARCHAR2 | CLOB)
   RETURN NUMBER;
     Deletes the table specified for *ctxHandle* with *xDoc* and returns the number of
     rows deleted.

PROCEDURE DBMS_XMLSAVE.propagateOriginalException
   (*ctxHandle* IN ctxType,
   flag IN BOOLEAN);
   Sets whether to throw exceptions rather than wrapping them with OracleXMLSQLException for *ctxHandle*.

PROCEDURE DBMS_XMLSAVE.getExceptionContent
   (*ctxHandle* IN ctxType,
   errNo OUT NUMBER,
   errMsg OUT VARCHAR2);
   Returns *errNo* and *errMsg* for exceptions for *ctxHandle*. Used to work around the fact that the JVM throws its own exception on top of the original exception.

DBMS_XMLSCHEMA

Provides procedures and functions to register and delete XML schemas. New with Oracle9*i*.

Calls

PROCEDURE DBMS_XMLSCHEMA.registerSchema
   (*schemaURL* IN VARCHAR2,
   schemaDoc IN {VARCHAR2 | CLOB | BFILE | SYS.XMLType | SYS.URIType},
   local IN BOOLEAN := TRUE,
   genTypes IN BOOLEAN := TRUE,
   genbean IN BOOLEAN := FALSE,
   [*genTables* IN BOOLEAN := TRUE,]
   force IN BOOLEAN := FALSE,
   owner IN VARCHAR2 := NULL);
   Registers *schemaDoc*, which has a datatype varying according to the type of schema being registered, with the URL of *schemaURL*. If *local*, the schema is local; if not, the schema is global. If *genTypes*, the schema compiler will generate object types. If *genbean*, the schema compiler will generate object types. If *force*, the schema registration will not raise errors and will instead create an invalid XML schema. *owner* is the database owner who owns the XML schema; if *owner* is NULL, the user owns the schema. *genTables* is used only for the VARCHAR2 datatype of *schemaDoc* and causes the schema compiler to generate tables.

PROCEDURE DBMS_XMLSCHEMA.registerURI
   (*schemaURL* IN VARCHAR2,
   schemaDocURI IN VARCHAR2,
   local IN BOOLEAN := TRUE,
   genTypes IN BOOLEAN := TRUE,
   genbean IN BOOLEAN := FALSE,
   genTables IN BOOLEAN := TRUE,
   force IN BOOLEAN := FALSE,
   owner IN VARCHAR2 := NULL);
   Registers the schema at *schemaDocURI* with the URL of *schemaURL*. If *local*, the schema is local; if not, the schema is global. If *genTypes*, the schema compiler will generate object types. If *genbean*, the schema compiler will generate object types. If *genTables*, the schema compiler will generate tables. If *force*, schema registration will not raise errors and will instead create an invalid XML schema. *owner* is the database owner who owns the XML schema; if *owner* is NULL, the user owns the schema.

```
PROCEDURE DBMS_XMLSCHEMA.deleteSchema
  (schemaURL IN VARCHAR2,
  delete_option IN PLS_INTEGER := DELETE_RESTRICT);
```
Deletes the schema at *schemaURL*. *delete_option* can be DELETE_RESTRICT, DELETE_INVALIDATE, DELETE_CASCADE, or DELETE_CASCADE_ FORCE.

```
PROCEDURE DBMS_XMLSCHEMA.generateBean
  (schemaURL IN VARCHAR2);
```
Generates JavaBeans code for *schemaURL*.

```
PROCEDURE DBMS_XMLSCHEMA.compileSchema
  (schemaURL IN VARCHAR2);
```
Recompiles schema *schemaURL*.

```
FUNCTION DBMS_XMLSCHEMA.generateSchema
  (schemaName IN VARCHAR2,
  typeName IN VARCHAR2,
  elementName IN VARCHAR2 := NULL,
  {schemaURL IN VARCHAR2 := NULL | recurse IN BOOLEAN := TRUE},
  annotate IN BOOLEAN := TRUE,
  embedCol IN BOOLEAN := TRUE)
  RETURN {SYS.XMLSequenceType | SYS.XMLType};
```
Generates a schema from *schemaName* of *typeName*. The top-level element is *elementName*. The *schemaURL* is the base URL for storing schemas. If *schemaURL* is used, the function returns one XMLSchema for each database schema. *recurse* indicates whether or not to also generate schemas for all types referred to. If *recurse*, the function returns all schemas in a single XMLType. If *annotate*, the function puts annotations in XMLSchema. If *embedCol*, the function embeds collections in the type that refers to them; if not, it creates a complex type.

DBMS_XPLAN

Provides a function to format the output of the EXPLAIN PLAN statement. New with Oracle9*i*. This function is used as part of a SQL statement, as in:
```
SELECT * FROM TABLE(DBMS_XPLAN.DISPLAY());
```

Call

```
FUNCTION DBMS_XPLAN.DISPLAY
  (table_name IN VARCHAR2 DEFAULT 'PLAN_TABLE',
  statement_id IN VARCHAR2 DEFAULT NULL,
  format IN VARCHAR2 DEFAULT 'TYPICAL');
```
Displays information from EXPLAIN PLAN stored in *table_name* with an optional *statement_id* for the plan. Valid values for *format* are BASIC, TYPICAL, and ALL, which offer increasing levels of information, and SERIAL, which excludes information about the parallelism of the plan.

DBMS_XSLPROCESSOR

Used to access the contents and structure of XML documents. New with Oracle9*i*.

Calls

FUNCTION DBMS_XSLPROCESSOR.newProcessor
  RETURN Processor;
    Creates a new XSL processor instance and returns a handle to it.

FUNCTION DBMS_XSLPROCESSOR.processXSL
  (*p* IN Processor,
  ss IN Stylesheet,
  {*xmldoc* IN DOMDoc | *url* IN VARCHAR})
  RETURN DOMDocumentFragment;
    Transforms *xmldoc* or the document at *url*, using *p* and *ss*.

PROCEDURE DBMS_XSLPROCESSOR.showWarnings
  (*p* IN Processor,
  yes IN BOOLEAN);
    Turns warnings on or off for *p*, depending on *yes*.

PROCEDURE DBMS_XSLPROCESSOR.setErrorLog
  (*p* IN Processor,
  fileName IN VARCHAR2);
    Sets the location for the error log for *p* to *fileName*.

FUNCTION DBMS_XSLPROCESSOR.newStylesheet
  ({*xmldoc* IN DOMDocument | *inp* IN VARCHAR2},
  ref IN VARCHAR2)
  RETURN Stylesheet;
    Creates and returns a new instance of a stylesheet, using either *xmldoc* or *inp*, which is a URL to use for construction of the stylesheet, and the reference URL of *ref*.

FUNCTION DBMS_XSLPROCESSOR.transformNode
  (*n* IN DOMNode,
  ss IN STYLESHEET)
  RETURN DOMDocumentFragment;
    Transforms node *n* using *ss* and returns result.

FUNCTION DBMS_XSLPROCESSOR.selectNodes
  (*n* IN DOMNode,
  pattern IN VARCHAR2)
  RETURN DOMNodeList;
    Selects and returns nodes from the XML tree with root *n* that match *pattern*.

FUNCTION DBMS_XSLPROCESSOR.selectNodes
  (*n* IN DOMNode,
  pattern IN VARCHAR2)
  RETURN DOMNode;
    Selects and returns the first node from the XML tree with root *n* that matches *pattern*.

```
PROCEDURE DBMS_XSLPROCESSOR.valueOf
    (n IN DOMNode,
    pattern IN VARCHAR2
    val OUT VARCHAR2);
```
Selects and returns the first node from the XML tree with root *n* that matches *pattern* and returns in *val*.

```
PROCEDURE DBMS_XSLPROCESSOR.setParam
    (ss IN STYLESHEET,
    name IN VARCHAR2,
    value IN VARCHAR2);
```
Sets parameter *name* in *ss* to *value*.

```
PROCEDURE DBMS_XSLPROCESSOR.setParam
    (ss IN STYLESHEET,
    name IN VARCHAR2);
```
Removes parameter *name* from *ss*.

```
PROCEDURE DBMS_XSLPROCESSOR.resetParams
    (ss IN Stylesheet);
```
Resets parameters for top-level stylesheet *ss*.

```
PROCEDURE DBMS_XSLPROCESSOR.freeStylesheet
    (ss IN Stylesheet);
```
Frees top-level stylesheet *ss*.

```
PROCEDURE DBMS_XSLPROCESSOR.freeProcessor
    (p IN Processor);
```
Frees processor *p*.

DEBUG_EXTPROC

Starts up the *extproc* agent for a session and helps you to debug external procedures. You must run *DBGEXTP.SQL* to install the package. New with Oracle9i.

Call

```
PROCEDURE DEBUG_EXTPROC;
```
Starts up the *extproc* process in the session, which lets you get the process ID (PID) for the executing process.

OUTLN_PKG

This package was replaced by DBMS_OUTLINE in Oracle9i.

UTL_COLL

Lets PL/SQL programs use collection locators to query and update. New with Oracle9i.

Call

```
FUNCTION UTL_COLL.IS_LOCATOR
    (collection IN ANY)
    RETURN BOOLEAN;
```
Returns whether *collection* is a locator.

UTL_ENCODE

Provides functions to encode RAW data for transport between hosts. New with Oracle9*i*.

Calls

FUNCTION UTL_ENCODE.BASE64_ENCODE
    (*r* IN RAW)
    RETURN RAW;
      Encodes and returns the RAW value, *r*, into base 64 elements.

FUNCTION UTL_ENCODE.BASE64_DECODE
    (*r* IN RAW)
    RETURN RAW;
      Decodes and returns the RAW value, *r*, from base 64 elements.

FUNCTION UTL_ENCODE.UUENCODE
    (*r* IN RAW,
    type IN PLS_INTEGER DEFAULT 1,
    filename IN VARCHAR2 DEFAULT NULL,
    permission IN VARCHAR2 DEFAULT NULL)
    RETURN RAW;
      Encodes and returns *r* in type. *type* can be COMPLETE (the default), HEADER_PIECE, MIDDLE_PIECE, or END_PIECE. *filename* is the optional *uuencode* filename.

FUNCTION UTL_ENCODE.UUDECODE
    (*r* IN RAW)
    RETURN RAW;
      Decodes from *uuencode* format and returns *r*.

FUNCTION UTL_ENCODE.QUOTED_PRINTABLE_ENCODE
    (*r* IN RAW)
    RETURN RAW;
      Encodes and returns *r* as a quoted printable format string.

FUNCTION UTL_ENCODE.QUOTED_PRINTABLE_DECODE
    (*r* IN RAW)
    RETURN RAW;
      Decodes and returns *r* from a quoted printable format string.

UTL_FILE

Allows PL/SQL programs to read from and write to operating system files on the server where the Oracle database resides.

Calls

PROCEDURE UTL_FILE.FCLOSE
    (*file* IN OUT FILE_TYPE);
      Closes the file identified by file handle *file* and sets the value of file ID to NULL.

PROCEDURE UTL_FILE.FCLOSE_ALL;
      Closes all opened files; however, the ID fields of any file handles will not be set to NULL.

PROCEDURE UTL_FILE.FCOPY
   (*location* IN VARCHAR2,
   filename IN VARCHAR2,
   dest_dir IN VARCHAR2,
   dest_file IN VARCHAR2,
   start_line IN PLS_INTEGER DEFAULT 1,
   end_line IN PLS_INTEGER DEFAULT NULL);

    Copies *filename* in location to *dest_file* in *dest_dir*. *start_line* and *end_line* are used to copy a portion of filename. New with Oracle9*i*.

PROCEDURE UTL_FILE.FFLUSH
   (*file* IN FILE_TYPE
   [, *invalid_maxlinesize* EXCEPTION]#);

    Forces any buffered data for file handle *file* to be written out immediately. *invalid_maxlinesize* (new with Oracle9*i*) can be INVALID_FILENAME, INVALID_OPERATION, or WRITE_ERROR.

PROCEDURE UTL_FILE.FGETATTR
   (*location* IN VARCHAR2,
   filename IN VARCHAR2,
   exists OUT BOOLEAN,
   file_length OUT NUMBER,
   blocksize OUT NUMBER);

    Returns attributes *exists*, *file_length,* and *blocksize* of *filename* in location. New with Oracle9*i*.

FUNCTION UTL_FILE.FGETPOS
   (*fileid* IN FILE_TYPE)
   RETURN PLS_INTEGER;

    Returns the current offset position in *fileid*, in bytes. New with Oracle9*i*.

PROCEDURE UTL_FILE.FREMOVE
   (*location* IN VARCHAR2,
   filename IN VARCHAR2);

    Deletes *filename* in directory *location*. New with Oracle9*i*.

PROCEDURE UTL_FILE.FRENAME
   (*location* IN VARCHAR2,
   filename IN VARCHAR2,
   dest_dir IN VARCHAR2,
   dest_file IN VARCHAR2,
   overwrite IN BOOLEAN DEFAULT FALSE);

    Renames *filename* in location to *dest_file* in *dest_dir*. If *overwrite*, overwrites an existing file with the same name. New with Oracle9*i*.

PROCEDURE UTL_FILE.FSEEK
   (*fid* IN UTL_FILE.FILE_TYPE,
   absolute_offset IN PLS_INTEGER DEFAULT NULL,
   relative_offset IN PLS_INTEGER DEFAULT NULL);

    Adjusts the file pointer for *fid* to either an *absolute_offset* or a *relative_offset*, which can be positive, negative, or NULL. New with Oracle9*i*.

FUNCTION UTL_FILE.FOPEN
   (*location* IN VARCHAR2,
   filename IN VARCHAR2,
   open_mode IN VARCHAR2

```
[, max_linesize IN BINARY_INTEGER]#);
RETURN FILE_TYPE;
```
Returns a file handle of type UTL_FILE.FILE_TYPE upon successfully opening file *filename* in directory *location* in mode *open_mode* or raises an exception. Valid *open_mode* values are:

R   open file in read-only mode.

W   open file in read-write mode and replace contents.

A   open file in read-write mode and append to contents.

Valid *location* values are directories specified by the Oracle initialization parameter UTL_FILE_DIR. *max_linesize* (new in Oracle9*i*) is the maximum number of characters per line, including the newline character, for the file.

```
FUNCTION UTL_FILE.FOPEN_NCHAR
    (location IN VARCHAR2,
    filename IN VARCHAR2,
    open_mode IN VARCHAR2
    [, max_linesize IN BINARY_INTEGER]#);
    RETURN FILE_TYPE;
```
Same parameters as FOPEN but used for Unicode files. New with Oracle9*i*.

```
PROCEDURE UTL_FILE.GET_LINE
    (file IN FILE_TYPE,
    buffer OUT VARCHAR2
    [,linesize IN NUMBER]#
    [,len IN PLS_INTEGER DEFAULT NULL]#);
```
Reads the next line in file handle *file* into *buffer*. Raises the NO_DATA_FOUND exception when reading past end-of-file and the VALUE_ERROR exception when *buffer* is too small for the data. The *linesize* (which specifies the maximum number of bytes to be read) and *len* (which is the number of bytes read from the file) parameters are new with Oracle9*i*.

```
PROCEDURE UTL_FILE.GET_LINE_NCHAR
    (file IN FILE_TYPE,
    buffer OUT VARCHAR2
    [,linesize IN NUMBER]#
    [,len IN PLS_INTEGER DEFAULT NULL]#);
```
Same parameter values as GET_LINE, but for Unicode files. New with Oracle9*i*.

```
FUNCTION UTL_FILE.IS_OPEN
    (file IN FILE_TYPE)
    RETURN BOOLEAN;
```
Returns TRUE if the file handle *file* is currently open in any mode and FALSE otherwise.

```
FUNCTION UTL_FILE.GET_RAW
    (fid IN UTL_FILE.FILE_TYPE,
    r OUT NOCOPY RAW,
    len IN PLS_INTEGER DEFAULT NULL);
```
Returns RAW string *r* with file ID *fid*. *len* is the number of bytes read from the file. New with Oracle9*i*.

```
PROCEDURE UTL_FILE.NEW_LINE
    (file IN FILE_TYPE,
    lines IN NATURAL := 1);
```
Places *lines* newline characters into file handle *file*.

PROCEDURE UTL_FILE.PUT
  (*file* IN FILE_TYPE,
  buffer IN VARCHAR2);
    Places the data in *buffer* into file handle *file* without a newline terminator.

PROCEDURE UTL_FILE.PUT_NCHAR
  (*file* IN FILE_TYPE,
  buffer IN VARCHAR2);
    Same parameters as PUT, but for Unicode characters. New with Oracle9*i*.

PROCEDURE UTL_FILE.PUT_RAW
  (*fid* IN UTL_FILE.FILE_TYPE,
  r IN RAW
  [,*autoflush* IN BOOLEAN DEFAULT FALSE]#);
    Writes RAW values in *r* to *fid*. If *autoflush* (new with Oracle9*i*), flushes after writing the value. New with Oracle9*i*.

PROCEDURE UTL_FILE.PUT_LINE
  (*file* IN FILE_TYPE,
  buffer IN VARCHAR2
  [, *autoflush* IN BOOLEAN DEFAULT FALSE]#);
    Places the data in *buffer* into file handle *file* with a newline character appended. If *autoflush* (new with Oracle9*i*), flushes after writing the value.

PROCEDURE UTL_FILE.PUT_LINE_NCHAR
  (*file* IN FILE_TYPE,
  buffer IN VARCHAR2);
    Same parameters as PUT_LINE, but for Unicode file. New with Oracle9*i*.

PROCEDURE UTL_FILE.PUTF
  (*file* IN FILE_TYPE,
  format IN VARCHAR2,
  arg1 IN VARCHAR2 DEFAULT NULL,
  arg2 IN VARCHAR2 DEFAULT NULL,
  arg3 IN VARCHAR2 DEFAULT NULL,
  arg4 IN VARCHAR2 DEFAULT NULL,
  arg5 IN VARCHAR2 DEFAULT NULL);
    Writes a formatted message out to file handle *file* using *format* as the template, replacing up to five %s format elements with the values of *arg1* through *arg5*. *format* can contain the following items: any literal text, %s indicating *argN* substitution (up to five allowed), or \n indicating newline (any number allowed).

PROCEDURE UTL_FILE.PUTF_NCHAR
  (*file* IN FILE_TYPE,
  format IN VARCHAR2,
  arg1 IN VARCHAR2 DEFAULT NULL,
  arg2 IN VARCHAR2 DEFAULT NULL,
  arg3 IN VARCHAR2 DEFAULT NULL,
  arg4 IN VARCHAR2 DEFAULT NULL,
  arg5 IN VARCHAR2 DEFAULT NULL);
    Same parameters as PUTF, but for Unicode *file*. New with Oracle9*i*.

UTL_HTTP

Provides procedures and functions to make HTTP callouts from SQL and PL/SQL. With Oracle8, this package contained only the REQUEST and REQUEST PIECES functions.

Calls

This section specifies the UTL_HTTP calls in several different categories: simple HTTP fetches, HTTP session settings, HTTP requests, HTTP responses, HTTP cookies, HTTP persistent connections, and HTTP error conditions.

Simple HTTP fetches

```
FUNCTION UTL_HTTP.REQUEST
   (url IN VARCHAR2,
   proxy IN VARCHAR2 DEFAULT NULL
   [,wallet_path IN VARCHAR2 DEFAULT NULL]#
   [,wallet_password IN VARCHAR2 DEFAULT NULL]#)
   RETURN VARCHAR2;
```
   Returns the first 2000 bytes of *url* through optional *proxy*, which was new with Oracle8*i*. Can include the *wallet_path* and *wallet_password* parameters, both new with Oracle9*i*.

```
FUNCTION UTL_HTTP.REQUEST_PIECES
   (url IN VARCHAR2,
   max_pieces IN NATURAL DEFAULT 32767,
   proxy IN VARCHAR2 DEFAULT NULL
   [,wallet_path IN VARCHAR2 DEFAULT NULL]#
   [,wallet_password IN VARCHAR2 DEFAULT NULL]#)
   RETURN VARCHAR2;
```
   Returns *max_pieces* of 2000 bytes of *url* through optional *proxy*. Can include the *wallet_path* and *wallet_password* parameters, both new with Oracle9*i*.

HTTP session settings

```
PROCEDURE UTL_HTTP.SET_PROXY
   (proxy IN VARCHAR2,
   no_proxy_domains IN VARCHAR2);
```
   Sets the *proxy* and can include the domains that will not use proxies at *no_proxy_domains*.

```
PROCEDURE UTL_HTTP.GET_PROXY
   (proxy OUT NOCOPY VARCHAR2,
   no_proxy_domains OUT NOCOPY VARCHAR2);
```
   Gets the *proxy* and can include the domains that will not use proxies at *no_proxy_domains*.

```
PROCEDURE UTL_HTTP.GET_COOKIE_SUPPORT
   (enable IN BOOLEAN,
   max_cookies IN PLS_INTEGER DEFAULT 300,
   max_cookies_per_site IN PLS_INTEGER DEFAULT 20);
```
   Sets whether or not cookies are *enabled*, the maximum number of cookies per session (*max_cookies*), and the maximum number of cookies per database (*max_cookies_per_site*).

PROCEDURE UTL_HTTP.SET_COOKIE_SUPPORT
(*enable* OUT BOOLEAN,
max_cookies OUT PLS_INTEGER,
max_cookies_per_site OUT PLS_INTEGER);

Gets whether or not cookies are *enabled*, the maximum number of cookies per session (*max_cookies*), and the maximum number of cookies per database (*max_cookies_per_site*).

PROCEDURE UTL_HTTP.SET_FOLLOW_REDIRECT
(*max_redirects* IN PLS_INTEGER DEFAULT 3);

Sets the maximum number of times a UTL_HTTP follows the HTTP redirect instruction.

PROCEDURE UTL_HTTP.GET_FOLLOW_REDIRECT
(*max_redirects* OUT PLS_INTEGER);

Gets the maximum number of times a UTL_HTTP follows the HTTP redirect instruction.

PROCEDURE UTL_HTTP.SET_BODY_CHARSET
(*charset* IN VARCHAR2 DEFAULT NULL);

Sets the default character set of the body of all future HTTP requests.

PROCEDURE UTL_HTTP.GET_BODY_CHARSET
(*charset* OUT VARCHAR2 NOCOPY);

Gets the default character set of the body of all future HTTP requests.

PROCEDURE UTL_HTTP.SET_PERSISTENT_CONN_SUPPORT
(*enable* IN BOOLEAN,
max_conns IN PLS_INTEGER DEFAULT 0);

Sets whether persistent connections are supported (*enable*) and how many (*max_conns*).

PROCEDURE UTL_HTTP.GET_PERSISTENT_CONN_SUPPORT
(*enable* OUT BOOLEAN,
max_conns OUT PLS_INTEGER);

Gets whether persistent connections are supported (*enable*) and how many (*max_conns*).

PROCEDURE UTL_HTTP.SET_RESPONSE_ERROR_CHECK
(*enable* IN BOOLEAN DEFAULT FALSE);

Sets whether GET_RESPONSE raises an exception on a web server error.

PROCEDURE UTL_HTTP.GET_RESPONSE_ERROR_CHECK
(*enable* IN BOOLEAN);

Gets whether GET_RESPONSE raises an exception on a web server error.

PROCEDURE UTL_HTTP.SET_DETAILED_EXCP_SUPPORT
(*enable* IN BOOLEAN DEFAULT FALSE);

Sets whether GET_RESPONSE raises a detailed exception on a web server error.

PROCEDURE UTL_HTTP.GET_DETAILED_EXCP_SUPPORT
(*enable* IN BOOLEAN);

Gets whether GET_RESPONSE raises a detailed exception on a web server error.

PROCEDURE UTL_HTTP.SET_WALLET
(*path* IN VARCHAR2,
password IN VARCHAR2 DEFAULT NULL);

Sets the *path* that contains the Oracle wallet and sends the *password* for the wallet used for HTTP requests over SSL.

PROCEDURE UTL_HTTP.SET_TRANSFER_TIMEOUT
    (*timeout* IN PLS_INTEGER DEFAULT 60);
      Sets the default *timeout* for all future UTL_HTTP requests attempted while reading HTTP responses from the web or proxy server.

HTTP requests

FUNCTION UTL_HTTP.BEGIN_REQUEST
    (*url* IN VARCHAR2,
    method IN VARCHAR2 DEFAULT 'GET',
    http_version IN VARCHAR2 DEFAULT NULL)
    RETURN REQ;
      Begins a new HTTP request to *url* with *method* and *http_version*. Returns the *req* handle.

PROCEDURE UTL_HTTP.SET_HEADER
    (*r* IN OUT NOCOPY REQ,
    name IN VARCHAR2,
    value IN VARCHAR2);
      Sets the request header *name* to *value* for request *r*.

PROCEDURE UTL_HTTP.SET_AUTHENTICATION
    (*r* IN OUT NOCOPY req,
    username IN VARCHAR2,
    password IN VARCHAR2,
    scheme IN VARCHAR2 DEFAULT 'Basic',
    for_proxy IN BOOLEAN DEFAULT FALSE);
      Sets *username/password* for HTTP authentication *scheme* for request *r*. If *for_proxy*, identifies that authentication is for proxy server.

PROCEDURE UTL_HTTP.SET_COOKIE_SUPPORT
    (*r* IN OUT NOCOPY REQ,
    enable IN BOOLEAN DEFAULT TRUE);
      Enables cookie support for request *r*.

PROCEDURE UTL_HTTP.SET_FOLLOW_REDIRECT
    (*r* IN OUT NOCOPY REQ,
    max_redirects IN PLS_INTEGER DEFAULT 3);
      Changes the *max_redirects* request *r* inherits from default session setting.

PROCEDURE UTL_HTTP.SET_BODY_CHARSET
    (*r* IN OUT NOCOPY REQ,
    charset IN VARCHAR2 DEFAULT NULL);
      Changes the *charset* request *r* inherits from default session setting.

PROCEDURE UTL_HTTP.SET_PERSISTENT_CONN_SUPPORT
    (*r* IN OUT NOCOPY REQ,
    enable IN BOOLEAN DEFAULT TRUE);
      Enables persistent connection support for request *r*.

PROCEDURE UTL_HTTP.WRITE_TEXT
    (*r* IN OUT NOCOPY REQ,
    data IN VARCHAR2);
      Writes data to HTTP request body for request *r*.

PROCEDURE UTL_HTTP.WRITE_LINE
    (*r* IN OUT NOCOPY REQ,
    data IN VARCHAR2);
      Writes data to HTTP request body for request *r* and ends the line with a newline.

```
)CEDURE UTL_HTTP.WRITE_RAW
  (r IN OUT NOCOPY REQ,
  data IN RAW);
```
Writes raw data to HTTP request body for request *r*.

```
PROCEDURE UTL_HTTP.END_REQUEST
  (r IN OUT NOCOPAY REQ);
```
Ends request *r*.

HTTP responses

```
FUNCTION UTL_HTTP.GET_RESPONSE
  (r IN OUT NOCOPY REQ)
  RETURN resp;
```
Returns handle to response for request *r*.

```
FUNCTION UTL_HTTP.GET_HEADER_COUNT
  (r IN OUT NOCOPY REQ)
  RETURN PLS_INTEGER;
```
Returns number of response headers for response *r*.

```
PROCEDURE UTL_HTTP.GET_HEADER
  (r IN OUT NOCOPY RESP,
  n IN PLS_INTEGER,
  name OUT NOCOPY VARCHAR2,
  value OUT NOCOPY VARCHAR2);
```
Returns *name* and *value* of *n*th response header for response *r*.

```
PROCEDURE UTL_HTTP.GET_HEADER_BY_NAME
  (r IN OUT NOCOPY RESP,
  name IN VARCHAR2,
  name OUT NOCOPY VARCHAR2,
  value OUT NOCOPY VARCHAR2);
```
Returns *name* and *value* of *name* response header for response *r*.

```
PROCEDURE UTL_HTTP.GET_AUTHENTICATION
  (r IN OUT NOCOPY RESP,
  scheme OUT VARCHAR2,
  realm OUT VARCHAR2,
  for_proxy IN BOOLEAN DEFAULT FALSE);
```
Returns *scheme* and *realm* for required HTTP authentication for response *r*. If *for_proxy*, information applies to access proxy server.

```
PROCEDURE UTL_HTTP.SET_BODY_CHARSET
  (r IN OUT NOCOPY RESP,
  charset IN VARCHAR2 DEFAULT NULL);
```
Sets *charset* for response *r* when media type is 'TEXT' but character set is not specified in the 'Content-Type' header.

```
PROCEDURE UTL_HTTP.READ_TEXT
  (r IN OUT NOCOPY RESP,
  data OUT NOCOPY VARCHAR2,
  len IN PLS_INTEGER DEFAULT NULL);
```
Returns response body of *r* in *data*, up to *len*. If *len* is NULL, will fill buffer.

```
PROCEDURE UTL_HTTP.READ_LINE
    (r IN OUT NOCOPY RESP,
    data OUT NOCOPY VARCHAR2,
    remove_crlf IN BOOLEAN DEFAULT FALSE);
```
Returns response body of *r* in *data*, up to the end of the line. If *remove_crls*, removes the newline characters.

```
PROCEDURE UTL_HTTP.READ_RAW
    (r IN OUT NOCOPY RESP,
    data OUT NOCOPY RAW,
    len IN PLS_INTEGER DEFAULT NULL);
```
Returns response body of *r* in *data*, up to *len*, and returns it as RAW data. If *len* is NULL, will fill buffer.

```
PROCEDURE UTL_HTTP.END_RESPONSE
    (r IN OUT NOCOPY RESP);
```
Ends response *r*.

HTTP cookies

```
FUNCTION UTL_HTTP.GET_COOKIE_COUNT
    RETURN PLS_INTEGER;
```
Returns the number of cookies currently maintained by the UTL_HTTP package for all servers.

```
PROCEDURE UTL_HTTP.GET_COOKIES
    (cookies IN OUT NOCOPY COOKIE_TABLE);
```
Returns the *cookies* currently maintained by the UTL_HTTP package for all servers.

```
PROCEDURE UTL_HTTP.ADD_COOKIES
    (cookies IN NOCOPY COOKIE_TABLE);
```
Adds *cookies* to be maintained by the UTL_HTTP package.

```
PROCEDURE UTL_HTTP.CLEAR_COOKIES;
```
Clears the *cookies* currently maintained by the UTL_HTTP package for all servers.

HTTP persistent connections

```
FUNCTION UTL_HTTP.GET_PERSISTENT_CONN_COUNT
    RETURN PLS_INTEGER;
```
Returns the number of persistent connections maintained by the UTL_HTTP package.

```
PROCEDURE UTL_HTTP.GET_PERSISTENT_CONN
    (connections IN OUT NOCOPY CONNECTION_TABLE);
```
Returns the persistent connection maintained by the UTL_HTTP package.

```
PROCEDURE UTL_HTTP.CLOSE_PERSISTENT_CONN
    (conn IN connection);
```
Closes the persistent connection *conn*.

```
PROCEDURE UTL_HTTP.CLOSE_PERSISTENT_CONNS
    (host IN VARCHAR2 DEFAULT NULL,
    port IN PLS_INTEGER DEFAULT NULL,
    proxy_host IN VARCHAR2 DEFAULT NULL,
```

```
proxy_port IN PLS_INTEGER DEFAULT NULL,
ssl IN BOOLEAN DEFAULT NULL);
```
Closes persistent connections for *port* on *host* or *proxy_port* on *proxy_host*. If *ssl*, closes persistent SSL connection. Making the call without any parameters closes all persistent connections.

HTTP error conditions

```
FUNCTION UTL_HTTP.GET_DETAILED_SQLCODE
    RETURN PLS_INTEGER;
```
Retrieves the detailed SQLCODE of the last exception.

```
FUNCTION UTL_HTTP.GET_DETAILED_SQLERRM
    RETURN VARCHAR2;
```
Retrieves the detailed SQLERRM of the last exception.

UTL_INADDR

Provides functions to support Internet addressing. New with Oracle9*i*.

Calls

```
FUNCTION UTL_INADDR.GET_HOST_NAME
    (ip IN VARCHAR2 DEFAULT NULL)
    RETURN VARCHAR2;
```
Returns the name of the local or remote host of *ip* address.

```
FUNCTION UTL_INADDR.GET_HOST_ADDRESS
    (name IN VARCHAR2 DEFAULT NULL)
    RETURN VARCHAR2;
```
Returns the address of the *name* host. If *name* is NULL, returns the address of the local host.

UTL_RAW

Provides routines for accessing and manipulating RAW datatypes. These routines perform conversions, divisions, combinations, and bitwise operations on RAW datatypes.

Calls

```
FUNCTION UTL_RAW.BIT_AND
    (r1 IN RAW,
    r2 IN RAW)
    RETURN RAW;
```
Returns the bitwise logical AND of *r1* and *r2*.

```
FUNCTION UTL_RAW.BIT_COMPLEMENT
    (r1 IN RAW,
    r2 IN RAW)
    RETURN RAW;
```
Returns the bitwise logical complement of *r1* and *r2*.

```
FUNCTION UTL_RAW.BIT_OR
   (r1 IN RAW,
   r2 IN RAW)
   RETURN RAW;
```
   Returns the bitwise logical OR of *r1* and *r2*.

```
FUNCTION UTL_RAW.BIT_XOR
   (r1 IN RAW,
   r2 IN RAW)
   RETURN RAW;
```
   Returns the bitwise logical XOR of *r1* and *r2*.

```
FUNCTION UTL_RAW.CAST_FROM_BINARY_INTEGER
   (n IN BINARY_INTEGER,
   endianess IN PLS_INTEGER DEFAULT BIG_ENDIAN)
   RETURN RAW;
```
   Returns the raw binary representation of *n*. *endianess* is either BIG_ENDIAN or LITTLE_ENDIAN. New with Oracle9*i*.

```
FUNCTION UTL_RAW.CAST_FROM_NUMBER
   (n IN BINARY_INTEGER,
   include_length IN BOOLEAN)
   RETURN RAW;
```
   Returns the raw binary representation of *n*. If not *include_length*, the return is variable length with a maximum length of 21 bytes. New with Oracle9*i*.

```
FUNCTION UTL_RAW.CAST_TO_BINARY_INTEGER
   (r IN RAW,
   endianess IN PLS_INTEGER DEFAULT BIG_ENDIAN)
   RETURN BINARY_INTEGER;
```
   Returns the binary representation of *r*. *endianess* is either BIG_ENDIAN or LITTLE_ENDIAN. New with Oracle9*i*.

```
FUNCTION UTL_RAW.CAST_TO_NUMBER
   (r IN RAW,
   include_length IN BOOLEAN)
   RETURN RAW;
```
   Returns the binary representation of *r*. If not *include_length*, the return is variable length with a maximum length of 21 bytes plus the length byte, which is the first byte of the return. New with Oracle9*i*.

```
FUNCTION UTL_RAW.CAST_TO_RAW
   (c IN VARCHAR2)
   RETURN RAW;
```
   Returns VARCHAR2 *c* to RAW, converting datatype only.

```
FUNCTION UTL_RAW.CAST_TO_VARCHAR2
   (r IN RAW)
   RETURN VARCHAR2;
```
   Returns RAW *c* to VARCHAR2, converting datatype only.

```
FUNCTION UTL_RAW.COMPARE
   (r1 IN RAW,
   r2 IN RAW,
   pad IN RAW DEFAULT NULL)
   RETURN NUMBER;
```
   Returns 0 if *r1* and *r2* are identical. Returns the first byte position of the difference in *r1* and *r2*. If *r1* and *r2* are different lengths, right-pads the shorter with *pad*.

```
FUNCTION UTL_RAW.CONCAT
   (r1 IN RAW DEFAULT NULL,
   r2 IN RAW DEFAULT NULL,
   r3 IN RAW DEFAULT NULL,
   r4 IN RAW DEFAULT NULL,
   r5 IN RAW DEFAULT NULL,
   r6 IN RAW DEFAULT NULL,
   r7 IN RAW DEFAULT NULL,
   r8 IN RAW DEFAULT NULL,
   r9 IN RAW DEFAULT NULL,
   r10 IN RAW DEFAULT NULL,
   r11 IN RAW DEFAULT NULL,
   r12 IN RAW DEFAULT NULL)
   RETURN RAW;
```

Returns the concatenation of *r1* through *r12*. The result must be less than 32K. *r3* through *r12* are optional.

```
FUNCTION UTL_RAW.CONVERT
   (r IN RAW,
   to_charset IN VARCHAR2,
   from_charset IN VARCHAR2)
   RETURN RAW;
```

Returns *r* in *to_charset* after conversion from *from_charset*. *from_ charset* and *to_ charset* are National Language Support (NLS) character sets.

```
FUNCTION UTL_RAW.COPIES
   (r IN RAW,
   n IN NUMBER)
   RETURN RAW;
```

Concatenates *r*, *n* number of times, and returns the result.

```
FUNCTION UTL_RAW.LENGTH
      (r IN RAW)
   RETURN NUMBER;
```

Returns the number of bytes in *r*.

```
FUNCTION UTL_RAW.OVERLAY
   (overlay_str IN RAW,
   target IN RAW,
   pos IN BINARY_INTEGER DEFAULT 1,
   len IN BINARY_INTEGER DEFAULT NULL,
   pad IN RAW DEFAULT NULL)
   RETURN RAW;
```

Returns the *target* overlaid with the *overlay_str* string beginning *pos* bytes into *target* and continuing for *len* bytes, right-padding with *pad* as necessary. If *pos* is greater than the length of *target*, fills the missing section with *pad*.

```
FUNCTION UTL_RAW.REVERSE
   (r IN RAW)
   RETURN RAW;
```

Returns the bytes in *r* in reverse order.

```
FUNCTION UTL_RAW.SUBSTR
   (r IN RAW,
   pos IN BINARY_INTEGER,
   len IN BINARY_INTEGER DEFAULT NULL)
   RETURN RAW;
```

Returns a portion of *r* beginning at *pos* and extending for *len* bytes.

```
FUNCTION UTL_RAW.TRANSLATE
   (r IN RAW,
   from_set IN RAW,
   to_set IN RAW)
   RETURN RAW;
```
Returns the contents of *r*, translating bytes found in *from_set* to *to_ set*. If *from_ set* is longer than *to_set*, the unmatched bytes are removed from *r*.

```
FUNCTION UTL_RAW.TRANSLITERATE
   (r IN RAW,
   to_set IN RAW DEFAULT NULL,
   from_set IN RAW DEFAULT NULL,
   pad IN RAW DEFAULT NULL)
   RETURN RAW;
```
Returns the contents of *r*, translating bytes found in *from_set* to *to_ set*. If *from_ set* is longer than *to_set*, the unmatched bytes are translated to *pad*.

```
FUNCTION UTL_RAW.XRANGE
   (start_byte IN RAW DEFAULT NULL,
   end_byte IN RAW DEFAULT NULL)
   RETURN RAW;
```
Returns a raw string containing all bytes in order between *start_byte* and *end_ byte*, inclusive. If *start_byte* is greater than *end_byte*, the result wraps from 0xFF to 0x00.

UTL_REF

Provides procedures for selecting and modifying instances of an object type in an object table. The name of the table does not have to be known. New with Oracle 8.0.4.

Calls

```
PROCEDURE UTL_REF.DELETE_OBJECT
   (reference IN REF ANY);
```
Deletes the object (actually the row containing the object) identified by *reference*.

```
PROCEDURE UTL_REF.LOCK_OBJECT
   (reference IN REF ANY
   [, object IN OUT ANY]#);
```
Locks the object referenced by the *reference.object* parameter (new with Oracle8*i*).

```
PROCEDURE UTL_REF.SELECT_OBJECT
   (reference IN REF ANY,
   object IN OUT ANY);
```
Retrieves the object referenced by *reference* into *object*.

```
PROCEDURE UTL_REF.UPDATE_OBJECT
   (reference IN REF ANY,
   object IN ANY);
```
Replaces an object in the database identified by *reference* with the object *object*.

UTL_SMTP

Provides an interface with the Simple Mail Transfer Protocol (SMTP) to allow email to be sent from the package. New with Oracle9*i*.

Calls

```
FUNCTION UTL_SMTP.OPEN_CONNECTION
  (host IN VARCHAR2,
   port IN PLS_INTEGER DEFAULT 25,
   [c OUT CONNECTION,]
   tx_timeout IN PLS_INTEGER DEFAULT NULL)
  RETURN {REPLY | CONNECTION};
```
Opens a connection to an SMTP server on *port* of *host* with *tx_timeout*. If connection *c* is passed with the call, the return is a reply record type; if not, a connection record type is returned.

```
FUNCTION UTL_SMTP.COMMAND
  (c IN CONNECTION,
   ord IN VARCHAR2,
   arg IN VARCHAR2 DEFAULT NULL)
  RETURN REPLY;
```

```
PROCEDURE UTL_SMTP.COMMAND
  (c IN CONNECTION,
   cmd IN VARCHAR2,
   arg IN VARCHAR2 DEFAULT NULL);
```

```
FUNCTION UTL_SMTP.COMMAND_REPLIES
  (c IN CONNECTION,
   ord IN VARCHAR2,
   arg IN VARCHAR2 DEFAULT NULL)
  RETURN REPLIES;
```
Performs *cmd* with *arg* for connection *c*. If *cmd* generates a reply, use the function. If *cmd* generates multiple replies, use the COMMAND_REPLIES function.

```
FUNCTION UTL_SMTP.HELO
  (c IN NOCOPY CONNECTION,
   domain IN NOCOPY)
  RETURN REPLY;
```

```
PROCEDURE UTL_SMTP.HELO
  (c IN NOCOPY CONNECTION,
   domain IN NOCOPY);
```
Performs handshaking with *c*. *domain* identifies the local host.

```
FUNCTION UTL_SMTP.EHLO
  (c IN NOCOPY CONNECTION,
   domain IN NOCOPY)
  RETURN REPLIES;
```

```
PROCEDURE UTL_SMTP.EHLO
  (c IN NOCOPY CONNECTION,
   domain IN NOCOPY);
```
Performs handshaking with *c* with extended information returned. *domain* identifies the local host.

```
FUNCTION UTL_SMTP.MAIL
  (c IN NOCOPY CONNECTION,
   sender IN OUT NOCOPY,
   parameters IN OUT NOCOPY)
  RETURN REPLY;
```

```
PROCEDURE UTL_SMTP.MAIL
    (c IN NOCOPY CONNECTION,
    sender IN OUT NOCOPY,
    parameters IN OUT NOCOPY);
```
   Specifies the *sender* of the email with *c* with *parameters*.

```
FUNCTION UTL_SMTP.RCPT
    (c IN NOCOPY CONNECTION,
    recipient IN OUT NOCOPY,
    parameters IN OUT NOCOPY)
    RETURN REPLY;
```

```
PROCEDURE UTL_SMTP.RCPT
    (c IN NOCOPY CONNECTION,
    recipient IN OUT NOCOPY,
    parameters IN OUT NOCOPY);
```
   Specifies the *recipient* of the email to *c* with *parameters*.

```
FUNCTION UTL_SMTP.DATA
    (c IN NOCOPY CONNECTION,
    body IN OUT NOCOPY)
    RETURN REPLY;
```

```
PROCEDURE UTL_SMTP.DATA
    (c IN NOCOPY CONNECTION,
    body IN OUT NOCOPY);
```
   Specifies the *body* of the email transaction with *c*.

```
FUNCTION UTL_SMTP.OPEN_DATA
    (c IN NOCOPY connection)
    RETURN REPLY;
```

```
PROCEDURE UTL_SMTP.OPEN_DATA
    (c IN NOCOPY CONNECTION);
```
   Sends the DATA command to *c*.

```
FUNCTION UTL_SMTP.WRITE_DATA
    (c IN NOCOPY CONNECTION,
    data IN OUT NOCOPY)
    RETURN REPLY;
```

```
PROCEDURE UTL_SMTP.WRITE_DATA
    (c IN NOCOPY CONNECTION,
    data IN OUT NOCOPY);
```
   Writes *data* to *c* after the OPEN_DATA command.

```
FUNCTION UTL_SMTP.WRITE_RAW_DATA
    (c IN NOCOPY CONNECTION,
    sender IN OUT NOCOPY);
```
   Writes raw *data* to *c* after the OPEN_DATA command.

```
FUNCTION UTL_SMTP.CLOSE_DATA
    (c IN NOCOPY CONNECTION)
    RETURN REPLY;
```

```
PROCEDURE UTL_SMTP.CLOSE_DATA
    (c IN NOCOPY CONNECTION);
```
    Closes the email message by sending the <CR><LF>.<CR><LF> sequence to *c*.

```
FUNCTION UTL_SMTP.RSET
    (c IN NOCOPY CONNECTION)
    RETURN REPLY;
```

```
PROCEDURE UTL_SMTP.WRITE_DATA
    (c IN NOCOPY CONNECTION);
```
    Aborts the current mail transaction to *c*.

```
FUNCTION UTL_SMTP.VRFY
    (c IN OUT NOCOPY CONNECTION,
    recipient IN OUT NOCOPY)
    RETURN REPLY;
```
    Verifies the validity of the *recipient* as an email address.

```
FUNCTION UTL_SMTP.NOOP
    (c IN NOCOPY CONNECTION)
    RETURN VARCHAR2;
```

```
PROCEDURE UTL_SMTP.NOOP
    (c IN NOCOPY CONNECTION);
```
    Provides a NULL command.

```
FUNCTION UTL_SMTP.QUIT
    (c IN OUT NOCOPY CONNECTION)
    RETURN VARCHAR2;
```
    Terminates *c*.

UTL_TCP

Used to communicate with external TCP/IP servers directly using TCP/IP. New with
Oracle9*i*.

Calls

```
FUNCTION UTL_TCP.OPEN_CONNECTION
    (remote_host IN VARCHAR2,
    remote_port IN PLS_INTEGER,
    local_host IN VARCHAR2 DEFAULT NULL,
    local_port IN PLS_INTEGER DEFAULT NULL,
    in_buffer_size IN PLS_INTEGER DEFAULT NULL,
    out_buffer_size IN PLS_INTEGER DEFAULT NULL,
    charset IN VARCHAR2 DEFAULT NULL,
    newline DEFAULT CRLF,
    tx_timeout IN PLS_INTEGER DEFAULT NULL)
    RETURN CONNECTION;
```
    Establishes a connection to *remote_port* on *remote_host*; if these parameters are
    NULL, uses *local_port* on *local_host*. Sets the sizes of the in and out buffers, the
    on-the-wire *charset*, the *newline* character sequence, and the *tx_timeout* (which is
    the amount of time the package will wait before abandoning a read or write oper-
    ation). Returns a connection handle.

FUNCTION UTL_TCP.AVAILABLE
  (c IN OUT NOCOPY CONNECTION,
  timeout IN PLS_INTEGER DEFAULT 0)
  RETURN PLS_INTEGER;

Determines the amount of data available to read on c. Will wait for *timeout* seconds.

FUNCTION UTL_TCP.READ_RAW
  (c IN OUT NOCOPY CONNECTION,
  data IN OUT NOCOPY RAW,
  len IN PLS_INTEGER DEFAULT 1,
  peek IN BOOLEAN DEFAULT FALSE)
  RETURN PLS_INTEGER;

Reads *slen* bytes of raw *data* on c. If *peek*, data is left in the input queue. Returns the actual number of bytes received.

FUNCTION UTL_TCP.WRITE_RAW
  (c IN OUT NOCOPY CONNECTION,
  data IN RAW,
  len IN PLS_INTEGER DEFAULT NULL)
  RETURN PLS_INTEGER;

Writes binary *data* on c of *len* bytes. If *len* is NULL, all *data* is sent. Returns the actual number of bytes transmitted.

FUNCTION UTL_TCP.READ_TEXT
  (c IN OUT NOCOPY CONNECTION,
  data IN OUT NOCOPY VARCHAR2,
  len IN PLS_INTEGER DEFAULT 1,
  peek IN BOOLEAN DEFAULT FALSE)
  RETURN PLS_INTEGER;

Reads *slen* bytes of *data* on c. If *peek*, *data* is left in the input queue. Returns the actual number of bytes received.

FUNCTION UTL_TCP.WRITE_TEXT
  (c IN OUT NOCOPY CONNECTION,
  data IN VARCHAR2,
  len IN PLS_INTEGER DEFAULT NULL)
  RETURN PLS_INTEGER;

Writes text *data* on c of *len* bytes. If *len* is NULL, all *data* is sent. Returns the actual number of bytes transmitted.

FUNCTION UTL_TCP.READ_LINE
  (c IN OUT NOCOPY CONNECTION,
  data IN OUT NOCOPY VARCHAR2,
  remove_crlf IN PLS_INTEGER DEFAULT 1,
  peek IN BOOLEAN DEFAULT FALSE)
  RETURN PLS_INTEGER;

Reads a text line of *data* on c. If *remove_crlf*, the trailing CR and LF characters are removed. If *peek*, data is left in the input queue. Returns the actual number of bytes received.

FUNCTION UTL_TCP.WRITE_LINE
  (c IN OUT NOCOPY CONNECTION,
  data IN VARCHAR2)
  RETURN PLS_INTEGER;

Writes text line *data* on c. Returns the actual number of bytes transmitted.

```
FUNCTION UTL_TCP.GET_RAW
   (c IN OUT NOCOPY CONNECTION,
   len IN PLS_INTEGER DEFAULT 1,
   peek IN BOOLEAN DEFAULT FALSE)
   RETURN RAW;

FUNCTION UTL_TCP.GET_TEXT
   (c IN OUT NOCOPY CONNECTION,
   len IN PLS_INTEGER DEFAULT 1,
   peek IN BOOLEAN DEFAULT FALSE)
   RETURN VARCHAR2;

FUNCTION UTL_TCP.GET_LINE
   (c IN OUT NOCOPY CONNECTION,
   remove_crlf IN BOOLEAN DEFAULT FALSE
   peek IN BOOLEAN DEFAULT FALSE)
   RETURN VARCHAR2;
```
   Different forms of READ functions that return actual data.

```
PROCEDURE UTL_TCP.FLUSH
   (c IN OUT NOCOPY CONNECTION);
```
   Transmits all data in output buffer to *c*.

```
PROCEDURE UTL_TCP.CLOSE_CONNECTION
   (c IN OUT NOCOPY connection);
```
   Closes connection *c*.

```
FUNCTION UTL_TCP.CLOSE_ALL_CONNECTIONS;
```
   Closes all open TCP/IP connections.

UTL_URL

Provides escape and unescape mechanisms for URL characters.

Calls

```
FUNCTION UTL_URL.ESCAPE
   (url IN VARCHAR2,
   escape_reserved_chars IN BOOLEAN DEFAULT FALSE,
   url_charset IN VARCHAR2 DEFAULT UTL_HTTP.BODY_CHARSET)
   RETURN VARCHAR2;
```
   If *escape_reserved_chars*, reserved and illegal URL characters in *url* are escaped; otherwise, only illegal characters are escaped. If there is a value for *url_charset*, used for target character set for escaped characters.

```
FUNCTION UTL_URL.UNESCAPE
   (url IN VARCHAR2,
   url_charset IN VARCHAR2 DEFAULT UTL_HTTP.BODY_CHARSET)
   RETURN VARCHAR2;
```
   Unescapes escaped URL characters in *url* to their original form. If there is a value for *url_charset*, used for target character set for escaped characters.

11

Java and Oracle

The growth in Java usage and popularity has been a key development in the computing world in recent years. Java's cross-platform capabilities and object-oriented functionality have given it broad acceptance as a development and runtime platform. Since the introduction of Oracle8*i*, Java has been an integral part of the overall Oracle environment.

There are two basic ways to access Oracle data from Java:

SQLJ
> A high-level language designed for embedding SQL statements into Java code. SQL statements used in SQLJ are checked at compile time. Up until Oracle9*i*, you could use SQLJ only for static SQL statements. With Oracle9*i*, you can now use SQLJ for both static and dynamic SQL statements.

JDBC
> A Java API that typically involves more coding than SQLJ. The SQL statements used in JDBC code are checked at runtime, so it is more loosely typed than SQLJ.

Both of these interfaces are established standards for Java, and each has its own virtues—fewer statements to code with SQLJ, more control with JDBC. To some extent, use of either interface is a matter of personal choice, although Java, with its low-level programming orientation, tends to appeal to developers who are not deterred by the more detailed coding required with JDBC. You can even mix JDBC calls with SQLJ in the same program if you wish.

This chapter focuses on using Java to interface with Oracle databases. It covers the following:

- Java drivers available for Oracle
- Using Java within the Oracle database
- Mapping between Java datatypes and Oracle datatypes
- SQLJ and JDBC interfaces to Oracle

The use of Java in general is beyond the scope of this book. However, for a very helpful summary of Java capabilities and syntax, we recommend *Java in a Nutshell* by David Flanagan (O'Reilly). For additional information about SQLJ and JDBC, see *Java Programming with Oracle SQLJ* by Jason Price and *Java Programming with Oracle JDBC* by Don Bales, also from O'Reilly. See also the Oracle documentation for these products.

Java Drivers

Oracle supplies two types of JDBC drivers:

- A JDBC Oracle Call Interface (OCI) *driver*, or *fat driver*, which is a Type 2 driver. This driver allows you to use the full capabilities of Oracle Net Services.

- A JDBC *thin driver*, a Type 4 driver that is 100% pure Java but does not provide all the capabilities of Oracle Net Services.

Each of these types of drivers has client-side and server-side versions.

Check the Oracle documentation for your version of Oracle for a compatibility listing for these drivers, the Oracle version number, and the supported versions of the JDK and JDBC code.

Java in the Oracle Database

Starting with Oracle8*i*, there is a Java Virtual Machine (JVM) that runs inside the Oracle database. You can use Java to write procedural code for Oracle in much the same way that you use PL/SQL.

The following sections summarize the manual steps for loading and using Java in the Oracle database. If you use JDeveloper, a development tool available from Oracle, you can create a deployment profile that will handle these steps for you automatically.

Compiling and Loading Java

If you are writing Java to run in the Oracle database, you should be aware of a few special conditions:

- With SQLJ, you do not need to import any of the standard Java libraries, like *oracle.sqlj.runtime.Oracle*. With JDBC, you do need to import the appropriate libraries.

- With SQLJ, you do not need to establish a connection to the database, because this is mediated by the JDBC KPRB driver. With JDBC, you do need to establish this connection.

- You cannot use autocommit with either SQLJ or JDBC.

Once you have written your Java code, you have to load it into the Oracle database using the *loadjava* program described in the next section.

---

loadjava

Once you have compiled the Java code, you use the *loadjava* program to load the classes or JAR archive files into the database. The syntax you use to invoke *loadjava* is:

```
loadjava -user user_name/password[@URL] [option_list] file_list
```

where *user_name* and *password* indicate the schema that will be used to load the classes, and *URL* is a database URL (described in more detail for the SQLJ connect function in the "SQLJ Methods" section later in this chapter). The *file_list* is a list of files to be loaded, and the *option_list* is one or more of the parameters listed here:

-action
>   Performs all actions. The default. New with Oracle9*i*.

-andresolve
>   Compiles the uploaded source files and resolves each as it is loaded. Mutually exclusive with –resolve.

-casesensitivepub
>   Publishing creates case-sensitive names. New with Oracle9*i*.

-cleargrants
>   Clears out any existing grants to classes, sources, and resources. Used with –grants to reset grant levels.

-debug
>   Generates and displays debugging information as load progresses.

-definer | d
>   Specifies that methods of classes being loaded be executed with the privileges of the definer, not the invoker.

-dirprefix *prefix*
>   Deletes prefix from the name before the name of the schema object is determined. New with Oracle9*i*.

-encoding | e
>   Specifies character set encoding for source files.

-fileout *file*
>   Prints all messages to *file*. New with Oracle9*i*.

-force | f
>   Forces loading of previously loaded Java class files.

-genmissing
>   Causes the generation of dummy definitions for any missing classes referred to in the methods. New with Oracle9*i*.

-genmissingjar *jar_file*
>   Works like -genmissing and creates a JAR file that contains the definitions. New with Oracle9*i*.

-grant | g

Grants EXECUTE privilege on classes to the comma-separated list of users and roles that follows.

-help

Displays options for the command.

-jararesource

Loads whole JAR file without unpacking it. New with Oracle9*i*.

-noaction

Takes no action on any files, except to determine if a JAR file contains a META-INF/loadjava-options entry, which will cause the options file to be processed. New with Oracle9*i*.

-nocasesensitivepub

Specifies that all lowercase characters be converted to uppercase, with underscores to denote transitions. New with Oracle9*i*.

-nocleargrants

Omits revoking of EXECUTE privilege to override -cleargrants. New with Oracle9*i*.

-nodefiner

Grants invoker rights on loaded classes. New with Oracle9*i*.

-nograant

Prevents granting of EXECUTE privilege to loaded classes. Default. New with Oracle9*i*.

-norecursivejars

Considers JARs in other JARs as resources. Default. New with Oracle9*i*.

-noschema

Puts loaded classes, sources, and resources into user's schema. Default. New with Oracle9*i*.

-noserverside

Forces the use of a server-side JDBC driver to access objects, rather than directly, which is the default. New with Oracle9*i*.

-nosynonym

Specifies that no public synonyns be created for classes. Default. New with Oracle9*i*.

-nousage

Suppresses usage messages for no option or –help. New with Oracle9*i*.

-noverify

Indicates that uploaded classes are not verified by bytecode verifyer. Used with -resolve option. New with Oracle9*i*.

-oci8 | o | oci

Uses the Oracle Call Interface (OCI) driver to access the database.

-optionfile *file*
   Specifies file with options, which are added to the end of the command line. New with Oracle9i.

-optiontable *table*
   Like -optionfile, but the source is a SQL table. New with Oracle9i.

-oracleresolver
   Detects missing classes referenced in the classes being loaded. Default. Only in Oracle8i.

-publish *package*
   Creates PL/SQL wrappers for eligible methods. See the Oracle documentation for rules of eligibility. New with Oracle9i.

-pubmain *number*
   Creates multiple variants of the procedures or function, each of which takes a different number of arguments of type VARCHAR, up to and including *number*. Applies to *main* and any methods with a single java.lang.String argument. New with Oracle9i.

-recursivejars
   Processes internal JARs as top-level JARs. New with Oracle9i.

-resolve | r
   Resolves references in classes that have been loaded and compiles if necessary. Mutually exclusive with –andresolve.

-R | resolver *"resolver_spec"*
   resolver_spec contains patterns used to compare against class schema objects to see if they should be created or replaced.

-resolveonly
   Skips the initial creation step. New with Oracle9i.

-schema *schema*
   Specifies database schema to load the Java objects. Default is login schema.

-stdout
   Specifies output to stdout, rather than stderr. New with Oracle9i.

-stoponerror
   Forces stop on processing or Java error. New with Oracle9i.

-synonym | s
   Creates public synonym for each loaded Java class.

-tableschema *schema*
   Creates *loadjava* internal tables in *schema*. New with Oracle9i.

-thin
   Specifies thin driver used to access the database. Mutually exclusive with –oci8, the default.

-time
   Includes timestamp with every message. New with Oracle9i.

-unresolvedok

> Ignores unresolved errors when combined with -resolve. New with Oracle9*i*.

-verbose

> Specifies detailed process messages during load.

Once you have loaded Java classes into the database, you can view them with the following SQL statement:

```
SELECT OBJECT_NAME FROM USER_OBJECTS WHERE OBJECT_TYPE = 'JAVA CLASS';
```

dropjava

To remove Java classes from the database, you use the *dropjava* program. The syntax you use to invoke *dropjava* is:

```
dropjava -user user_name/password[@URL] [option_list] file_list
```

The command-line options are the same as for the *loadjava* program, described in the previous section, but the *option_list* takes the following parameters:

-genmissingjar *jar-file*

> Treats operand of option as file to be processed. New with Oracle9*i*.

-help

> Displays the options for the command.

-jararesource

> Drops whole JAR file, previously loaded as resource. New with Oracle9*i*.

-oci8 | o | oci

> Uses the Oracle Call Interface (OCI) driver to access the database.

-optionfile *file*

> See the same parameter described for *loadjava*. New with Oracle9*i*.

-optiontable *table*

> See the same parameter described for *loadjava*. New with Oracle9*i*.

-schema | S *schema*

> Specifies *schema* from which objects are to be dropped.

-stdout

> See the same parameter described for *loadjava*. New with Oracle9*i*.

-synonym|s

> Drops public synonym for each loaded Java class. New with Oracle9*i*.

-thin | t

> Specifies thin driver used to acces the database. Mutually exclusive with —oci8, the default.

-time

> See the same parameter description for *loadjava*. New with Oracle9*i*.

-verbose

> Specifies detailed process messages during load.

Creating a PL/SQL Wrapper

Once the Java class is loaded into the database, you will need to create a PL/SQL wrapper procedure to call it.

Classes that will be called from PL/SQL have two restrictions:

- Methods published to SQL and PL/SQL must be declared static. PL/SQL has no mechanisms for instantiating nonstatic Java classes.
- The classes must not issue any GUI calls (for example, to the AWT, the Abstract Windowing Toolkit) at runtime.

The syntax for creating this procedure is:

```
CREATE [OR REPLACE] {
    PROCEDURE procedure_name [(param[, param ...])] |
    FUNCTION  function_name  [(param[, param ...])]
    RETURN plsql_type]}

    [AUTHID {DEFINER | CURRENT_USER}]
    [PARALLEL_ENABLE]
    [DETERMINISTIC]
    {IS | AS} LANGUAGE JAVA
    NAME 'java_method (java_type[, java_type] ...)
    [RETURN java_type];
```

where *param* is defined as:

```
        param := parameter_name [IN | OUT | IN OUT] plsql_type
```

where:

procedure_name/function_name
> Specifies the name you want to give to the PL/SQL wrapper procedure or wrapper function that you are creating.

plsql_type
> Specifies the PL/SQL type of a wrapper function's return value.

AUTHID {DEFINER | CURRENT_USER}
> Determines whether the stored subprogram runs with the database privileges of the user who created it (DEFINER) or of the user who invoked it (CURRENT_USER). The default is CURRENT_USER.

PARALLEL_ENABLE
> Indicates that the function can be used in slave sessions in parallel DML evaluations. Parallel DML allows DML operations to be spread across multiple processes running in parallel to improve performance.

DETERMINISTIC
> Tells the database optimizer to avoid redundant function calls, assuming that the function is deterministic, that is, if the return result is dependent only on the input values. If the DETERMINISTIC hint is used and the function has already been called once before with the same input values, then the previous result returned by the function is reused.

LANGUAGE JAVA clause
Indicates that the procedure or function invokes a Java method.

NAME clause
Identifies the Java method being wrapped and also its parameters. You can specify the following in the NAME clause:

java_method
Must uniquely identify the Java method being wrapped. The method must be specified using dot notation to identify both the class and the method.

java_type
Specifies the type of the Java method parameter, which must be compatible with the corresponding *plsql_type* database type.

parameter_name
Specifies the name of a PL/SQL parameter.

Once the PL/SQL wrapper is created, you can call it just like any other PL/SQL procedure.

Data Mapping

The datatypes used by an Oracle database are not exactly the same as the datatypes in Java. Table 11-1 summarizes the mapping from Java database datatypes to Oracle datatypes.

Some of the java.lang datatypes are wrapper classes for the Java primitive datatypes that can accept a NULL reference, because normal Java datatypes cannot. To retrieve a value from a wrapper class, use the appropriate method *type*Value() for each wrapper class.

Table 11-1. Datatype mapping between Java and Oracle

Java datatype	Oracle datatype
java.sql.Array	ARRAY
java.sqlBlob	BLOB
Boolean java.lang.Boolean	NUMBER
byte java.lang.byte	NUMBER
byte[]	RAW LONGRAW
java.slq.Clob	CLOB
java.sql.date	DATE
double java.lang.double	NUMBER
float java.lang.float	NUMBER

Table 11-1. *Datatype mapping between Java and Oracle (continued)*

Java datatype	Oracle datatype
int java.lang.Integer	NUMBER
long java.lang.Long	NUMBER
java.sql.Ref	REF
short java.lang.Short	NUMBER
java.lang.string	VARCHAR2 LONG RAW
java.sql.Struct	STRUCT
java.sql.time	DATE
java.sql.timestamp	DATE
java.math.BigDecimal (recommended)	NUMBER

There are also sets of Oracle extensions for the following Oracle datatypes. The oracle.sql.NUMBER extension allows you to store and retrieve Oracle NUMBER data without losing any precision.

oracle.sql.ARRAY   oracle.sql.NUMBER
oracle.sql.BFILE   oracle.sql.RAW
oracle.sql.BLOB   oracle.sql.REF
oracle.sql.CHAR   oracle.sql.ROWID
oracle.sql.CLOB   oracle.sql.STRUCT
oracle.sql.DATE

SQLJ

SQLJ consists of two basic components:

- Runtime libraries, which perform the actual database calls at runtime
- A translator, which translates SQLJ code into runtime calls in a compilation process

In order to run code with SQLJ, you will need the translator, as well as the Java Development Kit (JDK) and the Oracle JDBC drivers, on the development machine.

Imports

To use SQLJ to write applications that will run outside the Oracle database, you must have an import statement in your Java code for the following libraries:

- *java.sql.date*
- *java.sql.SQLExceptio*n
- *oracle.sqlj.runtime.Oracle*

The *oracle.sqlj.runtime.Oracle* library contains most of the specific calls you will use to access the Oracle database. We'll describe these calls in a later section.

Compiling SQLJ Code

Once you have created a Java program using SQLJ, you use the *sqlj* program to compile the code. You can invoke this program using the following syntax:

```
sqlj [option_list] file_list
```

The flags available for the option list are:

-cache [=True | False]
> Boolean indicating whether to enable caching of results of online semantics checking. Default is False.

-checkfilename [=True | False]
> Boolean indicating whether to display warnings if source filename does not match name in public class. Default is True.

-classpath
> Specifies Java CLASSPATH.

-codegen=oracle
> Suppresses creation of profile files. New with Oracle9i.

-compile [=True | False]
> Boolean indicating whether *.java* file produced should be compiled. Default is True.

-compiler-executable
> Executable name of Java compiler.

-compiler-output-file
> File for output from compiler. If not present, displayed on screen.

-Coption
> Option to be passed to Java compiler.

-d
> Directory for *.ser* and *.class* files produced.

-default-customizer
> Class name for profile customizer. Default is oracle.sqlj.runtime.util. OraCustomizer.

-dir
> Directory for *.java* files produced.

-driver
> Class name for JDBC driver to use. Default is oracle.jdbc.driver.OracleDriver.

-explain [=True | False]
> Boolean indicating whether to turn on detailed error messages. Default is False.

-g
> Causes compiler to include debugging code.

-help

    Displays list of options.

-Joption

    Option to be passed to JVM.

-linemap [=True | False]

    Boolean indicating whether to enable the mapping of line numbers between SQLJ and generated Java code. Default is False.

-n

    Boolean indicating whether to enable echoing command line rather than executing it.

-nowarn

    Turns off -warn Java compiler option.

-O

    Disables Java compiler's -linemap option.

-online

    Class name of online SQL checker. If used, also requires –user and –password options. Default is oracle.sqlj.checker.OracleChecker.

-Poption

    Option to be passed to SQLJ profile customizer.

-password

    Password to be passed to database for online semantics checking.

-profile [=True | False]

    Boolean indicating whether to enable profile customization. Default is True.

-props

    Specifies property file with command-line properties.

-ser2class [=True | False]

    Boolean indicating whether to enable translation of generated *.ser* profiles to *-class* files. Default is False.

-status

    Boolean indicating whether to enable display of status messages. Default is False.

-url

    Specifies database URL for online semantics checking.

-user

    Database user to use when connecting to database for online semantics checking.

-verbose

    Enables display of detailed status information and the –status option of Java compiler.

-version

    Displays version of SQLJ.

-version-long
> Displays more detailed version information.

-warn
> Specifies a comma-separated list of flags to enable SQLJ warnings. The possible flags are precision/noprecision, nulls/nonulls, portable/noportable, strict/nostrict, verbose/noverbose, and all/none. The last pair enables or disables all warnings. The defaults are precision, nulls, noportable, strict, and noverbose.

For more detailed information on parameters allowed with the *sqlj* command, see the Oracle documentation, as well as *Java Programming with Oracle SQL*.

Using SQL with SQLJ

Once you have established a connection to an Oracle database with the Oracle. connect() function (shown later), you can specify SQL statements with this syntax:

```
#sql{ [conn_context] [[,]exec_context] SQL_statement };
```

The variable *SQL_statement* can be virtually any SQL statement acceptable to the Oracle database. The optional variable *conn_context* specifies a particular connection context, and the optional variable *exec_context* specifies an execution context for that connection; see the descriptions of the *getConnection()* and *getExecutionContext()* functions in the later "SQL Methods" section for more information.

You can set the transaction isolation level of a SQL transaction with the following syntax:

```
#sql [conn_context] {SET TRANSACTION (READ ONLY | READ WRITE)
     ISOLATION LEVEL (SERIALIZATION | READ COMMITTED) }
```

If the SQL statement returns a value, you can receive the value with the following syntax:

```
#sql{ :host_variable = SQL_statement };
```

The *host_variable* can include a mode specifier of IN, OUT, or IN OUT. If the *host_variable* is part of an INTO list or an assignment with a SET statement (both discussed later in this section), the default mode is OUT; otherwise, the default mode is IN.

You can also use the following command:

```
#sql { SET :host_expression = expression };
```

to receive data into a host variable. If the expression is a PL/SQL function, you can use the VALUES clause described in the later section "PL/SQL in SQLJ."

With Oracle9*i*, you can use bind variables to represent column and table names to create dynamic SQL statements. If you are going to use a bind variable with the same name as the column or table, you can simply specify it with a colon (:) in front of it. If you are going to use a bind variable to replace a table or column with a different name, you must use the syntax:

```
:host_variable :: database_replacement
```

You cannot use a bind variable for a column or table name in an INTO clause or specify a value to a CALL, VALUES, SET, FETCH, or CAST statement.

If the SQL statement returns a single row, you can use the following syntax:

```
SELECT ... INTO :host_variable ...
```

to retrieve the data.

If the SQL statement returns more than one row, you will have to use a SQL iterator to receive the data, described in the next section.

SQL Iterators

A SQL iterator is used to process multiple rows returned from a SELECT statement. To use a SQL iterator, you must declare the iterator class, declare an iterator object, and then populate it with a SELECT statement. Once the iterator is populated, you can read rows from it. If you have a nested SELECT statement, you must use nested iterators to receive the data, one for each SELECT statement.

You can create an iterator and share it with a JDBC result set by assigning the result of getResultSet() to a JDBC result set.

There are two types of iterators: named iterators and positional iterators.

Named iterators

To declare a named iterator class, use the following syntax:

```
#sql [modifiers] iterator class_name
    [implements interface_class [, interface_class . . .]]
    [with constant_name = value [,constant_name = value . . .]]
    (java_type column_name [, java_type column_name ...]);
```

where:

modifiers
   Optional Java class modifier: public, private, protected, static.

class_name
   Name for the iterator class.

interface_class
   The interface(s) implemented by the iterator class. If the iterator implements the sqlj.runtime.Scrollable class (available with Oracle 8.1.7 and later), the iterator will support the following navigation functions:

   * previous()
   * first()
   * last()
   * absolute(*row_number*)
   * relative(*relative_number*): number of rows relative to current row
   * afterLast()
   * beforeFirst()

and these other functions:

- setFetchDirection(*direction*), where *direction* can be a constant in sqlj. runtime.ResultSetIterator of FETCH_FORWARD, FETCH_REVERSE, or FETCH_UNKNOWN as a hint
- getFetchDirection( )
- isFirst( )
- isLast( )
- isBeforeFirst( )
- isAfterLast( )

constant_name
Name of a constant that can be accessed in the iterator.

java_type
Java datatype of an iterator column.

column_name
Name of the column in the iterator. If this name is different from the column name, you should use AS to identify the iterator column.

Once you have declared a named iterator, you can select into it with this syntax:

```
#sql iterator_name = {sql_statement};
```

When the named iterator has been populated, you can move through the rows in the iterator by using the next method for the iterator. This method returns FALSE if there are no more rows in the iterator.

Each column in the named iterator has its own access method with the same name as the column.

Positional iterators

A positional iterator is similar to a named iterator, with two significant differences:

- You do not use a *column_name* in the declaration for a positional iterator. The columns retrieved by the SELECT statement place their values into the iterator columns in the same position.
- You use the following syntax to retrieve a row from the positional iterator into a series of host variables.:

```
#sql {
  FETCH :iterator_name INTO :host_expression [, :host_expression ...]
};
```

For a positional iterator that implements the sqlj.runtime.Scrollable interface, the FETCH clause can take the following forms:

FETCH PREVIOUS | PRIOR
FETCH FIRST
FETCH LAST

```
FETCH ABSOLUTE:(row_number)
FETCH RELATIVE:(relative_number)
```

The end_fetch method for the positional iterator returns a Boolean indicating whether the last row has been fetched.

With Oracle9i, you can implicitly declare a positional iterator by simply making it a host variable to receive the results of a SELECT statement. You retrieve data from the iterator with a FETCH CURRENT call.

PL/SQL in SQLJ

To call a PL/SQL procedure with SQLJ, use the following syntax:

```
#sql { CALL procedure_name([parameter_list])};
```

To call a PL/SQL function with SQLJ, use this syntax:

```
#sql host_variable = { VALUES (function_name([parameter_list])) }
```

If the return from a PL/SQL function is a REF CURSOR, the *host_variable* should be an iterator that matches the result set.

You can also use the SET command, discussed earlier, in SQLJ to receive data into host variables. In addition, you can include anonymous blocks of PL/SQL code within a SQLJ call.

Database Objects and JPublish

You can use Java objects to write data to database objects and a Java object to retrieve data from a database object with the INTO clause or with an iterator with the same structure as the database object.

JPublish is a utility that can create custom object classes in Java that will match the attributes and methods in an object class in an Oracle database. You can use JPublish from the command line or from within JDeveloper, a Java development tool from Oracle. See the Oracle documentation for further details.

SQLJ Methods

SQLJ is implemented with the library *oracle.sqlj.runtime.Oracle*, which you will have to include in any Java code that uses SQLJ. Note that some of the following methods are associated with subclasses of this main class.

---

connect

```
Oracle.connect(databaseURL,
    username,
    password
    [, autocommit]);
```

Establishes a connection to an Oracle database.

Variables

databaseURL

    Takes the form of:

        `driver_name@database_location`

    where *driver_name* is jdbc:oracle:*driver* and *driver* is one of the following:

- thin for the JDBC thin driver
- oci (Oracle9*i*), oci8 (Oracle8*i*), or oci7 (Oracle7) OCI JDBC driver

    The *database_location* can be specified as:

        `host_name:port:database_SID`

    for the JDBC thin driver or as:

        `(description=(address=(host=host_name)(protocol=tcp)(port=port))`
        `(connect_data=(sid=database_SID)))`

    for either type of JDBC drive. The entire *databaseURL* is enclosed in double quotes.

username

    Name of the user, enclosed in double quotes.

password

    User's password, enclosed in double quotes.

autocommit

    Optional Boolean value indicating whether autocommit is on for SQL statements for this connection.

close

```
Oracle.close([ CLOSE_CONNECTION | KEEP_CONNECTION]);
```

Disconnects from the Oracle database.

Variables

CLOSE_CONNECTION

    Closes the underlying JDBC connection

KEEP_CONNECTION

    Keeps the underlying JDBC connection open

The preceding call closes the active (default) connection. You can close a specific connection with the call:

    `conn_context.close( )`

getConnection

```
DefaultContext conn_context Oracle.getConnection databaseURL,
    username,
    password
    [, autocommit];
```

Creates and returns a connection context. If you are going to use more than one connection, use this function to create multiple contexts and a host variable instance of DefaultContext to hold it.

You can also use this function to return the underlying connection to a JDBC connection object, which can then be used for JDBC statements. You can also pass a JDBC connection to a SQLJ connection by creating a SQLJ connection object, which receives the value from the JDBC call getConnection().

Variables

See the variables described for the context() call earlier.

setDefaultRowPrefetch

(*(OracleConnection)* *conn_context*.getConnection()).
setDefaultRowPrefetch(*integer*);

Specifies the number of rows to fetch in each round-trip to the server.

Variables

(OracleConnection)
> Casts the JDBC connection to the class *OracleConnection*, which contains the setDefaultRowPrefetch() method.

> You can use the syntax DefaultContext.setDefaultContext. getConnection() with this function to set the number of rows to prefetch for the default connection.

setFetchSize

Replaces setDefaultRowPrefetch() in Oracle 8.1.7 and later.

getDefaultRowPrefetch

(*(OracleConnection)* *conn_context*.getConnection()).setDefaultRowPrefetch();

Retrieves the number of rows to fetch in each round trip to the server.

Variables

(OracleConnection)
> Casts the JDBC connection to the class *OracleConnection*, which contains the setDefaultRowPrefetch() method.

> You can use the syntax DefaultContext.getDefaultContext. getConnection() with this function to set the number of rows to prefetch for the default connection.

getFetchSize

Replaces getDefaultRowPrefetch() in Oracle 8.1.7 and later.

setDefaultContext

```
DefaultContext.setDefaultContext(conn_context);
```

Can be used to assign a default context to all subsequent SQL statements.

Variables

conn_context A context handle created with getConnection().

getExecutionContext

```
ExecutionContext exec_context =
    DefaultContext.getDefaultContext.getExecutionContext( );
```

Returns an execution context for a connection to an instance of ExecutionContext. The execution context must be retrieved before many of the methods described later, such as getMaxRows() and setMaxRows(), are used.

Variables

exec_context An instance of ExecutionContext to hold the context handle.

getMaxRows

```
exec_context.getMaxRows();
```

Sets the maximum number of rows to be returned to an iterator.

Variables

exec_context An instance of ExecutionContext to hold the context handle.

setMaxRows

```
exec_context.setMaxRows(integer);
```

Sets the maximum number of rows to be returned to an iterator.

Variables

exec_context An instance of ExecutionContext to hold the context handle.

getQueryTimeout

```
exec_context.getQueryTimeout( );
```

Sets the query timeout in seconds for an execution context.

Variables

exec_context An instance of ExecutionContext to hold the context handle.

setQueryTimeout

```
exec_context.setQueryTimeout(integer);
```

Sets the query timeout in seconds for an execution context.

Variables

exec_context   An instance of ExecutionContext to hold the context handle.

getResultSet

ResultSet *JDBC_ResultSet* = *iterator*.getResultSet( )

Shares an iterator with a JDBC result set.

You can share a JDBC result set with an iterator with the syntax:

    #sql *iterator* = {CAST *result_set*};

getSQLState

sql_warning.getSQLState( );

Returns a string with the warning message for an instance of the SQLWarning class retrieved with getWarnings.

getUpdateCount

exec_context.getUpdateCount( );

Returns the number of rows modified by the last SQL statement for an execution context.

Variables

exec_context   An instance of ExecutionContext to hold the context handle.

getWarnings

SQLWarning sql_warning=exec_context.getWarnings( )

Returns the first warning from an execution context to an instance of SQLWarning.

Variables

exec_context   An instance of ExecutionContext to hold the context handle.

setBatching

exec_context.setBatching(TRUE | FALSE);

Turns batch processing on and off for an execution context.

isBatching

Boolean *result exec_context*.isBatching( );

Returns whether batching is turned on or off for an execution context.

executeBatch

int *results exec_context*.executeBatch( );

Forces the execution of a batch job before the default number of SQL operations have accumulated for the job.

Variables

results An integer that receives -2 if the batch job was successful.

setBatchLimits

exec_context.setBatchLimits(*integer* | AUTO_BATCH | UNLIMITED);

Sets the default number of SQL operations accumulated before a batch is run.

Keywords

AUTO_BATCH
    Allows SQLJ to determine the best limit of operations
for the batch.

JDBC

JDBC is a standard, low-level Java API to databases. This section concentrates on the Oracle implementation of the JDBC standard set of interfaces.

Oracle uses a set of packages to implement the standard JDBC interface. In Oracle9*i*, the packages are:

oracle.jdbc
    Consists of interfaces that extend the java.sql.Connection, java.sql.Meta-Data, java.sql.PreparedStatement, and java.sql.Savepoint interfaces and the classes to implement them. This package is new in Oracle9*i*. In Oracle8*i*, some of the interfaces defined in this class were implemented as classes in a variety of different packages, as shown in Table 11-2. The interfaces and packages in this class, for both Oracle8*i* and Oracle9*i*, are covered in the following sections.

oracle.jdbc.driver
    In Oracle9*i*, handles the implementation of the interfaces of the oracle.jdbc library. Because the classes in this package simply implement the interfaces, this package is not documented in this chapter. In Oracle8*i*, the interfaces were not defined in the *oracle.jdbc* library.

oracle.jdbc.pool
    Used to manage Oracle Connection Pooling. Because relatively few developers use this feature of Oracle, this package is not documented in this chapter.

oracle.jdbc.xa*

New with Oracle9i. The oracle.jdbc.xa and oracle.jdbc.xa.client packages are relevant only to developers using the XA distributed transaction protocol and are therefore not documented in this chapter.

oracle.sql

Consists of interfaces used by classes in the library and to handle user-defined datatypes and classes to handle Oracle SQL datatypes.

The following sections cover the Oracle-specific interfaces and classes from the two most commonly used Oracle JDBC libraries—oracle.jdbc and oracle.sql. For documentation on the standard JDBC interfaces, see the JDBC documentation.

As we've mentioned, Oracle's implementation of the JDBC interface changed with Oracle9i. In the rest of this chapter, we use the Oracle9i standard as the basis for the discussion, but we note differences in the Oracle8i implementation as appropriate.

Table 11-2 provides a map from the Oracle8i classes to their counterparts in Oracle9i for cases in which there are differences in implementation or hierarchy. If a class or interface is not listed, that means it has the same name and place in the hierarchy in both releases. The interfaces are shown in italics.

Table 11-2. Oracle8i classes/interfaces and Oracle9i class/interfaces

Oracle8i class/interface	Oracle9i class/interface
CharacterSet [oracle.sql]	Not implemented
ClientDataSupport [oracle.jdbc.driver]	Not implemented
Const [oracle.jdbc.driver]	Not implemented
Mutable [oracle.sql]	Not implemented
OracleCallableStatement [oracle.jdbc.driver]	*OracleCallableStatement* [oracle.jdbc]
OracleConnection [oracle.jdbc.driver]	*OracleConnection* [oracle.Jdbc]
OracleDriver [oracle.jdbc.driver]	OracleDriver [oracle.jdbc]
OracleResultSet [oracle.jdbc.internal]	*OracleResultSet* [oracle.jdbc]
OracleResultSetCache [oracle.jdbc.internal]	*OracleResultSetCache* [oracle.jdbc]
OracleResultSetMetaData [oracle.jdbc.internal]	*OracleResultSetMetaData* [oracle.jdbc]
OracleTypes [oracle.jdbc.driver]	OracleTypes [oracle.jdbc]
StructMetaData [oracle.jdbc.driver]	*StructMetaData* [oracle.jdbc]
Not implemented	INTERVALYM [oracle.sql]
Not implemented	OracleOCIConnectionPool [oracle.jdbc.pool]
Not implemented	OracleXAConnectionCache [oracle.jdbc.pool]

Note that the oracle.jdbc.xa.client package is new for Oracle9i so there is no Oracle8i counterpart.

oracle.jdbc

The oracle.jdbc package contains 10 Oracle-specific interfaces and four Oracle-specific classes. The interfaces contain the basic extensions to the standard JDBC syntax that are Oracle-specific. The classes implement java.sql.driver, java.lang. object, and java.sql.DatabaseMetaData with Oracle-specific extensions. The other class implements the Oracle connection interface.

Interfaces

The interfaces described in the following entries are part of the oracle.jdbc package.

OracleCallableStatement

Extends the oracle.jdbc.OraclePreparedStatement interface and the java.sql.CallableStatement interface with Oracle9i. Extends the oracle.jdbc.driver.OraclePreparedStatement interface and implements the oracle.jdbc.internal.OracleCallableStatement interface with Oracle8i.

Inherited fields

The following fields are inherited from oracle.jdbc.PreparedStatement with Oracle9i:

> FORM CHAR
> FORM NCHAR

The following fields are inherited from oracle.jdbc.Statement with Oracle9i:

> EXPLICIT
> IMPLICIT
> NEW

The following fields are inherited from oracle.jdbc.driver.OracleStatement with Oracle8i:

> auto_rollback
> closed
> dbstmt
> defines
> EXPLICIT
> IMPLICIT
> NEW
> wait_option

Methods
addBatch( )
> Adds a set of parameters to the batch. Oracle8i only.

clearParameters( )
> Only with Oracle8i.

close( )
> Only with Oracle8i.

getAnyDataEmbeddedObject(int *parameterIndex*)
> Retrieves data of an embedded object within AnyData into a java.lang.Object object. New with Oracle9i.

getARRAY(int *parameterIndex*)
> Retrieves data into an oracle.sql.ARRAY object.

getAsciiStream(int *parameterIndex*)
    Retrieves data into a java.io.InputStream object.

getBFILE(int *parameterIndex*)
    Retrieves data into an oracle.sql.BFILE object.

getBigDecimal(int *parameterIndex*)
    Retrieves data into java.math.BigDecimal. Oracle8*i* only.

getBigDecimal(int *parameterIndex*, int *scale*)
    Retrieves data into java.math.BigDecimal. Oracle8*i* only.

getBinaryStream(int *parameterIndex*)
    Retrieves data into a java.io.InputStream object.

getBlob(int *parameterIndex*)
    Retrieves data into an oracle.jdbc2.Blob. Oracle8*i* only.

getBLOB(int *parameterIndex*)
    Retrieves data into an oracle.sql.BLOB object.

getByte(int *parameterIndex*)
    Retrieves data into byte. Oracle8*i* only.

getBytes(int *parameterIndex*)
    Retrieves data into a byte array. Oracle8*i* only.

getCHAR(int *parameterIndex*)
    Retrieves data into an oracle.sql.CHAR object.

getCharacterStream(int *parameterIndex*)
    Retrieves data into a java.io.Reader object. New with Oracle9*i*.

getClob(int *parameterIndex*)
    Retrieves data into an oracle.jdbc2.Clob object. Oracle8*i* only.

getCLOB(int *parameterIndex*)
    Retrieves data into an oracle.sql.CLOB object.

getCursor(int *parameterIndex*)
    Retrieves data into a java.sql.ResultSet object.

getCustomDatum(int *parameterIndex*, CustomDatumFactory *factory*)
    Deprecated with Oracle9*i*.

getDate(int *parameterIndex*)
    Retrieves data into a java.sql.Date object. Oracle8*i* only.

getDATE(int *parameterIndex*)
    Retrieves data into an oracle.sql.DATE object.

getDouble(int *parameterIndex*)
    Retrieves data into an oracle.sql.Double object. Oracle8i only.

getFloat(int *parameterIndex*)
    Retrieves data into an oracle.sql.Float object. Oracle8i only.

getInt(int *parameterIndex*)
    Retrieves data into an oracle.sql.Int object. Oracle8*i* only.

getINTERVALYM(int *parameterIndex*)
    Retrieves data into an oracle.sql.INTERVALYM object. New with Oracle9*i*.

getLong(int *parameterIndex*)
    Retrieves data into an oracle.sql.long object. Oracle8*i* only.

getNUMBER(int *parameterIndex*)
    Retrieves data into an oracle.sql.NUMBER object.

getObject(int *parameterIndex*)
    Retrieves data into a java.lang.object. Oracle8*i* only.

getObject(int *parameterIndex, java.util.Dictionary map*)
    Retrieves data into a java.lang.object. Oracle8*i* only.

getOPAQUE(int *parameterIndex*)
    Retrieves data into an oracle.sql.OPAQUE object. New with Oracle9*i*.

getOracleObject(int *parameterIndex*)
    Retrieves data into an oracle.sql.Datum object.

getOraclePlsqlIndexTable(int *paramIndex*)
    Retrieves a PL/SQL index table into oracle.sql.Datum. Oracle OCI driver-specific.

getORAData(int *parameterIndex, ORADataFactory factory*)
    Retrieves into java.lang.Object. New with Oracle9*i*.

getPlsqlIndexTable(int *paramIndex*)
    Retrieves a PL/SQL index table into java.lang.Object. Oracle OCI driver-specific.

getPlsqlIndexTable(int *paramIndex*, java.lang.Class *primitiveType*)
    Retrieves a PL/SQL index table into java.lang.Object. Oracle OCI driver-specific.

getRAW(int *parameterIndex*)
    Retrieves data into an oracle.sql.RAW object.

getRef(int *parameterIndex*)
    Retrieves data into an oracle.jdbc2.Ref object. Oracle8*i* only.

getREF(int *parameterIndex*)
    Retrieves data into an oracle.sql.REF object.

getROWID(int *parameterIndex*)
    Retrieves data into an oracle.sql.ROWID object.

getShort(int *parameterIndex*)
    Retrieves data into an oracle.sql.Short object. Oracle8*i* only.

getString(int *parameterIndex*)
    Retrieves data into a java.lang.string object. Oracle8*i* only.

getSTRUCT(int *parameterIndex*)
    Retrieves data into an oracle.sql.STRUCT object.

getTime(int *paramIdx*)
    Retrieves data into a java.sql.Time object. Oracle8*i* only.

getTime(int *paramIdx*, java.util.Calendar *cal*)
    Retrieves data into a java.sql.Time object. Oracle8*i* only.

getTimestamp(int *paramIdx*)
    Retrieves data into a java.sql.Timestamp object. Oracle8*i* only.

getTimestamp(int *paramIdx*, java.util.Calendar *cal*)
    Retrieves data into a java.sql.Timestamp object. Oracle8*i* only.

getTIMESTAMP(int *paramIdx*)
    Retrieves data into an oracle.sql.TIMESTAMP object. New with Oracle9*i*.

getTIMESTAMPLTZ(int *paramIdx*)
    Retrieves data into an oracle.sql.TIMESTAMPLTZ object. New with Oracle9*i*.

getTIMESTAMPTZ(int *paramIdx*)
> Retrieves data into an oracle.sql.TIMESTAMPTZ object. New with Oracle9*i*.

getUnicodeStream(int *parameterIndex*)
> Retrieves data into a java.io.InputStream object.

registerIndexTableOutParameter(int *paramIndex*, int *maxLen*, int *elemSqlType*, int *elemMaxLen*)
> Oracle OCI driver-specific.

registerOutParameter(int *paramIndex*, int *sqlType*)
> Registers Out parameters. Oracle8*i* only.

registerOutParameter(int *paramIndex*, int *sqlType*, int *scale*)
> Registers Out parameters. Oracle8*i* only.

registerOutParameter(int *paramIndex*, int *sqlType,* java.lang.String *sqlName*)
> Registers column objects as Out parameters. Oracle8*i* only.

registerOutParameter(int *paramIndex*, int *sqlType*, int *scale*, int *maxLength*)
> Special Oracle version of registerOutParameter for registering CHAR, VARCHAR, LONG, RAW, and LONG RAW columns.

registerOutParameterBytes(int *paramIndex*, int *sqlType*, int *scale*, int *maxLength*)
> Special Oracle version of registerOutParameter for registering CHAR, VARCHAR, LONG, RAW, and LONG RAW columns. New with Oracle9*i*.

registerOutParameterChars(int *paramIndex*, int *sqlType*, int *scale*, int *maxLength*)
> Special Oracle version of registerOutParameter for registering CHAR, VARCHAR, LONG, RAW, and LONG RAW columns. New with Oracle9*i*.

sendBatch( )
> Sends the sets of parameters batched (for Oracle-style batching only) and returns it.

setExecuteBatch(int *nrows*)
> Sets the batch value (for Oracle-style batching only).

wasNULL( )
> Returns Boolean. Oracle8*i* only.

Inherited methods

Inherits all methods from the java.sql.CallableStatement interface in Oracle9*i*, the oracle.jdbc.OraclePreparedStatement interface, and the oracle.jdbc.OracleStatement interface.

OracleConnection

Extends the java.sql.Connection interface.

The constructor for this class (in Oracle8*i*) is:

```
OracleConnection(oracle.jdbc.dbaccess.DBAccess access, java.lang.String ur,
java.lang.String us, java.lang.String p, java.lang.String db, java.util.
Properties info)
```

Fields

ASCII_TO_CHAR	Static int, Oracle8*i* only
CACHE_SIZE_NOT_SET	Static int, new with Oracle9*i*

CHAR_TO_ASCII	Static int, Oracle8*i* only
CHAR_TO_JAVACHAR	Static int, Oracle8*i* only
CHAR_TO_UNICODE	Static int, Oracle8*i* only
conversion	Oracle.jdbc.dbaccess.DBConversion, Oracle8*i* only
DATABASE_CLOSED	Static int, new with Oracle9*i*
DATABASE_NOTOK	Static int, new with Oracle9*i*
DATABASE_OK	Static int, new with Oracle9*i*
DATABASE_TIMEOUT	Static int, new with Oracle9*i*
dataSizeBytes	Static java.lang.String, new with Oracle9*i*
dataSizeChars	Static java.lang.String, new with Oracle9*i*
dataSizeUnitsPropertyName	Static java.lang.String, new with Oracle9*i*
db_access	Oracle.jdbc.dbaccess.DBAccess, Oracle8*i* only
DEBUG	Static Boolean, Oracle8*i* only
JAVACHAR_TO_CHAR	Static int, Oracle8*i* only
lob_dbaccess	Oracle.sql.LobDBACCESSImpl, Oracle8*i* only
NONE	Static int, Oracle8*i* only
RAW_TO_ASCII	Static int, Oracle8*i* only
RAW_TO_JAVACHAR	Static int, Oracle8*i* only
RAW_TO_UNICODE	Static int, Oracle8*i* only
UNICODE_TO_CHAR	Static int, Oracle8*i* only
UsingXA	Boolean, Oracle8*i* only
XA_wants_error	Boolean, Oracle8*i* only

Inherited fields

The following fields are inherited from java.sql.Connection with Oracle9*i*:

TRANSACTION_NONE
TRANSACTION_READ_COMMITTED
TRANSACTION_READ_UNCOMMITTED
TRANSACTION_REPEATABLE_READ
TRANSACTION_SERIALIZABLE

Methods

_getPC( )
Returns the underlying physical connection if this is a logical connection as java.sql.Connection. New with Oracle9*i*.

archive(int *mode*, int *aseq*, java.lang.String *acstext*)
Deprecated with Oracle9*i* and will be removed in a future release.

assertComplete( )
Oracle no longer supports Ultra. Deprecated and will be removed in a future release.

clearWarnings( )
Clear warnings for connection object. Oracle8*i* only.

close( )
Rolls back the current transaction. Oracle8*i* only.

commit( )
Commits changes for connection object. Oracle8*i* only.

createBfileDBAccess( )
> Returns oracle.sql.BfileDBAccess. Oracle8*i* only.

createBlobDBAccess( )
> Returns oracle.sql.BlobDBAccess. Oracle8*i* only.

createClobDBAccess( )
> Returns oracle.sql.ClobDBAccess. Oracle8*i* only.

createStatement( )
> Returns java.sql.Statement. Oracle8*i* only.

createStatement(int *resultSetType*, int *resultSetConcurrency*)
> JDBC 2.0. Returns a java.sql.Statement object that will generate ResultSet objects with the given type and concurrency. Oracle8*i* only.

createStatementWithKey(java.lang.String *key*)
> Returns java.sql.Statement. If a statement with the given *key* exists in the cache, then the statement is returned as it was when it was closed and cached with this *key*. Oracle8*i* only.

getAutoClose( )
> Returns a Boolean. The driver is always in autoclose mode.

getAutoCommit( )
> Returns a Boolean. Oracle8*i* only.

getCallWithKey(java.lang.String *key*)
> Searches the explicit cache for a match on *key* and returns java.sql.CallableStatement. New with Oracle9*i*.

getClientData(java.lang.Object *key*)
> Returns a java.lang.Object. Oracle8*i* only.

getCreateStatementAsRefCursor( )
> Retrieves the current Boolean setting of the createStatementAsRefCursor flag, which you can set with the setCreateStatementAsRefCursor method. New with Oracle9*i*.

getDatabaseProductionVersion( )
> Returns java.lang.String. Oracle8*i* only.

getDbCsId( )
> Returns short with Oracle identifier of character set. Oracle8*i* only.

getDefaultAutoRefetch( )
> Returns a Boolean. Oracle8*i* only.

getDefaultExecuteBatch( )
> Returns int as the overall connection batch value of this connection.

getDefaultRowPrefetch( )
> Retrieves the value of row prefetch as int for all statements associated with this connection and created after this value was set.

getDescriptor(java.lang.String *sql_name*)
> Gets a Descriptor object corresponding to a SQL type as java.lang.Object.

getExplicitCachingEnabled( )
> Returns True if the explicit cache is currently enabled, False otherwise. New with Oracle9*i*.

getImplicitCachingEnabled()
    Returns True if the implicit cache is currently enabled, False otherwise. New with Oracle9i.

getIncludeSynonyms()
    Returns Boolean indicating whether or not synonym information is included in DatabaseMetaData.getColumns.

getJavaObject(java.lang.String sql_name)
    Deprecated with Oracle9i.

getJdbcCsId()
    Returns short with Oracle ID of character set. Oracle8i only.

getMetaData()
    Returns java.sql.DatabaseMetaData. Oracle8i only.

getProperties()
    Determines the connection properties and returns as java.util.Properties. New with Oracle9i.

getRemarksReporting()
    Returns Boolean indicating whether or not a call of getTables or getColumns of the DatabaseMetaData interface will report the REMARKS column.

getReportRemarks()
    Returns Boolean. Oracle8i only.

getRestrictGetTables()
    Gets the restriction status as Boolean of the returned data in DatabaseMetaData. getTables.

getSessionTimeZone()
    Obtains Oracle session time zone region name as java.lang.String. New with Oracle9i.

getSQLType(java.lang.Object obj)
    Deprecated with Oracle9i.

getStatementCacheSize()
    Returns int, the current size of the application cache. New with Oracle9i.

getStatementWithKey(java.lang.String key)
    Searches the explicit cache for a match on key and returns java.sql.PreparedStatement. New with Oracle9i.

getStmtCacheSize()
    Deprecated with Oracle9i. Use getStatementCacheSize() instead.

getStructAttrCsId()
    Obtains the Oracle identifier of the character set used in STRUCT attributes as short

getSynchronousMode()
    Deprecated with Oracle9i Release 2. New with Oracle9i.

getTypeMap()
    Returns java.util.Dictionary. Oracle8i only.

getUserName()
    Gets the username of the current connection as java.lang.String.

getUsingXAFlag()
    Deprecated.

getVersionNumber( )
    Returns short. Oracle8i only.

getWarnings( )
    Returns java.sql.SQLWarning. Oracle8i only.

getXAErrorFlag( )
    Returns XA error flag. In OracleXAException class in Oracle9i.

holdLine(OracleStatement *stmt*)
    Oracle8i only.

initUserName( )
    Oracle8i only.

isClosed( )
    Returns Boolean. Oracle8i only.

isLogicalConnection( )
    Returns a Boolean indicating whether it's a logical connection or not. New with Oracle9i.

isReadOnly( )
    Returns Boolean. Oracle8i only.

nativeSQL(java.lang.String *sql*)
    Returns java.lang.String. Oracle8i only.

needLine( )
    Oracle8i only.

openJoltConnection(java.lang.String *apiName*, short *major*, short *minor*)
    New with Oracle9i. Deprecated with Oracle9i Release 2.

oracleReleaseSavepoint(OracleSavepoint *savepoint*)
    Removes the given OracleSavepoint object from the current transaction. New with Oracle9i.

oracleRollback(OracleSavepoint *savepoint*)
    Undoes all changes made after the given OracleSavepoint object was set. New with Oracle9i.

oracleSetSavepoint( )
    Creates an unnamed savepoint in the current transaction and returns the new OracleSavepoint object that represents it. New with Oracle9i.

oracleSetSavepoint(java.lang.String *name*)
    Creates a savepoint with the given name in the current transaction and returns the new OracleSavepoint object that represents it. New with Oracle9i.

pingDatabase(int *timeOut*)
    Pings Database and returns int. New with Oracle9i.

prepareCall(java.lang.String *sql*)
    Returns java.sql.CallableStatement. Oracle8i only.

prepareCall(java.lang.String *sql*, int *resultSetType*, int *resultSetConcurrency*)
    Returns java.sql.CallableStatement. Oracle8i only.

prepareCallWithKey(java.lang.String *key*)
    Deprecated with Oracle9i. This is the same as prepareCall, except that if a CallableStatement with the given *key* exists in the cache, then the statement is returned as it was when it was closed and cached with this *key*. An object returned from the Cache based on *key* will have its state set to "KEYED". If no such CallableStatement is found, then NULL is returned. The key cannot be NULL.

prepareStatement(java.lang.String *sql*)
  Returns java.sql.PreparedStatement. Oracle8*i* only.

prepareStatement(java.lang.String *sql*, int *resultSetType*, int *resultSetConcurrency*)
  Returns java.sql.PreparedStatement. Oracle8*i* only.

prepareStatementWithKey(java.lang.String *key*)
  Deprecated with Oracle9*i*. See prepareCallWithKey for details.

purgeExplicitCache( )
  Removes all existing statements from the explicit cache, after which it will be empty. New with Oracle9*i*.

purgeImplicitCache( )
  Removes all existing statements from the implicit cache, after which it will be empty. New with Oracle9*i*.

putDescriptor(java.lang.String *sql_name*, java.lang.Object *desc*)
  Stores the Object descriptor for later usage.

registerApiDescription(java.lang.String *apiName*, short *major*, short *minor*,
  java.lang.String *className*)
  New with Oracle9*i*. Deprecated with Oracle9*i* Release 2.

registerSQLType(java.lang.String *sql_name*, java.lang.Class *java_class*)
  Deprecated with Oracle9*i*.

registerSQLType(java.lang.String *sql_name*, java.lang.String *java_class_name*)
  Deprecated with Oracle9*i*.

registerTAFCallback(OracleOCIFailover *cbk*, java.lang.Object *obj*)
  Registers an application TAF callback instance that will be called when an application failover occurs. New with Oracle9*i*.

releaseLine( )
  Only with Oracle8*i*.

removeClientData(java.lang.Object *key*)
  Returns java.lang.Object. Oracle8*i* only.

rollback( )
  Drops changes since last commit or rollback and releases database locks. Oracle8*i* only.

setAutoClose(boolean *autoClose*)
  Always in autoclose mode.

setAutoCommit(boolean *autoCommit*)
  Oracle8*i* only.

setClientData(java.lang.Object *key*, java.lang.Object *value*)
  Returns java.lang.Object. Oracle8*i* only.

setCreateStatementAsRefCursor(boolean *value*)
  When this is set to true, any new statements created from this connection will be created as a REF CURSOR. New with Oracle9*i*.

setDefaultAutoRefetch(boolean *autoRefresh*)
  Sets default value of AutoRefresh, which causes automatic refetching of rows during update process. Oracle8*i* only.

setDefaultExecuteBatch(int *batch*)
  Sets a default batch value for the Oracle update batching model (the default value is 1).

setDefaultRowPrefetch(int *value*)
> Sets the value of the row prefetch for all statements associated with this connection and created after this value was set. The row-prefetching feature associates an integer row-prefetch setting with a given statement object.

setExplicitCachingEnabled(boolean *cache*)
> Enables or disables the explicit cache. New with Oracle9i.

setImplicitCachingEnabled(boolean *cache*)
> Enables or disables the implicit cache. New with Oracle9i.

setIncludeSynonyms(boolean *synonyms*)
> Turns on or off the retrieval of synonym information in DatabaseMetaData.

setReadOnly(boolean *readOnly*)
> Oracle8i only.

setRemarksReporting(boolean *reportRemarks*)
> Turns on or off the reporting of the REMARKS columns by the getTables and getColumns calls of the DatabaseMetaData interface. The DatabaseMetaData calls to getTables and getColumns are extremely slow if the REMARKS column has to be reported because this necessitates an expensive outer join. Thus, by default, the JDBC driver does not report the REMARKS columns.

setRestrictGetTables(boolean *restrict*)
> Turns on or off the restriction of the returned data in DatabaseMetaData.getTables. DatabaseMetaData.getTables returns information about all accessible tables, views, and synonyms.

setSessionTimeZone(java.lang.String *regionName*)
> Sets the session time zone. New with Oracle9i.

setStatementCacheSize(int *size*)
> Specifies *size* of the application cache (which will be used by both implicit and explicit caching). New with Oracle9i.

setStmtCacheSize(int *size*)
> Deprecated with Oracle9i. Use setStatementCacheSize( ) instead.

setStmtCacheSize(int *size*, boolean *clearMetaData*)
> Deprecated with Oracle9i. Use setStatementCacheSize( ) instead.

setSynchronousMode(boolean *isSynchronous*)
> New with Oracle9i. Deprecated with Oracle9i Release 2.

setTypeMap(java.util.Dictionary *map*)
> Installs *map* as type map for connection. Oracle8i only.

setUsingXAFlag(boolean *value*)
> Deprecated with Oracle9i.

setWrapper(OracleConnection *wrapper*)
> Sets the wrapping object. New with Oracle9i.

setXAErrorFlag(boolean *value*)
> Deprecated with Oracle9i.

shutdown(int *mode*)
> Deprecated with Oracle9i.

startup(java.lang.String *startup_str*, int *mode*)
> Deprecated with Oracle9i.

trace(java.lang.String *s*)
>   Oracle8*i* only.

unwrap( )
>   Returns the wrapping object as OracleConnection; otherwise, NULL. New with
>   Oracle9*i*.

Inherited methods

Inherits all methods from the java.sql.Connection interface.

Inherits all methods from java.lang.Object except clone, equals, and finalize.

OracleJdbc2SQLInput

Extends the java.lang.Object interface. Implements the oracle.jdbc2.SQLInput interface. Only in Oracle8*i*.

Methods

readArray( )
>   Returns oracle.jdbc2.Array from the stream.

readARRAY( )
>   Returns ARRAY, the next attribute in the stream, as a oracle.sql.ARRAY.

readAsciiStream( )
>   Returns java.io.InputStream as the next attribute in the stream.

readBFILE( )
>   Returns BFILE as the next attribute in the stream.

readBigDecimal( )
>   Returns java.math.BigDecimal as the next attribute in the stream.

readBinaryStream( )
>   Returns java.io.InputStream as the next attribute in the stream.

readBlob( )
>   Returns oracle.jdbc2.Blob as the next attribute in the stream.

readBLOB( )
>   Returns BLOB as the next attribute in the stream.

readBoolean( )
>   Returns Boolean as the next attribute in the stream.

readByte( )
>   Returns byte as the next attribute in the stream.

readBytes( )
>   Returns byte array as the next attribute in the stream.

readCHAR( )
>   Returns oracle.sql.CHAR as the next attribute in the stream.

readCharacterStream( )
>   Returns java.io.Reader as the next attribute in the stream.

readClob( )
>   Returns oracle.jdbc2.Clob as the next attribute in the stream.

readCLOB()
    Returns CLOB as the next attribute in the stream.
readDATE()
    Returns DATE as the next attribute in the stream.
readDouble()
    Returns Double as the next attribute in the stream.
readFloat()
    Returns float as the next attribute in the stream.
readInt()
    Returns int as the next attribute in the stream.
readLong()
    Returns long as the next attribute in the stream.
readNUMBER()
    Returns NUMBER as the next attribute in the stream.
readObject()
    Returns java.lang.Object as the datum at the head of the stream.
readOracleObject()
    Returns java.lang.Object as the next attribute in the stream.
readRAW()
    Returns RAW as the next attribute in the stream.
readRef()
    Returns oracle.jdbc2.Ref as the next attribute in the stream.
readREF()
    Returns REF as the next attribute in the stream.
readROWID()
    Returns ROWID as the next attribute in the stream.
readShort()
    Returns short as the next attribute in the stream.
readString()
    Returns java.lang.String as the next attribute in the stream.
readStruct()
    Returns oracle.jdbc2.Struct as the next attribute in the stream.
readSTRUCT()
    Returns STRUCT as the next attribute in the stream.
readTime()
    Returns java.sql.Time as the next attribute in the stream.
readTimestamp()
    Returns java.sql.Timestamp as the next attribute in the stream.
wasNull()
    Returns Boolean.

Inherited methods

Inherits all methods from java.lang.Object except clone and finalize.

OracleOCIFailover

Handles failover at the OCI level. New with Oracle9*i*.

Fields

FO_ABORT	Static int
FO_BEGIN	Static int
FO_END	Static int
FO_ERROR	Static int
FO_EVENT_UNKNOWN	Static int
FO_NONE	Static int
FO_REAUTH	Static int
FO_RETRY	Static int
FO_SELECT	Static int
FO_SESSION	Static int
FO_TYPE_UNKNOWN	Static int

Method

callbackFn(java.sql.Connection *conn*, java.lang.Object ctxt, int *type*, int *event*)
> Returns int.

OracleParameterMetaData

Extends the java.sql.ParameterMetaData interface. New with Oracle9*i*.

Fields

parameterModeIn	Static int
parameterModeInOut	Static int
parameterModeOut	Static int
parameterModeUnknown	Static int
parameterNoNulls	Static int
parameterNullable	Static int
parameterNullableUnknown	Static int

Methods

getParameterClassName(int *param*)
> Retrieves the fully qualified name of the Java class as java.lang.String whose instances should be passed to the method PreparedStatement.setObject.

getParameterCount( )
> Retrieves int as the number of parameters in the PreparedStatement object for which this OracleParameterMetaData object contains information.

getParameterMode(int *param*)
> Retrieves int as the designated parameter's mode.

getParameterType(int *param*)
> Retrieves int as the designated parameter's SQL type.

getParameterTypeName(int *param*)
> Retrieves java.lang.String as the designated parameter's database-specific type name.

getPrecision(int *param*)
> Retrieves int as the designated parameter's number of decimal digits.

getScale(int *param*)
> Retrieves int as the designated parameter's number of digits to the right of the decimal point.

isNullable(int *param*)
> Retrieves int indicating whether NULL values are allowed in the designated parameter.

isSigned(int *param*)
> Retrieves Boolean indicating whether values for the designated parameter can be signed numbers.

OraclePreparedStatement

Extends the java.sql.PreparedStatement interface with Oracle9*i*; extends OracleStatement with Oracle8*i*. With Oracle8*i*, implements oracle.jdbc.internal.OraclePreparedStatement.

Fields

FORM_CHAR   Static short, new with Oracle9*i*
FORM_NCHAR   Static short, new with Oracle9*i*

Inherited fields

The following fields are inherited from oracle.jdbc.OracleStatement:

auto_rollback	Only with Oracle8*i*
closed	Only with Oracle8*i*
dbstmt	Only with Oracle8*i*
defines	Only with Oracle8*i*
EXPLICIT	
IMPLICIT	
NEW	
wait_option	Only with Oracle8*i*.

Methods

closeWithKey(java.lang.String *key*)
> The underlying cursor is not closed and the statement handle is cached on the *key*, while the state, data, and metadata are not cleared. The statement can be retrieved with this key later. Oracle8*i* only.

defineParameterType(int *param_index*, int *type*, int *max_size*)
> Defines the type under which you will bind the parameter and the maximum size (in characters) of data you will bind in binds.

defineParameterTypeBytes(int *param_index*, int *type*, int *max_size*)
> Defines the type under which you will bind the parameter and the maximum size (in bytes) of data you will bind in binds. New with Oracle9*i*.

defineParameterTypeChars(int *param_index*, int *type*, int *max_size*)
> Defines the type under which you will bind the parameter and the maximum size (in characters) of data you will bind in binds. New with Oracle9*i*.

getExecuteBatch( )
> Retrieves the int batch value of this statement for the Oracle update batching model (default is set by the connection object).

OracleGetParameterMetaData( )
> Retrieves the number, types, and properties of this PreparedStatement object's parameters as OracleParameterMetaData.

sendBatch( )
> Sends any existing batch (for the Oracle update batching model) and returns int.

setARRAY(int *paramIndex*, ARRAY *arr*)
> Binds the designated parameter to a oracle.sql.ARRAY.

setBfile(int *paramIndex*, BFILE *file*)
> Binds the designated parameter to an oracle.sql.BFILE value.

setBFILE(int *paramIndex*, BFILE *file*)
> Binds the designated parameter to an oracle.sql.BFILE value.

setBLOB(int *paramIndex*, BLOB *lob*)
> Binds the designated parameter to an oracle.sql.BLOB value.

setCHAR(int *paramIndex*, CHAR *ch*)
> Binds the designated parameter to an oracle.sql.CHAR value.

setCheckBindTypes(boolean *flag*)
> Enables/disables bind type checking.

setCLOB(int *paramIndex*, CLOB *lob*)
> Binds the designated parameter to an oracle.sql.CLOB value.

setCursor(int *paramIndex*, java.sql.ResultSet *rs*)
> Deprecated with Oracle9*i*.

setCustomDatum(int *paramIndex*, CustomDatum *x*)
> Deprecated with Oracle9*i*.

setDATE(int *paramIndex*, DATE *date*)
> Binds the designated parameter to an oracle.sql.DATE value.

setDisableStmtCaching(boolean *cache*)
> Indicates that this object should not be cached even when the corresponding Connection is cache-enabled.

setExecuteBatch(int *batchValue*)
> Sets the batch value of this statement for the Oracle update batching model (the default value is set by the connection object).

setFixedCHAR(int *paramIndex*, java.lang.String *x*)
> Sets the designated parameter to a string and executes a nonpadded comparison with a SQL CHAR.

setFormOfUse(int *paramIndex*, short *formOfUse*)
> Specifies whether the data is bound for a SQL NCHAR datatype.

setINTERVALYM(int *paramIndex*, INTERVALYM *x*)
> Binds the designated parameter to an oracle.sql.INTERVALYM value.

setNUMBER(int *paramIndex*, NUMBER *num*)
> Binds the designated parameter to an oracle.sql.NUMBER value.

setOPAQUE(int *paramIndex*, OPAQUE *val*)
Binds the designated parameter to a oracle.sql.OPAQUE value.

setOracleObject(int *paramIndex*, Datum *x*)
Binds the designated parameter to an oracle.sql.Datum value.

setORAData(int *paramIndex*, ORAData *x*)
Binds the designated parameter to an oracle.sql.ORAData value.

setPlsqlIndexTable(int *paramIndex*, java.lang.Object *arrayData*, int *maxLen*, int *curLen*, int *elemSqlType*, int *elemMaxLen*)
Binds a PL/SQL associative array parameter in the IN parameter mode.

setRAW(int *paramIndex*, RAW *raw*)
Binds the designated parameter to an oracle.sql.RAW value.

setREF(int *paramIndex*, REF *ref*)
Binds the designated parameter to an oracle.sql.REF value.

setRefType(int *paramIndex*, REF *ref*)
Binds the designated parameter to an oracle.sql.REF value.

setROWID(int *paramIndex*, ROWID *rowid*)
Binds the designated parameter to an oracle.sql.RAWID value.

setSTRUCT(int *paramIndex*, STRUCT *struct*)
Binds the designated parameter to an oracle.sql.STRUCT value.

setStructDescriptor(int *paramIndex*, StructDescriptor *desc*)
Binds the bind type of the designated parameter from an oracle.sql.StructDescriptor.

setTIMESTAMP(int *paramIndex*, TIMESTAMP *x*)
Binds the designated parameter to an oracle.sql.TIMESTAMP value.

setTIMESTAMPLTZ(int *paramIndex*, TIMESTAMPLTZ *x*)
Binds the designated parameter to an oracle.sql.TIMESTAMPLTZ value.

setTIMESTAMPTZ(int *paramIndex*, TIMESTAMPTZ *x*)
Binds the designated parameter to an oracle.sql.TIMESTAMPTZ value.

Inherited methods
Inherits all methods from the java.sql.PreparedStatement interface except executeQuery.

Inherits all methods from the oracle.jdbc.OracleStatement interface.

OracleResultSet

Extends the java.sql.ResultSet interface.

Inherited fields
The following fields are inherited from java.sql.ResultSet:

    CONCUR_READ_ONLY
    CONCUR_UPDATABLE
    FETCH_FORWARD
    FETCH_REVERSE
    FETCH_UNKNOWN
    TYPE_FORWARD_ONLY
    TYPE_SCROLL_INSENSITIVE
    TYPE_SCROLL_SENSITIVE

Methods

getARRAY(int *columnIndex*)
   Returns ARRAY from *columnIndex* column.

getARRAY(java.lang.String *columnName*)
   Returns ARRAY from name *columnName*.

getBfile(int *columnIndex*)
   Returns BFILE from *columnIndex* column.

getBFILE(int *columnIndex*)
   Returns BFILE from *columnIndex* column.

getBfile(java.lang.String *columnName*)
   Returns BFILE from name *columnName*.

getBFILE(java.lang.String *columnName*)
   Returns BFILE from name *columnName*.

getBLOB(int *columnIndex*)
   Returns BLOB from *columnIndex* column.

getBLOB(java.lang.String *columnName*)
   Returns BLOB from name *columnName*.

getCHAR(int *columnIndex*)
   Returns CHAR from *columnIndex* column.

getCHAR(java.lang.String *columnName*)
   Returns CHAR from name *columnName*.

getCLOB(int *columnIndex*)
   Returns CLOB from *columnIndex* column.

getCLOB(java.lang.String *columnName*)
   Returns CLOB from name *columnName*.

getCursor(int *columnIndex*)
   Returns java.sql.ResultSet from *columnIndex* column.

getCursor(java.lang.String *columnName*)
   Returns java.sql.ResultSet from name *columnName*.

getCustomDatum(int *columnIndex*, CustomDatumFactory *factory*)
   Returns CustomDatum. Deprecated with Oracle9*i*.

getCustomDatum(java.lang.String *columnName*, CustomDatumFactory *factory*)
   Returns CustomDatum. Deprecated with Oracle9*i*.

getDATE(int *columnIndex*)
   Returns DATE from *columnIndex* column.

getDATE(java.lang.String *columnName*)
   Returns DATE from name *columnName*.

getINTERVALYM(int *columnIndex*)
   Returns an oracle.sql.INTERVALYM value from *columnIndex* column.

getINTERVALYM(java.lang.String *columnName*)
   Returns an oracle.sql.INTERVALYM value from name *columnName*.

getNUMBER(int *columnIndex*)
   Returns NUMBER from *columnIndex* column.

getNUMBER(java.lang.String *columnName*)
   Returns NUMBER from name *columnName*.

getOPAQUE(int *columnIndex*)
    Returns OPAQUE from *columnIndex* column.

getOPAQUE(java.lang.String *columnName*)
    Returns OPAQUE. from name *columnName*.

getOracleObject(int *columnIndex*)
    Returns Datum from *columnIndex* column.

getOracleObject(java.lang.String *columnName*)
    Returns Datum from name *columnName*.

getORAData(int *columnIndex*, ORADataFactory *factory*)
    Returns ORAData from *columnIndex* column.

getORAData(java.lang.String *columnName*, ORADataFactory *factory*)
    Returns ORAData from name *columnName*.

getRAW(int *columnIndex*)
    Returns RAW from *columnIndex* column.

getRAW(java.lang.String *columnName*)
    Returns RAW from name *columnName*.

getREF(int *columnIndex*)
    Returns REF from *columnIndex* column.

getREF(java.lang.String *columnName*)
    Returns REF from name *columnName*.

getROWID(int *columnIndex*)
    Returns ROWID from *columnIndex* column.

getROWID(java.lang.String *columnName*)
    Returns ROWID from name *columnName*.

getSTRUCT(int *columnIndex*)
    Returns STRUCT from *columnIndex* column.

getSTRUCT(java.lang.String *columnName*)
    Returns STRUCT from name *columnName*.

getTIMESTAMP(int *columnIndex*)
    Returns an oracle.sql.TIMESTAMP value from *columnIndex* column.

getTIMESTAMP(java.lang.String *colName*)
    Returns an oracle.sql.TIMESTAMP value from *colName*.

getTIMESTAMPLTZ(int *columnIndex*)
    Returns an oracle.sql.TIMESTAMPLTZ value from *columnIndex* column.

getTIMESTAMPLTZ(java.lang.String *colName*)
    Returns an oracle.sql.TIMESTAMPLTZ value from *colName*.

getTIMESTAMPTZ(int *columnIndex*)
    Returns an oracle.sql.TIMESTAMPTZ value from *columnIndex* column.

getTIMESTAMPTZ(java.lang.String *colName*)
    Returns an oracle.sql.TIMESTAMPTZ value from *colName*.

updateArray(int *columnIndex*, java.sql.Array *x*)
    Updates a java.sql.Array with *columnIndex*.

updateARRAY(int *columnIndex*, ARRAY *x*)
    Updates an ARRAY datatype with *columnIndex*.

updateArray(java.lang.String *columnName*, java.sql.Array *x*)
　　Updates a java.sql.Array with name columnName.

updateARRAY(java.lang.String *columnName*, ARRAY *x*)
　　Updates an ARRAY with name *columnName*.

updateBfile(int *columnIndex*, BFILE *x*)
　　Updates a BFILE datatype with *columnIndex*.

updateBFILE(int *columnIndex*, BFILE *x*)
　　Updates a BFILE datatype with *columnIndex*.

updateBfile(java.lang.String *columnName*, BFILE *x*)
　　Updates a BFILE with name *columnName*.

updateBFILE(java.lang.String *columnName*, BFILE *x*)
　　Updates a BFILE with name *columnName*.

updateBlob(int *columnIndex*, java.sql.Blob *x*)
　　Updates a java.sql.Blob with *columnIndex*.

updateBLOB(int *columnIndex*, BLOB *x*)
　　Updates a BLOB with *columnIndex*.

updateBlob(java.lang.String *columnName*, java.sql.Blob *x*)
　　Updates a java.sql.Blob datatype with *columnIndex*.

updateBLOB(java.lang.String *columnName*, BLOB *x*)
　　Updates a BLOB with name *columnName*.

updateCHAR(int *columnIndex*, CHAR *x*)
　　Updates a CHAR datatype with *columnIndex*.

updateCHAR(java.lang.String *columnName*, CHAR *x*)
　　Updates a CHAR with name *columnName*.

updateClob(int *columnIndex*, java.sql.Clob *x*)
　　Updates a java.sql.Clob datatype with *columnIndex*.

updateCLOB(int *columnIndex*, CLOB *x*)
　　Updates a CLOB datatype with *columnIndex*.

updateClob(java.lang.String *columnName*, java.sql.Clob *x*)
　　Updates a java.sql.Clob with name *columnName*.

updateCLOB(java.lang.String *columnName*, CLOB *x*)
　　Updates a CLOB with name *columnName*.

updateCustomDatum(int *columnIndex*, CustomDatum *x*)
　　Deprecated with Oracle9*i*.

updateCustomDatum(java.lang.String *columnName*, CustomDatum *x*)
　　Deprecated with Oracle9*i*.

updateDATE(int *columnIndex*, DATE *x*)
　　Updates a DATE datatype with *columnIndex*.

updateDATE(java.lang.String *columnName*, DATE *x*)
　　Updates a DATE with name *columnName*.

updateNUMBER(int *columnIndex*, NUMBER *x*)
　　Updates a NUMBER datatype with *columnIndex*.

updateNUMBER(java.lang.String *columnName*, NUMBER *x*)
　　Updates a NUMBER with name *columnName*.

updateOracleObject(int *columnIndex*, Datum *x*)
> Updates an OracleObject datatype with *columnIndex*.

updateOracleObject(java.lang.String *columnName*, Datum *x*)
> Updates an OracleObject with name *columnName*.

updateORAData(int *columnIndex*, ORAData *x*)
> Updates an OraData datatype with *columnIndex*.

updateORAData(java.lang.String *columnName*, ORAData *x*)
> Updates an OraData datatype with name *columnName*.

updateRAW(int *columnIndex*, RAW *x*)
> Updates a RAW datatype with *columnIndex*.

updateRAW(java.lang.String *columnName*, RAW *x*)
> Updates a RAW with name *columnName*.

updateRef(int *columnIndex*, java.sql.Ref *x*)
> Updates a java.sql.Ref datatype with *columnIndex*.

updateREF(int *columnIndex*, REF *x*)
> Updates a REF datatype with *columnIndex*.

updateRef(java.lang.String *columnName*, java.sql.Ref *x*)
> Updates a java.sql.Ref with name *columnName*.

updateREF(java.lang.String *columnName*, REF *x*)
> Updates a REF datatype with name *columnName*.

updateROWID(int *columnIndex*, ROWID *x*)
> Updates a ROWID datatype with *columnIndex*.

updateROWID(java.lang.String *columnName*, ROWID *x*)
> Updates a ROWID with name *columnName*.

updateSTRUCT(int *columnIndex*, STRUCT *x*)
> Updates a STRUCT datatype with *columnIndex*.

updateSTRUCT(java.lang.String *columnName*, STRUCT *x*)
> Updates a STRUCT with name *columnName*.

Inherited methods

Inherits all methods from java.sql.ResultSet except insertRow.

OracleResultSetCache

Provides an interface to the Oracle result set cache.

Methods

clear( )
> Removes all data from the result set cache.

close( )
> Closes the result set cache.

get(int *i*, int *j*)
> Returns the data stored in the *i*th row and *j*th column as a java.lang.Object..

put(int *i*, int *j*, java.lang.Object *value*)
> Saves the data in the *i*th row and *j*th column in java.lang.Object.

remove(int *i*)
> Removes the *i*th row from the result set cache.

remove(int *i*, int *j*)
> Removes the data stored in the *i*th row and *j*th column in the result set cache.

OracleResultSetMetaData

Extends the java.sql.ResultSetMetaData interface.

Inherited fields

The following fields are inherited from java.sql.ResultSetMetaData:

> columnNoNulls
> columnNullable
> columnNullableUnknown

Method

isNCHAR(int *index*)
> Returns a Boolean indicating whether the *index* entry is an NCHAR, NVAR-CHAR, or NCLOB.

Inherited methods

Inherits all methods from java.sql.ResultSetMetaData.

OracleSavepoint

Extends the java.sql.Savepoint interface.

Methods

getSavepointId( )
> Retrieves the generated ID as an int for the savepoint that this OracleSavepoint object represents.

getSavepointName( )
> Retrieves the name of the savepoint as a java.lang.String that this OracleSavepoint object represents. New with Oracle9*i*.

OracleStatement

Extends the java.sql.Statement interface. OracleCallableStatement and OraclePreparedStatement are subinterfaces. OracleStatement is a class in oracle.jdbc.driver in Oracle8*i*, with additional methods. See the Oracle documentation for details.

Fields

EXPLICIT	Static int
IMPLICIT	Static int
NEW	Static int

Methods

clearDefines()
> Clears previously defined types for the define columns of this statement.

closeWithKey(java.lang.String *key*)
> The underlying cursor is not closed and the statement handle is cached on the *key*, while the state, data, and metadata are not cleared. The statement can be retrieved with this key later. Oracle8*i* only.

creationState()
> Deprecated with Oracle9*i*.

defineColumnType(int *column_index*, int *type*)
> Defines the *type* you will use to retrieve data from a particular database table column *column_index*.

defineColumnType(int *column_index*, int type, int *max_size*)
> Defines the *type* you will use to retrieve data from a particular database table column *column_index* with a *max_ size*.

defineColumnType(int *column_index*, int *typeCode*, java.lang.String *typeName*)
> Defines the *typeCode* you will use to retrieve data from a particular database table column *column_index* with column name *typeName*.

defineColumnTypeBytes(int *column_index*, int *type*, int *max_size*)
> Defines the *type* you will use to retrieve data from a particular database table column *column_index* and the maximum size of data in bytes.

defineColumnTypeChars(int *column_index*, int *type*, int *max_size*)
> Defines the *type* you will use to retrieve data from a particular database table column *column_index* and the maximum size of data in characters.

getRowPrefetch()
> Retrieves int row prefetch for result sets created from this statement.

isNCHAR(int *index*)
> Returns Boolean indicating whether the *index* is NCHAR, NVARCHAR, or NCLOB.

setResultSetCache(OracleResultSetCache *cache*)
> Sets your own client-side *cache* implementation for scrollable result sets.

setRowPrefetch(int *value*)
> Sets the *value* of row prefetch for all result sets created from this statement.

Inherited methods

Inherits all methods from java.sql.Statement.

StructMetaData

Extends the OracleResultSetMetaData interface.

Inherited fields

The following fields are inherited from java.sql.ResultSetMetaData:

> columnNoNulls
> columnNullable
> columnNullableUnknown

Methods

getAttributeJavaName(int *column*)
> Gets a JAVA_STRUCT attribute's external name as java.lang.String.

getLocalColumnCount( )
> Gets the number of local attributes as int.

getOracleColumnClassName(int *column*)
> Returns the fully qualified name as java.lang.String of the Datum class whose instances are manufactured if the method OracleResultSet.getOracleObject is called to retrieve a value from a column.

isInherited(int *column*)
> Returns a Boolean indicating whether the attribute is inherited from its supertype.

Inherited methods

Inherits all methods from OracleResultSetMetaData.

Inherits all methods from java.sql.ResultSetMetaData.

Classes

The following classes are a part of the oracle.jdbc package.

OracleConnectionWrapper

Extends java.lang.Object and implements OracleConnection. New with Oracle9*i*.

The constructor for this class is:

```
OracleConnectionWrapper(OracleConnection toBeWrapped)
```

Methods

_getPC( )
> Returns java.sql.Connection.

archive(int mode, int *aseq*, java.lang.String *acstext*)
> Deprecated and will be removed in a future release.

assertComplete( )
> Oracle no longer supports Ultra. Deprecated and will be removed in a future release.

clearWarnings( )
> Clears warnings from the connection.

close( )
> Closes the connection.

commit( )
> Commits the connection.

createStatement( )
> Returns java.sql.Statement.

createStatement(int *resultSetType*, int *resultSetConcurrency*)
> Returns java.sql.Statement.

createStatement(int *resultSetType*, int *resultSetConcurrency*, int *resultSetHoldability*)
> Returns java.sql.Statement.

---

getAutoClose( )
    Returns the Boolean state of AutoClose.
getAutoCommit( )
    Returns the Boolean state of AutoCommit.
getCallWithKey(java.lang.String *key*)
    Returns java.sql.CallableStatement base on *key*.
getCatalog( )
    Returns catalog as java.lang.String.
getCreateStatementAsRefCursor( )
    Returns a Boolean indicating the current state of CreateStatementAsRefCursor.
getDefaultExecuteBatch( )
    Returns int of default number of batch operations.
getDefaultRowPrefetch( )
    Returns int of default number of rows prefetched.
getDescriptor(java.lang.String *sql_name*)
    Returns java.lang.Object of SQL type *sql_name*.
getExplicitCachingEnabled( )
    Returns a Boolean indicating the current state of explicit cache.
getHoldability( )
    Returns int for holdability.
getImplicitCachingEnabled( )
    Returns a Boolean indicating the current state of implicit cache.
getIncludeSynonyms( )
    Returns a Boolean indicating whether synonym information is included.
getJavaObject(java.lang.String *sql_name*)
    Returns java.lang.Object for *sql_name*.
getMetaData( )
    Returns java.sql.DatabaseMetaData.
getProperties( )
    Returns java.util.Properties.
getRemarksReporting( )
    Returns a Boolean indicating whether remarks are returned with metadata.
getRestrictGetTables( )
    Returns a Boolean indicating the state of restriction status.
getSessionTimeZone( )
    Returns java.lang.String with session time zone.
getSQLType(java.lang.Object *obj*)
    Returns java.lang.String with SQL type for *obj*.
getStatementCacheSize( )
    Returns int for statement cache size.
getStatementWithKey(java.lang.String *key*)
    Returns java.sql.PreparedStatement from explicit cache for statement with *key*.
getStmtCacheSize( )
    Returns int for statement cache size.

getStructAttrCsId( )
Returns short for Oracle identifier of character set for STRUCT attributes.

getSynchronousMode( )
Returns a Boolean indicating whether in synchronous mode.

getTransactionIsolation( )
Returns int for transaction isolation level.

getTypeMap( )
Returns java.util.Map.

getUserName( )
Returns java.lang.String for username.

getUsingXAFlag( )
Returns a Boolean indicating status of UsingXA flag.

getWarnings( )
Returns java.sql.SQLWarning.

getXAErrorFlag( )
Returns a Boolean indicating the status of the XAError flag.

isClosed( )
Returns a Boolean indicating the status of the connection.

isLogicalConnection( )
Returns a Boolean indicating whether the connection is a logical connection.

isReadOnly( )
Returns a Boolean indicating whether the connection is read-only.

nativeSQL(java.lang.String *sql*)
Returns java.lang.String.

openJoltConnection(java.lang.String *apiName*, short *major*, short *minor*)
Returns java.lang.Object. Deprecated with Oracle9*i*.

oracleReleaseSavepoint(OracleSavepoint *savepoint*)
Releases *savepoint*.

oracleRollback(OracleSavepoint *savepoint*)
Rolls back operations since *savepoint*.

oracleSetSavepoint( )
Creates and returns unnamed OracleSavepoint.

oracleSetSavepoint(java.lang.String *name*)
Creates and returns OracleSavepoint *name*.

pingDatabase(int *timeOut*)
Returns int result from database ping.

prepareCall(java.lang.String *sql*)
Returns java.sql.CallableStatement.

prepareCall(java.lang.String *sql*, int *resultSetType*, int *resultSetConcurrency*)
Returns java.sql.CallableStatement.

prepareCall(java.lang.String *sql*, int *resultSetType*, int *resultSetConcurrency*,
int *resultSetHoldability*)
Returns java.sql.CallableStatement.

prepareCallWithKey(java.lang.String *key*)
Returns java.sql.CallableStatement.

prepareStatement(java.lang.String *sql*)
    Returns java.sql.PreparedStatement.

prepareStatement(java.lang.String *sql*, int *autoGeneratedKeys*)
    Returns java.sql.PreparedStatement.

prepareStatement(java.lang.String *sql*, int[] *columnIndexes*)
    Returns java.sql.PreparedStatement.

prepareStatement(java.lang.String *sql*, int *resultSetType*, int *resultSetConcurrency*)
    Returns java.sql.PreparedStatement.

prepareStatement(java.lang.String *sql*, int *resultSetType*, int *resultSetConcurrency*,
    int *resultSetHoldability*)
    Returns java.sql.PreparedStatement.

prepareStatement(java.lang.String *sql*, java.lang.String[] *columnNames*)
    Returns java.sql.PreparedStatement.

prepareStatementWithKey(java.lang.String *key*)
    Returns java.sql.PreparedStatement.

purgeExplicitCache( )
    Purges explicit cache.

purgeImplicitCache( )
    Purges implicit cache.

putDescriptor(java.lang.String *sql_name*, java.lang.Object *desc*)
    Stores the object descriptor.

registerApiDescription(java.lang.String *apiName*, short *major*, short *minor*,
    java.lang.String *className*)
    Deprecated with Oracle9*i*.

registerSQLType(java.lang.String *sql_name*, java.lang.Class *java_class*)
    Deprecated with Oracle9*i*.

registerSQLType(java.lang.String *sql_name*, java.lang.String *java_class_name*)
    Deprecated with Oracle9*i*.

registerTAFCallback(OracleOCIFailover *cbk*, java.lang.Object *obj*)
    Registers TAF callback instance *cbk* with context object *obj*.

releaseSavepoint(java.sql.Savepoint *savepoint*)
    Releases *savepoint*.

rollback( )
    Rolls back operations.

rollback(java.sql.Savepoint *savepoint*)
    Rolls back operations to *savepoint*.

setAutoClose(boolean *autoClose*)
    Sets AutoClose to *autoClose*; the connection is always in autoClose.

setAutoCommit(boolean *autoCommit*)
    Sets AutoCommit to *autoCommit*.

setCatalog(java.lang.String *catalog*)
    Sets *catalog*.

setCreateStatementAsRefCursor(boolean *value*)
    Sets CreateStatementAsRefCursor flag.

setDefaultExecuteBatch(int *batch*)
    Sets batch as number of default operations in batch job.

setDefaultRowPrefetch(int *value*)
    Sets *value* as number of rows to prefetch by default.

setExplicitCachingEnabled(boolean *cache*)
    Sets ExplicitCachingEnabled flag.

setHoldability(int *holdability*)
    Sets holdability.

setImplicitCachingEnabled(boolean *cache*)
    Sets ImplicitCachingEnabled flag.

setIncludeSynonyms(boolean *synonyms*)
    Sets IncludeSynonyms flag.

setReadOnly(boolean *readOnly*)
    Sets ReadOnly flag.

setRemarksReporting(boolean *reportRemarks*)
    Sets RemarksReporting flag.

setRestrictGetTables(boolean *restrict*)
    Sets RestrictGetTables flag.

setSavepoint( )
    Creates and returns java.sql.Savepoint.

setSavepoint(java.lang.String *name*)
    Creates and returns java.sql.Savepoint with *name*.

setSessionTimeZone(java.lang.String *regionName*)
    Sets SessionTimeZone to *regionName*.

setStatementCacheSize(int *size*)
    Sets StatementCacheSize to *size*.

setStmtCacheSize(int *size*)
    Deprecated with Oracle9*i*. Use setStatementCacheSize instead.

setStmtCacheSize(int *size*, boolean *clearMetaData*)
    Deprecated with Oracle9*i*. Use setStatementCacheSize instead.

setSynchronousMode(boolean *isSynchronous*)
    Sets SynchronousMode flag.

setTransactionIsolation(int *level*)
    Sets transaction isolation level.

setTypeMap(java.util.Map *map*)
    Sets type map.

setUsingXAFlag(Boolean *value*)
    Sets UsingXA flag. Deprecated with Oracle9*i*.

setWrapper(OracleConnection *wrapper*)
    Sets a connection *wrapper* as the wrapper of this connection.

setXAErrorFlag(boolean *value*)
    Sets XAError flag. Deprecated with Oracle9*i*.

shutdown(int *mode*)
    Deprecated with Oracle9*i*.

startup(java.lang.String startup_str, int *mode*)
>   Deprecated with Oracle9*i*.

unwrap()
>   Returns OracleConnection, which is unwrapped one level.

Inherited methods

Inherits all methods from java.lang.Object except clone, equals, and finalize.

OracleDatabaseMetaData

Extends the java.lang.Object class and implements the java.sql.DatabaseMetaData JDBC 1.0 DatabaseMetaData interface.

The constructor for this class is:

```
OracleDatabaseMetaData(OracleConnection conn)
```

Methods

allProceduresAreCallable()
>   Returns a Boolean indicating whether all the procedures returned by getProcedures can be called by the current user.

allTablesAreSelectable()
>   Returns a Boolean indicating whether all the tables returned by getTable() are SELECTed by the current user.

dataDefinitionCausesTransactionCommit()
>   Returns a Boolean indicating whether a DDL statement within a transaction forces the transaction to commit.

dataDefinitionIgnoredInTransactions()
>   Returns a Boolean indicating whether a DDL statement within a transaction is ignored.

deletesAreDetected(int *type*)
>   Returns a Boolean. Implements JDBC 2.0 DatabaseMetaData.deletesAreDetected.

doesMaxRowSizeIncludeBlobs()
>   Returns a Boolean indicating whether the row contains LONGVARCHAR or LONGVARBINARY BLOBs.

getAttributes(java.lang.String *catalog*, java.lang.String *schemaPattern*, java.lang.String *typeNamePattern*, java.lang.String *attributeNamePattern*)
>   Returns java.sql.ResultSet that contains a description of the given attribute of the given type for a user-defined type (UDT) that is available in the given schema and catalog. JDBC 3.0. New with Oracle9*i*.

getBestRowIdentifier(java.lang.String *catalog*, java.lang.String *schema*,
>   java.lang.String *table*, int *scope*, boolean *nullable*)
>   Returns java.sqlResultSet that uniquely identifies a row.

getCatalogs()
>   Returns java.sqlResultSet with catalogs.

getCatalogSeparator()
>   Returns java.lang.String with catalog separator.

getCatalogTerm()
Returns java.lang.String with preferred term for catalog.

getColumnPrivileges(java.lang.String *catalog*, java.lang.String *schemaPattern*, java.lang.String *tableNamePattern*, java.lang.String *columnNamePattern*)
Returns java.sql.ResultSet with description of access rights for table's columns.

getColumns(java.lang.String *catalog*, java.lang.String *schemaPattern*, java.lang.String *tableNamePattern*, java.lang.String *columnNamePattern*)
Returns java.sql.ResultSet with description of table columns available in catalog.

getConnection()
Returns java.sql.Connection. Implements JDBC 2.0 DatabaseMetaData.getConnection.

getCrossReference(java.lang.String *primaryCatalog*, java.lang.String *primarySchema*, java.lang.String *primaryTable*, java.lang.String *foreignCatalog*, java.lang.String *foreignSchema*, java.lang.String *foreignTable*)
Returns java.sql.ResultSet with a description of the foreign key columns in the foreign key table that reference the primary key columns of the primary key table.

getDatabaseMajorVersion()
Returns int with major version of the database. JDBC 3.0. New with Oracle9*i*.

getDatabaseMinorVersion()
Returns int with major version of the database. JDBC 3.0. New with Oracle9*i*.

getDatabaseProductName()
Returns java.lang.String with name of database product.

getDatabaseProductVersion()
Returns java.lang.String with name of database product.

getDefaultTransactionIsolation()
Returns int with database's default transaction isolation level.

getDriverMajorVersion()
Returns int with JDBC driver's major version number.

getDriverMajorVersionInfo()
Returns int with JDBC driver's major version number. Static method

getDriverMinorVersion()
Returns int with JDBC driver's minor version number.

getDriverMinorVersionInfo()
Returns int with JDBC driver's minor version number. Static method.

getDriverName()
Returns java.lang.String with the name of this JDBC driver.

getDriverNameInfo()
Returns static.java.lang.String with the name of this JDBC driver.

getDriverVersion()
Returns java.lang.String with version of this JDBC driver.

getDriverVersionInfo()
Returns static.java.lang.String with version of this JDBC driver.

getExportedKeys(java.lang.String *catalog*, java.lang.String *schema*, java.lang.String *table*)
Returns java.sql.ResultSet with a description of a foreign key's columns that reference a table's primary key columns.

getExtraNameCharacters( )
> Returns java.lang.String with all "extra" characters that can be used in unquoted identifier names

getIdentifierQuoteString( )
> Returns java.lang.String used to quote SQL identifiers or space if not permitted.

getImportedKeys(java.lang.String *catalog*, java.lang.String *schema*, java.lang.String *table*)
> Returns java.sql.ResultSet with a description of the primary key columns that are referenced by a table's foreign key columns.

getIndexInfo(java.lang.String *catalog*, java.lang.String *schema*, java.lang.String *table*, boolean *unique*, boolean *approximate*)
> Returns java.sql.ResultSet with description of a table's indexes and statistics.

getJDBCMajorVersion( )
> Returns int with major JDBC version number for this driver. JDBC 3.0. New with Oracle9*i*.

getJDBCMinorVersion( )
> Returns int with minor JDBC version number for this driver. JDBC 3.0. static java.lang.String. New with Oracle9*i*.

getLobPrecision( )
> Returns static java.lang.String.

getMaxBinaryLiteralLength( )
> Returns int with number of hex characters allowed in an inline binary literal.

getMaxCatalogNameLength( )
> Returns int with maximum length of a catalog name.

getMaxCharLiteralLength( )
> Returns int with maximum length for a character literal.

getMaxColumnNameLength( )
> Returns int with limit on column name length.

getMaxColumnsInGroupBy( )
> Returns int with maximum number of columns in a GROUP BY clause.

getMaxColumnsInIndex( )
> Returns int with maximum number of columns allowed in an index.

getMaxColumnsInOrderBy( )
> Returns int with maximum number of columns in an ORDER BY clause.

getMaxColumnsInSelect( )
> Returns int with maximum number of columns in a select list.

getMaxColumnsInTable( )
> Returns int with maximum number of columns in a table.

getMaxConnections( )
> Returns int with maximum number of active connections to this database.

getMaxCursorNameLength( )
> Returns int with maximum cursor name length.

getMaxIndexLength( )
> Returns int with maximum length of an index (in bytes).

getMaxProcedureNameLength( )
> Returns int with maximum length of a procedure name.

getMaxRowSize( )
> Returns int with maximum length of a single row.

getMaxSchemaNameLength( )
> Returns int with maximum length allowed for a schema name.

getMaxStatementLength( )
> Returns int with maximum length of a SQL statement.

getMaxStatements( )
> Returns int with maximum number of active statements open at one time to the database.

getMaxTableNameLength( )
> Returns int with maximum length of a table name.

getMaxTablesInSelect( )
> Returns int with maximum number of tables in a SELECT.

getMaxUserNameLength( )
> Returns int with maximum length of a username.

getNumericFunctions( )
> Returns java.lang.String with comma-separated list of math functions.

getPrimaryKeys(java.lang.String *catalog*, java.lang.String *schema*, java.lang.String *table*)
> Returns java.sql.ResultSet with a description of table's primary key columns.

getProcedureColumns(java.lang.String *catalog*, java.lang.String *schemaPattern*, java.lang.String *procedureNamePattern*, java.lang.String *columnNamePattern*)
> Returns java.sql.ResultSet with a description of a catalog's stored procedure parameters and result columns.

getProcedures(java.lang.String *catalog*, java.lang.String *schemaPattern*, java.lang.String *procedureNamePattern*)
> Returns java.sql.ResultSet with a description of stored procedures available in a catalog.

getProcedureTerm( )
> Returns java.lang.String with database vendor's term for *procedure*.

getResultSetHoldability( )
> Returns int with the default holdability of this ResultSet object. JDBC 3.0.

getSchemas( )
> Returns java.sql.ResultSet with schema names available in this database.

getSchemaTerm( )
> Returns java.lang.String with the database vendor's term for *schema*.

getSearchStringEscape( )
> Returns java.lang.String with a string that can be used to escape '_' or '%' in the string pattern style catalog search parameters.

getSQLKeywords( )
> Returns java.lang.String with a comma-separated list of all of a database's SQL keywords that are *not* also SQL92 keywords.

getSQLStateType( )
> Returns int indicating whether the SQLSTATEs returned by SQLException. getSQLState is X/Open or Open Group SQL CLI or SQL99. JDBC 3.0. New with Oracle9i.

getStringFunctions( )
>   Returns java.lang.String with comma-separated list of string functions.

getSuperTables(java.lang.String *catalog*, java.lang.String *schemaPattern*,
java.lang.String *tableNamePattern*)
>   Returns java.sql.ResultSet with description of the table hierarchies defined in a particular schema in the database. JDBC 3.0. New with Oracle9*i*.

getSuperTypes(java.lang.String *catalog*, java.lang.String *schemaPattern*, java.lang.
String *typeNamePattern*)
>   Returns java.sql.ResultSet with a description of the user-defined type (UDT) hierarchies defined in a particular schema in this database. JDBC 3.0. New with Oracle9*i*.

getSystemFunctions( )
>   Returns java.lang.String with a comma-separated list of system functions.

getTablePrivileges(java.lang.String *catalog*, java.lang.String *schemaPattern*,
java.lang.String *tableNamePattern*)
>   Returns java.sql.ResultSet with a description of the access rights for each table available in a catalog.

getTables(java.lang.String *catalog*, java.lang.String *schemaPattern*,
java.lang.String tableNamePattern, java.lang.String[] types)
>   Returns java.sql.ResultSet with a description of tables available in a catalog.

getTableTypes( )
>   Returns java.sql.ResultSet with the table types available in this database.

getTimeDateFunctions( )
>   Returns java.lang.String with a comma-separated list of time/date functions.

getTypeInfo( )
>   Returns java.sql.ResultSet with a description of all the standard SQL types supported by this database.

getUDTs(java.lang.String *catalog*, java.lang.String *schemaPattern*, java.lang.String
typeNamePattern, int[] types)
>   Returns java.sql.ResultSet. Implements JDBC 2.0 DatabaseMetaData::getUDTs.

getURL( )
>   Returns java.lang.String with URL for this database.

getUserName( )
>   Returns java.lang.String with your username as known to the database.

getVersionColumns(java.lang.String *catalog*, java.lang.String *schema*,
java.lang.String *table*)
>   Returns java.sql.ResultSet with a description of a table's columns that are automatically updated when any value in a row is updated.

insertsAreDetected(int *type*)
>   Returns a Boolean and implements JDBC 2.0 DatabaseMetaData. insertsAreDetected.

isCatalogAtStart( )
>   Returns a Boolean indicating whether a catalog appears at the start of a qualified table name.

isReadOnly( )
>   Returns a Boolean indicating whether database is read-only mode.

nullPlusNonNullIsNull( )
> Returns a Boolean indicating whether concatenations between NULL and non-NULL values are NULL.

nullsAreSortedAtEnd( )
> Returns a Boolean indicating whether NULL values are sorted at the end regardless of sort order.

nullsAreSortedAtStart( )
> Returns a Boolean indicating whether NULL values are sorted at the start regardless of sort order.

nullsAreSortedHigh( )
> Returns a Boolean indicating whether NULL values are sorted high.

nullsAreSortedLow( )
> Returns a Boolean indicating whether NULL values are sorted low.

othersDeletesAreVisible(int *type*)
> Returns a Boolean and implements JDBC 2.0 DatabaseMetaData.

othersInsertsAreVisible(int *type*)
> Returns a Boolean and implements JDBC 2.0 DatabaseMetaData. othersInsertsAreVisible.

othersUpdatesAreVisible(int *type*)
> Returns a Boolean and implements JDBC 2.0 DatabaseMetaData..

ownDeletesAreVisible(int *type*)
> Returns a Boolean and implements JDBC 2.0 DatabaseMetaData. ownDeletesAreVisible.

ownInsertsAreVisible(int *type*)
> Returns a Boolean and implements JDBC 2.0 DatabaseMetaData. ownInsertsAreVisible.

ownUpdatesAreVisible(int *type*)
> Returns Boolean and implements JDBC 2.0 DatabaseMetaData. ownUpdatesAreVisible.

storesLowerCaseIdentifiers( )
> Returns a Boolean indicating whether the database treats mixed-case unquoted SQL identifiers as case-insensitive and stores them in lowercase.

storesLowerCaseQuotedIdentifiers( )
> Returns a Boolean indicating whether the database treats mixed-case quoted SQL identifiers as case-insensitive and stores them in lowercase.

storesMixedCaseIdentifiers( )
> Returns a Boolean indicating whether the database treats mixed-case unquoted SQL identifiers as case-insensitive and stores them in mixed case.

storesMixedCaseQuotedIdentifiers( )
> Returns a Boolean indicating whether the database treats mixed-case quoted SQL identifiers as case-insensitive and stores them in mixed case.

storesUpperCaseIdentifiers( )
> Returns a Boolean indicating whether the database treats mixed-case unquoted SQL identifiers as case-insensitive and stores them in uppercase.

storesUpperCaseQuotedIdentifiers( )
> Returns a Boolean indicating whether the database treats mixed-case quoted SQL identifiers as case-insensitive and stores them in uppercase.

supportsAlterTableWithAddColumn( )
> Returns a Boolean indicating whether ALTER TABLE with add column is supported.

supportsAlterTableWithDropColumn( )
> Returns Boolean indicating whether ALTER TABLE with drop column is supported.

supportsANSI92EntryLevelSQL( )
> Returns a Boolean indicating whether ANSI92 entry-level SQL grammar is supported.

supportsANSI92FullSQL( )
> Returns a Boolean indicating whether ANSI92 full SQL grammar is supported.

supportsANSI92IntermediateSQL( )
> Returns a Boolean indicating whether ANSI92 intermediate SQL grammar is supported.

supportsBatchUpdates( )
> Returns a Boolean indicating whether JDBC 2.0 DatabaseMetaData::supportBatchUpdates is implemented.

supportsCatalogsInDataManipulation( )
> Returns a Boolean indicating whether a catalog name can be used in a data manipulation statement.

supportsCatalogsInIndexDefinitions( )
> Returns a Boolean indicating whether a catalog name can be used in an index definition statement.

supportsCatalogsInPrivilegeDefinitions( )
> Returns a Boolean indicating whether a catalog name can be used in a privilege definition statement

supportsCatalogsInProcedureCalls( )
> Returns a Boolean indicating whether a catalog name can be used in a procedure call statement.

supportsCatalogsInTableDefinitions( )
> Returns a Boolean indicating whether a catalog name can be used in a table definition statement.

supportsColumnAliasing( )
> Returns a Boolean indicating whether column aliasing is supported.

supportsConvert( )
> Returns a Boolean indicating whether the CONVERT function between SQL types is supported.

supportsConvert(int *fromType*, int *toType*)
> Returns a Boolean indicating whether CONVERT between the given SQL types is supported.

supportsCoreSQLGrammar( )
> Returns a Boolean indicating whether the ODBC Core SQL grammar is supported.

supportsCorrelatedSubqueries( )
> Returns a Boolean indicating whether correlated subqueries are supported.

supportsDataDefinitionAndDataManipulationTransactions()
> Returns a Boolean indicating whether both data definition and data manipulation statements within a transaction are supported.

supportsDataManipulationTransactionsOnly()
> Returns a Boolean indicating whether only data manipulation statements within a transaction are supported.

supportsDifferentTableCorrelationNames()
> Returns a Boolean indicating whether table correlation names are supported, and whether they must be different from the names of the tables.

supportsExpressionsInOrderBy()
> Returns a Boolean indicating whether expressions in ORDER BY lists are supported.

supportsExtendedSQLGrammar()
> Returns a Boolean indicating whether the ODBC Extended SQL grammar is supported.

supportsFullOuterJoins()
> Returns a Boolean indicating whether full nested outer joins are supported.

supportsGetGeneratedKeys()
> Returns a Boolean indicating whether autogenerated keys can be retrieved after a statement has been executed. JDBC 3.0.

supportsGroupBy()
> Returns a Boolean indicating whether some form of GROUP BY clause is supported.

supportsGroupByBeyondSelect()
> Returns a Boolean indicating whether a GROUP BY clause's add columns are not in the SELECT, provided that it specifies all the columns in the SELECT.

supportsGroupByUnrelated()
> Returns a Boolean indicating whether a GROUP BY clause's use columns are not in the SELECT.

supportsIntegrityEnhancementFacility()
> Returns a Boolean indicating whether the SQL Integrity Enhancement Facility is supported.

supportsLikeEscapeClause()
> Returns a Boolean indicating whether the escape character in LIKE clauses is supported.

supportsLimitedOuterJoins()
> Returns a Boolean indicating whether there is limited support for outer joins.

supportsMinimumSQLGrammar()
> Returns a Boolean indicating whether the ODBC Minimum SQL grammar is supported.

supportsMixedCaseIdentifiers()
> Returns a Boolean indicating whether the database treats mixed-case unquoted SQL identifiers as case-sensitive and stores them in mixed case.

supportsMixedCaseQuotedIdentifiers()
> Returns a Boolean indicating whether the database treats mixed-case quoted SQL identifiers as case-sensitive and stores them in mixed case.

supportsMultipleOpenResults( )
> Returns a Boolean indicating whether it is possible to have multiple ResultSet objects returned from a CallableStatement object simultaneously. JDBC 3.0. New with Oracle9*i*.

supportsMultipleResultSets( )
> Returns a Boolean indicating whether multiple ResultSets from a single execute are supported.

supportsMultipleTransactions( )
> Returns a Boolean indicating whether multiple transactions can be open at once.

supportsNamedParameters( )
> Returns a Boolean indicating whether this database supports named parameters to callable statements. JDBC 3.0. New with Oracle9*i*.

supportsNonNullableColumns( )
> Returns a Boolean indicating whether columns can be defined as non-nullable.

supportsOpenCursorsAcrossCommit( )
> Returns a Boolean indicating whether cursors remain open across commits.

supportsOpenCursorsAcrossRollback( )
> Returns a Boolean indicating whether cursors remain open across rollbacks.

supportsOpenStatementsAcrossCommit( )
> Returns a Boolean indicating whether statements remain open across commits.

supportsOpenStatementsAcrossRollback( )
> Returns a Boolean indicating whether statements remain open across rollbacks.

supportsOrderByUnrelated( )
> Returns a Boolean indicating whether an ORDER BY clause's use columns are not in the SELECT.

supportsOuterJoins( )
> Returns a Boolean indicating whether some form of outer join is supported.

supportsPositionedDelete( )
> Returns a Boolean indicating whether positioned DELETE is supported.

supportsPositionedUpdate( )
> Returns a Boolean indicating whether positioned UPDATE is supported.

supportsResultSetConcurrency(int *type*, int *concurrency*)
> Returns a Boolean indicating whether the database implements JDBC 2.0 DatabaseMetaData.supportsResultSetConcurrency.

supportsResultSetHoldability(int *holdability*)
> Returns a Boolean indicating whether the database supports the given result set holdability. JDBC 3.0. New with Oracle9*i*.

supportsResultSetType(int *type*)
> Returns a Boolean indicating whether the database implements JDBC 2.0 DatabaseMetaData.supportsResultSetType.

supportsSavepoints( )
> Returns a Boolean indicating whether the database supports savepoints. JDBC 3.0. New with Oracle9*i*.

supportsSchemasInDataManipulation( )
> Returns a Boolean indicating whether a schema name can be used in a data manipulation statement.

supportsSchemasInIndexDefinitions( )
> Returns a Boolean indicating whether a schema name can be used in an index definition statement.

supportsSchemasInPrivilegeDefinitions( )
> Returns a Boolean indicating whether a schema name can be used in a privilege definition statement.

supportsSchemasInProcedureCalls( )
> Returns a Boolean indicating whether a schema name can be used in a procedure call statement.

supportsSchemasInTableDefinitions( )
> Returns a Boolean indicating whether a schema name can be used in a table definition statement.

supportsSelectForUpdate( )
> Returns a Boolean indicating whether SELECT for UPDATE is supported.

supportsStoredProcedures( )
> Returns a Boolean indicating whether stored procedure calls using the stored procedure escape syntax are supported.

supportsSubqueriesInComparisons( )
> Returns a Boolean indicating whether subqueries in comparison expressions are supported.

supportsSubqueriesInExists( )
> Returns a Boolean indicating whether subqueries in EXISTS expressions are supported.

supportsSubqueriesInIns( )
> Returns a Boolean indicating whether subqueries in IN statements are supported.

supportsSubqueriesInQuantifieds( )
> Returns a Boolean indicating whether subqueries in quantified expressions are supported.

supportsTableCorrelationNames( )
> Returns a Boolean indicating whether table correlation names are supported.

supportsTransactionIsolationLevel(int *level*)
> Returns a Boolean indicating whether the database supports the given transaction isolation level.

supportsTransactions( )
> Returns a Boolean indicating whether transactions are supported.

supportsUnion( )
> Returns a Boolean indicating whether SQL UNION is supported.

supportsUnionAll( )
> Returns a Boolean indicating whether SQL UNION ALL is supported.

updatesAreDetected(int *type*)
> Returns a Boolean indicating whether the database implements JDBC 2.0 DatabaseMetaData.updatesAreDetected.

usesLocalFilePerTable( )
> Returns a Boolean indicating whether the database uses a file for each table.

usesLocalFiles( )
> Returns a Boolean indicating whether the database stores tables in a local file.

Inherited methods

Inherits all methods from java.lang.Object except clone and finalize.

OracleDriver

Extends the oracle.jdbc.driver.OracleDriver class and implements the java.sql.Driver interface. The constructor for this class is:

    OracleDriver( )

Inherited fields

The following fields are inherited from oracle.jdbc.driver.OracleDriver:

> at_sign_character
> database_string
> dll_string
> dms_parent_name_string
> dms_parent_type_string
> logon_as_internal_str
> password_string
> process_escapes_string
> protocol_string
> slash_character
> user_string

Inherited methods

Inherits all methods from oracle.jdbc.driver.OracleDriver.

Inherits all methods from java.lang.Object except clone, equals and finalize. In Oracle8*i*, also inherits the equal method.

OracleTypes

Extends the java.lang.Object class.

The constructor for this class is:

    OracleTypes( )

Fields

ARRAY	Static int
BFILE	Static int
BIGINT	Static int
BINARY	Static int
BIT	Static int
BLOB	Static int
BOOLEAN	Static int, new with Oracle9*i*
CHAR	Static int
CLOB	Static int
CURSOR	Static int
DATALINK	Static int
DATE	Static int

DECIMAL	Static int
DOUBLE	Static int
FIXED_CHAR	Static int
FLOAT	Static int
INTEGER	Static int
INTERVALDS	Static int, new with Oracle9*i*
INTERVALYM	Static int, new with Oracle9*i*
JAVA_OBJECT	Static int, new with Oracle9*i*
JAVA_STRUCT	Static int, new with Oracle9*i*
LONGVARBINARY	Static int
LONGVARCHAR	Static int
NULL	Static int
NUMBER	Static int
NUMERIC	Static int
OPAQUE	Static int, new with Oracle9*i*
OTHER	Static int, indicates that the SQL type is database-specific and gets mapped to a Java object that can be accessed via getObject and setObject
PLSQL_INDEX_TABLE	Static int
RAW	Static int
REAL	Static int
REF	Static int
ROWID	Static int
SMALLINT	Static int
STRUCT	Static int
TIME	Static int
TIMESTAMP	Static int
TIMESTAMPLTZ	Static int, new with Oracle9*i*
TIMESTAMPNS	Static int, new with Oracle9*i*, deprecated since 9.2.0. Use OracleTypes.
TIMESTAMPTZ	Static int, new with Oracle9*i*
TINYINT	Static int
VARBINARY	Static int
VARCHAR	Static int

Inherited methods

Inherits all methods from java.lang.Object except clone, equals, and finalize. In Oracle8*i*, also inherits equals method.

oracle.sql

This package provides Java wrappers for raw SQL data, which allows the data to be used without losing information. The classes for SQL structured types, such as objects and arrays, also provide additional information about the structure and its conversion to other forms. Each of the classes extends the oracle.sql.Datum.

oracle.sql contains four Oracle-specific interfaces in Oracle9i and three in Oracle8i.

Interfaces

The following interfaces are part of the oracle.jdbc package.

CustomDatum

Used to return a category of Datum object. Deprecated and replaced with ORAData with Oracle9*i*.

Method
toDatum(OracleConnection *c*)
> Returns a datum when called by setOracleObject to extract a Datum.

CustomDatumFactory

Creates an Object from a SQL type. Deprecated and replaced with ORADataFactory with Oracle9*i*.

Method
create(Datum *d*, int *sqlType*)
> Creates and returns an Object from *sqlType* as CustomDatum. Datum is initialized as *d*.

Mutable

Used to move one type of object into another. Only in Oracle8*i*.

Method
copy(CustomDatum *cd*)
> Copies contents of *cd* into object.

ORAData

Interface for customized user-defined datatypes. Replacement for CustomDatum interface, which was deprecated with Oracle9*i*.

Method
toDatum(java.sql.Connection *c*)
> Extracts an oracle.sql.Datum object from connection *c*.

ORADataFactory

Interface for ORAData factory. Replacement for the CustomDatumFactory interface, which was deprecated with Oracle9*i*.

Method

create(Datum *d*, int *sqlType*)
> Creates and returns an Object from *sqlType* as CustomDatum. Datum is initialized as *d*.

Classes

The following classes are a part of the oracle.sql package.

ARRAY

Extends oracle.sql.DatumWithConnection. Implements java.sql.Array.

The constructor for this class is:

```
ARRAY(ArrayDescriptor type, java.sql.Connection conn,
java.lang.Object elements)
```

Fields

ACCESS_FORWARD   Static int
ACCESS_REVERSE   Static int
ACCESS_UNKNOWN   Static int

Methods

getAccessDirection( )
> Returns int as performance hint.

getArray( )
> Returns as java.lang.Object the contents of the SQL array designated by the object.

getArray(java.util.Map *map*)
> Returns as java.lang.Object the contents of the SQL array designated by the object.

getArray(long *index*, int *count*)
> Returns as java.lang.Object an array containing a slice of the SQL array, beginning with the given *index* and containing up to *count* successive elements of the SQL array.

getArray(long *index*, int *count*, java.util.Map *map*)
> Returns as java.lang.Object an array containing a slice of the SQL array, beginning with the given *index* and containing up to *count* successive elements of the SQL array.

getAutoBuffering( )
> Returns a Boolean.

getAutoIndexing( )
> Returns a Boolean.

getBaseType( )
> Returns int with the code, from java.sql.Types, of the type of the elements of the array.

getBaseTypeName()
> Returns as java.lang.String the SQL type name of the elements in the array designated by this Array object.

getConnection()
> Returns OracleConnection.

getDescriptor()
> Returns ArrayDescriptor.

getDoubleArray()
> Returns double[].

getDoubleArray(long *index*, int *count*)
> Returns double[] beginning with *index* for *count* entries.

getFloatArray()
> Returns float[]

getFloatArray(long *index*, int *count*)
> Returns float[] beginning with *index* for *count* entries.

getIntArray()
> Returns int[] beginning with *index* for *count* entries.

getIntArray(long *index*, int *count*)
> Returns int[].

getJavaSqlConnection()
> Returns java.sql.Connection.

getLongArray()
> Returns long [].

getLongArray(long *index*, int *count*)
> Returns int[] beginning with *index* for *count* entries.

getOracleArray()
> Returns Datum[].

getOracleArray(long *index*, int *count*)
> Returns int[] beginning with *index* for *count* entries.

getResultSet()
> Returns java.sql.ResultSet that contains the elements of the array.

getResultSet(java.util.Map *map*)
> Returns java.sql.ResultSet that contains the elements of the array designated by this Array object and uses the given *map* to map the array elements.

getResultSet(long *index*, int *count*)
> Returns java.sql.ResultSet holding the elements of the subarray that starts at index *index* and contains up to *count* successive elements.

getResultSet(long *index*, int *count*, java.util.Map *map*)
> Returns java.sql.ResultSet holding the elements of the subarray that starts at *index* and contains up to *count* successive elements.

getShortArray()
> Returns short[].

getShortArray(long *index*, int *count*)
> Returns int[] beginning with *index* for *count* entries.

getSQLTypeName( )
    Returns java.lang.String.
isConvertibleTo(java.lang.Class *jClass*)
    Returns Boolean.
length( )
    Returns int.
setAutoBuffering(boolean *enable*)
    Sets AutoBuffering flag to *enable*.
setAutoIndexing(boolean *enable*)
    Sets AutoBuffering flag to *enable*.
setAutoIndexing(boolean *enable*, int *direction*)
    Sets AutoIndexing flag to *enable* in *direction*.
toJdbc( )
    Returns java.lang.Object as JDBC representation of the Datum object.

Inherited methods

The following methods are inherited from oracle.sql.DatumWithConnection with Oracle9*i*:

    assertNotNull
    getOracleConnection

Inherits all methods from oracle.sql.Datum except isConvertibleTo and toJdbc.

Also inherits all methods from java.lang.Object except clone, equals, and finalize.

ArrayDescriptor

Extends TypeDescriptor. Implements java.io.Serializable.

Fields

CACHE_ALL
CACHE_LAST
CACHE_NONE
TYPE_NESTED_TABLE
TYPE_VARRAY

Inherited fields

The following field is inherited from oracle.sql.TypeDescriptor:

    DEBUG_SERIALIZATION

Methods

createDescriptor(java.lang.String *name*, java.sql.Connection *conn*)
    Returns ArrayDescriptor with type *name* Descriptor factory. Static method.
descType( )
    Returns java.lang.String, which describes the collection type.
getArrayType( )
    Returns int with the database type of the array.

getBaseName( )
> Returns java.lang.String with the fully qualified name of its type if elements are named types, or returns the type name used by the database

getBaseType( )
> Returns int with element's type code.

getMaxLength( )
> Returns long with the maximum number of elements Array object can hold.

getTypeCode( )
> Returns int. New with Oracle9i.

toResultSet(ARRAY *array*, long *index*, int *count*, java.util.Map *map*, boolean *saveLocalCopy*)
> Returns java.sql.ResultSet.

toResultSetFromImage(ARRAY *array*, long *index*, int *count*, java.util.Map *map*)
> Returns java.sql.ResultSet.

Inherited methods

Inherits all methods from oracle.sql.TypeDescriptor. Also inherits all methods from java.lang.Object except clone, equals, and finalize; in Oracle8i, also inherits equals.

BFILE

Extends oracle.sql.DatumWithConnection in Oracle9i, oracle.sql.Datum in Oracle8i.

Fields

MODE_READONLY   Static int. New with Oracle9i.
MODE_READWRITE   Static int. New with Oracle9i.

Methods

asciiStreamValue( )
> Returns java.io.InputStream, which is a converted ASCII stream representation of the Datum object.

close( )
> Closes a previously opened external LOB. New with Oracle9i.

closeFile( )
> Closes the file.

fileExists( )
> Returns a Boolean indicating whether the locator for a given BFILE points to a file that actually exists on the server's filesystem.

getBinaryStream( )
> Returns java.io.InputStream of the entire BFILE.

getBinaryStream(long *pos*)
> Returns java.io.InputStream as a stream from position *pos*. New with Oracle9i.

getBytes(long *pos*, int *length*)
> Returns byte[] as a copy of the contents of the BFILE at the requested position *pos* of *length*.

getBytes(long *pos*, int *length*, byte[] *buf*)
> Returns int; copies the contents of the BFILE from *pos* with *length* to *buf*.

getConnection( )
> Returns OracleConnection.

getDirAlias( )
> Returns java.lang.String, the BFILE's directory alias.

getJavaSqlConnection( )
> Returns java.sql.Connection. New with Oracle9*i*.

getName( )
> Returns java.lang.String with the BFILE's filename.

isConvertibleTo(java.lang.Class *jClass*)
> Returns a Boolean indicating whether this Data object can be converted to the specified Java datatype.

isFileOpen( )
> Returns a Boolean indicating whether a BFILE was opened with the given BFILE.

isOpen( )
> Returns a Boolean indicating whether the external LOB is opened. New with Oracle9*i*.

length( )
> Returns a LONG with the length of the BFILE in bytes.

open( )
> Opens an external LOB in read-only mode. New with Oracle9*i*.

open(int *mode*)
> Opens an external LOB in the specified *mode*. New with Oracle9*i*.

openFile( )
> Opens the FILE.

position(BFILE *pattern*, long *start*)
> Returns a LONG that determines the byte position at which the given *pattern* starts, starting from position *start*.

position(byte[] *pattern*, long *start*)
> Returns a LONG that determines the byte position at which the given *pattern* starts, starting from position *start*.

toJdbc( )
> Returns java.lang.Object with default Java object type.

Inherited methods

Inherits all methods from oracle.sql.TypeDescriptor.

Inherits all methods from oracle.sql.Datum except for asciiStreamValue and toJDBC.

Inherits all methods from java.lang.Object except clone, equals, and finalize.

BLOB

Extends oracle.sql.DatumWithConnection in Oracle9*i*, oracle.sql.Datum in Oracle8*i*. Implements java.sql.Blob in Oracle 9*i* and oracle.jdbc2.Blob in Oracle8*i*.

Fields

DURATION_CALL	Static int, new with Oracle9*i*
DURATION_SESSION	Static int, new with Oracle9*i*
MAX_CHUNK_SIZE	Static int
MODE_READONLY	Static int, new with Oracle9*i*
MODE_READWRITE	Static int, new with Oracle9*i*

Methods

close()
> Closes a previously opened BLOB. New with Oracle9*i*.

createTemporary(java.sql.Connection *conn*, Boolean *cache*, int *duration*)
> Returns BLOB as temporary BLOB. Static method. New with Oracle9*i*.

empty_lob()
> Returns BLOB as empty lob. Static method.

freeTemporary()
> Frees the contents and the locator of the temporary BLOB. New with Oracle9*i*.

freeTemporary(BLOB *temp_lob*)
> Frees the contents and the locator of the temporary BLOB. Static method. New with Oracle9*i*.

getBinaryOutputStream()
> Returns java.io.OutputStream.

getBinaryOutputStream(long *pos*)
> Returns java.io.OutputStream, a stream from *pos*. New with Oracle9*i*.

getBinaryStream()
> Returns java.io.InputStream as the BLOB interface function.

getBinaryStream(long *pos*)
> Returns java.io.InputStream as a stream from *pos*. New with Oracle9i.

getBufferSize()
> Returns int.

getBytes(long pos, int *length*)
> Returns byte[] as the BLOB interface function.

getBytes(long *pos*, int *length*, byte[] *buf*)
> Returns java.io.InputStream from *pos* in *buf* of *length*.

getChunkSize()
> Returns int.

getConnection()
> Returns OracleConnection.

getJavaSqlConnection()
> Returns java.sql.Connection. New with Oracle9*i*.

isConvertibleTo(java.lang.Class *jClass*)
> Returns a Boolean.

isEmptyLob()
> Returns a Boolean indicating whether the LOB locator points to an empty BLOB.

isOpen()
> Returns a Boolean indicating whether the BLOB is open. New with Oracle9*i*.

isTemporary( )
> Returns a Boolean indicating whether the LOB locator points to a temporary BLOB. New with Oracle9i.

isTemporary(BLOB *lob*)
> Returns a Boolean indicating whether the LOB locator points to a temporary BLOB. Static method. New with Oracle9i.

length( )
> Returns a LONG as length of BLOB.

open(int *mode*)
> Opens a BLOB in the indicated mode.

position(java.sql.Blob *pattern*, long *start*)
> Returns a LONG with the position of *pattern*, starting from *start*. *pattern* is oracle.jdbc2.Blob in Oracle8i.

position(byte[] *pattern*, long *start*)
> Returns a LONG with the position of *pattern*, starting from *start*.

putBytes(long *pos*, byte[] *bytes*)
> Returns int, the number of bytes written, to *pos* in the BLOB from *bytes*.

putBytes(long *pos*, byte[] *bytes*, int *length*)
> Returns int, the number of bytes written, to *pos* in the BLOB from *bytes* of *length*.

setBinaryStream(long *pos*)
> Returns java.io.OutputStream that can be used to write to the BLOB value that this BLOB object represents. JDBC 3.0. New with Oracle9i.

setBytes(long *pos*, byte[] *bytes*)
> Returns int, the number of bytes actually written, and writes the given array of *bytes* to the BLOB this object represents, starting at position *pos*. JDBC 3.0. New with Oracle9i.

setBytes(long *pos*, byte[] *bytes*, int *offset*, int *len*)
> Returns int, the number of bytes actually written, and writes the given array of *bytes* to the BLOB this object represents, starting at position *pos* for *len*. JDBC 3.0. New with Oracle9i Release 2.

toJdbc( )
> Returns java.lang.Object, the default Java object type.

trim(long *newlen*)
> Trims the value of the BLOB to *newlen*. New with Oracle9i.

truncate(long *len*)
> Truncates the BLOB value to be *len* bytes in length. JDBC 3.0. New with Oracle9i Release 2.

Inherited methods

The following methods are inherited from oracle.sql.DatumWithConnection in Oracle9i.

> assertNotNull
> getOracleConnection

Inherits all methods from oracle.sql.Datum except isConvertibleTo and toJdbc.

Inherits all methods from java.lang.Object except clone, equals, and finalize.

CHAR

Extends oracle.sql.Datum.

The constructors for this class are:

    CHAR(java.lang.Object obj, oracle.sql.CharacterSet charSet)

to construct a CHAR from an Object or:

    CHAR(java.lang.String str, oracle.sql.CharacterSet charSet)

to construct a CHAR from a CHAR.

Field

DEFAULT_CHARSET   Static oracle.sql.CharacterSet

Methods

asciiStreamValue( )
> Returns java.io.InputStream representation of the datum object.

bigDecimalValue( )
> Returns data object as java.math.BigDecimal.

binaryStreamValue( )
> Returns data object as java.io.InputStream.

booleanValue( )
> Returns data object as Boolean.

byteValue( )
> Returns data object as byte.

characterStreamValue( )
> Returns data object as java.io.Reader.

dateValue( )
> Returns data object as java.sql.Date.

doubleValue( )
> Returns data object as double.

floatValue( )
> Returns data object as float.

getString( )
> Returns data object as java.lang.String.

intValue( )
> Returns data object as int.

isConvertibleTo(java.lang.Class jClass)
> Returns a Boolean indicating whether this data object can be converted to jClass.

longValue( )
> Returns data object as long.

stringValue( )
> Returns data object as java.lang.String.

timestampValue( )
> Returns data object as java.sql.Timestamp.

timeValue( )
> Returns data object as java.sql.Time.

toJdbc( )
> Returns data object as default Java type in java.lang.Object.

toString( )
> Returns data object as java.lang.String.

Inherited methods

The following methods are inherited from oracle.sql.Datum:

> equals
> getBytes
> getLength
> getStream
> makeJdbcArray
> setBytes
> setShareBytes
> shareBytes

Inherits all methods from java.lang.Object except clone, equals, and finalize.

CharacterSet

Extends java.lang.Object. Oracle8*i* only.

Fields

This class has a field to support each character set. See the Oracle documentation for details.

Methods

convert(CharacterSet, byte[], int, int)
> Returns abstract byte array.

convert(java.lang.String)
> Returns abstract byte array.

convertUnshared(CharacterSet, byte[], int, int)
> Returns byte array.

convertWithReplacement(java.lang.String)
> Returns abstract byte array.

equals(java.lang.Object)
> Returns Boolean.

getOracleId( )
> Returns int.

getRatioTo(CharacterSet)
> Returns int.

hashCode( )
> Returns int.

isConvertibleFrom(CharacterSet)
> Returns Boolean.

isLossyFrom(CharacterSet)
    Returns abstract Boolean.
make(int)
    Returns CharacterSet. Static method.
toString( )
    Returns java.lang.String.
toString(byte[], int, int)
    Returns java.lang.String.
toStringWithReplacement(byte[], int, int)
    Returns abstract java.lang.String.

Inherited methods

The following methods are inherited from java.lang.Object:

    getClass
    notify
    notifyAll
    wait

CLOB

Extends oracle.sql.DatumWithConnection. Implements java.sql.Clob in Oracle9*i*, oracle.jdbc2.Clob in Oracle8*i*.

The constructor for this class is:

```
CLOB(OracleConnection conn, byte[] lob_descriptor, short csform)
```

Fields

DURATION_CALL	Static int, new in Oracle9*i*
DURATION_SESSION	Static int, new in Oracle9*i*
MAX_CHUNK_SIZE	Static int
MODE_READONLY	Static int, new in Oracle9*i*
MODE_READWRITE	Static int, new in Oracle9*i*

Methods

close( )
    Closes a previously opened CLOB. New with Oracle9*i*.
createTemporary(java.sql.Connection *conn*, boolean *cache*, int *duration*)
    Returns a static CLOB as a temporary CLOB. New with Oracle9*i*.
empty_lob( )
    Returns a CLOB as an empty LOB. Static method.
freeTemporary( )
    Frees the contents and the locator of the temporary CLOB. New with Oracle9*i*.
freeTemporary(CLOB *temp_lob*)
    Frees the contents and the locator of the temporary CLOB. Static method. New with Oracle9*i*.
getAsciiOutputStream( )
    Returns java.io.OutputStream.

getAsciiOutputStream(long *pos*)
    Returns java.io.OutputStream, a stream from *pos*. New with Oracle9*i*.

getAsciiStream( )
    Returns java.io.InputStream as the clob interface function.

getAsciiStream(long *pos*)
    Returns java.io.InputStream as a stream from *pos*. New with Oracle9*i*.

getBufferSize( )
    Returns int.

getCharacterOutputStream( )
    Returns java.io.Writer.

getCharacterOutputStream(long *pos*)
    Returns java.io.Reader as a stream from position *pos*. New with Oracle9*i*.

getCharacterStream( )
    Returns java.io.Reader.

getCharacterStream(long *pos*)
    Returns java.io.Reader as a stream from position *pos*. New with Oracle9*i*.

getChars(long *pos*, int *length*, char[] *buffer*)
    Returns int as number of characters read from *pos* in *buf* of *length*. New with Oracle9*i*.

getChunkSize( )
    Returns int.

getConnection( )
    Returns OracleConnection.

getJavaSqlConnection( )
    Returns java.sql.Connection. New with Oracle9*i*.

getSubString(long *pos*, int *length*)
    Returns java.lang.String of *length* from position *pos*.

isConvertibleTo(java.lang.Class *jClass*)
    Returns a Boolean.

isEmptyLob( )
    Returns a Boolean indicating whether the LOB locator points to an empty CLOB.

isNCLOB( )
    Returns a Boolean. New with Oracle9*i*.

isOpen( )
    Returns a Boolean indicating whether the CLOB is opened. New with Oracle9*i*.

isTemporary( )
    Returns a Boolean indicating whether the LOB locator points to a temporary CLOB. New with Oracle9*i*.

isTemporary(CLOB *lob*)
    Returns a Boolean indicating whether the *lob* locator points to a temporary CLOB. Static method. New with Oracle9*i*.

length( )
    Returns a LONG as the length of a CLOB.

open(int *mode*)
    Opens a CLOB in the indicated mode.

---

position(java.lang.String *pattern*, long *start*)
: Returns a LONG with the position of *pattern*, starting from *start*.

position(java.sql.Clob *pattern*, long *start*)
: Returns a LONG with the position of *pattern*, starting from *start*.

putChars(long *pos*, char[] *chars*)
: Returns int, the number of bytes written to *pos* in a CLOB from *chars*.

putChars(long *pos*, char[] *chars*, int *length*)
: Returns int, the number of bytes written to *pos* in a CLOB from *chars* of *length*. New with Oracle9*i*.

putString(long *pos*, java.lang.String *str*)
: Returns int, number of chars written to *pos* in CLOB from *str*.

setAsciiStream(long *pos*)
: Returns java.io.OutputStream that can be used to write to the CLOB value that this CLOB object represents. JDBC 3.0. New with Oracle9*i*.

setBytes(long *pos*, java.lang.String *str*, int *offset*, int *len*)
: Returns int, number of bytes actually written, and writes *str* to the CLOB value this CLOB object represents, starting at position *pos* for *len* JDBC 3.0. New with Oracle9*i* Release 2.

setCharacterStream(long *pos*)
: Returns java.io.Writer that can be used to write Unicode characters to the CLOB value that this CLOB object represents. JDBC 3.0. New with Oracle9*i*.

setString(long *pos*, java.lang.String *str*)
: Returns int, number of bytes actually written, and writes the given array of *str* to the CLOB value that this CLOB object represents, starting at position *pos*. JDBC 3.0. New with Oracle9*i*.

setString(long *pos*, java.lang.String *string*, int *offset*, int *length*)
: Returns int, number of bytes actually written, starting at *offset* for *length*, and writes the given array of *str* to the CLOB value that this CLOB represents, starting at position *pos*. JDBC 3.0. New with Oracle9*i*.

toJdbc( )
: Returns java.lang.Object, the default Java object type.

trim(long *newlen*)
: Trims the value of the CLOB to *newlen*. New with Oracle9*i*.

truncate(long *len*)
: Truncates the CLOB value to be *len* bytes in length. JDBC 3.0. New with Oracle9*i* Release 2.

Inherited methods

The following methods are inherited from oracle.sql.DatumWithConnection in Oracle9*i*:

    assertNotNull
    getOracleConnection

Inherits all methods from oracle.sql.Datum except isConvertibleTo and toJdbc.

Inherits all methods from java.lang.Object except clone, equals, and finalize.

DATE

Extends oracle.sql.Datum.

This class has many constructors, which can create dates from different types of information:

```
DATE()
DATE(byte[] date)
DATE(java.sql.Date date)
DATE(java.sql.Date date, java.util.Calendar cal)
DATE(java.lang.Object obj)
DATE(java.lang.Object obj, java.util.Calendar cal)
DATE(java.lang.String str)
DATE(java.lang.String str, java.util.Calendar cal) -- New with Oracle9i.
DATE(java.sql.Time time)
DATE(java.sql.Time time, java.util.Calendar cal)
DATE(java.sql.Timestamp timestamp)
DATE(java.sql.Timestamp timestamp, java.util.Calendar cal)
```

Fields

BDA	Static int
BDAL	Static int
BDT	Static int
BHR	Static int
BHRL	Static int
BMN	Static int
BMNL	Static int
BMO	Static int
BMOL	Static int
BSC	Static int
BSCL	Static int
BYR	Static int
BYRL	Static int
HRZERO	Static int
MIZERO	Static int
MSD	Static int
SEZERO	Static int
YR0	Static int

Methods

addJulianDays(int *julianDay*, int *julianSec*)
> Returns DATE, which is *julianDay* and *julianSec* later.

addMonths(int *months*)
> Returns DATE, which is *months* later.

checkValidity(byte[] *date*)
> Returns int, which is either 0 if valid or a combination of the fields listed earlier to designate the invalid portions of *date*. Static method.

compareTo(DATE *date*)
> Returns -1 if DATE is less than *date*, 0 if DATE and *date* are equal, 1 if DATE is greater than *date*.

dateValue( )
> Returns java.sql.Date of internal Oracle DATE.

dateValue(java.util.Calendar *cal*)
> Returns java.sql.Date of internal Oracle DATE.

diffInJulianDays(DATE *date*, int[] *julianDay*, int[] *julianSec*)
> Calculates the difference between *dates* in Julian days.

diffInMonths(DATE *date*)
> Returns a number that is the difference between two dates in months.

fromJulianDays(int *julianDay*, int *julianSec*)
> Returns a DATE that is the conversion in Julian days and seconds to an Oracle DATE. Static method.

fromText(java.lang.String *datestr*, java.lang.String *fmt*, java.lang.String *lang*)
> Returns a DATE converted from a string to a DATE object. Static method.

getCurrentDate( )
> Returns the current date and time as a DATE. Static method.

isConvertibleTo(java.lang.Class *cls*)
> Returns a Boolean indicating whether the object can be converted to a particular class.

lastDayOfMonth( )
> Returns a DATE object intialized to the last day of the month.

makeJdbcArray(int *arraySize*)
> Returns java.lang.Object as a representation of the datum.

numberToJulianDays(NUMBER *num*, int[] *julianDay*, int[] *julianSec*)
> Converts an Oracle NUMBER *num* to Julian days and seconds.

parseFormat(java.lang.String *fmt*, java.lang.String *lang*)
> Returns a static byte[] conversion of the *fmt* into tokens for use by toText( ). New with Oracle9i.

round(java.lang.String *prec*)
> Returns DATE with date rounded to specified precision *prec*.

setDayOfWeek(int *day*)
> Returns DATE object initialized to date advanced to the week of the *day* specified.

stringValue( )
> Returns java.lang.String as internal Oracle DATE converted to a Java String.

timestampValue( )
> Returns java.sql.Timestamp as internal Oracle DATE converted to a Java Timestamp.

timestampValue(java.util.Calendar *cal*)
> Returns java.sql.Timestamp as internal Oracle DATE and Calendar converted to a Java Timestamp.

timeValue( )
> Returns java.sql.Time as internal Oracle DATE converted to a Java Time.

timeValue(java.util.Calendar *cal*)
> Returns java.sql.Time as internal Oracle DATE and Calendar to a Java Time.

toBytes( )
: Returns byte[]. Static method.

toBytes(java.sql.Date *date*)
: Returns byte[], an Oracle DATE converted from *date*. Static method.

toBytes(java.sql.Date *date*, java.util.Calendar *cal*)
: Returns byte[], an Oracle DATE converted from *cal*. Static method.

toBytes(java.lang.String *str*)
: Returns byte[], an Oracle DATE converted from *str*. Static method.

toBytes(java.lang.String *str*, java.util.Calendar *cal*)
: Returns byte[], an Oracle DATE converted from *str* in *cal*. New with Oracle9*i*. Static method.

toBytes(java.sql.Time *time*)
: Returns byte[], an Oracle DATE converted from *time*. Static method.

toBytes(java.sql.Time *time*, java.util.Calendar *cal*)
: Returns byte[], an Oracle DATE converted from *time* in *cal*. Static method.

toBytes(java.sql.Timestamp *timestamp*)
: Returns byte[], an Oracle DATE converted from *timestamp*. Static method.

toBytes(java.sql.Timestamp *timestamp*, java.util.Calendar *cal*)
: Returns byte[], an Oracle DATE converted from *timestamp* in *cal*. Static method.

toDate(byte[] *date*)
: Returns java.sql.Date, an Oracle DATE from *date*. Static method.

toDate(byte[] *date*, java.util.Calendar *cal*)
: Returns java.sql.Date, an Oracle DATE from *date* in *cal*. Static method.

toJdbc( )
: Returns java.lang.Object representation of the datum object

toJulianDays(int[] *julianDay*, int[] *julianSec*)
: Converts to Julian days and seconds from the given date.

toNumber( )
: Returns NUMBER, conversion of date to an Oracle NUMBER.

toString(byte[] *date*)
: Returns static java.lang.String conversion of *date*.

toText(byte[] *pfmt*, java.lang.String *lang*)
: Returns java.lang.String of date in *pfmt* in language *lang*. New with Oracle9*i*.

toText(java.lang.String *fmt*, java.lang.String *lang*)
: Returns java.lang.String of date in *fmt* in language *lang*.

toTime(byte[] *date*)
: Returns static java.sql.Time of *date* converted from Oracle DATE.

toTime(byte[] *date*, java.util.Calendar *cal*)
: Returns static java.sql.Time of *date* in *cal* converted from Oracle DATE.

toTimestamp(byte[] *date*)
: Returns static java.sql.Timestamp of *date* converted from Oracle DATE.

toTimestamp(byte[] *date*, java.util.Calendar *cal*)
: Returns static java.sql.Time of *date* in *cal* converted from Oracle DATE.

truncate(java.lang.String *prec*)
: Returns a DATE object with date truncated to *prec*.

Inherited methods

The following methods are inherited from oracle.sql.Datum:

asciiStreamValue
bigDecimalValue
binaryStreamValue
BooleanValue
byteValue
characterStreamValue
doubleValue
equals
floatValue
getBytes
getLength
getStream
intValue
longValue
setBytes
setShareBytes
shareBytes

Inherits all methods from java.lang.Object except clone, equals, and finalize.

Datum

Extends java.sql.Object. Datum is the root class for subclasses CHAR, DATE, Datum-WithConnection, INTERVALYM, NUMBER, RAW, ROWID, TIMESTAMP, TIMES-TAMPLTZ, and TIMESTAMPTZ in Oracle9*i*; Datum is the root class for ARRAY, BFILE, BLOB, CHAR, CLOB, DATE, NUMBER, RAW, REF, ROWID, and STRUCT in Oracle8*i*.

The constructors for this class are:

```
Datum( )
```

which creates an empty datum or

```
Datum(byte[] newData)
```

which creates a new datum with *newData* as representation of datum.

Methods

asciiStreamValue()
    Returns java.io.InputStream representation as ASCII representation of the datum object.

bigDecimalValue()
    Returns java.math.BigDecimal representation of the datum object.

binaryStreamValue()
    Returns java.io.InputStream representation of the datum object.

booleanValue()
    Returns Boolean representation of the datum object.

byteValue()
    Returns byte representation of the datum object.

characterStreamValue()
> Returns representation of the datum object.

dateValue()
> Returns java.sql.Date representation of the datum object.

doubleValue()
> Returns a double representation of the datum object

equals(java.lang.Object *obj*)
> Returns Boolean with equality test result with a Datum.

floatValue()
> Returns float representation of the datum object.

getBytes()
> Returns byte array containing a copy of the RDBMS data.

getLength()
> Returns long representing the length of a datum.

getStream()
> Returns java.io.InputStream so the raw data may be read.

intValue()
> Returns int representation of the datum object.

isConvertibleTo(java.lang.Class *cls*)
> Returns abstract Boolean if datum object can be converted to *cls*.

longValue()
> Returns long representation of the datum object

makeJdbcArray(int *arraySize*)
> Returns abstract java.lang.Object representation of the datum.

setBytes(byte[] *array*)
> Sets datum value using a byte *array*.

setShareBytes(byte[] *array*)
> Sets datum value using a byte *array*.

shareBytes()
> Returns byte[].

stringValue()
> Returns java.lang.String representation of the datum object.

timestampValue()
> Returns java.sql.Timestamp representation of the datum object.

timeValue()
> Returns java.sql.Time representation of the datum object.

toJdbc()
> Returns the JDBC representation as abstract java.lang.Object of the datum object.

Inherited methods

Inherits all methods from java.lang.Object except clone, equals, and finalize.

DatumWithConnection

Extends Datum. DatumWithConnection is the parent of subclasses ARRAY, BFILE, BLOB, CLOB, OPAQUE, REF, and STRUCT. New with Oracle9i.

The constructors for this class are:

```
DatumWithConnection( )
```

or:

```
DatumWithConnection(byte[] elements)
```

Methods

assertNotNull(java.sql.Connection conn)
    Static method.

assertNotNull(TypeDescriptor desc)
    Static method.

getConnection( )
    Returns OracleConnection. Deprecated since 9.0.0. Use getJavaSqlConnection(),
    getInternalConnection(), or getOracleConnection() instead.

getJavaSqlConnection( )
    Returns the java.sql.Connection associated with the receiver.

getOracleConnection( )
    Returns OracleConnection associated with the receiver.

Inherited methods

Inherits all methods from oracle.sql.Datum.

INTERVALYM

Extends Datum. Used for measuring time differences. New with Oracle9i.

The constructors for this class are:

```
INTERVALYM( )
INTERVALYM(byte[] intervalYM)
INTERVALYM(java.lang.String str)
```

with the instance initialized to 0:0, intervalYM, or str.

Methods

isConvertibleTo(java.lang.Class cls)
    Returns Boolean if the object can be converted to cls.

makeJdbcArray(int arraySize)
    Returns java.lang.Object array of arraySize representation of the datum.

toBytes( )
    Returns INTERVALYM object as a byte array.

toBytes(java.lang.String str)
    Returns byte array as Java String conversion of INTERVALYM. Static method.

toJdbc( )
    Returns java.lang.Object as JDBC representation of the INTERVALYM object.

toString()
> Returns java.lang.String representation of INTERVALYM.

toString(byte[] *inparray*)
> Returns static java.lang.String representation of INTERVALYM *inparray*.

Inherited methods

Inherits all methods from oracle.sql.Datum except isConvertibleTo, makeJdbcArray, and toJdbc.

Inherits all methods from java.lang.Object except clone, equals, and finalize.

JAVA_STRUCT

Extends oracle.sql.struct. New with Oracle9*i*.

The constructor for this class is:

```
JAVA_STRUCT(StructDescriptor type, java.sql.Connection conn,
    java.lang.Object[] attributes)
```

Methods

toJdbc()
> Returns java.lang.Object.

Inherited methods

Inherits all methods from oracle.sql.STRUCT except for toJdbc.

The following methods are inherited from oracle.sql.DatumWithConnection:

> assertNotNull
> getOracleConnection

Inherits all methods from oracle.sql.Datum except isConvertibleTo and toJdbc.

Inherits all methods from java.lang.Object except clone, equals, and finalize.

NUMBER

Extends oracle.sql.Datum. Used for conversion between Oracle number types and Java number types.

The constructors for this class are:

```
NUMBER()
NUMBER(java.math.BigDecimal BigDecNum)
NUMBER(java.math.BigInteger BigIntNum)
NUMBER(boolean boolNum)
NUMBER(byte byteNum)
NUMBER(byte[] num)
NUMBER(double doubleNum)
NUMBER(float floatNum)
NUMBER(int intNum)
NUMBER(java.lang.Object obj)
NUMBER(java.lang.String StringNum, int scale)
NUMBER(long longNum)
NUMBER(short shortNum)
```

Each of these constructors uses the variable as the initialization value. The java.lang. String constructor uses *scale* for the scale of the converted number.

Methods

abs()
> Returns NUMBER initialized to the absolute value of NUMBER.

acos()
> Returns NUMBER initialized to the arc cosine value of NUMBER.

add(NUMBER *n*)
> Returns NUMBER initialized to the value of the NUMBER value and *n*.

asin()
> Returns NUMBER initialized to the arc sine value of NUMBER.

atan()
> Returns NUMBER initialized to the arc tangent value of NUMBER.

atan2(NUMBER *x*)
> Returns NUMBER initialized to the value of atan2(NUMBER/*x*).

bigDecimalValue()
> Returns java.math.BigDecimal conversion of internal Oracle Number.

bigIntegerValue()
> Returns java.math.BigInteger conversion of internal Oracle Number.

booleanValue()
> Returns Boolean conversion of internal Oracle Number.

byteValue()
> Returns byte conversion of internal Oracle Number.

ceil()
> Returns NUMBER initialized to the ceiling of NUMBER value.

compareTo(NUMBER n)
> Returns -1 if NUMBER is less than *n*, 0 if NUMBER and *n* are equal (==), 1 if NUMBER is greater than *n*.

cos()
> Returns NUMBER initialized to the cosine value of NUMBER.

cosh()
> Returns NUMBER initialized to the hyperbolic cosine value of NUMBER.

decrement()
> Returns NUMBER initialized to the NUMBER value decremented by 1.

div(NUMBER *n*)
> Returns NUMBER initialized to the division of NUMBER value by *n*.

doubleValue()
> Returns double conversion of internal Oracle NUMBER.

e()
> Returns NUMBER initialized to the value of *e*. Static method.

exp()
> Returns NUMBER initialized to the value of *e* raised to NUMBER value.

floatingPointRound(int *precision*)
> Returns NUMBER initialized to Number rounded to *precision* significant decimal digits.

floatValue( )
> Returns float conversion of internal Oracle Number.

floor( )
> Returns NUMBER initialized to the floor of NUMBER value.

formattedTextToNumber(java.lang.String *num*, java.lang.String *fmt*, java.lang.String *lang*)
> Returns NUMBER converted from *num* controlled by the format *fmt* in language *lang*. Static method.

increment( )
> Returns NUMBER initialized to the NUMBER value incremented by 1.

inInitialization( )
> Returns a Boolean indicating the state of initialization. Static method. Oracle8*i* only.

intValue( )
> Returns int conversion of internal Oracle Number.

isConvertibleTo(java.lang.Class *cls*)
> Returns a Boolean TRUE if object can be converted to *cls*.

isInf( )
> Returns a Boolean TRUE if NUMBER value is positive or negative infinity.

isInt( )
> Returns a Boolean TRUE if NUMBER value is finite and integral.

isNegInf( )
> Returns a Boolean TRUE if NUMBER is negative infinity.

isPosInf( )
> Returns a Boolean TRUE if NUMBER is positive infinity.

*is*Valid(byte[] *num*)
> Checks if Oracle Number *num* is valid. Static method.

isZero( )
> Returns a Boolean TRUE if NUMBER is 0.

ln( )
> Returns NUMBER initialized to the natural logarithm of NUMBER value.

ln10( )
> Returns NUMBER initialized to the value of ln(10).

log(NUMBER *base*)
> Returns NUMBER initialized to the logarithm of the *base* of NUMBER.

longValue( )
> Returns long conversion of internal Oracle Number.

makeJdbcArray(int *arraySize*)
> Returns java.lang.Object array representation of the datum of *arraySize*.

mod(NUMBER *n*)
> Returns NUMBER initialized to the remainder of NUMBER/*n*.

mul(NUMBER *n*)
>   Returns NUMBER initialized to product of NUMBER and *n*.

negate( )
>   Returns NUMBER initialized to the negated NUMBER value.

negInf( )
>   Returns NUMBER initialized to negative infinity. Static method.

pi( )
>   Returns NUMBER initialized to the value of pi. Static method.

posInf( )
>   Returns NUMBER initialized to positive infinity. Static method.

pow(int exp)
>   Returns NUMBER initialized to NUMBER raised to the *exp* power.

pow(NUMBER *exp*)
>   Returns NUMBER initialized to the NUMBER value raised to *exp* power.

round(int *decimal_place*)
>   Returns NUMBER initialized to the NUMBER value rounded to *decimal_place*.

scale(int *left*, int *right*, boolean[] *big*)
>   Returns NUMBER initialized to the value determined by rounding to the left and right. If there are too many digits on the left, *big* is TRUE.

shift(int *digits*)
>   Returns NUMBER initialized to the NUMBER value shifted *digits* decimal places.

shortValue( )
>   Returns short conversion of internal Oracle Number.

sign( )
>   Returns -1 if the sign of NUMBER is negative, 0 if NUMBER is 0, and > 0 if NUMBER is positive.

sin( )
>   Returns NUMBER initialized to the sine of the NUMBER.

sinh( )
>   Returns NUMBER initialized to the hyperbolic sine of NUMBER.

sqroot( )
>   Returns NUMBER initialized to the square root of NUMBER.

stringValue( )
>   Returns java.lang.String conversion of internal Oracle Number.

sub(NUMBER *n*)
>   Returns NUMBER initialized to the difference of NUMBER and *n*.

tan( )
>   Returns NUMBER initialized to the tangent of NUMBER.

tanh( )
>   Returns NUMBER initialized to the hyperbolic tangent of Number.

textToPrecisionNumber(java.lang.String *num*, boolean *precflag*, int *preclen*, boolean *scaleflag*, int *scalelen*, java.lang.String *lang*)
>   Returns NUMBER initialized to the value in *num* as indicated. Static method.

toBigDecimal(byte[] *num*)
>   Returns java.math.BigDecimal conversion of internal Oracle Number.

toBigInteger(byte[] *num*)
    Returns java.math.BigInteger conversion of internal Oracle Number.
toBoolean(byte[] *num*)
    Returns Boolean conversion of internal Oracle Number. Static method.
toByte(byte[] *num*)
    Returns byte conversion of internal Oracle Number. Static method.
toBytes( )
    Returns internal Oracle Number byte array.
toBytes(boolean *boolNum*)
    Converts *boolNum* to an Oracle Number byte array. Static method.
toBytes(byte *byteNum*)
    Converts *byteNum* to an Oracle Number byte array. Static method.
toBytes(double *doubleNum*)
    Converts *doubleNum* to an Oracle Number byte array. Static method.
toBytes(float *floatNum*)
    Converts *floatNum* to an Oracle Number byte array. Static method.
toBytes(int *intNum*)
    Converts *intNum* to an Oracle Number byte array. Static method.
toBytes(java.lang.String *StringNum*, int *scale*)
    Converts *StringNum* to an Oracle Number byte array of *scale*. Static method.
toBytes(java.math.BigDecimal *BigDecNum*)
    Converts *BigDecNum* to an Oracle Number byte array. Static method.
toBytes(java.math.BigInteger *BigIntNum*)
    Converts *BigIntNum* to an Oracle Number byte array. Static method.
toBytes(long *longNum*)
    Converts *longNum* to an Oracle Number byte array. Static method.
toBytes(short *shortNum*)
    Converts *shortNum* to an Oracle Number byte array. Static method.
toDouble(byte[] *num*)
    Returns double conversion of internal Oracle Number. Static method.
toFloat(byte[] *num*)
    Returns float conversion of internal Oracle Number. Static method.
toFormattedText(java.lang.String *fmt*, java.lang.String *lang*)
    Returns java.lang.String based on the format specified in *fmt* and *lang*.
toInt(byte[] *num*)
    Returns int conversion of internal Oracle Number. Static method.
toJdbc( )
    Returns java.lang.Object representation of the Datum object
toLong(byte[] *num*)
    Returns long conversion of internal Oracle Number. Static method.
toShort(byte[] *num*)
    Returns short conversion of internal Oracle Number. Static method.
toString(byte[] *num*)
    Returns java.lang.String conversion of internal Oracle Number. Static method.

toText(int *outStringLength*, java.lang.String *lang*)
> Returns java.lang.String with the unformatted representation of NUMBER.

truncate(int *decimal_place*)
> Returns NUMBER initialized to the NUMBER value truncated to *decimal_place*.

zero( )
> Returns NUMBER initialized to zero. Static method.

Inherited methods

The following methods are inherited from oracle.sql.Datum:

> asciiStreamValue
> binaryStreamValue
> characterStreamValue
> dateValue
> equals
> getBytes
> getLength
> getStream
> setBytes
> setShareBytes
> shareBytes
> timestampValue
> timeValue

Inherits all methods from java.lang.Object except clone, equals, and finalize.

OPAQUE

Extends DatumWithConnection. New with Oracle9*i*.

The constructor for this class is:

```
OPAQUE(OpaqueDescriptor type, java.sql.Connection conn,
    java.lang.Object value)
```

Methods

getBytesValue( )
> Returns a byte array that represents the attributes into the format that is actually used in the database.

getConnection( )
> Returns OracleConnection.

getDescriptor( )
> Returns OpaqueDescriptor.

getJavaSqlConnection( )
> Returns java.sql.Connection.

getSQLTypeName( )
> Returns java.lang.String SQL type name of the SQL-structured type this Struct object represents.

getValue( )
> Returns java.lang.Object with the Opaque value.

isConvertibleTo(java.lang.Class *jClass*)
: Returns Boolean TRUE if datum object can be converted to *jClass*.

toJdbc( )
: Returns java.lang.Object representation of the datum object.

Inherited methods

The following methods are inherited from oracle.sql.DatumWithConnection:

    assertNotNull
    getOracleConnection

Inherits all methods from oracle.sql.Datum except for isConvertibleTo and toJdbc.

Inherits all methods from java.lang.Object except clone, equals, and finalize.

OpaqueDescriptor

Extends oracle.sql.TypeDescriptor. Implements java.io.Serializable. New with Oracle9*i*.

The constructor for this class is:

    OpaqueDescriptor(oracle.sql.SQLName *name*, oracle.sql.OracleTypeOPAQUE *type*,
    java.sql.Connection *connection*)

Inherited fields

The following field is inherited from oracle.sql.TypeDescriptor:

    DEBUG_SERIALIZATION

Methods

createDescriptor(java.lang.String *name*, java.sql.Connection *conn*)
: Returns OpaqueDescriptor. Static method.

descType( )
: Returns java.lang.String with description of type.

getMaxLength( )
: Returns LONG with maximun number of bytes this opaque object can hold.

getTypeCode( )
: Returns int with the Opaque type code: OracleTypes.OPAQUE.

hasFixedSize( )
: Returns a Boolean indicating whether the Opaque type has fixed size.

hasUnboundedSize( )
: Returns a Boolean indicating whether the Opaque type has unbounded size.

isModeledInC( )
: Returns a Boolean indicating whether the Opaque type is modeled in the C language.

isTrustedLibrary( )
: Returns a Boolean indicating whether the Trusted Library implementing Support functions is specified for the Opaque type.

Inherited methods

The following methods are inherited from oracle.sql.TypeDescriptor:

> getName
> getSubtypeName
> getConnection

Inherits all methods from java.lang.Object except clone, equals, and finalize.

OracleSQLOutput

Extends java.lang.Object. Implements oracle.jdbc2.SQLOutput. Only in Oracle8*i*.

Methods

writeArray(ARRAY *x*)
> Writes an array *x* to the stream.

writeArray(oracle.jdbc2.Array *x*)
> Writes an array *x* to the stream.

writeAsciiStream(java.io.InputStream *x*)
> Writes the next attribute to the stream as a stream of ASCII character *x*.

writeBfile(BFILE x)
> Writes the next attribute to the stream as BFILE *x*.

writeBigDecimal(java.math.BigDecimal *x*)
> Writes the next attribute to the stream as a java.math.BigDecimal *x*.

writeBinaryStream(java.io.InputStream *x*)
> Writes the next attribute to the stream as a java.math.InputStream *x*.

writeBlob(BLOB *x*)
> Writes the next attribute to the stream as a BLOB *x*.

writeBlob(oracle.jdbc2.Blob *x*)
> Writes the next attribute to the stream as an oracle.jdbc2.Blob *x*.

writeBoolean(Boolean *x*)
> Writes the next attribute to the stream as a Java Boolean *x*.

writeByte(byte *x*)
> Writes the next attribute to the stream as a Java byte *x*.

writeBytes(byte[] *x*)
> Writes the next attribute to the stream as an array of bytes *x*.

writeCHAR(CHAR x)
> Writes the next attribute to the stream as a CHAR *x*.

writeCharacterStream(java.io.Reader *x*)
> Writes the next attribute to the stream as a java.io.Reader *x*.

writeClob(CLOB *x*)
> Writes the next attribute to the stream as a CLOB *x*.

writeClob(oracle.jdbc2.Clob *x*)
> Writes the next attribute to the stream as a Clob *x*.

writeDATE(DATE *x*)
> Writes the next attribute to the stream as a DATE *x*.

writeDate(java.sql.Date *x*)
> Writes the next attribute to the stream as a java.sql.Date *x*.

writeDouble(double *x*)
> Writes the next attribute to the stream as a Double *x*.

writeFloat(float *x*)
> Writes the next attribute to the stream as a Float *x*.

writeInt(int *x*)
> Writes the next attribute to the stream as an int *x*.

writeLong(long *x*)
> Writes the next attribute to the stream as a Java long *x*.

writeNUMBER(NUMBER *x*)
> Writes the next attribute to the stream as NUMBER *x*.

writeObject(java.lang.Object *x*)
> Writes the next attribute to the stream as a java.lang.Object *x*.

writeObject(oracle.jdbc2.SQLData *x*)
> Writes the next attribute to the stream as an oracle.jdbc2.SQLData *x*.

writeOracleObject(Datum *x*)
> Writes the next attribute to the stream as a Datum *x*.

writeRAW(RAW *x*)
> Writes the next attribute to the stream as a RAW *x*.

writeRef(oracle.jdbc2.Ref *x*)
> Writes the next attribute to the stream as an oracle.jdbc2.Ref *x*.

writeRef(REF *x*)
> Writes the next attribute to the stream as a REF *x*.

writeROWID(ROWID *x*)
> Writes the next attribute to the stream as a ROWID *x*.

writeShort(short *x*)
> Writes the next attribute to the stream as a Short *x*.

writeString(java.lang.String *x*)
> Writes the next attribute to the stream as a java.lang.String *x*.

writeStruct(oracle.jdbc2.Struct *x*)
> Writes the next attribute to the stream as an oracle.jdbc2.Struct *x*.

writeStruct(STRUCT *x*)
> Writes the next attribute to the stream as a STRUCT *x*.

writeTime(java.sql.Time *x*)
> Writes the next attribute to the stream as a java.sql.Time *x*.

writeTimestamp(java.sql.Timestamp *x*)
> Writes the next attribute to the stream as a java.sql.Timestamp *x*.

Inherited methods

Inherits all methods from java.lang.Object except clone and finalize.

RAW

Extends oracle.sql.Datum.

The contructors for this class are:

```
RAW(byte[] raw_bytes)
RAW(java.lang.Object val)
```

The second constructor is deprecated in Oracle9i Release 2.

Methods

hexString2Bytes(java.lang.String *hexString*)
> Returns byte array, which is a converted string of *hexString* digits. Static method.

isConvertibleTo(java.lang.Class *jClass*)
> Returns a Boolean indicating whether the data object can be converted to *jClass*.

newRAW(java.lang.Object *obj*)
> Returns RAW from *obj* in the manner of the RAW(Object) constructor beginning in the next major release after Oracle JDBC 9.2. Static method.

oldRAW(java.lang.Object *obj*)
> Returns RAW from *obj* in the manner of the RAW(Object) constructor in versions of Oracle JDBC 9.2 and earlier. Static method.

stringValue( )
> Returns java.lang.String converted from this data object.

toJdbc( )
> Returns java.lang.Object converted from this data object.

Inherited methods

Inherits all methods from oracle.sql.Datum except isConvertibleTo, stringValue, and toJdbc.

Inherits all methods from java.lang.Object except clone, equals, and finalize.

REF

Extends DatumWithConnection with Oracle9i, Datum in Oracle8i. Implements java.sql.Ref, java.io.Serializable, and java.lang.Cloneable in Oracle9i, oracle.jdbc2.Ref in Oracle8i.

Methods

clone()
> Returns java.lang.Object. New with Oracle9i.

equals(java.lang.Object *obj*)
> Returns Boolean. New with Oracle9i.

getBaseTypeName()
> Returns java.lang.String.

getConnection()
> Returns OracleConnection.

getDescriptor()
> Returns StructDescriptor.

getJavaSqlConnection()
> Returns java.sql.Connection. New with Oracle9*i*.

getObject()
> Returns java.lang.Object referenced by this Ref object. JDBC 3.0. New with Oracle9*i*.

getObject(java.util.Map *map*)
> Returns java.lang.Object. New with Oracle9*i*.

getSQLTypeName()
> Returns java.lang.String. New with Oracle9*i*.

getSTRUCT()
> Returns STRUCT.

getValue()
> Returns java.lang.Object.

getValue(java.util.Map *map*)
> Returns java.lang.Object.

hashCode()
> Returns int. New with Oracle9*i*.

isConvertibleTo(java.lang.Class *jClass*)
> Returns Boolean indicating whether this data object can be converted to *jClass*.

setObject(java.lang.Object *value*)
> Sets structured type value to the given instance of object. JDBC 3.0. New with Oracle9*i*.

setValue(java.lang.Object *value*)
> Sets value.

toJdbc()
> Returns java.lang.Object converted from this data object into its default Java object type.

Inherited methods

The following methods are inherited from DatumWithConnection in Oracle9*i*:

> assertNotNull
> assertNotNull
> getOracleConnection

Inherits all methods from oracle.sql.Datum except isConvertibleTo and toJdbc.

Inherits all methods from java.lang.Object except clone, equals, and finalize.

ROWID

Extends oracle.sql.Datum.

Methods

isConvertibleTo(java.lang.Class *jClass*)
> Returns a Boolean indicating whether this data object can be converted to *jClass*.

stringValue()
> Returns java.lang.String converted from this data object.

toJdbc()
> Returns java.lang.Object converted from this data object.

Inherited methods

Inherits all methods from oracle.sql.Datum except for isConvertibleTo, stringValue, and toJdbc.

Inherits all methods from java.lang.Object except clone, equals, and finalize.

STRUCT

Extends oracle.sql.DatumWithConnection. Implements java.sql.Struct. Parent class of JAVA_STRUCT.

The constructor for this class is:

```
STRUCT(StructDescriptor type, java.sql.Connection conn,
    java.lang.Object[] attributes)
```

Methods

getAttributes( )
> Returns java.lang.Object[] with attributes.

getAttributes(java.util.Map map)
> Returns java.lang.Object[] with attributes.

getAutoBuffering( )
> Returns a Boolean.

getConnection( )
> Returns OracleConnection.

getDescriptor( )
> Returns StructDescriptor.

getJavaSqlConnection( )
> Returns java.sql.Connection.

getOracleAttributes( )
> Returns Datum[].

getSQLTypeName( )
> Returns java.lang.String with SQL type name of SQL-structured type.

isConvertibleTo(java.lang.Class jClass)
> Returns a Boolean indicating whether datum object can be converted to jClass.

setAutoBuffering(Boolean enable)
> Returns a Boolean.

toJdbc( )
> Returns java.lang.Object.

Inherited methods

The following methods are inherited from oracle.sql.DatumWithConnection:

> assertNotNull
> getOracleConnection

Inherits all methods from oracle.sql.Datum except isConvertibleTo and toJdbc.

Inherits all methods from java.lang.Object except clone, equals, and finalize.

StructDescriptor

Extends oracle.sql.TypeDescripton. Implements java.io.Serializable.

The constructor for this class is:

```
StructDescriptor(oracle.sql.SQLName name, oracle.sql.OracleTypeADT type,
    java.sql.Connection connection)
```

Inherited fields

The following field is inherited from oracle.sql.TypeDescriptor:

DEBUG_SERIALIZATION

Methods

createDescriptor(java.lang.String *name*, java.sql.Connection *conn*)
    Returns StructDescriptor. Static method.

descType( )
    Returns java.lang.String description.

getJavaClassName( )
    Returns java.lang.String with external name of the JAVA_STRUCT type.

getLanguage( )
    Returns java.lang.String.

getLength( )
    Returns int with number of fields in the Object Type.

getLocalAttributeCount( )
    Returns int with the number of attributes defined in the subtype.

getMetaData( )
    Returns java.sql.ResultSetMetaData.

getSubtypeNames( )
    Returns java.lang.String[] with SQL type names of the direct subtypes.

getSupertypeName( )
    Returns java.lang.String with SQL type name of the direct supertype.

getTypeCode( )
    Returns int.

getTypeVersion( )
    Returns int.

isFinalType( )
    Returns a Boolean indicating whether the Object type is a final type.

isInstantiable( )
    Returns a Boolean indicating whether the Object type is instantiable.

isJavaObject( )
    Returns a Boolean indicating whether the Object type is JAVA_STRUCT or
    STRUCT.

isSubtype( )
    Returns a Boolean.

Inherited methods

The following methods are inherited from oracle.sql.TypeDescriptor:

> getName
> getSubtypeName
> setConnection

Inherits all methods from java.lang.Object except clone, equals, and finalize.

TIMESTAMP

Extends oracle.sql.Datum.

The constructors for this class are:

```
TIMESTAMP( )
TIMESTAMP(byte[] timestamp)
TIMESTAMP(DATE date)
TIMESTAMP(java.sql.Date date)
TIMESTAMP(java.lang.String str)
TIMESTAMP(java.sql.Time time)
TIMESTAMP(java.sql.Timestamp timestamp)
```

The variables in the constructors represent initial values for the created object.

Methods

isConvertibleTo(java.lang.Class *cls*)
> Returns a Boolean indicating whether the object can be converted to *cls*.

makeJdbcArray(int *arraySize*)
> Returns java.lang.Object representation of the datum.

timestampValue( )
> Returns java.sql.Timestamp conversion of internal Oracle.

TimeZoneConvert(java.sql.Connection *conn*, TIMESTAMP *tstamp*, java.util.TimeZone *tz1*, java.util.TimeZone *tz2*)
> Returns TIMESTAMP converted from *tz1* to *tz2*. Static method.

toBytes( )
> Returns byte array of converted Oracle Timestamp.

toBytes(DATE *date*)
> Returns byte array of converted Oracle DATE. Static method.

toBytes(java.lang.String *str*)
> Returns byte array of converted Java String. Static method.

toBytes(java.sql.Date *date*)
> Returns byte array of converted Java Date. Static method.

toBytes(java.sql.Time *time*)
> Returns byte array of converted Java Time. Static method.

toBytes(java.sql.Timestamp *timestamp*)
> Returns byte array of converted Java Timestamp. Static method.

toDate(byte[] *timestamp*)
> Returns java.sql.Date converted from byte array representing a TIMESTAMP object. Static method.

toDATE(byte[] *timestamp*)
  Returns DATE converted from byte array representing a TIMESTAMP object.
  Static method.
toJdbc()
  Returns java.lang.Object representation of the datum object.
toString(byte[] *timestamp*)
  Returns java.lang.String converted from a TIMESTAMP. Static method.
toTime(byte[] *timestamp*)
  Returns static java.sql.Time converted from byte array representing a
  TIMESTAMP object. Static method.
toTimestamp(byte[] *timestamp*)
  Returns static java.sql.Timestamp converted from byte array representing a
  TIMESTAMP object. Static method.

Inherited methods

Inherits all methods from oracle.sql.Datum except for isConvertibleTo, makeJdbcAray, timestampValue and toJdbc.

Inherits all methods from java.lang.Object except clone, equals, and finalize.

TIMESTAMPLTZ

Extends oracle.sql.Datum.

The constructors for this class are:

```
TIMESTAMPLTZ( )
TIMESTAMPLTZ(byte[] timestampltz)
TIMESTAMPLTZ(java.sql.Connection conn, java.util.Calendar sess,
    java.sql.Date date)
TIMESTAMPLTZ(java.sql.Connection conn, java.util.Calendar sess, DATE date)
TIMESTAMPLTZ(java.sql.Connection conn, java.util.Calendar sess,
    java.lang.String str) -- deprecated with Oracle9i
TIMESTAMPLTZ(java.sql.Connection conn, java.util.Calendar sess,
    java.sql.Time time)
TIMESTAMPLTZ(java.sql.Connection conn, java.util.Calendar sess,
    java.sql.Timestamp timestamp)
TIMESTAMPLTZ(java.sql.Connection conn, java.sql.Date date)
TIMESTAMPLTZ(java.sql.Connection conn, DATE date)
TIMESTAMPLTZ(java.sql.Connection conn, java.sql.Date date,
    java.util.Calendar dbtz) -- deprecated with Oracle9i
TIMESTAMPLTZ(java.sql.Connection conn, DATE date,
    java.util.Calendar dbtz) -- deprecated with Oracle9i
TIMESTAMPLTZ(java.sql.Connection conn,
    java.lang.String str) -- deprecated with Oracle9i
TIMESTAMPLTZ(java.sql.Connection conn, java.lang.String str,
    java.util.Calendar dbtz) -- deprecated with Oracle9i
TIMESTAMPLTZ(java.sql.Connection conn, java.sql.Time time)
TIMESTAMPLTZ(java.sql.Connection conn, java.sql.Time time,
    java.util.Calendar dbtz) -- deprecated with Oracle9i
TIMESTAMPLTZ(java.sql.Connection conn, java.sql.Timestamp timestamp)
TIMESTAMPLTZ(java.sql.Connection conn, java.sql.Timestamp timestamp,
    java.util.Calendar dbtz) -- deprecated with Oracle9i
```

Methods

isConvertibleTo(java.lang.Class *cls*)
> Returns a Boolean indicating whether the object can be converted to *cls*.

makeJdbcArray(int *arraySize*)
> Returns java.lang.Object representation of the datum.

timestampValue(java.sql.Connection *conn*, java.util.Calendar *dbtz*)
> Returns java.sql.Timestamp converted from internal Oracle.

toBytes( )
> Returns byte array of converted Oracle TIMESTAMPLTZ object.

toBytes(java.sql.Connection *conn*, DATE *date*, java.util.Calendar *dbtz*)
> Static method. Deprecated with Oracle9*i*.

toBytes(java.sql.Connection *conn*, java.lang.String *str*, java.util.Calendar *dbtz*)
> Returns byte array of converted Java String to Oracle TIMESTAMPLTZ. Static method.

toBytes(java.sql.Connection *conn*, java.sql.Date *date*, java.util.Calendar *dbtz*)
> Static method. Deprecated with Oracle9*i*.

toBytes(java.sql.Connection *conn*, java.sql.Time *time*, java.util.Calendar *dbtz*)
> Static method. Deprecated with Oracle9*i*.

toBytes(java.sql.Connection *conn*, java.util.Calendar cal, DATE *date*)
> Returns byte array of converted Oracle DATE to Oracle TIMESTAMPLTZ. Static method.

toBytes(java.sql.Connection *conn*, java.util.Calendar *cal*, java.sql.Date *date*)
> Returns byte array of converted Java Date to Oracle TIMESTAMPLTZ object. Static method.

toBytes(java.sql.Connection *conn*, java.util.Calendar *cal*, java.sql.Time *time*)
> Returns byte array of converted Java Time to Oracle TIMESTAMPLTZ. Static method.

toBytes(java.sql.Connection *conn*, java.util.Calendar *cal*, java.sql.Timestamp *timestamp*)
> Returns byte array of converted Java Timestamp to Oracle TIMESTAMPLTZ. Static method.

toBytes(java.sql.Connection *conn*, java.util.Calendar *sess*, java.lang.String *str*)
> Returns byte array of converted Java String to Oracle TIMESTAMPLTZ. Static method.

toBytes(java.sql.Connection *conn*, java.sql.Timestamp *timestamp*, java.util.Calendar *dbtz*)
> Static method. Deprecated with Oracle9*i*.

toDate(java.sql.Connection *conn*, byte[] *timestamp*)
> Returns byte array of TIMESTAMPLTZ converted to Java Date Object. Static method.

toDATE(java.sql.Connection *conn*, byte[] *timestamp*)
> Returns DATE converted from TIMESTAMPLTZ. Static method.

toDate(java.sql.Connection *conn*, byte[] *timestamp*, java.util.Calendar *dbtz*)
> Returns java.sql.Date converted from TIMESTAMPLTZ to a Java Date. Static method.

toDATE(java.sql.Connection *conn*, byte[] *timestamp*, java.util.Calendar *dbtz*)
> Returns DATE converted from TIMESTAMPLTZ to Oracle Date. Static method.

toJdbc( )
> Returns java.lang.Object representation of the datum object.

toString(java.sql.Connection *conn*, byte[] *timestamp*)
> Returns java.lang.String converted from TIMESTAMP. Static method.

toString(java.sql.Connection *conn*, byte[] *timestamp*, java.util.Calendar *dbtz*)
> Static method. Deprecated with Oracle9*i*.

toTime(java.sql.Connection *conn*, byte[] *timestamp*)
> Returns java.sql.Time converted from TIMESTAMPLTZ. Static method.

toTime(java.sql.Connection *conn*, byte[] *timestamp*, java.util.Calendar *dbtz*)
> Returns java.sql.Time converted from TIMESTAMPLTZ. Static method.

toTimestamp(java.sql.Connection *conn*, byte[] *timestamptz*)
> Returns java.sql.Timestamp converted a TIMESTAMP. Static method.

toTimestamp(java.sql.Connection *conn*, byte[] *timestamptz*, java.util.Calendar *dbtz*)
> Returns java.sql.Timestamp converted from a TIMESTAMP. Static method.

Inherited methods

Inherits all methods from oracle.sql.Datum except for isConvertibleTo, makeJdbcAray and toJdbc.

Inherits all methods from java.lang.Object except clone, equals, and finalize.

TIMESTAMPTZ

Extends oracle.sql.Datum.

The constructors for this class are:

```
TIMESTAMPTZ( )
TIMESTAMPTZ(byte[] timestamptz)
TIMESTAMPTZ(java.sql.Connection conn, java.sql.Date date)
TIMESTAMPTZ(java.sql.Connection conn, DATE date)
TIMESTAMPTZ(java.sql.Connection conn, java.sql.Date date,
    java.util.Calendar cal)
TIMESTAMPTZ(java.sql.Connection conn, java.lang.String str)
TIMESTAMPTZ(java.sql.Connection conn, java.lang.String str,
    java.util.Calendar cal)
TIMESTAMPTZ(java.sql.Connection conn, java.sql.Time time)
TIMESTAMPTZ(java.sql.Connection conn, java.sql.Time time,
    java.util.Calendar cal)
TIMESTAMPTZ(java.sql.Connection conn, java.sql.Timestamp timestamp)
TIMESTAMPTZ(java.sql.Connection conn, java.sql.Timestamp timestamp,
    java.util.Calendar cal)
```

Methods

isConvertibleTo(java.lang.Class *cls*)
> Returns a Boolean indicating whether the object can be converted to *cls*.

makeJdbcArray(int *arraySize*)
> Returns java.lang.Object representation of the datum.

---

timestampValue(java.sql.Connection *conn*)
Returns java.sql.Timestamp converted from Oracle TIMESTAMPLTZ.

toBytes()
Returns byte array converted from Oracle TIMESTAMPLTZ.

toBytes(java.sql.Connection *conn*, DATE *date*)
Returns byte array converted to Oracle TIMESTAMPTZ. Static method.

toBytes(java.sql.Connection *conn*, java.lang.String *str*)
Returns byte array converted to Oracle TIMESTAMPTZ. Static method.

toBytes(java.sql.Connection *conn*, java.lang.String *str*, java.util.Calendar *cal*)
Returns byte array converted to Oracle TIMESTAMPTZ. Static method.

toBytes(java.sql.Connection *conn*, java.sql.Date *date*)
Returns byte array converted to Oracle TIMESTAMPTZ. Static method.

toBytes(java.sql.Connection *conn*, java.sql.Date *date*, java.util.Calendar *cal*)
Returns byte array converted to Oracle TIMESTAMPTZ. Static method.

toBytes(java.sql.Connection *conn*, java.sql.Time *time*)
Returns byte array converted to Oracle TIMESTAMPTZ. Static method.

toBytes(java.sql.Connection *conn*, java.sql.Time *time*, java.util.Calendar *cal*)
Returns byte array converted to Oracle TIMESTAMPTZ. Static method.

toBytes(java.sql.Connection *conn*, java.sql.Timestamp *timestamp*)
Returns byte array converted to Oracle TIMESTAMPTZ. Static method.

toBytes(java.sql.Connection *conn*, java.sql.Timestamp *timestamp*, java.util.Calendar *cal*)
Returns byte array converted to Oracle TIMESTAMPTZ. Static method.

toDate(java.sql.Connection *conn*, byte[] *timestamptz*)
Returns java.sql.Date converted from TIMESTAMPTZ. Static method.

toDATE(java.sql.Connection *conn*, byte[] *timestamptz*)
Returns DATE converted from byte array representing a TIMESTAMPTZ. Static method.

toJdbc()
Returns java.lang.Object representation of the TIMESTAMPTZ object.

toString(java.sql.Connection *conn*, byte[] *timestamptz*)
Returns java.lang.String converted from a TIMESTAMPTZ. Static method.

toTime(java.sql.Connection *conn*, byte[] *timestamptz*)
Returns static java.sql.Time converted from a byte array representing a TIMESTAMPTZ object. Static method.

toTimestamp(java.sql.Connection *conn*, byte[] *timestamptz*)
Returns static java.sql.Timestamp converted from a byte array representing a TIMESTAMP object. Static method.

Inherited methods

Inherits all methods from oracle.sql.Datum except for isConvertibleTo, makeJdbcArray and toJdbc.

Inherits all methods from java.lang.Object except clone, equals, and finalize.

TypeDescriptor

Extends java.lang.Object. Implements java.io.Serializable. Parent of ArrayDescriptor, OpaqueDescriptor, and StructDescriptor.

Field
DEBUG_SERIALIZATION

Methods
getName( )
  Returns java.lang.String of fully qualified type name.

getSubtypeName(OracleConnection conn, byte[] image, long offset)
  Returns java.lang.String. Static method.

setConnection(java.sql.Connection *connection*)
  See Oracle documentation.

Inherited methods
Inherits all methods from java.lang.Object except clone and finalize.

Tools and Utilities

This part of the book summarizes the commands and file specifications for a variety of tools and utilities used to manage and interact with the Oracle database. It consists of the following chapters:

Chapter 12, *SQL*Plus*, summarizes the commands and formatting elements available with SQL*Plus, the command-line interface to the Oracle database that you use to enter SQL statements and PL/SQL code and execute script files.

Chapter 13, *Export and Import*, summarizes the commands available with the Export utility (which copies data from the database into a binary file) and the Import utility (which bring data into the Oracle database from a binary file). You can use these utilities to capture both the structures and the data in an Oracle database.

Chapter 14, *SQL*Loader*, summarizes the commands available with SQL*Loader, a utility that allows you to load data in standard operating system file formats into an Oracle database and to perform a variety of data manipulation and transformation operations during the load.

Chapter 15, *Backup and Recovery*, briefly describes Oracle backup and recovery concepts, outlines the procedures you can follow to perform user-managed backup and recovery, and summarizes the commands available with the Recovery Manager (RMAN), the Oracle backup and recovery utility.

Chapter 16, *Enterprise Manager*, summarizes the features of Enterprise Manager, a graphical user interface console that allows you to manage Oracle databases.

Chapter 17, *Performance*, summarizes the main Oracle tools that help you examine and improve Oracle performance. It describes the SQL optimizers and hints and provides syntax for using the Explain Plan, TKPROF, AUTOTRACE, UTLBSTAT, UTLESTAT, and Statspack optimization tools.

12

SQL*Plus

SQL*Plus is the command-line interface to the Oracle database and is probably the most frequently used Oracle utility. This utility allows you to enter SQL statements and PL/SQL code and execute script files. Although some of its functionality is also offered by other products, such as Recovery Manager, Enterprise Manager, and the various Oracle reporting tools, the longevity and wide-ranging capabilities of SQL*Plus keep it in most Oracle practitioners' toolkits.

SQL*Plus is also one of the oldest of the Oracle utilities. It actually started life as the User Friendly Interface (UFI), the command-line interface for IBM's System R, one of the first relational database systems. In the 1980s, Oracle started adding features to UFI and soon renamed it AUFI (for Advanced User Friendly Interface). When Oracle 5.0 was released in 1985, the name of the product was changed to SQL*Plus. With each new release of Oracle, new commands and options have been added to this venerable product, but the core of SQL*Plus is still fundamentally the same.

Running SQL*Plus

You almost always invoke SQL*Plus by issuing the *sqlplus* command from your operating system command prompt. On Microsoft Windows systems, use either *sqlplus* or *sqlplusw*, depending on whether you want SQL*Plus to run in a command prompt window or in its own window; you also have the option of selecting an icon from the Start menu. Early releases of SQL*Plus on Windows used executable names such as *PLUS33* and *PLUS80W*, depending on the specific release number and on whether the DOS version or the Windows version was to be invoked.

 Beware of passing your password as a command-line argument to SQL*Plus. On Linux and Unix systems, such passwords may be easily visible to other users.

Use the following syntax to invoke SQL*Plus. Note that the –RESTRICT and –MARKUP parameters were new in Oracle8*i*. –HELP and –VERSION were new in Oracle9*i*.

```
SQLPLUS [[-S[ILENT]] [-H[ELP]] [-V[ERSION]]
    [-R[ESTRICT] level] [L[OGON]]
    [-M[ARKUP] 'markup_options']
    [username[/password][@connect] | / [AS (SYSDBA | SYSOPER)]] | /NOLOG]
    [@scriptfile [arg1 arg2 arg3...]]] | - | -?
```

–S[ILENT]
: Tells SQL*Plus to run in silent mode, with no startup messages, command prompts, or echoed commands displayed.

–H[ELP]
: Causes SQL*Plus to display a short summary of this syntax. Prior to Oracle9*i*, use *sqlplus* to get the help summary.

–V[ERSION]
: Causes SQL*Plus to display version and copyright information. Prior to Oracle9*i*, use *sqlplus –?* to get version and copyright information.

–R[ESTRICT] *level*
: Restricts what the user can do from SQL*Plus. The *level* must be one of the following:

  1   Disables the EDIT, HOST, and ! commands.

  2   Disables the EDIT, HOST, !, SAVE, SPOOL, and STORE commands.

  3   Disables the EDIT, GET, HOST, SAVE, START, @, @@, SPOOL, and STORE commands.

       Level 3 also disables the reading of the *login.sql* file. The *glogin.sql* file will be read, but restricted commands won't be executed.

–L[OGON]
: Prevents SQL*Plus from reprompting for username and password in case the first username and password that you pass are incorrect. New in Oracle9*i* Release 2.

–M[ARKUP] *markup_options*
: Allows you to specify the markup language to use when generating output. Except for HTML, all markup options are optional. The following are valid markup options:

HTML { [ON | OFF] }
: Specifies the markup language to use and enables or disables the use of that markup language. In Oracle 8.1.6, this is a mandatory option.

HEAD text
: Specifies content for the <head> tag. The tag is written as <head>text</head>.

BODY text
: Specifies content for the <body> tag. The tag is written as <body text>.

TBLE text
> Specifies content for the <table> tag used to format query output. The tag is written as <table text >.

ENTMAP (ON | OFF)
> Controls whether SQL*Plus uses HTML equivalents such as < and > for special characters such as < and >.

SPOOL (ON | OFF)
> Controls whether SQL*Plus writes to the spool file using plain text or the specified markup language (currently HTML).

PRE[FORMAT] (ON | OFF)
> Controls whether spooled report output is enclosed within <pre> ... </pre> tags.

On some operating systems, you need to enclose the entire string of markup options within double quotes.

username [/password][@connect]
> Database login information.

/
> Connects you to a local database using operating system authentication.

AS (SYSDBA | SYSOPER)
> Connects you in an administrative role so that you can perform database administration tasks (e.g., starting and stopping a database instance). You may need to enclose the login within quotes:

```
sqlplus "sys/password as sysdba"
```

/NOLOG
> Tells SQL*Plus to start without connecting to a database first.

scriptfile
> Name of a SQL*Plus script file. Upon completion of this script file, SQL*Plus will terminate.

arg1 arg2 arg3
> Optional command-line arguments to pass to your script.

Entering SQL*Plus Commands

How you enter commands in SQL*Plus depends a bit on whether you are entering a command to SQL*Plus itself or are entering a SQL statement or a PL/SQL block.

Entering SQL*Plus commands

Commands such as DESCRIBE, COLUMN, TTITLE, SET, and all the others listed in the "Commands" section are commands to SQL*Plus itself. These must be entered on one line and are executed immediately after you enter them. For example:

```
SET ECHO ON
DESCRIBE employee
```

SQL*Plus commands may optionally be terminated by a semicolon. For example:

```
PROMPT This semicolon won't print.;
CONNECT system/manager;
```

You can change this behavior of SQL*Plus toward semicolons by changing the SQLTERMINATOR setting.

Long SQL*Plus commands may be continued onto multiple physical lines. The SQL*Plus continuation character is a hyphen (-). Use it at the end of a physical line to continue a long SQL*Plus command to the next line. The following three lines, for example, are treated as one by SQL*Plus:

```
COLUMN employee_id -
FORMAT 099999 -
HEADING 'Emp ID'
```

The space in front of the continuation character is optional. Quoted strings may also be continued. For example:

```
SELECT 'Hello-
World!' FROM dual;
```

When you are continuing a quoted string, any spaces before the continuation character will be included in the string. The line break also counts as one space.

Entering SQL statements

SQL statements may span multiple lines and must always be terminated. This may be done using either a semicolon (;) or a forward slash (/). For example:

```
SELECT user
FROM dual;

SELECT user
FROM dual
/
```

In both of these cases, the SQL statement will be entered into a buffer known as the *SQL buffer* and then will be executed. You may also terminate a SQL statement using either a blank line or a period, in which case the statement is stored in the buffer but not executed. For example:

```
SQL> SELECT user
  2  FROM dual
  3
SQL> SELECT user
  2  FROM dual
  3  .
```

Use the SET SQLTERMINATOR command to change the terminator from a semicolon to some other character. Use SET SQLBLANKLINES ON to allow blank lines within a SQL statement. To execute the statement currently in the buffer, enter a forward slash on a line by itself.

Entering PL /SQL blocks

PL/SQL blocks may span multiple lines and may contain blank lines. They must be terminated by either a forward slash or a period (.) on a line by itself. For example:

```
BEGIN
    DBMS_OUTPUT.PUT_LINE('Hello World!');
END;
/

BEGIN
    DBMS_OUTPUT.PUT_LINE('Hello World!');
END;
.
```

When a forward slash is used, the block is sent to the server and executed immediately. When a period is used, the block is only stored in the SQL buffer. Use the SET BLOCKTERMINATOR command to change the block terminator from a period to some other character.

Strings in SQL*Plus Commands

Many SQL*Plus-specific commands take string values as parameters. Simple strings containing no spaces or punctuation characters may be entered without quotes. Here's an example:

```
COLUMN employee_id HEADING emp_id
```

Generally, it's safer to use quoted strings. Either single or double quotes may be used. For example:

```
COLUMN employee_id HEADING 'Emp #'
COLUMN employee_id HEADING "Emp #"
```

To embed quotes in a string, either double them or use a different enclosing quote. The following two commands have equivalent results:

```
COLUMN employee_id HEADING '''Emp #'''
COLUMN employee_id HEADING "'Emp #'"
```

The single exception to these rules is the PROMPT command. All quotes used in a PROMPT command will appear in the output.

Specifying Filenames

Several SQL*Plus commands allow you to specify a filename. In all cases, you may also include a path and/or an extension with the name. For example:

```
SPOOL my_report
SPOOL c:\temp\my_report
SPOOL create_synonyms.sql
```

Most file-related commands assume a default extension if you don't supply one. The default varies by command.

Naming Variables

SQL*Plus allows you to declare two types of variables: user variables and bind variables. The rules for naming each type are different:

User variable names
> These names may contain letters, digits, and underscores (_) in any order. They are case-insensitive and are limited to 30 characters in length.

Bind variable names
> These names must begin with a letter, but after that may contain letters, digits, underscores, dollar signs ($), and number signs (#). They also are case-insensitive and are limited to 30 characters in length.

Formatting Text Reports

SQL*Plus reports are columnar in nature. SQL*Plus allows you to define column headings and display formats for each column in a report, as well as page headers and footers, page and line breaks, and summary calculations.

Column Headings

Specify column headings using the HEADING clause of the COLUMN command:

```
COLUMN employee_name HEADING "Employee Name"
```

Either single or double quotes may be used to enclose the heading text.

To specify a multiline heading, use the vertical bar, or pipe, character (|) to specify the location of the line break. For example:

```
COLUMN employee_name HEADING "Employee|Name"
```

Headings of text columns are aligned to the left. Headings of numeric columns are aligned to the right. Use the JUSTIFY clause to alter that behavior:

```
COLUMN employee_name HEADING "Employee|Name" -
    JUSTIFY RIGHT
COLUMN employee_name HEADING "Employee|Name" -
    JUSTIFY CENTER
```

Use SET HEADSEP to change the line-break character to something other than a vertical bar. Use SET UNDERLINE to change the underline character to something other than a hyphen.

Column Formats

Specify display formats using the FORMAT clause of the COLUMN command. For numeric fields, format specifications can be quite detailed—controlling the length, the number of decimal places, and the punctuation used in the number. For text and date fields, you can control the column width and whether the column wraps. The "SQL*Plus Format Elements" section, later in this chapter, shows you how to format different types of data.

Page Width and Length

Page width is controlled by the SET LINESIZE command. The default width is 80 characters. You can change it—to 60 characters, for example—by using the command like this:

```
SET LINESIZE 60
```

The LINESIZE setting is used by SQL*Plus to center and right-justify page headers and page footers.

Page length is controlled by the SET PAGESIZE command. The default is to print 24 lines per page, and this includes the page header and page footer lines. The following command changes the page length to 50 lines:

```
SET PAGESIZE 50
```

When using SET MARKUP HTML ON to generate HTML output, PAGESIZE controls the number of HTML table rows that display before column headings are repeated; each row may display as one or more physical lines depending on how the browser window is sized.

Setting PAGESIZE to 0 has a special meaning to SQL*Plus. A PAGESIZE of 0 will inhibit the display of page headers, page footers, and column headings.

Page Headers and Footers

Define page headers and footers using TTITLE for the top title and BTITLE for the bottom title. The syntax is identical for both commands

Defining a title

The following example defines a multiline page header with the company name on the left and the page number on the right:

```
TTITLE LEFT "My Company" CENTER "Current" -
RIGHT "Page" FORMAT 999 SQL.PNO SKIP 1 -
CENTER "Employee Listing" SKIP 4
```

The resulting title will look like this:

```
My Company          Current          Page    1
                Employee Listing
```

The final SKIP clause provides three blank lines between the page title and the column headers.

Getting the date into a title

To get the current date into a page title, you must get the date into a user variable and then place the user variable into your BTITLE or TTITLE command.

You can use the following commands in a SQL*Plus script to get the current date into a user variable:

```
SET TERMOUT OFF
COLUMN curdate NEW_VALUE report_date
```

```
SELECT TO_CHAR(SYSDATE,'dd-Mon-yyyy') curdate
   FROM DUAL;
SET TERMOUT ON
```

After executing the commands shown here, the date will be in a user variable named REPORT_DATE. The following command places that value into a page footer:

```
BTITLE LEFT "Report Date: " report_date
```

This same technique can also be used to retrieve other values from the database and place them in either a page header or page footer.

Page Breaks

By default, SQL*Plus will print one blank line between each page of output. That blank line, added to the PAGESIZE setting, must equal the physical size of the pages in your printer.

The SET PAGESIZE command may be used to control the number of lines SQL*Plus prints on a page. SET NEWPAGE controls the action of SQL*Plus when a page break occurs. You can change the number of blank lines between pages by using a command such as this:

```
SET NEWPAGE 10
```

You can tell SQL*Plus to display one form-feed character between pages by specifying SET NEWPAGE 0.

Newer releases of SQL*Plus also allow SET NEWPAGE NONE, which eliminates both blank lines and form-feed characters from between pages.

Report Breaks

The BREAK and COMPUTE commands may be used to define breaks and summary calculations for a report. BREAK also allows you to inhibit the display of repetitive column values.

BREAK command

To eliminate repetitive column values, use the BREAK command as shown in this example:

```
SQL> BREAK ON owner

SQL> SELECT owner, table_name
  2  FROM all_tables
  3  ORDER BY owner, table_name;

OWNER       TABLE_NAME
==========  ================
CTXSYS      DR$CLASS
            DR$DELETE
            DR$INDEX
DEMO        CUSTOMER
            DEPARTMENT
            EMPLOYEE
```

When you list a column in the BREAK command, SQL*Plus prints the value of the column only when it changes. For this to work properly, remember to sort the query results on the same column.

You can also use the BREAK command to skip lines or skip to a new page whenever a value changes. For example:

```
BREAK ON owner SKIP 1
BREAK ON owner SKIP PAGE
```

The first command results in printing a blank line whenever the owner changes. The second results in a page break each time the owner changes.

Multiple breaks may be specified for a report, but with the same command. The following example causes a page break to occur whenever an owner changes and a blank line to be printed whenever the object type changes:

```
BREAK ON owner SKIP PAGE ON object_type SKIP 1
SELECT owner, object_type, object_name
    FROM dba_objects
ORDER BY owner, object_type, object_name;
```

Before performing the break actions for a column, SQL*Plus will first perform the break actions for all inner columns. In this case, a change in the owner field would result in one skipped line and *then* a page break.

COMPUTE command

The COMPUTE command tells SQL*Plus to compute summary values for a group of records. COMPUTE is always used in tandem with BREAK. For example, to compute the number of tables owned by each user, you could do the following:

```
BREAK ON owner
COMPUTE COUNT OF table_name ON owner
SELECT owner, table_name
    FROM dba_tables
ORDER BY owner, table_name;
```

SQL*Plus counts the number of table names for each distinct owner value and displays the results whenever a break occurs in the owner field.

You can compute summaries on multiple columns at once by using multiple COMPUTE commands.

Notice that the display order—the order used in the SELECT list—does not need to match the sort order or the break order.

SQL*Plus Format Elements

The COLUMN, ACCEPT, SET NUMBER, TTITLE, BTITLE, REPHEADER, and REPFOOTER commands allow you to control data formats using what is called a *format specification*. A *format specification* is a string of characters that tells SQL*Plus exactly how to format a number, date, or text string when it is displayed.

Formatting Numbers

For a complete list of the format elements you can use when formatting numeric output, see Table C-1. That appendix also contains a variety of examples illustrating the use of the numeric format elements.

Formatting Character Strings

Character strings are formatted using only one element, A, followed by a number specifying the column width in terms of characters. For example:

```
SQL> COLUMN a FORMAT A40

SQL> SELECT 'An apple a day keeps the doctor away.' A
  2    FROM dual;

A
----------------------------------------
An apple a day keeps the doctor away.
```

By default, longer text values are wrapped within the column. You can use the WORD_WRAPPED, WRAPPED, and TRUNCATED parameters of the COLUMN command to control whether and how wrapping occurs. For example:

```
SQL> COLUMN a FORMAT A18 WORD_WRAPPED

SQL> SELECT 'An apple a day keeps the doctor away.' A
  2    FROM dual;

A
------------------
An apple a day
keeps the doctor
away.
```

When text columns wrap to multiple lines, SQL*Plus prints a blank line called a *record separator* following the record. Use SET RECSEP OFF to prevent that behavior.

When used with the ACCEPT command, a character format defines the maximum number of characters SQL*Plus will accept from the user.

Formatting Dates

For a complete list of the format elements you can use when formatting dates in output, see Table B-1. That appendix also contains a variety of examples illustrating the use of the date format elements, as well as a summary of time zone identifiers.

Use the date format elements listed in Appendix B in conjunction with Oracle's built-in TO_CHAR function to convert date values to character strings. For example:

```
SQL> SELECT TO_CHAR(SYSDATE, 'dd-Mon-yyyy hh:mi:ss PM')
  3      FROM dual;

TO_CHAR(SYSDATE,'DD-MON
-----------------------
13-Dec-1999 09:13:59 PM
```

When used with the ACCEPT command, a date format string requires the user to enter a date in the format specified.

Commands

This section contains an alphabetic listing of all of the SQL*Plus commands, with brief descriptions. The values for parameters shown in bold are the defaults.

SQL*Plus

/*...*/

`/* comment_text comment_text comment_text */`

The /* and */ delimiters set off a comment in SQL*Plus. Comments entered this way may span multiple lines. If you use /*...*/ in a script file, the comments will be displayed on the screen when the script is executed.

--
(Double Hyphen)

`--comment_text`

Specifying a double hyphen (--) allows you to place a single-line comment in a SQL*Plus script.

@
(At Sign)

`@script_file [argument...]`

Used to execute a SQL*Plus script file

Parameters

script_file

Name, or URL in Oracle9i and higher, of the file to execute. You may include a path as part of the name. If you do not specify a path, SQL*Plus will look in the current directory and then follow the SQL*Plus search path. The default extension is *.sql*.

In Oracle9i Release 1, only the Windows version of SQL*Plus allows you to identify a script file by its URL. In Release 2, all versions of SQL*Plus support this functionality. URLs may be HTTP or FTP. In iSQL*Plus, you must specify a URL in this command; you cannot specify a filename.

argument

Argument you wish to pass to the script. You may pass as many arguments as the script requires. Arguments must be separated from each other by at least one space.

| @@ | @@*script_file* [*argument*...] |
| **(Double At Sign)** | Used within a script file to execute another script file from the same directory as the first. See @ for parameter descriptions. |

| / | Executes the SQL statement or PL/SQL block that is currently in |
| **(Forward Slash)** | the buffer. |

ACCEPT	ACC[EPT] user_variable [NUM[BER] | **CHAR** | DATE]
	[FOR[MAT] format_specification]
	[DEF[AULT] default_value]
	[PROMPT prompt_text | **NOPR[OMPT]**] [HIDE]

Gets input from a user. ACCEPT is not supported in *i*SQL*Plus. The syntax for the ACCEPT command has evolved significantly with the past few releases of SQL*Plus. The syntax shown here is valid for Oracle8*i* and higher. Not all of the clauses are available when using prior versions.

Parameters

user_variable
> Name of the variable that you want to define.

NUM[BER] | **CHAR** | *DATE*
> Specifies the type of data you are after.

FOR[MAT] *format_specification*
> Specifies a format specification, which may be optionally enclosed in quotes.

DEF[AULT] *default_value*
> Provides a default value to assign to the variable.

PROMPT *prompt_text*
> Specifies the prompt text displayed to the user.

NOPR[OMPT]
> Indicates that you do not want the user to see a visible prompt.

HIDE
> Causes SQL*Plus not to echo the user's response back to the display. This is useful if you are prompting for a password.

| APPEND | A[PPEND] *text* |

Lets you add text onto the end of the current line in the SQL buffer. APPEND is an editing command and is not supported in *i*SQL*Plus. Note that you must use two spaces after the APPEND command if you want your appended string to begin with one space.

ARCHIVE LOG   ARCHIVE LOG {LIST | STOP | START [TO *destination*] |
NEXT [TO *destination*] | ALL [TO *destination*] |
log_sequence_number [TO *destination*]}

Controls—or displays information about—archive logging. You must be connected as SYSDBA, SYSOPER, or INTERNAL in order to use this command.

Parameters

LIST
> Causes SQL*Plus to display information about the current state of archiving.

STOP
> Stops log files from being automatically archived.

START
> Turns on automatic archiving of redo log files.

NEXT
> Manually archives the next log file group in the sequence, provided that it is filled. Use ARCHIVE LOG LIST to see the sequence number of this file.

ALL
> Manually archives all log file groups that have been filled but not previously archived.

log_sequence_number
> Manually archives a specific log file group, provided that the group is still online.

destination
> Specifies a destination for archived log files. If used with ARCHIVE LOG START, this becomes the destination for all log files as they are archived. If used with NEXT, ALL, or a specific sequence number, this becomes the destination for files archived by that one command. If you do not specify a destination when using ARCHIVE LOG START, the value from the LOG_ARCHIVE_DEST initialization parameter is used.

ATTRIBUTE   ATTRIBUTE [*object_type.attribute* | *attribute_alias* [ALI[AS]
alias |
CLE[AR]| FOR[MAT] *format_spec* |
LIKE *source_attribute* |
ON | OFF...]]

Formats attributes of an Oracle object type. Issuing the ATTRIBUTE command with no parameters gets you a list of all current attribute settings. Note that the ALIAS, CLEAR, FORMAT, LIKE, ON, and OFF clauses function just as they do in the COLUMN command.

Parameters

object_type
> Name of an Oracle object type.

attribute
> Name of an attribute of the specified object type and the attribute you are formatting. If you stop here and don't supply any other parameters, the current display settings for this attribute are shown.

BREAK

```
BRE[AK] [ON (column_name | ROW | REPORT)
    [SKI[P] (lines_to_skip | PAGE) |
    NODUP[LICATES] | DUP[LICATES]...]...]
```

Defines page breaks and line breaks based on changing column values in a report. It controls whether duplicate values print in a column, and it controls the printing of computed values such as totals and subtotals. Issuing the BREAK command with no parameters causes SQL*Plus to display the current break setting.

Parameters

column_name
> Specifies a report column to watch. When the value in the column changes, SQL*Plus executes the specified break actions.

ROW
> Causes SQL*Plus to break on each row.

REPORT
> Specifies a report-level break and is used to cause SQL*Plus to print grand totals at the end of the report. SKIP PAGE will be ignored if it is specified as a report break action, but, strangely enough, you can skip lines on a report break.

SKI[P] lines_to_skip
> Tells SQL*Plus to skip the specified number of lines when a break occurs.

SKI[P] PAGE
> Tells SQL*Plus to advance to a new page when a break occurs.

NODUP[LICATES]
> Tells SQL*Plus to print a column's value only when it changes. By default, whenever you put a break on a column, you get this behavior.

DUP[LICATES]
> Forces SQL*Plus to print a column's value in every line on the report, regardless of whether the value is the same as that printed for the previous record.

BTITLE

```
BTI[TLE] [[OFF | ON] |
    COL x | S[KIP] x | TAB x | LE[FT] | CE[NTER] | R[IGHT] |
    BOLD | FOR[MAT] format_spec | text | variable...]
```

Functions the same as TTITLE, except that BTITLE defines a page footer instead of a page header. See TTITLE for parameter descriptions.

CHANGE

```
C[HANGE] /old_text[/[new_text[/]]]
```

Allows you to do a search and replace on the current line in the SQL buffer. CHANGE is an editing command. You can use CHANGE to delete text as well as to change it. CHANGE is not supported in iSQL*Plus.

Parameters

old_text
> Text you want to change or delete.

new_text
> Replacement text.

/
> Commonly used to delimit the old and new text strings, but any other character may be used as long as it is not a number or letter—and as long as it is used consistently throughout the command.

CLEAR

```
CL[EAR] (BRE[AKS] | BUFF[ER] | COL[UMNS] | COMP[UTES] |
    SCR[EEN] | SQL | TIMI[NG])
```

Allows you to easily delete all column definitions, break settings, compute definitions, and so forth.

Parameters

BRE[AKS]
> Deletes any break setting you may have defined using the BREAK command.

BUFF[ER]
> Erases the contents of the buffer.

COL[UMNS]
> Deletes any column definitions you may have made using the COLUMN command.

COMP[UTES]
> Deletes any computations you may have defined using the COMPUTE command.

SCR[EEN]
> Clears the screen. Not supported in iSQL*Plus.

SQL

Erases the contents of the SQL buffer.

TIMI[NG]

Deletes any timers you may have created using the TIMING command.

COLUMN

```
COL[UMN] [column_name [ALI[AS] alias |
    CLE[AR] | ENTMAP (ON|OFF) |
    FOLD_A[FTER] | FOLD_B[EFORE] |
    FOR[MAT] format_spec | HEA[DING] heading_text |
    JUS[TIFY] (LEFT | CENTER | CENTRE | RIGHT) |
    LIKE source_column_name | NEWL[INE] |
    NEW_V[ALUE] user_variable | NOPRI[NT] |
    PRI[NT] | NUL[L] null_text |
    OLD_V[ALUE] user_variable | ON | OFF |
    TRU[NCATED] | WOR[D_WRAPPED] | WRA[PPED]...]]
```

Formats report output for columnar reports. Issuing the COLUMN command with no parameters gets you a list of all current column formats.

COLUMN commands are cumulative. Two COLUMN commands specifying two different settings for the same field are equivalent to one command specifying both parameters.

Parameters

column_name

Name of the column you are formatting. If it is a computed column, the expression is the name. If your SELECT statement aliases the column, you must use that alias name here. Issuing the command COLUMN *column_name* with no further parameters causes SQL*Plus to display the current format for that column.

ALI[AS]

Allows you to specify an alternate name for the column that is meaningful.

alias

Alternate name for the column that may be used in BREAK commands, COMPUTE commands, and other COLUMN commands.

CLE[AR]

Erases any format settings for the column in question.

ENTMAP (ON | OFF)

Controls whether characters such as < and > should be represented as < and > in HTML reports. The default is to use the ENTMAP setting specified with the SET MARKUP command or –M command-line option.

FOLD_A[FTER]

Causes SQL*Plus to advance to a new line after printing this column.

FOLD_B[EFORE]
> Causes SQL*Plus to advance to a new line before this column is printed.

FOR[MAT]
> Allows you to control how the data for the column is displayed.

format_spec
> String that specifies the display format for the column.

HEA[DING]
> Allows you to define a heading for the column.

heading_text
> Text you want for the column heading. This may optionally be enclosed in either single or double quotes.

JUS[TIFY] (LEFT | CENTER | CENTRE | RIGHT)
> Controls where the heading text prints relative to the column width. By default, headings for numeric fields print flush right, and headings for text fields print flush left. This parameter allows you to change that behavior.

LIKE
> Causes the column to be defined with the same format attributes as another column.

source_column_name
> Name of the source column used with the LIKE parameter.

NEWL[INE]
> Causes SQL*Plus to wrap to a new line before the column is printed.

NEW_V[ALUE]
> Causes SQL*Plus to keep a user variable updated with the current value of the column.

user_variable
> Name of a user variable for use with the NEW_VALUE and OLD_VALUE parameters.

NOPRI[NT]
> Tells SQL*Plus not to print the column.

PRI[NT]
> Enables the printing of a column.

NUL[L]
> Allows you to specify text to be displayed when the column value is null.

null_text
> Text you want displayed when the column in question is null.

OLD_V[ALUE]
> Causes SQL*Plus to keep a user variable updated with the previous value of the column.

ON
> Causes SQL*Plus to print the column using the format you have specified. This is the default behavior.

OFF
Disables the format settings for the column.

TRU[NCATED]
Causes the column text to be truncated to the width of the column. Longer values are not wrapped.

WOR[D_WRAPPED]
Causes SQL*Plus to word-wrap long column values.

WRA[PPED]
Causes SQL*Plus to wrap long column values. Line breaks occur exactly at the column boundary, even in the middle of a word.

COMPUTE

COMP[UTE] [(AVG | COU[NT] | MAX[IMUM] | MIN[IMUM] | NUM[BER] | STD | SUM | VAR[IANCE])... [LABEL *label_text*] OF *column_name*...
    ON (*group_column_name* | ROW | REPORT)...]

Defines summary calculations needed in a report. You can use COMPUTE in conjunction with BREAK to calculate and print column totals, averages, minimum and maximum values, and so forth. These calculations are performed by SQL*Plus as the report runs.

Issuing COMPUTE with no parameters causes SQL*Plus to list all currently defined computations.

Parameters

AVG
Computes the average of all non-NULL values for a numeric column.

COU[NT]
Computes the total number of non-NULL values for a column.

MAX[IMUM]
Computes the maximum value returned for a column. Applies to columns of type NUMBER, CHAR, VARCHAR2, NCHAR, and NVARCHAR2.

MIN[IMUM]
Computes the minimum value returned for a column. Applies to columns of type NUMBER, CHAR, VARCHAR2, NCHAR, and NVARCHAR2.

NUM[BER]
Performs a function similar to COUNT but computes the number of all values, including nulls.

STD
Computes the standard deviation of all non-NULL values for a numeric column.

SUM
> Computes the sum of all non-NULL values for a numeric column.

VAR[IANCE]
> Computes the variance of all non-NULL values for a numeric column.

LABEL
> Allows you to specify a label for the computed value. If possible, this label will be printed to the left of the computed value.

label_text
> Text you want to use as a label when the computed value is printed.

column_name
> Name of the column you are summarizing. If it's a computed column, the expression is the name. If your SELECT statement aliases the column, you must use that alias name here.

group_column_name
> Causes SQL*Plus to restart the calculation every time this column changes.

ROW
> Causes the computation to be performed once for each row returned by the query.

REPORT
> Causes the computation to be performed at the end of the report and to include values from all rows. REPORT is used for grand totals.

CONNECT

```
CONN[ECT] [username[/password][@connect] | / ]
          [AS (SYSOPER | SYSDBA)] | [INTERNAL]
```

Allows you to change your database connection, log in as a different user, or connect to the database in an administrative mode.

Parameters

username
> Database username.

password
> Database password.

connect
> Connect string or host string telling SQL*Plus the database to which you want to connect.

/

> Allows you to use a forward slash instead of your username, password, and connect string when you want to connect to a local database using operating system authentication.

AS

> Tells SQL*Plus you are connecting in an administrative role.

SYSOPER

> Tells SQL*Plus you are connecting as an operator.

SYSDBA

> Tells SQL*Plus you are connecting as a database administrator.

INTERNAL

> Tells SQL*Plus you want to connect internally. Beginning with Oracle9*i*, this is no longer a valid option.

COPY

```
COPY { FROM connection | TO connection}
   (APPEND | CREATE | INSERT | REPLACE)
   destination_table [(column_list)] USING select_statement
```

Allows you to use SQL*Plus as a conduit for transferring data between two Oracle databases.

The COPY command is now a deprecated feature. It will not handle new datatypes, including object types, introduced in Oracle8 and higher.

Parameters

FROM/TO

> Specifies either the target or the source database. You must be connected to one database. Use this clause to specify the other.

connection

> Login information to use when connecting to the other database. This must be in the typical *username/ password@connect_string* format.

APP[END]

> Causes SQL*Plus to insert the copied rows into the destination table. If necessary, SQL*Plus will create the destination table first.

CRE[ATE]

> Causes SQL*Plus to copy the data only if the destination table is a new table.

INSERT

> Causes SQL*Plus to insert the copied rows into the destination table only if it already exists.

REP[LACE]

> Causes SQL*Plus to delete and re-create the destination table if it currently exists.

destination_table

> Name of the table to which you want to copy the data.

column_list
> Specifies column names to use when the COPY command creates a new destination table. This is a comma-delimited list, and the number of column names must match the number of columns in the SELECT statement.

select_statement
> A SELECT statement that returns the data you want to COPY.

DEFINE

`DEF[INE] [variable_name [= text]]`

Allows you to create a user variable (or substitution variable) and to assign it a value or to list the value of one or more variables.

Parameters

variable_name
> Name of the variable you want to create. Issue the command with only a variable name, and SQL*Plus will display the current contents of that variable, if it exists.

text
> Text you want to assign to the variable.

DEL

`DEL [(b | * | LAST)[ (e | * | LAST)]]`

Used to delete one or more lines from the buffer. DEL is an editing command. Not supported in *i*SQL*Plus.

Parameters

b   Line number representing either a line to delete or the beginning of a range of lines to delete.

e   Line number representing the end of a range of lines to delete.

*   Refers to the current line.

LAST
> Refers to the last line in the buffer.

DESCRIBE

`DESC[RIBE] [schema.]object_name[@database_link_name]`

Displays information about a table, a view, an object type, a stored package, a stored procedure, a stored function, or a synonym. (See also SET DESCRIBE.)

Parameters

schema
> Name of the object's owner.

object_name
> Name of the object that you want to describe.

database_link_name
> Name of a database link pointing to the database where the object exists.

DISCONNECT	DISC[ONNECT]

Closes your database connection without terminating SQL*Plus.

EDIT	ED[IT] [*filename*]

Allows you to invoke an external editor to edit the contents of the SQL buffer (if you specify EDIT with no parameter) or to edit the contents of an operating system file (if you specify a *filename*). EDIT is not supported in *i*SQL*Plus.

You can specify the command used to invoke the external editor via the _EDITOR user variable. Use the DEFINE command to change _EDITOR's value.

EXECUTE	EXEC[UTE] *statement*

Allows you to execute a single PL/SQL statement.

EXIT	EXIT [**SUCCESS**	FAILURE	WARNING	*value*	*user_variable*	
	:*bind_variable*] [**COMMIT**	ROLLBACK]

Terminates a SQL*Plus session and returns you to the operating system.

Parameters

SUCCESS
> Returns a success status. This is the default.

FAILURE
> Returns a failure status.

WARNING
> Returns a warning status.

value
> Returns an arbitrary value as the status.

user_variable
> Returns the value of the specified user variable as the status.

:bind_variable
> Returns the value of the specified bind variable as the status.

COMMIT
> Causes SQL*Plus to commit before exiting. This is the default.

ROLLBACK
> Causes SQL*Plus to roll back any open transaction before exiting.

GET

```
GET filename [LIS[T] | NOL[IST]]
```

Reads a SQL statement from a file and loads it into the buffer. GET is not supported in *i*SQL*Plus.

Parameters

filename
> Name of the file containing the SQL statement you want to load.

LIST
> Causes SQL*Plus to display the buffer after loading the file. This is the default.

NOL[IST]
> Causes SQL*Plus to load the file without displaying it.

HELP

```
HELP [topic]
```

Gets help on SQL*Plus commands. Prior to the release of Oracle8*i*, HELP would also provide information on SQL and PL/SQL syntax. Note that some Windows versions of SQL*Plus, notably prior to Oracle9*i*, do not support online help.

Parameters

topic
> Help topic you want to read about. Entering HELP INDEX (HELP MENU in some older releases) will get you a complete list of valid topics.

HOST

```
HO[ST] [os_command]
```

Allows you to execute an operating system command or invoke the command interpreter so that you can execute several such commands. Issuing HOST without specifying a command will get you a command prompt from which you may enter several commands. To return to SQL*Plus, you typically issue the operating system *exit* command. HOST is not supported in *i*SQL*Plus.

INPUT

```
I[NPUT] [text]
```

Inserts one or more lines of text into the buffer. The lines are inserted after the current line. When you issue the INPUT command with no text after it, SQL*Plus puts you in insert mode, allowing you to type as many lines as you like. INPUT is not supported in *i*SQL*Plus.

LIST

L[IST] [(b | * | LAST)[(e | * | LAST)]]

Used to list the current line from the buffer. LIST is an editing command. Issuing LIST by itself will cause SQL*Plus to display all lines in the buffer.

Parameters

b Line number representing the beginning of a range of lines to list. If no ending line number is specified, only this one line will be listed.

e Line number representing the end of a range of lines to list.

* Refers to the current line number.

LAST
 Refers to the last line in the buffer.

PASSWORD

PASSW[ORD] [username]

Allows you to change your Oracle password using SQL*Plus. PASS-WORD is not supported in iSQL*Plus. After entering this command, you are prompted for your old password and then you must enter your new password twice.

Parameter

username
 User whose password you want to change. The default is to change your own password. You need the ALTER USER privilege to change another user's password.

PAUSE

PAU[SE] [pause_message]

Tells SQL*Plus to display the specified message and then pause. The user must then press the Enter key in order to continue. PAUSE is not supported in iSQL*Plus.

PRINT

PRI[NT] [bind_variable_name]

Displays the value of a bind variable.

Parameters

bind_variable_name
 Name of the bind variable you want to print. If you omit a name, the values of all bind variables are printed.

PROMPT

PRO[MPT] *text_to_be_displayed*

Displays a message for the user to see.

Parameters

text_to_be_displayed

    Text you want displayed to the user. The prompt string should not be quoted. If you include quotes, they will appear in the output.

QUIT

QUIT FAILURE ROLLBACK QUIT [**SUCCESS** | FAILURE | WARNING | *value* | *user_variable* | :*bind_variable*] | [**COMMIT** | ROLLBACK]

Same as the EXIT command. See EXIT for parameter descriptions.

RECOVER

Initiates media recovery on a database, tablespace, or datafile. You must be connected as SYSDBA, SYSOPER, or INTERNAL (INTERNAL is not supported beginning with Oracle9*i*) in order to use RECOVER. RECOVER is not supported in *i*SQL*Plus. The functionality that RECOVER implements can also be accomplished with Recovery Manager (see Chapter 15).

Do not use the RECOVER command unless you fully understand database recovery procedures.

RECOVER's syntax changes frequently. The following syntax is valid for Oracle9*i* Release 2:

```
RECOVER {general | managed | END BACKUP}

general ::=
    [AUTOMATIC] [FROM directory]
    { {full_database_recovery
     |partial_database_recovery
     |LOGFILE filename}
     [recovery_option [recovery_option...]]]
    |CONTINUE [DEFAULT] | CANCEL}

full_database_recovery ::=
    [STANDBY] DATABASE
    [UNTIL {CANCEL | TIME datetime | CHANGE scn}]
    [USING BACKUP CONTROLFILE]
or
    [STANDBY] DATABASE
    [USING BACKUP CONTROLFILE]
    [UNTIL {CANCEL | TIME datetime | CHANGE scn}]
```

```
partial_database_recovery ::=
    {TABLESPACE tablespace [, tablespace]...
    | DATAFILE datafilename [, datafilename]...
    | STANDBY {TABLESPACE tablespace [, tablespace]...
            | DATAFILE datafilename [, datafilename]...}
    UNTIL [CONSISTENT] [WITH] CONTROLFILE }

recovery_option ::=
    {TEST | ALLOW blocks CORRUPTION
    | PARALLEL [degree] | NOPARALLEL}

managed ::=
    MANAGED STANDBY DATABASE
    [ {NODELAY | [TIMEOUT] minutes
    | CANCEL [IMMEDIATE] [NOWAIT]}
    | [DISCONNECT [FROM SESSION] ] [FINISH [NOWAIT] ] ]
```

Parameters

AUTOMATIC

Causes Oracle to automatically determine the names of the redo log files to apply during recovery.

FROM directory

Specifies the directory in which archived redo log files can be found.

LOGFILE filename

Begins recovery using the specified archived redo log file.

TEST

Performs a trial recovery in which redo is read and applied in memory, but in which the database files themselves are left untouched.

ALLOW blocks CORRUPTION

Specifies the number of corrupt blocks to tolerate in the logfiles being applied during recovery. You can exceed only one block when also using the TEST option.

PARALLEL [degree]

Specifies that recovery be done in parallel and optionally the degree of parallelism to use. The default degree of parallelism is the number of CPUs available on all instances multiplied by the value of the PARALLEL_THREADS_PER_CPU initialization parameter.

NOPARALLEL

Specifies that the recovery be done serially.

CONTINUE [DEFAULT]

Continue an interrupted multi-instance recovery. Use CONTINUE DEFAULT to have Oracle determine the next logfile to apply.

CANCEL

Terminate cancel-based recovery.

STANDBY DATABASE

> Recovers the standby database using control and archived redo log files from the primary database.

DATABASE

> Initiates media recovery on the entire database. The database must be mounted but not open.

TABLESPACE tablespace

> Initiates media recovery on the specified tablespace or list of tablespaces (up to a maximum of 16). The tablespace(s) must be offline, and the database must be mounted and open.

DATAFILE datafile_name

> Initiates media recovery on the specified datafile or list of datafiles. The datafiles to be recovered must be offline. As long as none of the datafiles are part of the SYSTEM tablespace, the database may remain open.

STANDBY TABLESPACE tablespace

> Recovers specified tablespace(s) in the standby database.

STANDBY DATAFILE datafilename

> Recovers specified datafile(s) in the standby database.

UNTIL CANCEL

> Allows you to recover one log file at a time, with the opportunity to cancel after each log file has been processed.

UNTIL CHANGE scn

> Performs an incomplete recovery based on the System Change Number (SCN). Note that the transaction with the specified number is not recovered.

UNTIL TIME datetime

> Performs a time-based recovery. All transactions that were completed prior to the time specified are recovered.

USING BACKUP CONTROLFILE

> Causes recovery to use a backup control file.

UNTIL CONSISTENT WITH CONTROLFILE

> Recovers the standby database using the standby database's control file.

MANAGED STANDBY DATABASE

> Places the standby database into sustained recovery mode.

NODELAY

> Applies archived log files to the standby database without delay. Overrides any delay setting in LOG_ARCHIVE_DEST.

TIMEOUT minutes

> Specifies a timeout, after which standby recovery will terminate if no log file is available to be applied.

CANCEL [IMMEDIATE] [NOWAIT]

> Terminates standby recovery after applying the current archived redo log file. Use IMMEDIATE to terminate on the next log file read. NOWAIT functions like IMMEDIATE, except that the command returns control to you immediately.

SQL*Plus

DISCONNECT [FROM SESSION]
> Creates a background process to apply redo to the standby database, so that you can do other work in your session.

FINISH [NOWAIT]
> Use in the event the primary fails to finish applying all primary log files to the standby. By default the command waits for recovery to finish. Use NOWAIT to have control return to you immediately.

REMARK

REM[ARK] *comment_text*

Used to place comments in a SQL*Plus script.

REPFOOTER

```
REPF[OOTER] [OFF | ON] |
    [COL x | S[KIP] x | TAB x |
    LE[FT] | CE[NTER] | R[IGHT] | BOLD |
    FOR[MAT] format_spec | text | variable...]
```

Defines a report footer. Report footers print on the last page of a report—after the last detail line and before the bottom title. See TTITLE for parameter descriptions.

REPHEADER

```
REPH[EADER] [OFF | ON] |
    [COL x | S[KIP] x | TAB x |
    LE[FT] | CE[NTER] | R[IGHT] | BOLD |
    FOR[MAT] format_spec | text | variable...]
```

Defines a report header. Report headers print on the first page of a report—after the page title and before the first detail line. See TTITLE for parameter descriptions.

RUN

R[UN]

Displays and then executes the command currently in the SQL buffer.

SAVE

SAV[E] *filename* [CRE[ATE] | REP[LACE] | APP[END]]

Writes the contents of the SQL buffer to an operating system file. SAVE is not supported in *i*SQL*Plus.

Parameters

filename
> Name of the file to which you want to write the buffer contents. The default extension is *.sql*.

CRE[ATE]
> Causes the operation to succeed only if the file does not already exist. This is the default.

REP[LACE]
Overwrites any existing file of the same name.

APP[END]
Appends the contents of the buffer to the file.

SET Customizes the operations of SQL*Plus to your needs. The varieties of SET commands follow.

SET commands

SET APPI[NFO] (ON | OFF | app_text)
Controls automatic registration of command files using the DBMS_APPLICATION_INFO package.

SET ARRAY[SIZE] (15 | array_size)
Sets the number of rows that SQL*Plus will return at one time from the database when executing a query.

*SET AUTO[COMMIT] (ON | **OFF** | IMMEDIATE | statement_count)*
Controls whether SQL*Plus automatically commits your changes. Also specifies the number of statements to allow between commits.

*SET AUTOP[RINT] (ON | **OFF**)*
Controls whether SQL*Plus automatically prints the contents of bind variables after they have been referenced in a SQL statement or PL/SQL block.

*SET AUTORECOVERY (ON | **OFF**)*
When turned on, allows the RECOVER command to run without user intervention.

*SET AUTOT[RACE] (ON | **OFF** | TRACE[ONLY]) [EXP[LAIN]] [STAT[ISTICS]]*
Enables and disables the automatic display of the execution plan and execution statistics for a SQL statement.

*SET BLO[CKTERMINATOR] (. | term_char | **ON** | OFF)*
Sets the character used to terminate entry of a PL/SQL block. The default is a period.

*SET BUF[FER] (buffer_name | **SQL**)*
Allows you to switch between buffers. Note that only one buffer can be used for executing SQL statements.

*SET CLOSECUR[SOR] (ON | **OFF**)*
Controls whether SQL*Plus keeps the statement cursor open all the time.

*SET CMDS[EP] (ON | **OFF** | separator_char)*
Controls whether you can enter multiple SQL statements on one line and also sets the separator character. If you turn this option on, then the default separator character is a semicolon.

SET COLSEP column_separator
Controls the text used to separate columns of data. The default is to separate columns using one space.

*SET COM[PATIBILITY] (V7 | V8 | **NATIVE**)*
Specifies the Oracle release with which SQL*Plus should be compatible. The default behavior is to let SQL*Plus decide this automatically.

*SET CON[CAT] (**ON** | OFF | concat_char)*
Specifies the concatenation character, which marks the end of a substitution variable name in a SQL*Plus command, SQL statement, or PL/SQL block. The default character is a period.

SET COPYC[OMMIT] batch_count
Controls how often SQL*Plus commits during the execution of a COPY command. The default is 0.

*SET COPYTYPECHECK (**ON** | OFF)*
Controls whether type checking is done when using the COPY command to copy data from one table to another.

*SET DEF[INE] (**ON** | OFF | prefix_char)*
Specifies the character used to define a substitution variable. The default is the ampersand character (&).

*SET DESCRIBE [DEPTH (1 | n | ALL)] [LINENUM (ON | **OFF**)] [INDENT (**ON** | OFF)]*

Specifies behavior for the DESCRIBE command. DEPTH controls the level to which to recursively describe an object (e. g., a table might contain an object column which in turn might contain a nested table, etc.). LINENUM adds line numbers to DESCRIBE's output. INDENT causes descriptions of nested objects to be indented.

*SET DOC[UMENT] (**ON** | OFF)*
Controls whether SQL*Plus displays documentation demarcated by the DOCUMENT command.

*SET ECHO (ON | **OFF**)*
Controls whether SQL*Plus displays commands from a command file as they are executed.

SET EDITF[ILE] edit_filename
Specifies the name of the work file used when you invoke an external editor using the EDIT command. The default name is *afiedt.buf*. Not supported in *i*SQL*Plus.

*SET EMB[EDDED] (ON | **OFF**)*
Enables and disables the embedded report feature. This allows you to combine two reports into one without resetting the page numbering.

*SET ESC[APE] (ON | **OFF** | escape_char)*
Specifies the escape character, which is used in front of the substitution variable prefix character (usually an ampersand), when you want that character interpreted literally—not as part of a variable name. The default character is a backslash (\ ).

*SET FEED[BACK] (ON | OFF | **6** | row_threshold)*
Controls whether and when SQL*Plus displays the number of rows affected by a SQL statement. Setting *row_threshold* to 0 has the same effect as SET FEEDBACK OFF.

*SET FLAGGER (**OFF** | ENTRY | INTERMED[IATE] | FULL)*
>Controls whether SQL*Plus checks your statements for compliance with ANSI/ISO syntax.

*SET FLU[SH] (**ON** | OFF)*
>Controls whether output may be buffered. Not supported in *i*SQL*Plus.

*SET HEA[DING] (**ON** | OFF)*
>Controls whether column headings are displayed when selecting data.

*SET HEADS[EP] (**ON** | OFF | heading _separator)*
>Controls the character used to make a line break in a column heading. The default is a vertical bar (|).

*SET INSTANCE (service_name | **LOCAL**)*
>Specifies the default net service name to use with the CONNECT command.

SET LIN[ESIZE] line_width
>Specifies the size of a line in terms of characters. The default LINESIZE is 80 characters.

SET LOBOF[FSET] offset
>Is an index into a LONG column, specifying the first character to be displayed. The default is 1.

SET LOGSOURCE logpath
>Tells SQL*Plus where to find archive log files for recovery. There is no default.

SET LONG long _length
>Specifies the maximum number of characters to display from a column of type LONG. The default is 80.

SET LONGC[HUNKSIZE] size
>Controls the number of characters retrieved from a LONG column at one time. The default is 80.

SET MARK[UP] markup_options
>Allows you to specify the markup language to use when generating output. You must specify the HTML option; other options are optional.

*HTML [ON | **OFF**]*
>Specifies whether or not to use HTML as the markup language.

HEAD "text"
>Specifies content for the <head> tag. The tag is written as <head>*text*</head>.

BODY "text"
>Specifies content for the <body> tag. The tag is written as <body *text*>.

TABLE "text"
>Specifies content for the <table> tag used to format query output. The tag is written as <table *text* >.

SQL*Plus

*ENTMAP (**ON** | OFF)*

Controls whether SQL*Plus uses HTML equivalents such as < and > for special characters such as < and >.

*SPOOL (ON | **OFF**)*

Controls whether SQL*Plus writes <head> and <body> tags to the spool file when spooling HTML output.

*PRE[FORMAT] [(ON | **OFF**)*

Controls whether spooled report output is enclosed within <pre>...</pre> tags instead of being placed into an HTML table.

SET MAXD[ATA] max_row_width

Sets the maximum row length that SQL*Plus can handle. This is an obsolete setting, and there is no default.

SET NEWP[AGE] (lines_to_print | NONE)

Controls the number of lines that SQL*Plus prints between pages. A value of 0 causes SQL*Plus to print a form-feed character between each page. The default is 0. Not supported in *i*SQL*Plus.

SET NULL null_text

Controls the text that SQL*Plus uses to represent a null value. The default is to represent nulls by a space.

SET NUMF[ORMAT] format_spec

Sets the default display format for numbers. There is no default value for this setting.

*SET NUM[WIDTH] (**10** | width)*

Sets the default display width for numbers. SET NUMFORMAT takes precedence over this value.

SET PAGES[IZE] lines_on_page

Specifies the number of printable lines on a page. The default is 24.

*SET PAU[SE] (ON | **OFF** | pause_message)*

Controls whether SQL*Plus pauses after each page of output. Not supported in *i*SQL*Plus.

*SET RECSEP (**WR[APPED]** | EA[CH] | OFF)*

Controls whether a record-separator line is printed between lines of output. The default is to print separators only when one of the column values in a record has wrapped.

SET RECSEPCHAR separator_char

Controls the character to use for the record separator. The default record separator is a line of space characters.

SET SCAN [ON | OFF]

Enables and disables user variable substitution. This is obsolete in favor of SET DEFINE.

*SET SERVEROUT[PUT] (ON | **OFF**) [SIZE buffer_size]*
*[FOR[MAT] (WRA[PPED] | **WOR[D_WRAPPED]** |*
TRU[NCATED])
> Controls whether SQL*Plus prints output from PL/SQL blocks.

*SET SHIFT[INOUT] (VIS[IBLE] | **INV[ISIBLE]**)*
> Controls the display of shift characters on IBM 3270 terminals. Not supported in *i*SQL*Plus.

*SET SHOW[MODE] (ON | **OFF** | BOTH)*
> Controls whether SQL*Plus displays the before and after values when you change a setting. Not supported in *i*SQL*Plus.

SET SPACE num_of_spaces
> Specifies the number of spaces to print between columns. The default is 1. This is obsolete in favor of SET COLSEP.

*SET SQLBLANKLINES (ON | **OFF**)*
> Controls whether you may enter blank lines as part of a SQL statement. This feature was introduced in Release 8.1.5. Not supported in *i*SQL*Plus.

*SET SQLC[ASE] (**MIXED** | UPPER | LOWER)*
> Controls automatic case conversion of SQL statements and PL/SQL blocks.

SET SQLCO[NTINUE] continuation_prompt
> Allows you to change the continuation prompt used for multiline SQL statements. The default is greater-than (>). Not supported in *i*SQL*Plus.

*SET SQLN[UMBER] (**ON** | OFF)*
> Controls whether SQL*Plus uses the line number as a prompt when you enter a multiline SQL statement. Not supported in *i*SQL*Plus.

*SET SQLPLUSCOMPAT[IBILITY] (x.y[.z] | **8.1.7**)*
> Specifies that SQL*Plus act in a manner compatible with a prior release of the software. New in Oracle9*i*, this setting currently affects only the operation of the VARIABLE command when that command is used to declare NCHAR and NVARCHAR2 variables.

SET SQLPRE[FIX] prefix_char
> Specifies the SQL*Plus prefix character, which allows you to execute a SQL*Plus command while entering a SQL statement or PL/SQL block into the buffer. The default is a pound sign (#). Not supported in *i*SQL*Plus.

SET SQLP[ROMPT] prompt_text
> Allows you to change the SQL*Plus command prompt. The default is SQL>. Not supported in *i*SQL*Plus.

*SET SQLT[ERMINATOR] (**ON** | OFF | term_char)*
> Controls whether terminating a SQL statement using the semicolon causes it to be executed. Also allows you to change the termination character to something other than a semicolon.

SET SUF[FIX] extension

Specifies the default extension used for command files. The default is *.sql*. Not supported in *i*SQL*Plus.

SET TAB (ON | OFF)

Controls whether SQL*Plus uses tab characters to format whitespace. Not supported in *i*SQL*Plus.

SET TERM[OUT] (ON | OFF)

Controls whether SQL*Plus displays output generated from a SQL*Plus script file. Not supported in *i*SQL*Plus.

SET TI[ME] (ON | OFF)

Controls whether SQL*Plus displays the current time as part of the command prompt. Not supported in *i*SQL*Plus.

SET TIMI[NG] (ON | OFF)

Controls whether SQL*Plus displays the elapsed execution time for each SQL statement or PL/SQL block.

SET TRIM[OUT] (ON | OFF)

Controls whether SQL*Plus trims trailing spaces from lines displayed on the screen. Not supported in *i*SQL*Plus.

SET TRIMS[POOL] (ON | OFF)

Controls whether SQL*Plus trims trailing spaces from lines written to a spool file. Not supported in *i*SQL*Plus.

SET TRU[NCATE] (ON | OFF)

Controls whether SQL*Plus truncates long lines.

SET UND[ERLINE] (underline_char | (ON | OFF))

Sets the character used to underline column headings. The default is a hyphen.

SET VER[IFY] (ON | OFF)

Controls whether SQL*Plus displays before and after images of lines containing substitution variables.

SET WRA[P] (ON | OFF)

Controls whether SQL*Plus wraps or truncates long lines.

SHOW

SHO[W] [*setting* | ALL | BTI[TLE] | ERR[ORS] [(FUNCTION |
PROCEDURE | PACKAGE |PACKAGE BODY | TRIGGER | TYPE |
TYPE BODY | DIMENSION | JAVA CLASS) [*owner.*]*object_name*] |
LNO | PARAMETER[S] [*parameter_name*] | PNO | REL[EASE] |
REPF[OOTER] | REPH[EADER] | SGA | SPOO[L] |
SQLCODE | TTI[TLE] | USER]

Allows you to look at the current state of your SQL*Plus environment.

Parameters

setting

Any one of the settings you can set using the SET command.

ALL

Shows everything, except for errors and the System Global Area (SGA).

BTI[TLE]
> Displays the current page footer.

ERR[ORS]
> Displays an error listing for a stored object. The command SHOW ERRORS by itself causes the error listing for the most recently created object to be displayed. You can get the error listing for a specific object by specifying the object type (function, procedure, and so forth) and the object name.

FUNCTION | PROCEDURE | PACKAGE | PACKAGE BODY | TRIGGER | TYPE | TYPE BODY | DIMENSION | JAVA CLASS
> Used with SHOW ERRORS to specify the object type of interest.

[owner.] object_name
> Used with SHOW ERRORS to name the object for which you want to display an error listing.

LNO
> Displays the current line number.

PARAMETER[S] [parameter_name]
> Displays the current value of one or more database initialization parameters.

PNO
> Displays the current page number.

REL[EASE]
> Displays the release number (the version) of the Oracle database to which you are connected.

REPF[OOTER]
> Displays the current report footer.

REPH[EADER]
> Displays the current report header.

SGA
> Displays information about the current state of the System Global Area.

SPOO[L]
> Tells you whether output is currently being spooled to a file.

SQLCODE
> Displays the SQL code returned by the most recent SQL statement.

TTI[TLE]
> Displays the current page title.

USER
> Displays the current username.

SHUTDOWN

SHUTDOWN [**NORMAL** | IMMEDIATE | TRANSACTIONAL [LOCAL] | ABORT]

Allows you to stop an Oracle instance. In order to use SHUT-
DOWN, you must be connected as SYSDBA, SYSOPER, or
INTERNAL. (INTERNAL is not supported beginning with
Oracle9i.)

Parameters

NORMAL
> Oracle waits for all users to voluntarily disconnect before shut-
> ting down the instance. This is the default.

IMMEDIATE
> Oracle summarily disconnects each user as soon as his current
> SQL statement completes. Open transactions are rolled back.

TRANSACTIONAL [LOCAL]
> Oracle waits for each user to complete her current transaction
> and then disconnects her. Use LOCAL to wait for only local
> (as opposed to distributed) transactions.

ABORT
> All background processes for the instance are immediately
> aborted. Crash recovery will occur the next time the database
> is open or, if Oracle Parallel Server or Real Application Clus-
> ters is being used, one of the surviving instances will recover
> the one that was aborted.

SPOOL

SP[OOL] *filename* | OFF | OUT

Causes output to be written to a text file. SPOOL is not supported
in *i*SQL*Plus.

Parameters

filename
> Name of the file to which you want to write the output. The
> default extension depends on the operating system and will be
> either LST or LIS. Under Windows, it is LST. A path may be
> specified as part of the filename.

OFF
> Turns spooling off.

OUT
> Turns spooling off and prints the file on the default printer.
> This option is not available in the Windows versions of
> SQL*Plus.

START

STA[RT] *script_file* [*argument*...]

Executes a SQL*Plus script. START and @ function identically. See
@ for parameter descriptions.

```
STARTUP [FORCE] [RESTRICT] [PFILE=filename] [QUIET]
    [MOUNT [dbname] | OPEN [open_options] [dbname] | NOMOUNT]
    [EXCLUSIVE | {PARALLEL | SHARED}]
```

open_options ::=
```
    READ (ONLY | WRITE [RECOVER]) | RECOVER
```

An alternate form of STARTUP used for migration:
```
STARTUP [PFILE=filename] MIGRATE [QUIET]
```

Allows you to start an Oracle instance and open a database. To use STARTUP, you must be connected as SYSDBA, SYSOPER, or INTERNAL. (INTERNAL is not supported beginning with Oracle9i.)

Parameters

FORCE
> Forces the instance to start. If the instance is currently running, then FORCE will cause the equivalent of a SHUT-DOWN ABORT to be done first; the instance will then be restarted.

RESTRICT
> Opens the database in restricted session mode. Only users with the RESTRICTED SESSION privilege will be able to connect.

PFILE =_filename
> Tells SQL*Plus to use the specified initialization parameter file (*INIT.ORA* or *SPFILE*) when starting the instance. You may specify a path with the filename.

 SQL*Plus reads the parameter file, not the Oracle instance, so the path to the parameter file must be relative to the machine running SQL*Plus.

MIGRATE
> Starts the database in OPEN MIGRATE mode with intialization parameters set to allow upgrade or downgrade scripts to be run. Use this option only with a new version of the server.

QUIET
> Starts the instance without displaying information about memory allocation within the System Global Area.

MOUNT [dbname]
> Causes the database to be mounted but not opened.

[dbname]
> Optionally specifies a database name to override the DB_NAME initialization parameter.

OPEN [open_options] [dbname]
> Causes the database to be mounted and then opened for normal operation.

NOMOUNT
Starts the instance without mounting the database.

READ (ONLY | WRITE [RECOVER])
Use READ ONLY to open the database so that it can be read from, but not written to. Use READ WRITE to explicitly specify the default behavior.

RECOVER
Tells Oracle to perform media recovery, if necessary, before opening the database.

EXCLUSIVE
Causes the database to be opened or mounted exclusively by the current instance. No other instances may share it. This is the default setting and is used if neither SHARE nor PARALLEL is specified.

PARALLEL
Causes the database to be opened or mounted so as to allow multiple instances to access it simultaneously.

SHARED
Has the same effect as PARALLEL.

STORE

```
STORE SET filename [CRE[ATE] | REP[LACE] | APP[END]]
```

Generates a file of SET commands based on the current state of those settings. STORE is not supported in *i*SQL*Plus.

Parameters

filename
Name of the file to which you want to write the SET commands.

CRE[ATE]
Causes the command to fail if the file already exists. This is the default.

REP[LACE]
Causes SQL*Plus to overwrite any existing file with the same name.

APP[END]
Appends the SET commands to an existing file.

TIMING

```
TIMI[NG] [START [timer_name] | SHOW | STOP]
```

Lets you start, stop, or display the value of a timer in order to measure elapsed time.

Parameters

START [timer_name]
Starts a new timer and optionally gives it the name you provide.

SHOW

> Shows the current value of the most recently started timer.

STOP

> Stops the most recently started timer, shows its current value, and then deletes it.

TTITLE

```
TTI[TLE] [OFF | ON] |
    [COL x | S[KIP] x | TAB x | LE[FT] | CE[NTER] | R[IGHT] |
    BOLD | FOR[MAT] format_spec | text | variable...]
```

Defines page titles for a report. Issuing the TTITLE command with no parameters causes SQL*Plus to display the current setting.

Parameters

OFF

> Turns off the page title but does not erase its definition.

ON

> Turns on the printing of page titles.

COL x

> Causes any title text following this parameter to print at the specified column position.

S[KIP] x

> Inserts the specified number of line breaks before printing any subsequent title text.

TAB x

> Skips forward the specified number of character columns. Negative values cause SQL*Plus to skip backward.

LE[FT]

> Causes subsequent title text to be printed beginning at the left-most column of the current title line.

CE[NTER]

> Causes subsequent title text to be centered within the current line.

R[IGHT]

> Causes subsequent title text to be printed flush right.

BOLD

> Makes your title bold by printing it three times. Only title text following the BOLD command is repeated on each line.

FOR[MAT]

> Allows you to control how subsequent numeric data in the title is displayed.

format_spec

> String that specifies the display format to use for subsequent numeric data in the title.

text

    Any text you want to have in the title.

variable

    Inserts the value of the specified user variable. You may also use one of the system variables maintained by SQL*Plus. These are summarized in Table 12-1.

*Table 12-1. SQL*Plus system variables*

System variable	Value
SQL.PNO	The current page number
SQL.LNO	The current line number
SQL.RELEASE	The current Oracle release
SQL.SQLCODE	The error code returned by the most recent SQL query
SQL.USER	The Oracle username of the user running the report

UNDEFINE

UNDEF[INE] *variable_name* [*variable_name*...]

Deletes a user variable definition.

Parameter

variable_name

    Name of a user variable to delete. You can delete several variables with one command by listing them, separated by spaces.

VARIABLE

VAR[IABLE] [*variable_name* [*data_type*]]

Allows you to declare bind variables. Bind variables are real variables that can be used within a PL/SQL block or SQL statement. Issuing the VARIABLE command with no parameters generates a list of all currently defined bind variables.

Parameters

variable_name

    Name you want to give the variable. If you stop here and don't supply a datatype, SQL*Plus displays the datatype for the variable that you have named.

data_type

    Datatype of the variable. The following datatypes are allowed:

NUMBER

    Results in a floating-point number and is the same as a NUMBER variable in PL/SQL or a NUMBER column in a table. Unlike PL/SQL, SQL*Plus does not let you specify a length or a precision, so a declaration like NUMBER (9,2) is not allowed.

CHAR [(length [CHAR | BYTE])]

    Results in a fixed-length character string. The *length* is optional. If it is omitted, you get a one-byte string.

NCHAR [(length)]
>Results in a fixed-length character string in the national character set. The *length* is optional. If it is omitted, you get a one-character string.

VARCHAR2 (length [CHAR | BYTE])
>Results in a variable-length character string.

NVARCHAR2 (length)
>Results in a variable-length character string using the national language character set.

CLOB
>Results in a character large object variable.

NCLOB
>Results in a character large object variable using the national language character set.

REFCURSOR
>Gives you a cursor variable you can use to return the results of a SQL query from PL/SQL to SQL*Plus.

WHENEVER

```
WHENEVER (OSERROR | SQLERROR)
  (EXIT [SUCCESS | FAILURE | value | :bind_variable ]
  [COMMIT | ROLLBACK] | CONTINUE [COMMIT | ROLLBACK | NONE])
```

Controls the behavior of SQL*Plus when an operating system error or a SQL error occurs.

Parameters

WHENEVER OSERROR
>Use this form of the command to tell SQL*Plus what to do in the event of an operating system error.

WHENEVER SQLERROR
>Use this form of the command to tell SQL*Plus what to do when an error is returned from a SQL statement or a PL/SQL block.

EXIT SUCCESS
>Exit with a success status.

EXIT FAILURE
>Exit with a failure status.

EXIT value
>Exit and return the value specified as the status. The value may be a literal or a user variable.

EXIT :bind_variable
>Exit and return the value of the specified bind variable as the status.

CONTINUE
>Do not exit if an error occurs. This is the default behavior when you first start SQL*Plus.

COMMIT

May be used in conjunction with both EXIT and CONTINUE. It causes SQL*Plus to COMMIT the current transaction when an error occurs. This is the default behavior when you use the EXIT keyword.

ROLLBACK

May be used in conjunction with EXIT and CONTINUE and causes SQL*Plus to roll back the current transaction when an error occurs.

NONE

May be used only in conjunction with CONTINUE and causes SQL*Plus to neither commit nor roll back when an error occurs. This is the default behavior when you use the CONTINUE keyword.

13

Export and Import

The Oracle database stores information within the confines of its own datafiles, in its own format. Any user can access this data through the use of SQL.

The Oracle database also includes utilities that allow you to extract the data from the database into a binary file (the Export utility) and to bring data into the Oracle database from a binary file (the Import utility). You can use these utilities to capture both the structures and the data in an Oracle database. Import and Export are helpful in moving your data to a different database, as well as in backup and recovery operations. (Note, however, that Oracle provides more comprehensive backup and recovery utilities, described in Chapter 15.)

This chapter describes the syntax and basic operations of the Export and Import utilities.

Export/Import Fundamentals

The Export and Import utilities can be used in two different modes:

Interactive
> In this mode, the utility prompts the user for the information needed for the task.

Command line
> In this mode, the information needed for the task is included either on the command line or in a specified parameter file.

The interactive mode for the Export and Import utilities is essentially a legacy interface, left over from earlier releases of the software. Using the command-line interface gives you more flexibility.

If you use the Export and Import utilities for moving data between different versions of Oracle, you will need to pay attention to which version of the utilities you use. The Import utility used must be the same as the version of the database that is receiving the data, and the Export version must be the same as the lower of the two versions being used.

To run any version of Export or Import, you must run the *catexp.sql* or *catalog.sql* script to prepare the database for these operations.

 Throughout this chapter, we'll show the Export command and Import command names as *exp* and *imp*, respectively. Those will be the correct command names on most systems. Note, however, that in older Oracle releases on Windows systems, release numbers were embedded in the executable names, so on such systems you may encounter names like *imp80*, *exp73*, and so on. If you have any doubt, refer to your platform-specific documentation for the specific name used to invoke these utilities on your platform

Interactive Operation

You can invoke the Export and Import utilities with the commands:

```
exp [userid]
imp [userid]
```

where *userid* can be a username or a username/password combination or can be omitted entirely. If a password is not supplied, the interactive dialog prompts for the password. The *userid* can be qualified with the identifier *@net_service_name* or the keywords AS SYSDBA; these options are required for certain uses of the Export utility, such as tablespace point-in-time recovery for Oracle8.

Export prompts

The interactive prompts for the Export utility follow. In contrast to several other chapters in this book, we've shown the defaults between the prompt and the entry marker (>) as they appear during the interactive session. For clarity, the defaults are shown in bold type (e.g., SYSTEM is the default username).

Username: **SYSTEM** >
Username for this export session.

Password:
Password for the username supplied.

Enter array fetch buffer size: **4096** >
Size of the array fetch buffer, which can affect performance. For more information about this prompt, see the BUFFER keyword in the "Common Parameters" section later in this chapter.

Export file: **expdat.dmp** >
Name of the export file.

(1)E(ntire database), (2)U(sers), or (3)T(ables): **(2)U** >
Choice of the type of export. If you select U or T, Export will display additional prompts.

*Export grants (yes/no): **yes** >*
  Specifies whether to export security grants with the export.

*Export table data (yes/no): **yes** >*
  Specifies whether to include the actual table data in the export. If you do not include the table data, the export will simply export the definitions of the tables you specify.

*Compress extents (yes/no): **yes** >*
  Specifies whether to compress the extents while performing the export. For more information about this prompt, see COMPRESS in the "Export-Only Parameters" section later in this chapter.

Export may not necessarily display all of these prompts in all types of exports. For example, if you do not supply the username and password, the program will prompt you for this information. If you choose to export the entire database, you will not be prompted for the names of tables.

After you have responded to these prompts, the export job begins, and status information is shown in a series of responses. This status information includes messages about the entities being exported (such as which tables are being exported) and the size of these entities (such as the number of rows).

Import prompts

The interactive prompts for the Import utility follow, with the defaults between the prompt and the entry market (>). As with the Export prompts, we've shown the defaults between the prompt and the entry marker (>) as they appear during the interactive session. For clarity, the defaults are shown in bold type (e.g., SYSTEM is the default username).

*Username: **SYSTEM** >*
  Username for this import session.

Password:
  Password for the username supplied.

*Import file: **expdat.dmp** >*
  File to be imported.

*Enter insert buffer size (minimum is 4096): **30720**>*
  Size of the array fetch buffer, which can affect performance. For more information about this prompt, see the BUFFER keyword in the "Common Parameters" section later in this chapter.

*List contents of import file only (yes/no): **no** >*
  Can be used to determine the contents of an import file without actually importing any of the data.

*Ignore create error due to object existence (yes/no): **no** >*
  If an object being imported already exists, this setting controls how the Import utility responds. If the setting is 'no', the default, the create error is reported, and rows for the object are not imported. If the setting is 'yes', the create error is not reported, and the rows are imported. The object is never replaced if it already exists.

Import grants (yes/no): **yes** >
   Specifies whether to import the grants in the export file.

Import table data (yes/no): **yes** >
   Specifies whether to import the table data in the export file.

Import entire export file (yes/no): **no** >
   Specifies whether to import the entire export file.

Username: **SCOTT** >
   If the entire export file is not to be imported, allows you to specify which schemas are to be imported.

Enter table(T) or partition (T:P) names: Null list means all tables for user >
   Specifies a list of all tables or partitions to import. If you provide a null response, all tables or partitions are imported.

As with the Export utility, not all prompts are displayed in all situations. The specific prompts will depend upon the information already supplied.

Command-Line Operation

Invoke the Export and Import utilities from the command-line interface with this basic syntax:

```
exp | imp userid {parametername = value ... | PARFILE = filename expModes }
```

The *userid* is the username or the username/password combination, combined with the *@net_service_name* keyword to identify the instance, if necessary. If a password is not specified, the utilities will prompt for it.

This syntax can be used to specify the parameters as part of the command. Each parameter specified on the command line is separated from other parameters with a space or comma. A single *value* for a parameter can be in parentheses. Multiple *value*s for a parameter are in parentheses, separated by commas. The total length of the command cannot exceed the maximum length for a command on the platform-specific operating system.

Alternatively, you can store parameter values in a parameter file. In this case, specify the name of that file in the PARFILE *filename* clause as shown here:

```
exp greenie/****@bailey FULL=Y FILE=EXP.DMP ROWS=Y PARFILE=parms.dat
```

Even if you specify a parameter file, you can also include parameters on the command line. If a parameter file and a command-line parameter both refer to the same parameter, the last mention in the command line takes precedence. For example, if a parameter is mentioned both on the command line and in the parameter file, the value in the parameter file will take precedence if the PARFILE clause referencing this file comes after the command-line keyword. In the previous example, if the PARFILE contained the parameter listing of FULL=N, the command would not perform a full database export even though the full database export has been specified with FULL=Y on the command line.

The following sections describe the common identifiers and parameters (those that apply to both the Export and the Import utilities), followed by sections with the parameters specific to each utility.

Common Parameters

The following identifier is used for many different Export and Import commands:

filename
Name for an export file or log file. The default filename for an export file is *expdat.dmp*. The default extension is *.dmp* for an export file and *.log* for a log file.

The following parameters can also be used with both the Export and Import utilities:

BUFFER = buffersize
Specifies the size, in bytes, of the buffer used to fetch or load rows. This parameter determines the maximum number of rows in an array fetched by the Export utility as:

> rows = buffer / maximum_row_size

If you specify 0, Export fetches one row at a time, or Import loads one row at a time. Tables with LONG, LOB, BFILE, REF, ROWID, or type columns are always fetched or loaded one row at a time. BUFFER applies only to conventional path export and has no effect on a direct path export. The default is operating system dependent.

CONSTRAINTS = Y | N
Specifies whether table constraints are exported or imported. The default is Y.

FEEDBACK = n
When set greater than 0, specifies that Export or Import should display a progress meter in the form of a dot for each *n* number of rows exported. The default is 0.

FILE = filename
Specifies the name of the export file or the file created by the Export utility that is the source of the import. This parameter can take multiple filenames if the size of the file is limited by the FILESIZE parameter, as of Oracle8*i*. *filename* is a common identifier, defined earlier.

FILESIZE = n
Limits the size of an individual export file. If the export is larger than this specified size, Export will create multiple files, and multiple files can be specified in the FILES parameter to support this. The maximum number of bytes represented by *n* is limited by the operating system and version of Oracle. You must use the FILESIZE parameter when importing from an export file that was created using the FILESIZE parameter. New with Oracle8*i*.

FULL = Y | N
When set to Y, Export performs a full database export, which exports all objects from the entire database, or Import imports the entire export file. The default is FULL=N. The EXP_FULL_DATABASE role is required to export in this mode.

GRANTS = Y | N

Specifies whether the Export utility exports grants or whether the Import utility imports grants that were previously exported. The grants that are exported depend on whether you export in full database or user mode. In full database mode, all grants on a table are exported; in user mode, only those granted by the owner of the table are exported. The default is GRANTS=Y.

HELP = Y | N

Determines whether a help message with descriptions of the export and import parameters is displayed. The default is HELP=N. If you specify HELP=Y, you will not also be able to perform an export in the same command.

INDEXES = Y | N

Specifies whether Export will export all indexes or whether indexes will be created or updated after a table is imported. The default is INDEXES=Y. INDEXES=N specifies that indexes are not to be exported. The use of INDEXES=Y for import assumes that the same parameter was used in the creation of the export file. System-generated indexes such as LOB indexes, OID indexes, or unique constraint indexes are re-created by Import regardless of the setting of this parameter.

LOG =filename

Specifies the name of an operating system file to receive informational and error messages. If LOG is not specified, messages will not be sent to a file. *filename* is a common identifier, defined earlier.

PARFILE = filename

If used, specifies the name of an operating system file that contains a list of Export or Import parameters. *filename* is a common identifier, defined earlier.

POINT_IN_TIME_RECOVER = Y | N

Determines whether the Export utility will export one or more tablespaces in an Oracle database so that when running Import you can recover the tablespace to a prior point in time without affecting the rest of the database. In order to do point-in-time recovery with the Import utility, you must have specified this parameter (set to Y) in the Export process and specified this parameter (set to Y) as part of the *imp* command. The default is POINT_IN_TIME_RECOVER=N. Not supported after Oracle8.

RECORDLENGTH = length

Specifies the record length for the export file or the file to be imported. The value for *n* defaults to the standard for the host operating system. If you are transferring an export file for import on another system, you can use this parameter to match the default record length on the other system. You may also be able to improve the performance of a direct path export (DIRECT=Y) by increasing the RECORDLENGTH.

RESUMABLE = N | Y

Used to enable and disable resumable space allocation. The default is N. This feature lets Oracle9*i* pause in the middle of an operation if the operation fails because it has run out of space.

RESUMABLE_NAME = *name*

Used to identify the resumable operation for the operator. Requires RESUMABLE to be Y. New with Oracle9i.

RESUMABLE_TIMEOUT = *n*

Specifies the time, in seconds, that the operation will wait for the operator to resume it after allocating more space. The default is 7200. New with Oracle9i.

ROWS = Y | N

Specifies whether the rows of data in tables are written to the export file or imported during the import process. The default is ROWS=Y. Specify ROWS=N to export the structure of all objects without their contents or to create the structures on import without any data.

TABLES = *(tablename[,tablename...])*

For export, specifies that Export is to be run in table mode, and lists the table and partition names to export. There is no default. Tables or partitions may be specified as *schema.table:partition_name*. For the import, specifies a list of table names to import; note that for import, table names cannot be qualified by a schema name.

schema

Specifies the name of the user's schema from which to export the table or partition. If omitted, the schema specified by USERID is used, except when FULL=Y is specified.

table

Indicates the name of a table to be exported. If a table in the list is partitioned and you do not specify a partition name, all its partitions are exported.

partition_name

Indicates that the export is a partition-level export. Partition-level export lets you export one or more specified partitions within a table. If this value is omitted for a partitioned table, all partitions will be exported.

TABLESPACES = *(tablespace_name[, tablespace_name . . .])*

For export, exports all tables that exist in the listed tablespace or that have a partition in a listed tablespace. For import, specifies a list of the tablespaces to be imported. New with Oracle8i.

USERID = *username/password@net_service_name*

Specifies the *username/password@net_service_name* of the user initiating the export or the import if it is not specified on the command line. *password* and *@net_service_name* are optional; if you do not include them as part of the parameter, the utility will prompt you for them.

VOLSIZE = *n*

Specifies the maximum number of bytes in an export file on a tape. New in Oracle8i.

Export-Only Parameters

The following parameters can only be used with the Export utility:

COMPRESS = Y | N
> Specifies how Export manages the initial extent for table data. The default, COMPRESS=Y, causes export to write a CREATE object statement for use in a subsequent import that will cause the object to be created with all the exported data in a single initial extent. If you specify COMPRESS=N, Export uses the current storage parameters, including the values of the INITIAL extent size and the NEXT extent size.

CONSISTENT = Y | N
> Specifies whether Export uses the SET TRANSACTION READ ONLY statement to ensure that the data seen by Export is consistent to a single point in time and does not change during the execution of the *exp* command. You should specify CONSISTENT=Y when you anticipate that other applications will update the database after an export has started. The default is CONSISTENT=N.

DIRECT = Y | N
> Specifies direct path or conventional path export. Direct path exports extract data by reading the data directly, bypassing the SQL processing layer, which can be much faster than a conventional path export. The default is DIRECT=N. Direct path export cannot be used to export tables containing any of the following column types: REF, LOB, BFILE, or object type columns, which include VARRAYs and nested tables.

FLASHBACK_SCN = n
> Indicates the System Change Number used for flashback on the export. New with Oracle9i.

FLASHBACK_SCN = time
> Indicates the time used for flashback on the export. Oracle identifies the SCN closest to this time and uses that for the export. New with Oracle9i.

INCTYPE = INCREMENTAL | CUMULATIVE | COMPLETE
> If used, specifies that one of the following types of incremental export is to be run:
>
> *INCREMENTAL*
> > Exports all database objects that have changed since the last incremental, cumulative, or complete export, as tracked by the table SYS. INCEXP, then updates the table with a new ITIME and EXPID.
>
> *CUMULATIVE*
> > Exports all database objects that have changed since the last cumulative or complete export, as tracked by the table SYS.INCEXP, then updates the table with a new CTIME, ITIME, and EXPID.
>
> *COMPLETE*
> > Exports all objects, then updates the tables SYS.INCEXP and SYS. INCVID. (A FULL=Y export does not update these tables unless you specify the INCTYPE parameter.) This parameter is no longer supported in Oracle9i.

OBJECT_CONSISTENT = Y | N

Causes each object to be exported in its own transaction, as opposed to CONSISTENT, which uses a single transaction for the export. The default is OBJECT_CONSISTENT=N. New with Oracle9i Release 2.

QUERY = query_clause

The *query_clause* is a WHERE clause that is amended to the SELECT for each table or partition listed in the TABLE clause. The *query_clause* is a string, so it should be preceded and ended with the characters \". If you need to use single quotes to delimit character strings in the query, use \'. New with Oracle8i.

OWNER = (username[,username…])

If used, indicates that the export is a user-mode export and lists the users whose objects will be exported.

RECORD = Y | N

Determines whether Export will create a record of an incremental or cumulative export in the system tables SYS.INCEXP, SYS.INCFIL, and SYS.INCVID. The default is RECORD=Y. Not available with Oracle9i.

RECOVERY_TABLESPACES = (tablespace_name[,tablespace_name…])

Specifies the tablespaces to be exported for recovery using point-in-time recovery. There is no default. Not available starting with Oracle8.

*STATISTICS = **ESTIMATE** | COMPUTE | NONE*

Specifies the type of SQL ANALYZE statements to generate when the exported data is restored using the Import utility. The default is STATISTICS=ESTIMATE. New with Oracle8i.

TRANSPORTABLE_TABLESPACE = Y | N

Allows the export of metadata for transportable tablespaces. Used in conjunction with the TABLESPACES parameter. The default is TRANSPORTABLE_TABLESPACE=N. New with Oracle8i.

TRIGGERS = Y | N

Causes triggers to be exported. The default is TRIGGERS=Y. New with Oracle9i.

*TTS_FULL_CHECK = **FALSE** | TRUE*

When TTS_FULL_CHECK is TRUE, Export makes sure that the tablespaces specified have no dependencies outside of the export. The default is TTS_FULL_CHECK=FALSE. New with Oracle9i.

Import-Only Parameters

The following parameters can be used only with the Import utility.

*ANALYZE = **Y** | N*

Specifies whether the Import utility executes SQL ANALYZE statements found in the export file. The default is ANALYZE=Y. This feature is not supported with Oracle9i.

CHARSET = charsetname

Applies to Oracle Version 6 export files only and specifies the actual character set used at the time of export. The Import utility will verify whether the specified character set is ASCII or EBCDIC based on the character set in the export file. If that file was created with Oracle7 or Oracle8, the character set is specified within the export file, and conversion to the current database's character set is automatic.

COMMIT = Y | N

Specifies whether the import process should commit after each array insert. The default is N, which causes Import to commit after loading each table. If COMMIT=N and a table is partitioned, each partition in the export file is imported in a separate transaction. Specifying COMMIT=Y prevents rollback segments from growing too large. This setting is advisable if the table has a uniqueness constraint, because if the import is restarted, any rows that have already been imported are rejected with a nonfatal error. If a table does not have a uniqueness constraint and COMMIT=Y is specified, import could produce duplicate rows when the data is reimported.

*COMPILE = **Y** | N*

Specifies whether the import process should compile packages, procedures, and functions when they are imported. The default is COMPILE=Y. New with Oracle9*i*.

DATAFILES = (filename [filename . . .])

When transportable tablespaces are used, this parameter gives a list of the datafiles that will be transported. New with Oracle8*i*.

DESTROY = Y | N

Specifies whether existing datafiles making up the database should be reused if tablespaces are being re-created by import. The default is DESTROY=N.

 If datafiles are stored on a raw device, DESTROY=N does not prevent files from being overwritten.

FROMUSER = (username[,username...])

Specifies a list of schemas containing objects to import. The default for users without the IMP_FULL_DATABASE role is a user-mode import, in which objects for the current user are imported. If the specified user does not exist in the database, the objects will be imported into the schema of the current user unless TOUSER is also specified.

IGNORE = Y | N

Specifies how object creation errors are handled. If IGNORE=Y is specified, Import does not log creation errors when it attempts to create database objects, and the objects are imported. The default is IGNORE=N, which causes Import to log and/or display the object creation error before continuing and to not import the objects.

INCTYPE = {*SYSTEM* | *RESTORE*}

Specifies that one of the following types of incremental import is to be run. The default is INCTYPE=RESTORE. Not supported with Oracle9*i*.

SYSTEM
Imports the most recent version of system objects, including foreign function libraries and object type definitions but does not import user data or objects.

RESTORE
Imports all user database objects and data contained in the export file.

INDEXFILE = *filename*

Specifies a file to receive table, index, and cluster creation commands. Table and cluster commands are included as remarks but can be edited. *filename* is a common identifier, defined earlier. There is no default for this parameter, and it can be used only with the FULL=Y, FROMUSER, TOUSER, or TABLES parameters.

SHOW = *Y* | *N*

If SHOW=Y* is specified, the SQL statements contained in the export file are listed to the display only, and objects are not imported. SHOW=Y can be used only with the FULL=Y, FROMUSER, TOUSER, or TABLES parameters. The default is SHOW=N.

SKIP_UNUSABLE_INDEXES = *Y* | *N*

Specifies whether Import skips building indexes set to the Index Unusable state. Without this parameter, row insertions that attempt to update unusable indexes fail. The default is SKIP_UNUSABLE_INDEXES=N.

STREAMS_CONFIGURATION = *Y* | *N*

Specifies whether to import any general streams-related metadata in the dump file. The default is STREAMS_CONFIGURATION=N. New with Oracle9*i*.

STREAMS_INSTANTIATION = *Y* | *N*

Specifies whether to import any streams instantiation metadata in the dump file. The default is STREAMS_INSTANTIATION=N. New with Oracle9*i*.

TOID_NOVALIDATE

Suppresses the validation of types with existing type IDs in the import database. New with Oracle8*i*.

TOUSER = (*username*[,*username*. . .])

Specifies a list of usernames whose schemas will be the target of the import. If multiple schemas are specified, the schema names must be paired with schema names in a corresponding FROMUSER parameter, such as:

```
FROMUSER=(scott,harry) TOUSER=(dave,brian)
```

TTS_OWNERS = (*ownername*[,*ownername* . . .])

Specifies the owners of an imported transportable tablespace. New with Oracle8*i*.

---

* You can use SHOW to regenerate DDL. Do an export followed by an import with SHOW=Y, and then redirect the output to a file. Edit the file to get rid of messages that are not DDL, and you have your DDL again.

14

SQL*Loader

Chapter 13 described how you can use the Export and Import utilities to move data from an Oracle database and into an Oracle database. The file used for this transfer is a binary file. SQL*Loader, described in this chapter, is another Oracle utility that is designed to load data in standard operating system file formats into an Oracle database.

SQL*Loader offers many options for manipulating and transforming the data that it loads. For example, you can:

- Read from multiple files and load into multiple database tables; in addition to standard relational tables, these tables may be object tables, nested tables, varying arrays (VARRAYs), and large object (LOB) columns
- Handle files with fixed-length, variable-length, and stream-oriented data of many different datatypes
- Manipulate the data being loaded by dealing with null data and various delimiters and performing character set translation

Five basic files may be involved in a SQL*Loader job:

Input data file(s)
   Operating system files containing the actual data; these may be fixed-length or delimited files.

Control file
   Text file that contains all the information SQL*Loader needs to load the data from the data file.

Log file
   Logs the results of SQL*Loader operations.

Bad file
   Created if errors result from bad data in the input file(s). This file holds the records containing bad data (e.g., data with datatype mismatches, constraint

violations, etc.). If the SQL*Loader run completes successfully, no bad file is created. Each input file can have its own bad file.

Discard file

Holds any rows that are discarded during SQL*Loader operations as a result of WHEN comparisons. The discard file is optional. Each input file can have its own discard file.

For more detailed information on SQL*Loader and its capabilities, see *Oracle SQL*Loader: The Definitive Guide* by Jonathan Gennick and Sanjay Mishra (O'Reilly & Associates), as well as the Oracle documentation.

Running SQL*Loader

SQL*Loader can be invoked from the command line in two different ways. Simply typing the following:

```
sqlldr
```

causes SQL*Loader to display a list of valid command-line parameters. You can also invoke the program as follows:

```
sqlldr keyword=value [keyword=value ...]
```

For example:

```
sqlldr system/manager CONTROL=product.ctl LOG=product.log
```

You can specify values without associated keywords, if you wish, but if you do, the order of the values must match the order in which the parameters are listed in the help file (or in the Oracle documentation). You must include values for all parameters up to the last one you will specify in this manner. You may also mix techniques; you could, for example, simply provide the username value without the USERID keyword (because this is the first-position parameter) and then use keyword/value pairs for the rest.

You can also specify all of the command-line parameters as part of a parameter file; you specify the name of this file in the PARFILE parameter on the *sqlldr* command line.

Command-Line Parameters

Command-line parameters are separated by commas, spaces, or both. All *file-name* parameters can either use a specific filename or include a path.

BAD = path_filename

Specifies the name of the bad file. By default, the bad file takes the name of the control file, but with a *.bad* extension, and is written to the same directory as the control file. If you specify a different name, the default extension is still *.bad*. However, if you use the BAD parameter to specify a bad-file name, the default directory becomes your current working directory. If you are loading data from multiple files, then this bad-file name gets associated only with the first file being loaded.

BINDSIZE = bytes_in_bind_array

Specifies the maximum size, in bytes, of the bind array. This parameter overrides any bind array size computed as a result of using the ROWS parameter. The default bind array size is 65,536 bytes, or 64K.

COLUMNARRAYROWS = integer

Specifies the number of rows to allocate for direct path column arrays. New with Oracle9i.

CONTROL = control_filename

Specifies the name, which may include the path, of the control file. The default extension is *.ctl*. If a control file is not specified, you will be prompted for one.

DATA = path_filename

Specifies the name of the file containing the data to load. By default, the name of the control file is used, but with the *.dat* extension. If you specify a different name, the default extension is still *.dat*. If you are loading from multiple files, you can specify only the first filename using this parameter. Place the names of the other files in their respective INFILE clauses in the control file.

DATE_CACHE = integer

Specifies the size of the data cache, which is used in direct load jobs to reduce the overhead of date conversion. The default value is 1000. New with Oracle9i Release 2.

DIRECT = TRUE | FALSE

Determines the data path used for the load. Direct load puts data directly into the datafiles, rather than creating INSERT statements to do the job, which can improve performance by reducing overhead. See the Oracle documentation for restrictions on the type of data that can be loaded with the direct path, the use of constraints and triggers during the load, and other issues.

A value of FALSE results in a conventional path load. A value of TRUE results in a direct path load. The default is DIRECT=FALSE.

DISCARD = path_filename

Specifies the name of the discard file. By default, the discard file takes the name of the control file, but it has a *.dis* extension. If you specify a different name, the default extension is still *.dis*. If you are loading data from multiple files, then this discard file name gets associated with only the first file being loaded.

DISCARDMAX = logical_record_count

Sets an upper limit on the number of logical records that can be discarded before a load will terminate. When the number of discarded records becomes equal to the value specified for DISCARDMAX, the load will terminate. The default is to allow an unlimited number of discards.

ERRORS = insert_error_count

Specifies a limit on the number of errors to tolerate before the load is aborted. The default is to abort a load when the error count exceeds 50.

*EXTERNAL_TABLE = **NOT_USED** | GENERATE_ONLY | EXECUTE*

Specifies whether to use external tables to load data. The default, NOT_ USED, performs the load using either direct path or conventional path load mode. GENERATE_ONLY generates the SQL statements necessary for the load into the log file, where they can be edited and run. EXECUTE creates the SQL statements and executes them. New with Oracle9*i*.

FILE = database_datafile_name

Specifies the database datafile from which to allocate extents. Use this parameter when doing parallel loads, to ensure that each load session is using a different disk. If you are not doing a direct path load, this parameter will be ignored.

LOAD = logical_record_count

Specifies a limit on the number of logical records to load. The default is to load all records.

LOG = path_filename

Specifies the name of the log file to generate for a load session. By default, the log file takes on the name of the control file, but with a *.log* extension, and is written to the same directory as the control file. If you specify a different name, the default extension is still *.log*. However, if you use the LOG parameter to specify a name for the log file, the log file will no longer be written automatically to the directory that contains the control file; instead, it will be written to the path you specify. If you do not specify a path, the log file will be written to the current working directory.

MULTITHREADING = TRUE | FALSE

Specifies whether to use multithreading on a direct path load. On single-CPU systems, the default is FALSE. On systems with multiple CPUs, the default is TRUE. New with Oracle9*i*.

*PARALLEL = TRUE | **FALSE***

Indicates whether or not you are doing a direct path parallel load. If you are loading the same object from multiple direct path load sessions, then set this parameter to TRUE. The default is PARALLEL=FALSE.

PARFILE = path_file_name

Tells SQL*Loader to read command-line parameter values from a text file. This text file is referred to as a *parameter file*, and contains keyword/value pairs. Usually, the keyword/value pairs are separated by line breaks. Use of the PARFILE parameter can save a lot of typing if you need to perform the same load several times, because you won't need to retype all the command-line parameters each time. There is no default extension for parameter files.

READSIZE = bytes_in_read_buffer

Specifies the size of the buffer used by SQL*Loader when reading data from the input file. The default value is 64K. The values of the READSIZE and BINDSIZE parameters should match. If you supply values for these two parameters that do not match, SQL*Loader will increase the lower of the two parameters so that they do match.

ROWS = rows_in_bind_array

The precise meaning of this parameter depends on whether you are doing a direct path load or a conventional path load. With a conventional path load, this parameter is used to control the number of rows in the bind array. This represents the number of rows that SQL*Loader loads with each INSERT statement, and also represents the commit frequency. The default is 64 rows. The BINDSIZE must be big enough to hold the number of rows specified. If the space required to hold the number of rows is less than the BINDSIZE, the memory used by the bind array is reduced. If the space required to hold the number of rows is more than the BINDSIZE, the bind array will hold a smaller number of rows than the number you specify.

With a direct path load, ROWS specifies the number of rows to read from the input file before saving the data to the database. SQL*Loader will round up the ROWS value to coincide with an even number of database blocks. The default, when a direct path load is done, is to do one save at the completion of the load.

SILENT = [(]keyword[,keyword...][)]

Allows you to suppress various header and feedback messages that SQL*Loader normally displays during a load session. These keywords are:

ALL

Suppresses all messages, the equivalent of specifying all the rest of the keywords

DISCARDS

Suppresses the message that is written to the log file each time a record is discarded

ERRORS

Suppresses the error messages that are written to a log file each time a record generates an Oracle error

FEEDBACK

Suppresses the "commit point reached" messages that are displayed each time SQL*Loader reaches a commit or save

HEADER

Suppresses the initial messages written to the screen but does not suppress these messages in the log file

PARTITIONS

Suppresses the per-partition statistics that are written to the log file when doing a direct path load of a partitioned table

SKIP = logical_record_count

Allows you to continue an interrupted load by skipping the specified number of logical records added to the database. For a conventional path load that fails, you can find the number of logical records added by looking at the last "commit point reached" message on the display. If you are continuing a multiple-table direct path load, you may need to use the CONTINUE_LOAD clause in the control file, which allows you to specify a different number of rows to skip for each table you are loading, rather than the SKIP parameter on the command line.

SKIP_INDEX_MAINTENANCE = TRUE | FALSE
Controls whether or not index maintenance is done for a direct path load. This parameter does not apply to conventional path loads. A value of TRUE causes index maintenance to be skipped. Any index segments (partitions) that should have been updated will be marked as unusable. A value of FALSE causes indexes to be maintained as they normally would be. The default is SKIP_INDEX_MAINTENANCE = FALSE.

SKIP_UNUSABLE_INDEXES = TRUE | FALSE
Controls the manner in which a load is done when a table being loaded has indexes in an unusable state. A value of TRUE causes SQL*Loader to load data into tables even when those tables have indexes marked as unusable. The indexes will remain unusable at the end of the load. If a UNIQUE index is marked as unusable, the load will not be allowed to proceed.

A value of FALSE causes SQL*Loader not to insert records when those records need to be recorded in an index marked as unusable. For a conventional path load, this means that any records that require an unusable index to be updated will be rejected as errors. For a direct path load, this means that the load will be aborted the first time such a record is encountered. The default is SKIP_UNUSABLE_INDEXES = FALSE.

STREAMSIZE = integer
Specifies the size, in bytes, for direct path streams. This feature was new with Oracle9i.

USERID = {username[/password][@net_service_name]|/}
Specifies the username and password to use when connecting to the database. The *net_service_name* parameter optionally allows you to connect to a remote database. Use a forward-slash character (/) to connect to a local database using operating system authentication. If you omit both the username and the password, SQL*Loader will prompt you for both.

Control File

The control file tells SQL*Loader how to load the data. In constructing the control file, you place each control file parameter on its own line in the file. You can include comments in the control file by preceding the comment text with a double dash (--).

If you have to include a SQL*Loader reserved word in the control file, you must enclose it in double quotes. On Unix systems, you can include special characters by preceding them with the escape character (\).

The basic command that begins the control file is the LOAD command. The LOAD can have one or more INFILE clauses to specify input data files, as well as one or more INTO TABLE clauses to indicate the target tables.

A control file may also include the data to be loaded. If included, this data comes after the LOAD command and starts with the BEGINDATA keyword.

The following sections describe the basic control file keywords; the INFILE, INTO TABLE, and other clauses; and the concatenation rules that can be specified with the control file.

LOAD

```
[OPTIONS keyword_pair [,keyword_pair]...] [UNRECOVERABLE | RECOVERABLE]
   LOAD | CONTINUE_LOAD [DATA]
   [CHARACTERSET character_set] [BYTEORDER]
   [INFILE clause [INFILE clause...]]
   [MAXRECORDSIZE bytes]
   [READBUFFERS integer]
   [INSERT | APPEND | REPLACE | TRUNCATE]
   [concatenate_rules]
   [PRESERVE BLANKS]
   INTO TABLE clause [INTO TABLE clause...]
   [BEGINDATA]
```

Specifies what data to load, the locations of the input and the output, and how to interpret the data being loaded.

Keywords

OPTIONS

Specifies keyword_pair pairs (described in the previous section). Keywords can include:

```
SKIP
LOAD
ERRORS
ROWS
BINDSIZE
SILENT
DIRECT
PARALLEL
READSIZE
```

If a keyword/value pair is specified both on the command line and as part of the OPTIONS statement in the control file, the command-line argument overrides the value in the control file.

If you specify a command-line parameter that is not in this list, SQL*Loader will simply ignore it without generating an error.

This keyword must precede the LOAD keyword in the command file. For more details on these parameters, see the preceding section.

UNRECOVERABLE | RECOVERABLE

Specifies whether the load is recorded in the database redo log. UNRECOVERABLE improves performance but requires you to reload the data in the event that any affected database files are lost and subsequently restored and recovered. This option is applicable only to direct path loads. The default is RECOVERABLE.

LOAD [DATA] | CONTINUE_LOAD [DATA]

Basic keyword to start the LOAD command. The CONTINUE_LOAD keyword replaces LOAD when you have a failed direct path load and you want to restart from the point of failure with a different number of SKIPped rows for each table.

CHARACTERSET character_set

Specifies the character set used for the input data.

BYTEORDER

Indicates that binary integers, including those used in VARCHAR-type fields to specify field length, were generated on a machine with a byte order opposite to the one on which SQL*Loader is currently running. This keyword is available only in the Oracle9*i* release of SQL*Loader.

INFILE clause

A clause identifying a file containing data that you want to load. You can have one or more INFILE clauses in a LOAD command. See the following section for a description of the syntax of this clause.

MAXRECORDSIZE bytes

Specifies the maximum logical record size in bytes.

READBUFFERS integer

Specifies the number of buffers to use during a direct path load. The default value is 4. You should increase the number of buffers only in response to an ORA-02374 error. Obsolete in Oracle9*i*.

INSERT | APPEND | REPLACE | TRUNCATE

Specifies at a global level what is to be done to any existing data in the tables that you are loading. You can specify these options at the table level (using the INFILE clause) rather than globally. The default is INSERT.

INSERT

Requires that all tables being loaded be empty to begin with. If any table is not empty, SQL*Loader will abort the load with an error.

APPEND

Preserves any existing data in the tables being loaded.

REPLACE

Uses a SQL DELETE statement to delete all existing data from the tables being loaded.

TRUNCATE

Uses a SQL TRUNCATE statement to delete all existing data from the tables being loaded.

PRESERVE BLANKS

Specifies whether to preserve leading and trailing blanks in the input record fields. The manner in which SQL*Loader handles whitespace depends on whether you are loading fixed-width or delimited data.

INTO TABLE clause

Identifies a table that you are loading. You may specify multiple occurrences of the INTO TABLE clause if you need to distribute the data that you are loading over multiple tables.

BEGINDATA

Marks the end of a LOAD command when you are including data in the control file. The data then begins with the line immediately following the BEGINDATA keyword.

INFILE CLAUSE

```
INFILE | INDDN filename|* [os_specific_options]
   [BADFILE | BADDN bad_filename]
   [DISCARDFILE | DISCARDDN discard_filename]
   [DISCARDS | DISCARDMAX discardmax]
   [FIELDS TERMINATED BY character]
```

Specifies the file containing the data to be loaded.

The BADDN, INDDN, and DISCARDDN keywords are provided for compatibility with DB2 syntax. Each INFILE can have its own bad file and discard file, as well as its own limit on the number of discards. If you omit the BADFILE or DISCARDFILE parameter and the job requires one, SQL*Loader will create a file with the name of the INFILE and either the *.bad* or *.dis* extension.

Keywords

filename
> Name of the file containing the data to be loaded.

*
> Indicates that the data is included in the control file.

BADFILE
> Specifies the location of the bad file, which is created if errors result from bad data in the object file(s).

DISCARDFILE
> Specifies the location of the discard file, which holds any rows discarded during operation.

DISCARDS, DISCARDMAX
> Specifies the maximum number of records to discard before terminating the load.

FIELDS TERMINATED BY
> Include before any of the fields in a FIELDS clause to specify a standard terminator for all fields. The global termination can be overridden in the individual field definitions or in an operating system–specific "str" clause for the INFILE. For more details on termination, see the description of the Datatype clause.

os_specific_options
> See the Oracle documentation for your specific platform.

INTO TABLE Clause

```
INTO TABLE table_name
   [PARTITION | SUBPARTITION (partition_name)]
   [{INSERT | REPLACE | TRUNCATE | APPEND}]
   [SORTED [INDEXES] (index_list)] [SINGLEROW]
   [{INSERT | REPLACE | TRUNCATE | APPEND}]
   [OPTIONS (FILE=database_filename)]
   [REENABLE [DISABLED_CONSTRAINTS][EXCEPTIONS exception_table_name]]
   [WHEN field_conditions]
   [OID(fieldname) | SID(fieldname)]
   [FIELDS [delimiter_description]]
   [TRAILING [NULLCOLS]]
   [SKIP skip_count]
   (field_list)
```

Specifies the table being loaded. You can use one or more INTO TABLE clauses to load data into one or more tables. All *_filename variables may have either the file-name or the file and pathname.

Keywords

table_name
> Name of the table that you are loading. You may optionally specify an owner name using the *owner.table_name* format.

partition_name
> Specifies the name of a partition, or subpartition, of the table being loaded. Use the PARTITION clause if you are loading a partitioned table and if all the data goes into the same partition.

INSERT | REPLACE | TRUNCATE | APPEND
> Specifies the load method on a table-specific basis. This overrides the load method specified for the load as a whole (in the LOAD statement). There are two possible locations in the INTO TABLE clause where these keywords may appear: after the PARTITION specification or after the SORTED specification.

SORTED [INDEXES] (index_list)
> Specifies the name of one or more indexes that match the way in which the input data is sorted on a direct path load. If you specify more than one index name, use a comma-separated list.

SINGLEROW
> Used only with direct path loads with APPEND. This keyword specifies that each index entry should be inserted directly into the index, one row at a time. Normally, when loading with APPEND, index entries are accumulated in a temporary storage area and merged into the existing index at the end of the load.

database_filename
> Name of a datafile in the tablespace of the table or partition being loaded. This applies only to parallel, direct path loads. When such a load is performed, SQL*Loader uses the specified datafile for any temporary segments that it creates during the load. This allows you to have multiple parallel loads against the same table (or partition), but using separate datafiles.

REENABLE [DISABLED_CONSTRAINTS]
> Causes SQL*Loader to reenable any disabled constraints at the end of a direct path load.

exception_table_name
> Name of a table to hold rows that violate constraints that have been reenabled as a result of your use of the REENABLE clause. This table name is used in the SQL statement that SQL*Loader executes in order to enable constraints.

field_conditions
> Conditions that an input data record must meet in order to be loaded. Field conditions are specified in a manner similar to the WHERE clause of a SQL SELECT statement. See the Field Clause for more information.

OID(fieldname) | SID(fieldname)
> Field in the input file that contains a 32-digit Oracle system-generated object identifier in hexadecimal format or the set identifier for a nested table. This clause is used only when loading object tables. Prior to Oracle9i, this clause could be used only in conventional path loads. Beginning with Oracle9i, this clause can also be used in direct path loads.

delimiter_description

Delimiters and enclosing characters used for delimited data. This clause functions at the table level and should be used only when the same delimiters and enclosing characters apply to all fields in the input file. See Field Clause for more information.

TRAILING [NULLCOLS]

Applies when delimited data is being loaded and tells SQL*Loader to treat missing fields at the end of a record as nulls.

skip_count

Number of logical records to skip before beginning the load. The SKIP clause is used to continue a load that has previously failed.

field_list

List of fields in the input data record that includes datatypes and lengths. See the "Field clause" entry for more information.

Field Clause

```
column_name {[[BOUND] FILLER] | [generated]}
    [POSITION({start|*[+offset]}[{:|-}end])]
    [datatype clause] [PIECED]
    WHEN [(]condition[)] [AND [(]condition[)]]...]
    [NULLIF condition [AND condition...]]
    [DEFAULTIF condition [AND condition...]]
    ["sql_expression"]
```

Describes the fields that SQL*Loader is to extract from the input record. The field clause is enclosed in parentheses and can contain one or more field definitions, separated by commas.

Keywords

column_name

Name of the database column into which you want data for the field to be loaded.

[BOUND] FILLER

Indicates that a field in the INFILE is not loaded into the target table. This keyword was introduced with Oracle8i. A bound filler field, new in Oracle9i, is a filler field that can be used with the NULLIF or DEFAULTIF clauses.

generated

Causes SQL*Loader to use a generated value for the field. The options for generation are:

RECNUM

The record number for the record

SYSDATE

CONSTANT "string"

SEQUENCE

Similar to RECNUM, but does not include a sequence number for bad records. The SEQUENCE specification can include the following: the keyword COUNT, which starts the sequence with a number higher than the count of the records already in the table; the keyword MAX, which starts the sequence with the integer higher than the maximum value of the column; an integer, which is the integer with which to start the sequence; and an increment, which is a positive integer greater than 1, indicating how the sequence should be incremented for each record.

*start | ***

Starting position of the field in the input record. The first byte is position one. Using * in this position indicates that this field starts immediately after the previous field or with the first byte of the record for the first field.

offset

Optional offset that you can have SQL*Loader add to the position represented by the * character.

end

Position of the last byte of data in the field. This is optional. If you omit the ending position, SQL*Loader determines it based on information that you supply in your datatype specification.

datatype clause

Datatype specification for the field. This may include information about delimiters and enclosing characters. See the later "Datatype clause" entry for more information.

PIECED

An option that causes SQL*Loader to load a field one piece at a time This option is relevant only for a direct path load and for the last field in the record.

WHEN

A Boolean condition that is evaluated for each instance of the field. The *condition* for this clause (as well as the NULLIF and DEFAULTIF clauses) consists of a field name or position clause, an equality or inequality operator, and a string or hex value. The WHEN keyword can also use the keyword BLANKS as a comparison, which indicates that the field is entirely composed of blanks. If a record fails this test, it is placed in the discard file.

NULLIF and DEFAULTIF

A Boolean condition for either the NULLIF or DEFAULTIF clause. When the specified conditions are met, these clauses cause SQL*Loader to store NULL or 0 into the database column instead of the value that the field actually contains. You can reference other fields in these condition clauses. If a record fails this test, it is placed in the discard file.

If you are using either of these clauses on a field within an object or collection, you will have to use dot notation to specify the qualified name for any fields in the clause.

sql_expression

An SQL expression, the result of which is stored in the database column. You can use any valid Oracle SQL function, any user-written function, and any non-filler field. Field names should be preceded by a colon (:). Prior to Oracle9*i*, a direct path load would not execute this expression.

LOB, BFILE, Object, and Collection Clauses

You must specify special SQL*Loader syntax for LOB data, for data stored in BFILEs, for object data, and for collections:

LOB Data Syntax

The special syntax for LOB data that you are loading from an external file is:

```
column_name LOBFILE (fieldname | CONSTANT filename
    [CHARACTERSET charsetname])
```

where *fieldname* is the name of a field in the INFILE that has the filename for the LOB data, which is usually a filler field. The *filename* is the filename of the file that contains the LOB data. If you load LOBs from an external file, SQL*Loader does not have to allocate memory for their temporary storage.

BFILE Data Syntax

For data stored in BFILEs, the SQL*Loader syntax is:

```
column_name BFILE({dirfield | CONSTANT dirname},
    {filefield | CONSTANT filename})
```

where *dirfield* or *dirname* are the names of the field in the INFILE that contains Oracle directory alias, and *filefield* or *filename* are the names of the operating system file that contains the data.

Object Data Syntax

For object data, you use the keywords OBJECT DATA after the field name and then specify another field list following the keywords.

Collection Data Syntax

For collections, you use the following syntax:

```
column_name {VARRAY | NESTED TABLE | secondary_data_file} {COUNT(fieldname)
    | COUNT(CONSTANT integer)
```

where COUNT is the number of items in the collection and *fieldname* is the name of a field in the INFILE that contains that count. The *secondary_data_file* is the name of an external file that holds the collection with the following syntax:

```
SDF({fieldname|CONSTANT 'file_name'}) os_specific_options
    [MAXRECORDSIZE bytes] [CHARACTERSET 'charsetname']
```

where *fieldname* is the name of a field in the INFILE that contains the name of the external file. For information on *os_specific_options*, see the Oracle documentation for your specific platform.

Datatype Clause

datatype_name datatype_clauses

Describes the type of data in the INFILE.

Keywords

datatype_name

Name of one of the datatypes described later. Different datatype clauses apply to different datatypes. Two parts of the datatype clause are common across multiple datatypes: *enclosure* and *termination*.

enclosure

The syntax for this clause is:

```
[OPTIONAL] ENCLOSED [BY] ['string' | X'hex_value'] [AND 'string' |
    X'hex_value']
```

You can also use the OPTIONAL keyword to indicate that the enclosing characters are optional, but only following the TERMINATED BY clause. The AND keyword indicates a different ending character from the initial character.

termination

The syntax for this clause is:

```
{DELIMITED [BY]}|{TERMINATED [BY]} WHITESPACE|X'hex_value' |
    'string' | EOF
```

where WHITESPACE indicates that the termination of the field is any type of whitespace, including space characters, tab characters, and newline characters. EOF stands for end-of-file, and is primarily used for loading LOBs.

The *datatype_names* and their syntax are:

```
CHAR length enclosure termination
DATE length mask enclosure termination
```

where *mask* is the date mask used by the Oracle TO_DATE function to convert the incoming date.

```
{INTEGER | DECIMAL | FLOAT | ZONED} [EXTERNAL]
 length enclosure termination
GRAPHIC [EXTERNAL] length
```

where *length* is the length of the raw graphic file in terms of double bytes. The EXTERNAL keyword indicates that the graphic is enclosed by shift-in and shift-out characters.

```
RAW length
VARCHARC | VARRAWC (length[,max_bytes])
```

For these datatypes, the length of the field is indicated in the first bytes of the field. The number of bytes indicating the length of the field is *length*, and *max_bytes* indicates the maximum number of bytes possible in the field. The VARRAWC loads the data without conversion.

The datatypes listed previously are called *portable datatypes*, because they are platform independent. SQL*Loader also supports a number of *nonportable datatypes*, which are binary representations that are platform-specific. For more information about these nonportable datatypes, see the Oracle documentation.

Concatenation Clauses

Concatenation rules tell SQL*Loader to combine two or more records from the INFILE into a single row in the database. You can specify concatenation in two ways. The first way is with the CONCATENATE clause:

```
CONCATENATE record_number
```

where *record_number* indicates a fixed number of records in the INFILE. The second is with the CONTINUEIF clause.

The THIS keyword indicates that the continuation character is in the current record. The NEXT keyword indicates that the continuation character is in the next record, which will be concatenated to this record. The PRESERVE keyword indicates that the continuation character(s) are preserved in the data loaded. The PRESERVE keyword was new in Oracle8*i*. The remainder of the clause is used to identify the position and value of the continuation characters.

An alternative syntax for the CONTINUEIF clause for non–fixed length is:

```
CONTINUEIF LAST [(]{= | <>}{'char' | X'hex_digits'}[)]
```

which tells SQL*Loader to check the last character in the record for a continuation character. With this syntax, the continuation character is always preserved in the row.

If you use concatenation, the position information for the fields refers to the combined row.

15

Backup and Recovery

No database is flawless, and no environment is fail-safe. These hard facts collide with the need for absolute reliability and data integrity in an Oracle database. A variety of backup and recovery techniques are available to safeguard an Oracle database and its data from unforeseen problems that could result in the loss of some or all of its data.

This chapter describes the methods commonly used to back up and restore Oracle databases. Before presenting the details of backup and recovery, we'll summarize the most important backup and recovery terms and concepts and provide a comparison of the available Oracle backup and recovery methods.

There are three basic methods for backing up and restoring Oracle databases:

Export/Import
> Oracle provides command-line utilities for exporting data from a database (Export) and importing data into a database (Import). The Export and Import processes produce binary files, which can be transported between machines. Although the Export and Import utilities can be used for backup and recovery operations, they are more frequently used for moving data between different Oracle databases. Chapter 13 describes the details of using these utilities.

User-managed operations
> Oracle provides a recommended sequence of operations for backing up and recovering a database using a combination of operating system commands (to back up the database) and SQL*Plus (to restore the database from these backups). If you use this approach, the backup actually happens outside the realm of the Oracle instance, so your log file may have to contain additional information about the changes that are occurring to the data while the backup is taking place. We describe user-managed backup and recovery methods later in this chapter.

Recovery Manager

Oracle Recovery Manager, known far and wide as RMAN, was introduced with Oracle8. RMAN operates from inside an Oracle instance, which removes the need for the additional log file information required for user-managed backup and recovery. RMAN provides additional capabilities not available through user-managed backup and recovery. For example, with RMAN, you can perform incremental backups; with such backups, only the blocks that have been changed—rather than the entire file—are backed up. RMAN also provides a simplified set of commands and can be used with a recovery catalog, which removes some of the administrative burden of managing backup sets. We describe RMAN later in this chapter.

Oracle now strongly recommends RMAN as the preferred database backup and recovery method. For this reason, some new Oracle recovery features, such as point-in-time recovery for tablespaces, are currently available only through RMAN.

Backup and Recovery Fundamentals

The common Oracle backup and recovery methods can be differentiated in a number of ways, based on the type of backup and recovery available and the steps necessary to recover from a failure. The following list summarizes the concepts and terms that are fundamental to the backup and recovery process.

Instance/media recovery

An Oracle database can fail in two basic ways: instance failure and media failure. When *instance failure* occurs, something happens that prevents the processes that make up an Oracle instance from servicing database requests. The Oracle database can automatically recover itself from this type of failure as soon as the instance is restarted, with roll-forward and rollback operations. Because instance recovery is automatic, we don't cover it in this chapter.

An Oracle database can also experience a *media failure*. This occurs when the underlying storage for the files used by an Oracle database fails or experiences a corruption. Oracle does not provide automatic recovery from this type of failure, because there may very well be other actions that you need to take before you attempt recovery, such as replacing a failed disk drive. The backup and recovery operations described in the remainder of this chapter are used to address media failure.

Consistent/inconsistent

An Oracle backup can be either consistent or inconsistent. A *consistent backup* is a complete backup of an Oracle database that is in a consistent state. A consistent backup does not need additional modifications after it has been restored. Typically, a consistent backup is obtained only if the backup has been done when the database is offline or in a quiescent state.

An *inconsistent backup* is a backup in which the data has changed since the time the backup was originally made. An inconsistent backup will need log files applied to the backup in order to restore the consistency of the database. Because database failures have an unfortunate habit of happening at unplanned intervals, you'll generally find yourself recovering from inconsistent backups.

Logical/physical

One of the key qualities of any relational database is the ability to keep logical data, organized by tables and columns, separate from the physical storage of that data in files on disk. A *logical backup* of an Oracle database is a backup of data that maintains the logical structure of the data in tables. A *physical backup* of an Oracle database is a backup that is made of the actual files, such as the individual datafiles and log files, that make up the complete database.

Full/incremental

A *full backup* is a backup of a complete database at a particular point in time. An *incremental backup* is a backup that includes only those parts of the database that have changed since the time of the last full or incremental backup. An incremental backup is almost always smaller than a full backup, so it takes less time to create. However, the recovery process using incremental backups can take longer, because you will have to restore the full backup and then apply the incremental backup(s) before you can initiate any other recovery process.

Whole database/tablespace

A backup can consist of either the whole Oracle database, which includes all of the files used in the database—datafiles, archived log files, and control files—or just one or more tablespaces. Because an Oracle database may contain many tablespaces, a tablespace backup may be smaller than a full backup and take less time to produce. A backup may also consist of individual datafiles or control files.

An Oracle database may have some tablespaces marked as read-only. A *read-only tablespace backup* is always a consistent backup, because the data in a read-only tablespace does not change. For this reason, a read-only tablespace can be backed up once and then eliminated from future backups, which can speed the overall backup process.

 This process is effective only if you make a tablespace backup of the read-only tablespace after it has been marked as read-only. If a read-only tablespace is changed to a normal tablespace, backup and recovery procedures will have to be changed to protect the now-dynamic data.

Complete/incomplete recovery

A *complete recovery* is a recovery process that restores an Oracle database to its most complete state, prior to failure. *An incomplete recovery* is a recovery process that cannot complete. There are a number of reasons why a recovery process cannot complete—for example, a missing log file.

Starting with Oracle8i, you can take advantage of the *point-in-time recovery* (PITR) feature for the database, which allows you to recover your database to a specific point in time. PITR is useful in recovering a database to a point in time just before a log file went missing or to recover to a point just before a user-induced error (e.g., an inadvertent drop of a table) damaged the data. PITR can work with a specific time or with a specific System Change Number (SCN). Oracle9i offers PITR for an individual tablespace as well.

Datafile/block media recovery

For all versions of Oracle prior to Oracle9i, a recovery from a media failure could work only at the level of *datafile recovery*. Beginning with Oracle9i, when you are using RMAN for backup and recovery, you can specify that you want to recover only the specific blocks in a datafile that have been lost. *Block media recovery* can be much faster than datafile recovery, because the scope of recovery is often much smaller.

Table 15-1 compares the different backup and recovery methods with regard to these backup and recovery characteristics.

Table 15-1. Comparison of backup and recovery methods

Characteristic	Export/Import	User-managed backup/recovery	RMAN
Consistent/inconsistent	Consistent, but only with database activity stopped or suspended for the table	Either	Either
Logical/physical	Logical	Physical	Physical
Full/incremental	Full	Full	Either; can back up only changed data blocks
Whole database/tablespace	Tables only	Either	Either
Complete/incomplete recovery	Complete only	Either	Either
Datafile/block media recovery	Table-based recovery	Datafile only	Either

User-Managed Backup and Recovery

User-managed backup and recovery is a process that allows you to back up and restore your Oracle database by issuing an appropriate combination of operating system commands, SQL*Plus commands, and custom Oracle utility commands.

At this time, Recovery Manager (RMAN), described later in this chapter, has largely replaced user-managed backup and recovery, and Oracle Corporation is no longer enhancing its older user-managed backup and recovery processes. RMAN provides all of the capabilities of user-managed backup and recovery, offers quite a few additional features, and is easier to use than user-managed backup and recovery.

Nevertheless, user-managed backup and recovery still works, and there may be reasons why you may prefer to use this method. For example, you may be supporting Oracle databases prior to Oracle8, when RMAN was introduced; your staff may not be as familiar with RMAN as with these older procedures; or your own administrative plan may not yet have been changed to embrace RMAN.

With user-managed backup and recovery, you can make either consistent or inconsistent backups. The processes differ depending on what type of backup you are performing:

Consistent backup

> To make a consistent backup, you must shut down the database normally. Consistent backups are the only type of backup supported in NOARCHIVELOG mode, because recovery cannot be performed in this mode.

Inconsistent backup

> You can make an inconsistent backup with the database (or tablespace) either online or offline. Because user-managed backup operations are issued by the operating system, the backup process is unaware of changes that may be made to the database or log files by Oracle processes while the backup is underway. To compensate for this, you must issue SQL commands to begin and end your user-managed backup to add the appropriate information to the log files.

How to Perform User-Managed Backup

To back up your datafiles, your archived log files and your configuration files, you use the appropriate operating system commands. To back up control files and initialization files, you use the appropriate SQL*Plus commands.

There are a number of steps in the complete user-managed backup process, described in the following sections.

Determining the files to back up

Because your Oracle database is always changing, your first step in performing a user-managed backup is to determine the files you will need to back up. You can identify these files by running queries against the various V$ views, as shown in Table 15-2.

Table 15-2. V$ views used in user-managed backup

Type of file	V$ view	SQL
Datafile	V$DATAFILE	SELECT NAME FROM V$DATAFILE;
Online redo log files	V$LOGFILE	SELECT MEMBER FROM V$LOGFILE;
Archived redo log files	V$ARCHIVED_LOG	SELECT THREAD#, SEQUENCE#, NAME FROM V$ARCHIVED_LOG;
Control files	V$CONTROLFILE	SELECT NAME FROM V$CONTROLFILE;

Make sure to save a list of the datafiles and archived log files with the control file. The structure of your database may change between the time you make your backup and the time you have to use it, in which case the current control file for that database might not match up with the files you backed up.

When performing a user-managed backup, you need to back up four types of files:

- Datafiles
- Log files

- Control files
- Miscellaneous files

Because you need all of these types of files for recovery operations, make sure that your user-managed backup routines include backups of all four file types.

Backing up datafiles

You can make a user-managed consistent backup of your complete Oracle database after you have shut down the database with the NORMAL, IMMEDIATE, or TRANSACTIONAL keyword. Once the database is shut down, you use the appropriate operating system command to back up or copy the datafiles.

You can also back up individual tablespaces and datafiles. If a tablespace is offline, you can use the appropriate operating system command to back up the datafiles. If the tablespace is online, you must first put the tablespace into BACKUP mode by issuing the following command in SQL*Plus:

```
ALTER TABLESPACE tablespace_name BEGIN BACKUP;
```

Once the backup is complete, you issue either of the following commands:

```
ALTER TABLESPACE tablespace_name END BACKUP;
ALTER DATABASE END BACKUP;
```

to return to normal operation. Because there is extra overhead involved in writing the extra information to the log files while in BACKUP mode, you should always end the mode as soon as your backup completes successfully.

 You may need to use the ALTER DATABASE END BACKUP command if your database is still in BACKUP mode when it fails. Oracle will not reopen a tablespace in BACKUP mode, so you will need to mount the database, run this command, and then open the database.

You may find that it makes more sense to back up your tablespaces serially, rather than in a single job. By backing up your tablespaces one at a time, you avoid having to put all the tablespaces in BACKUP mode for the duration of the complete backup—you will need to do this only for the amount of time needed to back up a single tablespace. This reduces the overall impact of the extra information needed for the log files in BACKUP mode.

Backing up log files

If you are running in ARCHIVELOG mode, your log files are being archived as soon as they are filled. The archiving process automatically backs up the filled log to another location. You may want to copy these archived files to a backup media to protect against the possibility of media corruption.

Typically, you want to force the archiving of the current log after you have backed up your datafiles. To do this, you execute the following command in SQL*Plus:

```
ALTER SYSTEM ARCHIVE LOG CURRENT;
```

Backing up the control file

The control file contains essential information about the current state of the database. You should always back up your control file when you make a user-managed backup. You do this by executing the following command in SQL*Plus:

```
ALTER DATABASE BACKUP CONTROLFILE TO filename | TO TRACE
```

You can back up a control file in binary format to a binary location or to a trace file. Backing up the control file to a binary location includes more information and is the method recommended by Oracle. Backing up a control file to a trace file allows you to re-create the control file from the trace file with the CREATE CONTROLFILE command.

Backing up miscellaneous files

Other files, such as initialization files (*INIT.ORA* and *SPFILE*), networking files (*TNSNAMES.ORA* and *LISTENER.ORA*), and password files, are an essential part of your Oracle environment.

You should be sure to back up these files, either as a part of your normal user-managed backup or whenever they are changed.

How to Perform User-Managed Recovery

In the event of a media failure, you will have to use the files created with your user-managed backup to restore the database.

Restoring datafiles

The restore process for datafiles has three basic steps: determining which datafiles need recovery, copying the relevant backup files, and then restoring the database to a workable state.

Determining the files to recover. If your control file has not been corrupted by the media failure, you can run the following command in SQL*Plus to obtain a list of the datafiles that need recovery:

```
SELECT * FROM V$RECOVER_FILE;
```

This query will return a set of numbers that indicates the files needing recovery.

To determine which datafiles and tablespaces these file numbers represent, run the following command:

```
SELECT d.NAME, t.NAME AS Tablespace_Name
    FROM V$DATAFILE d, V$TABLESPACE
    WHERE d.TS# = t.TS# AND
    d.FILE# IN (filenumbers);
```

where *filenumbers* is a comma-separated list of the file numbers returned from the previous query.

Copying backup files. Once you have determined the datafiles that need recovery, you need to copy the backups of these files. To accomplish this, take the tablespace of the damaged datafile offline and copy the backup to the appropriate location.

If the default location is no longer available as a result of the media failure, you will have to modify the control file to recognize these new locations.

Restoring the database. Once the backup copy of the datafile is in place, you must restore the tablespace that contains it. You can restore the database using SQL*Plus by following these steps:

1. Ensure that the database has been shut down:

    SQL> **SHUTDOWN IMMEDIATE;**

    or

    SQL> **SHUTDOWN ABORT;**

2. Copy your datafile from a good backup.

3. Start the database in mount mode.

    SQL> **STARUP MOUNT;**

4. Recover the corrupt datafile through SQL*Plus:

    SQL> **RECOVER TABLESPACE <tablespace_name>;**

    or

    SQL> **RECOVER DATAFILE <datafile_name>;**

5. Open the database:

    SQL> **ALTER DATABASE OPEN;**

Restoring the control file

If you have specified multiple copies of your control file with the initialization parameter CONTROL_FILES, you can restore an individual copy of it by shutting down the database with the SHUTDOWN ABORT command, copying one of your other, undamaged control files to replace the damaged copy, and bringing the database back up.

If a media failure has made the location of the damaged control file unavailable, you follow the same procedure but edit the CONTROL_FILES initialization parameter to reflect the new location while the database is shut down.

If you have to restore a single copy of a control file or if all copies of a multiplexed control file have been damaged, you must perform the following steps:

1. Shut down the database with the SHUTDOWN ABORT command.

2. Copy the backup of the control file to the appropriate location.

3. Mount the database with the STARTUP MOUNT command.

4. Issue the command:

    RECOVER DATABASE USING BACKUP CONTROLFILE;

5. Apply the archive log files as you are prompted to do so. (See the later RECOVER entry for more information.)

If an archived log is not available, or if the recovery requires changes from the online redo log and it is not available, you will have to perform an incomplete recovery. To perform an incomplete recovery, add the keywords UNTIL CANCEL to the RECOVER command specified in the previous step.

6. Open the database and reset the log files with the command:

```
ALTER DATABASE OPEN RESETLOGS;
```

After completing this process, you should immediately perform a complete backup of your database.

Tablespace Point-in-Time Recovery

Oracle provides another type of recovery operation known as *tablespace point-in-time recovery* (TSPITR). TSPITR is most commonly used with transportable tablespaces to recover from a variety of errors, such as mistakenly dropping a table or a tablespace, or encountering a logically corrupted table.

Transportable tablespaces are an efficient way to move tablespaces from one database to another. You can copy the actual tablespace files, rather than having to back up and restore them or use Import and Export to move the data.

To accomplish this type of recovery, you perform the following steps:

1. Take tablespaces that are to be recovered offline in the original database.
2. Set up an auxiliary database.
3. Recover the tablespace in the auxiliary database to the appropriate point in time.
4. Make the target tablespaces read-only in the auxiliary database.
5. Export the transportable tablespace information from the auxiliary database.
6. Drop the tablespace in the original database.
7. Copy the tablespace files from the auxiliary database to the original database.
8. Import the transportable tablespace information into the original database.
9. Use transportable tablespaces to move the recovered tablespace to the original database.
10. Enable read-write access for the new tablespaces.

Backup and Recovery Commands

As discussed in earlier sections, some of the steps required for user-managed backup and recovery are implemented with operating system commands, some with Oracle's SQL*Plus commands, and some with special-purpose Oracle backup/recovery utility commands. See the documentation for your particular operating system for information on the operating system commands.

The following sections summarize the syntax of the Oracle commands used for backup and recovery. These commands are common to Oracle across all operating system platforms. Most of the following commands are SQL*Plus commands. Note, however, that only the options that apply to user-managed backup and recovery are shown here; for complete SQL*Plus command syntax, see Chapter 12. For additional documentation on these other commands, see the index for the location of the complete definition and description.

Two of the commands listed here are unique to backup and recovery. Oracle provides the DBVERIFY and the OCOPY utilities to allow you to test the validity of a backup and back up raw Windows partitions, respectively. For detailed information on these utilities, see the Oracle documentation.

ALTER DATABASE BACKUP CONTROLFILE

ALTER DATABASE BACKUP CONTROLFILE *TO filename* | TO TRACE

SQL*Plus command. Creates a backup of the current control file for the database.

Keywords

to_filename   Specifies the location of a copy of the current control file.

TO TRACE   Causes the information in the control file to be written as SQL statements to a file in the database's trace directory. You can use this information to re-create the control file with the CREATE CONTROL-FILE command.

ALTER DATABASE OPEN

ALTER DATABASE OPEN *dbname* [NORESETLOGS | RESETLOGS]

SQL*Plus command. Opens the database after performing user-managed recovery.

Keywords

dbname   Specifies the name of the database to be opened.

NORESETLOGS

Continues numbering the archive logs from the last set. This is the default value and is used after a complete recovery of the database.

RESETLOGS

Needed after incomplete recovery or use of a backup control file to ensure that old archived logs are not used to recover the new incarnation of the database.

ALTER SYSTEM SUSPEND/RESUME

ALTER SYSTEM SUSPEND | RESUME

SQL*Plus command. Suspends all I/O operations to the database to accommodate third-party products that require this type of pause.

At many sites, third-party tools are used to mirror an Oracle database. You can back up the mirrored database without affecting online operations by splitting the mirror and then backing it up. However, some mirrored systems cannot be split while there are I/O operations occurring, so in these cases you will have to suspend I/O while you are splitting the mirror.

Make sure to put the relevant tablespaces in BACKUP mode before you suspend I/O and take them back out of BACKUP mode after you resume I/O operations.

Note that there are many other options for the ALTER SYSTEM command in addition to those shown here. That command is described in Chapter 7. See the index for specific pointers to the discussion of additional command keywords.

Keywords

SUSPEND   Suspends all I/O operations to all database files.

RESUME   Resumes I/O operations to all database files.

CREATE CONTROLFILE

```
CREATE CONTROLFILE [REUSE] [SET]
    DATABASE database_name
    {LOGFILE {[GROUP integer] filename}...}
    [RESETLOGS | NORESETLOGS]
    [DATAFILE filename]
    [MAXLOGFILES integer]
    [MAXLOGMEMBERS integer]
    [MAXLOGHISTORY integer]
    [MAXDATAFILES integer]
    [MAXINSTANCES integer]
    [ARCHIVELOG | NOARCHIVELOG]
    [CHARACTER SET character_set]
```

SQL*Plus command. Allows you to re-create the control file. You can create the control file by manually entering the values for the control file or by using the text file created with a previous BACKUP CONTROLFILE TO TRACE command.

For any parameters for which you don't specify values with the CREATE CONTROL-FILE statement, Oracle will use the default values for the parameters.

Keywords

REUSE

> Causes the control file named in the CONTROL_FILE initialization parameter to become the new control file. If the control file named in the initialization file exists and the REUSE keyword is not used, an error will be returned.

SET

> Indicates that the *database_name* is the new name for the database.

DATABASE database_name

> Specifies the name of the database for the control file.

LOGFILE filename

> Specifies the name of the log file to be used for the database. You must list all members of all redo log groups.

GROUP integer

> Specifies the number of the log file group.

RESETLOGS | NORESETLOGS

> Indicates whether the database should ignore any log files listed for the log file clause. These keywords are used to prevent log file conflicts in the event of an incomplete recovery.

DATAFILE filename
> Specifies the datafiles for the database. You must list all datafiles for the database.

MAXLOGFILES integer
> Specifies the maximum number of log files that can ever be created for the database.

MAXLOGMEMBERS integer
> Specifies the maximum number of members for a redo log file. A member is an identical copy of a redo log file.

MAXLOGHISTORY integer
> Specifies the maximum number of archived redo log file groups for automatic media recovery with Oracle Parallel Server or Real Application Clusters.

MAXDATAFILES integer
> Specifies the maximum number of datafiles used initially for the database; this value is used to size the datafile section of the control file.

MAXINSTANCES integer
> Specifies the maximum number of instances that can have the database simultaneously mounted and open.

ARCHIVELOG | NOARCHIVELOG
> Indicates whether the database will be in ARCHIVELOG mode. The default is NOARCHIVELOG.

CHARACTER SET character_set
> Specifies the character set that is reconstructed in the control file, where it can be used to interpret the tablespace names for the database properly.

DBVERIFY

```
DBV FILE=filename
```

Oracle utility command. The DBVERIFY utility is specifically designed to test the validity of your backup.

Keywords

filename   Name of the backup file you wish to verify.

OCOPY

```
OCOPY from_rawfile to_file |
OCOPY /b from_file to_drive |
OCOPY /r from_drive to_rawfile |
```

Oracle utility command. The OCOPY utility is specifically designed to back up raw partitions on Windows systems.

Keywords

from_rawfile Filename of the raw partition.

to_file   Filename to receive the backup of the raw partition.

/b   Indicates that Oracle is to back up a raw partition to span multiple copies of media on a drive, such as a disk drive.

to_drive   Drive to receive the backup of the raw partition.

/r	Specifies recovery of a raw partition that has been backed up to multiple copies of media, such as a disk drive.
from_drive	Drive that will contain the multiple copies of media.
to_rawfile	Name of the raw partition that will be restored using the information from the multiple copies of media.

RECOVER

```
RECOVER {general_clause | managed_clause | END BACKUP}

general_clause :=
[AUTOMATIC] [FROM location]
    {{full_database_recovery_options |
    partial_database_recovery_options |
    LOGFILE filename}
    {[TEST | ALLOW integer CORRUPTION]} ... |
    CONTINUE [DEFAULT] | CANCEL}
    [PARALLEL [integer]]

full_database_recovery_options :=
[STANDBY] DATABASE
    [{UNTIL {CANCEL | TIME date | CHANGE integer} |
    USING BACKUP CONTROLFILE]

partial_database_recovery_options :=
TABLESPACE tablespace_name [, tablespace_name] . . . |
    DATAFILE datafile_name [, datafile_name] . . . |
    STANDBY {TABLESPACE tablespace_name [, tablespace_name] . . . |
        DATAFILE datafile_name [, datafile_name] . . .}
        UNTIL [CONSISTENT WITH] CONTROLFILE

managed_clause :=
    MANAGED STANDBY DATABASE
    [{NODELAY | [TIMEOUT] integer | CANCEL [IMMEDIATE] [NOWAIT]} |
    [DISCONNECT [FROM SESSION]] [FINISH [NOWAIT]]]
```

SQL*Plus command. Applies the appropriate log files to a datafile to restore the database. This operation rolls forward the transactions from the logs and then rolls back the uncommitted transactions.

You can use the RECOVER option of the SQL ALTER DATABASE statement to perform the same operations.

Keywords

END BACKUP

Takes the database out of online backup mode.

AUTOMATIC

Causes the name of the next archived redo file to be automatically generated, based on the LOG_ARCHIVE_DEST and LOG_ARCHIVE_FORMAT parameters. If no file matching the automatically generated name exists, SQL*Plus prompts you for the name of the file. This functionality can also be implemented with the SET AUTORECOVERY ON statement.

FROM location
> The location of the archived log file group. If this parameter is missing, SQL*Plus uses the value specified in the LOG_ARCHIVE_DEST initialization parameter.

LOGFILE filename
> Specifies the name of the log file to be used for recovery.

TEST
> Lets you run a trial recovery to determine if there are problems with the files that will be used in the recovery process. A trial recovery reads through the required files but does not write the specified changes to disk.

ALLOW integer CORRUPTION
> Specifies how many corrupt blocks can be found without canceling the entire recovery or trial recovery process.

CONTINUE
> Used to continue multi-instance recovery after the process has been interrupted to disable a thread.

CONTINUE DEFAULT
> Indicates that recovery should continue with automatically generated archived log file names.

CANCEL
> Cancels the current recovery process.

PARALLEL [integer]
> Allows recovery to continue in parallel. This option may not help in all situations—for example, if the I/O bottleneck is in the actual disk hardware. If you do not specify an integer, Oracle will calculate the degree of parallelism using the number of CPUs and the PARALLEL_THREADS_PER_CPU parameter.

DATABASE
> Recovers the entire database.

STANDBY DATABASE
> Recovers the standby database with the control file and archived log files.

UNTIL CANCEL | TIME | CHANGE
> Causes the recovery process to continue until you enter ALTER DATABASE RECOVER CANCEL, until a specified time, or until a specified SCN number.

TABLESPACE
> Follow this keyword with the name of the tablespace(s) you wish to recover.

DATAFILE
> Follow this keyword with the name of the datafile(s) you wish to recover.

UNTIL CONSISTENT WITH CONTROLFILE
> Specifies that the recovery should continue until the datafile or tablespace is consistent with the current standby database control file.

MANAGED STANDBY DATABASE
> Starts automated standby recovery mode.

NODELAY
> Overrides any DELAY setting to immediately apply an archived log file to the standby database.

TIMEOUT integer
> Specifies the time in minutes a managed recovery operation will wait for an archived log file. If this time is exceeded, the recovery operation terminates and you must reissue the RECOVER command to restart the managed recovery operation.

CANCEL
> Terminates the managed recovery operation and returns session control after the recovery process terminates.

CANCEL IMMEDIATE
> Terminates the managed recovery operation after applying all redo information in the current log or after the next log file read. Session control returns after the recovery process has terminated.

CANCEL IMMEDIATE NOWAIT
> Like CANCEL IMMEDIATE, but session control returns immediately.

CANCEL NOWAIT
> Cancels the managed recovery operation after the next log file read and returns control to the session immediately.

DISCONNECT [FROM SESSION]
> Runs the managed recovery operation as a background process.

FINISH
> Causes the managed recovery process to recover the current log files of the standby database. When used with the NOWAIT keyword, returns control immediately to the session.

STARTUP MOUNT

STARTUP MOUNT *dbname*

SQL*Plus command. Used to mount the database, but not open it. To perform a user-managed recovery operation, you must use this command.

Keywords
dbname   Name of the database to be mounted.

Recovery Manager (RMAN)

Oracle's Recovery Manager (RMAN), introduced with Oracle8, is a utility that allows you to create backups of your Oracle database and to restore your Oracle database from these backups. Although many of RMAN's operations can be performed with the other methods described in this chapter, RMAN provides some significant advantages over user-managed backup and recovery, including:

- Performing a backup without having to put the database in backup mode
- Performing an incremental backup of only changed data blocks
- Automatically tracking and logging backup operations
- Automatically detecting block corruption during backup
- Reporting on backup operations
- Performing block media recovery

RMAN is clearly the backup and recovery strategy of the future. Recently, Oracle has been adding such backup features as block media recovery and tablespace point-in-time recovery only to RMAN.

The following sections describe the use of RMAN. We'll look briefly at basic RMAN concepts, the command-line options used to start and use RMAN, and a sample RMAN command script that you can use to perform a backup of an Oracle database. We'll then describe the RMAN commands.

RMAN Fundamentals

You need to be familiar with a few RMAN concepts as you read the following sections:

Server processes
> RMAN uses a number of server processes to operate. These server processes are started whenever you start RMAN or use one of its features—for example, when you connect to a catalog or allocate a channel for backup.

Channel
> A channel is an RMAN server process that communicates with a particular backup device. You must allocate a channel before you can begin any backup operations.

Target and catalog
> RMAN can interact with two different Oracle databases. The *target* database is the database for which you are performing backup or recovery operations. The *catalog* is a database that acts as a repository for information about RMAN activities. The catalog is normally another Oracle database on a different Oracle host; using a different host prevents a failure from destroying the very catalog information that will be needed to recover from that failure.
>
> The catalog includes a specific schema that will hold the relevant information. To create a catalog for RMAN, you first connect to the catalog database with RMAN and issue the CREATE CATALOG command. If you want to use a catalog for RMAN, you will have to register any target databases using RMAN's REGISTER command before those databases will be able to use the catalog.
>
> You don't have to use a catalog, because RMAN includes information about any backup in the target database's control files. However, the catalog gives you more management flexibility by maintaining a greater amount of historical data about all the backups done on a database.

Media Management Layer
> If you will be using a tape drive for your RMAN backups, you will have to use a Media Management Layer (MML) to communicate with the tape drive. The MML is third-party software that generally comes from the hardware vendor.

Backup sets
> Whenever you create a backup with RMAN, you are actually creating one or more *backup sets*. A backup set is a logical entity composed of one or more physical *backup pieces*, the physical files that make up a backup set. Datafiles

and control files can be in the same backup set, but archived log files must be in a different backup set. The only way to restore a database from backup pieces is through RMAN.

Running RMAN

In order to run RMAN, you must have SYSDBA privileges, either through operating system authentication or by use of a password file. If you are using OS authentication, you must also properly establish the following target environment variables:

ORACLE_SID
ORACLE_HOME

To run Recovery Manager, you call the RMAN executable at the command prompt with the following command:

```
> RMAN
```

RMAN displays the following prompt:

```
RMAN>
```

You can connect to a target database and a recovery catalog within RMAN by issuing the CONNECT command, described later in this section.

You can specify the following options when invoking the RMAN executable:

TARGET
Specifies a string containing the connect string for the target database. If you do not include a connect string, RMAN connects to the Oracle database specified by the ORACLE_SID environment variable.

CATALOG
Specifies a string containing the connect string for the recovery catalog database. If you do not specify a recovery catalog when you connect or within RMAN, backup operations will proceed without a catalog.

NOCATALOG
Indicates that RMAN will not start with a particular recovery catalog. With Oracle9*i*, this is the default.

AUXILARY
Specifies a string containing the connect string for the recovery catalog database. Auxiliary databases are used to create duplicate standby databases (see the DUPLICATE command entry later in this section) or to implement tablespace point-in-time recovery.

CMDFILE
Specifies a string containing the filename specifying RMAN commands. Once the commands in the file have completed, RMAN terminates.

LOG
Specifies a string containing the path and filename for the output message log file.

MSGNO

Causes the RMAN message number to be included in all output from commands.

APPEND

Indicates that RMAN should append new messages onto the end of the existing message file. If you do not specify this keyword and the log file name is the name of a file that already exists, the existing file is overwritten.

DEBUG

Activates debug mode for RMAN, which produces verbose messages for each RMAN command. With Oracle9*i*, you can specify the type and level of debug messages produced.

TRACE

Specifies a string containing the path and filename of the output debug message file.

SEND

Specifies a string containing a command that is sent to the destinations of all allocated channels. Support of this feature is provided by the MML for a particular device.

PIPE

Specifies a string containing the name of a pipe that can be used to pass commands to RMAN. Pipes can be used in conjunction with the PL/SQL built-in package DBMS_PIPE. New with Oracle9*i*.

TIMEOUT

Specifies the amount of time (in seconds) that a pipe will wait for input. If this time limit is exceeded, RMAN will terminate. New with Oracle9*i*.

If you use more than one of these keywords as part of your RMAN command, you will have to separate them with spaces, as shown here:

```
> RMAN TARGET SYS/syspassword NOCATALOG
> RMAN TARGET / CATALOG SYS/syspassword
> RMAN TARGET SYS/syspassword CATALOG CAT/meow APPEND
```

Using RMAN Scripts

When you specify the backup or recovery operations to be performed by RMAN, you will frequently need to include several commands. If you make a mistake entering one of these commands, RMAN will abort the entire job. Because of this behavior, many DBAs use scripts containing a ready-made, correct set of RMAN commands.

You may wish to create operating system scripts containing all the commands needed to run an RMAN job, from setting the environment variables to actually backing up or restoring the database. You may also wish to create operating system scripts that pass variables to RMAN. The syntax for these scripts is the standard syntax for scripts for your operating system.

You can also create scripts to run within RMAN. The @ command calls an operating system script from within RMAN. The @@ command calls another script

---

from within a called script. The @@ command must reference a script in the same directory as the originally called script.

You can store scripts in the recovery catalog with the following command syntax:

```
RMAN> CREATE SCRIPT script_name {scriptbody}
```

To edit an existing script, use the same syntax, but begin with the keywords REPLACE SCRIPT.

You can run a script stored in the catalog using the syntax:

```
RMAN> RUN {EXECUTE SCRIPT script_name;}
```

You can delete a script from the catalog as follows:

```
RMAN> DELETE SCRIPT script_name;
```

You can view a script stored in the catalog in two ways. You can use the PRINT command, followed by the script name, in RMAN, or you can query the actual tables used to store the script. The following SQL query on the catalog database will retrieve all the scripts stored in the database:

```
SELECT a.script_name, a.text
    FROM rc_stored_script_line a, rc_stored_script b
    WHERE a.db_key = b.db_key
```

RMAN includes commands that shape the operation of your Oracle database, but you can also call any SQL statement by specifying the SQL statement within RMAN, followed by a quoted string containing the SQL syntax.

Using RMAN Commands

The main purpose of Recovery Manager is to make it easy to perform backup and recovery operations. With Oracle9i Recovery Manager, the command needed to do a full online backup of your database is quite simple. The following examples assume that you have already connected to the target database and that you are using defaults for all options.

```
RMAN> BACKUP DATABASE FORMAT
2> '/d99/rmanback/brdstn/rman_%d_%t_%U.bus';
```

Oracle8i RMAN required you to issue the RUN command and explicitly allocate a channel. To perform the same backup shown previously, you would need the following, more complex set of commands with Oracle8i:

```
RMAN> RUN {
2> ALLOCATE CHANNEL d1 TYPE DISK;
3> BACKUP DATABASE FORMAT
4> '/d99/rmanback/brdstn/rman_%d_%t_%U.bus';
5> }
```

To perform a normal recovery operation with Oracle9i RMAN, use the following commands, assuming that the database is already closed:

```
RMAN> RESTORE DATABASE;
RMAN> RECOVER DATABASE;
RMAN> ALTER DATABASE OPEN;
```

The same basic recovery operation with RMAN in Oracle8*i* requires the following commands:

```
RMAN> RUN{
2> ALLOCATE CHANNEL d1 TYPE DISK;
3> RESTORE DATABASE;
4> RECOVER DATABASE;
5> ALTER DATABASE OPEN; }
```

RMAN provides a lot of flexibility for shaping the way you perform backup and recovery operations, as the commands in the remainder of this chapter will show.

Common RMAN Parameters and Identifiers

The following keywords and parameters are used for many different RMAN commands. The later command syntax entries show which of the common keywords can be included in the commands but do not repeat the detailed descriptions.

channel_id
Case-sensitive name of a channel; follows the CHANNEL keyword.

ConnectStringSpec
Connects to an Oracle database with RMAN; specify as following:

['][*userid*][/[*password*]][@*net_service_name*]['']

datafileSpec
Specifies a datafile by its fully qualified filename or by its file number; specify as following:

'*filename*' | *file_number*

deviceSpecifier
Storage type that will be the destination of a backup or copy. The value is either DISK or the name of a media device specified by the vendor of the backup tape drive being used.

filename
Name of a file to be used as part of an RMAN command. The filename can include the complete path for the file. If it does not contain the complete path, RMAN assumes that the file is in the directory from which RMAN was started.

format_string
Quoted string that specifies the format for a particular set of filenames. Because most filenames for backup pieces have to be unique, the *format_string* generally includes a pathname and one or more wildcard indicators. Wildcard indicators are preceded by a % and apply either a unique generated value (%u) or a more meaningful value, such as a copy number or a date-based value. For more detailed information, see the RMAN documentation.

media_handle
Complete name of a backup piece.

PARMS

Parameters for a nondisk device that has been allocated. You can specify PARMS '*channel_parms*' or PARMS='*channel_parms*'. For more detailed information, see the RMAN documentation.

primary_key

Unique primary key value assigned to a backup piece.

tablespace_name

Names of one or more tablespaces in the specified Oracle database.

tag_name

One or more tag names, which identify datafile copies. If multiple copies with a tag exist, RMAN uses the most recent copy. The tag name is assigned during a backup operation.

Common RMAN Clauses

The following clauses may be included in many different RMAN commands. The later command syntax entries show which of the common clauses can be included in the commands but do not repeat the detailed descriptions.

allocOperand Clause

```
allocOperand :=
{ PARMS [=] 'channel_parms'
| CONNECT [=] ConnectStringSpec
| DEBUG [=] integer
| FORMAT [=] 'format_string' [,'format_string' ...]
| TRACE [=] integer
| { MAXPIECESIZE [=] integer
  | RATE [=] integer } [ K | M | G ]
| MAXOPENFILES [=] integer
| SEND 'command'
}
```

Allows you to change the characteristics of a channel.

Keywords

ConnectStringSpec

Indicates an alternate database that will be the target of backup and restore operations. See the previous section for this clause's syntax.

DEBUG integer

Logs debugging information to an output file for backup, copy, or restore commands that use the channel. The *integer* specifies the level of information logged.

TRACE integer

Specifies the level of trace information that is logged to an output file. The exact meaning of the integer is defined by the MML software.

MAXPIECESIZE integer

Specifies the maximum size for a backup piece. New with Oracle9*i*.

RATE integer

Specifies the maximum number of bytes that RMAN will read per channel in bytes, kilobytes (K), megabytes (M), or gigabytes (G). New with Oracle9*i*.

MAXOPENFILES integer

Specifies the maximum number of files that RMAN is allowed to have open at any given time. New with Oracle9*i*.

SEND command

Sends a vendor-specific command to all of the allocated channels. New with Oracle9*i*.

archivelogRecordSpecifier Clause

```
ARCHIVELOG
    { ALL
    | LIKE 'string_pattern'
    | archlogRange
      [LIKE 'string_pattern' [THREAD [=] integer]]
    }

archlogRange for Oracle9i :=
{ { { UNTIL TIME | FROM TIME } [=] 'date_string'
  | { TIME BETWEEN 'date_string' AND
    | FROM TIME [=] 'date_string' UNTIL TIME [=]
    }
    'date_string'
  | UNTIL SCN [=] integer
  | SCN BETWEEN integer AND integer
  | FROM SCN [=] integer [UNTIL SCN [=] integer]
  }
  [THREAD [=] integer]
  | { UNTIL SEQUENCE [=] integer
  | FROM SEQUENCE [=] integer [UNTIL SEQUENCE [=] integer]
  | SEQUENCE [BETWEEN integer AND] integer
  }
  [THREAD [=] integer]
}

archlogRange for Oracle8i :=
{ { UNTIL TIME | FROM TIME } [=]'date_string'
  | FROM TIME [=]'date_string' UNTIL TIME [=]'date_string'
  | UNTIL SCN [=]integer
  | FROM SCN [=] integer [UNTIL SCN [=] integer]
  | UNTIL LOGSEQ [=] integer [THREAD [=] integer]
  | FROM LOGSEQ [=] integer [UNTIL LOGSEQ [=] integer]
    [THREAD [=] integer]
}
```

Provides flexibility in specifying the archived redo log files that will be included in backup, restore, and maintenance operations.

Keywords

ALL

Specifies that all logs should be included in the specified operation.

LIKE 'string_pattern'

Includes logs that match the specified pattern.

archlogRange

Includes logs that match specified criteria for time, SCN, or sequence number.

THREAD integer

Specifies a redo thread and is used only with Oracle Parallel Server or Real Application Clusters.

completedTimeSpec Clause

```
completedTimeSpec :=
COMPLETED
{ AFTER [=]
| BETWEEN 'date_string' AND
| BEFORE [=] } 'date_string'
```

Specifies the time or time range when a backup or copy operation completed.

Keywords

AFTER 'date_string'

Specifies a time after which a backup or copy occurred.

BETWEEN 'date_string' AND 'date_string'

Specifies a date range during which backups or copies occurred.

BEFORE 'date_string'

Specifies a time before a backup or copy occurred.

keepOption Clause

```
{ KEEP { UNTIL TIME [=] 'date_string' | FOREVER } { LOGS |
    NOLOGS }
| NOKEEP
}
```

Specifies that a backup or copy is considered exempt from a specified retention policy.

Keywords

UNTIL TIME 'date_string'

Specifies that the backup or copy should be kept until the specified date.

FOREVER   Specifies that the backup will be kept indefinitely. This requires the use of a recovery catalog because the backup or copy will never expire.

LOGS   Keeps all archived redo log files associated with a backup or copy.

NOLOGS   Specifies that archived redo log files associated with a backup or copy will not be kept. Consequently, the database can be restored only to the point in time when the backup or copy was made.

listObjList Clause

```
listObjList :=
{ DATAFILE datafileSpec [, datafileSpec ...]
| TABLESPACE [']tablespace_name[']
  [, [']tablespace_name['] ...]
| archivelogRecordSpecifier
| DATABASE [SKIP TABLESPACE
  [']tablespace_name['] [, [']tablespace_name[']]...]
| CONTROLFILE
}
[ DATAFILE datafileSpec [, datafileSpec]...
| TABLESPACE [']tablespace_name[']
  [, [']tablespace_name['] ...]
| archivelogRecordSpecifier
| DATABASE [SKIP TABLESPACE
  [']tablespace_name['] [, [']tablespace_name[']]...]
| CONTROLFILE
]...
```

Specifies the database elements that will be included in backup, restore, and maintenance operations.

See the earlier sections for descriptions of these keywords and clauses.

mntQualifier Clause

```
mntQualifier :=
{ TAG [=] [']tag_name[']
| completedTimeSpec
| LIKE 'string_pattern'
| DEVICE TYPE deviceSpecifier [, deviceSpecifier ...]
}
```

Allows additional options to be included when performing maintenance operations on database files and archived redo log files. Valid only for Oracle9*i*.

See the earlier sections for descriptions of these keywords and clauses.

obsoleteOpersList Clause

```
obsoleteOpersList :=
{ REDUNDANCY [=] integer
| RECOVERY WINDOW OF integer DAYS | ORPHAN }
[ REDUNDANCY [=] integer
| RECOVERY WINDOW OF integer DAYS | ORPHAN }...
```

Specifies the backups that can be considered obsolete. Valid only for Oracle9*i*.

Keywords

REDUNDANCY integer
    Specifies a number of redundant backups or copies that must be kept available.

ORPHAN
    Indicates that a backup is obsolete.

recordSpec Clause

```
recordSpec :=
{ { BACKUPPIECE | PROXY }
  { 'media_handle' [,'media_handle' ...]
  | primary_key [, primary_key ...]
  | TAG [=] [']tag_name[']
  }
| BACKUPSET primary_key [, primary_key ...]
| { CONTROLFILECOPY | DATAFILECOPY }
  { { primary_key [, primary_key ...]
    | 'filename' [, 'filename' ...]
    }
  | TAG [=] [']tag_name['] [, [']tag_name['] ...]
  }
| ARCHIVELOG
  { primary_key [, primary_key ...]
  | 'filename' [, 'filename' ...]
  }
| archivelogRecordSpecifier
}
```

Specifies types of objects on which to operate when performing maintenance. Valid only for Oracle9*i*.

Keywords

BACKUPPIECE
> Specifies the physical backup piece by its filename, primary key, or tag name.

PROXY
> Specifies a proxy copy by its filename, primary key, or tag name.

CONTROLFILECOPY
> Specifies a control file copy by its filename, primary key, or tag name.

DATAFILECOPY
> Specifies a datafile copy by its filename, primary key, or tag name.

until Clause

```
until :=
{ UNTIL TIME [=] 'date_string'
| UNTIL SCN [=] integer
| UNTIL SEQUENCE [=] integer THREAD [=] integer
}
```

Used by various RMAN commands to specify an upper limit for time, SCN, or log sequence numbers.

RMAN Commands

This section contains an alphabetical listing of all RMAN commands. You can enter each of these commands at the RMAN prompt. You can stop the execution of a command at any time with the Ctrl-C keystroke combination.

Each command description contains a brief description, shows the syntax of the command, describes the keywords and parameters specific to that command, and references any common keywords, parameters, and/or clauses described earlier.

@ (At Sign)

`@ filename`

Used to call a script file of RMAN commands.

Common keywords and clauses: *filename*.

@@ (Double At Sign)

`@@ filename`

References a command file from within another command file. The file is assumed to be located in the same directory as the command file containing this command

Common keywords and clauses: *filename*.

ALLOCATE CHANNEL

```
ALLOCATE [AUXILIARY] CHANNEL ['] channel_id [']
    { DEVICE TYPE [=] deviceSpecifier | NAME [=] 'channel_name'}
    [ allocOperand [allocOperand . . .]];
```

Creates a communication channel between RMAN and an output device. You can execute the ALLOCATE CHANNEL command only from within the RUN command.

Keywords

AUXILIARY   Specifies that the channel will be to an auxiliary database. Used for the DUPLICATE command and for tablespace point-in-time recovery.

NAME   Precedes the name of a particular device. Note that this syntax is not supported on any Oracle platform as of Oracle9*i*.

Common keywords and clauses: *allocOperand, channel_id, deviceSpecifier*.

ALLOCATE CHANNEL FOR MAINTENANCE

```
ALLOCATE CHANNEL FOR MAINTENANCE
    { DEVICE TYPE [=] deviceSpecifier | NAME [=] 'channel_name'}
    [ allocOperand [allocOperand . . .]];
```

Creates a communication channel between RMAN and an output device in preparation for issuing a CHANGE, CROSSCHECK, or DELETE command.

Keywords

NAME   Precedes the name of a particular device. Not supported in Oracle9*i*.

Common keywords and clauses: *allocOperand, deviceSpecifier*.

ALTER DATABASE

```
ALTER DATABASE { MOUNT | OPEN [RESETLOGS] } |
    { MOUNT | OPEN [RESETLOGS] DATABASE };
```

Same as the ALTER DATABASE statement in SQL. You can use this command to mount and open a database from an RMAN prompt. You can include the command within a RUN command or by itself.

Keywords

MOUNT   Mounts the database without opening it.

OPEN   Opens the database.

RESETLOGS Resets the online redo logs to start at sequence number 1. If you specify the RMAN ALTER DATABASE command, the target database is automatically reset within the catalog. If you specify the SQL*Plus version of the command, you must execute the RMAN RESET DATABASE command in order to reset the target database within the catalog.

BACKUP

Oracle9i syntax:
```
BACKUP [ FULL | INCREMENTAL LEVEL [=] integer ]
[backupOperand [backupOperand ...]]
backupSpec [backupSpec]...
[PLUS ARCHIVELOG
[backupSpecOperand [backupSpecOperand ...]]];

backupOperand :=
{ FORMAT [=] 'format_string' [,'format_string' ...]
| CHANNEL [']channel_id[']
| CUMULATIVE
| MAXSETSIZE [=] integer [ K | M | G ]
| FILESPERSET [=] integer
| PARMS [=] 'channel_parms'
| POOL [=] integer
| TAG [=] [']tag_name[']
| keepOption
| SKIP { OFFLINE | READONLY | INACCESSIBLE }
| NOEXCLUDE
| PROXY [ONLY]
| VALIDATE
| FORCE
| DISKRATIO [=] integer
| NOT BACKED UP [SINCE TIME [=] 'date_string']
| NOCHECKSUM
| CHECK LOGICAL
| COPIES [=] integer
| DEVICE TYPE deviceSpecifier
}

backupSpec :=
[(]
```

```
{ BACKUPSET
  { { ALL | completedTimeSpec }
  | primary_key [,primary_key ...]
  }
| DATAFILE datafileSpec [, datafileSpec ...]
| DATAFILECOPY 'filename' [,'filename' ...]
| DATAFILECOPY TAG [=] [']tag_name['] [,
    [']tag_name['] ...]
| TABLESPACE [']tablespace_name[']
    [, [']tablespace_name['] ...]
| DATABASE
| archivelogRecordSpecifier
| CURRENT CONTROLFILE [FOR STANDBY]
| CONTROLFILECOPY 'filename'
}
[backupSpecOperand [backupSpecOperand]...]
[)]

backupSpecOperand :=
{ FORMAT [=] 'format_string' [, 'format_string' ...]
| CHANNEL [']channel_id[']
| MAXSETSIZE [=] integer [ K | M | G ]
| FILESPERSET [=] integer
| PARMS [=]'channel_parms'
| POOL [=] integer
| TAG [=] [']tag_name[']
| keepOption
| SKIP { OFFLINE | READONLY | INACCESSIBLE }
| NOEXCLUDE
| FORCE
| DISKRATIO [=] integer
| NOT BACKED UP [SINCE TIME [=] 'date_string']
| INCLUDE CURRENT CONTROLFILE [FOR STANDBY]
| DELETE [ALL] INPUT
}
```

Oracle8i syntax:
```
BACKUP [ FULL | INCREMENTAL LEVEL [=] integer ]
[backupOperand [backupOperand]...]
backupSpec [backupSpec];

backupOperand :=
{ FORMAT [=] 'format_string' [, 'format_string' ...]
| CHANNEL [']channel_id[']
| CUMULATIVE
| FILESPERSET [=] integer
| PARMS [=] 'channel_parms'
| POOL [=] integer
| TAG [=] [']tag_name[']
| keepOption
| SKIP { OFFLINE | READONLY | INACCESSIBLE }
| PROXY [ONLY]
| DISKRATIO [=] integer
```

```
| NOCHECKSUM
| CHECK LOGICAL
| SETSIZE [=] integer
}

backupSpec :=
[(]
{ DATAFILE datafileSpec [, datafileSpec ...]
| DATAFILECOPY 'filename' [, 'filename' ...]
| DATAFILECOPY TAG [=] [']tag_name['] [,\
  [']tag_name['] ...]
| TABLESPACE [']tablespace_name['] [,\
  [']tablespace_name['] ...]
| DATABASE
| archivelogRecordSpecifier
| CURRENT CONTROLFILE
| CONTROLFILECOPY 'filename'
}
[backupSpecOperand [backupSpecOperand]...]
[)]

backupSpecOperand :=
{ FORMAT [=] 'format_string' [,'format_string' ...]
| CHANNEL [']channel_id[']
| FILESPERSET [=] integer
| PARMS [=] 'channel_parms'
| POOL [=] integer
| TAG [=] [']tag_name[']
| SKIP { OFFLINE | READONLY | INACCESSIBLE }
| DISKRATIO [=] integer
| INCLUDE CURRENT CONTROLFILE
| DELETE INPUT
| SETSIZE [=] integer
}
```

Creates a backup of a database of a physical component (e.g., a database file), an archived redo log file, or a logical component (e.g., a tablespace). For Oracle8*i*, you can execute this command only from within the RUN command.

Keywords

INCREMENTAL

> The integer that follows this keyword indicates the level of incremental backup. You can specify a level from 0 (which indicates a full backup) to 4. The incremental backup will back up all the changes made since the last backup made at the same level. For instance, doing a level 2 incremental backup will back up all the changes made since the last level 2, level 1, or level 0 backup and will include any and all changes made in level 3 backups since that last level 2 backup.

CURRENT CONTROLFILE [FOR STANDBY]

> Indicates that the current control file should also be backed up. If you include the FOR STANDBY option, a control file that can be used for the creation of a standby database will be created.

CUMULATIVE
Causes RMAN to back up only those blocks that have changed since the most recent backup taken at a prior level.

MAXSETSIZE integer
Limits a backup set to a specified size. You may specify the size in bytes, kilobytes (K), megabytes (M), or gigabytes (G).

FILESPERSET integer
Limits a backup set to the specified number of files.

PARMS 'channel_parms'
Sends operating system–specific information to the operating system layer each time a backup piece is created.

POOL Specifies a media management pool where the backup should be kept. This option is used in conjunction with the MML software.

SKIP Skips datafiles that are read-only, offline, or inaccessible.

NOEXCLUDE
Overrides default settings that have previously been established with CONFIGURE EXCLUDE.

PROXY Allows the media manager to make decisions on when and how data is to be transferred.

VALIDATE Validates files for physical and logical errors.

FORCE Allows the backup to ignore optimization settings specified with CONFIGURE.

DISKRATIO integer
Load-balances the backup across disks.

NOT BACKED UP [SINCE TIME 'date_string']
Backs up those files that have not been backed up or have not been backed up since a specific date and time.

NO CHECKSUM
Prevents block checksums from being computed.

COPIES integer
Specifies the number of backup copies to be created. The default is 1.

DELETE Deletes the backup set, datafile copy, or archived log input file upon successful completion of the backup.

Common keywords and clauses: *archivelogRecordSpecifier, channel_id, datafileSpec, deviceSpecifier, filename, format_string, keepOption*, PARMS, *primary_key, tablespace_name, tag_name*.

BLOCKRECOVER

```
BLOCKRECOVER
[DEVICE TYPE deviceSpecifier [, deviceSpecifier]...]
blockSpec [blockSpec]... [blockOption [blockOption]...];

blockSpec :=
{ DATAFILE datafileSpec BLOCK integer [, integer ...]
| TABLESPACE tablespace_name DBA integer [, integer ...]
| CORRUPTION LIST
}
```

```
blockOption :=
{ FROM { BACKUPSET | DATAFILECOPY }
| FROM TAG [=] [']tag_name[']
| RESTORE until
}
```

Allows for a fine-grained level of recovery by specifying a small list of corrupt blocks rather than an entire datafile. This option is available only for Oracle9i.

Keywords

BLOCK integer
> Specifies the block(s) that require recovery.

DBA
> Specifies the data block address of a block to recover.

CORRUPTION LIST
> Recovers blocks that are listed in the dictionary views V$COPY_CORRUPTION and V$BACKUP_CORRUPTION.

FROM
> Specifies that restoration should be from either a backup set or a datafile copy.

FROM TAG tag_name
> Specifies the backup set that needs to be restored and from which you want to perform block-level recovery.

RESTORE until
> Specifies that backup sets created before a given time are to be restored

Common keywords and clauses: *datafileSpec, deviceSpecifier, tablespace_name, tag_ name, until.*

CATALOG

```
CATALOG { CONTROLFILECOPY | DATAFILECOPY | ARCHIVELOG }
    'filename' [, 'filename' ...]
[TAG [=] [']tag_name['] | LEVEL [=] integer ]
[ TAG [=] [']tag_name['] | LEVEL [=] integer ]...;
```

Adds information pertaining to user-managed COPY commands to the recovery catalog. Use this command if a COPY was performed before a connection to the recovery catalog was established.

Keywords

CONTROLFILECOPY 'filename'
> Specifies the filename of the copied control file that should be added to the recovery catalog.

DATEFILECOPY 'filename'
> Specifies the filename of the copied datafile that should be added to the recovery catalog.

ARCHIVELOG 'filename'
> Specifies the filename of an archived redo log file that should be added to the recovery catalog.

TAG tag_name

Specifies a tag name that will be assigned to the file within the recovery catalog.

LEVEL integer

Specifies that the file copy should be recorded within the recovery catalog with the specified increment level.

Common keywords and clauses: *filename, tag_name*.

CHANGE

Oracle9*i* syntax:
```
CHANGE
    { { BACKUP | COPY } [OF listObjList]
      [mntQualifer [mntQualifer]...}
    | recordSpec
      [DEVICE TYPE deviceSpecifier [, deviceSpecifier]...]
    }
    { AVAILABLE | UNAVAILABLE | UNCATALOG | keepOption }
    [DEVICE TYPE deviceSpecifier [, deviceSpecifier]...];
```
Oracle8*i* syntax:
```
CHANGE
    { ARCHIVELOG
        { primary_key [, primary_key...]
        | 'filename' [,'filename' ...] }
    | archivelogRecordSpecifier
    | BACKUPPIECE { 'media_handle' [,'media_handle' ...]
                  | primary_key [, primary_key ...]
                  | TAG [=] [']tag_name['] }
    | BACKUPSET primary_key [, primary_key ...]
    | { CONTROLFILECOPY | DATAFILECOPY }
      { primary_key [, primary_key ...]
      | 'filename' [,'filename' ...]
      | TAG [=] [']tag_name['] [, [']tag_name ['] ... ] }
    | PROXY { 'media_handle' [,'media_handle' ...]
           | primary_key [, primary_key ...]
           | TAG [=] [']tag_name['] }
    }
    { DELETE | AVAILABLE | UNAVAILABLE
    | UNCATAOG | CROSSCHECK };
```

Enables you to perform maintenance on backup sets or their associated backup pieces. Such maintenance might include changing the status repository records for backup sets and backup pieces or deleting backup pieces from disk or tape media; the latter would also remove the associated records from the target database's control files and from the optional recovery catalog

Keywords

AVAILABLE

Changes the status of backups or copies to AVAILABLE.

UNAVAILABLE

Changes the status of backups or copies to UNAVAILABLE. Backups marked as UNAVAILABLE are not used by RMAN. Therefore, a subsequent recovery operation will look for a prior available backup.

UNCATALOG

Deletes records associated with datafile copies and archived redo log files from the catalog and marks that information as DELETED in the target database's control file.

Common keywords and clauses: *archivelogRecordSpecifier*, *filename*, *listObjList*, *media_handle*, *mntQualifier*, *primary_key*, *recordSpec*, *tag_name*.

CONFIGURE

```
CONFIGURE
{ configureDevice
| configureBackup
| { AUXNAME FOR DATAFILE datafileSpec
  | SNAPSHOT CONTROLFILE NAME
  }
  { TO 'filename' | CLEAR }
| configureCtlfile
};

configureDevice :=
{ DEFAULT DEVICE TYPE { TO deviceSpecifier | CLEAR }
| DEVICE TYPE deviceSpecifier
  { PARALLELISM integer | CLEAR }
| [AUXILIARY] CHANNEL [integer]
  DEVICE TYPE deviceSpecifier { allocOperand | CLEAR }
}

configureBackup :=
{ RETENTION POLICY { TO { RECOVERY WINDOW OF integer DAYS
                        | REDUNDANCY [=] integer
                        | NONE
                        }
                   | CLEAR
                   }
| MAXSETSIZE { TO { integer [ K | M | G ]
                  | UNLIMITED
                  }
            | CLEAR
            }
| { ARCHIVELOG | DATAFILE }
  BACKUP COPIES FOR DEVICE TYPE deviceSpecifier
  { TO integer | CLEAR }
| BACKUP OPTIMIZATION { ON | OFF | CLEAR }
| EXCLUDE FOR TABLESPACE tablespace_name [CLEAR]
}

configureCtlfile :=
CONTROLFILE AUTOBACKUP
{ ON
| OFF
| CLEAR
| FORMAT FOR DEVICE TYPE
    deviceSpecifier { TO 'format_string' | CLEAR }
}
```

Sets configuration values that persist for an RMAN session. This command is valid only for Oracle9i.

Keywords

SNAPSHOT CONTROLFILE NAME
> Defines the name and path of the snapshot control file. Default is platform-specific. In Unix, the default is *$ORACLE_ HOME/dbs*.

DEFAULT DEVICE TYPE
> Specifies the default media type as disk or tape.

PARALLELISM integer
> Establishes the number of automatic channels for the device. Default is 1.

RETENTION POLICY
> Defines a retention policy whereby RMAN flags backup sets as obsolete so that they can subsequently be manually deleted.

RECOVERY WINDOW OF
> Defines a recovery window based on SYSDATE minus a specified number of days. Backups taken prior to the computed date are marked as obsolete.

REDUNDANCY
> Defines the redundant number of backups or copies that RMAN should not consider as obsolete. Default is 1.

MAXSETSIZE integer
> Defines the maximum size of a backup piece for each channel in bytes, kilobytes (K), megabytes (M), or gigabytes (G). Default is UNLIMITED.

CONTROLFILE AUTOBACKUP
> Specifies whether autobackup of the control file is enabled. Default is OFF.

FORMAT FOR DEVICE TYPE
> Defines the filename and location for the control file. Default is %F.

CLEAR
> Reestablishes the default value.

Common keywords and clauses: *allocOperand, datafileSpec, deviceSpecifier, filename, format_string, tablespace_name*.

CONNECT

```
{ CONNECT TARGET | CATALOG | AUXILIARY [connectStringSpec] [;]
| { CONNECT CATALOG | CONNECT AUXILIARY } connectStringSpec [;]
}
```

Establishes a connection to a particular database, recovery catalog, or auxiliary database from within RMAN.

Keywords

TARGET   Specifies a connection to a target database.

CATALOG   Specifies a connection to a recovery catalog.

AUXILIARY   Specifies a connection to an auxiliary database.

Common keywords and clauses: *connectStringSpec*.

COPY

```
COPY [copyOption [copyOption]...]
{ copyInputfile TO
  { AUXNAME | 'filename' [copyOption [copyOption]...] }
  [, copy_inputfile TO
   { AUXNAME | 'filename' [copyOption [copyOption]...] }
  ]...
| (copyInputfile TO
   { AUXNAME | 'filename' [copyOption [copyOption]...] }
  )
  [(copy_inputfile TO
    { AUXNAME | 'filename' [copyOption [copyOption]...] }
   )
  ]...
};
```

Oracle9i syntax:
```
copyOption :=
{ TAG [=] [']tag_name[']
| LEVEL [=] integer
| NOCHECKSUM
| CHECK LOGICAL
| keepOption
}

copyInputFile :=
{ DATAFILE datafileSpec
| DATAFILECOPY
  { 'filename' | TAG [=] [']tag_name['] }
| ARCHIVELOG 'filename'
| CURRENT CONTROLFILE [FOR STANDBY]
| CONTROLFILECOPY
  { 'filename' | TAG [=] [']tag_name['] }
}
```

Oracle8i syntax:
```
copyOption :=
{ TAG [=] [']tag_name[']
| LEVEL [=] integer
| NOCHECKSUM
| CHECK LOGICAL
}

copyInputFile :=
{ DATAFILE datafileSpec
| DATAFILECOPY
  { 'filename' | TAG [=] [']tag_name['] }
| ARCHIVELOG 'filename'
| CURRENT CONTROLFILE
| CONTROLFILECOPY
  { 'filename' | TAG [=] [']tag_name['] }
}
```

Creates image file copies of database files. For Oracle8i, you must execute this command from within the RUN command.

Keywords

AUXNAME
> Specifies that the result of the COPY command is an alternate name for a file that was previously defined through the SET command.

NO CHECKSUM
> Prevents block checksums from being computed.

Common keywords and clauses: *datafileSpec, filename, keepOption, tag_name*.

CREATE CATALOG

```
CREATE CATALOG [TABLESPACE [']tablespace_name['']][;]
```

Creates the required schema for a recovery catalog. You must be connected to the recovery catalog before executing this command.

Common keywords and clauses: *tablespace_name*.

CREATE SCRIPT

```
CREATE SCRIPT [']script_name[']
{
   { backupCommands
   | restoreCommands
   | maintenanceCommands
   | miscellaneousCommands
   }
   [ backupCommands
   | restoreCommands
   | maintenanceCommands
   | miscellaneousCommands
   ...
   ]
}

backupCommands :=
{ BACKUP
| COPY
}

restoreCommands :=
{ REPLICATE
| RESTORE
| RECOVER
| BLOCKRECOVER
| DUPLICATE
| SWITCH
}

maintenanceCommands :=
{ CATALOG
| CHANGE
| CONFIGURE
| CROSSCHECK
```

```
| DELETE
| VALIDATE
| REPORT
| DELETE
| SHOW
}

miscellaneousCommands :=
{ ALLOCATE
| ALTERDATABASE
| BEGINLINE
| DEBUG
| EXECUTESCRIPT
| HOST
| RELEASE
| RESYNC
| SEND
| SET
| SHUTDOWN
| SQL
| STARTUP
}
```

Creates a script, which is then stored in the recovery catalog.

CROSSCHECK

Oracle9i syntax:
```
CROSSCHECK
    { { BACKUP | COPY }
      [OF listObjList] [mntQualifer [mntQualifer]...]
    | recordSpec
      [DEVICE TYPE deviceSpecifier [, deviceSpecifier]...]
    };
```

Oracle8i syntax:
```
CROSSCHECK BACKUP
    [ OF listObjList ]
    [ checkOptions [ checkOptions...]]];
```

```
checkOptions :=
{ TAG [=] [']tag_name[']
| completedTimeSpec }
```

Determines whether a backup set and its related pieces still exist on media. If a backup piece exists in the location recorded in the control file of the target database or in the optional recovery catalog, its status is marked as AVAILABLE. If it is not at the specified location, it is marked as EXPIRED.

Common keywords and clauses: *completedTimeSpec*, *listObjList*, *mntQualifier*, *tag_name*.

DELETE

Oracle9*i* syntax:
```
DELETE [NOPROMPT]
   { [EXPIRED]
     { { BACKUP | COPY }
        [OF listObjList] [mntQualifer [mntQualifer]...]
     | recordSpec
       [DEVICE TYPE deviceSpecifier [, deviceSpecifier]...]
     }
   | OBSOLETE [obsoleteOpersList]
     [DEVICE TYPE [deviceSpecifier [, deviceSpecifier]...]
   };
```

Oracle8*i* syntax:
```
DELETE EXPIRED BACKUP
   [ OF listObjList ]
   [ deleteOptions [ deleteOptions...]]];

deleteOptions :=
   { TAG [=] [']tag_name[']
   | completedTimeSpec }
```

For Oracle9*i*, deletes the physical files associated with backup sets and datafile copies, updates their status in the control file, and removes their information from the optional recovery catalog (if one is used).

In Oracle8*i* and Oracle9*i*, backups are flagged as EXPIRED if they cannot be found at their recorded location. Deletion of EXPIRED backups removes their information from the control file and from the optional recovery catalog (if one is used).

Keywords

NOPROMPT Deletes the specified files without confirmation.

EXPIRED Deletes files that have been marked as EXPIRED in the catalog.

OBSOLETE Deletes files that are no longer needed for recovery.

Common keywords and clauses: *completedTimeSpec, listObjList, obsoleteOpersList, tag_name*.

DELETE SCRIPT

```
DELETE SCRIPT [']script_name['];
```

Deletes a script from the recovery catalog.

DROP CATALOG

```
DROP CATALOG;
```

Drops all the objects associated with a recovery catalog.

DUPLICATE

Oracle9*i* syntax:
```
DUPLICATE TARGET DATABASE
   { TO [']database_name[']
     [ [dupOptionList] [dupOptionList ...] ]
   | FOR STANDBY [ [dupsbyOptionList]
        [dupOptionList ...] ]
   };

dupOptionList :=
{ LOGFILE logSpec [, logSpec]...
| NOFILENAMECHECK
| SKIP READONLY
| DEVICE TYPE deviceSpecifier [, deviceSpecifier ...]
| PFILE [=] [']filename[']
}

logSpec :=
{ 'filename' [SIZE integer [ K | M ] [REUSE]]
| GROUP integer ('filename' [, 'filename' ...])
   [SIZE integer [ K | M ] [REUSE]] }

dupsbyOptionList :=
{ DORECOVER | NOFILENAMECHECK }
```

Oracle8*i* syntax:
```
DUPLICATE TARGET DATABASE TO [']database_name[']
   [ LOGFILE logSpec [, logSpec ...]]
   [ NOFILENAMECHECK ]
   [ SKIP READONLY ];

logSpec :=
   { 'filename' [SIZE integer [ K | M ] [REUSE]]
   | GROUP integer ('filename' [, 'filename' ...])
      [SIZE integer [ K | M ] [REUSE]] }
```

Creates a duplicate database, or a standby database, from the backups of a target database. For Oracle8*i*, you must execute this command from within the RUN command.

Keywords

NOFILENAMECHECK

Causes RMAN not to check to see if the target database filenames are the same as those in the duplicate database. Use this option only when duplicating a database to a different host, in which case it is acceptable for the directory names and the filenames to be the same.

PFILE

Specifies the location of the parameter file for the duplicated database. RMAN uses the parameter file at this location, which you must have previously created, to start the duplicated database. You must specify this option if the location of the parameter file is not in the default location (*$ORACLE_HOME/dbs*).

DORECOVER
> Causes RMAN to recover the standby database after creating it. Archived redo logs will be applied as necessary.

Common keywords and clauses: *deviceSpecifier, filename*.

EXECUTE SCRIPT

```
EXECUTE SCRIPT [']script_name['];
```

Executes a script stored in the recovery catalog.

EXIT

```
EXIT[;]
```

Exits RMAN.

HOST

```
HOST [{' | "}command{' | "}];
```

Executes an operating system command. When the command completes, control is returned to the RMAN environment. Issuing the command with no command string opens up an operating system session.

LIST

Oracle9*i* syntax:
```
LIST
   { INCARNATION [OF DATABASE [[']database_name[']]]
   | [EXPIRED]
     { listObjectSpec
       [ mntQualifer | RECOVERABLE [until] ]
       [ mntQualifer | RECOVERABLE [until] ]...
     | recordSpec
     }
   };

listObjectSpec :=
{ BACKUP [OF listObjList] [listBackupOption]
| COPY [OF listObjList]
}

listBackupOption :=
[ [BY BACKUP] [VERBOSE]
| SUMMARY
| BY { BACKUP SUMMARY | FILE }
]
```

Oracle8*i* syntax:
```
LIST
   { INCARNATION [OF DATABASE [ [']database_name['] ] ]
   | { BACKUP | COPY } [OF listObjList]
     [ listOptions [listOptions ...] ]
   };
```

```
listOptions :=
{ { TAG [=] [']tag_name[']
  | completedTimeSpec }
| RECOVERABLE [ until ]
| DEVICE TYPE deviceSpecifier [, deviceSpecifier ...]
| LIKE 'string_pattern' }
```

Produces a list of backups or image copies.

Keywords

EXPIRED   Lists backup sets that have been marked as EXPIRED in the control files of the target database of the recovery catalog.

BY BACKUP   Lists backup sets and their contents.

VERBOSE   Lists detailed backup set information.

SUMMARY   Lists a one-line summary for backup sets or files and summary information for backup sets or files.

Common keywords and clauses: *completedTimeSpec, deviceSpecifier listObjList, mntQualifier, recordSpec, tag_name, until.*

PRINT SCRIPT

```
PRINT SCRIPT [']script_name['];
```

Displays a script stored in the recovery catalog.

QUIT

```
QUIT[;]
```

Exits RMAN.

RECOVER

Oracle9i syntax:
```
RECOVER [DEVICE TYPE deviceSpecifier
    [, deviceSpecifier]...]
recoverObject [recoverOptionList];

recoverObject :=
{ DATABASE
  [ until
  | [until] SKIP [FOREVER] TABLESPACE
    [']tablespace_name['] [, [']tablespace_name['] ...]
  ]
| TABLESPACE [']tablespace_name[']
  [, [']tablespace_name['] ...]
| DATAFILE datafileSpec [, datafileSpec ...]
}

recoverOptionList :=
{ DELETE ARCHIVELOG
| CHECK READONLY
```

```
| NOREDO
| CHECK LOGICAL
| { FROM TAG | ARCHIVELOG TAG } [=] [']tag_name[']
}
[, { DELETE ARCHIVELOG
   | CHECK READONLY
   | NOREDO
   | CHECK LOGICAL
   | { FROM TAG | ARCHIVELOG TAG } [=] [']tag_name[']
   }
]...
```

Oracle8i syntax:
```
RECOVER recoverObject [recoverOptionList];

recoverOptionList :=
{ DELETE ARCHIVELOG
| CHECK READONLY
| NOREDO
| CHECK LOGICAL
}
[, { DELETE ARCHIVELOG
   | CHECK READONLY
   | NOREDO
   | CHECK LOGICAL
   }
] ...
```

Recovers a database or one of its physical components. This command uses either incremental backups, if available, or archived redo log files to recover the datafiles. For Oracle8i, you must execute this command from within the RUN command.

Keywords

DELETE ARCHIVELOG
> Removes archived redo log files that are no longer necessary.

CHECK READONLY
> Excludes read-only tablespaces from the recovery process if their datafiles are current.

NOREDO
> Forces the recovery to be performed using only incremental backups. No archived redo log files are applied. This option is valid when recovering a database operating in NOARCHIVELOG mode.

CHECK LOGICAL
> Checks database for logical corruption and logs results in *alert.log* and server session trace files.

Common keywords and clauses: *datafileSpec, deviceSpecifier, tablespace_name, tag_name, until.*

REGISTER

```
REGISTER DATABASE;
```

Registers a target database with a repository catalog. You must connect to the catalog and to the target that you wish to register before issuing this command.

RELEASE CHANNEL

```
RELEASE CHANNEL [']channel_id['];
```

Releases a channel that has been allocated for I/O purposes. Once allocated, channels remain open until the job has finished execution or until they have specifically been released. You can use this command to release a specified channel while RMAN maintains a connection to the target database. For Oracle8*i*, you must execute this command from within the RUN command.

Using this command without specifying a *channel_id* releases the maintenance channel created with the ALLOCATE CHANNEL FOR MAINTENANCE command.

Common keywords and clauses: *channel_id*.

REPLACE SCRIPT

```
REPLACE SCRIPT [']script_name[']
{
 { backupCommands
 | restoreCommands
 | maintenanceCommands
 | miscellaneousCommands
 }
 [ backupCommands
 | restoreCommands
 | maintenanceCommands
 | miscellaneousCommands
 ]...
}
```

Replaces an existing script in the recovery catalog. If a script with the specified *script_name* does not exist, it will be created.

The commands indicated in the following syntax are listed in the earlier entry for the CREATE SCRIPT command.

REPLICATE

```
REPLICATE CONTROLFILE FROM 'filename';
```

Replicates control files to those locations specified by the CONTROL_FILES initialization parameter for the target database. You must execute this command from within the RUN command.

Common keywords and clauses: *filename*.

REPORT

Oracle9i syntax:
```
REPORT
{ { NEED BACKUP [ { INCREMENTAL | DAYS } [=] integer
                 | REDUNDANCY [=] integer
                 | RECOVERY WINDOW OF integer DAYS
             } ]
  | UNRECOVERABLE
  }
  reportObject
| SCHEMA [atClause]
| OBSOLETE [obsoleteOpersList]
}
[ DEVICE TYPE deviceSpecifier [, deviceSpecifier ...]];

reportObject :=
[ DATAFILE datafileSpec [, datafileSpec]...
| TABLESPACE [']tablespace_name[']
  [, [']tablespace_name['] ...]
| DATABASE [SKIP TABLESPACE
    [']tablespace_name['] [, [']tablespace_name[']]...]
]

atClause :=
{ AT TIME [=] 'date_string'
| AT SCN [=] integer
| AT SEQUENCE [=] integer THREAD [=] integer
}
```

Oracle8i syntax:
```
REPORT
{ { NEED BACKUP [ { INCREMENTAL | DAYS } [=] integer
                 | REDUNDANCY [=] integer ]
  | UNRECOVERABLE
  }
  reportObject
| SCHEMA [atClause]
| OBSOLETE [obsoleteOpersList]
}

reportObject :=
[ DATAFILE datafileSpec [, datafileSpec]...
| TABLESPACE [']tablespace_name[']
  [, [']tablespace_name['] ...]
| DATABASE [SKIP TABLESPACE
    [']tablespace_name['] [, [']tablespace_name[']]...]
]

atClause :=
{ AT TIME [=] 'date_string'
| AT SCN [=] integer
| AT LOGSEQ [=] integer THREAD [=] integer
}
```

Provides detailed reports on database backup activity. These reports can provide information on backups that are required for restoration, that require a specified number of incremental backups for restoration, or that may be considered for deletion.

You can also use this command to display datafiles that require the application of a specified number of days worth of archived redo log files in order to recover.

Keywords
NEED BACKUP
> Reports on datafiles that require a backup based on a redundancy factor, incremental level, or recovery window.

UNRECOVERABLE
> Reports on all unrecoverable datafiles.

SCHEMA [atClause]
> Reports on tablespaces and datafiles at a specific point in time.

OBSOLETE [obsoleteOpersList]
> Displays backups and copies that are no longer required and therefore can be removed.

Common keywords and clauses: *datafileSpec, deviceSpecifier, obsoleteOpersList, tablespace_name.*

RESET DATABASE

RESET DATABASE [TO INCARNATION *incarnation_key*];

Creates a new incarnation of the target database, or resets the target database to a previous incarnation within the recovery catalog. This command is needed only when the target database has been opened with the RESET_LOGS option of the SQL ALTER DATABASE statement. If you use the RMAN ALTER DATABASE statement to reset logs, the target database is automatically reset within the catalog.

Keyword
INCARNATION incarnation_key
> Specifies that an older incarnation of the database should be the current incarnation.

RESTORE

Oracle9i syntax:
```
RESTORE
[(] restoreObject [(restoreSpecOperand [restoreSpecOperand]...]) [)]
[(] restoreObject [(restoreSpecOperand [restoreSpecOperand]...]) [)]...
[ CHANNEL [']channel_id[']
| PARMS [=] 'channel_parms'
| FROM { BACKUPSET | DATAFILECOPY }
| until
| FROM TAG [=] [']tag_name[']
| VALIDATE
| CHECK LOGICAL
| CHECK READONLY
| DEVICE TYPE deviceSpecifier [, deviceSpecifier ...]
| FORCE
```

```
]
[ CHANNEL [']channel_id[']
| PARMS [=] 'channel_parms'
| FROM { BACKUPSET | DATAFILECOPY }
| until
| FROM TAG [=] [']tag_name[']
| VALIDATE
| CHECK LOGICAL
| CHECK READONLY
| DEVICE TYPE deviceSpecifier [, deviceSpecifier ...]
| FORCE
]...;

restoreObject :=
{ CONTROLFILE [TO 'filename']
| DATABASE
  [SKIP [FOREVER] TABLESPACE
  [']tablespace_name['] [, [']tablespace_name['] ...]
  ]
| DATAFILE datafileSpec [, datafileSpec ...]
| TABLESPACE [']tablespace_name[']
  [, [']tablespace_name[']]...
| archivelogRecordSpecifier
}

restoreSpecOperand :=
{ CHANNEL [']channel_id[']
| FROM TAG [=] [']tag_name[']
| PARMS [=] 'channel_parms'
| FROM
  { AUTOBACKUP
    [{ MAXSEQ | MAXDAYS } [=] integer]
    [{ MAXSEQ | MAXDAYS } [=] integer] ...]]
  | 'media_handle'
  }
}
```

Oracle8i syntax:
```
RESTORE
[(] restoreObject [(restoreSpecOperand [restoreSpecOperand]...) [)]]
[(] restoreObject [(restoreSpecOperand [restoreSpecOperand]...) [)]]...
[ CHANNEL [']channel_id[']
| PARMS [=] 'channel_parms'
| FROM { BACKUPSET | DATAFILECOPY }
| until
| FROM TAG [=] [']tag_name[']
| VALIDATE
| CHECK LOGICAL
| CHECK READONLY
]
[ CHANNEL [']channel_id[']
| PARMS [=] 'channel_parms'
| FROM { BACKUPSET | DATAFILECOPY }
| untilC
```

```
|  FROM TAG [=] [']tag_name[']
|  VALIDATE
|  CHECK LOGICAL
|  CHECK READONLY
]...;

restoreSpecOperand :=
{ CHANNEL [']channel_id[']
|  FROM TAG [=] [']tag_name[']
|  PARMS [=] 'channel_parms'
}
```

Restores an entire backup, or a component of a backup, to the target database. For Oracle8*i*, you must execute this command from within the RUN command.

Keywords

PARMS   Specifies parameters for a nondisk device that has been allocated.

VALIDATE   Used to ask RMAN to decide which backups need to be restored and validates their contents. This option does not result in any restore activity but is used to check existing backups.

CHECK LOGICAL
                 Checks database for logical corruption and logs results in *alert.log* and server session trace files.

CHECK READONLY
                 Normally, RECOVER does not restore read-only databases. This keyword causes RECOVER to check read-only datafiles to make sure they exist, are readable, and contain the proper checkpoints. If any of these conditions are not met, the datafile is recovered.

FORCE   Normally, RMAN recovers files only if their header information does not match the control file information. The FORCE keyword forces recovery of all datafiles.

SKIP   Instructs RMAN to skip a particular tablespace.

FROM AUTOBACKUP
                 Restores a control file from an autobackup. RMAN looks at the current day and then goes back through the number of days specified with the MAXDAYS keyword.

Common keywords and clauses: *archivelogRecordSpecifier, channel_id, media_handle, PARMS, tag_name, until.*

RESYNC

```
RESYNC CATALOG [FROM CONTROLFILECOPY 'filename'];
```

Resynchronizes the catalog with the control files of the target database. For example, you use RESYNC when the recovery catalog has been down for maintenance or other reasons and needs to be synchronized with the target database. In general, most RMAN operations synchronize the catalog with the target database. For Oracle8*i*, you must execute this command from within the RUN command.

Common keywords and clauses: *filename.*

RUN

```
RUN {
    RMAN_commands . . .
}
```

Executes a series of commands. With Oracle8*i*, most commands can only be executed within the punctuation (the braces, or {} characters) following the RUN command. In many cases, that requirement has been removed with Oracle9*i*. However, even with Oracle9*i*, a few commands still must be executed from within the braces of RUN:

ALLOCATE CHANNEL
EXECUTE SCRIPT
REPLICATE
SWITCH

SEND

```
SEND
[ DEVICE TYPE deviceSpecifier [, deviceSpecifier]...]
| CHANNEL [']channel_id['] [, [']channel_id['] ...]
]
'command' [PARMS [=] 'channel_parms'];
```

Sends vendor-specific commands to one or more channels when using a Media Management Layer. For Oracle8*i*, you must execute this command from within the RUN command.

Keywords

Common keywords and clauses: *channel_id, deviceSpecifier*, PARMS.

SET

Oracle9*i* syntax:
```
SET { setRmanOption [;] | setRunOption; }

setRmanOption :=
{ ECHO { ON | OFF }
| DBID [=] integer
| CONTROLFILE AUTOBACKUP FORMAT
  FOR DEVICE TYPE deviceSpecifier TO 'format_string' }

setRunOption :=
{ NEWNAME FOR DATAFILE datafileSpec TO { 'filename' | NEW }
| MAXCORRUPT FOR DATAFILE datafileSpec
  [, datafileSpec ...] TO integer
| ARCHIVELOG DESTINATION TO 'log_archive_dest'
| until
| BACKUP COPIES [=] integer
| COMMAND ID TO 'string'
| AUTOLOCATE { ON | OFF }
| CONTROLFILE AUTOBACKUP
  FORMAT FOR DEVICE TYPE deviceSpecifier TO
      'format_string'
}
```

Oracle8*i* syntax:

```
SET { setRmanOption [;] | setRunOption;}

setRmanOption :=
 {{ AUXNAME FOR DATAFILE datafileSpec TO { 'filename' | NULL }
    | DBID [=] integer
    | SNAPSHOT CONTROLFILE NAME TO 'filename'
    }
  | ECHO { ON | OFF }
  };

setRunOption :=
{ { NEWNAME FOR DATAFILE datafileSpec TO 'filename'
  | MAXCORRUPT FOR DATAFILE datafileSpec
      [, datafileSpec ...]
    TO integer
  | ARCHIVELOG DESTINATION TO 'log_archive_dest'
  | until
  | DUPLEX [=] { ON | OFF | integer }
  | COMMAND ID TO 'string'
  | AUTOLOCATE { ON | OFF }
  }
| LIMIT CHANNEL [']channel_id[']
  limitOptions [limitOptions ...]
}

limitOptions :=
{ KBYTES [=] integer
| READRATE [=] integer
| MAXOPENFILES [=] integer
}
```

Establishes values for settings for the current RMAN session.

Keywords

ECHO
> Controls whether RMAN commands are echoed in the message log. By default, commands entered at the prompt are not echoed, while script commands are.

DBID
> Specifies a unique 32-bit identification number that is created when an Oracle database is installed. Normally used only when not connected to a target database.

CONTROLFILE AUTOBACKUP FORMAT
> Overrides the default format for the name of the autobackup control file.

NEWNAME FOR DATAFILE
> Sets the default datafile name for all subsequent RESTORE or SWITCH commands for the existing RMAN session. With Oracle8*i*, this setting lasts only for the extent of the current RUN command.

MAXCORRUPT FOR DATAFILE
> Sets the limit for newly discovered physical block corruptions during a BACKUP or RESTORE command. If this number is exceeded, the job terminates. With Oracle8*i*, this setting lasts only for the extent of the current RUN command.

ARCHIVELOG DESTINATION

Overrides the default log destination file specified in the LOG_ARCHIVE_DEST_1 initialization parameter for all RESTORE and RECOVER operations in the session. With Oracle8*i*, this setting lasts only for the extent of the current RUN command.

BACKUP COPIES

Sets the number of copies of each backup piece during a database backup. The value can be an integer from 1 to 4.

COMMAND ID

Enters the specified string into the V$SESSION.CLIENT_INFO column to identify which server sessions relate to which RMAN channel. With Oracle8*i*, this setting lasts only for the extent of the current RUN command.

AUTOLOCATE

Tells RMAN to automatically locate which nodes of a Real Application Clusters database have the backups you want to restore. Without this setting, RMAN will try to restore each of the nodes.

AUXNAME FOR DATAFILE

Sets the name of the target database to the name of the auxiliary database for use with the DUPLICATE command or tablespace-point-in-time recovery.

SNAPSHOT CONTROLFILE NAME TO

Sets the snapshot control file name to a particular name.

DUPLEX

With Oracle8*i*, this setting lasts only for the extent of the current RUN command.

LIMIT CHANNEL

Sets the limits for any BACKUP or COPY command that uses this channel. The limits are size (KBYTES), maximum number of buffers per second (READRATE), or maximum number of open files for a BACKUP operation. With Oracle8*i*, this setting lasts only for the extent of the current RUN command.

Common keywords and clauses: *channel_id, datafileSpec, deviceSpecifier, filename, format_string, until.*

SHOW

```
SHOW
{ RETENTION POLICY
| [DEFAULT] DEVICE TYPE
| [AUXILIARY] CHANNEL [FOR DEVICE TYPE deviceSpecifier]
| MAXSETSIZE
| { DATAFILE | ARCHIVELOG } BACKUP COPIES
| BACKUP OPTIMIZATION
| SNAPSHOT CONTROLFILE NAME
| AUXNAME
| EXCLUDE
| CONTROLFILE AUTOBACKUP [FORMAT]
| ALL
};
```

Displays the current configuration settings. Valid only for Oracle9*i*.

Keywords

The keywords are described in the earlier CONFIGURE command entry.

Common keywords and clauses: *deviceSpecifier*.

SHUTDOWN

```
SHUTDOWN [ NORMAL | ABORT | IMMEDIATE | TRANSACTIONAL ][;]
```

Shuts down the target database. NORMAL is the default.

Keywords

ABORT

> Shuts down the database immediately and indicates crash recovery the next time the database is started.

IMMEDIATE

> Shuts down the database immediately.

TRANSACTIONAL

> Allows all clients to complete current transactions, prevents any new transactions from initiating, and disconnects users after all transactions have terminated. After this process, shuts down the database.

SPOOL

```
SPOOL LOG { OFF | TO filename } [APPEND][;]
```

Sends output from RMAN to the log file. Valid only for Oracle9*i*.

Common keywords and clauses: *filename*.

SQL

```
SQL {' | "}command{' | "};
```

Executes a SQL statement.

STARTUP

```
STARTUP
[ FORCE
| { NOMOUNT | MOUNT }
| DBA
| PFILE [=] [']filename[']
]
[ FORCE
| { NOMOUNT | MOUNT }
| DBA
| PFILE [=] [']filename[']
]... [;]
```

Starts a database from within RMAN, like the SQL statement STARTUP.

Keywords

FORCE If the database is open, forces a shutdown, then starts it up again.

MOUNT Starts the instance and mounts it without opening it.

NOMOUNT   Starts the instance and does not mount or open it.

DBA   Restricts access to users with RESTRICTED SESSION privilege.

PFILE   Specifies a particular initialization (*INIT.ORA*) file.

Common keywords and clauses: *filename*.

SWITCH

```
SWITCH
{ DATAFILE datafileSpec
  [ TO DATAFILECOPY { 'filename' | TAG [=] [']tag_name['] }]
| DATAFILE ALL
};
```

Specifies that a datafile copy is now the current datafile and must be run from within the RUN command. This command is analogous to the SQL ALTER DATABASE RENAME *filename* statement.

Common keywords and clauses: *filename*.

UPGRADE CATALOG

```
UPGRADE CATALOG [TABLESPACE [']tablespace_name[']] [;]
```

Upgrades a recovery catalog schema to a newer version that is required by the RMAN executable. You cannot use an RMAN binary against a catalog that was created with a lesser version. For example, you cannot use an Oracle 9.0.1 RMAN binary to connect to an Oracle 8.1.7 catalog.

Common keywords and clauses: *tablespace_name*.

VALIDATE

Oracle9*i* Syntax:
```
VALIDATE BACKUPSET primary_key [, primary_key ...]
[ CHECK LOGICAL
| DEVICE TYPE deviceSpecifier [, deviceSpecifier ...]
]
[ CHECK LOGICAL
| DEVICE TYPE deviceSpecifier [, deviceSpecifier ...]
]...;
```

Oracle8*i* Syntax:
```
VALIDATE BACKUPSET primary_key [, primary_key ...]
[ CHECK LOGICAL ];
```

Checks the integrity of a backup. RMAN examines all of the associated backup pieces to determine whether their contents can be restored, if necessary, and if they are free of physical corruption. For Oracle8*i*, you must execute this command from within the RUN command.

Keywords

CHECK LOGICAL
   Validates that there are no logical corruptions, such as corruption of an index entry.

Common keywords and clauses: *deviceSpecifier, primary_key*.

16

Enterprise Manager

Oracle Enterprise Manager (EM) is a graphical user interface console that allows you to manage Oracle databases. In addition, EM also provides a number of services used to help manage and monitor your database instances, including:

Discovery Wizard
Finds all active instances available to Enterprise Manager.

Job system
Allows you to schedule maintenance tasks or the running of SQL scripts. This system tracks the outcome of jobs and notifies you of their completion status or any intervening errors. A job can be implemented with any SQL or operating system commands.

Event system
Monitors target instances for events, such as outages or resource problems.

Alert system
Notifies you of the status of jobs or events through the Enterprise Manager Console, email, or your pager. EM gives you the option of disabling the alert system to prevent excessive messaging for planned events.

Security
Provides security implementation options for administrators, target databases, and objects.

System reporting
Reports on status, usage, and configuration of target systems, as well as on the contents of the Enterprise Manager repository.

This chapter provides an overview of this basic Oracle utility. For the most part, the screens used to navigate EM are easy to follow. Therefore, in this chapter, we don't attempt to show all the EM screens and describe the details of their interactions. Instead, we will focus on the architecture and structure of the EM environment. For detailed information on individual screens and options, see the Oracle documentation.

Architecture

Enterprise Manager, starting with Version 2.0 (which coincided with Oracle8*i*) can be run in either a three-tier or a two-tier architectural configuration.

Three-Tier Configuration

When Enterprise Manager is run on a three-tier architecture, the components are:

Enterprise Manager Console
Can be run from a browser, personal computer, or Unix workstation. The Console is run from a browser on Windows machines and accesses the Enterprise Manager home page, which is available at the URL:

http://<webserver hostname>.<port_number>

with the default port number of 3339. Note that not all of the functionality of the Enterprise Manager Console is available from a browser.

Oracle Management Server
Runs on a middle tier of machines and includes a repository. The Oracle Management Server is responsible for implementing the job system, event system, and groups. You can have multiple Oracle Management Server servers for redundancy and load balancing. The Oracle Management Server uses a repository, which is an Oracle database.

Intelligent Agents
Run on each database server managed by the Oracle Management Server, implement tasks as local jobs, and monitor the state and operations of the database instances on the server. Intelligent Agents operate asynchronously with the Oracle Management Server. For instance, if a job is scheduled from a client, the Oracle Management Server passes the job off to the Intelligent Agent for the target database. Even if there is a network interruption between the Oracle Management Server machine and the target database, the job will still run on the target server.

Jobs can be run on target nodes via Intelligent Agents through the use of Preferred Credentials. Preferred Credentials give Enterprise Manager privileges to operate management tasks on target nodes, without having the high level of privileges necessary for them to be granted to the individual users of Enterprise Manager.

With Oracle9*i*, Intelligent Agents are automatically restarted in the event of a failure.

Two-Tier Configuration

If you run Enterprise Manager on a two-tier architecture, you will have a version of the Enterprise Manager Console running standalone on a client machine with direct access to the database server. Although you can use Enterprise Manager to perform a variety of maintenance operations in a two-tier architecture, the job system, event system, and groups are not available without the Oracle Management Server (available only in the three-tier configuration).

The two-tier configuration does not require a repository, but some types of applications, such as the Change Manager, Expert, SQL Analyze, Index Tuning Wizard, and LogMiner Viewer, do require a standalone repository.

Running Enterprise Manager

To start the Enterprise Manager Console, enter the command:

```
oemapp console
```

on the machine that will be the Console or select it from the Programs listing on a Windows machine. You will be prompted for a username and password and will be asked whether you want to run the Console standalone or with the Oracle Management Server.

The default username and password for the master administrator is SYSMAN/ OEM_TEMP. You can create other username/password pairs for other users once you enter the Console.

If you are running the three-tier configuration, you also have to start the Oracle Management Server. Startup can be part of the boot sequence for the middle-tier server, or you can start the Management Server by invoking the OEMCTRL utility with the command:

```
oemctrl start oms
```

on the server on which the Management Server runs.

The OEMCTRL utility also provides the following commands:

oemctrl ping oms
> Checks to see if the Management Server is running

oemctrl status oms
> Returns the status for the Management Server

oemctrl stop oms
> Shuts down the Management Server

Enterprise Manager Interface

The Enterprise Manager Console provides an interface to the functionality of Enterprise Manager. A typical view of the Console for Oracle8i is shown in Figure 16-1.

Console Areas

There are four basic areas in the Console:

Toolbar
> Located at the top of the lefthand side of the window. Provides access to common functions for objects in the Navigator pane to its right. The six icons represent, from top to bottom, viewing Enterprise Manager reports, refreshing the Navigator view, creating a new object, creating a new object

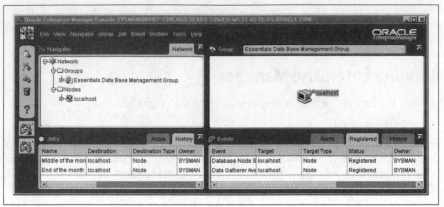

Figure 16-1. Enterprise Manager Console for Oracle8i

from an existing object, deleting an object, and displaying the master contents page of the help system. Not all of these choices are enabled at all times; display depends on the object selected in the Navigator.

Tool drawers

Located just below the toolbar. Used to launch different applications. Each drawer can contain several applications. These applications can include (if installed):

*SQL*Plus Worksheet*
An interface to SQL*Plus with an input window at the top and a results window at the bottom. You can have multiple SQL*Plus worksheets open at the same time.

SQL Scratchpad
New with Oracle9i; allows you to enter SQL code in the top window and see the results in the bottom window. This tool can also show a graphical version of EXPLAIN PLAN output and statistics on the return and execution of a SQL statement.

Oracle Enterprise Security Manager
Comes with Oracle Advanced Security.

Oracle Text
Helps to manage and search text in an Oracle database.

Oracle Spatial Index Advisor
Used with the Oracle Spatial option.

Oracle Directory Manager
Used with the Oracle Internet Directory.

Oracle Forms Server Manager
Manages and monitors the various servers that work with Oracle Forms.

Oracle Policy Manager
Administers label security.

Oracle Net Manager
> Configures and manages Oracle Net Services.

Oracle Data Guard Manager
> Implements and manages Data Guard, a high-availability configuration option.

Oracle LogMiner Viewer
> Provides an interface to use with LogMiner files for investigating database activity.

Navigator pane
> Located to the right of the toolbar and tool drawers. Presents an Explorer-like interface to objects and views in the Console. Right-click on a database object to bring up a list of actions you can perform on that object. You can also copy objects, when appropriate, by dragging them from one spot in the Navigator hierarchy and dropping them in another.

Detail pane
> Each leaf object selected in the Navigator brings up a detail pane on the right of the Console. The detail pane can be a property sheet or listing and can also be a tabbed page for additional information.

In addition, there is a series of menus along the top of the Enterprise Manager Console, including File, Navigator, Object, Event, Job, Tools, Configuration, and Help menus. Some of the menu choices for these menus may not be active at a particular time; display depends upon the object currently selected in the Navigator.

The version of Enterprise Manager that came with Oracle8*i* had a default view with four detail panes: the Navigator, Group, Event, and Job panes. Objects could be viewed in the Navigator pane by creating a split view, which created a tabbed page in that pane. With Oracle9*i*, this default view has been changed so that the Navigator pane is on the left, and each of these different areas can be included in the single detail pane on the right by selecting them in the Navigator hierarchy. The effect is a view similar to that presented by the DBA Studio feature of the prior version of Enterprise Manager.

Views

There are four basic ways you can view information in the Navigator pane:

Standard view
> This view is a hierarchical view, which is called Databases in the Navigator near the top of the pane. With this view, subobjects can be shown or hidden by clicking on the icon to the left of the parent object.

Group view
> This view, which is below the Databases hierarchical view in the Navigator, gives you the ability to organize collections of objects into groups and navigate through these groups. You can use groups to reduce the complexity of your environment or increase your productivity. For instance, you can run a job against a group, which will cause the job to run against all members of a group. You can also use groups to aggregate the display of status for all the

members of a group. You can add objects to a group by dragging and dropping them from the Navigator into the Group detail pane.

Job view

This view is the interface to the job system, which is used for running and monitoring maintenance jobs. The detail pane for the Job view is a tabbed page with a list of active jobs and a history page showing completed jobs and their status. You can check a log that provides details about the progress of a job from either page.

Event view

This view shows the events that have been registered for monitoring by Enterprise Manager. The detail pane for the Event view contains a tabbed page that can show alerts that have occurred and have not been cleared, a list of events that have been registered, and a history page that shows events that have occurred and been cleared.

Table 16-1 provides a list of the pages that appear in the detail pane for each type of folder for a database in the Navigator pane. If no tabbed pages are specified, the option displays a list of objects. Selecting an object brings up a property sheet for the object.

Table 16-1. Detail pane options

Folder	Option in Navigator	Tabbed pages
Instance	Configuration	General
		Memory
		Recovery
		Resource Managers
		Undo
	Stored Configurations (available only when using the Management Server)	
	Sessions	
	Resource Consumer Groups	
	Resource Plans	
Schemas	Tables	
	Indexes	
	Views	
	Synonyms	
	Sequences	
	Clusters	
	Source types	
	User-defined types	Array types
		Object types
		Table types
Security	Users	
	Roles	
	Profiles	

Table 16-1. Detail pane options (continued)

Folder	Option in Navigator	Tabbed pages
Storage	Control file	
	Tablespace	
	Datafile	General
		Storage
	Rollback segments	
	Redo logs	
	Archive logs	
Distributed	In-doubt transactions	
	Database links	
	Streams	Available only with Oracle9*i* Release 2
	Queue tables	
	Advanced replication	Topology
		Errors
		Transactions
		Schedule
		Configurations
		DBMS jobs
Warehouse	OLAP	Measure folders
		Cubes folders
		Dimensions folders
	Summaries	Dimensions
		Materialized view folders
		Materialized view logs folders
		Refresh group folders
Workspace	Version-enabled tables	
	Workspaces	
XML Database	Configuration	
	Resources	
	XML Schema Links	

In addition to these database objects, the Navigator pane can include entries for groups, listeners, nodes, and web servers.

Enterprise Manager Administration

The primary purpose of Enterprise Manager is to perform and monitor administrative tasks on an Oracle database. Enterprise Manager includes a number of wizards to help you manage a database. Enterprise Manager can provide reports on a database, monitor changes to the database, or search for database objects.

Enterprise Manager can define multiple administrative users. For each user, you can specify a variety of attributes, including what nodes, schemas, or objects they can access and manage and how and when to notify them with alerts.

Enterprise Manager comes with a standard set of reports, but you can also define your own custom reports. Reports can be accessed from an automatically created and maintained web site.

You can access the functionality of Recovery Manager (RMAN, covered in Chapter 15) through Enterprise Manager via property sheets and the Backup and Recovery Wizards.

Jobs

Enterprise Manager can handle the creation, scheduling, and management of jobs. A *job* is any operation that can be performed with SQL statements, operating system commands, or scripts.

Through the Enterprise Manager Console, you can create a job and schedule it for multiple sites. You can also create a job for servers on different platforms, because Enterprise Manager uses Tool Command Language (Tcl), a platform-neutral language, for its internal scripts.

Enterprise Manager comes with some predefined tasks, which mainly relate to database management. You can use these tasks in creating jobs, as well as SQL*Plus, operating system, or Tcl scripts.

The Oracle Management Server passes a specific job to a specific Intelligent Agent at a scheduled time. If the Intelligent Agent is not available, the Oracle Management Server continues to try to pass the job along until the agent comes back up.

Enterprise Manager also tracks the status of jobs, both during operation and after the operation completes.

Events

An *event* occurs as the result of an event test run by Enterprise Manager. Enterprise Manager comes with a number of predefined events, which can monitor conditions for the databases, the listeners, the HTTP servers, the Connection Manager, and each specific node.

The base Enterprise Manager product comes with a simple set of UpDown events, used to check to see if a database, listener, or node is available. You can add additional events with some of the expansion packs detailed in the later "Expansion Packs" section. You can also add your own unsolicited events; these are events that take place outside the scope of the Enterprise Manager system and specifically notify Enterprise Manager of their occurrence.

You can create your own events, which are then implemented by the Oracle Management Server. When you define an event, you define event tests and schedules for the event, as well as parameters and security settings for the event, which limit how administrators can access and modify it. If you create an event that detects some kind of failure, you can assign a "fixit" script that will run automatically and try to correct the failure.

When an event occurs, it modifies the status of the event. The four possible levels of status for an event are:

- Unknown, which means that the event test could not be run
- Critical
- Warning
- Error, which indicates that the event test did not successfully complete

When you define an event, you also specify what values returned from the event will result in the status of Critical or Warning.

The Event tabbed page in the detail pane contains pages for Alerts, History, and Registered events. You can call up the Event Viewer, which gives details on a selected event, in either the Alerts or History page. The Alerts and History pages mark events with flags to denote their status—a gray flag for Unknown, a yellow flag for Warning, a red flag for Critical, and a yellow hexagon with an exclamation point for Error.

Enterprise Manager also has an Event Handler, which was included in a pre-production version with Oracle8*i* and a full production version with Oracle9*i*. The Event Handler logs events and can automatically take actions based on the results of an event test. Filters on the Event Handler limit the events that are logged or responded to.

Wizards

A *wizard* is an automated tool that is used to perform specific tasks, with minimal input from the user. Enterprise Manager comes with the following wizards:

Analyze Wizard
Collects and manages statistics.

Backup and Recovery Management Wizards
Help to back up and restore databases and subsidiary entities, such as tablespaces, datafiles, and archive logs. These Wizards provide a wide range of functionality and act as an interface to RMAN, the Recovery Manager, covered in Chapter 15.

Create Table Wizard
Guides you through the creation of tables and columns.

Cube Wizard
Helps to build multidimensional data cubes.

Data Management Wizard
Performs imports, exports, and data loads.

Dimension Creation Wizard
Used to build dimensions for a data warehouse.

Resource Plan Wizard
Groups user sessions for creating resource groups.

Summary Advisor Wizard
    Provides advice on creating and dropping materialized views.

View Wizard
    Guides you through the creation of views.

Expansion Packs

Enterprise Manager can be extended by adding expansion packs to it. Oracle's expansion packs are an extra-charge option, designed to provide specific management capabilities for certain types of work.

With the version of Enterprise Manager that came with Oracle8*i*, the following applications were integrated with Enterprise Manager:

    Oracle Applications Manager
    Oracle Enterprise Security Manager
    Oracle8I *inter*Media Text Manager
    Oracle Parallel Server Manager
    Oracle Spatial Index Advisor
    Oracle Directory Manager
    Oracle Distributed Access Manager
    Oracle Developer Server Forms Manager

This version of Enterprise Manager also came with the DBA Management Pack, described in a later section, as standard. The functionality of most of these applications is also included in the standard version of Enterprise Manager that comes with Oracle9*i*.

Diagnostics Pack

This pack includes these applications:

Advanced Events
    A set of predefined events used to test for conditions like excessive resource use and performance degradation for the databases, listeners, nodes, and HTTP servers. There are even events to check to see if Microsoft SQL Server is running.

Performance Manager
    Creates graphs and charts to help monitor the performance of the database in real time.

Capacity Planner
    Uses information gathered by Performance Manager to predict future capacity needs.

TopSessions
    Displays the sessions using the most of a particular resource and detailed information about them.

Trace Data Viewer
    Views data collected by Oracle Trace.

With Oracle8*i*, there was a separate tool for managing Apache and Oracle *i*AS Version 1.0 web servers.

Tuning Pack

This pack includes these applications:

Expert
Helps with the initial configuration of an Oracle database and makes recommendations for modifications to the database to improve performance. Expert also generates scripts to implement these recommendations.

Index Tuning Wizard
Generates suggestions concerning tables that could use additional indexes and the scripts for implementing those recommendations.

SQL Analyze
Analyzes and compares optimization plans for SQL statements, as well as helps to improve the performance with hints.

Tablespace Map and Analysis
Displays information about tablespaces and an analysis that can detect potential space management problems.

Reorg Wizard
Can reorganize specific schema objects or tablespaces or repair migrated rows. This application is new as a standalone application with Oracle9*i*.

Outline Management
Helps to manage stored outlines. This application is new as a standalone application with Oracle9i.

Outline Editor
Allows easy editing of stored outlines. This application is new as a standalone application with Oracle9i.

Auto Analyze
Automatically maintains the statistics for an Oracle8*i* database. This application was not offered as of Oracle9*i*.

Change Management Pack

This pack is a set of applications used to track and implement changes in one or more databases. This pack contains Change Manager, which allows you to:

- Create a baseline for a database
- Compare two different sets of database definitions
- Synchronize two sets of database definitions
- Make quick changes to an object through a property sheet
- Make alterations to one or more objects in a database
- Propagate changes from one database to others
- Edit generated plans for any of these types of changes

Standard Management Pack

This pack is a subset of the applications in the other three packs, designed for use with smaller installations. The applications included in this pack are:

Performance Manager
Provides real-time, graphical monitoring of Oracle and hosts

Index Tuning Wizard
Proactively optimizes indexes

Create Baseline
Captures definitions of existing schema objects

Compare Database Objects
Compares two databases, two schemas, or two sets of object definitions

Advanced Events for Databases and Nodes
Provides a subset of Advanced Events

Management Pack for Oracle Applications

This pack contains applications designed specifically for managing Oracle Applications, including:

Performance Manager
Displays performance information from multiple instances of Oracle Applications

Capacity Planner
Uses historical data to predict future capacity requirements

Concurrent Processing Tuning Assistant
Analyzes batch job execution records and makes tuning suggestions

Oracle Applications Advanced Events
Defines events for Oracle Applications

Management Pack for SAP R/3

This pack contains applications designed specifically for managing SAP R/3, including:

Performance Manager
Can display performance information from multiple instances of Oracle Applications

Capacity Planner
Uses historical data to predict future capacity requirements

Oracle Applications Advanced Events
Defines events for SAP R/3

DBA Management Pack and DBA Studio

The DBA Management Pack was a group of standard applications included with Enterprise Manager in Oracle8*i*. These applications have been integrated with Enterprise Manager in Oracle9*i*.

DBA Studio was part of the DBA Management Pack available with the version of Enterprise Manager that was a part of Oracle8*i*. DBA Studio was a standalone interface for the following tasks that were a part of the DBA Management Pack:

- Instance management
- Schema management
- Security management
- Storage management
- Replication management
- JServer management
- Cache management
- SQL*Plus worksheet

and a number of wizards for backup, recovery, table and view creation, and analyze.

Prior to this version of Enterprise Manager, this functionality was provided by a variety of different tools. With Oracle9*i* Enterprise Manager, the functionality in DBA Studio is integrated into the core product.

OEMUTIL

OEMUTIL is a command-line utility, new with Oracle9*i*, that can be used to perform job- and event-related activities. The command-line interface can be submitted as part of a batch job.

Running OEMUTIL

To run a single command with OEMUTIL, use the command:

```
oemapp oemutil username/password@oms command parameters
```

where *oms* is the name of the server running the Oracle Management Server. All of the commands described in the next section will need the *username/ password@oms* prefix if they are run at the command line.

To run OEMUTIL with a list of commands, use the command:

```
oemapp oemutil –cmdfile commandfile
```

where *commandfile* is a file containing the necessary OEMUTIL commands, including login information.

OEMUTIL Commands

The commands for OEMUTIL are summarized in the following entries. Note that if you include whitespace or any special characters in any of these parameters, you will need to enclose the parameters in quotes, if you are entering the command from the command line.

changeCredentials

changeCredentials *EMusername targetname user password role*

Changes credentials for database targets in the Enterprise Manager repository.

Keywords

EMusername Enterprise Manager administrator whose credentials are to be changed.

targetName Database target for the change.

user Database user.

password Database password.

role Role associated with the database user: NORMAL, SYSDBA, or SYSOPER.

deregisterEvent

deregisterEvent *eventname owner targetname targettype*

Deregisters an event.

Keywords

eventname Name of the event to be submitted.

owner Owner of the event.

targetname Node or group against which the event is to be deregistered.

targettype Type of target to deregister event. Valid types are:

        oracle_sysman_database
        oracle_sysman_node
        oracle_sysman_listener
        oracle_sysman_cmanager
        oracle_sysman_ops
        oracle_sysman_webserver
        oracle_sysman_hotstandby

omsCredentials

omsCredentials *username/password*

Specifies the username and password for an Enterprise Manager user. This command is required when using a batch file.

registerEventFromLibrary

registerEventFromLibrary *eventname ownername targetname* [*admin*]

Registers an event defined in the Event Library.

Keywords

eventname Name of the event to be submitted.

ownername Owner of the event.

targetname Node or group against which the event is to be registered.

admin Optional name for the Enterprise Manager administrator to receive notifications from the job.

submitJob

submitJob *jobName nodeName osCommand osParameters*

Submits a job against a node immediately.

Keywords

jobName Name assigned to the job.

nodeName Target node or group. Uses one of the following forms:

    groupOwner:groupName
        You must specify the group name in quotes.

    oracle_sysman_group
        A literal following the group owner and group name.

osCommand Operating system command to run.

osParameters Parameters associated with the command.

submitJobFromLibrary

submitJobFromLibrary *jobname ownername targetname* [*admin*]

Submits a job that has been saved in a job library. This job will run as it is defined in the library, including the schedule specified.

Keywords

jobname Name of the job.

ownername Owner of the job.

targetname Target for the job; this can be a node or group name, as specified for submitJob.

admin Optional name for the Enterprise Manager administrator to receive notifications from the job.

17

Performance

Achieving optimal performance from your Oracle database is an art, not a science. Using the appropriate data structures, ensuring that there are adequate resources available, and leveraging the features of the Oracle database can help you to avoid bottlenecks that reduce the performance of your system.

This chapter provides an overview of some of the tools within an Oracle database that will help you understand how Oracle optimizes performance for its operations. Specifically, this chapter covers:

- SQL optimization, including types of optimizers and hints
- EXPLAIN PLAN, TKPROF, and AUTOTRACE, various Oracle utilities that help you to understand how SQL is being optimized
- UTLBSTAT, UTLESTAT, and Statspack, various statistical packages that help you to collect performance statistics and identify bottlenecks.

Of course, understanding the tools and syntax covered in this chapter is only the beginning; there is much more to achieving the highest possible performance. For more information, consult the Oracle documentation and some of the books available on Oracle internals and performance tuning. (See Appendix E for suggestions).

SQL Optimization

One of the great virtues of a relational database is its ability to access data without predefining the access paths to the data. When a SQL query is submitted to an Oracle database, Oracle must decide how to access the data. The process of making this decision is called *query optimization*, because Oracle looks for the optimal way to retrieve the data, using the execution path. The trick behind query optimization is to choose the most efficient way to get the data, because many different options may be available.

The query optimizer has to determine which execution path will be the fastest. When you submit a rather involved query, such as one involving many tables that must be joined together efficiently, or one that has complex selection criteria and multiple levels of sorting, the query optimizer has a very complex task.

Query optimizers are one of the keys to delivering optimal performance for SQL queries. Prior to Oracle7, Oracle had only a rule-based optimizer. A cost-based optimizer was introduced with Oracle7.

Rule-based Optimizer

The rule-based optimizer, as the name implies, uses a set of predefined rules to determine query optimization.

The rule-based optimizer uses the set of rules summarized in Table 17-1, in the order shown in the table, to select an execution path.

Table 17-1. Rule precedence for the rule-based optimizer

Rule	Meaning
Single row by ROWID	Use ROWID in the WHERE clause, or CURRENT OF CURSOR
Single row by cluster join	Use cluster key in the WHERE clause; query returns only one row
Single row by hash cluster key with a unique or primary key	Use all columns in hash cluster key in the WHERE clause; query returns only one row
Single row by unique or primary key	Use unique or primary key in the WHERE clause; query returns only single row
Clustered join	Use when all tables are in cluster and all columns in the cluster key are in the WHERE clause with equality condition
Hash cluster key	Use when all columns in hash cluster key are in the WHERE clause with equality condition
Indexed cluster key	Use when all columns In Indexed cluster key are in the WHERE clause with equality condition
Composite index	Use when all columns in composite index are in the WHERE clause with equality condition
Single-column index	Use when all columns in single-column index are in the WHERE clause with equality condition
Bounded range search on an indexed column	Use when indexed column is in the WHERE clause with bounded values specified
Unbounded range search on an indexed column	Use when indexed column is in the WHERE clause without bounded values specified
Sort merge join	Use when columns from join of tables are in the WHERE clause with equality condition
MAX or MIN on indexed column	Use MAX or MIN on an indexed column and when no WHERE or GROUP BY clause
ORDER BY on indexed column	Use a single-column index or the leading portion of a multicolumn index in the ORDER BY clause when there is a PRIMARY KEY or NOT NULL clause on at least one column to ensure a value for all rows
Full table scan	Scan whole table if no prior rules apply

The rule-based optimizer is better than a random optimization of SQL queries, but it does have some weaknesses. One weakness is the simplistic set of rules. In a complex database, a query can easily involve several tables, each with several indexes and complex selection conditions and ordering. This complexity means that there will be a lot of options, and the simple set of rules used by the rule-based optimizer might not make the best choice.

The rule-based optimizer decides which of the rules in the table apply to a query. It then uses the rule with the highest precedence in the list. But for a complex query, there may be several single-column indexes to choose from in the tables used. In this scenario, the rule-based optimizer looks to the syntax of the SQL statement to resolve the tie. The winning execution path is based on the order in which the tables occur in the SQL statement. This means that the same functional SQL statement might end up with two different execution paths, depending on table order.

Cost-based Optimizer

To improve the optimization of SQL statements, Oracle introduced the cost-based optimizer in Oracle7. As the name implies, the cost-based optimizer does more than simply look at a set of optimization rules. It selects the execution path that requires the least number of logical I/O operations and thus the lowest cost for the completion of the query. This approach avoids the potential problems discussed in the previous section.

Oracle8 and later versions will use the cost-based optimizer to identify the optimal execution plan if any statistics for any table or index are present.

Statistics

The cost of any particular portion of an execution plan depends on the composition of the target data structures. The cost-based optimizer uses statistics about the data (e.g., information about the size and uniqueness of data in tables and indexes) to create optimal execution plans.

The types of statistics used by the cost-based optimizer are shown in Table 17-2.

Table 17-2. Statistics used by cost-based analyzer

Entity	Type of statistic
Table	Number of rows
	Number of blocks
	Number of unused blocks
	Average available free space per block
	Number of chained rows
	Average row length
	Remote average row length
Column	Number of distinct values per column (cardinality)
	Remote cardinality
	Second lowest column value
	Second highest column value
	Column density factor
	Number of NULLs for the column
	Data distribution factor

Table 17-2. Statistics used by cost-based analyzer (continued)

Entity	Type of statistic
Index	Depth of index B*-tree structure
	Number of leaf blocks
	Number of distinct values
	Average number of leaf blocks per key
	Average number of data blocks per key
	Clustering factor
System	I/O performance and utilization (new in Oracle9*i*)
	CPU performance and utilization (new in Oracle9*i*)

Gathering statistics

Any cost-based optimization is a reflection of the validity of the statistics on which it is based. To ensure that the statistics in your Oracle database are valid, you should periodically collect these statistics.

Prior to Oracle8*i*, the ANALYZE command was used to collect statistics. Oracle8*i* introduced the DBMS_STATS package, which offers a number of advantages over ANALYZE, such as collecting statistics in parallel and collecting statistics for global and partitioned objects. For more information on this package, see Chapter 10.

When you collect statistics, you can either collect statistics for the complete database or a data structure or use a sampling method to estimate the statistics for the complete data structure based on a smaller portion of data.

In general, you should gather statistics whenever the amount or composition of data in the database changes significantly, such as after creating a new index or doing a data load. Updating statistics should be a part of a general maintenance routine. You can also specify that statistics are automatically gathered for a particular table with procedures from the DBMS_STATS package.

Stored statistics

The cost-based optimizer can select different execution plans based on different statistics. If you feel that the cost-based optimizer is working appropriately and you don't want new statistics to change execution plans, you can store the statistics for the database with the DBMS_STATS.EXPORT_SCHEMA_STATS procedure to save them before you update the statistics.

If the new set of statistics does not deliver the desired performance or better, you can use the DBMS_STATS.IMPORT_SCHEMA_STATS procedure to reimport the saved statistics.

You can also store multiple versions of statistics in a statistics table you specify.

Performance

Histograms

The cost-based optimizer assumes that the values for a column are evenly distributed. For instance, if there are two distinct values in a column, the cost-based optimizer assumes that each value applies to 50% of the entries in the column.

This assumption can be incorrect for columns with extreme data value skew and can result in the optimizer's making the wrong choice for an execution plan. You can create histograms to avoid this potential problem.

Introduced with Oracle8i, *histograms* give the optimizer a more detailed view of the distribution of data values in the column. You can create a histogram with procedures in the DBMS_STATS package. Histograms require some overhead, so you should not use them, by default, for all columns, but they can help to improve the accuracy of execution plans involving some columns with low selectivity.

Histograms were

Optimizer Modes

You can specify which optimizer to use and how to use the cost-based optimizer by selecting from the following optimizer modes:

RULE
> The rule-based optimizer is used.

CHOOSE
> If there are no statistics for any table in the query, the rule-based optimizer is used. If there are statistics for some of the tables in the query, the optimizer uses those statistics and guesses at the statistics for the rest of the tables.

ALL_ROWS
> The cost-based optimizer chooses the execution path that will return all the rows in the query the fastest. This mode is most appropriate for data warehousing queries.

FIRST_ROWS[(n)]
> The cost-based optimizer chooses the path that will return the first *n* rows that satisfy a query the fastest. The *n* portion of the keyword, introduced with Oracle9i, can have a value of 1, 10, 100, or 1000. This mode is most appropriate for OLTP type queries, where there may be user interaction after some rows are retrieved.

These modes can be set in various ways. You can set the initialization parameter OPTIMIZER_MODE. You can set the mode interactively, using the command:

```
ALTER SESSION SET OPTIMIZER_GOAL = optimizer_mode
```

Or you can specify a hint in an individual SQL statement, as explained in the next section.

Although you still have the choice of which optimizer mode to use, we recommend that you always use the cost-based optimizer. Although the cost-based optimizer got somewhat of a bad name in its initial releases, it has been significantly improved in the years since then. Not only is the cost-based optimizer better in theory and practice, but new Oracle features, such as materialized views, are considered in the cost-based optimizer, whereas the rule-based optimizer does not recognize them.

If your SQL uses certain features, such as querying a partitioned table, the cost-based optimizer will be used even if you have set the optimizer mode to RULE or if you have set the optimizer mode to CHOOSE and have no statistics. When Oracle invokes the cost-based optimizer in the absence of statistics, default statistics are used.

Hints

Hints can be used to direct the Oracle query optimizer to use a specific optimization technique for a query.

Hints are embedded as comments in a SQL query, with the following syntax:

    sql_action /*+ hint */

or

    sql_action --+ hint

where *sql_action* is a SELECT, INSERT, UPDATE, or DELETE statement. The hint can also include a text comment for documentation purposes. Any statement can have multiple hints. If a hint is incorrect or invalid, Oracle ignores the hint without causing an error.

The following sections describe hints in a variety of categories: optimizer mode hints, access path hints, query transformation hints, join hints, parallel execution hints, and miscellaneous hints.

Optimizer mode hints

You can specify any of the optimizer modes described in the earlier list (RULE, CHOOSE, ALL_ROWS, FIRST_ROWS) as hints.

Access path hints

The following hints direct the query optimizer to a specific type of access path, if available:

FULL(table)
:   Specifies a full table span for *table*.

ROWID(table)
:   Specifies a table scan by ROWID for *table*.

CLUSTER(table)
Specifies a cluster scan for *table*.

HASH(table)
Specifies a hash scan for *table*.

INDEX(table [index . . .])
Specifies using an index. If a single index is in the hint, that index is used. If multiple indexes are specified in the hint, the SQL optimizer determines the lowest cost for an index listed. If no indexes are listed, the SQL optimizer uses the index on the table with the lowest cost.

INDEX_ASC(table [index . .])
Specifies an index to be used in ascending order. The syntax is identical to that of the INDEX hint.

INDEX_COMBINE(table [index . . .])
Specifes the use of the bitmapped indexes listed. The syntax is identical to that of the INDEX hint.

INDEX_JOIN(table [index . . .])
Specifies using an index join for access. The syntax is identical to that of the INDEX hint. New with Oracle8*i*.

INDEX_DESC(table [index . . .])
Specifies an index to be used in descending order. The syntax is identical to that of the INDEX hint.

INDEX_FFS(table [index . . .])
Specifies a fast full index scan to be used instead of a table scan. The syntax is identical to that of the INDEX hint.

NO_INDEX(table [index . . .])
Explicitly disallows the use of the specified indexes. New with Oracle8*i*.

AND_EQUAL(table index index [index . . .])
Specifies using a merged index scan on the single-column indexes specified.

Query transformation hints

The following hints direct the optimizer to transform the submitted query:

USE_CONCAT
Forces an OR list to be transformed into a UNION ALL compound query.

NO_EXPAND
Prevents OR expansion for the query. New with Oracle8*i*.

REWRITE
Forces the use of materialized views. New with Oracle8*i*.

EXPAND_GSET_TO_UNION
Forces query using grouping sets to be transformed into a UNION ALL compound query. New with Oracle9*i*.

NOREWRITE
Prevents query rewrite for materialized views. New with Oracle8*i*.

MERGE(table)
Specifies merging a view with a query. Complex view merging must be enabled for this hint to operate.

NO_MERGE(table)
Disallows complex view merging.

STAR_TRANSFORMATION
Suggests, but does not force, a transformation of the query into a star query.

FACT(table)
Specifies that the table is used as the fact table in a star transformation. New with Oracle9i.

NO_FACT(table)
Specifies that the table should not be used as the fact table in a star transformation. New with Oracle9i.

Join hints

The following hints suggest a join order or a type of join operation:

ORDERED
Forces tables to be joined in the order they are listed in the FROM clause.

STAR
Forces a star query plan.

USE_NL(table [table . . .])
Forces the use of a nested loop join, with the specified table(s) as the inner table.

USE_MERGE(table [table . . .])
Forces the use of a sort merge join, with the specfied table(s) as the driver.

USE_HASH(table [table . . .])
Specifies the use of a hash join with the specified table.

DRIVING_SITE(table)
Forces the join to be performed at the site containing the specified table.

LEADING(table)
Specifies the table to be used as the first table in a join. New with Oracle9i.

HASH_AJ, MERGE_AJ, NL_AJ
Used in a NOT IN subquery to specify a hash, merge, or nested loop anti-join. The NL_AJ hint is new with Oracle9i.

HASH_SJ, MERGE_SJ, NL_SJ
Specifies a hash, merge, or nested loop semijoin. The NL_SJ hint is new with Oracle9i.

Parallel execution hints

The following hints control the use of parallel execution for data warehousing type queries:

PARALLEL(*table*, [*integer* | DEFAULT][,{*integer* | DEFAULT}])
> Specifies the degree of parallelism of the SQL operation on *table*. The first parameter specifies the degree of parallelism on the table; the second, optional parameter (new with Oracle 9*i*) specifies how the table is to be split between instances of the database in a Real Application Clusters implementation. The value DEFAULT indicates that the query should use the degree of parallelism set with the initialization parameter.

NOPARALLEL(*table*)
> Overrides any parallelism setting and prevenst parallel operations on *table*.

PQ_DISTRIBUTE(*table*[,] *outer_distribution, inner_distribution*)
> Specifies how rows of joined tables should be distributed between producer and consumer query servers. The *outer_distribution* and *inner_distribution* keyword pair can have six value combinations:

> Hash, Hash
> Broadcast, None
> None, Broadcast
> Partition, None
> None, Partition
> None, None

PARALLEL_INDEX(*table*, [*integer* | DEFAULT][,{*integer* | DEFAULT}])
> Specifies the number of concurrent servers that can be used for parallel index range scans. The keywords have the same meaning as the keywords for the PARALLEL hint.

NOPARALLEL_INDEX(*table*)
> Overrides any parallel setting and prevents parallel index scans.

Miscellaneous hints

The following hints cover other types of optimization choices:

APPEND
> Enables direct-path INSERTs if you are running in serial mode (i.e., you are not running Enterprise Edition).

NOAPPEND
> Disables direct-path INSERTs for the statement.

CACHE(*table*)
> Places *table* in the buffer cache at the most recently used end of the least recently used (LRU) list when a full table scan is performed, as for a small lookup table.

NOCACHE

Places *table* in the buffer cache at the least recently used end of the LRU list when a full table scan is performed. With Oracle9i Release 2, small tables are automatically cached.

UNNEST

Specifies that a subquery is merged with the parent query. This hint is new with Oracle9i.

NO_UNNEST

Turns off UNNEST for specific query blocks. This hint is new with Oracle9i.

PUSH_PRED(table)

Pushes a join predicate into a view. This hint was called PUSH_JOIN_PRED in Oracle8.

NO_PUSH_PRED(table)

Prevents pushing a join predicate into a view. This hint was called NO_PUSH_JOIN_PRED in Oracle8.

PUSH_SUBQ

Forces nonmerged subqueries to be evaluated at the earliest possible step in the optimization process. Appropriate if the subquery is inexpensive and limits the number of rows evaluated.

NO_PUSH_SUBQ

Forces nonmerged subqueries to be evaluated at the earliest possible step in the optimization process. New with Oracle9i.

ORDERED_PREDICATES

Forces optimizer to preserve the order of the predicates in the WHERE clause. This hint is specified in the WHERE clause. New with Oracle8i.

CURSOR_SHARING_EXACT

Disables the replacing of literals with bind variables. This type of optimization is enabled with the CURSOR_SHARING initialization parameter. New with Oracle9i.

DYNAMIC_SAMPLING([table] integer)

Determines selectivity and cardinality estimates more accurately. You can set the level of dynamic sampling from 0 to 10, for the statement or for an individual table in the statement. For more information on these levels, see the Oracle documentation. New with Oracle9i.

Stored Outlines and Plan Stability

The cost-based optimizer evaluates SQL statements based on the current cost of operations. The cost calculations are based on the known statistics about the database and its data.

You may decide that the optimizations for your SQL statements are appropriate and that you do not want them to change in the future. If so, you can create a stored outline, which uses hints to direct the optimization of the statement.

With a *stored outline*, changes in the composition of the database that might result in a different optimal execution path will not affect the optimization of the statement. A stored outline can ensure that all installations of a system use the same optimization. You might also create and use stored outlines before upgrading your Oracle system to ensure that the new version of the optimizer delivered at least equivalent performance.

Oracle refers to the use of stored outlines as *plan stability*.

Creating outlines

Outlines are automatically created for all SQL statements if the parameter CREATE_STORED_OUTLINE is set to TRUE.

You can create a stored outline for an individual statement by using the following syntax:

```
CREATE [OR REPLACE] [PUBLIC | PRIVATE] OUTLINE outline_name
    [FROM {PUBLIC | PRIVATE} source_outline]
    FOR CATEGORY category
    ON SQL_statement
```

The CATEGORY clause allows you to group outlines into specific categories. If no category is specified, the outlines are placed in a default category. PUBLIC outlines, the default, are available to all users who are part of the PUBLIC security group. PRIVATE outlines are described shortly.

Outlines can be created and edited with the DBMS_OUTLN and DBMS_OUTLIN_EDIT packages. (See Chapter 10 for more information on these packages.) You can also use Enterprise Manager to create and edit outlines with Oracle9i. Outlines are stored in tables in the SYS schema and are visible through the *_OUTLINES and *_OUTLINE_HINTS views. For more information on these views, see Chapter 6.

Using outlines

To use stored outlines, you must set the parameter USE_STORED_OUTLINES to TRUE. This parameter can be followed by a category name, which will cause Oracle to look for the stored outline in the specified category and then in the default category. If no category name is specified, Oracle looks only in the default category.

Private outlines

A private outline is one that is seen only by the current session. The parameter USE_PRIVATE_OUTLINE controls the use of private outlines.

To use private outlines, you have to have outline tables in the current schema. You can create these tables with the *UTLEDITOL.SQL* script or the DBMS_OUTLN_EDIT.CREATE_EDIT_TABLES procedure.

EXPLAIN PLAN

The Oracle optimizer should select the best execution plan for SQL statements. If there is a problem with the performance of a SQL statement, you may want to see the execution path choices the optimizer made for the statement. The EXPLAIN PLAN statement can produce this information.

 The execution plan produced by the EXPLAIN PLAN statement may not exactly match the execution plan used at runtime, because of differences in the two environments. The SQL_PLAN data dictionary views, new in Oracle9i, contain information about the actual execution plan used at runtime. See Chapter 6 for more information about these views.

Preparing to Run EXPLAIN PLAN

The EXPLAIN PLAN statement needs a table to store the information it gathers. By default, this table is called PLAN_TABLE and it is created by running the script *UTLXPLAN.SQL* in your schema.

If you want to use a different table for the information produced by EXPLAIN PLAN, Oracle recommends that you use the *UTLXPLAN.SQL* script and then rename the table.

Because the output of the EXPLAIN PLAN statement may change with new releases, Oracle recommends that you drop and re-create the PLAN_TABLE table with each major upgrade.

Executing EXPLAIN PLAN

You can execute the EXPLAIN PLAN statement using the following syntax:

```
EXPLAIN PLAN [SET STATEMENT_ID = 'id_label']
    [INTO [schema.]table [@dblink]] FOR statement
```

The STATEMENT_ID clause can be used to identify the plan for a particular statement. The INTO clause can target a table other than the PLAN_TABLE for storage of the plan information; that table must exist before you issue this command. *statement* is the SQL statement to be explained.

To display execution plans, you can create your own SQL statement on the PLAN_TABLE table or use the script *UTLXPLS.SQL*, for serial execution, or *UTLXPLP.SQL*, for parallel execution.

PLAN_TABLE Columns

The information gathered from the EXPLAIN PLAN statement is stored in the PLAN_TABLE table or another table as specified in the command. This table contains the following columns. Each column description also shows the column's datatype (e.g., VARCHAR2, DATE, etc.).

STATEMENT_ID
Identifies the information for a particular statement. VARCHAR2(30).

TIMESTAMP
Time the EXPLAIN PLAN was run. DATE.

REMARKS
Contains any remarks you want to add to a row. VARCHAR2(80).

OPERATION
The first row in the PLAN_TABLE contains one of the following values:

```
DELETE STATEMENT
INSERT STATEMENT
SELECT STATEMENT
UPDATE STATEMENT
```

Subsequent rows in the PLAN_TABLE contain a combination for this column and the OPTION column, which are listed in Table 17-3. VARCHAR2(30).

OPTION
Describes variations on the OPERATION column. VARCHAR2(225). The value pairs for these two columns are shown in Table 17-3.

Table 17-3. OPERATION and OPTION values

OPERATION	OPTION	Meaning
AND-EQUAL		Intersection of sets of data.
BITMAP	CONVERSION (TO ROWIDS | FROM ROWIDS | COUNT)	Uses bitmapped indexes. AND and KEY ITERA-TION are new with Oracle9i.
	INDEX (SINGLE VALUE | RANGE SCAN | FULL SCAN)	
	MERGE	
	MINUS	
	OR	
	AND	
	KEY ITERATION	
CONCATENATION		Union of multiple sets of data.
CONNECT BY		Uses CONNECT BY clause for hierarchical retrieval.
COUNT		Counts number of rows.
	STOPKEY	Count limited by ROWNUM expression in the WHERE clause.
DOMAIN INDEX		Uses domain to retrieve ROWIDs. New with Oracle8i.
FILTER		Eliminates some rows in a set.
FIRST ROW		Returns first row of query.
FOR UPDATE		Retrieves and locks rows.
HASH JOIN	ANTI	Types of hash join.
	SEMI	

Table 17-3. OPERATION and OPTION values (continued)

OPERATION	OPTION	Meaning
INDEX	RANGE SCAN [DESCENDING] FULL SCAN [DESCENDING] FAST FULL SCAN SKIP SCAN UNIQUE SCAN	Uses index. FULL SCAN, FAST FULL SCAN, and SKIP SCAN are new with Oracle9*i*. UNIQUE SCAN was not included with Oracle9*i*.
INLIST ITERATOR		Uses values in IN list iteratively.
INTERSECTION		Eliminates duplicates from two sets of rows.
MERGE JOIN	OUTER ANTI SEMI CARTESIAN	Types of merge joins. CARTESIAN is new with Oracle9*i*.
MINUS		Returns rows in first set but not in the second.
NESTED LOOPS	OUTER	Compares each member of outer set with each member of inner set and returns those that match condition.
PARTITION	SINGLE ITERATOR ALL INLIST INVALID CONCATENATED	Accesses partitions. The only valid option was CONCATENATED with Oracle8.
PROJECTION		An internal operation that was not included with Oracle9*i*.
REMOTE		Retrieves data from remote database.
SEQUENCE		Accesses values of a sequence.
SORT	AGGREGATE UNIQUE GROUP BY JOIN ORDER BY	Types of sort operations.
TABLE ACCESS	FULL SAMPLE CLUSTER HASH BY ROWID BY ROWID RANGE SAMPLE BY ROWID RANGE BY USER ROWID BY INDEX ROWID BY GLOBAL INDEX ROWID BY LOCAL INDEX ROWID	Types of data retrieval from a table. SAMPLE and SAMPLE BY ROWID RANGE were new with Oracle9*i*. BY ROWID, BY ROWID RANGE, BY USER ROWID, BY INDEX ROWID, BY GLOBAL INDEX ROWID, and BY LOCAL INDEX ROWID were new with Oracle8*i*. BY ROWID was not included after Oracle8.
UNION		Uses UNION.
VIEW		Uses view.

OBJECT_NODE

Used for the name of the database link used to reference the object or the order in which the output from this operation is consumed for local parallel queries. VARCHAR2(128).

OB JECT_OWNER

Name of the owner of the schema that contains the table or index. VARCHAR2(30).

OBJECT_NAME

Name of the object. VARCHAR2(30).

OBJECT_INSTANCE

Ordinal position of the object in the original statement. NUMERIC.

OBJECT_TYPE

Descriptive information about the object. VARCHAR2(30).

OPTIMIZER

Optimizer mode used. VARCHAR2(255).

SEARCH_COLUMNS

Not used for Oracle9*i*. NUMERIC.

ID

ID number of the step in the execution plan. NUMERIC.

PARENT_ID

ID number of the step that operates on the output of this step. NUMERIC.

POSITION

For the first row of the EXPLAIN PLAN output, estimated cost of executing the statement. For subsequent rows, the position relative to the other children of the same plan step. NUMERIC.

COST

Internal cost of the operation as determined by optimizer. Used for relative comparisons to other costs. NUMERIC.

CARDINALITY

Estimate of rows accessed by operation. NUMERIC.

BYTES

Estimate of bytes accessed by the operation. NUMERIC.

OTHER_TAG

Can contain one of the following values:

```
Blank
SERIAL_FROM_REMOTE (S → R)
SERIAL_TO_PARALLEL (S → P)
PARALLEL_TO_PARALLEL (P → P)
PARALLEL_TO_SERIAL (P → S)
PARALLEL_COMBINED_WITH_PARENT (PWP)
PARALLEL_COMBINED_WITH_CHILD (PWC)
```

For more information about these values, see the Oracle documentation. VARCHAR2(255).

PARTITION_START

Starting position for a range of accessed partitions. Can be an integer representing partition number, KEY indicating that a key value will be identified at runtime, ROW_REMOVE_LOCATION indicating that the location of a record at runtime will be used, or INVALID indicating that the range of accessed partitions is empty. VARCHAR2(255).

PARTITION_STOP

End position for a range of accessed partitions. Uses the same keywords as PARTITION_START. VARCHAR2(255).

PARTITION_ID

ID number of the step that computed PARTITION_START and PARTITION_STOP. NUMERIC. This column was called PID in Oracle8*i*.

OTHER

Additional information about a step. LONG.

DISTRIBUTION

Method used to distribute rows from producer query servers to consumer query servers. VARCHAR2(30). Can contain the following values:

```
PARTITION (ROWID)
PARTITION (KEY)
HASH
RANGE
ROUND-ROBIN
BROADCAST
QC (ORDER)
QC (RANDOM)
```

For more information on these values, see the Oracle documentation.

CPU_COST

Cost in terms of CPU cycles. NUMERIC. New with Oracle9*i*.

IO_COST

Cost in terms of I/O operations. NUMERIC. New with Oracle9*i*.

TEMP_SPACE

Estimate of temporary space needed by the operation. NUMERIC. New with Oracle9*i*.

TKPROF

The EXPLAIN PLAN statement can help you to understand what execution paths were used for individual SQL statements. TKPROF is used in conjunction with files created by the SQL Trace utility, which collects information about SQL statements that have been executed. The TKPROF utility formats information gathered by SQL Trace into a readable format.

Performance

Preparing for a Trace

Before you can use TKPROF, you must collect information about SQL statements into a trace file. To use the SQL Trace utility, you must have the following settings in the initialization file for the target Oracle database:

- TIMED_STATISTICS must be set to TRUE. For Oracle9i Release 2, setting the STATISTICS_LEVEL parameter to TYPICAL or ALL will also collect timing statistics, and the value of DB_CACHE_ADVICE.TIMED_STATISTICS or TIMED_OS_STATISTICS will override the value set for STATISTICS_LEVEL.
- MAX_DUMP_FILE_SIZE must be big enough to hold all the information written to the trace file.
- USER_DUMP_DEST must point to a valid directory.

 The SQL Trace utility writes all trace files to the USER_DUMP_DEST directory, so make sure you have a way to recognize your particular trace file.

All of these parameters are session parameters and can be changed dynamically with Oracle9i.

Collecting Trace Information

You can start collecting SQL trace information either by running the DBMS_SESSION.SET_SQL_TRACE procedure or by issuing the statement:

```
ALTER SESSION SET SQL_TRACE = TRUE;
```

You can turn SQL tracing off by setting SQL_TRACE to FALSE.

You can turn on SQL Trace for a session other than your current one with the DBMS_SYSTEM.SET_SQL_TRACE_IN_SESSION procedure.

To turn on SQL Trace for the entire instance, you can either set the SQL_TRACE initialization parameter to TRUE or issue the following statement:

```
ALTER SYSTEM SET SQL_TRACE = TRUE;
```

Use this method with care, because collecting trace information does add overhead to the operation of the instance.

For more detailed information on Oracle Trace, the statistics it collects, and how it can be used by itself, see the Oracle documentation.

Running TKPROF

Call TKPROF from the command line using the following syntax.

Syntax

```
TKPROF filename1 filename2
    [WAITS = YES | NO ]
    [SORT = option (, option . . .)]
```

```
[PRINT = integer]
[AGGREGATE = YES | NO]
[INSERT = filename3]
[SYS = YES | NO]
[[TABLE = schema.table] EXPLAIN = username/password]
[RECORD = filename4]
[WIDTH = integer]
```

Keywords

filename1
> Input SQL trace file.

filename2
> Filename for output of TKPROF.

WAITS
> Specifies whether to record summary for wait events. New with Oracle9*i*.

SORT
> Sorts SQL statements in descending order for the listed *options*. Values for these options are:

PRSCNT	number of times parsed
PRSCPU	CPU time spent parsing
PRSELA	elapsed time spent parsing
PRSDSK	number of disk reads during parsing
PRSQRY	number of consistent mode block reads during parsing
PRSCU	number of current mode block reads during parsing
PRSMIS	number of library cache misses during parsing
EXECNT	[pnumber of times statement is executed
EXECPU	CPU time spent executing
EXEELA	elapsed time spent executing
EXEDSK	number of disk reads during execution
EXEQRY	number of consistent mode block reads during execution
EXECU	number of current mode block reads during execution
EXEROW	number of rows processed during execution
EXESMIS	number of library cache misses during execution
FCHCNT	number of fetches
FCHCPU	CPU time spent fetching
FCHELA	elapsed time spent fetching
FCHDSK	number of disk reads during fetch
FCHQRY	number of consistent mode block reads during fetch
FCHCU	number of current mode block reads during fetch
FCHROW	number of rows fetched

> Consistent mode block reads are done for SELECT statements and do not place locks on the data. Current mode block reads are done for writes to the database and do place locks on the data.

PRINT

Lists only *integer* number of sorted SQL statements.

AGGREGATE

If NO, does not aggregate statistics for multiple users of the same SQL text.

INSERT

Creates a SQL script *filename3* that is run to store the trace file statistics in the database. The default name for the table used to store this data is TKPROF_TABLE, but you can edit the CREATE TABLE statement in *filename3*.

SYS

If NO, does not list SQL statements issued by user SYS or recursive SQL statements.

TABLE

Specifies temporary *schema.table* in which to store execution plan before writing it to the output file, which allows more than one person to run TKPROF with the same value for *username*.

EXPLAIN

Writes the execution plan in the output file by issuing the EXPLAIN PLAN statement as *username* with *password*. Will make the overall execution of TKPROF slower.

RECORD

Creates a SQL script with all the nonrecursive SQL in the trace file, which can be used to replay the user events.

WIDTH

Specifies the width of the output line of TKPROF to *integer*. New with Oracle9*i*.

Running TKPROF without any parameters will display online help.

TKPROF Output

The output from TKPROF contains the following items:

- The SQL statement.
- Statistics for the statement. There are three lines of statistics for each SQL statement: parse, execute, and fetch, as listed in the call column of the output. For each of these lines are seven additional fields in the following columns:

count

Number of times the step was performed

cpu

Total CPU time for the step

elapsed

Elapsed time for the step

disk
Number of disk blocks read

query
Number of buffers accessed in consistent mode, which is used for SELECT operations and does not apply to locks

current
Number of buffers accessed in current mode, which is used for INSERT, UPDATE, and DELETE operations and applies to locks

rows
Number of rows processed by the SQL statement

These three rows are followed by a summary row with the totals for all three phases:

- Information about the statement's execution. This information can include the number of library cache misses in each portion of the call, the optimizer goal for the statement, and the ID of the user executing the statement. If there are no library cache misses, this information is not reported.
- The execution plan, if specified in the command-line argument.

The TKPROF report begins with information on any SQL statements that generated an error and ends with a summary of all of the information presented, divided into nonrecursive SQL statements and recursive SQL statements. The summary also includes information about the trace file used to generate the report.

AUTOTRACE

AUTOTRACE, introduced in Oracle8*i*, enables automatic reporting on statements issued in SQL*Plus. To use AUTOTRACE, a PLAN_TABLE must exist (for the storage of EXPLAIN PLAN information) and the user must have been granted the PLUSTRACE role. The PLUSTRACE role is created by running the *PLUS-TRACE.SQL* script as DBA; it may then be granted to other users.

You can control AUTOTRACE operations by issuing the following statement:

```
SET AUTOTRACE ON | OFF | TRACEONLY option
```

where *option* can be EXPLAIN or STATISTICS. Without an option, AUTOTRACE returns information on the optimization (EXPLAIN) and the statistics used by the statement. If you specify TRACEONLY, the statement returns the optimizer plan and the statistics but does not return any result.

The statistics that are created by AUTOTRACE are:

Recursive calls
DB block – gets number of times a CURRENT block was requested
Consistent – gets number of times a consistent read was requested for a block
Physical reads – number of datablocks read from disk
Redo size – amount of redo generated, listed in bytes
Bytes sent via Oracle Net Services to client

Bytes sent via Oracle Net Services from client
SQL*Net round-trips to and from clients
Sorts in memory
Sorts in disk
Rows processed

Statistics Collection

Statistics about the operation of an Oracle database are kept in the dynamic V$ data dictionary views (described in Chapter 6). Because the information in these dynamic views is lost when an instance is stopped, Oracle provides packages for saving the performance statistics gathered for these views.

Prior to Oracle8*i*, the UTLBSTAT and UTLESTAT scripts were used for this purpose. With Oracle8*i*, the Statspack package was introduced as an improvement on UTLBSTAT and UTLESTAT.

 In addition to these packages, you can use Oracle Enterprise Manager and its Diagnostic Pack add-on for monitoring performance-related statistics. See Chapter 16.

Collecting statistics is the first step to understanding performance problems. It is beyond the scope of this book to help you to learn the delicate art of performance tuning, but there are many fine books on the topic.

UTLBSTAT/UTLESTAT

These two scripts collect data from the V$ data dictionary views and save it to tables in the database.

The UTLBSTAT script collects the initial statistics into a set of tables and also creates tables for the ending statistics. The UTLESTAT script collects the ending statistics and creates a set of tables that show the differences between the beginning and ending statistics.

The tables created have the names shown in the following list. Unless otherwise noted, the beginning statistics tables use the name format of STATS$BEGIN_*, the ending statistics tables use the format of STATS$END_*, and the differences tables use the format of STATS$*.

*DC
> For dictionary cache statistics.

*EVENT
> For wait statistics.

*FILE
> For file I/O statistics. The difference table is named STATS$FILES.

*LATCH
> For latch statistics. The difference table is named STATS$LATCHES.

LIB
> For library cache statistics.

ROLL
> For rollback segment statistics.

STATS
> For system statistics.

STATS$DATES
> Contains beginning date and time after running UTLBSTAT and both beginning and ending time after running UTLESTAT.

UTLBSTAT and UTLESTAT always use the same tables for saving the statistics, so you can look at only one set of differences at a time with them. If you want to look at multiple sets of differences, you can save the information in the DIF tables to another set of tables or create reports from them, for comparison with other sets of statistics.

Statspack

Statspack, introduced in Oracle8*i*, performs a function that's similar to that performed by the UTLBSTAT/UTLESTAT scripts. Statspack differs from these earlier gathering tools in that it collects more data, computes some of the ratios between data automatically, and stores the data in an Oracle database.

Statspack also accounts for transactions that end with either a COMMIT or a ROLLBACK.

Installing Statspack

The objects used by Statspack are owned by the user PERFSTAT. You can either create this user and then call the script *SPCREATE.SQL* as a user with SYSDBA privilege or run the script as a batch job in SQL*Plus, after first assigning the variables DEFAULT_TABLESPACE and TEMPORARY_TABLESPACE.

In either case, the *SPCREATE.SQL* script calls the *SPCUSR.SQL*, *SPCTAB.SQL*, and *SPCPKG.SQL* scripts and saves the results of these scripts in their corresponding *.LIS* files.

Using Statspack

Statspack works by creating a snapshot view of performance statistics at a particular point in time. The snapshot is identified by a SNAP_ID, a DBID, and an INSTANCE_ID.

To create a snapshot, log into SQL*Plus as PERFSTAT/PERFSTAT and use the command:

```
EXECUTE STATSPACK.SNAP;
```

You can also call the SNAP procedure to return the SNAP_ID of the most recent snapshot.

You can use the procedures in the DBMS_JOB built-in package to schedule snapshots to run at specific intervals.

Reporting on Statspack data

To get a report on the differences between two snapshots, use the script *SPRE-PORT.SQL* in SQL*Plus while logged on as PERFSTAT. The script reports on the existing snapshots for the current instance and prompts you to enter the starting snapshot, the ending snapshot, and the name of the file in which to store the resulting report.

 If there is a blank line in between snapshots listed, it means that the instance has been restarted between the two snapshots, so they should not be used for comparison.

You can also run this script in batch mode by assigning a value to the variables BEGIN_SNAP, END_SNAP, and REPORT_NAME.

The output generated in the report from *SPREPORT.SQL* includes a hash value for identifying a particular SQL statement. You can get a detailed report on the performance statistics for that particular statement by running the *SPREPSQL.SQL* report, which will prompt you for the same values and the hash number of the statement. You can also run this in batch by assigning the values for *SPREPORT. SQL* and the HASH_VALUE variable.

Statspack also includes a script called *SPREPINS.SQL*, which creates a report on database and instance statistics.

Statspack levels and thresholds

You can adjust the amount of information collected by Statspack by specifying a level or adjusting the threshold for data collection. A SQL statement must surpass the specified threshold for a statistic before it is captured by Statspack.

Statspack supports the following levels:

- 0 or greater collects general statistics such as wait and system statistics, rollback segment data, row cache and SGA information, system, background, and session events, as well as lock, buffer pool, and parent latch statistics
- 5 or greater also includes performance data on SQL statements that exceed the thresholds specified
- 6 or greater also includes information about whether the execution plan has changed.
- 10 or greater also includes information about child and parent latches

The thresholds that can be specified for a statement, with their defaults, are:

I_EXECUTIONS_TH
 Number of times executed (100)

I_DISK_READS_TH
 Number of disk reads (1000)

I_PARSE_CALLS_TH
 Number of parse calls (1000)

I_BUFFER_GETS_TH
> Number of buffer gets (10,000)

I_SHARABLE_MEM_TH
> Amount of sharable memory (1,048,576)

I_VERSION_COUNT_TH
> Number of versions (20)

To change a parameter for an individual session, include the threshold or level number identifier followed by => and the new value as a parameter to the SNAP procedure. To set the level, you use the parameter name I_SNAP_LEVEL. You can also include I_UCOMMENT to add a user comment and I_SESSION_ID for the ID of the session to use to gather session-specific information.

To change these parameters permanently, either set the I_MODIFY_PARAM-ETER to TRUE when you call the SNAP procedure or use the MODIFY_STATSPACK_PARAMETER call with the same parameter syntax.

Removing Statspack data

To remove snapshot data collected by Statspack from the database, use the *SPPURGE.SQL* script. If you run this script interactively in SQL*Plus, you will get a list of the existing snapshots and then be prompted for the lowest snapshot number and the highest snapshot number, which will mark the boundaries of the snapshots deleted. You can also define values for the variables LOSNAPID and HISNAPID and run the script in batch mode.

To remove all snapshot statistics from the database, use the *SPTRUNC.SQL* script.

IV

Appendixes

This part of the book contains summary information. It consists of the following appendixes:

Appendix A, *Datatypes,* summarizes the Oracle datatypes and conversion rules.

Appendix B, *Expressions, Operators, and Conditions*, lists the valid expressions, operators, and conditions that can be included in SQL, PL/SQL, and SQL*Plus statements.

Appendix C, *Numeric Formats*, lists numeric format elements that can be included in SQL, PL/SQL, and SQL*Plus statements.

Appendix D, *Date Formats*, lists date format elements that can be included in SQL, PL/SQL, and SQL*Plus statements.

Appendix E, *Additional Resources*, provides a list of books and online resources containing additional information on the topics included in this book.

A

Datatypes

The *datatype* is one of the attributes for a column in a table or for a variable in a stored procedure. A datatype describes and limits the type of information stored in a column, as well as some of the operations that you can perform on that column.

You can logically divide Oracle datatype support into two categories—scalar datatypes (datatypes that return a single value) and collection datatypes (datatypes that hold or point to a collection of data). PL/SQL also supports reference datatypes that contain pointers to other objects.

Scalar Datatypes

There are five basic varieties of scalar datatypes: character datatypes, numeric datatypes, datetime datatypes, large object (LOB) datatypes, and datatypes that represent other types of data. This appendix summarizes the characteristics of each of these varieties.

Unless otherwise noted, all scalar datatypes described in the following sections are valid for both the database and for PL/SQL declarations. (Note, however, that some of the datatypes listed under "Collection Datatypes" later in this appendix are valid only for PL/SQL.)

Character Datatypes

Character datatypes can store any string value, including the string representations of numeric values. Assigning a value larger than the length specified for a character datatype results in a runtime error. You can use string functions, such as UPPER, LOWER, SUBSTR, and SOUNDEX, on standard character value types (but not on large character value types, which we describe under "Large Object Datatypes").

The character datatypes are:

CHAR/CHARACTER[(n [CHAR | BYTE])]

Stores character values with a fixed length. A CHAR datatype can have between 1 and 2000 characters. If you don't explicitly specify a length for a CHAR, it assumes the default length of 1. If you assign a value that's shorter than the length specified for the CHAR datatype, Oracle will automatically pad the value with blanks. With Oracle9*i*, you can specify *n* with the keywords of BYTE or CHAR.

VARCHAR2(n [CHAR | BYTE]) and VARCHAR(n [CHAR | BYTE])

Store variable-length character strings. Although you must assign a length to a VARCHAR2 datatype, the length is the maximum length for a value, rather than the required length. Values assigned to a VARCHAR2 datatype are not padded with blanks. The VARCHAR2 datatype can have up to 4000 characters.

At this time, the VARCHAR datatype and the VARCHAR2 datatype are synonymous in Oracle8 and later versions, but Oracle recommends the use of VARCHAR2, because future changes may cause VARCHAR and VARCHAR2 to diverge.

With Oracle9*i*, you can specify *n* with the keywords of BYTE or CHAR.

With PL/SQL, you can use STRING as the keyword for this datatype.

NCHAR2(n) and NVARCHAR2(n)

Store fixed-length or variable-length character data using a different character set from the one used by the rest of the database. When you create a database, you specify a character set used for encoding the various characters stored in the database. You can optionally specify a secondary character set as well. (This is known as the National Language Set, or NLS.) This secondary character set is used for NCHAR and NVARCHAR2 columns. For example, you may have a description field in which you want to store Japanese characters while the rest of the database uses English encoding. You would specify a secondary character set that supports Japanese characters when you create the database and then use the NCHAR or NVARCHAR2 datatype for the columns in question.

With Oracle9*i*, you can specify that you want to indicate the length of NCHAR and NVARCHAR2 columns in terms of characters, rather than bytes. This means that if you indicate that one of these datatypes is seven characters, the Oracle9*i* database will automatically make the conversion to 14 bytes if the characters require double-byte storage.

LONG

Stores up to 2 GB of character data. The LONG datatype is regarded as a legacy datatype from earlier versions of Oracle. If you want to store large amounts of character data, Oracle now recommends that you use the CLOB and NCLOB datatypes. There are many restrictions on the use of LONG datatypes in tables and within SQL statements; for example, you cannot use LONGs in WHERE, GROUP BY, ORDER BY, or CONNECT BY clauses or in SQL statements with the DISTINCT qualifier. You also cannot create an index on a LONG column.

Numeric Datatypes

The Oracle database uses a standard, variable-length internal format for storing numbers. This internal format can maintain a precision of up to 38 digits.

The only numeric datatype within the database for Oracle8 and later versions is NUMBER. (However, see the later discussion of PL/SQL numeric types.) Declaring a column or variable as NUMBER will automatically provide a precision of 38 digits. The NUMBER datatype can also accept two qualifiers, as in:

```
column NUMBER(precision, scale)
```

The *precision* of the datatype is the total number of significant digits in the number and can be any integer up to 38; the default *precision* is 38. *scale* represents the number of digits to the right of the decimal point; the default *scale* is 0. If you assign a negative number to *scale*, Oracle will round the number up to the designated place to the left of the decimal point.

The NUMBER datatype is the only datatype that stores numeric values in Oracle8 and later versions. The ANSI datatypes of DECIMAL/DEC, NUMBER, INTEGER/INT, SMALLINT, FLOAT, DOUBLE PRECISION, and REAL are all stored in the NUMBER datatype. These are all defined datatypes in PL/SQL and other languages.

PL/SQL supports the BINARY_INTEGER, which stores signed integers between -2^{31} and 2^{31}. This datatype has the following subtypes:

NATURAL
  Non-negative integers

NATURALN
  Non-negative integers and no NULLs

POSITIVE
  Positive integers

POSITIVEN
  Positive integers and no NULLs

SIGNTYPE
  Accepts only -1, 0, or 1, which is useful in three-state logic

PL/SQL also supports the PLS_INTEGER datatype. This datatype stores signed integers between -2^{31} and 2^{31}, like BINARY_INTEGER. But PLS_INTEGER requires less storage space than BINARY_INTEGER and performs machine arithmetic, which is faster than BINARY_INTEGER's library arithmetic.

Datetime Datatypes

Historically, Oracle has supported a single date datatype, known as DATE. With Oracle9*i*, additional interval and timestamp types are supported.

DATE datatype

Oracle stores all dates and times in a standard internal format that includes the year, month, day, hour, minute, and second. The default format for inserting dates is DD-MON-RR, where RR automatically assigns years in the 50–99 range as 1950–1999 and assigns other years to the 2000–2049 range. You can change the format you use for inserting dates for an instance by changing the NLS_DATE_FORMAT initialization parameter for that instance. You do this for a session by using the ALTER SESSION SQL statement. To change the format for a specific value, you can include the appropriate parameters with the TO_DATE expression in your SQL statement.

Date and Time Ranges

All datetime and interval datatypes described in this appendix are made up of the following fields:

YEAR
> Can be between -4712 and 9999 (except year 0) for datetimes; can be any positive or negative number for intervals

MONTH
> Can be between 01 and 12 for datetimes; can be between 0 and 11 for intervals

DAY
> Is limited by the particular month for datetimes

HOUR
> Can be between 00 and 12 for datetimes; can be between 0 and 12 for intervals

MINUTE
> Can be between 00 and 59 for datetimes; can be between 0 and 59 for intervals

SECOND
> Can be between 00 and 59.9 for datetimes; can be between 0 and 59.9 for intervals

TIMEZONE_HOUR
> Can be between 12 and 13 for datetimes; not valid for intervals

TIMEZONE_MINUTE
> Can be between 00 and 59 for datetimes; not valid for intervals

You can use the EXTRACT function (see Chapter 8) to extract the value of any of these fields from a datetime or interval datatype.

Oracle SQL supports date arithmetic in which integers represent days, and fractions represent the fractional component represented by hours, minutes, and seconds. For example, adding .5 to a date value results in a date and time combination 12 hours later than the initial value. Some examples of date arithmetic are:

```
12-DEC-99 + 10 = 22-DEC-99
31-DEC-1999:23:59:59 + .25 = 1-JAN-2000:5:59:59
```

INTERVAL datatypes

Oracle9*i* introduces two new interval datatypes:

INTERVAL YEAR TO MONTH
Stores a period of time using the year and month datetime fields with the following syntax:

INTERVAL YEAR (*year_precision*) TO MONTH

where *year_precision* is the number of digits used to specify the number of years, with a default value of 2.

INTERVAL DAY TO SECOND
Stores a period of time using the day, hour, minute, and seconds datetime fields. Defined with the following syntax:

INTERVAL DAY (*day_precision*) TO SECOND (*fractional_second_precision*)

where *day_precision* is the number of digits used to specify the number of days, from 0 to 9, with a default value of 2. *fractional_second_precision* specifies the number of digits in the fractional portion of the seconds, from 0 to 9, with a default of 6.

For more information on assigning values to INTERVAL datatypes, see the descriptions of the INTERVAL functions in Chapter 8.

TIMESTAMP datatypes

There are three new TIMESTAMP datatypes in Oracle9*i*:

TIMESTAMP
An extension of the DATE datatype that includes year, month, day, hour, minute, and second values with the following syntax:

TIMESTAMP [(*fractional_second_precision*)]

where *fractional_second_precision* specifies the number of digits in the fractional portion of the seconds, from 0 to 9, with a default of 2.

TIMESTAMP WITH TIMEZONE
A variant of TIMESTAMP than includes a time zone displacement from UTC (Coordinated Universal Time, which is essentially Greenwich Mean Time). The syntax for this datatype is:

TIMESTAMP [(*fractional_second_precision*)] WITH TIMEZONE

TIMESTAMP WITH LOCAL TIME ZONE
Similar to TIMESTAMP WITH TIMEZONE, but the time is normalized to the local time zone for the database, and the displacement from UTC is not stored as part of the column data. The syntax for this datatype is:

TIMESTAMP [(*fractional_second_precision*)] WITH LOCAL TIMEZONE

Large Object Datatypes

Large objects are most often used to store large amounts (up to 4 gigabytes) of binary data (such as images) or character text data. LOBs have a couple of common characteristics: they typically have sizes that may exceed the limits of other datatypes or formatting that falls outside the understanding of these standard datatypes.

Oracle supports several different datatypes for handling large objects:

BLOB
> Stores up to 4 GBs of binary data. BLOB stands for binary large object. This datatype does not translate values stored in it. It can be used in a transaction.

CLOB
> Stores up to 4 GBs of character data. CLOB stands for character large object. This datatype is used to store a large block of single-byte, fixed-width character data stored inside the database. This datatype does not translate values stored in it. It can be used in a transaction.

NCLOB
> Stores up to 4 GBs of character data. NCLOB stands for National Language Support (NLS) character large object. This datatype does not translate values stored in it. It can be used in a transaction.

BFILE
> The BFILE datatype acts as a pointer to a file stored outside of the Oracle database. Because of this, columns or variables with BFILE datatypes do not participate in transactions, and the data stored in these columns is available only for reading. Oracle treats the data in the outside file as binary data. The file size limitations of the underlying operating system limit the size of data in a BFILE.

Other Scalar Datatypes

Oracle also supports a number of specialized datatypes:

BOOLEAN
> Holds a Boolean value (TRUE, FALSE, or NULL).

RAW and LONG RAW
> Normally, the Oracle database server not only stores data, but also interprets that data. When data is exported from the database or requested from the database, the Oracle database sometimes needs to convert the character set or perform blank padding on the data.
>
> The RAW and LONG RAW datatypes circumvent any interpretation on the part of the Oracle database. When you specify one of these datatypes, Oracle will store the data as the exact series of bytes presented to it. The RAW datatypes typically store objects with their own internal format, such as bitmaps. A RAW datatype can hold 2000 bytes, while a LONG RAW datatype can hold 2 GBs.

ROWID
> The ROWID is a special type of column known as a *pseudocolumn*. The ROWID pseudocolumn can be accessed just like a column in a SQL SELECT statement. There is a ROWID pseudocolumn for every row in an Oracle database. The ROWID represents the specific address of a particular row. You can define the ROWID pseudocolumn with a ROWID datatype.

The ROWID relates to a specific location on a disk drive. For this reason, the ROWID is the fastest way to retrieve an individual row. However, the ROWID for a row can change as the result of dumping and reloading the database. As a consequence, we don't recommend using the value for the ROWID pseudocolumn across transaction boundaries.

You cannot set the value of the standard ROWID pseudocolumn with any SQL statement. You can define a column or variable with a ROWID datatype, but Oracle8 and later versions do not guarantee that any value placed in this column or variable is a valid ROWID.

UROWID

Some types of tables, such as index-organized tables or foreign tables (in other types of databases) have row IDs that are not physical, permanent, or generated by Oracle. The UROWID holds the logical, physical, or non-Oracle row ID for these tables. Such tables have UROWIDs as the datatype for the ROWID pseudocolumn. A UROWID datatype can hold up to 4000 bytes.

XMLType

As part of its support for XML, Oracle9*i* includes the new XMLType datatype. A column defined as this type of data can store an XML document. Associated built-in functions allow you to extract individual nodes from the datatype (see the XML functions in Chapter 8.). You can also build indexes on any particular node in an XMLType document.

SYS.AnyType, SYS.AnyData, SYS.AnyDataSet

Oracle9*i* includes three new Any datatypes, which can be used to explicitly define datatypes that can hold any type of data:

SYS.AnyType

Can contain any type description

SYS.AnyData

Can contain any data and its type description

SYS.AnyDataSet

Can contain any set of data and its type description

You will have to define each instance of these types with program units that let Oracle9*i* know how to process specific implementations of each of these datatypes.

UriType

Oracle9*i* introduces several URITypes, which are used to store uniform resource identifiers. All of these types allow you to retrieve information based on some type of URI. Four of these datatypes are available:

URIType

Parent object type of all of these types, which can be used to store data for any of the other URI types.

HTTPURIType

Used to store URIs for information outside the database. Access to these pages is performed with HTTP.

XDBURIType
> Used to store XML database hierarchies.

DBURIType
> Used to store DBURI REFs that reference data in the database through an Xpath-like representation.

User-defined data
> Oracle also allows users to define their own complex datatypes, which are created as combinations of the basic Oracle datatypes previously discussed. Oracle also allows users to create objects composed from both basic datatypes and user-defined data types. For more information about the creation of user-defined datatypes, see the entry for the SQL statement, CREATE TYPE, in Chapter 7.

Collection Datatypes

In addition to the scalar datatypes described in the previous sections, there are a number of additional datatypes that can hold or point to a collection of data:

RECORD
> Used only in PL/SQL. Composed of fields with datatypes, just like a table in the database. You can insert or update RECORDs into matching tables in the database or use the RETURNING clause to retrieve values from a table after an INSERT, UPDATE, or DELETE statement.

TABLE
> A nested table. Cannot be of datatype REF CURSOR in PL/SQL or the PL/SQL datatypes, such as BINARY_INTEGER or POSITIVE, when stored in the database. You can delete individual values in a TABLE. When stored in the database, preserves order as stored.
>
> In PL/SQL, you can use an INDEX BY clause, which adds an index that can be used to access the data in the table. The INDEX BY clause can specify BINARY_INTEGER, PLS_INTEGER, a VARCHAR2(n), or a key type.
>
> A TABLE can be part of an object type, which would make it a nested table. For more information on object types, see Chapter 7.

VARRAY(n)
> An array of values with n values. You reference individual values in a VARRAY with a subscript. You cannot delete individual values in a VARRAY, because values must be consecutive. When stored in the database, does not preserve order as stored.

Collection Operators

You can use the following operators on collections of data in PL/SQL:

COUNT
> Returns count.

DELETE[([*m*,]*n*)]

Deletes all elements (if no parameters), element *n* (if only *n* present), or between element *m* and *n* (if both present).

EXISTS(*n*)

Returns TRUE if element *n* exists.

EXTEND

Increases the size of a collection.

FIRST

Returns first element.

LAST

Returns last element.

LIMIT

For VARRAYs, returns limit.

NEXT

Returns next element.

PRIOR

Returns previous element.

TRIM[(*n*)]

Removes *n* elements from end of collection. If *n* is not present, removes one element.

For more information about using collections with PL/SQL, see the collection sections in Chapter 9. For more information about creating collection types in the database, see the CREATE TYPE entry in Chapter 7.

Reference Datatypes

The datatypes in this category contain references to other data sets:

REF CURSOR

A PL/SQL pointer to a SQL cursor that can return a row from the database. After an instance of this datatype is OPENed, you can FETCH rows with it. You should CLOSE the REF CURSOR when finished with it.

REF object

Points to an instance of *object*. Used to share access to the object between subprograms in PL/SQL or between reference objects in SQL.

B

Expressions, Operators, and Conditions

SQL (Structured Query Language), which we describe in Chapter 7, is the common language used to access the Oracle database. You frequently use some type of logic to specify the data affected by a SQL statement. To implement this logic, you need expressions, operators, and conditions:

Expressions
> Used to define values, for example:
>
> ```
> 2+2
> SYSDATE
> TO_CHAR(SYSDATE)
> ```

Operators
> Used to compare two values, for example:
>
> ```
> a = b
> a != b
> a AND b
> ```

Conditions
> Used to specify acceptable values, for example:
>
> ```
> a > b
> a EXISTS
> a IS NOT NULL
> ```

Expressions, operators, and conditions may be included in a variety of SQL statements, as well as in PL/SQL code. This appendix summarizes the various options available for specifying expressions, operators, and conditions. For a more detailed description of where they can be specified, see Chapter 7 for SQL and Chapter 9 for PL/SQL.

Expressions

An expression is the basic unit of information in an SQL statement or function. Oracle supports several different types of expressions:

Simple expression

> May be any of the following:
>
> - Text within quotes
> - A number
> - A ROWID for a row specified as part of a table, a schema and table, or a query
> - A column value for a row specified as part of a table, a schema and table, or a query
> - ROWNUM
> - A sequence followed by .NEXTVAL or .CURRVAL
> - NULL

Compound expression

> Consists of multiple expressions, joined by a standard operator, such as +, -, *, /, or || where applicable. Compound expressions can also be the result of a function.

CASE expression

> Returns a single value, based on the result of a logical comparison. A CASE expression takes one of the following two forms:
>
> ```
> CASE expression WHEN comparison_expression THEN RETURN return_expression
>     [WHEN comparison_expression THEN RETURN return_expression . . .]
> END
> ```
>
> or
>
> ```
> CASE WHEN condition THEN RETURN return_expression
>     [WHEN condition THEN RETURN return_expression . . .]
> END
> ```
>
> CASE expressions are new with Oracle9*i*. Both of the forms shown here can take an ELSE clause in the form:
>
> ```
> ELSE else_expression
> ```
>
> You specify this clause before the END keyword, where *else_expression* is returned if none of the comparisons or conditions return a value.

CURSOR expression

> Returns a nested cursor, the equivalent of a PL/SQL REF CURSOR (see Chapter 9). The form of this expression is:
>
> ```
> CURSOR(subquery)
> ```
>
> CURSOR expressions are new with Oracle9*i*.

DATETIME expression

> Returns a datetime value, with the following syntax:
>
> ```
> datetime_expression [ AT [LOCAL |
> ```

```
TIME ZONE [DBTIMEZONE | SESSIONTIMEZONE | '+/-HH:MM' |
         'time_zone_name' | expr]]]
```

where '*time_zone_name*' is one of the time zone names listed in Table 8-2.
DATETIME expressions are new with Oracle9*i*.

Function expression
  A function that returns a value with an appropriate datatype. This capability
  allows for nested functions.

INTERVAL expression
  Returns a time interval. You can specify the following syntax:

```
interval_expression [YEAR TO MONTH | DAY TO SECOND]
```

  For more information on intervals, see Appendix A. INTERVAL expressions
  are new with Oracle9*i*.

Object access expression
  Returns a value. You can specify the following syntax:

```
{table_alias.column | object_table_alias|(expression) }
{attribute[.method ([argument[, argument . . .]]) |
method ([.argument])}}
```

Scalar subquery expression
  A value returned from a subquery that returns either one or zero rows. If one
  row is returned, the value is the select list of the subquery. If no rows are
  returned, the value is NULL. Scalar subquery expressions are new with
  Oracle9*i*.

Type constructor expression
  Returns an object type from the constructor method for that object. The
  syntax is:

```
[NEW] [schema.]type_name([expression[, expression . . .]])
```

Host variable
  Specifies a host variable, preceded by a colon (:), optionally followed by a
  host indicator variable, also preceded by a colon. The syntax is:

```
:host_variable [INDICATOR :host_indicator_variable]
```

Expression list
  A list of comma-separated expressions, used for comparisons and member-
  ship conditions and in the GROUP BY clause of a query.

Operators

Oracle supports the following standard operators:

- Arithmetic: + - * /
- Concatenation: ||
- Set operators, which work on groups of rows:
  UNION
      All rows selected by either query
  UNION ALL
      All rows selected by either query including duplicates

INTERSECT
> All distinct rows selected by both queries

MINUS
> All distinct rows selected by the first query but not the second

- User-defined operators: You can create your own special-purpose operators with the CREATE OPERATOR statement. New with Oracle9*i*.

Operators are evaluated according to the precedence level of the operator, where operators with precedence level 1 are evaluated first. Table B-1 lists the precedence levels of operators and conditions. All operators with the same precedence are evaluated left to right within an expression. Oracle will evaluate all operators within a set of parentheses first.

Table B-1. Precedence levels for operators and conditions

Precedence	Operator/condition
1	+ (positive), - (negative), PRIOR
2	*, /
3	+ (addition), - (subtraction), || (concatenation)
4	=, != (not equals), <, >, <=, >=
5	IS [NOT] NULL, [NOT] LIKE, [NOT] BETWEEN, [NOT] IN, EXISTS, IS [NOT] OF *type*
6	NOT
7	AND
8	OR

All set and user-defined operators have equal precedence and are evaluated from left to right after the expressions used in the operations have been evaluated.

Conditions

A condition is a logical operation that returns TRUE, FALSE, or UNKNOWN. Conditions can be used in the WHERE clause of a DML statement such as SELECT, INSERT, UPDATE, or DELETE, as well as in the START WITH, CONNECT BY, or HAVING clause of a SELECT statement.

Simple Conditions

A simple condition compares an expression with another expression or with a single result of a subquery. Oracle supports the following simple conditions:

- =   Equal to
- !=   Not equal to
- <   Less than
- >   Greater than
- <> Either less than or greater than, but not equal to
- <= Less than or equal to
- >= Greater than or equal to

Group Conditions

A group condition compares an expression to a group of results. The syntax for a group comparison is:

```
[(]expr[, expr . . .][)] simple_condition ANY | SOME | ALL | IN| NOT IN
    (subquery|expression_list
    [,subquery | expression_list . . .])
```

If you use multiple expressions on the left of the condition, you must have an equal number of values, with matching datatypes, on the right of the condition.

If any values on the right of the NOT IN condition evaluate to NULL, then the condition always evaluates to FALSE. If the values on the right of the NOT IN condition constitute a subquery that returns no rows, all rows in the parent query containing the condition are returned.

Logical Conditions

A logical condition is a condition that can return one of three values—TRUE, FALSE, or UNKNOWN (which, in Oracle, is known as NULL). The three logical conditions supported by Oracle are NOT, AND, and OR.

The results of the NOT conditions for three-state logic (TRUE, FALSE, and UNKNOWN or NULL) are:

NOT TRUE = FALSE
NOT FALSE = TRUE
NOT UNKNOWN = UNKNOWN (NULL)

Table B-2 provides the results of comparisons with combinations of these conditions:

Table B-2. Combinations of logical conditions

Comparison	Value	TRUE	FALSE	UNKNOWN
AND	TRUE	TRUE	FALSE	UNKNOWN
	FALSE	FALSE	FALSE	FALSE
	UNKNOWN	UNKNOWN	FALSE	UNKNOWN
OR	TRUE	TRUE	TRUE	TRUE
	FALSE	TRUE	FALSE	UNKNOWN
	UNKNOWN	TRUE	UNKNOWN	UNKNOWN

Other Conditions

Oracle also allows you to specify a number of additional conditions:

Range condition
    Returns a value based on whether *expr* falls between two other values. The syntax is:

```
expr [NOT] BETWEEN comparison_expr1 AND comparison_expr2
```

NULL

Returns a value based on whether the expression is NULL or NOT NULL. The syntax is:

    expr IS [NOT] NULL

EXISTS

Returns TRUE if *subquery* returns at least one row. The syntax is:

    EXISTS (subquery)

LIKE

Returns TRUE if *char1* is in *char2*. Can use wildcards: underscore (_) to represent a single character or percent (%) for multiple characters. *escape_char* must be specified before the wildcard characters if these characters are to be treated as actual characters. The syntax is:

    char1 [NOT] LIKE | LIKEC | LIKE2 | LIKE4 char2 [ESCAPE escape_char]

Note that for the comparison:

> LIKEC uses Unicode complete characters.
> LIKE2 uses UCS2 codepoints.
> LIKE4 uses UCS4 codepoints.

EQUALS_PATH

Returns whether an XML document can be found at a specified path in the database. This type of condition is used with the views RESOURCE_VIEW and PATH_VIEW. It is new with Oracle9*i* Release 2. The syntax is:

    EQUALS_PATH (column, path_string[, correlation_integer])

correlation_integer is used to correlate this condition with the DEPTH and PATH functions.

UNDER_PATH

Returns whether an XML document can be found under a specified path in the database. This type of condition is used with the views RESOURCE_VIEW and PATH_VIEW. It is new with Oracle9*i* Release 2. The syntax is:

    UNDER_PATH (column, [levels,] path_string[, correlation_integer])

where *levels* is used to limit the number of levels down that Oracle should search. *correlation_integer* is used to correlate this condition with the DEPTH and PATH functions.

IS OF

Tests object types to see if they match a particular object type. This condition is new with Oracle9*i* Release 1. The syntax is:

    expr IS [NOT] OF [TYPE] ([ONLY] [schema.]type[,
        [ONLY] [schema.]type ...])

C

Numeric Formats

This appendix summarizes the numeric format elements that may be used in a variety of Oracle tools (e.g., SQL*Plus), in the built-in packages, and in format specifications within SQL statements.

Table C-1 lists all numeric format elements. Table C-2 contains examples illustrating the use of many of these elements

Table C-1. Numeric format elements

Format element	Function
9	Represents a digit in the output.
0	Marks the spot at which you want to begin displaying leading zeros.
$	Includes a leading dollar sign in the output.
,	Places a comma in the output.
.	Marks the location of the decimal point.
B	Forces zero values to be displayed as blanks.
C	Marks the place where you want the ISO currency indicator to appear. For U.S. dollars, this will be USD.
D	Marks the location of the decimal point.
MI	Adds a trailing negative sign to a number and may be used only at the end of a format string.
S	Adds a + or - sign[a] to the number and may be used at either the beginning or end of a format string.
PR	Causes negative values to be displayed within angle brackets. For example, -123.99 will be displayed as <123.99>.
G	Places a group separator (usually a comma) in the output.
L	Marks the place where you want the local currency indicator to appear. For U.S. dollars, this will be the dollar sign character.
V	Displays scaled values. The number of digits to the right of the V indicates how many places to the right the decimal point is shifted before the number is displayed.
EEEE	Uses scientific notation to display a value. You must use exactly four Es, and they must appear at the right end of the format string.

Table C-1. Numeric format elements (continued)

Format element	Function
RN or rn	Displays a number using Roman numerals. An uppercase RN yields uppercase Roman numerals, while a lowercase rn yields lowercase Roman numerals. Numbers displayed as Roman numerals must be integers and must be between 1 and 3999, inclusive.
DATE	Assumes that the number represents a Julian date and displays it in MM/DD/YY format.

a SQL*Plus always allows for a sign somewhere when you display a number. The default is for the sign to be positioned to the left of the number and to be displayed only when the number is negative. Positive numbers will have a blank space in the leftmost position.

Table C-2. Numeric format examples

Value	Format	Result
123	9999	123
1234.01	9,999.99	1,234.01
23456	$999,999.99	$23,456.00
1	0999	0001
1	99099	001
-1000.01	9,999.99mi	1,000.01-
1001	S9,999	+1,001
-1001	9,999PR	<1,001>
1001	9,999PR	1,001

D

Date Formats

This appendix summarizes the date format elements that may be used in a variety of Oracle tools (e.g., SQL*Plus), in the built-in packages, and in format specifications within SQL statements.

Table D-1 lists all date format elements. Table D-2 contains examples illustrating the use of many of these elements.

Table D-1. Date format elements

Format element	Function
- / , . ; :	Punctuation to be included in the output.
'text'	Quoted text to be reproduced in the output.
AD or A.D. BC or B.C.	AD, A.D., BC, or B.C. indicator included with the date.
AM or A.M. PM or P.M.	AM, A.M., PM, or P.M. printed, whichever applies.
CC	The century number. This will be 20 for years 1900 through 1999.
SCC	Same as CC, but negative for BC dates.
D	The number of the day of the week—1 through 7.
DAY	The full name of the day.
DD	The day of the month.
DDD	The day of the year.
DY	The abbreviated name of the day.
E	The abbreviated era name. Valid only for Japanese Imperial, ROC Official, and Thai Buddha calendars.
EE	The full era name. See E.
FF	The fractional seconds. Valid only for TIMESTAMP types.
FM	Suppresses extra blanks and zeros in the character string representation of a date. For example, use 'FMMonth DD' to get 'July 4' rather than 'July 04'.

Table D-1. Date format elements (continued)

Format element	Function
HH	The hour of the day on a 12-hour clock.
HH12	The hour of the day on a 12-hour clock.
HH24	The hour of the day on a 24-hour clock.
IW	The ISO week number, which can be from 1 to 53. See IYYY.
IYYY	The four-digit ISO year. The ISO year begins on January 1 only when January 1 falls on a Monday; it begins on the previous Monday when January 1 falls on a Tuesday through Thursday; it begins on the subsequent Monday when January 1 falls on a Friday through Sunday.
IYY	The last three digits of the ISO year number.
IY	The last two digits of the ISO year number.
I	The last digit of the year number.
J	The Julian day. Day one is equivalent to Jan. 1, 4712 BC.
MI	The minute.
MM	The month number.
MON	The three-letter month abbreviation.
MONTH	The month name, fully spelled out.
Q	The quarter of the year. Quarter one is January–March, quarter two is April–June, and so forth.
RM	The month number in Roman numerals.
RR	The two-digit year.
RRRR	The four-digit year.
SP	A suffix that converts a number to its spelled format (e.g., ONE, FOUR).
SS	The second.
SSSSS	The number of seconds since midnight.
TH	A suffix, which can appear at the end of any format element resulting in a number (e.g., DDth), and which results in the ordinal version of the number (e.g., 1st, 4th).
SPTH	A suffix that converts a number to its spelled and ordinal format (e.g., FIRST, FOURTH). See TH.
TZD	The abbreviated time zone name (e.g., EST, PST, etc.).
TZH	The hour portion of the time zone displacement from UTC (e.g., -05 for U.S. EST).
TZM	The minute portion of the time zone displacement from UTC (usually zero).
TZR	The time zone region (e.g., US/Eastern).
WW	The week of the year.
W	The week of the month. Week one starts on the first of the month, week two starts on the eighth of the month, and so forth.
X	The local radix character (e.g., the period (.) in American-English).
Y,YYY	The four-digit year with a comma after the first digit.
YEAR	The year spelled out in words.
SYEAR	The year spelled out in words with a leading negative sign when the year is BC. See YEAR.
YYYY	The four-digit year.
SYYYY	The four-digit year with a leading negative sign when the year is BC.
YYY	The last three digits of the year number.
YY	The last two digits of the year number.
Y	The last digit of the year number.

When you use a date format element that displays a text value, such as the name of a month, the case used for the format element determines the case used in the output.

Table D-2. Date format examples

Format	Result
dd-mon-yyyy	13-dec-2002
dd-Mon-yyyy	13-Dec-2002
DD-MON-YYYY	13-DEC-2002
Month dd, yyyy	December 13, 2002
mm/dd/yyyy	12/13/2002
Day	Sunday

E

Additional Resources

There is a lot more to learn about all of the topics discussed in this book. This appendix provides some suggestions for further reading.

Web Sites

Oracle Corporation

This site is the online home of the company. It contains the latest information and marketing, as well as some helpful technical and packaging information.

http://www.oracle.com/

Oracle Technology Network

The Oracle Technology Network (OTN), sometimes called TechNet, is full of resources for every aspect of Oracle technology. It's a great place to download Oracle software, documentation, and lots of sample code. Search by topic at:

http://technet.us.oracle.com/

Oracle FAQ

Independent of Oracle Corporation, this site provides a wide variety of useful Oracle information, including FAQs, scripts, tips, news, jobs, message forums, chat boards, and more.

http://www.orafaq.com

Oraclezone

This site provides a wealth of Oracle information, including news, scripts, tips, and tricks especially for Oracle DBAs.

http://www.oraclezone.com

Ixora

Maintained by Steve Adams, this site offers a lot of information on Oracle internals and tips on Oracle performance tuning.

http://www.ixora.com.au

OraPub

Maintained by Craig Shallahamer, a long-time Oracle employee in the performance analysis group, this site provides helpful Oracle performance tuning information.

http://www.orapub.com

Quest Pipelines

This site provides a community resource for Oracle developers and DBAs, hosted by Quest Software. The PL/SQL and DBA pipelines are regularly monitored by many Oracle authors and other experts. Both pipelines provide archives of training materials and useful code. The Pipetalk forum features many active discussions and what is in essence free consulting for developers and DBAs.

http://www.quest-pipelines.com

PL/Net.org

Designed mainly for PL/SQL developers and maintained by Bill Pribyl, this site is a repository of open source software that is written in PL/SQL or is otherwise for the benefit of PL/SQL developers. The site contains a FAQ and links to a variety of excellent software, including utPLSQL, the unit-testing framework for PL/SQL developers.

http://plnet.org

Oracle Professional from Pinnacle Publishing

This site contains information about this monthly, printed newsletter (with accompanying online edition), which offers in-depth articles on Oracle technology.

http://www.oracleprofessionalnewsletter.com/

Oracle Magazine from Oracle Corporation

This site contains information about this monthly, printed publication, which covers a wide variety of Oracle technology and often introduces new Oracle functionality.

http://www.oramag.com/

O'Reilly Resources

The Oracle area of the O'Reilly web site contains detailed descriptions of Oracle books, articles describing Oracle technologies, and other helpful links. You might also want to check out the O'Reilly home page, which offers links to all of the various book areas and other resources, as well as the O'Reilly Network, which provides articles, forums, and other resources especially for open and emerging technologies.

http://oracle.oreilly.com
http://www.oreilly.com
http://oreillynet.com

Books

The following books provide additional information on the various topics covered in this book.

First, a note about Oracle documentation. Oracle's standard documentation has improved a great deal over the years. Now distributed exclusively online or on CD-ROM, these documents are an excellent source of information.

General

The books in this section contain a wide range of information on Oracle products and features. More specific references are included in later sections.

Greenwald, Rick, *Oracle Essentials: Oracle9i, Oracle8i, and Oracle8* (O'Reilly & Associates, Inc.).

Kreines, David C., and Brian Laskey, *Oracle Database Administration: The Essential Reference* (O'Reilly & Associates, Inc.).

Kyte, Thomas, *Expert One-on-One: Oracle* (Wrox Press).

Lewis, Jonathan, *Practical Oracle8i: Building Efficient Databases* (Addison Wesley).

Loney, Kevin, and George Koch, *Oracle9i: The Complete Reference* (Osborne-McGraw Hill).

Thakkar, Meghraj, *e-Business for the Oracle DBA* (Sams Publishing).

Loney, Kevin and Marlene Theriault, *Oracle9i DBA Handbook* (Osborne-McGraw Hill).

Theriault, Marlene, et al., *Oracle DBA 101* (Osborne-McGraw Hill).

Security

Theriault, Marlene, and Aaron Newman, *Oracle Security Handbook* (Osborne-McGraw Hill).

Networking

Gennick, Jonathan, and Hugo Toledo, *Oracle Net8 Configuration and Troubleshooting* (O'Reilly & Associates).

Theriault, Marlene, *Oracle Networking 101* (Osborne-McGraw Hill).

SQL

Kreines, David C., *Oracle SQL: The Essential Reference* (O'Reilly & Associates, Inc.).

Mishra, Sanjay, and Alan Beaulieu, *Mastering Oracle SQL* (O'Reilly & Associates, Inc.).

PL/SQL

Feuerstein, Steven, *Oracle PL/SQL Best Practices* (O'Reilly & Associates, Inc.).

Feuerstein, Steven, with Andrew Odewahn, *Oracle PL/SQL Developer's Workbook* (O'Reilly & Associates, Inc.).

Feuerstein, Steven, with Bill Pribyl, *Oracle PL/SQL Programming*, 3d ed. (O'Reilly & Associates, Inc.).

Feuerstein, Steven, Bill Pribyl, and Chip Dawes, *Oracle PL/SQL Language Pocket Reference* (O'Reilly & Associates, Inc.).

Pribyl, Bill, and Steven Feuerstein, *Learning Oracle PL/SQL,* (O'Reilly & Associates, Inc.).

Trezzo, Joseph C., *Oracle PL/SQL Tips and Techniques* (Osborne-McGraw Hill).

Packages

Feuerstein, Steven, John Beresniewicz, and Chip Dawes, *Oracle PL/SQL Built-ins Pocket Reference* (O'Reilly & Associates, Inc.).

Feuerstein, Steven, Charles Dye, and John Beresniewicz, *Oracle Built-in Packages* (O'Reilly & Associates, Inc.).

Java

Bales, Don, *Java Programming with Oracle JDBC* (O'Reilly & Associates, Inc.).

Flanagan, David, *Java in a Nutshell* (O'Reilly & Associates, Inc.).

Flanagan, David, Jim Farley, and William Crawford, *Java Enterprise in a Nutshell* (O'Reilly & Associates, Inc.).

McLaughlin, Brett, *Building Java Enterprise Applications* (O'Reilly & Associates, Inc.).

Morisseau-Leroy, Nirva et. al., *Oracle8i SQLJ Programming* (Osborne-McGraw Hill)

Niemeyer, Pat, and Jonathan Knudsen, *Learning Java* (O'Reilly & Associates, Inc.).

Price, Jason, *Java Programming with Oracle SQLJ* (O'Reilly & Associates, Inc.).

Reese, George, *Database Programming with JDBC and Java* (O'Reilly & Associates, Inc.).

SQL*Plus

Gennick, Jonathan, *Oracle SQL*Plus: The Definitive Guide* (O'Reilly & Associates, Inc.).

Gennick, Jonathan, *Oracle SQL*Plus Pocket Reference* (O'Reilly & Associates, Inc.).

SQL*Loader

Gennick, Jonathan, and Sanjay Mishra, *Oracle SQL*Loader: The Definitive Guide* (O'Reilly & Associates, Inc.).

Backup and Recovery

Freeman, Robert G. and Hart, Matthew, *Oracle9i RMAN Backup and Recovery* (Osborne-McGraw Hill)

Kuhn, Darl, and Scott Schulze, *Oracle RMAN Pocket Reference* (O'Reilly & Associates, Inc.).

Smith, Kenny, and Stephan Haisley, *Oracle Backup and Recovery 101* (Osborne-McGraw Hill).

Velpuri, Rama, et al., *Oracle8i Backup and Recovery* (Osborne-McGraw Hill).

Enterprise Manager

Vanting, Lars Bo, and Dirk Schepanik, *Oracle Enterprise Manager 101* (Osborne-McGraw Hill).

Performance

Adams, Steve, *Oracle8i Internal Services* (O'Reilly & Associates, Inc.).

Alomari, Ahmed, *Oracle8i and UNIX Performance Tuning* (Prentice Hall)

Burleson, Don, *Oracle9i High-Performance Tuning with STATSPACK* (Osborne-McGraw Hill).

Gurry, Mark, *Oracle SQL Tuning Pocket Reference* (O'Reilly & Associates, Inc.).

Gurry, Mark, and Peter Corrigan, *Oracle Performance Tuning* (O'Reilly & Associates, Inc.).

Harrison, Guy, *Oracle SQL High-Performance Tuning* (Prentice-Hall).

Morle, James, *Scaling Oracle8i: Building Highly Scalable OLTP System Architectures* (Addison Wesley)

Niemiec, Rich, et al., *Oracle Performance Tuning Tips and Techniques* (Osborne-McGraw Hill).

Vaidyanatha, Gaja Krishna, Kirtikumar Deshpande, and John A. Kostelac, *Oracle Performance Tuning 101* (Osborne-McGraw Hill).

Index

We'd like to hear your suggestions for improving our indexes. Send email to *index@oreilly.com*.

CREATE PROCEDURE statement, 228, 376

CREATE PROFILE statement, 88, 228

CREATE ROLE statement, 106, 230

CREATE ROLLBACK SEGMENT statement, 231

CREATE SCHEMA statement, 232

CREATE SCRIPT command, RMAN, 772

CREATE SEQUENCE statement, 233

CREATE SNAPSHOT LOG statement, 235

CREATE SNAPSHOT statement, 234

CREATE SPFILE statement, 235

CREATE SYNONYM statement, 236

CREATE TABLE statement
 object syntax, 247
 relational syntax, 236
 XML syntax, 252

CREATE TABLESPACE statement, 253

CREATE TEMPORARY TABLESPACE statement, 255

CREATE TRIGGER statement, 256, 369

CREATE TYPE BODY statement, 259

CREATE TYPE statement, 256

CREATE TYPE system role, 105

CREATE USER statement, 86, 260

CREATE VIEW statement, 261

CREATE_BITMAP_AREA_SIZE parameter, 42

CROSSCHECK command, RMAN, 773

CUME_DIST function, 292

CURRENT ROW parameter, 291

*$CURRENT_BUCKET dynamic dictionary view, 172

CURRENT_DATE function, 308

CURRENT_TIMESTAMP function, 308, 311

CURSOR expression, 841

cursor expressions, 351

cursor FOR loop, 347

cursor parameters, 28

cursor variables, PL/SQL, 336

cursor-based records, PL/SQL, 339

cursors, dynamic (SQL), 350

CURSOR_SHARING parameter, 28

CURSOR_SHARING_EXACT optimizer hint, 813

CURSOR_SPACE_FOR_TIME parameter, 28

CustomDatum interface, oracle.sql package, 629

CustomDatumFactory interface, oracle. sql package, 629

D

D (numeric format element), 846

dash (-) date format element, 848

Data Definition Language (see DDL)

data dictionary
 cache, dynamic data dictionary views, 164
 dynamic performance data dictionary views, 145
 static data dictionary views, 145–161
 views, 148
  dynamic data dictionary views, 161–175
 (see also dynamic data dictionary views; static data dictionary views)

data gateways, static data dictionary views, 159

Data Guard, 15

Data Manipulation Language (see DML)

data mapping, Java, 576

Data Mining option, Enterprise Edition, 16

DATA parameter, SQL*Loader, 724

database buffer cache, instance memory, 11

*$DATABASE dynamic dictionary view, 164

database events, PL/SQL triggers, 372

database link parameters, 29

DATABASE LINKS privilege, 92

DATABASE privilege, 92

Database Resource Manager, privilege maintenance package, 473

Database Workspace Manager, interface package, 515

databases, 3
 creating/altering, 208
 dynamic data dictionary views, 164
 files, 5
 Java objects, 583
 recovery, 744
 tablespaces, 4

*$DATAFILE dynamic dictionary view, 164

datafile recovery, 740

*$DATAFILE_COPY dynamic dictionary view, 169

*$DATAFILE_HEADER dynamic dictionary view, 164

I

identifiers
  PL/SQL, 330
  RMAN, 756–757
IFILE parameter, 57
IF-THEN-ELSE statement, 344
IMP_FULL_DATABASE system
    role, 105
Import utility
  backups and, 737
  command-line operation, 714
  invoking, 712
  overview, 711–714
  parameters, 715–717
    ANALYZE, 719
    BUFFER, 715
    CHARSET, 720
    COMMIT, 720
    COMPILE, 720
    CONSTRAINTS, 715
    DATAFILES, 720
    DESTROY, 720
    FEEDBACK, 715
    FILE, 715
    FILESIZE, 715
    FROMUSER, 720
    FULL, 715
    GRANTS, 716
    HELP, 716
    IGNORE, 720
    Import only, 719–721
    INCTYPE, 721
    INDEXES, 716
    INDEXFILE, 721
    LOG, 716
    PARFILE, 716
    POINT_IN_TIME_
      RECOVER, 716
    RECORDLENGTH, 716
    RESUMABLE_NAME, 717
    RESUMABLE_TIMEOUT, 717
    ROWS, 717
    SHOW, 721
    SKIP_UNUSABLE_
      INDEXES, 721
    STREAMS_
      CONFIGURATION, 721
    STREAMS_
      INSTANTIATION, 721
    TABLES, 717
    TABLESPACES, 717
    TOID_NOVALIDATE, 721
    TOUSER, 721
    TTS_OWNERS, 721
    USERID, 717
    VOLSIZE, 717
  prompts, 713
  recovery and, 737
  static data dictionary views, 159
importing, SQLJ and, 577
incomplete recovery, 739
inconsistent backups, 738, 741
incremental backups, 15, 739
*_IND_COLUMNS static dictionary
    view, 149
INDEX optimizer access path hint, 810
INDEX privilege, 93
INDEX_ASC optimizer access path
    hint, 810
Index_Attributes_Clause, SQL, 185
INDEX_COMBINE optimizer access
    path hint, 810
INDEX_DESC optimizer access path
    hint, 810
*$INDEXED_FIXED_COLUMN
    dynamic dictionary view, 175
indexes
  bitmapped, 15
  creating/modifying/removing, 220
  static data dictionary views, 149
*_INDEXES static dictionary view, 149
INDEX_FFS optimizer access path
    hint, 810
INDEX_HISTOGRAM static dictionary
    view, 149
INDEX_JOIN optimizer access path
    hint, 810
INDEX_STATS static dictionary
    view, 149
indextype object, creating/
    removing, 222
INDEXTYPE privilege, 93
indextypes schema object, 100
*_IND_PARTITIONS static dictionary
    view, 152
INFILE clause, SQL*Loader, 730
INITCAP function, 303
initialization
  collections, 353
  packages, PL/SQL, 369
  parameters
    overview, 17, 20
    text file containing, creating, 228
initialization file example, 17
INIT.ORA initialization file, 19
INIT.ORA parameters, 17
  (see also parameters, initialization)
INPUT command, SQL*Plus, 691

M

N

name parameters, 47
named iterators, SQL in SQLJ, 581
namesctl (Oracle Names Control
 utility), 140
NAMES.ORA file, 121
namespaces, creating/dropping, 204
naming service, 117–118
naming variables, SQL*Plus, 674
native compilation, PL/SQL, 374–375
nested collections, 355
nested records, PL/SQL, 339
nested tables, PL/SQL, 340
*_NESTED_TABLES static dictionary
 view, 151
networking
 addresses, translation, 120
 Connection Manager, 120
 connections, 117
 load balancing, 119
 management utilities, 140–144
 multiple sessions, 120
 Oracle Net Configuration
  Assistant, 144
 Oracle Net Manager, 144
 Oracle Net Services, 116
  failover, 118
 overview, 116
 protocols, translation, 120
 servers, Shared, 119
 static data dictionary views, 151
Newman, Aaron, 853
NEW_TIME function, 311
NEXT_DAY function, 312
Niemeyer, Pat, 854
Niemiec, Rich, 855
NL_AJ optimizer join hint, 811
NLS (National Language Support)
 parameters, 49
NLS_CALENDAR parameter, 49
NLS_CHARSET_DECL_LEN
 function, 324
NLS_CHARSET_ID function, 324
NLS_CHARSET_NAME function, 325
NLS_COMP parameter, 49
NLS_CURRENCY parameter, 49
NLS_DATABASE_PARAMETERS static
 dictionary view, 156
NLS_DATE_FORMAT parameter, 49
NLS_DATE_LANGUAGE
 parameter, 49
NLS_DUAL_CURRENCY
 parameter, 50
NLS_INITCAP function, 304

NLS_INSTANCE_PARAMETERS static
 dictionary view, 156
NLS_ISO_CURRENCY parameter, 50
NL_SJ optimizer join hint, 811
NLS_LANGUAGE parameter, 50
NLS_LENGTH_SEMANTICS
 parameter, 50
NLS_LOWER function, 304
NLS_NUMERIC_CHARACTERS
 parameter, 50
*$NLS_PARAMETERS dynamic
 dictionary view, 163
NLS_SESSION_PARAMETERS static
 dictionary view, 156
NLSSORT function, 305
NLS_SORT parameter, 51
NLS_TERRITORY parameter, 51
NLS_TIMESTAMP_FORMAT
 parameter, 51
NLS_TIMESTAMP_TZ_FORMAT
 parameter, 51
NLS_UPPER function, 304
*$NLS_VALID_VALUES dynamic
 dictionary view, 163
NOAPPEND optimizer hint, 812
NOAUDIT (schema objects)
 statement, 112, 265
NOAUDIT (SQL statements)
 statement, 112, 265
NOCACHE optimizer hint, 813
NOCATALOG option, RMAN, 753
NO_EXPAND optimizer query
 transformation hint, 810
NO_FACT optimizer query
 transformation hint, 811
NO_INDEX optimizer access path
 hint, 810
/NOLOG parameter (SQL*Plus), 671
NO_MERGE optimizer query
 transformation hint, 811
nonescalating row locks, 82
nonrepeatable reads, 80
NOPARALLEL optimizer parallel
 execution hint, 812
NOPARALLEL_INDEX optimizer
 parallel execution hint, 812
NO_PUSH_PRED optimizer hint, 813
NO_PUSH_SUBQ optimizer hint, 813
NOREWRITE optimizer query
 transformation hint, 810
NO_UNNEST optimizer hint, 813
NTILE function, 295
NULL statement, 346
NULLIF function, 325

parameters, initialization (*continued*)
NLS_DUAL_CURRENCY, 50
NLS_ISO_CURRENCY, 50
NLS_LANGUAGE, 50
NLS_LENGTH_SEMANTICS, 50
NLS_NUMERIC_
CHARACTERS, 50
NLS_SORT, 51
NLS_TERRITORY, 51
NLS_TIMESTAMP_
FORMAT, 51
NLS_TIMESTAMP_TZ_
FORMAT, 51
O7_DICTIONARY_
ACCESSIBILITY, 62
OBJECT_CACHE_MAX_SIZE_
PERCENT, 44
OBJECT_CACHE_OPTIMAL_
SIZE, 45
OPEN_CURSORS, 29
OPEN_LINKS, 30
OPEN_LINKS_PER_
INSTANCE, 30
OPS_ADMIN_GROUP, 27
OPTIMIZER_FEATURES_
ENABLE, 52
OPTIMIZER_INDEX_
CACHING, 52
OPTIMIZER_INDEX_COST_
ADJ, 53
OPTIMIZER_MAX_
PERMUTATIONS, 53
OPTIMIZER_MODE, 53
OPTIMIZER_PERCENT_
PARALLEL, 53
OPTIMIZER_SEARCH_
LIMIT, 53
ORACLE_TRACE_
COLLECTION_NAME, 74
ORACLE_TRACE_
COLLECTION_PATH, 74
ORACLE_TRACE_
COLLECTION_SIZE, 74
ORACLE_TRACE_ENABLE, 74
ORACLE_TRACE_FACILITY_
NAME, 75
ORACLE_TRACE_FACILITY_
PATH, 75
OS_AUTHENT_PREFIX, 62
OS_ROLES, 63
overview, 17, 20
PARALLEL_ADAPTIVE_MULTI_
USER, 55
PARALLEL_AUTOMATIC_
TUNING, 55
PARALLEL_BROADCAST_
ENABLED, 55
PARALLEL_DEFAULT_MAX_
INSTANCES, 55
PARALLEL_EXECUTION_
MESSAGE_SIZE, 56
PARALLEL_INSTANCE_
GROUP, 56
PARALLEL_MAX_SERVERS, 56
PARALLEL_MIN_MESSAGE_
POOL, 56
PARALLEL_MIN_PERCENT, 56
PARALLEL_MIN_SERVERS, 56
PARALLEL_SERVER, 27
PARALLEL_SERVER_IDLE_
TIME, 27
PARALLEL_SERVER_
INSTANCES, 28
PARALLEL_THREADS_PER_
CPU, 57
PARALLEL_TRANSACTION_
RESOURCE_TIMEOUT, 57
PARTITION_VIEW_
ENABLED, 53
PGA_AGGREGATE_
TARGET, 45
PLSQL_COMPILER_FLAGS, 57
PLSQL_LOAD_WITHOUT_
COMPILE, 58
PLSQL_NATIVE_C_
COMPILER, 58
PLSQL_NATIVE_LIBRARY_
DIR, 58
PLSQL_NATIVE_LIBRARY_
SUBDIR_COUNT, 58
PLSQL_NATIVE_LINKER, 58
PLSQL_NATIVE_MAKE_
UTILITY, 58
PLSQL_V2_
COMPATIBILITY, 58
PRE_PAGE_SGA, 45
PROCESSES, 72
QUERY_REWRITE_
ENABLED, 54
QUERY_REWRITE_
INTEGRITY, 54
RDBMS_SERVER_DN, 63
READ_ONLY_OPEN_
DELAYED, 54
RECOVERY_PARALLELISM, 23
REMOTE_ARCHIVE_
ENABLE, 41

TO_TIMESTAMP_TZ function, 313
TO_YMINTERVAL function, 314, 319
TRACE option, RMAN, 754
Trace utility, TKPROF, 819
  collecting information, 820
  output, 822
  preparation, 820
  running, 820
TRACE_ENABLED parameter, 75
TRACEFILE_IDENTIFIER
    parameter, 75
tracing, package for, 508
*$TRANSACTION dynamic dictionary
    view, 175
transaction parameters, 35
transaction statements
  COMMIT, 356
  LOCK TABLE, 358
  ROLLBACK, 357
  SAVEPOINT, 357
  SET TRANSACTION, 357
TRANSACTION_AUDITING
    parameter, 22
transaction-based notification package
    (DBMS_ALERT), 379
*$TRANSACTION_ENQUEUE dynamic
    dictionary view, 175
transactions
  autonomous, 358
  concurrency condsiderations, 78
  distributed, static data dictionary
    views, 151
  locks, 79
    contention, 80
    integrity problems, 80
  management package, 509
  managing, PL/SQL and, 356–359
  SCN (System Change Number), 82
TRANSACTIONS parameter, 36
TRANSACTIONS_PER_ROLLBACK_
    SEGMENT parameter, 36
TRANSLATE function, 307, 319
transportable tablespaces, exporting, 16
TREAT function, 307
Trezzo, Joseph C., 854
trial recovery, 15
TRIGGER privilege, 97
*_TRIGGER_COLS static dictionary
    view, 153
triggers
  creating/modifying/removing, 256
  PL/SQL, 363, 369–372
    event sequences, 371
    predicates, 372
*_TRIGGERS static dictionary view, 153

TRIM function, 307
TRUNC function, 301, 314
TRUNCATE statement, 285
Trusted Server maintenance, package
    for, 400
TRUSTED_SERVERS static dictionary
    view, 151
TSPITR (tablespace point-in-time
    recovery), 745
*_TS_QUOTAS static dictionary
    view, 157
TTITLE command, SQL*Plus, 707
tuning pack, EM expansion, 799
two-tier architecture, EM, 790
type bodies, creating/removing, 259
type constructor expression, 842
*_TYPE_ATTRS static dictionary
    view, 152
TypeDescriptor class, oracle.sql
    package, 666
*_TYPE_METHODS static dictionary
    view, 152
TYPES privilege, 97
*_TYPES static dictionary view, 152
*$TYPE_SIZE dynamic dictionary
    view, 164
TZ_OFFSET function, 314

U

UFI (User Friendly Interface), 669
UID function, 328
UNBOUNDED FOLLOWING
    parameter, 291
UNBOUNDED PRECEDING
    parameter, 291
unconstrained declarations, PL/
    SQL, 335
UNDEFINE command, SQL*Plus, 708
UNDER privilege, schema object
    privileges, 99
UNDO_MANAGEMENT parameter, 61
UNDO_RETENTION parameter, 62
*$UNDOSTAT dynamic dictionary
    view, 165
UNDO_SUPPRESS_ERRORS
    parameter, 62
UNDO_TABLESPACE parameter, 62
UNISTR function, 319
UNNEST optimizer hint, 813
until clause, RMAN, 761
*_UPDATABLE_COLUMNS static
    dictionary view, 158
UPDATE privilege, schema object
    privileges, 99

X

XML (Extensible Markup Language)
 document access, 549
 functions, 320–328
XML interface package, 522
XML schemas, package for, 547
XMLAGG function, 321
XMLCOLATTVAL function, 321

XMLCONCAT function, 321
XMLELEMENT function, 322
XMLFOREST function, 322
XMLSEQUENCE function, 322
XMLTRANSFORM function, 322
XMLType datatype, 837
XMLType objects, accessing, 526

About the Authors

Rick Greenwald has been active in the world of computer software for nearly two decades, including stints with Data General, Cognos, and Gupta. He is currently an analyst with Oracle Corporation. He has published seven books and countless articles on a variety of technical topics, and has spoken at conferences and training sessions across six continents. In addition to *Oracle in a Nutshell*, Rick's books include *Oracle Essentials: Oracle9i, Oracle8i, and Oracle8* (principal author with Robert Stackowiak and Jonathan Stern), (O'Reilly & Associates, 2001); *Oracle Power Objects Developer's Guide* (principal author with Kasu Sista and Richard Finklestein, Oracle Press, 1995); *Mastering Oracle Power Objects* (principal author with Robert Hoskins, O'Reilly & Associates, 1996); *Using Oracle Web Server* (principal author with many others, Que Publishing, 1997); *The Oracle WebDB Bible* (principal author with Jim Milbery, IDG Books Worldwide, 1999); and *Administering Exchange Server* (principal author with Walter Glenn, Microsoft Press, 1999).

David C. Kreines is the Manager of Database Services for Rhodia, Inc., and author of *Oracle SQL: The Essential Reference* (O'Reilly & Associates, 2000) and coauthor of *Oracle Database Administration: The Essential Reference* (with Brian Laskey) (O'Reilly & Associates, 1999) and *Oracle Scripts* (with Brian Lomasky) (O'Reilly & Associates, 1998). Dave has worked with Oracle as a developer and database administrator since 1985, on a wide variety of platforms from PCs to mainframes. He is an Oracle Certified Professional, is certified as a DBA, and has been a frequent contributor to Oracle conferences, user groups, and publications, both in the United States and in Europe. Dave served two terms as president of the International Oracle Users Group-Americas (IOUG-A), and spent ten years on the board of directors.

Colophon

Our look is the result of reader comments, our own experimentation, and feedback from distribution channels. Distinctive covers complement our distinctive approach to technical topics, breathing personality and life into potentially dry subjects.

The animal on the cover of *Oracle in a Nutshell* is a myrmeleon, an insect found in abundance throughout the world. Adults have a long, slender abdomen that can grow to nearly two inches in length, and the longer of their two pairs of wings can span two and a half inches. These wings contain elaborate patterns of cross-veined nerves that resemble those of small dragonflies, but myrmeleon belong to an entirely different family. Unlike dragonflies, myrmeleon are nocturnal and have a pair of clubbed antennae. They undergo a complete metamorphosis with egg, larval, pupal, and winged adult stages. In its larval stage, the myrmeleon is commonly referred to as a "doodlebug" or "antlion." These strange-looking wingless creatures have oversized heads with long spiny jaws, short legs, and bristled bodies. They are primarily known for constructing sand pits in riverbeds or the soft areas surrounding tree roots. When ants and other small insects wander into these pits, the antlion digs deeper into the hole, causing miniature landslides that bury the intruder in sand. The myrmeleon larva then sucks bodily fluid from the trapped insect, tosses its carcass from the pit, and patiently prepares for another unlucky victim.

When first hatched, antlions specialize in capturing very small insects, but they usually graduate to larger pits in order to catch more substantial prey. The larval growing process can take over two years, during which the antlion consumes hundreds of insects. Eventually, the myrmeleon larva instinctively moves deeper into the sand to build a cocoon. Silky white threads expelled from its abdomen form a sphere around the antlion that is held in place by the surrounding sand. After a month in this pupal stage, a tiny-winged myrmeleon emerges from the cocoon and climbs to the surface. It waits a short time for its wings to dry and night to fall before flying off in search of a mate. During this full-grown stage, they may nibble on small flies or nectar, but are just as likely to eat nothing. Myrmeleon rarely survive more than a few weeks, and their primary objective as adults is to breed. Like other nocturnal insects, myrmeleon often find their mates lingering at a lit window or flitting around a campfire. The female returns to sandy areas to lay her eggs and, in an ironic twist, is often eaten by antlions if she should happen to stumble into one of their pits.

Philip Dangler was the production editor, and Norma Emory was the copyeditor for *Oracle in a Nutshell*. Emily Quill and Jane Ellin provided quality control. Tom Dinse and Johnna VanHoose Dinse wrote the index.

Ellie Volckhausen designed the cover of this book, based on a series design by Edie Freedman. The cover image is a 19th-century engraving from the Dover Pictorial Archive. Emma Colby produced the cover layout with QuarkXPress 4.1 using Adobe's ITC Garamond font.

David Futato designed the interior layout. This book was converted to FrameMaker 5.5.6 with a format conversion tool created by Erik Ray, Jason McIntosh, Neil Walls, and Mike Sierra that uses Perl and XML technologies. The text font is Linotype Birka; the heading font is Adobe Myriad Condensed; and the code font is LucasFont's TheSans Mono Condensed. The illustrations that appear in the book were produced by Robert Romano and Jessamyn Read using Macromedia FreeHand 9 and Adobe Photoshop 6. The tip and warning icons were drawn by Christopher Bing. This colophon was written by Philip Dangler.

Other Titles Available from O'Reilly

Oracle

Building Oracle XML Applications

By Steve Muench
1st Edition September 2000
810 pages, Includes CD-ROM
ISBN 1-56592-691-9

Building Oracle XML Applications gives Java and PL/SQL developers a rich and detailed look at the many tools Oracle ~des to support XML development. It shows how to ~bine the power of XML and XSLT with the speed, ~tionality, and reliability of the Oracle database. The ~or delivers nearly 800 pages of entertaining text, ~ful and timesaving hints, and extensive examples ~ developers can put to use immediately to build cus-XML applications. The accompanying CD-ROM ~tains JDeveloper 3.1, an integrated development envi-~ment for Java developers.

Oracle Essentials: Oracle9i, Oracle8i & Oracle8

By Rick Greenwald, Robert Stackowiak
& Jonathan Stern
2nd Edition June 2001
381 pages, ISBN 0-596-00179-7

Updated for Oracle's latest release, Oracle9i, *Oracle Essentials* is a concise and readable technical introduction to ~acle features and technologies, including the Oracle ~hitecture, data structures, configuration, networking, ~ning, and data warehousing. It introduces such major ~acle9i features as Real Application clusters, flashback ~eries, clickstream intelligence, Oracle Database and ~eb Cache, XML integration, the Oracle9i Application ~rver, Oracle9i Portal, and much more.

Java Programming with Oracle JDBC

By Donald K. Bales
1st Edition December 2001
496 pages, ISBN 0-596-00088-X

Learn how to leverage JDBC, a key Java technology used to access rela-tional data from Java programs, in an Oracle environment. Author Don Bales ~egins by teaching you the mysteries of establishing ~atabase connections, and how to issue SQL queries and ~et results back. You'll move on to advanced topics such ~s streaming large objects, calling PL/SQL procedures, ~nd working with Oracle9i's object-oriented features, ~hen finish with a look at transactions, concurrency ~management, and performance.

Perl for Oracle DBAs

By Andy Duncan & Jared Still
1st Edition August 2002
620 pages, ISBN 0-596-00210-6

Perl is a very helpful tool for Oracle database administrators, but too few DBAs realize how powerful Perl can be. *Perl for Oracle DBAs* describes what DBAs need to know about Perl and explains how they can use this popular open source language to man-age, monitor, and tune their Oracle databases. The book also describes the Oracle/Perl software modules that tie these two environments together—for example, Oracle Call Interface (OCI), Perl DataBase Interface (DBI), DBD-Oracle, and mod_perl, etc. The book comes with a toolk-it containing more than 100 ready-to-use programs that DBAs can put to immediate use in their Linux or Win-dows systems.

TOAD Pocket Reference for Oracle

By Jim McDaniel & Patrick McGrath
1st Edition August 2002
128 pages, ISBN 0-596-00337-4

This handy little book provides data-base developers and administrators with quick access to TOAD feature summaries, hot keys, productivity tips and tricks, and much more. A perfect pocket-sized guide that's easy to take anywhere, *TOAD Pocket Reference for Oracle* focuses on the major TOAD components, including the SQL Editor, Data Grid, Schema Browser, SQL Tuning module, and DBA tools (for database administration, user administra-tion, and database performance).

How to stay in touch with O'Reilly

1. Visit our award-winning web site

http://www.oreilly.com/

★ "Top 100 Sites on the Web"—PC Magazine
★ CIO Magazine's Web Business 50 Awards

Our web site contains a library of comprehensive product information (including book excerpts and tables of contents), downloadable software, background articles, interviews with technology leaders, links to relevant sites, book cover art, and more. File us in your bookmarks or favorites!

2. Join our email mailing lists

Sign up to get email announcements of new books and conferences, special offers, and O'Reilly Network technology newsletters at:

http://elists.oreilly.com

It's easy to customize your free elists subscription so you'll get exactly the O'Reilly news you want.

3. Get examples from our books

To find example files for a book, go to:

http://www.oreilly.com/catalog

select the book, and follow the "Examples" link.

4. Work with us

Check out our web site for current employment opportunities:

http://jobs.oreilly.com/

5. Register your book

Register your book at:

http://register.oreilly.com

6. Contact us

O'Reilly & Associates, Inc.
1005 Gravenstein Hwy North
Sebastopol, CA 95472 USA
TEL: 707-827-7000 or 800-998-9938
          (6am to 5pm PST)
FAX: 707-829-0104

order@oreilly.com
For answers to problems regarding your order o
products. To place a book order online visit:

http://www.oreilly.com/order_new/

catalog@oreilly.com
To request a copy of our latest catalog.

booktech@oreilly.com
For book content technical questions or correcti

corporate@oreilly.com
For educational, library, government, and corpor
sales.

proposals@oreilly.com
To submit new book proposals to our editors an
product managers.

international@oreilly.com
For information about our international distribu
or translation queries. For a list of our distributo
outside of North America check out:

http://international.oreilly.com/distributors.html

adoption@oreilly.com
For information about academic use of
O'Reilly books, visit:

http://academic.oreilly.com

O'REILLY®